Family Maps of Jefferson County, Alabama

Deluxe Edition

With Homesteads, Roads, Waterways, Towns, Cemeteries, Railroads, and More

Family Maps of Jefferson County, Alabama

Deluxe Edition

With Homesteads, Roads, Waterways, Towns, Cemeteries, Railroads, and More

by Gregory A. Boyd, J.D.

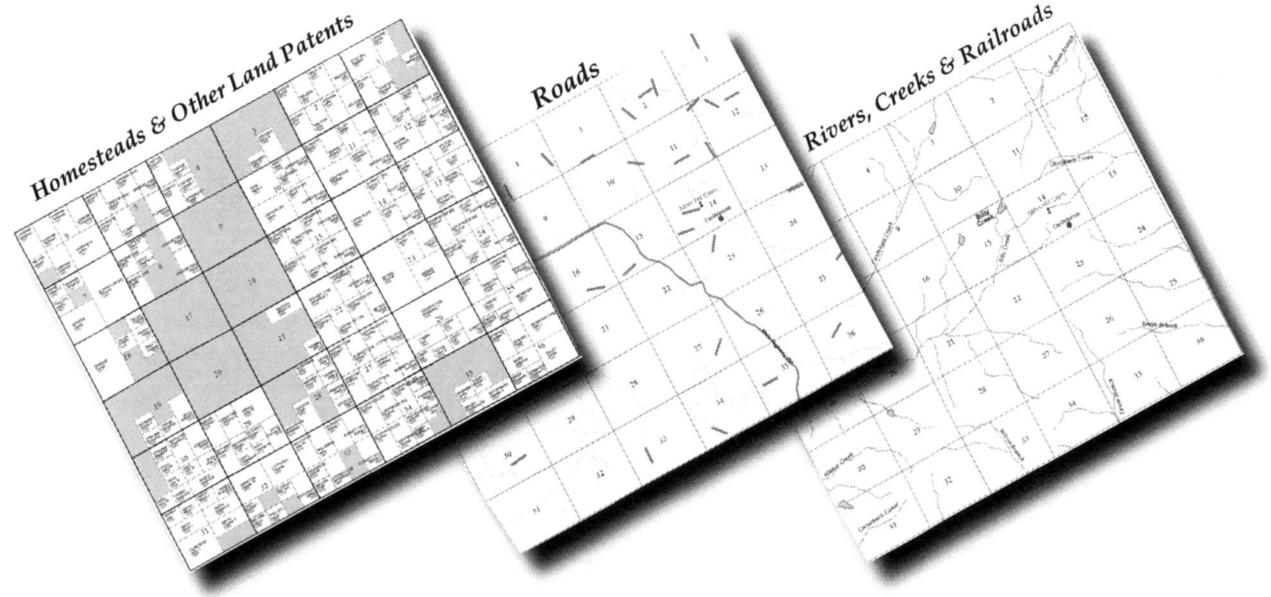

Featuring 3 Maps Per Township...

Arphax Publishing Co.
www.arphax.com

Family Maps of Jefferson County, Alabama, Deluxe Edition: With Homesteads, Roads, Waterways, Towns, Cemeteries, Railroads, and More.
by Gregory A. Boyd, J.D.

ISBN 1-4203-1280-4

Printed in the United States of America

Published by Arphax Publishing Co., 2210 Research Park Blvd., Norman, Oklahoma, USA 73069
www.arphax.com

First Edition

ATTENTION HISTORICAL & GENEALOGICAL SOCIETIES, UNIVERSITIES, COLLEGES, CORPORATIONS, FAMILY REUNION COORDINATORS, AND PROFESSIONAL ORGANIZATIONS: Quantity discounts are available on bulk purchases of this book. For information, please contact Arphax Publishing Co., at the address listed above, or at (405) 366-6181, or visit our web-site at www.arphax.com and contact us through the "Bulk Sales" link.

This book is dedicated to my wonderful family:

Vicki, Jordan, & Amy Boyd

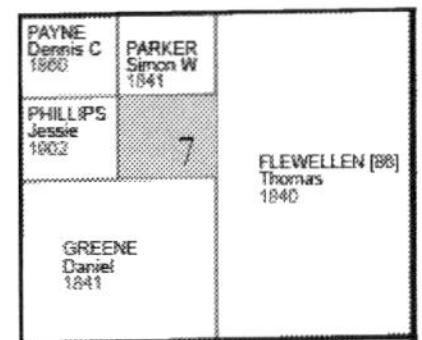
PAYNE
Dennis C
1860
PARKER
Simon W
1841
PHILLIPS
Jessie
1902
7
FLEWELLEN [86]
Thomas
1840
GREENE
Daniel
1841

Contents

Appendices

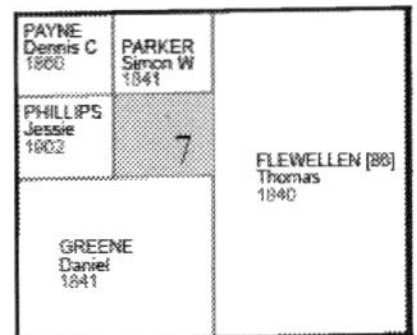

Preface

The quest for the discovery of my ancestors' origins, migrations, beliefs, and life-ways has brought me rewards that I could never have imagined. The *Family Maps* series of books is my first effort to share with historical and genealogical researchers, some of the tools that I have developed to achieve my research goals. I firmly believe that this effort will allow many people to reap the same sorts of treasures that I have.

Our Federal government's General Land Office of the Bureau of Land Management (the "GLO") has given genealogists and historians an incredible gift by virtue of its enormous database housed on its web-site at glorecords.blm.gov. Here, you can search for and find millions of parcels of land purchased by our ancestors in about thirty states.

This GLO web-site is one of the best FREE on-line tools available to family researchers. But, it is not for the faint of heart, nor is it for those unwilling or unable to to sift through and analyze the thousands of records that exist for most counties.

My immediate goal with this series is to spare you the hundreds of hours of work that it would take you to map the Land Patents for this county. Every Jefferson County homestead or land patent that I have gleaned from public GLO databases is mapped here. Consequently, I can usually show you in an instant, where your ancestor's land is located, as well as the names of nearby land-owners.

Originally, that was my primary goal. But after speaking to other genealogists, it became clear that there was much more that they wanted. Taking their advice set me back almost a full year, but I think you will agree it was worth the wait. Because now, you can learn so much more.

Now, this book answers these sorts of questions:

- Are there any variant spellings for surnames that I have missed in searching GLO records?
- Where is my family's traditional home-place?
- What cemeteries are near Grandma's house?
- My Granddad used to swim in such-and-such-Creek—where is that?
- How close is this little community to that one?
- Are there any other people with the same surname who bought land in the county?
- How about cousins and in-laws—did they buy land in the area?

And these are just for starters!

The rules for using the *Family Maps* books are simple, but the strategies for success are many. Some techniques are apparent on first use, but many are gained with time and experience. Please take the time to notice the roads, cemeteries, creek-names, family names, and unique first-names throughout the whole county. You cannot imagine what YOU might be the first to discover.

I hope to learn that many of you have answered age-old research questions within these pages or that you have discovered relationships previously not even considered. When these sorts of things happen to you, will you please let me hear about it? I would like nothing better. My contact information can always be found at www.arphax.com.

One more thing: please read the "How To Use This Book" chapter; it starts on the next page. This will give you the very best chance to find the treasures that lie within these pages.

My family and I wish you the very best of luck, both in life, and in your research. Greg Boyd

How to Use This Book - A Graphical Summary

Part I
"The Big Picture"

Map A ▸ *Counties in the State*
Map B ▸ *Surrounding Counties*
Map C ▸ *Congressional Townships (Map Groups) in the County*
Map D ▸ *Cities & Towns in the County*
Map E ▸ *Cemeteries in the County*
Surnames in the County ▸ *Number of Land-Parcels for Each Surname*
Surname/Township Index ▸ Directs you to Township Map Groups in Part II

The Surname/Township Index can direct you to any number of **Township Map Groups**

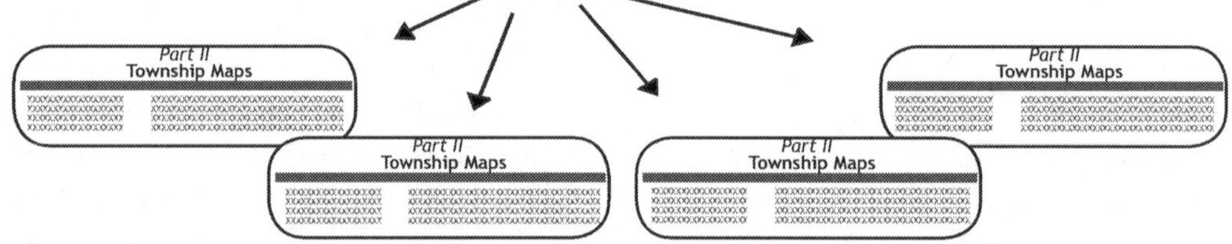

Part II
Township Map Groups
(1 for each Township in the County)

Each Township Map Group contains all four of of the following tools . . .

Land Patent Index ▸ *Every-name Index of Patents Mapped in this Township*
Land Patent Map ▸ *Map of Patents as listed in above Index*
Road Map ▸ *Map of Roads, City-centers, and Cemeteries in the Township*
Historical Map ▸ *Map of Railroads, Lakes, Rivers, Creeks, City-Centers, and Cemeteries*

Appendices

Appendix A ▸ *Congressional Authority enabling Patents within our Maps*
Appendix B ▸ *Section-Parts / Aliquot Parts (a comprehensive list)*
Appendix C ▸ *Multi-patentee Groups (Individuals within Buying Groups)*

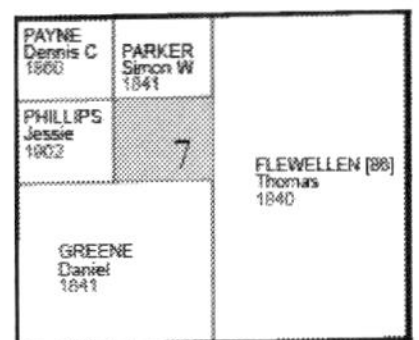

How to Use This Book

The two "Parts" of this *Family Maps* volume seek to answer two different types of questions. Part I deals with broad questions like: what counties surround Jefferson County, are there any ASHCRAFTs in Jefferson County, and if so, in which Townships or Maps can I find them? Ultimately, though, Part I should point you to a particular Township Map Group in Part II.

Part II concerns itself with details like: where exactly is this family's land, who else bought land in the area, and what roads and streams run through the land, or are located nearby. The Chart on the opposite page, and the remainder of this chapter attempt to convey to you the particulars of these two "parts", as well as how best to use them to achieve your research goals.

Part I
"The Big Picture"

Within Part I, you will find five "Big Picture" maps and two county-wide surname tools.

These include:

- Map A - Where Jefferson County lies within the state
- Map B - Counties that surround Jefferson County
- Map C - Congressional Townships of Jefferson County (+ Map Group Numbers)
- Map D - Cities & Towns of Jefferson County (with Index)
- Map E - Cemeteries of Jefferson County (with Index)
- Surnames in Jefferson County Patents (with Parcel-counts for each surname)
- Surname/Township Index (with Parcel-counts for each surname by Township)

The five "Big-Picture" Maps are fairly self-explanatory, yet should not be overlooked. This is particularly true of Maps "C", "D", and "E", all of which show Jefferson County and its Congressional Townships (and their assigned Map Group Numbers).

Let me briefly explain this concept of Map Group Numbers. These are a device completely of our own invention. They were created to help you quickly locate maps without having to remember the full legal name of the various Congressional Townships. It is simply easier to remember "Map Group 1" than a legal name like: "Township 9-North Range 6-West, 5th Principal Meridian." But the fact is that the TRUE legal name for these Townships IS terribly important. These are the designations that others will be familiar with and you will need to accurately record them in your notes. This is why both Map Group numbers AND legal descriptions of Townships are almost always displayed together.

Map "C" will be your first intoduction to "Map Group Numbers", and that is all it contains: legal Township descriptions and their assigned Map Group Numbers. Once you get further into your research, and more immersed in the details, you will likely want to refer back to Map "C" from time to time, in order to regain your bearings on just where in the county you are researching.

Remember, township boundaries are a completely artificial device, created to standardize land descriptions. But do not let them become a boundary in your mind when choosing which townships to research. Your relative's in-laws, children, cousins, siblings, and mamas and papas, might just as easily have lived in the township next to the one your grandfather lived in—rather than in the one where he actually lived. So Map "C" can be your guide to which other Townships/ Map Groups you likewise ought to analyze.

Of course, the same holds true for County lines; this is the purpose behind Map "B". It shows you surrounding counties that you may want to consider for further reserarch.

Map "D", the Cities and Towns map, is the first map with an index. Map "E" is the second (Cemeteries). Both, Maps "D" and "E" give you broad views of City (or Cemetery) locations in the County. But they go much further by pointing you toward pertinent Township Map Groups so you can locate the patents, roads, and waterways located near a particular city or cemetery.

Once you are familiar with these *Family Maps* volumes and the county you are researching, the "Surnames In Jefferson County" chapter (or its sister chapter in other volumes) is where you'll likely start your future research sessions. Here, you can quickly scan its few pages and see if anyone in the county possesses the surnames you are researching. The "Surnames in Jefferson County" list shows only two things: surnames and the number of parcels of land we have located for that surname in Jefferson County. But whether or not you immediately locate the surnames you are researching, please do not go any further without taking a few moments to scan ALL the surnames in these very few pages.

You cannot imagine how many lost ancestors are waiting to be found by someone willing to take just a little longer to scan the "Surnames In Jefferson County" list. Misspellings and typographical errors abound in most any index of this sort. Don't miss out on finding your Kinard that was written Rynard or Cox that was written Lox. If it looks funny or wrong, it very often is. And one of those little errors may well be your relative.

Now, armed with a surname and the knowledge that it has one or more entries in this book, you are ready for the "Surname/Township Index." Unlike the "Surnames In Jefferson County", which has only one line per Surname, the "Surname/Township Index" contains one line-item for each Township Map Group in which each surname is found. In other words, each line represents a different Township Map Group that you will need to review.

Specifically, each line of the Surname/Township Index contains the following four columns of information:

1. Surname
2. Township Map Group Number (these Map Groups are found in Part II)
3. Parcels of Land (number of them with the given Surname within the Township)
4. Meridian/Township/Range (the legal description for this Township Map Group)

The key column here is that of the Township Map Group Number. While you should definitely record the Meridian, Township, and Range, you can do that later. Right now, you need to dig a little deeper. That Map Group Number tells you where in Part II that you need to start digging.

But before you leave the "Surname/Township Index", do the same thing that you did with the "Surnames in Jefferson County" list: take a moment to scan the pages of the Index and see if there are similarly spelled or misspelled surnames that deserve your attention. Here again, is an easy opportunity to discover grossly misspelled family names with very little effort. Now you are ready to turn to . . .

Part II
"Township Map Groups"

You will normally arrive here in Part II after being directed to do so by one or more "Map Group Numbers" in the Surname/Township Index of Part I.

Each Map Group represents a set of four tools dedicated to a single Congressional Township that is either wholly or partially within the county. If you are trying to learn all that you can about a particular family or their land, then these tools should usually be viewed in the order they are presented.

These four tools include:

1. a Land Patent Index
2. a Land Patent Map
3. a Road Map, and
4. an Historical Map

As I mentioned earlier, each grouping of this sort is assigned a Map Group Number. So, let's now move on to a discussion of the four tools that make up one of these Township Map Groups.

Land Patent Index

Each Township Map Group's Index begins with a title, something along these lines:

MAP GROUP 1: Index to Land Patents
Township 16-North Range 5-West (2nd PM)

The Index contains seven (7) columns. They are:

1. ID (a unique ID number for this Individual and a corresponding Parcel of land in this Township)
2. Individual in Patent (name)
3. Sec. (Section), and
4. Sec. Part (Section Part, or Aliquot Part)
5. Date Issued (Patent)
6. Other Counties (often means multiple counties were mentioned in GLO records, or the section lies within multiple counties).
7. For More Info . . . (points to other places within this index or elsewhere in the book where you can find more information)

While most of the seven columns are self-explanatory, I will take a few moments to explain the "Sec. Part." and "For More Info" columns.

The "Sec. Part" column refers to what surveryors and other land professionals refer to as an Aliquot Part. The origins and use of such a term mean little to a non-surveyor, and I have chosen to simply call these sub-sections of land what they are: a "Section Part". No matter what we call them, what we are referring to are things like a quarter-section or half-section or quarter-quarter-section. See Appendix "B" for most of the "Section Parts" you will come across (and many you will not) and what size land-parcel they represent.

The "For More Info" column of the Index may seem like a small appendage to each line, but please recognize quickly that this is not so. And to understand the various items you might find here, you need to become familiar with the Legend that appears at the top of each Land Patent Index.

Here is a sample of the Legend . . .

LEGEND

"For More Info . . . " column

A = Authority (Legislative Act, See Appendix "A")
B = Block or Lot (location in Section unknown)
C = Cancelled Patent
F = Fractional Section
G = Group (Multi-Patentee Patent, see Appendix "C")
V = Overlaps another Parcel
R = Re-Issued (Parcel patented more than once)

Most parcels of land will have only one or two of these items in their "For More Info" columns, but when that is not the case, there is often some valuable information to be gained from further investigation. Below, I will explain what each of these items means to you you as a researcher.

A = Authority
<u>(Legislative Act, See Appendix "A")</u>

All Federal Land Patents were issued because some branch of our government (usually the U.S. Congress) passed a law making such a transfer of title possible. And therefore every patent within these pages will have an "A" item next to it in the index. The number after the "A" indicates which item in Appendix "A" holds the citation to the particular law which authorized the transfer of land to the public. As it stands, most of the Public Land data compiled and released by our government, and which serves as the basis for the patents mapped here, concerns itself with "Cash Sale" homesteads. So in some Counties, the law which authorized cash sales will be the primary, if not the only, entry in the Appendix.

<u>B = Block or Lot (location in Section unknown)</u>

A "B" designation in the Index is a tip-off that the EXACT location of the patent within the map is not apparent from the legal description. This Patent will nonetheless be noted within the proper

Section along with any other Lots purchased in the Section. Given the scope of this project (many states and many Counties are being mapped), trying to locate all relevant plats for Lots (if they even exist) and accurately mapping them would have taken one person several lifetimes. But since our primary goal from the onset has been to establish relationships between neighbors and families, very little is lost to this goal since we can still observe who all lived in which Section.

C = Cancelled Patent

A Cancelled Patent is just that: cancelled. Whether the original Patentee forfeited his or her patent due to fraud, a technicality, non-payment, or whatever, the fact remains that it is significant to know who received patents for what parcels and when. A cancellation may be evidence that the Patentee never physically re-located to the land, but does not in itself prove that point. Further evidence would be required to prove that. *See also*, Re-issued Patents, *below*.

F = Fractional Section

A Fractional Section is one that contains less than 640 acres, almost always because of a body of water. The exact size and shape of land-parcels contained in such sections may not be ascertainable, but we map them nonetheless. Just keep in mind that we are not mapping an actual parcel to scale in such instances. Another point to consider is that we have located some fractional sections that are not so designated by the Bureau of Land Management in their data. This means that not all fractional sections have been so identified in our indexes.

G = Group
(Multi-Patentee Patent, see Appendix "C")

A "G" designation means that the Patent was issued to a GROUP of people (Multi-patentees). The "G" will always be followed by a number. Some such groups were quite large and it was impractical if not impossible to display each individual in our maps without unduly affecting readability. EACH person in the group is named in the Index, but they won't all be found on the Map. You will find the name of the first person in such a Group on the map with the Group number next to it, enclosed in [square brackets].

To find all the members of the Group you can either scan the Index for all people with the same Group Number or you can simply refer to Appendix "C" where all members of the Group are listed next to their number.

O = Overlaps another Parcel

An Overlap is one where PART of a parcel of land gets issued on more than one patent. For genealogical purposes, both transfers of title are important and both Patentees are mapped. If the ENTIRE parcel of land is re-issued, that is what we call it, a Re-Issued Patent (*see below*). The number after the "O" indicates the ID for the overlapping Patent(s) contained within the same Index. Like Re-Issued and Cancelled Patents, Overlaps may cause a map-reader to be confused at first, but for genealogical purposes, all of these parties' relationships to the underlying land is important, and therefore, we map them.

R = Re-Issued (Parcel patented more than once)

The label, "Re-issued Patent" describes Patents which were issued more than once for land with the EXACT SAME LEGAL DESCRIPTION. Whether the original patent was cancelled or not, there were a good many parcels which were patented more than once. The number after the "R" indicates the ID for the other Patent contained within the same Index that was for the same land. A quick glance at the map itself within the relevant Section will be the quickest way to find the other Patentee to whom the Parcel was transferred. They should both be mapped in the same general area.

I have gone to some length describing all sorts of anomalies either in the underlying data or in their representation on the maps and indexes in this book. Most of this will bore the most ardent reseracher, but I do this with all due respect to those researchers who will inevitably (and rightfully) ask: *"Why isn't so-and-so's name on the exact spot that the index says it should be?"*

In most cases it will be due to the existence of a Multi-Patentee Patent, a Re-issued Patent, a Cancelled Patent, or Overlapping Parcels named in separate Patents. I don't pretend that this discussion will answer every question along these lines, but I hope it will at least convince you of the complexity of the subject.

Not to despair, this book's companion web-site will offer a way to further explain "odd-ball" or errant data. Each book (County) will have its own web-page or pages to discuss such situations. You can go to www.arphax.com to find the relevant web-page for Jefferson County.

Land Patent Map

On the first two-page spread following each Township's Index to Land Patents, you'll find the corresponding Land Patent Map. And here lies the real heart of our work. For the first time anywhere, researchers will be able to observe and analyze, on a grand scale, most of the original land-owners for an area AND see them mapped in proximity to each one another.

We encourage you to make vigorous use of the accompanying Index described above, but then later, to abandon it, and just stare at these maps for a while. This is a great way to catch misspellings or to find collateral kin you'd not known were in the area.

Each Land Patent Map represents one Congressional Township containing approximately 36-square miles. Each of these square miles is labeled by an accompanying Section Number (1 through 36, in most cases). Keep in mind, that this book concerns itself solely with Jefferson County's patents. Townships which creep into one or more other counties will not be shown in their entirety in any one book. You will need to consult other books, as they become available, in order to view other countys' patents, cities, cemeteries, etc.

But getting back to Jefferson County: each Land Patent Map contains a Statistical Chart that looks like the following:

Township Statistics

Parcels Mapped	:	173
Number of Patents	:	163
Number of Individuals	:	152
Patentees Identified	:	151
Number of Surnames	:	137
Multi-Patentee Parcels	:	4
Oldest Patent Date	:	11/27/1820
Most Recent Patent	:	9/28/1917
Block/Lot Parcels	:	0
Parcels Re-Issued	:	3
Parcels that Overlap	:	8
Cities and Towns	:	6
Cemeteries	:	6

This information may be of more use to a social statistician or historian than a genealogist, but I think all three will find it interesting.

Most of the statistics are self-explanatory, and what is not, was described in the above discussion of the Index's Legend, but I do want to mention a few of them that may affect your understanding of the Land Patent Maps.

First of all, Patents often contain more than one Parcel of land, so it is common for there to be more Parcels than Patents. Also, the Number of Individuals will more often than not, not match the number of Patentees. A Patentee is literally the person or PERSONS named in a patent. So, a Patent may have a multi-person Patentee or a single-person patentee. Nonetheless, we account for all these individuals in our indexes.

On the lower-righthand side of the Patent Map is a Legend which describes various features in the map, including Section Boundaries, Patent (land) Boundaries, Lots (numbered), and Multi-Patentee Group Numbers. You'll also find a "Helpful Hints" Box that will assist you.

One important note: though the vast majority of Patents mapped in this series will prove to be reasonably accurate representations of their actual locations, we cannot claim this for patents lying along state and county lines, or waterways, or that have been platted (lots).

Shifting boundaries and sparse legal descriptions in the GLO data make this a reality that we have nonetheless tried to overcome by estimating these patents' locations the best that we can.

Road Map

On the two-page spread following each Patent Map you will find a Road Map covering the exact same area (the same Congressional Township).

For me, fully exploring the past means that every once in a while I must leave the library and travel to the actual locations where my ancestors once walked and worked the land. Our Township Road Maps are a great place to begin such a quest.

Keep in mind that the scaling and proportion of these maps was chosen in order to squeeze hundreds of people-names, road-names, and place-names into tinier spaces than you would traditionally see. These are not professional road-maps, and like any secondary genealogical source, should be looked upon as an entry-way to original sources—in this case, original patents and applications, professionally produced maps and surveys, etc.

Both our Road Maps and Historical Maps contain cemeteries and city-centers, along with a listing of these on the left-hand side of the map. I should note that I am showing you city center-points, rather than city-limit boundaries, because in many instances, this will represent a place where settlement began. This may be a good time to mention that many cemeteries are located on private property, Always check with a local historical or genealogical society to see if a particular cemetery is publicly accessible (if it is not obviously so). As a final point, look for your surnames among the road-names. You will often be surprised by what you find.

Historical Map

The third and final map in each Map Group is our attempt to display what each Township might have looked like before the advent of modern roads. In frontier times, people were usually more determined to settle near rivers and creeks than they were near roads, which were often few and far between. As was the case with the Road Map, we've included the same cemeteries and city-centers. We've also included railroads, many of which came along before most roads.

While some may claim "Historical Map" to be a bit of a misnomer for this tool, we settled for this label simply because it was almost as accurate as saying "Railroads, Lakes, Rivers, Cities, and Cemeteries," and it is much easier to remember.

In Closing . . .

By way of example, here is *A Really Good Way to Use a Township Map Group.* First, find the person you are researching in the Township's Index to Land Patents, which will direct you to the proper Section and parcel on the Patent Map. But before leaving the Index, scan all the patents within it, looking for other names of interest. Now, turn to the Patent Map and locate your parcels of land. Pay special attention to the names of patent-holders who own land surrounding your person of interest. Next, turn the page and look at the same Section(s) on the Road Map. Note which roads are closest to your parcels and also the names of nearby towns and cemeteries. Using other resources, you may be able to learn of kin who have been buried here, plus, you may choose to visit these cemeteries the next time you are in the area.

Finally, turn to the Historical Map. Look once more at the same Sections where you found your research subject's land. Note the nearby streams, creeks, and other geographical features. You may be surprised to find family names were used to name them, or you may see a name you haven't heard mentioned in years and years—and a new research possibility is born.

Many more techniques for using these *Family Maps* volumes will no doubt be discovered. If from time to time, you will navigate to Jefferson County's web-page at www.arphax.com (use the "Research" link), you can learn new tricks as they become known (or you can share ones you have employed). But for now, you are ready to get started. So, go, and good luck.

– Part I –

The Big Picture

Map A - Where Jefferson County, Alabama Lies Within the State

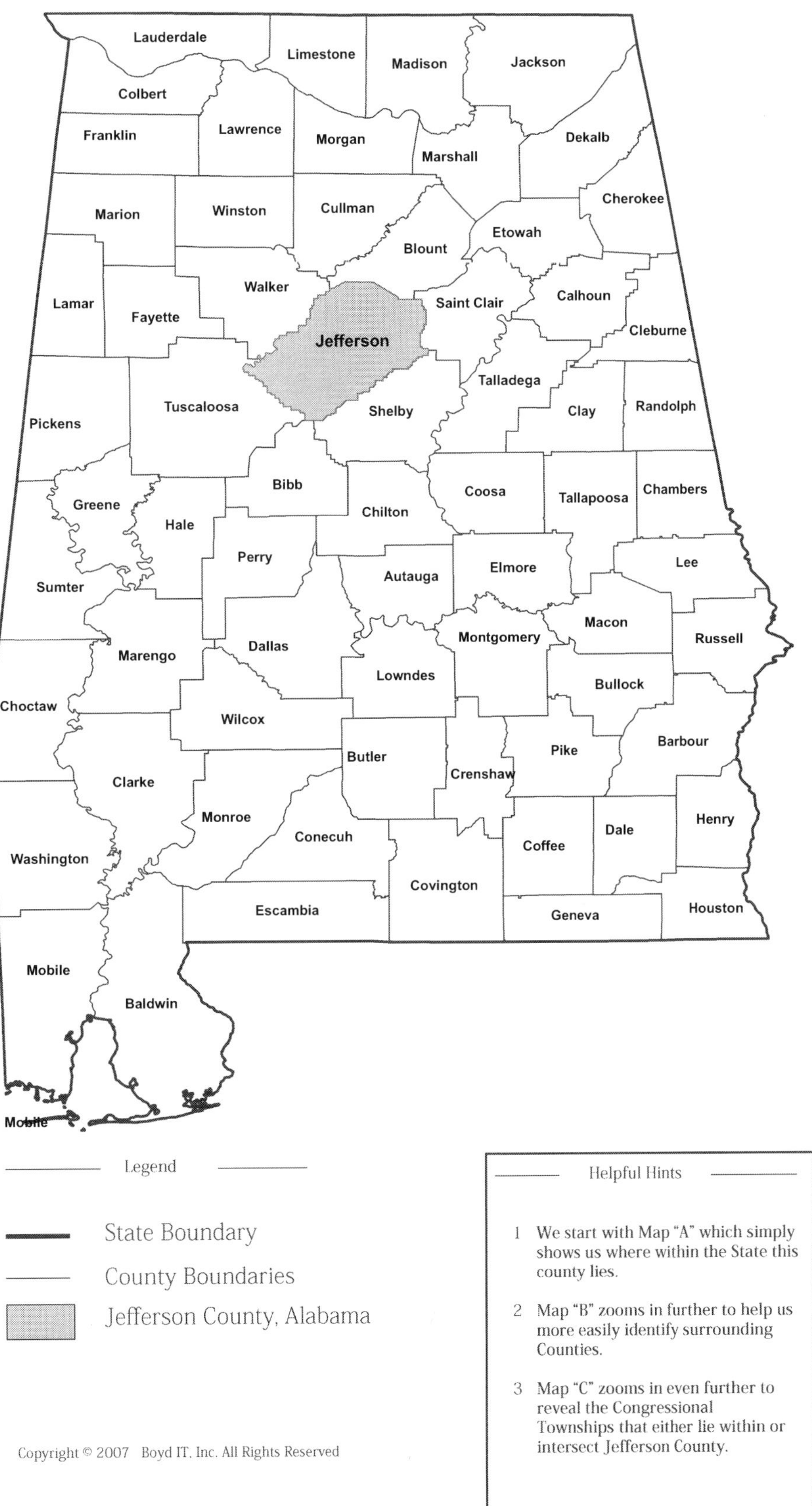

Helpful Hints

1 We start with Map "A" which simply shows us where within the State this county lies.

2 Map "B" zooms in further to help us more easily identify surrounding Counties.

3 Map "C" zooms in even further to reveal the Congressional Townships that either lie within or intersect Jefferson County.

Map B - Jefferson County, Alabama and Surrounding Counties

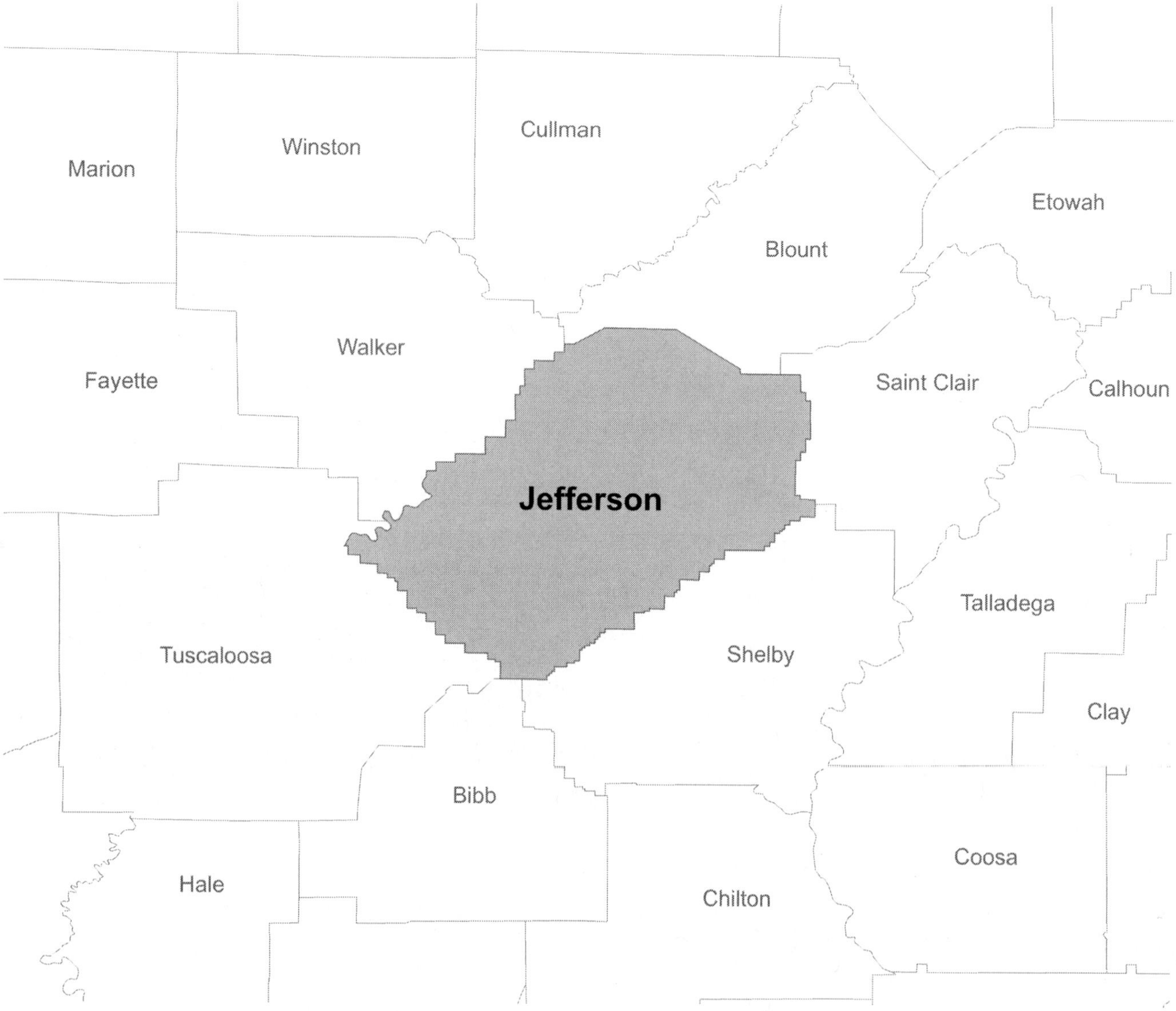

Marion
Winston
Cullman
Etowah
Blount
Walker
Saint Clair
Calhoun
Fayette
Jefferson
Talladega
Tuscaloosa
Shelby
Clay
Bibb
Coosa
Hale
Chilton

Legend

- State Boundaries (when applicable)
- County Boundary

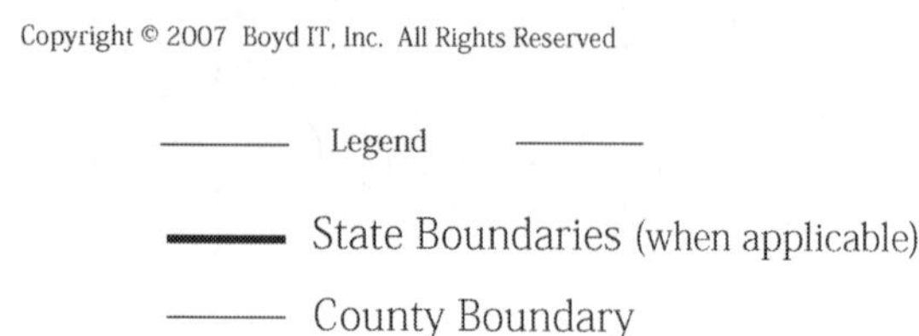

Helpful Hints

1 Many Patent-holders and their families settled across county lines. It is always a good idea to check nearby counties for your families.

2 Refer to Map "A" to see a broader view of where this County lies within the State, and Map "C" to see which Congressional Townships lie within Jefferson County.

Map C - Congressional Townships of Jefferson County, Alabama

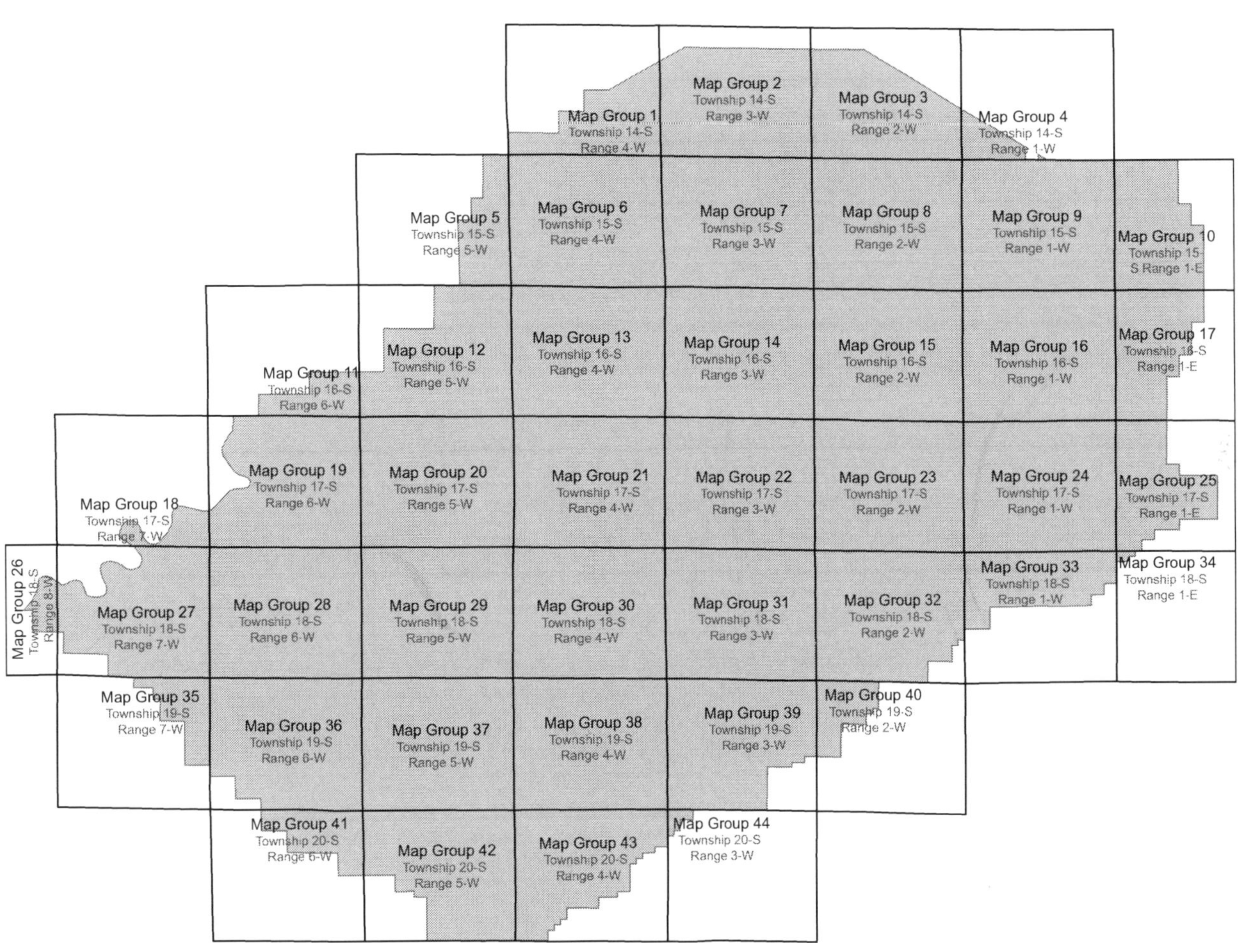

Legend

Jefferson County, Alabama

Congressional Townships

Helpful Hints

1 Many Patent-holders and their families settled across county lines. It is always a good idea to check nearby counties for your families (See Map "B").

2 Refer to Map "A" to see a broader view of where this county lies within the State, and Map "B" for a view of the counties surrounding Jefferson County.

Map D Index: Cities & Towns of Jefferson County, Alabama

The following represents the Cities and Towns of Jefferson County, along with the corresponding Map Group in which each is found. Cities and Towns are displayed in both the Road and Historical maps in the Group.

City/Town	Map Group No.
Adamsville	13
Adger	37
Alton	24
Bessemer	38
Birmingham	22
Brookside	13
Bullard Shoals (historical)	37
Cardiff	13
Cedar Grove (historical)	25
Clay	9
Docena	21
Dolomite	30
Fairfield	30
Fultondale	15
Gardendale	14
Graysville	13
Kimberly	2
Leeds	25
McCalla	37
Morris	7
Mount Olive	14
Mulga	21
New Castle	15
Palmerdale	9
Pinson	9
Pleasant Grove	30
Sayre	6
Shannon	39
Trafford	3
Trussville	16
Warrior	2
Watson	14

Map D - Cities & Towns of Jefferson County, Alabama

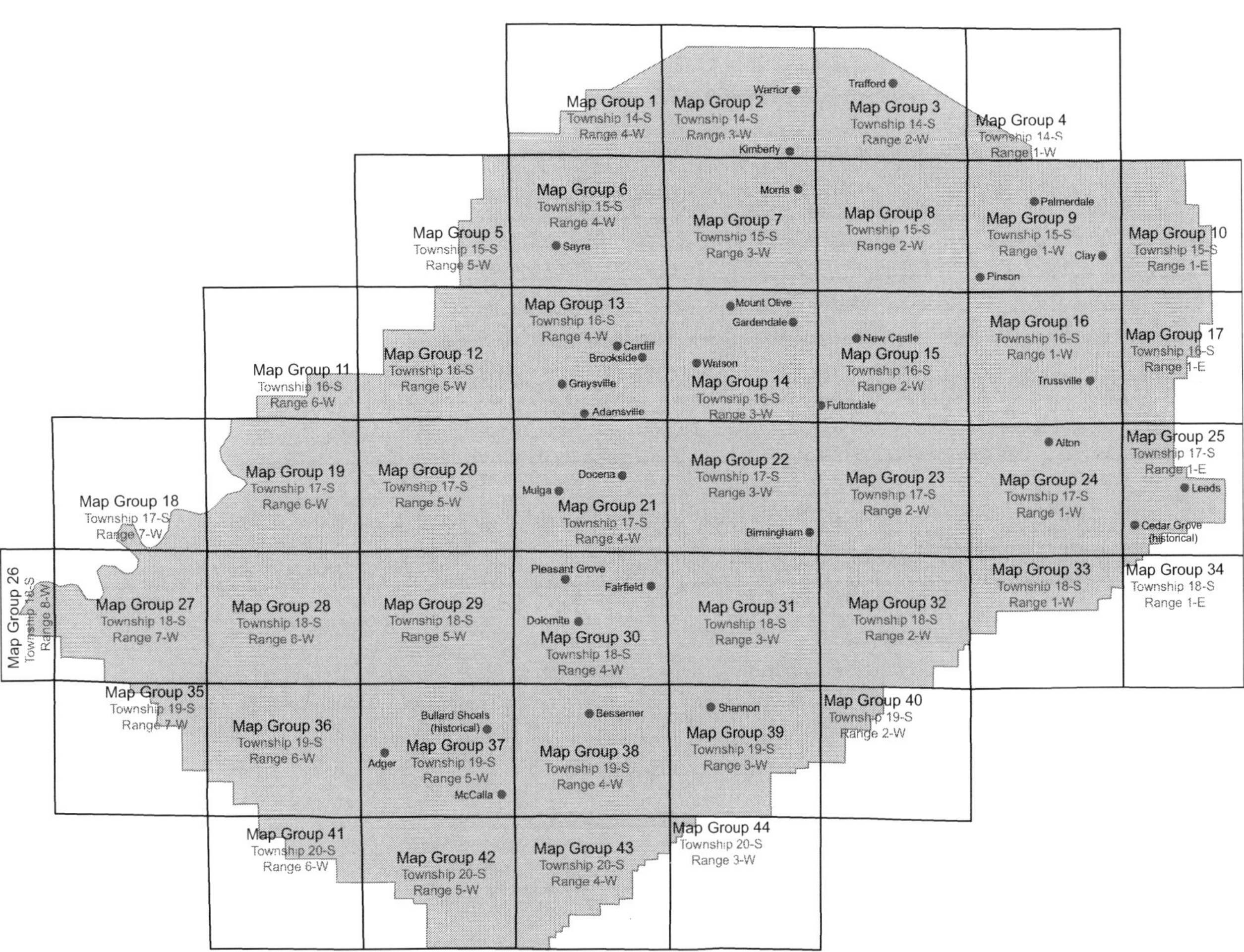

Legend

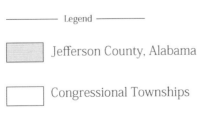

Jefferson County, Alabama

Congressional Townships

Helpful Hints

1 Cities and towns are marked only at their center-points as published by the USGS and/or NationalAtlas.gov. This often enables us to more closely approximate where these might have existed when first settled.

2 To see more specifically where these Cities & Towns are located within the county, refer to both the Road and Historical maps in the Map-Group referred to above. See also, the Map "D" Index on the opposite page.

Map E Index: Cemeteries of Jefferson County, Alabama

The following represents many of the Cemeteries of Jefferson County, along with the corresponding Township Map Group in which each is found. Cemeteries are displayed in both the Road and Historical maps in the Map Groups referred to below.

Cemetery	Map Group No.
Adams Cem.	12
Adger Cem.	37
Atwood Cem.	19
Bagley Bend Cem.	12
Bass Cem.	23
Bass Cem.	24
Beth-El Cem.	38
Bibb Cem.	7
Bivens Chapel Cem.	13
Brewer Cem.	2
Brighton Cem.	30
Bush Cem.	23
Cahaba Heights Cem.	32
Cain Creek Cem.	2
Cardiff Cem.	13
Castle Heights Memorial Gardens	8
Cedar Hill Cem.	38
Creel Cem.	8
Crooked Creek Cem.	7
Crumley Chapel Cem.	21
Dug Hill Cem.	19
Earltown Cem.	24
East Lake Cem.	23
Edward Cem.	7
Elmwood Cem.	31
Emanuel Cem.	22
Fairington Cem.	43
Forest Crest Cem.	24
Forest Hill Cem.	23
Fraternal Cem.	22
George Cem.	43
George Washington Memorial Gardens	21
Glasgow Hill Cem.	13
Grace Hill Cem.	31
Greenwood Cem.	23
Higgins Cem.	23
Highland Memorial Gardens	30
Hodges Cem.	14
Hughes Cem.	8
Inglenook Cem.	23
Jefferson Garden of Memories	39
Jefferson Memorial Gardens	16
Joley Cem.	30
Knesses Israel Cem.	22
Lakeview Cem.	21
Lawler Cem.	5
Lincoln Cem.	37
Linn Cem.	13
Linns Crossing Cem.	13
Maben Cem.	12
Martin Luther King Junior Memorial	30
Mason Cem.	30
Massey Cem.	43
McCombs Cem.	24
McElwain Cem.	23
Midway Cem.	21
Moncrief Cem.	14
Morris Cem.	7
Mount Calvary Cem.	10

Cemetery	Map Group No.
Mount Hebron Cem.	33
Mount Nebo Cem.	16
Mount Olive Cem.	14
Mount Zion Cem.	23
Narl Cem.	7
New Horizon Memorial Gardens	5
Oak Hill Cem.	22
Oakdale Cem.	30
Oakland Cem.	31
Pine Hill Cem.	37
Pinson Cem.	9
Prescott Cem.	19
Providence Cem.	27
Reed Cem.	16
Roberts Cem.	22
Sadlers Cem.	38
Saint Michaels Cem.	13
Salter Cem.	20
Shadowlawn Memorial Park	31
Shady Grove Cem.	20
Sheritt Cem.	15
Shiloh Cem.	25
Smithson Cem.	43
Taylors Chapel Cem.	16
Toadvine Cem.	28
Trussville Cem.	16
Union Cem.	30
Union Cem.	38
Union Grove Cem.	5
Union Grove Cem.	21
Union Hill Cem.	32
Valhalla Cem.	30
Valley Creek Cem.	29
Village Falls Cem.	21
Virginia Mines Cem.	29
Walker Cem.	14
Weaver Cem.	19
Wise Cem.	32

Map E - Cemeteries of Jefferson County, Alabama

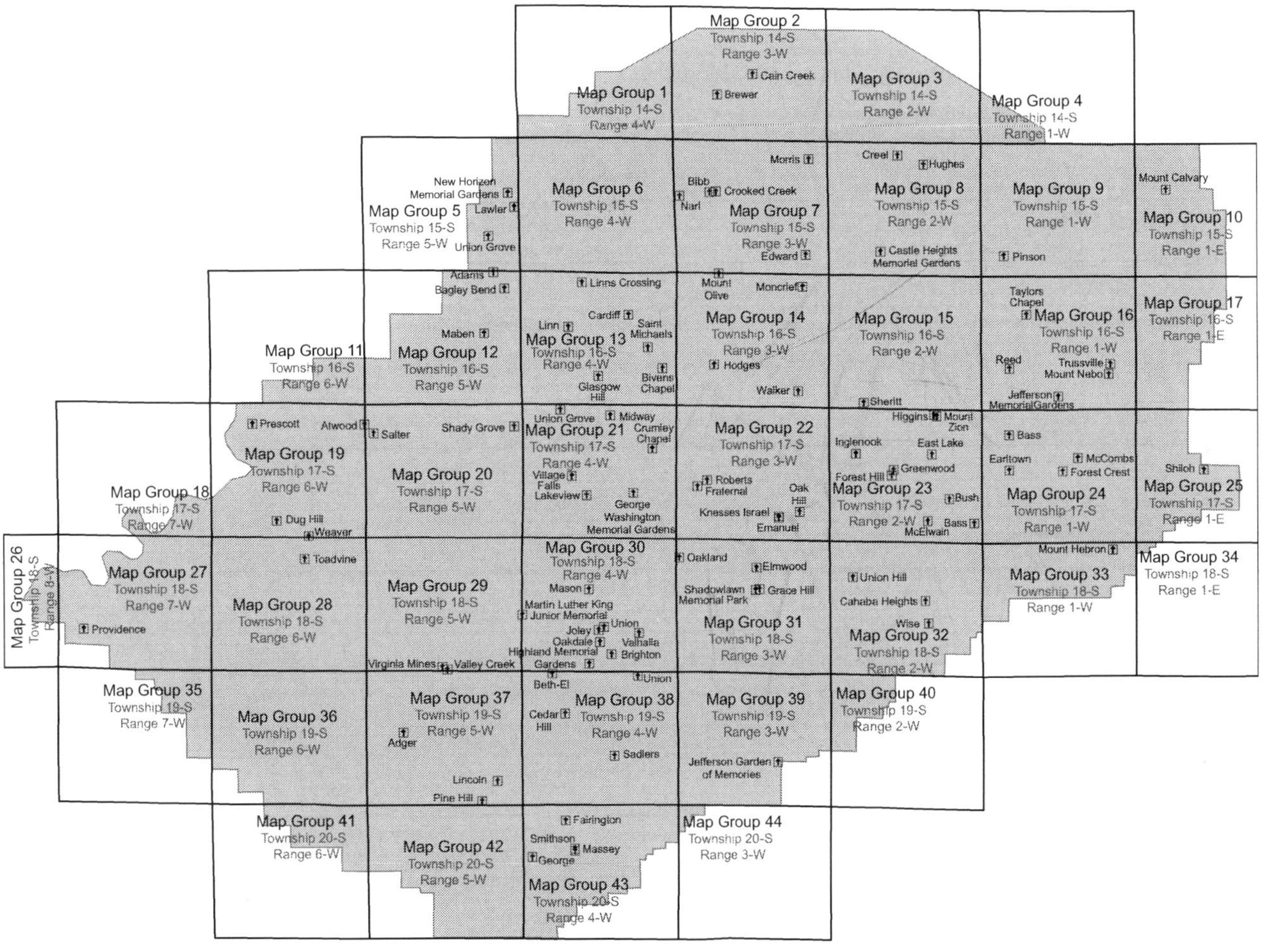

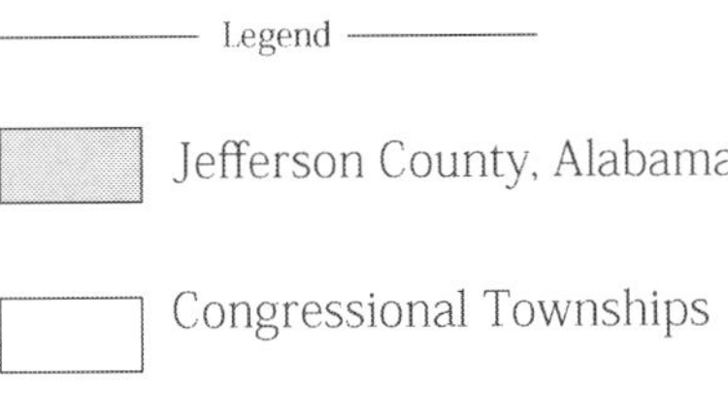

Helpful Hints

1 Cemeteries are marked at locations as published by the USGS and/or NationalAtlas.gov.

2 To see more specifically where these Cemeteries are located, refer to the Road & Historical maps in the Map-Group referred to above. See also, the Map "E" Index on the opposite page to make sure you don't miss any of the Cemeteries located within this Congressional township.

Surnames in Jefferson County, Alabama Patents

The following list represents the surnames that we have located in Jefferson County, Alabama Patents and the number of parcels that we have mapped for each one. Here is a quick way to determine the existence (or not) of Patents to be found in the subsequent indexes and maps of this volume.

Surname	# of Land Parcels	Surname	# of Land Parcels	Surname	# of Land Parcels	Surname	# of Land Parcels
AARON	3	BARGER	1	BRASWELL	7	CARMICHEAL	2
ABANATHY	2	BARKSDALE	2	BRAZIER	1	CARMICLE	2
ABARNATHY	4	BARNETT	1	BREWER	11	CARPENTER	1
ABEL	1	BARR	3	BRIDGES	3	CARRINGTON	3
ABELS	1	BARRY	3	BRIDGMON	2	CARROL	1
ABERCROMBIE	1	BARTON	14	BRITT	1	CARROLL	6
ABERNATHY	14	BASS	26	BROCK	6	CARTER	4
ABSTEN	1	BATES	4	BROOKS	8	CARZELIUS	1
ABSTON	1	BATSON	13	BROTHERS	2	CASE	4
ACKER	1	BAYLES	4	BROWN	102	CASH	3
ACTON	29	BAYLESS	2	BROWNE	1	CAST	1
ADAMS	19	BEAM	3	BROWNLEE	4	CASTE	3
ADCOCK	4	BEARD	4	BRUCE	1	CAWOOD	3
ADKINS	10	BEARDEN	6	BRYANT	3	CEMP	1
ADKINSON	2	BEARDIN	3	BUCK	1	CHAMBLEE	9
AGERTON	3	BEASLEY	3	BUCKALEW	3	CHAMLESS	1
AIKIN	5	BEASLY	1	BUCKELEW	3	CHAPEL	1
AKERS	2	BEAZLEY	2	BUCKLEY	1	CHAPMAN	5
AKINS	1	BECKHAM	1	BUFFINGTON	8	CHAPPELL	6
ALABAMA	3	BEERS	2	BULLARD	3	CHENNAULT	1
ALEXANDER	2	BELCHER	15	BULLOCK	3	CHILDERS	1
ALLEN	8	BELL	14	BURCHFIELD	15	CHILDRESS	7
ALLEY	1	BELSHER	1	BURFORD	10	CHILTON	4
ALLINDER	7	BENNETT	1	BURGIN	11	CHOAT	2
ALLMAN	2	BETTER	1	BURKS	1	CHRISTIAN	2
ALLRED	1	BIBB	17	BURLASON	1	CLARK	9
ALLSOP	1	BILLINGSLEA	1	BURLESON	1	CLARKE	1
ALMON	1	BILLINGSLEY	2	BURLESSON	1	CLATON	1
ALRED	1	BIRD	1	BURLINSON	2	CLAYTON	5
ANDERSON	21	BIRKETT	1	BURNS	8	CLEMENTS	18
ANDREWS	1	BISHOP	9	BURRELL	6	CLICK	2
ANTHONY	3	BIVEN	2	BURTON	12	CLIFT	5
APPLEBERRY	1	BIVENS	10	BURWELL	6	CLINE	2
ARCHER	1	BIVINS	4	BUSBY	1	CLOPTON	4
ARMSTEAD	2	BLACK	21	BUSH	4	CLOWER	1
ARMSTRONG	39	BLACKBURN	5	BUTLER	11	COBB	2
ARNETT	5	BLACKWELL	2	BUTTLER	2	COBELL	1
ARNOLD	3	BLALOCK	1	BYARS	20	COCHRAN	2
ASHLEY	3	BLANKINGSHIP	1	BYERS	9	COCKE	1
ASKEW	2	BLANKINSHIP	1	BYRAM	8	CODDELL	1
ATTAWAY	2	BLAYLOCK	1	BYRD	1	COKER	8
ATWOOD	2	BLITON	2	CADDELL	1	COLDWELL	1
AUSTIN	2	BLUDWORTH	1	CAIN	8	COLE	6
AVERY	5	BLYTHE	2	CALDWELL	23	COLEMAN	3
AYERS	3	BOOKER	3	CALLAWAY	2	COLLEY	3
AYRES	10	BOOKOUT	3	CAMAK	3	COLLIER	2
AYRS	1	BOONE	1	CAMERON	8	COLLINS	3
BAGBY	4	BOYD	7	CAMMEL	2	COLLMAN	1
BAGGETT	1	BOYLES	1	CAMP	8	COLLY	1
BAGLEY	30	BRACKNER	1	CAMPBELL	21	COLWELL	3
BAGWELL	7	BRADFORD	14	CANADAY	1	COMPANY	2
BAILEY	27	BRADLEY	2	CANNON	14	CONDEN	1
BAIRD	13	BRADSHAW	2	CANTERBERRY	2	CONDRAY	1
BAKER	17	BRAGG	3	CANTRELL	3	CONDRY	2
BALCOM	2	BRAKE	4	CAPERS	1	CONNER	11
BALL	1	BRAMLET	2	CAPPS	1	CONWAY	2
BALLARD	1	BRAMLETT	1	CAREY	2	COOK	4
BANKS	1	BRANHAM	1	CARGILE	11	COOKE	1
BANKSTON	1	BRANTLEY	1	CARITHERS	1	COOLEY	7
BARBEAU	1	BRASFIELD	2	CARLILE	2	COOPER	21
BARBOUR	1	BRASHER	2	CARLISLE	12	COPELAND	1
BARFORD	1	BRASSFIELD	2	CARMICHAEL	10	CORLEY	7

Surname	# of Land Parcels
CORNELIUS	3
COSBY	3
COTNAM	1
COTTON	1
COUNTS	1
COWARD	4
COWDEN	11
COWEN	1
COWLEY	5
COX	12
COZBY	2
CRAIGER	1
CRAIK	1
CRANE	8
CRANNEY	3
CRAUSWELL	1
CRAWFORD	1
CREEL	9
CREWS	1
CROCKER	21
CROCKETT	2
CROOKS	13
CROSS	6
CROTWELL	2
CROW	1
CRUM	4
CRUMLY	2
CRUMP	4
CULBERTSON	3
CULP	1
CULPEPPER	3
CUMMING	1
CUMMINGS	3
CUMMINS	9
CUNINGHAM	1
CUNNINGHAM	13
CURRY	4
DABBS	5
DACUS	2
DAILEY	2
DANIEL	9
DANIELL	1
DAVENPORT	6
DAVIDSON	6
DAVIS	22
DAWSON	1
DEAN	3
DEASE	1
DEATON	7
DEAVENPORT	2
DEAVOURS	1
DEES	6
DELANY	2
DELASHAW	1
DELLASHAW	2
DEMENT	1
DEMOTT	2
DENTON	3
DEPOISTER	2
DESHAZO	1
DEVERNEY	1
DICKENSON	1
DICKEY	7
DICKINSON	5
DIFFEY	1
DILL	1
DILLARD	1
DILLASHAW	1
DIMMICK	3
DISON	2
DOBBS	3
DOCKENS	2
DOCKINGS	2
DODD	6
DOGGET	2
DOLLAR	1
DONELSON	8
DORMAN	5
DORNING	6
DOROUGH	4
DOSS	13
DOTSON	3
DOUGLASS	1
DOWNEY	10
DOWNS	2
DOXEY	5
DRAKE	2
DRAPER	8
DRENNON	1
DUFF	2
DUKE	4
DULANY	12
DUMAS	5
DUNN	11
DUPEY	6
DUPREY	1
DUPUY	16
DUTTON	6
DYER	4
EARL	1
EARLE	15
EARLEY	6
EARLY	3
EARNEST	1
EASTIN	6
EASTIS	13
EATON	10
ECHOLS	19
EDENS	5
EDMUNDSON	1
EDWARDS	26
ELLARD	10
ELLERD	1
ELLICOTT	1
ELLINGTON	3
ELLIOTT	5
ELLIS	6
EMOND	1
ENDSLEY	4
ENGLISH	1
EPPERSON	2
EPPES	2
ERNEST	1
ERWIN	4
ESKEW	2
ESPEY	2
ETHRIDGE	1
EUBANK	10
EUBANKS	4
EVANS	4
EVERETT	1
EZEKIAL	1
EZEKIEL	7
FAGASON	1
FAGERSON	1
FALKNER	1
FALKS	4
FANCHER	3
FARLEY	1
FARR	1
FARRAR	1
FARRINGTON	2
FARRIS	1
FASON	3
FATIO	2
FAUCETT	4
FEENKER	1
FENDLEY	3
FERGUSON	4
FERRINGTON	2
FIELDS	38
FINCH	1
FINDLEY	1
FINLEY	2
FISHER	2
FLANAGAN	4
FLEMING	1
FLORENCE	3
FLOWERS	9
FORBIS	2
FORD	1
FORMAN	1
FORREST	1
FORRESTER	4
FORTNER	2
FOSSETT	3
FOSTER	17
FOUST	2
FOWLER	2
FOX	1
FRANKLIN	63
FRANKS	1
FRAZER	1
FRAZIER	19
FREELAND	6
FREEMAN	3
FRENCH	1
FRETWELL	2
FRIEDMAN	1
FRIEL	1
FRIERSON	3
FRIES	1
FULLER	5
FULMER	3
FULTON	1
FURGASON	1
GABLE	1
GAFFORD	1
GALLAGHER	1
GALLAWAY	1
GALLOWAY	4
GAMMAGE	2
GANONS	1
GANUS	3
GARNER	13
GARRETT	11
GARRITT	2
GARY	1
GEE	2
GEESLIN	1
GENTRY	1
GEORGE	14
GERMAN	2
GESNER	1
GILBERT	29
GILL	25
GILLASPIE	1
GILLEN	3
GILLESPIE	22
GILLEY	1
GILLIAN	2
GILLILAND	1
GILLMORE	1
GILMER	8
GILMORE	10
GILPIN	1
GINERY	2
GIVENS	3
GLASGOW	9
GLASS	14
GLAZE	10
GLENN	32
GLOVER	14
GOAS	1
GODFREY	3
GODWIN	4
GOGGANS	5
GOING	1
GOINS	1
GOLDEN	14
GOLDING	1
GOLDSBY	2
GOODE	18
GOODMAN	1
GOODWIN	86
GOOLD	3
GOOLSBY	8
GORE	6
GORMAN	6
GOSSET	4
GOSSETT	3
GOULSBY	4
GOWEN	1
GOWIN	2
GOWINS	1
GOYENS	1
GOYNE	5
GRACE	16
GRAHAM	15
GRANT	2
GRAVES	2
GRAVETTE	1
GRAY	4
GRAYHAM	8
GREEN	47
GREENBERG	1
GREENE	8
GREER	1
GRIFFIN	9
GRIFFITHS	1
GRIMES	9
GRUBBS	1
GUNNELL	1
GURLEY	6
GUTHERY	3
GUTHREY	1
GUTTERY	2
GWIN	7
HAACK	2
HADEN	5
HAGELGANS	1
HAGER	2
HAGOOD	45
HAGWOOD	1
HAIL	3
HALCOMBE	1
HALE	9
HALL	38
HALLMARK	2
HAMAKER	33

Surname	# of Land Parcels
HAMIL	1
HAMILTON	11
HAMMER	1
HAMMOND	1
HAMMONDS	4
HAMNER	7
HANBY	25
HANCOCK	6
HAND	9
HANEY	1
HANLY	4
HANNA	3
HARAN	2
HARD	1
HARDEN	5
HARDIMAN	1
HARDIN	9
HARDING	5
HARDYMAN	4
HARIS	1
HARISON	2
HARKEY	1
HARKNESS	1
HARMAN	1
HARMON	9
HARPER	7
HARRIS	20
HARRISON	10
HARTGROVES	1
HARVEY	2
HASKETT	1
HASTINGS	2
HAUGHEY	3
HAWKINS	40
HAYGOOD	1
HAYS	6
HEARD	3
HEATON	4
HEFNER	3
HEIFNER	1
HEMBREE	1
HEMPHILL	1
HENDERSON	5
HENDLEY	1
HENDON	1
HENLEY	3
HENLY	4
HENRY	5
HERREN	2
HERRING	19
HEWBERRY	1
HEWITT	5
HICKMAN	6
HICKS	16
HIGGINBOTHAM	12
HIGGINBOTHOM	1
HIGGINS	9
HILL	17
HINTON	2
HITT	3
HIX	4
HOBBS	2
HODGE	1
HODGES	12
HOFFMAN	1
HOGAN	9
HOLCOMB	3
HOLCOMBE	6
HOLLEY	1
HOLLIGAN	2

Surname	# of Land Parcels
HOLLINGSWORTH	4
HOLLIS	8
HOLLY	3
HOLMES	7
HOLT	1
HOOD	20
HOOPER	1
HOPKINS	5
HOPPER	4
HORN	1
HORNE	3
HORTON	7
HOSMER	1
HOUGHTON	1
HOUK	4
HOUSTON	5
HOWARD	6
HOWEL	1
HOWELL	1
HOWEN	1
HOWTON	39
HUBBARD	6
HUCHINGSON	1
HUCKABEE	1
HUDSON	2
HUEY	10
HUFFMAN	2
HUFFSTUTTER	1
HUGHES	13
HULL	1
HULSEY	1
HUMBER	17
HUNEYCUTT	1
HUNT	3
HUNTER	1
HURST	1
HUTCHINS	3
HUTSON	1
HYCH	1
HYDE	3
IGOW	2
INGLE	2
INGRAM	7
INZER	2
IRION	1
ISAACS	2
ISRAEL	2
IVEANS	1
IVY	1
JACK	3
JACKS	9
JACKSON	10
JACOBS	5
JAMES	14
JEFFERSON	2
JENKINS	2
JENNINGS	2
JOHN	1
JOHNSON	33
JOHNSTON	9
JOLLEY	1
JOLLY	2
JONES	61
JORDAN	32
JORDON	5
JOURDEN	1
JUDD	1
JUSTICE	21
KEATON	2
KEETH	1

Surname	# of Land Parcels
KEITH	15
KELLEY	2
KELLY	21
KELSO	1
KEMP	8
KENNEBREW	1
KENNEDY	15
KENNON	3
KEVELING	1
KILE	2
KILLAUGH	2
KILLOUGH	43
KIMBREL	3
KING	3
KIRKPATRICK	1
KITCHENS	3
KNABE	2
KNIGHT	3
KNOX	1
KYLE	1
LACEY	4
LACY	4
LAFOY	3
LAIRD	3
LAMBERT	1
LAND	3
LANDIFER	1
LANDRUM	2
LANE	15
LANEY	1
LANG	1
LANGFORD	2
LANIER	2
LANINGHAM	1
LASETER	2
LASITER	3
LATHAM	6
LATHEM	8
LAWLER	1
LAWLESS	4
LAWLEY	10
LAWSON	10
LE FEVRE	1
LEATHERWOOD	5
LEDLOW	2
LEDYARD	4
LEE	23
LEMMONS	1
LESLEY	2
LETSON	1
LEWIS	5
LIGHTHALL	3
LINDSEY	5
LINEMAN	1
LINN	12
LINTHICUM	3
LITTLE	6
LIVELY	1
LIVERMAN	1
LIVERMORE	2
LLOYD	1
LOCKHART	10
LOLLER	5
LOLLY	1
LONG	2
LOONEY	2
LOVE	2
LOVELESS	24
LOVEMAN	1
LOVETT	8

Surname	# of Land Parcels
LOWE	1
LOWERY	4
LOWRY	1
LUCKIE	1
LYKES	1
MACKEY	1
MADDOX	7
MADISON	5
MAHAN	1
MAJOR	2
MAJORS	1
MALLORY	1
MALONE	3
MANN	4
MANSON	1
MARCH	1
MARKE	1
MARKS	2
MARSHALL	2
MARTIN	39
MASKE	2
MASON	6
MASSENGILL	1
MASSEY	43
MASTERS	3
MATHENY	2
MATHIS	1
MATTHEWS	1
MATTISON	2
MAULDIN	3
MAVERICK	6
MAXWELL	2
MAYFIELD	8
MCADAMS	4
MCADOREY	1
MCADORY	61
MCANALLY	3
MCASHAN	2
MCBRIDE	3
MCCABE	2
MCCALL	1
MCCALLA	1
MCCARSON	1
MCCARTEY	1
MCCARTNEY	17
MCCARTY	13
MCCAY	5
MCCLAIN	8
MCCLELEN	1
MCCLENDON	2
MCCLERKIN	1
MCCLINTOCK	4
MCCLINTON	4
MCCLURE	2
MCCOLLUM	1
MCCOMAK	3
MCCOMBE	2
MCCOMBS	23
MCCOO	1
MCCORMACK	1
MCCOW	1
MCCOY	6
MCCRARY	2
MCCRAW	1
MCCULLOUGH	2
MCCURRY	1
MCDANAL	12
MCDANIEL	7
MCDONALD	9
MCDOUGAL	2

Surname	# of Land Parcels	Surname	# of Land Parcels	Surname	# of Land Parcels	Surname	# of Land Parcels
MCDOWEL	1	MUDD	5	PEELER	1	REID	24
MCDUFF	1	MULLINGS	1	PEIRCE	1	REIVES	1
MCELROY	5	MULVEHILL	2	PENN	2	RETALLACK	2
MCFALL	3	MUNKUS	1	PENWELL	1	RHEA	7
MCFALLS	2	MURPHEY	1	PERKINS	13	RHODY	1
MCFERRIN	4	MURPHREE	3	PERRY	7	RICE	1
MCGEE	3	MURPHY	4	PERSONS	3	RICHARDS	4
MCGEHEE	6	MURRAY	7	PERTEET	1	RICHARDSON	9
MCGHEE	1	MURRY	1	PETERSON	13	RICHEY	2
MCGILL	2	MYRICK	7	PHELAN	1	RICHMOND	1
MCGOWEN	1	MYRICKE	1	PHILIPS	15	RICKEY	3
MCGUIRE	3	MYROCK	2	PHILLIPS	7	RIDDLE	1
MCKAY	1	NABERS	13	PHILYAW	4	RIED	1
MCKEEVER	2	NABORS	11	PIERCE	10	RILEY	10
MCKENNEY	1	NABOURS	7	PIERSON	4	RINEHART	2
MCKENZIE	1	NAIL	19	PILLARS	1	RITCHEY	1
MCKINNEY	3	NASH	13	PITTS	13	RITCHIE	4
MCLAUGHLIN	15	NATIONS	10	PLEDGER	4	RIVERS	5
MCLEOD	1	NAVE	1	POE	1	ROBBINS	22
MCLINTOCK	3	NEAL	5	POINIER	2	ROBERSON	1
MCLUER	4	NEIGHBOURS	1	POOL	9	ROBERTS	20
MCMAHON	2	NEILSON	2	POOLE	4	ROBERTSON	29
MCMATH	9	NELMS	1	PORTER	1	ROBINS	6
MCMEANS	1	NELSION	1	POSEY	7	ROBINSON	10
MCMICHENS	1	NELSON	5	POTEETE	1	ROBISON	1
MCMICKEN	2	NEVES	1	POTTER	4	ROCKETT	15
MCMILLAN	2	NEWBERRY	4	POTTS	3	RODGERS	10
MCMILLION	2	NEWMAN	2	POWELL	12	ROEBUCK	13
MCPHAUL	1	NICHOLAS	7	PRATT	1	ROGERS	23
MCPHERRIN	1	NICHOLS	19	PRAYTOR	8	ROPER	3
MCPHERSON	2	NIELSON	2	PRESCOAT	3	ROSS	9
MCWILLIAMS	13	NORMENT	4	PRESCOTT	7	ROTH	1
MEDLEN	3	NORRIS	3	PRESLEY	3	ROTTON	2
MEEKS	3	NORTON	1	PRICE	13	ROUNSLEY	3
MEIGS	1	NORWOOD	3	PRIDE	1	ROUSE	10
MELTON	7	NUNLEY	1	PRINCE	1	ROWAN	10
MELVIN	6	OATES	3	PRUDE	5	ROWE	7
MERKEL	1	OBAR	2	PRYOR	2	ROY	4
MERRICK	1	OBARR	3	PULLEN	2	RUCKER	1
MERRIKEN	2	ODAM	1	PULLIAM	1	RUDER	1
MERRITT	1	ODEN	1	PURCELL	2	RUPE	1
MICHAEL	1	ODOM	3	PUTTEET	1	RUSSELL	25
MIKELLS	2	OGLESBERRY	2	PYBAS	4	RUTH	3
MILES	8	OGLETREE	1	PYBUS	2	RUTHERFORD	1
MILLENDER	2	OGWIN	3	QUIN	1	RUTLEDGE	1
MILLER	18	OLDHAM	2	QUINN	15	RYAN	3
MILLWOOD	2	OLIVER	3	RAGAN	5	RYLANT	1
MILNE	2	ONEAL	1	RAGIN	1	SADBERRY	1
MILNER	4	ORR	5	RAGLAN	1	SADDLER	23
MILSTEAD	2	OTTS	1	RAGLAND	1	SADLER	14
MINOR	3	OWEN	46	RAGLIN	2	SALMONS	3
MINTER	7	OWENS	11	RAGSDALE	1	SALTER	21
MITCHEL	3	PAGE	1	RAIMER	2	SAMPLES	1
MITCHELL	17	PAIN	1	RANDOLPH	2	SANDERS	12
MONCRIEF	3	PALMER	4	RANEY	10	SANDIFORD	5
MONFEE	2	PALMORE	4	RATLIFF	2	SANSON	5
MONTGOMERY	13	PARKER	10	RAY	6	SARGENT	6
MOONEY	5	PARRIS	5	READ	1	SAULSBURY	3
MOOR	7	PARRISH	1	READING	1	SAVAGE	3
MOORE	49	PARRY	2	REAM	1	SCHLEY	2
MORELAND	2	PARSONS	116	REAVES	5	SCOTT	29
MORGAN	5	PARTAIN	3	REAVIS	2	SEAL	2
MORRIS	2	PASLEY	1	REDDING	2	SELF	31
MORRISON	4	PATTEN	2	REDER	2	SELFE	1
MORROW	13	PATTERSON	9	REED	37	SELLARS	4
MORTON	1	PATTON	23	REEDER	7	SELLENGER	1
MOSES	18	PAULLING	1	REESE	5	SELLERS	21
MOSS	1	PAYNE	18	REEVES	4	SENTELL	1
MOTE	3	PEARCE	1	REGAN	1	SHACKELFORD	3
MOTTE	4	PEARSON	5	REGIN	1	SHACKLEFORD	1

Surname	# of Land Parcels
SHAGER	1
SHAMBLIN	1
SHARIT	10
SHARP	14
SHAW	5
SHEDD	1
SHELTON	1
SHEPHERD	5
SHERMAN	1
SHIPMAN	2
SHIPP	6
SHIRL	2
SHOEMAKER	34
SHOOK	1
SHORT	11
SHUGART	8
SHULTS	1
SHUTTLESWORTH	1
SIDES	1
SIMMONS	2
SIMPSON	6
SIMS	54
SKAGGS	1
SKELTON	11
SLAPPY	2
SLOAN	6
SMITH	92
SMITHSON	8
SNEAD	3
SNELL	4
SNOW	17
SOUTH	1
SOUTHERLAND	1
SPARKES	3
SPARKS	5
SPAULDING	3
SPEAKMAN	1
SPEAR	1
SPEARS	3
SPEER	6
SPENCER	41
SPERRY	1
SPRADLEY	1
SPRADLING	20
SPRUELL	4
SQUIRE	7
STACKS	2
STAGG	2
STAGGS	20
STALNAKER	2
STANDIFER	4
STANDLAND	1
STARKY	1
STARNES	4
STATEM	1
STATHAM	1
STATON	2
STATUM	6
STEALE	1
STEEDMAN	4
STEEL	12
STEELE	1
STEPHENS	6
STEWART	1
STIVENDER	1
STONE	7
STOUT	1
STOVALL	10
STRINGFELLOW	3
STROUP	1
STUBBS	3
STURDIVANT	1
SULLIVAN	14
SULLIVANT	3
SWINNEY	1
TACKET	2
TADLOCK	1
TALLEY	12
TANKERSLY	1
TANNAHILL	3
TANNEHILL	9
TANNER	3
TARRANT	11
TATE	7
TATUM	5
TAYLOR	64
TEAGUE	2
TEASLEY	1
TEDMORE	1
TERRIL	1
TERRY	2
THACK	1
THACKER	1
THOMAS	49
THOMPSON	51
THORINGTON	1
THORNE	3
THORP	2
THURSTON	5
TIDWELL	4
TILERSON	1
TILLISON	1
TILLMAN	3
TILLOTSON	1
TIMMONS	1
TORRENT	1
TOURY	1
TOWERS	1
TOWERY	1
TOWNBY	1
TOWNLEY	1
TOWNLY	1
TRAMMELL	3
TRASS	2
TRAVIS	1
TREADAWAY	4
TRUETT	1
TRUSS	45
TUCKER	9
TUMBOUGH	1
TUNE	2
TUNNELL	1
TURKENET	1
TURNBOUGH	6
TURNER	40
TURNHAM	3
TUTHILL	4
TUTTLE	1
TUTWILER	1
TYLER	15
TYLOR	5
USTICK	1
VAN HAUSE	1
VAN HOOSE	1
VANCE	3
VANDEVIR	2
VANDIFORD	1
VANDIVER	3
VANHOOSE	1
VANHOUSE	1
VANN	27
VANZANDT	3
VARNON	8
VARNUM	1
VEAZEY	1
VEITCH	1
VENS	1
VIENS	4
VINCENT	1
VINES	87
VINING	2
VINSON	3
VON MINDIN	2
VOSE	1
WADE	3
WAIT	1
WALD	2
WALDROP	60
WALDRUP	1
WALKER	31
WALLACE	2
WALLS	1
WALTERS	2
WALTON	1
WARD	3
WARE	22
WARNICK	2
WARREN	3
WASHINGTON	1
WATHEN	1
WATKINS	7
WATSON	11
WATTS	1
WEAR	14
WEBB	1
WEDGEWORTH	2
WEED	6
WEEMS	11
WEISMAN	3
WELCH	1
WELDON	3
WEST	1
WETHERS	1
WHARTON	2
WHATLEY	1
WHEELER	6
WHISENANT	7
WHISNANT	2
WHITBY	1
WHITE	23
WHITEFIELD	1
WHITEHEAD	4
WHITEHOUSE	2
WHITTINGTON	3
WIDEMAN	13
WILDER	1
WILEY	6
WILKES	4
WILKEY	7
WILKINS	1
WILKS	7
WILLARD	8
WILLIAMS	69
WILLIAMSON	1
WILLINGHAM	2
WILLIS	8
WILSON	29
WINCHESTER	3
WINES	3
WINFIELD	3
WINGO	2
WINSTEAD	1
WINTER	3
WIRE	5
WISE	2
WOBARR	1
WOLF	1
WOMACK	1
WOOD	89
WOODALL	3
WOODARD	3
WOODDIEL	1
WOODRUFF	3
WOODS	6
WOODSON	2
WOODWARD	3
WOOTEN	1
WOOTTEN	1
WORNICK	2
WORTHINGTON	26
WORTHY	2
WRIGHT	10
WRITE	1
WYATT	3
WYLIE	2
YANCEY	1
YANCY	1
YEAGER	1
YORK	2
YORKE	3
YOUNG	7
YOUNGBLOOD	11

Surname/Township Index

This Index allows you to determine which *Township Map Group(s)* contain individuals with the following surnames. Each *Map Group* has a corresponding full-name index of all individuals who obtained patents for land within its Congressional township's borders. After each index you will find the Patent Map to which it refers, and just thereafter, you can view the township's Road Map and Historical Map, with the latter map displaying streams, railroads, and more.

So, once you find your Surname here, proceed to the Index at the beginning of the **Map Group** indicated below.

Surname	Map Group	Parcels of Land	Meridian/Township/Range		
AARON	**35**	3	Huntsville	19-S	7-W
ABANATHY	**38**	2	Huntsville	19-S	4-W
ABARNATHY	**38**	4	Huntsville	19-S	4-W
ABEL	**9**	1	Huntsville	15-S	1-W
ABELS	**6**	1	Huntsville	15-S	4-W
ABERCROMBIE	**22**	1	Huntsville	17-S	3-W
ABERNATHY	**38**	8	Huntsville	19-S	4-W
" "	**39**	3	Huntsville	19-S	3-W
" "	**43**	2	Huntsville	20-S	4-W
" "	**42**	1	Huntsville	20-S	5-W
ABSTEN	**27**	1	Huntsville	18-S	7-W
ABSTON	**27**	1	Huntsville	18-S	7-W
ACKER	**38**	1	Huntsville	19-S	4-W
ACTON	**32**	15	Huntsville	18-S	2-W
" "	**40**	14	Huntsville	19-S	2-W
ADAMS	**12**	9	Huntsville	16-S	5-W
" "	**38**	3	Huntsville	19-S	4-W
" "	**3**	1	Huntsville	14-S	2-W
" "	**7**	1	Huntsville	15-S	3-W
" "	**5**	1	Huntsville	15-S	5-W
" "	**22**	1	Huntsville	17-S	3-W
" "	**20**	1	Huntsville	17-S	5-W
" "	**19**	1	Huntsville	17-S	6-W
" "	**31**	1	Huntsville	18-S	3-W
ADCOCK	**1**	3	Huntsville	14-S	4-W
" "	**13**	1	Huntsville	16-S	4-W
ADKINS	**31**	7	Huntsville	18-S	3-W
" "	**32**	2	Huntsville	18-S	2-W
" "	**22**	1	Huntsville	17-S	3-W
ADKINSON	**13**	2	Huntsville	16-S	4-W
AGERTON	**2**	2	Huntsville	14-S	3-W
" "	**1**	1	Huntsville	14-S	4-W
AIKIN	**13**	4	Huntsville	16-S	4-W
" "	**7**	1	Huntsville	15-S	3-W
AKERS	**2**	2	Huntsville	14-S	3-W
AKINS	**14**	1	Huntsville	16-S	3-W
ALABAMA	**27**	2	Huntsville	18-S	7-W
" "	**29**	1	Huntsville	18-S	5-W
ALEXANDER	**12**	1	Huntsville	16-S	5-W
" "	**38**	1	Huntsville	19-S	4-W
ALLEN	**5**	4	Huntsville	15-S	5-W
" "	**25**	1	Huntsville	17-S	1-E
" "	**24**	1	Huntsville	17-S	1-W
" "	**30**	1	Huntsville	18-S	4-W

Surname	Map Group	Parcels of Land	Meridian/Township/Range		
ALLEN (Cont'd)	**44**	1	Huntsville	20-S	3-W
ALLEY	**39**	1	Huntsville	19-S	3-W
ALLINDER	**38**	7	Huntsville	19-S	4-W
ALLMAN	**28**	2	Huntsville	18-S	6-W
ALLRED	**9**	1	Huntsville	15-S	1-W
ALLSOP	**7**	1	Huntsville	15-S	3-W
ALMON	**35**	1	Huntsville	19-S	7-W
ALRED	**21**	1	Huntsville	17-S	4-W
ANDERSON	**3**	9	Huntsville	14-S	2-W
" "	**9**	6	Huntsville	15-S	1-W
" "	**8**	3	Huntsville	15-S	2-W
" "	**5**	1	Huntsville	15-S	5-W
" "	**16**	1	Huntsville	16-S	1-W
" "	**15**	1	Huntsville	16-S	2-W
ANDREWS	**22**	1	Huntsville	17-S	3-W
ANTHONY	**21**	2	Huntsville	17-S	4-W
" "	**30**	1	Huntsville	18-S	4-W
APPLEBERRY	**24**	1	Huntsville	17-S	1-W
ARCHER	**38**	1	Huntsville	19-S	4-W
ARMSTEAD	**15**	2	Huntsville	16-S	2-W
ARMSTRONG	**42**	9	Huntsville	20-S	5-W
" "	**32**	7	Huntsville	18-S	2-W
" "	**39**	6	Huntsville	19-S	3-W
" "	**25**	5	Huntsville	17-S	1-E
" "	**43**	5	Huntsville	20-S	4-W
" "	**23**	3	Huntsville	17-S	2-W
" "	**41**	3	Huntsville	20-S	6-W
" "	**38**	1	Huntsville	19-S	4-W
ARNETT	**9**	2	Huntsville	15-S	1-W
" "	**20**	2	Huntsville	17-S	5-W
" "	**21**	1	Huntsville	17-S	4-W
ARNOLD	**43**	3	Huntsville	20-S	4-W
ASHLEY	**3**	2	Huntsville	14-S	2-W
" "	**4**	1	Huntsville	14-S	1-W
ASKEW	**14**	2	Huntsville	16-S	3-W
ATTAWAY	**1**	2	Huntsville	14-S	4-W
ATWOOD	**20**	1	Huntsville	17-S	5-W
" "	**30**	1	Huntsville	18-S	4-W
AUSTIN	**12**	2	Huntsville	16-S	5-W
AVERY	**39**	5	Huntsville	19-S	3-W
AYERS	**12**	1	Huntsville	16-S	5-W
" "	**24**	1	Huntsville	17-S	1-W
" "	**23**	1	Huntsville	17-S	2-W
AYRES	**30**	4	Huntsville	18-S	4-W
" "	**23**	2	Huntsville	17-S	2-W
" "	**22**	2	Huntsville	17-S	3-W
" "	**6**	1	Huntsville	15-S	4-W
" "	**38**	1	Huntsville	19-S	4-W
AYRS	**23**	1	Huntsville	17-S	2-W
BAGBY	**12**	3	Huntsville	16-S	5-W
" "	**14**	1	Huntsville	16-S	3-W
BAGGETT	**16**	1	Huntsville	16-S	1-W
BAGLEY	**14**	9	Huntsville	16-S	3-W
" "	**12**	6	Huntsville	16-S	5-W
" "	**33**	4	Huntsville	18-S	1-W
" "	**32**	3	Huntsville	18-S	2-W
" "	**23**	2	Huntsville	17-S	2-W
" "	**22**	2	Huntsville	17-S	3-W
" "	**21**	2	Huntsville	17-S	4-W
" "	**13**	1	Huntsville	16-S	4-W

Surname	Map Group	Parcels of Land	Meridian/Township/Range		
BAGLEY (Cont'd)	**30**	1	Huntsville	18-S	4-W
BAGWELL	**32**	4	Huntsville	18-S	2-W
" "	**23**	3	Huntsville	17-S	2-W
BAILEY	**39**	15	Huntsville	19-S	3-W
" "	**40**	10	Huntsville	19-S	2-W
" "	**14**	1	Huntsville	16-S	3-W
" "	**13**	1	Huntsville	16-S	4-W
BAIRD	**9**	9	Huntsville	15-S	1-W
" "	**8**	3	Huntsville	15-S	2-W
" "	**7**	1	Huntsville	15-S	3-W
BAKER	**23**	7	Huntsville	17-S	2-W
" "	**42**	3	Huntsville	20-S	5-W
" "	**32**	2	Huntsville	18-S	2-W
" "	**31**	2	Huntsville	18-S	3-W
" "	**38**	2	Huntsville	19-S	4-W
" "	**22**	1	Huntsville	17-S	3-W
BALCOM	**2**	2	Huntsville	14-S	3-W
BALL	**30**	1	Huntsville	18-S	4-W
BALLARD	**39**	1	Huntsville	19-S	3-W
BANKS	**30**	1	Huntsville	18-S	4-W
BANKSTON	**6**	1	Huntsville	15-S	4-W
BARBEAU	**44**	1	Huntsville	20-S	3-W
BARBOUR	**38**	1	Huntsville	19-S	4-W
BARFORD	**15**	1	Huntsville	16-S	2-W
BARGER	**38**	1	Huntsville	19-S	4-W
BARKSDALE	**30**	1	Huntsville	18-S	4-W
" "	**39**	1	Huntsville	19-S	3-W
BARNETT	**36**	1	Huntsville	19-S	6-W
BARR	**7**	3	Huntsville	15-S	3-W
BARRY	**23**	2	Huntsville	17-S	2-W
" "	**22**	1	Huntsville	17-S	3-W
BARTON	**23**	6	Huntsville	17-S	2-W
" "	**2**	5	Huntsville	14-S	3-W
" "	**4**	1	Huntsville	14-S	1-W
" "	**8**	1	Huntsville	15-S	2-W
" "	**15**	1	Huntsville	16-S	2-W
BASS	**24**	21	Huntsville	17-S	1-W
" "	**43**	2	Huntsville	20-S	4-W
" "	**16**	1	Huntsville	16-S	1-W
" "	**31**	1	Huntsville	18-S	3-W
" "	**30**	1	Huntsville	18-S	4-W
BATES	**15**	2	Huntsville	16-S	2-W
" "	**2**	1	Huntsville	14-S	3-W
" "	**7**	1	Huntsville	15-S	3-W
BATSON	**29**	5	Huntsville	18-S	5-W
" "	**21**	4	Huntsville	17-S	4-W
" "	**28**	4	Huntsville	18-S	6-W
BAYLES	**23**	3	Huntsville	17-S	2-W
" "	**24**	1	Huntsville	17-S	1-W
BAYLESS	**6**	2	Huntsville	15-S	4-W
BEAM	**12**	1	Huntsville	16-S	5-W
" "	**22**	1	Huntsville	17-S	3-W
" "	**31**	1	Huntsville	18-S	3-W
BEARD	**16**	3	Huntsville	16-S	1-W
" "	**9**	1	Huntsville	15-S	1-W
BEARDEN	**32**	3	Huntsville	18-S	2-W
" "	**23**	2	Huntsville	17-S	2-W
" "	**24**	1	Huntsville	17-S	1-W
BEARDIN	**23**	3	Huntsville	17-S	2-W
BEASLEY	**7**	3	Huntsville	15-S	3-W

Surname	Map Group	Parcels of Land	Meridian/Township/Range		
BEASLY	**7**	1	Huntsville	15-S	3-W
BEAZLEY	**15**	1	Huntsville	16-S	2-W
" "	**14**	1	Huntsville	16-S	3-W
BECKHAM	**24**	1	Huntsville	17-S	1-W
BEERS	**25**	2	Huntsville	17-S	1-E
BELCHER	**14**	7	Huntsville	16-S	3-W
" "	**7**	5	Huntsville	15-S	3-W
" "	**8**	2	Huntsville	15-S	2-W
" "	**16**	1	Huntsville	16-S	1-W
BELL	**38**	7	Huntsville	19-S	4-W
" "	**40**	2	Huntsville	19-S	2-W
" "	**15**	1	Huntsville	16-S	2-W
" "	**24**	1	Huntsville	17-S	1-W
" "	**19**	1	Huntsville	17-S	6-W
" "	**28**	1	Huntsville	18-S	6-W
" "	**43**	1	Huntsville	20-S	4-W
BELSHER	**7**	1	Huntsville	15-S	3-W
BENNETT	**31**	1	Huntsville	18-S	3-W
BETTER	**31**	1	Huntsville	18-S	3-W
BIBB	**2**	4	Huntsville	14-S	3-W
" "	**31**	4	Huntsville	18-S	3-W
" "	**7**	3	Huntsville	15-S	3-W
" "	**23**	3	Huntsville	17-S	2-W
" "	**8**	1	Huntsville	15-S	2-W
" "	**22**	1	Huntsville	17-S	3-W
" "	**39**	1	Huntsville	19-S	3-W
BILLINGSLEA	**22**	1	Huntsville	17-S	3-W
BILLINGSLEY	**14**	2	Huntsville	16-S	3-W
BIRD	**37**	1	Huntsville	19-S	5-W
BIRKETT	**17**	1	Huntsville	16-S	1-E
BISHOP	**10**	4	Huntsville	15-S	1-E
" "	**7**	2	Huntsville	15-S	3-W
" "	**44**	2	Huntsville	20-S	3-W
" "	**6**	1	Huntsville	15-S	4-W
BIVEN	**14**	1	Huntsville	16-S	3-W
" "	**13**	1	Huntsville	16-S	4-W
BIVENS	**13**	8	Huntsville	16-S	4-W
" "	**21**	2	Huntsville	17-S	4-W
BIVINS	**13**	4	Huntsville	16-S	4-W
BLACK	**13**	7	Huntsville	16-S	4-W
" "	**12**	5	Huntsville	16-S	5-W
" "	**6**	3	Huntsville	15-S	4-W
" "	**25**	3	Huntsville	17-S	1-E
" "	**42**	2	Huntsville	20-S	5-W
" "	**8**	1	Huntsville	15-S	2-W
BLACKBURN	**2**	3	Huntsville	14-S	3-W
" "	**7**	1	Huntsville	15-S	3-W
" "	**6**	1	Huntsville	15-S	4-W
BLACKWELL	**20**	2	Huntsville	17-S	5-W
BLALOCK	**6**	1	Huntsville	15-S	4-W
BLANKINGSHIP	**43**	1	Huntsville	20-S	4-W
BLANKINSHIP	**43**	1	Huntsville	20-S	4-W
BLAYLOCK	**6**	1	Huntsville	15-S	4-W
BLITON	**33**	2	Huntsville	18-S	1-W
BLUDWORTH	**7**	1	Huntsville	15-S	3-W
BLYTHE	**10**	2	Huntsville	15-S	1-E
BOOKER	**8**	3	Huntsville	15-S	2-W
BOOKOUT	**1**	3	Huntsville	14-S	4-W
BOONE	**11**	1	Huntsville	16-S	6-W
BOYD	**12**	3	Huntsville	16-S	5-W

Surname	Map Group	Parcels of Land	Meridian/Township/Range
BOYD (Cont'd)	**13**	2	Huntsville 16-S 4-W
" "	**9**	1	Huntsville 15-S 1-W
" "	**27**	1	Huntsville 18-S 7-W
BOYLES	**23**	1	Huntsville 17-S 2-W
BRACKNER	**42**	1	Huntsville 20-S 5-W
BRADFORD	**2**	4	Huntsville 14-S 3-W
" "	**17**	4	Huntsville 16-S 1-E
" "	**10**	2	Huntsville 15-S 1-E
" "	**16**	2	Huntsville 16-S 1-W
" "	**24**	1	Huntsville 17-S 1-W
" "	**31**	1	Huntsville 18-S 3-W
BRADLEY	**18**	2	Huntsville 17-S 7-W
BRADSHAW	**21**	2	Huntsville 17-S 4-W
BRAGG	**32**	3	Huntsville 18-S 2-W
BRAKE	**14**	3	Huntsville 16-S 3-W
" "	**2**	1	Huntsville 14-S 3-W
BRAMLET	**3**	2	Huntsville 14-S 2-W
BRAMLETT	**3**	1	Huntsville 14-S 2-W
BRANHAM	**9**	1	Huntsville 15-S 1-W
BRANTLEY	**23**	1	Huntsville 17-S 2-W
BRASFIELD	**12**	2	Huntsville 16-S 5-W
BRASHER	**33**	2	Huntsville 18-S 1-W
BRASSFIELD	**12**	2	Huntsville 16-S 5-W
BRASWELL	**39**	7	Huntsville 19-S 3-W
BRAZIER	**32**	1	Huntsville 18-S 2-W
BREWER	**1**	7	Huntsville 14-S 4-W
" "	**14**	3	Huntsville 16-S 3-W
" "	**2**	1	Huntsville 14-S 3-W
BRIDGES	**37**	3	Huntsville 19-S 5-W
BRIDGMON	**6**	2	Huntsville 15-S 4-W
BRITT	**23**	1	Huntsville 17-S 2-W
BROCK	**39**	5	Huntsville 19-S 3-W
" "	**14**	1	Huntsville 16-S 3-W
BROOKS	**3**	2	Huntsville 14-S 2-W
" "	**7**	2	Huntsville 15-S 3-W
" "	**13**	2	Huntsville 16-S 4-W
" "	**8**	1	Huntsville 15-S 2-W
" "	**39**	1	Huntsville 19-S 3-W
BROTHERS	**22**	2	Huntsville 17-S 3-W
BROWN	**30**	20	Huntsville 18-S 4-W
" "	**29**	12	Huntsville 18-S 5-W
" "	**15**	10	Huntsville 16-S 2-W
" "	**23**	10	Huntsville 17-S 2-W
" "	**22**	6	Huntsville 17-S 3-W
" "	**31**	6	Huntsville 18-S 3-W
" "	**28**	6	Huntsville 18-S 6-W
" "	**13**	4	Huntsville 16-S 4-W
" "	**21**	4	Huntsville 17-S 4-W
" "	**32**	4	Huntsville 18-S 2-W
" "	**2**	3	Huntsville 14-S 3-W
" "	**9**	3	Huntsville 15-S 1-W
" "	**12**	3	Huntsville 16-S 5-W
" "	**1**	2	Huntsville 14-S 4-W
" "	**7**	2	Huntsville 15-S 3-W
" "	**6**	2	Huntsville 15-S 4-W
" "	**36**	2	Huntsville 19-S 6-W
" "	**16**	1	Huntsville 16-S 1-W
" "	**24**	1	Huntsville 17-S 1-W
" "	**33**	1	Huntsville 18-S 1-W
BROWNE	**3**	1	Huntsville 14-S 2-W

Surname	Map Group	Parcels of Land	Meridian/Township/Range		
BROWNLEE	**23**	3	Huntsville	17-S	2-W
" "	**43**	1	Huntsville	20-S	4-W
BRUCE	**31**	1	Huntsville	18-S	3-W
BRYANT	**33**	2	Huntsville	18-S	1-W
" "	**36**	1	Huntsville	19-S	6-W
BUCK	**42**	1	Huntsville	20-S	5-W
BUCKALEW	**21**	3	Huntsville	17-S	4-W
BUCKELEW	**22**	2	Huntsville	17-S	3-W
" "	**21**	1	Huntsville	17-S	4-W
BUCKLEY	**39**	1	Huntsville	19-S	3-W
BUFFINGTON	**31**	4	Huntsville	18-S	3-W
" "	**23**	3	Huntsville	17-S	2-W
" "	**39**	1	Huntsville	19-S	3-W
BULLARD	**1**	2	Huntsville	14-S	4-W
" "	**19**	1	Huntsville	17-S	6-W
BULLOCK	**32**	2	Huntsville	18-S	2-W
" "	**8**	1	Huntsville	15-S	2-W
BURCHFIELD	**35**	5	Huntsville	19-S	7-W
" "	**27**	4	Huntsville	18-S	7-W
" "	**28**	3	Huntsville	18-S	6-W
" "	**9**	2	Huntsville	15-S	1-W
" "	**36**	1	Huntsville	19-S	6-W
BURFORD	**31**	8	Huntsville	18-S	3-W
" "	**22**	2	Huntsville	17-S	3-W
BURGIN	**15**	4	Huntsville	16-S	2-W
" "	**30**	3	Huntsville	18-S	4-W
" "	**14**	2	Huntsville	16-S	3-W
" "	**7**	1	Huntsville	15-S	3-W
" "	**38**	1	Huntsville	19-S	4-W
BURKS	**31**	1	Huntsville	18-S	3-W
BURLASON	**8**	1	Huntsville	15-S	2-W
BURLESON	**8**	1	Huntsville	15-S	2-W
BURLESSON	**4**	1	Huntsville	14-S	1-W
BURLINSON	**16**	2	Huntsville	16-S	1-W
BURNS	**1**	3	Huntsville	14-S	4-W
" "	**8**	1	Huntsville	15-S	2-W
" "	**12**	1	Huntsville	16-S	5-W
" "	**39**	1	Huntsville	19-S	3-W
" "	**43**	1	Huntsville	20-S	4-W
" "	**41**	1	Huntsville	20-S	6-W
BURRELL	**13**	4	Huntsville	16-S	4-W
" "	**1**	1	Huntsville	14-S	4-W
" "	**5**	1	Huntsville	15-S	5-W
BURTON	**27**	10	Huntsville	18-S	7-W
" "	**15**	1	Huntsville	16-S	2-W
" "	**14**	1	Huntsville	16-S	3-W
BURWELL	**15**	4	Huntsville	16-S	2-W
" "	**23**	2	Huntsville	17-S	2-W
BUSBY	**12**	1	Huntsville	16-S	5-W
BUSH	**9**	2	Huntsville	15-S	1-W
" "	**6**	2	Huntsville	15-S	4-W
BUTLER	**9**	4	Huntsville	15-S	1-W
" "	**22**	3	Huntsville	17-S	3-W
" "	**12**	2	Huntsville	16-S	5-W
" "	**31**	1	Huntsville	18-S	3-W
" "	**43**	1	Huntsville	20-S	4-W
BUTTLER	**23**	2	Huntsville	17-S	2-W
BYARS	**31**	12	Huntsville	18-S	3-W
" "	**32**	3	Huntsville	18-S	2-W
" "	**4**	2	Huntsville	14-S	1-W

Surname	Map Group	Parcels of Land	Meridian/Township/Range
BYARS (Cont'd)	**15**	2	Huntsville 16-S 2-W
" "	**23**	1	Huntsville 17-S 2-W
BYERS	**32**	3	Huntsville 18-S 2-W
" "	**16**	2	Huntsville 16-S 1-W
" "	**24**	2	Huntsville 17-S 1-W
" "	**15**	1	Huntsville 16-S 2-W
" "	**33**	1	Huntsville 18-S 1-W
BYRAM	**39**	4	Huntsville 19-S 3-W
" "	**40**	3	Huntsville 19-S 2-W
" "	**24**	1	Huntsville 17-S 1-W
BYRD	**9**	1	Huntsville 15-S 1-W
CADDELL	**3**	1	Huntsville 14-S 2-W
CAIN	**9**	3	Huntsville 15-S 1-W
" "	**8**	2	Huntsville 15-S 2-W
" "	**18**	1	Huntsville 17-S 7-W
" "	**28**	1	Huntsville 18-S 6-W
" "	**27**	1	Huntsville 18-S 7-W
CALDWELL	**39**	6	Huntsville 19-S 3-W
" "	**29**	3	Huntsville 18-S 5-W
" "	**40**	3	Huntsville 19-S 2-W
" "	**37**	3	Huntsville 19-S 5-W
" "	**32**	2	Huntsville 18-S 2-W
" "	**30**	2	Huntsville 18-S 4-W
" "	**43**	2	Huntsville 20-S 4-W
" "	**33**	1	Huntsville 18-S 1-W
" "	**38**	1	Huntsville 19-S 4-W
CALLAWAY	**32**	2	Huntsville 18-S 2-W
CAMAK	**32**	3	Huntsville 18-S 2-W
CAMERON	**25**	4	Huntsville 17-S 1-E
" "	**24**	2	Huntsville 17-S 1-W
" "	**33**	2	Huntsville 18-S 1-W
CAMMEL	**14**	2	Huntsville 16-S 3-W
CAMP	**2**	3	Huntsville 14-S 3-W
" "	**6**	3	Huntsville 15-S 4-W
" "	**15**	2	Huntsville 16-S 2-W
CAMPBELL	**2**	8	Huntsville 14-S 3-W
" "	**6**	6	Huntsville 15-S 4-W
" "	**14**	4	Huntsville 16-S 3-W
" "	**10**	1	Huntsville 15-S 1-E
" "	**12**	1	Huntsville 16-S 5-W
" "	**24**	1	Huntsville 17-S 1-W
CANADAY	**16**	1	Huntsville 16-S 1-W
CANNON	**5**	10	Huntsville 15-S 5-W
" "	**6**	4	Huntsville 15-S 4-W
CANTERBERRY	**23**	2	Huntsville 17-S 2-W
CANTRELL	**24**	3	Huntsville 17-S 1-W
CAPERS	**22**	1	Huntsville 17-S 3-W
CAPPS	**30**	1	Huntsville 18-S 4-W
CAREY	**6**	2	Huntsville 15-S 4-W
CARGILE	**28**	6	Huntsville 18-S 6-W
" "	**36**	5	Huntsville 19-S 6-W
CARITHERS	**31**	1	Huntsville 18-S 3-W
CARLILE	**16**	2	Huntsville 16-S 1-W
CARLISLE	**16**	5	Huntsville 16-S 1-W
" "	**1**	4	Huntsville 14-S 4-W
" "	**8**	3	Huntsville 15-S 2-W
CARMICHAEL	**21**	7	Huntsville 17-S 4-W
" "	**20**	2	Huntsville 17-S 5-W
" "	**22**	1	Huntsville 17-S 3-W
CARMICHEAL	**21**	2	Huntsville 17-S 4-W

Surname	Map Group	Parcels of Land	Meridian/Township/Range		
CARMICLE	**21**	2	Huntsville	17-S	4-W
CARPENTER	**19**	1	Huntsville	17-S	6-W
CARRINGTON	**28**	3	Huntsville	18-S	6-W
CARROL	**38**	1	Huntsville	19-S	4-W
CARROLL	**1**	4	Huntsville	14-S	4-W
" "	**2**	1	Huntsville	14-S	3-W
" "	**42**	1	Huntsville	20-S	5-W
CARTER	**39**	2	Huntsville	19-S	3-W
" "	**5**	1	Huntsville	15-S	5-W
" "	**31**	1	Huntsville	18-S	3-W
CARZELIUS	**24**	1	Huntsville	17-S	1-W
CASE	**3**	4	Huntsville	14-S	2-W
CASH	**13**	2	Huntsville	16-S	4-W
" "	**15**	1	Huntsville	16-S	2-W
CAST	**25**	1	Huntsville	17-S	1-E
CASTE	**25**	3	Huntsville	17-S	1-E
CAWOOD	**9**	3	Huntsville	15-S	1-W
CEMP	**23**	1	Huntsville	17-S	2-W
CHAMBLEE	**9**	4	Huntsville	15-S	1-W
" "	**16**	2	Huntsville	16-S	1-W
" "	**10**	1	Huntsville	15-S	1-E
" "	**8**	1	Huntsville	15-S	2-W
" "	**15**	1	Huntsville	16-S	2-W
CHAMLESS	**25**	1	Huntsville	17-S	1-E
CHAPEL	**37**	1	Huntsville	19-S	5-W
CHAPMAN	**24**	2	Huntsville	17-S	1-W
" "	**20**	2	Huntsville	17-S	5-W
" "	**30**	1	Huntsville	18-S	4-W
CHAPPELL	**2**	6	Huntsville	14-S	3-W
CHENNAULT	**15**	1	Huntsville	16-S	2-W
CHILDERS	**15**	1	Huntsville	16-S	2-W
CHILDRESS	**15**	3	Huntsville	16-S	2-W
" "	**8**	2	Huntsville	15-S	2-W
" "	**12**	1	Huntsville	16-S	5-W
" "	**28**	1	Huntsville	18-S	6-W
CHILTON	**43**	2	Huntsville	20-S	4-W
" "	**42**	2	Huntsville	20-S	5-W
CHOAT	**10**	2	Huntsville	15-S	1-E
CHRISTIAN	**21**	2	Huntsville	17-S	4-W
CLARK	**17**	3	Huntsville	16-S	1-E
" "	**29**	3	Huntsville	18-S	5-W
" "	**7**	2	Huntsville	15-S	3-W
" "	**23**	1	Huntsville	17-S	2-W
CLARKE	**36**	1	Huntsville	19-S	6-W
CLATON	**10**	1	Huntsville	15-S	1-E
CLAYTON	**10**	2	Huntsville	15-S	1-E
" "	**16**	2	Huntsville	16-S	1-W
" "	**9**	1	Huntsville	15-S	1-W
CLEMENTS	**23**	6	Huntsville	17-S	2-W
" "	**31**	5	Huntsville	18-S	3-W
" "	**7**	2	Huntsville	15-S	3-W
" "	**15**	2	Huntsville	16-S	2-W
" "	**6**	1	Huntsville	15-S	4-W
" "	**13**	1	Huntsville	16-S	4-W
" "	**30**	1	Huntsville	18-S	4-W
CLICK	**21**	1	Huntsville	17-S	4-W
" "	**30**	1	Huntsville	18-S	4-W
CLIFT	**22**	4	Huntsville	17-S	3-W
" "	**14**	1	Huntsville	16-S	3-W
CLINE	**33**	2	Huntsville	18-S	1-W

Surname	Map Group	Parcels of Land	Meridian/Township/Range		
CLOPTON	**10**	4	Huntsville	15-S	1-E
CLOWER	**2**	1	Huntsville	14-S	3-W
COBB	**23**	1	Huntsville	17-S	2-W
" "	**22**	1	Huntsville	17-S	3-W
COBELL	**17**	1	Huntsville	16-S	1-E
COCHRAN	**15**	1	Huntsville	16-S	2-W
" "	**19**	1	Huntsville	17-S	6-W
COCKE	**3**	1	Huntsville	14-S	2-W
CODDELL	**1**	1	Huntsville	14-S	4-W
COKER	**16**	3	Huntsville	16-S	1-W
" "	**23**	3	Huntsville	17-S	2-W
" "	**28**	1	Huntsville	18-S	6-W
" "	**38**	1	Huntsville	19-S	4-W
COLDWELL	**38**	1	Huntsville	19-S	4-W
COLE	**8**	4	Huntsville	15-S	2-W
" "	**15**	1	Huntsville	16-S	2-W
" "	**20**	1	Huntsville	17-S	5-W
COLEMAN	**9**	1	Huntsville	15-S	1-W
" "	**8**	1	Huntsville	15-S	2-W
" "	**13**	1	Huntsville	16-S	4-W
COLLEY	**39**	3	Huntsville	19-S	3-W
COLLIER	**21**	2	Huntsville	17-S	4-W
COLLINS	**9**	2	Huntsville	15-S	1-W
" "	**39**	1	Huntsville	19-S	3-W
COLLMAN	**16**	1	Huntsville	16-S	1-W
COLLY	**31**	1	Huntsville	18-S	3-W
COLWELL	**38**	2	Huntsville	19-S	4-W
" "	**43**	1	Huntsville	20-S	4-W
COMPANY	**37**	2	Huntsville	19-S	5-W
CONDEN	**23**	1	Huntsville	17-S	2-W
CONDRAY	**37**	1	Huntsville	19-S	5-W
CONDRY	**38**	1	Huntsville	19-S	4-W
" "	**37**	1	Huntsville	19-S	5-W
CONNER	**21**	7	Huntsville	17-S	4-W
" "	**13**	4	Huntsville	16-S	4-W
CONWAY	**22**	2	Huntsville	17-S	3-W
COOK	**14**	2	Huntsville	16-S	3-W
" "	**15**	1	Huntsville	16-S	2-W
" "	**19**	1	Huntsville	17-S	6-W
COOKE	**17**	1	Huntsville	16-S	1-E
COOLEY	**42**	3	Huntsville	20-S	5-W
" "	**20**	2	Huntsville	17-S	5-W
" "	**43**	2	Huntsville	20-S	4-W
COOPER	**8**	6	Huntsville	15-S	2-W
" "	**7**	5	Huntsville	15-S	3-W
" "	**20**	3	Huntsville	17-S	5-W
" "	**31**	3	Huntsville	18-S	3-W
" "	**16**	2	Huntsville	16-S	1-W
" "	**12**	2	Huntsville	16-S	5-W
COPELAND	**25**	1	Huntsville	17-S	1-E
CORLEY	**7**	3	Huntsville	15-S	3-W
" "	**5**	3	Huntsville	15-S	5-W
" "	**6**	1	Huntsville	15-S	4-W
CORNELIUS	**14**	2	Huntsville	16-S	3-W
" "	**13**	1	Huntsville	16-S	4-W
COSBY	**9**	3	Huntsville	15-S	1-W
COTNAM	**2**	1	Huntsville	14-S	3-W
COTTON	**8**	1	Huntsville	15-S	2-W
COUNTS	**22**	1	Huntsville	17-S	3-W
COWARD	**39**	3	Huntsville	19-S	3-W

Surname	Map Group	Parcels of Land	Meridian/Township/Range		
COWARD (Cont'd)	**38**	1	Huntsville	19-S	4-W
COWDEN	**8**	5	Huntsville	15-S	2-W
" "	**9**	2	Huntsville	15-S	1-W
" "	**23**	2	Huntsville	17-S	2-W
" "	**24**	1	Huntsville	17-S	1-W
" "	**33**	1	Huntsville	18-S	1-W
COWEN	**36**	1	Huntsville	19-S	6-W
COWLEY	**36**	4	Huntsville	19-S	6-W
" "	**42**	1	Huntsville	20-S	5-W
COX	**37**	9	Huntsville	19-S	5-W
" "	**33**	1	Huntsville	18-S	1-W
" "	**38**	1	Huntsville	19-S	4-W
" "	**36**	1	Huntsville	19-S	6-W
COZBY	**9**	2	Huntsville	15-S	1-W
CRAIGER	**39**	1	Huntsville	19-S	3-W
CRAIK	**2**	1	Huntsville	14-S	3-W
CRANE	**37**	6	Huntsville	19-S	5-W
" "	**42**	2	Huntsville	20-S	5-W
CRANNEY	**7**	3	Huntsville	15-S	3-W
CRAUSWELL	**22**	1	Huntsville	17-S	3-W
CRAWFORD	**24**	1	Huntsville	17-S	1-W
CREEL	**1**	4	Huntsville	14-S	4-W
" "	**2**	3	Huntsville	14-S	3-W
" "	**8**	2	Huntsville	15-S	2-W
CREWS	**15**	1	Huntsville	16-S	2-W
CROCKER	**12**	16	Huntsville	16-S	5-W
" "	**13**	3	Huntsville	16-S	4-W
" "	**24**	1	Huntsville	17-S	1-W
" "	**23**	1	Huntsville	17-S	2-W
CROCKETT	**6**	2	Huntsville	15-S	4-W
CROOKS	**30**	6	Huntsville	18-S	4-W
" "	**28**	4	Huntsville	18-S	6-W
" "	**36**	2	Huntsville	19-S	6-W
" "	**37**	1	Huntsville	19-S	5-W
CROSS	**17**	3	Huntsville	16-S	1-E
" "	**6**	1	Huntsville	15-S	4-W
" "	**33**	1	Huntsville	18-S	1-W
" "	**43**	1	Huntsville	20-S	4-W
CROTWELL	**13**	1	Huntsville	16-S	4-W
" "	**39**	1	Huntsville	19-S	3-W
CROW	**14**	1	Huntsville	16-S	3-W
CRUM	**21**	4	Huntsville	17-S	4-W
CRUMLY	**21**	2	Huntsville	17-S	4-W
CRUMP	**15**	3	Huntsville	16-S	2-W
" "	**25**	1	Huntsville	17-S	1-E
CULBERTSON	**38**	3	Huntsville	19-S	4-W
CULP	**31**	1	Huntsville	18-S	3-W
CULPEPPER	**11**	3	Huntsville	16-S	6-W
CUMMING	**22**	1	Huntsville	17-S	3-W
CUMMINGS	**8**	2	Huntsville	15-S	2-W
" "	**23**	1	Huntsville	17-S	2-W
CUMMINS	**23**	5	Huntsville	17-S	2-W
" "	**32**	3	Huntsville	18-S	2-W
" "	**37**	1	Huntsville	19-S	5-W
CUNINGHAM	**7**	1	Huntsville	15-S	3-W
CUNNINGHAM	**15**	4	Huntsville	16-S	2-W
" "	**7**	3	Huntsville	15-S	3-W
" "	**2**	2	Huntsville	14-S	3-W
" "	**31**	2	Huntsville	18-S	3-W
" "	**6**	1	Huntsville	15-S	4-W

Surname	Map Group	Parcels of Land	Meridian/Township/Range		
CUNNINGHAM (Cont'd)	**20**	1	Huntsville	17-S	5-W
CURRY	**42**	2	Huntsville	20-S	5-W
" "	**41**	2	Huntsville	20-S	6-W
DABBS	**29**	4	Huntsville	18-S	5-W
" "	**30**	1	Huntsville	18-S	4-W
DACUS	**22**	1	Huntsville	17-S	3-W
" "	**21**	1	Huntsville	17-S	4-W
DAILEY	**10**	1	Huntsville	15-S	1-E
" "	**38**	1	Huntsville	19-S	4-W
DANIEL	**16**	5	Huntsville	16-S	1-W
" "	**23**	2	Huntsville	17-S	2-W
" "	**43**	2	Huntsville	20-S	4-W
DANIELL	**2**	1	Huntsville	14-S	3-W
DAVENPORT	**40**	4	Huntsville	19-S	2-W
" "	**2**	1	Huntsville	14-S	3-W
" "	**8**	1	Huntsville	15-S	2-W
DAVIDSON	**3**	2	Huntsville	14-S	2-W
" "	**13**	2	Huntsville	16-S	4-W
" "	**43**	2	Huntsville	20-S	4-W
DAVIS	**42**	10	Huntsville	20-S	5-W
" "	**36**	3	Huntsville	19-S	6-W
" "	**3**	1	Huntsville	14-S	2-W
" "	**9**	1	Huntsville	15-S	1-W
" "	**6**	1	Huntsville	15-S	4-W
" "	**17**	1	Huntsville	16-S	1-E
" "	**11**	1	Huntsville	16-S	6-W
" "	**19**	1	Huntsville	17-S	6-W
" "	**30**	1	Huntsville	18-S	4-W
" "	**27**	1	Huntsville	18-S	7-W
" "	**40**	1	Huntsville	19-S	2-W
DAWSON	**36**	1	Huntsville	19-S	6-W
DEAN	**4**	1	Huntsville	14-S	1-W
" "	**3**	1	Huntsville	14-S	2-W
" "	**8**	1	Huntsville	15-S	2-W
DEASE	**29**	1	Huntsville	18-S	5-W
DEATON	**21**	4	Huntsville	17-S	4-W
" "	**12**	3	Huntsville	16-S	5-W
DEAVENPORT	**14**	2	Huntsville	16-S	3-W
DEAVOURS	**10**	1	Huntsville	15-S	1-E
DEES	**29**	6	Huntsville	18-S	5-W
DELANY	**16**	2	Huntsville	16-S	1-W
DELASHAW	**10**	1	Huntsville	15-S	1-E
DELLASHAW	**10**	2	Huntsville	15-S	1-E
DEMENT	**22**	1	Huntsville	17-S	3-W
DEMOTT	**43**	2	Huntsville	20-S	4-W
DENTON	**38**	2	Huntsville	19-S	4-W
" "	**37**	1	Huntsville	19-S	5-W
DEPOISTER	**24**	2	Huntsville	17-S	1-W
DESHAZO	**33**	1	Huntsville	18-S	1-W
DEVERNEY	**24**	1	Huntsville	17-S	1-W
DICKENSON	**30**	1	Huntsville	18-S	4-W
DICKEY	**42**	4	Huntsville	20-S	5-W
" "	**37**	2	Huntsville	19-S	5-W
" "	**43**	1	Huntsville	20-S	4-W
DICKINSON	**30**	4	Huntsville	18-S	4-W
" "	**38**	1	Huntsville	19-S	4-W
DIFFEY	**31**	1	Huntsville	18-S	3-W
DILL	**6**	1	Huntsville	15-S	4-W
DILLARD	**37**	1	Huntsville	19-S	5-W
DILLASHAW	**10**	1	Huntsville	15-S	1-E

Surname	Map Group	Parcels of Land	Meridian/Township/Range		
DIMMICK	**32**	3	Huntsville	18-S	2-W
DISON	**31**	2	Huntsville	18-S	3-W
DOBBS	**29**	3	Huntsville	18-S	5-W
DOCKENS	**1**	2	Huntsville	14-S	4-W
DOCKINGS	**2**	2	Huntsville	14-S	3-W
DODD	**32**	4	Huntsville	18-S	2-W
" "	**2**	1	Huntsville	14-S	3-W
" "	**19**	1	Huntsville	17-S	6-W
DOGGET	**5**	2	Huntsville	15-S	5-W
DOLLAR	**22**	1	Huntsville	17-S	3-W
DONELSON	**31**	4	Huntsville	18-S	3-W
" "	**23**	3	Huntsville	17-S	2-W
" "	**39**	1	Huntsville	19-S	3-W
DORMAN	**9**	2	Huntsville	15-S	1-W
" "	**3**	1	Huntsville	14-S	2-W
" "	**33**	1	Huntsville	18-S	1-W
" "	**39**	1	Huntsville	19-S	3-W
DORNING	**3**	6	Huntsville	14-S	2-W
DOROUGH	**25**	4	Huntsville	17-S	1-E
DOSS	**6**	5	Huntsville	15-S	4-W
" "	**2**	4	Huntsville	14-S	3-W
" "	**3**	3	Huntsville	14-S	2-W
" "	**7**	1	Huntsville	15-S	3-W
DOTSON	**24**	3	Huntsville	17-S	1-W
DOUGLASS	**7**	1	Huntsville	15-S	3-W
DOWNEY	**21**	6	Huntsville	17-S	4-W
" "	**31**	2	Huntsville	18-S	3-W
" "	**30**	2	Huntsville	18-S	4-W
DOWNS	**14**	2	Huntsville	16-S	3-W
DOXEY	**9**	5	Huntsville	15-S	1-W
DRAKE	**30**	2	Huntsville	18-S	4-W
DRAPER	**43**	5	Huntsville	20-S	4-W
" "	**14**	1	Huntsville	16-S	3-W
" "	**13**	1	Huntsville	16-S	4-W
" "	**30**	1	Huntsville	18-S	4-W
DRENNON	**43**	1	Huntsville	20-S	4-W
DUFF	**38**	1	Huntsville	19-S	4-W
" "	**37**	1	Huntsville	19-S	5-W
DUKE	**32**	4	Huntsville	18-S	2-W
DULANY	**16**	10	Huntsville	16-S	1-W
" "	**17**	2	Huntsville	16-S	1-E
DUMAS	**10**	5	Huntsville	15-S	1-E
DUNN	**27**	10	Huntsville	18-S	7-W
" "	**18**	1	Huntsville	17-S	7-W
DUPEY	**38**	3	Huntsville	19-S	4-W
" "	**39**	2	Huntsville	19-S	3-W
" "	**31**	1	Huntsville	18-S	3-W
DUPREY	**12**	1	Huntsville	16-S	5-W
DUPUY	**31**	5	Huntsville	18-S	3-W
" "	**23**	4	Huntsville	17-S	2-W
" "	**22**	4	Huntsville	17-S	3-W
" "	**6**	1	Huntsville	15-S	4-W
" "	**30**	1	Huntsville	18-S	4-W
" "	**39**	1	Huntsville	19-S	3-W
DUTTON	**2**	5	Huntsville	14-S	3-W
" "	**3**	1	Huntsville	14-S	2-W
DYER	**9**	1	Huntsville	15-S	1-W
" "	**7**	1	Huntsville	15-S	3-W
" "	**14**	1	Huntsville	16-S	3-W
" "	**22**	1	Huntsville	17-S	3-W

Surname	Map Group	Parcels of Land	Meridian/Township/Range		
EARL	**22**	1	Huntsville	17-S	3-W
EARLE	**31**	7	Huntsville	18-S	3-W
" "	**22**	3	Huntsville	17-S	3-W
" "	**39**	2	Huntsville	19-S	3-W
" "	**14**	1	Huntsville	16-S	3-W
" "	**12**	1	Huntsville	16-S	5-W
" "	**24**	1	Huntsville	17-S	1-W
EARLEY	**5**	3	Huntsville	15-S	5-W
" "	**22**	2	Huntsville	17-S	3-W
" "	**37**	1	Huntsville	19-S	5-W
EARLY	**13**	1	Huntsville	16-S	4-W
" "	**21**	1	Huntsville	17-S	4-W
" "	**30**	1	Huntsville	18-S	4-W
EARNEST	**31**	1	Huntsville	18-S	3-W
EASTIN	**42**	6	Huntsville	20-S	5-W
EASTIS	**14**	4	Huntsville	16-S	3-W
" "	**23**	4	Huntsville	17-S	2-W
" "	**33**	2	Huntsville	18-S	1-W
" "	**13**	1	Huntsville	16-S	4-W
" "	**22**	1	Huntsville	17-S	3-W
" "	**32**	1	Huntsville	18-S	2-W
EATON	**20**	7	Huntsville	17-S	5-W
" "	**7**	3	Huntsville	15-S	3-W
ECHOLS	**22**	15	Huntsville	17-S	3-W
" "	**21**	3	Huntsville	17-S	4-W
" "	**14**	1	Huntsville	16-S	3-W
EDENS	**16**	3	Huntsville	16-S	1-W
" "	**17**	2	Huntsville	16-S	1-E
EDMUNDSON	**24**	1	Huntsville	17-S	1-W
EDWARDS	**16**	8	Huntsville	16-S	1-W
" "	**7**	7	Huntsville	15-S	3-W
" "	**17**	3	Huntsville	16-S	1-E
" "	**8**	2	Huntsville	15-S	2-W
" "	**38**	2	Huntsville	19-S	4-W
" "	**10**	1	Huntsville	15-S	1-E
" "	**15**	1	Huntsville	16-S	2-W
" "	**23**	1	Huntsville	17-S	2-W
" "	**32**	1	Huntsville	18-S	2-W
ELLARD	**23**	7	Huntsville	17-S	2-W
" "	**24**	2	Huntsville	17-S	1-W
" "	**14**	1	Huntsville	16-S	3-W
ELLERD	**24**	1	Huntsville	17-S	1-W
ELLICOTT	**33**	1	Huntsville	18-S	1-W
ELLINGTON	**24**	2	Huntsville	17-S	1-W
" "	**33**	1	Huntsville	18-S	1-W
ELLIOTT	**14**	3	Huntsville	16-S	3-W
" "	**9**	2	Huntsville	15-S	1-W
ELLIS	**42**	6	Huntsville	20-S	5-W
EMOND	**12**	1	Huntsville	16-S	5-W
ENDSLEY	**3**	4	Huntsville	14-S	2-W
ENGLISH	**30**	1	Huntsville	18-S	4-W
EPPERSON	**25**	2	Huntsville	17-S	1-E
EPPES	**16**	2	Huntsville	16-S	1-W
ERNEST	**26**	1	Huntsville	18-S	8-W
ERWIN	**15**	3	Huntsville	16-S	2-W
" "	**8**	1	Huntsville	15-S	2-W
ESKEW	**7**	2	Huntsville	15-S	3-W
ESPEY	**19**	1	Huntsville	17-S	6-W
" "	**18**	1	Huntsville	17-S	7-W
ETHRIDGE	**16**	1	Huntsville	16-S	1-W

Surname	Map Group	Parcels of Land	Meridian/Township/Range		
EUBANK	13	5	Huntsville	16-S	4-W
" "	21	2	Huntsville	17-S	4-W
" "	22	1	Huntsville	17-S	3-W
" "	31	1	Huntsville	18-S	3-W
" "	30	1	Huntsville	18-S	4-W
EUBANKS	12	2	Huntsville	16-S	5-W
" "	30	2	Huntsville	18-S	4-W
EVANS	12	3	Huntsville	16-S	5-W
" "	14	1	Huntsville	16-S	3-W
EVERETT	10	1	Huntsville	15-S	1-E
EZEKIAL	14	1	Huntsville	16-S	3-W
EZEKIEL	14	4	Huntsville	16-S	3-W
" "	21	3	Huntsville	17-S	4-W
FAGASON	24	1	Huntsville	17-S	1-W
FAGERSON	24	1	Huntsville	17-S	1-W
FALKNER	25	1	Huntsville	17-S	1-E
FALKS	16	3	Huntsville	16-S	1-W
" "	17	1	Huntsville	16-S	1-E
FANCHER	31	3	Huntsville	18-S	3-W
FARLEY	14	1	Huntsville	16-S	3-W
FARR	19	1	Huntsville	17-S	6-W
FARRAR	39	1	Huntsville	19-S	3-W
FARRINGTON	43	2	Huntsville	20-S	4-W
FARRIS	22	1	Huntsville	17-S	3-W
FASON	12	2	Huntsville	16-S	5-W
" "	11	1	Huntsville	16-S	6-W
FATIO	24	2	Huntsville	17-S	1-W
FAUCETT	4	2	Huntsville	14-S	1-W
" "	3	1	Huntsville	14-S	2-W
" "	9	1	Huntsville	15-S	1-W
FEENKER	44	1	Huntsville	20-S	3-W
FENDLEY	4	3	Huntsville	14-S	1-W
FERGUSON	22	2	Huntsville	17-S	3-W
" "	12	1	Huntsville	16-S	5-W
" "	23	1	Huntsville	17-S	2-W
FERRINGTON	43	2	Huntsville	20-S	4-W
FIELDS	13	25	Huntsville	16-S	4-W
" "	29	4	Huntsville	18-S	5-W
" "	6	2	Huntsville	15-S	4-W
" "	21	2	Huntsville	17-S	4-W
" "	43	2	Huntsville	20-S	4-W
" "	14	1	Huntsville	16-S	3-W
" "	30	1	Huntsville	18-S	4-W
" "	28	1	Huntsville	18-S	6-W
FINCH	12	1	Huntsville	16-S	5-W
FINDLEY	3	1	Huntsville	14-S	2-W
FINLEY	42	2	Huntsville	20-S	5-W
FISHER	39	2	Huntsville	19-S	3-W
FLANAGAN	6	2	Huntsville	15-S	4-W
" "	14	1	Huntsville	16-S	3-W
" "	22	1	Huntsville	17-S	3-W
FLEMING	42	1	Huntsville	20-S	5-W
FLORENCE	1	3	Huntsville	14-S	4-W
FLOWERS	32	5	Huntsville	18-S	2-W
" "	15	4	Huntsville	16-S	2-W
FORBIS	28	1	Huntsville	18-S	6-W
" "	36	1	Huntsville	19-S	6-W
FORD	39	1	Huntsville	19-S	3-W
FORMAN	15	1	Huntsville	16-S	2-W
FORREST	31	1	Huntsville	18-S	3-W

Surname	Map Group	Parcels of Land	Meridian/Township/Range
FORRESTER	28	4	Huntsville 18-S 6-W
FORTNER	2	1	Huntsville 14-S 3-W
" "	12	1	Huntsville 16-S 5-W
FOSSETT	3	3	Huntsville 14-S 2-W
FOSTER	24	5	Huntsville 17-S 1-W
" "	16	4	Huntsville 16-S 1-W
" "	7	3	Huntsville 15-S 3-W
" "	6	3	Huntsville 15-S 4-W
" "	9	2	Huntsville 15-S 1-W
FOUST	24	2	Huntsville 17-S 1-W
FOWLER	34	2	Huntsville 18-S 1-E
FOX	27	1	Huntsville 18-S 7-W
FRANKLIN	28	22	Huntsville 18-S 6-W
" "	16	10	Huntsville 16-S 1-W
" "	27	9	Huntsville 18-S 7-W
" "	8	4	Huntsville 15-S 2-W
" "	21	4	Huntsville 17-S 4-W
" "	25	3	Huntsville 17-S 1-E
" "	29	2	Huntsville 18-S 5-W
" "	9	1	Huntsville 15-S 1-W
" "	17	1	Huntsville 16-S 1-E
" "	24	1	Huntsville 17-S 1-W
" "	23	1	Huntsville 17-S 2-W
" "	22	1	Huntsville 17-S 3-W
" "	19	1	Huntsville 17-S 6-W
" "	18	1	Huntsville 17-S 7-W
" "	33	1	Huntsville 18-S 1-W
" "	35	1	Huntsville 19-S 7-W
FRANKS	13	1	Huntsville 16-S 4-W
FRAZER	10	1	Huntsville 15-S 1-E
FRAZIER	17	10	Huntsville 16-S 1-E
" "	10	6	Huntsville 15-S 1-E
" "	28	2	Huntsville 18-S 6-W
" "	19	1	Huntsville 17-S 6-W
FREELAND	28	5	Huntsville 18-S 6-W
" "	27	1	Huntsville 18-S 7-W
FREEMAN	10	2	Huntsville 15-S 1-E
" "	22	1	Huntsville 17-S 3-W
FRENCH	23	1	Huntsville 17-S 2-W
FRETWELL	21	2	Huntsville 17-S 4-W
FRIEDMAN	8	1	Huntsville 15-S 2-W
FRIEL	22	1	Huntsville 17-S 3-W
FRIERSON	27	2	Huntsville 18-S 7-W
" "	19	1	Huntsville 17-S 6-W
FRIES	33	1	Huntsville 18-S 1-W
FULLER	25	3	Huntsville 17-S 1-E
" "	17	1	Huntsville 16-S 1-E
" "	16	1	Huntsville 16-S 1-W
FULMER	14	3	Huntsville 16-S 3-W
FULTON	43	1	Huntsville 20-S 4-W
FURGASON	24	1	Huntsville 17-S 1-W
GABLE	38	1	Huntsville 19-S 4-W
GAFFORD	14	1	Huntsville 16-S 3-W
GALLAGHER	39	1	Huntsville 19-S 3-W
GALLAWAY	38	1	Huntsville 19-S 4-W
GALLOWAY	17	2	Huntsville 16-S 1-E
" "	38	2	Huntsville 19-S 4-W
GAMMAGE	3	2	Huntsville 14-S 2-W
GANONS	43	1	Huntsville 20-S 4-W
GANUS	27	3	Huntsville 18-S 7-W

Surname	Map Group	Parcels of Land	Meridian/Township/Range		
GARNER	**17**	6	Huntsville	16-S	1-E
" "	**16**	4	Huntsville	16-S	1-W
" "	**10**	2	Huntsville	15-S	1-E
" "	**36**	1	Huntsville	19-S	6-W
GARRETT	**7**	7	Huntsville	15-S	3-W
" "	**15**	4	Huntsville	16-S	2-W
GARRITT	**14**	1	Huntsville	16-S	3-W
" "	**23**	1	Huntsville	17-S	2-W
GARY	**22**	1	Huntsville	17-S	3-W
GEE	**9**	2	Huntsville	15-S	1-W
GEESLIN	**42**	1	Huntsville	20-S	5-W
GENTRY	**42**	1	Huntsville	20-S	5-W
GEORGE	**43**	14	Huntsville	20-S	4-W
GERMAN	**14**	2	Huntsville	16-S	3-W
GESNER	**15**	1	Huntsville	16-S	2-W
GILBERT	**33**	11	Huntsville	18-S	1-W
" "	**27**	10	Huntsville	18-S	7-W
" "	**2**	4	Huntsville	14-S	3-W
" "	**26**	3	Huntsville	18-S	8-W
" "	**24**	1	Huntsville	17-S	1-W
GILL	**39**	11	Huntsville	19-S	3-W
" "	**31**	7	Huntsville	18-S	3-W
" "	**8**	3	Huntsville	15-S	2-W
" "	**7**	2	Huntsville	15-S	3-W
" "	**2**	1	Huntsville	14-S	3-W
" "	**22**	1	Huntsville	17-S	3-W
GILLASPIE	**4**	1	Huntsville	14-S	1-W
GILLEN	**20**	1	Huntsville	17-S	5-W
" "	**19**	1	Huntsville	17-S	6-W
" "	**30**	1	Huntsville	18-S	4-W
GILLESPIE	**8**	10	Huntsville	15-S	2-W
" "	**9**	4	Huntsville	15-S	1-W
" "	**15**	3	Huntsville	16-S	2-W
" "	**4**	2	Huntsville	14-S	1-W
" "	**3**	2	Huntsville	14-S	2-W
" "	**7**	1	Huntsville	15-S	3-W
GILLEY	**11**	1	Huntsville	16-S	6-W
GILLIAN	**26**	2	Huntsville	18-S	8-W
GILLILAND	**21**	1	Huntsville	17-S	4-W
GILLMORE	**28**	1	Huntsville	18-S	6-W
GILMER	**31**	4	Huntsville	18-S	3-W
" "	**23**	3	Huntsville	17-S	2-W
" "	**39**	1	Huntsville	19-S	3-W
GILMORE	**19**	6	Huntsville	17-S	6-W
" "	**28**	3	Huntsville	18-S	6-W
" "	**31**	1	Huntsville	18-S	3-W
GILPIN	**16**	1	Huntsville	16-S	1-W
GINERY	**43**	2	Huntsville	20-S	4-W
GIVENS	**25**	3	Huntsville	17-S	1-E
GLASGOW	**21**	7	Huntsville	17-S	4-W
" "	**20**	2	Huntsville	17-S	5-W
GLASS	**24**	6	Huntsville	17-S	1-W
" "	**33**	5	Huntsville	18-S	1-W
" "	**32**	3	Huntsville	18-S	2-W
GLAZE	**19**	7	Huntsville	17-S	6-W
" "	**11**	2	Huntsville	16-S	6-W
" "	**28**	1	Huntsville	18-S	6-W
GLENN	**39**	9	Huntsville	19-S	3-W
" "	**8**	8	Huntsville	15-S	2-W
" "	**3**	4	Huntsville	14-S	2-W

Surname	Map Group	Parcels of Land	Meridian/Township/Range
GLENN (Cont'd)	**30**	4	Huntsville 18-S 4-W
" "	**31**	3	Huntsville 18-S 3-W
" "	**16**	2	Huntsville 16-S 1-W
" "	**17**	1	Huntsville 16-S 1-E
" "	**32**	1	Huntsville 18-S 2-W
GLOVER	**12**	8	Huntsville 16-S 5-W
" "	**6**	4	Huntsville 15-S 4-W
" "	**5**	1	Huntsville 15-S 5-W
" "	**19**	1	Huntsville 17-S 6-W
GOAS	**33**	1	Huntsville 18-S 1-W
GODFREY	**21**	3	Huntsville 17-S 4-W
GODWIN	**16**	3	Huntsville 16-S 1-W
" "	**24**	1	Huntsville 17-S 1-W
GOGGANS	**6**	5	Huntsville 15-S 4-W
GOING	**22**	1	Huntsville 17-S 3-W
GOINS	**7**	1	Huntsville 15-S 3-W
GOLDEN	**28**	6	Huntsville 18-S 6-W
" "	**12**	5	Huntsville 16-S 5-W
" "	**33**	2	Huntsville 18-S 1-W
" "	**19**	1	Huntsville 17-S 6-W
GOLDING	**28**	1	Huntsville 18-S 6-W
GOLDSBY	**16**	1	Huntsville 16-S 1-W
" "	**21**	1	Huntsville 17-S 4-W
GOODE	**39**	7	Huntsville 19-S 3-W
" "	**14**	5	Huntsville 16-S 3-W
" "	**32**	5	Huntsville 18-S 2-W
" "	**31**	1	Huntsville 18-S 3-W
GOODMAN	**9**	1	Huntsville 15-S 1-W
GOODWIN	**16**	16	Huntsville 16-S 1-W
" "	**24**	15	Huntsville 17-S 1-W
" "	**36**	10	Huntsville 19-S 6-W
" "	**28**	9	Huntsville 18-S 6-W
" "	**3**	8	Huntsville 14-S 2-W
" "	**19**	4	Huntsville 17-S 6-W
" "	**15**	3	Huntsville 16-S 2-W
" "	**20**	3	Huntsville 17-S 5-W
" "	**39**	3	Huntsville 19-S 3-W
" "	**38**	3	Huntsville 19-S 4-W
" "	**8**	2	Huntsville 15-S 2-W
" "	**14**	2	Huntsville 16-S 3-W
" "	**10**	1	Huntsville 15-S 1-E
" "	**9**	1	Huntsville 15-S 1-W
" "	**17**	1	Huntsville 16-S 1-E
" "	**13**	1	Huntsville 16-S 4-W
" "	**12**	1	Huntsville 16-S 5-W
" "	**22**	1	Huntsville 17-S 3-W
" "	**32**	1	Huntsville 18-S 2-W
" "	**41**	1	Huntsville 20-S 6-W
GOOLD	**2**	3	Huntsville 14-S 3-W
GOOLSBY	**21**	5	Huntsville 17-S 4-W
" "	**20**	2	Huntsville 17-S 5-W
" "	**12**	1	Huntsville 16-S 5-W
GORE	**24**	5	Huntsville 17-S 1-W
" "	**23**	1	Huntsville 17-S 2-W
GORMAN	**16**	6	Huntsville 16-S 1-W
GOSSET	**21**	4	Huntsville 17-S 4-W
GOSSETT	**21**	2	Huntsville 17-S 4-W
" "	**12**	1	Huntsville 16-S 5-W
GOULSBY	**21**	4	Huntsville 17-S 4-W
GOWEN	**7**	1	Huntsville 15-S 3-W

Surname	Map Group	Parcels of Land	Meridian/Township/Range		
GOWIN	**14**	2	Huntsville	16-S	3-W
GOWINS	**14**	1	Huntsville	16-S	3-W
GOYENS	**15**	1	Huntsville	16-S	2-W
GOYNE	**30**	3	Huntsville	18-S	4-W
" "	**31**	2	Huntsville	18-S	3-W
GRACE	**31**	14	Huntsville	18-S	3-W
" "	**24**	2	Huntsville	17-S	1-W
GRAHAM	**7**	8	Huntsville	15-S	3-W
" "	**14**	5	Huntsville	16-S	3-W
" "	**5**	1	Huntsville	15-S	5-W
" "	**23**	1	Huntsville	17-S	2-W
GRANT	**44**	2	Huntsville	20-S	3-W
GRAVES	**11**	2	Huntsville	16-S	6-W
GRAVETTE	**2**	1	Huntsville	14-S	3-W
GRAY	**24**	2	Huntsville	17-S	1-W
" "	**1**	1	Huntsville	14-S	4-W
" "	**42**	1	Huntsville	20-S	5-W
GRAYHAM	**7**	6	Huntsville	15-S	3-W
" "	**14**	2	Huntsville	16-S	3-W
GREEN	**15**	12	Huntsville	16-S	2-W
" "	**23**	10	Huntsville	17-S	2-W
" "	**31**	6	Huntsville	18-S	3-W
" "	**43**	4	Huntsville	20-S	4-W
" "	**25**	3	Huntsville	17-S	1-E
" "	**24**	3	Huntsville	17-S	1-W
" "	**14**	2	Huntsville	16-S	3-W
" "	**39**	2	Huntsville	19-S	3-W
" "	**6**	1	Huntsville	15-S	4-W
" "	**17**	1	Huntsville	16-S	1-E
" "	**36**	1	Huntsville	19-S	6-W
" "	**44**	1	Huntsville	20-S	3-W
" "	**42**	1	Huntsville	20-S	5-W
GREENBERG	**24**	1	Huntsville	17-S	1-W
GREENE	**15**	3	Huntsville	16-S	2-W
" "	**43**	2	Huntsville	20-S	4-W
" "	**8**	1	Huntsville	15-S	2-W
" "	**17**	1	Huntsville	16-S	1-E
" "	**23**	1	Huntsville	17-S	2-W
GREER	**36**	1	Huntsville	19-S	6-W
GRIFFIN	**31**	4	Huntsville	18-S	3-W
" "	**39**	4	Huntsville	19-S	3-W
" "	**24**	1	Huntsville	17-S	1-W
GRIFFITHS	**2**	1	Huntsville	14-S	3-W
GRIMES	**7**	9	Huntsville	15-S	3-W
GRUBBS	**7**	1	Huntsville	15-S	3-W
GUNNELL	**38**	1	Huntsville	19-S	4-W
GURLEY	**4**	5	Huntsville	14-S	1-W
" "	**3**	1	Huntsville	14-S	2-W
GUTHERY	**3**	3	Huntsville	14-S	2-W
GUTHREY	**22**	1	Huntsville	17-S	3-W
GUTTERY	**8**	2	Huntsville	15-S	2-W
GWIN	**28**	3	Huntsville	18-S	6-W
" "	**27**	2	Huntsville	18-S	7-W
" "	**35**	2	Huntsville	19-S	7-W
HAACK	**24**	2	Huntsville	17-S	1-W
HADEN	**4**	5	Huntsville	14-S	1-W
HAGELGANS	**42**	1	Huntsville	20-S	5-W
HAGER	**30**	2	Huntsville	18-S	4-W
HAGOOD	**15**	16	Huntsville	16-S	2-W
" "	**9**	10	Huntsville	15-S	1-W

Surname	Map Group	Parcels of Land	Meridian/Township/Range
HAGOOD (Cont'd)	**16**	8	Huntsville 16-S 1-W
" "	**8**	5	Huntsville 15-S 2-W
" "	**4**	2	Huntsville 14-S 1-W
" "	**3**	2	Huntsville 14-S 2-W
" "	**24**	2	Huntsville 17-S 1-W
HAGWOOD	**25**	1	Huntsville 17-S 1-E
HAIL	**10**	3	Huntsville 15-S 1-E
HALCOMBE	**38**	1	Huntsville 19-S 4-W
HALE	**23**	5	Huntsville 17-S 2-W
" "	**10**	3	Huntsville 15-S 1-E
" "	**24**	1	Huntsville 17-S 1-W
HALL	**31**	9	Huntsville 18-S 3-W
" "	**23**	6	Huntsville 17-S 2-W
" "	**38**	4	Huntsville 19-S 4-W
" "	**10**	3	Huntsville 15-S 1-E
" "	**9**	3	Huntsville 15-S 1-W
" "	**29**	3	Huntsville 18-S 5-W
" "	**37**	3	Huntsville 19-S 5-W
" "	**16**	2	Huntsville 16-S 1-W
" "	**3**	1	Huntsville 14-S 2-W
" "	**24**	1	Huntsville 17-S 1-W
" "	**30**	1	Huntsville 18-S 4-W
" "	**39**	1	Huntsville 19-S 3-W
" "	**43**	1	Huntsville 20-S 4-W
HALLMARK	**8**	1	Huntsville 15-S 2-W
" "	**15**	1	Huntsville 16-S 2-W
HAMAKER	**29**	23	Huntsville 18-S 5-W
" "	**37**	8	Huntsville 19-S 5-W
" "	**33**	1	Huntsville 18-S 1-W
" "	**30**	1	Huntsville 18-S 4-W
HAMIL	**15**	1	Huntsville 16-S 2-W
HAMILTON	**23**	7	Huntsville 17-S 2-W
" "	**25**	2	Huntsville 17-S 1-E
" "	**2**	1	Huntsville 14-S 3-W
" "	**15**	1	Huntsville 16-S 2-W
HAMMER	**7**	1	Huntsville 15-S 3-W
HAMMOND	**28**	1	Huntsville 18-S 6-W
HAMMONDS	**36**	4	Huntsville 19-S 6-W
HAMNER	**22**	4	Huntsville 17-S 3-W
" "	**23**	3	Huntsville 17-S 2-W
HANBY	**8**	11	Huntsville 15-S 2-W
" "	**9**	6	Huntsville 15-S 1-W
" "	**3**	5	Huntsville 14-S 2-W
" "	**16**	1	Huntsville 16-S 1-W
" "	**20**	1	Huntsville 17-S 5-W
" "	**31**	1	Huntsville 18-S 3-W
HANCOCK	**7**	3	Huntsville 15-S 3-W
" "	**9**	1	Huntsville 15-S 1-W
" "	**22**	1	Huntsville 17-S 3-W
" "	**19**	1	Huntsville 17-S 6-W
HAND	**13**	9	Huntsville 16-S 4-W
HANEY	**22**	1	Huntsville 17-S 3-W
HANLY	**3**	1	Huntsville 14-S 2-W
" "	**7**	1	Huntsville 15-S 3-W
" "	**12**	1	Huntsville 16-S 5-W
" "	**20**	1	Huntsville 17-S 5-W
HANNA	**32**	2	Huntsville 18-S 2-W
" "	**22**	1	Huntsville 17-S 3-W
HARAN	**25**	2	Huntsville 17-S 1-E
HARD	**39**	1	Huntsville 19-S 3-W

Surname	Map Group	Parcels of Land	Meridian/Township/Range		
HARDEN	**13**	3	Huntsville	16-S	4-W
" "	**8**	1	Huntsville	15-S	2-W
" "	**20**	1	Huntsville	17-S	5-W
HARDIMAN	**28**	1	Huntsville	18-S	6-W
HARDIN	**13**	6	Huntsville	16-S	4-W
" "	**21**	2	Huntsville	17-S	4-W
" "	**30**	1	Huntsville	18-S	4-W
HARDING	**24**	3	Huntsville	17-S	1-W
" "	**25**	2	Huntsville	17-S	1-E
HARDYMAN	**36**	2	Huntsville	19-S	6-W
" "	**28**	1	Huntsville	18-S	6-W
" "	**27**	1	Huntsville	18-S	7-W
HARIS	**33**	1	Huntsville	18-S	1-W
HARISON	**15**	2	Huntsville	16-S	2-W
HARKEY	**41**	1	Huntsville	20-S	6-W
HARKNESS	**43**	1	Huntsville	20-S	4-W
HARMAN	**39**	1	Huntsville	19-S	3-W
HARMON	**43**	8	Huntsville	20-S	4-W
" "	**39**	1	Huntsville	19-S	3-W
HARPER	**10**	4	Huntsville	15-S	1-E
" "	**2**	2	Huntsville	14-S	3-W
" "	**17**	1	Huntsville	16-S	1-E
HARRIS	**27**	4	Huntsville	18-S	7-W
" "	**14**	3	Huntsville	16-S	3-W
" "	**19**	3	Huntsville	17-S	6-W
" "	**16**	2	Huntsville	16-S	1-W
" "	**22**	2	Huntsville	17-S	3-W
" "	**17**	1	Huntsville	16-S	1-E
" "	**24**	1	Huntsville	17-S	1-W
" "	**18**	1	Huntsville	17-S	7-W
" "	**33**	1	Huntsville	18-S	1-W
" "	**32**	1	Huntsville	18-S	2-W
" "	**37**	1	Huntsville	19-S	5-W
HARRISON	**4**	3	Huntsville	14-S	1-W
" "	**15**	2	Huntsville	16-S	2-W
" "	**30**	2	Huntsville	18-S	4-W
" "	**10**	1	Huntsville	15-S	1-E
" "	**9**	1	Huntsville	15-S	1-W
" "	**23**	1	Huntsville	17-S	2-W
HARTGROVES	**9**	1	Huntsville	15-S	1-W
HARVEY	**24**	1	Huntsville	17-S	1-W
" "	**20**	1	Huntsville	17-S	5-W
HASKETT	**5**	1	Huntsville	15-S	5-W
HASTINGS	**5**	2	Huntsville	15-S	5-W
HAUGHEY	**9**	3	Huntsville	15-S	1-W
HAWKINS	**22**	22	Huntsville	17-S	3-W
" "	**31**	10	Huntsville	18-S	3-W
" "	**30**	5	Huntsville	18-S	4-W
" "	**21**	2	Huntsville	17-S	4-W
" "	**42**	1	Huntsville	20-S	5-W
HAYGOOD	**9**	1	Huntsville	15-S	1-W
HAYS	**13**	3	Huntsville	16-S	4-W
" "	**10**	1	Huntsville	15-S	1-E
" "	**9**	1	Huntsville	15-S	1-W
" "	**22**	1	Huntsville	17-S	3-W
HEARD	**19**	2	Huntsville	17-S	6-W
" "	**27**	1	Huntsville	18-S	7-W
HEATON	**13**	3	Huntsville	16-S	4-W
" "	**21**	1	Huntsville	17-S	4-W
HEFNER	**10**	2	Huntsville	15-S	1-E

Surname	Map Group	Parcels of Land	Meridian/Township/Range
HEFNER (Cont'd)	**17**	1	Huntsville 16-S 1-E
HEIFNER	**31**	1	Huntsville 18-S 3-W
HEMBREE	**21**	1	Huntsville 17-S 4-W
HEMPHILL	**15**	1	Huntsville 16-S 2-W
HENDERSON	**7**	3	Huntsville 15-S 3-W
" "	**21**	1	Huntsville 17-S 4-W
" "	**36**	1	Huntsville 19-S 6-W
HENDLEY	**38**	1	Huntsville 19-S 4-W
HENDON	**27**	1	Huntsville 18-S 7-W
HENLEY	**31**	3	Huntsville 18-S 3-W
HENLY	**30**	3	Huntsville 18-S 4-W
" "	**23**	1	Huntsville 17-S 2-W
HENRY	**24**	2	Huntsville 17-S 1-W
" "	**9**	1	Huntsville 15-S 1-W
" "	**8**	1	Huntsville 15-S 2-W
" "	**39**	1	Huntsville 19-S 3-W
HERREN	**24**	1	Huntsville 17-S 1-W
" "	**33**	1	Huntsville 18-S 1-W
HERRING	**25**	5	Huntsville 17-S 1-E
" "	**24**	4	Huntsville 17-S 1-W
" "	**33**	3	Huntsville 18-S 1-W
" "	**41**	3	Huntsville 20-S 6-W
" "	**10**	2	Huntsville 15-S 1-E
" "	**36**	2	Huntsville 19-S 6-W
HEWBERRY	**12**	1	Huntsville 16-S 5-W
HEWITT	**15**	3	Huntsville 16-S 2-W
" "	**2**	1	Huntsville 14-S 3-W
" "	**14**	1	Huntsville 16-S 3-W
HICKMAN	**9**	3	Huntsville 15-S 1-W
" "	**23**	3	Huntsville 17-S 2-W
HICKS	**20**	8	Huntsville 17-S 5-W
" "	**21**	3	Huntsville 17-S 4-W
" "	**4**	2	Huntsville 14-S 1-W
" "	**42**	2	Huntsville 20-S 5-W
" "	**9**	1	Huntsville 15-S 1-W
HIGGINBOTHAM	**4**	7	Huntsville 14-S 1-W
" "	**9**	2	Huntsville 15-S 1-W
" "	**7**	2	Huntsville 15-S 3-W
" "	**8**	1	Huntsville 15-S 2-W
HIGGINBOTHOM	**38**	1	Huntsville 19-S 4-W
HIGGINS	**20**	4	Huntsville 17-S 5-W
" "	**28**	4	Huntsville 18-S 6-W
" "	**21**	1	Huntsville 17-S 4-W
HILL	**22**	5	Huntsville 17-S 3-W
" "	**21**	4	Huntsville 17-S 4-W
" "	**12**	3	Huntsville 16-S 5-W
" "	**13**	2	Huntsville 16-S 4-W
" "	**10**	1	Huntsville 15-S 1-E
" "	**38**	1	Huntsville 19-S 4-W
" "	**43**	1	Huntsville 20-S 4-W
HINTON	**43**	2	Huntsville 20-S 4-W
HITT	**17**	3	Huntsville 16-S 1-E
HIX	**20**	3	Huntsville 17-S 5-W
" "	**4**	1	Huntsville 14-S 1-W
HOBBS	**16**	2	Huntsville 16-S 1-W
HODGE	**31**	1	Huntsville 18-S 3-W
HODGES	**30**	6	Huntsville 18-S 4-W
" "	**14**	3	Huntsville 16-S 3-W
" "	**23**	2	Huntsville 17-S 2-W
" "	**32**	1	Huntsville 18-S 2-W

Surname	Map Group	Parcels of Land	Meridian/Township/Range		
HOFFMAN	**42**	1	Huntsville	20-S	5-W
HOGAN	**21**	4	Huntsville	17-S	4-W
" "	**29**	2	Huntsville	18-S	5-W
" "	**3**	1	Huntsville	14-S	2-W
" "	**2**	1	Huntsville	14-S	3-W
" "	**20**	1	Huntsville	17-S	5-W
HOLCOMB	**30**	1	Huntsville	18-S	4-W
" "	**38**	1	Huntsville	19-S	4-W
" "	**42**	1	Huntsville	20-S	5-W
HOLCOMBE	**38**	5	Huntsville	19-S	4-W
" "	**42**	1	Huntsville	20-S	5-W
HOLLEY	**16**	1	Huntsville	16-S	1-W
HOLLIGAN	**14**	2	Huntsville	16-S	3-W
HOLLINGSWORTH	**43**	3	Huntsville	20-S	4-W
" "	**17**	1	Huntsville	16-S	1-E
HOLLIS	**5**	8	Huntsville	15-S	5-W
HOLLY	**16**	3	Huntsville	16-S	1-W
HOLMES	**17**	4	Huntsville	16-S	1-E
" "	**22**	2	Huntsville	17-S	3-W
" "	**10**	1	Huntsville	15-S	1-E
HOLT	**10**	1	Huntsville	15-S	1-E
HOOD	**19**	8	Huntsville	17-S	6-W
" "	**11**	7	Huntsville	16-S	6-W
" "	**12**	5	Huntsville	16-S	5-W
HOOPER	**39**	1	Huntsville	19-S	3-W
HOPKINS	**37**	3	Huntsville	19-S	5-W
" "	**18**	2	Huntsville	17-S	7-W
HOPPER	**33**	2	Huntsville	18-S	1-W
" "	**2**	1	Huntsville	14-S	3-W
" "	**9**	1	Huntsville	15-S	1-W
HORN	**22**	1	Huntsville	17-S	3-W
HORNE	**23**	1	Huntsville	17-S	2-W
" "	**28**	1	Huntsville	18-S	6-W
" "	**43**	1	Huntsville	20-S	4-W
HORTON	**36**	4	Huntsville	19-S	6-W
" "	**43**	3	Huntsville	20-S	4-W
HOSMER	**27**	1	Huntsville	18-S	7-W
HOUGHTON	**29**	1	Huntsville	18-S	5-W
HOUK	**22**	3	Huntsville	17-S	3-W
" "	**14**	1	Huntsville	16-S	3-W
HOUSTON	**38**	2	Huntsville	19-S	4-W
" "	**44**	2	Huntsville	20-S	3-W
" "	**37**	1	Huntsville	19-S	5-W
HOWARD	**32**	3	Huntsville	18-S	2-W
" "	**42**	2	Huntsville	20-S	5-W
" "	**33**	1	Huntsville	18-S	1-W
HOWEL	**42**	1	Huntsville	20-S	5-W
HOWELL	**37**	1	Huntsville	19-S	5-W
HOWEN	**33**	1	Huntsville	18-S	1-W
HOWTON	**28**	16	Huntsville	18-S	6-W
" "	**36**	15	Huntsville	19-S	6-W
" "	**27**	7	Huntsville	18-S	7-W
" "	**29**	1	Huntsville	18-S	5-W
HUBBARD	**39**	3	Huntsville	19-S	3-W
" "	**19**	2	Huntsville	17-S	6-W
" "	**12**	1	Huntsville	16-S	5-W
HUCHINGSON	**25**	1	Huntsville	17-S	1-E
HUCKABEE	**2**	1	Huntsville	14-S	3-W
HUDSON	**7**	1	Huntsville	15-S	3-W
" "	**22**	1	Huntsville	17-S	3-W

Surname	Map Group	Parcels of Land	Meridian/Township/Range
HUEY	**28**	9	Huntsville 18-S 6-W
" "	**20**	1	Huntsville 17-S 5-W
HUFFMAN	**42**	2	Huntsville 20-S 5-W
HUFFSTUTTER	**3**	1	Huntsville 14-S 2-W
HUGHES	**3**	5	Huntsville 14-S 2-W
" "	**8**	3	Huntsville 15-S 2-W
" "	**30**	3	Huntsville 18-S 4-W
" "	**7**	1	Huntsville 15-S 3-W
" "	**22**	1	Huntsville 17-S 3-W
HULL	**9**	1	Huntsville 15-S 1-W
HULSEY	**6**	1	Huntsville 15-S 4-W
HUMBER	**27**	7	Huntsville 18-S 7-W
" "	**18**	5	Huntsville 17-S 7-W
" "	**28**	3	Huntsville 18-S 6-W
" "	**19**	1	Huntsville 17-S 6-W
" "	**38**	1	Huntsville 19-S 4-W
HUNEYCUTT	**24**	1	Huntsville 17-S 1-W
HUNT	**10**	1	Huntsville 15-S 1-E
" "	**38**	1	Huntsville 19-S 4-W
" "	**42**	1	Huntsville 20-S 5-W
HUNTER	**9**	1	Huntsville 15-S 1-W
HURST	**25**	1	Huntsville 17-S 1-E
HUTCHINS	**28**	3	Huntsville 18-S 6-W
HUTSON	**22**	1	Huntsville 17-S 3-W
HYCH	**36**	1	Huntsville 19-S 6-W
HYDE	**7**	3	Huntsville 15-S 3-W
IGOW	**32**	1	Huntsville 18-S 2-W
" "	**31**	1	Huntsville 18-S 3-W
INGLE	**15**	2	Huntsville 16-S 2-W
INGRAM	**9**	6	Huntsville 15-S 1-W
" "	**1**	1	Huntsville 14-S 4-W
INZER	**10**	1	Huntsville 15-S 1-E
" "	**33**	1	Huntsville 18-S 1-W
IRION	**30**	1	Huntsville 18-S 4-W
ISAACS	**14**	1	Huntsville 16-S 3-W
" "	**22**	1	Huntsville 17-S 3-W
ISRAEL	**21**	2	Huntsville 17-S 4-W
IVEANS	**12**	1	Huntsville 16-S 5-W
IVY	**38**	1	Huntsville 19-S 4-W
JACK	**9**	3	Huntsville 15-S 1-W
JACKS	**14**	7	Huntsville 16-S 3-W
" "	**15**	2	Huntsville 16-S 2-W
JACKSON	**6**	6	Huntsville 15-S 4-W
" "	**27**	3	Huntsville 18-S 7-W
" "	**33**	1	Huntsville 18-S 1-W
JACOBS	**31**	5	Huntsville 18-S 3-W
JAMES	**7**	13	Huntsville 15-S 3-W
" "	**15**	1	Huntsville 16-S 2-W
JEFFERSON	**32**	2	Huntsville 18-S 2-W
JENKINS	**13**	1	Huntsville 16-S 4-W
" "	**12**	1	Huntsville 16-S 5-W
JENNINGS	**30**	2	Huntsville 18-S 4-W
JOHN	**3**	1	Huntsville 14-S 2-W
JOHNSON	**21**	6	Huntsville 17-S 4-W
" "	**7**	3	Huntsville 15-S 3-W
" "	**16**	3	Huntsville 16-S 1-W
" "	**14**	3	Huntsville 16-S 3-W
" "	**25**	3	Huntsville 17-S 1-E
" "	**18**	3	Huntsville 17-S 7-W
" "	**36**	3	Huntsville 19-S 6-W

Surname	Map Group	Parcels of Land	Meridian/Township/Range
JOHNSON (Cont'd)	**30**	2	Huntsville 18-S 4-W
" "	**28**	2	Huntsville 18-S 6-W
" "	**9**	1	Huntsville 15-S 1-W
" "	**8**	1	Huntsville 15-S 2-W
" "	**32**	1	Huntsville 18-S 2-W
" "	**31**	1	Huntsville 18-S 3-W
" "	**43**	1	Huntsville 20-S 4-W
JOHNSTON	**18**	2	Huntsville 17-S 7-W
" "	**33**	2	Huntsville 18-S 1-W
" "	**9**	1	Huntsville 15-S 1-W
" "	**22**	1	Huntsville 17-S 3-W
" "	**27**	1	Huntsville 18-S 7-W
" "	**37**	1	Huntsville 19-S 5-W
" "	**36**	1	Huntsville 19-S 6-W
JOLLEY	**2**	1	Huntsville 14-S 3-W
JOLLY	**2**	2	Huntsville 14-S 3-W
JONES	**2**	8	Huntsville 14-S 3-W
" "	**39**	8	Huntsville 19-S 3-W
" "	**38**	8	Huntsville 19-S 4-W
" "	**7**	5	Huntsville 15-S 3-W
" "	**37**	5	Huntsville 19-S 5-W
" "	**36**	5	Huntsville 19-S 6-W
" "	**32**	4	Huntsville 18-S 2-W
" "	**14**	3	Huntsville 16-S 3-W
" "	**22**	3	Huntsville 17-S 3-W
" "	**9**	2	Huntsville 15-S 1-W
" "	**19**	2	Huntsville 17-S 6-W
" "	**10**	1	Huntsville 15-S 1-E
" "	**6**	1	Huntsville 15-S 4-W
" "	**13**	1	Huntsville 16-S 4-W
" "	**25**	1	Huntsville 17-S 1-E
" "	**21**	1	Huntsville 17-S 4-W
" "	**31**	1	Huntsville 18-S 3-W
" "	**27**	1	Huntsville 18-S 7-W
" "	**40**	1	Huntsville 19-S 2-W
JORDAN	**30**	10	Huntsville 18-S 4-W
" "	**27**	9	Huntsville 18-S 7-W
" "	**29**	7	Huntsville 18-S 5-W
" "	**19**	4	Huntsville 17-S 6-W
" "	**32**	1	Huntsville 18-S 2-W
" "	**37**	1	Huntsville 19-S 5-W
JORDON	**38**	3	Huntsville 19-S 4-W
" "	**37**	2	Huntsville 19-S 5-W
JOURDEN	**29**	1	Huntsville 18-S 5-W
JUDD	**43**	1	Huntsville 20-S 4-W
JUSTICE	**29**	20	Huntsville 18-S 5-W
" "	**30**	1	Huntsville 18-S 4-W
KEATON	**17**	1	Huntsville 16-S 1-E
" "	**16**	1	Huntsville 16-S 1-W
KEETH	**10**	1	Huntsville 15-S 1-E
KEITH	**10**	15	Huntsville 15-S 1-E
KELLEY	**9**	2	Huntsville 15-S 1-W
KELLY	**22**	10	Huntsville 17-S 3-W
" "	**23**	2	Huntsville 17-S 2-W
" "	**19**	2	Huntsville 17-S 6-W
" "	**31**	2	Huntsville 18-S 3-W
" "	**39**	2	Huntsville 19-S 3-W
" "	**9**	1	Huntsville 15-S 1-W
" "	**30**	1	Huntsville 18-S 4-W
" "	**38**	1	Huntsville 19-S 4-W

Surname	Map Group	Parcels of Land	Meridian/Township/Range
KELSO	**14**	1	Huntsville 16-S 3-W
KEMP	**20**	5	Huntsville 17-S 5-W
" "	**12**	2	Huntsville 16-S 5-W
" "	**31**	1	Huntsville 18-S 3-W
KENNEBREW	**9**	1	Huntsville 15-S 1-W
KENNEDY	**42**	13	Huntsville 20-S 5-W
" "	**21**	2	Huntsville 17-S 4-W
KENNON	**7**	3	Huntsville 15-S 3-W
KEVELING	**38**	1	Huntsville 19-S 4-W
KILE	**1**	2	Huntsville 14-S 4-W
KILLAUGH	**15**	1	Huntsville 16-S 2-W
" "	**31**	1	Huntsville 18-S 3-W
KILLOUGH	**15**	14	Huntsville 16-S 2-W
" "	**22**	9	Huntsville 17-S 3-W
" "	**23**	6	Huntsville 17-S 2-W
" "	**16**	4	Huntsville 16-S 1-W
" "	**9**	3	Huntsville 15-S 1-W
" "	**7**	2	Huntsville 15-S 3-W
" "	**31**	2	Huntsville 18-S 3-W
" "	**14**	1	Huntsville 16-S 3-W
" "	**40**	1	Huntsville 19-S 2-W
" "	**42**	1	Huntsville 20-S 5-W
KIMBREL	**41**	2	Huntsville 20-S 6-W
" "	**42**	1	Huntsville 20-S 5-W
KING	**10**	1	Huntsville 15-S 1-E
" "	**23**	1	Huntsville 17-S 2-W
" "	**32**	1	Huntsville 18-S 2-W
KIRKPATRICK	**5**	1	Huntsville 15-S 5-W
KITCHENS	**1**	3	Huntsville 14-S 4-W
KNABE	**9**	2	Huntsville 15-S 1-W
KNIGHT	**19**	2	Huntsville 17-S 6-W
" "	**18**	1	Huntsville 17-S 7-W
KNOX	**42**	1	Huntsville 20-S 5-W
KYLE	**22**	1	Huntsville 17-S 3-W
LACEY	**31**	2	Huntsville 18-S 3-W
" "	**30**	1	Huntsville 18-S 4-W
" "	**38**	1	Huntsville 19-S 4-W
LACY	**12**	2	Huntsville 16-S 5-W
" "	**16**	1	Huntsville 16-S 1-W
" "	**31**	1	Huntsville 18-S 3-W
LAFOY	**27**	3	Huntsville 18-S 7-W
LAIRD	**8**	2	Huntsville 15-S 2-W
" "	**28**	1	Huntsville 18-S 6-W
LAMBERT	**11**	1	Huntsville 16-S 6-W
LAND	**22**	3	Huntsville 17-S 3-W
LANDIFER	**38**	1	Huntsville 19-S 4-W
LANDRUM	**1**	1	Huntsville 14-S 4-W
" "	**31**	1	Huntsville 18-S 3-W
LANE	**16**	6	Huntsville 16-S 1-W
" "	**24**	2	Huntsville 17-S 1-W
" "	**22**	2	Huntsville 17-S 3-W
" "	**31**	2	Huntsville 18-S 3-W
" "	**38**	2	Huntsville 19-S 4-W
" "	**37**	1	Huntsville 19-S 5-W
LANEY	**39**	1	Huntsville 19-S 3-W
LANG	**16**	1	Huntsville 16-S 1-W
LANGFORD	**7**	2	Huntsville 15-S 3-W
LANIER	**8**	2	Huntsville 15-S 2-W
LANINGHAM	**2**	1	Huntsville 14-S 3-W
LASETER	**3**	2	Huntsville 14-S 2-W

Surname	Map Group	Parcels of Land	Meridian/Township/Range		
LASITER	**3**	3	Huntsville	14-S	2-W
LATHAM	**23**	2	Huntsville	17-S	2-W
" "	**2**	1	Huntsville	14-S	3-W
" "	**17**	1	Huntsville	16-S	1-E
" "	**16**	1	Huntsville	16-S	1-W
" "	**25**	1	Huntsville	17-S	1-E
LATHEM	**17**	4	Huntsville	16-S	1-E
" "	**16**	2	Huntsville	16-S	1-W
" "	**24**	1	Huntsville	17-S	1-W
" "	**23**	1	Huntsville	17-S	2-W
LAWLER	**14**	1	Huntsville	16-S	3-W
LAWLESS	**9**	2	Huntsville	15-S	1-W
" "	**16**	1	Huntsville	16-S	1-W
" "	**42**	1	Huntsville	20-S	5-W
LAWLEY	**43**	5	Huntsville	20-S	4-W
" "	**38**	3	Huntsville	19-S	4-W
" "	**17**	2	Huntsville	16-S	1-E
LAWSON	**42**	5	Huntsville	20-S	5-W
" "	**12**	3	Huntsville	16-S	5-W
" "	**36**	2	Huntsville	19-S	6-W
LE FEVRE	**31**	1	Huntsville	18-S	3-W
LEATHERWOOD	**43**	4	Huntsville	20-S	4-W
" "	**39**	1	Huntsville	19-S	3-W
LEDLOW	**37**	2	Huntsville	19-S	5-W
LEDYARD	**20**	2	Huntsville	17-S	5-W
" "	**7**	1	Huntsville	15-S	3-W
" "	**12**	1	Huntsville	16-S	5-W
LEE	**40**	6	Huntsville	19-S	2-W
" "	**32**	4	Huntsville	18-S	2-W
" "	**8**	3	Huntsville	15-S	2-W
" "	**7**	2	Huntsville	15-S	3-W
" "	**20**	2	Huntsville	17-S	5-W
" "	**3**	1	Huntsville	14-S	2-W
" "	**9**	1	Huntsville	15-S	1-W
" "	**19**	1	Huntsville	17-S	6-W
" "	**30**	1	Huntsville	18-S	4-W
" "	**29**	1	Huntsville	18-S	5-W
" "	**28**	1	Huntsville	18-S	6-W
LEMMONS	**43**	1	Huntsville	20-S	4-W
LESLEY	**17**	1	Huntsville	16-S	1-E
" "	**16**	1	Huntsville	16-S	1-W
LETSON	**37**	1	Huntsville	19-S	5-W
LEWIS	**16**	2	Huntsville	16-S	1-W
" "	**30**	2	Huntsville	18-S	4-W
" "	**31**	1	Huntsville	18-S	3-W
LIGHTHALL	**33**	3	Huntsville	18-S	1-W
LINDSEY	**15**	2	Huntsville	16-S	2-W
" "	**24**	2	Huntsville	17-S	1-W
" "	**10**	1	Huntsville	15-S	1-E
LINEMAN	**7**	1	Huntsville	15-S	3-W
LINN	**13**	9	Huntsville	16-S	4-W
" "	**15**	2	Huntsville	16-S	2-W
" "	**23**	1	Huntsville	17-S	2-W
LINTHICUM	**31**	2	Huntsville	18-S	3-W
" "	**39**	1	Huntsville	19-S	3-W
LITTLE	**8**	3	Huntsville	15-S	2-W
" "	**7**	2	Huntsville	15-S	3-W
" "	**31**	1	Huntsville	18-S	3-W
LIVELY	**6**	1	Huntsville	15-S	4-W
LIVERMAN	**8**	1	Huntsville	15-S	2-W

Surname	Map Group	Parcels of Land	Meridian/Township/Range
LIVERMORE	**8**	2	Huntsville 15-S 2-W
LLOYD	**23**	1	Huntsville 17-S 2-W
LOCKHART	**9**	3	Huntsville 15-S 1-W
" "	**6**	3	Huntsville 15-S 4-W
" "	**22**	2	Huntsville 17-S 3-W
" "	**25**	1	Huntsville 17-S 1-E
" "	**42**	1	Huntsville 20-S 5-W
LOLLER	**6**	3	Huntsville 15-S 4-W
" "	**5**	2	Huntsville 15-S 5-W
LOLLY	**38**	1	Huntsville 19-S 4-W
LONG	**9**	1	Huntsville 15-S 1-W
" "	**5**	1	Huntsville 15-S 5-W
LOONEY	**16**	1	Huntsville 16-S 1-W
" "	**33**	1	Huntsville 18-S 1-W
LOVE	**16**	1	Huntsville 16-S 1-W
" "	**30**	1	Huntsville 18-S 4-W
LOVELESS	**23**	10	Huntsville 17-S 2-W
" "	**43**	5	Huntsville 20-S 4-W
" "	**42**	5	Huntsville 20-S 5-W
" "	**30**	3	Huntsville 18-S 4-W
" "	**38**	1	Huntsville 19-S 4-W
LOVEMAN	**8**	1	Huntsville 15-S 2-W
LOVETT	**21**	6	Huntsville 17-S 4-W
" "	**36**	2	Huntsville 19-S 6-W
LOWE	**42**	1	Huntsville 20-S 5-W
LOWERY	**34**	2	Huntsville 18-S 1-E
" "	**33**	1	Huntsville 18-S 1-W
" "	**32**	1	Huntsville 18-S 2-W
LOWRY	**33**	1	Huntsville 18-S 1-W
LUCKIE	**7**	1	Huntsville 15-S 3-W
LYKES	**14**	1	Huntsville 16-S 3-W
MACKEY	**17**	1	Huntsville 16-S 1-E
MADDOX	**18**	5	Huntsville 17-S 7-W
" "	**19**	2	Huntsville 17-S 6-W
MADISON	**15**	4	Huntsville 16-S 2-W
" "	**16**	1	Huntsville 16-S 1-W
MAHAN	**42**	1	Huntsville 20-S 5-W
MAJOR	**9**	2	Huntsville 15-S 1-W
MAJORS	**8**	1	Huntsville 15-S 2-W
MALLORY	**42**	1	Huntsville 20-S 5-W
MALONE	**8**	3	Huntsville 15-S 2-W
MANN	**10**	3	Huntsville 15-S 1-E
" "	**17**	1	Huntsville 16-S 1-E
MANSON	**23**	1	Huntsville 17-S 2-W
MARCH	**12**	1	Huntsville 16-S 5-W
MARKE	**32**	1	Huntsville 18-S 2-W
MARKS	**15**	2	Huntsville 16-S 2-W
MARSHALL	**9**	1	Huntsville 15-S 1-W
" "	**23**	1	Huntsville 17-S 2-W
MARTIN	**17**	12	Huntsville 16-S 1-E
" "	**21**	7	Huntsville 17-S 4-W
" "	**15**	3	Huntsville 16-S 2-W
" "	**31**	3	Huntsville 18-S 3-W
" "	**30**	3	Huntsville 18-S 4-W
" "	**23**	2	Huntsville 17-S 2-W
" "	**22**	2	Huntsville 17-S 3-W
" "	**36**	2	Huntsville 19-S 6-W
" "	**44**	2	Huntsville 20-S 3-W
" "	**8**	1	Huntsville 15-S 2-W
" "	**24**	1	Huntsville 17-S 1-W

Surname	Map Group	Parcels of Land	Meridian/Township/Range		
MARTIN (Cont'd)	**37**	1	Huntsville	19-S	5-W
MASKE	**24**	2	Huntsville	17-S	1-W
MASON	**25**	2	Huntsville	17-S	1-E
" "	**33**	2	Huntsville	18-S	1-W
" "	**24**	1	Huntsville	17-S	1-W
" "	**22**	1	Huntsville	17-S	3-W
MASSENGILL	**25**	1	Huntsville	17-S	1-E
MASSEY	**15**	10	Huntsville	16-S	2-W
" "	**17**	8	Huntsville	16-S	1-E
" "	**31**	7	Huntsville	18-S	3-W
" "	**10**	6	Huntsville	15-S	1-E
" "	**9**	6	Huntsville	15-S	1-W
" "	**32**	2	Huntsville	18-S	2-W
" "	**43**	2	Huntsville	20-S	4-W
" "	**14**	1	Huntsville	16-S	3-W
" "	**23**	1	Huntsville	17-S	2-W
MASTERS	**17**	1	Huntsville	16-S	1-E
" "	**14**	1	Huntsville	16-S	3-W
" "	**22**	1	Huntsville	17-S	3-W
MATHENY	**39**	2	Huntsville	19-S	3-W
MATHIS	**8**	1	Huntsville	15-S	2-W
MATTHEWS	**15**	1	Huntsville	16-S	2-W
MATTISON	**8**	1	Huntsville	15-S	2-W
" "	**15**	1	Huntsville	16-S	2-W
MAULDIN	**12**	3	Huntsville	16-S	5-W
MAVERICK	**22**	6	Huntsville	17-S	3-W
MAXWELL	**14**	1	Huntsville	16-S	3-W
" "	**39**	1	Huntsville	19-S	3-W
MAYFIELD	**1**	4	Huntsville	14-S	4-W
" "	**29**	4	Huntsville	18-S	5-W
MCADAMS	**15**	2	Huntsville	16-S	2-W
" "	**24**	1	Huntsville	17-S	1-W
" "	**23**	1	Huntsville	17-S	2-W
MCADOREY	**32**	1	Huntsville	18-S	2-W
MCADORY	**38**	40	Huntsville	19-S	4-W
" "	**37**	15	Huntsville	19-S	5-W
" "	**23**	3	Huntsville	17-S	2-W
" "	**43**	2	Huntsville	20-S	4-W
" "	**32**	1	Huntsville	18-S	2-W
MCANALLY	**3**	3	Huntsville	14-S	2-W
MCASHAN	**37**	2	Huntsville	19-S	5-W
MCBRIDE	**42**	3	Huntsville	20-S	5-W
MCCABE	**7**	1	Huntsville	15-S	3-W
" "	**32**	1	Huntsville	18-S	2-W
MCCALL	**15**	1	Huntsville	16-S	2-W
MCCALLA	**10**	1	Huntsville	15-S	1-E
MCCARSON	**9**	1	Huntsville	15-S	1-W
MCCARTEY	**22**	1	Huntsville	17-S	3-W
MCCARTNEY	**15**	4	Huntsville	16-S	2-W
" "	**22**	4	Huntsville	17-S	3-W
" "	**23**	3	Huntsville	17-S	2-W
" "	**31**	3	Huntsville	18-S	3-W
" "	**16**	1	Huntsville	16-S	1-W
" "	**25**	1	Huntsville	17-S	1-E
" "	**19**	1	Huntsville	17-S	6-W
MCCARTY	**19**	9	Huntsville	17-S	6-W
" "	**11**	2	Huntsville	16-S	6-W
" "	**20**	2	Huntsville	17-S	5-W
MCCAY	**9**	5	Huntsville	15-S	1-W
MCCLAIN	**29**	7	Huntsville	18-S	5-W

Surname	Map Group	Parcels of Land	Meridian/Township/Range
MCCLAIN (Cont'd)	**23**	1	Huntsville 17-S 2-W
MCCLELEN	**39**	1	Huntsville 19-S 3-W
MCCLENDON	**10**	1	Huntsville 15-S 1-E
" "	**43**	1	Huntsville 20-S 4-W
MCCLERKIN	**29**	1	Huntsville 18-S 5-W
MCCLINTOCK	**31**	2	Huntsville 18-S 3-W
" "	**39**	2	Huntsville 19-S 3-W
MCCLINTON	**29**	2	Huntsville 18-S 5-W
" "	**37**	2	Huntsville 19-S 5-W
MCCLURE	**8**	2	Huntsville 15-S 2-W
MCCOLLUM	**2**	1	Huntsville 14-S 3-W
MCCOMAK	**13**	3	Huntsville 16-S 4-W
MCCOMBE	**24**	2	Huntsville 17-S 1-W
MCCOMBS	**8**	11	Huntsville 15-S 2-W
" "	**24**	10	Huntsville 17-S 1-W
" "	**3**	1	Huntsville 14-S 2-W
" "	**16**	1	Huntsville 16-S 1-W
MCCOO	**22**	1	Huntsville 17-S 3-W
MCCORMACK	**14**	1	Huntsville 16-S 3-W
MCCOW	**22**	1	Huntsville 17-S 3-W
MCCOY	**2**	2	Huntsville 14-S 3-W
" "	**10**	2	Huntsville 15-S 1-E
" "	**23**	1	Huntsville 17-S 2-W
" "	**22**	1	Huntsville 17-S 3-W
MCCRARY	**2**	1	Huntsville 14-S 3-W
" "	**1**	1	Huntsville 14-S 4-W
MCCRAW	**38**	1	Huntsville 19-S 4-W
MCCULLOUGH	**2**	2	Huntsville 14-S 3-W
MCCURRY	**3**	1	Huntsville 14-S 2-W
MCDANAL	**24**	7	Huntsville 17-S 1-W
" "	**33**	5	Huntsville 18-S 1-W
MCDANIEL	**22**	2	Huntsville 17-S 3-W
" "	**33**	2	Huntsville 18-S 1-W
" "	**37**	2	Huntsville 19-S 5-W
" "	**43**	1	Huntsville 20-S 4-W
MCDONALD	**30**	3	Huntsville 18-S 4-W
" "	**2**	2	Huntsville 14-S 3-W
" "	**12**	2	Huntsville 16-S 5-W
" "	**5**	1	Huntsville 15-S 5-W
" "	**24**	1	Huntsville 17-S 1-W
MCDOUGAL	**2**	2	Huntsville 14-S 3-W
MCDOWEL	**33**	1	Huntsville 18-S 1-W
MCDUFF	**22**	1	Huntsville 17-S 3-W
MCELROY	**19**	5	Huntsville 17-S 6-W
MCFALL	**38**	2	Huntsville 19-S 4-W
" "	**39**	1	Huntsville 19-S 3-W
MCFALLS	**38**	2	Huntsville 19-S 4-W
MCFERRIN	**20**	3	Huntsville 17-S 5-W
" "	**36**	1	Huntsville 19-S 6-W
MCGEE	**14**	2	Huntsville 16-S 3-W
" "	**9**	1	Huntsville 15-S 1-W
MCGEHEE	**30**	3	Huntsville 18-S 4-W
" "	**9**	2	Huntsville 15-S 1-W
" "	**16**	1	Huntsville 16-S 1-W
MCGHEE	**14**	1	Huntsville 16-S 3-W
MCGILL	**42**	2	Huntsville 20-S 5-W
MCGOWEN	**9**	1	Huntsville 15-S 1-W
MCGUIRE	**25**	2	Huntsville 17-S 1-E
" "	**22**	1	Huntsville 17-S 3-W
MCKAY	**10**	1	Huntsville 15-S 1-E

Surname	Map Group	Parcels of Land	Meridian/Township/Range		
MCKEEVER	**32**	2	Huntsville	18-S	2-W
MCKENNEY	**42**	1	Huntsville	20-S	5-W
MCKENZIE	**2**	1	Huntsville	14-S	3-W
MCKINNEY	**42**	2	Huntsville	20-S	5-W
" "	**43**	1	Huntsville	20-S	4-W
MCLAUGHLIN	**25**	12	Huntsville	17-S	1-E
" "	**34**	2	Huntsville	18-S	1-E
" "	**38**	1	Huntsville	19-S	4-W
MCLEOD	**42**	1	Huntsville	20-S	5-W
MCLINTOCK	**39**	3	Huntsville	19-S	3-W
MCLUER	**38**	3	Huntsville	19-S	4-W
" "	**39**	1	Huntsville	19-S	3-W
MCMAHON	**14**	2	Huntsville	16-S	3-W
MCMATH	**23**	3	Huntsville	17-S	2-W
" "	**42**	2	Huntsville	20-S	5-W
" "	**41**	2	Huntsville	20-S	6-W
" "	**32**	1	Huntsville	18-S	2-W
" "	**43**	1	Huntsville	20-S	4-W
MCMEANS	**43**	1	Huntsville	20-S	4-W
MCMICHENS	**1**	1	Huntsville	14-S	4-W
MCMICKEN	**29**	2	Huntsville	18-S	5-W
MCMILLAN	**20**	1	Huntsville	17-S	5-W
" "	**30**	1	Huntsville	18-S	4-W
MCMILLION	**11**	1	Huntsville	16-S	6-W
" "	**22**	1	Huntsville	17-S	3-W
MCPHAUL	**43**	1	Huntsville	20-S	4-W
MCPHERRIN	**13**	1	Huntsville	16-S	4-W
MCPHERSON	**2**	2	Huntsville	14-S	3-W
MCWILLIAMS	**22**	9	Huntsville	17-S	3-W
" "	**31**	2	Huntsville	18-S	3-W
" "	**6**	1	Huntsville	15-S	4-W
" "	**28**	1	Huntsville	18-S	6-W
MEDLEN	**18**	3	Huntsville	17-S	7-W
MEEKS	**29**	2	Huntsville	18-S	5-W
" "	**7**	1	Huntsville	15-S	3-W
MEIGS	**28**	1	Huntsville	18-S	6-W
MELTON	**17**	4	Huntsville	16-S	1-E
" "	**10**	2	Huntsville	15-S	1-E
" "	**9**	1	Huntsville	15-S	1-W
MELVIN	**3**	3	Huntsville	14-S	2-W
" "	**15**	3	Huntsville	16-S	2-W
MERKEL	**32**	1	Huntsville	18-S	2-W
MERRICK	**6**	1	Huntsville	15-S	4-W
MERRIKEN	**9**	1	Huntsville	15-S	1-W
" "	**8**	1	Huntsville	15-S	2-W
MERRITT	**43**	1	Huntsville	20-S	4-W
MICHAEL	**4**	1	Huntsville	14-S	1-W
MIKELLS	**1**	2	Huntsville	14-S	4-W
MILES	**13**	2	Huntsville	16-S	4-W
" "	**12**	2	Huntsville	16-S	5-W
" "	**43**	2	Huntsville	20-S	4-W
" "	**5**	1	Huntsville	15-S	5-W
" "	**22**	1	Huntsville	17-S	3-W
MILLENDER	**12**	2	Huntsville	16-S	5-W
MILLER	**21**	5	Huntsville	17-S	4-W
" "	**28**	5	Huntsville	18-S	6-W
" "	**15**	3	Huntsville	16-S	2-W
" "	**20**	2	Huntsville	17-S	5-W
" "	**16**	1	Huntsville	16-S	1-W
" "	**13**	1	Huntsville	16-S	4-W

Surname	Map Group	Parcels of Land	Meridian/Township/Range
MILLER (Cont'd)	**23**	1	Huntsville 17-S 2-W
MILLWOOD	**9**	2	Huntsville 15-S 1-W
MILNE	**16**	2	Huntsville 16-S 1-W
MILNER	**32**	2	Huntsville 18-S 2-W
" "	**15**	1	Huntsville 16-S 2-W
" "	**23**	1	Huntsville 17-S 2-W
MILSTEAD	**39**	2	Huntsville 19-S 3-W
MINOR	**3**	2	Huntsville 14-S 2-W
" "	**14**	1	Huntsville 16-S 3-W
MINTER	**3**	3	Huntsville 14-S 2-W
" "	**2**	2	Huntsville 14-S 3-W
" "	**1**	2	Huntsville 14-S 4-W
MITCHEL	**23**	3	Huntsville 17-S 2-W
MITCHELL	**23**	5	Huntsville 17-S 2-W
" "	**1**	4	Huntsville 14-S 4-W
" "	**22**	3	Huntsville 17-S 3-W
" "	**7**	1	Huntsville 15-S 3-W
" "	**14**	1	Huntsville 16-S 3-W
" "	**31**	1	Huntsville 18-S 3-W
" "	**36**	1	Huntsville 19-S 6-W
" "	**42**	1	Huntsville 20-S 5-W
MONCRIEF	**14**	3	Huntsville 16-S 3-W
MONFEE	**39**	2	Huntsville 19-S 3-W
MONTGOMERY	**23**	13	Huntsville 17-S 2-W
MOONEY	**13**	5	Huntsville 16-S 4-W
MOOR	**25**	7	Huntsville 17-S 1-E
MOORE	**37**	16	Huntsville 19-S 5-W
" "	**43**	8	Huntsville 20-S 4-W
" "	**8**	7	Huntsville 15-S 2-W
" "	**42**	7	Huntsville 20-S 5-W
" "	**9**	3	Huntsville 15-S 1-W
" "	**16**	3	Huntsville 16-S 1-W
" "	**38**	2	Huntsville 19-S 4-W
" "	**17**	1	Huntsville 16-S 1-E
" "	**14**	1	Huntsville 16-S 3-W
" "	**32**	1	Huntsville 18-S 2-W
MORELAND	**9**	2	Huntsville 15-S 1-W
MORGAN	**34**	3	Huntsville 18-S 1-E
" "	**14**	1	Huntsville 16-S 3-W
" "	**33**	1	Huntsville 18-S 1-W
MORRIS	**32**	2	Huntsville 18-S 2-W
MORRISON	**6**	2	Huntsville 15-S 4-W
" "	**14**	2	Huntsville 16-S 3-W
MORROW	**38**	6	Huntsville 19-S 4-W
" "	**12**	3	Huntsville 16-S 5-W
" "	**39**	2	Huntsville 19-S 3-W
" "	**16**	1	Huntsville 16-S 1-W
" "	**21**	1	Huntsville 17-S 4-W
MORTON	**3**	1	Huntsville 14-S 2-W
MOSES	**31**	4	Huntsville 18-S 3-W
" "	**42**	4	Huntsville 20-S 5-W
" "	**23**	3	Huntsville 17-S 2-W
" "	**37**	3	Huntsville 19-S 5-W
" "	**41**	3	Huntsville 20-S 6-W
" "	**39**	1	Huntsville 19-S 3-W
MOSS	**2**	1	Huntsville 14-S 3-W
MOTE	**1**	2	Huntsville 14-S 4-W
" "	**8**	1	Huntsville 15-S 2-W
MOTTE	**7**	4	Huntsville 15-S 3-W
MUDD	**22**	2	Huntsville 17-S 3-W

Surname	Map Group	Parcels of Land	Meridian/Township/Range		
MUDD (Cont'd)	**5**	1	Huntsville	15-S	5-W
" "	**12**	1	Huntsville	16-S	5-W
" "	**20**	1	Huntsville	17-S	5-W
MULLINGS	**3**	1	Huntsville	14-S	2-W
MULVEHILL	**3**	2	Huntsville	14-S	2-W
MUNKUS	**31**	1	Huntsville	18-S	3-W
MURPHEY	**17**	1	Huntsville	16-S	1-E
MURPHREE	**6**	3	Huntsville	15-S	4-W
MURPHY	**8**	2	Huntsville	15-S	2-W
" "	**22**	2	Huntsville	17-S	3-W
MURRAY	**23**	6	Huntsville	17-S	2-W
" "	**7**	1	Huntsville	15-S	3-W
MURRY	**23**	1	Huntsville	17-S	2-W
MYRICK	**6**	4	Huntsville	15-S	4-W
" "	**14**	2	Huntsville	16-S	3-W
" "	**2**	1	Huntsville	14-S	3-W
MYRICKE	**6**	1	Huntsville	15-S	4-W
MYROCK	**6**	2	Huntsville	15-S	4-W
NABERS	**31**	6	Huntsville	18-S	3-W
" "	**38**	4	Huntsville	19-S	4-W
" "	**29**	2	Huntsville	18-S	5-W
" "	**30**	1	Huntsville	18-S	4-W
NABORS	**23**	3	Huntsville	17-S	2-W
" "	**31**	3	Huntsville	18-S	3-W
" "	**39**	2	Huntsville	19-S	3-W
" "	**30**	1	Huntsville	18-S	4-W
" "	**38**	1	Huntsville	19-S	4-W
" "	**44**	1	Huntsville	20-S	3-W
NABOURS	**38**	4	Huntsville	19-S	4-W
" "	**22**	2	Huntsville	17-S	3-W
" "	**31**	1	Huntsville	18-S	3-W
NAIL	**29**	8	Huntsville	18-S	5-W
" "	**6**	5	Huntsville	15-S	4-W
" "	**7**	3	Huntsville	15-S	3-W
" "	**37**	2	Huntsville	19-S	5-W
" "	**2**	1	Huntsville	14-S	3-W
NASH	**15**	12	Huntsville	16-S	2-W
" "	**8**	1	Huntsville	15-S	2-W
NATIONS	**22**	5	Huntsville	17-S	3-W
" "	**32**	4	Huntsville	18-S	2-W
" "	**8**	1	Huntsville	15-S	2-W
NAVE	**24**	1	Huntsville	17-S	1-W
NEAL	**15**	3	Huntsville	16-S	2-W
" "	**25**	2	Huntsville	17-S	1-E
NEIGHBOURS	**15**	1	Huntsville	16-S	2-W
NEILSON	**12**	2	Huntsville	16-S	5-W
NELMS	**39**	1	Huntsville	19-S	3-W
NELSION	**25**	1	Huntsville	17-S	1-E
NELSON	**36**	3	Huntsville	19-S	6-W
" "	**32**	1	Huntsville	18-S	2-W
" "	**30**	1	Huntsville	18-S	4-W
NEVES	**15**	1	Huntsville	16-S	2-W
NEWBERRY	**13**	4	Huntsville	16-S	4-W
NEWMAN	**9**	2	Huntsville	15-S	1-W
NICHOLAS	**43**	5	Huntsville	20-S	4-W
" "	**42**	2	Huntsville	20-S	5-W
NICHOLS	**12**	13	Huntsville	16-S	5-W
" "	**20**	4	Huntsville	17-S	5-W
" "	**43**	2	Huntsville	20-S	4-W
NIELSON	**12**	2	Huntsville	16-S	5-W

Surname	Map Group	Parcels of Land	Meridian/Township/Range
NORMENT	**31**	4	Huntsville 18-S 3-W
NORRIS	**20**	3	Huntsville 17-S 5-W
NORTON	**23**	1	Huntsville 17-S 2-W
NORWOOD	**42**	2	Huntsville 20-S 5-W
" "	**38**	1	Huntsville 19-S 4-W
NUNLEY	**33**	1	Huntsville 18-S 1-W
OATES	**32**	3	Huntsville 18-S 2-W
OBAR	**25**	1	Huntsville 17-S 1-E
" "	**20**	1	Huntsville 17-S 5-W
OBARR	**25**	3	Huntsville 17-S 1-E
ODAM	**6**	1	Huntsville 15-S 4-W
ODEN	**16**	1	Huntsville 16-S 1-W
ODOM	**1**	2	Huntsville 14-S 4-W
" "	**7**	1	Huntsville 15-S 3-W
OGLESBERRY	**42**	2	Huntsville 20-S 5-W
OGLETREE	**1**	1	Huntsville 14-S 4-W
OGWIN	**22**	3	Huntsville 17-S 3-W
OLDHAM	**42**	2	Huntsville 20-S 5-W
OLIVER	**25**	3	Huntsville 17-S 1-E
ONEAL	**31**	1	Huntsville 18-S 3-W
ORR	**16**	4	Huntsville 16-S 1-W
" "	**23**	1	Huntsville 17-S 2-W
OTTS	**32**	1	Huntsville 18-S 2-W
OWEN	**38**	17	Huntsville 19-S 4-W
" "	**22**	10	Huntsville 17-S 3-W
" "	**23**	6	Huntsville 17-S 2-W
" "	**7**	3	Huntsville 15-S 3-W
" "	**33**	3	Huntsville 18-S 1-W
" "	**15**	2	Huntsville 16-S 2-W
" "	**30**	2	Huntsville 18-S 4-W
" "	**19**	1	Huntsville 17-S 6-W
" "	**31**	1	Huntsville 18-S 3-W
" "	**37**	1	Huntsville 19-S 5-W
OWENS	**32**	3	Huntsville 18-S 2-W
" "	**2**	2	Huntsville 14-S 3-W
" "	**33**	2	Huntsville 18-S 1-W
" "	**1**	1	Huntsville 14-S 4-W
" "	**9**	1	Huntsville 15-S 1-W
" "	**23**	1	Huntsville 17-S 2-W
" "	**38**	1	Huntsville 19-S 4-W
PAGE	**3**	1	Huntsville 14-S 2-W
PAIN	**9**	1	Huntsville 15-S 1-W
PALMER	**32**	2	Huntsville 18-S 2-W
" "	**4**	1	Huntsville 14-S 1-W
" "	**20**	1	Huntsville 17-S 5-W
PALMORE	**28**	4	Huntsville 18-S 6-W
PARKER	**15**	4	Huntsville 16-S 2-W
" "	**24**	2	Huntsville 17-S 1-W
" "	**23**	1	Huntsville 17-S 2-W
" "	**20**	1	Huntsville 17-S 5-W
" "	**33**	1	Huntsville 18-S 1-W
" "	**32**	1	Huntsville 18-S 2-W
PARRIS	**2**	3	Huntsville 14-S 3-W
" "	**1**	2	Huntsville 14-S 4-W
PARRISH	**1**	1	Huntsville 14-S 4-W
PARRY	**7**	2	Huntsville 15-S 3-W
PARSONS	**37**	43	Huntsville 19-S 5-W
" "	**36**	32	Huntsville 19-S 6-W
" "	**29**	13	Huntsville 18-S 5-W
" "	**28**	13	Huntsville 18-S 6-W

Surname	Map Group	Parcels of Land	Meridian/Township/Range		
PARSONS (Cont'd)	41	5	Huntsville	20-S	6-W
" "	20	3	Huntsville	17-S	5-W
" "	22	2	Huntsville	17-S	3-W
" "	19	2	Huntsville	17-S	6-W
" "	12	1	Huntsville	16-S	5-W
" "	27	1	Huntsville	18-S	7-W
" "	35	1	Huntsville	19-S	7-W
PARTAIN	31	2	Huntsville	18-S	3-W
" "	7	1	Huntsville	15-S	3-W
PASLEY	2	1	Huntsville	14-S	3-W
PATTEN	27	2	Huntsville	18-S	7-W
PATTERSON	38	5	Huntsville	19-S	4-W
" "	37	3	Huntsville	19-S	5-W
" "	30	1	Huntsville	18-S	4-W
PATTON	39	10	Huntsville	19-S	3-W
" "	27	5	Huntsville	18-S	7-W
" "	26	3	Huntsville	18-S	8-W
" "	8	1	Huntsville	15-S	2-W
" "	25	1	Huntsville	17-S	1-E
" "	19	1	Huntsville	17-S	6-W
" "	18	1	Huntsville	17-S	7-W
" "	32	1	Huntsville	18-S	2-W
PAULLING	30	1	Huntsville	18-S	4-W
PAYNE	6	8	Huntsville	15-S	4-W
" "	14	5	Huntsville	16-S	3-W
" "	19	3	Huntsville	17-S	6-W
" "	8	1	Huntsville	15-S	2-W
" "	28	1	Huntsville	18-S	6-W
PEARCE	9	1	Huntsville	15-S	1-W
PEARSON	23	3	Huntsville	17-S	2-W
" "	10	1	Huntsville	15-S	1-E
" "	39	1	Huntsville	19-S	3-W
PEELER	31	1	Huntsville	18-S	3-W
PEIRCE	30	1	Huntsville	18-S	4-W
PENN	20	2	Huntsville	17-S	5-W
PENWELL	20	1	Huntsville	17-S	5-W
PERKINS	17	6	Huntsville	16-S	1-E
" "	16	6	Huntsville	16-S	1-W
" "	19	1	Huntsville	17-S	6-W
PERRY	16	3	Huntsville	16-S	1-W
" "	24	2	Huntsville	17-S	1-W
" "	11	1	Huntsville	16-S	6-W
" "	19	1	Huntsville	17-S	6-W
PERSONS	37	3	Huntsville	19-S	5-W
PERTEET	7	1	Huntsville	15-S	3-W
PETERSON	43	6	Huntsville	20-S	4-W
" "	12	3	Huntsville	16-S	5-W
" "	38	3	Huntsville	19-S	4-W
" "	37	1	Huntsville	19-S	5-W
PHELAN	32	1	Huntsville	18-S	2-W
PHILIPS	38	12	Huntsville	19-S	4-W
" "	43	2	Huntsville	20-S	4-W
" "	19	1	Huntsville	17-S	6-W
PHILLIPS	26	3	Huntsville	18-S	8-W
" "	20	2	Huntsville	17-S	5-W
" "	39	1	Huntsville	19-S	3-W
" "	42	1	Huntsville	20-S	5-W
PHILYAW	14	4	Huntsville	16-S	3-W
PIERCE	32	3	Huntsville	18-S	2-W
" "	17	2	Huntsville	16-S	1-E

Surname	Map Group	Parcels of Land	Meridian/Township/Range
PIERCE (Cont'd)	**31**	2	Huntsville 18-S 3-W
" "	**24**	1	Huntsville 17-S 1-W
" "	**38**	1	Huntsville 19-S 4-W
" "	**43**	1	Huntsville 20-S 4-W
PIERSON	**23**	3	Huntsville 17-S 2-W
" "	**42**	1	Huntsville 20-S 5-W
PILLARS	**40**	1	Huntsville 19-S 2-W
PITTS	**43**	5	Huntsville 20-S 4-W
" "	**16**	3	Huntsville 16-S 1-W
" "	**31**	2	Huntsville 18-S 3-W
" "	**4**	1	Huntsville 14-S 1-W
" "	**15**	1	Huntsville 16-S 2-W
" "	**38**	1	Huntsville 19-S 4-W
PLEDGER	**32**	2	Huntsville 18-S 2-W
" "	**40**	2	Huntsville 19-S 2-W
POE	**24**	1	Huntsville 17-S 1-W
POINIER	**2**	2	Huntsville 14-S 3-W
POOL	**24**	4	Huntsville 17-S 1-W
" "	**19**	2	Huntsville 17-S 6-W
" "	**13**	1	Huntsville 16-S 4-W
" "	**20**	1	Huntsville 17-S 5-W
" "	**32**	1	Huntsville 18-S 2-W
POOLE	**32**	3	Huntsville 18-S 2-W
" "	**24**	1	Huntsville 17-S 1-W
PORTER	**44**	1	Huntsville 20-S 3-W
POSEY	**9**	4	Huntsville 15-S 1-W
" "	**4**	2	Huntsville 14-S 1-W
" "	**7**	1	Huntsville 15-S 3-W
POTEETE	**7**	1	Huntsville 15-S 3-W
POTTER	**22**	2	Huntsville 17-S 3-W
" "	**38**	2	Huntsville 19-S 4-W
POTTS	**15**	3	Huntsville 16-S 2-W
POWELL	**3**	3	Huntsville 14-S 2-W
" "	**8**	3	Huntsville 15-S 2-W
" "	**22**	3	Huntsville 17-S 3-W
" "	**6**	2	Huntsville 15-S 4-W
" "	**7**	1	Huntsville 15-S 3-W
PRATT	**23**	1	Huntsville 17-S 2-W
PRAYTOR	**17**	5	Huntsville 16-S 1-E
" "	**10**	2	Huntsville 15-S 1-E
" "	**16**	1	Huntsville 16-S 1-W
PRESCOAT	**11**	2	Huntsville 16-S 6-W
" "	**19**	1	Huntsville 17-S 6-W
PRESCOTT	**19**	6	Huntsville 17-S 6-W
" "	**18**	1	Huntsville 17-S 7-W
PRESLEY	**17**	3	Huntsville 16-S 1-E
PRICE	**9**	5	Huntsville 15-S 1-W
" "	**16**	3	Huntsville 16-S 1-W
" "	**29**	2	Huntsville 18-S 5-W
" "	**15**	1	Huntsville 16-S 2-W
" "	**14**	1	Huntsville 16-S 3-W
" "	**30**	1	Huntsville 18-S 4-W
PRIDE	**38**	1	Huntsville 19-S 4-W
PRINCE	**37**	1	Huntsville 19-S 5-W
PRUDE	**42**	4	Huntsville 20-S 5-W
" "	**37**	1	Huntsville 19-S 5-W
PRYOR	**9**	2	Huntsville 15-S 1-W
PULLEN	**32**	2	Huntsville 18-S 2-W
PULLIAM	**2**	1	Huntsville 14-S 3-W
PURCELL	**7**	2	Huntsville 15-S 3-W

Surname	Map Group	Parcels of Land	Meridian/Township/Range		
PUTTEET	**7**	1	Huntsville	15-S	3-W
PYBAS	**10**	4	Huntsville	15-S	1-E
PYBUS	**10**	2	Huntsville	15-S	1-E
QUIN	**12**	1	Huntsville	16-S	5-W
QUINN	**11**	11	Huntsville	16-S	6-W
" "	**12**	4	Huntsville	16-S	5-W
RAGAN	**29**	5	Huntsville	18-S	5-W
RAGIN	**20**	1	Huntsville	17-S	5-W
RAGLAN	**2**	1	Huntsville	14-S	3-W
RAGLAND	**2**	1	Huntsville	14-S	3-W
RAGLIN	**2**	2	Huntsville	14-S	3-W
RAGSDALE	**43**	1	Huntsville	20-S	4-W
RAIMER	**33**	2	Huntsville	18-S	1-W
RANDOLPH	**8**	1	Huntsville	15-S	2-W
" "	**31**	1	Huntsville	18-S	3-W
RANEY	**37**	5	Huntsville	19-S	5-W
" "	**36**	5	Huntsville	19-S	6-W
RATLIFF	**9**	1	Huntsville	15-S	1-W
" "	**24**	1	Huntsville	17-S	1-W
RAY	**39**	2	Huntsville	19-S	3-W
" "	**2**	1	Huntsville	14-S	3-W
" "	**14**	1	Huntsville	16-S	3-W
" "	**25**	1	Huntsville	17-S	1-E
" "	**41**	1	Huntsville	20-S	6-W
READ	**16**	1	Huntsville	16-S	1-W
READING	**39**	1	Huntsville	19-S	3-W
REAM	**24**	1	Huntsville	17-S	1-W
REAVES	**41**	5	Huntsville	20-S	6-W
REAVIS	**17**	1	Huntsville	16-S	1-E
" "	**23**	1	Huntsville	17-S	2-W
REDDING	**40**	1	Huntsville	19-S	2-W
" "	**39**	1	Huntsville	19-S	3-W
REDER	**38**	2	Huntsville	19-S	4-W
REED	**16**	18	Huntsville	16-S	1-W
" "	**9**	4	Huntsville	15-S	1-W
" "	**15**	4	Huntsville	16-S	2-W
" "	**23**	4	Huntsville	17-S	2-W
" "	**10**	3	Huntsville	15-S	1-E
" "	**7**	2	Huntsville	15-S	3-W
" "	**3**	1	Huntsville	14-S	2-W
" "	**8**	1	Huntsville	15-S	2-W
REEDER	**13**	7	Huntsville	16-S	4-W
REESE	**8**	3	Huntsville	15-S	2-W
" "	**23**	2	Huntsville	17-S	2-W
REEVES	**28**	3	Huntsville	18-S	6-W
" "	**1**	1	Huntsville	14-S	4-W
REGAN	**22**	1	Huntsville	17-S	3-W
REGIN	**30**	1	Huntsville	18-S	4-W
REID	**14**	5	Huntsville	16-S	3-W
" "	**2**	4	Huntsville	14-S	3-W
" "	**26**	4	Huntsville	18-S	8-W
" "	**8**	3	Huntsville	15-S	2-W
" "	**3**	2	Huntsville	14-S	2-W
" "	**9**	2	Huntsville	15-S	1-W
" "	**10**	1	Huntsville	15-S	1-E
" "	**7**	1	Huntsville	15-S	3-W
" "	**17**	1	Huntsville	16-S	1-E
" "	**27**	1	Huntsville	18-S	7-W
REIVES	**29**	1	Huntsville	18-S	5-W
RETALLACK	**14**	2	Huntsville	16-S	3-W

Surname	Map Group	Parcels of Land	Meridian/Township/Range		
RHEA	**18**	7	Huntsville	17-S	7-W
RHODY	**7**	1	Huntsville	15-S	3-W
RICE	**1**	1	Huntsville	14-S	4-W
RICHARDS	**14**	2	Huntsville	16-S	3-W
" "	**6**	1	Huntsville	15-S	4-W
" "	**30**	1	Huntsville	18-S	4-W
RICHARDSON	**19**	3	Huntsville	17-S	6-W
" "	**18**	3	Huntsville	17-S	7-W
" "	**36**	2	Huntsville	19-S	6-W
" "	**27**	1	Huntsville	18-S	7-W
RICHEY	**10**	1	Huntsville	15-S	1-E
" "	**9**	1	Huntsville	15-S	1-W
RICHMOND	**2**	1	Huntsville	14-S	3-W
RICKEY	**9**	2	Huntsville	15-S	1-W
" "	**16**	1	Huntsville	16-S	1-W
RIDDLE	**9**	1	Huntsville	15-S	1-W
RIED	**27**	1	Huntsville	18-S	7-W
RILEY	**28**	4	Huntsville	18-S	6-W
" "	**29**	3	Huntsville	18-S	5-W
" "	**32**	1	Huntsville	18-S	2-W
" "	**30**	1	Huntsville	18-S	4-W
" "	**38**	1	Huntsville	19-S	4-W
RINEHART	**33**	2	Huntsville	18-S	1-W
RITCHEY	**10**	1	Huntsville	15-S	1-E
RITCHIE	**10**	3	Huntsville	15-S	1-E
" "	**9**	1	Huntsville	15-S	1-W
RIVERS	**6**	3	Huntsville	15-S	4-W
" "	**2**	2	Huntsville	14-S	3-W
ROBBINS	**6**	17	Huntsville	15-S	4-W
" "	**14**	3	Huntsville	16-S	3-W
" "	**1**	2	Huntsville	14-S	4-W
ROBERSON	**17**	1	Huntsville	16-S	1-E
ROBERTS	**28**	9	Huntsville	18-S	6-W
" "	**2**	6	Huntsville	14-S	3-W
" "	**15**	2	Huntsville	16-S	2-W
" "	**1**	1	Huntsville	14-S	4-W
" "	**7**	1	Huntsville	15-S	3-W
" "	**14**	1	Huntsville	16-S	3-W
ROBERTSON	**30**	10	Huntsville	18-S	4-W
" "	**36**	4	Huntsville	19-S	6-W
" "	**13**	3	Huntsville	16-S	4-W
" "	**12**	3	Huntsville	16-S	5-W
" "	**2**	2	Huntsville	14-S	3-W
" "	**7**	2	Huntsville	15-S	3-W
" "	**16**	2	Huntsville	16-S	1-W
" "	**10**	1	Huntsville	15-S	1-E
" "	**6**	1	Huntsville	15-S	4-W
" "	**18**	1	Huntsville	17-S	7-W
ROBINS	**6**	5	Huntsville	15-S	4-W
" "	**27**	1	Huntsville	18-S	7-W
ROBINSON	**17**	6	Huntsville	16-S	1-E
" "	**7**	2	Huntsville	15-S	3-W
" "	**15**	2	Huntsville	16-S	2-W
ROBISON	**36**	1	Huntsville	19-S	6-W
ROCKETT	**38**	8	Huntsville	19-S	4-W
" "	**31**	7	Huntsville	18-S	3-W
RODGERS	**12**	2	Huntsville	16-S	5-W
" "	**36**	2	Huntsville	19-S	6-W
" "	**2**	1	Huntsville	14-S	3-W
" "	**8**	1	Huntsville	15-S	2-W

" "	**36**	3	Huntsville	19-S	6-W
" "	**24**	2	Huntsville	17-S	1-W
ROTH	**32**	1	Huntsville	18-S	2-W
ROTTON	**15**	2	Huntsville	16-S	2-W
ROUNSLEY	**43**	3	Huntsville	20-S	4-W
ROUSE	**2**	9	Huntsville	14-S	3-W
" "	**5**	1	Huntsville	15-S	5-W
ROWAN	**24**	6	Huntsville	17-S	1-W
" "	**17**	2	Huntsville	16-S	1-E
" "	**25**	1	Huntsville	17-S	1-E
" "	**32**	1	Huntsville	18-S	2-W
ROWE	**2**	5	Huntsville	14-S	3-W
" "	**8**	1	Huntsville	15-S	2-W
" "	**7**	1	Huntsville	15-S	3-W
ROY	**38**	3	Huntsville	19-S	4-W
" "	**40**	1	Huntsville	19-S	2-W
RUCKER	**9**	1	Huntsville	15-S	1-W
RUDER	**13**	1	Huntsville	16-S	4-W
RUPE	**42**	1	Huntsville	20-S	5-W
RUSSELL	**21**	6	Huntsville	17-S	4-W
" "	**30**	6	Huntsville	18-S	4-W
" "	**42**	3	Huntsville	20-S	5-W
" "	**14**	2	Huntsville	16-S	3-W
" "	**13**	2	Huntsville	16-S	4-W
" "	**22**	2	Huntsville	17-S	3-W
" "	**43**	2	Huntsville	20-S	4-W
" "	**2**	1	Huntsville	14-S	3-W
" "	**38**	1	Huntsville	19-S	4-W
RUTH	**12**	3	Huntsville	16-S	5-W
RUTHERFORD	**32**	1	Huntsville	18-S	2-W
RUTLEDGE	**30**	1	Huntsville	18-S	4-W
RYAN	**24**	3	Huntsville	17-S	1-W
RYLANT	**15**	1	Huntsville	16-S	2-W
SADBERRY	**43**	1	Huntsville	20-S	4-W
SADDLER	**42**	12	Huntsville	20-S	5-W
" "	**43**	4	Huntsville	20-S	4-W
" "	**23**	2	Huntsville	17-S	2-W
" "	**38**	2	Huntsville	19-S	4-W
" "	**37**	2	Huntsville	19-S	5-W

Surname	Map Group	Parcels of Land	Meridian/Township/Range		
SADDLER (Cont'd)	**24**	1	Huntsville	17-S	1-W
SADLER	**43**	4	Huntsville	20-S	4-W
" "	**42**	4	Huntsville	20-S	5-W
" "	**38**	3	Huntsville	19-S	4-W
" "	**37**	3	Huntsville	19-S	5-W
SALMONS	**42**	2	Huntsville	20-S	5-W
" "	**41**	1	Huntsville	20-S	6-W
SALTER	**19**	14	Huntsville	17-S	6-W
" "	**11**	3	Huntsville	16-S	6-W
" "	**20**	3	Huntsville	17-S	5-W
" "	**29**	1	Huntsville	18-S	5-W
SAMPLES	**21**	1	Huntsville	17-S	4-W
SANDERS	**30**	5	Huntsville	18-S	4-W
" "	**38**	3	Huntsville	19-S	4-W
" "	**29**	2	Huntsville	18-S	5-W
" "	**7**	1	Huntsville	15-S	3-W
" "	**6**	1	Huntsville	15-S	4-W
SANDIFORD	**31**	4	Huntsville	18-S	3-W
" "	**39**	1	Huntsville	19-S	3-W
SANSON	**25**	3	Huntsville	17-S	1-E
" "	**24**	2	Huntsville	17-S	1-W
SARGENT	**14**	6	Huntsville	16-S	3-W
SAULSBURY	**7**	3	Huntsville	15-S	3-W
SAVAGE	**1**	3	Huntsville	14-S	4-W
SCHLEY	**1**	2	Huntsville	14-S	4-W
SCOTT	**15**	11	Huntsville	16-S	2-W
" "	**16**	8	Huntsville	16-S	1-W
" "	**31**	3	Huntsville	18-S	3-W
" "	**25**	2	Huntsville	17-S	1-E
" "	**9**	1	Huntsville	15-S	1-W
" "	**8**	1	Huntsville	15-S	2-W
" "	**32**	1	Huntsville	18-S	2-W
" "	**29**	1	Huntsville	18-S	5-W
" "	**37**	1	Huntsville	19-S	5-W
SEAL	**25**	2	Huntsville	17-S	1-E
SELF	**9**	13	Huntsville	15-S	1-W
" "	**16**	8	Huntsville	16-S	1-W
" "	**4**	3	Huntsville	14-S	1-W
" "	**8**	2	Huntsville	15-S	2-W
" "	**21**	2	Huntsville	17-S	4-W
" "	**3**	1	Huntsville	14-S	2-W
" "	**10**	1	Huntsville	15-S	1-E
" "	**15**	1	Huntsville	16-S	2-W
SELFE	**9**	1	Huntsville	15-S	1-W
SELLARS	**39**	2	Huntsville	19-S	3-W
" "	**42**	2	Huntsville	20-S	5-W
SELLENGER	**42**	1	Huntsville	20-S	5-W
SELLERS	**37**	8	Huntsville	19-S	5-W
" "	**42**	6	Huntsville	20-S	5-W
" "	**41**	5	Huntsville	20-S	6-W
" "	**5**	2	Huntsville	15-S	5-W
SENTELL	**22**	1	Huntsville	17-S	3-W
SHACKELFORD	**32**	3	Huntsville	18-S	2-W
SHACKLEFORD	**31**	1	Huntsville	18-S	3-W
SHAGER	**24**	1	Huntsville	17-S	1-W
SHAMBLIN	**15**	1	Huntsville	16-S	2-W
SHARIT	**7**	7	Huntsville	15-S	3-W
" "	**2**	1	Huntsville	14-S	3-W
" "	**1**	1	Huntsville	14-S	4-W
" "	**14**	1	Huntsville	16-S	3-W

Surname	Map Group	Parcels of Land	Meridian/Township/Range		
SHARP	**37**	9	Huntsville	19-S	5-W
" "	**31**	2	Huntsville	18-S	3-W
" "	**21**	1	Huntsville	17-S	4-W
" "	**30**	1	Huntsville	18-S	4-W
" "	**41**	1	Huntsville	20-S	6-W
SHAW	**5**	2	Huntsville	15-S	5-W
" "	**38**	2	Huntsville	19-S	4-W
" "	**37**	1	Huntsville	19-S	5-W
SHEDD	**8**	1	Huntsville	15-S	2-W
SHELTON	**11**	1	Huntsville	16-S	6-W
SHEPHERD	**42**	4	Huntsville	20-S	5-W
" "	**33**	1	Huntsville	18 S	1 W
SHERMAN	**34**	1	Huntsville	18-S	1-E
SHIPMAN	**24**	2	Huntsville	17-S	1-W
SHIPP	**1**	3	Huntsville	14-S	4-W
" "	**2**	2	Huntsville	14-S	3-W
" "	**5**	1	Huntsville	15-S	5-W
SHIRL	**7**	2	Huntsville	15-S	3-W
SHOEMAKER	**21**	19	Huntsville	17-S	4-W
" "	**20**	11	Huntsville	17-S	5-W
" "	**29**	3	Huntsville	18-S	5-W
" "	**23**	1	Huntsville	17-S	2-W
SHOOK	**25**	1	Huntsville	17-S	1-E
SHORT	**19**	10	Huntsville	17-S	6-W
" "	**6**	1	Huntsville	15-S	4-W
SHUGART	**14**	7	Huntsville	16-S	3-W
" "	**15**	1	Huntsville	16-S	2-W
SHULTS	**3**	1	Huntsville	14-S	2-W
SHUTTLESWORTH	**23**	1	Huntsville	17-S	2-W
SIDES	**15**	1	Huntsville	16-S	2-W
SIMMONS	**14**	1	Huntsville	16-S	3-W
" "	**22**	1	Huntsville	17-S	3-W
SIMPSON	**15**	3	Huntsville	16-S	2-W
" "	**7**	1	Huntsville	15-S	3-W
" "	**38**	1	Huntsville	19-S	4-W
" "	**43**	1	Huntsville	20-S	4-W
SIMS	**15**	10	Huntsville	16-S	2-W
" "	**23**	10	Huntsville	17-S	2-W
" "	**22**	6	Huntsville	17-S	3-W
" "	**31**	6	Huntsville	18-S	3-W
" "	**33**	5	Huntsville	18-S	1-W
" "	**16**	4	Huntsville	16-S	1-W
" "	**10**	2	Huntsville	15-S	1-E
" "	**17**	2	Huntsville	16-S	1-E
" "	**25**	2	Huntsville	17-S	1-E
" "	**9**	1	Huntsville	15-S	1-W
" "	**14**	1	Huntsville	16-S	3-W
" "	**13**	1	Huntsville	16-S	4-W
" "	**24**	1	Huntsville	17-S	1-W
" "	**19**	1	Huntsville	17-S	6-W
" "	**38**	1	Huntsville	19-S	4-W
" "	**37**	1	Huntsville	19-S	5-W
SKAGGS	**17**	1	Huntsville	16-S	1-E
SKELTON	**11**	8	Huntsville	16-S	6-W
" "	**9**	1	Huntsville	15-S	1-W
" "	**12**	1	Huntsville	16-S	5-W
" "	**19**	1	Huntsville	17-S	6-W
SLAPPY	**17**	2	Huntsville	16-S	1-E
SLOAN	**2**	3	Huntsville	14-S	3-W
" "	**1**	3	Huntsville	14-S	4-W

Surname	Map Group	Parcels of Land	Meridian/Township/Range
SMITH	**28**	12	Huntsville 18-S 6-W
" "	**19**	10	Huntsville 17-S 6-W
" "	**25**	9	Huntsville 17-S 1-E
" "	**3**	8	Huntsville 14-S 2-W
" "	**30**	8	Huntsville 18-S 4-W
" "	**39**	8	Huntsville 19-S 3-W
" "	**14**	7	Huntsville 16-S 3-W
" "	**21**	4	Huntsville 17-S 4-W
" "	**31**	4	Huntsville 18-S 3-W
" "	**2**	3	Huntsville 14-S 3-W
" "	**8**	3	Huntsville 15-S 2-W
" "	**23**	3	Huntsville 17-S 2-W
" "	**22**	3	Huntsville 17-S 3-W
" "	**6**	2	Huntsville 15-S 4-W
" "	**5**	2	Huntsville 15-S 5-W
" "	**18**	2	Huntsville 17-S 7-W
" "	**38**	2	Huntsville 19-S 4-W
" "	**17**	1	Huntsville 16-S 1-E
" "	**16**	1	Huntsville 16-S 1-W
SMITHSON	**43**	8	Huntsville 20-S 4-W
SNEAD	**20**	3	Huntsville 17-S 5-W
SNELL	**14**	3	Huntsville 16-S 3-W
" "	**23**	1	Huntsville 17-S 2-W
SNOW	**30**	5	Huntsville 18-S 4-W
" "	**19**	3	Huntsville 17-S 6-W
" "	**28**	3	Huntsville 18-S 6-W
" "	**23**	2	Huntsville 17-S 2-W
" "	**37**	2	Huntsville 19-S 5-W
" "	**15**	1	Huntsville 16-S 2-W
" "	**21**	1	Huntsville 17-S 4-W
SOUTH	**32**	1	Huntsville 18-S 2-W
SOUTHERLAND	**12**	1	Huntsville 16-S 5-W
SPARKES	**38**	2	Huntsville 19-S 4-W
" "	**6**	1	Huntsville 15-S 4-W
SPARKS	**33**	2	Huntsville 18-S 1-W
" "	**25**	1	Huntsville 17-S 1-E
" "	**38**	1	Huntsville 19-S 4-W
" "	**43**	1	Huntsville 20-S 4-W
SPAULDING	**29**	3	Huntsville 18-S 5-W
SPEAKMAN	**2**	1	Huntsville 14-S 3-W
SPEAR	**1**	1	Huntsville 14-S 4-W
SPEARS	**28**	2	Huntsville 18-S 6-W
" "	**14**	1	Huntsville 16-S 3-W
SPEER	**14**	2	Huntsville 16-S 3-W
" "	**13**	2	Huntsville 16-S 4-W
" "	**23**	2	Huntsville 17-S 2-W
SPENCER	**31**	13	Huntsville 18-S 3-W
" "	**30**	10	Huntsville 18-S 4-W
" "	**38**	9	Huntsville 19-S 4-W
" "	**29**	6	Huntsville 18-S 5-W
" "	**37**	2	Huntsville 19-S 5-W
" "	**22**	1	Huntsville 17-S 3-W
SPERRY	**33**	1	Huntsville 18-S 1-W
SPRADLEY	**40**	1	Huntsville 19-S 2-W
SPRADLING	**9**	9	Huntsville 15-S 1-W
" "	**7**	5	Huntsville 15-S 3-W
" "	**15**	3	Huntsville 16-S 2-W
" "	**10**	2	Huntsville 15-S 1-E
" "	**8**	1	Huntsville 15-S 2-W
SPRUELL	**14**	3	Huntsville 16-S 3-W

Surname	Map Group	Parcels of Land	Meridian/Township/Range		
SPRUELL (Cont'd)	**7**	1	Huntsville	15-S	3-W
SQUIRE	**10**	4	Huntsville	15-S	1-E
" "	**42**	3	Huntsville	20-S	5-W
STACKS	**39**	2	Huntsville	19-S	3-W
STAGG	**14**	1	Huntsville	16-S	3-W
" "	**21**	1	Huntsville	17-S	4-W
STAGGS	**22**	5	Huntsville	17-S	3-W
" "	**7**	3	Huntsville	15-S	3-W
" "	**36**	3	Huntsville	19-S	6-W
" "	**6**	2	Huntsville	15-S	4-W
" "	**27**	2	Huntsville	18-S	7-W
" "	**15**	1	Huntsville	16-S	2-W
" "	**14**	1	Huntsville	16-S	3-W
" "	**23**	1	Huntsville	17-S	2-W
" "	**29**	1	Huntsville	18-S	5-W
" "	**37**	1	Huntsville	19-S	5-W
STALNAKER	**33**	2	Huntsville	18-S	1-W
STANDIFER	**33**	4	Huntsville	18-S	1-W
STANDLAND	**44**	1	Huntsville	20-S	3-W
STARKY	**16**	1	Huntsville	16-S	1-W
STARNES	**23**	3	Huntsville	17-S	2-W
" "	**14**	1	Huntsville	16-S	3-W
STATEM	**13**	1	Huntsville	16-S	4-W
STATHAM	**21**	1	Huntsville	17-S	4-W
STATON	**3**	1	Huntsville	14-S	2-W
" "	**21**	1	Huntsville	17-S	4-W
STATUM	**12**	3	Huntsville	16-S	5-W
" "	**13**	2	Huntsville	16-S	4-W
" "	**6**	1	Huntsville	15-S	4-W
STEALE	**31**	1	Huntsville	18-S	3-W
STEEDMAN	**43**	4	Huntsville	20-S	4-W
STEEL	**12**	6	Huntsville	16-S	5-W
" "	**5**	3	Huntsville	15-S	5-W
" "	**7**	2	Huntsville	15-S	3-W
" "	**6**	1	Huntsville	15-S	4-W
STEELE	**2**	1	Huntsville	14-S	3-W
STEPHENS	**20**	4	Huntsville	17-S	5-W
" "	**12**	1	Huntsville	16-S	5-W
" "	**19**	1	Huntsville	17-S	6-W
STEWART	**30**	1	Huntsville	18-S	4-W
STIVENDER	**13**	1	Huntsville	16-S	4-W
STONE	**35**	4	Huntsville	19-S	7-W
" "	**36**	2	Huntsville	19-S	6-W
" "	**18**	1	Huntsville	17-S	7-W
STOUT	**2**	1	Huntsville	14-S	3-W
STOVALL	**24**	9	Huntsville	17-S	1-W
" "	**22**	1	Huntsville	17-S	3-W
STRINGFELLOW	**36**	2	Huntsville	19-S	6-W
" "	**28**	1	Huntsville	18-S	6-W
STROUP	**42**	1	Huntsville	20-S	5-W
STUBBS	**8**	2	Huntsville	15-S	2-W
" "	**10**	1	Huntsville	15-S	1-E
STURDIVANT	**43**	1	Huntsville	20-S	4-W
SULLIVAN	**8**	9	Huntsville	15-S	2-W
" "	**6**	4	Huntsville	15-S	4-W
" "	**9**	1	Huntsville	15-S	1-W
SULLIVANT	**8**	3	Huntsville	15-S	2-W
SWINNEY	**16**	1	Huntsville	16-S	1-W
TACKET	**27**	2	Huntsville	18-S	7-W
TADLOCK	**9**	1	Huntsville	15-S	1-W

Surname	Map Group	Parcels of Land	Meridian/Township/Range
TALLEY	**16**	6	Huntsville 16-S 1-W
" "	**10**	3	Huntsville 15-S 1-E
" "	**17**	3	Huntsville 16-S 1-E
TANKERSLY	**22**	1	Huntsville 17-S 3-W
TANNAHILL	**7**	1	Huntsville 15-S 3-W
" "	**37**	1	Huntsville 19-S 5-W
" "	**43**	1	Huntsville 20-S 4-W
TANNEHILL	**42**	7	Huntsville 20-S 5-W
" "	**22**	1	Huntsville 17-S 3-W
" "	**32**	1	Huntsville 18-S 2-W
TANNER	**6**	3	Huntsville 15-S 4-W
TARRANT	**23**	3	Huntsville 17-S 2-W
" "	**30**	3	Huntsville 18-S 4-W
" "	**38**	2	Huntsville 19-S 4-W
" "	**15**	1	Huntsville 16-S 2-W
" "	**22**	1	Huntsville 17-S 3-W
" "	**39**	1	Huntsville 19-S 3-W
TATE	**6**	3	Huntsville 15-S 4-W
" "	**20**	3	Huntsville 17-S 5-W
" "	**19**	1	Huntsville 17-S 6-W
TATUM	**8**	2	Huntsville 15-S 2-W
" "	**37**	2	Huntsville 19-S 5-W
" "	**9**	1	Huntsville 15-S 1-W
TAYLOR	**10**	19	Huntsville 15-S 1-E
" "	**9**	16	Huntsville 15-S 1-W
" "	**16**	11	Huntsville 16-S 1-W
" "	**19**	4	Huntsville 17-S 6-W
" "	**8**	3	Huntsville 15-S 2-W
" "	**28**	3	Huntsville 18-S 6-W
" "	**24**	2	Huntsville 17-S 1-W
" "	**38**	2	Huntsville 19-S 4-W
" "	**37**	2	Huntsville 19-S 5-W
" "	**3**	1	Huntsville 14-S 2-W
" "	**15**	1	Huntsville 16-S 2-W
TEAGUE	**16**	2	Huntsville 16-S 1-W
TEASLEY	**9**	1	Huntsville 15-S 1-W
TEDMORE	**7**	1	Huntsville 15-S 3-W
TERRIL	**31**	1	Huntsville 18-S 3-W
TERRY	**3**	2	Huntsville 14-S 2-W
THACK	**15**	1	Huntsville 16-S 2-W
THACKER	**18**	1	Huntsville 17-S 7-W
THOMAS	**2**	10	Huntsville 14-S 3-W
" "	**38**	10	Huntsville 19-S 4-W
" "	**37**	8	Huntsville 19-S 5-W
" "	**1**	5	Huntsville 14-S 4-W
" "	**42**	5	Huntsville 20-S 5-W
" "	**6**	3	Huntsville 15-S 4-W
" "	**8**	2	Huntsville 15-S 2-W
" "	**21**	2	Huntsville 17-S 4-W
" "	**3**	1	Huntsville 14-S 2-W
" "	**9**	1	Huntsville 15-S 1-W
" "	**15**	1	Huntsville 16-S 2-W
" "	**30**	1	Huntsville 18-S 4-W
THOMPSON	**19**	15	Huntsville 17-S 6-W
" "	**29**	8	Huntsville 18-S 5-W
" "	**27**	6	Huntsville 18-S 7-W
" "	**18**	5	Huntsville 17-S 7-W
" "	**43**	4	Huntsville 20-S 4-W
" "	**42**	4	Huntsville 20-S 5-W
" "	**24**	3	Huntsville 17-S 1-W

Surname	Map Group	Parcels of Land	Meridian/Township/Range		
THOMPSON (Cont'd)	**3**	1	Huntsville	14-S	2-W
" "	**8**	1	Huntsville	15-S	2-W
" "	**25**	1	Huntsville	17-S	1-E
" "	**22**	1	Huntsville	17-S	3-W
" "	**38**	1	Huntsville	19-S	4-W
" "	**37**	1	Huntsville	19-S	5-W
THORINGTON	**43**	1	Huntsville	20-S	4-W
THORNE	**37**	3	Huntsville	19-S	5-W
THORP	**16**	2	Huntsville	16-S	1-W
THURSTON	**23**	5	Huntsville	17-S	2-W
TIDWELL	**2**	2	Huntsville	14-S	3-W
" "	**10**	1	Huntsville	15-S	1 E
" "	**16**	1	Huntsville	16-S	1-W
TILERSON	**32**	1	Huntsville	18-S	2-W
TILLISON	**12**	1	Huntsville	16-S	5-W
TILLMAN	**17**	2	Huntsville	16-S	1-E
" "	**38**	1	Huntsville	19-S	4-W
TILLOTSON	**12**	1	Huntsville	16-S	5-W
TIMMONS	**32**	1	Huntsville	18-S	2-W
TORRENT	**38**	1	Huntsville	19-S	4-W
TOURY	**38**	1	Huntsville	19-S	4-W
TOWERS	**37**	1	Huntsville	19-S	5-W
TOWERY	**38**	1	Huntsville	19-S	4-W
TOWNBY	**17**	1	Huntsville	16-S	1-E
TOWNLEY	**17**	1	Huntsville	16-S	1-E
TOWNLY	**17**	1	Huntsville	16-S	1-E
TRAMMELL	**2**	3	Huntsville	14-S	3-W
TRASS	**16**	2	Huntsville	16-S	1-W
TRAVIS	**36**	1	Huntsville	19-S	6-W
TREADAWAY	**6**	4	Huntsville	15-S	4-W
TRUETT	**13**	1	Huntsville	16-S	4-W
TRUSS	**16**	30	Huntsville	16-S	1-W
" "	**3**	4	Huntsville	14-S	2-W
" "	**17**	4	Huntsville	16-S	1-E
" "	**2**	3	Huntsville	14-S	3-W
" "	**10**	2	Huntsville	15-S	1-E
" "	**23**	1	Huntsville	17-S	2-W
" "	**38**	1	Huntsville	19-S	4-W
TUCKER	**16**	3	Huntsville	16-S	1-W
" "	**17**	2	Huntsville	16-S	1-E
" "	**29**	2	Huntsville	18-S	5-W
" "	**10**	1	Huntsville	15-S	1-E
" "	**9**	1	Huntsville	15-S	1-W
TUMBOUGH	**10**	1	Huntsville	15-S	1-E
TUNE	**16**	2	Huntsville	16-S	1-W
TUNNELL	**9**	1	Huntsville	15-S	1-W
TURKENET	**6**	1	Huntsville	15-S	4-W
TURNBOUGH	**10**	6	Huntsville	15-S	1-E
TURNER	**31**	8	Huntsville	18-S	3-W
" "	**10**	7	Huntsville	15-S	1-E
" "	**6**	7	Huntsville	15-S	4-W
" "	**23**	5	Huntsville	17-S	2-W
" "	**5**	3	Huntsville	15-S	5-W
" "	**3**	2	Huntsville	14-S	2-W
" "	**15**	2	Huntsville	16-S	2-W
" "	**9**	1	Huntsville	15-S	1-W
" "	**7**	1	Huntsville	15-S	3-W
" "	**16**	1	Huntsville	16-S	1-W
" "	**36**	1	Huntsville	19-S	6-W
" "	**43**	1	Huntsville	20-S	4-W

Surname	Map Group	Parcels of Land	Meridian/Township/Range
TURNER (Cont'd)	**42**	1	Huntsville 20-S 5-W
TURNHAM	**7**	3	Huntsville 15-S 3-W
TUTHILL	**20**	2	Huntsville 17-S 5-W
" "	**7**	1	Huntsville 15-S 3-W
" "	**12**	1	Huntsville 16-S 5-W
TUTTLE	**2**	1	Huntsville 14-S 3-W
TUTWILER	**15**	1	Huntsville 16-S 2-W
TYLER	**43**	11	Huntsville 20-S 4-W
" "	**20**	2	Huntsville 17-S 5-W
" "	**9**	1	Huntsville 15-S 1-W
" "	**16**	1	Huntsville 16-S 1-W
TYLOR	**42**	3	Huntsville 20-S 5-W
" "	**9**	2	Huntsville 15-S 1-W
USTICK	**15**	1	Huntsville 16-S 2-W
VAN HAUSE	**28**	1	Huntsville 18-S 6-W
VAN HOOSE	**28**	1	Huntsville 18-S 6-W
VANCE	**20**	3	Huntsville 17-S 5-W
VANDEVIR	**13**	2	Huntsville 16-S 4-W
VANDIFORD	**42**	1	Huntsville 20-S 5-W
VANDIVER	**13**	3	Huntsville 16-S 4-W
VANHOOSE	**39**	1	Huntsville 19-S 3-W
VANHOUSE	**28**	1	Huntsville 18-S 6-W
VANN	**16**	24	Huntsville 16-S 1-W
" "	**15**	3	Huntsville 16-S 2-W
VANZANDT	**22**	2	Huntsville 17-S 3-W
" "	**23**	1	Huntsville 17-S 2-W
VARNON	**22**	4	Huntsville 17-S 3-W
" "	**9**	2	Huntsville 15-S 1-W
" "	**21**	2	Huntsville 17-S 4-W
VARNUM	**13**	1	Huntsville 16-S 4-W
VEAZEY	**32**	1	Huntsville 18-S 2-W
VEITCH	**38**	1	Huntsville 19-S 4-W
VENS	**39**	1	Huntsville 19-S 3-W
VIENS	**20**	3	Huntsville 17-S 5-W
" "	**21**	1	Huntsville 17-S 4-W
VINCENT	**15**	1	Huntsville 16-S 2-W
VINES	**19**	46	Huntsville 17-S 6-W
" "	**20**	31	Huntsville 17-S 5-W
" "	**29**	3	Huntsville 18-S 5-W
" "	**28**	3	Huntsville 18-S 6-W
" "	**12**	2	Huntsville 16-S 5-W
" "	**42**	2	Huntsville 20-S 5-W
VINING	**42**	2	Huntsville 20-S 5-W
VINSON	**8**	3	Huntsville 15-S 2-W
VON MINDIN	**24**	2	Huntsville 17-S 1-W
VOSE	**33**	1	Huntsville 18-S 1-W
WADE	**10**	2	Huntsville 15-S 1-E
" "	**22**	1	Huntsville 17-S 3-W
WAIT	**6**	1	Huntsville 15-S 4-W
WALD	**24**	2	Huntsville 17-S 1-W
WALDROP	**28**	17	Huntsville 18-S 6-W
" "	**19**	14	Huntsville 17-S 6-W
" "	**29**	14	Huntsville 18-S 5-W
" "	**23**	6	Huntsville 17-S 2-W
" "	**12**	2	Huntsville 16-S 5-W
" "	**24**	2	Huntsville 17-S 1-W
" "	**37**	2	Huntsville 19-S 5-W
" "	**13**	1	Huntsville 16-S 4-W
" "	**20**	1	Huntsville 17-S 5-W
" "	**43**	1	Huntsville 20-S 4-W

Surname	Map Group	Parcels of Land	Meridian/Township/Range		
WALDRUP	**19**	1	Huntsville	17-S	6-W
WALKER	**9**	8	Huntsville	15-S	1-W
" "	**31**	7	Huntsville	18-S	3-W
" "	**14**	6	Huntsville	16-S	3-W
" "	**6**	3	Huntsville	15-S	4-W
" "	**16**	2	Huntsville	16-S	1-W
" "	**15**	2	Huntsville	16-S	2-W
" "	**3**	1	Huntsville	14-S	2-W
" "	**32**	1	Huntsville	18-S	2-W
" "	**38**	1	Huntsville	19-S	4-W
WALLACE	**25**	2	Huntsville	17-S	1-E
WALLS	**16**	1	Huntsville	16-S	1-W
WALTERS	**15**	2	Huntsville	16-S	2-W
WALTON	**39**	1	Huntsville	19-S	3-W
WARD	**1**	2	Huntsville	14-S	4-W
" "	**6**	1	Huntsville	15-S	4-W
WARE	**9**	6	Huntsville	15-S	1-W
" "	**38**	4	Huntsville	19-S	4-W
" "	**31**	3	Huntsville	18-S	3-W
" "	**37**	3	Huntsville	19-S	5-W
" "	**2**	2	Huntsville	14-S	3-W
" "	**24**	2	Huntsville	17-S	1-W
" "	**10**	1	Huntsville	15-S	1-E
" "	**27**	1	Huntsville	18-S	7-W
WARNICK	**10**	2	Huntsville	15-S	1-E
WARREN	**39**	2	Huntsville	19-S	3-W
" "	**38**	1	Huntsville	19-S	4-W
WASHINGTON	**37**	1	Huntsville	19-S	5-W
WATHEN	**3**	1	Huntsville	14-S	2-W
WATKINS	**32**	7	Huntsville	18-S	2-W
WATSON	**9**	4	Huntsville	15-S	1-W
" "	**1**	2	Huntsville	14-S	4-W
" "	**25**	2	Huntsville	17-S	1-E
" "	**24**	2	Huntsville	17-S	1-W
" "	**29**	1	Huntsville	18-S	5-W
WATTS	**22**	1	Huntsville	17-S	3-W
WEAR	**9**	9	Huntsville	15-S	1-W
" "	**10**	3	Huntsville	15-S	1-E
" "	**16**	2	Huntsville	16-S	1-W
WEBB	**2**	1	Huntsville	14-S	3-W
WEDGEWORTH	**7**	2	Huntsville	15-S	3-W
WEED	**42**	4	Huntsville	20-S	5-W
" "	**43**	2	Huntsville	20-S	4-W
WEEMS	**16**	4	Huntsville	16-S	1-W
" "	**24**	3	Huntsville	17-S	1-W
" "	**15**	2	Huntsville	16-S	2-W
" "	**4**	1	Huntsville	14-S	1-W
" "	**31**	1	Huntsville	18-S	3-W
WEISMAN	**3**	1	Huntsville	14-S	2-W
" "	**2**	1	Huntsville	14-S	3-W
" "	**6**	1	Huntsville	15-S	4-W
WELCH	**39**	1	Huntsville	19-S	3-W
WELDON	**32**	3	Huntsville	18-S	2-W
WEST	**39**	1	Huntsville	19-S	3-W
WETHERS	**33**	1	Huntsville	18-S	1-W
WHARTON	**31**	1	Huntsville	18-S	3-W
" "	**40**	1	Huntsville	19-S	2-W
WHATLEY	**7**	1	Huntsville	15-S	3-W
WHEELER	**13**	3	Huntsville	16-S	4-W
" "	**21**	3	Huntsville	17-S	4-W

Surname	Map Group	Parcels of Land	Meridian/Township/Range
WHISENANT	**3**	6	Huntsville 14-S 2-W
" "	**8**	1	Huntsville 15-S 2-W
WHISNANT	**3**	2	Huntsville 14-S 2-W
WHITBY	**33**	1	Huntsville 18-S 1-W
WHITE	**33**	13	Huntsville 18-S 1-W
" "	**3**	4	Huntsville 14-S 2-W
" "	**1**	1	Huntsville 14-S 4-W
" "	**6**	1	Huntsville 15-S 4-W
" "	**17**	1	Huntsville 16-S 1-E
" "	**25**	1	Huntsville 17-S 1-E
" "	**32**	1	Huntsville 18-S 2-W
" "	**38**	1	Huntsville 19-S 4-W
WHITEFIELD	**33**	1	Huntsville 18-S 1-W
WHITEHEAD	**11**	2	Huntsville 16-S 6-W
" "	**6**	1	Huntsville 15-S 4-W
" "	**32**	1	Huntsville 18-S 2-W
WHITEHOUSE	**9**	2	Huntsville 15-S 1-W
WHITTINGTON	**15**	2	Huntsville 16-S 2-W
" "	**22**	1	Huntsville 17-S 3-W
WIDEMAN	**32**	8	Huntsville 18-S 2-W
" "	**39**	4	Huntsville 19-S 3-W
" "	**23**	1	Huntsville 17-S 2-W
WILDER	**39**	1	Huntsville 19-S 3-W
WILEY	**12**	5	Huntsville 16-S 5-W
" "	**32**	1	Huntsville 18-S 2-W
WILKES	**16**	3	Huntsville 16-S 1-W
" "	**21**	1	Huntsville 17-S 4-W
WILKEY	**28**	5	Huntsville 18-S 6-W
" "	**18**	1	Huntsville 17-S 7-W
" "	**27**	1	Huntsville 18-S 7-W
WILKINS	**12**	1	Huntsville 16-S 5-W
WILKS	**21**	7	Huntsville 17-S 4-W
WILLARD	**37**	3	Huntsville 19-S 5-W
" "	**41**	3	Huntsville 20-S 6-W
" "	**35**	2	Huntsville 19-S 7-W
WILLIAMS	**12**	17	Huntsville 16-S 5-W
" "	**42**	10	Huntsville 20-S 5-W
" "	**19**	7	Huntsville 17-S 6-W
" "	**9**	6	Huntsville 15-S 1-W
" "	**31**	6	Huntsville 18-S 3-W
" "	**39**	6	Huntsville 19-S 3-W
" "	**8**	3	Huntsville 15-S 2-W
" "	**16**	3	Huntsville 16-S 1-W
" "	**24**	3	Huntsville 17-S 1-W
" "	**5**	2	Huntsville 15-S 5-W
" "	**22**	2	Huntsville 17-S 3-W
" "	**11**	1	Huntsville 16-S 6-W
" "	**20**	1	Huntsville 17-S 5-W
" "	**32**	1	Huntsville 18-S 2-W
" "	**27**	1	Huntsville 18-S 7-W
WILLIAMSON	**3**	1	Huntsville 14-S 2-W
WILLINGHAM	**9**	1	Huntsville 15-S 1-W
" "	**31**	1	Huntsville 18-S 3-W
WILLIS	**15**	2	Huntsville 16-S 2-W
" "	**14**	2	Huntsville 16-S 3-W
" "	**32**	2	Huntsville 18-S 2-W
" "	**33**	1	Huntsville 18-S 1-W
" "	**39**	1	Huntsville 19-S 3-W
WILSON	**16**	5	Huntsville 16-S 1-W
" "	**13**	4	Huntsville 16-S 4-W

Surname	Map Group	Parcels of Land	Meridian/Township/Range		
WILSON (Cont'd)	**23**	4	Huntsville	17-S	2-W
" "	**4**	3	Huntsville	14-S	1-W
" "	**3**	3	Huntsville	14-S	2-W
" "	**10**	2	Huntsville	15-S	1-E
" "	**43**	2	Huntsville	20-S	4-W
" "	**5**	1	Huntsville	15-S	5-W
" "	**15**	1	Huntsville	16-S	2-W
" "	**24**	1	Huntsville	17-S	1-W
" "	**22**	1	Huntsville	17-S	3-W
" "	**21**	1	Huntsville	17-S	4-W
" "	**37**	1	Huntsville	19-S	5-W
WINCHESTER	**27**	3	Huntsville	18-S	7-W
WINES	**20**	3	Huntsville	17-S	5-W
WINFIELD	**39**	3	Huntsville	19-S	3-W
WINGO	**7**	2	Huntsville	15-S	3-W
WINSTEAD	**32**	1	Huntsville	18-S	2-W
WINTER	**3**	3	Huntsville	14-S	2-W
WIRE	**32**	5	Huntsville	18-S	2-W
WISE	**32**	2	Huntsville	18-S	2-W
WOBARR	**20**	1	Huntsville	17-S	5-W
WOLF	**39**	1	Huntsville	19-S	3-W
WOMACK	**15**	1	Huntsville	16-S	2-W
WOOD	**23**	27	Huntsville	17-S	2-W
" "	**36**	14	Huntsville	19-S	6-W
" "	**6**	12	Huntsville	15-S	4-W
" "	**15**	12	Huntsville	16-S	2-W
" "	**16**	6	Huntsville	16-S	1-W
" "	**13**	3	Huntsville	16-S	4-W
" "	**29**	3	Huntsville	18-S	5-W
" "	**38**	3	Huntsville	19-S	4-W
" "	**35**	3	Huntsville	19-S	7-W
" "	**37**	2	Huntsville	19-S	5-W
" "	**2**	1	Huntsville	14-S	3-W
" "	**1**	1	Huntsville	14-S	4-W
" "	**14**	1	Huntsville	16-S	3-W
" "	**28**	1	Huntsville	18-S	6-W
WOODALL	**10**	2	Huntsville	15-S	1-E
" "	**24**	1	Huntsville	17-S	1-W
WOODARD	**13**	2	Huntsville	16-S	4-W
" "	**6**	1	Huntsville	15-S	4-W
WOODDIEL	**27**	1	Huntsville	18-S	7-W
WOODRUFF	**12**	1	Huntsville	16-S	5-W
" "	**22**	1	Huntsville	17-S	3-W
" "	**21**	1	Huntsville	17-S	4-W
WOODS	**16**	3	Huntsville	16-S	1-W
" "	**2**	2	Huntsville	14-S	3-W
" "	**29**	1	Huntsville	18-S	5-W
WOODSON	**28**	1	Huntsville	18-S	6-W
" "	**36**	1	Huntsville	19-S	6-W
WOODWARD	**6**	3	Huntsville	15-S	4-W
WOOTEN	**32**	1	Huntsville	18-S	2-W
WOOTTEN	**32**	1	Huntsville	18-S	2-W
WORNICK	**10**	2	Huntsville	15-S	1-E
WORTHINGTON	**16**	10	Huntsville	16-S	1-W
" "	**10**	4	Huntsville	15-S	1-E
" "	**25**	4	Huntsville	17-S	1-E
" "	**17**	2	Huntsville	16-S	1-E
" "	**23**	2	Huntsville	17-S	2-W
" "	**24**	1	Huntsville	17-S	1-W
" "	**33**	1	Huntsville	18-S	1-W

Surname	Map Group	Parcels of Land	Meridian/Township/Range
WORTHINGTON (Cont'd)	**30**	1	Huntsville 18-S 4-W
" "	**38**	1	Huntsville 19-S 4-W
WORTHY	**25**	1	Huntsville 17-S 1-E
" "	**33**	1	Huntsville 18-S 1-W
WRIGHT	**27**	4	Huntsville 18-S 7-W
" "	**32**	3	Huntsville 18-S 2-W
" "	**42**	2	Huntsville 20-S 5-W
" "	**28**	1	Huntsville 18-S 6-W
WRITE	**39**	1	Huntsville 19-S 3-W
WYATT	**24**	1	Huntsville 17-S 1-W
" "	**19**	1	Huntsville 17-S 6-W
" "	**43**	1	Huntsville 20-S 4-W
WYLIE	**12**	2	Huntsville 16-S 5-W
YANCEY	**10**	1	Huntsville 15-S 1-E
YANCY	**9**	1	Huntsville 15-S 1-W
YEAGER	**2**	1	Huntsville 14-S 3-W
YORK	**23**	2	Huntsville 17-S 2-W
YORKE	**23**	3	Huntsville 17-S 2-W
YOUNG	**13**	4	Huntsville 16-S 4-W
" "	**21**	2	Huntsville 17-S 4-W
" "	**29**	1	Huntsville 18-S 5-W
YOUNGBLOOD	**6**	8	Huntsville 15-S 4-W
" "	**8**	1	Huntsville 15-S 2-W
" "	**7**	1	Huntsville 15-S 3-W
" "	**16**	1	Huntsville 16-S 1-W

– Part II –

Township Map Groups

Map Group 1: Index to Land Patents

Township 14-South Range 4-West (Huntsville)

After you locate an individual in this Index, take note of the Section and Section Part then proceed to the Land Patent map on the pages immediately following. You should have no difficulty locating the corresponding parcel of land.

The "For More Info" Column will lead you to more information about the underlying Patents. See the *Legend* at right, and the "How to Use this Book" chapter, for more information.

LEGEND

"For More Info . . . " column

A = Authority (Legislative Act, See Appendix "A")
B = Block or Lot (location in Section unknown)
C = Cancelled Patent
F = Fractional Section
G = Group (Multi-Patentee Patent, see Appendix "C")
V = Overlaps another Parcel
R = Re-Issued (Parcel patented more than once)

(A & G items require you to look in the Appendixes referred to above. All other Letter-designations followed by a number require you to locate line-items in this index that possess the ID number found after the letter).

ID	Individual in Patent	Sec.	Sec. Part	Date Issued	Other Counties	For More Info . . .
100	ADCOCK, Wilson	34	NESW	1890-05-17		A4
101	" "	34	SWNW	1890-05-17		A4
102	" "	34	W½SW	1890-05-17		A4
36	AGERTON, James P	25	SESE	1858-03-01		A1
96	ATTAWAY, William M	28	N½SW	1893-07-31		A4
97	" "	28	W½NW	1893-07-31		A4
42	BOOKOUT, Jesse T	24	N½NW	1890-05-21		A4
43	" "	24	NWNE	1890-05-21		A4
44	" "	24	SWNW	1890-05-21		A4
10	BREWER, Benjamin A	14	SESE	1888-03-10	Blount	A4
11	" "	14	SESW	1888-03-10	Blount	A4
12	" "	14	W½SE	1888-03-10	Blount	A4
37	BREWER, James P	22	E½NE	1890-03-12		A4
38	" "	22	E½SE	1890-03-12		A4
54	BREWER, Joseph H	34	E½NW	1890-05-21		A4
55	" "	34	W½NE	1890-05-21		A4
24	BROWN, George	35	SENE	1834-09-10		A1
25	" "	36	SWNW	1838-09-10		A1
29	BULLARD, James A	26	SE	1890-05-17		A4
32	BULLARD, James M	12	E½NW	1884-11-01	Blount	A1
2	BURNS, Alexander H	13	NWSW	1860-09-01	Blount	A1
3	" "	13	SWNW	1860-09-01	Blount	A1
4	" "	14	NESE	1860-09-01	Blount	A1
9	BURRELL, Asa	33	W½NW	1858-03-01		A1
72	CARLISLE, Richard	24	E½NE	1890-05-21		A4
73	" "	24	NESE	1890-05-21		A4
74	" "	24	SWNE	1890-05-21		A4
94	CARLISLE, William G	24	SENW	1901-08-24		A4
67	CARROLL, Moses	36	NWSE	1852-04-01		A1
68	" "	36	SENE	1852-04-01		A1
65	" "	36	E½SE	1858-03-01		A1
66	" "	36	NESW	1858-03-01		A1
16	CODDELL, Elizabeth	26	E½NE	1890-05-21		A4
14	CREEL, Elijah N	32	S½SE	1890-05-17		A4
15	" "	32	S½SW	1890-05-17		A4
63	CREEL, Mathew M	22	SESW	1889-07-16		A4
64	" "	22	SWSE	1889-07-16		A4
49	DOCKENS, John M	32	E½NE	1885-05-04		A4
50	" "	32	N½SE	1885-05-04		A4
5	FLORENCE, Andrew J	22	E½NW	1890-05-17		A4
6	" "	22	NESW	1890-05-17		A4
7	" "	22	NWNE	1890-05-17		A4
62	GRAY, Marion C	34	NENE	1891-11-02		A4
80	INGRAM, Solomon	36	SESW	1852-04-01		A1
56	KILE, Joseph J	26	N½SW	1890-05-17		A4
57	" "	26	W½NW	1890-05-17		A4

ID	Individual in Patent	Sec.	Sec. Part	Date Issued	Other Counties	For More Info . . .
58	KITCHENS, Leander D	34	N½SE	1890-05-21		A4
59	" "	34	SENE	1890-05-21		A4
60	" "	34	SESE	1890-05-21		A4
21	LANDRUM, Felix	26	S½SW	1890-05-21		A4
87	MAYFIELD, William A	26	NENW	1883-07-03		A4
88	" "	26	NWNE	1883-07-03		A4
89	" "	26	SENW	1890-05-17		A4
90	" "	26	SWNE	1890-05-17		A4
95	MCCRARY, William J	36	N½NW	1858-03-01		A1
48	MCMICHENS, John D	34	NWNW	1891-11-02		A4
39	MIKELLS, James R	14	E½NE	1895-06-08	Blount	A4
40	" "	14	SWNE	1895-06-08	Blount	A4
91	MINTER, William E	35	E½SE	1858-03-01		A1
92	" "	35	W½NE	1858-03-01		A1
33	MITCHELL, James M	14	NESW	1888-03-10	Blount	A4
34	" "	14	SWNW	1888-03-10	Blount	A4
35	" "	14	W½SW	1888-03-10	Blount	A4
93	MITCHELL, William F	28	E½SE	1895-06-08		A4
75	MOTE, Richard	12	W½NW	1888-03-10	Blount	A4
76	" "	12	W½SW	1888-03-10	Blount	A4
19	ODOM, Emma L	12	E½SE	1890-05-17	Blount	A4 G184
20	" "	12	NWSE	1890-05-17	Blount	A4 G184
19	ODOM, James P	12	E½SE	1890-05-17	Blount	A4 G184
20	" "	12	NWSE	1890-05-17	Blount	A4 G184
1	OGLETREE, Absalom T	24	SW	1891-11-02		A4
30	OWENS, James A	24	W½SE	1890-03-12		A4
52	PARRIS, John T	28	S½SW	1890-05-17		A4
53	" "	28	W½SE	1890-05-17		A4
45	PARRISH, Joel	32	NWNW	1895-01-24		A4
31	REEVES, James H	28	NE	1889-07-16		A4
99	RICE, William	32	W½NE	1858-03-01		A1
46	ROBBINS, John B	35	E½SW	1858-03-01		A1
47	" "	35	SWSW	1858-03-01		A1
51	ROBERTS, John	24	SESE	1900-07-21		A4
84	SAVAGE, Thomas J	32	E½NW	1890-05-21		A4
85	" "	32	NESW	1890-05-21		A4
86	" "	32	SWNW	1890-05-21		A4
27	SCHLEY, Jacob H	22	W½NW	1890-05-17		A4
28	" "	22	W½SW	1890-05-17		A4
71	SHARIT, R G	36	SWSE	1896-04-23		A4
77	SHIPP, Rolley J	14	E½NW	1888-03-10	Blount	A4
78	" "	14	NWNE	1888-03-10	Blount	A4
79	" "	14	NWNW	1888-03-10	Blount	A4
81	SLOAN, Sterling W	36	N½NE	1858-03-01		A1
82	" "	36	SENW	1858-03-01		A1
83	" "	36	SWNE	1858-03-01		A1
26	SPEAR, George	36	W½SW	1821-09-05		A1
13	THOMAS, David	27	E½NW	1858-03-01		A1
61	THOMAS, Linsey	27	W½NE	1858-03-01		A1
69	THOMAS, Nathan T	22	NWSE	1883-07-03		A4
70	" "	22	SWNE	1883-07-03		A4
98	THOMAS, William R	12	NE	1888-03-10	Blount	A4
17	WARD, Emanuel R	34	SESW	1895-11-05		A4
18	" "	34	SWSE	1895-11-05		A4
22	WATSON, Francis M	12	E½SW	1888-03-10	Blount	A4
23	" "	12	SWSE	1888-03-10	Blount	A4
41	WHITE, James W	28	E½NW	1893-07-31		A4
8	WOOD, Andrew J	32	NWSW	1902-07-03		A4

Patent Map

T14-S R4-W
Huntsville Meridian

Map Group 1

Township Statistics

Parcels Mapped	:	102
Number of Patents	:	61
Number of Individuals	:	57
Patentees Identified	:	56
Number of Surnames	:	47
Multi-Patentee Parcels	:	2
Oldest Patent Date	:	9/5/1821
Most Recent Patent	:	7/3/1902
Block/Lot Parcels	:	0
Parcels Re - Issued	:	0
Parcels that Overlap	:	0
Cities and Towns	:	0
Cemeteries	:	0

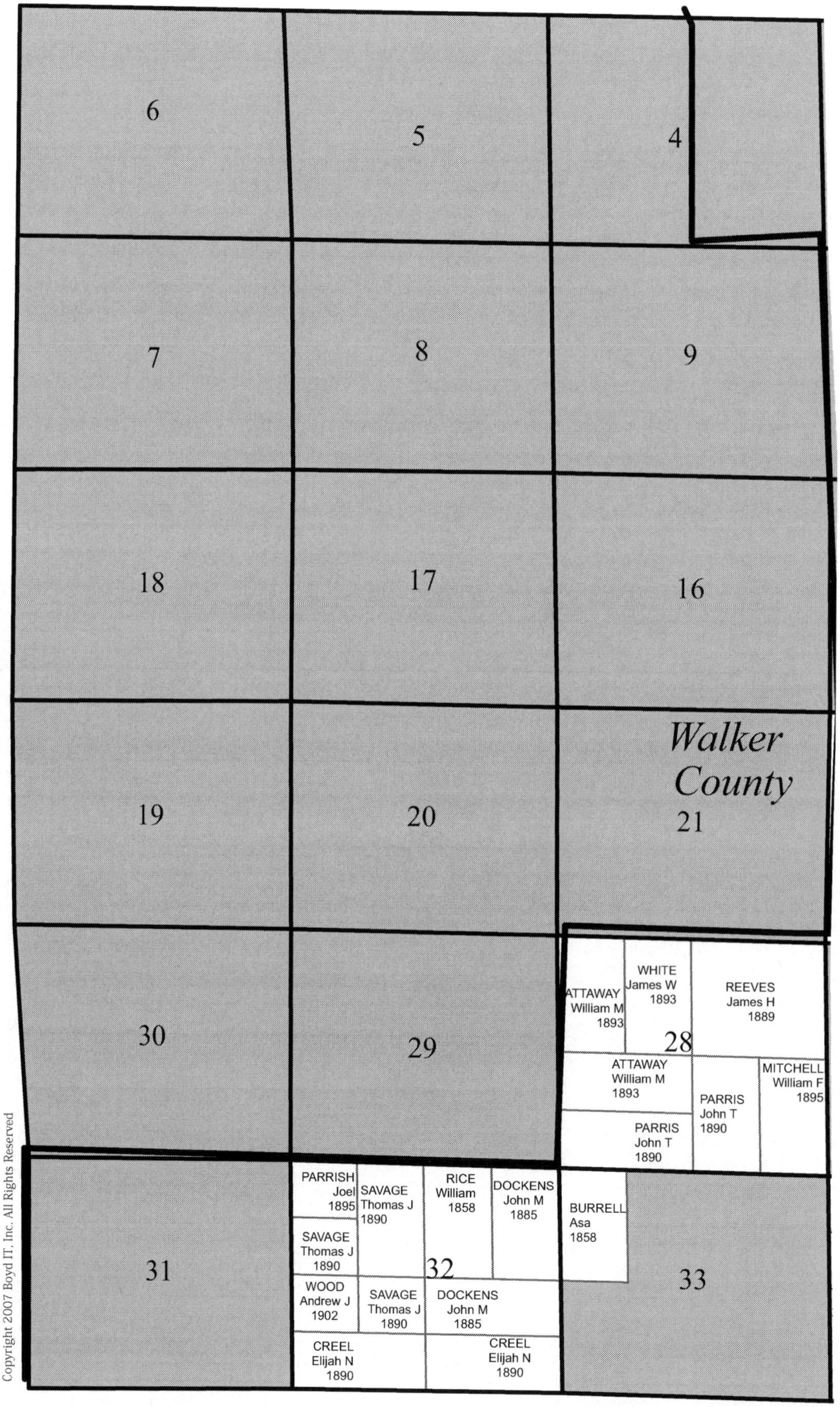

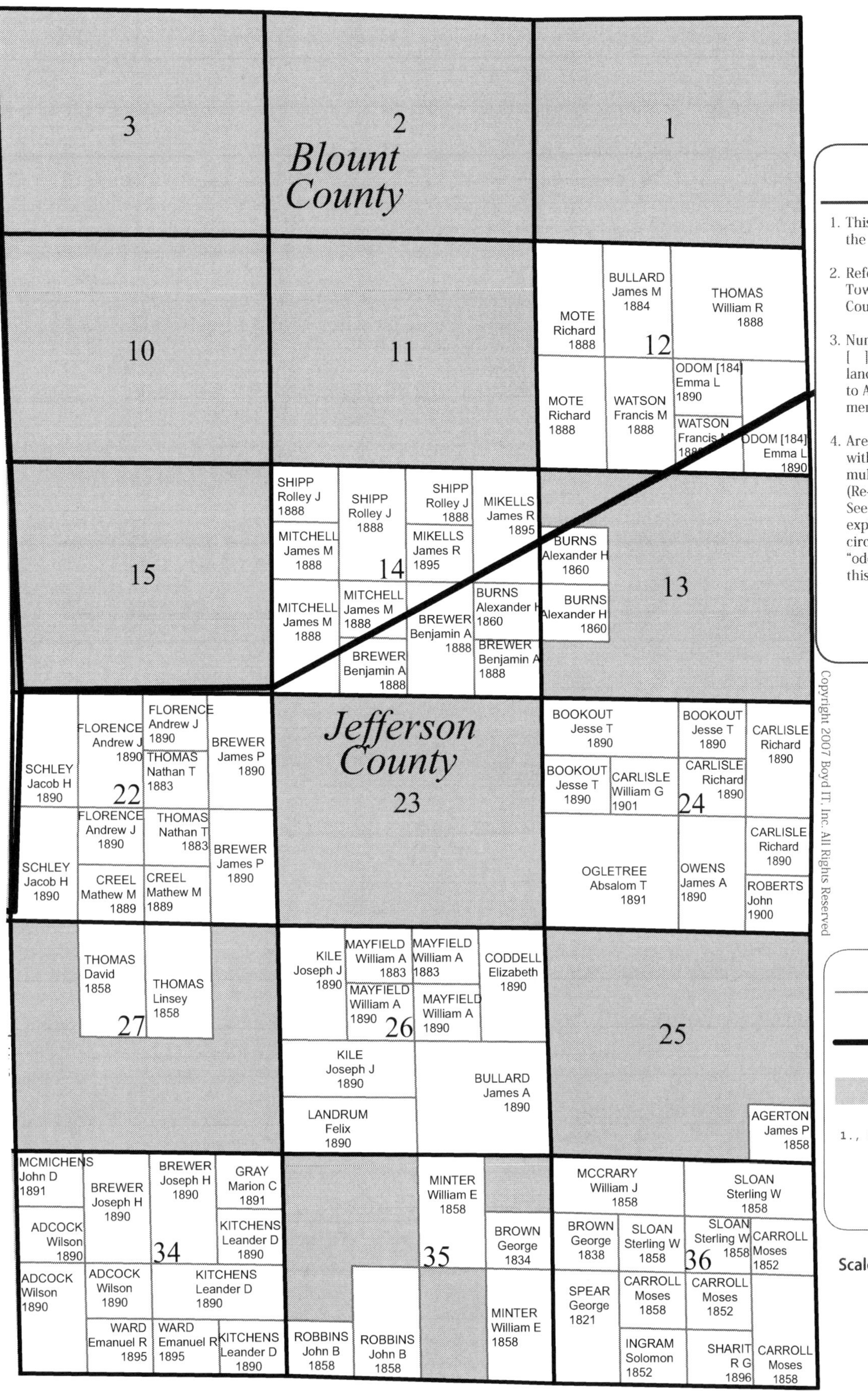

Helpful Hints

1. This Map's INDEX can be found on the preceding pages.
2. Refer to Map "C" to see where this Township lies within Jefferson County, Alabama.
3. Numbers within square brackets [ ] denote a multi-patentee land parcel (multi-owner). Refer to Appendix "C" for a full list of members in this group.
4. Areas that look to be crowded with Patentees usually indicate multiple sales of the same parcel (Re-issues) or Overlapping parcels. See this Township's Index for an explanation of these and other circumstances that might explain "odd" groupings of Patentees on this map.

Legend

- Patent Boundary
- Section Boundary
- No Patents Found (or Outside County)
- 1., 2., 3., ... Lot Numbers (when beside a name)
- [ ] Group Number (see Appendix "C")

Scale: Section = 1 mile X 1 mile (generally, with some exceptions)

Road Map

T14-S R4-W
Huntsville Meridian

Map Group 1

Cities & Towns

None

Cemeteries

None

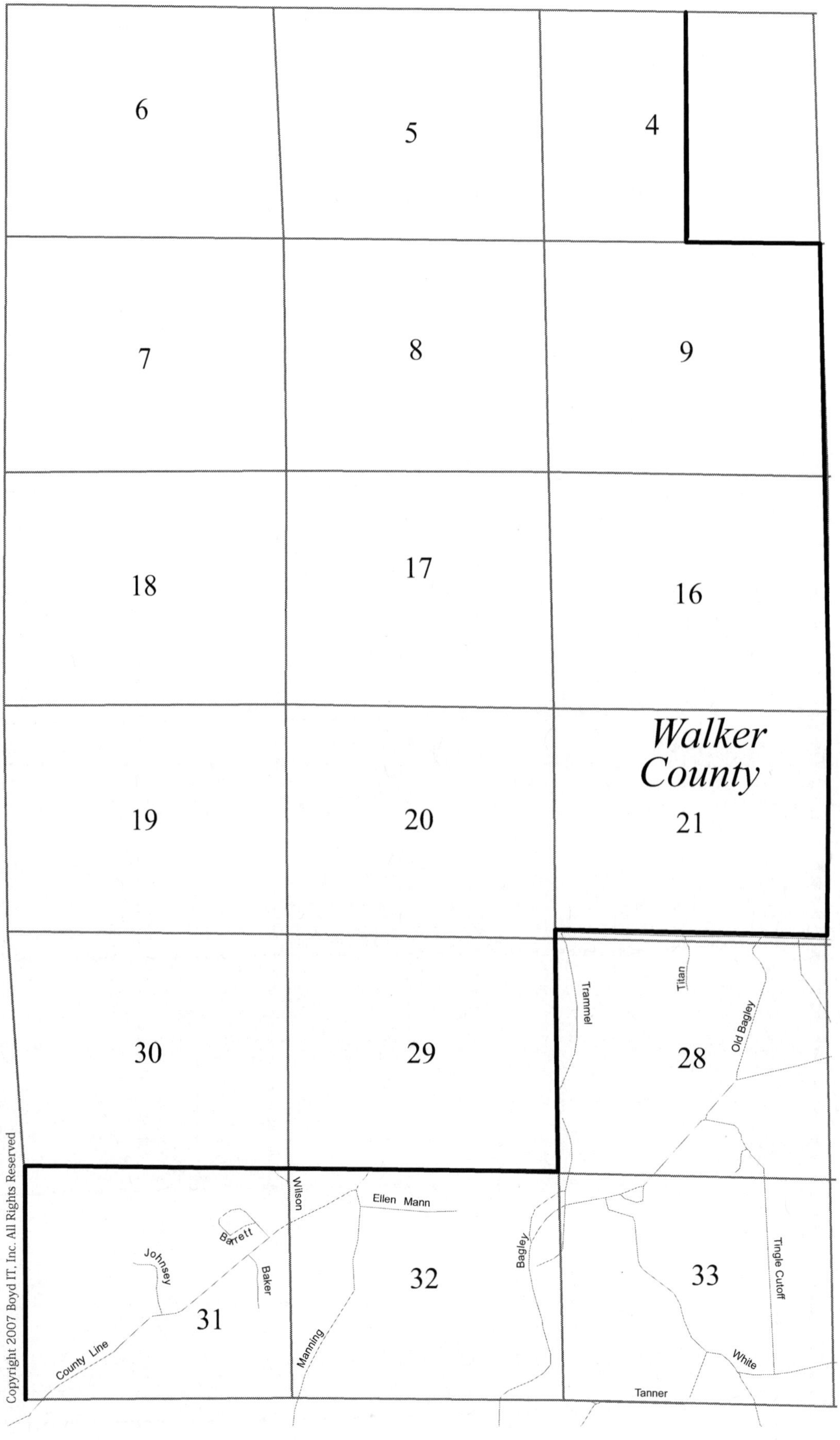

6
5
4
7
8
9
18
17
16
19
20
Walker County
21
30
29
28
Trammel
Titan
Old Bagley
31
32
33
Wilson
Ellen Mann
Barrett
Johnsey
Baker
Bagley
Tingle Cutoff
County Line
Manning
White
Tanner
Copyright 2007 Boyd IT, Inc. All Rights Reserved

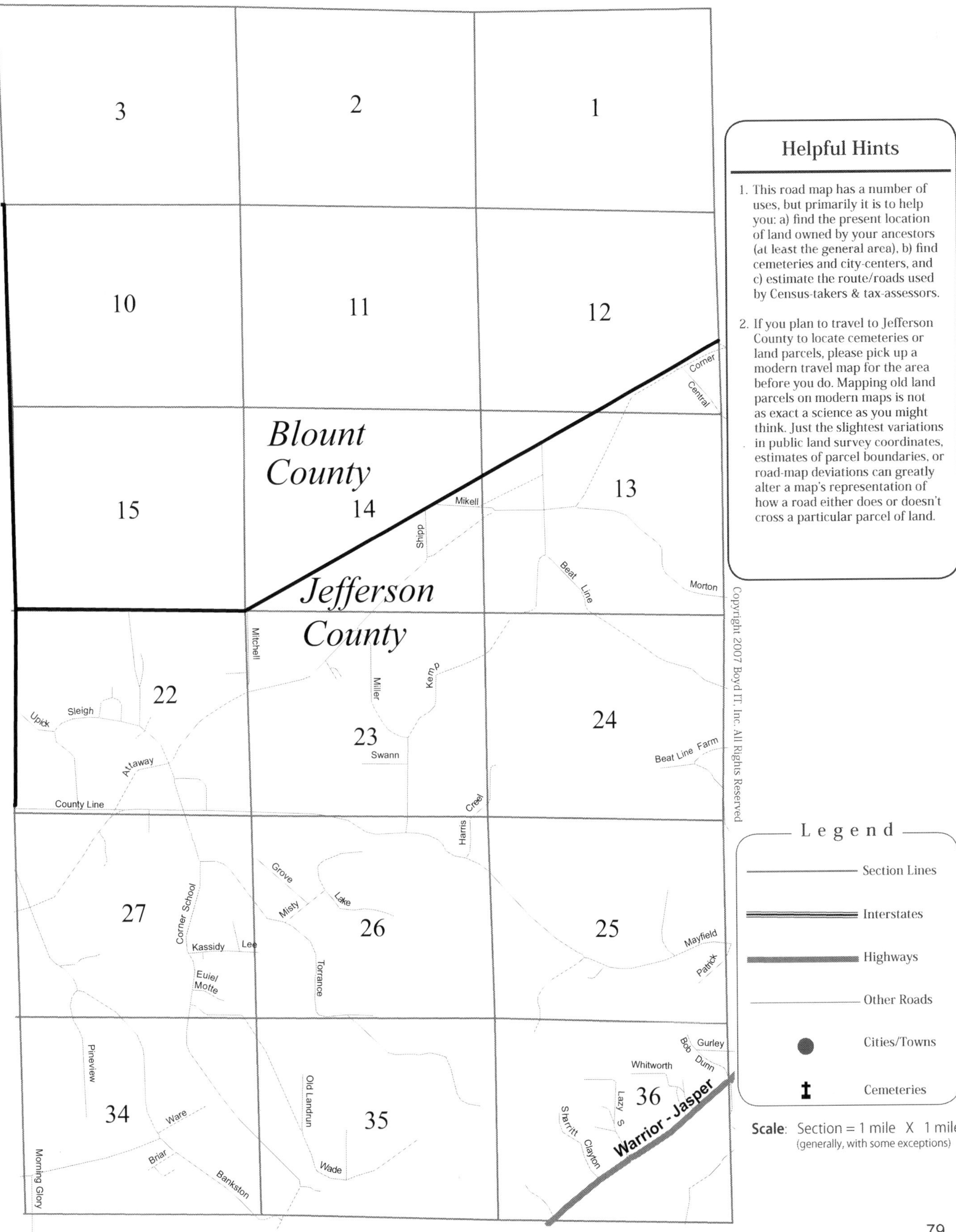
3
2
1
10
11
12
15
14
13
Blount County
Jefferson County
Corner
Central
Mikell
Shipp
Beat Line
Morton
22
23
24
Mitchell
Miller
Kemp
Upick
Sleigh
Attaway
Swann
Beat Line Farm
County Line
Creel
Harris
27
26
25
Grove
Misty
Lake
Corner School
Kassidy
Lee
Euiel Motte
Torrance
Mayfield
Patrick
34
35
36
Pineview
Ware
Briar
Bankston
Morning Glory
Old Landrun
Wade
Bob Dunn
Gurley
Whitworth
Lazy S
Starritt
Clayton
Warrior - Jasper
Helpful Hints
1. This road map has a number of uses, but primarily it is to help you: a) find the present location of land owned by your ancestors (at least the general area), b) find cemeteries and city-centers, and c) estimate the route/roads used by Census-takers & tax-assessors.
2. If you plan to travel to Jefferson County to locate cemeteries or land parcels, please pick up a modern travel map for the area before you do. Mapping old land parcels on modern maps is not as exact a science as you might think. Just the slightest variations in public land survey coordinates, estimates of parcel boundaries, or road-map deviations can greatly alter a map's representation of how a road either does or doesn't cross a particular parcel of land.
Legend
Section Lines
Interstates
Highways
Other Roads
Cities/Towns
Cemeteries
Scale: Section = 1 mile X 1 mile
(generally, with some exceptions)

Historical Map

T14-S R4-W
Huntsville Meridian

Map Group 1

Cities & Towns
None

Cemeteries
None

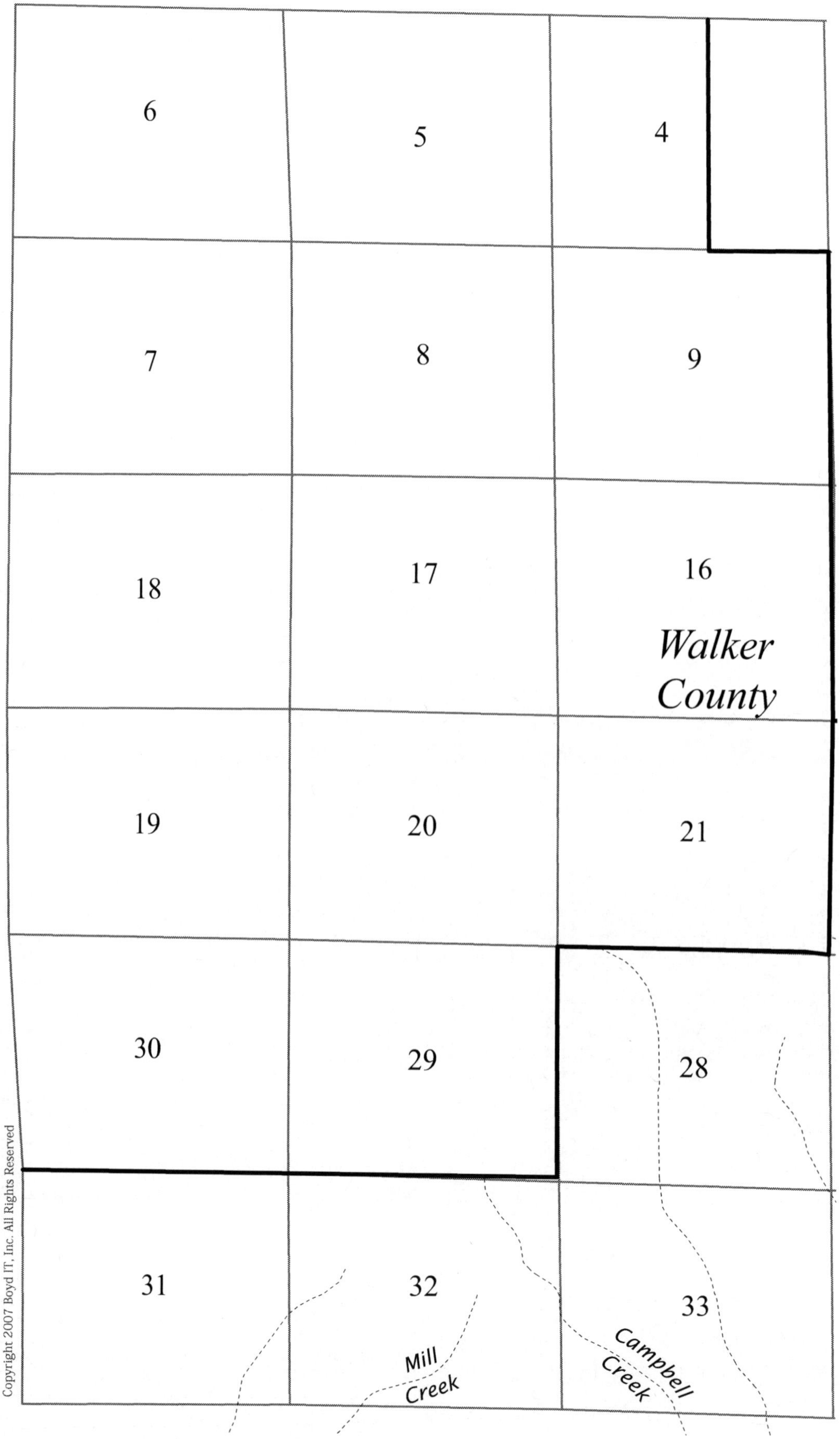

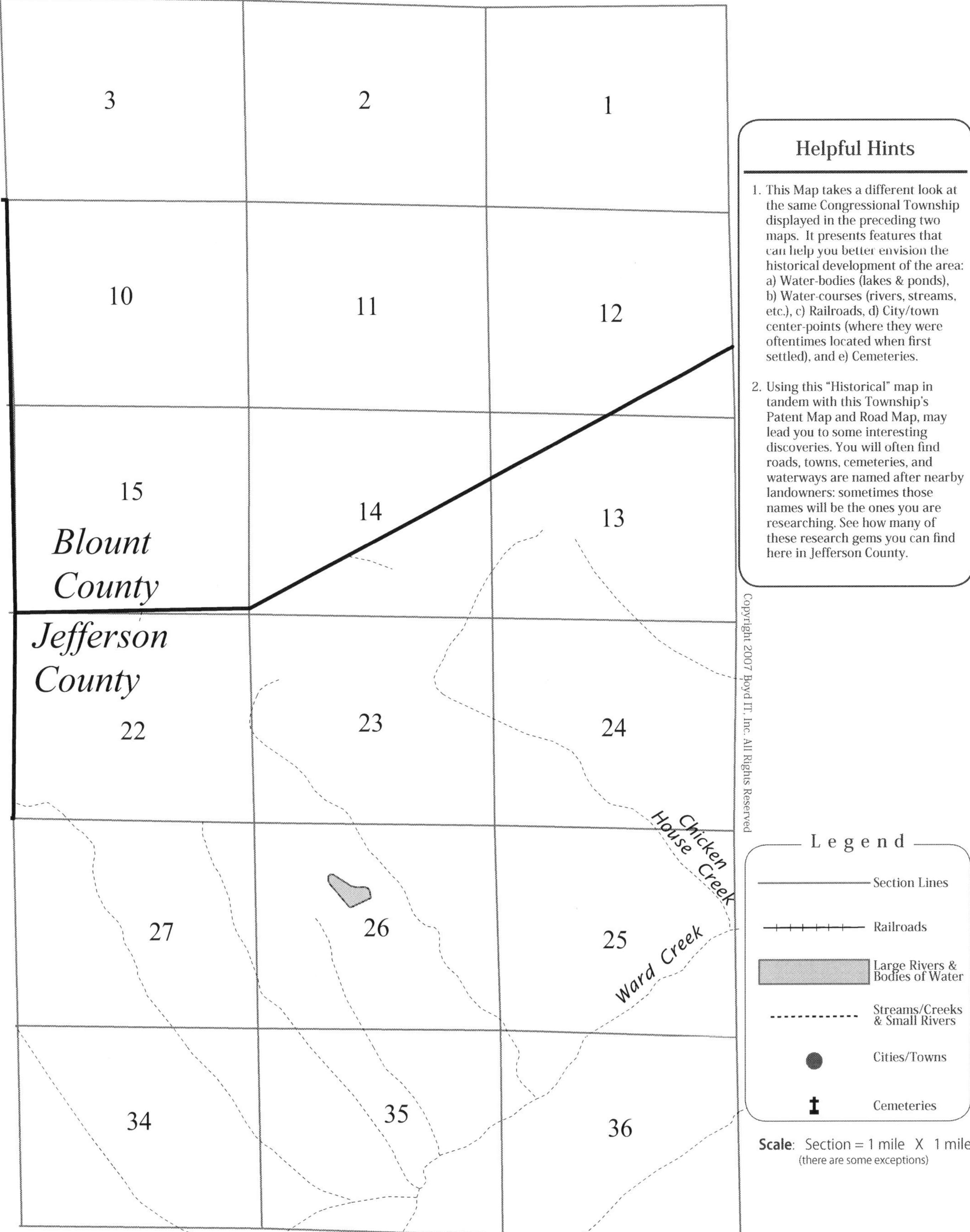
3
2
1
10
11
12
15
14
13
Blount County
Jefferson County
22
23
24
27
26
25
34
35
36
Chicken House Creek
Ward Creek
Copyright 2007 Boyd IT, Inc. All Rights Reserved
Helpful Hints
1. This Map takes a different look at the same Congressional Township displayed in the preceding two maps. It presents features that can help you better envision the historical development of the area: a) Water-bodies (lakes & ponds), b) Water-courses (rivers, streams, etc.), c) Railroads, d) City/town center-points (where they were oftentimes located when first settled), and e) Cemeteries.
2. Using this "Historical" map in tandem with this Township's Patent Map and Road Map, may lead you to some interesting discoveries. You will often find roads, towns, cemeteries, and waterways are named after nearby landowners: sometimes those names will be the ones you are researching. See how many of these research gems you can find here in Jefferson County.
Legend
Section Lines
Railroads
Large Rivers & Bodies of Water
Streams/Creeks & Small Rivers
Cities/Towns
Cemeteries
Scale: Section = 1 mile X 1 mile
(there are some exceptions)

Map Group 2: Index to Land Patents

Township 14-South Range 3-West (Huntsville)

After you locate an individual in this Index, take note of the Section and Section Part then proceed to the Land Patent map on the pages immediately following. You should have no difficulty locating the corresponding parcel of land.

The "For More Info" Column will lead you to more information about the underlying Patents. See the *Legend* at right, and the "How to Use this Book" chapter, for more information.

LEGEND

"For More Info . . . " column

A = Authority (Legislative Act, See Appendix "A")
B = Block or Lot (location in Section unknown)
C = Cancelled Patent
F = Fractional Section
G = Group (Multi-Patentee Patent, see Appendix "C")
V = Overlaps another Parcel
R = Re-Issued (Parcel patented more than once)

(A & G items require you to look in the Appendixes referred to above. All other Letter-designations followed by a number require you to locate line-items in this index that possess the ID number found after the letter).

ID	Individual in Patent	Sec.	Sec. Part	Date Issued	Other Counties	For More Info . . .
178	AGERTON, James P	30	SWSW	1858-03-01		A1
177	" "	30	SESW	1860-03-01		A1
193	AKERS, John J	8	NESE	1882-06-30		A1
194	" "	8	S½SE	1883-07-03		A4
255	BALCOM, Stephen	26	SENW	1884-02-20		A4
256	" "	26	SWNE	1884-02-20		A4
252	BARTON, Sarah	21	SENW	1839-08-01		A1
259	BARTON, Thomas	20	W½NE	1828-06-12		A1
258	" "	15	W½SW	1831-10-04		A1
260	" "	21	SWSW	1834-09-04		A1
261	" "	28	NENW	1838-09-10		A1
169	BATES, James	35	SWSE	1837-08-05		A1
128	BIBB, Charles B	22	SESW	1911-03-23		A1
197	BIBB, John M	34	NWNW	1883-07-03		A4
270	BIBB, William	27	NESW	1858-03-01		A1
271	" "	27	NWSE	1858-03-01		A1
118	BLACKBURN, Arrena	15	E½SE	1858-03-01		A1
158	BLACKBURN, Harden H	23	W½SW	1857-04-02		A1
272	BLACKBURN, William	22	NWNE	1839-08-01		A1
144	BRADFORD, Ezekiel H	8	NWSW	1890-12-31		A4
145	" "	8	S½SW	1890-12-31		A4
146	" "	8	SWNW	1890-12-31		A4
247	BRADFORD, Robert A	8	SENW	1906-05-14		A4
166	BRAKE, Jacob	35	W½NW	1857-04-02		A1
216	BREWER, Joseph	18	E½NW	1884-12-05		A4
122	BROWN, Benjamin	11	NWSW	1839-08-01		A1
123	" "	23	NESW	1839-08-01		A1
131	BROWN, Crawford	10	SENE	1835-09-04		A1
191	CAMP, John	17	W½NE	1840-10-10		A1
264	CAMP, Thompson	20	NESW	1839-08-01		A1
265	" "	20	NWSW	1839-08-01		A1
171	CAMPBELL, James H	18	W½NW	1888-03-10		A4
190	CAMPBELL, John B	23	SWNW	1858-03-01		A1
189	" "	23	N½NW	1860-09-01		A1
274	CAMPBELL, William	22	W½SE	1858-03-01		A1
283	CAMPBELL, William H	32	NWSE	1884-11-01		A4
285	" "	32	SWNE	1884-11-01		A4
282	" "	32	NESE	1890-03-12		A4
284	" "	32	SENE	1890-03-12		A4
237	CARROLL, Moses	31	NW	1858-03-01		A1
248	CHAPPELL, Robert	19	S½SE	1858-03-01		A1
249	" "	30	E½NE	1858-03-01		A1
253	CHAPPELL, Secretary W	30	NENW	1875-06-15		A4
254	" "	30	NWNE	1875-06-15		A4
266	CHAPPELL, William A	32	E½NW	1890-02-07		A1
267	" "	32	N½NE	1890-02-07		A1

ID	Individual in Patent	Sec.	Sec. Part	Date Issued	Other Counties	For More Info . . .
160	CLOWER, Hillery R	17	SESW	1858-03-01		A1
286	COTNAM, William H	29	NWNE	1838-09-10		A1
275	CRAIK, William	36	N½NE	1876-04-05		A1
170	CREEL, James F	32	S½SE	1884-11-01		A1
220	CREEL, Joshua A	28	W½SW	1884-11-01		A4
219	" "	28	SWNW	1893-07-06		A4
152	CUNNINGHAM, George	36	NENW	1839-08-01		A1
188	CUNNINGHAM, Jesse	33	NWSE	1850-05-01		A1
238	DANIELL, Moses N	22	N½SW	1884-11-01		A4
153	DAVENPORT, George	35	E½SE	1860-03-01		A1
276	DOCKINGS, William	32	W½NW	1884-11-20		A4
277	" "	32	W½SW	1884-11-20		A4
278	DODD, William	24	SESW	1884-11-05		A1
110	DOSS, Ambrose	36	E½SW	1858-03-01		A1
111	" "	36	NWSW	1858-03-01		A1
112	" "	36	SWNW	1858-03-01		A1
113	" "	36	W½SE	1858-03-01		A1
106	DUTTON, Aaron	15	W½SE	1823-10-20		A1
103	" "	10	E½SE	1825-11-30		A1
104	" "	10	SWSE	1838-09-10		A1 R212
105	" "	14	NWNW	1839-08-01		A1
157	DUTTON, Harden	15	SESW	1835-10-16		A1
116	FORTNER, Ansel	28	W½SE	1883-07-03		A4 R117
117	" "	28	W½SE	1890-11-11		A4 R116
243	GILBERT, Oliver L	20	NWSE	1860-09-01		A1
244	" "	20	SESE	1860-09-01		A1
245	" "	20	SESW	1883-07-03		A4
281	GILBERT, William	20	E½NE	1884-12-05		A4
287	GILL, William H	35	E½SW	1833-07-30		A1
182	GOOLD, James S	36	SENW	1875-08-30		A1
183	" "	36	SWNE	1875-08-30		A1
268	GOOLD, William A	36	NWNW	1875-08-30		A1
185	GRAVETTE, James W	22	SENW	1919-09-22		A4
263	GRIFFITHS, Thomas S	10	N½NW	1885-05-20		A1
143	HAMILTON, Elizabeth S	24	N½NE	1884-02-13		A4
224	HARPER, Lewis	18	S½SW	1890-03-12		A4
225	" "	18	SWSE	1890-03-12		A4
172	HEWITT, James H	36	SENE	1850-04-01		A1
130	HOGAN, Christopher	14	E½NE	1875-10-05		A4
173	HOPPER, James	10	NWSE	1839-08-01		A1
109	HUCKABEE, Amanda	20	SWSW	1893-07-19		A4
164	JOLLEY, Hosea B	14	NENW	1890-05-21		A4
176	JOLLY, James L	22	S½NE	1884-03-10		A4
175	" "	22	NENE	1884-11-20		A4
174	JONES, James	18	SESE	1895-10-16		A4
211	JONES, John W	12	S½NW	1883-07-03		A4
288	JONES, William J	24	NWNW	1858-03-01		A1
289	" "	24	S½SE	1858-03-01		A1
294	JONES, William T	24	NENW	1850-05-01		A1
296	" "	25	NWNE	1850-05-01		A1
293	" "	24	N½SE	1858-03-01		A1
295	" "	24	S½NE	1858-03-01		A1
135	LANINGHAM, David	8	NESW	1858-03-01		A1
196	LATHAM, John	27	SWNW	1858-03-01		A1
290	MCCOLLUM, William L	27	NWSW	1839-08-01		A1
223	MCCOY, Lewis C	10	SESW	1890-05-17		A4
250	MCCOY, Robert	8	S½NE	1875-06-30		A4
165	MCCRARY, Isaac C	30	S½SE	1883-07-03		A4
212	MCCULLOUGH, John W	10	SWSE	1858-03-01		A1 R104
213	" "	15	W½NE	1858-03-01		A1
132	MCDONALD, Daniel	36	E½SE	1885-06-25		A4
269	MCDONALD, William B	26	W½SE	1884-12-05		A4
114	MCDOUGAL, Ananias	26	N½NE	1875-08-30		A1
149	MCDOUGAL, Francis M	34	N½NE	1883-09-10		A4
262	MCKENZIE, Thomas	12	N½NW	1890-05-17		A4 R137
133	MCPHERSON, Daniel	20	SWSE	1834-09-10		A1
134	" "	21	SESW	1834-09-10		A1
279	MINTER, William E	34	E½SE	1858-03-01		A1
280	" "	35	E½NW	1858-03-01		A1
129	MOSS, Charles W	12	SE	1875-06-15		A4
257	MYRICK, Thomas B	14	W½NE	1891-01-30		A4
198	NAIL, John	32	E½SW	1883-09-10		A4
156	OWENS, Green A	30	S½NW	1883-09-15		A4

ID	Individual in Patent	Sec.	Sec. Part	Date Issued	Other Counties	For More Info . . .
155	OWENS, Green A (Cont'd)	30	NWSW	1891-06-30		A4
240	PARRIS, Nathan	18	N½SW	1884-11-01		A4
241	" "	18	NWSE	1884-11-01		A4
242	" "	18	SWNE	1884-11-01		A4
273	PASLEY, William C	14	E½SE	1883-09-10		A4
167	POINIER, Jacob	34	SWNW	1884-11-01		A4
168	" "	34	W½SW	1884-11-01		A4
115	PULLIAM, Andrew J	15	E½NE	1858-03-01		A1
192	RAGLAN, John H	28	W½NE	1884-11-01		A1
108	RAGLAND, Alexander	14	S½NW	1884-03-10		A4
124	RAGLIN, Benjamin C	10	SENW	1883-09-15		A4
125	" "	10	SWNE	1883-09-15		A4
195	RAY, John J	34	SENE	1884-11-01		A4
179	REID, James	23	S½NE	1858-03-01		A1
180	" "	24	SWSW	1858-03-01		A1
181	" "	25	NWNW	1858-03-01		A1
214	REID, Jonathan	36	SWSW	1852-04-01		A1
246	RICHMOND, Orlin D	26	W½NW	1884-02-20		A4
136	RIVERS, Dempsey	12	E½SW	1883-07-03		A4
151	RIVERS, Frederick J	20	S½NW	1875-06-15		A4
161	ROBERTS, Hiram	10	NESW	1858-03-01		A1
162	" "	10	W½SW	1858-03-01		A1
163	" "	9	SESE	1858-03-01		A1
230	ROBERTS, Martin	22	N½NW	1884-03-10		A4
303	ROBERTS, Zion Y	28	E½NE	1891-06-30		A4
304	" "	28	E½SE	1891-06-30		A4
232	ROBERTSON, Mathew	34	E½NW	1886-03-20		A4
233	" "	34	E½SW	1886-03-20		A4
217	RODGERS, Joseph	23	E½SE	1826-02-01		A1
126	ROUSE, Benjamin F	10	SWNW	1914-07-13		A4
138	ROUSE, Eli	10	N½NE	1857-04-02		A1
186	ROUSE, James W	28	E½SW	1858-03-01		A1
187	" "	33	N½NW	1858-03-01		A1
199	ROUSE, John	21	N½NW	1858-03-01		A1
200	" "	21	NWNE	1858-03-01		A1
234	ROUSE, Miles	11	E½NW	1858-03-01		A1
235	" "	11	SWNE	1858-03-01		A1
236	" "	11	SWNW	1858-03-01		A1
203	ROWE, John	14	SESW	1849-08-01		A1
202	" "	14	NWSW	1858-03-01		A1
205	" "	14	W½SE	1858-03-01		A1
201	" "	14	NESW	1860-03-01		A1
204	" "	14	SWSW	1860-03-01		A1
229	RUSSELL, Marquis H	11	E½NE	1858-03-01		A1
142	SHARIT, Elihugh V	34	W½SE	1883-07-03		A4
291	SHIPP, William	8	N½NE	1888-03-10		A4
292	" "	8	N½NW	1888-03-10		A4
139	SLOAN, Elihu G	30	N½SE	1857-04-02		A1
140	" "	30	NESW	1857-04-02		A1
141	" "	30	SWNE	1857-04-02		A1
127	SMITH, Benjamin F	22	E½SE	1891-04-22		A4
227	SMITH, Malinda J	26	NESE	1858-03-01		A1
228	" "	26	SENE	1858-03-01		A1
184	SPEAKMAN, James	30	NWNW	1858-03-01		A1
215	STEELE, Jonathan	27	E½SE	1840-10-10		A1
107	STOUT, Abraham	26	SESE	1838-09-10		A1
150	THOMAS, Franklin C	12	S½NE	1876-04-01		A4
154	THOMAS, George	26	SWSW	1834-09-10		A1
209	THOMAS, John	21	NWSW	1857-04-02		A1
210	" "	21	SWNW	1857-04-02		A1
239	THOMAS, Nancy	26	NENW	1849-09-01		A1
251	THOMAS, Samuel	8	NWSE	1896-04-07		A4
300	THOMAS, William	33	NESE	1850-05-01		A1
297	" "	28	NWNW	1857-04-02		A1
298	" "	28	SENW	1858-03-01		A1
299	" "	29	NENW	1858-03-01		A1
226	TIDWELL, Lucius L	20	N½NW	1890-04-05		A1
231	TIDWELL, Mary E	12	W½SW	1883-07-03		A4
206	TRAMMELL, John T	18	N½NE	1893-10-13		A4
207	" "	18	NESE	1893-10-13		A4
208	" "	18	SENE	1893-10-13		A4
119	TRUSS, Arthur	27	SWSE	1849-09-01		A1 G221
120	" "	33	SWSE	1849-09-01		A1 G221

ID	Individual in Patent	Sec.	Sec. Part	Date Issued	Other Counties	For More Info . . .
121	TRUSS, Arthur (Cont'd)	34	SWNE	1850-05-01		A1 G221
119	TRUSS, John	27	SWSE	1849-09-01		A1 G221
120	" "	33	SWSE	1849-09-01		A1 G221
121	" "	34	SWNE	1850-05-01		A1 G221
119	TRUSS, Thomas K	27	SWSE	1849-09-01		A1 G221
120	" "	33	SWSE	1849-09-01		A1 G221
121	" "	34	SWNE	1850-05-01		A1 G221
159	TUTTLE, Henry	35	W½SW	1822-11-28		A1
147	WARE, Francis A	24	NESW	1884-02-13		A4
148	" "	24	SENW	1884-02-13		A4
222	WEBB, Julius	23	SENW	1858-03-01		A1
218	WEISMAN, Joseph	35	NWSE	1838-09-10		A1
221	WOOD, Joshua	23	SWSE	1834-09-10		A1
301	WOODS, William	20	NESE	1839-08-01		A1
302	" "	23	NWSE	1839-08-01		A1
137	YEAGER, Eldridge J	12	N½NW	1891-06-30		A4 R262

Patent Map

T14-S R3-W
Huntsville Meridian

Map Group 2

Township Statistics

Parcels Mapped	:	202
Number of Patents	:	157
Number of Individuals	:	132
Patentees Identified	:	130
Number of Surnames	:	91
Multi-Patentee Parcels	:	3
Oldest Patent Date	:	11/28/1822
Most Recent Patent	:	9/22/1919
Block/Lot Parcels	:	0
Parcels Re - Issued	:	3
Parcels that Overlap	:	0
Cities and Towns	:	2
Cemeteries	:	2

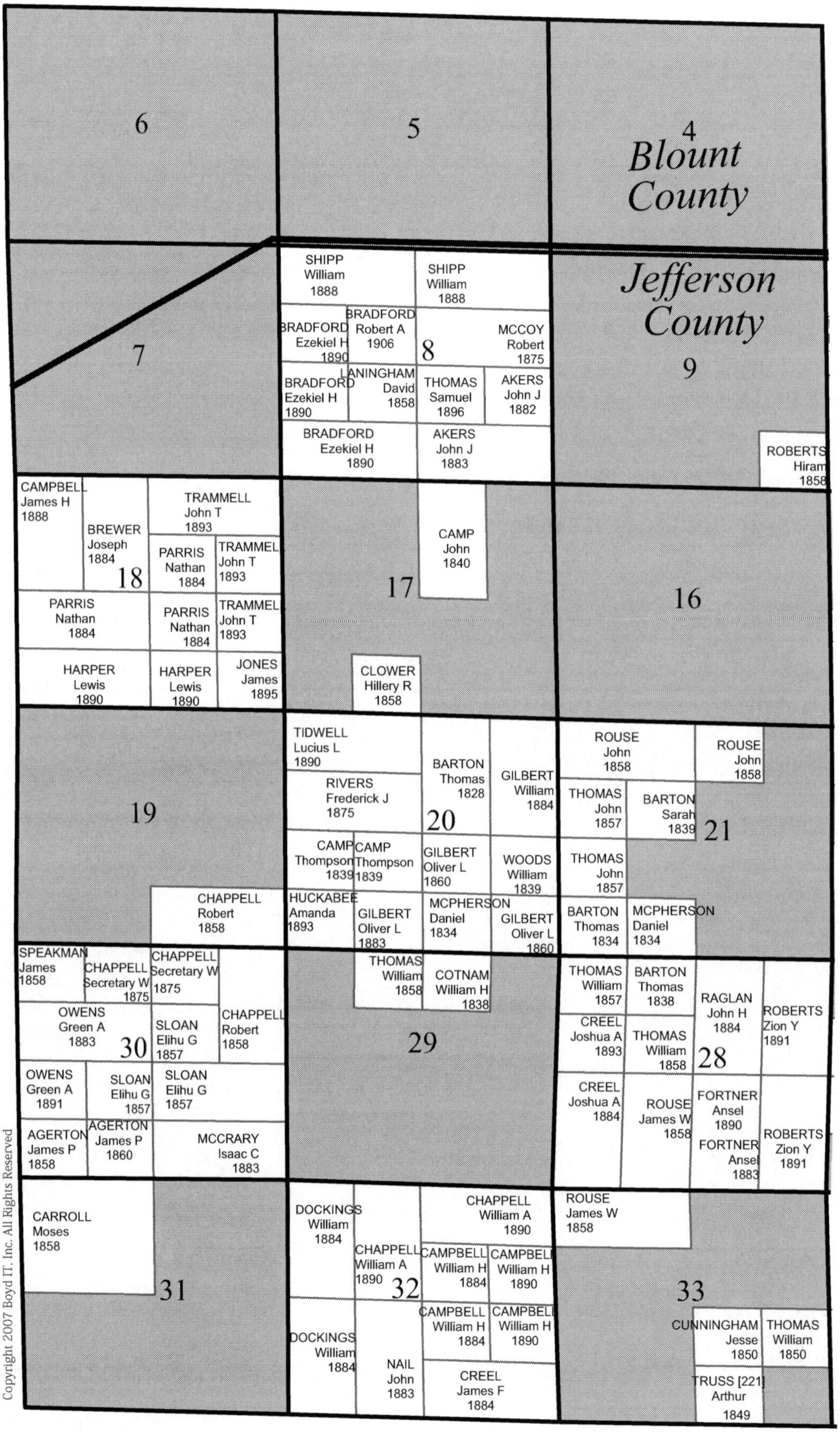

Helpful Hints

1. This Map's INDEX can be found on the preceding pages.
2. Refer to Map "C" to see where this Township lies within Jefferson County, Alabama.
3. Numbers within square brackets [ ] denote a multi-patentee land parcel (multi-owner). Refer to Appendix "C" for a full list of members in this group.
4. Areas that look to be crowded with Patentees usually indicate multiple sales of the same parcel (Re-issues) or Overlapping parcels. See this Township's Index for an explanation of these and other circumstances that might explain "odd" groupings of Patentees on this map.

Legend

- Patent Boundary
- Section Boundary
- No Patents Found (or Outside County)
- 1., 2., 3., ... Lot Numbers (when beside a name)
- [ ] Group Number (see Appendix "C")

Scale: Section = 1 mile X 1 mile (generally, with some exceptions)

Road Map

T14-S R3-W
Huntsville Meridian

Map Group 2

Cities & Towns

- Kimberly
- Warrior

Cemeteries

- Brewer Cemetery
- Cain Creek Cemetery

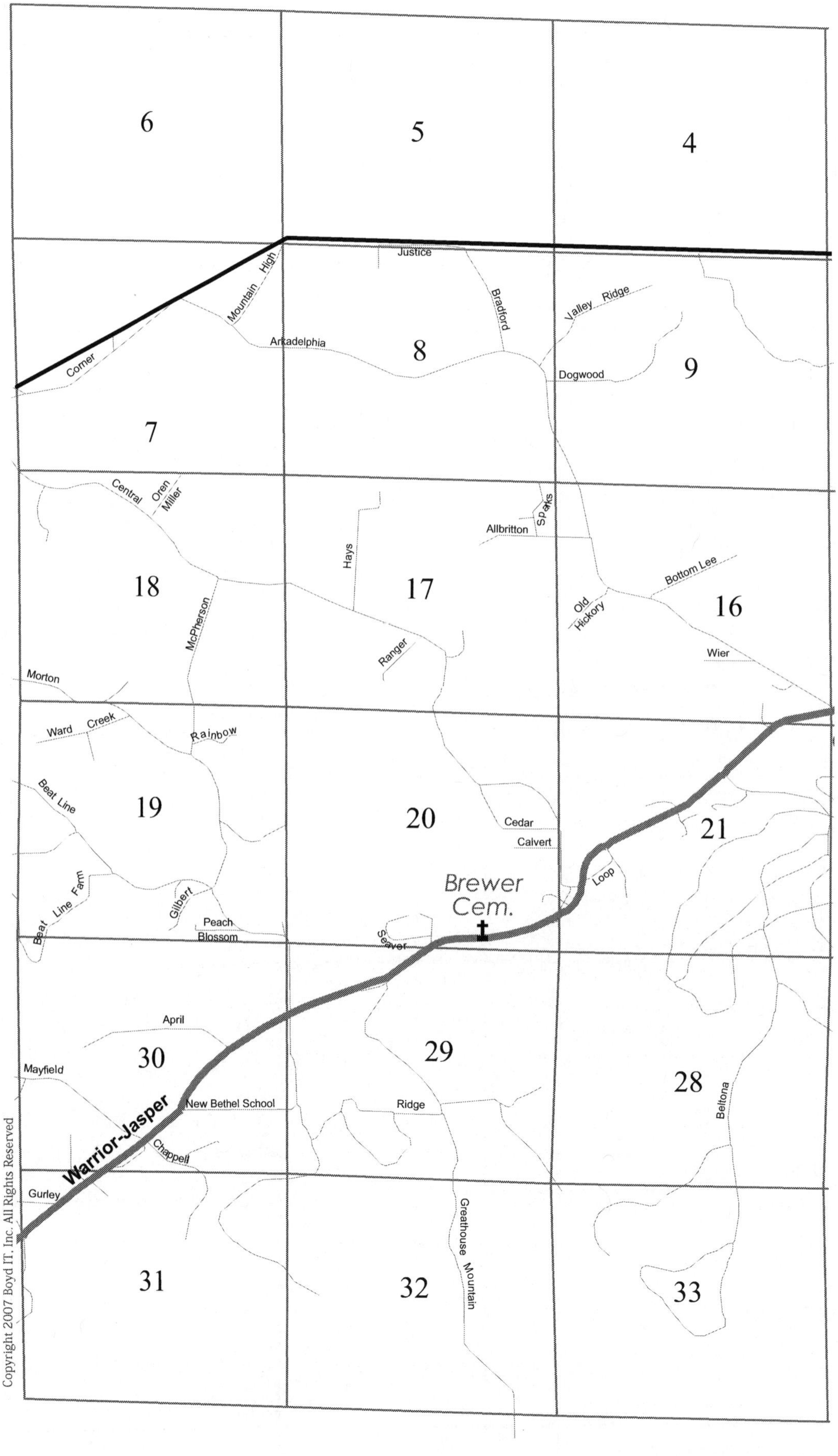

6 5 4

7 8 9

18 17 16

19 20 21

30 29 28

31 32 33

Justice
Mountain High
Bradford
Valley Ridge
Arkadelphia
Corner
Dogwood
Central
Oren Miller
Sparks
Allbritton
Hays
Bottom Lee
Old Hickory
McPherson
Ranger
Wier
Morton
Ward Creek
Rainbow
Beat Line
Cedar
Calvert
Loop
Brewer Cem.
Beat Line Farm
Gilbert
Peach Blossom
Seaver
April
Mayfield
New Bethel School
Ridge
Beltona
Warrior-Jasper
Chappell
Gurley
Greathouse Mountain

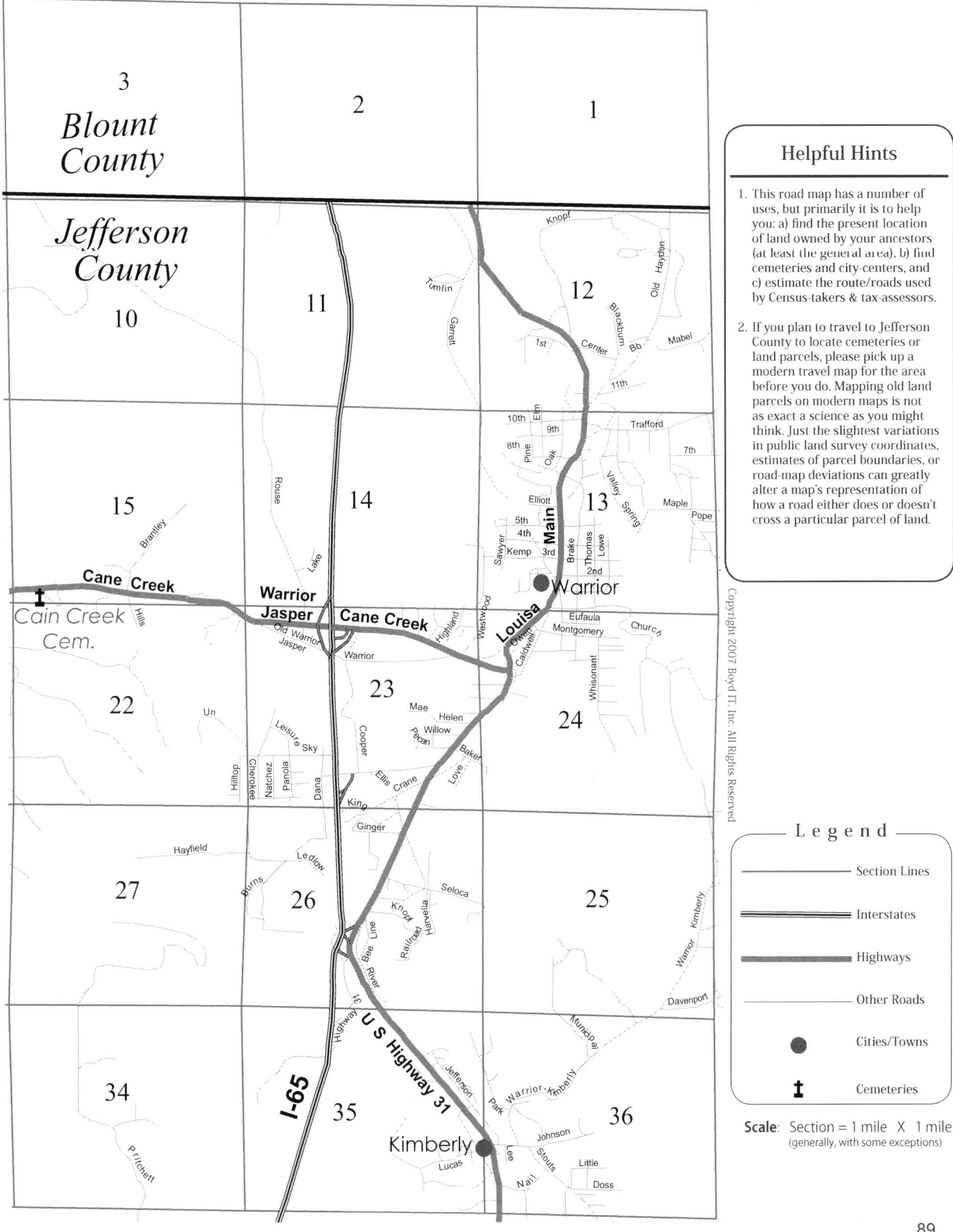

Helpful Hints

1. This road map has a number of uses, but primarily it is to help you: a) find the present location of land owned by your ancestors (at least the general area), b) find cemeteries and city-centers, and c) estimate the route/roads used by Census-takers & tax-assessors.

2. If you plan to travel to Jefferson County to locate cemeteries or land parcels, please pick up a modern travel map for the area before you do. Mapping old land parcels on modern maps is not as exact a science as you might think. Just the slightest variations in public land survey coordinates, estimates of parcel boundaries, or road-map deviations can greatly alter a map's representation of how a road either does or doesn't cross a particular parcel of land.

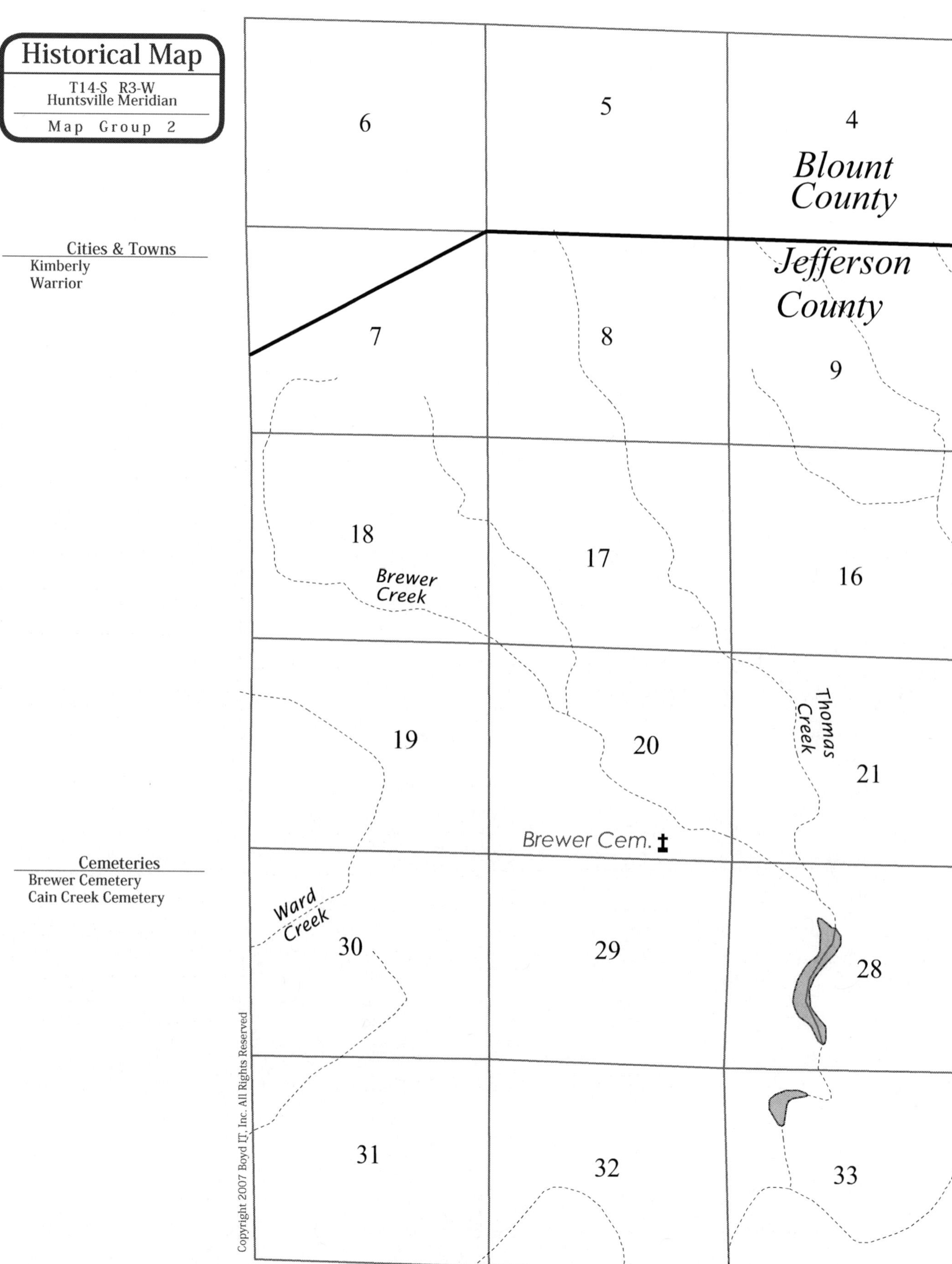
Historical Map
T14-S R3-W
Huntsville Meridian
Map Group 2
Cities & Towns
Kimberly
Warrior
Cemeteries
Brewer Cemetery
Cain Creek Cemetery
6
5
4
Blount County
Jefferson County
7
8
9
18
17
16
Brewer Creek
19
20
21
Thomas Creek
Brewer Cem.
Ward Creek
30
29
28
31
32
33
Copyright 2007 Boyd IT, Inc. All Rights Reserved

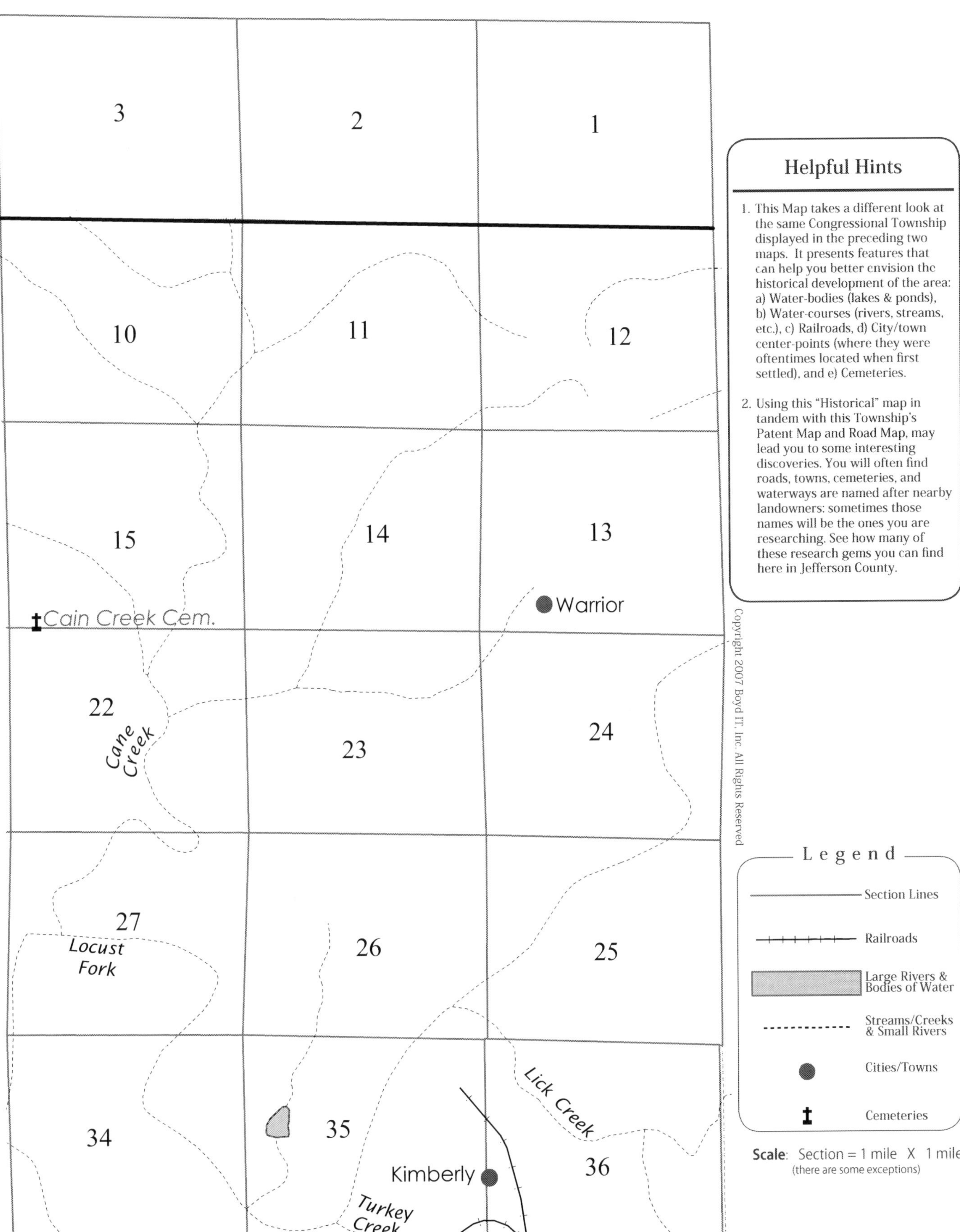

Helpful Hints

1. This Map takes a different look at the same Congressional Township displayed in the preceding two maps. It presents features that can help you better envision the historical development of the area: a) Water-bodies (lakes & ponds), b) Water-courses (rivers, streams, etc.), c) Railroads, d) City/town center-points (where they were oftentimes located when first settled), and e) Cemeteries.

2. Using this "Historical" map in tandem with this Township's Patent Map and Road Map, may lead you to some interesting discoveries. You will often find roads, towns, cemeteries, and waterways are named after nearby landowners: sometimes those names will be the ones you are researching. See how many of these research gems you can find here in Jefferson County.

Legend

- Section Lines
- Railroads
- Large Rivers & Bodies of Water
- Streams/Creeks & Small Rivers
- Cities/Towns
- Cemeteries

Scale: Section = 1 mile X 1 mile
(there are some exceptions)

Map Group 3: Index to Land Patents

Township 14-South Range 2-West (Huntsville)

After you locate an individual in this Index, take note of the Section and Section Part then proceed to the Land Patent map on the pages immediately following. You should have no difficulty locating the corresponding parcel of land.

The "For More Info" Column will lead you to more information about the underlying Patents. See the *Legend* at right, and the "How to Use this Book" chapter, for more information.

LEGEND

"For More Info . . . " column

A = Authority (Legislative Act, See Appendix "A")
B = Block or Lot (location in Section unknown)
C = Cancelled Patent
F = Fractional Section
G = Group (Multi-Patentee Patent, see Appendix "C")
V = Overlaps another Parcel
R = Re-Issued (Parcel patented more than once)

(A & G items require you to look in the Appendixes referred to above. All other Letter-designations followed by a number require you to locate line-items in this index that possess the ID number found after the letter).

ID	Individual in Patent	Sec.	Sec. Part	Date Issued	Other Counties	For More Info . . .
430	ADAMS, Richard B	8	E½SE	1858-03-01		A1
364	ANDERSON, Harrison	24	W½SW	1858-03-01	Blount	A1
387	ANDERSON, John	24	NESW	1857-04-02	Blount	A1
388	" "	24	S½NW	1857-04-02	Blount	A1
386	" "	14	N½NW	1875-06-15	Blount	A4
443	ANDERSON, Thomas	24	SWSE	1852-03-10	Blount	A1
444	" "	25	NENE	1852-03-10		A1
440	" "	14	S½SE	1857-04-02	Blount	A1
442	" "	24	NWNW	1857-04-02	Blount	A1
441	" "	23	W½NE	1858-03-01		A1
308	ASHLEY, Andrew J	25	SENE	1854-06-15		A1
309	" "	25	SWNE	1858-03-01		A1
306	BRAMLET, Alonzo	18	NESW	1883-09-15		A4
307	" "	18	NWSE	1883-09-15		A4
375	BRAMLETT, James	8	W½SW	1884-11-01		A1
414	BROOKS, Margaret	18	NENW	1888-11-02		A1
415	" "	18	NWNE	1888-11-02		A1
371	BROWNE, Isaac	7	E½SE	1823-10-20		A1
372	CADDELL, Isaac J	20	N½NW	1884-03-10		A4
400	CASE, Joseph D	19	SENE	1858-03-01		A1
451	CASE, William	18	SWSE	1837-08-05		A1
453	" "	30	SENE	1838-09-10		A1
452	" "	19	NENE	1839-08-01		A1
454	COCKE, William	22	S½SE	1883-07-03		A4
398	DAVIDSON, John W	22	NENW	1885-06-25		A4
399	" "	22	NWNE	1885-06-25		A4
395	DAVIS, John R	18	S½NE	1883-07-03		A4
437	DEAN, Sarah E	36	NE	1884-11-01		A4
368	DORMAN, Hiram T	36	NESW	1895-08-08		A4
394	DORNING, John P	28	SWNE	1839-08-01		A1
391	" "	28	NESW	1858-03-01		A1
392	" "	28	NWSE	1858-03-01		A1
393	" "	28	SENW	1858-03-01		A1
455	DORNING, William	26	NENW	1858-03-01		A1
456	" "	26	W½NW	1858-03-01		A1
403	DOSS, Lafayette A	30	N½SE	1891-06-30		A4
404	" "	30	SENW	1891-06-30		A4
405	" "	30	SWNE	1891-06-30		A4
305	DUTTON, Aaron	7	W½NE	1823-10-01		A1
350	ENDSLEY, Francis M	14	SESW	1894-09-25	Blount	A4
351	" "	14	W½SW	1894-09-25	Blount	A4
413	ENDSLEY, Marcus J	10	S½NE	1884-11-01	Blount	A4
416	ENDSLEY, Martha S	34	SWSW	1891-11-23		A1
428	FAUCETT, Nancy	36	S½SW	1883-07-03		A4
457	FINDLEY, William G	36	SE	1888-10-11		A4
432	FOSSETT, Samuel	23	NESW	1857-04-02		A1

ID	Individual in Patent	Sec.	Sec. Part	Date Issued	Other Counties	For More Info . . .
434	FOSSETT, Samuel (Cont'd)	23	S½SW	1857-04-02		A1
433	" "	23	NWSW	1858-03-01		A1
348	GAMMAGE, Floyd	10	E½SW	1858-03-01	Blount	A1
349	" "	10	SE	1858-03-01	Blount	A1
369	GILLESPIE, Ira P	24	N½NE	1890-05-17	Blount	A4
370	" "	24	NENW	1890-05-17	Blount	A4
352	GLENN, Francis M	34	NENE	1857-04-02		A1
354	" "	34	SWNE	1857-04-02		A1
353	" "	34	NWNE	1858-03-01		A1
355	" "	35	SWNW	1858-03-01		A1
315	GOODWIN, Benjamin	22	SENW	1858-03-01		A1
316	" "	22	SWNE	1858-03-01		A1
342	GOODWIN, Elijah	22	N½SE	1858-03-01		A1
410	GOODWIN, Mannon	28	N½NW	1858-03-01		A1
411	" "	28	NWNE	1858-03-01		A1
412	GOODWIN, Manon	21	SESW	1854-06-15		A1
458	GOODWIN, William	21	NWSE	1858-03-01		A1
459	" "	21	SWNE	1858-03-01		A1
374	GURLEY, James A	24	SESE	1923-02-06	Blount	A1
337	GUTHERY, Eli	18	S½SW	1883-09-10		A4
338	" "	30	W½NW	1891-06-30		A4
438	GUTHERY, Sarah	30	SW	1891-06-30		A4
358	HAGOOD, George M	24	SESW	1854-06-15	Blount	A1
431	HAGOOD, Robert I	25	NWNW	1854-06-15		A1
435	HALL, Samuel	20	NENE	1888-11-02		A1
328	HANBY, David	10	SWNW	1850-04-01	Blount	A1
329	" "	17	NESE	1850-04-01		A1
330	" "	21	NESW	1854-06-15		A1
331	" "	8	SESW	1857-04-02		A1
332	" "	8	SWSE	1857-04-02		A1
333	HANLY, David	17	NWSE	1850-04-01		A1
324	HOGAN, Christopher	18	W½NW	1875-10-05		A4
460	HUFFSTUTTER, William	8	W½NW	1884-11-01		A1
361	HUGHES, George W	34	SESW	1850-08-10		A1
377	HUGHES, James M	20	E½SE	1883-09-15		A4
384	HUGHES, Jesse	27	SW	1857-04-02		A1
383	" "	27	S½NW	1858-03-01		A1
385	" "	28	E½SE	1858-03-01		A1
310	JOHN, Andrew	9	NESE	1838-09-10	Blount	A1
317	LASETER, Benjamin	26	NWSW	1857-04-02		A1
318	" "	34	NENW	1857-04-02		A1
319	LASITER, Benjamin	33	SENE	1858-03-01		A1
320	" "	34	NWSW	1858-03-01		A1
321	" "	34	SENW	1858-03-01		A1
336	LEE, Edmond F	36	S½NW	1889-07-16		A4
346	MCANALLY, Elizabeth	8	NESW	1889-12-31		A4 G164
347	" "	8	NWSE	1889-12-31		A4 G164
425	MCANALLY, Monroe	8	E½NE	1891-06-30		A4
346	MCANALLY, William	8	NESW	1889-12-31		A4 G164
347	" "	8	NWSE	1889-12-31		A4 G164
334	MCCOMBS, David	36	NWSW	1854-06-15		A1
396	MCCURRY, John R	26	E½NE	1884-03-10		A4
359	MELVIN, George N	24	NESE	1885-03-10	Blount	A4
360	" "	24	S½NE	1885-03-10	Blount	A4
445	MELVIN, Thomas G	10	SWSW	1895-01-24	Blount	A4
462	MINOR, William	20	NESW	1884-02-13		A4
463	" "	20	SENW	1884-02-13		A4
390	MINTER, John J	32	NE	1891-06-30		A4
420	MINTER, Mary E	32	N½SW	1884-11-01		A4
421	" "	32	S½SW	1899-04-01		A4
325	MORTON, Dallas	22	SW	1890-04-05		A1
436	MULLINGS, Samuel	10	NENW	1835-11-07	Blount	A1
365	MULVEHILL, Henry	34	SE	1891-11-23		A1
422	MULVEHILL, Mary	32	N½NW	1891-06-30		A4 G177
422	MULVEHILL, Peter E	32	N½NW	1891-06-30		A4 G177
429	PAGE, Perry	10	N½NE	1884-11-01	Blount	A1
373	POWELL, Isaac W	32	W½SE	1875-06-15		A4 V426
426	POWELL, Moses	32	S½SE	1875-06-15		A4 V373
461	POWELL, William M	36	N½NW	1888-11-02		A1
379	REED, James	17	SWNW	1854-06-15		A1
380	REID, James	18	NENE	1839-08-01		A1
381	" "	7	NWSE	1839-08-01		A1
376	ROPER, James D	24	NWSE	1923-02-06	Blount	A1

ID	Individual in Patent	Sec.	Sec. Part	Date Issued	Other Counties	For More Info . . .
464	SELF, William P	10	NWNW	1898-06-23	Blount	A4
335	SHULTS, David	22	W½NW	1884-11-20		A4
339	SMITH, Elijah E	14	NESW	1894-09-25	Blount	A4
340	" "	14	S½NW	1894-09-25	Blount	A4
341	" "	14	SWNE	1894-09-25	Blount	A4
389	SMITH, John E	14	NWSE	1890-05-21	Blount	A4
409	SMITH, Louis J	28	E½NE	1893-07-31		A4
417	SMITH, Martha	14	N½NE	1885-03-10	Blount	A4
418	" "	14	NESE	1892-05-31	Blount	A4
419	" "	14	SENE	1892-05-31	Blount	A4
323	STATON, Christopher C	10	SENW	1885-05-20	Blount	A1
446	TAYLOR, Thomas R	26	NWNE	1884-11-01		A4
378	TERRY, James M	26	S½SE	1890-03-12		A4
439	TERRY, Stephen L	26	S½SW	1890-02-07		A1
427	THOMAS, Moses	9	N½NW	1858-03-01	Blount	A1
397	THOMPSON, John	18	SESE	1884-11-20		A4
311	TRUSS, Arthur	10	NWSW	1849-09-01	Blount	A1 G221
314	" "	9	NWSE	1849-09-01	Blount	A1 G221
312	" "	23	NENE	1850-04-01		A1 G221
313	" "	23	SENE	1850-08-10		A1 G221
311	TRUSS, John	10	NWSW	1849-09-01	Blount	A1 G221
314	" "	9	NWSE	1849-09-01	Blount	A1 G221
312	" "	23	NENE	1850-04-01		A1 G221
313	" "	23	SENE	1850-08-10		A1 G221
311	TRUSS, Thomas K	10	NWSW	1849-09-01	Blount	A1 G221
314	" "	9	NWSE	1849-09-01	Blount	A1 G221
312	" "	23	NENE	1850-04-01		A1 G221
313	" "	23	SENE	1850-08-10		A1 G221
326	TURNER, Darby	20	NWSW	1860-09-01		A1 V363
327	" "	25	NESE	1860-09-01		A1
447	WALKER, Thomas	18	SENW	1914-01-17		A4
322	WATHEN, Carl	18	NWSW	1896-01-03		A4
401	WEISMAN, Joseph	9	SESW	1838-09-10	Blount	A1
366	WHISENANT, Henry	29	SWNW	1850-08-10		A1
367	" "	32	S½NW	1858-03-01		A1
402	WHISENANT, L D	20	SESW	1884-11-05		A1
406	WHISENANT, Lorenzo D	18	NESE	1838-09-10		A1
407	" "	30	N½NE	1858-03-01		A1
408	" "	30	S½SE	1891-06-30		A4
356	WHISNANT, George E	17	SWSE	1854-06-15		A1
357	" "	20	NWNE	1858-03-01		A1
362	WHITE, Harden H	20	SWNW	1915-02-26		A4
363	" "	20	W½SW	1915-02-26		A4 V326
423	WHITE, Milton D	8	E½NW	1891-06-30		A4
424	" "	8	W½NE	1891-06-30		A4
382	WILLIAMSON, James	22	E½NE	1884-11-01		A1
343	WILSON, Elijah L	26	N½SE	1890-02-07		A1
344	" "	26	SENW	1890-02-07		A1
345	" "	26	SWNE	1890-02-07		A1
448	WINTER, William C	28	NWSW	1892-06-30		A4
449	" "	28	S½SW	1892-06-30		A4
450	" "	28	SWNW	1892-06-30		A4

Patent Map

T14-S R2-W
Huntsville Meridian

Map Group 3

Township Statistics

Parcels Mapped	:	160
Number of Patents	:	125
Number of Individuals	:	102
Patentees Identified	:	98
Number of Surnames	:	71
Multi-Patentee Parcels	:	7
Oldest Patent Date	:	10/1/1823
Most Recent Patent	:	2/6/1923
Block/Lot Parcels	:	0
Parcels Re - Issued	:	0
Parcels that Overlap	:	4
Cities and Towns	:	1
Cemeteries	:	0

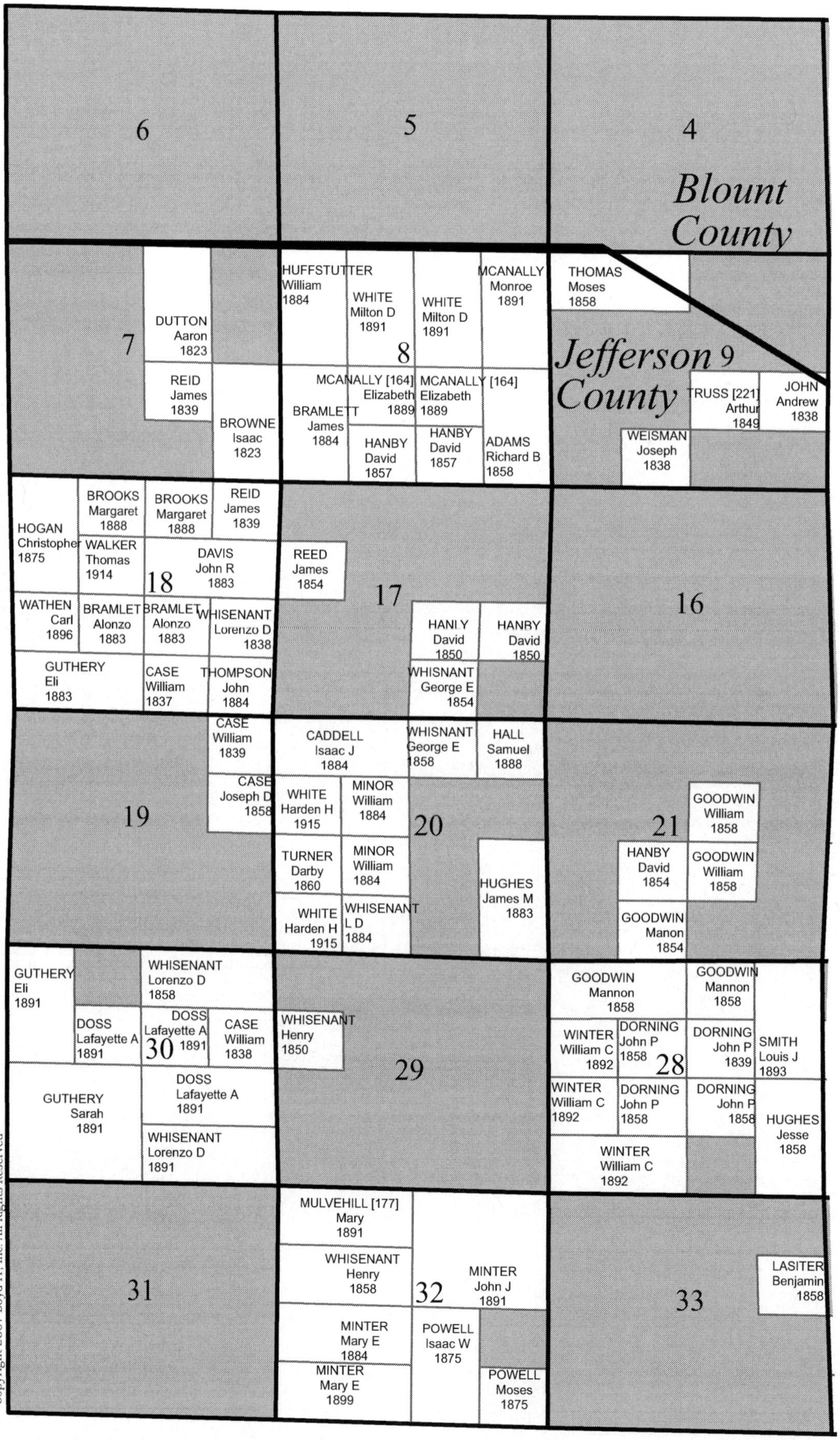

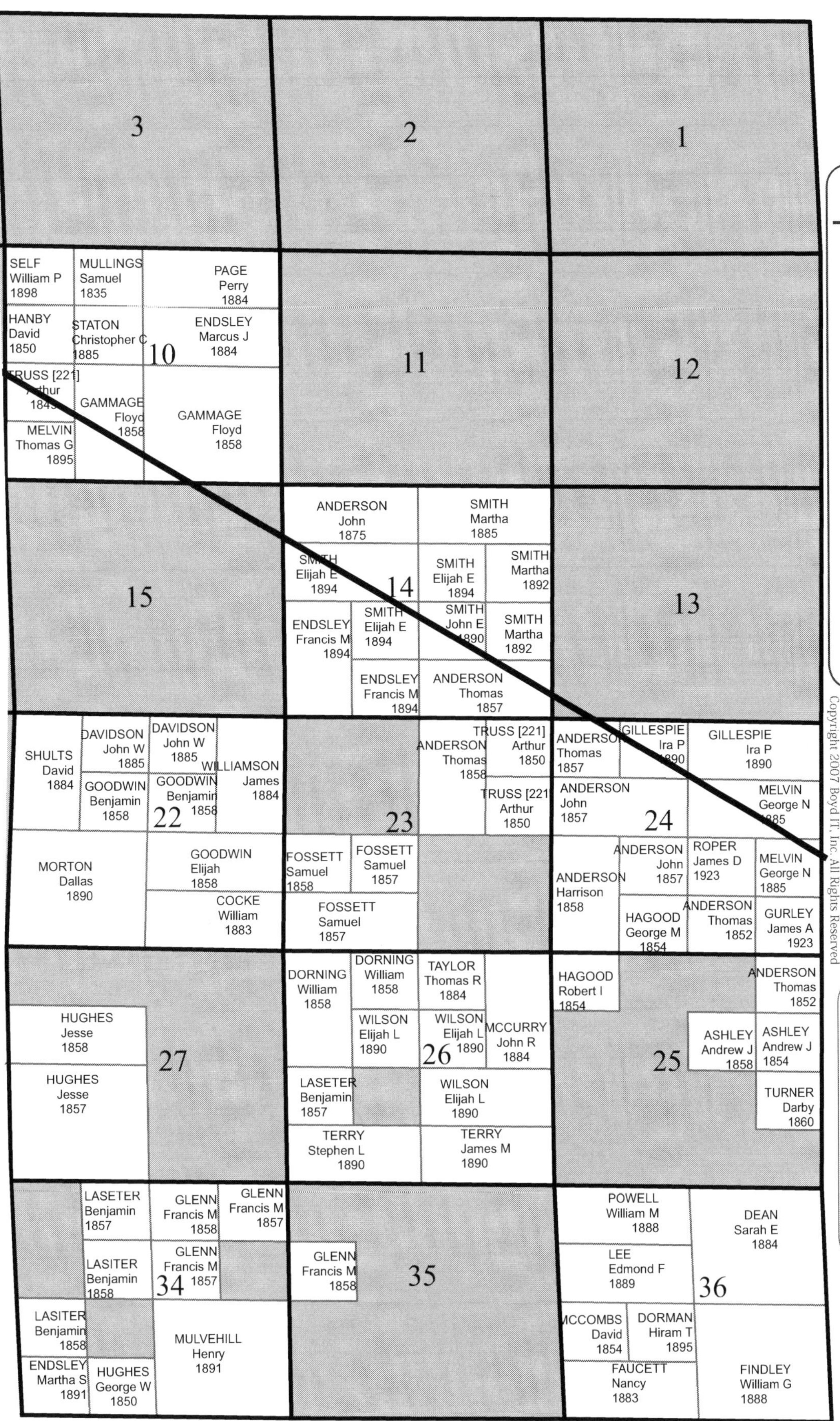

Helpful Hints

1. This Map's INDEX can be found on the preceding pages.
2. Refer to Map "C" to see where this Township lies within Jefferson County, Alabama.
3. Numbers within square brackets [ ] denote a multi-patentee land parcel (multi-owner). Refer to Appendix "C" for a full list of members in this group.
4. Areas that look to be crowded with Patentees usually indicate multiple sales of the same parcel (Re-issues) or Overlapping parcels. See this Township's Index for an explanation of these and other circumstances that might explain "odd" groupings of Patentees on this map.

Legend

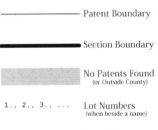

- Patent Boundary
- Section Boundary
- No Patents Found (or Outside County)
- 1., 2., 3., ... Lot Numbers (when beside a name)
- [ ] Group Number (see Appendix "C")

Scale: Section = 1 mile X 1 mile (generally, with some exceptions)

Road Map

T14-S R2-W
Huntsville Meridian

Map Group 3

Cities & Towns

Trafford

Cemeteries

None

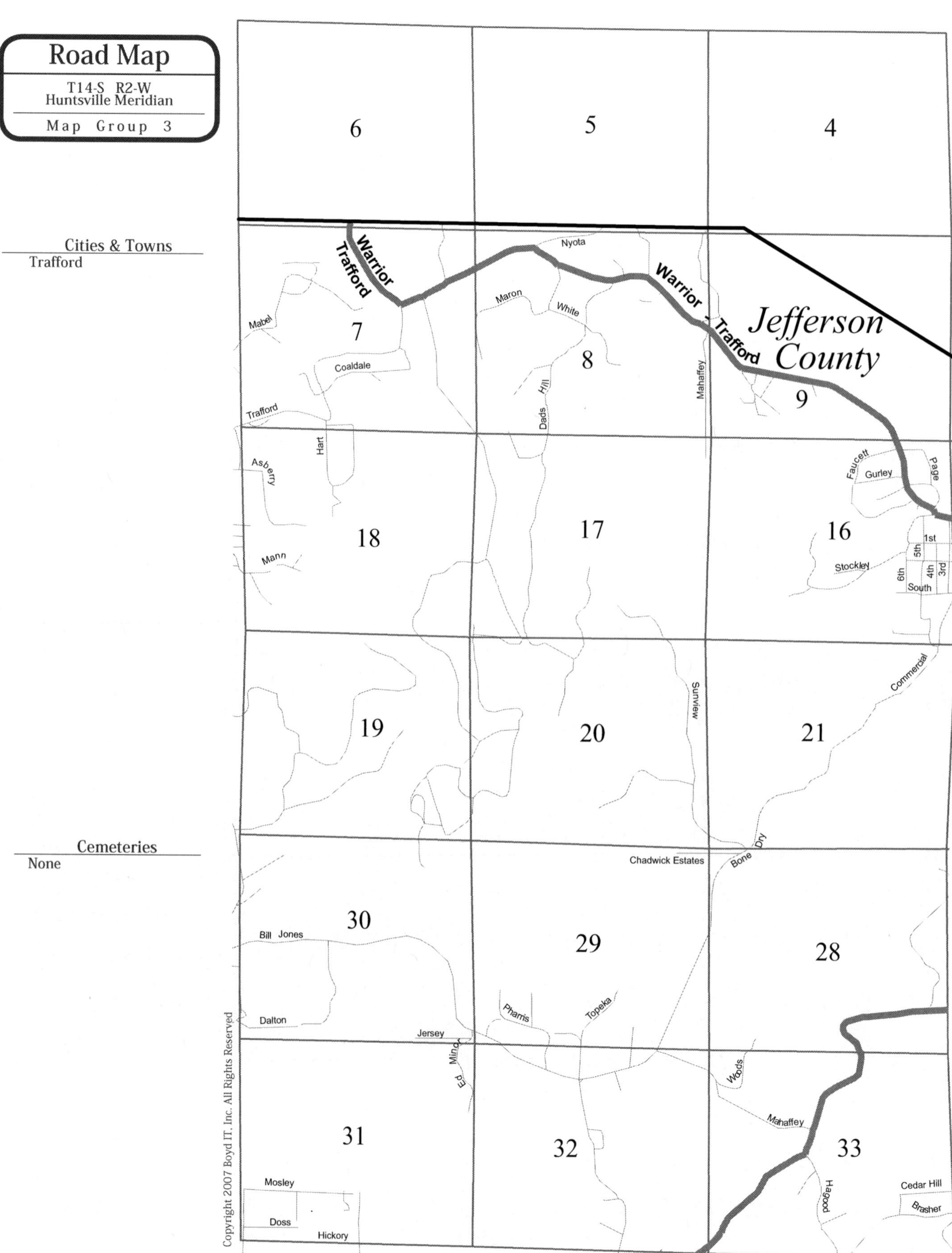

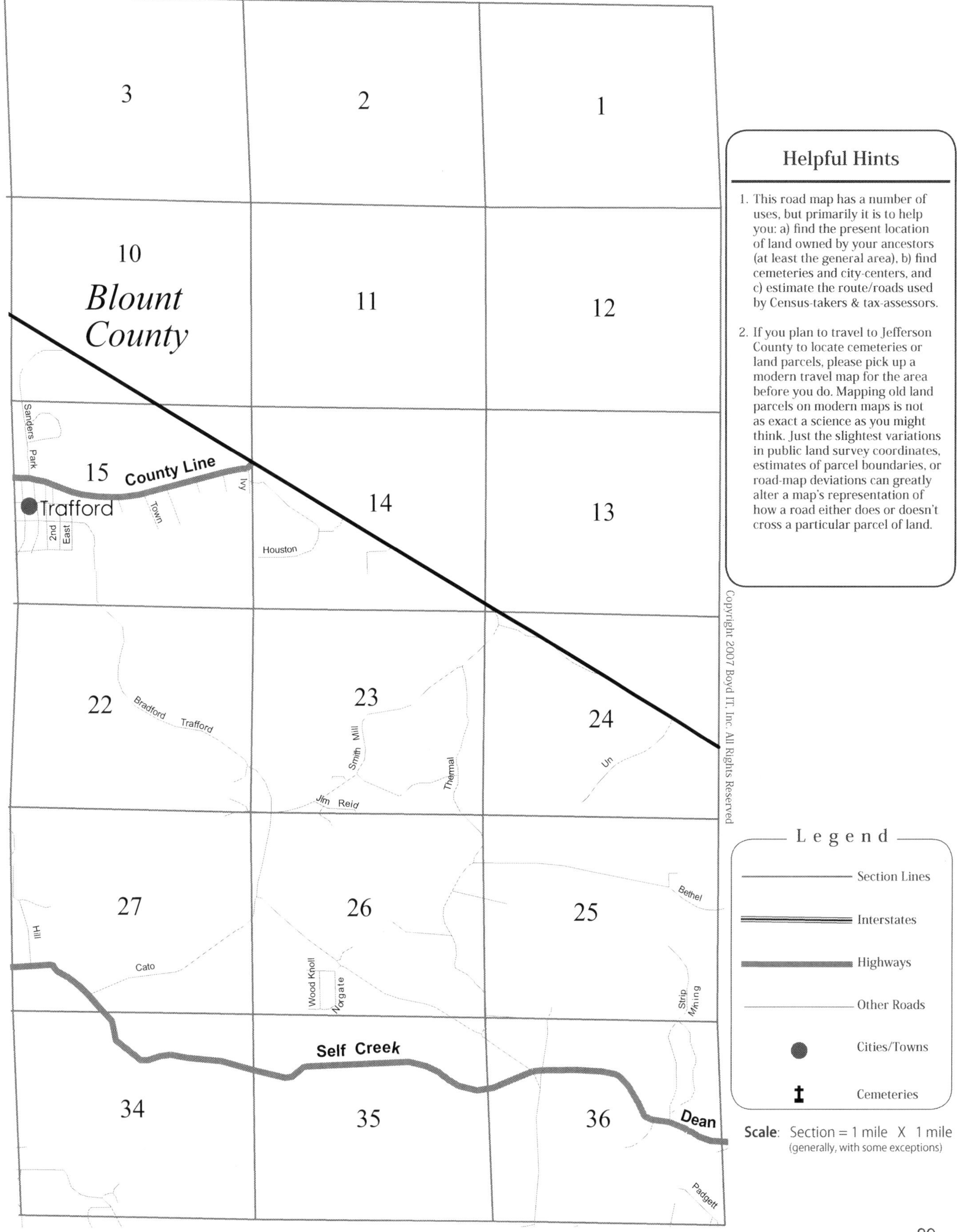
3
2
1
10
Blount County
11
12
Sanders
Park
15
County Line
Ivy
Trafford
Town
2nd
East
14
13
Houston
22
Bradford
Trafford
23
Smith Mill
Thermal
24
Un
Jim Reid
27
Hill
Cato
26
Wood Knoll
Norgate
25
Bethel
Strip Mining
Self Creek
34
35
36
Dean
Padgett
Copyright 2007 Boyd IT, Inc. All Rights Reserved
Helpful Hints
1. This road map has a number of uses, but primarily it is to help you: a) find the present location of land owned by your ancestors (at least the general area), b) find cemeteries and city-centers, and c) estimate the route/roads used by Census-takers & tax-assessors.
2. If you plan to travel to Jefferson County to locate cemeteries or land parcels, please pick up a modern travel map for the area before you do. Mapping old land parcels on modern maps is not as exact a science as you might think. Just the slightest variations in public land survey coordinates, estimates of parcel boundaries, or road-map deviations can greatly alter a map's representation of how a road either does or doesn't cross a particular parcel of land.
Legend
Section Lines
Interstates
Highways
Other Roads
Cities/Towns
Cemeteries
Scale: Section = 1 mile X 1 mile
(generally, with some exceptions)

Historical Map

T14-S R2-W
Huntsville Meridian

Map Group 3

Cities & Towns

Trafford

Cemeteries

None

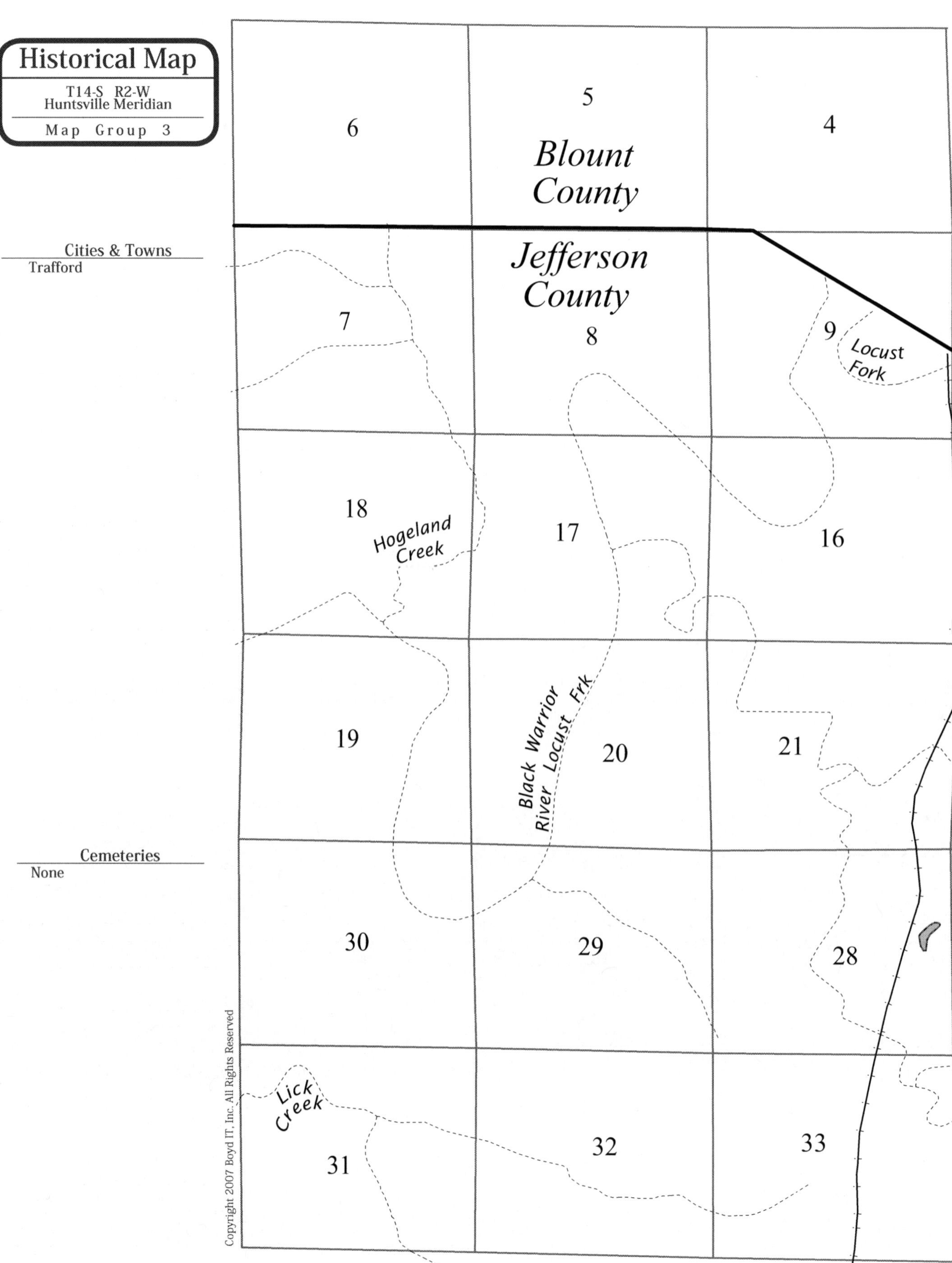

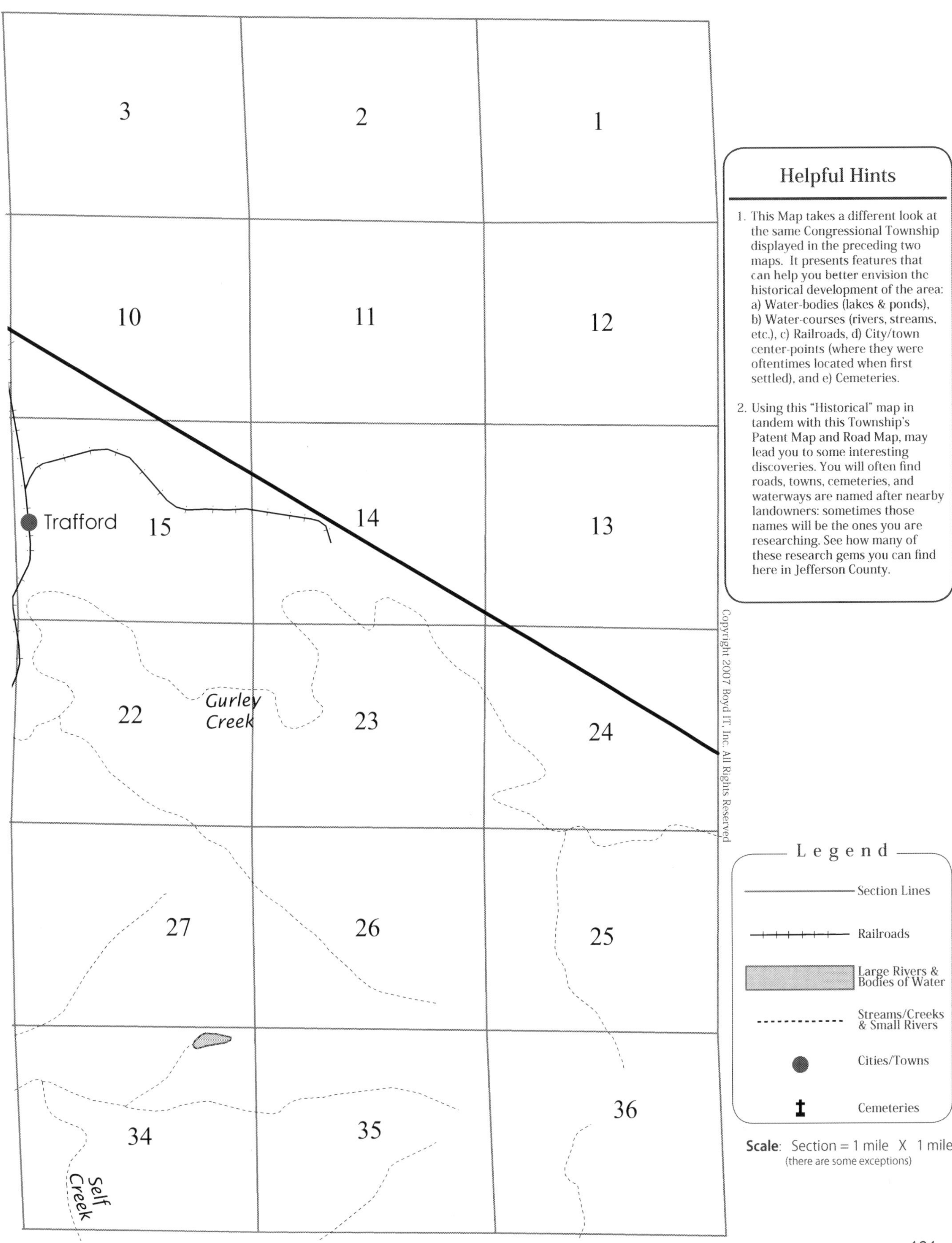

Helpful Hints

1. This Map takes a different look at the same Congressional Township displayed in the preceding two maps. It presents features that can help you better envision the historical development of the area: a) Water-bodies (lakes & ponds), b) Water-courses (rivers, streams, etc.), c) Railroads, d) City/town center-points (where they were oftentimes located when first settled), and e) Cemeteries.

2. Using this "Historical" map in tandem with this Township's Patent Map and Road Map, may lead you to some interesting discoveries. You will often find roads, towns, cemeteries, and waterways are named after nearby landowners: sometimes those names will be the ones you are researching. See how many of these research gems you can find here in Jefferson County.

Map Group 4: Index to Land Patents

Township 14-South Range 1-West (Huntsville)

After you locate an individual in this Index, take note of the Section and Section Part then proceed to the Land Patent map on the pages immediately following. You should have no difficulty locating the corresponding parcel of land.

The "For More Info" Column will lead you to more information about the underlying Patents. See the *Legend* at right, and the "How to Use this Book" chapter, for more information.

LEGEND

"For More Info . . . " column

- **A** = Authority (Legislative Act, See Appendix "A")
- **B** = Block or Lot (location in Section unknown)
- **C** = Cancelled Patent
- **F** = Fractional Section
- **G** = Group (Multi-Patentee Patent, see Appendix "C")
- **V** = Overlaps another Parcel
- **R** = Re-Issued (Parcel patented more than once)

(A & G items require you to look in the Appendixes referred to above. All other Letter-designations followed by a number require you to locate line-items in this index that possess the ID number found after the letter).

ID	Individual in Patent	Sec.	Sec. Part	Date Issued	Other Counties	For More Info . . .
467	ASHLEY, Andrew J	19	NWSW	1858-03-01	Blount	A1
469	BARTON, Catharine	33	E½NE	1835-09-04	Blount	A1
509	BURLESSON, William	31	W½SE	1826-06-15		A1
492	BYARS, John W	30	NENE	1857-04-02	Blount	A1
493	" "	30	SWNE	1857-04-02	Blount	A1
496	DEAN, Joseph	30	SE	1883-07-03	Blount	A4
512	FAUCETT, William R	32	SESE	1860-03-01		A1
513	" "	33	SWSW	1860-03-01	Blount	A1
500	FENDLEY, Rebecca	29	SESE	1858-03-01	Blount	A1
501	" "	32	NENE	1858-03-01		A1
502	" "	33	NWNW	1858-03-01	Blount	A1
471	GILLASPIE, David	34	SENE	1837-08-05	Blount	A1
472	GILLESPIE, David	34	NWSE	1834-10-14	Blount	A1
490	GILLESPIE, John C	34	SWNE	1838-09-10	Blount	A1
465	GURLEY, Aaron	19	SESW	1838-09-10	Blount	A1
466	GURLEY, Alonzo	19	NESW	1849-08-01	Blount	A1
494	GURLEY, John W	19	NESE	1849-08-01	Blount	A1
499	GURLEY, Nathaniel	19	SWSW	1838-09-10	Blount	A1
508	GURLEY, West	30	E½SW	1826-06-15	Blount	A1
476	HADEN, George L	31	NESE	1858-03-01		A1
479	HADEN, George S	31	NWNE	1850-04-01		A1
477	" "	31	E½NE	1860-03-01		A1
478	" "	31	E½NW	1860-03-01		A1
480	" "	31	SWNE	1860-03-01		A1
514	HAGOOD, Zachariah	19	NWSE	1854-06-15	Blount	A1
515	HAGOOD, Zackariah	19	SWSE	1854-06-15	Blount	A1
481	HARRISON, Greenberry H	33	SWSE	1835-09-04	Blount	A1
495	HARRISON, Joseph D	33	E½SE	1915-08-09	Blount	A1 G126
504	HARRISON, Robert P	34	NWSW	1838-09-10	Blount	A1
473	HICKS, Elisha	29	NWNW	1838-09-10	Blount	A1
474	" "	30	NWNE	1838-09-10	Blount	A1
470	HIGGINBOTHAM, Clemens C	32	NW	1885-05-09		A4
482	HIGGINBOTHAM, James	33	SWNW	1852-11-15	Blount	A1
485	HIGGINBOTHAM, James W	32	NESE	1894-09-11		A4
486	" "	32	SENE	1894-09-11		A4
487	" "	32	W½NE	1894-09-11		A4
505	HIGGINBOTHAM, Shannon K	34	E½NW	1858-03-01	Blount	A1
506	" "	34	NWNE	1858-03-01	Blount	A1
475	HIX, Faraby	30	SENE	1860-09-01	Blount	A1
495	MICHAEL, Barney	33	E½SE	1915-08-09	Blount	A1 G126
507	PALMER, Solomon	33	E½NW	1833-07-30	Blount	A1
491	PITTS, John C	30	SWSW	1858-03-01	Blount	A1
497	POSEY, Moses M	33	NWSE	1858-03-01	Blount	A1
498	" "	33	W½NE	1858-03-01	Blount	A1
503	ROGERS, Robert H	34	SWSW	1835-10-16	Blount	A1
483	SELF, James P	32	E½SW	1895-06-27		A4

ID	Individual in Patent	Sec.	Sec. Part	Date Issued	Other Counties	For More Info . . .
484	SELF, James P (Cont'd)	32	W½SE	1895-06-27		A4
489	SELF, Jesse E	32	W½SW	1883-09-10		A4
488	WEEMS, James	33	NWSW	1839-08-01	Blount	A1
468	WILSON, Benjamin R	34	NENE	1840-10-10	Blount	A1
510	WILSON, William L	34	E½SE	1860-03-01	Blount	A1
511	" "	34	SWSE	1860-03-01	Blount	A1

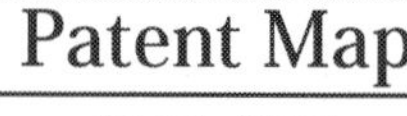

T14-S R1-W
Huntsville Meridian

Map Group 4

Township Statistics

Parcels Mapped	:	51
Number of Patents	:	39
Number of Individuals	:	38
Patentees Identified	:	37
Number of Surnames	:	24
Multi-Patentee Parcels	:	1
Oldest Patent Date	:	6/15/1826
Most Recent Patent	:	8/9/1915
Block/Lot Parcels	:	0
Parcels Re - Issued	:	0
Parcels that Overlap	:	0
Cities and Towns	:	0
Cemeteries	:	0

Note: the area contained in this map amounts to far less than a full Township. Therefore, its contents are completely on this single page (instead of a "normal" 2-page spread).

N

19
ASHLEY Andrew J 1858
GURLEY Alonzo 1849
GURLEY Nathaniel 1838
GURLEY Aaron 1838
HAGOOD Zachariah 1854
HAGOOD Zackariah 1854
GURLEY John W 1849
HICKS Elisha 1838
BYARS John W 1857

30
PITTS John C 1858
GURLEY West 1826
DEAN Joseph 1883
BYARS John W 1857
HIX Faraby 1860

31
HADEN George S 1860
HADEN George S 1850
HADEN George S 1860
HADEN George S 1860
BURLESSON William 1826
HADEN George L 1858

Jefferson County
Blount County

20

29
HICKS Elisha 1838
FENDLEY Rebecca 1858

32
HIGGINBOTHAM Clemens C 1885
SELF Jesse E 1883
SELF James P 1895
HIGGINBOTHAM James W 1894
SELF James P 1895
HIGGINBOTHAM James W 1894
HIGGINBOTHAM James W 1894
HIGGINBOTHAM James W 1894
FENDLEY Rebecca 1858
FAUCETT William R 1860

33
FENDLEY Rebecca 1858
HIGGINBOTHAM James 1852
WEEMS James 1839
FAUCETT William R 1860
PALMER Solomon 1833
POSEY Moses M 1858
POSEY Moses M 1858
HARRISON Greenberry H 1835
HARRISON [126] Joseph D 1915
BARTON Catharine 1835

28
21

34
HARRISON Robert P 1838
ROGERS Robert H 1835
HIGGINBOTHAM Shannon K 1858
HIGGINBOTHAM Shannon K 1858
GILLESPIE John C 1838
GILLESPIE David 1834
WILSON William L 1860
WILSON William L 1860
WILSON Benjamin R 1840
GILLASPIE David 1837

27
22
35
26
23
36
25
24

Legend

Patent Boundary
Section Boundary
No Patents Found (or Outside County)
1., 2., 3., ... Lot Numbers (when beside a name)
[ ] Group Number (see Appendix "C")

Scale: Section = 1 mile X 1 mile (generally, with some exceptions)

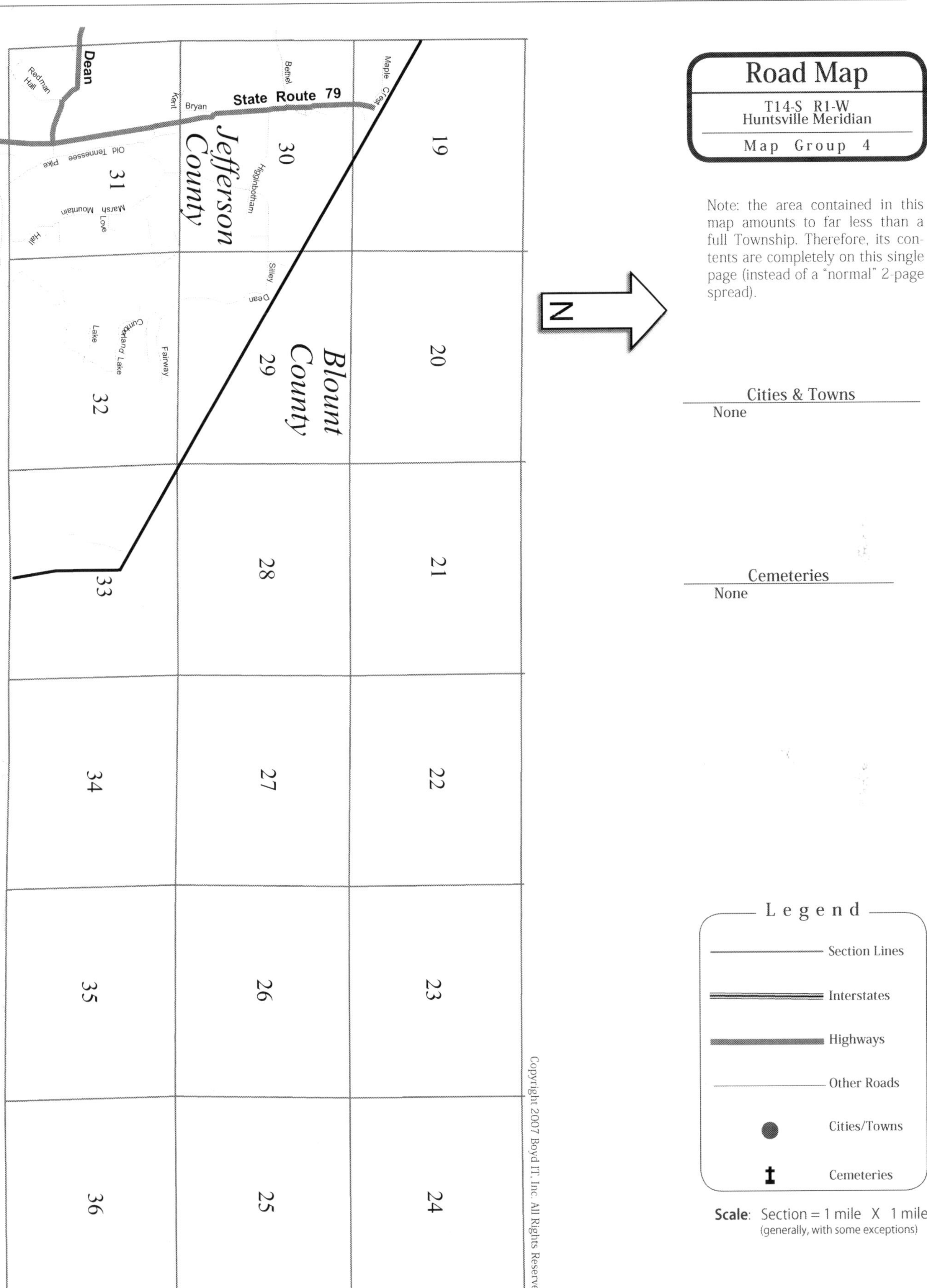
Road Map
T14-S R1-W
Huntsville Meridian
Map Group 4
Note: the area contained in this map amounts to far less than a full Township. Therefore, its contents are completely on this single page (instead of a "normal" 2-page spread).
Cities & Towns
None
Cemeteries
None
N
Dean
Redman Hall
State Route 79
Bryan
Kent
Bethel
Maple Crest
Old Tennessee Pike
Marsh Mountain
Love
Hall
Higginbotham
Jefferson County
Blount County
Silley
Dean
Cumberland Lake
Lake
Fairway
19
20
21
22
23
24
30
29
28
27
26
25
31
32
33
34
35
36
Legend
Section Lines
Interstates
Highways
Other Roads
Cities/Towns
Cemeteries
Scale: Section = 1 mile X 1 mile
(generally, with some exceptions)

Historical Map

T14-S R1-W
Huntsville Meridian

Map Group 4

Note: the area contained in this map amounts to far less than a full Township. Therefore, its contents are completely on this single page (instead of a "normal" 2-page spread).

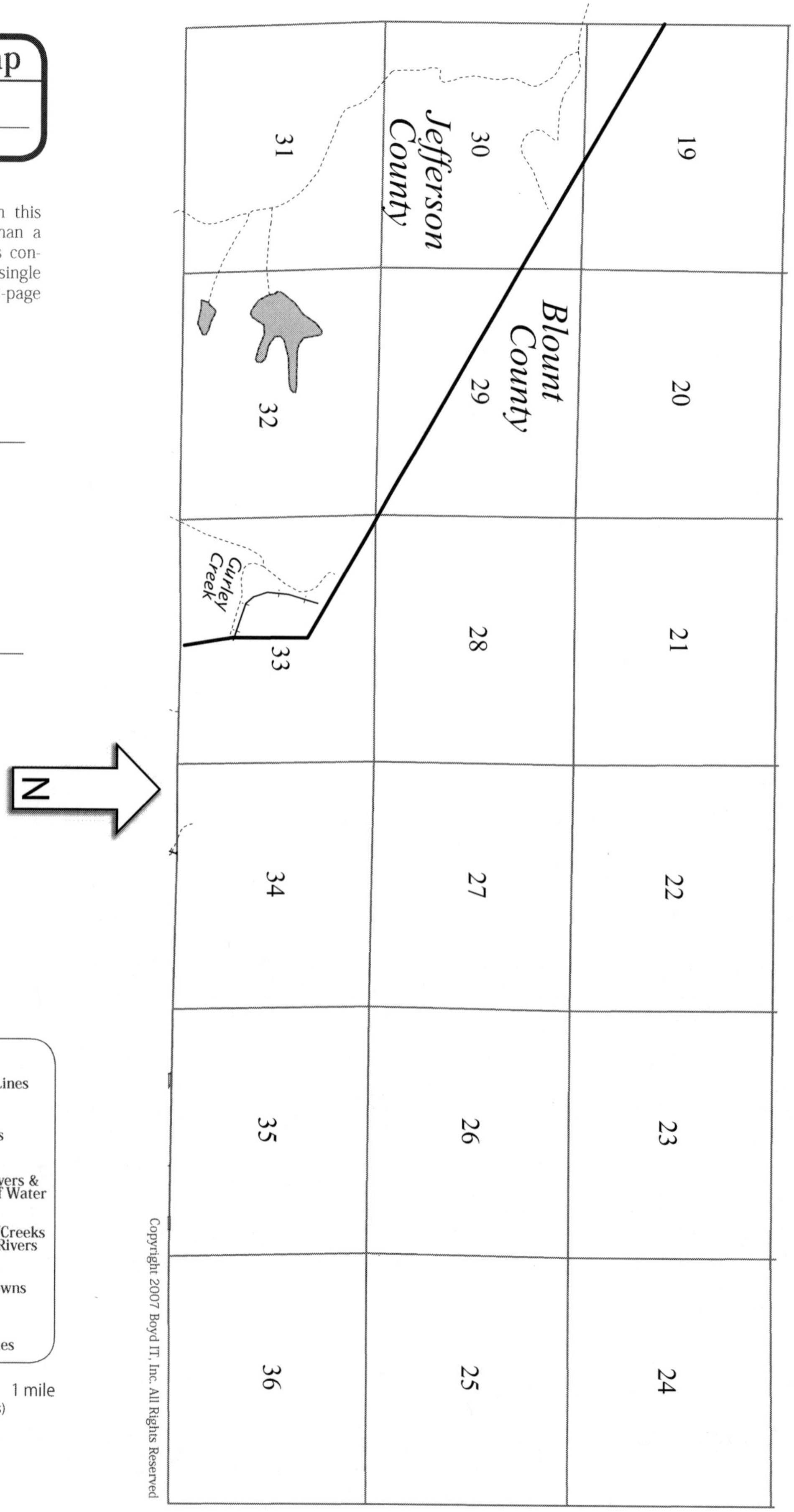

Cities & Towns

None

Cemeteries

None

19 20 21 22 23 24
30 29 28 27 26 25
31 32 33 34 35 36
Jefferson County
Blount County
Gurley Creek

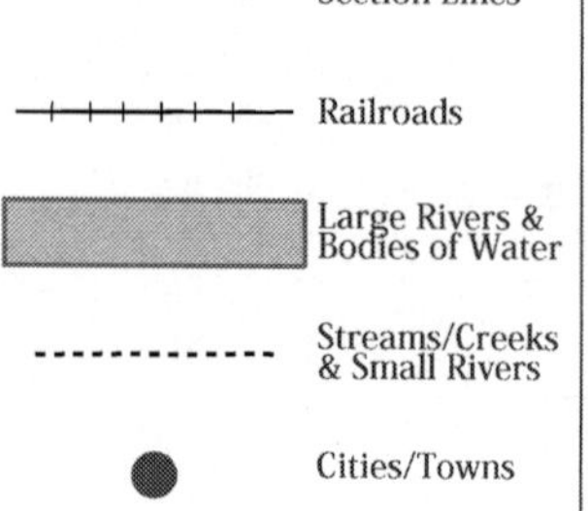

Scale: Section = 1 mile X 1 mile
(there are some exceptions)

Map Group 5: Index to Land Patents

Township 15-South Range 5-West (Huntsville)

After you locate an individual in this Index, take note of the Section and Section Part then proceed to the Land Patent map on the pages immediately following. You should have no difficulty locating the corresponding parcel of land.

The "For More Info" Column will lead you to more information about the underlying Patents. See the *Legend* at right, and the "How to Use this Book" chapter, for more information.

LEGEND

"For More Info . . . " column

A = Authority (Legislative Act, See Appendix "A")
B = Block or Lot (location in Section unknown)
C = Cancelled Patent
F = Fractional Section
G = Group (Multi-Patentee Patent, see Appendix "C")
V = Overlaps another Parcel
R = Re-Issued (Parcel patented more than once)

(A & G items require you to look in the Appendixes referred to above. All other Letter-designations followed by a number require you to locate line-items in this index that possess the ID number found after the letter).

ID	Individual in Patent	Sec.	Sec. Part	Date Issued	Other Counties	For More Info . . .
557	ADAMS, Madison P	36	SESW	1858-06-01		A1
516	ALLEN, Benjamin J	12	NW	1884-11-13		A1
535	ALLEN, Jeremiah	12	NWSW	1891-09-15		A4
536	" "	12	S½SW	1891-09-15		A4
537	" "	12	SWSE	1891-09-15		A4
560	ANDERSON, Peter	23	SESE	1850-09-02		A1
524	BURRELL, Elias A	13	SENE	1858-06-01		A1
520	CANNON, Daniel	25	NWSE	1850-09-02		A1
521	" "	25	SWSE	1858-06-01		A1
522	" "	36	E½NE	1858-06-01		A1
528	CANNON, Elisha M	13	SWSW	1839-09-20		A1
529	" "	24	SWNE	1839-09-20		A1
541	CANNON, John	36	E½SE	1858-06-01		A1
570	CANNON, Thomas	24	NESW	1839-09-20		A1
571	" "	24	W½SW	1839-09-20		A1
579	CANNON, William N	25	SESE	1841-01-09		A1
578	" "	24	SESE	1858-06-01		A1
553	CARTER, Lloyd	23	SWSE	1852-01-01		A1
574	CORLEY, William B	12	NESW	1858-06-01		A1
575	" "	12	NWSE	1858-06-01		A1
576	" "	12	SWNE	1858-06-01		A1
568	DOGGET, Tarrents	23	SESW	1858-06-01		A1
569	" "	26	N½NE	1858-06-01		A1
538	EARLEY, Jesse	26	NW	1890-07-03		A4
542	EARLEY, John	35	NESW	1859-12-10		A1
543	" "	35	W½SW	1859-12-10		A1
544	GLOVER, John F	36	W½SE	1890-07-03		A4
561	GRAHAM, Ransom	14	NWSE	1839-09-20	Walker	A1
532	HASKETT, Evelina	36	W½SW	1858-06-01		A1
545	HASTINGS, John H	13	NWNW	1839-09-20		A1
546	" "	13	SWNW	1848-07-01		A1
517	HOLLIS, Caroline	14	SESW	1883-07-03	Walker	A4
518	" "	14	SWSE	1883-07-03	Walker	A4
523	HOLLIS, Daniel	26	SWSE	1858-06-01		A1
526	HOLLIS, Elijah V	13	SESW	1858-06-01		A1
527	" "	36	SENW	1858-06-01		A1
547	HOLLIS, John H	36	NENW	1889-08-02		A4
548	" "	36	NESW	1889-08-02		A4
550	HOLLIS, Jonathan M	14	N½NE	1890-07-03	Walker	A4
533	KIRKPATRICK, James	24	N½SE	1875-11-20		A4
540	LOLLER, Joab	24	NWNE	1858-06-01		A1
539	" "	24	NENW	1861-08-01		A1
556	LONG, Lyndsa B	12	SESE	1895-09-04		A4
577	MCDONALD, William	24	W½NW	1884-03-20		A4
551	MILES, Jonathan Y	14	SWNE	1839-09-20	Walker	A1
534	MUDD, James	14	NESE	1834-10-14	Walker	A1

ID	Individual in Patent	Sec.	Sec. Part	Date Issued	Other Counties	For More Info . . .
564	ROGERS, Samuel	36	W½NE	1834-10-01		A1
549	ROUSE, John	14	E½NW	1890-03-19	Walker	A4
554	SELLERS, Luther	24	SESW	1875-11-20		A4
555	" "	24	SWSE	1875-11-20		A4
572	SHAW, Wiley	14	NESW	1839-09-20	Walker	A1
573	" "	14	SESE	1839-09-20	Walker	A1
519	SHIPP, Cary W	12	NWNE	1901-01-23		A4
530	SMITH, Emily A	14	W½NW	1884-03-20	Walker	A4
531	" "	14	W½SW	1884-03-20	Walker	A4
565	STEEL, Sylvester	26	SESE	1839-09-20		A1
566	" "	35	E½NE	1839-09-20		A1
567	" "	36	W½NW	1839-09-20		A1
525	TURNER, Elihu	24	SENW	1839-09-20		A1
562	TURNER, Richard	12	E½NE	1859-12-10		A1
563	" "	12	NESE	1859-12-10		A1
558	WILLIAMS, Nancy	26	N½SE	1885-04-27		A4
559	" "	26	SWNE	1885-04-27		A4
552	WILSON, Josiah	26	SW	1890-08-29		A4

Patent Map

T15-S R5-W
Huntsville Meridian

Map Group 5

Township Statistics

Parcels Mapped	:	64
Number of Patents	:	51
Number of Individuals	:	41
Patentees Identified	:	41
Number of Surnames	:	30
Multi-Patentee Parcels	:	0
Oldest Patent Date	:	10/1/1834
Most Recent Patent	:	1/23/1901
Block/Lot Parcels	:	0
Parcels Re - Issued	:	0
Parcels that Overlap	:	0
Cities and Towns	:	0
Cemeteries	:	3

Note: the area contained in this map amounts to far less than a full Township. Therefore, its contents are completely on this single page (instead of a "normal" 2-page spread).

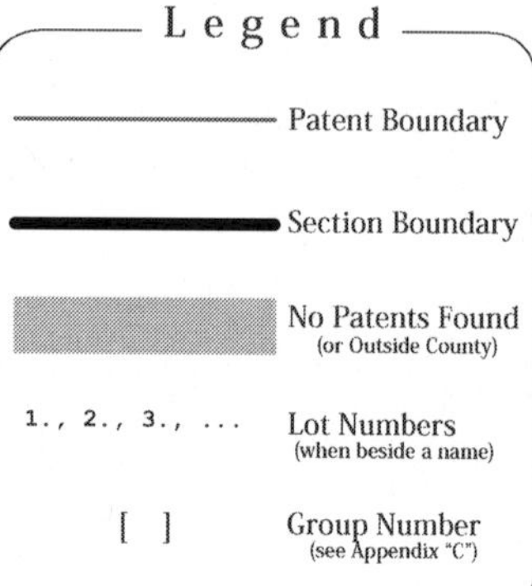

Scale: Section = 1 mile X 1 mile
(generally, with some exceptions)

3

2

1
Jefferson County

10

11

12
ALLEN Benjamin J 1884
SHIPP Cary W 1901
CORLEY William B 1858
TURNER Richard 1859
ALLEN Jeremiah 1891
CORLEY William B 1858
CORLEY William B 1858
TURNER Richard 1859
ALLEN Jeremiah 1891
ALLEN Jeremiah 1891
LONG Lyndsa B 1895

15

14
SMITH Emily A 1884
ROUSE John 1890
SMITH Emily A 1884
SHAW Wiley 1839
HOLLIS Caroline 1883
HOLLIS Jonathan M 1890
MILES Jonathan Y 1839
GRAHAM Ransom 1839
MUDD James 1834
HOLLIS Caroline 1883
SHAW Wiley 1839

13
HASTINGS John H 1839
HASTINGS John H 1848
BURRELL Elias A 1858
CANNON Elisha M 1839
HOLLIS Elijah V 1858

22

23
DOGGET Tarrents 1858
CARTER Lloyd 1852
ANDERSON Peter 1850

24
MCDONALD William 1884
LOLLER Joab 1861
LOLLER Joab 1858
TURNER Elihu 1839
CANNON Elisha M 1839
CANNON Thomas 1839
CANNON Thomas 1839
KIRKPATRICK James 1875
SELLERS Luther 1875
SELLERS Luther 1875
CANNON William N 1858

27

26
EARLEY Jesse 1890
DOGGET Tarrents 1858
WILLIAMS Nancy 1885
WILLIAMS Nancy 1885
WILSON Josiah 1890
HOLLIS Daniel 1858
STEEL Sylvester 1839

25
CANNON Daniel 1850
CANNON Daniel 1858
CANNON William N 1841

34
Walker County

35
STEEL Sylvester 1839
EARLEY John 1859
EARLEY John 1859

36
STEEL Sylvester 1839
HOLLIS John H 1889
HOLLIS Elijah V 1858
ROGERS Samuel 1834
CANNON Daniel 1858
HASKETT Evelina 1858
HOLLIS John H 1889
ADAMS Madison P 1858
GLOVER John F 1890
CANNON John 1858

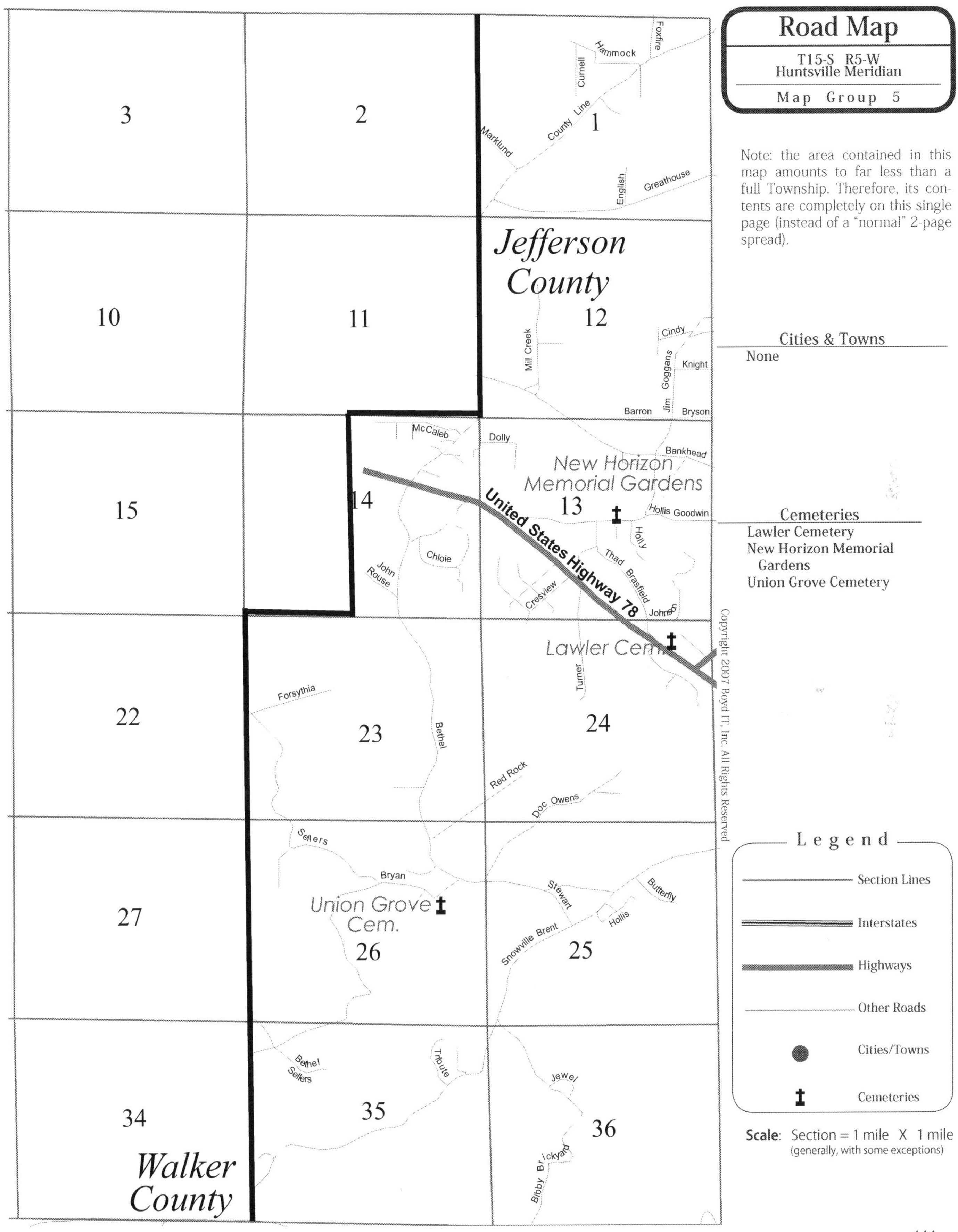

Road Map
T15-S R5-W
Huntsville Meridian
Map Group 5
Note: the area contained in this map amounts to far less than a full Township. Therefore, its contents are completely on this single page (instead of a "normal" 2-page spread).
Cities & Towns
None
Cemeteries
Lawler Cemetery
New Horizon Memorial Gardens
Union Grove Cemetery
Legend
Section Lines
Interstates
Highways
Other Roads
Cities/Towns
Cemeteries
Scale: Section = 1 mile X 1 mile
(generally, with some exceptions)
Jefferson County
Walker County
United States Highway 78
New Horizon Memorial Gardens
Lawler Cem.
Union Grove Cem.
3
2
1
10
11
12
15
14
13
22
23
24
27
26
25
34
35
36
Hammock
Foxfire
Curnell
County Line
Marklund
English
Greathouse
Mill Creek
Cindy
Knight
Jim Goggans
Barron
Bryson
McCaleb
Dolly
Bankhead
Hollis Goodwin
Holly
Chloie
John Rouse
Thad Brasfield
Cresview
Johnson
Turner
Forsythia
Bethel
Red Rock
Doc Owens
Sellers
Bryan
Stewart
Butterfly
Hollis
Snowville Brent
Bethel
Sellers
Tribute
Jewel
Bibby Brickyard

Historical Map

T15-S R5-W
Huntsville Meridian

Map Group 5

Note: the area contained in this map amounts to far less than a full Township. Therefore, its contents are completely on this single page (instead of a "normal" 2-page spread).

Cities & Towns

None

Cemeteries

Lawler Cemetery
New Horizon Memorial Gardens
Union Grove Cemetery

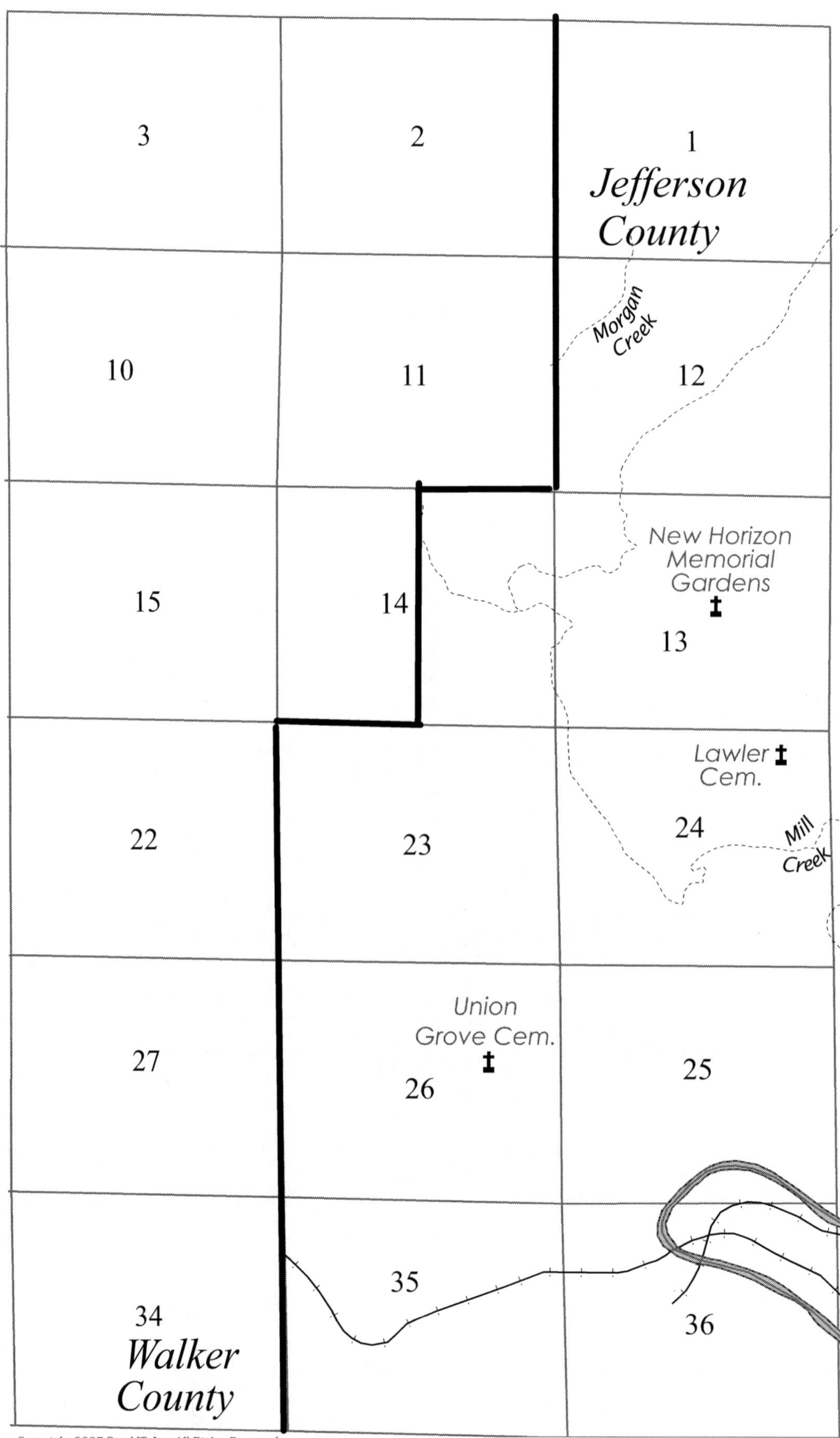

Legend

Section Lines
Railroads
Large Rivers & Bodies of Water
Streams/Creeks & Small Rivers
Cities/Towns
Cemeteries

Scale: Section = 1 mile X 1 mile
(there are some exceptions)

Map Group 6: Index to Land Patents

Township 15-South Range 4-West (Huntsville)

After you locate an individual in this Index, take note of the Section and Section Part then proceed to the Land Patent map on the pages immediately following. You should have no difficulty locating the corresponding parcel of land.

The "For More Info" Column will lead you to more information about the underlying Patents. See the *Legend* at right, and the "How to Use this Book" chapter, for more information.

LEGEND

"For More Info . . . " column

A = Authority (Legislative Act, See Appendix "A")
B = Block or Lot (location in Section unknown)
C = Cancelled Patent
F = Fractional Section
G = Group (Multi-Patentee Patent, see Appendix "C")
V = Overlaps another Parcel
R = Re-Issued (Parcel patented more than once)

(A & G items require you to look in the Appendixes referred to above. All other Letter-designations followed by a number require you to locate line-items in this index that possess the ID number found after the letter).

ID	Individual in Patent	Sec.	Sec. Part	Date Issued	Other Counties	For More Info . . .
689	ABELS, John S	14	S½NW	1858-06-01		A1
687	AYRES, John G	19	NENW	1839-09-20		A1
732	BANKSTON, Sarah A C	10	N½NE	1895-06-19		A4 G11
626	BAYLESS, George W	31	NESW	1839-09-20		A1
627	" "	31	NWNW	1839-09-20		A1
596	BISHOP, Caroline	28	SENW	1858-06-01		A1
694	BLACK, Joseph A	10	N½NW	1858-06-01		A1
695	" "	3	SESW	1858-06-01		A1
696	" "	3	SWSE	1858-06-01		A1
586	BLACKBURN, Andrew J	2	NENE	1852-01-01		A1
779	BLALOCK, Zachariah T	12	NENE	1889-11-21		A4
780	BLAYLOCK, Zachariah T	12	S½NE	1883-07-03		A4
600	BRIDGMON, Daniel W	21	NENW	1858-06-01		A1
601	" "	21	NWNE	1858-06-01		A1
605	BROWN, Early A	1	NWSW	1837-11-07		A1
606	" "	1	W½NW	1839-09-20		A1
666	BUSH, James W	34	E½NE	1893-04-03		A4
667	" "	34	N½SE	1893-04-03		A4
650	CAMP, James E	14	N½NW	1890-04-15		A1
651	" "	14	NWNE	1890-04-15		A1
729	CAMP, Robert M	2	W½SE	1883-07-03		A4 V622, 613
742	CAMPBELL, Thomas	4	SWSE	1858-06-01		A1
743	" "	9	NENE	1858-06-01		A1
744	" "	9	SENW	1858-06-01		A1
763	CAMPBELL, William H	10	NWSE	1883-07-03		A4
764	" "	10	S½SE	1883-07-03		A4
765	" "	10	SWNE	1883-07-03		A4
679	CANNON, John	19	SWNW	1839-09-20		A1
680	" "	30	SWSW	1839-09-20		A1
681	" "	31	SWSW	1850-09-02		A1
745	CANNON, Thomas	18	SWNW	1839-09-20		A1
746	CAREY, Thomas J	30	E½SE	1883-07-03		A4
747	" "	30	SWSE	1883-07-03		A4
730	CLEMENTS, Salathiel P	34	E½SW	1875-11-20		A4
758	CORLEY, William B	10	S½SW	1883-07-03		A4
768	CROCKETT, William J	36	E½SW	1888-02-04		A4
769	" "	36	N½SE	1888-02-04		A4
711	CROSS, Monroe C	4	NE	1890-07-03		A4
610	CUNNINGHAM, Elijah	14	NENE	1839-09-20		A1
602	DAVIS, David J	24	SWNW	1913-03-25		A4
649	DILL, James	14	S½NE	1875-11-20		A4
674	DOSS, Joel	13	SW	1860-07-02		A1
675	" "	14	E½SE	1860-07-02		A1
676	" "	24	E½NW	1860-07-02		A1
682	DOSS, John	2	SENE	1839-09-20		A1
683	" "	2	SWNE	1839-09-20		A1

ID	Individual in Patent	Sec.	Sec. Part	Date Issued	Other Counties	For More Info . . .
688	DUPUY, John M	30	W½NW	1840-11-10		A1
635	FIELDS, Hampton	34	W½SW	1858-06-01		A1
652	FIELDS, James	31	SENE	1839-09-20		A1
707	FLANAGAN, Mary A	9	NWNE	1839-09-20		A1
753	FLANAGAN, William A	31	NWSW	1837-04-01		A1
684	FOSTER, John F	30	E½NE	1880-02-20		A4
685	" "	30	SENW	1885-06-20		A4
686	" "	30	SWNE	1885-06-20		A4
580	GLOVER, Abner W	32	N½NE	1884-03-20		A1
724	GLOVER, Richard W	28	NE	1858-06-01		A1
725	" "	28	SESW	1860-04-02		A1
726	" "	28	W½SE	1860-04-02		A1
636	GOGGANS, Henry M	22	SE	1885-06-12		A4
706	GOGGANS, Manco	20	NWNW	1916-01-19		A4
761	GOGGANS, William D	20	SWNW	1858-06-01		A1
760	" "	20	NESW	1883-07-03		A4
766	GOGGANS, William H	20	NESE	1885-03-16		A1
727	GREEN, Robert J	4	N½SE	1883-07-03		A4
713	HULSEY, Needham W	12	S½NW	1875-11-20		A4
734	JACKSON, Solomon A	34	S½SE	1875-11-20		A4
754	JACKSON, William A	26	NWNW	1883-04-10		A4
755	" "	26	NWSW	1883-04-10		A4
756	" "	26	SWNW	1883-04-10		A4
757	" "	26	SWSW	1883-04-10		A4
776	JACKSON, Woody T	8	NESW	1858-06-01		A1
777	JONES, Zachariah	18	SWSE	1839-09-20		A1
671	LIVELY, Jemima	14	W½SE	1891-06-29		A4
653	LOCKHART, James H	18	N½NW	1885-03-16		A1
654	" "	18	NWNE	1885-03-16		A1
655	" "	18	SENW	1885-03-16		A1
640	LOLLER, Isaac M	18	SESW	1883-07-03		A4
641	" "	18	W½SW	1883-07-03		A4
673	LOLLER, Joab	19	NWNW	1858-06-01		A1
773	MCWILLIAMS, William	29	NENE	1839-09-20		A1
637	MERRICK, Henry	28	NWNW	1839-09-20		A1
661	MORRISON, James	8	N½NW	1861-07-01		A1 R748
662	" "	8	NWNE	1861-07-01		A1 V668
611	MURPHREE, Elizabeth J	2	E½SE	1884-12-05		A4
612	" "	2	SESW	1884-12-05		A4
613	" "	2	SWSE	1884-12-05		A4 V729
608	MYRICK, Eli	29	NWNE	1858-06-01		A1
614	MYRICK, Elizabeth	20	SESE	1858-06-01		A1
692	MYRICK, John W	26	E½NE	1890-01-08		A4
774	MYRICK, William	9	SWNE	1858-06-01		A1
701	MYRICKE, Levi	31	SWNE	1859-04-01		A1
638	MYROCK, Henry	20	SENW	1834-10-01		A1
639	" "	20	W½SE	1839-09-20		A1
702	NAIL, Luke	1	SWSE	1849-08-01		A1
703	" "	13	E½NE	1860-07-02		A1
704	" "	13	NWNE	1860-07-02		A1
705	" "	36	W½SW	1884-12-05		A4
714	NAIL, Nicholas	2	SENW	1848-07-01		A1
672	ODAM, Jennings	5	W½NW	1858-06-01		A1
643	PAYNE, James C	19	E½SW	1860-10-01		A1
644	" "	19	SENW	1860-10-01		A1
645	" "	19	SWNE	1860-10-01		A1 V646
646	" "	19	W½NE	1860-10-01		A1 V645
647	" "	30	NENW	1860-10-01		A1
648	" "	30	NWNE	1860-10-01		A1
691	PAYNE, John T	29	W½NW	1858-06-01		A1
759	PAYNE, William C	18	E½SE	1858-06-01		A1
633	POWELL, Greene B	10	NWSW	1888-02-04		A4
634	" "	10	SWNW	1888-02-04		A4
628	RICHARDS, George W	3	NENW	1858-06-01		A1
620	RIVERS, Frederick W	2	NESW	1858-06-01		A1
621	" "	2	NWNE	1858-06-01		A1
622	" "	2	NWSE	1858-06-01		A1 V729
599	ROBBINS, Columbus A	20	W½SW	1891-06-29		A4
617	ROBBINS, Ephraim N	20	NWNE	1884-03-20		A4
663	ROBBINS, James R	6	E½SW	1891-06-29		A4
664	" "	6	SENW	1891-06-29		A4
665	" "	6	SWNE	1891-06-29		A4
699	ROBBINS, Levi M	20	NENW	1858-06-01		A1

ID	Individual in Patent	Sec.	Sec. Part	Date Issued	Other Counties	For More Info . . .
700	ROBBINS, Levi M (Cont'd)	20	SWNE	1858-06-01		A1
708	ROBBINS, Michael	20	SESW	1839-09-20		A1
709	" "	29	NENW	1839-09-20		A1
737	ROBBINS, Thomas B	18	NENE	1849-09-01		A1
736	" "	17	N½NW	1858-06-01		A1
738	" "	18	NESW	1858-06-01		A1
739	" "	18	S½NE	1858-06-01		A1
740	" "	9	NWSE	1858-06-01		A1
770	ROBBINS, William L	8	NWSW	1884-03-20		A4
771	" "	8	S½SW	1884-03-20		A4
772	" "	8	SWNW	1884-03-20		A4
767	ROBERTSON, William H	11	E½SE	1840-11-10		A1 G202
618	ROBINS, Ephraim	6	W½SW	1858-06-01		A1
677	ROBINS, John B	2	NWNW	1858-06-01		A1
678	" "	3	N½NE	1858-06-01		A1
710	ROBINS, Michael	28	NENW	1852-01-01		A1
741	ROBINS, Thomas B	30	NWSE	1839-09-20		A1
731	RODGERS, Samuel	31	E½SE	1824-05-19		A1
715	SANDERS, Nicholas P	12	N½NW	1875-11-20		A4
716	SHORT, Obediah B	12	NWSW	1890-01-08		A4
668	SMITH, James W	8	NE	1858-06-01		A1 V662
669	" "	9	NWNW	1858-06-01		A1
762	SPARKES, William E	2	NENW	1883-07-03		A4
690	STAGGS, John	12	NWNE	1840-11-10		A1
778	STAGGS, Zachariah	12	E½SW	1840-11-10		A1
585	STATUM, Ambrose C	28	E½SE	1884-03-20		A1
767	STEEL, Jonathan	11	E½SE	1840-11-10		A1 G202
591	SULLIVAN, Arthur P	24	NE	1884-12-05		A4
712	SULLIVAN, Nancy A	24	N½SE	1891-06-29		A1
721	SULLIVAN, Rasbell	14	N½SW	1890-03-19		A4
735	SULLIVAN, Susan	14	S½SW	1883-07-03		A4
587	TANNER, Andrew J	10	NESW	1889-06-05		A4
588	" "	10	SENW	1889-06-05		A4
619	TANNER, Francis M	6	SE	1890-07-03		A4
670	TATE, James W	8	SE	1876-04-01		A4
748	TATE, Thomas M	8	N½NW	1890-07-03		A4 R661
749	" "	8	SENW	1890-07-03		A4
603	THOMAS, David W	10	NESE	1883-07-03		A4
604	" "	10	SENE	1883-07-03		A4
732	" "	10	N½NE	1895-06-19		A4 G11
732	THOMAS, Sarah A C	10	N½NE	1895-06-19		A4 G11
629	TREADAWAY, George W	2	SWNW	1858-06-01		A1
630	" "	3	NWSE	1858-06-01		A1
631	" "	3	SENE	1858-06-01		A1
632	" "	3	SWNE	1858-06-01		A1
642	TURKENET, Jacob	9	NENW	1839-09-20		A1
592	TURNER, Benjamin	22	SW	1884-03-20		A4 G223
597	TURNER, Collins	34	S½NW	1884-03-20		A4
598	" "	34	W½NE	1884-03-20		A4
592	TURNER, Elijah	22	SW	1884-03-20		A4 G223
718	TURNER, Rachel	26	E½SW	1880-02-20		A4 G224
719	" "	26	NWSE	1880-02-20		A4 G224
720	" "	26	SENW	1880-02-20		A4 G224
723	TURNER, Richard	7	W½NW	1859-12-10		A1
718	" "	26	E½SW	1880-02-20		A4 G224
719	" "	26	NWSE	1880-02-20		A4 G224
720	" "	26	SENW	1880-02-20		A4 G224
592	TURNER, Sarah	22	SW	1884-03-20		A4 G223
722	WAIT, Richard H	12	SWSW	1889-03-02		A1
623	WALKER, George M	6	N½NW	1891-11-23		A4
624	" "	6	NWNE	1891-11-23		A4
625	" "	6	SWNW	1891-11-23		A4
717	WARD, Otho	4	NW	1890-07-03		A4
698	WEISMAN, Joseph	11	E½SW	1840-11-10		A1
697	WHITE, Joseph R	12	W½SE	1884-03-20		A4
607	WHITEHEAD, Edmond	12	E½SE	1891-06-08		A4
584	WOOD, Abner	32	SWNE	1834-10-01		A1
583	" "	32	SENE	1837-03-30		A1
582	" "	32	E½SE	1839-09-20		A1
581	" "	21	E½SE	1858-06-01		A1
609	WOOD, Elias	6	E½NE	1890-07-03		A4
615	WOOD, Elizabeth	32	E½SW	1884-03-20		A4
616	" "	32	W½SE	1884-03-20		A4

ID	Individual in Patent	Sec.	Sec. Part	Date Issued	Other Counties	For More Info . . .
656	WOOD, James H	28	N½SW	1884-03-20		A1
657	" "	28	SWNW	1884-03-20		A1
658	" "	28	SWSW	1884-03-20		A1
693	WOOD, John	33	SWSW	1860-07-02		A1
728	WOOD, Robert J	4	SW	1883-07-03		A4
775	WOODARD, Wilson	26	S½SE	1889-08-16		A4
593	WOODWARD, Byrd	36	NENW	1889-08-13		A4
594	" "	36	NWNE	1889-08-13		A4
595	" "	36	S½NW	1889-08-13		A4
589	YOUNGBLOOD, Andrew M	20	E½NE	1839-09-20		A1
590	" "	29	NWSW	1839-09-20		A1
659	YOUNGBLOOD, James H	15	W½SW	1858-06-01		A1
660	" "	22	NWNW	1858-06-01		A1
733	YOUNGBLOOD, Sarah	31	NWSE	1849-08-01		A1
752	YOUNGBLOOD, Thomas P	31	SENW	1849-08-01		A1
750	" "	31	NENW	1858-06-01		A1
751	" "	31	NWNE	1858-06-01		A1

Patent Map

T15-S R4-W
Huntsville Meridian

Map Group 6

Township Statistics

Parcels Mapped	:	201
Number of Patents	:	146
Number of Individuals	:	126
Patentees Identified	:	122
Number of Surnames	:	78
Multi-Patentee Parcels	:	6
Oldest Patent Date	:	5/19/1824
Most Recent Patent	:	1/19/1916
Block/Lot Parcels	:	0
Parcels Re - Issued	:	1
Parcels that Overlap	:	7
Cities and Towns	:	1
Cemeteries	:	0

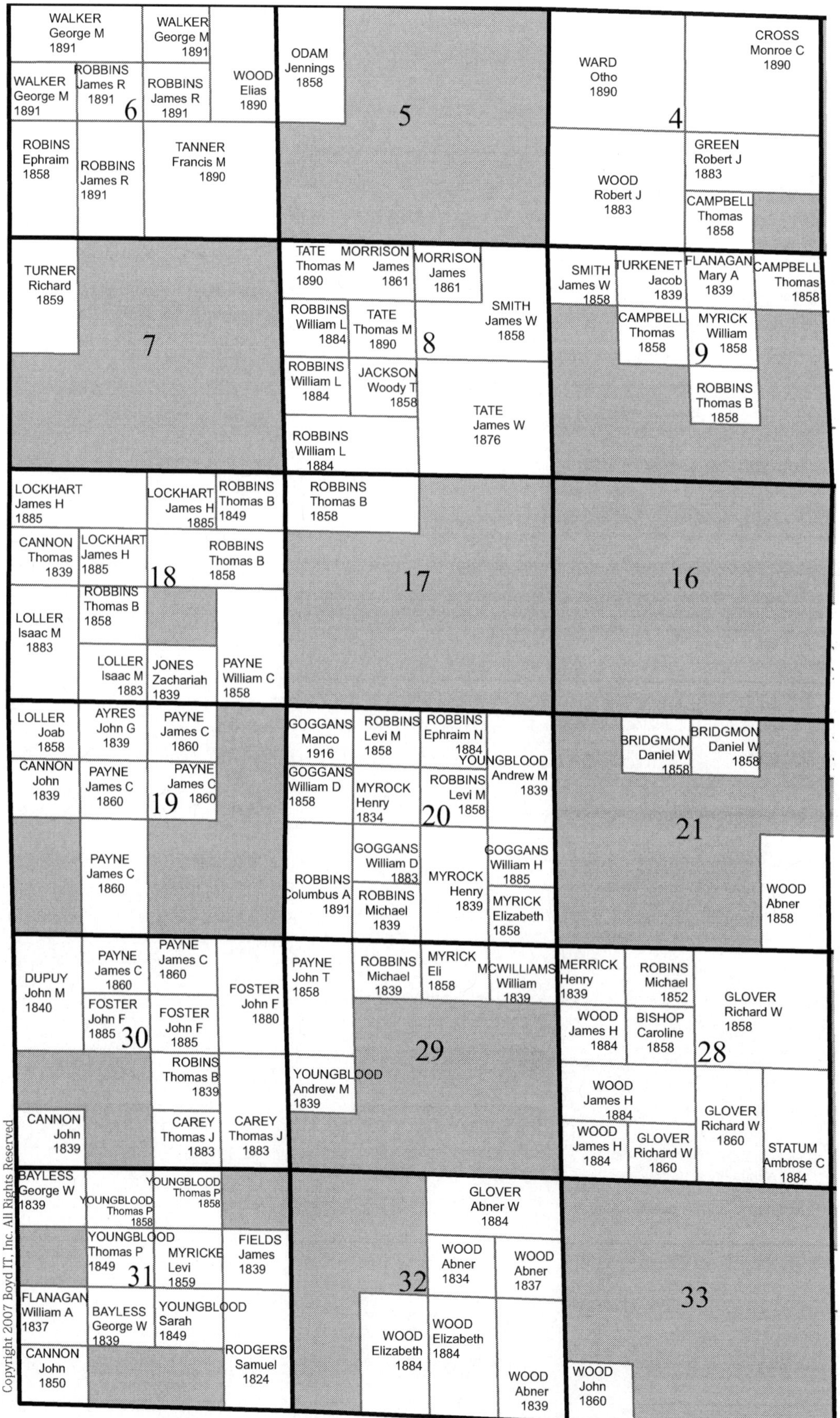

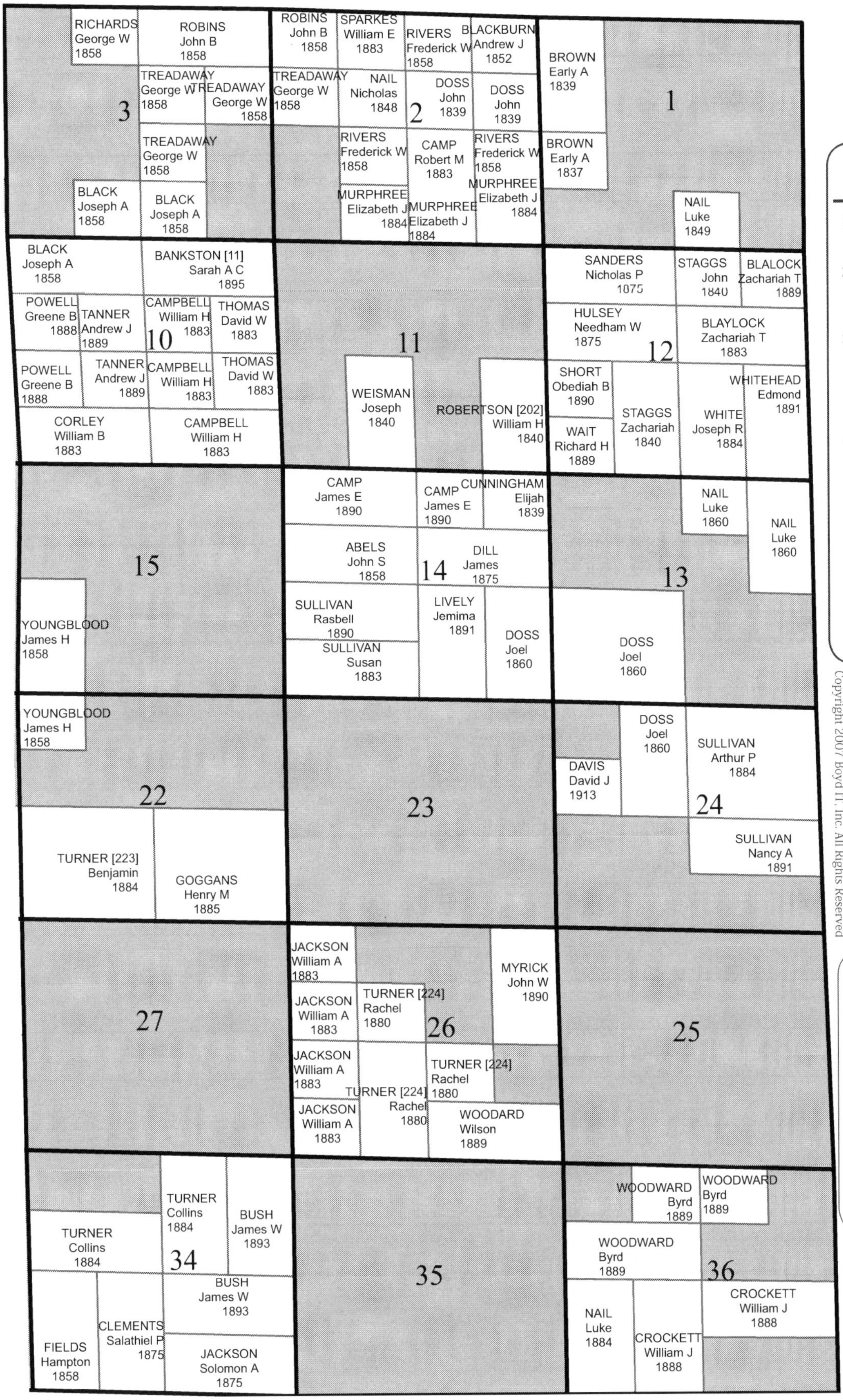

Helpful Hints

1. This Map's INDEX can be found on the preceding pages.
2. Refer to Map "C" to see where this Township lies within Jefferson County, Alabama.
3. Numbers within square brackets [ ] denote a multi-patentee land parcel (multi-owner). Refer to Appendix "C" for a full list of members in this group.
4. Areas that look to be crowded with Patentees usually indicate multiple sales of the same parcel (Re-issues) or Overlapping parcels. See this Township's Index for an explanation of these and other circumstances that might explain "odd" groupings of Patentees on this map.

Legend

- Patent Boundary
- Section Boundary
- No Patents Found (or Outside County)
- 1., 2., 3., ... Lot Numbers (when beside a name)
- [ ] Group Number (see Appendix "C")

Scale: Section = 1 mile X 1 mile (generally, with some exceptions)

Road Map

T15-S R4-W
Huntsville Meridian

Map Group 6

Cities & Towns

Sayre

Cemeteries

None

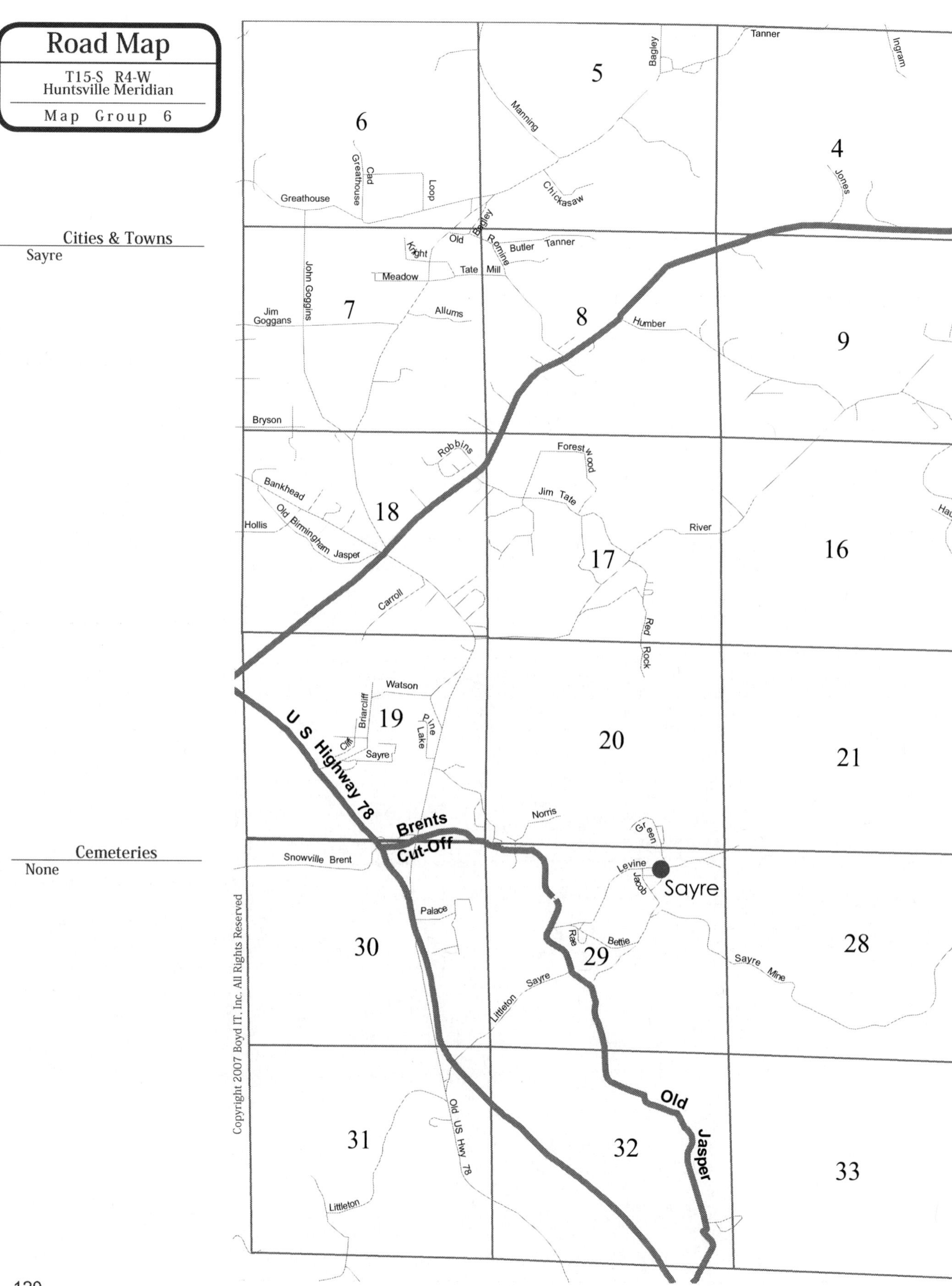

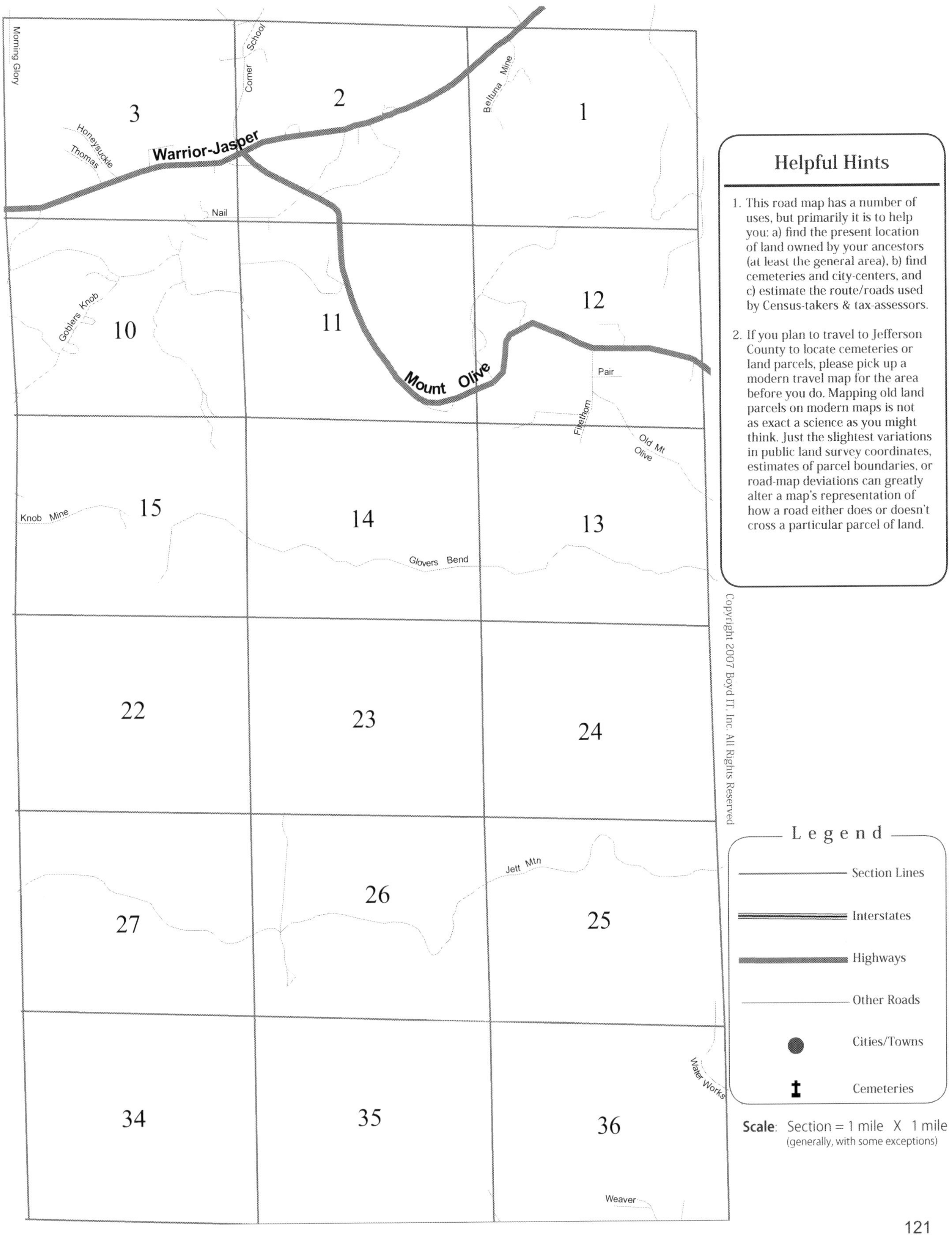
Morning Glory
Corner
School
Beltuna Mine
3
2
1
Honeysuckle
Thomas
Warrior-Jasper
Nail
Gobiers Knob
10
11
12
Mount Olive
Pair
Firethorn
Old Mt Olive
Knob Mine
15
14
13
Glovers Bend
22
23
24
Jett Mtn
26
27
25
Water Works
34
35
36
Weaver
Helpful Hints
1. This road map has a number of uses, but primarily it is to help you: a) find the present location of land owned by your ancestors (at least the general area), b) find cemeteries and city-centers, and c) estimate the route/roads used by Census-takers & tax-assessors.
2. If you plan to travel to Jefferson County to locate cemeteries or land parcels, please pick up a modern travel map for the area before you do. Mapping old land parcels on modern maps is not as exact a science as you might think. Just the slightest variations in public land survey coordinates, estimates of parcel boundaries, or road-map deviations can greatly alter a map's representation of how a road either does or doesn't cross a particular parcel of land.
Copyright 2007 Boyd IT, Inc. All Rights Reserved
Legend
Section Lines
Interstates
Highways
Other Roads
Cities/Towns
Cemeteries
Scale: Section = 1 mile X 1 mile
(generally, with some exceptions)

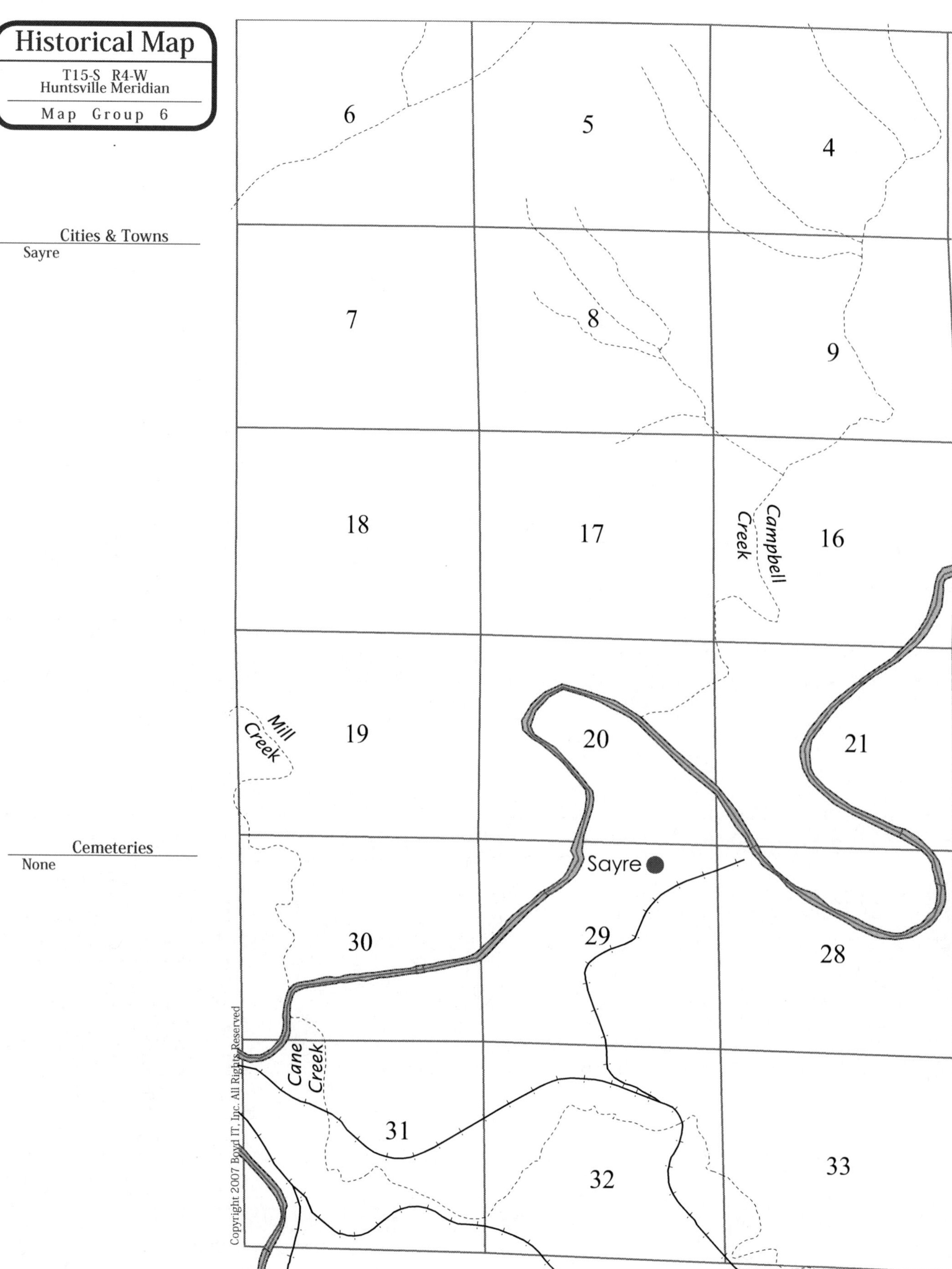
Historical Map
T15-S R4-W
Huntsville Meridian
Map Group 6
Cities & Towns
Sayre
Cemeteries
None
6
5
4
7
8
9
18
17
16
Campbell Creek
19
20
21
Mill Creek
Sayre
30
29
28
Cane Creek
31
32
33
Copyright 2007 Boyd IT, Inc. All Rights Reserved

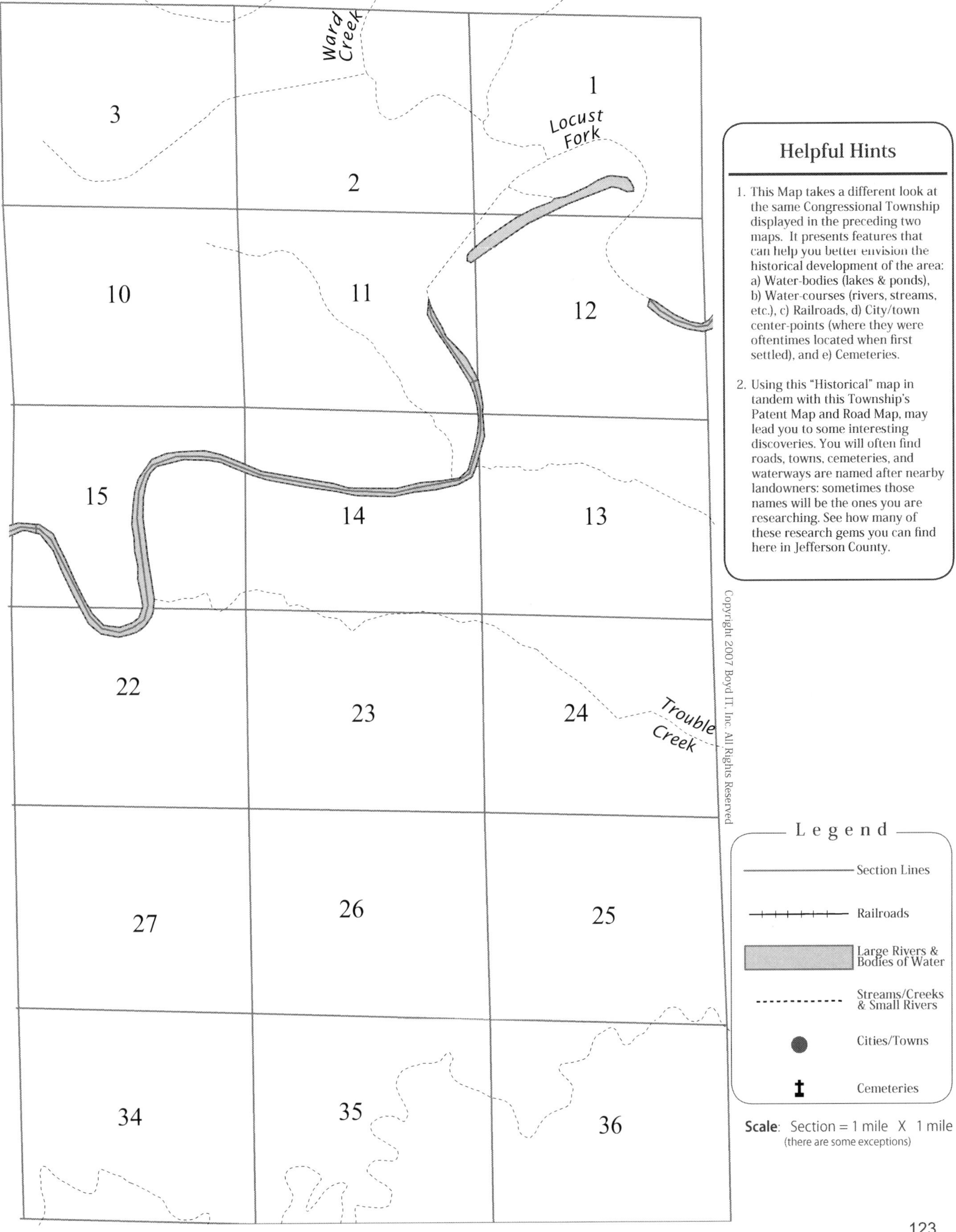

Helpful Hints

1. This Map takes a different look at the same Congressional Township displayed in the preceding two maps. It presents features that can help you better envision the historical development of the area: a) Water-bodies (lakes & ponds), b) Water-courses (rivers, streams, etc.), c) Railroads, d) City/town center-points (where they were oftentimes located when first settled), and e) Cemeteries.

2. Using this "Historical" map in tandem with this Township's Patent Map and Road Map, may lead you to some interesting discoveries. You will often find roads, towns, cemeteries, and waterways are named after nearby landowners: sometimes those names will be the ones you are researching. See how many of these research gems you can find here in Jefferson County.

Map Group 7: Index to Land Patents

Township 15-South Range 3-West (Huntsville)

After you locate an individual in this Index, take note of the Section and Section Part then proceed to the Land Patent map on the pages immediately following. You should have no difficulty locating the corresponding parcel of land.

The "For More Info" Column will lead you to more information about the underlying Patents. See the *Legend* at right, and the "How to Use this Book" chapter, for more information.

LEGEND

"For More Info . . . " column

A = Authority (Legislative Act, See Appendix "A")
B = Block or Lot (location in Section unknown)
C = Cancelled Patent
F = Fractional Section
G = Group (Multi-Patentee Patent, see Appendix "C")
V = Overlaps another Parcel
R = Re-Issued (Parcel patented more than once)

(A & G items require you to look in the Appendixes referred to above. All other Letter-designations followed by a number require you to locate line-items in this index that possess the ID number found after the letter).

ID	Individual in Patent	Sec.	Sec. Part	Date Issued	Other Counties	For More Info . . .
973	ADAMS, William	13	W½NE	1824-04-28		A1
974	AIKIN, William B	33	E½SE	1831-01-04		A1
937	ALLSOP, Samson	24	E½SE	1878-04-09		A4
934	BAIRD, Robert F	26	NW	1895-08-08		A4
868	BARR, John	8	N½SE	1889-10-07		A1
869	" "	8	N½SW	1889-10-07		A1
932	BARR, Robert	8	NW	1892-06-10		A4
870	BATES, John	1	S½SW	1858-06-01		A1
844	BEASLEY, Isaiah	34	E½SW	1889-11-21		A4
871	BEASLEY, John	34	NESE	1885-05-20		A4
872	" "	34	SENE	1885-05-20		A4
845	BEASLY, Isaiah	34	W½SW	1883-07-03		A4
873	BELCHER, John	24	E½NE	1824-05-04		A1
874	" "	26	W½SW	1883-07-03		A4
883	BELCHER, John H	24	NWSE	1860-07-02		A1
884	" "	24	SENW	1860-07-02		A1
885	" "	24	SWNE	1860-07-02		A1
967	BELSHER, Thomas R	24	SW	1889-08-13		A4
979	BIBB, William	15	SENW	1850-09-02		A1
980	" "	3	NWNW	1861-06-01		A1
981	" "	4	NENE	1861-06-01		A1
892	BISHOP, Joseph	12	N½NW	1839-09-20		A1
893	" "	12	SWSE	1839-09-20		A1 V950
875	BLACKBURN, John	24	SWSE	1839-09-20		A1
911	BLUDWORTH, Martha C	14	E½SE	1883-07-03		A4
820	BROOKS, Francis M	14	N½SW	1885-03-30		A4
821	" "	14	W½NW	1885-03-30		A4
846	BROWN, Jack	2	NENW	1875-06-01		A4
847	" "	2	NWNE	1875-06-01		A4
860	BURGIN, James H	30	SENW	1905-01-19		A1
912	CLARK, Mary	34	N½NE	1892-06-10		A4
913	" "	34	N½NW	1892-06-10		A4
984	CLEMENTS, William G	32	E½NE	1892-06-10		A4
985	" "	32	NESE	1892-06-10		A4
795	COOPER, Craft P	2	SENW	1839-09-20		A1
796	COOPER, Dabney	1	NWSW	1839-09-20		A1
822	COOPER, George H	26	SESE	1839-09-20		A1
876	COOPER, John	11	E½SE	1834-10-14		A1
877	" "	14	NENE	1837-04-01		A1
975	CORLEY, William B	30	N½NW	1891-06-29		A4
976	" "	30	NWSW	1891-06-29		A4
977	" "	30	SWNW	1891-06-29		A4
854	CRANNEY, James	10	SENW	1892-01-18		A4
855	" "	10	SWNE	1892-01-18		A4
856	" "	10	W½NW	1892-01-18		A4
865	CUNINGHAM, Jesse	12	NESW	1839-09-20		A1

ID	Individual in Patent	Sec.	Sec. Part	Date Issued	Other Counties	For More Info . . .
857	CUNNINGHAM, James	12	SESW	1839-03-15		A1
929	CUNNINGHAM, Reuben	13	NENW	1834-10-16		A1
933	CUNNINGHAM, Robert	12	SWNW	1835-10-01		A1
867	DOSS, John A	4	SENW	1885-12-10		A4
861	DOUGLASS, James L	1	SWNW	1852-01-01		A1
923	DYER, Otis	35	W½SE	1826-06-10		A1 G79
850	EATON, Jackson	14	W½SE	1875-06-01		A4
848	" "	14	SENW	1889-11-21		A4
849	" "	14	SWNE	1889-11-21		A4
812	EDWARDS, Eli H	26	NESE	1883-07-03		A4
813	" "	26	SENE	1883-07-03		A4
811	" "	26	NENE	1884-12-05		A4
878	EDWARDS, John	25	SWSW	1858-06-01		A1
879	" "	36	NWNW	1858-06-01		A1
899	EDWARDS, Joseph R	26	W½SE	1883-10-01		A4
898	" "	26	E½SW	1884-12-05		A4
943	ESKEW, Simeon J	20	NESW	1885-03-16		A1
944	" "	20	SENW	1885-03-16		A1
926	FOSTER, Rebeca J	34	NWSE	1893-05-05		A4
927	" "	34	S½SE	1893-05-05		A4
928	" "	34	SWNE	1893-05-05		A4
800	GARRETT, David	10	SW	1885-03-16		A4
807	GARRETT, Edward	11	NWNE	1834-10-14		A1
805	" "	11	E½NW	1858-06-01		A1
806	" "	11	NESW	1858-06-01		A1
808	" "	11	SWNE	1858-06-01		A1
809	" "	2	E½SW	1858-06-01		A1
810	" "	2	S½SE	1858-06-01		A1
896	GILL, Joseph M	1	SESE	1858-06-01		A1
897	" "	11	W½SE	1858-06-01		A1
858	GILLESPIE, James	14	S½SW	1899-05-22		A4
859	GOINS, James	33	NWNE	1839-09-20		A1
953	GOWEN, Thomas	15	SWNW	1858-06-01		A1
880	GRAHAM, John	32	NESW	1891-11-23		A4 G102
881	" "	32	SENW	1891-11-23		A4 G102
882	" "	32	W½SW	1891-11-23		A4 G102
880	GRAHAM, Permelia A	32	NESW	1891-11-23		A4 G102
881	" "	32	SENW	1891-11-23		A4 G102
882	" "	32	W½SW	1891-11-23		A4 G102
954	GRAHAM, Thomas	26	NWNE	1839-09-20		A1
955	" "	28	SWNE	1858-06-01		A1 V992
956	" "	28	SWSE	1858-06-01		A1
957	" "	29	W½SE	1860-07-02		A1
986	GRAHAM, William	28	NWSE	1839-09-20		A1
840	GRAYHAM, Isaac G	28	E½SW	1885-03-30		A4
842	GRAYHAM, Isaac J	28	W½SW	1889-11-21		A4
917	GRAYHAM, Nancy A	28	SESE	1889-10-07		A1
918	GRAYHAM, Nelley C	20	N½SE	1889-11-21		A4
919	" "	20	SESW	1889-11-21		A4
920	" "	20	SWSE	1889-11-21		A4
958	GRIMES, Thomas	21	NWNW	1844-07-10		A1
959	" "	29	NESE	1844-07-10		A1
987	GRIMES, William	21	SWNW	1834-10-14		A1
989	" "	27	SWNW	1853-08-01		A1
991	" "	28	NESE	1853-08-01		A1
988	" "	27	NWNW	1858-06-01		A1
993	" "	29	SESE	1858-06-01		A1
990	" "	28	E½NW	1878-04-09		A4
992	" "	28	W½NE	1889-11-21		A4 V955
841	GRUBBS, Isaac	11	E½NE	1824-10-20		A1
832	HAMMER, Granville	13	NWSE	1839-09-20		A1
939	HANCOCK, Sarah	32	SESE	1890-03-19		A4
940	" "	32	SESW	1890-03-19		A4
941	" "	32	W½SE	1890-03-19		A4
801	HANLY, David	4	SWNW	1850-04-01		A1 G122
835	HENDERSON, Hugh M	1	NWNW	1858-06-01		A1
836	" "	2	NESE	1858-06-01		A1
837	" "	2	SENE	1858-06-01		A1
930	HIGGINBOTHAM, Robert B	36	N½SW	1890-07-03		A4
931	" "	36	S½NW	1890-07-03		A4
972	HUDSON, Tony	36	SWSW	1900-04-21		A4
968	HUGHES, Thomas R	2	W½SW	1878-06-13		A4
825	HYDE, George W	10	NENW	1885-03-16		A4

ID	Individual in Patent	Sec.	Sec. Part	Date Issued	Other Counties	For More Info . . .
826	HYDE, George W (Cont'd)	10	NWNE	1885-03-16		A4
824	" "	10	E½NE	1888-01-21		A4
802	JAMES, David J	6	NESW	1883-07-03		A4
803	" "	6	NWSE	1885-03-30		A4
804	" "	6	S½NE	1885-03-30		A4
823	JAMES, George H	6	SWSW	1894-06-15		A4
843	JAMES, Isaac J	20	SESE	1896-02-19		A4
960	JAMES, Thomas	17	E½SE	1825-06-20		A1
961	" "	17	N½NW	1837-03-20		A1
962	" "	17	NWNE	1839-09-20		A1
963	" "	20	NENE	1839-09-20		A1
964	" "	6	SESW	1850-09-02		A1
969	JAMES, Thomas R	17	NWSW	1860-07-02		A1
970	" "	18	NESE	1860-07-02		A1
971	" "	18	SENE	1860-07-02		A1
946	JOHNSON, Stephen	30	E½SW	1884-12-05		A4
947	" "	30	S½SE	1884-12-05		A4 V793
996	JOHNSON, William R	30	W½NE	1891-06-08		A4 G140
996	JOHNSON, Zama P	30	W½NE	1891-06-08		A4 G140
827	JONES, George W	8	S½SE	1885-08-05		A1
828	" "	8	S½SW	1885-08-05		A1
924	JONES, Owen L	22	SE	1892-05-26		A1
997	JONES, William R	6	E½SE	1892-06-10		A4
998	" "	6	SWSE	1892-06-10		A4
815	KENNON, Emily H	36	E½SE	1883-04-10		A4
816	" "	36	SESW	1884-03-20		A4
817	" "	36	SWSE	1884-03-20		A4
781	KILLOUGH, Allen	36	NWSE	1860-07-02		A1
782	" "	36	SWNE	1860-07-02		A1
949	LANGFORD, Thomas A	12	E½NE	1889-08-16		A4
950	" "	12	S½SE	1889-08-16		A4 V893, 938
801	LEDYARD, William J	4	SWNW	1850-04-01		A1 G122
951	LEE, Thomas A	18	S½SE	1894-07-17		A4
952	" "	18	SESW	1894-07-17		A4
814	LINEMAN, Eli H	12	SWNE	1839-09-20		A1
935	LITTLE, Robert J	22	S½NE	1891-06-29		A4
936	" "	22	S½NW	1891-06-29		A4
851	LUCKIE, James B	2	W½NW	1883-07-03		A4
886	MCCABE, John	10	SE	1889-12-28		A1
942	MEEKS, Sidney W	12	NWNE	1885-03-16		A1
923	MITCHELL, Thomas	35	W½SE	1826-06-10		A1 G79
852	MOTTE, James C	6	NENW	1884-12-05		A4
853	" "	6	SENW	1884-12-05		A4
894	MOTTE, Joseph D	6	NWSW	1885-03-30		A4
895	" "	6	W½NW	1885-03-30		A4
914	MURRAY, Michael J	22	SW	1892-05-26		A1
903	NAIL, Julian	18	NESW	1860-07-02		A1
904	" "	18	NWSE	1860-07-02		A1
905	" "	18	SWNE	1860-07-02		A1
864	ODOM, Jennings	18	W½SW	1885-03-30		A4
908	OWEN, Martha A	24	NENW	1883-07-03		A4
909	" "	24	NWNE	1883-07-03		A4
910	" "	24	W½NW	1883-07-03		A4
965	PARRY, Thomas	32	NENW	1892-05-26		A1
966	" "	32	W½NW	1892-05-26		A1
783	PARTAIN, Amanda	32	W½NE	1885-05-25		A4
862	PERTEET, James	13	W½NW	1833-08-12		A1
891	POSEY, John W	2	NWSE	1890-07-03		A4
945	POTEETE, Squire L	14	SENE	1834-10-21		A1
833	POWELL, Green	13	E½NE	1829-04-01		A1
838	PURCELL, Ignatius	18	SENW	1891-06-10		A4
839	" "	18	W½NW	1891-06-10		A4
863	PUTTEET, James	12	W½SW	1824-05-19		A1
921	REED, Nicholas	22	N½NE	1890-03-08		A1
922	" "	22	N½NW	1890-03-08		A1
797	REID, Daniel	9	SESW	1839-09-20		A1
791	RHODY, Charles E	34	S½NW	1906-05-14		A4
889	ROBERTS, John	6	N½NE	1883-07-03		A4
994	ROBERTSON, William H	5	E½NW	1840-11-10		A1 G202
995	" "	7	W½NW	1840-11-10		A1 G202
915	ROBINSON, Milus J	18	N½NE	1891-06-29		A4
916	" "	18	NENW	1899-11-04		A4
938	ROGERS, Samuel	12	SESE	1858-06-01		A1 V950

ID	Individual in Patent	Sec.	Sec. Part	Date Issued	Other Counties	For More Info . . .
925	ROWE, Pearson	1	NENE	1858-06-01		A1
792	SANDERS, Charles L	28	W½NW	1892-06-10		A4
900	SAULSBURY, Joseph	36	E½NE	1883-04-10		A4
901	" "	36	NENW	1904-04-04		A4
902	" "	36	NWNE	1904-04-04		A4
786	SHARIT, Asa J	4	W½SW	1883-07-03		A4
785	" "	4	NESW	1889-11-21		A4
788	SHARIT, Benjamin M	4	SESW	1858-06-01		A1
789	" "	4	SWSE	1858-06-01		A1
790	" "	9	NWNE	1858-06-01		A1
787	" "	4	SESE	1880-02-20		A4
978	SHARIT, William B	14	NENW	1902-09-02		A1
798	SHIRL, David D	20	W½NW	1889-08-02		A4
799	" "	20	W½SW	1889-08-02		A4
948	SIMPSON, Terrance	2	NENE	1883-07-03		A4
887	SPRADLING, John R	4	N½NW	1885-03-30		A4
888	" "	4	NWNE	1885-03-30		A4
1000	SPRADLING, William	4	NWSE	1858-06-01		A1
1001	" "	4	S½NE	1858-06-01		A1
999	" "	4	NESE	1883-10-01		A4
890	SPRUELL, John T	28	E½NE	1894-07-17		A4
818	STAGGS, Ezekiel	17	S½NW	1837-03-20		A1
819	" "	26	SWNE	1839-09-20		A1
1002	STAGGS, Zacheriah	21	W½SW	1826-06-10		A1
994	STEEL, Jonathan	5	E½NW	1840-11-10		A1 G202
995	" "	7	W½NW	1840-11-10		A1 G202
794	TANNAHILL, Charleton T	12	SENW	1834-11-04		A1
834	TEDMORE, Henry	13	E½SE	1824-04-28		A1
793	TURNER, Charles	30	E½SE	1884-03-20		A4 V947, 983
829	TURNHAM, George W	20	NENW	1889-10-07		A1
830	" "	20	SENE	1889-10-07		A1
831	" "	20	W½NE	1889-10-07		A1
801	TUTHILL, George A	4	SWNW	1850-04-01		A1 G122
906	WEDGEWORTH, Louisa	8	E½NE	1885-03-16		A4
907	" "	8	W½NE	1891-06-08		A4
866	WHATLEY, Jesse D	14	NWNE	1839-09-20		A1
982	WINGO, William C	30	E½NE	1891-06-29		A4
983	" "	30	N½SE	1891-06-29		A4 V793
784	YOUNGBLOOD, Andrew M	2	SWNE	1840-11-10		A1

Patent Map

T15-S R3-W
Huntsville Meridian

Map Group 7

Township Statistics

Parcels Mapped	:	222
Number of Patents	:	159
Number of Individuals	:	132
Patentees Identified	:	126
Number of Surnames	:	101
Multi-Patentee Parcels	:	8
Oldest Patent Date	:	4/28/1824
Most Recent Patent	:	5/14/1906
Block/Lot Parcels	:	0
Parcels Re - Issued	:	0
Parcels that Overlap	:	8
Cities and Towns	:	1
Cemeteries	:	5

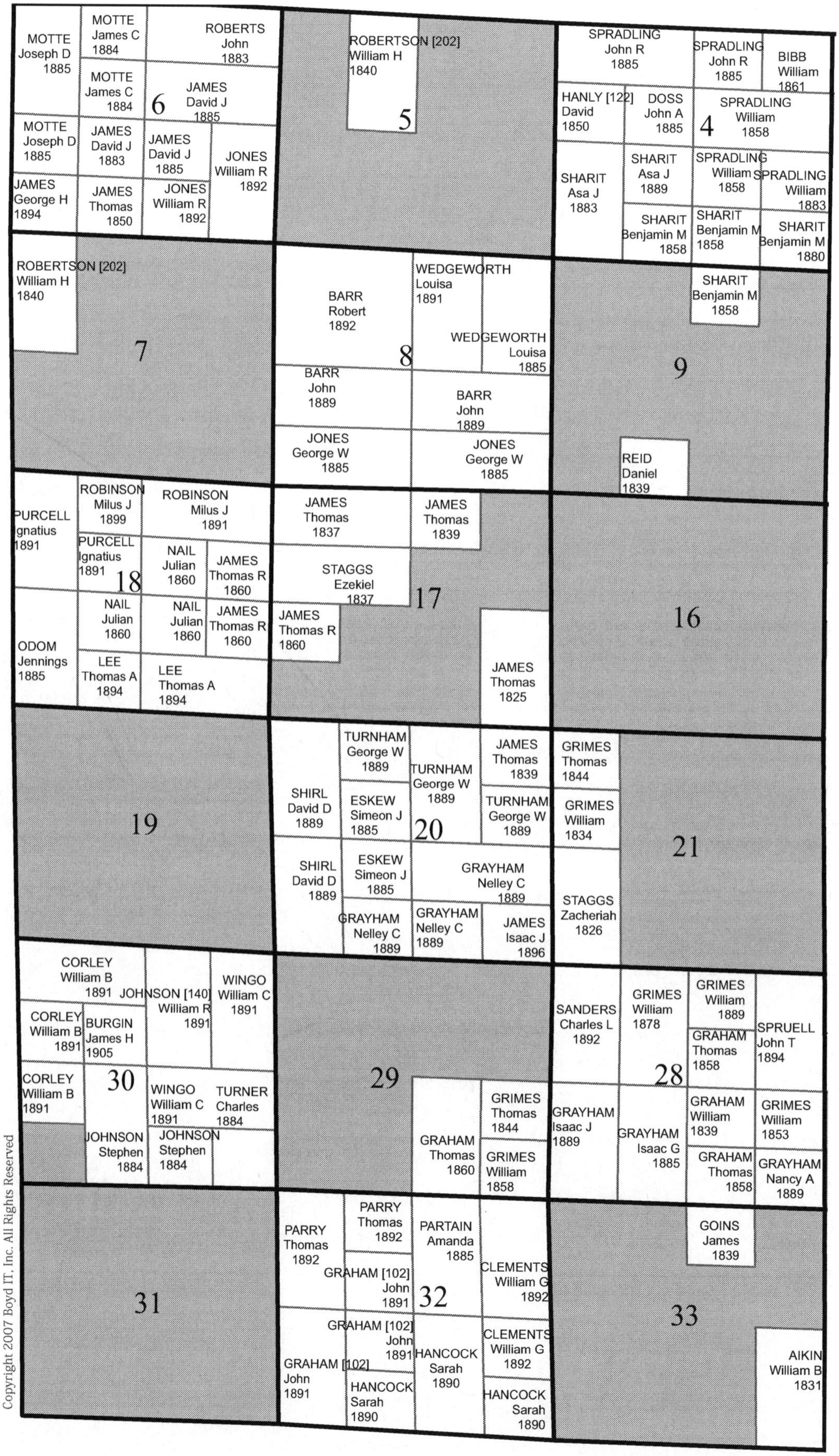

6
MOTTE Joseph D 1885
MOTTE James C 1884
ROBERTS John 1883
MOTTE James C 1884
JAMES David J 1885
MOTTE Joseph D 1885
JAMES David J 1883
JAMES David J 1885
JONES William R 1892
JAMES George H 1894
JAMES Thomas 1850
JONES William R 1892

5
ROBERTSON [202] William H 1840

4
SPRADLING John R 1885
SPRADLING John R 1885
BIBB William 1861
HANLY [122] David 1850
DOSS John A 1885
SPRADLING William 1858
SHARIT Asa J 1883
SHARIT Asa J 1889
SPRADLING William 1858
SPRADLING William 1883
SHARIT Benjamin M 1858
SHARIT Benjamin M 1858
SHARIT Benjamin M 1880

7
ROBERTSON [202] William H 1840

8
BARR Robert 1892
WEDGEWORTH Louisa 1891
WEDGEWORTH Louisa 1885
BARR John 1889
BARR John 1889
JONES George W 1885
JONES George W 1885

9
SHARIT Benjamin M 1858
REID Daniel 1839

18
PURCELL Ignatius 1891
ROBINSON Milus J 1899
ROBINSON Milus J 1891
PURCELL Ignatius 1891
NAIL Julian 1860
JAMES Thomas R 1860
NAIL Julian 1860
NAIL Julian 1860
JAMES Thomas R 1860
ODOM Jennings 1885
LEE Thomas A 1894
LEE Thomas A 1894

17
JAMES Thomas 1837
JAMES Thomas 1839
STAGGS Ezekiel 1837
JAMES Thomas R 1860
JAMES Thomas 1825

16

19

20
TURNHAM George W 1889
TURNHAM George W 1889
JAMES Thomas 1839
SHIRL David D 1889
ESKEW Simeon J 1885
TURNHAM George W 1889
SHIRL David D 1889
ESKEW Simeon J 1885
GRAYHAM Nelley C 1889
GRAYHAM Nelley C 1889
GRAYHAM Nelley C 1889
JAMES Isaac J 1896

21
GRIMES Thomas 1844
GRIMES William 1834
STAGGS Zacheriah 1826

30
CORLEY William B 1891
JOHNSON [140] William R 1891
WINGO William C 1891
CORLEY William B 1891
BURGIN James H 1905
CORLEY William B 1891
WINGO William C 1891
TURNER Charles 1884
JOHNSON Stephen 1884
JOHNSON Stephen 1884

29
GRIMES Thomas 1844
GRAHAM Thomas 1860
GRIMES William 1858

28
SANDERS Charles L 1892
GRIMES William 1878
GRIMES William 1889
GRAHAM Thomas 1858
SPRUELL John T 1894
GRAYHAM Isaac J 1889
GRAYHAM Isaac G 1885
GRAHAM William 1839
GRIMES William 1853
GRAHAM Thomas 1858
GRAYHAM Nancy A 1889

31

32
PARRY Thomas 1892
PARRY Thomas 1892
PARTAIN Amanda 1885
GRAHAM [102] John 1891
CLEMENTS William G 1892
GRAHAM [102] John 1891
CLEMENTS William G 1892
GRAHAM [102] John 1891
HANCOCK Sarah 1890
HANCOCK Sarah 1890
HANCOCK Sarah 1890

33
GOINS James 1839
AIKIN William B 1831

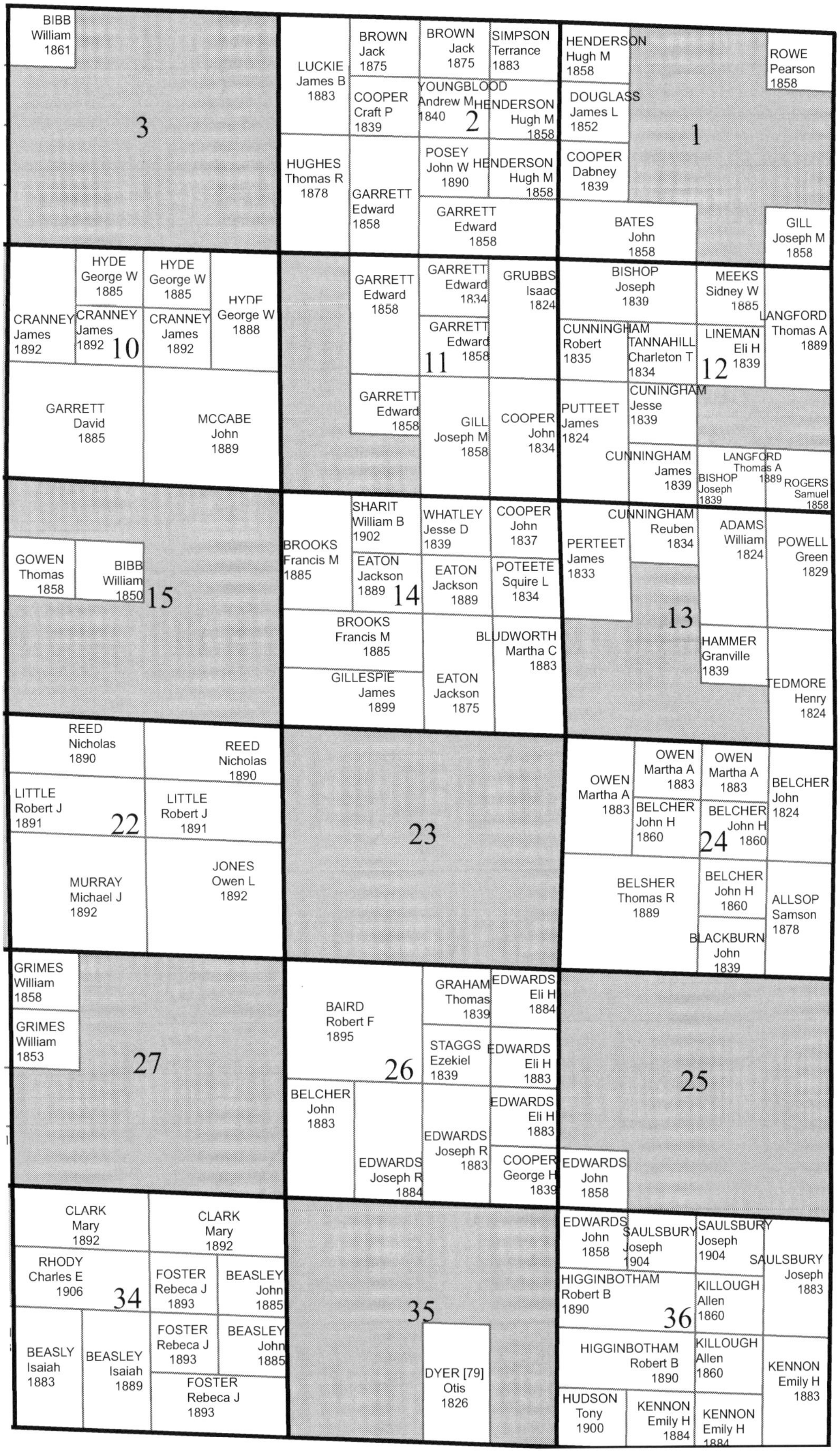

BIBB William 1861
3

LUCKIE James B 1883
BROWN Jack 1875
BROWN Jack 1875
SIMPSON Terrance 1883
COOPER Craft P 1839
YOUNGBLOOD Andrew M 1840
HENDERSON Hugh M 1858
2
HUGHES Thomas R 1878
GARRETT Edward 1858
POSEY John W 1890
HENDERSON Hugh M 1858
GARRETT Edward 1858

HENDERSON Hugh M 1858
ROWE Pearson 1858
DOUGLASS James L 1852
1
COOPER Dabney 1839
BATES John 1858
GILL Joseph M 1858

HYDE George W 1885
HYDE George W 1885
HYDE George W 1888
CRANNEY James 1892
CRANNEY James 1892
CRANNEY James 1892
10
GARRETT David 1885
MCCABE John 1889

GARRETT Edward 1858
GARRETT Edward 1834
GRUBBS Isaac 1824
GARRETT Edward 1858
11
GARRETT Edward 1858
GILL Joseph M 1858
COOPER John 1834

BISHOP Joseph 1839
MEEKS Sidney W 1885
LANGFORD Thomas A 1889
CUNNINGHAM Robert 1835
TANNAHILL Charleton T 1834
LINEMAN Eli H 1839
12
CUNINGHAM Jesse 1839
PUTTEET James 1824
CUNNINGHAM James 1839
LANGFORD Thomas A 1889
BISHOP Joseph 1839
ROGERS Samuel 1858

GOWEN Thomas 1858
BIBB William 1850
15

SHARIT William B 1902
WHATLEY Jesse D 1839
COOPER John 1837
BROOKS Francis M 1885
EATON Jackson 1889
14
EATON Jackson 1889
POTEETE Squire L 1834
BROOKS Francis M 1885
BLUDWORTH Martha C 1883
GILLESPIE James 1899
EATON Jackson 1875

CUNNINGHAM Reuben 1834
PERTEET James 1833
ADAMS William 1824
POWELL Green 1829
13
HAMMER Granville 1839
TEDMORE Henry 1824

REED Nicholas 1890
REED Nicholas 1890
LITTLE Robert J 1891
LITTLE Robert J 1891
22
MURRAY Michael J 1892
JONES Owen L 1892

23

OWEN Martha A 1883
OWEN Martha A 1883
OWEN Martha A 1883
BELCHER John 1824
BELCHER John H 1860
BELCHER John H 1860
24
BELSHER Thomas R 1889
BELCHER John H 1860
ALLSOP Samson 1878
BLACKBURN John 1839

GRIMES William 1858
GRIMES William 1853
27

BAIRD Robert F 1895
GRAHAM Thomas 1839
EDWARDS Eli H 1884
STAGGS Ezekiel 1839
EDWARDS Eli H 1883
26
BELCHER John 1883
EDWARDS Eli H 1883
EDWARDS Joseph R 1883
EDWARDS Joseph R 1884
COOPER George H 1839

EDWARDS John 1858
25

CLARK Mary 1892
CLARK Mary 1892
RHODY Charles E 1906
34
FOSTER Rebeca J 1893
BEASLEY John 1885
FOSTER Rebeca J 1893
BEASLEY John 1885
BEASLY Isaiah 1883
BEASLEY Isaiah 1889
FOSTER Rebeca J 1893

35
DYER [79] Otis 1826

EDWARDS John 1858
SAULSBURY Joseph 1904
SAULSBURY Joseph 1904
SAULSBURY Joseph 1883
HIGGINBOTHAM Robert B 1890
KILLOUGH Allen 1860
36
HIGGINBOTHAM Robert B 1890
KILLOUGH Allen 1860
KENNON Emily H 1883
HUDSON Tony 1900
KENNON Emily H 1884
KENNON Emily H 1884

Helpful Hints

1. This Map's INDEX can be found on the preceding pages.
2. Refer to Map "C" to see where this Township lies within Jefferson County, Alabama.
3. Numbers within square brackets [ ] denote a multi-patentee land parcel (multi-owner). Refer to Appendix "C" for a full list of members in this group.
4. Areas that look to be crowded with Patentees usually indicate multiple sales of the same parcel (Re-issues) or Overlapping parcels. See this Township's Index for an explanation of these and other circumstances that might explain "odd" groupings of Patentees on this map.

Legend

- Patent Boundary
- Section Boundary
- No Patents Found (or Outside County)
- 1., 2., 3., ... Lot Numbers (when beside a name)
- [ ] Group Number (see Appendix "C")

Scale: Section = 1 mile X 1 mile (generally, with some exceptions)

Road Map

T15-S R3-W
Huntsville Meridian

Map Group 7

Cities & Towns

Morris

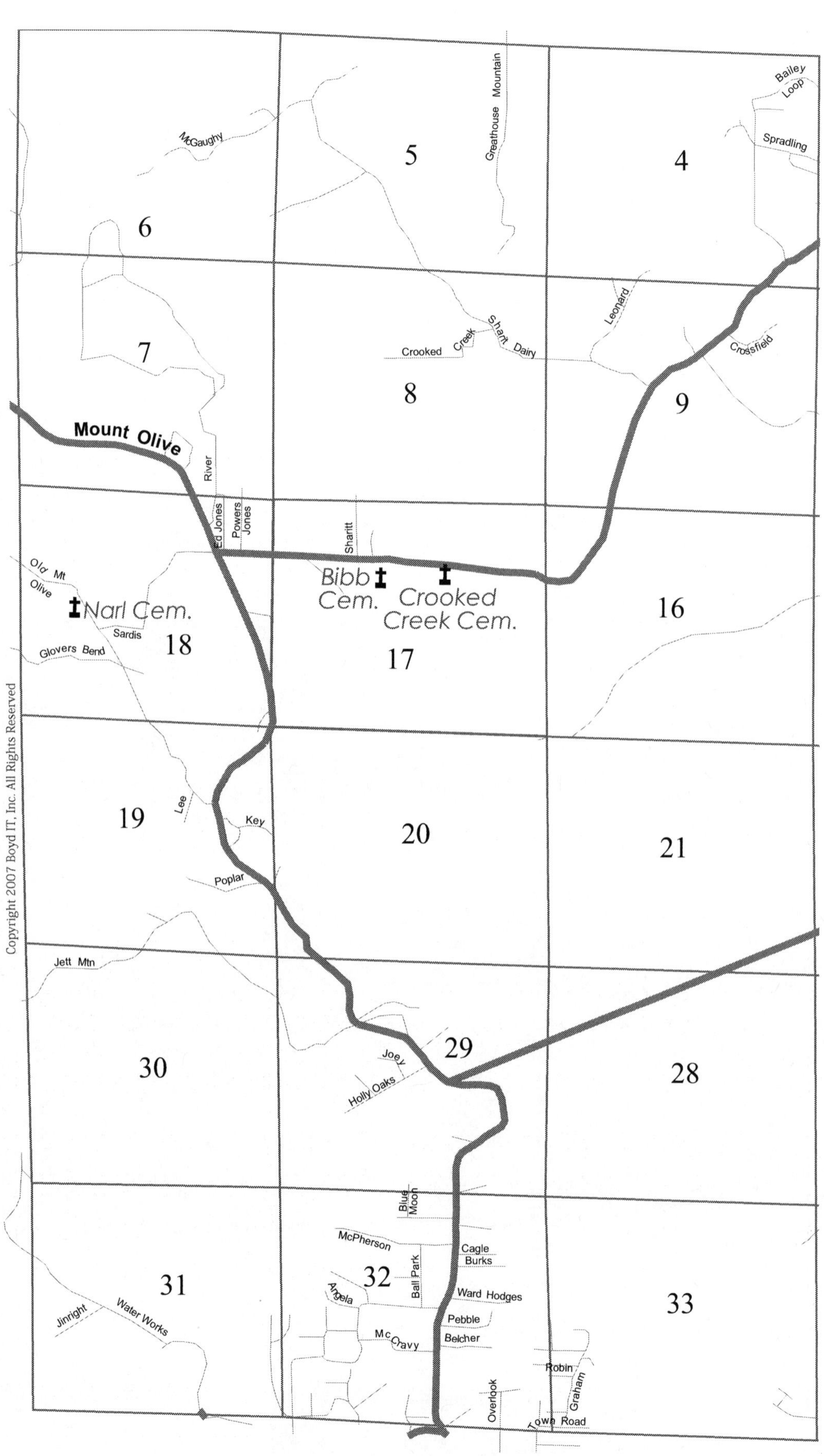

Cemeteries

Bibb Cemetery
Crooked Creek Cemetery
Edward Cemetery
Morris Cemetery
Narl Cemetery

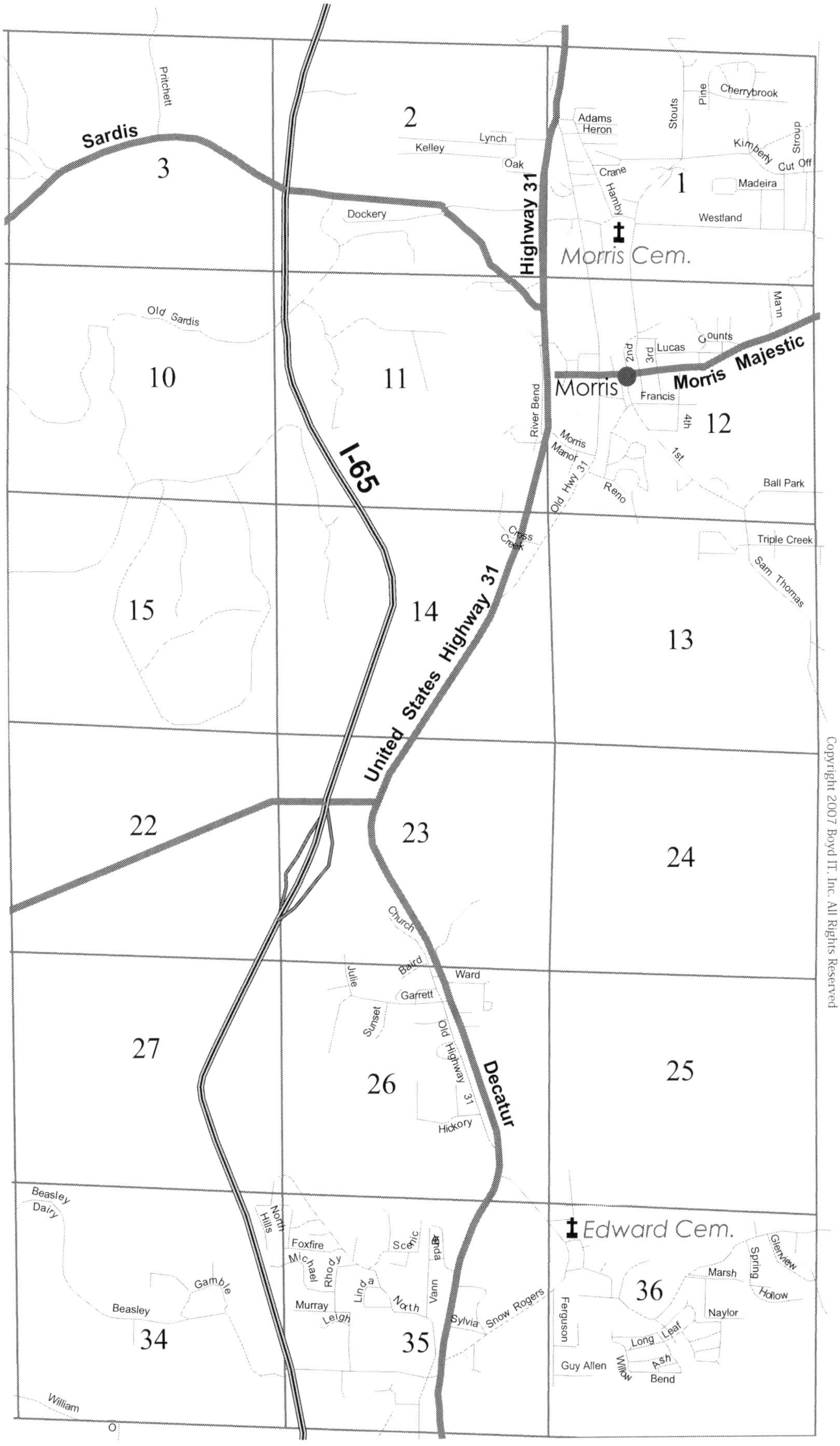

Sardis
Pritchett
3
2
Kelley
Lynch
Oak
Dockery
Highway 31
Adams
Heron
Crane
Hamby
Morris Cem.
Stouts
Pine
Cherrybrook
Kimberly
Cut Off
Stroup
1
Madeira
Westland
Old Sardis
10
11
I-65
River Bend
Morris
2nd
3rd
Lucas
Counts
Morris Majestic
Francis
4th
12
Mann
1st
Morris Manor
Old Hwy 31
Reno
Ball Park
Cross Creek
Triple Creek
Sam Thomas
15
14
13
United States Highway 31
22
23
24
Church
Baird
Ward
Julie
Garrett
Sunset
Old Highway 31
Decatur
27
26
25
Hickory
Beasley Dairy
North Hills
Foxfire
Michael
Rhody
Scenic
Brenda
Edward Cem.
Spring
Glenview
Hollow
Marsh
36
Gamble
Beasley
Murray
Leigh
Linda
North
Vann
Sylvia
Snow Rogers
Ferguson
Naylor
Long Leaf
Ash
Guy Allen
Willow
Bend
34
35
William

Helpful Hints

1. This road map has a number of uses, but primarily it is to help you: a) find the present location of land owned by your ancestors (at least the general area), b) find cemeteries and city-centers, and c) estimate the route/roads used by Census-takers & tax-assessors.

2. If you plan to travel to Jefferson County to locate cemeteries or land parcels, please pick up a modern travel map for the area before you do. Mapping old land parcels on modern maps is not as exact a science as you might think. Just the slightest variations in public land survey coordinates, estimates of parcel boundaries, or road-map deviations can greatly alter a map's representation of how a road either does or doesn't cross a particular parcel of land.

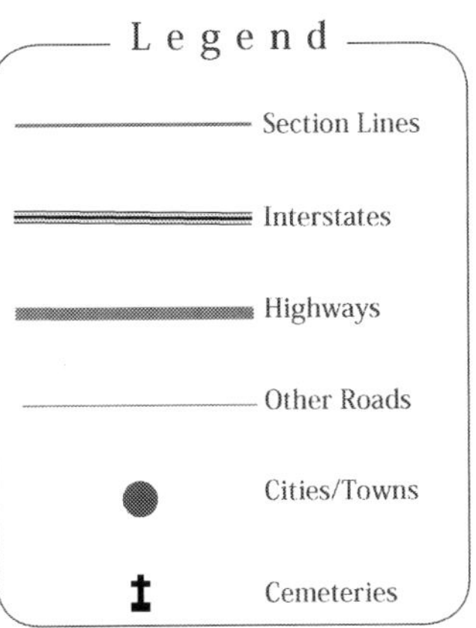

Scale: Section = 1 mile X 1 mile
(generally, with some exceptions)

Historical Map

T15-S R3-W
Huntsville Meridian

Map Group 7

Cities & Towns

Morris

Cemeteries

Bibb Cemetery
Crooked Creek Cemetery
Edward Cemetery
Morris Cemetery
Narl Cemetery

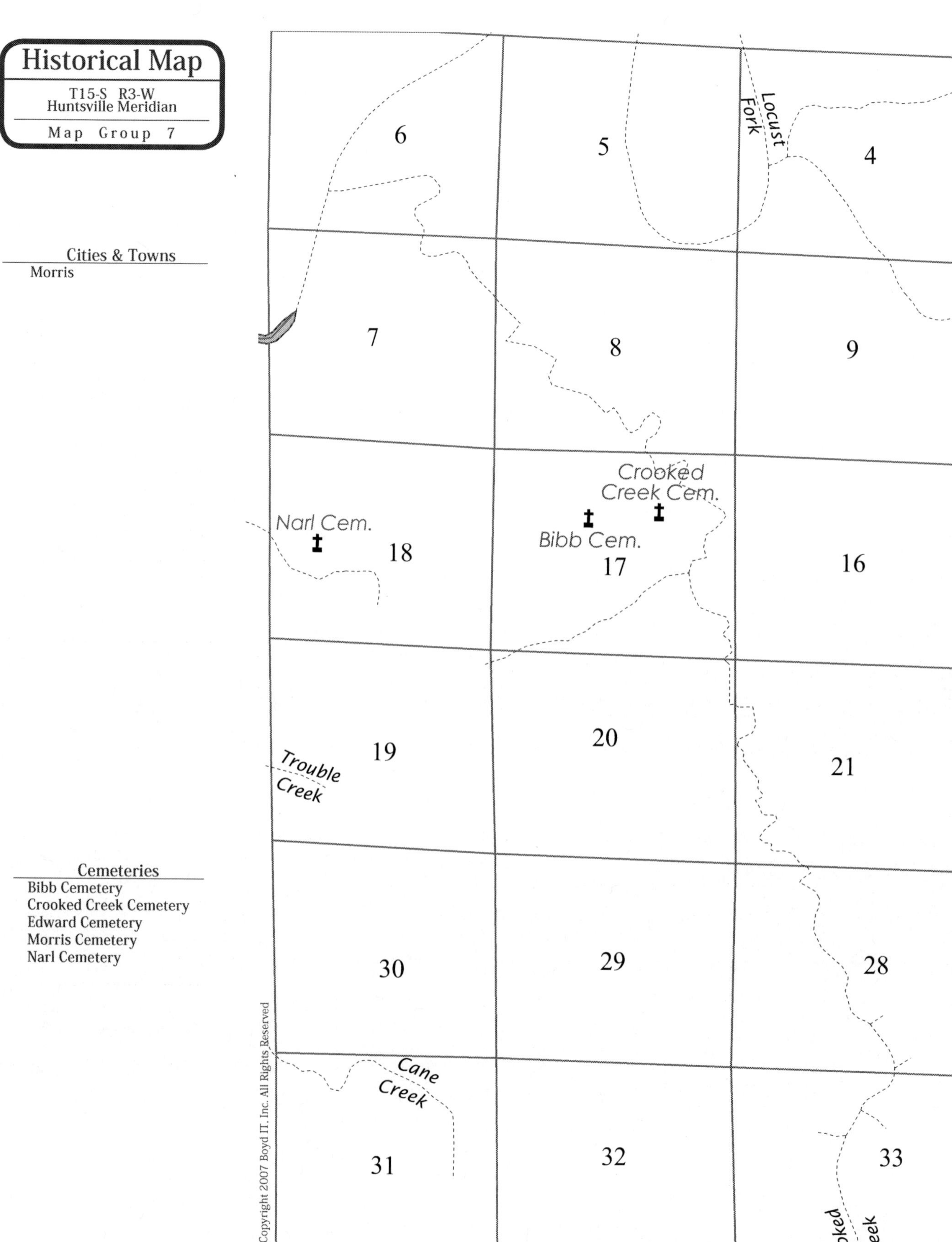

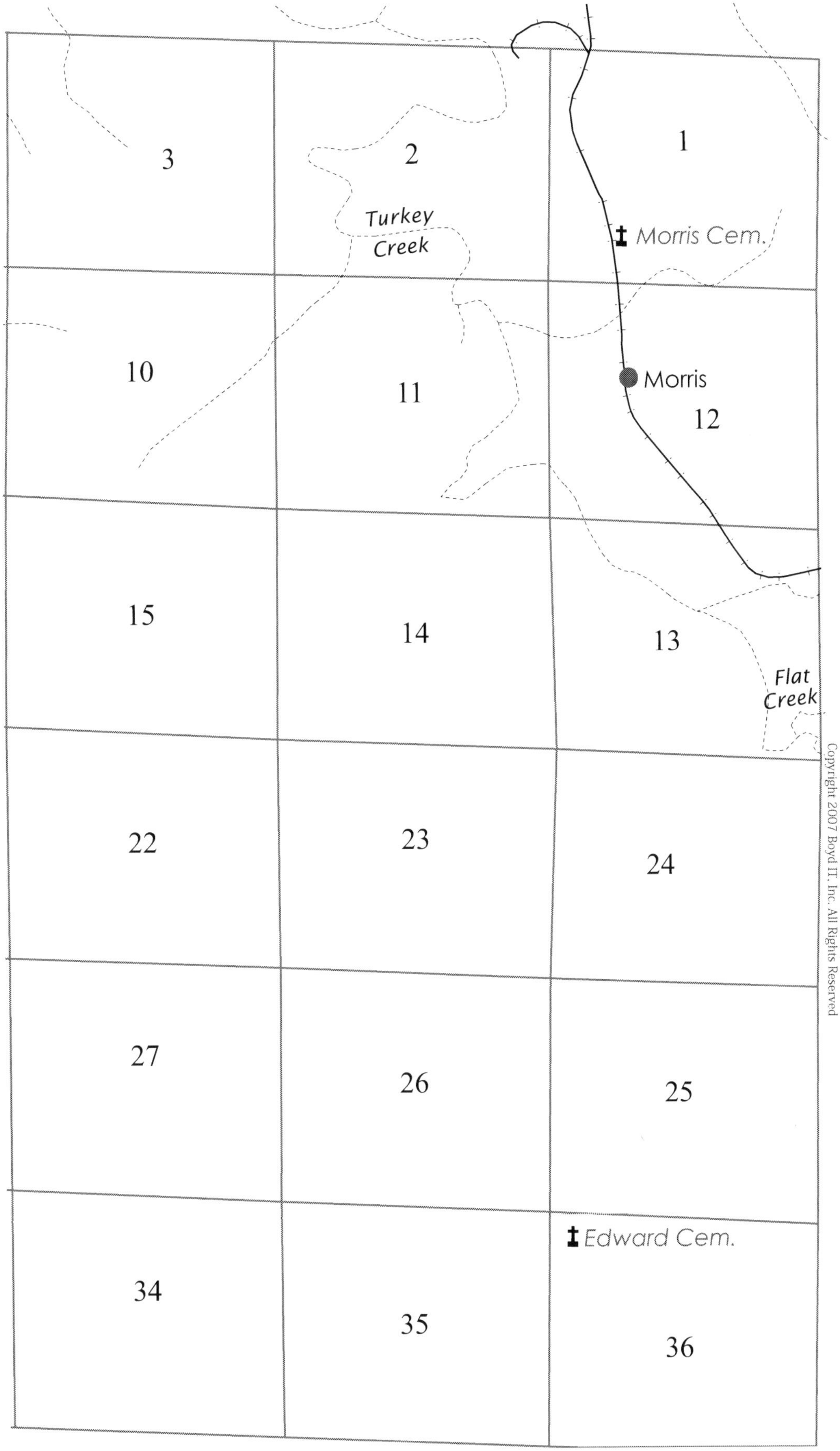

3 2 1

Turkey Creek

Morris Cem.

10 11 12

Morris

15 14 13

Flat Creek

22 23 24

27 26 25

34 35 36

Edward Cem.

Helpful Hints

1. This Map takes a different look at the same Congressional Township displayed in the preceding two maps. It presents features that can help you better envision the historical development of the area: a) Water-bodies (lakes & ponds), b) Water-courses (rivers, streams, etc.), c) Railroads, d) City/town center-points (where they were oftentimes located when first settled), and e) Cemeteries.

2. Using this "Historical" map in tandem with this Township's Patent Map and Road Map, may lead you to some interesting discoveries. You will often find roads, towns, cemeteries, and waterways are named after nearby landowners: sometimes those names will be the ones you are researching. See how many of these research gems you can find here in Jefferson County.

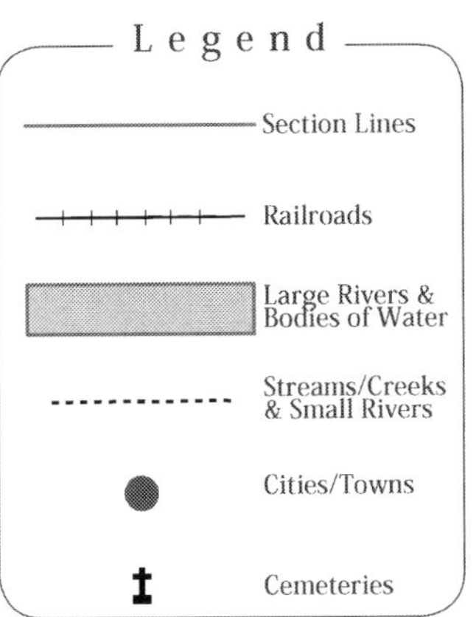

Scale: Section = 1 mile X 1 mile
(there are some exceptions)

Map Group 8: Index to Land Patents

Township 15-South Range 2-West (Huntsville)

After you locate an individual in this Index, take note of the Section and Section Part then proceed to the Land Patent map on the pages immediately following. You should have no difficulty locating the corresponding parcel of land.

The "For More Info" Column will lead you to more information about the underlying Patents. See the *Legend* at right, and the "How to Use this Book" chapter, for more information.

LEGEND

"For More Info . . . " column

- **A** = Authority (Legislative Act, See Appendix "A")
- **B** = Block or Lot (location in Section unknown)
- **C** = Cancelled Patent
- **F** = Fractional Section
- **G** = Group (Multi-Patentee Patent, see Appendix "C")
- **V** = Overlaps another Parcel
- **R** = Re-Issued (Parcel patented more than once)

(A & G items require you to look in the Appendixes referred to above. All other Letter-designations followed by a number require you to locate line-items in this index that possess the ID number found after the letter).

ID	Individual in Patent	Sec.	Sec. Part	Date Issued	Other Counties	For More Info . . .
1123	ANDERSON, John P	10	SE	1885-06-30		A4
1181	ANDERSON, Salina M	8	NENE	1891-06-10		A4
1182	" "	8	S½NE	1891-06-10		A4
1173	BAIRD, Robert B	20	N½NE	1858-06-01		A1
1174	" "	20	NENW	1858-06-01		A1
1175	" "	20	S½NE	1858-06-01		A1
1101	BARTON, John	30	E½NW	1824-05-04		A1
1102	BELCHER, John	18	W½SW	1831-01-04		A1
1103	" "	19	NWSW	1834-10-16		A1
1212	BIBB, William J	32	N½SE	1888-11-08		A1
1056	BLACK, Fannie F	32	N½NW	1899-09-07		A4 G24
1056	BLACK, Jacob	32	N½NW	1899-09-07		A4 G24
1196	BOOKER, Thomas M	28	SESW	1885-08-05		A4
1197	" "	28	SWSE	1885-08-05		A4
1198	" "	28	W½SW	1885-08-05		A4
1093	BROOKS, James P	10	W½SW	1889-10-07		A1
1073	BULLOCK, Howell C	30	E½NE	1885-03-16		A1
1133	BURLASON, Jonathan	2	NWSW	1840-11-10		A1
1055	BURLESON, Ezekiel	12	E½NW	1826-06-10		A1
1170	BURNS, Polly A	6	NE	1891-06-29		A4 G36
1170	BURNS, Thomas W	6	NE	1891-06-29		A4 G36
1210	CAIN, William H	24	NESE	1860-07-02		A1
1211	" "	24	S½NE	1860-07-02		A1
1165	CARLISLE, Philip G	14	SESE	1858-06-01		A1
1164	" "	13	SWSW	1860-04-02		A1
1166	" "	24	NWNW	1860-04-02		A1
1072	CHAMBLEE, Horton B	36	SWSE	1837-11-07		A1
1099	CHILDRESS, Joel	17	NENE	1839-09-20		A1
1154	CHILDRESS, Merideth	18	NESW	1834-10-16		A1
1057	COLE, George H	36	SENW	1854-07-15		A1
1058	" "	36	SESW	1854-07-15		A1
1113	COLE, John H	32	S½NE	1884-03-20		A4
1112	" "	22	S½NW	1885-03-30		A4 V1034, 1033
1204	COLEMAN, William	22	W½SW	1883-07-03		A4
1004	COOPER, Ambrose B	12	N½SW	1883-07-03		A4
1005	" "	12	SWNW	1889-11-21		A4
1006	" "	12	SWSW	1889-11-21		A4
1018	COOPER, Daniel V	12	S½NE	1885-08-05		A4
1046	COOPER, David V	12	N½NE	1883-07-03		A4
1156	COOPER, Nathaniel	19	W½NW	1824-05-10		A1
1151	COTTON, Marion L	10	S½NE	1889-03-01		A4
1064	COWDEN, George W	28	NESW	1883-10-01		A4
1065	" "	28	SENW	1883-10-01		A4
1143	COWDEN, Josiah J	28	SWNE	1885-03-16		A1
1172	COWDEN, Richard V	20	SESE	1884-12-05		A4
1178	COWDEN, Robert E	34	N½SW	1885-08-05		A1

ID	Individual in Patent	Sec.	Sec. Part	Date Issued	Other Counties	For More Info . . .
1048	CREEL, Early W	4	E½SW	1890-03-19		A4
1131	CREEL, John V	4	SE	1885-06-20		A4
1079	CUMMINGS, James A	34	E½SE	1891-06-18		A1
1080	" "	34	SWSE	1891-06-18		A1
1144	DAVENPORT, Lafayette	18	N½NW	1875-04-20		A1
1078	DEAN, J H	1	S½NE	1891-10-07		A1
1106	EDWARDS, John	30	NESW	1834-10-21		A1
1127	EDWARDS, John S	30	SWSE	1883-07-03		A4
1206	ERWIN, William	36	W½SW	1824-04-05		A1 V1160
1111	FRANKLIN, John	15	NWNE	1854-07-15		A1
1115	FRANKLIN, John M	15	SENW	1858-06-01		A1
1116	" "	15	SWNE	1858-06-01		A1
1117	" "	15	W½NW	1858-06-01		A1
1012	FRIEDMAN, Bernard	21	NWNE	1888-06-30		A1 G88
1014	GILL, Charles	18	SESW	1876-03-15		A1
1015	" "	18	SWSE	1876-03-15		A1
1141	GILL, Joseph	6	N½SE	1878-04-09		A4 G94 V1167
1141	GILL, Louisa	6	N½SE	1878-04-09		A4 G94 V1167
1022	GILLESPIE, David	17	S½SW	1860-04-02		A1
1023	" "	20	W½NW	1889-08-02		A4
1074	GILLESPIE, Hughey B	17	N½SW	1860-07-02		A1
1075	" "	18	NESE	1860-07-02		A1
1090	GILLESPIE, James M	34	E½NW	1876-04-01		A4
1091	" "	34	NWSE	1889-11-21		A4
1092	" "	34	SWNE	1889-11-21		A4
1104	GILLESPIE, John C	18	S½NW	1894-06-15		A4
1132	GILLESPIE, John W	18	SESE	1890-08-29		A4
1199	GILLESPIE, Thomas M	34	W½NW	1880-02-20		A4
1025	GLENN, David	14	N½SW	1858-06-01		A1
1028	" "	14	SWNE	1858-06-01		A1
1029	" "	14	SWSE	1858-06-01		A1
1030	" "	23	NWNE	1858-06-01		A1
1024	" "	14	N½NE	1885-06-12		A4
1026	" "	14	NESE	1885-06-12		A4
1027	" "	14	SENE	1885-06-12		A4
1142	GLENN, Joseph	22	E½SW	1883-07-03		A4
1003	GOODWIN, Aaron V	26	S½SE	1910-07-18		A1
1070	GOODWIN, Henry	30	W½SW	1824-05-19		A1
1010	GREENE, Augustus C	32	N½NE	1878-04-09		A4 G106
1010	GREENE, Sarah	32	N½NE	1878-04-09		A4 G106
1208	GUTTERY, William	4	S½NW	1885-06-20		A4
1209	" "	4	W½SW	1885-06-20		A4
1061	HAGOOD, George M	36	NWSE	1854-07-15		A1
1118	HAGOOD, John M	20	SESW	1889-08-16		A4
1119	" "	20	W½SW	1889-08-16		A4
1179	HAGOOD, Robert I	25	SESE	1839-09-20		A1
1180	" "	36	NENE	1839-09-20		A1
1059	HALLMARK, George	35	E½SE	1826-10-05		A1
1037	HANBY, David	25	W½NE	1824-04-12		A1
1031	" "	15	W½SW	1839-09-20		A1
1034	" "	22	SWNW	1839-09-20		A1 V1112
1032	" "	21	NENE	1858-06-01		A1
1033	" "	22	SENW	1858-06-01		A1 V1112
1035	" "	24	N½SW	1858-06-01		A1
1036	" "	25	NESE	1858-06-01		A1
1038	" "	9	SWNW	1858-06-01		A1
1107	HANBY, John F	36	E½SE	1839-03-15		A1
1109	" "	36	SWNE	1839-09-20		A1
1108	" "	36	NWNE	1854-07-15		A1
1207	HARDEN, William G	6	E½NW	1892-01-18		A4
1060	HENRY, George L	34	S½SW	1873-08-01		A1
1083	HIGGINBOTHAM, James C	1	N½NE	1895-01-31		A4
1066	HUGHES, George W	3	E½NW	1858-06-01		A1
1097	HUGHES, Jesse	11	NWNE	1839-09-20		A1
1098	" "	12	NWNW	1839-09-20		A1
1128	JOHNSON, John S	24	N½NE	1883-07-03		A4
1176	LAIRD, Robert B	20	NESW	1885-06-12		A4
1177	" "	20	SENW	1885-06-12		A4
1016	LANIER, Clifford A	32	SESE	1889-02-20		A1
1149	LANIER, Lucy J	32	NESW	1889-10-07		A1 G156
1149	LANIER, William B	32	NESW	1889-10-07		A1 G156
1063	LEE, George N	22	S½NE	1878-04-09		A4
1062	" "	22	N½NE	1884-12-05		A4

ID	Individual in Patent	Sec.	Sec. Part	Date Issued	Other Counties	For More Info . . .
1138	LEE, Jonathan W	22	SE	1889-08-16		A4
1218	LITTLE, William W	2	NESW	1890-04-15		A1
1219	" "	2	SWNW	1890-04-15		A1
1220	" "	2	SWSW	1890-04-15		A1
1134	LIVERMAN, Jonathan	8	E½SE	1824-04-14		A1
1135	LIVERMORE, Jonathan	9	NWSW	1839-09-20		A1
1136	" "	9	SWSW	1840-11-10		A1
1012	LOVEMAN, Emanuel	21	NWNE	1888-06-30		A1 G88
1137	MAJORS, Jonathan	18	NE	1885-06-20		A4
1145	MALONE, Lafayette	32	SESW	1884-12-05		A4
1146	" "	32	SWSE	1884-12-05		A4
1147	" "	32	W½SW	1884-12-05		A4
1202	MARTIN, Warren J	35	SWSE	1858-06-01		A1 R1159
1213	MATHIS, William	18	NWSE	1839-09-20		A1
1011	MATTISON, Benjamin	25	E½NE	1823-06-02		A1
1159	MCCLURE, Patience E	35	SWSE	1858-06-01		A1 R1202
1160	" "	36	NWSW	1858-06-01		A1 V1206
1009	MCCOMBS, Anthony C	14	S½SW	1894-05-04		A4
1042	MCCOMBS, David	12	NWSE	1854-07-15		A1
1039	" "	1	SWNW	1858-06-01		A1
1040	" "	1	W½SW	1858-06-01		A1
1041	" "	11	NENW	1858-06-01		A1
1043	" "	2	SENE	1858-06-01		A1
1044	" "	2	SESW	1858-06-01		A1
1045	" "	2	W½SE	1858-06-01		A1
1082	MCCOMBS, James A	14	S½NW	1883-07-03		A4
1081	" "	14	N½NW	1885-04-27		A4
1203	MCCOMBS, William B	1	SE	1894-11-28		A4
1100	MERRIKEN, John A	10	E½SW	1883-07-03		A4
1008	MOORE, Andrew	28	N½NE	1876-04-01		A4
1007	" "	26	SW	1889-03-01		A4
1124	MOORE, John R	12	E½SE	1889-10-07		A1
1125	" "	12	SESW	1889-10-07		A1
1126	" "	12	SWSE	1889-10-07		A1
1152	MOORE, Martha V	4	N½NW	1885-06-12		A4
1153	" "	4	W½NE	1885-06-12		A4
1047	MOTE, Demancil	10	NW	1885-06-20		A4
1122	MURPHY, John	24	SWSW	1891-06-29		A4
1114	MURPHY, John H	24	SESW	1891-01-15		A4
1017	NASH, Cooper B	27	NENW	1839-09-20		A1
1076	NATIONS, Isaac	15	E½SW	1824-04-28		A1
1110	PATTON, John F	26	E½NE	1884-12-05		A4
1157	PAYNE, Newton	36	SENE	1854-07-15		A1
1069	POWELL, Green	8	W½SE	1824-05-24		A1
1067	" "	7	NESE	1834-10-16		A1
1068	" "	8	NWSW	1834-10-16		A1
1096	RANDOLPH, Jeremiah	24	E½NW	1850-04-01		A1
1215	REED, William	30	NWNE	1835-10-01		A1
1162	REESE, Perry M	36	N½NW	1885-06-12		A4
1163	" "	36	SWNW	1885-06-12		A4
1214	REESE, William N	24	SWNW	1878-04-09		A4
1171	REID, Reuben	15	NENW	1839-09-20		A1
1217	REID, William	19	SWSW	1837-11-07		A1
1216	" "	19	SWSE	1839-09-20		A1
1155	RODGERS, Moses	22	N½NW	1884-03-10		A4
1094	ROGERS, James	7	NWSE	1839-09-20		A1
1095	" "	8	SENW	1839-09-20		A1
1086	ROGERS, James G	8	NENW	1850-09-02		A1
1084	" "	17	NENW	1858-06-01		A1
1085	" "	7	SWNE	1861-08-01		A1
1087	" "	8	NWNE	1861-08-01		A1
1088	" "	8	SWSW	1861-08-01		A1
1089	" "	8	W½NW	1861-08-01		A1
1183	ROGERS, Samuel	17	NWNE	1839-09-20		A1
1187	" "	8	E½SW	1839-09-20		A1
1184	" "	7	NESW	1858-06-01		A1
1185	" "	7	SENW	1858-06-01		A1
1186	" "	7	W½SW	1858-06-01		A1
1161	ROWE, Pearson	6	W½NW	1858-06-01		A1
1195	SCOTT, Thomas J	30	W½NW	1889-10-07		A1
1077	SELF, Isaac	2	E½SE	1824-05-25		A1
1130	SELF, John T	24	SESE	1891-06-10		A4
1205	SHEDD, William E	36	NESW	1839-09-20		A1

ID	Individual in Patent	Sec.	Sec. Part	Date Issued	Other Counties	For More Info . . .
1051	SMITH, Ervin C	26	N½SE	1889-08-02		A4
1052	" "	26	SENW	1889-08-02		A4
1053	" "	26	SWNE	1889-08-02		A4
1158	SPRADLING, Oliver J	23	SENW	1858-06-01		A1
1193	STUBBS, Susan E	28	W½NW	1885-06-20		A4
1194	STUBBS, Thomas E	20	SWSE	1906-05-14		A4
1129	SULLIVAN, John	10	N½NE	1885-05-20		A4
1191	SULLIVAN, Stephen	3	E½SE	1858-06-01		A1
1192	" "	3	NWSE	1858-06-01		A1
1189	" "	2	SENW	1885-03-30		A4
1190	" "	2	SWNE	1885-03-30		A4
1200	SULLIVAN, Walton G	1	E½NW	1891-10-07		A1
1201	" "	1	E½SW	1891-10-07		A1
1221	SULLIVAN, William W	2	N½NE	1885-03-16		A4
1222	" "	2	N½NW	1885-03-16		A4
1167	SULLIVANT, Pleasant	6	SE	1860-04-02		A1 V1141
1168	" "	7	NWNE	1860-04-02		A1
1169	" "	7	SENE	1860-04-02		A1
1120	TATUM, John M	30	NWSE	1883-07-03		A4
1121	" "	30	SWNE	1883-07-03		A4
1013	TAYLOR, Bethana B	26	W½NW	1884-03-10		A4
1049	TAYLOR, Embary F	34	NENE	1889-10-07		A1
1150	TAYLOR, Madison	20	N½SE	1883-07-03		A4
1139	THOMAS, Joseph B	28	NESE	1883-10-01		A4
1140	" "	28	SENE	1883-10-01		A4
1050	THOMPSON, Ephraim	19	E½SW	1824-05-04		A1
1020	VINSON, Daniel	31	SWNE	1834-11-04		A1
1019	" "	31	NESW	1839-09-20		A1
1021	" "	31	W½SE	1839-09-20		A1
1148	WHISENANT, Lorenzo D	6	S½SW	1885-06-20		A4
1054	WILLIAMS, Evans W	30	E½SE	1889-12-28		A1
1071	WILLIAMS, Hiram	34	NWNE	1839-09-20		A1
1105	WILLIAMS, John C	34	SENE	1889-03-02		A1
1188	YOUNGBLOOD, Samuel W	7	NENE	1839-09-20		A1

Patent Map

T15-S R2-W
Huntsville Meridian

Map Group 8

Township Statistics

Parcels Mapped	:	220
Number of Patents	:	166
Number of Individuals	:	139
Patentees Identified	:	133
Number of Surnames	:	89
Multi-Patentee Parcels	:	6
Oldest Patent Date	:	6/2/1823
Most Recent Patent	:	7/18/1910
Block/Lot Parcels	:	0
Parcels Re - Issued	:	1
Parcels that Overlap	:	7
Cities and Towns	:	0
Cemeteries	:	3

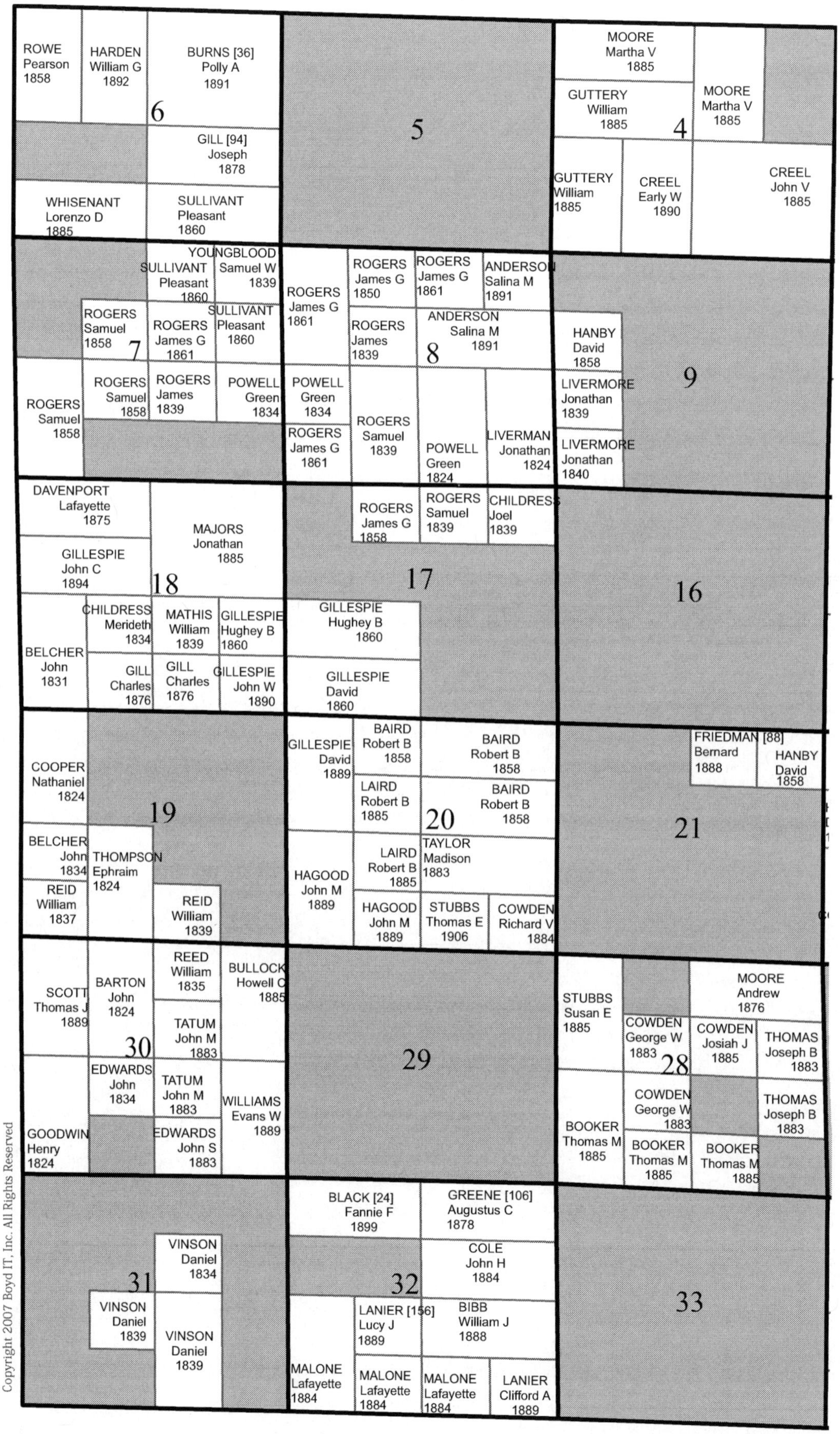

6
ROWE Pearson 1858
HARDEN William G 1892
BURNS [36] Polly A 1891
GILL [94] Joseph 1878
WHISENANT Lorenzo D 1885
SULLIVANT Pleasant 1860

5

4
MOORE Martha V 1885
GUTTERY William 1885
MOORE Martha V 1885
GUTTERY William 1885
CREEL Early W 1890
CREEL John V 1885

7
YOUNGBLOOD Samuel W 1839
SULLIVANT Pleasant 1860
ROGERS Samuel 1858
ROGERS James G 1861
SULLIVANT Pleasant 1860
ROGERS Samuel 1858
ROGERS Samuel 1858
ROGERS James 1839
POWELL Green 1834

8
ROGERS James G 1861
ROGERS James G 1850
ROGERS James G 1861
ANDERSON Salina M 1891
ROGERS James 1839
ANDERSON Salina M 1891
POWELL Green 1834
ROGERS James G 1861
ROGERS Samuel 1839
POWELL Green 1824
LIVERMAN Jonathan 1824

9
HANBY David 1858
LIVERMORE Jonathan 1839
LIVERMORE Jonathan 1840

18
DAVENPORT Lafayette 1875
MAJORS Jonathan 1885
GILLESPIE John C 1894
CHILDRESS Merideth 1834
MATHIS William 1839
GILLESPIE Hughey B 1860
BELCHER John 1831
GILL Charles 1876
GILL Charles 1876
GILLESPIE John W 1890

17
ROGERS James G 1858
ROGERS Samuel 1839
CHILDRESS Joel 1839
GILLESPIE Hughey B 1860
GILLESPIE David 1860

16

19
COOPER Nathaniel 1824
BELCHER John 1834
THOMPSON Ephraim 1824
REID William 1837
REID William 1839

20
GILLESPIE David 1889
BAIRD Robert B 1858
BAIRD Robert B 1858
LAIRD Robert B 1885
BAIRD Robert B 1858
LAIRD Robert B 1885
TAYLOR Madison 1883
HAGOOD John M 1889
HAGOOD John M 1889
STUBBS Thomas E 1906
COWDEN Richard V 1884

21
FRIEDMAN [88] Bernard 1888
HANBY David 1858

30
SCOTT Thomas J 1889
BARTON John 1824
REED William 1835
BULLOCK Howell C 1885
TATUM John M 1883
EDWARDS John 1834
TATUM John M 1883
WILLIAMS Evans W 1889
GOODWIN Henry 1824
EDWARDS John S 1883

29

28
STUBBS Susan E 1885
MOORE Andrew 1876
COWDEN George W 1883
COWDEN Josiah J 1885
THOMAS Joseph B 1883
COWDEN George W 1883
THOMAS Joseph B 1883
BOOKER Thomas M 1885
BOOKER Thomas M 1885
BOOKER Thomas M 1885

31
VINSON Daniel 1834
VINSON Daniel 1839
VINSON Daniel 1839

32
BLACK [24] Fannie F 1899
GREENE [106] Augustus C 1878
COLE John H 1884
LANIER [156] Lucy J 1889
BIBB William J 1888
MALONE Lafayette 1884
MALONE Lafayette 1884
MALONE Lafayette 1884
LANIER Clifford A 1889

33

Helpful Hints

1. This Map's INDEX can be found on the preceding pages.
2. Refer to Map "C" to see where this Township lies within Jefferson County, Alabama.
3. Numbers within square brackets [ ] denote a multi-patentee land parcel (multi-owner). Refer to Appendix "C" for a full list of members in this group.
4. Areas that look to be crowded with Patentees usually indicate multiple sales of the same parcel (Re-issues) or Overlapping parcels. See this Township's Index for an explanation of these and other circumstances that might explain "odd" groupings of Patentees on this map.

Legend

- Patent Boundary
- Section Boundary
- No Patents Found (or Outside County)
- 1., 2., 3., ... Lot Numbers (when beside a name)
- [ ] Group Number (see Appendix "C")

Scale: Section = 1 mile X 1 mile (generally, with some exceptions)

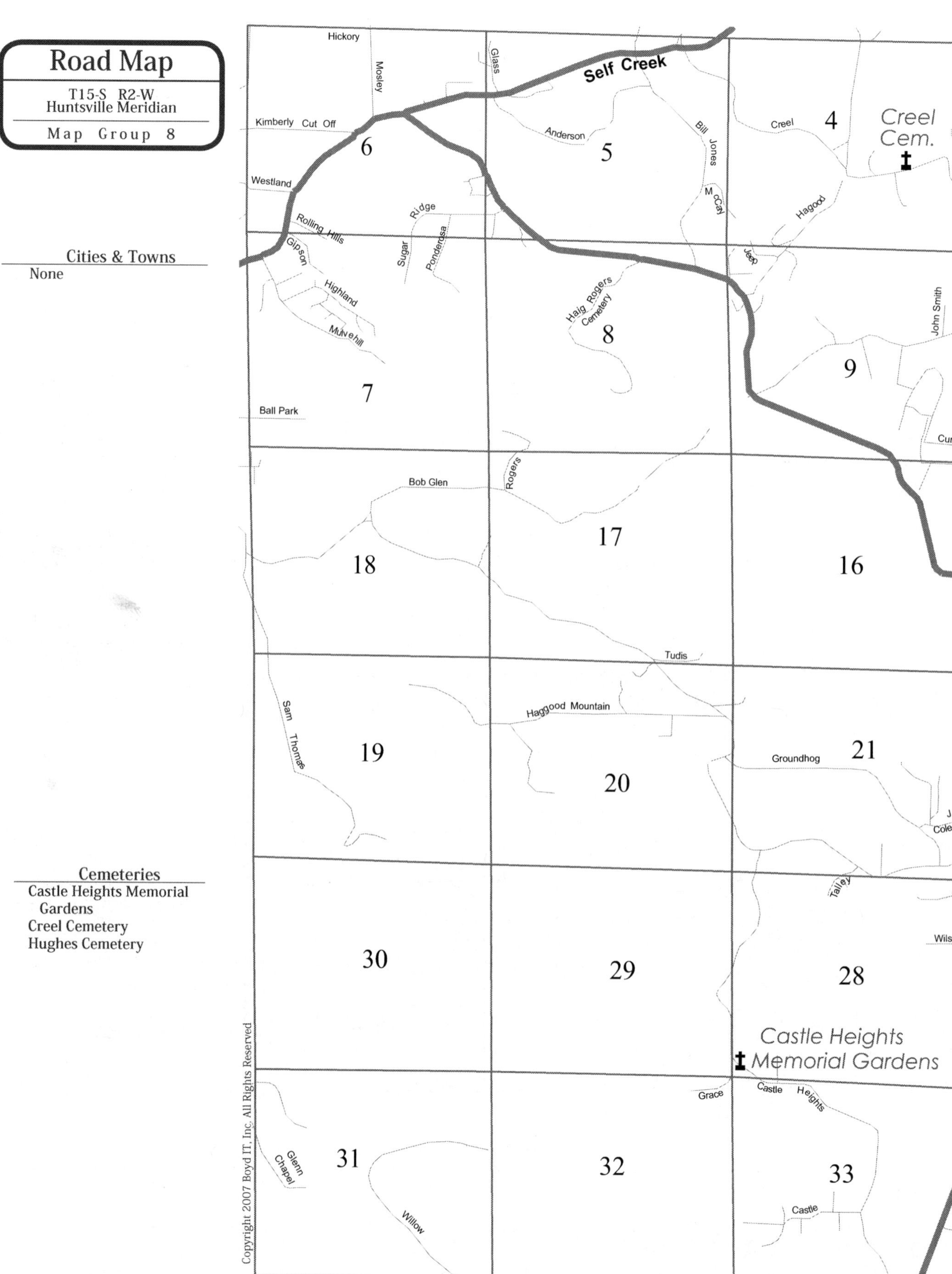
Road Map
T15-S R2-W
Huntsville Meridian
Map Group 8
Cities & Towns
None
Cemeteries
Castle Heights Memorial Gardens
Creel Cemetery
Hughes Cemetery
Hickory
Mosley
Glass
Self Creek
Kimberly Cut Off
Anderson
Bill Jones
Creel
Creel Cem.
Westland
M cCay
Hagood
Ridge
Rolling Hills
Sugar
Ponderosa
Gipson
Highland
Mulvehill
Jeep
Haig Rogers Cemetery
John Smith
Ball Park
Curry
Bob Glen
Rogers
Tudis
Sam Thomas
Haggood Mountain
Groundhog
J D Coleman
Talley
Wilson
Castle Heights Memorial Gardens
Grace
Castle Heights
Glenn Chapel
Willow
Castle
4
5
6
7
8
9
16
17
18
19
20
21
28
29
30
31
32
33
Copyright 2007 Boyd IT, Inc. All Rights Reserved

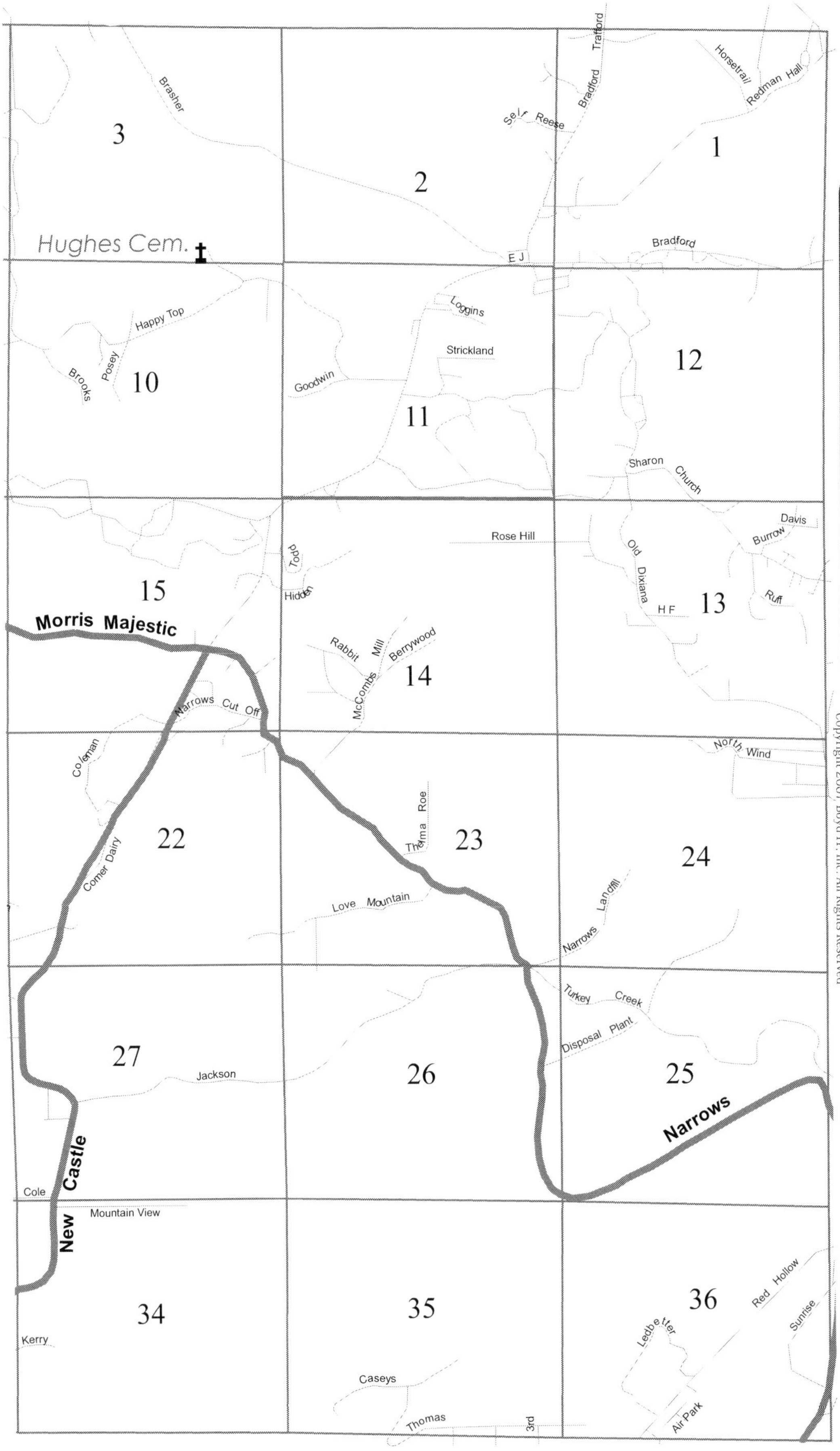

3
Brasher
2
Self
Reese
Bradford
Trafford
Horsetrail
Redman Hall
1
Hughes Cem.
EJ
Bradford
Happy Top
Posey
Brooks
10
Goodwin
Loggins
Strickland
11
12
Sharon
Church
15
Todd
Hidden
Rose Hill
Old
Dixiana
HF
13
Davis
Burrow
Ruff
Morris Majestic
Rabbit
Mill
Berrywood
McCombs
14
Narrows
Cut Off
Coleman
22
Comer Dairy
Thelma Roe
23
Love Mountain
North Wind
24
Narrows
Landfill
27
Jackson
26
Turkey
Creek
Disposal
Plant
25
Narrows
Cole
Castle
New
Mountain View
34
Kerry
35
Caseys
Thomas
3rd
36
Red Hollow
Sunrise
Ledbetter
Air Park

Helpful Hints

1. This road map has a number of uses, but primarily it is to help you: a) find the present location of land owned by your ancestors (at least the general area), b) find cemeteries and city-centers, and c) estimate the route/roads used by Census-takers & tax-assessors.

2. If you plan to travel to Jefferson County to locate cemeteries or land parcels, please pick up a modern travel map for the area before you do. Mapping old land parcels on modern maps is not as exact a science as you might think. Just the slightest variations in public land survey coordinates, estimates of parcel boundaries, or road-map deviations can greatly alter a map's representation of how a road either does or doesn't cross a particular parcel of land.

Legend
Section Lines
Interstates
Highways
Other Roads
Cities/Towns
Cemeteries

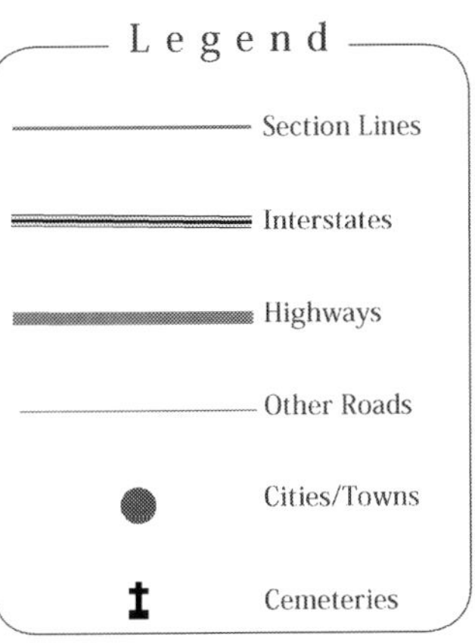

Scale: Section = 1 mile X 1 mile
(generally, with some exceptions)

Historical Map

T15-S R2-W
Huntsville Meridian

Map Group 8

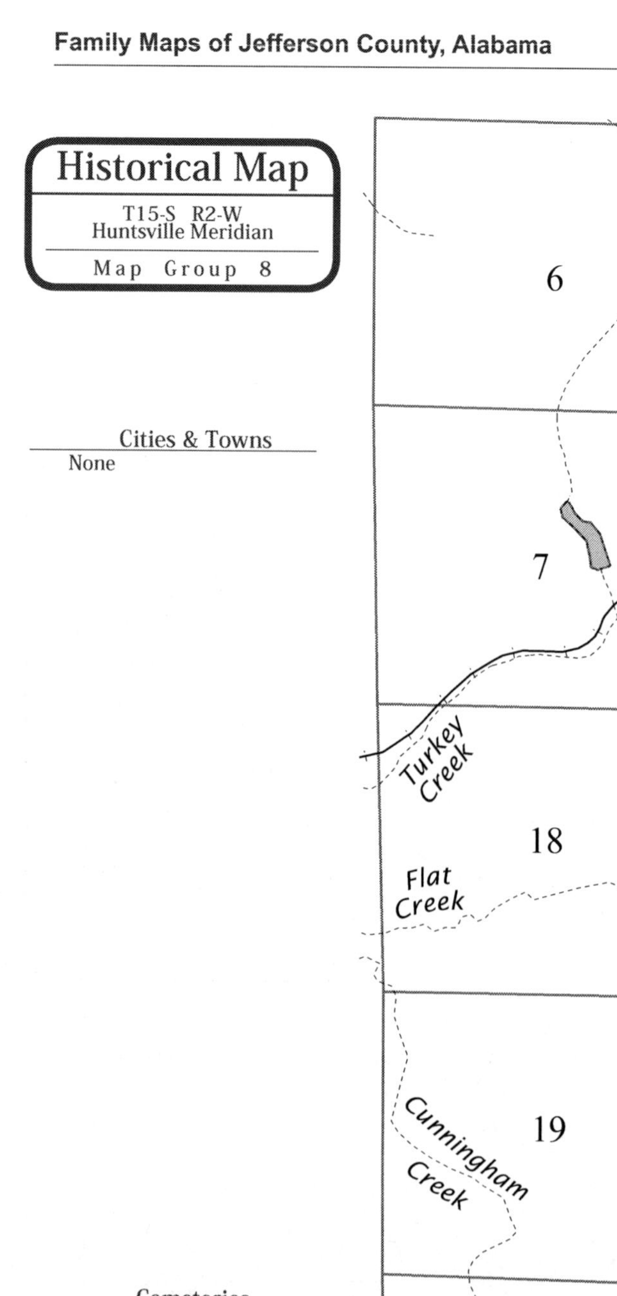

Cities & Towns

None

Cemeteries

Castle Heights Memorial Gardens
Creel Cemetery
Hughes Cemetery

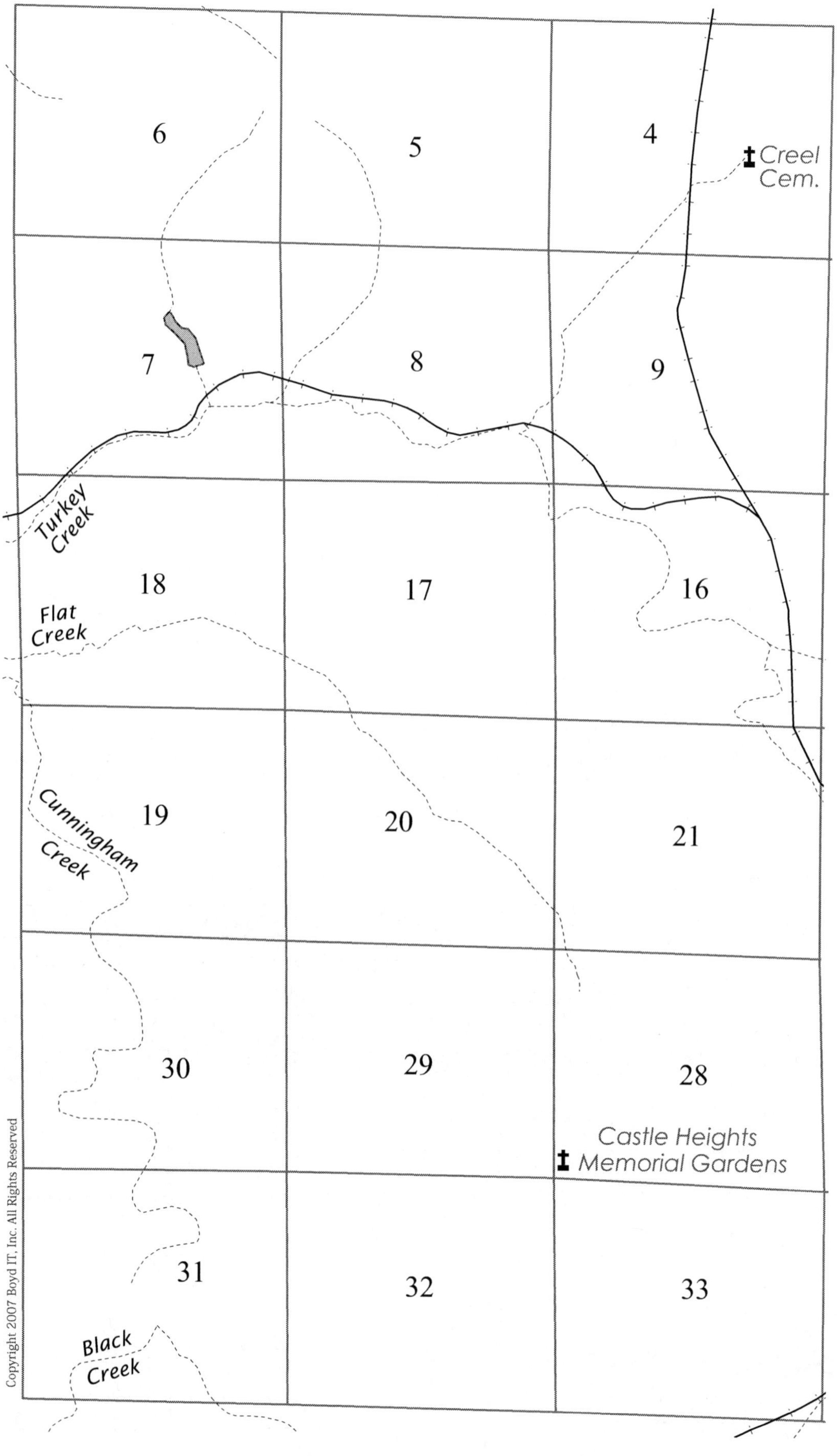

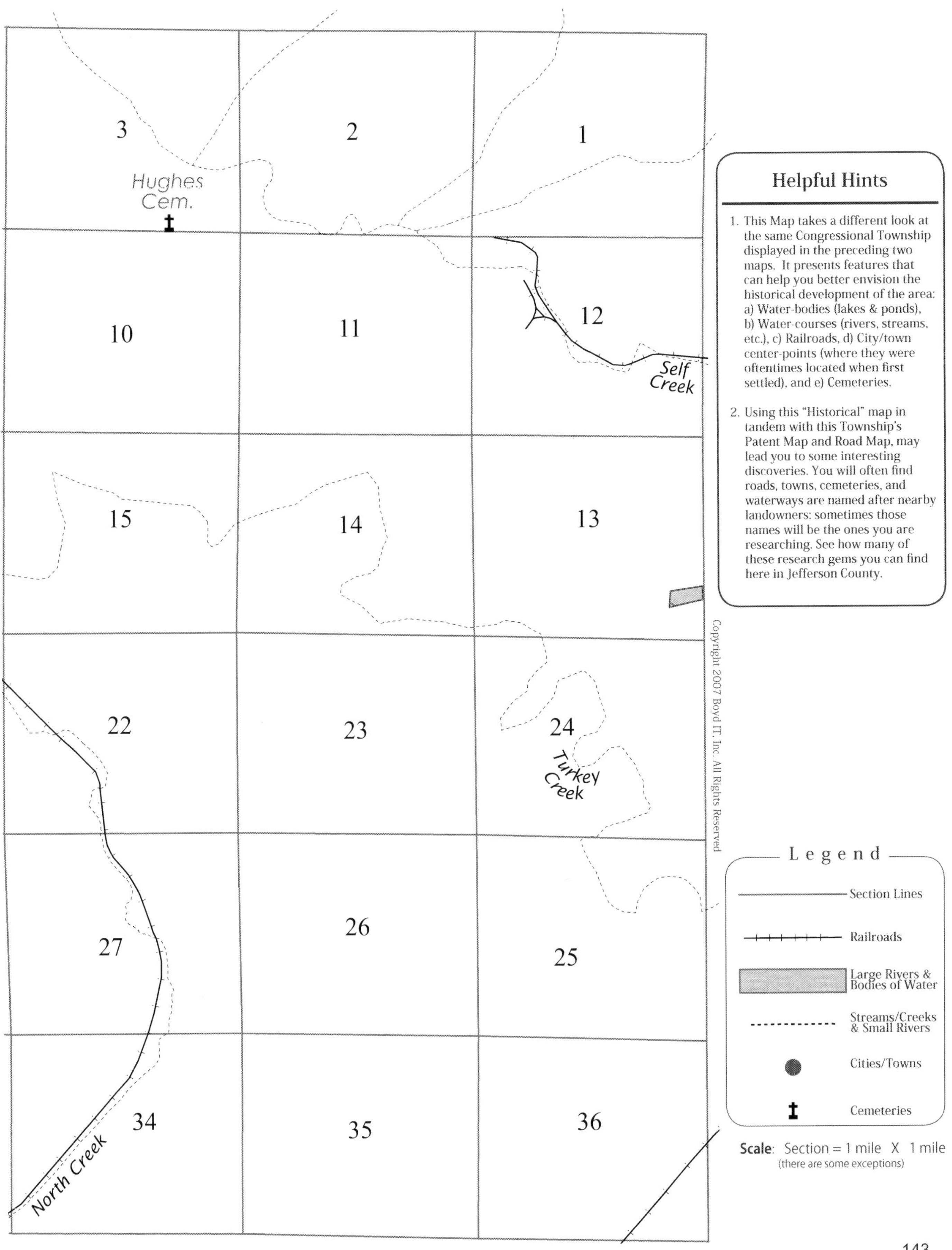

Helpful Hints

1. This Map takes a different look at the same Congressional Township displayed in the preceding two maps. It presents features that can help you better envision the historical development of the area: a) Water-bodies (lakes & ponds), b) Water-courses (rivers, streams, etc.), c) Railroads, d) City/town center-points (where they were oftentimes located when first settled), and e) Cemeteries.

2. Using this "Historical" map in tandem with this Township's Patent Map and Road Map, may lead you to some interesting discoveries. You will often find roads, towns, cemeteries, and waterways are named after nearby landowners: sometimes those names will be the ones you are researching. See how many of these research gems you can find here in Jefferson County.

Map Group 9: Index to Land Patents

Township 15-South Range 1-West (Huntsville)

After you locate an individual in this Index, take note of the Section and Section Part then proceed to the Land Patent map on the pages immediately following. You should have no difficulty locating the corresponding parcel of land.

The "For More Info" Column will lead you to more information about the underlying Patents. See the *Legend* at right, and the "How to Use this Book" chapter, for more information.

LEGEND

"For More Info . . . " column

A = Authority (Legislative Act, See Appendix "A")
B = Block or Lot (location in Section unknown)
C = Cancelled Patent
F = Fractional Section
G = Group (Multi-Patentee Patent, see Appendix "C")
V = Overlaps another Parcel
R = Re-Issued (Parcel patented more than once)

(A & G items require you to look in the Appendixes referred to above. All other Letter-designations followed by a number require you to locate line-items in this index that possess the ID number found after the letter).

ID	Individual in Patent	Sec.	Sec. Part	Date Issued	Other Counties	For More Info . . .
1366	ABEL, John W	2	E½NW	1883-07-03		A4
1442	ALLRED, Thomas	5	E½SE	1826-06-10		A1
1249	ANDERSON, Daniel W	18	NESE	1859-04-01		A1
1250	" "	7	NWSW	1859-04-01		A1
1384	ANDERSON, Margaret	31	W½NW	1823-05-01		A1
1385	" "	31	W½SW	1823-05-01		A1
1383	" "	31	E½SW	1824-05-25		A1
1443	ANDERSON, Thomas	18	NE	1849-05-01		A1
1392	ARNETT, Martha J	18	SESE	1891-06-29		A4
1393	" "	18	W½SE	1891-06-29		A4
1299	BAIRD, James	32	S½NE	1858-06-01		A1
1305	BAIRD, James L	21	SESW	1839-09-20		A1
1427	BAIRD, Robert	30	SWNE	1839-09-20		A1 G10
1458	BAIRD, Washington M	20	NESW	1854-07-15		A1
1459	" "	21	NESW	1854-07-15		A1
1460	" "	21	NWSE	1858-06-01		A1
1461	" "	21	SWNW	1858-06-01		A1
1462	" "	28	N½NW	1858-06-01		A1
1463	" "	28	NWNE	1858-06-01		A1
1401	BEARD, Milton A	20	SESW	1837-04-01		A1
1248	BOYD, Cornelius	29	W½SE	1826-12-01		A1
1261	BRANHAM, Elijah L	10	NENW	1885-06-12		A4
1275	BROWN, George	15	W½NW	1823-05-01		A1
1276	" "	8	E½SE	1826-06-10		A1
1277	" "	9	W½NW	1826-06-10		A1
1421	BURCHFIELD, Presley	2	NWSW	1890-10-11		A4
1422	" "	2	SWNW	1890-10-11		A4
1242	BUSH, Brooks	34	N½SW	1858-06-01		A1
1243	" "	34	S½NW	1858-06-01		A1
1428	BUTLER, Robert C	13	SWSW	1858-06-01		A1
1429	" "	24	NWNW	1858-06-01		A1
1468	BUTLER, William	23	NENE	1858-06-01		A1
1469	" "	23	NWNE	1858-06-01		A1
1255	BYRD, Dona	4	NESE	1902-02-03		A4 G40
1255	BYRD, Hilliard D	4	NESE	1902-02-03		A4 G40
1482	CAIN, William H	19	N½SW	1860-07-02		A1
1483	" "	19	S½NW	1860-07-02		A1
1484	" "	19	SWNE	1860-07-02		A1
1404	CAWOOD, Moses	29	W½SW	1823-05-01		A1 G46
1405	" "	30	E½SE	1823-05-01		A1 G46
1403	" "	29	E½SW	1824-05-04		A1
1476	CHAMBLEE, William F	17	SWSE	1854-07-15		A1
1477	" "	20	SENW	1854-07-15		A1
1475	" "	17	SESE	1858-06-01		A1
1478	" "	20	SWNE	1858-06-01		A1
1245	CLAYTON, Charles C	26	SESE	1839-09-20		A1

ID	Individual in Patent	Sec.	Sec. Part	Date Issued	Other Counties	For More Info . . .
1426	COLEMAN, Ren	33	SWNW	1852-01-01		A1
1452	COLLINS, Thompson	22	E½NE	1824-04-14		A1
1453	" "	9	E½NE	1824-04-14		A1
1225	COSBY, Abner	4	NWNE	1839-09-20		A1
1301	COSBY, James	8	W½SE	1824-04-30		A1
1302	" "	9	SWNE	1839-09-20		A1
1471	COWDEN, William D	10	SESW	1858-06-01		A1
1472	" "	10	SWSE	1858-06-01		A1
1293	COZBY, Isaac	10	NWSE	1839-09-20		A1
1303	COZBY, James	9	NWNE	1837-04-01		A1
1257	DAVIS, Edward J	6	SWNE	1858 06 01		A1
1289	DORMAN, George W	6	W½NW	1896-05-21		A4
1290	" "	6	W½SW	1896-05-21		A4
1359	DOXEY, John S	3	E½NW	1823-05-01		A1
1360	" "	9	E½SE	1823-05-01		A1
1361	" "	9	E½SW	1823-05-01		A1
1362	" "	9	W½SE	1823-05-01		A1
1363	" "	9	W½SW	1823-05-01		A1
1413	DYER, Otis	4	E½SW	1826-06-10		A1
1330	ELLIOTT, James W	36	E½NE	1885-06-12		A4
1331	" "	36	E½SE	1885-06-12		A4
1480	FAUCETT, William	4	NWNW	1858-06-01		A1
1235	FOSTER, Anthony	25	SWNW	1850-04-01		A1
1236	" "	6	NWNE	1858-06-01		A1
1268	FRANKLIN, Elisha	32	SESW	1858-06-01		A1
1490	GEE, William J	20	SWSW	1838-08-28		A1
1427	" "	30	SWNE	1839-09-20		A1 G10
1306	GILLESPIE, James L	10	NWNW	1858-06-01		A1
1307	" "	4	SWSE	1858-06-01		A1
1449	GILLESPIE, Thomas M	3	NWSW	1839-09-20		A1
1491	GILLESPIE, William J	14	NESW	1885-06-20		A4
1441	GOODMAN, Starling	18	W½SW	1915-04-02		A4
1444	GOODWIN, Thomas	11	W½SE	1823-05-01		A1
1312	HAGOOD, James M	21	NESE	1854-07-15		A1
1314	" "	21	SWSE	1854-07-15		A1
1313	" "	21	SESE	1858-06-01		A1
1315	" "	22	SWSW	1858-06-01		A1
1386	HAGOOD, Mark	17	SENE	1858-06-01		A1
1387	" "	9	NENW	1858-06-01		A1
1430	HAGOOD, Robert I	32	NWSW	1858-06-01		A1
1431	" "	32	SWNW	1858-06-01		A1
1508	HAGOOD, Zachariah	31	NESE	1850-04-01		A1
1509	" "	32	SWSW	1850-04-01		A1
1226	HALL, Abraham	14	SWNE	1858-06-01		A1
1377	HALL, Lent	24	SENE	1840-11-10		A1
1378	HALL, Levi	6	SE	1884-12-05		A4
1274	HANBY, Gabriel	31	W½NE	1823-05-01		A1 G119
1292	HANBY, Henry	8	S½NE	1878-04-09		A4
1344	HANBY, John	20	W½SE	1824-05-18		A1 G120
1339	HANBY, John F	19	NWNW	1850-04-01		A1
1340	" "	19	SWSE	1854-07-15		A1
1341	" "	30	NWNE	1854-07-15		A1
1373	HANCOCK, Josiah	29	W½NE	1823-05-01		A1 G121
1373	HARRISON, Joseph D	29	W½NE	1823-05-01		A1 G121
1345	HARTGROVES, John	5	E½NE	1826-12-01		A1
1446	HAUGHEY, Thomas	3	SWSW	1853-08-01		A1
1445	" "	21	NWNW	1854-07-15		A1
1447	" "	4	SESE	1858-06-01		A1
1376	HAYGOOD, Lafayette	2	W½NE	1894-03-17		A4
1406	HAYS, Nathaniel E	12	E½SW	1880-02-20		A4
1346	HENRY, John	31	E½NW	1823-05-01		A1 G128
1369	HICKMAN, Joseph B	26	NESE	1853-08-01		A1
1370	" "	35	NENE	1858-06-01		A1
1371	" "	36	NWNW	1858-06-01		A1
1436	HICKS, Robert W	10	SESE	1890-07-03		A4
1439	HIGGINBOTHAM, Shannon M	8	E½NW	1885-03-30		A4
1440	" "	8	N½NE	1885-03-30		A4
1448	HOPPER, Thomas	25	W½SW	1824-05-10		A1
1479	HULL, William F	28	SENE	1892-03-07		A4
1507	HUNTER, Willis	3	W½NW	1839-09-20		A1
1416	INGRAM, Philip E	14	SESW	1894-06-20		A4
1415	" "	14	S½SE	1901-12-04		A4
1486	INGRAM, William H	32	NESW	1884-03-20		A4

ID	Individual in Patent	Sec.	Sec. Part	Date Issued	Other Counties	For More Info . . .
1487	INGRAM, William H (Cont'd)	32	NWSE	1884-03-20		A4
1485	" "	32	NESE	1889-11-21		A4
1488	" "	32	SWSE	1889-11-21		A4
1278	JACK, George G	24	W½SW	1837-03-30		A1
1280	" "	34	SWSE	1853-08-01		A1
1279	" "	34	SESE	1858-06-01		A1
1395	JOHNSON, Matthew	31	SESE	1837-11-07		A1
1396	JOHNSTON, Matthew	31	W½SE	1824-04-26		A1
1246	JONES, Charles P	20	NWNW	1885-06-03		A1
1247	" "	20	NWSW	1885-06-03		A1
1348	KELLEY, John	14	E½NE	1858-06-01		A1
1347	KELLEY, John K	22	N½SW	1891-01-15		A4
1349	KELLY, John	13	SWNW	1849-05-01		A1
1432	KENNEBREW, Robert	8	NESW	1895-06-19		A4
1295	KILLOUGH, Isaac R	14	N½SE	1902-09-02		A1
1489	KILLOUGH, William H	36	E½NW	1884-12-05		A4
1497	KILLOUGH, William R	36	W½NE	1876-04-01		A4
1374	KNABE, Julius P	2	NWNW	1888-08-17		A1
1375	" "	2	SWSW	1888-08-17		A1
1342	LAWLESS, John H	36	N½SW	1889-12-28		A1
1343	" "	36	SWNW	1889-12-28		A1
1300	LEE, James C	18	E½SW	1884-03-20		A4
1240	LOCKHART, Benjamin	29	W½NW	1823-05-01		A1 G159
1238	" "	30	E½NE	1824-04-05		A1 R1239
1239	" "	30	E½NE	1921-11-04		A1 R1238
1354	LOCKHART, John P	21	W½SW	1824-04-30		A1
1241	LONG, Benjamin	14	E½NW	1826-05-15		A1
1399	MAJOR, Miles C	17	NWNE	1858-06-01		A1
1400	" "	8	SESW	1858-06-01		A1
1273	MARSHALL, Frank	14	NWNW	1901-12-04		A4
1281	MASSEY, George P	4	NENW	1885-07-27		A1
1282	" "	4	NWSW	1885-07-27		A1
1283	" "	4	SWNW	1885-07-27		A1
1350	MASSEY, John	29	NENE	1861-06-01		A1
1450	MASSEY, Thomas M	32	E½NW	1858-06-01		A1
1451	" "	32	NWNW	1858-06-01		A1
1495	MCCARSON, William	20	E½NE	1824-04-28		A1
1237	MCCAY, Archibald	1	SESE	1861-08-01		A1
1423	MCCAY, Ransom	12	NENE	1858-06-01		A1
1424	" "	12	NENW	1858-06-01		A1
1425	" "	12	W½NE	1858-06-01		A1
1481	MCCAY, William G	13	NWNE	1858-06-01		A1
1316	MCGEE, James	33	SENW	1839-09-20		A1
1346	MCGEHEE, William	31	E½NW	1823-05-01		A1 G128
1274	" "	31	W½NE	1823-05-01		A1 G119
1271	MCGOWEN, Francis A	23	NWNW	1860-04-02		A1
1470	MELTON, William C	34	SENE	1834-10-14		A1
1496	MERRIKEN, William P	26	NESW	1885-04-27		A4
1409	MILLWOOD, Noah	22	NENW	1893-07-19		A4
1410	" "	22	W½NW	1893-07-19		A4
1234	MOORE, Andrew J	26	SWSE	1882-11-20		A4
1408	MOORE, Nickelson M	35	S½NW	1852-01-01		A1
1407	" "	35	NWSW	1858-06-01		A1
1367	MORELAND, Jonathan	34	SESW	1834-10-01		A1
1368	MORELAND, Jonothan	35	E½SW	1823-07-09		A1
1259	NEWMAN, Elbert S	34	N½NW	1891-05-29		A4
1260	" "	34	NWNE	1891-05-29		A4
1414	OWENS, Owen	12	NWSW	1861-07-01		A1
1294	PAIN, Isaac	24	W½SE	1824-10-20		A1
1284	PEARCE, George	11	E½NE	1823-05-01		A1
1379	POSEY, Marcus P	4	E½NE	1861-08-01		A1
1380	" "	4	NWSE	1861-08-01		A1
1381	" "	4	SENW	1861-08-01		A1
1382	" "	4	SWNE	1861-08-01		A1
1335	PRICE, Jesse I	28	SWSE	1853-11-15		A1
1464	PRICE, William A	28	NWSW	1858-06-01		A1
1465	" "	28	SWNW	1858-06-01		A1
1466	" "	29	NESE	1858-06-01		A1
1467	" "	29	SENE	1858-06-01		A1
1355	PRYOR, John	7	NESW	1839-09-20		A1
1356	" "	7	NWSE	1839-09-20		A1
1334	RATLIFF, Jeremiah	12	SWSE	1858-06-01		A1
1434	REED, Robert	33	NWSE	1854-07-15		A1

ID	Individual in Patent	Sec.	Sec. Part	Date Issued	Other Counties	For More Info . . .
1433	REED, Robert (Cont'd)	33	NESE	1858-06-01		A1
1435	" "	33	SWNE	1858-06-01		A1
1498	REED, William	29	SESE	1852-01-01		A1
1332	REID, Jarrard R	6	E½NW	1880-02-20		A4
1333	" "	6	E½SW	1880-02-20		A4
1493	RICHEY, William M	34	SWSW	1854-07-15		A1
1317	RICKEY, James	33	S½SE	1858-06-01		A1
1357	RICKEY, John	25	NENW	1837-03-30		A1
1256	RIDDLE, Edward D	32	SESE	1899-08-03		A4
1318	RITCHIE, James	25	E½NE	1823-05-01		A1
1372	ROGERS, Joseph	30	W½SW	1824-04-14		A1
1358	RUCKER, John	1	SWNW	1858-06-01		A1
1240	SCOTT, David	29	W½NW	1823-05-01		A1 G159
1264	SELF, Elijah	25	SENW	1835-10-01		A1
1266	" "	35	SE	1837-03-20		A1 G213
1263	" "	25	NWNW	1850-04-01		A1
1265	" "	26	S½NE	1899-12-07		A1
1272	SELF, Francis	15	E½SE	1823-06-02		A1
1296	SELF, Isaac T	34	NENE	1858-06-01		A1
1337	SELF, Jesse	12	W½NW	1823-06-02		A1
1336	" "	1	W½SW	1824-05-04		A1
1352	SELF, John N	35	S½NE	1858-06-01		A1
1351	" "	26	NWSE	1876-04-01		A4
1266	SELF, Nathaniel	35	SE	1837-03-20		A1 G213
1454	SELF, Vincent	13	SESW	1858-06-01		A1
1455	" "	24	NESE	1858-06-01		A1
1456	" "	24	SWNW	1858-06-01		A1
1457	SELFE, Vincent	24	NENE	1850-04-01		A1
1258	SIMS, Edward	30	W½SE	1823-05-01		A1
1267	SKELTON, Elijah	11	W½NE	1826-06-01		A1
1254	SPRADLING, David	10	SWSW	1837-03-30		A1
1325	SPRADLING, James	17	NENE	1839-09-20		A1
1365	SPRADLING, John	14	SWNW	1834-11-04		A1
1364	" "	14	NWSW	1839-09-20		A1
1411	SPRADLING, Oliver	12	SENW	1839-09-20		A1
1412	SPRADLING, Oliver W	12	N½SE	1890-07-03		A4
1500	SPRADLING, William	2	E½SE	1823-05-01		A1
1499	" "	2	E½NE	1824-04-28		A1
1501	" "	5	NWSE	1850-09-02		A1
1394	SULLIVAN, Mathew L	12	SWSW	1895-07-17		A4
1229	TADLOCK, Albert J	6	E½NE	1884-03-20		A4
1344	TATUM, Jesse	20	W½SE	1824-05-18		A1 G120
1223	TAYLOR, Aaron	14	SWSW	1839-09-20		A1
1224	" "	15	NWSW	1858-06-01		A1
1285	TAYLOR, George	25	E½SE	1825-09-01		A1
1286	" "	25	W½NE	1825-09-01		A1
1287	" "	26	S½SW	1858-06-01		A1
1288	" "	35	NWNW	1858-06-01		A1
1326	TAYLOR, James	8	W½NW	1892-06-30		A4
1327	" "	8	W½SW	1892-06-30		A4
1298	TAYLOR, James A	18	NW	1891-11-23		A4
1353	TAYLOR, John N	28	SESW	1858-06-01		A1
1502	TAYLOR, William	11	E½SE	1824-04-05		A1
1504	" "	25	W½SE	1825-09-01		A1
1503	" "	24	SESE	1839-09-20		A1
1473	TAYLOR, William E	34	NWSE	1853-08-01		A1
1474	" "	34	SWNE	1858-06-01		A1
1494	TAYLOR, William M	22	NWNE	1876-04-01		A4
1492	TEASLEY, William J	28	SESE	1897-08-30		A4
1291	THOMAS, George W	32	N½NE	1858-06-01		A1
1338	TUCKER, John A	36	NWSE	1885-06-12		A4
1244	TUNNELL, Catharine	24	W½NE	1828-02-20		A1
1251	TURNER, Darby	25	E½SW	1835-10-01		A1
1230	TYLER, Anderson	15	SWSW	1839-09-20		A1
1505	TYLOR, William	15	SESW	1860-04-02		A1
1506	" "	15	SWSE	1860-04-02		A1
1328	VARNON, James	10	E½NE	1824-05-27		A1
1329	" "	10	W½NE	1826-05-15		A1
1319	WALKER, James S	20	E½SE	1823-05-01		A1
1320	" "	29	E½NW	1823-05-01		A1
1404	" "	29	W½SW	1823-05-01		A1 G46
1321	" "	30	E½NW	1823-05-01		A1
1405	" "	30	E½SE	1823-05-01		A1 G46

ID	Individual in Patent	Sec.	Sec. Part	Date Issued	Other Counties	For More Info . . .
1322	WALKER, James S (Cont'd)	30	E½SW	1823-05-01		A1
1323	" "	30	W½NW	1823-05-01		A1
1324	" "	31	E½NE	1823-05-01		A1
1231	WARE, Andrew B	27	NWNW	1858-06-01		A1
1232	" "	28	NENE	1858-06-01		A1
1297	WARE, Jacob	24	E½NW	1823-07-09		A1
1417	WARE, Pleasant D	22	NWSE	1852-01-01		A1
1418	" "	22	S½SE	1858-06-01		A1
1438	WARE, Samuel	24	E½SW	1824-05-18		A1
1308	WATSON, James L	28	NESW	1890-07-03		A4
1309	" "	28	NWSE	1890-07-03		A4
1310	" "	28	SENW	1890-07-03		A4
1311	" "	28	SWNE	1890-07-03		A4
1233	WEAR, Andrew B	22	SESW	1876-04-01		A4
1252	WEAR, David H	22	SENW	1876-04-01		A4
1253	" "	22	SWNE	1876-04-01		A4
1262	WEAR, Elijah S	26	SENW	1884-12-05		A4
1398	WEAR, Matthew T	26	W½NW	1886-04-10		A4
1397	" "	26	NWSW	1904-09-16		A4
1419	WEAR, Pleasant D	22	NESE	1848-07-01		A1
1420	" "	23	NWSW	1858-06-01		A1
1437	WEAR, Robert	35	SWSW	1858-06-01		A1
1269	WHITEHOUSE, Elisha	36	S½SW	1898-10-04		A4
1270	" "	36	SWSE	1898-10-04		A4
1227	WILLIAMS, Albert H	20	NENW	1885-07-27		A1
1228	" "	20	SWNW	1885-07-27		A1
1388	WILLIAMS, Mark	10	N½SW	1858-06-01		A1
1389	" "	10	NESE	1858-06-01		A1
1390	" "	10	S½NW	1858-06-01		A1
1391	" "	3	SESE	1858-06-01		A1
1304	WILLINGHAM, James H	14	NWNE	1891-06-29		A4
1402	YANCY, Mines	13	SENE	1840-11-10		A1

Patent Map

T15-S R1-W
Huntsville Meridian

Map Group 9

Township Statistics

Parcels Mapped	:	287
Number of Patents	:	233
Number of Individuals	:	179
Patentees Identified	:	176
Number of Surnames	:	119
Multi-Patentee Parcels	:	10
Oldest Patent Date	:	5/1/1823
Most Recent Patent	:	11/4/1921
Block/Lot Parcels	:	0
Parcels Re - Issued	:	1
Parcels that Overlap	:	0
Cities and Towns	:	3
Cemeteries	:	1

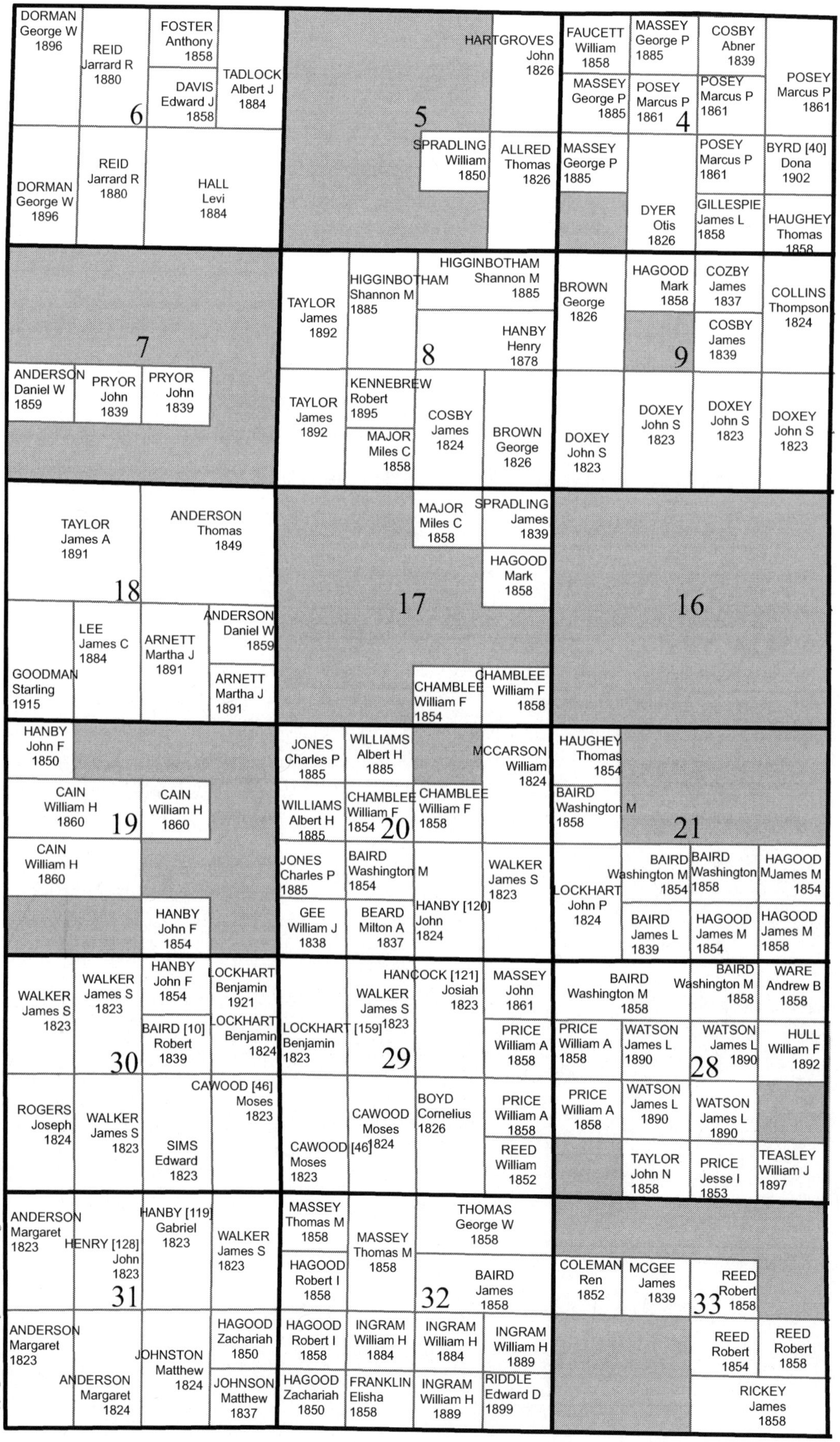

6
DORMAN George W 1896
REID Jarrard R 1880
FOSTER Anthony 1858
DAVIS Edward J 1858
TADLOCK Albert J 1884
DORMAN George W 1896
REID Jarrard R 1880
HALL Levi 1884

5
HARTGROVES John 1826
SPRADLING William 1850
ALLRED Thomas 1826

4
FAUCETT William 1858
MASSEY George P 1885
COSBY Abner 1839
MASSEY George P 1885
POSEY Marcus P 1861
POSEY Marcus P 1861
POSEY Marcus P 1861
MASSEY George P 1885
POSEY Marcus P 1861
BYRD [40] Dona 1902
DYER Otis 1826
GILLESPIE James L 1858
HAUGHEY Thomas 1858

7
ANDERSON Daniel W 1859
PRYOR John 1839
PRYOR John 1839

8
TAYLOR James 1892
HIGGINBOTHAM Shannon M 1885
HIGGINBOTHAM Shannon M 1885
HANBY Henry 1878
TAYLOR James 1892
KENNEBREW Robert 1895
MAJOR Miles C 1858
COSBY James 1824
BROWN George 1826

9
BROWN George 1826
HAGOOD Mark 1858
COZBY James 1837
COLLINS Thompson 1824
COSBY James 1839
DOXEY John S 1823
DOXEY John S 1823
DOXEY John S 1823
DOXEY John S 1823

18
TAYLOR James A 1891
ANDERSON Thomas 1849
LEE James C 1884
ARNETT Martha J 1891
ANDERSON Daniel W 1859
GOODMAN Starling 1915
ARNETT Martha J 1891

17
MAJOR Miles C 1858
SPRADLING James 1839
HAGOOD Mark 1858
CHAMBLEE William F 1854
CHAMBLEE William F 1858

16

19
HANBY John F 1850
CAIN William H 1860
CAIN William H 1860
CAIN William H 1860
HANBY John F 1854

20
JONES Charles P 1885
WILLIAMS Albert H 1885
MCCARSON William 1824
WILLIAMS Albert H 1885
CHAMBLEE William F 1854
CHAMBLEE William F 1858
JONES Charles P 1885
BAIRD Washington M 1854
WALKER James S 1823
GEE William J 1838
BEARD Milton A 1837
HANBY [120] John 1824

21
HAUGHEY Thomas 1854
BAIRD Washington M 1858
LOCKHART John P 1824
BAIRD Washington M 1854
BAIRD Washington M 1858
HAGOOD James M 1854
BAIRD James L 1839
HAGOOD James M 1854
HAGOOD James M 1858

30
WALKER James S 1823
WALKER James S 1823
HANBY John F 1854
LOCKHART Benjamin 1921
BAIRD [10] Robert 1839
LOCKHART Benjamin 1824
ROGERS Joseph 1824
WALKER James S 1823
CAWOOD [46] Moses 1823
SIMS Edward 1823

29
LOCKHART Benjamin 1823
HANCOCK [121] Josiah 1823
WALKER James S [159] 1823
MASSEY John 1861
PRICE William A 1858
CAWOOD Moses [46] 1824
BOYD Cornelius 1826
PRICE William A 1858
CAWOOD Moses 1823
REED William 1852

28
BAIRD Washington M 1858
BAIRD Washington M 1858
WARE Andrew B 1858
PRICE William A 1858
WATSON James L 1890
WATSON James L 1890
HULL William F 1892
PRICE William A 1858
WATSON James L 1890
WATSON James L 1890
TAYLOR John N 1858
PRICE Jesse I 1853
TEASLEY William J 1897

31
ANDERSON Margaret 1823
HENRY [128] John 1823
HANBY [119] Gabriel 1823
WALKER James S 1823
ANDERSON Margaret 1823
JOHNSTON Matthew 1824
ANDERSON Margaret 1824
HAGOOD Zachariah 1850
JOHNSON Matthew 1837

32
MASSEY Thomas M 1858
MASSEY Thomas M 1858
THOMAS George W 1858
HAGOOD Robert I 1858
BAIRD James 1858
HAGOOD Robert I 1858
INGRAM William H 1884
INGRAM William H 1884
INGRAM William H 1889
HAGOOD Zachariah 1850
FRANKLIN Elisha 1858
INGRAM William H 1889
RIDDLE Edward D 1899

33
COLEMAN Ren 1852
MCGEE James 1839
REED Robert 1858
REED Robert 1854
REED Robert 1858
RICKEY James 1858

HUNTER Willis 1839
DOXEY John S 1823
GILLESPIE Thomas M 1839
HAUGHEY Thomas 1853
WILLIAMS Mark 1858
3
KNABE Julius P 1888
ABEL John W 1883
HAYGOOD Lafayette 1894
SPRADLING William 1824
BURCHFIELD Presley 1890
BURCHFIELD Presley 1890
KNABE Julius P 1888
SPRADLING William 1823
2
RUCKER John 1858
SELF Jesse 1824
MCCAY Archibald 1861
1
GILLESPIE James L 1858
BRANHAM Elijah L 1885
VARNON James 1826
VARNON James 1824
WILLIAMS Mark 1858
WILLIAMS Mark 1858
COZBY Isaac 1839
WILLIAMS Mark 1858
SPRADLING David 1837
COWDEN William D 1858
COWDEN William D 1858
HICKS Robert W 1890
10
SKELTON Elijah 1826
PEARCE George 1823
GOODWIN Thomas 1823
TAYLOR William 1824
11
SELF Jesse 1823
MCCAY Ransom 1858
MCCAY Ransom 1858
MCCAY Ransom 1858
SPRADLING Oliver 1839
OWENS Owen 1861
HAYS Nathaniel E 1880
SPRADLING Oliver W 1890
SULLIVAN Mathew L 1895
RATLIFF Jeremiah 1858
12
BROWN George 1823
TAYLOR Aaron 1858
TYLER Anderson 1839
TYLOR William 1860
TYLOR William 1860
SELF Francis 1823
15
MARSHALL Frank 1901
LONG Benjamin 1826
WILLINGHAM James H 1891
KELLEY John 1858
SPRADLING John 1834
HALL Abraham 1858
SPRADLING John 1839
GILLESPIE William J 1885
KILLOUGH Isaac R 1902
TAYLOR Aaron 1839
INGRAM Philip E 1894
INGRAM Philip E 1901
14
MCCAY William G 1858
KELLY John 1849
YANCY Mines 1840
BUTLER Robert C 1858
SELF Vincent 1858
13
MILLWOOD Noah 1893
MILLWOOD Noah 1893
TAYLOR William M 1876
WEAR David H 1876
WEAR David H 1876
COLLINS Thompson 1824
KELLEY John K 1891
WARE Pleasant D 1852
WEAR Pleasant D 1848
HAGOOD James M 1858
WEAR Andrew B 1876
WARE Pleasant D 1858
22
MCGOWEN Francis A 1860
BUTLER William 1858
BUTLER William 1858
WEAR Pleasant D 1858
23
BUTLER Robert C 1858
WARE Jacob 1823
TUNNELL Catharine 1828
SELFE Vincent 1850
SELF Vincent 1858
HALL Lent 1840
SELF Vincent 1858
JACK George G 1837
WARE Samuel 1824
PAIN Isaac 1824
TAYLOR William 1839
24
WARE Andrew B 1858
27
WEAR Matthew T 1886
WEAR Elijah S 1884
SELF Elijah 1899
WEAR Matthew T 1904
MERRIKEN William P 1885
SELF John N 1876
HICKMAN Joseph B 1853
TAYLOR George 1858
MOORE Andrew J 1882
CLAYTON Charles C 1839
26
SELF Elijah 1850
RICKEY John 1837
TAYLOR George 1825
RITCHIE James 1823
FOSTER Anthony 1850
SELF Elijah 1835
HOPPER Thomas 1824
TURNER Darby 1835
TAYLOR William 1825
TAYLOR George 1825
25
NEWMAN Elbert S 1891
NEWMAN Elbert S 1891
SELF Isaac T 1858
BUSH Brooks 1858
TAYLOR William E 1858
MELTON William C 1834
BUSH Brooks 1858
TAYLOR William E 1853
RICHEY William M 1854
MORELAND Jonathan 1834
JACK George G 1853
JACK George G 1858
34
TAYLOR George 1858
HICKMAN Joseph B 1858
MOORE Nickelson M 1852
SELF John N 1858
MOORE Nickelson M 1858
MORELAND Jonothan 1823
SELF [213] Elijah 1837
WEAR Robert 1858
35
HICKMAN Joseph B 1858
KILLOUGH William H 1884
ELLIOTT James W 1885
KILLOUGH William R 1876
LAWLESS John H 1889
LAWLESS John H 1889
TUCKER John A 1885
ELLIOTT James W 1885
WHITEHOUSE Elisha 1898
WHITEHOUSE Elisha 1898
36

Helpful Hints

1. This Map's INDEX can be found on the preceding pages.
2. Refer to Map "C" to see where this Township lies within Jefferson County, Alabama.
3. Numbers within square brackets [ ] denote a multi-patentee land parcel (multi-owner). Refer to Appendix "C" for a full list of members in this group.
4. Areas that look to be crowded with Patentees usually indicate multiple sales of the same parcel (Re-issues) or Overlapping parcels. See this Township's Index for an explanation of these and other circumstances that might explain "odd" groupings of Patentees on this map.

Legend

- Patent Boundary
- Section Boundary
- No Patents Found (or Outside County)
- 1., 2., 3., ... Lot Numbers (when beside a name)
- [ ] Group Number (see Appendix "C")

Scale: Section = 1 mile X 1 mile (generally, with some exceptions)

Road Map

T15-S R1-W
Huntsville Meridian

Map Group 9

Cities & Towns

Clay
Palmerdale
Pinson

Cemeteries

Pinson Cemetery

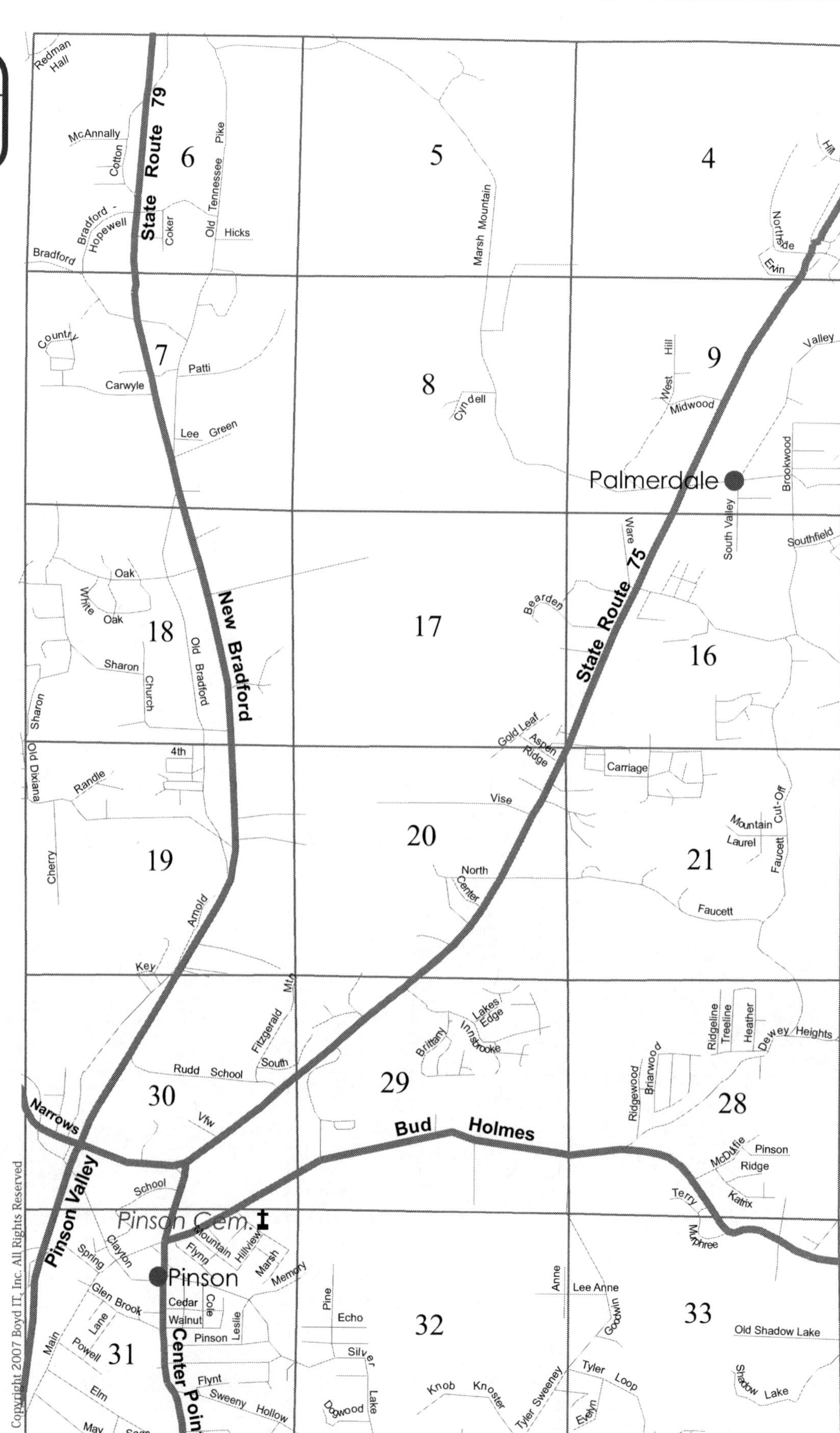

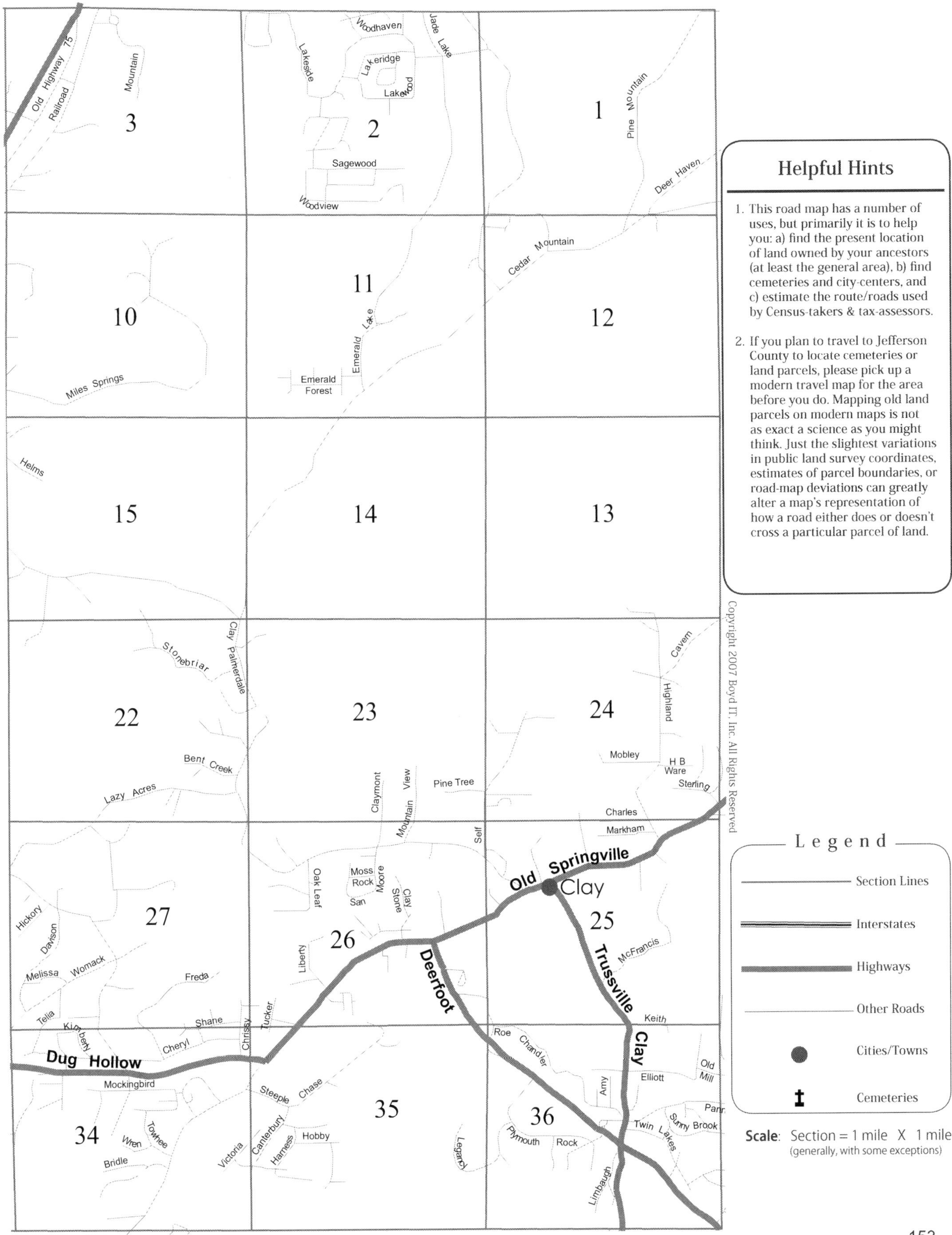

Helpful Hints

1. This road map has a number of uses, but primarily it is to help you: a) find the present location of land owned by your ancestors (at least the general area), b) find cemeteries and city-centers, and c) estimate the route/roads used by Census-takers & tax-assessors.

2. If you plan to travel to Jefferson County to locate cemeteries or land parcels, please pick up a modern travel map for the area before you do. Mapping old land parcels on modern maps is not as exact a science as you might think. Just the slightest variations in public land survey coordinates, estimates of parcel boundaries, or road-map deviations can greatly alter a map's representation of how a road either does or doesn't cross a particular parcel of land.

Legend

- Section Lines
- Interstates
- Highways
- Other Roads
- Cities/Towns
- Cemeteries

Scale: Section = 1 mile X 1 mile
(generally, with some exceptions)

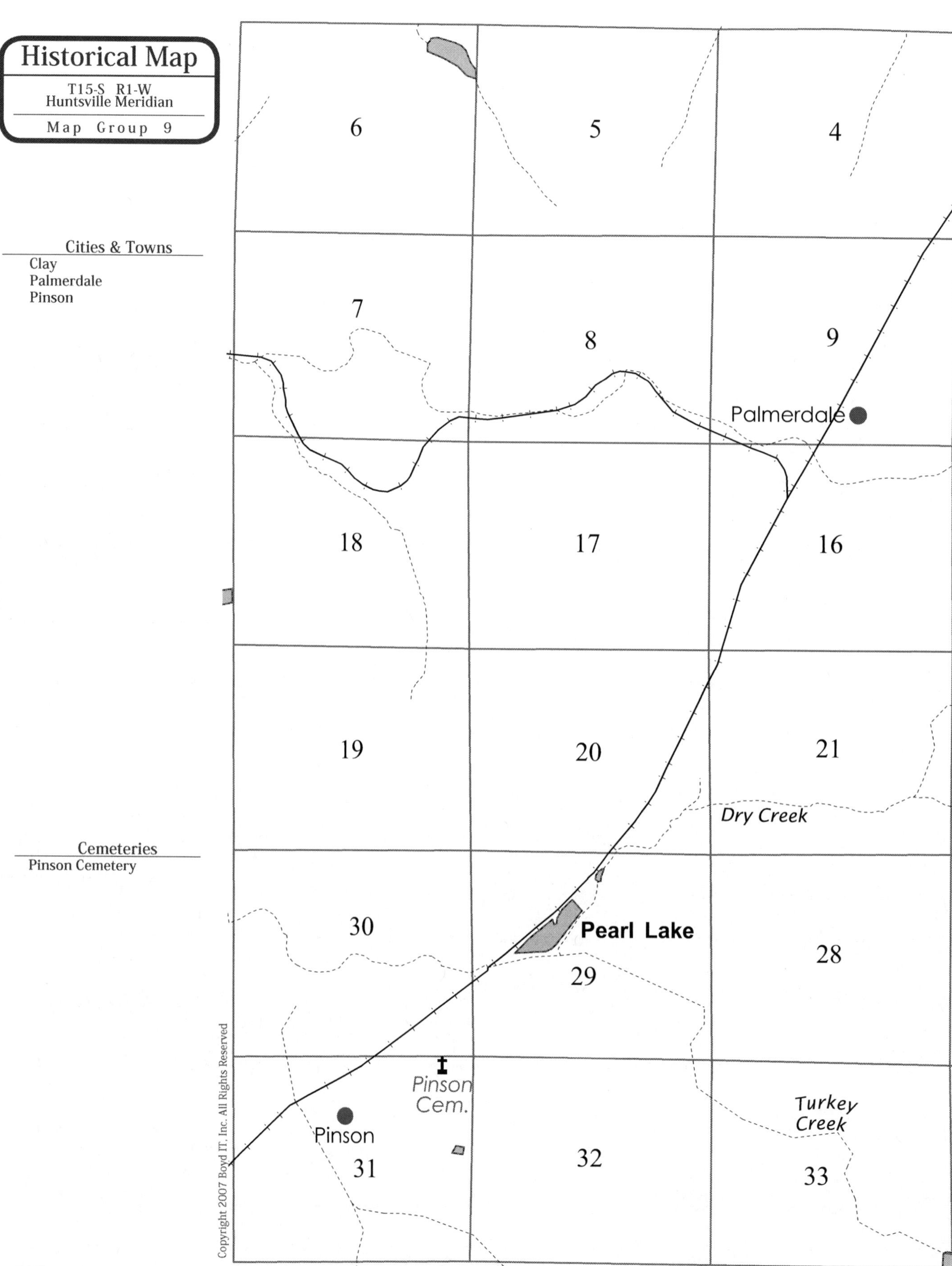
Historical Map
T15-S R1-W
Huntsville Meridian
Map Group 9
Cities & Towns
Clay
Palmerdale
Pinson
Cemeteries
Pinson Cemetery
6
5
4
7
8
9
Palmerdale
18
17
16
19
20
21
Dry Creek
30
Pearl Lake
29
28
Pinson Cem.
Pinson
31
32
Turkey Creek
33
Copyright 2007 Boyd IT, Inc. All Rights Reserved

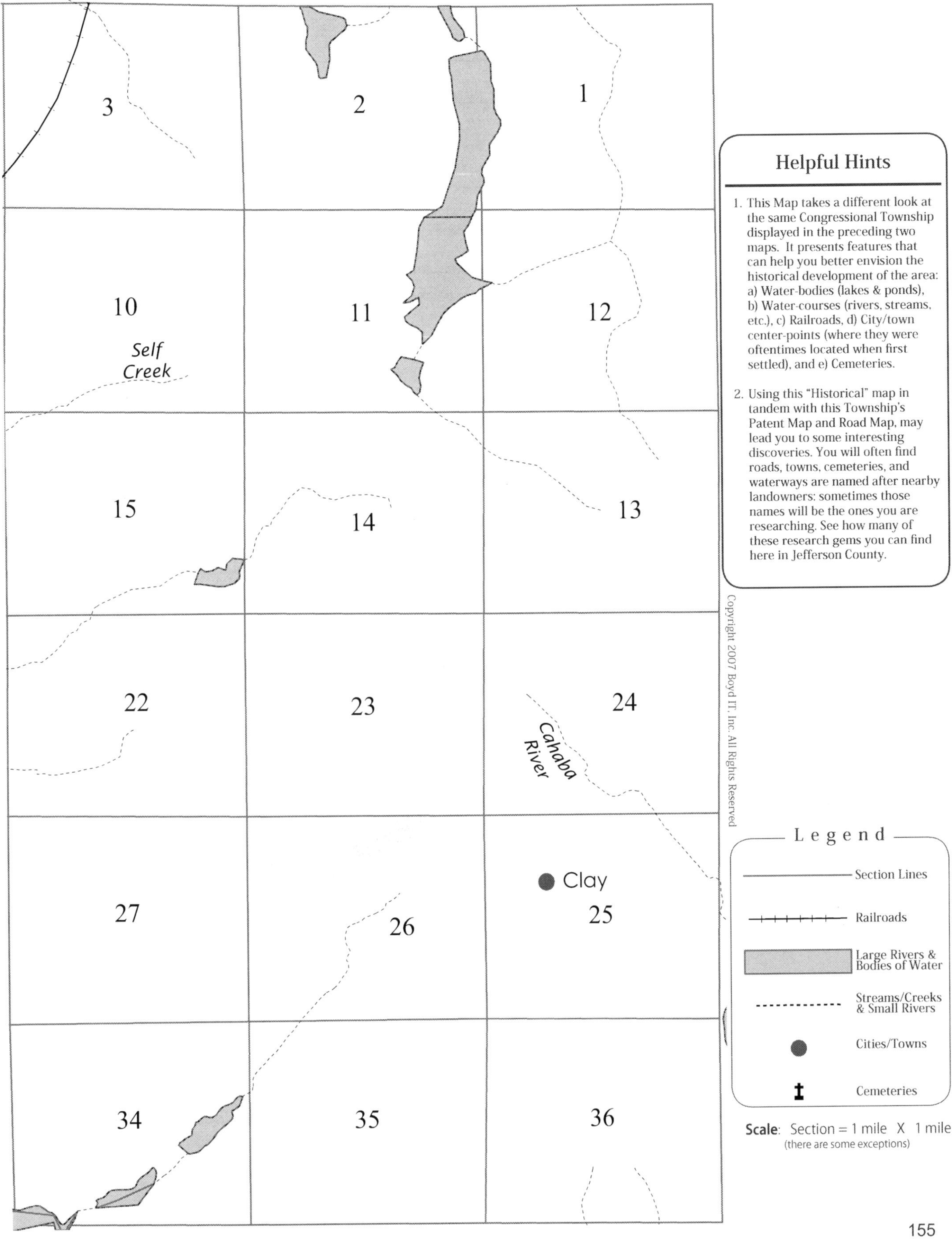

Helpful Hints

1. This Map takes a different look at the same Congressional Township displayed in the preceding two maps. It presents features that can help you better envision the historical development of the area: a) Water-bodies (lakes & ponds), b) Water-courses (rivers, streams, etc.), c) Railroads, d) City/town center-points (where they were oftentimes located when first settled), and e) Cemeteries.
2. Using this "Historical" map in tandem with this Township's Patent Map and Road Map, may lead you to some interesting discoveries. You will often find roads, towns, cemeteries, and waterways are named after nearby landowners: sometimes those names will be the ones you are researching. See how many of these research gems you can find here in Jefferson County.

Map Group 10: Index to Land Patents

Township 15-South Range 1-East (Huntsville)

After you locate an individual in this Index, take note of the Section and Section Part then proceed to the Land Patent map on the pages immediately following. You should have no difficulty locating the corresponding parcel of land.

The "For More Info" Column will lead you to more information about the underlying Patents. See the *Legend* at right, and the "How to Use this Book" chapter, for more information.

LEGEND

"For More Info . . . " column

- **A** = Authority (Legislative Act, See Appendix "A")
- **B** = Block or Lot (location in Section unknown)
- **C** = Cancelled Patent
- **F** = Fractional Section
- **G** = Group (Multi-Patentee Patent, see Appendix "C")
- **V** = Overlaps another Parcel
- **R** = Re-Issued (Parcel patented more than once)

(A & G items require you to look in the Appendixes referred to above. All other Letter-designations followed by a number require you to locate line-items in this index that possess the ID number found after the letter).

ID	Individual in Patent	Sec.	Sec. Part	Date Issued	Other Counties	For More Info . . .
1540	BISHOP, Elias S	19	NWSE	1837-03-20		A1
1538	" "	17	W½SW	1839-09-20		A1
1539	" "	18	SESE	1839-09-20		A1
1594	BISHOP, John	18	NWNE	1839-09-20		A1
1527	BLYTHE, Charles	21	NWNE	1858-06-01		A1
1647	BLYTHE, Rickets	21	NWNW	1858-06-01		A1
1645	BRADFORD, Philemon	8	W½NE	1823-07-09		A1
1662	BRADFORD, Thomas C	17	W½SE	1824-10-20		A1
1583	CAMPBELL, Jasper C	8	NWNW	1893-05-05		A4
1688	CHAMBLEE, William J	5	SESW	1858-06-01		A1
1691	CHOAT, William L	22	NWSE	1884-12-05	St. Clair	A4
1692	" "	22	SWNE	1884-12-05	St. Clair	A4
1528	CLATON, Charles	9	W½SW	1823-07-09	St. Clair	A1
1635	CLAYTON, Little B	4	SESE	1858-06-01	St. Clair	A1
1636	" "	9	NENE	1858-06-01	St. Clair	A1
1532	CLOPTON, Devrix	22	S½SW	1858-06-01	St. Clair	A1
1533	" "	22	SWSE	1858-06-01	St. Clair	A1
1534	" "	27	NW	1858-06-01	St. Clair	A1
1535	" "	27	NWNE	1858-06-01	St. Clair	A1
1552	DAILEY, George	6	W½NE	1826-06-10		A1 V1661
1531	DEAVOURS, Christopher	7	E½SW	1824-04-05		A1
1613	DELASHAW, Joseph G	28	NWSW	1850-09-02		A1
1614	DELLASHAW, Joseph G	21	SWSW	1860-04-02		A1
1615	" "	28	NWNW	1860-04-02		A1
1616	DILLASHAW, Joseph G	34	NWSW	1839-09-20	St. Clair	A1
1516	DUMAS, Andrew J	5	NENE	1858-06-01		A1
1521	DUMAS, Azariah	5	W½NW	1858-06-01		A1
1522	" "	6	NWSE	1858-06-01		A1
1523	" "	6	SENE	1858-06-01		A1
1638	DUMAS, Mathew A	4	N½SE	1889-12-28	St. Clair	A1
1683	EDWARDS, William	20	NWSW	1858-06-01		A1
1637	EVERETT, Martha	20	SESW	1899-07-15		A1
1630	FRAZER, Lewis	32	SENE	1834-10-16		A1
1569	FRAZIER, James H	32	SESE	1858-06-01		A1
1570	" "	33	NWSW	1858-06-01		A1
1571	" "	33	SWNW	1858-06-01		A1
1572	FRAZIER, James M	34	SESW	1849-08-01	St. Clair	A1
1646	FRAZIER, Richardson	32	NENW	1849-08-01		A1
1684	FRAZIER, William	19	E½NW	1852-01-01		A1
1564	FREEMAN, Jacob	28	SENW	1834-10-01		A1
1563	" "	21	NESE	1834-10-16		A1
1673	GARNER, Vinson	29	SESW	1858-06-01		A1
1674	" "	29	SWSE	1858-06-01		A1
1663	GOODWIN, Thomas	8	E½SE	1823-05-01		A1
1658	HAIL, Stephen	20	SWSW	1858-06-01		A1
1659	" "	29	NWNW	1858-06-01		A1

ID	Individual in Patent	Sec.	Sec. Part	Date Issued	Other Counties	For More Info . . .
1660	HAIL, Stephen (Cont'd)	30	N½NE	1858-06-01		A1
1524	HALE, Benjamin H	30	E½SW	1889-08-02		A4
1547	HALE, Ezekiel A	30	NESE	1884-12-05		A4
1548	" "	30	SENE	1884-12-05		A4
1541	HALL, Elijah	4	S½NE	1837-03-20	St. Clair	A1
1640	HALL, Nathaniel	4	N½NE	1837-03-20	St. Clair	A1
1685	HALL, William	19	NWNW	1850-04-01		A1
1632	HARPER, Lewis	30	NWSE	1858-06-01		A1
1633	" "	30	SWNE	1858-06-01		A1
1675	HARPER, Warren	4	S½NW	1858-06-01	St. Clair	A1
1676	" "	4	SWSE	1858-06-01	St. Clair	A1
1664	HARRISON, Thomas	22	W½NW	1824-05-25	St. Clair	A1
1686	HAYS, William	5	W½NE	1858-06-01		A1
1597	HEFNER, John	33	SESW	1858-06-01		A1
1595	HEFNER, John H	34	SWSW	1849-08-01	St. Clair	A1
1560	HERRING, Ibzan	19	W½NE	1835-10-01		A1
1561	" "	20	NENW	1835-10-01		A1
1529	HILL, Charles	22	NESE	1854-07-15	St. Clair	A1
1598	HOLMES, John	6	NENE	1840-11-10		A1
1530	HOLT, Charles	8	W½SW	1823-05-01		A1
1687	HUNT, William	27	E½SW	1824-04-26	St. Clair	A1
1648	INZER, Robert M	32	NENE	1894-05-04		A4
1689	JONES, William J	28	SWSE	1891-06-29		A4
1625	KEETH, Lemuel	28	NESE	1839-09-20		A1
1510	KEITH, Alexander M	34	E½NE	1884-03-20	St. Clair	A4
1511	" "	34	SWNE	1884-03-20	St. Clair	A4
1602	KEITH, John	28	SWNE	1849-05-01		A1
1599	" "	21	NENE	1858-06-01		A1
1600	" "	22	N½SW	1858-06-01	St. Clair	A1
1601	" "	22	NENW	1858-06-01	St. Clair	A1
1627	KEITH, Lemuel	27	NWSE	1849-05-01	St. Clair	A1
1626	" "	27	NESE	1858-06-01	St. Clair	A1
1628	" "	27	SWSE	1858-06-01	St. Clair	A1
1629	" "	34	NWNE	1858-06-01	St. Clair	A1
1650	KEITH, Samuel F	28	NESW	1880-02-20		A4
1655	KEITH, Samuel T	28	NENW	1891-11-23		A4
1657	KEITH, Simeon L	20	S½SE	1890-03-19		A4
1678	KEITH, William C	28	NWSE	1889-08-16		A4
1693	KEITH, William L	22	SENW	1853-08-01	St. Clair	A1
1690	KING, William	22	N½NE	1889-03-01	St. Clair	A4
1694	LINDSEY, William	28	N½NE	1860-04-02		A1
1566	MANN, James D	33	NESW	1858-06-01		A1
1567	" "	33	SENW	1858-06-01		A1
1568	" "	33	W½NE	1858-06-01		A1
1581	MASSEY, James T	34	S½SE	1858-06-01	St. Clair	A1
1580	" "	34	N½SE	1860-04-02	St. Clair	A1
1679	MASSEY, William D	28	SENE	1840-11-10		A1
1680	" "	28	SESE	1848-07-01		A1
1681	" "	32	SWSW	1858-06-01		A1
1682	" "	33	SWSW	1858-06-01		A1
1656	MCCALLA, Samuel W	6	N½NW	1902-09-15		A4
1649	MCCLENDON, Samuel A	22	SENE	1883-10-01	St. Clair	A4
1554	MCCOY, Henry	20	SENW	1884-12-05		A4
1555	" "	20	SWNE	1884-12-05		A4
1517	MCKAY, Archibald	6	SWSW	1852-01-01		A1
1553	MELTON, George W	28	S½SW	1891-09-15		A4
1668	MELTON, Thomas	20	W½NW	1824-05-04		A1
1593	PEARSON, John B	6	S½SE	1890-01-08		A4 G195
1593	PEARSON, Lucresy	6	S½SE	1890-01-08		A4 G195
1526	PRAYTOR, Bezaleel	32	NESE	1834-10-01		A1
1603	PRAYTOR, John L	32	SESW	1834-10-01		A1
1556	PYBAS, Henry	27	E½NE	1824-05-24	St. Clair	A1
1574	PYBAS, James M	21	NWSE	1853-08-01		A1
1573	" "	21	NESW	1858-06-01		A1
1575	" "	21	SWSE	1858-06-01		A1
1558	PYBUS, Henry	27	SWNE	1834-10-01	St. Clair	A1
1557	" "	22	SESE	1834-10-21	St. Clair	A1
1651	REED, Samuel	17	E½NE	1823-05-01		A1
1652	" "	8	E½NE	1823-05-01		A1
1653	" "	8	W½SE	1823-05-01		A1
1654	REID, Samuel	5	W½SE	1824-05-20		A1
1576	RICHEY, James	19	NESW	1837-03-30		A1
1577	RITCHEY, James	19	SESW	1834-10-01		A1

ID	Individual in Patent	Sec.	Sec. Part	Date Issued	Other Counties	For More Info . . .
1578	RITCHIE, James	19	W½SW	1823-06-02		A1
1579	" "	30	W½NW	1823-06-02		A1
1606	RITCHIE, John	19	E½NE	1824-04-14		A1
1565	ROBERTSON, James B	4	N½NW	1889-10-07	St. Clair	A1
1672	SELF, Vincent	19	SWNW	1858-06-01		A1
1536	SIMS, Edward	27	W½SW	1823-05-01	St. Clair	A1
1537	" "	34	W½NW	1823-05-01	St. Clair	A1
1644	SPRADLING, Oliver W	6	NWSW	1849-08-01		A1
1677	SPRADLING, William A	17	NESE	1848-07-01		A1
1617	SQUIRE, Joseph	30	S½SE	1881-06-01		A1
1618	" "	32	N½SW	1881-06-01		A1
1619	" "	32	SENW	1881-06-01		A1
1620	" "	32	W½NW	1881-06-01		A1
1665	STUBBS, Thomas J	5	E½SE	1858-06-01		A1
1642	TALLEY, Nicholas	33	E½SE	1823-05-01		A1
1643	" "	33	W½SE	1823-05-01		A1
1641	" "	33	E½NE	1824-10-20		A1
1512	TAYLOR, Alford	7	NWSE	1858-06-01		A1
1513	" "	7	SWNE	1858-06-01		A1
1514	" "	7	W½SW	1858-06-01		A1
1519	TAYLOR, Asberry	18	N½SW	1858-06-01		A1
1520	" "	18	W½NW	1858-06-01		A1
1562	TAYLOR, Isaac	30	SWSW	1839-09-20		A1
1582	TAYLOR, James	20	NENE	1891-06-29		A4 G219
1584	TAYLOR, Jesse	17	W½NE	1834-10-01		A1
1585	" "	18	NENE	1839-09-20		A1
1588	" "	18	SWNE	1852-01-01		A1
1589	" "	7	NESE	1852-01-01		A1
1586	" "	18	NWSE	1858-06-01		A1
1587	" "	18	SENE	1858-06-01		A1
1590	" "	7	SENE	1858-06-01		A1
1591	" "	7	SESE	1858-06-01		A1
1592	" "	8	SWNW	1858-06-01		A1
1582	TAYLOR, Penina	20	NENE	1891-06-29		A4 G219
1661	TAYLOR, Susan M	6	SWNE	1890-08-29		A4 V1552
1671	TAYLOR, Tilford	7	SENW	1858-06-01		A1
1700	TAYLOR, William	18	E½NW	1824-04-05		A1
1559	TIDWELL, Henry	5	NESW	1858-06-01		A1
1669	TRUSS, Thomas W	15	NW	1858-06-01	St. Clair	A1
1670	" "	15	W½NE	1858-06-01	St. Clair	A1
1515	TUCKER, Anderson B	31	E½SW	1858-06-01		A1
1621	TUMBOUGH, Joseph	4	E½SW	1824-04-26	St. Clair	A1
1544	TURNBOUGH, Elizabeth	17	SESW	1853-08-01		A1
1545	" "	18	SWSE	1859-04-01		A1
1546	" "	20	NWNE	1859-04-01		A1
1622	TURNBOUGH, Joseph	4	W½SW	1823-05-01	St. Clair	A1
1624	" "	9	W½NW	1823-05-01	St. Clair	A1
1623	" "	9	E½NW	1824-05-10	St. Clair	A1
1631	TURNER, Lewis H	17	NWNW	1852-01-01		A1
1634	TURNER, Lewis M	17	SESE	1858-06-01		A1
1699	TURNER, William S	8	E½SW	1826-06-01		A1
1695	" "	17	E½NW	1839-09-20		A1
1696	" "	17	NESW	1858-06-01		A1
1697	" "	17	SWNW	1858-06-01		A1
1698	" "	8	E½NW	1858-06-01		A1
1607	WADE, John W	20	NESW	1880-02-20		A4
1608	" "	20	NWSE	1889-11-21		A4
1604	WARE, John M	30	SENW	1853-08-01		A1
1549	WARNICK, Francis M	5	NWSW	1858-06-01		A1
1550	" "	6	NESE	1858-06-01		A1
1518	WEAR, Arthur	30	NENW	1894-12-07		A4
1596	WEAR, John H	18	SESW	1858-06-01		A1
1605	WEAR, John N	30	NWSW	1861-08-01		A1
1666	WILSON, Thomas M	20	NESE	1885-03-16		A1
1667	" "	20	SENE	1885-03-16		A1
1542	WOODALL, Elisha	6	NESW	1839-09-20		A1
1543	" "	6	SENW	1839-09-20		A1
1551	WORNICK, Francis M	5	SENW	1858-06-01		A1
1609	WORNICK, John	6	SESW	1858-06-01		A1
1525	WORTHINGTON, Benjamin	32	W½NE	1853-08-01		A1
1611	WORTHINGTON, John	32	W½SE	1824-05-20		A1
1612	" "	34	E½NW	1824-10-20	St. Clair	A1
1610	" "	21	SENE	1850-09-01		A1

ID	Individual in Patent	Sec.	Sec. Part	Date Issued	Other Counties	For More Info . . .
1639	YANCEY, Mines	19	NESE	1858-06-01		A1

Patent Map

T15-S R1-E
Huntsville Meridian

Map Group 10

Township Statistics

Parcels Mapped	:	191
Number of Patents	:	150
Number of Individuals	:	121
Patentees Identified	:	119
Number of Surnames	:	79
Multi-Patentee Parcels	:	2
Oldest Patent Date	:	5/1/1823
Most Recent Patent	:	9/15/1902
Block/Lot Parcels	:	0
Parcels Re - Issued	:	0
Parcels that Overlap	:	2
Cities and Towns	:	0
Cemeteries	:	1

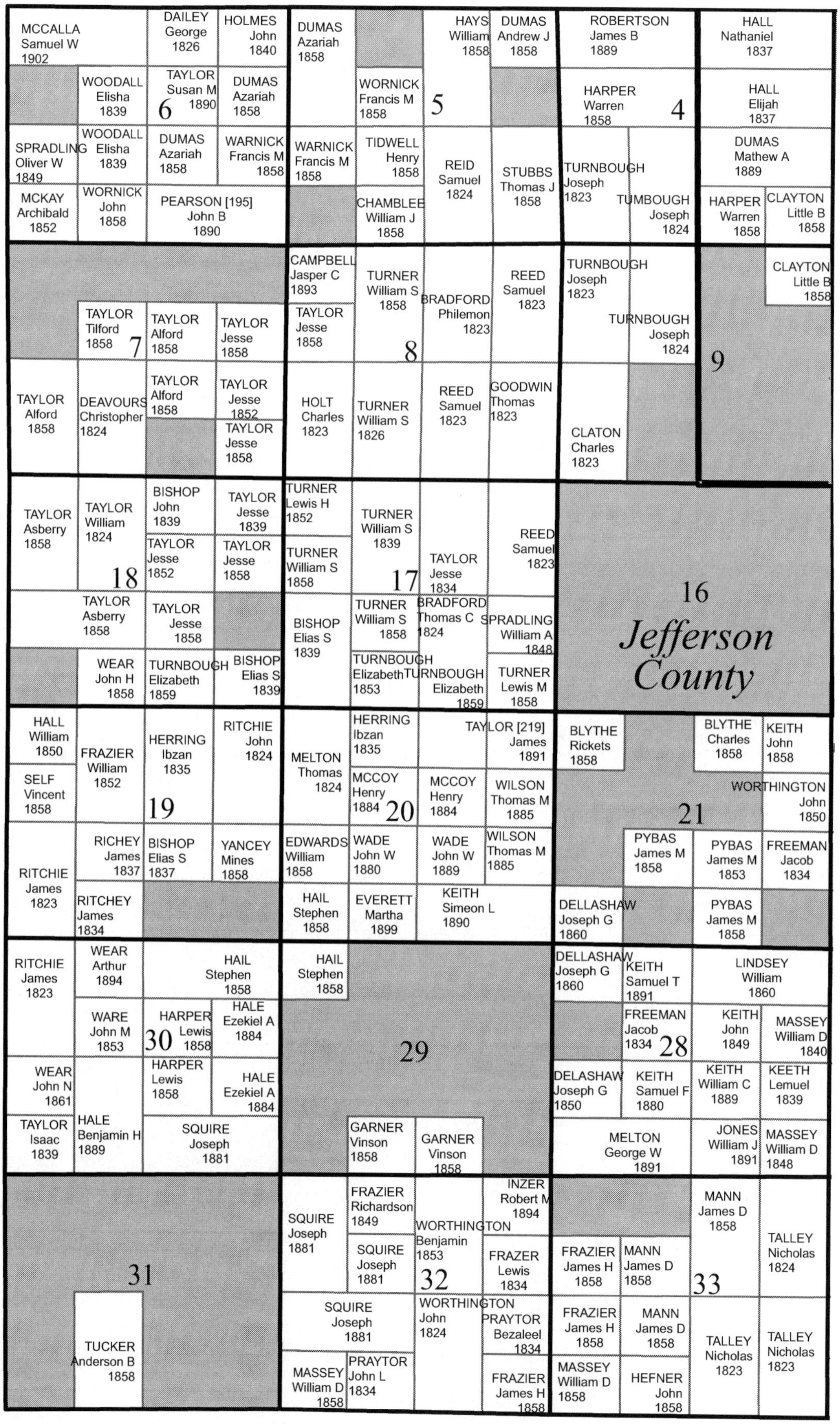

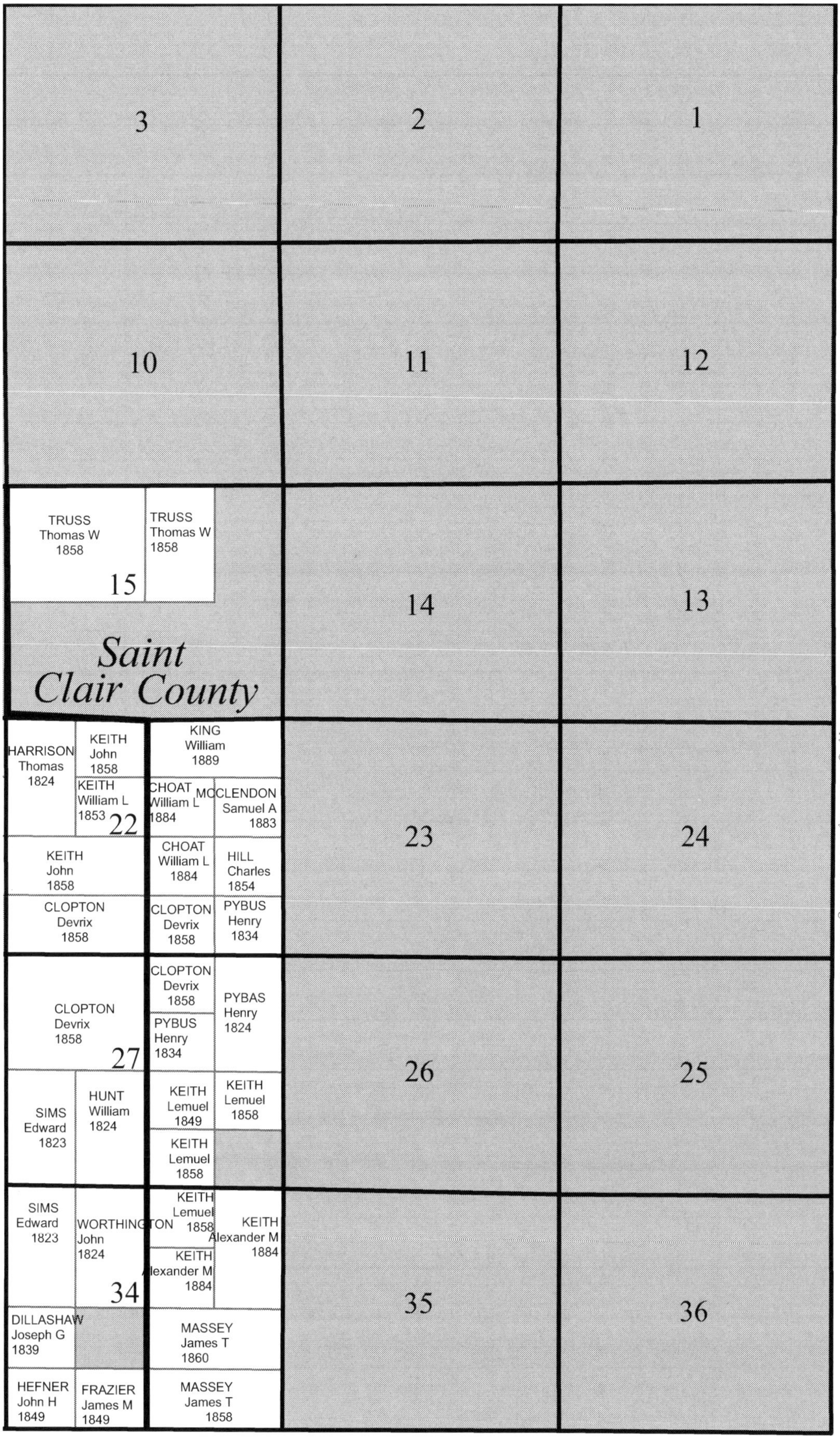

3
2
1
10
11
12

TRUSS
Thomas W
1858

TRUSS
Thomas W
1858

15
14
13

Saint Clair County

HARRISON
Thomas
1824

KEITH
John
1858

KEITH
William L
1853

22

KING
William
1889

CHOAT
William L
1884

MCCLENDON
Samuel A
1883

KEITH
John
1858

CHOAT
William L
1884

HILL
Charles
1854

CLOPTON
Devrix
1858

CLOPTON
Devrix
1858

PYBUS
Henry
1834

23
24

CLOPTON
Devrix
1858

27

CLOPTON
Devrix
1858

PYBUS
Henry
1834

PYBAS
Henry
1824

SIMS
Edward
1823

HUNT
William
1824

KEITH
Lemuel
1849

KEITH
Lemuel
1858

KEITH
Lemuel
1858

26
25

SIMS
Edward
1823

WORTHINGTON
John
1824

34

KEITH
Lemuel
1858

KEITH
Alexander M
1884

KEITH
Alexander M
1884

DILLASHAW
Joseph G
1839

MASSEY
James T
1860

HEFNER
John H
1849

FRAZIER
James M
1849

MASSEY
James T
1858

35
36

Helpful Hints

1. This Map's INDEX can be found on the preceding pages.
2. Refer to Map "C" to see where this Township lies within Jefferson County, Alabama.
3. Numbers within square brackets [ ] denote a multi-patentee land parcel (multi-owner). Refer to Appendix "C" for a full list of members in this group.
4. Areas that look to be crowded with Patentees usually indicate multiple sales of the same parcel (Re-issues) or Overlapping parcels. See this Township's Index for an explanation of these and other circumstances that might explain "odd" groupings of Patentees on this map.

Legend

Patent Boundary

Section Boundary

No Patents Found (or Outside County)

1., 2., 3., ... Lot Numbers (when beside a name)

[ ] Group Number (see Appendix "C")

Scale: Section = 1 mile X 1 mile
(generally, with some exceptions)

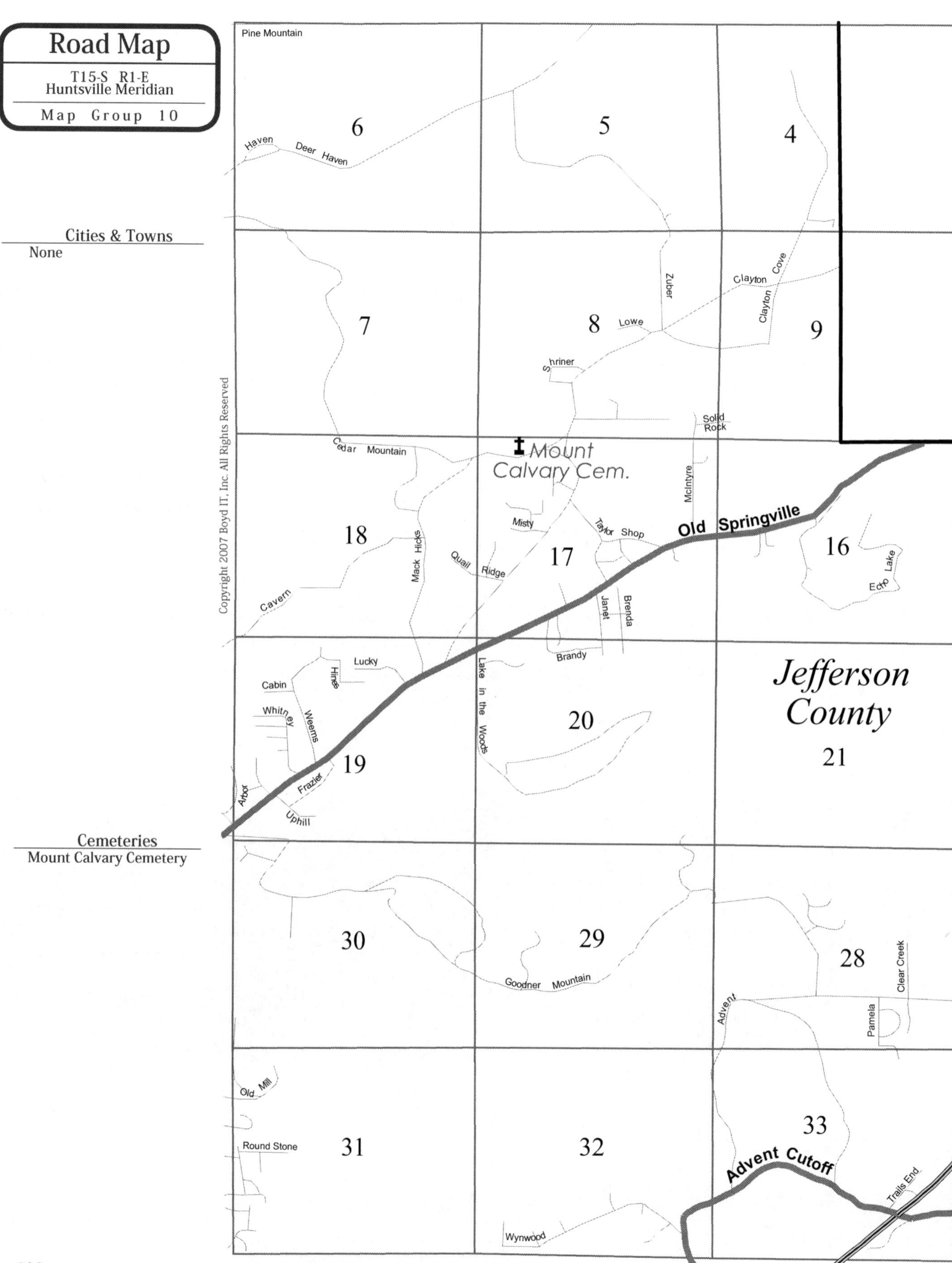
Road Map
T15-S R1-E
Huntsville Meridian
Map Group 10
Cities & Towns
None
Cemeteries
Mount Calvary Cemetery
Copyright 2007 Boyd IT, Inc. All Rights Reserved
Pine Mountain
6
5
4
Haven
Deer Haven
7
8
9
Zuber
Clayton
Cove
Clayton
Lowe
Shriner
Solid Rock
Cedar Mountain
Mount Calvary Cem.
McIntyre
18
17
16
Old Springville
Taylor Shop
Misty
Quail Ridge
Mack Hicks
Cavern
Janet
Brenda
Echo Lake
Brandy
Lucky
Hines
Cabin
Whitney
Weems
Lake in the Woods
20
Jefferson County
21
19
Arbor
Frazier
Uphill
30
29
28
Goodner Mountain
Advent
Clear Creek
Pamela
Old Mill
Round Stone
31
32
33
Advent Cutoff
Trails End
Wynwood

3
2
1
10
11
12
15
Saint Clair County
14
13
22
23
24
27
26
25
34
35
36

Keith
Skyline
Keith
Honor
Liles
Glenn
I-59
Gadsden
Meadow Run
Micklewright

Helpful Hints

1. This road map has a number of uses, but primarily it is to help you: a) find the present location of land owned by your ancestors (at least the general area), b) find cemeteries and city-centers, and c) estimate the route/roads used by Census-takers & tax-assessors.
2. If you plan to travel to Jefferson County to locate cemeteries or land parcels, please pick up a modern travel map for the area before you do. Mapping old land parcels on modern maps is not as exact a science as you might think. Just the slightest variations in public land survey coordinates, estimates of parcel boundaries, or road-map deviations can greatly alter a map's representation of how a road either does or doesn't cross a particular parcel of land.

Legend

- Section Lines
- Interstates
- Highways
- Other Roads
- Cities/Towns
- Cemeteries

Scale: Section = 1 mile X 1 mile (generally, with some exceptions)

Historical Map

T15-S R1-E
Huntsville Meridian

Map Group 10

Cities & Towns
None

Cemeteries
Mount Calvary Cemetery

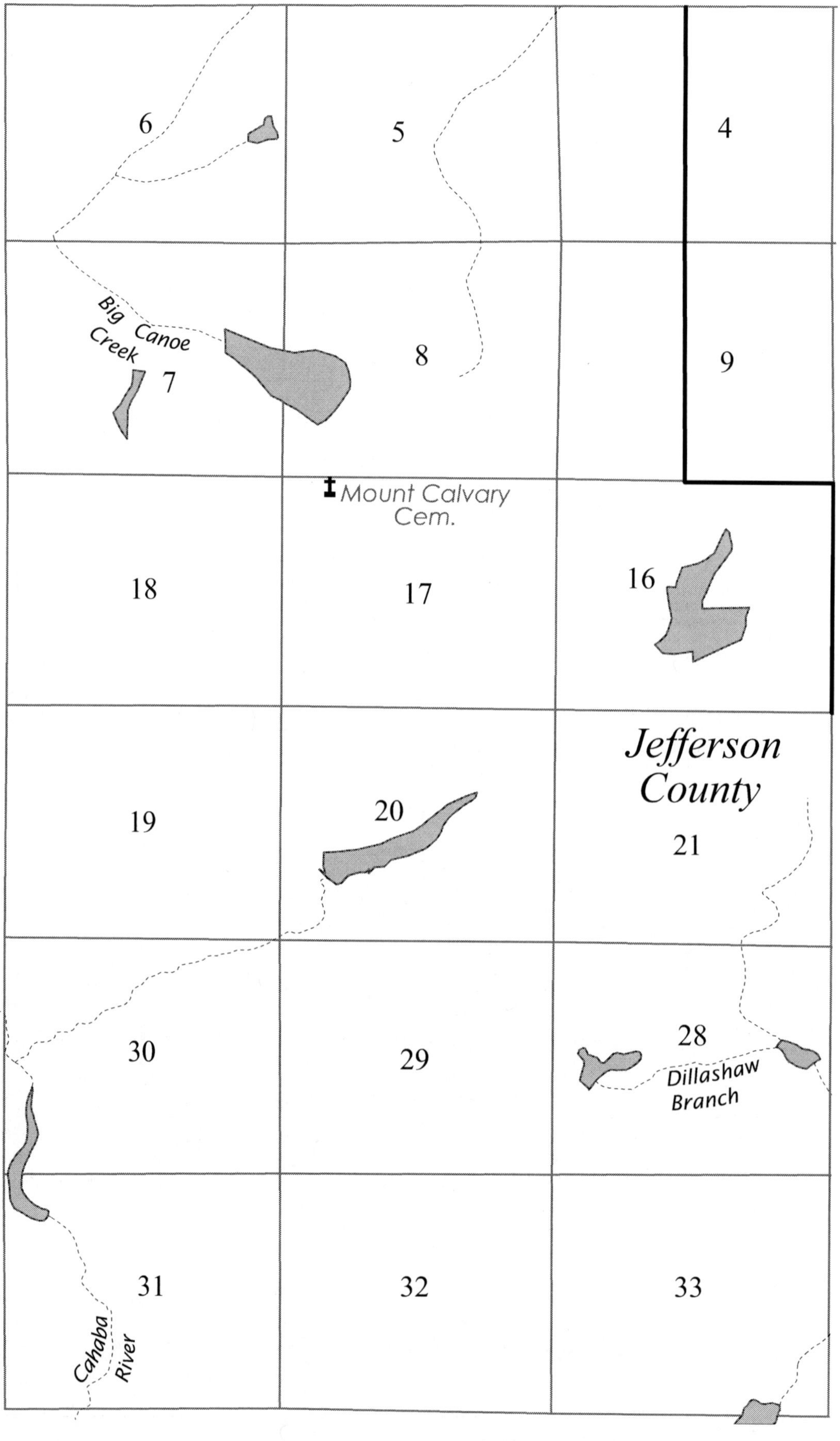

3
2
1
10
11
12
Saint Clair County
15
14
13
22
23
24
27
26
25
Clear Branch
34
35
36
Little Cahaba Creek

Helpful Hints

1. This Map takes a different look at the same Congressional Township displayed in the preceding two maps. It presents features that can help you better envision the historical development of the area: a) Water-bodies (lakes & ponds), b) Water-courses (rivers, streams, etc.), c) Railroads, d) City/town center-points (where they were oftentimes located when first settled), and e) Cemeteries.

2. Using this "Historical" map in tandem with this Township's Patent Map and Road Map, may lead you to some interesting discoveries. You will often find roads, towns, cemeteries, and waterways are named after nearby landowners: sometimes those names will be the ones you are researching. See how many of these research gems you can find here in Jefferson County.

Legend

Section Lines
Railroads
Large Rivers & Bodies of Water
Streams/Creeks & Small Rivers
Cities/Towns
Cemeteries

Scale: Section = 1 mile X 1 mile
(there are some exceptions)

Map Group 11: Index to Land Patents

Township 16-South Range 6-West (Huntsville)

After you locate an individual in this Index, take note of the Section and Section Part then proceed to the Land Patent map on the pages immediately following. You should have no difficulty locating the corresponding parcel of land.

The "For More Info" Column will lead you to more information about the underlying Patents. See the *Legend* at right, and the "How to Use this Book" chapter, for more information.

LEGEND

"For More Info . . . " column

A = Authority (Legislative Act, See Appendix "A")
B = Block or Lot (location in Section unknown)
C = Cancelled Patent
F = Fractional Section
G = Group (Multi-Patentee Patent, see Appendix "C")
V = Overlaps another Parcel
R = Re-Issued (Parcel patented more than once)

(A & G items require you to look in the Appendixes referred to above. All other Letter-designations followed by a number require you to locate line-items in this index that possess the ID number found after the letter).

ID	Individual in Patent	Sec.	Sec. Part	Date Issued	Other Counties	For More Info . . .
1734	BOONE, John W	35	NENW	1858-06-01		A1
1718	CULPEPPER, Hudson W	26	NENW	1889-10-07		A1
1719	" "	26	NWSW	1889-10-07		A1
1720	" "	26	W½NW	1889-10-07		A1
1744	DAVIS, Ruth	33	NE	1837-03-20		A1 G72
1721	FASON, James M	36	SENE	1890-04-15		A1
1717	GILLEY, Hiram	33	SESW	1839-09-20		A1
1744	GLAZE, William	33	NE	1837-03-20		A1 G72
1749	" "	33	NWSE	1839-09-20		A1
1722	GRAVES, Jesse	26	SWSW	1860-10-01		A1
1723	" "	35	NWNW	1860-10-01		A1
1709	HOOD, David	36	NWSW	1839-09-20		A1
1710	HOOD, Edmond P	25	W½NW	1860-10-01		A1
1711	" "	25	W½SW	1860-10-01		A1
1712	" "	26	E½NE	1860-10-01		A1
1713	" "	26	E½SE	1860-10-01		A1
1732	HOOD, John R	33	NESW	1861-01-01		A1
1733	" "	33	SWSW	1861-01-01		A1
1746	LAMBERT, Washington	35	NESW	1839-09-20		A1
1742	MCCARTY, Owen A	34	E½SE	1884-03-20		A4
1743	" "	35	W½SW	1884-03-20		A4
1745	MCMILLION, Tilmon	34	N½SW	1894-07-17		A4
1750	PERRY, William	33	NW	1889-10-07		A1
1747	PRESCOAT, Wesley	33	E½SE	1862-12-20		A1
1748	" "	33	SWSE	1862-12-20		A1
1704	QUINN, Anderson	35	SENW	1858-06-01		A1
1706	" "	35	SWNE	1858-06-01		A1
1702	" "	35	E½NE	1860-10-01		A1
1703	" "	35	NWNE	1860-10-01		A1
1705	" "	35	SESW	1860-10-01		A1
1701	" "	26	SESW	1861-01-01		A1
1725	QUINN, John G	26	NESW	1861-01-01		A1
1728	" "	26	SENW	1861-01-01		A1
1726	" "	26	NWNE	1894-06-09		A4
1727	" "	26	NWSE	1894-06-09		A4
1729	" "	26	SWNE	1894-06-09		A4
1714	SALTER, Elve	34	SENW	1884-03-20		A4
1715	" "	34	SWNE	1884-03-20		A4
1716	" "	34	W½SE	1884-03-20		A4
1737	SHELTON, Nelson	36	W½NW	1858-06-01		A1
1707	SKELTON, David F	25	E½SW	1888-02-04		A4
1708	" "	25	W½SE	1888-02-04		A4
1730	SKELTON, John P	25	SESE	1885-03-16		A1
1731	" "	36	NENE	1885-03-16		A1
1741	SKELTON, Nelson	36	SWSW	1849-05-01		A1
1738	" "	36	NENW	1860-10-01		A1

ID	Individual in Patent	Sec.	Sec. Part	Date Issued	Other Counties	For More Info . . .
1739	SKELTON, Nelson (Cont'd)	36	NESW	1860-10-01		A1
1740	" "	36	NWNE	1860-10-01		A1
1735	WHITEHEAD, Mathew W	34	N½NE	1884-03-20		A4
1736	" "	34	NENW	1884-03-20		A4
1724	WILLIAMS, John E	25	NE	1889-10-07		A1

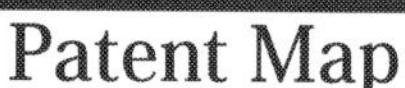

Patent Map

T16-S R6-W
Huntsville Meridian

Map Group 11

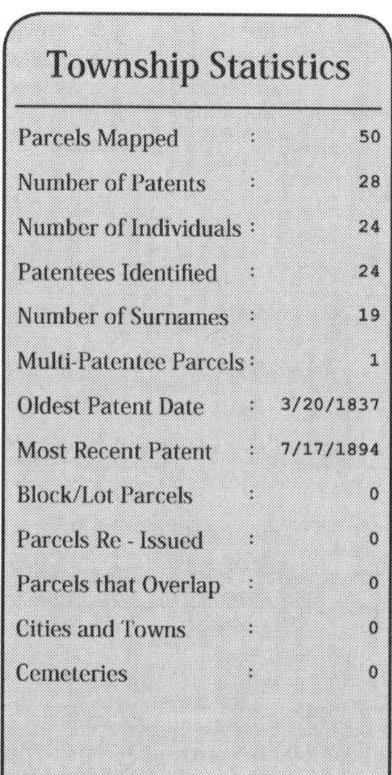

Township Statistics

Parcels Mapped	:	50
Number of Patents	:	28
Number of Individuals	:	24
Patentees Identified	:	24
Number of Surnames	:	19
Multi-Patentee Parcels	:	1
Oldest Patent Date	:	3/20/1837
Most Recent Patent	:	7/17/1894
Block/Lot Parcels	:	0
Parcels Re - Issued	:	0
Parcels that Overlap	:	0
Cities and Towns	:	0
Cemeteries	:	0

Note: the area contained in this map amounts to far less than a full Township. Therefore, its contents are completely on this single page (instead of a "normal" 2-page spread).

N

31 30 32 29 28 27

33
HOOD John R 1861
PERRY William 1889
HOOD John R 1861
GILLEY Hiram 1839
GLAZE William 1839
PRESCOAT Wesley 1862
DAVIS [72] Ruth 1837
PRESCOAT Wesley 1862

34
WHITEHEAD Mathew W 1884
SALTER Elve 1884
MCMILLION Tilmon 1894
SALTER Elve 1884
SALTER Elve 1884
WHITEHEAD Mathew W 1884
MCCARTY Owen A 1884

Walker County

35
GRAVES Jesse 1860
MCCARTY Owen A 1884
BOONE John W 1858
QUINN Anderson 1858
LAMBERT Washington 1839
QUINN Anderson 1860
QUINN Anderson 1860
QUINN Anderson 1858
QUINN Anderson 1860

26
CULPEPPER Hudson W 1889
CULPEPPER Hudson W 1889
CULPEPPER Hudson W 1889
GRAVES Jesse 1860
QUINN Anderson 1861
QUINN John G 1861
QUINN John G 1861
QUINN John G 1894
QUINN John G 1894
QUINN John G 1894
HOOD Edmond P 1860
HOOD Edmond P 1860

36
SHELTON Nelson 1858
HOOD David 1839
SKELTON Nelson 1849
SKELTON Nelson 1860
SKELTON Nelson 1860
SKELTON Nelson 1860
FASON James M 1890
SKELTON John P 1885

25
HOOD Edmond P 1860
HOOD Edmond P 1860
SKELTON David F 1888
SKELTON David F 1888
WILLIAMS John E 1889
SKELTON John P 1885

Jefferson County

Legend

Patent Boundary

Section Boundary

No Patents Found (or Outside County)

1., 2., 3., ... Lot Numbers (when beside a name)

[ ] Group Number (see Appendix "C")

Scale: Section = 1 mile X 1 mile
(generally, with some exceptions)

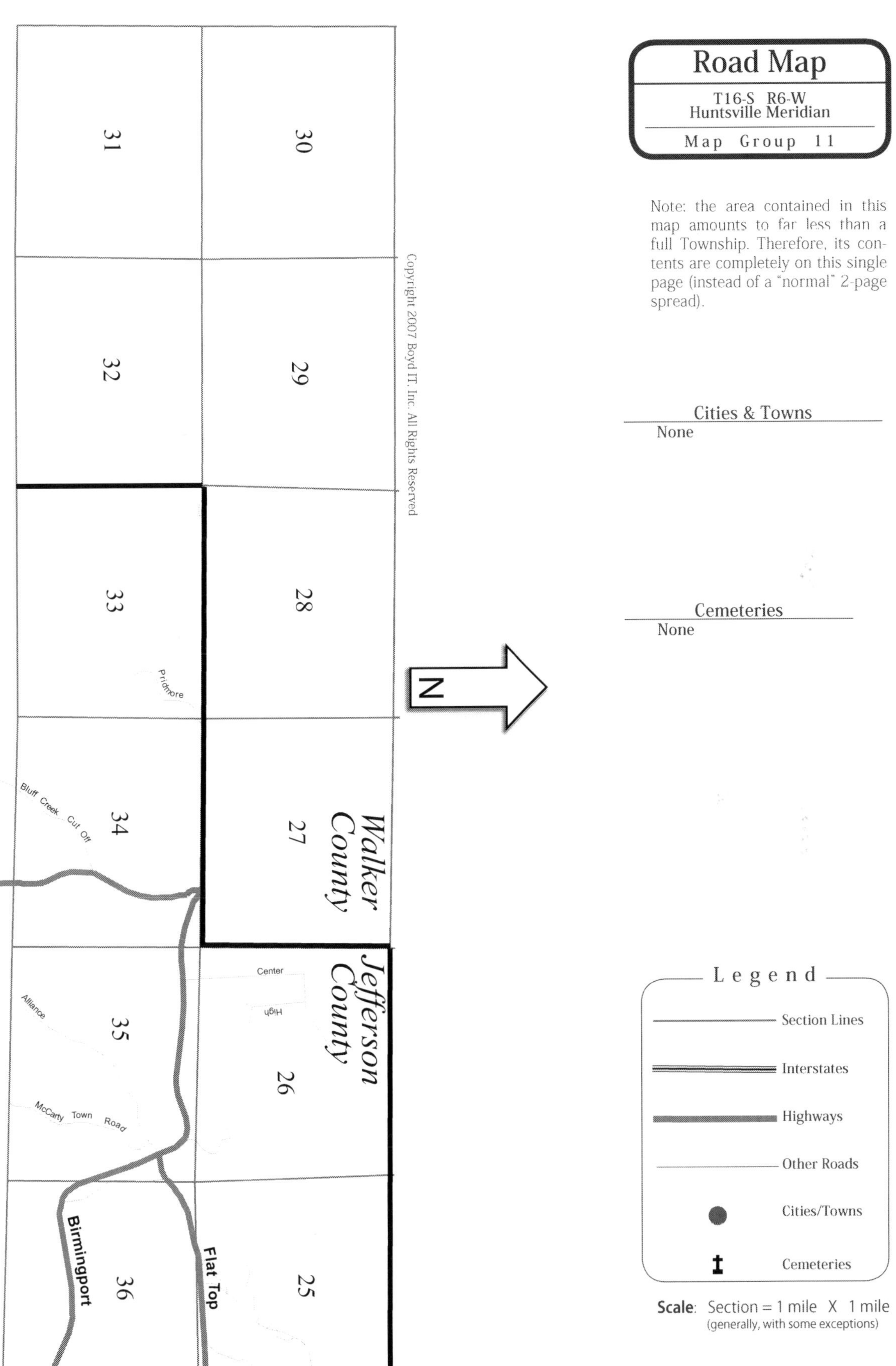
Road Map
T16-S R6-W
Huntsville Meridian
Map Group 11
Note: the area contained in this map amounts to far less than a full Township. Therefore, its contents are completely on this single page (instead of a "normal" 2-page spread).
Cities & Towns
None
Cemeteries
None
31
30
32
29
33
28
34
27
35
26
36
25
Pridmore
Bluff Creek Cut Off
Walker County
Jefferson County
Center
High
Alliance
McCarty Town Road
Birmingport
Flat Top
Flat Creek
N
Copyright 2007 Boyd IT, Inc. All Rights Reserved
Legend
Section Lines
Interstates
Highways
Other Roads
Cities/Towns
Cemeteries
Scale: Section = 1 mile X 1 mile
(generally, with some exceptions)

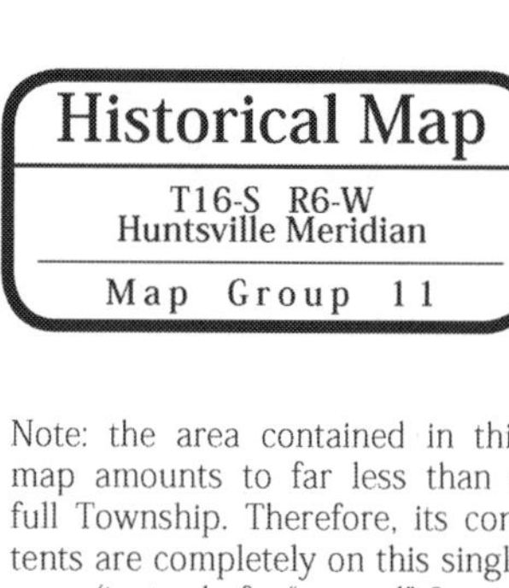

Note: the area contained in this map amounts to far less than a full Township. Therefore, its contents are completely on this single page (instead of a "normal" 2-page spread).

Cities & Towns
None

Cemeteries
None

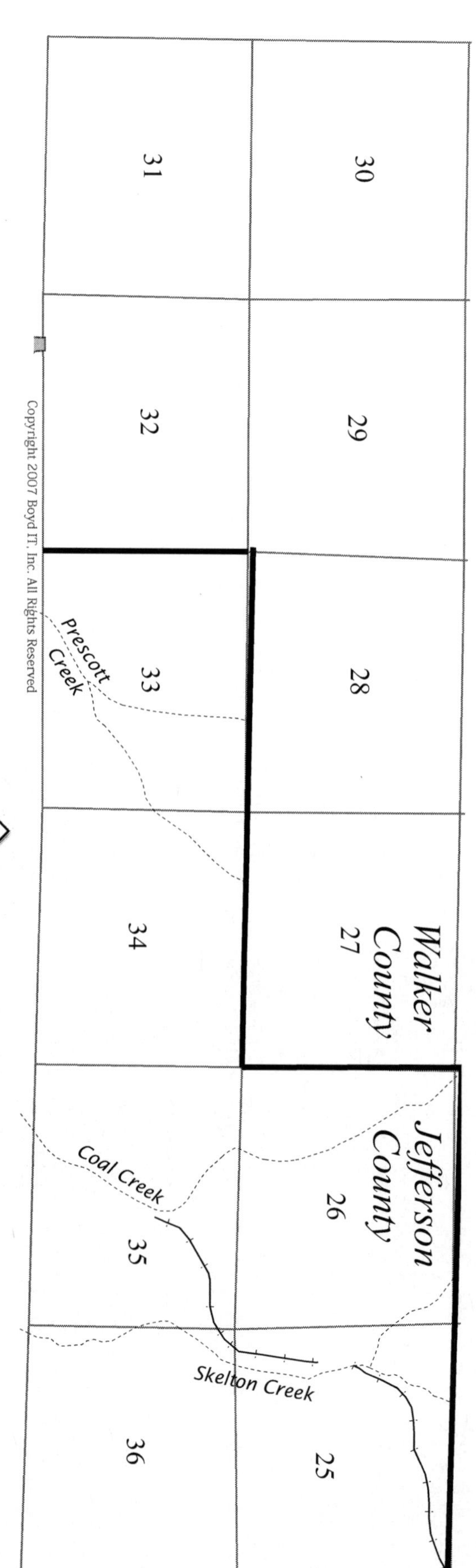

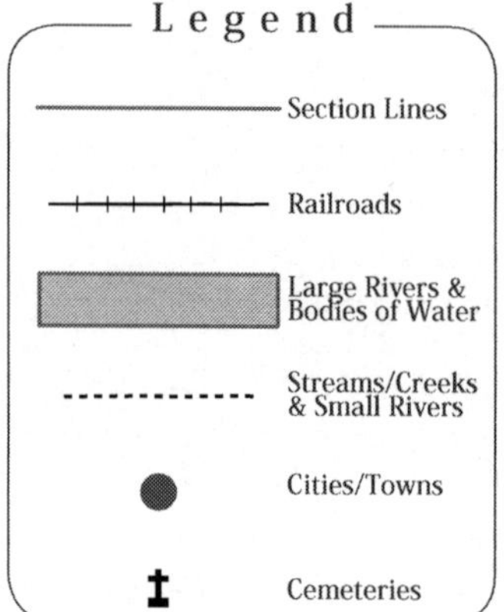

Scale: Section = 1 mile X 1 mile
(there are some exceptions)

Map Group 12: Index to Land Patents

Township 16-South Range 5-West (Huntsville)

After you locate an individual in this Index, take note of the Section and Section Part then proceed to the Land Patent map on the pages immediately following. You should have no difficulty locating the corresponding parcel of land.

The "For More Info" Column will lead you to more information about the underlying Patents. See the *Legend* at right, and the "How to Use this Book" chapter, for more information.

LEGEND

"For More Info . . . " column

A = Authority (Legislative Act, See Appendix "A")
B = Block or Lot (location in Section unknown)
C = Cancelled Patent
F = Fractional Section
G = Group (Multi-Patentee Patent, see Appendix "C")
V = Overlaps another Parcel
R = Re-Issued (Parcel patented more than once)

(A & G items require you to look in the Appendixes referred to above. All other Letter-designations followed by a number require you to locate line-items in this index that possess the ID number found after the letter).

ID	Individual in Patent	Sec.	Sec. Part	Date Issued	Other Counties	For More Info . . .
1791	ADAMS, Elias	1	N½SW	1858-06-01		A1
1792	" "	1	SWNW	1858-06-01		A1
1885	ADAMS, Madison F	1	NENW	1858-06-01		A1
1904	ADAMS, Richard	2	SESE	1839-03-15		A1
1900	" "	1	NWNW	1839-09-20		A1
1901	" "	11	N½NE	1858-06-01		A1
1902	" "	2	NESE	1858-06-01		A1
1903	" "	2	SENE	1858-06-01		A1
1905	" "	2	SWSE	1858-06-01		A1
1894	ALEXANDER, Milton	22	SWNE	1839-09-20		A1
1906	AUSTIN, Richard	20	NESE	1839-09-20		A1
1907	" "	21	NESW	1839-09-20		A1
1855	AYERS, John G	12	NENW	1839-09-20		A1
1846	BAGBY, Joab	10	NENW	1839-09-20		A1
1847	" "	3	E½NE	1839-09-20		A1
1848	" "	3	E½SW	1839-09-20		A1
1821	BAGLEY, James C	1	SESW	1852-01-01		A1
1820	" "	1	N½SE	1858-06-01		A1
1822	" "	12	SE	1858-06-01		A1
1849	BAGLEY, Joab	10	NWNE	1853-08-01		A1
1850	" "	3	W½SE	1858-06-01		A1
1941	BAGLEY, William M	12	W½NW	1858-06-01		A1
1812	BEAM, Jacob	29	NWNW	1839-09-20		A1
1819	BLACK, James	27	W½NE	1824-04-12		A1
1818	" "	27	E½NE	1824-05-10		A1
1840	BLACK, James T	36	E½SE	1889-08-16		A4
1841	" "	36	SESW	1889-08-16		A4
1842	" "	36	SWSE	1889-08-16		A4
1770	BOYD, Archibald C	14	E½SW	1883-07-03		A4 G25
1771	" "	14	SWSE	1883-07-03		A4 G25
1772	" "	14	SWSW	1883-07-03		A4 G25
1770	BOYD, Martha J	14	E½SW	1883-07-03		A4 G25
1771	" "	14	SWSE	1883-07-03		A4 G25
1772	" "	14	SWSW	1883-07-03		A4 G25
1852	BRASFIELD, John C	21	NENE	1858-06-01		A1
1853	" "	22	SWNW	1858-06-01		A1
1782	BRASSFIELD, Calvin	15	SESW	1850-04-01		A1
1783	" "	22	NWNW	1850-04-01		A1
1879	BROWN, Lida	31	E½SW	1893-12-26		A1 G32
1880	" "	31	SENW	1893-12-26		A1 G32
1881	" "	31	SWNE	1893-12-26		A1 G32
1928	BURNS, Wade C	2	NWSE	1858-06-01		A1
1875	BUSBY, Lethie J	24	SW	1891-12-01		A1
1947	BUTLER, William T	17	E½SW	1888-02-04		A4
1948	" "	20	N½NW	1888-02-04		A4
1823	CAMPBELL, James	29	SESE	1837-11-07		A1

ID	Individual in Patent	Sec.	Sec. Part	Date Issued	Other Counties	For More Info . . .
1876	CHILDRESS, Levi	1	E½NE	1833-08-12		A1
1752	COOPER, Alexander	26	E½NE	1885-05-25		A4
1753	" "	26	E½SE	1885-05-25		A4
1766	CROCKER, Andrew W	11	SESW	1858-06-01		A1
1767	" "	14	NENW	1858-06-01		A1
1768	" "	14	NWNE	1858-06-01		A1
1809	CROCKER, Jackson	11	SESE	1839-09-20		A1
1808	" "	11	NWSE	1850-09-02		A1
1810	" "	12	W½SW	1858-06-01		A1
1811	" "	13	SWNE	1858-06-01		A1
1813	CROCKER, Jacob	2	E½NW	1884-03-20		A4
1814	" "	2	SWNE	1884-03-20		A4
1815	" "	2	SWNW	1884-03-20		A4
1826	CROCKER, James	14	NWSW	1834-10-14		A1
1827	" "	14	SENW	1837-03-30		A1
1824	" "	11	NESE	1852-01-01		A1
1825	" "	14	NWSE	1858-06-01		A1
1886	CROCKER, Mary A	14	E½SE	1884-03-20		A4
1887	" "	14	S½NE	1884-03-20		A4
1828	DEATON, James	28	W½NW	1823-05-01		A1
1919	DEATON, Thomas	29	W½NE	1837-03-20		A1
1918	" "	29	NESE	1839-09-20		A1
1940	DUPREY, William L	15	NESW	1850-04-01		A1
1914	EARLE, Samuel S	1	W½NE	1839-09-20		A1
1912	EMOND, Robert T	26	SWNE	1849-09-01		A1
1760	EUBANKS, Andrew	29	NWSE	1839-09-20		A1
1929	EUBANKS, William C	27	NESE	1853-08-01		A1
1829	EVANS, James	36	NENW	1883-07-03		A4
1830	" "	36	NWNE	1883-07-03		A4
1831	" "	36	W½NW	1883-07-03		A4
1834	FASON, James M	31	SWNW	1890-04-15		A1
1835	" "	31	W½SW	1890-04-15		A1
1804	FERGUSON, Henry	1	S½SE	1839-09-20		A1
1759	FINCH, Allen B	27	E½SW	1890-04-15		A1
1769	FORTNER, Ansel	29	NWSW	1850-04-01		A1
1862	GLOVER, John L	11	NENW	1858-06-01		A1
1863	" "	11	NESW	1858-06-01		A1
1864	" "	11	SWNW	1858-06-01		A1
1860	" "	10	E½NE	1883-10-01		A4
1861	" "	10	SWNE	1883-10-01		A4
1889	GLOVER, Mary N	2	SW	1891-01-15		A4
1943	GLOVER, William P	20	W½NE	1858-06-01		A1
1944	" "	3	W½NE	1858-06-01		A1
1761	GOLDEN, Andrew J	15	S½NW	1889-08-02		A4
1762	" "	15	W½SW	1889-08-02		A4
1913	GOLDEN, Robert T	17	N½NE	1913-10-22		A4
1931	GOLDEN, William	20	NESW	1884-03-20		A4
1932	" "	20	NWSE	1884-03-20		A4
1856	GOODWIN, John H	32	SWSW	1858-06-01		A1
1899	GOOLSBY, Reuben L	34	NW	1885-03-16		A1
1867	GOSSETT, John S	31	SE	1891-04-16		A1
1788	HANLY, David	1	SENW	1850-04-01		A1 G122
1874	HEWBERRY, Julia A	24	NE	1890-04-15		A1 R1949
1857	HILL, John	25	SESE	1858-06-01		A1
1858	" "	25	SWSE	1858-06-01		A1
1859	" "	36	NENE	1858-06-01		A1
1775	HOOD, Austin	20	S½SE	1858-06-01		A1
1776	" "	20	SESW	1858-06-01		A1
1930	HOOD, William G	21	W½SW	1885-03-30		A4
1945	HOOD, William P	17	SWSW	1858-06-01		A1
1946	" "	21	NW	1861-01-01		A1
1789	HUBBARD, David	26	NESW	1848-04-15		A1
1839	IVEANS, James R	26	S½SW	1889-10-07		A1
1785	JENKINS, Daniel	17	NENW	1883-07-03		A4
1921	KEMP, Thomas	21	W½SE	1823-06-02		A1
1920	KEMP, Thomas H	21	E½SE	1823-05-01		A1
1764	LACY, Andrew N	26	NWSW	1884-03-20		A4
1765	" "	26	W½NW	1884-03-20		A4 R1938
1799	LAWSON, Gilbert B	17	E½SE	1890-03-19		A4
1800	" "	20	E½NE	1890-03-19		A4
1866	LAWSON, John R	17	NWSW	1884-03-10		A4
1788	LEDYARD, William J	1	SENW	1850-04-01		A1 G122
1917	MARCH, Thomas C	12	SENW	1839-09-20		A1

ID	Individual in Patent	Sec.	Sec. Part	Date Issued	Other Counties	For More Info . . .
1868	MAULDIN, John W	20	NWSW	1858-06-01		A1
1869	" "	20	SWNW	1858-06-01		A1
1870	" "	30	N½NE	1858-06-01		A1
1806	MCDONALD, J	17	S½NE	1884-12-05		A4
1807	" "	17	W½SE	1884-12-05		A4
1773	MILES, Arron E	29	E½SW	1909-05-24		A1
1774	" "	29	SWSW	1909-05-24		A1
1877	MILLENDER, Levi	31	N½NE	1891-06-29		A4
1878	" "	31	N½NW	1891-06-29		A4
1925	MORROW, Valentine C	36	N½SW	1890-04-15		A1
1926	" "	36	SENW	1890-04-15		A1
1927	" "	36	SWSW	1890-04-15		A1
1816	MUDD, James A	15	SWNE	1850-04-01		A1
1836	NEILSON, James	22	W½SW	1919-02-10		A1 R1837
1890	NEILSON, Mary	28	E½NE	1824-05-10		A1
1758	NICHOLS, Alfred W	34	SW	1883-08-13		A4
1763	NICHOLS, Andrew J	34	SE	1882-06-30		A1
1793	NICHOLS, Elizabeth J	33	N½NE	1889-10-07		A1
1794	" "	33	SWNE	1889-10-07		A1
1801	NICHOLS, Harlin H	33	NWSW	1889-10-07		A1
1802	" "	33	S½SW	1889-10-07		A1
1803	" "	33	SWNW	1889-10-07		A1
1891	NICHOLS, Matthew M	32	E½SE	1883-10-01		A4
1892	" "	32	SESW	1883-10-01		A4
1893	" "	32	SWSE	1883-10-01		A4
1908	NICHOLS, Robert B	33	N½SE	1891-06-29		A1
1909	" "	33	SESE	1891-06-29		A1
1922	NICHOLS, Thomas	33	SWSE	1858-06-01		A1
1837	NIELSON, James	22	W½SW	1824-04-12		A1 R1836
1838	" "	27	W½NW	1824-04-12		A1
1790	PARSONS, David	28	SWSW	1839-09-20		A1
1933	PETERSON, William H	10	SESW	1891-06-30		A4
1934	" "	15	N½NW	1891-06-30		A4
1935	" "	15	NWNE	1891-06-30		A4
1895	QUIN, Noah	30	NENW	1858-06-01		A1
1777	QUINN, Benjamin	20	SWSW	1885-03-30		A4
1817	QUINN, James A	29	SENW	1891-11-23		A4
1896	QUINN, Noah	30	NWNW	1852-01-01		A1
1936	QUINN, William H	29	SWNW	1850-04-01		A1
1937	ROBERTSON, William H	15	W½SE	1840-11-10		A1 G202
1938	" "	26	W½NW	1840-11-10		A1 G202 R1765
1939	" "	26	W½SE	1840-11-10		A1 G202
1910	RODGERS, Robert M	17	SENW	1858-06-01		A1
1911	" "	17	W½NW	1858-06-01		A1
1882	RUTH, Lucinda	31	SENE	1884-12-05		A4
1883	" "	32	N½SW	1884-12-05		A4
1884	" "	32	SWNW	1884-12-05		A4
1865	SKELTON, John P	30	S½SW	1885-03-16		A1
1751	SOUTHERLAND, Adam	22	E½NW	1832-01-10		A1
1851	STATUM, Job N	12	E½SW	1886-02-10		A1
1888	STATUM, Mary C	24	SE	1889-03-02		A1
1949	STATUM, William W	24	NE	1891-06-29		A4 R1874
1873	STEEL, Jonathan	27	NENW	1838-08-28		A1
1872	" "	11	SENW	1839-09-20		A1
1937	" "	15	W½SE	1840-11-10		A1 G202
1938	" "	26	W½NW	1840-11-10		A1 G202 R1765
1939	" "	26	W½SE	1840-11-10		A1 G202
1915	STEEL, Sylvester	1	SWSW	1839-09-20		A1
1784	STEPHENS, Coleman C	10	W½SW	1885-07-27		A1
1845	TILLISON, Jesse	33	SENW	1837-04-01		A1
1796	TILLOTSON, Frances	33	NESW	1852-01-01		A1
1788	TUTHILL, George A	1	SENW	1850-04-01		A1 G122
1786	VINES, Daniel	36	NWSE	1858-06-01		A1
1787	" "	36	S½NE	1858-06-01		A1
1795	WALDROP, Ferrel F	22	E½SW	1858-06-01		A1
1916	WALDROP, Terril F	22	SE	1889-10-07		A4 G228
1916	WALDROP, Thomas L	22	SE	1889-10-07		A4 G228
1755	WILEY, Alexander	10	NWSE	1850-04-01		A1
1756	" "	10	SESE	1853-11-15		A1
1754	" "	10	NESE	1858-06-01		A1
1757	" "	10	SWSE	1858-06-01		A1
1797	WILEY, Francis	21	SENE	1838-08-28		A1
1843	WILKINS, James	29	E½NE	1837-03-20		A1

ID	Individual in Patent	Sec.	Sec. Part	Date Issued	Other Counties	For More Info . . .
1781	WILLIAMS, Calvary	33	NENW	1839-09-20		A1
1778	" "	27	NWSW	1848-07-01		A1
1780	" "	28	SESW	1858-06-01		A1
1779	" "	28	N½SW	1883-10-01		A4
1805	WILLIAMS, Hezekiah	28	E½NW	1824-04-26		A1
1844	WILLIAMS, James	21	SESW	1838-08-28		A1
1833	WILLIAMS, James H	28	S½SE	1837-03-20		A1
1832	" "	27	SWSW	1858-06-01		A1
1871	WILLIAMS, John	28	W½NE	1824-04-30		A1
1854	WILLIAMS, John E	32	NE	1891-01-07		A1
1879	WILLIAMS, Lida	31	E½SW	1893-12-26		A1 G32
1880	" "	31	SENW	1893-12-26		A1 G32
1881	" "	31	SWNE	1893-12-26		A1 G32
1897	WILLIAMS, Owen	28	N½SE	1837-03-20		A1
1898	" "	29	SWSE	1837-11-07		A1
1923	WILLIAMS, Thomas	29	NENW	1850-04-01		A1
1924	" "	33	SENE	1853-08-01		A1
1950	WOODRUFF, William W	34	NE	1883-08-13		A4
1798	WYLIE, George N	21	W½NE	1824-05-25		A1
1942	WYLIE, William M	14	W½NW	1884-03-20		A4

Patent Map

T16-S R5-W
Huntsville Meridian

Map Group 12

Township Statistics

Parcels Mapped	:	200
Number of Patents	:	152
Number of Individuals	:	122
Patentees Identified	:	117
Number of Surnames	:	77
Multi-Patentee Parcels	:	11
Oldest Patent Date	:	5/1/1823
Most Recent Patent	:	2/10/1919
Block/Lot Parcels	:	0
Parcels Re - Issued	:	3
Parcels that Overlap	:	0
Cities and Towns	:	0
Cemeteries	:	3

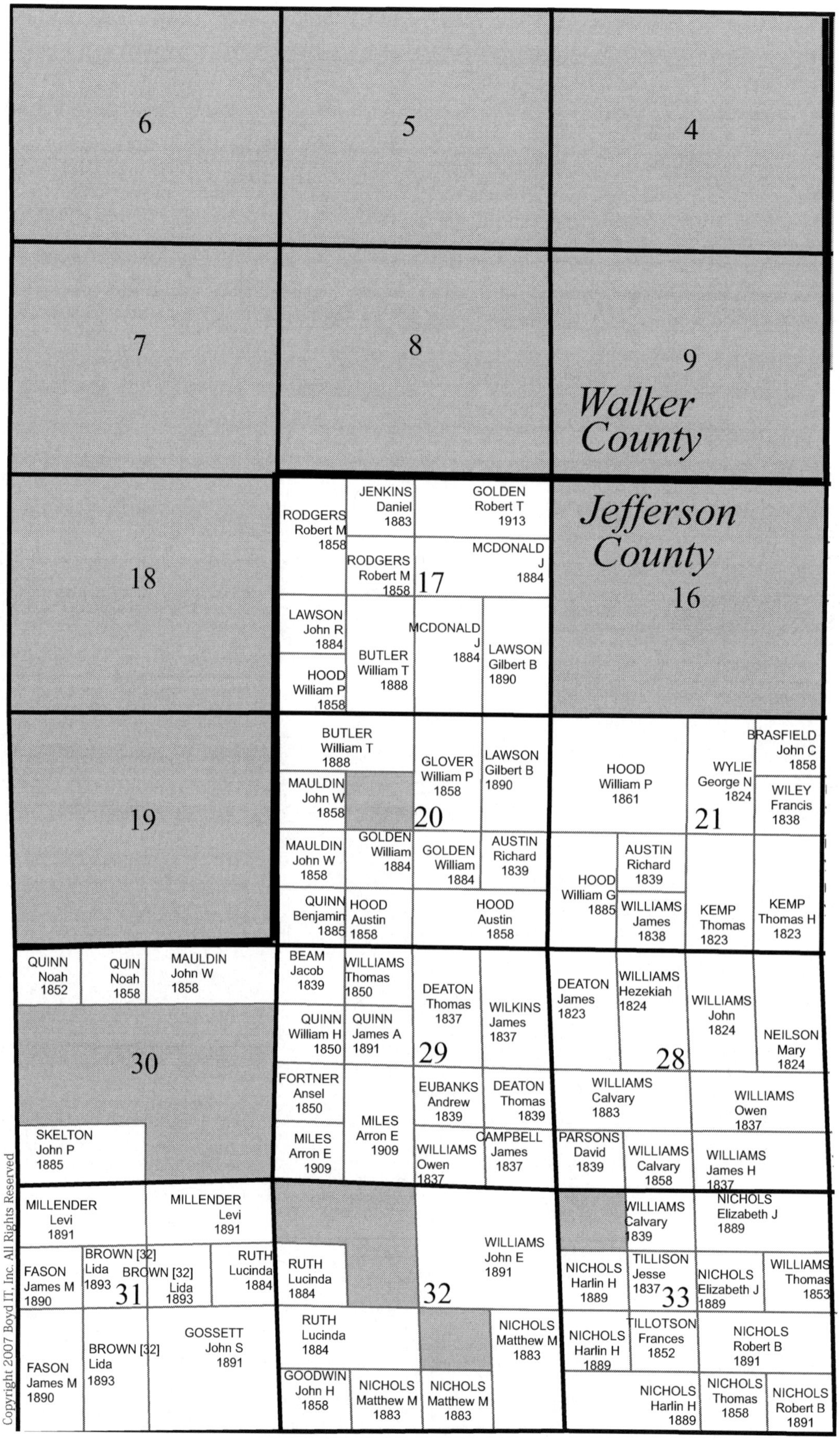

6
5
4
7
8
9
Walker County
Jefferson County
18
17
16

RODGERS Robert M 1858
JENKINS Daniel 1883
GOLDEN Robert T 1913
RODGERS Robert M 1858
MCDONALD J 1884
LAWSON John R 1884
MCDONALD J 1884
LAWSON Gilbert B 1890
BUTLER William T 1888
HOOD William P 1858

19
20
21

BUTLER William T 1888
GLOVER William P 1858
LAWSON Gilbert B 1890
HOOD William P 1861
BRASFIELD John C 1858
WYLIE George N 1824
WILEY Francis 1838
MAULDIN John W 1858
MAULDIN John W 1858
GOLDEN William 1884
GOLDEN William 1884
AUSTIN Richard 1839
AUSTIN Richard 1839
HOOD William G 1885
QUINN Benjamin 1885
HOOD Austin 1858
HOOD Austin 1858
WILLIAMS James 1838
KEMP Thomas 1823
KEMP Thomas H 1823

30
29
28

QUINN Noah 1852
QUIN Noah 1858
MAULDIN John W 1858
BEAM Jacob 1839
WILLIAMS Thomas 1850
DEATON Thomas 1837
WILKINS James 1837
DEATON James 1823
WILLIAMS Hezekiah 1824
WILLIAMS John 1824
NEILSON Mary 1824
QUINN William H 1850
QUINN James A 1891
FORTNER Ansel 1850
EUBANKS Andrew 1839
DEATON Thomas 1839
WILLIAMS Calvary 1883
WILLIAMS Owen 1837
MILES Arron E 1909
MILES Arron E 1909
SKELTON John P 1885
WILLIAMS Owen 1837
CAMPBELL James 1837
PARSONS David 1839
WILLIAMS Calvary 1858
WILLIAMS James H 1837

31
32
33

MILLENDER Levi 1891
MILLENDER Levi 1891
WILLIAMS John E 1891
WILLIAMS Calvary 1839
NICHOLS Elizabeth J 1889
FASON James M 1890
BROWN [32] Lida 1893
BROWN [32] Lida 1893
RUTH Lucinda 1884
RUTH Lucinda 1884
NICHOLS Harlin H 1889
TILLISON Jesse 1837
NICHOLS Elizabeth J 1889
WILLIAMS Thomas 1853
FASON James M 1890
BROWN [32] Lida 1893
GOSSETT John S 1891
RUTH Lucinda 1884
NICHOLS Matthew M 1883
NICHOLS Harlin H 1889
TILLOTSON Frances 1852
NICHOLS Robert B 1891
GOODWIN John H 1858
NICHOLS Matthew M 1883
NICHOLS Matthew M 1883
NICHOLS Harlin H 1889
NICHOLS Thomas 1858
NICHOLS Robert B 1891

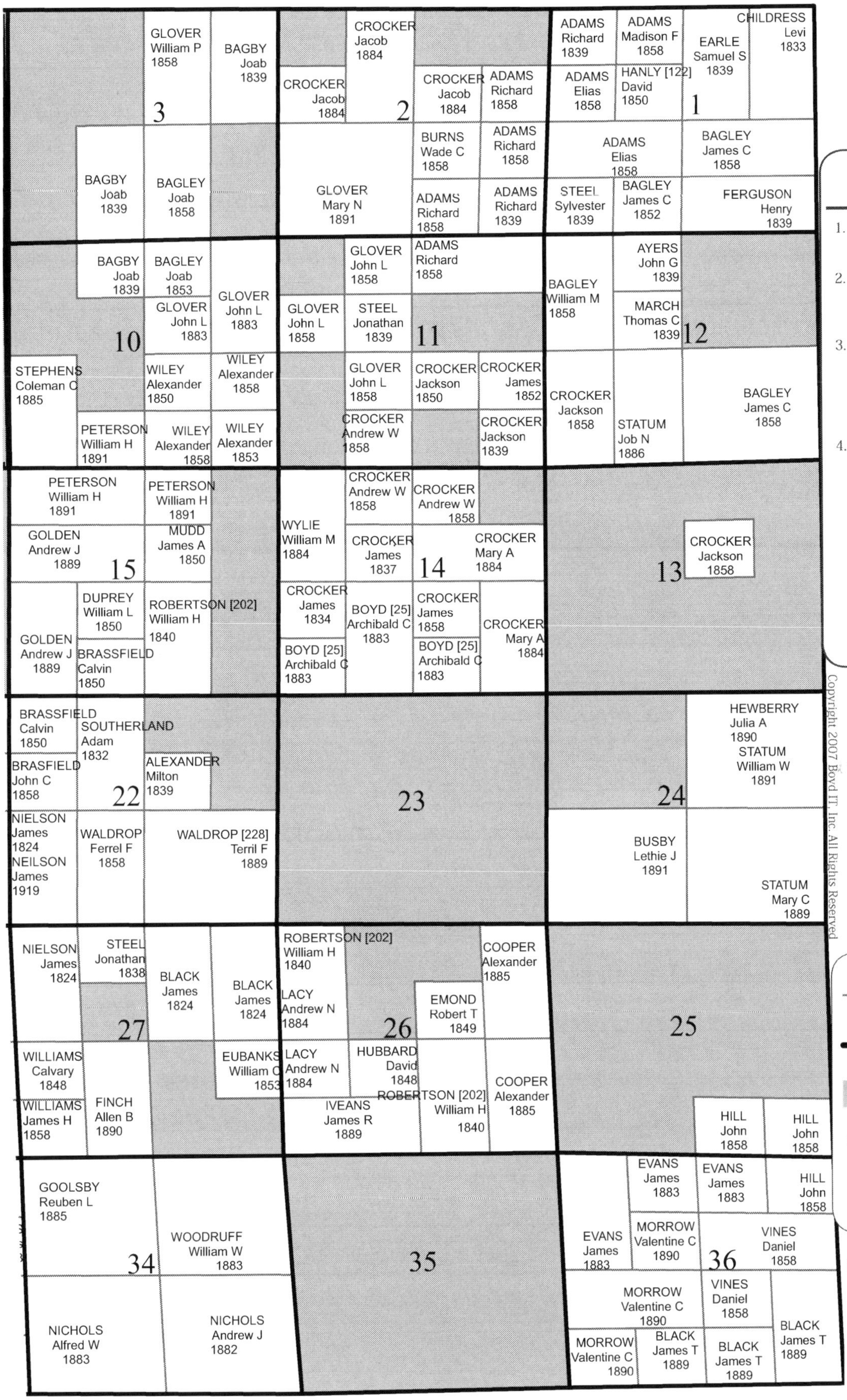

Helpful Hints

1. This Map's INDEX can be found on the preceding pages.
2. Refer to Map "C" to see where this Township lies within Jefferson County, Alabama.
3. Numbers within square brackets [ ] denote a multi-patentee land parcel (multi-owner). Refer to Appendix "C" for a full list of members in this group.
4. Areas that look to be crowded with Patentees usually indicate multiple sales of the same parcel (Re-issues) or Overlapping parcels. See this Township's Index for an explanation of these and other circumstances that might explain "odd" groupings of Patentees on this map.

Legend

- Patent Boundary
- Section Boundary
- No Patents Found (or Outside County)
- 1., 2., 3., ... Lot Numbers (when beside a name)
- [ ] Group Number (see Appendix "C")

Scale: Section = 1 mile X 1 mile (generally, with some exceptions)

Road Map

T16-S R5-W
Huntsville Meridian

Map Group 12

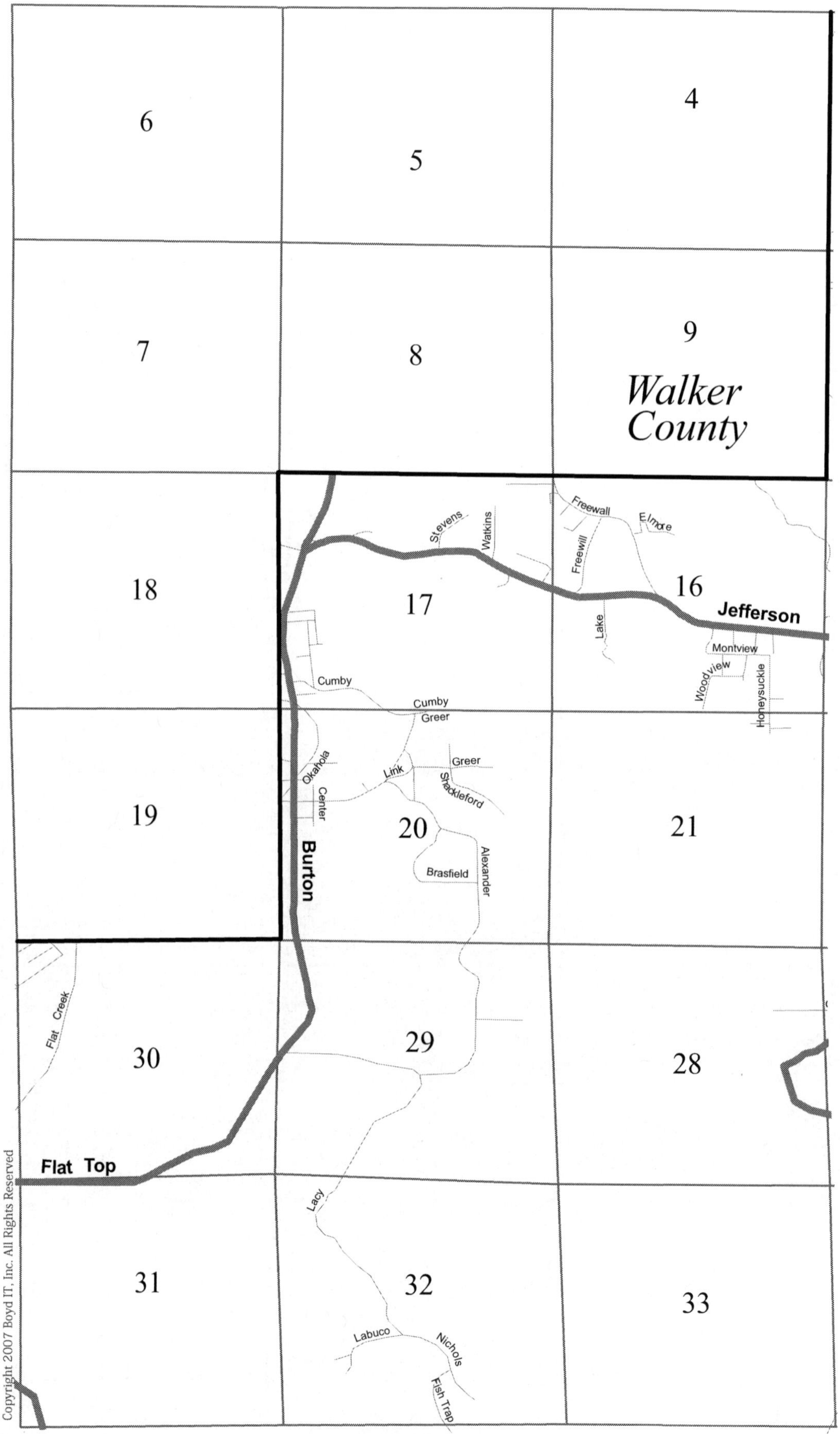

Cities & Towns
None

Cemeteries
Adams Cemetery
Bagley Bend Cemetery
Maben Cemetery

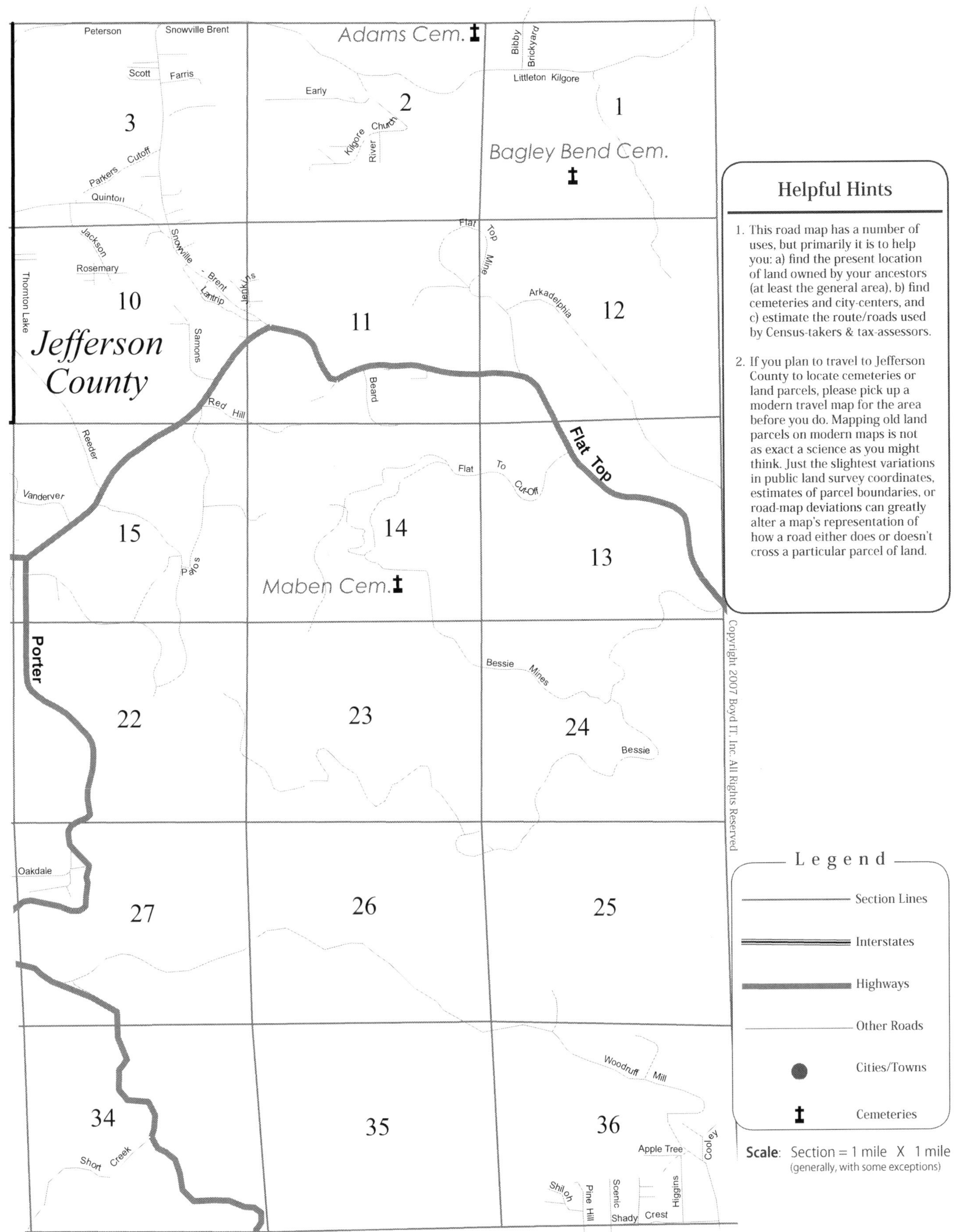
Peterson
Snowville Brent
Adams Cem.
Bibby
Brickyard
Scott
Farris
Littleton Kilgore
Early
2
1
3
Kilgore Church
River
Bagley Bend Cem.
Parkers Cutoff
Quinton
Jackson
Snowville - Brent
Flat Top Mine
Rosemary
Jenkins
Lantrip
Arkadelphia
Thornton Lake
10
11
12
Jefferson County
Samons
Beard
Red Hill
Flat Top
Reeder
Flat To Cut-Off
Vanderver
14
15
13
Paos
Maben Cem.
Porter
Bessie Mines
22
23
24
Bessie
Oakdale
27
26
25
Woodruff Mill
34
35
36
Short Creek
Apple Tree
Cooley
Shiloh
Pine Hill
Scenic
Higgins
Shady Crest
Helpful Hints
1. This road map has a number of uses, but primarily it is to help you: a) find the present location of land owned by your ancestors (at least the general area), b) find cemeteries and city-centers, and c) estimate the route/roads used by Census-takers & tax-assessors.
2. If you plan to travel to Jefferson County to locate cemeteries or land parcels, please pick up a modern travel map for the area before you do. Mapping old land parcels on modern maps is not as exact a science as you might think. Just the slightest variations in public land survey coordinates, estimates of parcel boundaries, or road-map deviations can greatly alter a map's representation of how a road either does or doesn't cross a particular parcel of land.
Copyright 2007 Boyd IT, Inc. All Rights Reserved
Legend
Section Lines
Interstates
Highways
Other Roads
Cities/Towns
Cemeteries
Scale: Section = 1 mile X 1 mile
(generally, with some exceptions)

Historical Map

T16-S R5-W
Huntsville Meridian

Map Group 12

Cities & Towns
None

Cemeteries
Adams Cemetery
Bagley Bend Cemetery
Maben Cemetery

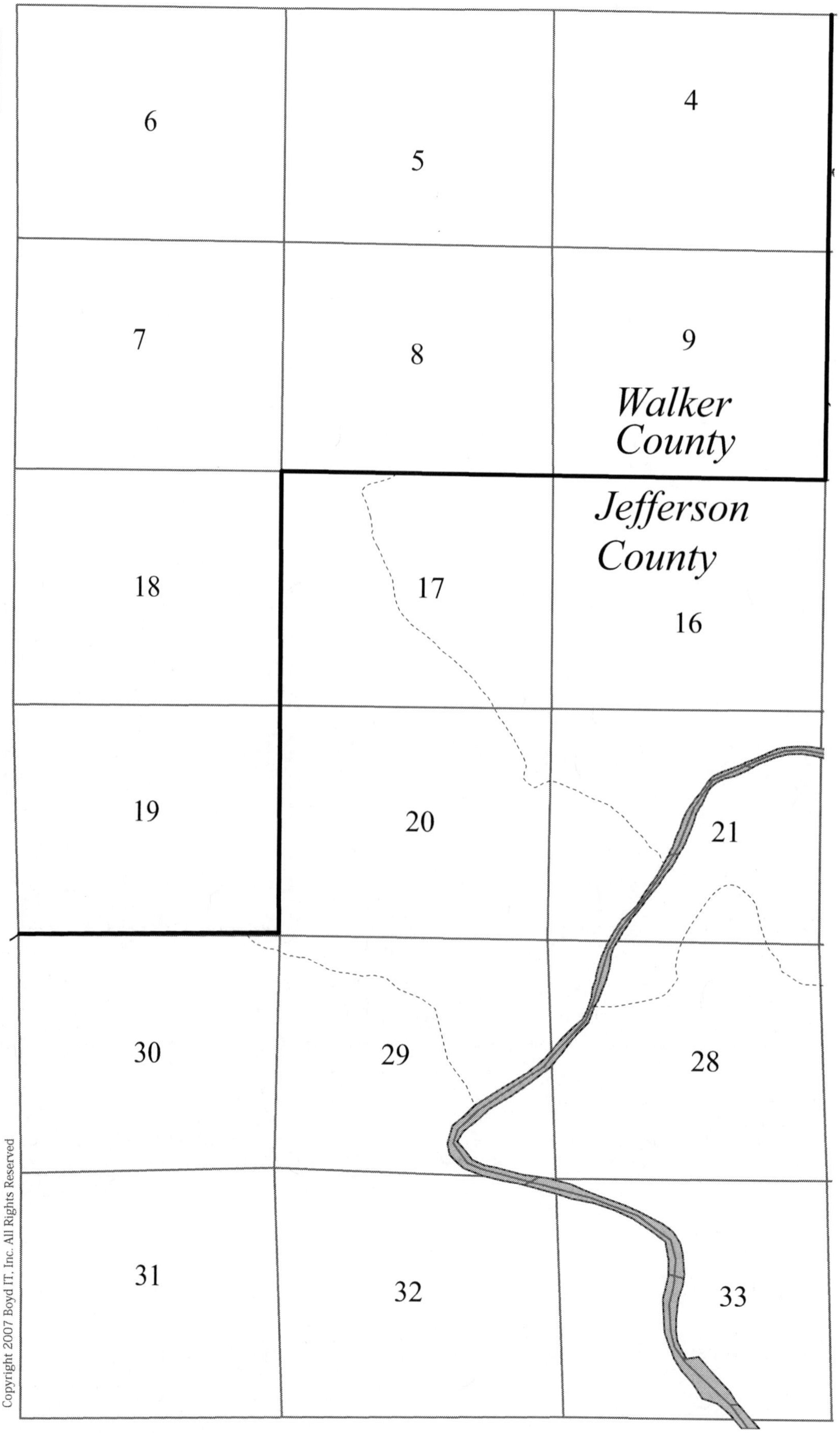

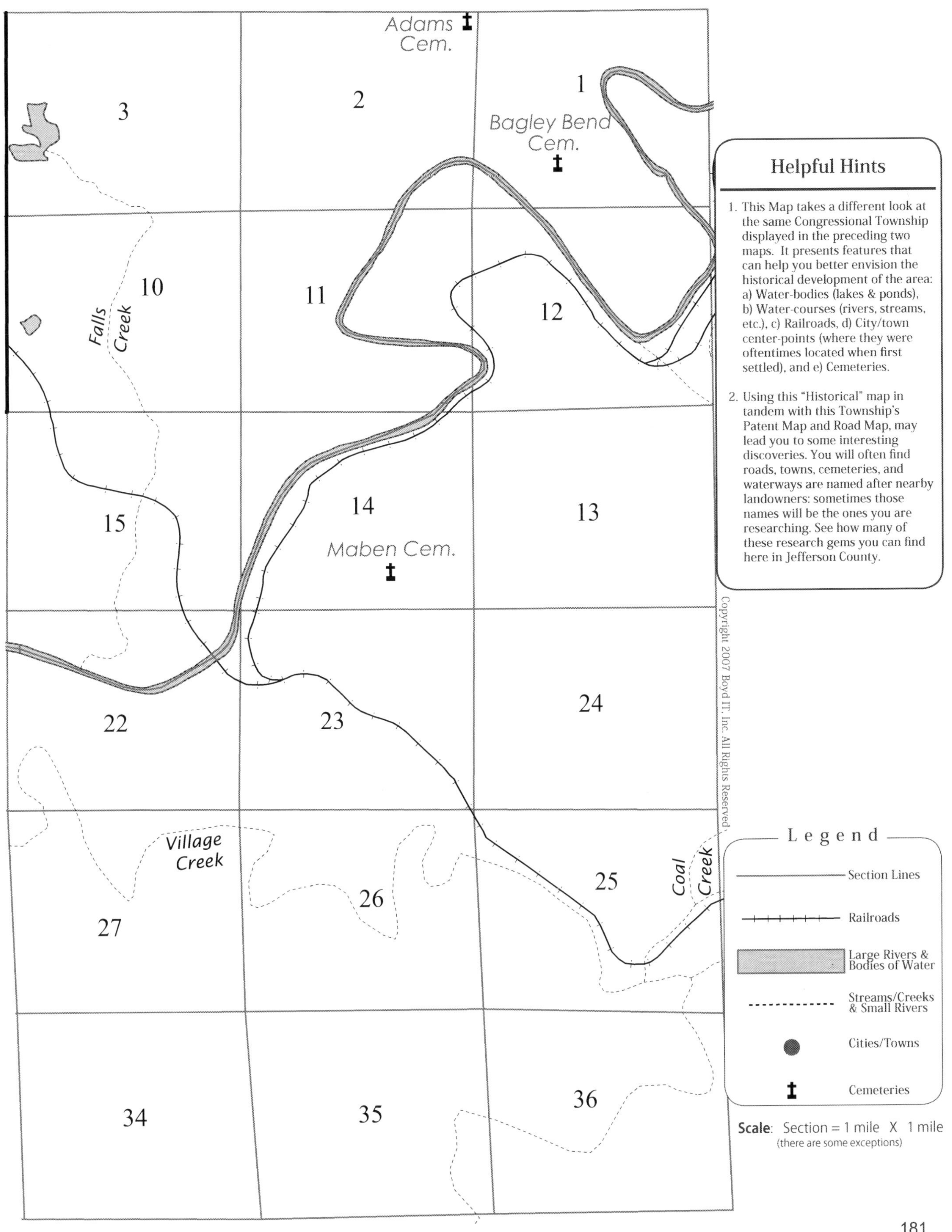

Helpful Hints

1. This Map takes a different look at the same Congressional Township displayed in the preceding two maps. It presents features that can help you better envision the historical development of the area: a) Water-bodies (lakes & ponds), b) Water-courses (rivers, streams, etc.), c) Railroads, d) City/town center-points (where they were oftentimes located when first settled), and e) Cemeteries.

2. Using this "Historical" map in tandem with this Township's Patent Map and Road Map, may lead you to some interesting discoveries. You will often find roads, towns, cemeteries, and waterways are named after nearby landowners: sometimes those names will be the ones you are researching. See how many of these research gems you can find here in Jefferson County.

Scale: Section = 1 mile X 1 mile
(there are some exceptions)

Map Group 13: Index to Land Patents

Township 16-South Range 4-West (Huntsville)

After you locate an individual in this Index, take note of the Section and Section Part then proceed to the Land Patent map on the pages immediately following. You should have no difficulty locating the corresponding parcel of land.

The "For More Info" Column will lead you to more information about the underlying Patents. See the *Legend* at right, and the "How to Use this Book" chapter, for more information.

LEGEND

"For More Info . . . " column

- **A** = Authority (Legislative Act, See Appendix "A")
- **B** = Block or Lot (location in Section unknown)
- **C** = Cancelled Patent
- **F** = Fractional Section
- **G** = Group (Multi-Patentee Patent, see Appendix "C")
- **V** = Overlaps another Parcel
- **R** = Re-Issued (Parcel patented more than once)

(A & G items require you to look in the Appendixes referred to above. All other Letter-designations followed by a number require you to locate line-items in this index that possess the ID number found after the letter).

ID	Individual in Patent	Sec.	Sec. Part	Date Issued	Other Counties	For More Info . . .
2066	ADCOCK, Mary	26	S½SW	1884-11-13		A1
2120	ADKINSON, William	25	NESW	1839-09-20		A1
2121	" "	25	SWNW	1839-09-20		A1
2029	AIKIN, John	25	NWNW	1834-10-01		A1
2031	AIKIN, John G	15	SWSW	1834-10-01		A1
2085	AIKIN, Samuel	15	W½NW	1826-10-05		A1
2084	" "	10	SWSW	1834-10-01		A1
2002	BAGLEY, James C	6	SWSW	1858-06-01		A1
1984	BAILEY, Fannie	34	SE	1885-03-30		A4 G9
1984	BAILEY, Livingston	34	SE	1885-03-30		A4 G9
2080	BIVEN, Robert	25	W½NE	1831-07-01		A1
1967	BIVENS, Calaway	36	W½SW	1878-06-13		A4
1969	BIVENS, Caloway	22	SENW	1837-11-07		A1 R2095
1968	" "	22	NWSE	1840-11-10		A1
1970	" "	22	SWSE	1858-06-01		A1
1999	BIVENS, James A	24	W½NW	1858-06-01		A1
1998	" "	24	SE	1883-07-03		A4
2116	BIVENS, Valentine	25	NWSE	1839-09-20		A1
2129	BIVENS, William E	26	E½NE	1883-08-13		A4
1971	BIVINS, Caloway	21	SESE	1852-01-01		A1
1972	" "	35	SENE	1858-06-01		A1
1973	" "	36	SWNW	1858-06-01		A1
2081	BIVINS, Robert	24	SW	1837-03-20		A1 G23
2015	BLACK, James W	32	E½NE	1882-10-30		A1
2016	" "	32	SWNE	1882-10-30		A1
2040	BLACK, John W	28	S½SW	1891-06-29		A1
2067	BLACK, Mary F	32	SE	1876-04-01		A4
2130	BLACK, William F	28	N½SW	1876-04-01		A4
2131	" "	28	SENW	1876-04-01		A4
2132	" "	28	SWNE	1876-04-01		A4
1974	BOYD, Charles L	20	NWSW	1884-11-13		A1
1975	" "	20	S½SW	1884-11-13		A1
2000	BROOKS, James	12	E½NW	1884-03-20		A4
2001	" "	12	W½NE	1884-03-20		A4
1976	BROWN, David O	20	E½NE	1884-03-20		A4 V2023
1977	" "	20	NESE	1884-03-20		A4
1978	" "	20	SWNE	1884-03-20		A4 V2023
1990	BROWN, Isaac	10	SESW	1850-09-02		A1
1980	BURRELL, Eli C	6	N½SW	1891-06-30		A4
1981	" "	6	SESW	1891-06-30		A4
1982	" "	6	SWSE	1891-06-30		A4
2061	BURRELL, Martin	8	NE	1891-12-01		A1
2056	CASH, Linsey C	20	N½NW	1889-08-16		A4
2057	" "	20	NWNE	1889-08-16		A4
2083	CLEMENTS, Salathiel	10	NWNW	1880-02-20		A4
2128	COLEMAN, William	35	NW	1839-09-20		A1 F

ID	Individual in Patent	Sec.	Sec. Part	Date Issued	Other Counties	For More Info . . .
2023	CONNER, John A	20	S½NE	1858-06-01		A1 V1976, 1978
2024	" "	29	E½NE	1858-06-01		A1
2025	" "	29	NWSE	1858-06-01		A1
2026	" "	29	SWNE	1858-06-01		A1
2119	CORNELIUS, West C	24	NE	1888-01-21		A4
2003	CROCKER, James D	30	E½SW	1883-07-03		A4
2004	" "	30	S½SE	1883-07-03		A4
2060	CROCKER, Marshall M	7	SWSW	1860-07-02		A1
2021	CROTWELL, Jeremiah	26	SESE	1839-09-20		A1
2036	DAVIDSON, John J	6	E½NE	1882-06-30		A1
2037	" "	6	E½SE	1882-06-30		A1
2030	DRAPER, John B	36	N½NE	1858-06-01		A1
2041	EARLY, John W	32	NW	1876-04-01		A4
1961	EASTIS, Balas E	24	E½NW	1891-06-08		A4 G82
1961	EASTIS, Mary L	24	E½NW	1891-06-08		A4 G82
2123	EUBANK, William C	29	SWSE	1858-06-01		A1
2126	" "	32	NWNE	1858-06-01		A1
2122	" "	29	E½SW	1860-04-02		A1
2124	" "	29	SWSW	1860-04-02		A1
2125	" "	30	NWSE	1860-04-02		A1
1957	FIELDS, Andrew J	28	W½NW	1888-02-04		A4
1979	FIELDS, Edward G	8	SW	1891-12-01		A1
1993	FIELDS, Isaac	26	SWNE	1834-10-21		A1
1991	" "	22	NWSW	1858-06-01		A1
1992	" "	22	SWSW	1858-06-01		A1
1996	FIELDS, Isaac W	12	S½SE	1890-08-16		A1
1997	" "	12	S½SW	1890-08-16		A1
2068	FIELDS, Mary M	6	NWSE	1883-04-10		A4
2069	" "	6	SENW	1883-04-10		A4
2070	" "	6	SWNE	1883-04-10		A4
2072	FIELDS, Moses	23	NENE	1839-09-20		A1
2073	" "	26	NWSE	1839-09-20		A1
2075	FIELDS, Nancy M	14	NWSE	1915-03-30		A4 G85 R2127
2094	FIELDS, Samuel	23	W½NE	1831-07-01		A1
2088	" "	14	SESW	1839-09-20		A1
2093	" "	23	NENW	1839-09-20		A1
2090	" "	14	SWSE	1852-01-01		A1
2091	" "	15	NWSE	1852-01-01		A1
2086	" "	14	NESW	1858-06-01		A1
2087	" "	14	S½NW	1858-06-01		A1
2089	" "	14	SWNE	1858-06-01		A1
2092	" "	22	NENE	1858-06-01		A1
2096	FIELDS, Samuel J	22	SESE	1854-07-15		A1
2097	" "	26	NESE	1858-06-01		A1
2098	" "	26	SENW	1858-06-01		A1
2127	FIELDS, William C	14	NWSE	1896-09-04		A4 C R2075
2075	" "	14	NWSE	1915-03-30		A4 G85 R2127
2095	FRANKS, Samuel	22	SENW	1839-09-20		A1 R1969
1985	GOODWIN, Francis M	8	W½NW	1875-11-20		A4
2050	HAND, Joseph I	12	E½NE	1891-06-29		A1
2051	" "	12	N½SE	1891-06-29		A1
2052	HAND, Joseph S	4	NENE	1884-03-20		A4
2053	" "	4	NESE	1884-03-20		A4
2054	" "	4	S½NE	1884-03-20		A4
2102	HAND, Simeon	10	SWNW	1859-12-10		A1
2103	" "	9	E½NW	1859-12-10		A1
2104	" "	9	SENE	1859-12-10		A1
2105	" "	9	W½NE	1859-12-10		A1
2034	HARDEN, John	27	SESE	1858-06-01		A1
2035	" "	34	NWNE	1858-06-01		A1
2074	HARDEN, Moses R	2	SW	1890-12-31		A1
1955	HARDIN, Ambrose J	23	SWSW	1858-06-01		A1
1956	" "	26	NWNW	1858-06-01		A1
1986	HARDIN, Hampton G	22	SENE	1883-07-03		A4
1987	" "	22	W½NE	1883-07-03		A4
2081	HARDIN, John	24	SW	1837-03-20		A1 G23
2137	HARDIN, William P	35	SESW	1858-06-01		A1
2012	HAYS, James T	10	NWSE	1884-03-20		A4
2013	" "	10	SENE	1884-03-20		A4
2014	" "	10	W½NE	1884-03-20		A4
1989	HEATON, Henry O	33	SWSE	1858-06-01		A1
1994	HEATON, Isaac J	34	E½SW	1884-03-20		A4
2101	HEATON, Sarah E	34	W½SW	1875-11-20		A4

ID	Individual in Patent	Sec.	Sec. Part	Date Issued	Other Counties	For More Info . . .
2109	HILL, Thomas	28	NENW	1860-04-02		A1
2110	" "	28	NWNE	1860-04-02		A1
1988	JENKINS, Henry C	32	SW	1876-04-01		A4
2133	JONES, William F	8	SE	1891-06-29		A1 R2108
1954	LINN, Alpheus C	4	SWNW	1888-01-21		A4
1960	LINN, Andrew J	15	NESW	1852-01-01		A1
1958	" "	10	NESW	1883-07-03		A4
1959	" "	10	SENW	1883-07-03		A4
1983	LINN, Elizabeth R	10	NWSW	1891-07-28		A4
2005	LINN, James J	4	SESE	1893-01-13		A1
2059	LINN, Margaret J	18	NW	1886-03-10		A1
2100	LINN, Samuel	18	NE	1884-11-13		A1
2099	LINN, Samuel J	18	SW	1885-09-10		A1
2134	MCCOMAK, William J	6	N½NW	1884-03-20		A4
2135	" "	6	NWNE	1884-03-20		A4
2136	" "	6	SWNW	1884-03-20		A4
2079	MCPHERRIN, Richard	28	NENE	1839-09-20		A1
2048	MILES, Jonathan Y	15	SESW	1839-09-20		A1
2049	" "	9	E½SW	1839-09-20		A1
2006	MILLER, James L	30	NW	1891-06-29		A4
1951	MOONEY, Alfred J	14	E½NE	1882-06-30		A1
1952	" "	14	E½SE	1882-06-30		A1
1953	MOONEY, Allen S	2	NE	1884-11-13		A1
2027	MOONEY, John A	14	N½NW	1890-07-03		A4
2028	" "	14	NWNE	1890-07-03		A4
2020	NEWBERRY, Jane	36	S½NE	1881-09-01		A1
2055	NEWBERRY, Lawrence W	36	SE	1881-04-11		A4
2077	NEWBERRY, Rhoda F	36	E½NW	1890-03-08		A1
2078	" "	36	E½SW	1890-03-08		A1
2082	POOL, Roswell	7	SWNW	1839-09-20		A1
2038	REEDER, John R	34	NENE	1891-06-08		A4
2076	REEDER, Newton J	22	NESE	1891-06-08		A4
2115	REEDER, Thomas	27	SWNE	1852-01-01		A1
2111	" "	27	NENE	1858-06-01		A1
2112	" "	27	NWNE	1858-06-01		A1
2113	" "	27	NWSE	1858-06-01		A1
2114	" "	27	SENE	1858-06-01		A1
1962	ROBERTSON, Benjamin A	20	NESW	1883-07-03		A4
1963	" "	20	NWSE	1883-07-03		A4
1964	" "	20	S½NW	1883-07-03		A4
1995	RUDER, Isaac	25	NESE	1834-10-01		A1
2032	RUSSELL, John H	34	E½NW	1883-08-13		A4
2033	" "	34	S½NE	1883-08-13		A4
2108	SIMS, Stephen M	8	SE	1883-07-03		A4 R2133
2138	SPEER, William	25	SESE	1839-09-20		A1
2139	" "	25	SWSW	1839-09-20		A1
2009	STATEM, James	28	W½SE	1880-02-20		A4
2010	STATUM, James	28	NESE	1858-06-01		A1
2011	" "	28	SENE	1858-06-01		A1
2039	STIVENDER, John	9	E½SE	1858-06-01		A1
2019	TRUETT, Jane E	10	S½SE	1889-12-28		A1
2044	VANDEVIR, Johnston	21	NENE	1858-06-01		A1
2045	" "	22	NWNW	1858-06-01		A1
1965	VANDIVER, Bryson	22	NESW	1850-09-02		A1
1966	" "	22	SESW	1858-06-01		A1
2046	VANDIVER, Johnston	15	NWSW	1858-06-01		A1
2058	VARNUM, Lurany	10	NENW	1886-02-10		A1
2071	WALDROP, Mercer R	4	W½SW	1883-07-03		A4
2017	WHEELER, James W	26	NENW	1885-03-16		A1
2018	" "	26	NWNE	1885-03-16		A1
2047	WHEELER, Jonas	26	N½SW	1884-03-20		A4
2106	WILSON, Smith B	4	SESW	1875-11-20		A4
2107	" "	4	SWSE	1875-11-20		A4
2117	WILSON, Virgil A	4	NESW	1884-11-13		A1
2118	" "	4	NWSE	1884-11-13		A1
2042	WOOD, John	4	NWNW	1860-07-02		A1
2043	" "	5	N½NE	1860-07-02		A1
2062	WOOD, Martin L	4	E½NW	1883-10-01		A4
2007	WOODARD, James L	30	NWSW	1891-06-30		A4
2008	" "	30	SWSW	1891-06-30		A4
2022	YOUNG, Jesse T	2	SE	1885-03-30		A4
2063	YOUNG, Martin	26	SWSE	1858-06-01		A1
2064	" "	35	NENE	1858-06-01		A1

ID	Individual in Patent	Sec.	Sec. Part	Date Issued	Other Counties	For More Info . . .
2065	YOUNG, Martin (Cont'd)	35	NWNE	1858-06-01		A1

Patent Map

T16-S R4-W
Huntsville Meridian

Map Group 13

Township Statistics

Parcels Mapped	:	189
Number of Patents	:	133
Number of Individuals	:	112
Patentees Identified	:	109
Number of Surnames	:	63
Multi-Patentee Parcels	:	4
Oldest Patent Date	:	10/5/1826
Most Recent Patent	:	3/30/1915
Block/Lot Parcels	:	0
Parcels Re - Issued	:	3
Parcels that Overlap	:	3
Cities and Towns	:	4
Cemeteries	:	6

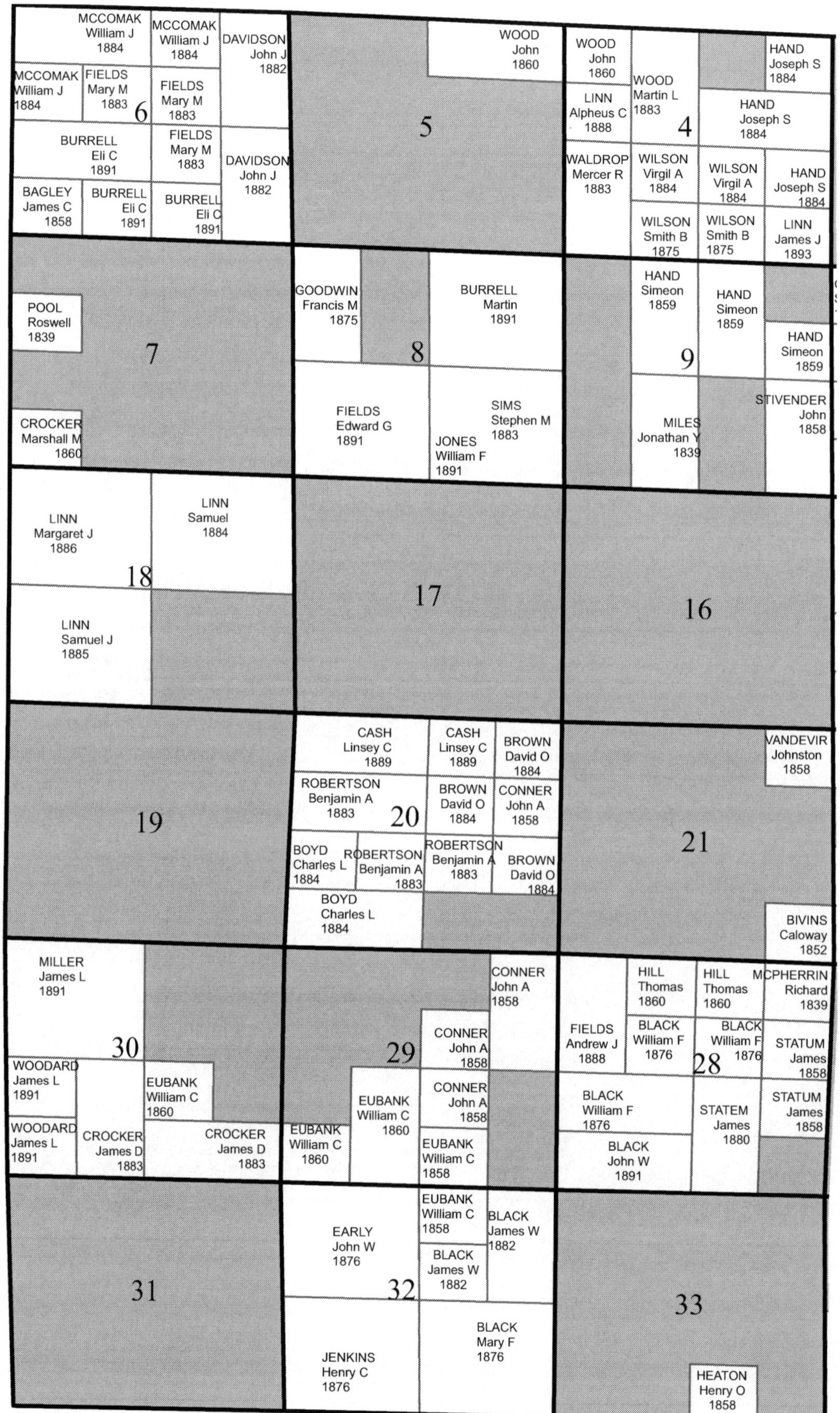

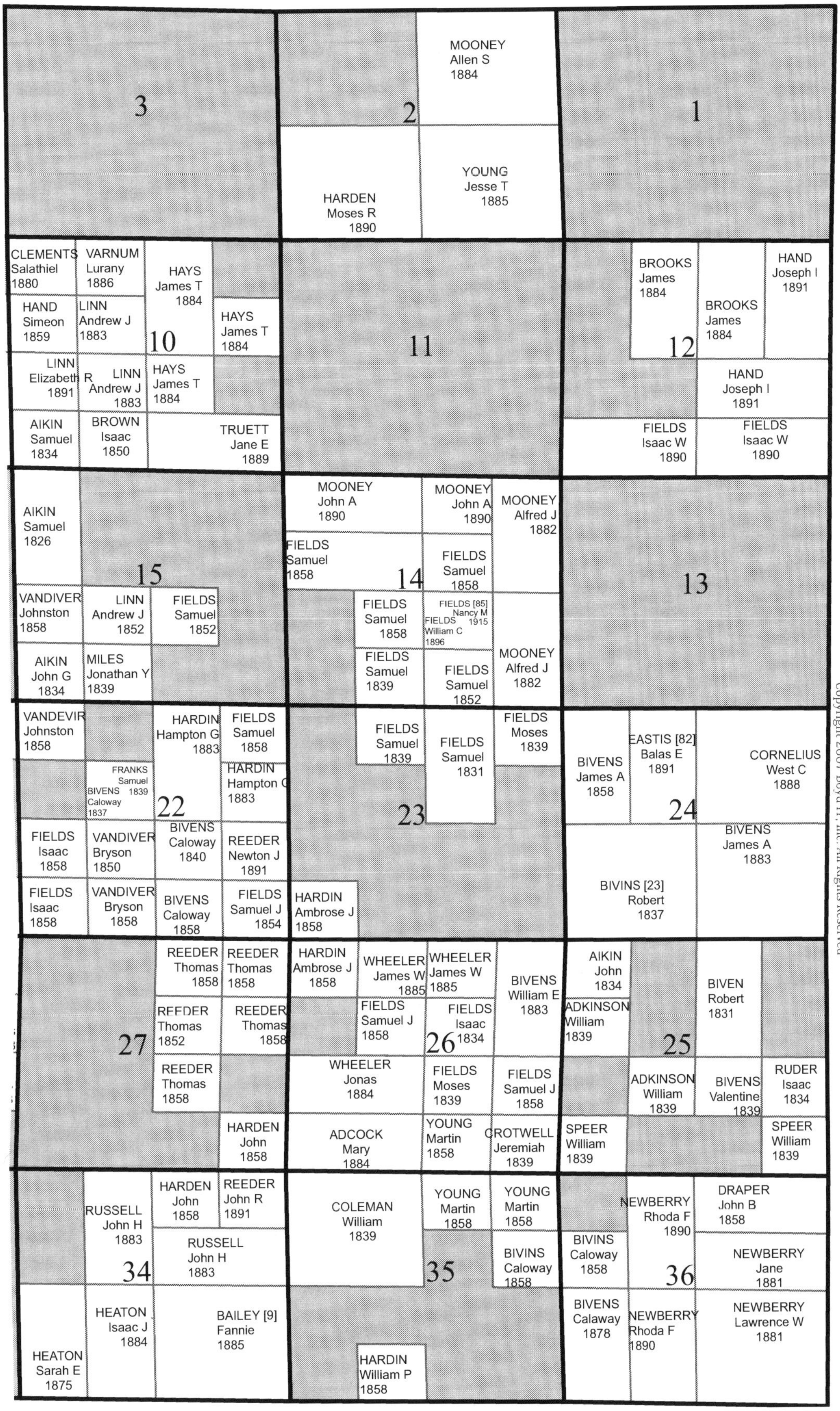

Helpful Hints

1. This Map's INDEX can be found on the preceding pages.
2. Refer to Map "C" to see where this Township lies within Jefferson County, Alabama.
3. Numbers within square brackets [ ] denote a multi-patentee land parcel (multi-owner). Refer to Appendix "C" for a full list of members in this group.
4. Areas that look to be crowded with Patentees usually indicate multiple sales of the same parcel (Re-issues) or Overlapping parcels. See this Township's Index for an explanation of these and other circumstances that might explain "odd" groupings of Patentees on this map.

Legend

Patent Boundary

Section Boundary

No Patents Found (or Outside County)

1., 2., 3., ... Lot Numbers (when beside a name)

[ ] Group Number (see Appendix "C")

Scale: Section = 1 mile X 1 mile (generally, with some exceptions)

Road Map

T16-S R4-W
Huntsville Meridian

Map Group 13

Cities & Towns
- Adamsville
- Brookside
- Cardiff
- Graysville

Cemeteries
- Bivens Chapel Cemetery
- Cardiff Cemetery
- Glasgow Hill Cemetery
- Linn Cemetery
- Linns Crossing Cemetery
- Saint Michaels Cemetery

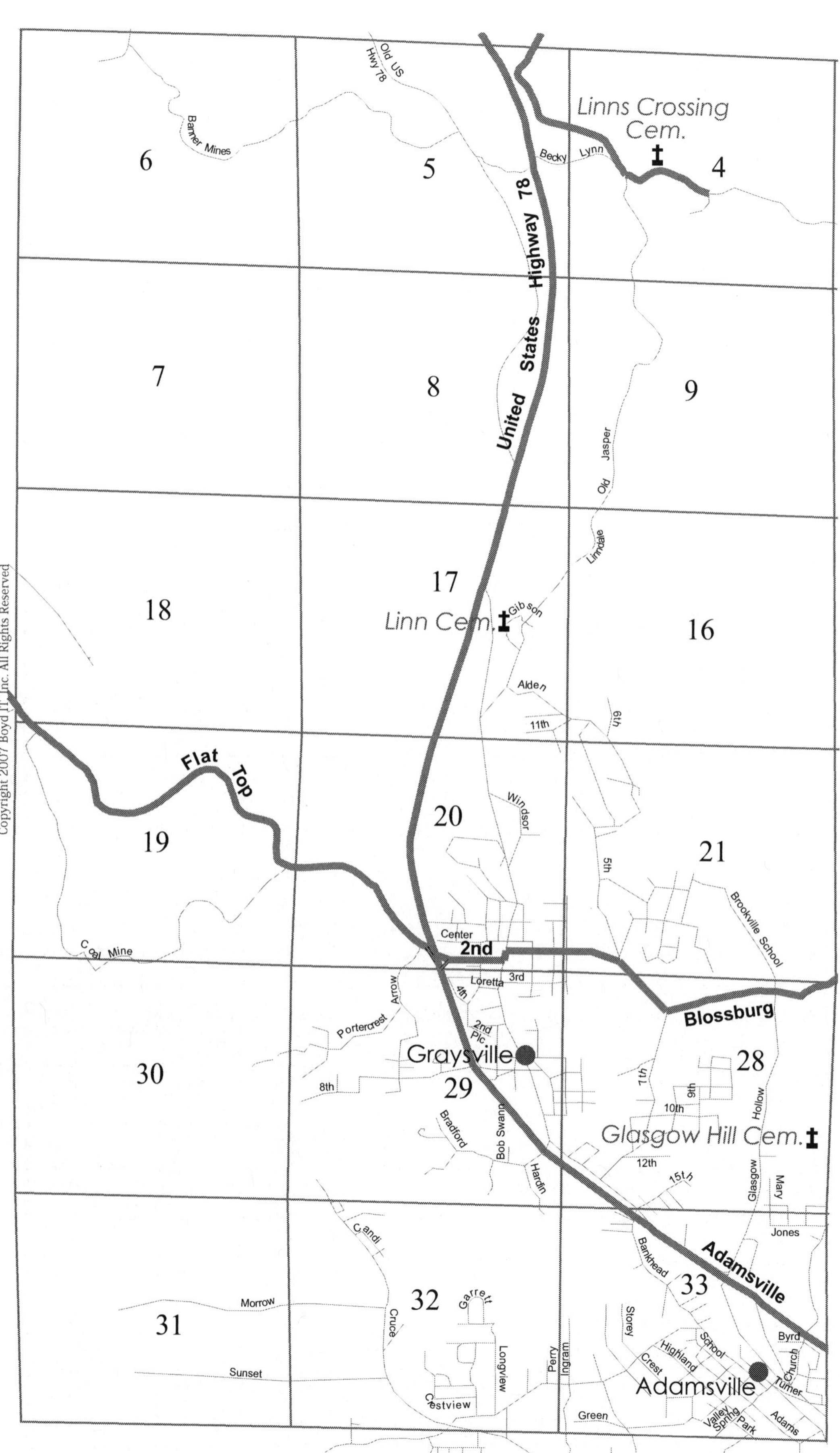

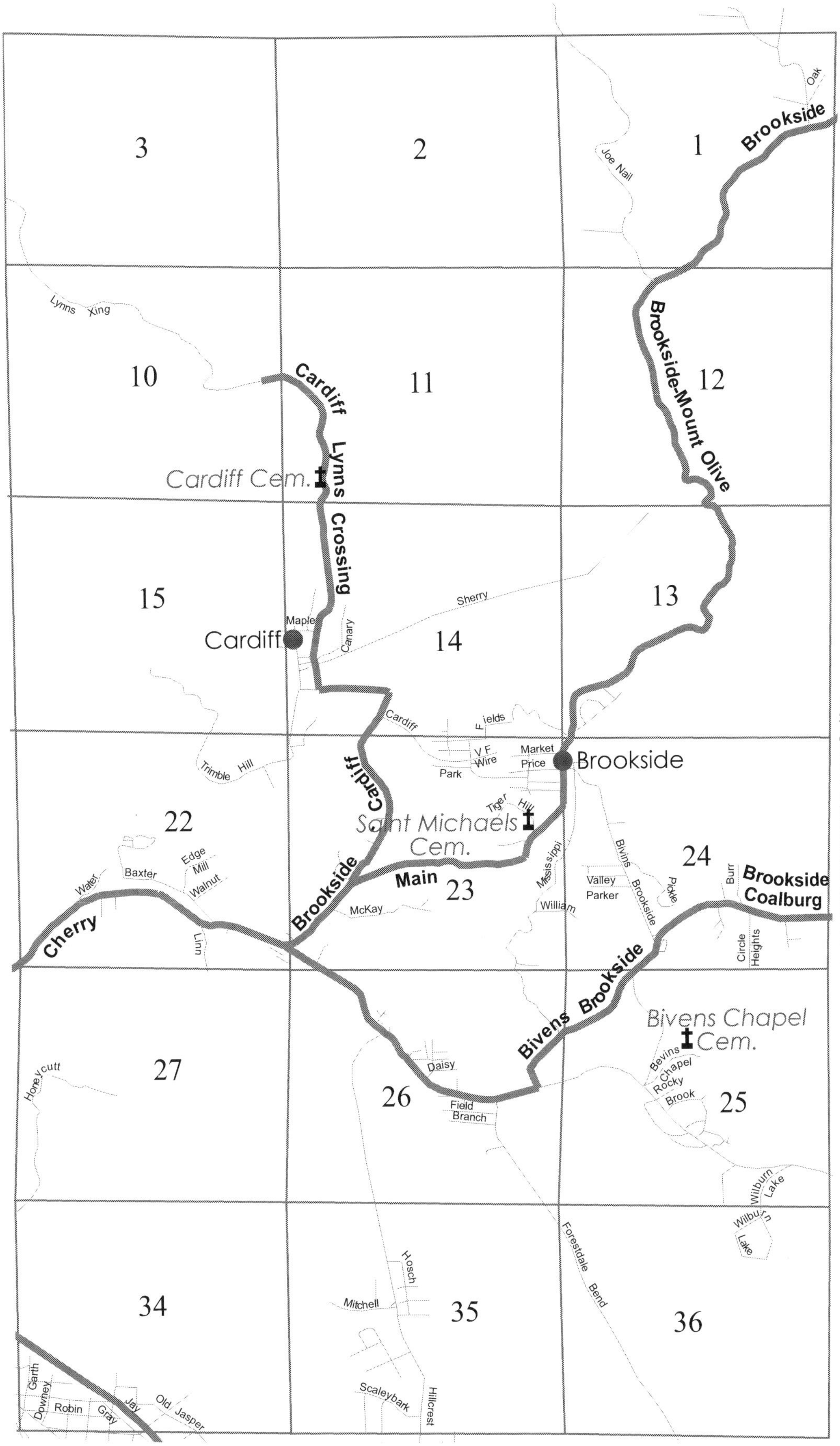

Helpful Hints

1. This road map has a number of uses, but primarily it is to help you: a) find the present location of land owned by your ancestors (at least the general area), b) find cemeteries and city-centers, and c) estimate the route/roads used by Census-takers & tax-assessors.

2. If you plan to travel to Jefferson County to locate cemeteries or land parcels, please pick up a modern travel map for the area before you do. Mapping old land parcels on modern maps is not as exact a science as you might think. Just the slightest variations in public land survey coordinates, estimates of parcel boundaries, or road-map deviations can greatly alter a map's representation of how a road either does or doesn't cross a particular parcel of land.

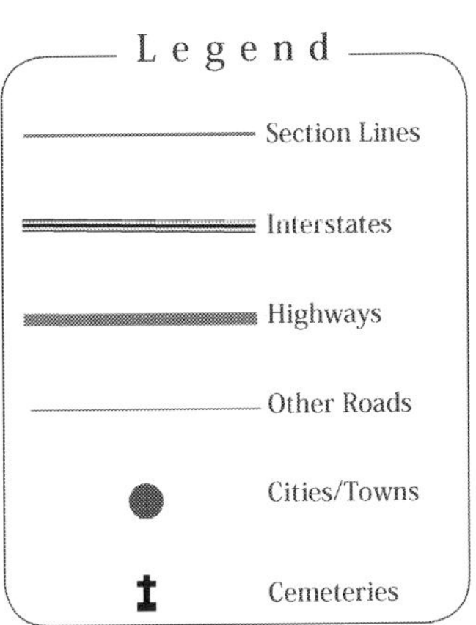

Scale: Section = 1 mile X 1 mile
(generally, with some exceptions)

Historical Map

T16-S R4-W
Huntsville Meridian

Map Group 13

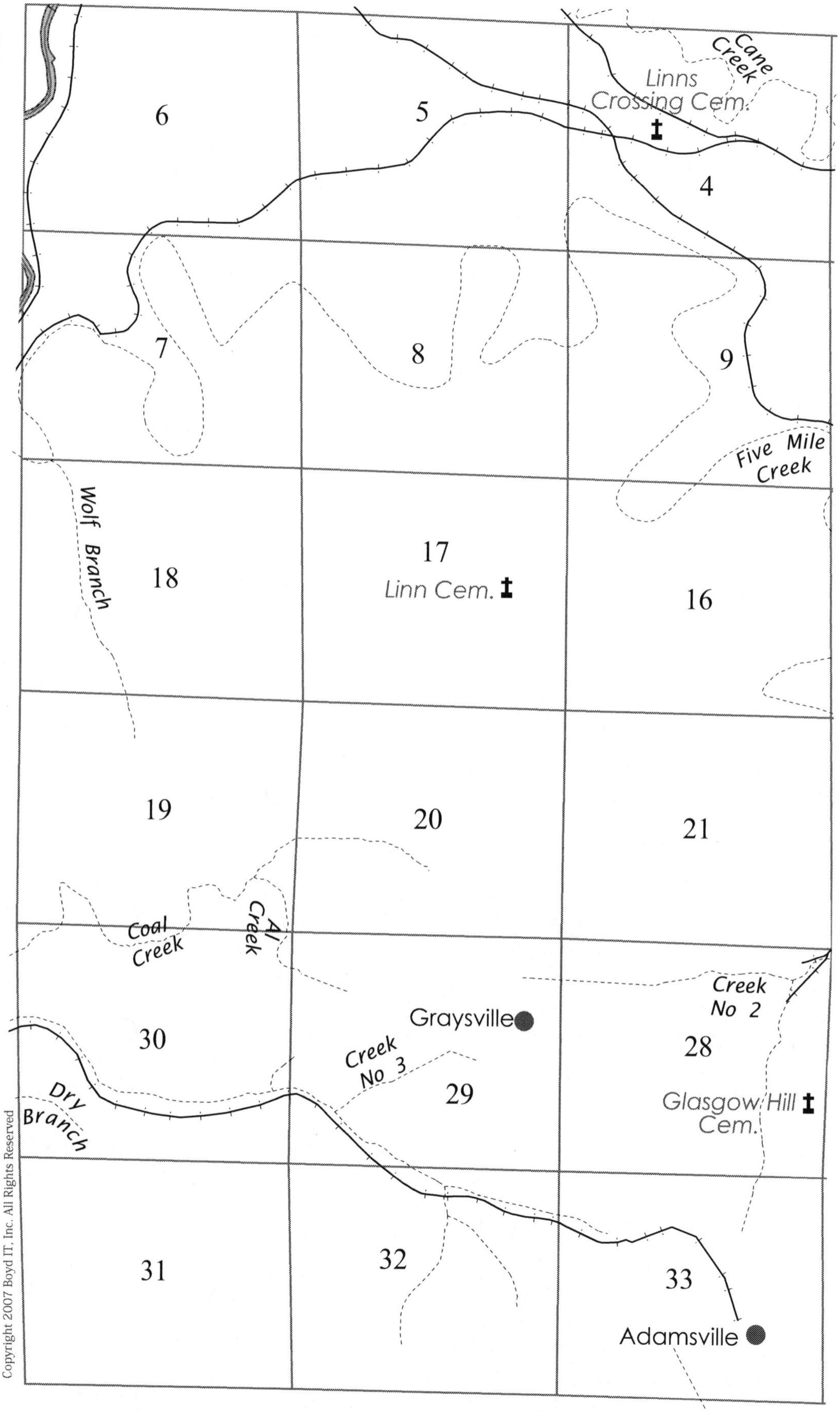

Cities & Towns

Adamsville
Brookside
Cardiff
Graysville

Cemeteries

Bivens Chapel Cemetery
Cardiff Cemetery
Glasgow Hill Cemetery
Linn Cemetery
Linns Crossing Cemetery
Saint Michaels Cemetery

6
5
Cane Creek
Linns Crossing Cem.
4
7
8
9
Five Mile Creek
Wolf Branch
18
17
Linn Cem.
16
19
20
21
Coal Creek
Al Creek
Creek No 2
Graysville
30
Creek No 3
28
29
Glasgow Hill Cem.
Dry Branch
31
32
33
Adamsville

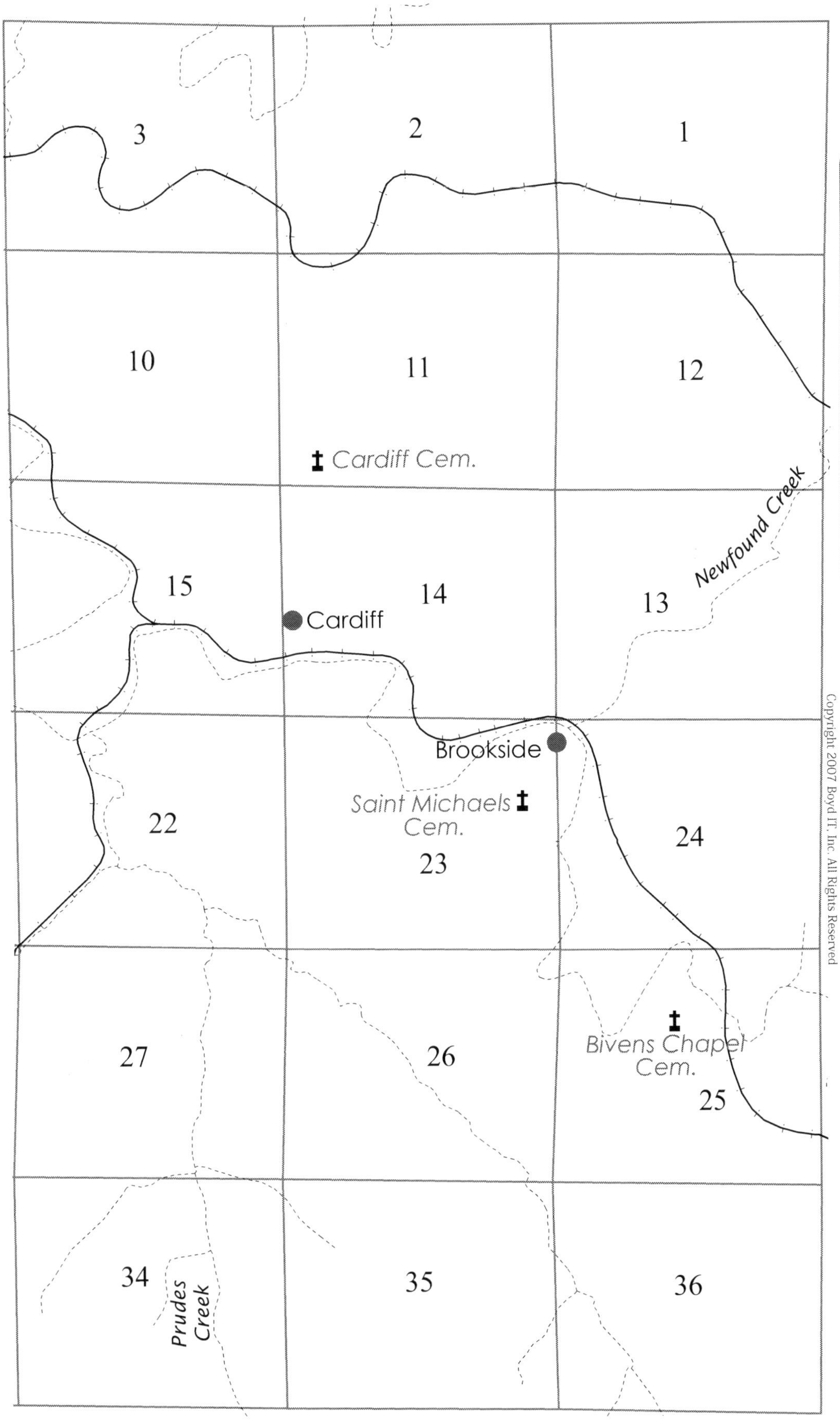

3
2
1
10
11
12
Cardiff Cem.
Newfound Creek
15
Cardiff
14
13
Brookside
Saint Michaels Cem.
22
23
24
Bivens Chapel Cem.
27
26
25
34
Prudes Creek
35
36

Helpful Hints

1. This Map takes a different look at the same Congressional Township displayed in the preceding two maps. It presents features that can help you better envision the historical development of the area: a) Water-bodies (lakes & ponds), b) Water-courses (rivers, streams, etc.), c) Railroads, d) City/town center-points (where they were oftentimes located when first settled), and e) Cemeteries.

2. Using this "Historical" map in tandem with this Township's Patent Map and Road Map, may lead you to some interesting discoveries. You will often find roads, towns, cemeteries, and waterways are named after nearby landowners: sometimes those names will be the ones you are researching. See how many of these research gems you can find here in Jefferson County.

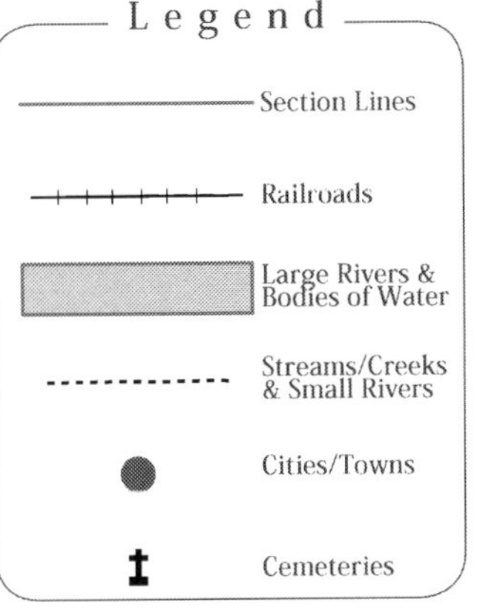

Scale: Section = 1 mile X 1 mile
(there are some exceptions)

Map Group 14: Index to Land Patents

Township 16-South Range 3-West (Huntsville)

After you locate an individual in this Index, take note of the Section and Section Part then proceed to the Land Patent map on the pages immediately following. You should have no difficulty locating the corresponding parcel of land.

The "For More Info" Column will lead you to more information about the underlying Patents. See the *Legend* at right, and the "How to Use this Book" chapter, for more information.

LEGEND

"For More Info . . . " column

- **A** = Authority (Legislative Act, See Appendix "A")
- **B** = Block or Lot (location in Section unknown)
- **C** = Cancelled Patent
- **F** = Fractional Section
- **G** = Group (Multi-Patentee Patent, see Appendix "C")
- **V** = Overlaps another Parcel
- **R** = Re-Issued (Parcel patented more than once)

(A & G items require you to look in the Appendixes referred to above. All other Letter-designations followed by a number require you to locate line-items in this index that possess the ID number found after the letter).

ID	Individual in Patent	Sec.	Sec. Part	Date Issued	Other Counties	For More Info . . .
2284	AKINS, Nathan B	28	E½SE	1875-07-01		A4
2330	ASKEW, William	2	SESW	1892-06-10		A4
2331	" "	2	W½SW	1892-06-10		A4
2207	BAGBY, Isaiah	30	SWSE	1839-09-20		A1
2173	BAGLEY, Elizabeth	32	NENW	1858-06-01		A1
2208	BAGLEY, Isaiah	31	E½NE	1824-05-27		A1
2209	" "	32	E½SW	1824-05-27		A1
2210	" "	32	SENW	1834-10-01		A1
2211	" "	32	SWSE	1834-10-01		A1
2212	BAGLEY, Isaih	32	W½NW	1824-05-24		A1
2233	BAGLEY, Joab	31	NWNE	1854-07-15		A1
2280	BAGLEY, Minus	30	E½SE	1858-06-01		A1
2332	BAGLEY, William	31	NESE	1834-10-01		A1
2327	BAILEY, Wiley J	36	W½NE	1890-04-15		A1
2174	BEAZLEY, Elizabeth	36	E½NE	1858-06-01		A1
2151	BELCHER, Benjamin H	8	SENW	1895-06-19		A4
2152	" "	8	SWNE	1895-06-19		A4
2172	BELCHER, Elizabeth A	2	S½NW	1885-03-30		A4
2170	" "	2	NESW	1889-11-21		A4
2171	" "	2	NWSE	1889-11-21		A4
2213	BELCHER, J A	28	E½SW	1885-08-05		A1 G20
2235	BELCHER, John A	4	SWSW	1897-07-03		A4
2283	BILLINGSLEY, Nancy	22	NENE	1889-08-16		A4
2341	BILLINGSLEY, William M	22	SWSW	1893-07-19		A4
2301	BIVEN, Robert	33	W½NW	1831-01-04		A1
2154	BRAKE, Bennett	30	NWNW	1834-10-01		A1
2155	" "	30	SWNW	1839-09-20		A1
2175	BRAKE, Elizabeth	19	S½SW	1858-06-01		A1
2187	BREWER, George N	10	NESW	1885-06-12		A4
2188	" "	10	NWSE	1885-06-12		A4
2189	" "	10	W½NE	1885-06-12		A4
2247	BROCK, John H	28	SWNE	1891-06-30		A4
2243	BURGIN, John G	31	SWNE	1854-07-15		A1
2242	" "	31	E½SW	1858-06-01		A1
2288	BURTON, Peyton C	26	SESE	1891-06-18		A1
2281	CAMMEL, Moses	21	NESE	1858-06-01		A1
2282	" "	22	NWSW	1858-06-01		A1
2229	CAMPBELL, James L	12	E½NE	1885-04-27		A4
2230	" "	12	NENW	1885-04-27		A4
2231	" "	12	NWNE	1885-04-27		A4
2232	CAMPBELL, Jane	34	SWSW	1860-07-02		A1
2191	CLIFT, George W	36	W½SE	1858-06-01		A1
2160	COOK, Calliedonia A	24	E½NE	1889-08-16		A4 G58
2161	" "	24	E½SE	1889-08-16		A4 G58
2160	COOK, James R	24	E½NE	1889-08-16		A4 G58
2161	" "	24	E½SE	1889-08-16		A4 G58

ID	Individual in Patent	Sec.	Sec. Part	Date Issued	Other Counties	For More Info . . .
2140	CORNELIUS, Aaron B	28	S½NW	1875-07-01		A4
2213	CORNELIUS, William P	28	E½SW	1885-08-05		A1 G20
2236	CROW, John B	32	W½SW	1890-07-03		A4
2182	DEAVENPORT, George	26	SWSE	1839-09-20		A1
2183	" "	35	NWNE	1839-09-20		A1
2274	DOWNS, Martha	24	E½SW	1883-07-03		A4
2309	DOWNS, Stephen W	24	W½NW	1891-06-30		A4
2237	DRAPER, John B	31	SWNW	1858-06-01		A1
2285	DYER, Otis	25	W½NE	1826-06-10		A1 G79
2305	EARLE, Samuel S	34	NWNE	1853-08-01		A1 C R2142
2307	EASTIS, Samuel W	18	E½NE	1888-10-25		A4
2350	EASTIS, William W	18	E½SE	1884-12-05		A4
2352	EASTIS, Willis	33	SWSW	1834-10-14		A1
2351	" "	20	S½NW	1876-02-01		A4
2224	ECHOLS, James F	30	NESW	1894-05-08		A1
2180	ELLARD, Felix J	34	SE	1885-03-16		A4
2310	ELLIOTT, Stephen W	12	N½SE	1890-04-15		A1
2311	ELLIOTT, Thomas A	12	E½SW	1891-06-08		A4
2312	" "	12	S½SE	1891-06-08		A4
2316	EVANS, Thomas	36	N½NW	1889-11-21		A4
2149	EZEKIAL, Ann E	22	S½NE	1883-07-03		A4
2159	EZEKIEL, Bridgett	22	SESE	1892-06-30		A4
2217	EZEKIEL, Jacob	14	NESE	1885-03-30		A4
2218	" "	14	S½SE	1885-03-30		A4
2271	EZEKIEL, Malinda	22	N½SE	1876-04-01		A4
2333	FARLEY, William	28	SENE	1858-06-01		A1
2275	FIELDS, Martha S	30	E½NW	1875-06-01		A4
2206	FLANAGAN, Hiram M	32	NWSE	1834-10-01		A1
2201	FULMER, Henry R	6	E½NW	1884-03-20		A4
2202	" "	6	NESW	1884-03-20		A4
2203	" "	6	SWNW	1884-03-20		A4
2181	GAFFORD, Frank H	32	NE	1891-11-16		A1
2262	GARRITT, Joseph	35	NENW	1839-09-20		A1
2334	GERMAN, William	22	N½NW	1884-11-13		A1
2335	" "	22	NWNE	1884-11-13		A1
2239	GOODE, John E	6	E½SE	1891-06-08		A4
2240	" "	6	SESW	1891-06-08		A4
2241	" "	6	SWSE	1891-06-08		A4
2317	GOODE, Thomas	31	E½NW	1833-08-12		A1
2336	GOODE, William	6	NWSE	1891-07-28		A4
2272	GOODWIN, Mannon A	2	N½NW	1890-08-29		A4
2273	" "	2	W½NE	1890-08-29		A4
2325	GOWIN, Thompson	4	S½NE	1883-07-03		A4
2324	" "	4	N½NE	1884-12-05		A4
2150	GOWINS, Benjamin F	10	E½NW	1884-03-20		A4
2244	GRAHAM, John	3	W½SW	1858-06-01		A1
2245	" "	4	E½SE	1858-06-01		A1
2246	" "	9	NE	1858-06-01		A1
2321	GRAHAM, Thomas R	4	E½SW	1891-06-29		A4
2322	" "	4	W½SE	1891-06-29		A4
2199	GRAYHAM, Henry H	4	NWSW	1889-03-02		A1
2200	" "	4	SWNW	1889-03-02		A1
2184	GREEN, George L	25	SENE	1839-09-20		A1
2185	" "	34	E½SW	1839-09-20		A1
2248	HARRIS, John	32	NESE	1858-06-01		A1
2249	" "	33	NWSW	1858-06-01		A1
2250	" "	33	SESW	1858-06-01		A1
2186	HEWITT, George L	14	SW	1884-03-20		A4
2267	HODGES, Leroy H	20	S½SW	1876-02-01		A4
2313	HODGES, Thomas D	20	N½NW	1876-02-01		A4
2314	" "	20	W½NE	1883-04-10		A4
2286	HOLLIGAN, Patrick	10	NWSW	1890-01-08		A4
2287	" "	10	W½NW	1890-01-08		A4
2166	HOUK, David	25	NENE	1834-10-01		A1
2147	ISAACS, Allen M	31	SESE	1854-07-15		A1 G137
2147	ISAACS, John W	31	SESE	1854-07-15		A1 G137
2193	JACKS, Gilbert C	24	NWNE	1858-06-01		A1
2192	" "	24	NENW	1883-07-03		A4
2194	" "	24	SENW	1888-02-04		A4
2195	" "	24	SWNE	1888-02-04		A4
2225	JACKS, James K	12	W½SW	1858-06-01		A1
2226	" "	14	SENE	1858-06-01		A1
2227	" "	22	S½NW	1889-01-31		A1

ID	Individual in Patent	Sec.	Sec. Part	Date Issued	Other Counties	For More Info . . .
2297	JOHNSON, Richard C	8	E½SW	1895-02-23		A4
2298	" "	8	NWSE	1895-02-23		A4
2315	JOHNSON, Thomas D	8	SWSE	1903-12-04		A1
2318	JONES, Thomas P	8	NENW	1860-12-01		A1
2319	" "	8	NWNE	1860-12-01		A1
2320	" "	8	W½NW	1860-12-01		A1
2228	KELSO, James	24	W½SE	1885-09-10		A1
2146	KILLOUGH, Allen	1	NENE	1858-06-01		A1
2234	LAWLER, Joab	27	SESW	1839-09-20		A1
2153	LYKES, Benjamin H	28	NWNW	1884-12-05		A1
2162	MASSEY, Caroline	24	W½SW	1876-04-01		A4
2303	MASTERS, Robert	32	SESE	1834-10-14		A1
2292	MAXWELL, Rebecca	20	SESE	1889-10-07		A1
2238	MCCORMACK, John B	6	NE	1889-08-02		A4
2289	MCGEE, Ralph	33	SENE	1834-10-01		A1
2290	" "	33	SWSE	1834-10-01		A1
2291	MCGHEE, Ralph	33	W½NE	1823-07-09		A1
2251	MCMAHON, John R	26	NENW	1889-03-01		A4
2252	" "	26	W½NW	1889-03-01		A4
2326	MINOR, Warren W	14	NWNW	1895-02-23		A4
2285	MITCHELL, Thomas	25	W½NE	1826-06-10		A1 G79
2219	MONCRIEF, James A	2	NESE	1890-07-03		A4
2220	" "	2	S½SE	1890-07-03		A4
2221	" "	2	SENE	1890-07-03		A4
2168	MOORE, David W	34	SENW	1876-02-01		A4
2167	MORGAN, David	28	W½SW	1858-06-01		A1
2222	MORRISON, James E	30	E½NE	1884-03-10		A4
2223	" "	30	NWNE	1884-03-20		A4
2278	MYRICK, Milton	10	E½NE	1890-03-19		A4
2279	" "	10	NESE	1890-03-19		A4
2156	PAYNE, Berry	20	E½NE	1858-06-01		A1
2157	" "	20	NESE	1858-06-01		A1
2158	" "	21	NWSW	1858-06-01		A1
2345	PAYNE, William	28	NENW	1858-06-01		A1
2346	" "	28	NWNE	1858-06-01		A1
2337	PHILYAW, William J	22	E½SW	1858-06-01		A1
2338	" "	22	SWSE	1858-06-01		A1
2339	" "	27	NENW	1858-06-01		A1
2340	" "	27	NWNE	1858-06-01		A1
2169	PRICE, Doc F	28	NENE	1884-12-05		A1
2163	RAY, Charles A	36	E½SE	1880-06-23		A4
2176	REID, Elizabeth J	18	N½SW	1889-03-01		A4
2177	" "	18	SESW	1889-03-01		A4
2178	" "	18	SWNW	1889-03-01		A4
2293	REID, Reuben T	18	E½NW	1884-11-13		A1
2294	" "	18	NWNW	1884-11-13		A1
2204	RETALLACK, Henry	4	E½NW	1889-10-07		A1
2205	" "	4	NWNW	1889-10-07		A1
2276	RICHARDS, Mathew T	30	NWSE	1884-11-13		A1
2277	" "	30	SWNE	1884-11-13		A1
2268	ROBBINS, Levi	8	E½NE	1897-11-05		A4
2269	" "	8	E½SE	1897-11-05		A4
2308	ROBBINS, Silvester B	8	W½SW	1891-06-30		A4
2253	ROBERTS, John	25	E½NW	1858-06-01		A1
2304	RUSSELL, Robert	26	W½SW	1878-04-09		A4
2302	RUSSELL, Robert C	34	NENE	1884-03-10		A4
2164	SARGENT, Cooper B	15	NWSW	1858-06-01		A1
2165	" "	15	SWNW	1858-06-01		A1
2263	SARGENT, Joseph	11	SESW	1858-06-01		A1
2264	" "	14	E½NW	1860-03-01		A1
2265	" "	14	SWNW	1860-03-01		A1
2266	" "	15	SENE	1860-03-01		A1
2148	SHARIT, Amos L	36	SWNW	1883-10-01		A4
2254	SHUGART, John	20	NESW	1858-06-01		A1
2255	" "	20	NWSW	1858-06-01		A1
2256	" "	20	W½SE	1858-06-01		A1
2258	" "	29	NWNE	1858-06-01		A1
2257	" "	28	W½SE	1875-06-01		A4
2259	SHUGART, John T	10	S½SE	1889-08-16		A4
2260	" "	10	S½SW	1889-08-16		A4
2323	SIMMONS, Thomas	26	NE	1888-01-21		A4
2306	SIMS, Samuel	36	SW	1885-03-16		A1
2198	SMITH, Henry G	12	W½NW	1889-03-01		A4

ID	Individual in Patent	Sec.	Sec. Part	Date Issued	Other Counties	For More Info . . .
2196	SMITH, Henry G (Cont'd)	12	SENW	1889-08-13		A4
2197	" "	12	SWNE	1889-08-13		A4
2214	SMITH, Jackson	27	NESW	1858-06-01		A1
2215	" "	27	SENW	1858-06-01		A1
2216	" "	27	SWNE	1858-06-01		A1
2270	SMITH, Lucresy J	2	NENE	1894-10-22		A4
2141	SNELL, Adam	34	NENW	1884-03-20		A4
2142	" "	34	NWNE	1884-03-20		A4 R2305
2143	" "	34	W½NW	1884-03-20		A4
2347	SPEARS, William	31	NWSE	1854-07-15		A1
2348	SPEER, William	30	SESW	1839-09-20		A1
2349	" "	31	NWNW	1839-09-20		A1
2342	SPRUELL, William N	14	N½NE	1889-11-21		A4
2343	" "	14	NWSE	1889-11-21		A4
2344	" "	14	SWNE	1889-11-21		A4
2353	STAGG, Zachariah	13	NWSW	1834-10-14		A1
2179	STAGGS, Ezekiel	1	SENE	1839-09-20		A1
2190	STARNES, George	36	SENW	1839-09-20		A1
2295	WALKER, Richard B	33	SENW	1858-06-01		A1
2296	" "	34	NWSW	1858-06-01		A1
2299	WALKER, Richard D	33	NESW	1858-06-01		A1
2300	" "	33	NWSE	1858-06-01		A1
2329	WALKER, William A	33	NENW	1834-10-01		A1
2328	" "	26	SESW	1858-06-01		A1
2144	WILLIS, Alexander L	13	NESE	1858-06-01		A1
2145	" "	13	SENE	1858-06-01		A1
2261	WOOD, John	30	W½SW	1823-06-02		A1

Patent Map

T16-S R3-W
Huntsville Meridian

Map Group 14

Township Statistics

Parcels Mapped	:	214
Number of Patents	:	156
Number of Individuals	:	135
Patentees Identified	:	131
Number of Surnames	:	99
Multi-Patentee Parcels	:	5
Oldest Patent Date	:	6/2/1823
Most Recent Patent	:	12/4/1903
Block/Lot Parcels	:	0
Parcels Re - Issued	:	1
Parcels that Overlap	:	0
Cities and Towns	:	3
Cemeteries	:	4

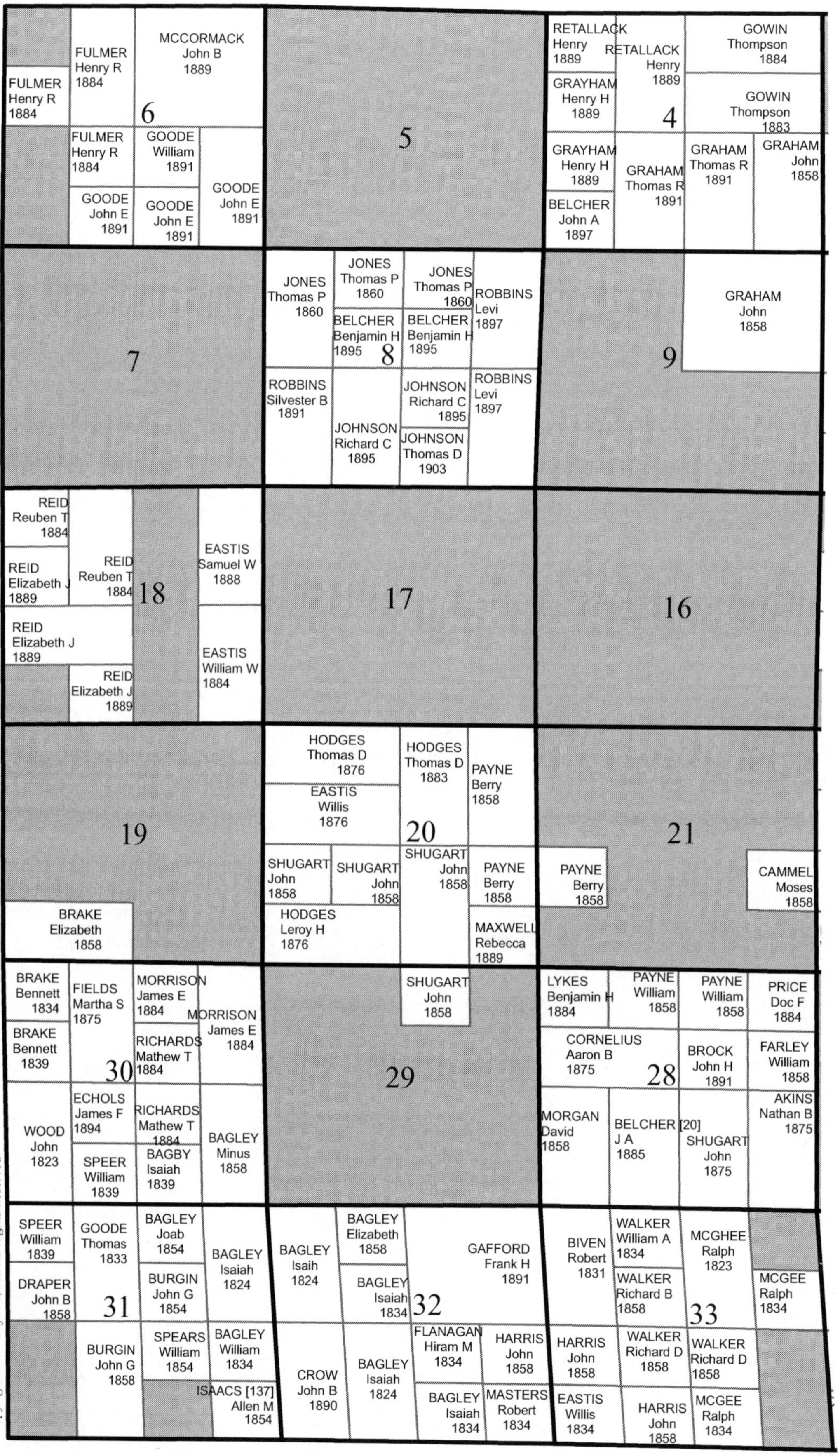

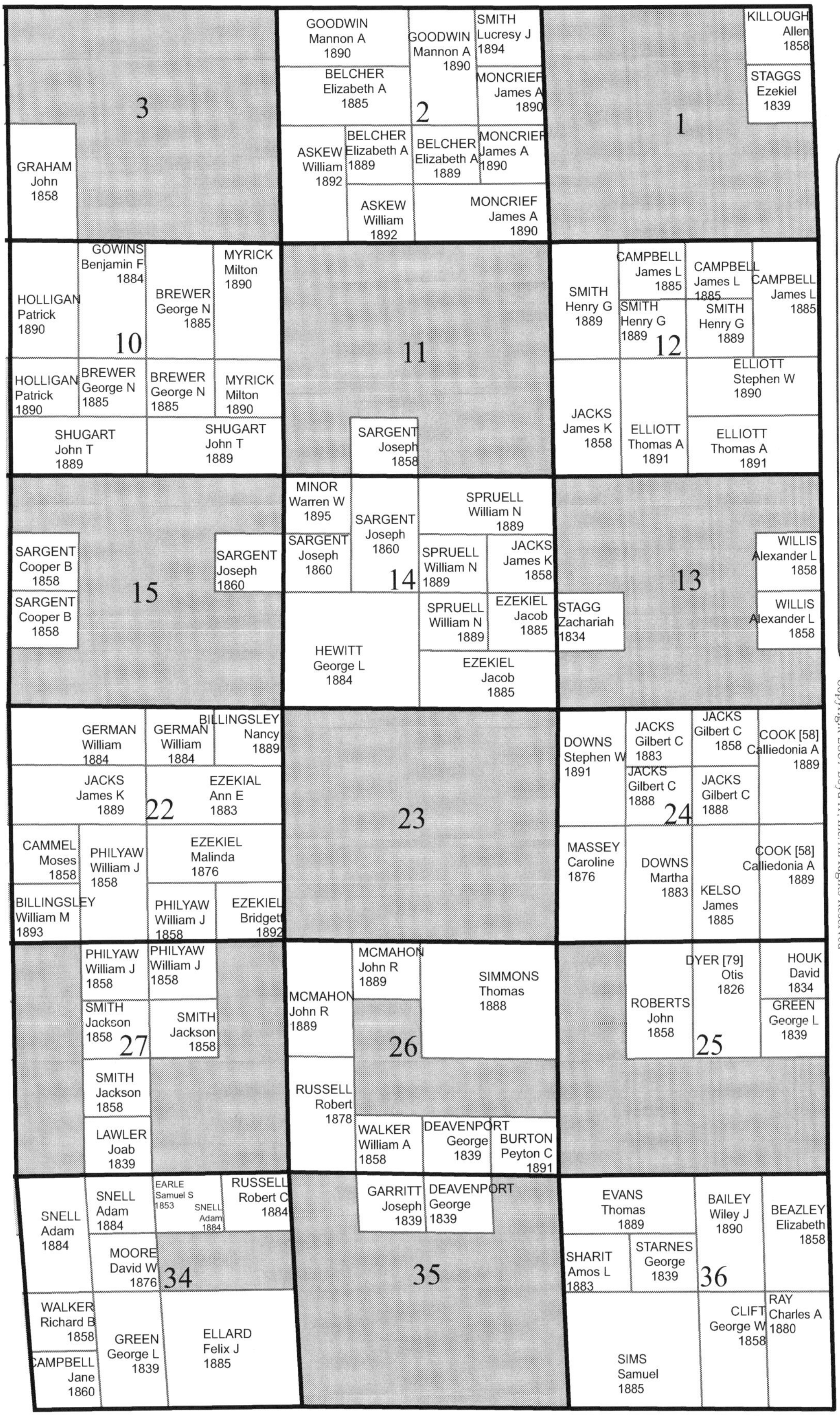

3
GRAHAM John 1858

2
GOODWIN Mannon A 1890
GOODWIN Mannon A 1890
SMITH Lucresy J 1894
BELCHER Elizabeth A 1885
MONCRIEF James A 1890
ASKEW William 1892
BELCHER Elizabeth A 1889
BELCHER Elizabeth A 1889
MONCRIEF James A 1890
ASKEW William 1892
MONCRIEF James A 1890

1
KILLOUGH Allen 1858
STAGGS Ezekiel 1839

10
HOLLIGAN Patrick 1890
GOWINS Benjamin F 1884
BREWER George N 1885
MYRICK Milton 1890
HOLLIGAN Patrick 1890
BREWER George N 1885
BREWER George N 1885
MYRICK Milton 1890
SHUGART John T 1889
SHUGART John T 1889

11
SARGENT Joseph 1858

12
SMITH Henry G 1889
CAMPBELL James L 1885
CAMPBELL James L 1885
CAMPBELL James L 1885
SMITH Henry G 1889
SMITH Henry G 1889
ELLIOTT Stephen W 1890
JACKS James K 1858
ELLIOTT Thomas A 1891
ELLIOTT Thomas A 1891

15
SARGENT Cooper B 1858
SARGENT Cooper B 1858
SARGENT Joseph 1860

14
MINOR Warren W 1895
SARGENT Joseph 1860
SARGENT Joseph 1860
SPRUELL William N 1889
SPRUELL William N 1889
JACKS James K 1858
SPRUELL William N 1889
EZEKIEL Jacob 1885
HEWITT George L 1884
EZEKIEL Jacob 1885

13
STAGG Zachariah 1834
WILLIS Alexander L 1858
WILLIS Alexander L 1858

22
GERMAN William 1884
GERMAN William 1884
BILLINGSLEY Nancy 1889
JACKS James K 1889
EZEKIAL Ann E 1883
CAMMEL Moses 1858
PHILYAW William J 1858
EZEKIEL Malinda 1876
BILLINGSLEY William M 1893
PHILYAW William J 1858
EZEKIEL Bridget 1892

23

24
DOWNS Stephen W 1891
JACKS Gilbert C 1883
JACKS Gilbert C 1858
COOK [58] Calliedonia A 1889
JACKS Gilbert C 1888
JACKS Gilbert C 1888
MASSEY Caroline 1876
DOWNS Martha 1883
KELSO James 1885
COOK [58] Calliedonia A 1889

27
PHILYAW William J 1858
PHILYAW William J 1858
SMITH Jackson 1858
SMITH Jackson 1858
SMITH Jackson 1858
LAWLER Joab 1839

26
MCMAHON John R 1889
MCMAHON John R 1889
SIMMONS Thomas 1888
RUSSELL Robert 1878
WALKER William A 1858
DEAVENPORT George 1839
BURTON Peyton C 1891

25
ROBERTS John 1858
DYER [79] Otis 1826
HOUK David 1834
GREEN George L 1839

34
SNELL Adam 1884
SNELL Adam 1884
EARLE Samuel S 1853
SNELL Adam 1884
RUSSELL Robert C 1884
MOORE David W 1876
WALKER Richard B 1858
GREEN George L 1839
ELLARD Felix J 1885
CAMPBELL Jane 1860

35
GARRITT Joseph 1839
DEAVENPORT George 1839

36
EVANS Thomas 1889
BAILEY Wiley J 1890
BEAZLEY Elizabeth 1858
SHARIT Amos L 1883
STARNES George 1839
RAY Charles A 1880
CLIFT George W 1858
SIMS Samuel 1885

Helpful Hints

1. This Map's INDEX can be found on the preceding pages.
2. Refer to Map "C" to see where this Township lies within Jefferson County, Alabama.
3. Numbers within square brackets [ ] denote a multi-patentee land parcel (multi-owner). Refer to Appendix "C" for a full list of members in this group.
4. Areas that look to be crowded with Patentees usually indicate multiple sales of the same parcel (Re-issues) or Overlapping parcels. See this Township's Index for an explanation of these and other circumstances that might explain "odd" groupings of Patentees on this map.

Legend

Patent Boundary
Section Boundary
No Patents Found (or Outside County)
1., 2., 3., ... Lot Numbers (when beside a name)
[ ] Group Number (see Appendix "C")

Scale: Section = 1 mile X 1 mile (generally, with some exceptions)

Road Map

T16-S R3-W
Huntsville Meridian

Map Group 14

Cities & Towns

Gardendale
Mount Olive
Watson

Cemeteries

Hodges Cemetery
Moncrief Cemetery
Mount Olive Cemetery
Walker Cemetery

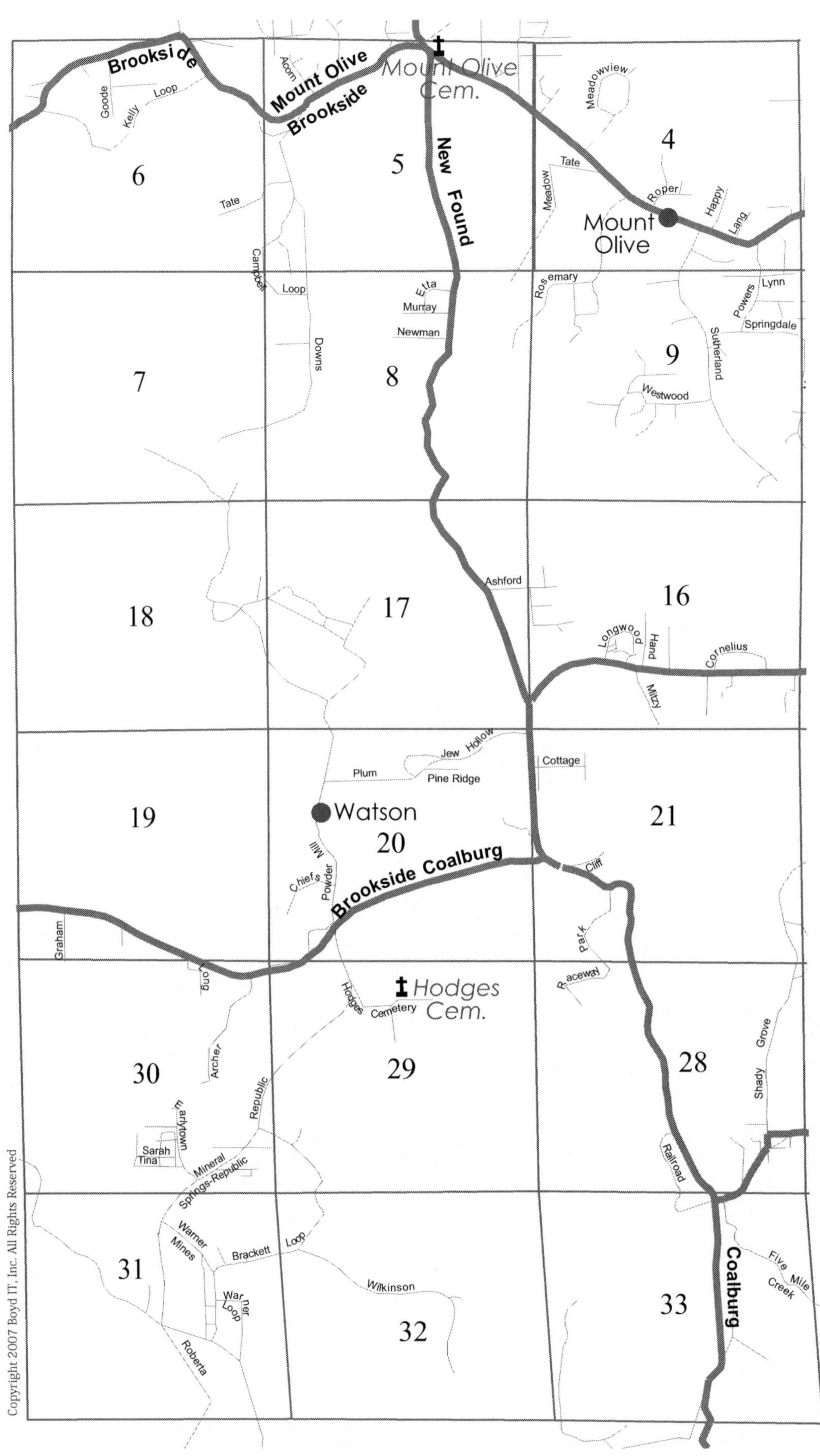

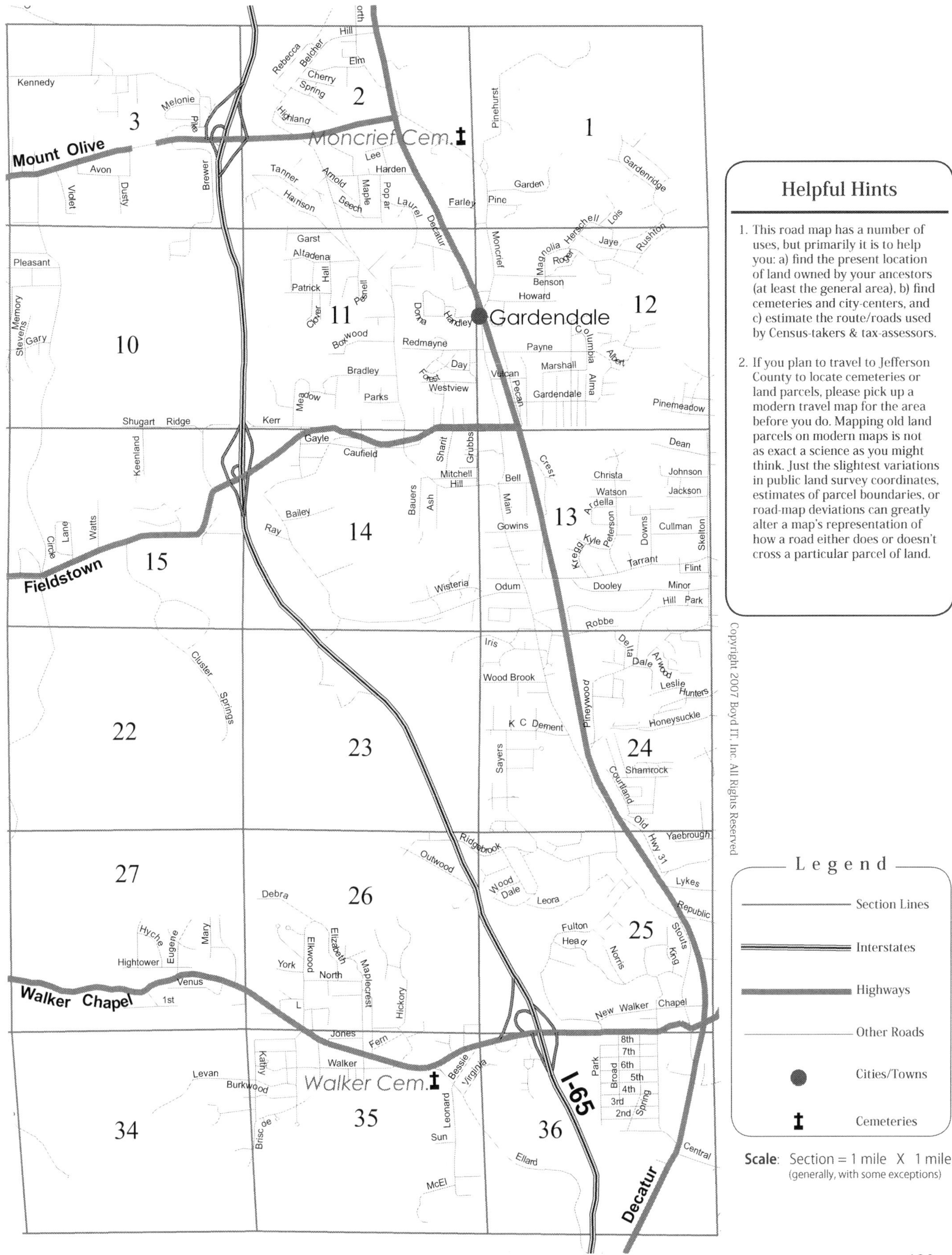
Helpful Hints
1. This road map has a number of uses, but primarily it is to help you: a) find the present location of land owned by your ancestors (at least the general area), b) find cemeteries and city-centers, and c) estimate the route/roads used by Census-takers & tax-assessors.
2. If you plan to travel to Jefferson County to locate cemeteries or land parcels, please pick up a modern travel map for the area before you do. Mapping old land parcels on modern maps is not as exact a science as you might think. Just the slightest variations in public land survey coordinates, estimates of parcel boundaries, or road-map deviations can greatly alter a map's representation of how a road either does or doesn't cross a particular parcel of land.
Legend
Section Lines
Interstates
Highways
Other Roads
Cities/Towns
Cemeteries
Scale: Section = 1 mile X 1 mile
(generally, with some exceptions)
Copyright 2007 Boyd IT, Inc. All Rights Reserved
Mount Olive
Fieldstown
Walker Chapel
New Walker Chapel
Decatur
I-65
Gardendale
Moncrief Cem.
Walker Cem.
1
2
3
10
11
12
13
14
15
22
23
24
25
26
27
34
35
36
Kennedy
Melonie
Pike
Avon
Violet
Dusty
Brewer
Rebecca
Belcher
Hill
Elm
Cherry
Spring
Highland
Lee
Harden
Tanner
Arnold
Maple
Poplar
Harrison
Beech
Laurel
Farley
Pine
Pinehurst
Garden
Gardenridge
Pleasant
Memory
Stevens
Gary
Garst
Altadena
Hall
Patrick
Clover
Boxwood
Donna
Handley
Redmayne
Bradley
Day
Forest
Westview
Meadow
Parks
Moncrief
Magnolia
Herschell
Lois
Jaye
Rushton
Roger
Benson
Howard
Payne
Columbia
Albert
Marshall
Vulcan
Pecan
Alma
Pinemeadow
Shugart Ridge
Kerr
Gayle
Caufield
Sharit
Grubbs
Mitchell Hill
Keenland
Bailey
Ray
Bauers
Ash
Bell
Main
Crest
Christa
Watson
Ardella
Dean
Johnson
Jackson
Gowins
Peterson
Kyle
Kregg
Downs
Cullman
Skelton
Tarrant
Flint
Lane
Circle
Watts
Wisteria
Odum
Dooley
Minor
Hill Park
Robbe
Iris
Delta
Dale
Arwood
Leslie
Hunters
Wood Brook
Pineywood
Cluster Springs
K C Dement
Honeysuckle
Sayers
Shamrock
Courtland
Old Hwy 31
Yaebrough
Ridgebrook
Outwood
Wood Dale
Leora
Lykes
Republic
Debra
Fulton
Head
Norris
Stouts
King
Hyche
Eugene
Mary
Hightower
Venus
1st
York
Elkwood
Elizabeth
North
Maplecrest
Hickory
L
Jones
Fern
Walker
Kathy
Levan
Burkwood
Briscoe
Bessie
Virginia
Leonard
Sun
McEl
Ellard
Park
Broad
8th
7th
6th
5th
4th
3rd
2nd
Spring
Central

Historical Map

T16-S R3-W
Huntsville Meridian

Map Group 14

Cities & Towns

Gardendale
Mount Olive
Watson

Cemeteries

Hodges Cemetery
Moncrief Cemetery
Mount Olive Cemetery
Walker Cemetery

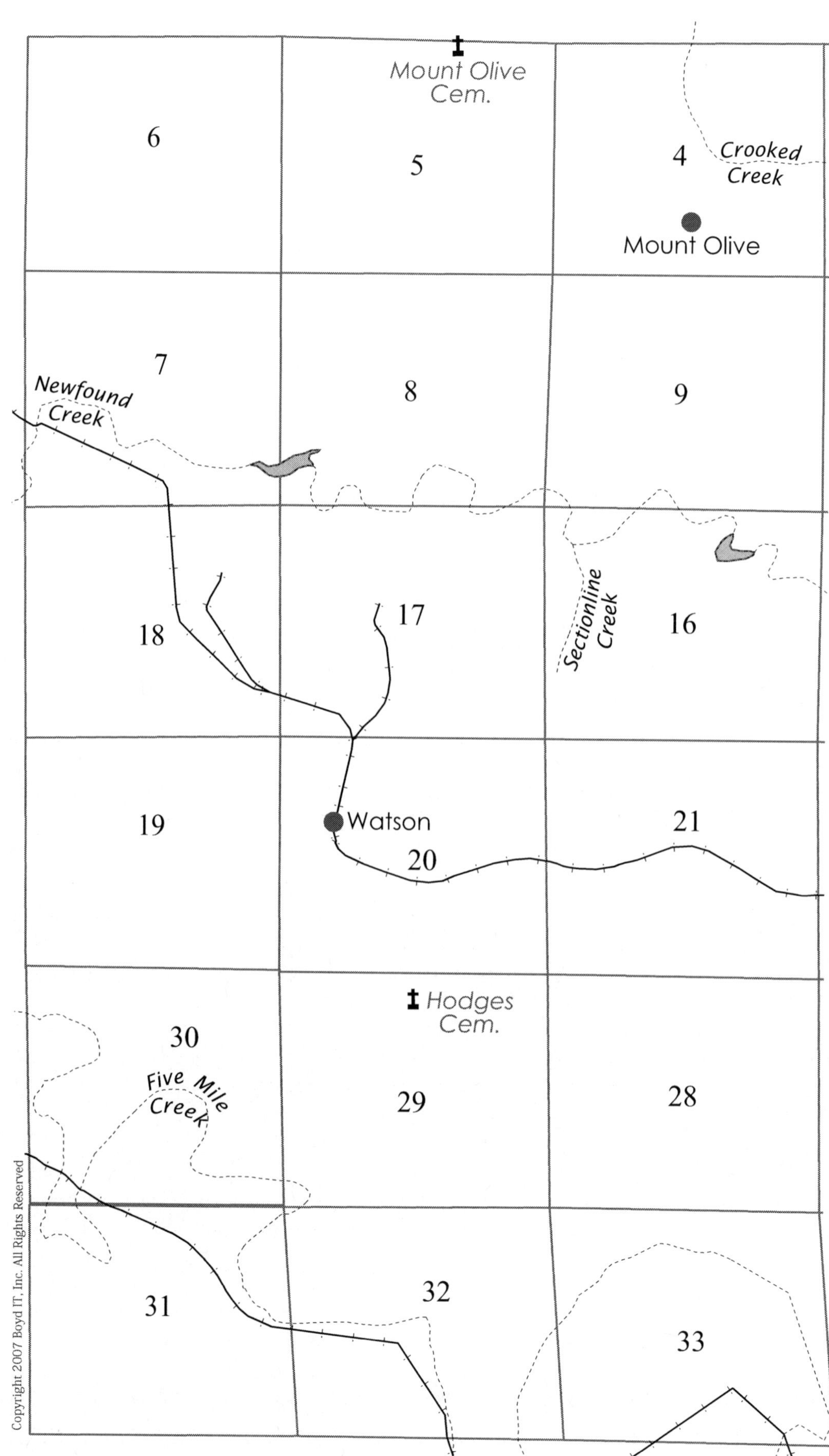

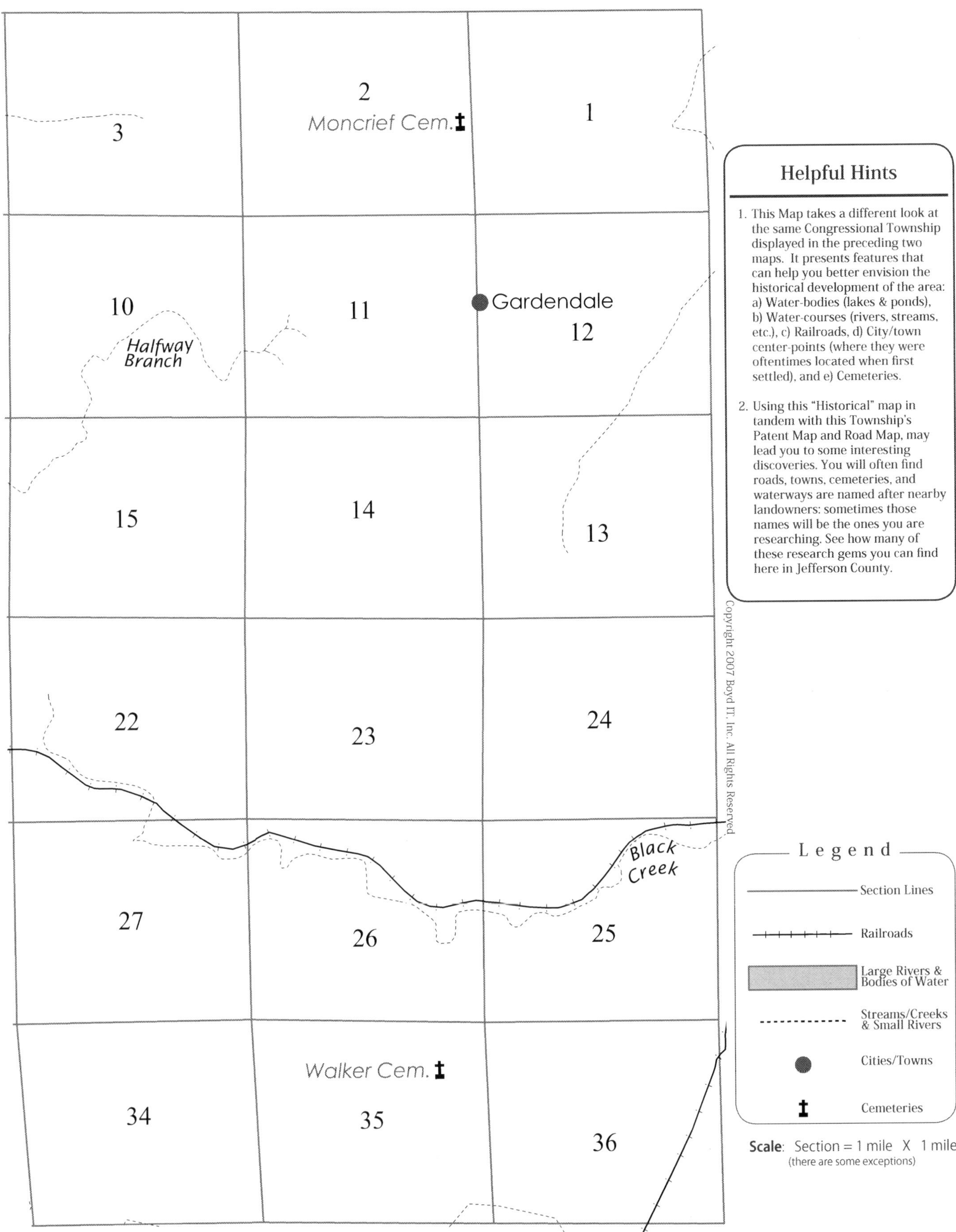

Helpful Hints

1. This Map takes a different look at the same Congressional Township displayed in the preceding two maps. It presents features that can help you better envision the historical development of the area: a) Water-bodies (lakes & ponds), b) Water-courses (rivers, streams, etc.), c) Railroads, d) City/town center-points (where they were oftentimes located when first settled), and e) Cemeteries.

2. Using this "Historical" map in tandem with this Township's Patent Map and Road Map, may lead you to some interesting discoveries. You will often find roads, towns, cemeteries, and waterways are named after nearby landowners: sometimes those names will be the ones you are researching. See how many of these research gems you can find here in Jefferson County.

Legend

- Section Lines
- Railroads
- Large Rivers & Bodies of Water
- Streams/Creeks & Small Rivers
- Cities/Towns
- Cemeteries

Scale: Section = 1 mile X 1 mile
(there are some exceptions)

Map Group 15: Index to Land Patents

Township 16-South Range 2-West (Huntsville)

After you locate an individual in this Index, take note of the Section and Section Part then proceed to the Land Patent map on the pages immediately following. You should have no difficulty locating the corresponding parcel of land.

The "For More Info" Column will lead you to more information about the underlying Patents. See the *Legend* at right, and the "How to Use this Book" chapter, for more information.

LEGEND

"For More Info . . . " column

A = Authority (Legislative Act, See Appendix "A")
B = Block or Lot (location in Section unknown)
C = Cancelled Patent
F = Fractional Section
G = Group (Multi-Patentee Patent, see Appendix "C")
V = Overlaps another Parcel
R = Re-Issued (Parcel patented more than once)

(A & G items require you to look in the Appendixes referred to above. All other Letter-designations followed by a number require you to locate line-items in this index that possess the ID number found after the letter).

ID	Individual in Patent	Sec.	Sec. Part	Date Issued	Other Counties	For More Info . . .
2567	ANDERSON, William	20	N½SW	1885-03-16		A4 V2582
2483	ARMSTEAD, John R	6	S½SE	1891-11-23		A4
2484	" "	6	S½SW	1891-11-23		A4
2489	BARFORD, John W	32	W½NW	1872-09-18		A1
2554	BARTON, Thomas	27	W½SE	1838-08-28		A1
2355	BATES, Adam	24	N½NE	1884-12-05		A4
2555	BATES, Thomas	14	S½SE	1889-08-16		A4
2401	BEAZLEY, Elizabeth	31	W½NW	1858-06-01		A1
2588	BELL, William P	20	S½NW	1891-06-29		A1
2354	BROWN, Aaron	34	SWNW	1889-10-07		A1
2382	BROWN, Demilins	34	E½SW	1884-03-20		A4
2398	BROWN, Elijah	34	E½NW	1823-05-01		A1 G29
2395	" "	27	E½SW	1824-04-14		A1
2396	" "	32	SENW	1839-09-20		A1
2397	" "	33	NENE	1839-09-20		A1
2409	BROWN, George	28	E½SE	1823-05-01		A1 G30
2407	" "	28	W½SE	1824-04-05		A1
2408	" "	34	W½NE	1824-05-18		A1
2438	BROWN, James A	34	SWSW	1891-07-28		A4
2439	BURGIN, James A	4	N½SW	1889-10-07		A1
2460	BURGIN, Jeremiah G	4	S½SE	1889-10-07		A1
2478	BURGIN, John M	4	S½SW	1889-10-07		A1
2557	BURGIN, Thomas J	6	NENE	1858-06-01		A1
2556	BURTON, Thomas	35	NENW	1834-11-04		A1
2522	BURWELL, Orrin S	35	E½SW	1858-06-01		A1
2523	" "	35	N½NE	1858-06-01		A1
2524	" "	35	S½NW	1858-06-01		A1
2525	" "	35	W½SE	1858-06-01		A1
2374	BYARS, Catharine	34	SESE	1860-04-02		A1
2444	BYARS, James H	35	NWSW	1854-07-15		A1
2477	BYERS, John L	34	NESE	1850-04-01		A1
2465	CAMP, John	26	W½SW	1828-02-20		A1
2466	" "	28	SWNW	1835-10-01		A1
2391	CASH, Elbert D	24	S½SW	1885-12-10		A4
2436	CHAMBLEE, Horton B	12	NWSW	1854-07-15		A1
2568	CHENNAULT, William	1	W½NW	1823-06-02		A1
2569	CHILDERS, William	28	W½SW	1824-05-04		A1
2570	CHILDRESS, William	32	E½SW	1823-05-01		A1
2572	" "	33	W½NE	1823-06-02		A1
2571	" "	33	E½NW	1824-04-28		A1
2428	CLEMENTS, Hardy	22	E½NW	1823-05-01		A1 G52
2429	" "	22	W½NW	1823-05-01		A1 G52
2435	COCHRAN, Hiram P	25	E½NE	1823-06-02		A1 G57
2500	COLE, Joseph H	34	NWNW	1839-09-20		A1
2375	COOK, Charles M	30	SW	1890-08-29		A4 G59 V2470
2375	COOK, Skiddie V	30	SW	1890-08-29		A4 G59 V2470

ID	Individual in Patent	Sec.	Sec. Part	Date Issued	Other Counties	For More Info . . .
2496	CREWS, Joseph G	34	NWSW	1902-10-11		A4
2467	CRUMP, John	27	W½NW	1823-05-01		A1 G64
2468	" "	28	E½NE	1823-05-01		A1 G64
2469	" "	28	W½NE	1823-05-01		A1 G64
2442	CUNNINGHAM, James	11	W½SW	1823-05-01		A1 G69
2441	" "	14	W½NW	1823-05-01		A1 G70
2440	" "	10	E½SE	1824-05-27		A1
2529	CUNNINGHAM, Robert	2	W½NE	1826-06-01		A1
2470	EDWARDS, John	30	SESW	1834-11-04		A1 V2375
2472	ERWIN, John	10	E½NE	1823-05-01		A1 G83
2473	" "	10	W½NE	1823-05-01		A1 G83
2471	" "	10	W½SE	1826-06-10		A1
2405	FLOWERS, Francis A	8	N½SW	1873-08-01		A1
2443	FLOWERS, James D	8	N½NW	1873-08-01		A1
2476	FLOWERS, John J	8	N½NE	1873-08-01		A1
2574	FLOWERS, William H	8	S½NE	1873-08-01		A1
2490	FORMAN, John W	29	W½NW	1824-04-14		A1
2497	GARRETT, Joseph	10	NESW	1858-06-01		A1
2498	" "	15	SENW	1858-06-01		A1
2499	" "	15	W½NW	1858-06-01		A1
2595	GARRETT, Willson	10	SESW	1850-04-01		A1
2573	GESNER, William	20	N½NW	1885-03-16		A1
2464	GILLESPIE, John C	6	SWNW	1878-06-13		A4
2462	" "	6	NESW	1883-04-10		A4
2463	" "	6	SENW	1883-04-10		A4
2474	GOODWIN, John	35	SENE	1838-08-28		A1
2513	GOODWIN, Mount V	30	NENW	1889-12-28		A1
2514	" "	30	NWNE	1889-12-28		A1
2356	GOYENS, Alexander	32	NENW	1885-12-10		A4
2411	GREEN, George L	33	NESW	1839-09-20		A1
2539	GREEN, Robert H	14	SWSW	1849-09-01		A1
2532	" "	11	SENW	1853-08-01		A1
2534	" "	12	SWSW	1853-08-01		A1
2531	" "	11	NESE	1854-07-15		A1
2537	" "	14	NESW	1854-07-15		A1
2533	" "	11	SESE	1858-06-01		A1
2535	" "	13	NWNW	1858-06-01		A1
2536	" "	14	NENE	1858-06-01		A1
2538	" "	14	SESW	1858-06-01		A1
2540	" "	14	W½NE	1858-06-01		A1
2541	" "	23	W½NW	1858-06-01		A1
2413	GREENE, George L	32	W½SW	1827-09-20		A1 R2414
2412	" "	32	NWNE	1835-10-01		A1
2414	" "	32	W½SW	1918-01-21		A1 R2413
2542	GREENE, Robert H	14	NWSW	1835-10-01		A1
2415	HAGOOD, George M	2	NESW	1848-07-01		A1
2604	HAGOOD, Zachariah	12	NWNW	1835-10-01		A1
2597	" "	1	NESE	1839-09-20		A1
2599	" "	11	NWNW	1849-09-01		A1
2602	" "	12	NENW	1849-09-01		A1
2607	" "	2	SENW	1849-09-01		A1
2608	" "	2	SESW	1849-09-01		A1
2611	" "	3	SESE	1849-09-01		A1
2600	" "	11	SWNW	1854-07-15		A1
2609	" "	2	SWSE	1854-07-15		A1
2610	" "	2	SWSW	1858-06-01		A1
2598	" "	1	SESE	1861-08-01		A1
2601	" "	12	NENE	1861-08-01		A1
2603	" "	12	NESW	1861-08-01		A1
2605	" "	12	SENW	1861-08-01		A1
2606	" "	12	W½NE	1861-08-01		A1
2410	HALLMARK, George	15	W½SW	1825-06-20		A1
2363	HAMIL, Augustus F	8	S½NW	1873-08-01		A1
2362	HAMILTON, Audley	35	E½SE	1839-09-20		A1
2575	HARISON, William H	26	NWSE	1860-04-02		A1 V2386
2576	" "	26	SWNE	1860-04-02		A1
2577	HARRISON, William H	26	NESE	1858-06-01		A1
2578	" "	26	NESW	1858-06-01		A1
2475	HEMPHILL, John	27	W½SW	1829-04-01		A1
2406	HEWITT, Francis A	28	NESW	1849-08-01		A1
2445	HEWITT, James H	21	SESW	1839-09-20		A1
2446	" "	28	NWNW	1839-09-20		A1
2527	INGLE, Peter	1	E½NE	1823-05-01		A1 G136

ID	Individual in Patent	Sec.	Sec. Part	Date Issued	Other Counties	For More Info . . .
2526	INGLE, Peter (Cont'd)	1	E½NW	1824-04-05		A1
2547	JACKS, Samuel F	18	N½NW	1890-03-19		A4
2548	" "	18	SENW	1890-03-19		A4
2558	JAMES, Thomas	29	E½SE	1824-04-14		A1
2582	KILLAUGH, William	20	NWSW	1850-04-01		A1 V2567
2359	KILLOUGH, Allen	6	NWNW	1858-06-01		A1
2380	KILLOUGH, David	27	NENE	1852-01-01		A1
2376	" "	26	NENW	1854-07-15		A1
2379	" "	26	SWNW	1854-07-15		A1
2377	" "	26	NWNW	1858-06-01		A1
2378	" "	26	SENW	1858-06-01		A1
2458	KILLOUGH, Jeremiah B	34	E½NE	1858-06-01		A1
2459	" "	35	NWNW	1858-06-01		A1
2518	KILLOUGH, Newton C	25	SWSW	1839-03-15		A1
2519	" "	36	NWNW	1839-03-15		A1
2584	KILLOUGH, William	25	S½NW	1853-11-15		A1
2583	" "	25	N½NW	1858-06-01		A1
2585	" "	26	S½SE	1858-06-01		A1 V2386
2586	" "	26	SENE	1858-06-01		A1
2515	LINDSEY, Nancy C	12	NWSE	1889-03-01		A4
2516	" "	12	S½SE	1889-03-01		A4
2504	LINN, Joseph	27	E½SE	1837-03-20		A1
2503	" "	26	SESW	1837-04-01		A1
2367	MADISON, Benjamin	15	E½SE	1823-05-01		A1
2369	" "	15	W½SE	1823-05-01		A1
2370	" "	22	W½NE	1823-05-01		A1 G161
2368	" "	15	W½NE	1824-05-24		A1
2409	MARKS, Nicholas M	28	E½SE	1823-05-01		A1 G30
2398	" "	34	E½NW	1823-05-01		A1 G29
2530	MARTIN, Robert G	15	NENW	1854-07-15		A1
2564	MARTIN, Warren J	11	NENW	1849-09-01		A1
2565	" "	2	NWSE	1858-06-01		A1
2365	MASSEY, Benjamin F	27	NWNE	1853-08-01		A1
2366	" "	27	S½NE	1858-06-01		A1
2479	MASSEY, John	22	NESE	1853-08-01		A1
2480	" "	22	SESE	1858-06-01		A1
2481	" "	23	SESW	1858-06-01		A1
2482	" "	23	W½SW	1858-06-01		A1
2495	MASSEY, Jonathan	22	E½SW	1823-05-01		A1 G163
2493	" "	27	E½NW	1823-06-02		A1
2494	" "	28	E½NW	1824-04-05		A1
2492	" "	22	W½SE	1824-05-25		A1
2370	MATTHEWS, Charles L	22	W½NE	1823-05-01		A1 G161
2371	MATTISON, Benjamin	15	E½SW	1823-05-01		A1
2447	MCADAMS, James	25	E½SE	1823-05-01		A1
2448	" "	25	W½SE	1823-05-01		A1
2563	MCCALL, Tristram B	4	S½NW	1878-04-09		A4
2449	MCCARTNEY, James	1	E½SW	1823-05-01		A1 G166
2495	" "	22	E½SW	1823-05-01		A1 G163
2451	" "	22	W½SW	1823-05-01		A1 G167
2450	" "	36	E½SW	1823-05-01		A1 G169
2559	MELVIN, Thomas	23	NESW	1858-06-01		A1
2560	" "	23	NWSE	1858-06-01		A1
2561	" "	23	SENW	1858-06-01		A1
2404	MILLER, Fannie	24	SENE	1890-07-03		A4 G174
2404	MILLER, Jasper	24	SENE	1890-07-03		A4 G174
2520	MILLER, Newton	24	NWSE	1884-12-05		A4
2521	" "	24	SWNE	1884-12-05		A4
2364	MILNER, Benjamin C	8	S½SW	1873-12-10		A1
2449	NASH, George	1	E½SW	1823-05-01		A1 G166
2416	" "	1	W½SW	1823-05-01		A1
2418	" "	11	E½SW	1823-05-01		A1
2420	" "	11	W½SE	1823-05-01		A1
2421	" "	14	E½NW	1823-05-01		A1
2424	" "	21	E½NE	1823-05-01		A1 G181
2425	" "	21	E½SE	1823-05-01		A1 G181
2426	" "	21	W½SE	1823-05-01		A1 G182
2419	" "	11	W½NE	1823-06-02		A1
2422	" "	2	E½SE	1824-04-05		A1
2417	" "	11	E½NE	1824-05-25		A1
2423	" "	1	W½SE	1835-05-01		A1 G180
2428	NEAL, Zacheriah	22	E½NW	1823-05-01		A1 G52
2429	" "	22	W½NW	1823-05-01		A1 G52

ID	Individual in Patent	Sec.	Sec. Part	Date Issued	Other Counties	For More Info . . .
2451	NEAL, Zacheriah (Cont'd)	22	W½SW	1823-05-01		A1 G167
2587	NEIGHBOURS, William	1	W½NE	1823-05-01		A1 G183
2553	NEVES, Thimothy	21	SWNE	1834-10-14		A1
2550	OWEN, Stephen	33	W½NW	1823-05-01		A1 G190
2549	OWEN, Stephen M	33	W½SW	1823-05-01		A1
2551	PARKER, Tan	24	NESW	1884-12-05		A4
2552	" "	24	SENW	1884-12-05		A4
2580	PARKER, William H	18	N½SE	1873-08-01		A1
2579	" "	18	E½SW	1884-03-10		A4
2392	PITTS, Eli B	10	SENW	1858-06-01		A1
2454	POTTS, James	10	SWNW	1839-09-20		A1
2453	" "	10	NWSW	1852-01-01		A1
2452	" "	10	NWNW	1858-06-01		A1
2507	PRICE, Malinda C	4	W½NE	1889-03-02		A1
2442	REED, Robert	11	W½SW	1823-05-01		A1 G69
2544	" "	15	E½NE	1823-05-01		A1 G200
2543	" "	22	E½NE	1823-05-01		A1
2589	REED, William	36	E½NE	1823-05-01		A1
2486	ROBERTS, John	30	SENW	1858-06-01		A1
2487	" "	30	W½NW	1858-06-01		A1
2508	ROBINSON, Martha O	6	NENW	1891-06-08		A4
2509	" "	6	NWNE	1891-06-08		A4
2510	ROEBUCK, Mattie	24	N½NW	1895-12-26		A4 G204
2596	ROEBUCK, York	34	W½SE	1890-08-29		A4
2593	ROTTON, William T	12	NESE	1889-03-01		A4
2594	" "	12	SENE	1889-03-01		A4
2403	RYLANT, Erasimus R	4	E½NE	1891-05-29		A4
2527	SCOTT, David	1	E½NE	1823-05-01		A1 G136
2587	" "	1	W½NE	1823-05-01		A1 G183
2472	" "	10	E½NE	1823-05-01		A1 G83
2473	" "	10	W½NE	1823-05-01		A1 G83
2467	" "	27	W½NW	1823-05-01		A1 G64
2468	" "	28	E½NE	1823-05-01		A1 G64
2469	" "	28	W½NE	1823-05-01		A1 G64
2381	" "	32	E½SE	1823-05-01		A1 G210
2550	" "	33	W½NW	1823-05-01		A1 G190
2423	" "	1	W½SE	1835-05-01		A1 G180
2488	SCOTT, John	17	SWNW	1837-11-07		A1
2581	SELF, William H	2	NENW	1890-03-08		A1
2437	SHAMBLIN, Horton B	12	SWNW	1849-09-01		A1
2517	SHUGART, Nancy J	6	NWSW	1894-10-22		A4
2501	SIDES, Joseph H	8	N½SE	1878-04-09		A4
2373	SIMPSON, Beverly	20	S½SW	1883-07-03		A4
2430	SIMPSON, Henry	30	NWSE	1884-12-05		A4
2431	" "	30	SWNE	1884-12-05		A4
2441	SIMS, Edward	14	W½NW	1823-05-01		A1 G70
2424	" "	21	E½NE	1823-05-01		A1 G181
2425	" "	21	E½SE	1823-05-01		A1 G181
2385	" "	25	E½SW	1823-05-01		A1
2386	" "	26	W½SE	1823-05-01		A1 V2585, 2575
2390	" "	32	W½SE	1823-05-01		A1 G214
2387	" "	36	E½NW	1823-05-01		A1
2388	" "	36	W½NE	1823-05-01		A1
2389	" "	36	W½SW	1823-05-01		A1
2426	SIMS, Francis	21	W½SE	1823-05-01		A1 G182
2394	SNOW, Eli	32	E½NE	1823-05-01		A1
2590	SPRADLING, William	5	NWNW	1839-09-20		A1
2591	" "	5	SESE	1839-09-20		A1
2592	" "	9	NWNW	1839-09-20		A1
2381	STAGGS, Ezekiel	32	E½SE	1823-05-01		A1 G210
2372	TARRANT, Benjamin	29	S½SW	1858-06-01		A1
2485	TAYLOR, John R	2	W½NW	1889-10-07		A1
2427	THACK, George W	10	NENW	1891-06-19		A4
2505	THOMAS, Kate	4	N½SE	1878-04-09		A4 G220
2505	THOMAS, William H	4	N½SE	1878-04-09		A4 G220
2461	TURNER, Jesse	36	SWNW	1839-09-20		A1
2544	TURNER, William S	15	E½NE	1823-05-01		A1 G200
2393	TUTWILER, Eli E	20	S½SE	1891-04-16		A1
2528	USTICK, Robert B	30	E½NE	1891-06-18		A1
2457	VANN, James W	8	S½SE	1875-06-01		A4 G225
2502	VANN, Joseph J	18	N½NE	1889-10-07		A1
2506	VANN, Lemuel G	18	S½NE	1882-10-30		A1
2457	VANN, Mary A	8	S½SE	1875-06-01		A4 G225

ID	Individual in Patent	Sec.	Sec. Part	Date Issued	Other Counties	For More Info . . .
2562	VINCENT, Thomas	2	E½NE	1824-04-26		A1
2455	WALKER, James S	36	E½SE	1823-05-01		A1
2450	" "	36	E½SW	1823-05-01		A1 G169
2400	WALTERS, Elizabeth A	20	N½NE	1883-07-03		A4 G229
2399	" "	20	S½NE	1885-09-10		A4
2400	WALTERS, Robert B	20	N½NE	1883-07-03		A4 G229
2360	WEEMS, Anderson	30	E½SE	1839-03-15		A1
2361	" "	30	SWSE	1839-09-20		A1
2511	WHITTINGTON, Melvin P	23	S½SE	1858-06-01		A1
2512	" "	26	N½NE	1858-06-01		A1
2357	WILLIS, Alexander L	18	SWNW	1858-06-01		A1
2358	" "	18	W½SW	1858-06-01		A1
2510	WILSON, Mattie	24	N½NW	1895-12-26		A4 G204
2510	WILSON, Toney	24	N½NW	1895-12-26		A4 G204
2456	WOMACK, James S	4	N½NW	1878-04-09		A4
2383	WOOD, Edmond	24	E½SE	1899-12-07		A1
2384	" "	24	SWSE	1899-12-07		A1
2402	WOOD, Ely	10	SWSW	1889-10-07		A1
2432	WOOD, Henry	32	SWNE	1834-11-04		A1
2433	WOOD, Henson	24	NWSW	1880-02-20		A4
2434	" "	24	SWNW	1880-02-20		A4
2435	WOOD, John	25	E½NE	1823-06-02		A1 G57
2491	" "	29	SWSE	1835-10-01		A1
2390	WOOD, Joshua	32	W½SE	1823-05-01		A1 G214
2545	WOOD, Robert	14	N½SE	1894-03-30		A4
2546	" "	14	SENE	1894-03-30		A4
2566	WOOD, Washington	28	SESW	1894-06-20		A4

Patent Map

T16-S R2-W
Huntsville Meridian

Map Group 15

Township Statistics

Parcels Mapped	:	258
Number of Patents	:	219
Number of Individuals	:	156
Patentees Identified	:	158
Number of Surnames	:	106
Multi-Patentee Parcels	:	33
Oldest Patent Date	:	5/1/1823
Most Recent Patent	:	1/21/1918
Block/Lot Parcels	:	0
Parcels Re - Issued	:	1
Parcels that Overlap	:	7
Cities and Towns	:	2
Cemeteries	:	1

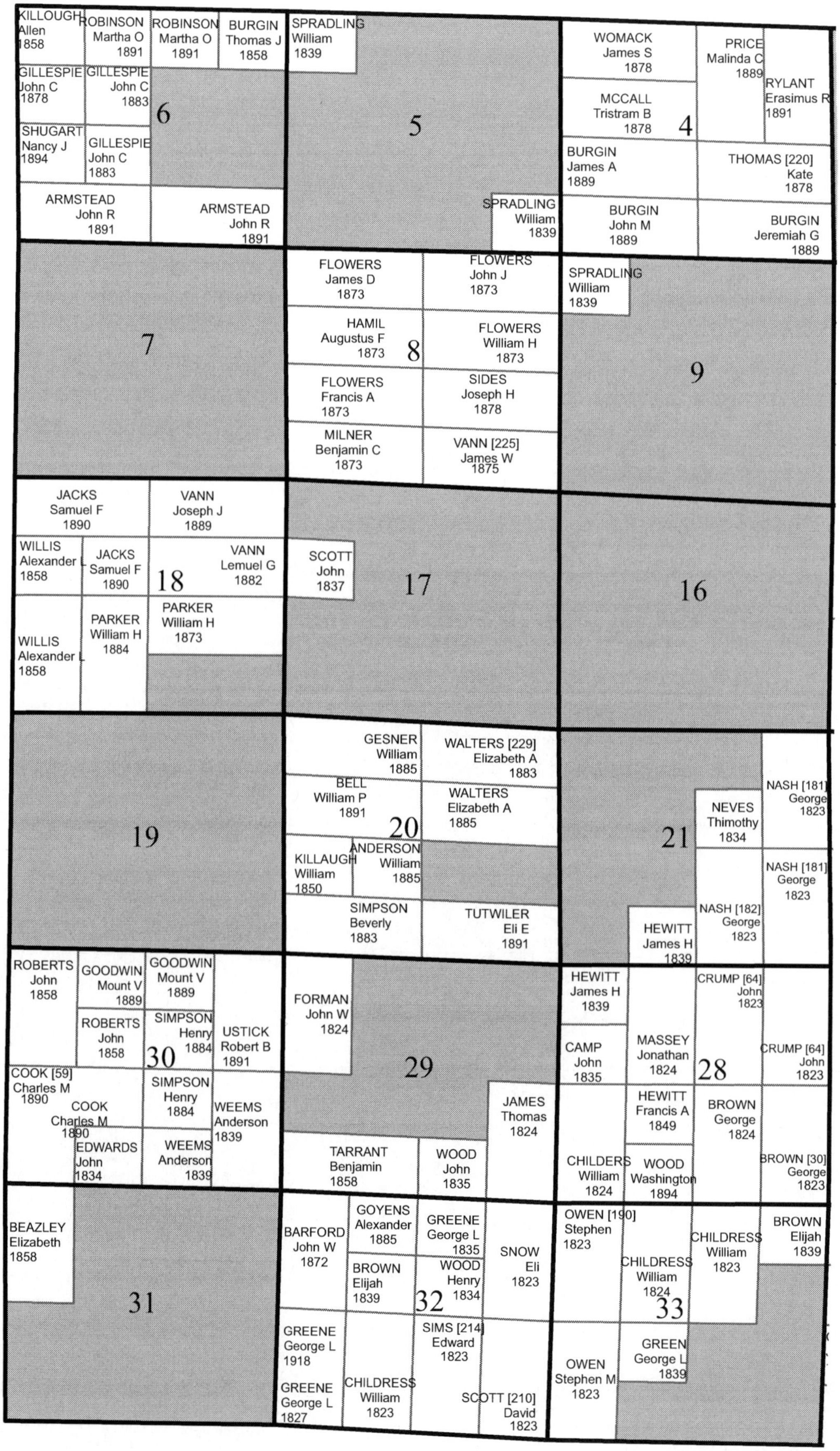

6
KILLOUGH Allen 1858
ROBINSON Martha O 1891
ROBINSON Martha O 1891
BURGIN Thomas J 1858
GILLESPIE John C 1878
GILLESPIE John C 1883
SHUGART Nancy J 1894
GILLESPIE John C 1883
ARMSTEAD John R 1891
ARMSTEAD John R 1891

5
SPRADLING William 1839
SPRADLING William 1839

4
WOMACK James S 1878
PRICE Malinda C 1889
RYLANT Erasimus R 1891
MCCALL Tristram B 1878
BURGIN James A 1889
THOMAS [220] Kate 1878
BURGIN John M 1889
BURGIN Jeremiah G 1889

7

8
FLOWERS James D 1873
FLOWERS John J 1873
HAMIL Augustus F 1873
FLOWERS William H 1873
FLOWERS Francis A 1873
SIDES Joseph H 1878
MILNER Benjamin C 1873
VANN [225] James W 1875

9
SPRADLING William 1839

18
JACKS Samuel F 1890
VANN Joseph J 1889
WILLIS Alexander L 1858
JACKS Samuel F 1890
VANN Lemuel G 1882
PARKER William H 1873
PARKER William H 1884
WILLIS Alexander L 1858

17
SCOTT John 1837

16

19

20
GESNER William 1885
WALTERS [229] Elizabeth A 1883
BELL William P 1891
WALTERS Elizabeth A 1885
KILLAUGH William 1850
ANDERSON William 1885
SIMPSON Beverly 1883
TUTWILER Eli E 1891

21
NASH [181] George 1823
NEVES Thimothy 1834
NASH [181] George 1823
NASH [182] George 1823
HEWITT James H 1839

30
ROBERTS John 1858
GOODWIN Mount V 1889
GOODWIN Mount V 1889
ROBERTS John 1858
SIMPSON Henry 1884
USTICK Robert B 1891
COOK [59] Charles M 1890
COOK Charles M 1890
SIMPSON Henry 1884
WEEMS Anderson 1839
EDWARDS John 1834
WEEMS Anderson 1839

29
FORMAN John W 1824
JAMES Thomas 1824
TARRANT Benjamin 1858
WOOD John 1835

28
HEWITT James H 1839
CRUMP [64] John 1823
CAMP John 1835
MASSEY Jonathan 1824
CRUMP [64] John 1823
HEWITT Francis A 1849
BROWN George 1824
CHILDERS William 1824
WOOD Washington 1894
BROWN [30] George 1823

31
BEAZLEY Elizabeth 1858

32
BARFORD John W 1872
GOYENS Alexander 1885
GREENE George L 1835
BROWN Elijah 1839
WOOD Henry 1834
SNOW Eli 1823
GREENE George L 1918
SIMS [214] Edward 1823
GREENE George L 1827
CHILDRESS William 1823
SCOTT [210] David 1823

33
OWEN [190] Stephen 1823
CHILDRESS William 1823
BROWN Elijah 1839
CHILDRESS William 1824
GREEN George L 1839
OWEN Stephen M 1823

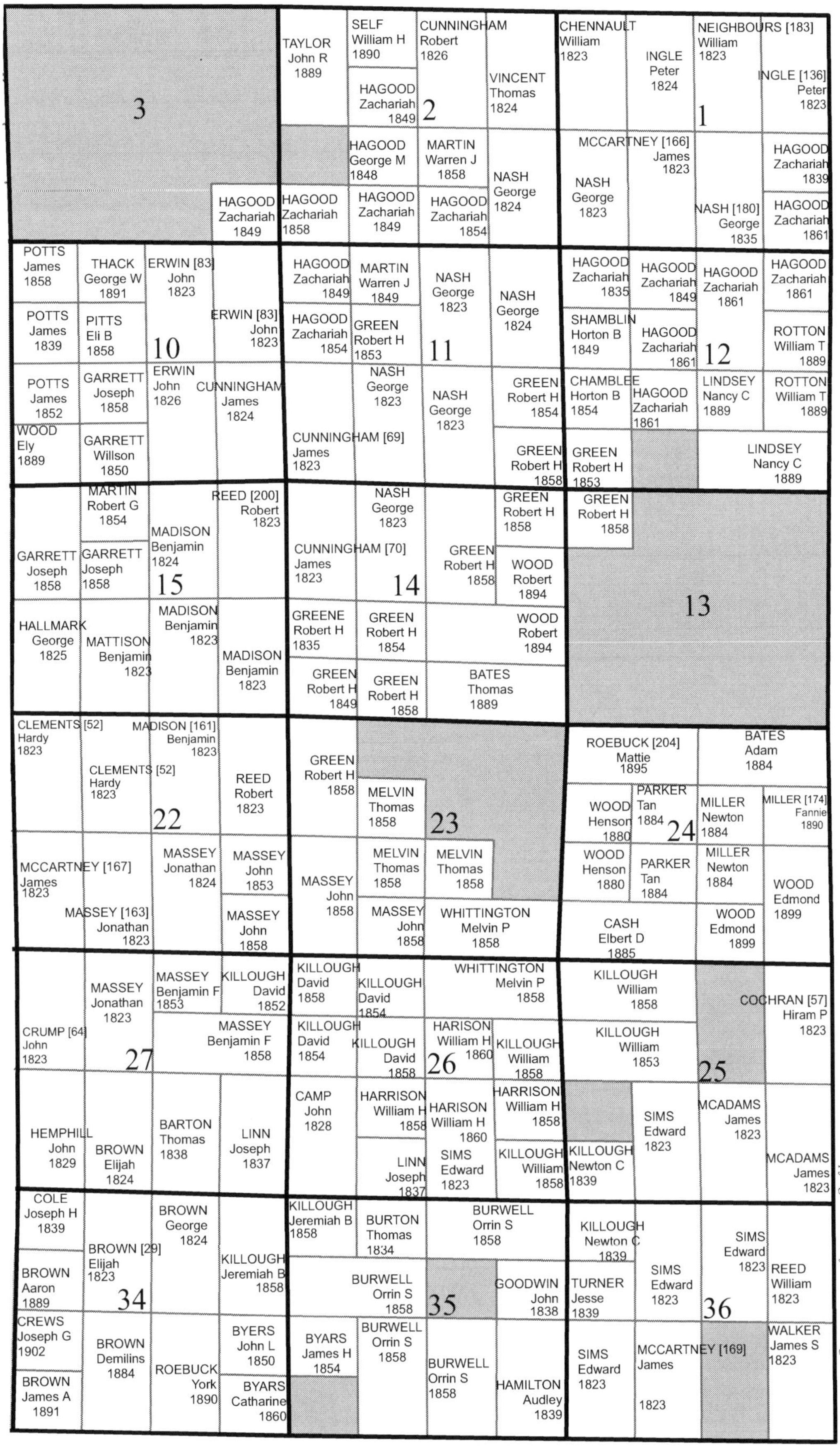

3

TAYLOR John R 1889
SELF William H 1890
CUNNINGHAM Robert 1826
HAGOOD Zachariah 1849
2
VINCENT Thomas 1824
HAGOOD George M 1848
MARTIN Warren J 1858
NASH George 1824
HAGOOD Zachariah 1849
HAGOOD Zachariah 1858
HAGOOD Zachariah 1849
HAGOOD Zachariah 1854

CHENNAULT William 1823
INGLE Peter 1824
NEIGHBOURS [183] William 1823
INGLE [136] Peter 1823
1
MCCARTNEY [166] James 1823
NASH George 1823
HAGOOD Zachariah 1839
NASH [180] George 1835
HAGOOD Zachariah 1861

POTTS James 1858
THACK George W 1891
ERWIN [83] John 1823
POTTS James 1839
PITTS Eli B 1858
ERWIN [83] John 1823
10
POTTS James 1852
GARRETT Joseph 1858
ERWIN John 1826
CUNNINGHAM James 1824
WOOD Ely 1889
GARRETT Willson 1850

HAGOOD Zachariah 1849
MARTIN Warren J 1849
NASH George 1823
NASH George 1824
HAGOOD Zachariah 1854
GREEN Robert H 1853
11
NASH George 1823
NASH George 1823
GREEN Robert H 1854
CUNNINGHAM [69] James 1823
GREEN Robert H 1858

HAGOOD Zachariah 1835
HAGOOD Zachariah 1849
HAGOOD Zachariah 1861
HAGOOD Zachariah 1861
SHAMBLIN Horton B 1849
HAGOOD Zachariah 1861
12
ROTTON William T 1889
CHAMBLEE Horton B 1854
HAGOOD Zachariah 1861
LINDSEY Nancy C 1889
ROTTON William T 1889
GREEN Robert H 1853
LINDSEY Nancy C 1889

MARTIN Robert G 1854
REED [200] Robert 1823
MADISON Benjamin 1824
GARRETT Joseph 1858
GARRETT Joseph 1858
15
HALLMARK George 1825
MATTISON Benjamin 1823
MADISON Benjamin 1823
MADISON Benjamin 1823

NASH George 1823
GREEN Robert H 1858
CUNNINGHAM [70] James 1823
GREEN Robert H 1858
WOOD Robert 1894
14
GREENE Robert H 1835
GREEN Robert H 1854
WOOD Robert 1894
GREEN Robert H 1849
GREEN Robert H 1858
BATES Thomas 1889

GREEN Robert H 1858
13

CLEMENTS [52] Hardy 1823
MADISON [161] Benjamin 1823
CLEMENTS [52] Hardy 1823
REED Robert 1823
22
MCCARTNEY [167] James 1823
MASSEY Jonathan 1824
MASSEY John 1853
MASSEY [163] Jonathan 1823
MASSEY John 1858

GREEN Robert H 1858
MELVIN Thomas 1858
23
MELVIN Thomas 1858
MELVIN Thomas 1858
MASSEY John 1858
MASSEY John 1858
WHITTINGTON Melvin P 1858

ROEBUCK [204] Mattie 1895
BATES Adam 1884
PARKER Tan 1884
WOOD Henson 1880
24
MILLER Newton 1884
MILLER [174] Fannie 1890
WOOD Henson 1880
PARKER Tan 1884
MILLER Newton 1884
WOOD Edmond 1899
CASH Elbert D 1885
WOOD Edmond 1899

MASSEY Jonathan 1823
MASSEY Benjamin F 1853
KILLOUGH David 1852
CRUMP [64] John 1823
MASSEY Benjamin F 1858
27
HEMPHILL John 1829
BROWN Elijah 1824
BARTON Thomas 1838
LINN Joseph 1837

KILLOUGH David 1858
KILLOUGH David 1854
WHITTINGTON Melvin P 1858
KILLOUGH David 1854
KILLOUGH David 1858
HARISON William H 1860
26
KILLOUGH William 1858
CAMP John 1828
HARRISON William H 1858
HARISON William H 1860
HARRISON William H 1858
LINN Joseph 1837
SIMS Edward 1823
KILLOUGH William 1858

KILLOUGH William 1858
COCHRAN [57] Hiram P 1823
KILLOUGH William 1853
25
SIMS Edward 1823
MCADAMS James 1823
KILLOUGH Newton C 1839
MCADAMS James 1823

COLE Joseph H 1839
BROWN George 1824
BROWN [29] Elijah 1823
KILLOUGH Jeremiah B 1858
BROWN Aaron 1889
34
CREWS Joseph G 1902
BROWN Demilins 1884
BYERS John L 1850
ROEBUCK York 1890
BYARS Catharine 1860
BROWN James A 1891

KILLOUGH Jeremiah B 1858
BURTON Thomas 1834
BURWELL Orrin S 1858
BURWELL Orrin S 1858
35
GOODWIN John 1838
BYARS James H 1854
BURWELL Orrin S 1858
BURWELL Orrin S 1858
HAMILTON Audley 1839

KILLOUGH Newton C 1839
SIMS Edward 1823
TURNER Jesse 1839
SIMS Edward 1823
REED William 1823
36
SIMS Edward 1823
MCCARTNEY [169] James 1823
WALKER James S 1823

Helpful Hints

1. This Map's INDEX can be found on the preceding pages.
2. Refer to Map "C" to see where this Township lies within Jefferson County, Alabama.
3. Numbers within square brackets [ ] denote a multi-patentee land parcel (multi-owner). Refer to Appendix "C" for a full list of members in this group.
4. Areas that look to be crowded with Patentees usually indicate multiple sales of the same parcel (Re-issues) or Overlapping parcels. See this Township's Index for an explanation of these and other circumstances that might explain "odd" groupings of Patentees on this map.

Legend

Patent Boundary
Section Boundary
No Patents Found (or Outside County)
1., 2., 3., ... Lot Numbers (when beside a name)
[ ] Group Number (see Appendix "C")

Scale: Section = 1 mile X 1 mile (generally, with some exceptions)

Road Map

T16-S R2-W
Huntsville Meridian

Map Group 15

Cities & Towns

Fulltondale
New Castle

Cemeteries

Sheritt Cemetery

6
5
4
7
8
9
18
17
16
19
20
21
30
29
28
31
32
33
New Castle
Fultondale
Sheritt Cem.
Willow
Paradise Valley
Quail Ridge
Ridgecrest
Berrywood
Grimmett
Short Leaf
Pineneedle
Pinemeadow
McCormack
Oakhill
Mulberry
Cottonwood
Holly
Skelton
Parker
Tarante
Brookview
Hillside
Cardi
Country Club
Twin Ridge
Hickory
Spruce
Carson
Mohawk
Shepherd
Dakota
Ottawa
Osage
Red Wing
Yuma
Hewitt
Tishamingo
Pawnee Village
Chenoer
Pawnee
Rosa
Hunters
Tambay
Krystal
Tarrant
Jew Hill
Pine
Elm
Sandra
Honeysuckle
Fox
Teresa
Church
Gann
Darlene
Oak
Northwood
Cone
Lual
Walker
Yaebrough
Nelda
Georgetown
Fulton
Lykes
Republic
Black Creek Valley
Franklin
Mann
Pine Hill
Headrick
Industrial
Indian Valley
12th
11th
3rd
5th
8th
6th
4th
1st
2nd
1st
County Shop
Cedar Hill
Lee
Oak Leaf
Bell
Murphree
West Park
Mountain
Whaley
Park
Central
Belcher
Howell
Oak Forest
Skyline
Pleasant Valley
Jacqueline
Gayle
Shady
Rushing Springs
Ketona
Pine Hill
Clow
Edna
Medco
Springdale
Pinson Valley
Old Pinson
Highland
Magnolia
Valley View
Treadwell
Ward
Toles
Cedar
Evergreen
Lane
Weatherly
Spice
Oak
McClaney
Cunningham

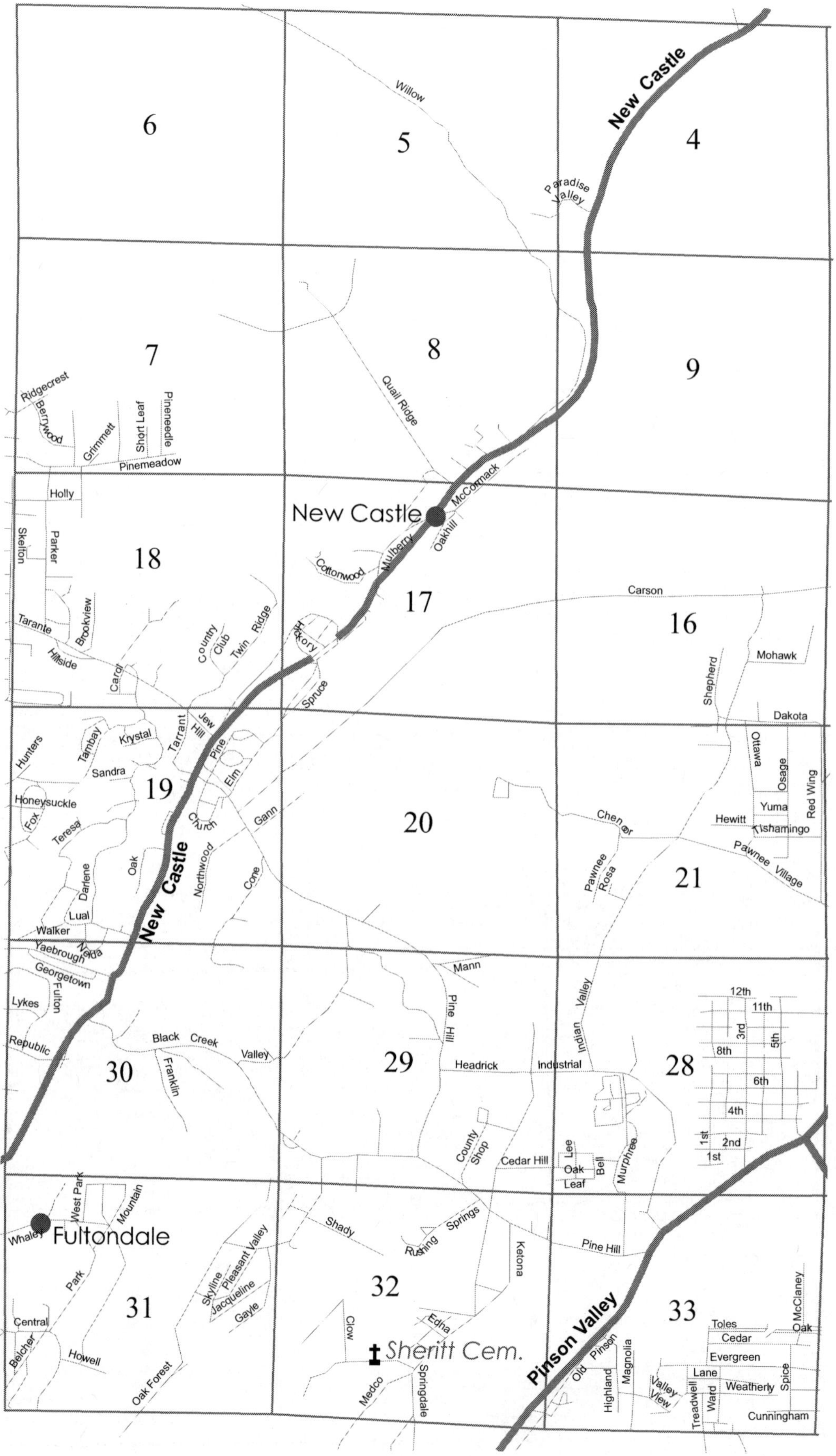

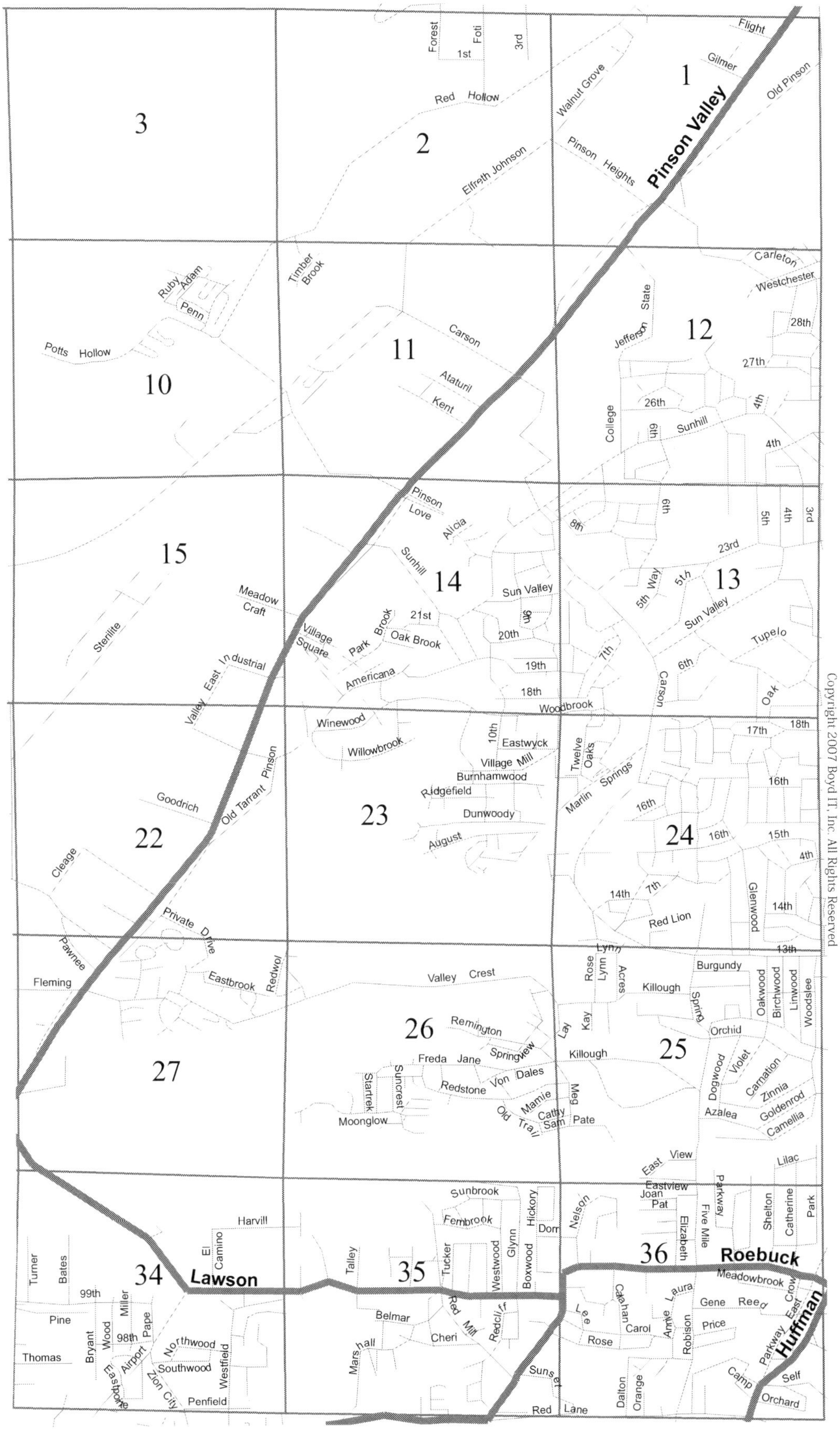

3

2
Forest 1st Foti 3rd
Red Hollow
Elfreth Johnson

1
Flight
Gilmer
Old Pinson
Walnut Grove
Pinson Heights
Pinson Valley

10
Ruby Adam Penn
Potts Hollow

11
Timber Brook
Carson
Ataturk
Kent

12
Carleton
Westchester
State
Jefferson
28th
27th
26th
College
6th
Sunhill
4th

15
Meadow Craft
Sterilite
East Industrial

14
Pinson Love
Alicia
Sunhill
Sun Valley
21st
Brook
Oak Brook
Park
Village Square
Americana
20th
19th
18th
Woodbrook
8th
7th

13
6th
5th 4th 3rd
23rd
5th Way
5th
Sun Valley
Tupelo
6th
Carson
Oak

22
Valley East
Pinson
Old Tarrant
Goodrich
Cleage
Private Drive

23
Winewood
Willowbrook
10th
Eastwyck
Village Mill
Burnhamwood
Ridgefield
Dunwoody
August

24
Twelve Oaks
Marlin Springs
17th
18th
16th
16th
16th
15th
4th
14th
7th
Red Lion
Glenwood
14th
13th

27
Pawnee
Fleming
Eastbrook
Redwol

26
Valley Crest
Remington
Springview
Freda Jane
Startrek
Suncrest
Redstone
Von Dales
Mamie
Old Trail
Cathy
Sam
Moonglow
Lay
Kay

25
Lynn
Rose Lynn
Acres
Killough
Burgundy
Spring
Oakwood
Birchwood
Linwood
Woodslee
Orchid
Killough
Meg
Pate
Dogwood
Violet
Carnation
Zinnia
Azalea
Goldenrod
Camellia
East View
Lilac

34
Harvill
El Camino
Lawson
Turner
Bates
99th
Pine
Miller
Bryant
Wood
98th
Pape
Airport
Thomas
Northwood
Southwood
Westfield
Eastbrook
Zion City
Penfield

35
Sunbrook
Fernbrook
Talley
Tucker
Westwood
Glynn
Boxwood
Hickory
Dorr
Belmar
Red Mill
Redcliff
Cheri
Marshall
Sunset
Red Lane

36
Nelson
Eastview
Joan
Pat
Parkway
Five Mile
Elizabeth
Shelton
Catherine
Park
Roebuck
Meadowbrook
Crow
Laura
Gene
Reed
Lee
Cahan
Carol
Annie
Robison
Price
Rose
East Parkway
Huffman
Dalton
Orange
Camp
Self
Orchard

Helpful Hints

1. This road map has a number of uses, but primarily it is to help you: a) find the present location of land owned by your ancestors (at least the general area), b) find cemeteries and city-centers, and c) estimate the route/roads used by Census-takers & tax-assessors.

2. If you plan to travel to Jefferson County to locate cemeteries or land parcels, please pick up a modern travel map for the area before you do. Mapping old land parcels on modern maps is not as exact a science as you might think. Just the slightest variations in public land survey coordinates, estimates of parcel boundaries, or road-map deviations can greatly alter a map's representation of how a road either does or doesn't cross a particular parcel of land.

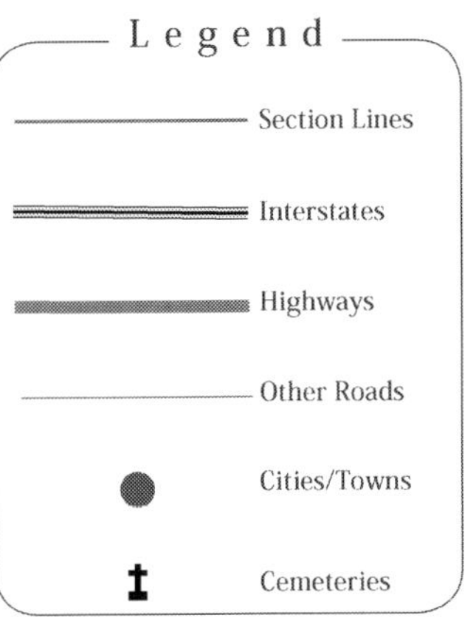

Scale: Section = 1 mile X 1 mile (generally, with some exceptions)

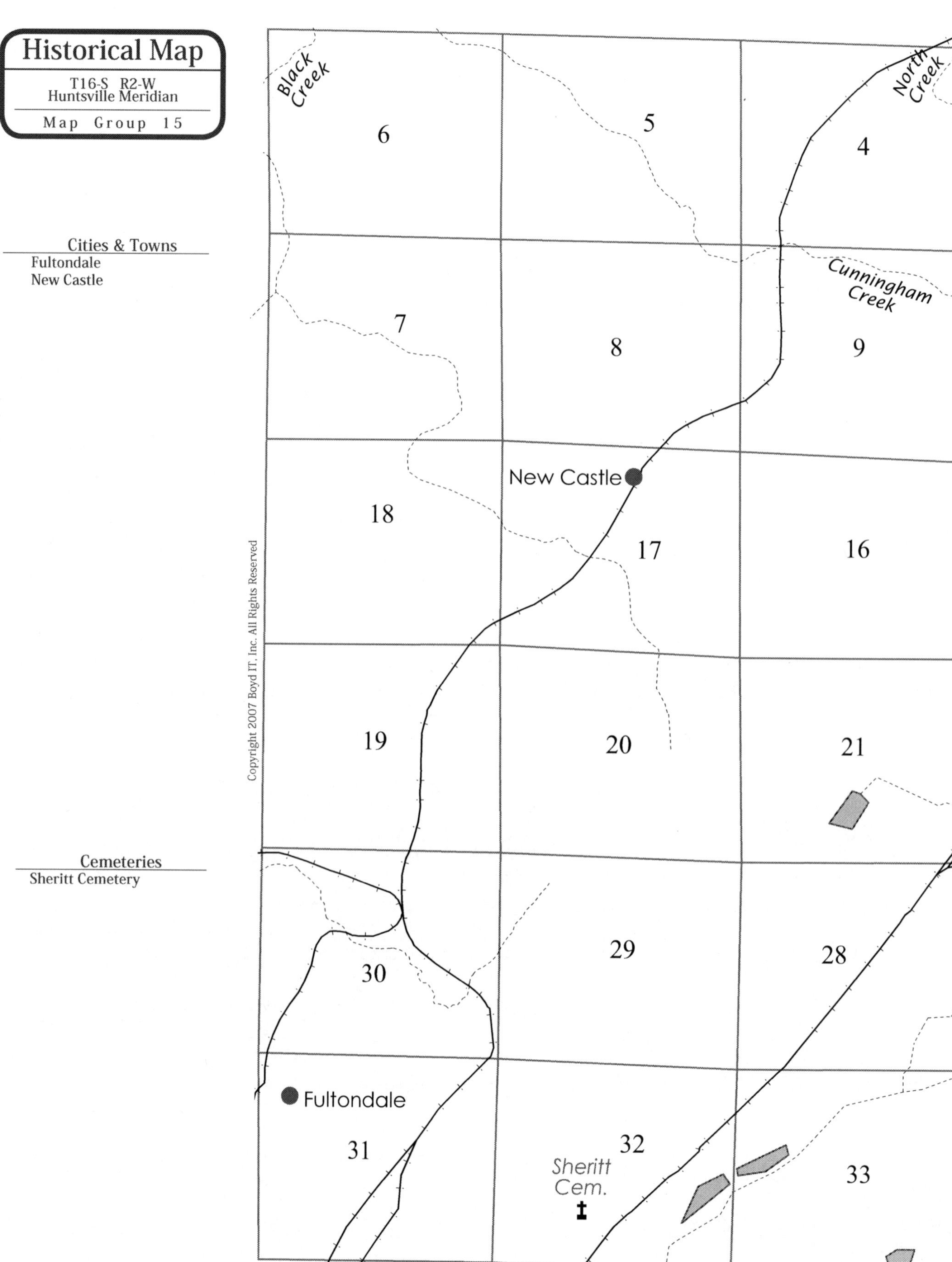
Historical Map
T16-S R2-W
Huntsville Meridian
Map Group 15
Cities & Towns
Fultondale
New Castle
Cemeteries
Sheritt Cemetery
Black Creek
North Creek
Cunningham Creek
New Castle
Fultondale
Sheritt Cem.
6
5
4
7
8
9
18
17
16
19
20
21
30
29
28
31
32
33
Copyright 2007 Boyd IT, Inc. All Rights Reserved

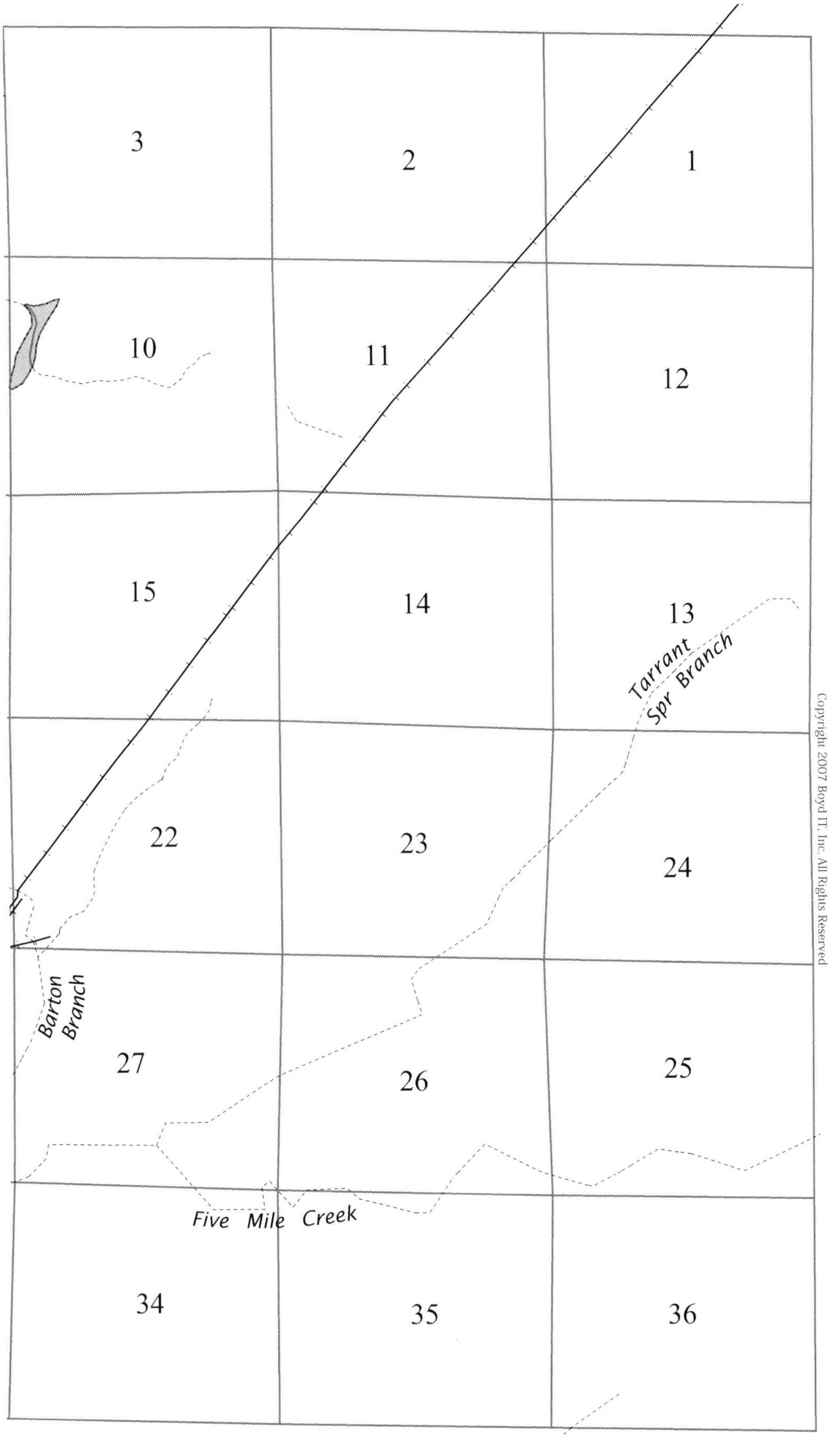

3

2

1

10

11

12

15

14

13

Tarrant Spr Branch

22

23

24

Barton Branch

27

26

25

Five Mile Creek

34

35

36

Helpful Hints

1. This Map takes a different look at the same Congressional Township displayed in the preceding two maps. It presents features that can help you better envision the historical development of the area: a) Water-bodies (lakes & ponds), b) Water-courses (rivers, streams, etc.), c) Railroads, d) City/town center-points (where they were oftentimes located when first settled), and e) Cemeteries.

2. Using this "Historical" map in tandem with this Township's Patent Map and Road Map, may lead you to some interesting discoveries. You will often find roads, towns, cemeteries, and waterways are named after nearby landowners: sometimes those names will be the ones you are researching. See how many of these research gems you can find here in Jefferson County.

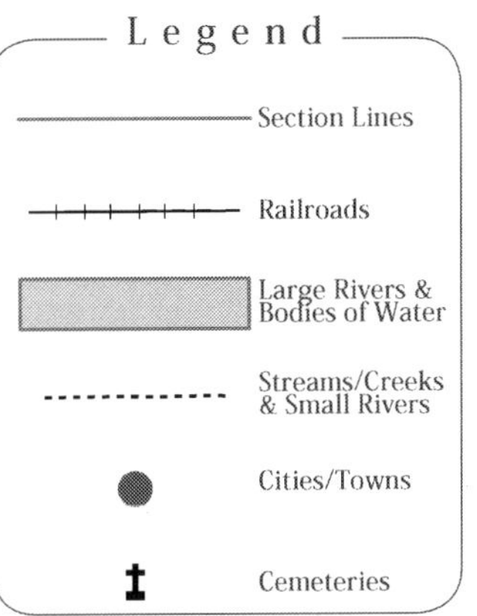

Scale: Section = 1 mile X 1 mile
(there are some exceptions)

Map Group 16: Index to Land Patents

Township 16-South Range 1-West (Huntsville)

After you locate an individual in this Index, take note of the Section and Section Part then proceed to the Land Patent map on the pages immediately following. You should have no difficulty locating the corresponding parcel of land.

The "For More Info" Column will lead you to more information about the underlying Patents. See the *Legend* at right, and the "How to Use this Book" chapter, for more information.

LEGEND

"For More Info . . . " column

A = Authority (Legislative Act, See Appendix "A")
B = Block or Lot (location in Section unknown)
C = Cancelled Patent
F = Fractional Section
G = Group (Multi-Patentee Patent, see Appendix "C")
V = Overlaps another Parcel
R = Re-Issued (Parcel patented more than once)

(A & G items require you to look in the Appendixes referred to above. All other Letter-designations followed by a number require you to locate line-items in this index that possess the ID number found after the letter).

ID	Individual in Patent	Sec.	Sec. Part	Date Issued	Other Counties	For More Info . . .
2813	ANDERSON, Margaret	33	E½SW	1823-06-02		A1
2652	BAGGETT, Berrin D	4	SW	1889-11-21		A4
2720	BASS, Jane	21	NWNW	1858-06-01		A1
2618	BEARD, Alexander	27	E½NE	1823-05-01		A1 G19
2619	" "	27	E½SE	1823-05-01		A1 G19
2617	" "	27	W½SE	1823-05-01		A1
2735	BELCHER, John	9	W½SW	1832-01-02		A1
2829	BRADFORD, Phelemon	1	SESE	1839-09-20		A1
2899	BRADFORD, William	15	W½NW	1823-05-01		A1 G27
2655	BROWN, David	30	W½NE	1823-05-01		A1
2736	BURLINSON, John	3	W½SW	1824-04-05		A1
2820	BURLINSON, Moses	3	NW	1824-04-05		A1
2802	BYERS, Joseph J	21	SENW	1848-07-01		A1
2803	" "	21	SWNE	1848-07-01		A1
2616	CANADAY, Adam E	23	NWNW	1839-09-20		A1
2672	CARLILE, Edward J	21	NENW	1839-09-20		A1
2673	" "	29	SENE	1858-06-01		A1
2674	CARLISLE, Edward J	20	NWSE	1858-06-01		A1
2675	" "	20	S½NE	1858-06-01		A1
2723	CARLISLE, Joel	13	NESE	1858-06-01		A1
2724	" "	13	SENE	1858-06-01		A1
2725	" "	13	SWSE	1858-06-01		A1
2702	CHAMBLEE, Horton B	6	NWNW	1839-09-20		A1 V2853
2701	" "	6	NENW	1858-06-01		A1 V2853
2737	CLAYTON, John	8	SESE	1839-09-20		A1
2894	CLAYTON, Warren	9	NENE	1834-10-01		A1
2714	COKER, James L	31	E½SE	1858-06-01		A1
2715	" "	31	SENE	1858-06-01		A1
2716	" "	31	SWSE	1858-06-01		A1
2699	COLLMAN, Henry	9	SWNE	1839-09-20		A1
2693	COOPER, Greenberry J	18	NESW	1858-06-01		A1
2694	" "	18	SENW	1858-06-01		A1
2753	DANIEL, John L	18	NWSW	1884-12-05		A4
2754	" "	18	SWNW	1884-12-05		A4
2799	DANIEL, Joseph H	21	SESW	1858-06-01		A1
2800	" "	28	NWNW	1858-06-01		A1
2801	" "	29	NENE	1858-06-01		A1
2641	DELANY, Baker	12	W½NE	1823-05-01		A1 G73
2640	" "	23	W½NE	1824-04-26		A1
2643	DULANY, Baker	13	E½SW	1823-05-01		A1
2644	" "	13	W½SW	1823-05-01		A1
2645	" "	23	E½NE	1823-05-01		A1 G77
2646	" "	24	W½NW	1823-05-01		A1 G76
2642	" "	12	E½NW	1824-04-12		A1
2738	DULANY, John	1	W½SE	1824-10-20		A1
2893	DULANY, Uriah	12	W½SE	1823-05-01		A1

ID	Individual in Patent	Sec.	Sec. Part	Date Issued	Other Counties	For More Info . . .
2900	DULANY, William	12	E½SE	1823-05-01		A1
2901	" "	12	E½SW	1823-05-01		A1
2902	" "	13	W½NW	1823-05-01		A1
2709	EDENS, Isreal S	25	NESE	1858-06-01		A1
2710	" "	25	SENE	1858-06-01		A1
2711	" "	25	W½SE	1858-06-01		A1
2614	EDWARDS, Abram	10	E½NE	1875-11-20		A4
2691	EDWARDS, George S	34	SENE	1889-12-28		A1
2756	EDWARDS, John M	27	E½NW	1858-06-01		A1
2762	EDWARDS, John S	27	W½NE	1839-09-20		A1
2763	" "	28	S½NW	1890-12-31		A1
2794	EDWARDS, Joseph B	28	SWNE	1891-06-29		A1
2890	EDWARDS, Thomas T	28	NENW	1876-02-01		A4
2891	" "	28	NWNE	1876-02-01		A4
2740	EPPES, John H	4	NWSE	1893-09-23		A4
2741	" "	4	S½NE	1893-09-23		A4
2819	ETHRIDGE, Morgan	36	N½NW	1888-03-01		A4
2636	FALKS, Anna	17	SENW	1858-06-01		A1
2637	" "	18	NESE	1858-06-01		A1
2807	FALKS, Lewis	17	N½SW	1839-09-20		A1
2878	FOSTER, Thomas J	3	SESE	1858-06-01		A1
2912	FOSTER, William H	2	NWNW	1854-07-15		A1
2913	" "	2	NWSW	1858-06-01		A1
2914	" "	2	SWNW	1858-06-01		A1
2662	FRANKLIN, David W	18	S½SW	1883-10-01		A4
2666	FRANKLIN, Edmond	4	SWNW	1858-06-01		A1
2668	FRANKLIN, Edmund	14	NWNE	1835-10-01		A1
2870	FRANKLIN, Thomas	14	E½NE	1823-05-01		A1
2871	" "	14	E½SW	1824-10-20		A1
2872	" "	14	NWSE	1834-10-01		A1
2873	" "	14	SENW	1835-10-01		A1
2875	" "	14	W½SW	1839-09-20		A1
2874	" "	14	SWNE	1858-06-01		A1
2876	" "	5	NWSE	1858-06-01		A1
2892	FULLER, Trion	11	E½SE	1823-05-01		A1 G90
2633	GARNER, Andrew J	36	E½SW	1890-03-19		A4
2634	" "	36	NWSE	1890-03-19		A4
2635	" "	36	SWNE	1890-03-19		A4
2869	GARNER, Stephen	25	W½NE	1858-06-01		A1
2676	GILPIN, Elijah P	4	N½NE	1891-06-19		A4
2798	GLENN, Joseph	19	SENE	1834-10-16		A1
2797	" "	19	NWSE	1839-03-15		A1
2746	GODWIN, John J	9	NESE	1858-06-01		A1
2745	" "	23	NENW	1860-04-02		A1
2830	GODWIN, Pinckney	34	E½SE	1858-06-01		A1 V2903
2706	GOLDSBY, Isaac	13	NWSE	1839-09-20		A1
2625	GOODWIN, Alexander	29	SESW	1854-07-15		A1
2621	" "	29	NESW	1858-06-01		A1
2622	" "	29	NWSE	1858-06-01		A1
2623	" "	29	NWSW	1858-06-01		A1
2624	" "	29	SENW	1858-06-01		A1
2626	" "	29	SWSE	1858-06-01		A1
2627	" "	32	NENW	1858-06-01		A1
2628	" "	32	NWNE	1858-06-01		A1
2629	" "	32	W½NW	1885-03-16		A1
2700	GOODWIN, Henry	29	E½SE	1824-05-04		A1
2707	GOODWIN, Isaac	28	SESE	1858-06-01		A1
2708	" "	28	W½SE	1858-06-01		A1
2808	GOODWIN, Manning	29	SWSW	1850-09-02		A1
2809	" "	9	SWSE	1852-01-01		A1
2831	GOODWIN, Pinckney	34	SWSE	1858-06-01		A1
2877	GOODWIN, Thomas	32	SENW	1858-06-01		A1
2910	GORMAN, William	33	E½NE	1823-05-01		A1 G101
2909	" "	34	E½NW	1823-05-01		A1
2911	" "	34	W½NW	1823-05-01		A1 G101
2906	" "	27	E½SW	1824-04-14		A1
2907	" "	33	E½SE	1824-05-10		A1
2908	" "	33	W½NE	1824-05-10		A1
2687	HAGOOD, George M	6	NESW	1854-07-15		A1
2686	" "	6	N½SE	1858-06-01		A1
2688	" "	6	NWSW	1858-06-01		A1
2689	" "	6	S½NE	1858-06-01		A1
2690	" "	6	SENW	1858-06-01		A1

ID	Individual in Patent	Sec.	Sec. Part	Date Issued	Other Counties	For More Info . . .
2748	HAGOOD, John K	24	NWNE	1839-09-20		A1
2837	HAGOOD, Robert I	5	S½NW	1854-07-15		A1
2836	" "	5	NWNW	1858-06-01		A1
2630	HALL, Alexander	25	SESE	1837-11-07		A1
2631	" "	36	NWNE	1839-09-20		A1
2739	HANBY, John F	6	SWNW	1839-09-20		A1
2860	HARRIS, Sarah	5	S½NE	1837-03-20		A1
2916	HARRIS, William	5	SWSE	1858-06-01		A1
2917	HOBBS, William	10	E½SW	1824-05-04		A1
2918	" "	10	SWNE	1835-10-01		A1
2717	HOLLEY, James M	13	E½NW	1824-04-14		A1
2863	HOLLY, Sherod	12	W½NW	1824-10-20		A1
2864	HOLLY, Sherwood	13	W½NE	1824-04-30		A1
2865	" "	23	W½SW	1824-04-30		A1
2747	JOHNSON, John	36	NENE	1889-10-07		A1
2853	JOHNSON, Salley	6	N½NW	1852-01-01		A1 V2702, 2701
2861	JOHNSON, Sarah	6	SESW	1858-06-01		A1
2832	KEATON, Reuben	24	E½SW	1823-06-02		A1
2749	KILLOUGH, John	28	NWSW	1854-07-15		A1
2750	" "	28	SWSW	1858-06-01		A1
2751	" "	32	NENE	1858-06-01		A1
2752	" "	33	NWNW	1858-06-01		A1
2828	LACY, Peter	10	E½SE	1875-11-20		A4
2778	LANE, John W	23	W½SE	1823-05-01		A1 G152
2646	" "	24	W½NW	1823-05-01		A1 G76
2779	" "	26	W½NE	1823-05-01		A1 G152
2618	" "	27	E½NE	1823-05-01		A1 G19
2619	" "	27	E½SE	1823-05-01		A1 G19
2777	" "	31	W½NW	1823-05-01		A1 G153
2755	LANG, John	26	W½SW	1823-07-09		A1
2815	LATHAM, Mary	22	NENW	1894-09-25		A4
2867	LATHEM, Sinkler	35	NENW	1860-04-02		A1
2868	" "	35	W½NW	1860-04-02		A1
2905	LAWLESS, William G	2	SENW	1888-09-29		A1
2613	LESLEY, Abel	24	SESE	1858-06-01		A1
2683	LEWIS, Frank P	8	N½NE	1883-10-20		A1
2684	" "	8	N½SW	1883-10-20		A1
2615	LOONEY, Absalom	24	SWSE	1839-09-20		A1 V2787
2915	LOVE, William H	7	NENE	1858-06-01		A1
2647	MADISON, Benjamin	19	E½SE	1823-05-01		A1
2641	MCCARTNEY, James	12	W½NE	1823-05-01		A1 G73
2656	MCCOMBS, David	5	NESW	1854-07-15		A1
2921	MCGEHEE, William	15	E½NW	1823-05-01		A1 G172
2677	MILLER, Ellick	6	SWSW	1894-10-22		A4
2697	MILNE, Henry A	24	S½SE	1883-05-25		A4 C
2698	" "	24	SESW	1883-05-25		A4 C
2757	MOORE, John	6	SWSE	1858-06-01		A1
2759	" "	7	NWNE	1858-06-01		A1
2758	" "	7	NENW	1899-12-07		A1
2946	MORROW, Wolsey P	28	E½SW	1891-06-29		A1
2665	ODEN, Edley J	22	W½NW	1880-02-20		A4
2788	ORR, Jonathan	12	W½SW	1823-05-01		A1 G185
2787	" "	24	W½SE	1823-05-01		A1 G186 V2615
2789	" "	30	E½SW	1823-05-01		A1 G187
2790	" "	30	W½SW	1823-05-01		A1 G187
2733	PERKINS, John B	11	SENE	1852-01-01		A1
2734	" "	14	NESE	1852-01-01		A1
2892	PERKINS, William	11	E½SE	1823-05-01		A1 G90
2788	" "	12	W½SW	1823-05-01		A1 G185
2922	" "	11	SWNE	1853-08-01		A1
2923	" "	11	SWSE	1858-06-01		A1
2705	PERRY, Hugh T	34	S½SW	1883-10-01		A4
2703	" "	34	NESW	1884-12-05		A4
2704	" "	34	NWSE	1884-12-05		A4
2780	PITTS, John W	8	SENW	1889-11-21		A4
2781	" "	8	SWNE	1889-11-21		A4
2782	" "	8	W½NW	1889-11-21		A4
2653	PRAYTOR, Bezaleel	13	SESE	1858-06-01		A1
2721	PRICE, Jesse J	3	W½SE	1858-06-01		A1
2722	" "	4	NESE	1858-06-01		A1
2919	PRICE, William J	9	N½NW	1858-06-01		A1
2924	READ, William	20	E½SW	1826-12-01		A1
2761	REED, John	21	NWNE	1852-01-01		A1

ID	Individual in Patent	Sec.	Sec. Part	Date Issued	Other Counties	For More Info . . .
2760	REED, John (Cont'd)	21	E½NE	1858-06-01		A1
2846	REED, Robert	17	W½SE	1823-07-09		A1
2844	" "	17	SESW	1839-09-20		A1
2843	" "	17	NESE	1840-11-10		A1
2850	" "	19	W½NE	1853-11-15		A1
2851	" "	20	NWNE	1853-11-15		A1
2845	" "	17	SWSW	1858-06-01		A1
2847	" "	18	SESE	1858-06-01		A1
2848	" "	19	NENE	1858-06-01		A1
2849	" "	19	SENW	1858-06-01		A1
2927	REED, William	20	W½SW	1823-05-01		A1
2929	" "	29	W½NW	1823-05-01		A1
2930	" "	30	E½NE	1823-05-01		A1
2925	" "	20	NW	1823-07-09		A1
2931	" "	31	NWSW	1840-11-10		A1
2926	" "	20	SWSE	1850-09-02		A1
2928	" "	29	NENW	1850-09-02		A1
2654	RICKEY, Daniel	3	E½SW	1832-01-10		A1
2632	ROBERTSON, Anderson	24	E½NE	1823-05-01		A1
2787	" "	24	W½SE	1823-05-01		A1 G186 V2615
2645	SCOTT, David	23	E½NE	1823-05-01		A1 G77
2657	" "	23	E½SW	1823-05-01		A1 G211
2658	" "	26	E½NE	1823-05-01		A1 G211
2659	" "	26	E½NW	1823-05-01		A1 G211
2660	" "	26	W½NW	1823-05-01		A1 G211
2661	" "	30	E½NW	1823-05-01		A1 G212
2910	" "	33	E½NE	1823-05-01		A1 G101
2911	" "	34	W½NW	1823-05-01		A1 G101
2695	SELF, Harris G	18	NWSE	1858-06-01		A1
2696	" "	18	SWNE	1858-06-01		A1
2822	SELF, Nathaniel H	17	NWNW	1853-08-01		A1
2821	" "	17	NENW	1858-06-01		A1
2823	" "	18	SENE	1858-06-01		A1
2932	SELF, William	5	SESW	1854-07-15		A1
2933	" "	5	SWSW	1858-06-01		A1
2934	" "	6	SESE	1858-06-01		A1
2888	SIMS, Thomas	32	SESE	1854-07-15		A1
2886	" "	32	NESE	1858-06-01		A1
2887	" "	32	S½NE	1858-06-01		A1
2889	" "	33	SWNW	1858-06-01		A1
2692	SMITH, George T	36	W½SW	1895-06-03		A4
2732	STARKY, Johan	36	S½NW	1894-06-20		A4
2764	SWINNEY, John	5	N½NE	1837-03-20		A1
2663	TALLEY, Dyer	26	E½SW	1858-06-01		A1
2664	" "	26	W½SE	1858-06-01		A1
2826	TALLEY, Nicholas	1	SWNE	1854-07-15		A1
2824	" "	1	NESW	1858-06-01		A1
2825	" "	1	S½NW	1858-06-01		A1
2827	" "	1	W½SW	1858-06-01		A1
2612	TAYLOR, Aaron	3	W½NE	1826-10-05		A1
2765	TAYLOR, John	17	SESE	1858-06-01		A1
2766	" "	20	NENE	1858-06-01		A1
2935	TAYLOR, William	17	NWNE	1854-07-15		A1
2936	" "	18	N½NE	1858-06-01		A1
2937	" "	8	NESE	1858-06-01		A1
2938	" "	8	SENE	1858-06-01		A1
2939	" "	8	SESW	1858-06-01		A1
2940	" "	8	SWSW	1858-06-01		A1
2941	" "	8	W½SE	1858-06-01		A1
2903	TAYLOR, William E	34	NESE	1853-08-01		A1 V2830
2805	TEAGUE, Lemuel O	2	N½SE	1883-10-20		A1
2806	" "	2	SWSW	1883-10-20		A1
2795	THORP, Joseph E	2	E½NE	1883-10-20		A1
2796	" "	4	E½NW	1883-10-20		A1
2742	TIDWELL, John H	2	NESW	1858-06-01		A1
2680	TRASS, Enos	10	SWSE	1834-11-04		A1
2681	" "	10	SWSW	1834-11-04		A1
2638	TRUSS, Arthur	24	NESE	1837-11-07		A1
2639	" "	25	NWNW	1839-09-20		A1
2770	TRUSS, John	14	SWSE	1844-07-10		A1
2769	" "	14	SESE	1852-01-01		A1
2773	" "	24	NENW	1854-07-15		A1
2775	" "	34	NWSW	1854-07-15		A1

ID	Individual in Patent	Sec.	Sec. Part	Date Issued	Other Counties	For More Info . . .
2767	TRUSS, John (Cont'd)	13	NENE	1858-06-01		A1
2768	" "	14	NENW	1858-06-01		A1
2771	" "	14	W½NW	1858-06-01		A1
2772	" "	15	NE	1858-06-01		A1
2774	" "	24	SENW	1858-06-01		A1
2879	TRUSS, Thomas K	10	NWSE	1852-01-01		A1
2880	" "	11	NWSE	1852-01-01		A1
2881	TRUSS, Thomas R	10	NWSW	1858-06-01		A1
2882	" "	10	SENW	1858-06-01		A1
2883	" "	10	SWNW	1858-06-01		A1
2884	" "	22	NWSE	1858-06-01		A1
2885	" "	25	NENW	1858-06-01		A1
2921	TRUSS, Warren	15	E½NW	1823-05-01		A1 G172
2899	" "	15	W½NW	1823-05-01		A1 G27
2896	" "	23	E½SE	1823-05-01		A1
2657	" "	23	E½SW	1823-05-01		A1 G211
2778	" "	23	W½SE	1823-05-01		A1 G152
2658	" "	26	E½NE	1823-05-01		A1 G211
2659	" "	26	E½NW	1823-05-01		A1 G211
2779	" "	26	W½NE	1823-05-01		A1 G152
2660	" "	26	W½NW	1823-05-01		A1 G211
2897	" "	24	W½SW	1823-07-09		A1
2895	" "	15	W½SW	1824-05-04		A1
2898	TRUSS, Wiley	1	SESW	1839-09-20		A1
2862	TUCKER, Sarah	2	S½SE	1889-03-01		A4
2904	TUCKER, William E	2	SESW	1876-04-01		A4
2943	TUCKER, William W	2	W½NE	1878-04-09		A4
2719	TUNE, James	32	S½SW	1837-03-20		A1
2942	TUNE, William	32	N½SW	1837-03-20		A1
2776	TURNER, John	17	E½NE	1829-04-01		A1
2685	TYLER, Frank	4	NWNW	1902-02-03		A4
2678	VANN, Enos T	10	NWNW	1858-06-01		A1
2679	" "	4	SESE	1858-06-01		A1
2728	VANN, Joel K	9	E½SW	1850-04-01		A1
2730	" "	9	SENE	1850-04-01		A1
2727	" "	17	SWNW	1852-01-01		A1
2729	" "	9	NWNE	1854-07-15		A1
2731	" "	9	SENW	1854-07-15		A1
2726	" "	17	SWNE	1858-06-01		A1
2804	VANN, King	23	SWNW	1839-09-20		A1
2816	VANN, Michael K	21	NESW	1850-04-01		A1
2817	" "	21	NWSW	1853-08-01		A1
2818	" "	21	W½SE	1858-06-01		A1
2835	VANN, Richard K	27	NWNW	1849-05-01		A1
2839	VANN, Robert J	27	SWNW	1854-07-15		A1
2841	" "	28	NESE	1854-07-15		A1
2838	" "	22	W½SW	1858-06-01		A1
2840	" "	28	NENE	1858-06-01		A1
2842	VANN, Robert M	9	NWSE	1852-01-01		A1
2854	VANN, Samuel S	22	NENE	1848-04-15		A1
2858	VANN, Samuel T	22	SWNE	1850-04-01		A1
2855	" "	15	SESE	1850-09-02		A1
2856	" "	22	NWNE	1858-06-01		A1
2857	" "	22	SENW	1858-06-01		A1
2920	VANN, William J	4	SWSE	1889-03-02		A1
2718	WALKER, James S	12	E½NE	1823-05-01		A1
2777	" "	31	W½NW	1823-05-01		A1 G153
2682	WALLS, Francis C	8	NENW	1892-01-18		A4
2852	WEAR, Robert	10	NENW	1852-01-01		A1 R2712
2859	WEAR, Samuel	3	NENE	1839-09-20		A1
2620	WEEMS, Alexander G	18	N½NW	1891-06-19		A4
2712	WEEMS, James J	10	NENW	1880-02-20		A4 R2852
2713	" "	10	NWNE	1880-02-20		A4
2814	WEEMS, Martin	32	W½SE	1875-11-20		A4
2783	WILKES, John	22	E½SW	1839-09-20		A1
2744	WILKES, John H	22	SWSE	1838-08-28		A1
2743	" "	22	SENE	1839-09-20		A1
2793	WILLIAMS, Jordan	34	W½NE	1824-05-10		A1
2792	" "	33	W½SW	1825-09-10		A1
2791	" "	23	SENW	1834-10-01		A1
2661	WILSON, William	30	E½NW	1823-05-01		A1 G212
2789	" "	30	E½SW	1823-05-01		A1 G187
2790	" "	30	W½SW	1823-05-01		A1 G187

ID	Individual in Patent	Sec.	Sec. Part	Date Issued	Other Counties	For More Info . . .
2944	WILSON, William (Cont'd)	30	W½NW	1824-10-20		A1
2945	" "	31	E½NW	1828-02-20		A1
2667	WOOD, Edmond	30	E½SE	1899-12-07		A1
2670	WOOD, Edmund	19	SWSE	1834-10-21		A1
2671	" "	30	W½SE	1839-09-20		A1
2669	" "	19	N½SW	1854-07-15		A1
2833	WOOD, Richard H	31	E½SW	1858-06-01		A1
2834	" "	31	SWNE	1858-06-01		A1
2947	WOODS, Young A	36	NESE	1891-12-01		A1
2948	" "	36	S½SE	1891-12-01		A1
2949	" "	36	SENE	1891-12-01		A1
2649	WORTHINGTON, Benjamin	27	SWSW	1838-08-28		A1
2650	" "	33	W½SE	1838-08-28		A1
2651	" "	34	NENE	1838-08-28		A1
2648	WORTHINGTON, Benjamin P	33	SENW	1844-07-10		A1
2786	WORTHINGTON, John	22	E½SE	1839-09-20		A1
2785	" "	21	SWNW	1849-09-01		A1
2784	" "	20	SESE	1850-09-02		A1
2810	WORTHINGTON, Marcus A	25	S½NW	1858-06-01		A1
2811	" "	25	SW	1858-06-01		A1
2812	" "	26	E½SE	1858-06-01		A1
2866	YOUNGBLOOD, Simon	28	SENE	1839-09-20		A1

Patent Map

T16-S R1-W
Huntsville Meridian

Map Group 16

Township Statistics

Parcels Mapped	:	338
Number of Patents	:	272
Number of Individuals	:	170
Patentees Identified	:	178
Number of Surnames	:	103
Multi-Patentee Parcels	:	22
Oldest Patent Date	:	5/1/1823
Most Recent Patent	:	2/3/1902
Block/Lot Parcels	:	0
Parcels Re - Issued	:	1
Parcels that Overlap	:	7
Cities and Towns	:	1
Cemeteries	:	5

CHAMBLEE Horton B 1839
JOHNSON Salley 1852
CHAMBLEE Horton B 1858
HAGOOD Robert I 1858
SWINNEY John 1837
TYLER Frank 1902
THORP Joseph E 1883
GILPIN Elijah P 1891
HANBY John F 1839
HAGOOD George M 1858
6
HAGOOD George M 1858
HAGOOD Robert I 1854
5
HARRIS Sarah 1837
FRANKLIN Edmond 1858
4
EPPES John H 1893
HAGOOD George M 1858
HAGOOD George M 1854
HAGOOD George M 1858
MCCOMBS David 1854
FRANKLIN Thomas 1858
BAGGETT Berrin D 1889
EPPES John H 1893
PRICE Jesse J 1858
MILLER Ellick 1894
JOHNSON Sarah 1858
MOORE John 1858
SELF William 1858
SELF William 1858
SELF William 1854
HARRIS William 1858
VANN William J 1889
VANN Enos T 1858
MOORE John 1899
MOORE John 1858
LOVE William H 1858
PITTS John W 1889
WALLS Francis C 1892
LEWIS Frank P 1883
PRICE William J 1858
VANN Joel K 1854
CLAYTON Warren 1834
7
PITTS John W 1889
8
PITTS John W 1889
TAYLOR William 1858
VANN Joel K 1854
9
COLLMAN Henry 1839
VANN Joel K 1850
LEWIS Frank P 1883
TAYLOR William 1858
TAYLOR William 1858
VANN Robert M 1852
GODWIN John J 1858
BELCHER John 1832
VANN Joel K 1850
TAYLOR William 1858
TAYLOR William 1858
CLAYTON John 1839
GOODWIN Manning 1852
WEEMS Alexander G 1891
TAYLOR William 1858
SELF Nathaniel H 1853
SELF Nathaniel H 1858
TAYLOR William 1854
TURNER John 1829
DANIEL John L 1884
COOPER Greenberry J 1858
18
SELF Harris G 1858
SELF Nathaniel H 1858
VANN Joel K 1852
FALKS Anna 1858
17
VANN Joel K 1858
16
DANIEL John L 1884
COOPER Greenberry J 1858
SELF Harris G 1858
FALKS Anna 1858
FALKS Lewis 1839
REED Robert 1823
REED Robert 1840
FRANKLIN David W 1883
REED Robert 1858
REED Robert 1858
REED Robert 1839
TAYLOR John 1858
REED Robert 1858
REED Robert 1853
REED Robert 1858
19
GLENN Joseph 1834
REED William 1823
20
REED Robert 1853
TAYLOR John 1858
CARLISLE Edward J 1858
BASS Jane 1858
CARLILE Edward J 1839
REED John 1852
REED John 1858
WORTHINGTON John 1849
BYERS Joseph J 1848
BYERS Joseph J 1848
21
WOOD Edmund 1854
GLENN Joseph 1839
MADISON Benjamin 1823
WOOD Edmund 1834
REED William 1823
READ William 1826
CARLISLE Edward J 1858
WORTHINGTON John 1850
REED William 1850
VANN Michael K 1853
VANN Michael K 1850
DANIEL Joseph H 1858
VANN Michael K 1858
WILSON William 1824
SCOTT [212] David 1823
30
BROWN David 1823
REED William 1823
REED William 1823
REED William 1850
GOODWIN Alexander 1858
29
DANIEL Joseph H 1858
CARLILE Edward J 1858
DANIEL Joseph H 1858
EDWARDS Thomas T 1876
EDWARDS Thomas T 1876
VANN Robert J 1858
EDWARDS John S 1890
28
YOUNGBLOOD Simon 1839
EDWARDS Joseph B 1891
ORR [187] Jonathan 1823
ORR [187] Jonathan 1823
WOOD Edmund 1839
WOOD Edmond 1899
GOODWIN Alexander 1858
GOODWIN Alexander 1858
GOODWIN Alexander 1858
GOODWIN Henry 1824
GOODWIN Manning 1850
GOODWIN Alexander 1854
GOODWIN Alexander 1858
KILLOUGH John 1854
KILLOUGH John 1858
MORROW Wolsey P 1891
GOODWIN Isaac 1858
VANN Robert J 1854
GOODWIN Isaac 1858
LANE [153] John W 1823
WILSON William 1828
WOOD Richard H 1858
31
COKER James L 1858
GOODWIN Alexander 1885
GOODWIN Alexander 1858
GOODWIN Alexander 1858
KILLOUGH John 1858
GOODWIN Thomas 1858
32
SIMS Thomas 1858
KILLOUGH John 1858
SIMS Thomas 1858
WORTHINGTON Benjamin P 1844
33
GORMAN William 1824
GORMAN [101] William 1823
REED William 1840
WOOD Richard H 1858
COKER James L 1858
COKER James L 1858
TUNE William 1837
TUNE James 1837
WEEMS Martin 1875
SIMS Thomas 1858
SIMS Thomas 1854
WILLIAMS Jordan 1825
ANDERSON Margaret 1823
WORTHINGTON Benjamin 1838
GORMAN William 1824

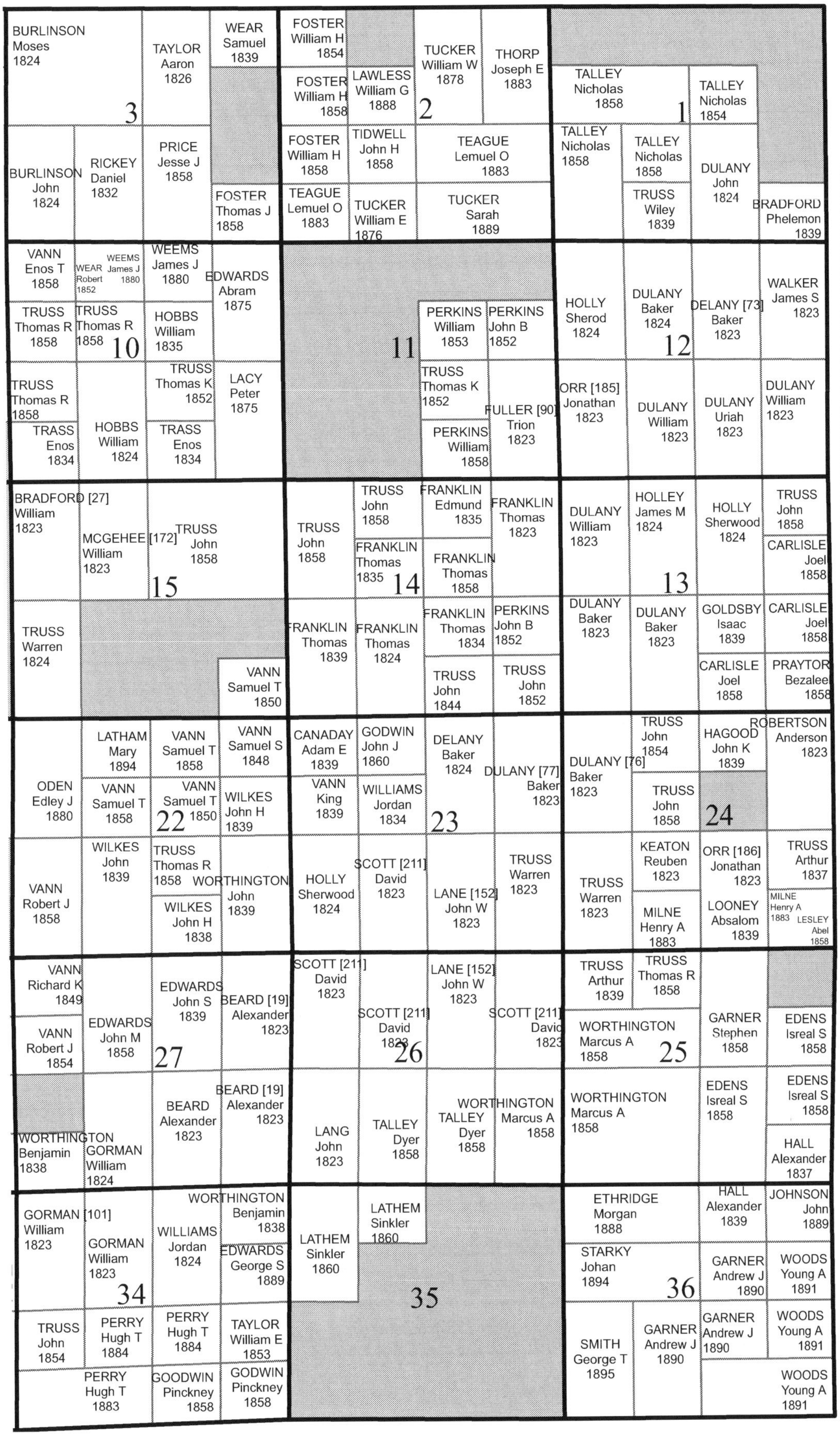

3
BURLINSON Moses 1824
TAYLOR Aaron 1826
WEAR Samuel 1839
BURLINSON John 1824
RICKEY Daniel 1832
PRICE Jesse J 1858
FOSTER Thomas J 1858

2
FOSTER William H 1854
FOSTER William H 1858
LAWLESS William G 1888
TUCKER William W 1878
THORP Joseph E 1883
FOSTER William H 1858
TIDWELL John H 1858
TEAGUE Lemuel O 1883
TEAGUE Lemuel O 1883
TUCKER William E 1876
TUCKER Sarah 1889

1
TALLEY Nicholas 1858
TALLEY Nicholas 1854
TALLEY Nicholas 1858
TALLEY Nicholas 1858
DULANY John 1824
TRUSS Wiley 1839
BRADFORD Phelemon 1839

10
VANN Enos T 1858
WEAR Robert 1852
WEEMS James J 1880
WEEMS James J 1880
EDWARDS Abram 1875
TRUSS Thomas R 1858
TRUSS Thomas R 1858
HOBBS William 1835
TRUSS Thomas R 1858
TRUSS Thomas K 1852
LACY Peter 1875
TRASS Enos 1834
HOBBS William 1824
TRASS Enos 1834

11
PERKINS William 1853
PERKINS John B 1852
TRUSS Thomas K 1852
FULLER [90] Trion 1823
PERKINS William 1858

12
HOLLY Sherod 1824
DULANY Baker 1824
DELANY [73] Baker 1823
WALKER James S 1823
ORR [185] Jonathan 1823
DULANY William 1823
DULANY Uriah 1823
DULANY William 1823

15
BRADFORD [27] William 1823
MCGEHEE [172] William 1823
TRUSS John 1858
TRUSS Warren 1824
VANN Samuel T 1850

14
TRUSS John 1858
TRUSS John 1858
FRANKLIN Edmund 1835
FRANKLIN Thomas 1823
FRANKLIN Thomas 1835
FRANKLIN Thomas 1858
FRANKLIN Thomas 1839
FRANKLIN Thomas 1824
FRANKLIN Thomas 1834
PERKINS John B 1852
TRUSS John 1844
TRUSS John 1852

13
DULANY William 1823
HOLLEY James M 1824
HOLLY Sherwood 1824
TRUSS John 1858
CARLISLE Joel 1858
DULANY Baker 1823
DULANY Baker 1823
GOLDSBY Isaac 1839
CARLISLE Joel 1858
CARLISLE Joel 1858
PRAYTOR Bezaleel 1858

22
LATHAM Mary 1894
VANN Samuel T 1858
VANN Samuel S 1848
ODEN Edley J 1880
VANN Samuel T 1858
VANN Samuel T 1850
WILKES John H 1839
VANN Robert J 1858
WILKES John 1839
TRUSS Thomas R 1858
WORTHINGTON John 1839
WILKES John H 1838

23
CANADAY Adam E 1839
GODWIN John J 1860
DELANY Baker 1824
DULANY [77] Baker 1823
VANN King 1839
WILLIAMS Jordan 1834
HOLLY Sherwood 1824
SCOTT [211] David 1823
LANE [152] John W 1823
TRUSS Warren 1823

24
DULANY [76] Baker 1823
TRUSS John 1854
HAGOOD John K 1839
ROBERTSON Anderson 1823
TRUSS John 1858
TRUSS Warren 1823
KEATON Reuben 1823
ORR [186] Jonathan 1823
TRUSS Arthur 1837
MILNE Henry A 1883
LOONEY Absalom 1839
MILNE Henry A 1883
LESLEY Abel 1858

27
VANN Richard K 1849
EDWARDS John S 1839
BEARD [19] Alexander 1823
VANN Robert J 1854
EDWARDS John M 1858
BEARD Alexander 1823
BEARD [19] Alexander 1823
WORTHINGTON Benjamin 1838
GORMAN William 1824

26
SCOTT [211] David 1823
LANE [152] John W 1823
SCOTT [211] David 1823
SCOTT [211] David 1823
LANG John 1823
TALLEY Dyer 1858
TALLEY Dyer 1858
WORTHINGTON Marcus A 1858

25
TRUSS Arthur 1839
TRUSS Thomas R 1858
WORTHINGTON Marcus A 1858
GARNER Stephen 1858
EDENS Isreal S 1858
WORTHINGTON Marcus A 1858
EDENS Isreal S 1858
EDENS Isreal S 1858
HALL Alexander 1837

34
GORMAN [101] William 1823
WORTHINGTON Benjamin 1838
GORMAN William 1823
WILLIAMS Jordan 1824
EDWARDS George S 1889
TRUSS John 1854
PERRY Hugh T 1884
PERRY Hugh T 1884
TAYLOR William E 1853
PERRY Hugh T 1883
GOODWIN Pinckney 1858
GODWIN Pinckney 1858

35
LATHEM Sinkler 1860
LATHEM Sinkler 1860

36
ETHRIDGE Morgan 1888
HALL Alexander 1839
JOHNSON John 1889
STARKY Johan 1894
GARNER Andrew J 1890
WOODS Young A 1891
SMITH George T 1895
GARNER Andrew J 1890
GARNER Andrew J 1890
WOODS Young A 1891
WOODS Young A 1891

Helpful Hints

1. This Map's INDEX can be found on the preceding pages.
2. Refer to Map "C" to see where this Township lies within Jefferson County, Alabama.
3. Numbers within square brackets [ ] denote a multi-patentee land parcel (multi-owner). Refer to Appendix "C" for a full list of members in this group.
4. Areas that look to be crowded with Patentees usually indicate multiple sales of the same parcel (Re-issues) or Overlapping parcels. See this Township's Index for an explanation of these and other circumstances that might explain "odd" groupings of Patentees on this map.

Legend

Patent Boundary
Section Boundary
No Patents Found (or Outside County)
1., 2., 3., ... Lot Numbers (when beside a name)
[ ] Group Number (see Appendix "C")

Scale: Section = 1 mile X 1 mile (generally, with some exceptions)

Road Map

T16-S R1-W
Huntsville Meridian

Map Group 16

Cities & Towns

Trussville

Cemeteries

Jefferson Memorial Gardens
Mount Nebo Cemetery
Reed Cemetery
Taylors Chapel Cemetery
Trussville Cemetery

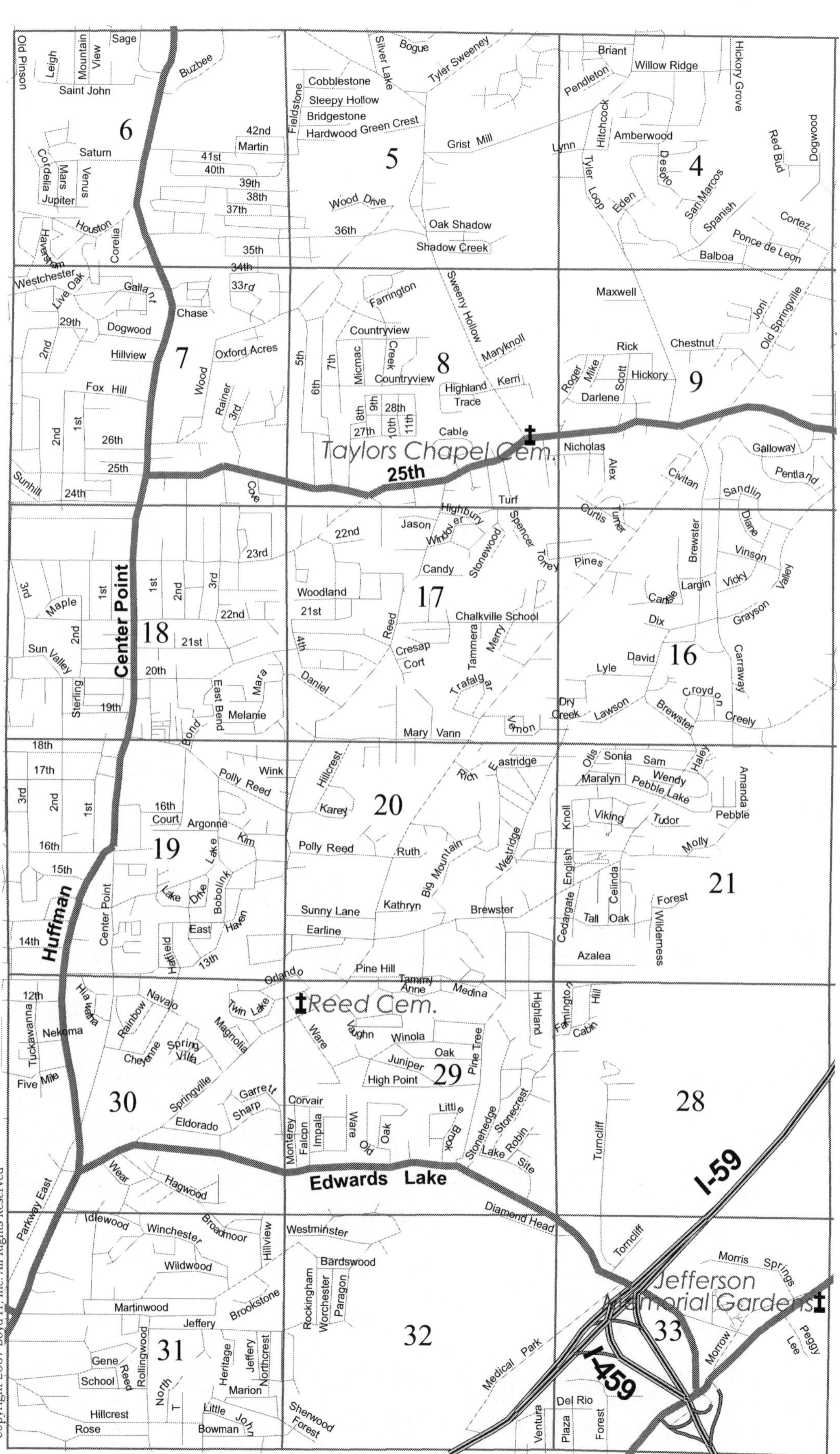

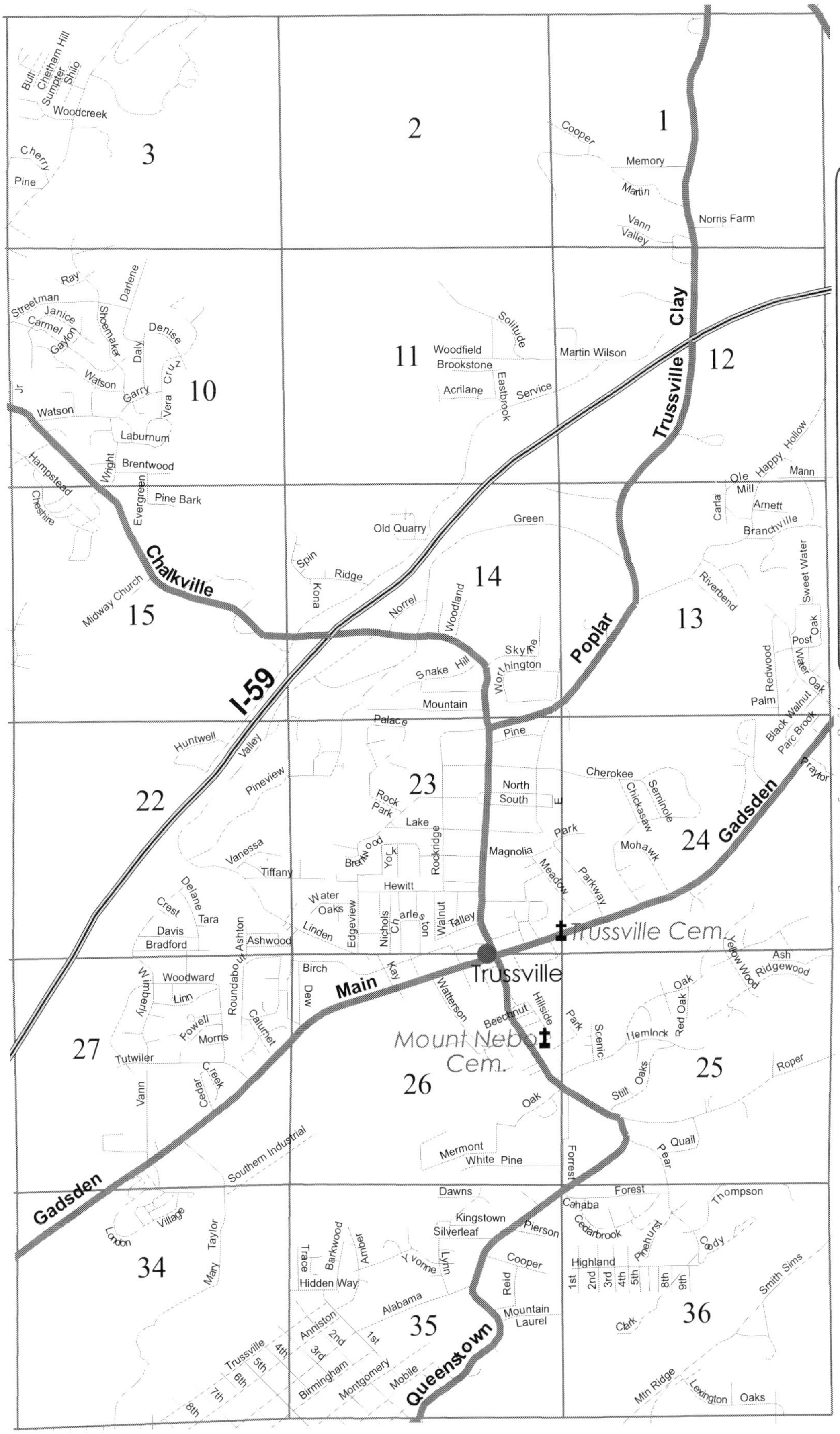

Helpful Hints

1. This road map has a number of uses, but primarily it is to help you: a) find the present location of land owned by your ancestors (at least the general area), b) find cemeteries and city-centers, and c) estimate the route/roads used by Census-takers & tax-assessors.

2. If you plan to travel to Jefferson County to locate cemeteries or land parcels, please pick up a modern travel map for the area before you do. Mapping old land parcels on modern maps is not as exact a science as you might think. Just the slightest variations in public land survey coordinates, estimates of parcel boundaries, or road-map deviations can greatly alter a map's representation of how a road either does or doesn't cross a particular parcel of land.

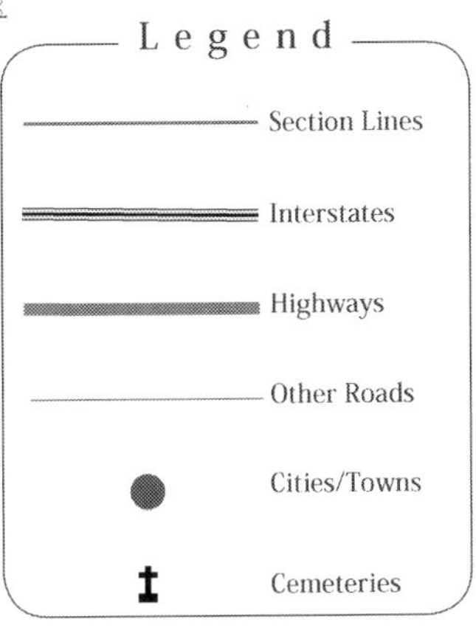

Scale: Section = 1 mile X 1 mile
(generally, with some exceptions)

Historical Map

T16-S R1-W
Huntsville Meridian

Map Group 16

Cities & Towns

Trussville

Cemeteries

Jefferson Memorial Gardens
Mount Nebo Cemetery
Reed Cemetery
Taylors Chapel Cemetery
Trussville Cemetery

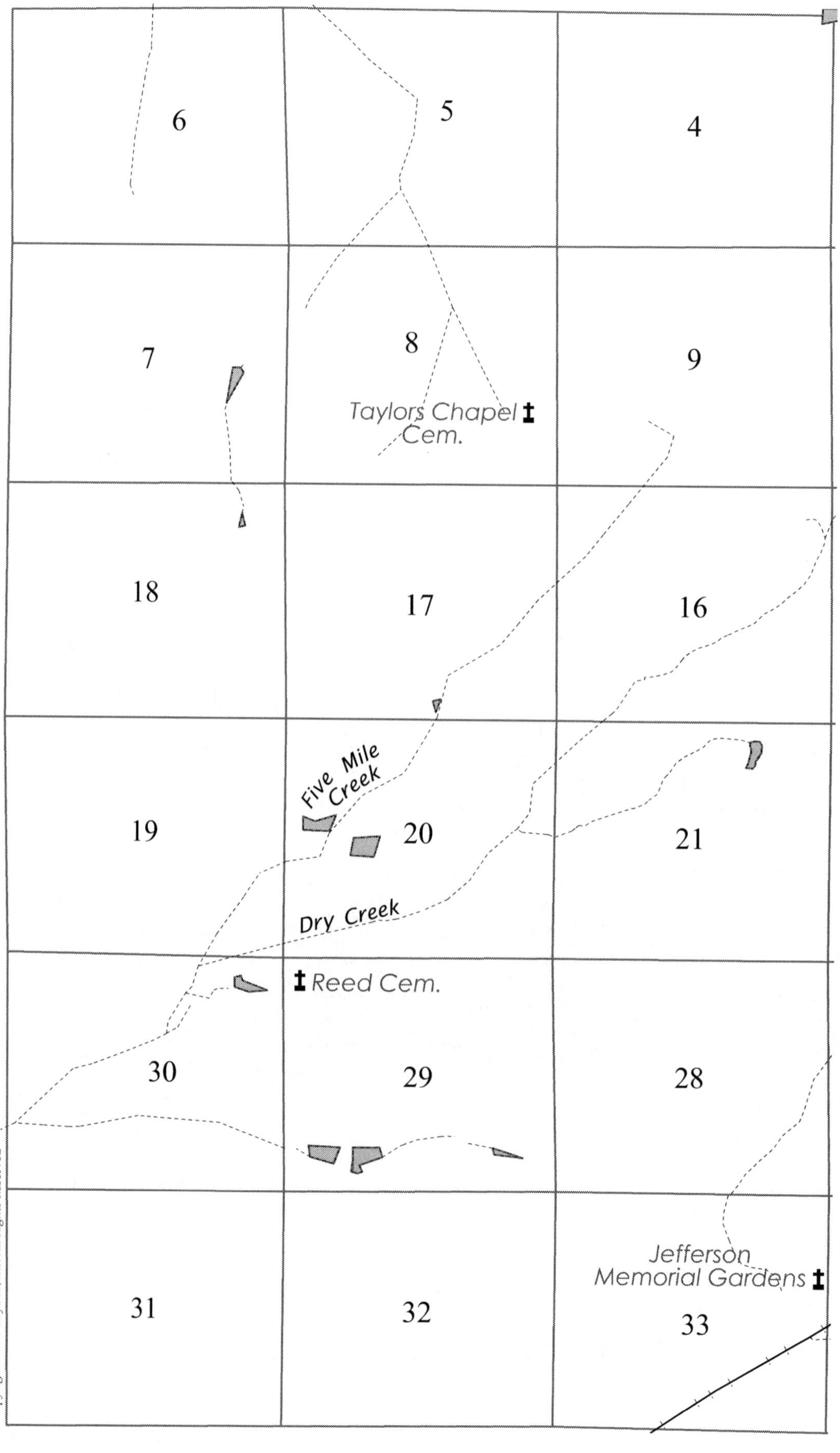

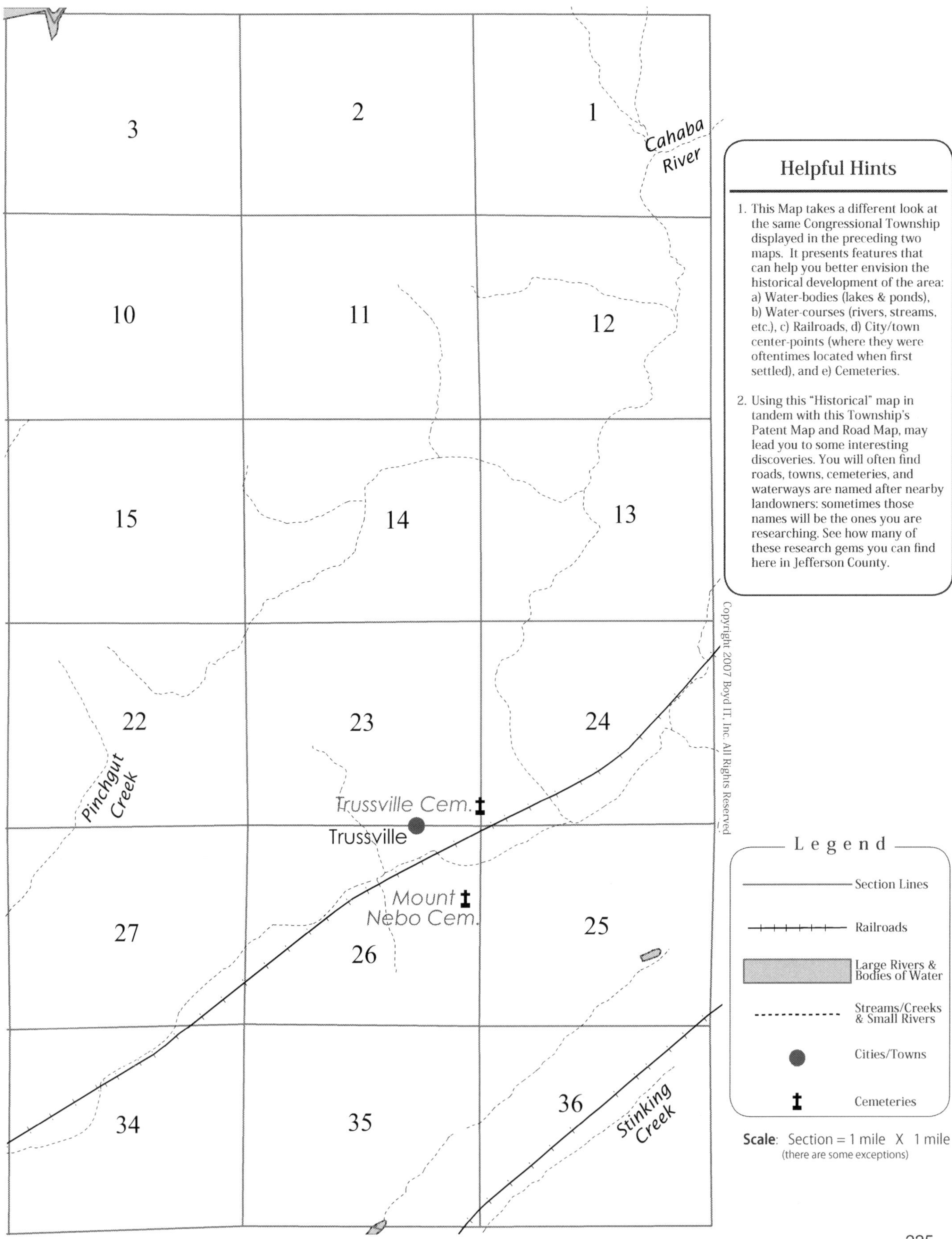
3
2
1
Cahaba River
10
11
12
15
14
13
22
23
24
Pinchgut Creek
Trussville Cem.
Trussville
Mount Nebo Cem.
27
26
25
34
35
36
Stinking Creek
Helpful Hints
1. This Map takes a different look at the same Congressional Township displayed in the preceding two maps. It presents features that can help you better envision the historical development of the area: a) Water-bodies (lakes & ponds), b) Water-courses (rivers, streams, etc.), c) Railroads, d) City/town center-points (where they were oftentimes located when first settled), and e) Cemeteries.
2. Using this "Historical" map in tandem with this Township's Patent Map and Road Map, may lead you to some interesting discoveries. You will often find roads, towns, cemeteries, and waterways are named after nearby landowners: sometimes those names will be the ones you are researching. See how many of these research gems you can find here in Jefferson County.
Copyright 2007 Boyd IT, Inc. All Rights Reserved
Legend
Section Lines
Railroads
Large Rivers & Bodies of Water
Streams/Creeks & Small Rivers
Cities/Towns
Cemeteries
Scale: Section = 1 mile X 1 mile
(there are some exceptions)

Map Group 17: Index to Land Patents

Township 16-South Range 1-East (Huntsville)

After you locate an individual in this Index, take note of the Section and Section Part then proceed to the Land Patent map on the pages immediately following. You should have no difficulty locating the corresponding parcel of land.

The "For More Info" Column will lead you to more information about the underlying Patents. See the *Legend* at right, and the "How to Use this Book" chapter, for more information.

LEGEND

"For More Info . . . " column

A = Authority (Legislative Act, See Appendix "A")
B = Block or Lot (location in Section unknown)
C = Cancelled Patent
F = Fractional Section
G = Group (Multi-Patentee Patent, see Appendix "C")
V = Overlaps another Parcel
R = Re-Issued (Parcel patented more than once)

(A & G items require you to look in the Appendixes referred to above. All other Letter-designations followed by a number require you to locate line-items in this index that possess the ID number found after the letter).

ID	Individual in Patent	Sec.	Sec. Part	Date Issued	Other Counties	For More Info . . .
2985	BIRKETT, James M	6	SE	1908-07-27		A4
3053	BRADFORD, Thomas C	4	E½SE	1823-05-01		A1 G26
3054	" "	4	E½SW	1823-05-01		A1 G26
3055	" "	4	W½SE	1823-05-01		A1 G26
3062	BRADFORD, William D	9	W½NE	1823-05-01		A1
3039	CLARK, Samuel	7	W½SE	1823-06-02		A1 G48
3038	" "	7	E½SW	1826-12-01		A1
3061	CLARK, William	7	NESE	1834-10-21		A1
3019	COBELL, Milton	32	SW	1882-09-15		A1
2966	COOKE, Elias J	29	SENW	1834-10-01		A1
2974	CROSS, George W	18	NWNW	1884-03-20		A4
2975	" "	18	SENW	1884-03-20		A4
2976	" "	18	SWNW	1884-03-20		A4
2964	DAVIS, Christopher I	3	SENW	1839-09-20	St. Clair	A1
3066	DULANY, William	17	W½NW	1824-05-24		A1
3067	" "	9	W½SW	1824-05-24		A1
2983	EDENS, Isreal S	30	N½SW	1858-06-01		A1
2984	" "	30	S½NW	1858-06-01		A1
3005	EDWARDS, John S	18	E½SW	1839-09-20		A1
3006	" "	18	NWSE	1839-09-20		A1
3007	" "	8	E½SW	1839-09-20		A1
2996	FALKS, John J	19	NENW	1839-09-20		A1
2994	FRANKLIN, John	30	N½NW	1880-02-20		A4
2986	FRAZIER, James M	3	NESW	1858-06-01	St. Clair	A1
2997	FRAZIER, John L	29	SWNW	1858-06-01		A1
2998	" "	30	N½NE	1858-06-01		A1
2999	" "	5	SWNW	1860-07-02		A1
3000	" "	6	SENE	1860-07-02		A1
3015	FRAZIER, Lewis	8	E½NW	1827-07-02		A1
3025	FRAZIER, Richardson	9	NENE	1850-04-01		A1
3027	FRAZIER, Richerson	3	SWSW	1854-07-15	St. Clair	A1
3026	" "	3	SESW	1859-04-01	St. Clair	A1
3028	" "	9	SENE	1859-04-01		A1
3020	FULLER, Mordecai	3	W½NW	1823-05-01	St. Clair	A1
3021	GALLOWAY, Patrick C	10	E½NE	1884-12-05	St. Clair	A4
3022	" "	10	E½SE	1884-12-05	St. Clair	A4
3068	GARNER, William	18	SWSE	1858-06-01		A1
3069	" "	19	E½NE	1858-06-01		A1
3070	" "	19	NWNE	1858-06-01		A1
3071	" "	20	NENW	1858-06-01		A1
3072	" "	20	SWNE	1858-06-01		A1
3073	" "	20	W½NW	1858-06-01		A1
2993	GLENN, Jane	4	NENE	1850-04-01		A1
2980	GOODWIN, Henry	19	W½SE	1858-06-01		A1
3009	GREEN, Joseph	10	SWSW	1915-11-10	St. Clair	A4
3056	GREENE, Thomas E	20	NWNE	1912-10-12		A1

ID	Individual in Patent	Sec.	Sec. Part	Date Issued	Other Counties	For More Info . . .
3074	HARPER, William	18	NENW	1839-09-20		A1
3052	HARRIS, Susan	18	NWNE	1882-11-20		A4
2995	HEFNER, John	3	NENW	1849-08-01	St. Clair	A1
3029	HITT, Robert	7	NWSW	1854-07-15		A1
3030	" "	7	S½NW	1858-06-01		A1
3031	" "	7	SWSW	1858-06-01		A1
3010	HOLLINGSWORTH, Larkin B	10	E½SW	1891-06-08	St. Clair	A4
2953	HOLMES, Ambrose	29	SW	1860-07-02		A1
2954	" "	30	SESE	1860-07-02		A1
2955	" "	31	NENE	1860-07-02		A1
2956	" "	32	W½NW	1860-07-02		A1
3024	KEATON, Reuben	18	E½NE	1824-05-21		A1
3047	LATHAM, Sinkler	9	NWSE	1853-08-01		A1
3050	LATHEM, Sinkler	18	SWNE	1839-09-20		A1
3049	" "	18	NESE	1848-07-01		A1
3048	" "	17	NWSW	1858-06-01		A1
3051	" "	8	NWSW	1858-06-01		A1
3016	LAWLEY, Lewis	5	E½SW	1824-04-30		A1
3017	" "	8	W½NW	1826-10-05		A1
2950	LESLEY, Abel	10	SWSE	1858-06-01	St. Clair	A1
2951	MACKEY, Alexander J	5	SENE	1839-09-20		A1
3058	MANN, Thomas R	20	E½NE	1890-03-19		A4
2988	MARTIN, James	9	E½SW	1823-07-09		A1
2987	" "	8	E½SE	1824-10-20		A1
3003	MARTIN, John	8	SENE	1839-09-20		A1
3032	MARTIN, Robert N	19	NESE	1852-01-01		A1
3034	" "	20	SWSW	1852-01-01		A1
3033	" "	20	NESE	1858-06-01		A1
3035	" "	21	SW	1858-06-01	St. Clair	A1
3078	MARTIN, William	9	E½NW	1823-05-01		A1
3079	" "	9	W½NW	1823-05-01		A1
3075	" "	29	S½SE	1858-06-01		A1
3076	" "	32	E½NW	1858-06-01		A1
3077	" "	32	W½NE	1858-06-01		A1
3041	MASSEY, Samuel	4	E½NW	1823-05-01		A1
3044	" "	4	W½SW	1823-05-01		A1
3045	" "	5	E½SE	1823-05-01		A1
3042	" "	4	W½NE	1824-04-26		A1
3043	" "	4	W½NW	1824-05-10		A1
3064	MASSEY, William D	5	NWNW	1850-04-01		A1
3063	" "	5	NENE	1858-06-01		A1
3065	" "	6	NENE	1858-06-01		A1
2989	MASTERS, James	5	W½NE	1824-05-04		A1
3011	MELTON, Laura J	10	NWNE	1884-12-05	St. Clair	A4 G173
3012	" "	10	NWSE	1884-12-05	St. Clair	A4 G173
3013	" "	10	SENW	1884-12-05	St. Clair	A4 G173
3014	" "	10	SWNE	1884-12-05	St. Clair	A4 G173
3011	MELTON, Thomas J	10	NWNE	1884-12-05	St. Clair	A4 G173
3012	" "	10	NWSE	1884-12-05	St. Clair	A4 G173
3013	" "	10	SENW	1884-12-05	St. Clair	A4 G173
3014	" "	10	SWNE	1884-12-05	St. Clair	A4 G173
3080	MOORE, William	18	SESE	1852-01-01		A1
3046	MURPHEY, Samuel	32	E½NE	1825-06-20		A1
3084	PERKINS, William	7	N½NW	1854-07-15		A1
3086	" "	8	SWNE	1854-07-15		A1
3083	" "	6	SWSW	1858-06-01		A1
3085	" "	8	NENE	1858-06-01		A1
3081	" "	6	E½SW	1859-04-01		A1
3082	" "	6	S½NW	1859-04-01		A1
3036	PIERCE, Salmon	30	SWNE	1884-01-15		A1
3037	" "	6	NWNW	1884-01-15		A1
2963	PRAYTOR, Bezaleel	29	NWNW	1852-01-01		A1
2959	" "	18	NWSW	1858-06-01		A1
2960	" "	19	NESW	1858-06-01		A1
2961	" "	19	SENW	1858-06-01		A1
2962	" "	19	SWNE	1858-06-01		A1
3004	PRESLEY, John	3	NWSW	1839-09-20	St. Clair	A1
3087	PRESLEY, William R	20	E½SW	1858-06-01		A1
3088	" "	29	SWNE	1858-06-01		A1
2952	REAVIS, Allen	29	NESE	1858-06-01		A1
2965	REID, Davis	10	N½NW	1891-05-29	St. Clair	A4
2967	ROBERSON, George	7	SESE	1854-07-15		A1
2972	ROBINSON, George	8	SWSW	1839-09-20		A1

ID	Individual in Patent	Sec.	Sec. Part	Date Issued	Other Counties	For More Info . . .
2973	ROBINSON, George (Cont'd)	8	W½SE	1848-07-01		A1
2968	" "	17	N½SE	1858-06-01		A1
2969	" "	17	NE	1858-06-01		A1
2970	" "	17	NESW	1858-06-01		A1
2971	" "	17	SENW	1858-06-01		A1
2977	ROPER, George W	20	NWSE	1889-11-21		A4
2978	" "	20	S½SE	1889-11-21		A4
3090	ROWAN, William	19	NWNW	1834-10-01		A1
3089	" "	18	SWSW	1838-08-28		A1
2990	SIMS, James T	30	S½SW	1894-04-19		A4
2991	" "	30	W½SE	1894-04-19		A4
2979	SKAGGS, George W	32	S½SE	1885-06-20		A4
3091	SLAPPY, William	30	NESE	1894-12-07		A4
3092	" "	30	SENE	1894-12-07		A4
3023	SMITH, Redden	8	NWNE	1839-09-20		A1
3053	TALLEY, Nicholas	4	E½SE	1823-05-01		A1 G26
3054	" "	4	E½SW	1823-05-01		A1 G26
3055	" "	4	W½SE	1823-05-01		A1 G26
3001	TILLMAN, John L	10	NWSW	1889-08-16	St. Clair	A4
3002	" "	10	SWNW	1889-08-16	St. Clair	A4
3039	TOWNBY, John	7	W½SE	1823-06-02		A1 G48
2982	TOWNLEY, Henry W	29	NENW	1852-01-01		A1
2981	TOWNLY, Henry M	19	SESE	1839-09-20		A1
2992	TRUSS, James	7	W½NE	1824-05-25		A1
3057	TRUSS, Thomas K	5	SWSW	1852-01-01		A1
3059	TRUSS, Thomas R	19	SWNW	1858-06-01		A1
3060	TRUSS, Warren	5	W½SE	1823-07-09		A1
2957	TUCKER, Anderson B	6	NENW	1858-06-01		A1
2958	" "	6	W½NE	1858-06-01		A1
3040	WHITE, Samuel M	32	N½SE	1884-11-13		A1
3008	WORTHINGTON, John	5	E½NW	1824-05-25		A1
3018	WORTHINGTON, Marcus A	19	NWSW	1858-06-01		A1

Patent Map

T16-S R1-E
Huntsville Meridian

Map Group 17

Township Statistics

Parcels Mapped	:	143
Number of Patents	:	107
Number of Individuals	:	78
Patentees Identified	:	76
Number of Surnames	:	62
Multi-Patentee Parcels	:	8
Oldest Patent Date	:	5/1/1823
Most Recent Patent	:	11/10/1915
Block/Lot Parcels	:	0
Parcels Re - Issued	:	0
Parcels that Overlap	:	0
Cities and Towns	:	0
Cemeteries	:	0

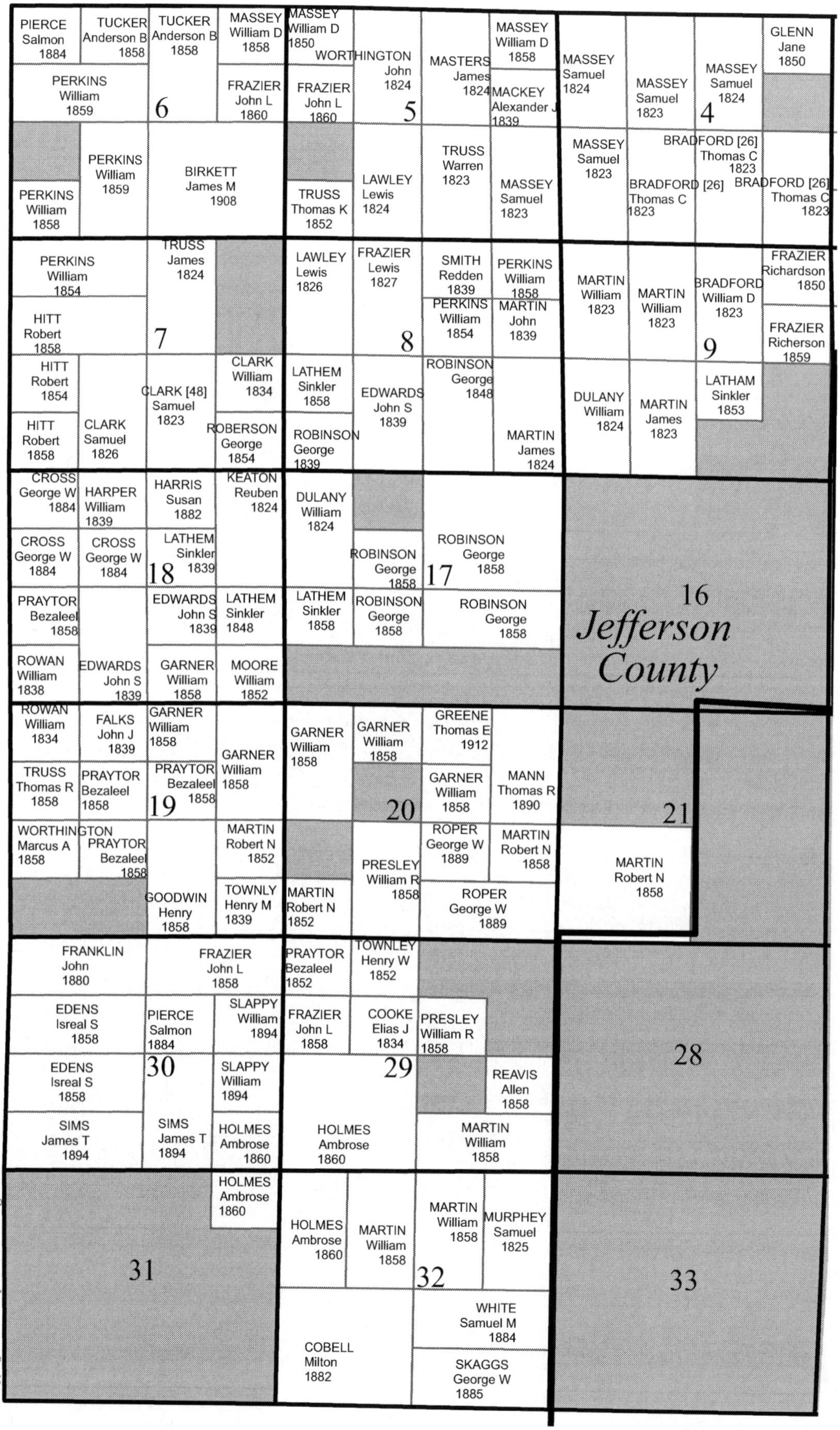

6
PIERCE Salmon 1884
TUCKER Anderson B 1858
TUCKER Anderson B 1858
MASSEY William D 1858
PERKINS William 1859
FRAZIER John L 1860
PERKINS William 1859
BIRKETT James M 1908
PERKINS William 1858

5
MASSEY William D 1850
WORTHINGTON John 1824
FRAZIER John L 1860
MASTERS James 1824
MASSEY William D 1858
MACKEY Alexander J 1839
TRUSS Thomas K 1852
LAWLEY Lewis 1824
TRUSS Warren 1823
MASSEY Samuel 1823

4
MASSEY Samuel 1824
MASSEY Samuel 1823
MASSEY Samuel 1824
GLENN Jane 1850
MASSEY Samuel 1823
BRADFORD [26] Thomas C 1823
BRADFORD [26] Thomas C 1823
BRADFORD [26] Thomas C 1823

7
PERKINS William 1854
TRUSS James 1824
HITT Robert 1858
HITT Robert 1854
CLARK [48] Samuel 1823
CLARK William 1834
HITT Robert 1858
CLARK Samuel 1826
ROBERSON George 1854

8
LAWLEY Lewis 1826
FRAZIER Lewis 1827
SMITH Redden 1839
PERKINS William 1858
PERKINS William 1854
MARTIN John 1839
LATHEM Sinkler 1858
EDWARDS John S 1839
ROBINSON George 1848
ROBINSON George 1839
MARTIN James 1824

9
MARTIN William 1823
MARTIN William 1823
BRADFORD William D 1823
FRAZIER Richardson 1850
FRAZIER Richerson 1859
DULANY William 1824
MARTIN James 1823
LATHAM Sinkler 1853

18
CROSS George W 1884
HARPER William 1839
HARRIS Susan 1882
KEATON Reuben 1824
CROSS George W 1884
CROSS George W 1884
LATHEM Sinkler 1839
PRAYTOR Bezaleel 1858
EDWARDS John S 1839
LATHEM Sinkler 1848
ROWAN William 1838
EDWARDS John S 1839
GARNER William 1858
MOORE William 1852

17
DULANY William 1824
ROBINSON George 1858
ROBINSON George 1858
LATHEM Sinkler 1858
ROBINSON George 1858
ROBINSON George 1858

16
Jefferson County

19
ROWAN William 1834
FALKS John J 1839
GARNER William 1858
GARNER William 1858
TRUSS Thomas R 1858
PRAYTOR Bezaleel 1858
PRAYTOR Bezaleel 1858
WORTHINGTON Marcus A 1858
PRAYTOR Bezaleel 1858
MARTIN Robert N 1852
GOODWIN Henry 1858
TOWNLY Henry M 1839

20
GARNER William 1858
GARNER William 1858
GREENE Thomas E 1912
GARNER William 1858
MANN Thomas R 1890
ROPER George W 1889
MARTIN Robert N 1858
PRESLEY William R 1858
MARTIN Robert N 1852
ROPER George W 1889

21
MARTIN Robert N 1858

30
FRANKLIN John 1880
FRAZIER John L 1858
EDENS Isreal S 1858
PIERCE Salmon 1884
SLAPPY William 1894
EDENS Isreal S 1858
SLAPPY William 1894
SIMS James T 1894
SIMS James T 1894
HOLMES Ambrose 1860

29
PRAYTOR Bezaleel 1852
TOWNLEY Henry W 1852
FRAZIER John L 1858
COOKE Elias J 1834
PRESLEY William R 1858
REAVIS Allen 1858
HOLMES Ambrose 1860
MARTIN William 1858

28

31
HOLMES Ambrose 1860

32
HOLMES Ambrose 1860
MARTIN William 1858
MARTIN William 1858
MURPHEY Samuel 1825
WHITE Samuel M 1884
COBELL Milton 1882
SKAGGS George W 1885

33

FULLER Mordecai 1823
HEFNER John 1849
DAVIS Christopher 1839
PRESLEY John 1839
FRAZIER James M 1858
FRAZIER Richerson 1854
FRAZIER Richerson 1859
3
2
1
REID Davis 1891
MELTON [173] Laura J 1884
GALLOWAY Patrick C 1884
TILLMAN John L 1889
MELTON [173] Laura J 1884
MELTON [173] Laura J 1884
TILLMAN John L 1889
10
MELTON [173] Laura J 1884
HOLLINGSWORTH Larkin B 1891
GREEN Joseph 1915
LESLEY Abel 1858
GALLOWAY Patrick C 1884
11
12
15
14
13
Saint Clair County
22
23
24
27
26
25
34
35
36

Helpful Hints

1. This Map's INDEX can be found on the preceding pages.
2. Refer to Map "C" to see where this Township lies within Jefferson County, Alabama.
3. Numbers within square brackets [ ] denote a multi-patentee land parcel (multi-owner). Refer to Appendix "C" for a full list of members in this group.
4. Areas that look to be crowded with Patentees usually indicate multiple sales of the same parcel (Re-issues) or Overlapping parcels. See this Township's Index for an explanation of these and other circumstances that might explain "odd" groupings of Patentees on this map.

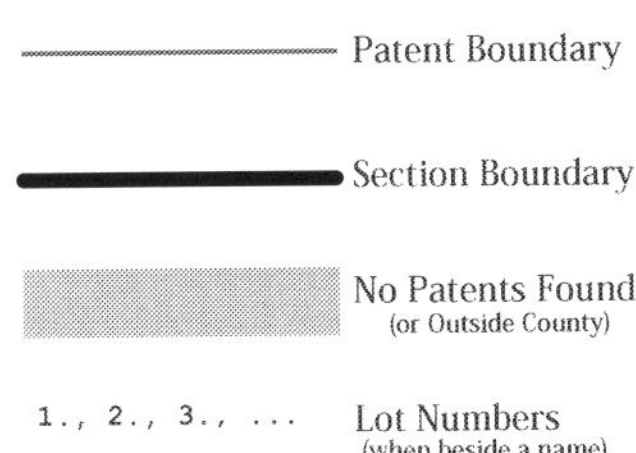

Legend

Patent Boundary
Section Boundary
No Patents Found (or Outside County)
1., 2., 3., ... Lot Numbers (when beside a name)
[ ] Group Number (see Appendix "C")

Scale: Section = 1 mile X 1 mile (generally, with some exceptions)

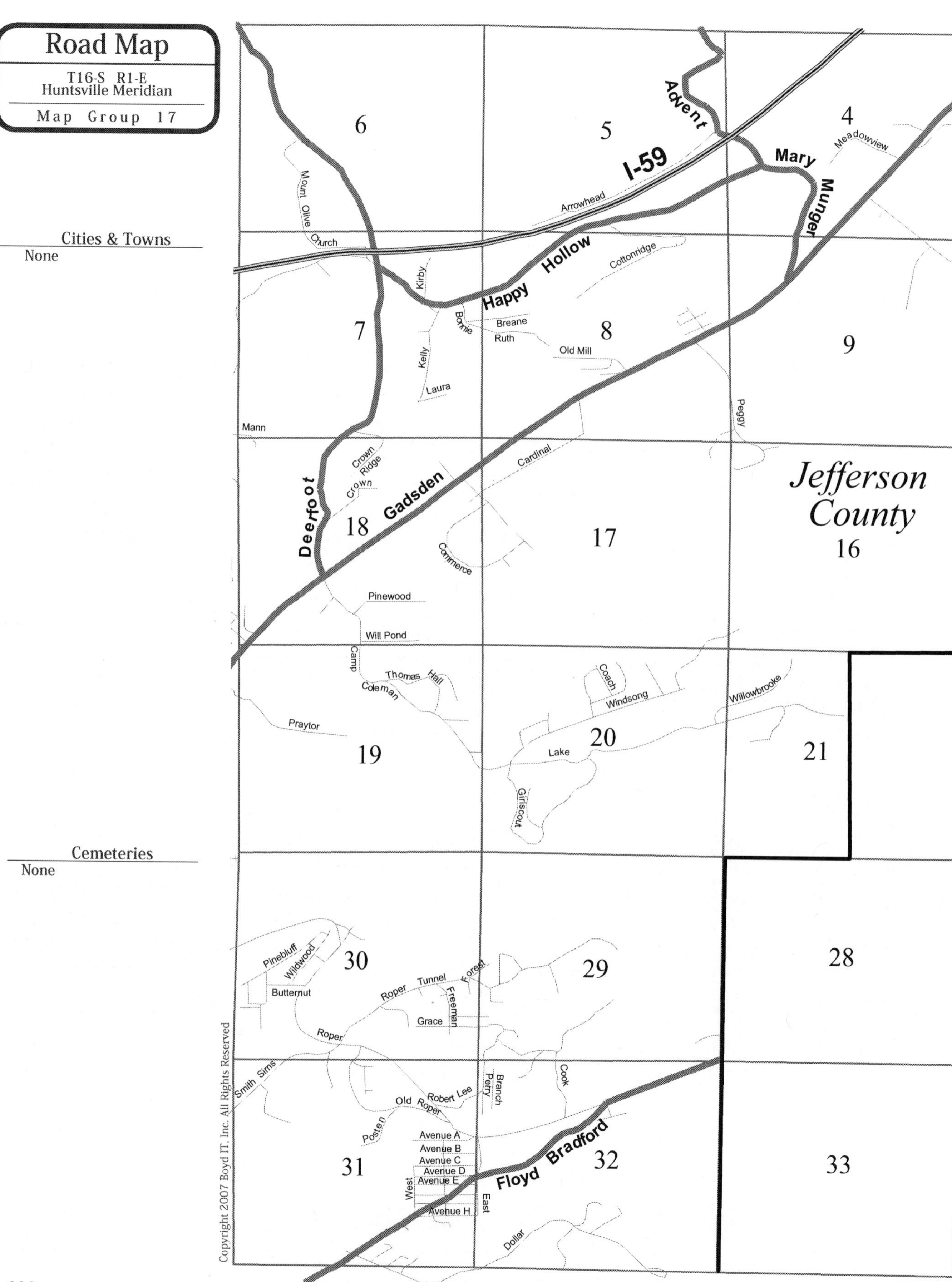
Road Map
T16-S R1-E
Huntsville Meridian
Map Group 17
Cities & Towns
None
Cemeteries
None
Jefferson County
I-59
Advent
Mary
Munger
Meadowview
Arrowhead
Mount Olive Church
Happy Hollow
Cottonridge
Kirby
Bonnie
Breane
Ruth
Old Mill
Kelly
Laura
Mann
Peggy
Crown Ridge
Crown
Deerfoot
Gadsden
Cardinal
Commerce
Pinewood
Will Pond
Camp
Thomas
Hall
Coleman
Praytor
Coach
Windsong
Willowbrooke
Lake
Girlscout
Pinebluff
Wildwood
Butternut
Roper
Tunnel
Forest
Freeman
Grace
Smith
Sims
Robert Lee
Old Roper
Branch
Perry
Cook
Posten
Avenue A
Avenue B
Avenue C
Avenue D
Avenue E
Avenue H
West
East
Floyd Bradford
Dollar
1
4
5
6
7
8
9
16
17
18
19
20
21
28
29
30
31
32
33
Copyright 2007 Boyd IT, Inc. All Rights Reserved

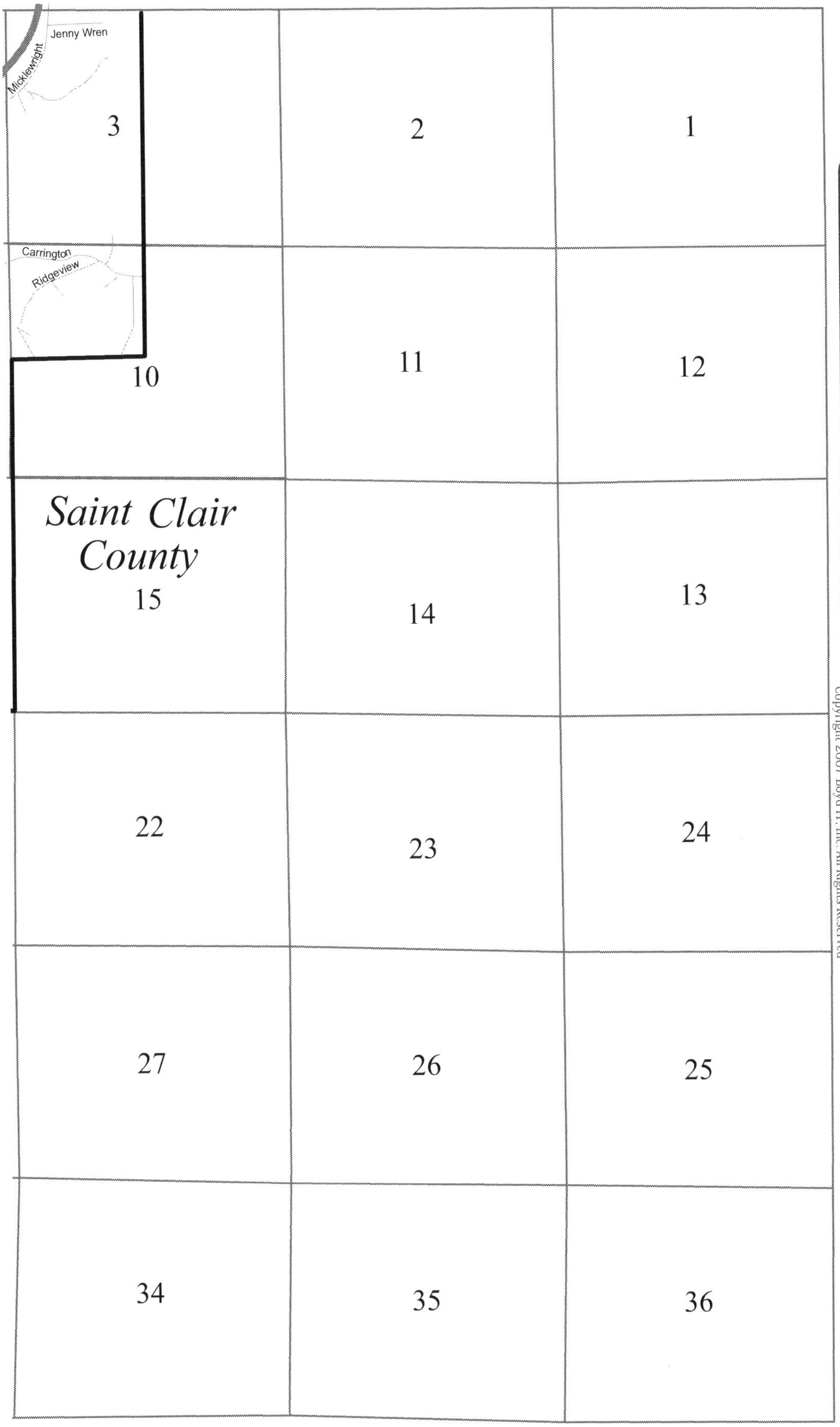

Helpful Hints

1. This road map has a number of uses, but primarily it is to help you: a) find the present location of land owned by your ancestors (at least the general area), b) find cemeteries and city-centers, and c) estimate the route/roads used by Census-takers & tax-assessors.

2. If you plan to travel to Jefferson County to locate cemeteries or land parcels, please pick up a modern travel map for the area before you do. Mapping old land parcels on modern maps is not as exact a science as you might think. Just the slightest variations in public land survey coordinates, estimates of parcel boundaries, or road-map deviations can greatly alter a map's representation of how a road either does or doesn't cross a particular parcel of land.

Legend

Section Lines

Interstates

Highways

Other Roads

Cities/Towns

Cemeteries

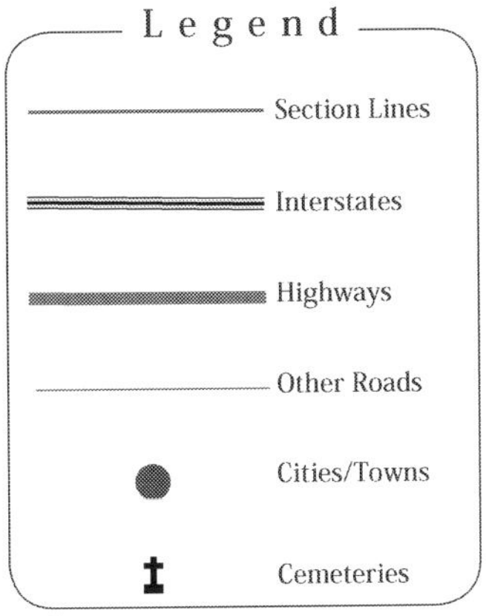

Scale: Section = 1 mile X 1 mile (generally, with some exceptions)

Historical Map

T16-S R1-E
Huntsville Meridian

Map Group 17

Cities & Towns
None

Cemeteries
None

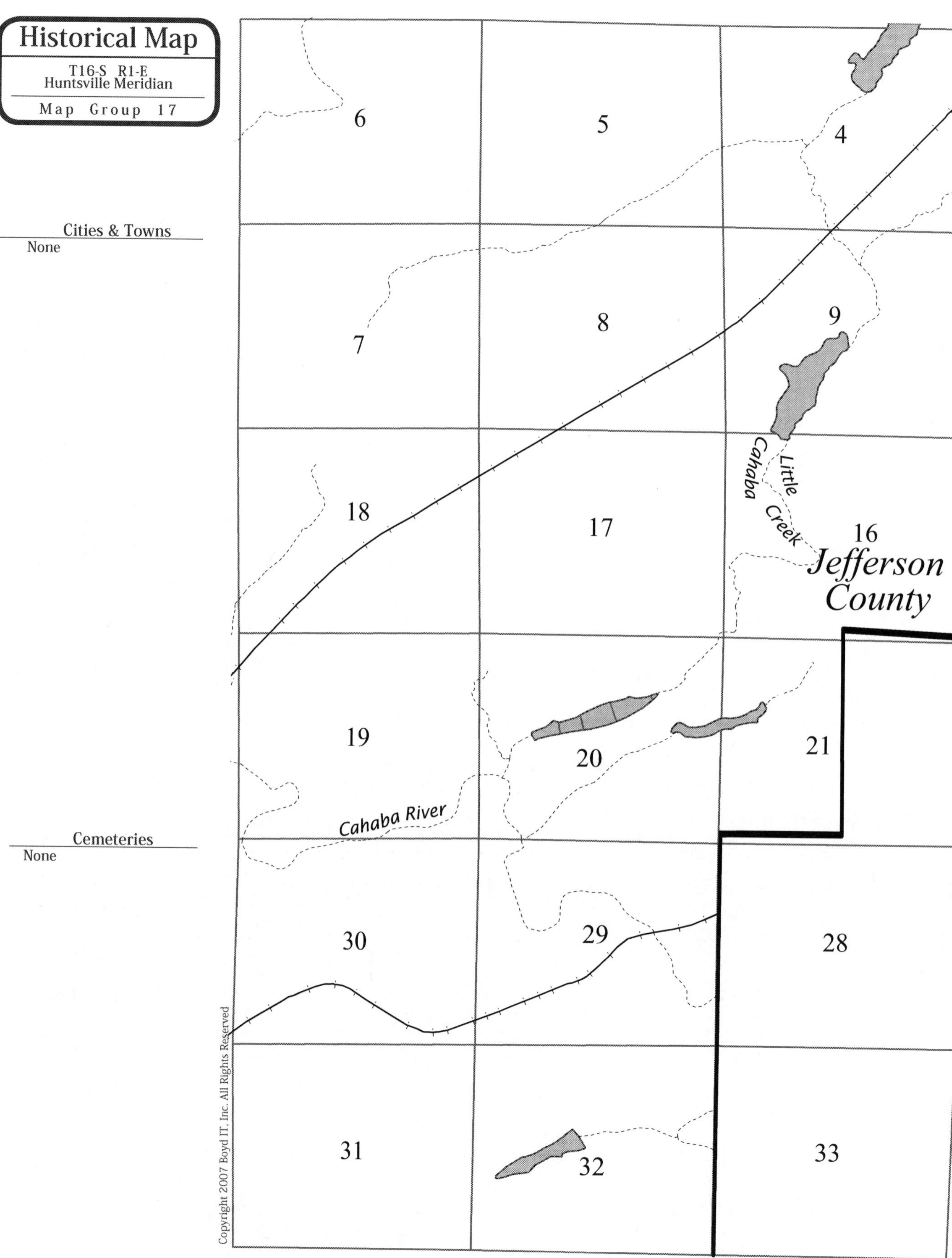

3
2
1
10
11
12
Saint Clair County
15
14
13
22
23
24
27
26
25
34
35
36

Helpful Hints

1. This Map takes a different look at the same Congressional Township displayed in the preceding two maps. It presents features that can help you better envision the historical development of the area: a) Water-bodies (lakes & ponds), b) Water-courses (rivers, streams, etc.), c) Railroads, d) City/town center-points (where they were oftentimes located when first settled), and e) Cemeteries.

2. Using this "Historical" map in tandem with this Township's Patent Map and Road Map, may lead you to some interesting discoveries. You will often find roads, towns, cemeteries, and waterways are named after nearby landowners: sometimes those names will be the ones you are researching. See how many of these research gems you can find here in Jefferson County.

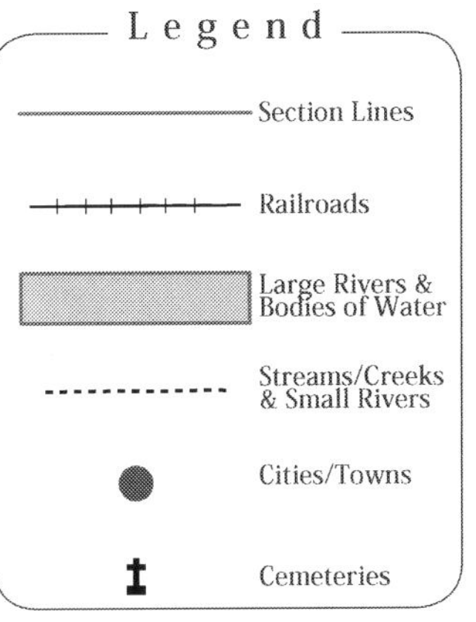

Scale: Section = 1 mile X 1 mile
(there are some exceptions)

Map Group 18: Index to Land Patents

Township 17-South Range 7-West (Huntsville)

After you locate an individual in this Index, take note of the Section and Section Part then proceed to the Land Patent map on the pages immediately following. You should have no difficulty locating the corresponding parcel of land.

The "For More Info" Column will lead you to more information about the underlying Patents. See the *Legend* at right, and the "How to Use this Book" chapter, for more information.

LEGEND

"For More Info . . . " column

A = Authority (Legislative Act, See Appendix "A")
B = Block or Lot (location in Section unknown)
C = Cancelled Patent
F = Fractional Section
G = Group (Multi-Patentee Patent, see Appendix "C")
V = Overlaps another Parcel
R = Re-Issued (Parcel patented more than once)

(A & G items require you to look in the Appendixes referred to above. All other Letter-designations followed by a number require you to locate line-items in this index that possess the ID number found after the letter).

ID	Individual in Patent	Sec.	Sec. Part	Date Issued	Other Counties	For More Info . . .
3097	BRADLEY, Francis M	28	W½NE	1883-10-01	Walker	A4
3098	" "	28	W½SE	1883-10-01	Walker	A4 F
3106	CAIN, James	36	NWSW	1850-04-01		A1
3107	DUNN, James M	33	SESW	1904-07-27	Walker	A4
3094	ESPEY, Andrew J	36	NESE	1882-06-30		A1
3134	FRANKLIN, Thomas J	27	N½SE	1890-07-03	Walker	A4
3133	HARRIS, Thomas C	25	NESW	1891-06-18	Walker	A1
3104	HOPKINS, Isaac T	25	SESW	1839-09-20	Walker	A1
3122	HOPKINS, Robert	27	SWNW	1840-11-10	Walker	A1
3095	HUMBER, Charles C	27		1839-09-20	Walker	A1 F
3111	HUMBER, John	33	SWE½	1837-03-30	Walker	A1 F
3112	" "	34	S½	1839-09-20	Walker	A1 F
3115	HUMBER, Joseph E	36	S½SW	1891-06-29		A4
3116	" "	36	W½SE	1891-06-29		A4
3125	JOHNSON, Samuel J	28	E½SW	1883-10-01	Walker	A4
3126	" "	28	SENW	1883-10-01	Walker	A4
3127	" "	28	SWSW	1883-10-01	Walker	A4
3093	JOHNSTON, Allen H	28	N½NW	1858-06-01	Walker	A1
3110	JOHNSTON, Jesse	33	B	1858-06-01	Walker	A1 F
3135	KNIGHT, Thomas M	26	S½SW	1885-03-16	Walker	A1 F
3096	MADDOX, Elizabeth	35	E½NE	1884-03-20	Walker	A4 G160
3099	MADDOX, George W	35	SESE	1891-06-29	Walker	A1
3108	MADDOX, Jeremiah	35	N½SE	1884-03-20	Walker	A4
3109	" "	35	W½NE	1884-03-20	Walker	A4
3096	MADDOX, John	35	E½NE	1884-03-20	Walker	A4 G160
3120	MADDOX, Marion D	25	W½SW	1887-07-01	Walker	A1
3140	MEDLEN, William R	28	NENE	1858-06-01	Walker	A1
3141	" "	28	NESE	1858-06-01	Walker	A1 F
3142	" "	28	SENE	1858-06-01	Walker	A1
3123	PATTON, Samuel B	25		1824-10-20	Walker	A1 F R3100, 3124
3124	" "	25		1915-08-12	Walker	A1 F R3100, 3123
3113	PRESCOTT, John	34	SE	1834-10-21	Walker	A1 F
3114	RHEA, John S	27	NENE	1891-11-23	Walker	A4
3117	RHEA, Joseph W	27	NWNW	1891-06-08	Walker	A4
3118	" "	27	SENW	1891-06-08	Walker	A4
3145	RHEA, William	27	SENE	1858-06-01	Walker	A1
3146	" "	27	W½NE	1858-06-01	Walker	A1
3143	" "	26	N½SW	1861-07-01	Walker	A1 F
3144	" "	26	SWNW	1861-07-01	Walker	A1
3100	RICHARDSON, Hiram	25		1839-09-20	Walker	A1 F R3123, 3124
3101	" "	26	NE	1839-09-20	Walker	A1 F R3119
3102	" "	26	SE	1839-09-20	Walker	A1 F
3119	RICHARDSON, Josiah	26	NE	1834-10-21	Walker	A1 F R3101
3128	ROBERTSON, Samuel J	26	NWNW	1891-06-29	Walker	A4
3137	ROGERS, William B	36	SWNW	1835-10-01		A1
3138	SMITH, William B	27	S½SE	1887-07-01	Walker	A1

ID	Individual in Patent	Sec.	Sec. Part	Date Issued	Other Counties	For More Info . . .
3139	SMITH, William B (Cont'd)	34	E½NE	1887-07-01	Walker	A1
3121	STONE, Richard	33	E½NE	1861-07-01	Walker	A1
3103	THACKER, Isaac A	25	SE	1916-01-19	Walker	A4
3131	THOMPSON, Samuel	35	NW	1834-10-21	Walker	A1 F
3129	" "	27	SW	1837-03-30	Walker	A1 F
3130	" "	34	NW	1839-09-20	Walker	A1 F
3132	" "	35	SW	1839-09-20	Walker	A1 F
3136	THOMPSON, Thomas	28		1824-05-28	Walker	A1 F
3105	WILKEY, Isham	36	E½NW	1895-08-08		A4

Patent Map

T17-S R7-W
Huntsville Meridian

Map Group 18

Township Statistics

Parcels Mapped	:	54
Number of Patents	:	44
Number of Individuals	:	36
Patentees Identified	:	35
Number of Surnames	:	24
Multi-Patentee Parcels	:	1
Oldest Patent Date	:	5/28/1824
Most Recent Patent	:	1/19/1916
Block/Lot Parcels	:	1
Parcels Re - Issued	:	2
Parcels that Overlap	:	0
Cities and Towns	:	0
Cemeteries	:	0

Note: the area contained in this map amounts to far less than a full Township. Therefore, its contents are completely on this single page (instead of a "normal" 2-page spread).

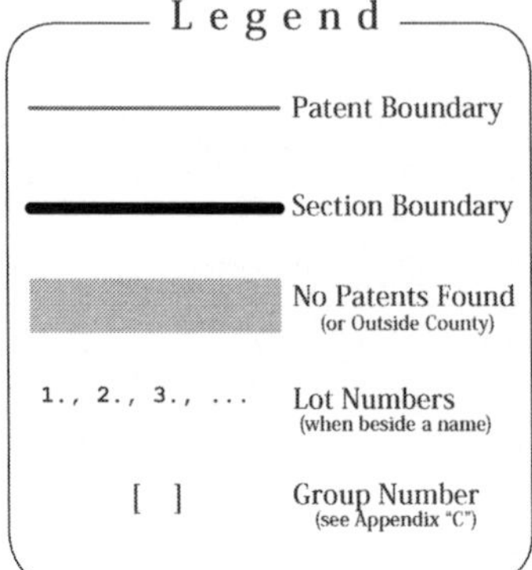

Scale: Section = 1 mile X 1 mile
(generally, with some exceptions)

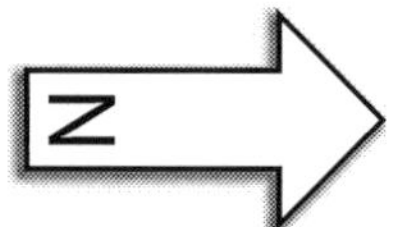

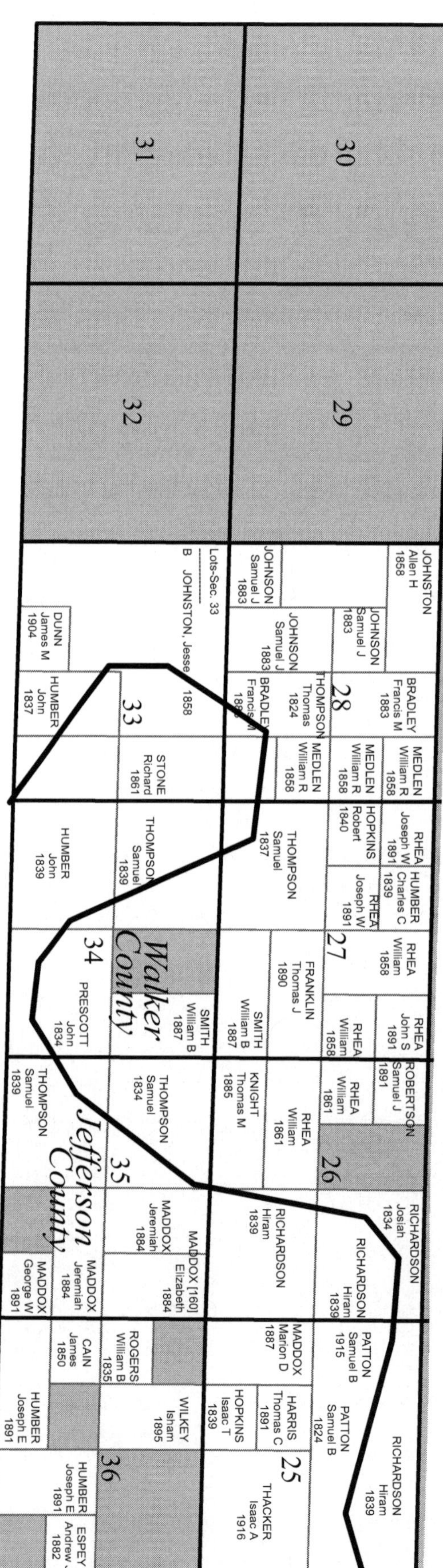

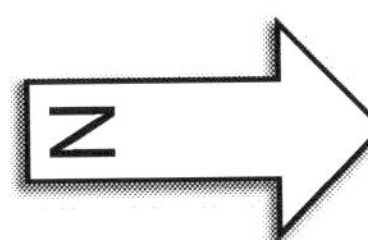

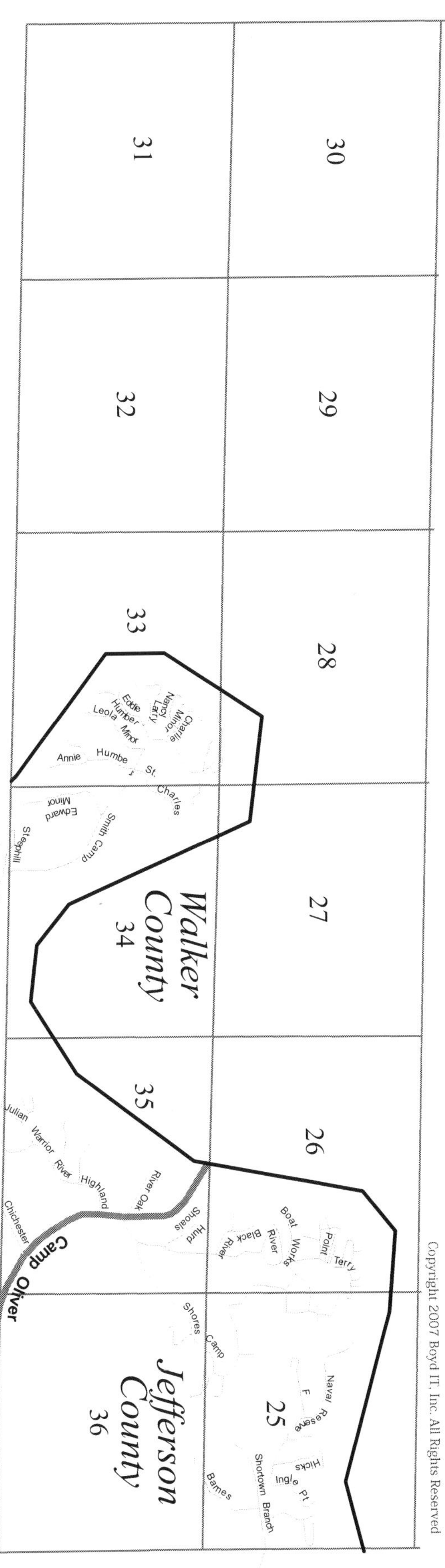

Road Map

T17-S R7-W
Huntsville Meridian

Map Group 18

Note: the area contained in this map amounts to far less than a full Township. Therefore, its contents are completely on this single page (instead of a "normal" 2-page spread).

Cities & Towns

None

Cemeteries

None

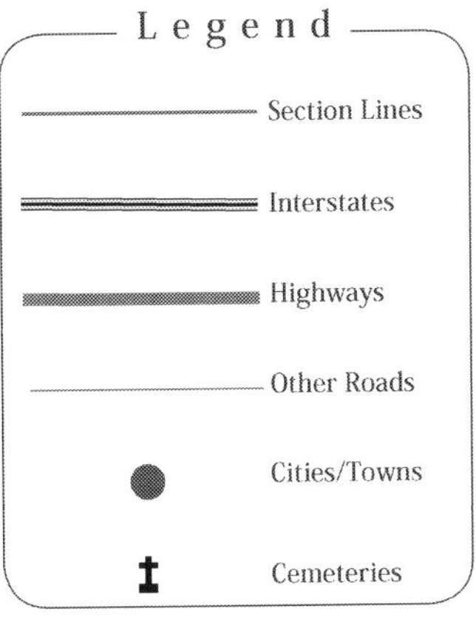

Scale: Section = 1 mile X 1 mile
(generally, with some exceptions)

Historical Map

T17-S R7-W
Huntsville Meridian

Map Group 18

Note: the area contained in this map amounts to far less than a full Township. Therefore, its contents are completely on this single page (instead of a "normal" 2-page spread).

Cities & Towns

None

Cemeteries

None

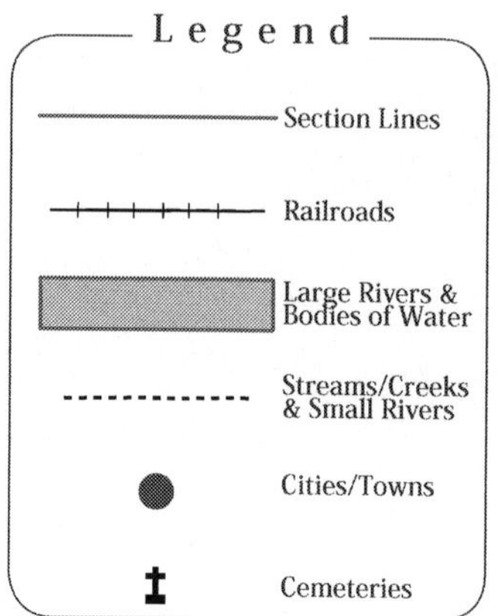

Scale: Section = 1 mile X 1 mile
(there are some exceptions)

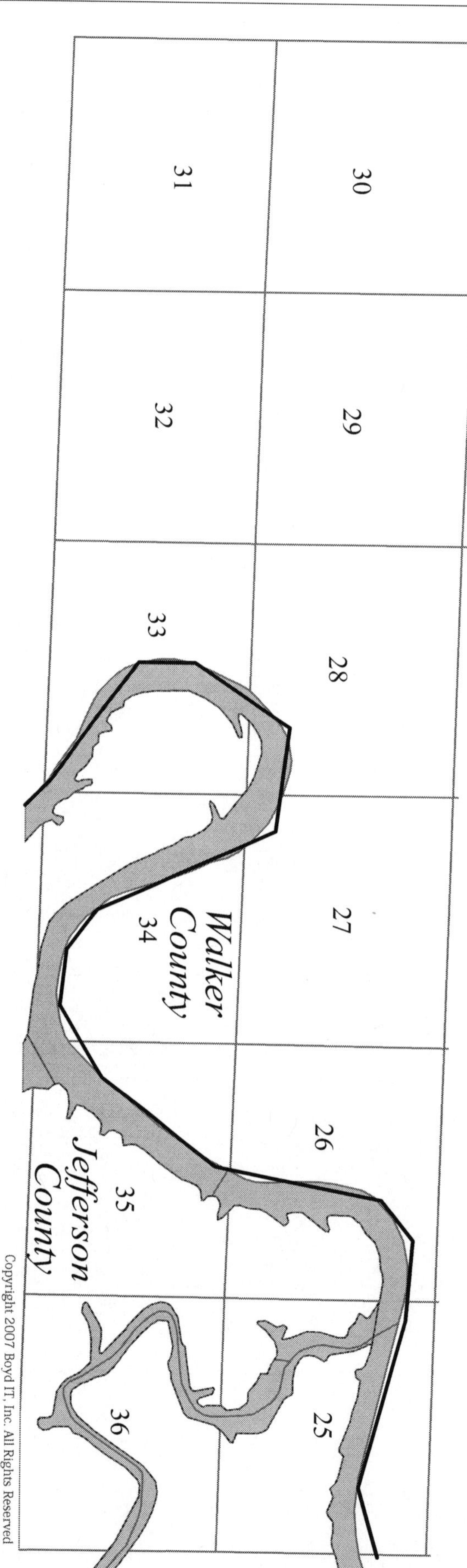

Map Group 19: Index to Land Patents

Township 17-South Range 6-West (Huntsville)

After you locate an individual in this Index, take note of the Section and Section Part then proceed to the Land Patent map on the pages immediately following. You should have no difficulty locating the corresponding parcel of land.

The "For More Info" Column will lead you to more information about the underlying Patents. See the *Legend* at right, and the "How to Use this Book" chapter, for more information.

LEGEND

"For More Info . . . " column

A = Authority (Legislative Act, See Appendix "A")
B = Block or Lot (location in Section unknown)
C = Cancelled Patent
F = Fractional Section
G = Group (Multi-Patentee Patent, see Appendix "C")
V = Overlaps another Parcel
R = Re-Issued (Parcel patented more than once)

(A & G items require you to look in the Appendixes referred to above. All other Letter-designations followed by a number require you to locate line-items in this index that possess the ID number found after the letter).

ID	Individual in Patent	Sec.	Sec. Part	Date Issued	Other Counties	For More Info . . .
3279	ADAMS, Lindley	24	N½SE	1860-10-01		A1
3154	BELL, Anthony F	6	SE	1839-09-20	Walker	A1 G21 F
3170	BULLARD, Christopher	5	E½SE	1826-12-01		A1 G35
3313	CARPENTER, Philip	11	E½NE	1823-06-02		A1
3205	COCHRAN, Hiram P	17	E½SE	1823-06-02	Walker	A1 G56 F
3237	COOK, John	17	S½	1837-03-20		A1 G60 F
3227	DAVIS, James T	17	E½NE	1890-03-19	Walker	A4
3364	DODD, Willis	5	NWNW	1858-06-01		A1
3151	ESPEY, Andrew J	31	NWSW	1882-06-30		A1
3172	FARR, David	1	E½SE	1823-06-02		A1 G84
3310	FRANKLIN, Owen	23	SENE	1850-09-02		A1
3295	FRAZIER, Nancy E	36	S½SW	1890-07-03		A4
3350	FRIERSON, William	21	SWNE	1850-04-01		A1
3172	GILLEN, John	1	E½SE	1823-06-02		A1 G84
3283	GILMORE, Mary	20	NESW	1891-09-15	Walker	A4 G95
3284	" "	20	SWSE	1891-09-15	Walker	A4 G95
3285	" "	29	NENW	1891-09-15		A4 G95
3296	GILMORE, Nancy	14	S½SW	1884-03-20		A4 G96
3297	" "	14	SWSE	1884-03-20		A4 G96
3298	" "	15	SESE	1884-03-20		A4 G96
3296	GILMORE, Samuel W	14	S½SW	1884-03-20		A4 G96
3297	" "	14	SWSE	1884-03-20		A4 G96
3298	" "	15	SESE	1884-03-20		A4 G96
3283	GILMORE, William C	20	NESW	1891-09-15	Walker	A4 G95
3284	" "	20	SWSE	1891-09-15	Walker	A4 G95
3285	" "	29	NENW	1891-09-15		A4 G95
3171	GLAZE, Daniel	21	W½NW	1858-06-01		A1
3311	GLAZE, Patrick	22	NWSW	1891-12-01		A1
3312	" "	22	S½NW	1891-12-01		A1
3328	GLAZE, Thomas	34	SE	1860-10-01		A1
3351	GLAZE, William	21	E½SE	1860-10-01		A1
3352	" "	22	S½SW	1860-10-01		A1
3353	" "	28	NENE	1860-10-01		A1
3355	GLOVER, William J	33	NW	1890-03-19		A4
3286	GOLDEN, Mary T	36	SE	1889-11-21		A4
3181	GOODWIN, Elizabeth	26	NWSW	1891-09-15		A4
3182	" "	26	W½NW	1891-09-15		A4
3326	GOODWIN, Theopholus	10	NWSE	1839-09-20		A1 G100
3327	" "	10	SESE	1839-09-20		A1 G100
3217	HANCOCK, James F	26	S½SE	1913-01-23		A4
3190	HARRIS, George C	22	N½NE	1890-07-03		A4
3191	" "	22	NESE	1890-07-03		A4
3192	" "	22	SENE	1890-07-03		A4
3154	HEARD, John K	6	SE	1839-09-20	Walker	A1 G21 F
3244	" "	7	NE	1839-09-20	Walker	A1 F
3211	HOOD, Isaac J	28	E½SE	1885-03-16		A1

ID	Individual in Patent	Sec.	Sec. Part	Date Issued	Other Counties	For More Info . . .
3212	HOOD, Isaac J (Cont'd)	28	SENE	1885-03-16		A1 R3247
3213	" "	28	SWSE	1885-03-16		A1
3248	HOOD, John R	4	NESW	1858-06-01		A1
3249	" "	4	NWSE	1858-06-01		A1
3250	" "	4	SESW	1858-06-01		A1
3251	" "	4	SWSE	1858-06-01		A1
3252	" "	4	SWSW	1861-01-01		A1
3253	HUBBARD, John R	20	C	1891-12-01	Walker	A1 F
3254	" "	20	N½NE	1891-12-01	Walker	A1 F
3243	HUMBER, John	21	NENE	1849-08-01		A1
3326	JONES, Reuben	10	NWSE	1839-09-20		A1 G100
3327	" "	10	SESE	1839-09-20		A1 G100
3275	JORDAN, Julia	30	N½SE	1884-03-20	Walker	A4
3276	" "	30	N½SW	1884-03-20	Walker	A4
3289	JORDAN, Mathew M	29	S½NW	1887-09-07		A4 G143
3290	" "	29	W½SW	1887-09-07		A4 G143
3289	JORDAN, Nancy	29	S½NW	1887-09-07		A4 G143
3290	" "	29	W½SW	1887-09-07		A4 G143
3322	KELLY, Sarah E	21	SENE	1850-04-01		A1
3323	" "	29	SENE	1850-04-01		A1
3330	KNIGHT, Thomas M	19	S½SW	1885-03-16	Walker	A1 F
3329	" "	18	SWSW	1889-10-07	Walker	A1
3319	LEE, Samuel	12	NWSE	1839-09-20		A1
3173	MADDOX, Dorcas	30	S½SW	1882-07-25	Walker	A4
3174	" "	31	N½NW	1882-07-25		A4
3220	MCCARTNEY, James	20	NW	1823-06-02	Walker	A1 G168 F
3155	MCCARTY, Bannager	2	SENE	1852-01-01		A1
3158	MCCARTY, Benajah	11	W½NE	1837-03-20		A1 G170
3202	MCCARTY, Henry	3	NESE	1858-06-01		A1
3203	" "	3	SENE	1858-06-01		A1
3204	" "	4	E½SE	1858-06-01		A1
3158	MCCARTY, James	11	W½NE	1837-03-20		A1 G170
3222	" "	2	W½NW	1839-09-20		A1
3221	" "	2	E½SE	1840-11-10		A1
3291	MCCARTY, Mike	2	W½NE	1884-03-20		A4
3292	" "	2	W½SE	1884-03-20		A4
3205	MCELROY, John	17	E½SE	1823-06-02	Walker	A1 G56 F
3245	" "	18	NE	1825-09-10	Walker	A1 F
3242	MCELROY, John H	8	SWSE	1835-10-01		A1
3237	" "	17	S½	1837-03-20		A1 G60 F
3241	" "	19	NE	1839-09-20	Walker	A1 F
3209	OWEN, Hopson	7	SE	1826-06-10	Walker	A1 G188
3246	PARSONS, John	28	NWSE	1861-07-01		A1
3247	" "	28	SENE	1861-07-01		A1 R3212
3318	PATTON, Samuel B	17	SW	1825-06-20	Walker	A1 F
3315	PAYNE, Preston F	3	SESE	1858-06-01		A1
3314	" "	2	SWSW	1860-10-01		A1
3316	" "	3	W½SE	1860-10-01		A1
3325	PERKINS, Solomon	4	W½NW	1839-09-20		A1
3354	PERRY, William I	19	N½SW	1885-06-20	Walker	A4
3201	PHILIPS, Henry J	13	W½NW	1858-06-01		A1
3365	POOL, Wilson P	10	E½NE	1839-09-20		A1
3366	" "	10	W½NE	1839-09-20		A1
3293	PRESCOAT, Moses	8	SESW	1834-11-04		A1
3170	PRESCOTT, Aaron	5	E½SE	1826-12-01		A1 G35
3147	" "	5	W½SE	1837-03-20		A1 G199
3214	PRESCOTT, Isham	5	S½SW	1884-03-20		A4
3215	" "	8	NENW	1884-03-20		A4
3294	PRESCOTT, Moses	4	NWSW	1838-08-28		A1
3147	PRESCOTT, Thomas	5	W½SE	1837-03-20		A1 G199
3331	" "	8	NWNE	1838-08-28		A1
3206	RICHARDSON, Hiram	19	W½NW	1839-09-20	Walker	A1
3207	" "	30		1839-09-20	Walker	A1 F
3208	" "	30	NW	1839-09-20	Walker	A1 F
3345	RODGERS, William B	28	NWNE	1850-04-01		A1
3157	SALTER, Benager	12	W½SW	1858-06-01		A1
3156	" "	11	E½SE	1860-12-01		A1
3195	SALTER, Getar	11	NESW	1891-06-30		A4
3196	" "	11	NWSE	1891-06-30		A4
3223	SALTER, James	11	SESW	1884-03-20		A4
3224	" "	11	SWSE	1884-03-20		A4
3225	" "	14	NENW	1884-03-20		A4
3226	" "	14	NWNE	1884-03-20		A4

ID	Individual in Patent	Sec.	Sec. Part	Date Issued	Other Counties	For More Info . . .
3238	SALTER, John D	34	NESW	1883-04-10		A4
3239	" "	34	SENW	1883-04-10		A4
3240	" "	34	W½SW	1883-04-10		A4
3341	SALTER, Tillman	21	E½SW	1852-01-01		A1
3342	" "	21	NWSE	1852-01-01		A1
3343	SALTER, Tilmon	8	SESE	1852-01-01		A1
3183	SHORT, Elizabeth	29	NWNW	1858-06-01		A1
3187	SHORT, Frederick T	20	SESE	1885-08-05	Walker	A4
3188	" "	28	NWNW	1885-08-05		A4
3189	" "	29	N½NE	1885-08-05		A4
3193	SHORT, George W	29	SESW	1895-06-19		A4
3194	" "	29	SWSE	1895-06-19		A4
3277	SHORT, Lewis	19	SE	1885-03-30	Walker	A4 F
3278	" "	20	NWSW	1885-03-30	Walker	A4
3346	SHORT, William B	20	SESW	1858-06-01	Walker	A1
3347	" "	32	NW	1885-12-10		A4
3220	SIMS, Edward	20	NW	1823-06-02	Walker	A1 G168 F
3308	SKELTON, Nelson	1	NWNW	1849-05-01		A1
3197	SMITH, Henry G	31	S½SE	1858-06-01		A1
3198	" "	31	SESW	1858-06-01		A1
3199	" "	32	S½SW	1858-06-01		A1
3200	" "	32	SWSE	1858-06-01		A1
3257	SMITH, John	23	SE	1837-03-20		A1 G215
3255	" "	12	NENE	1839-09-20		A1
3256	" "	12	SENW	1839-09-20		A1
3267	SMITH, John W	19	E½NW	1887-07-01	Walker	A1
3348	SMITH, William C	17	SENW	1889-03-02	Walker	A1
3349	" "	17	SWNE	1889-03-02	Walker	A1
3218	SNOW, James M	8	NESE	1890-03-08		A1
3219	" "	8	SENE	1890-03-08		A1
3233	SNOW, Joel J	29	SWNE	1913-01-06		A4
3180	STEPHENS, Eliza	4	S½NE	1891-06-29		A1
3301	TATE, Nathaniel	12	E½SE	1839-09-20		A1
3307	TAYLOR, Nehemiah	10	SENW	1834-10-01		A1
3257	" "	23	SE	1837-03-20		A1 G215
3324	TAYLOR, Sarah	18	SE	1883-07-03	Walker	A4 F
3344	TAYLOR, Urious	32	NWNE	1859-12-10		A1
3232	THOMPSON, Jerusha	7	NWNW	1883-08-13	Walker	A4
3271	THOMPSON, Joseph T	7	NWNE	1858-06-01	Walker	A1 F
3269	" "	6	SW	1860-10-01	Walker	A1 F
3270	" "	7	NENW	1860-10-01	Walker	A1
3309	THOMPSON, Oliver W	17	NWNE	1854-07-15	Walker	A1
3320	THOMPSON, Samuel	6	E½NW	1839-09-20	Walker	A1
3321	" "	6	W½NW	1839-09-20	Walker	A1 F
3209	THOMPSON, Thomas	7	SE	1826-06-10	Walker	A1 G188
3334	" "	8	NESW	1837-04-01		A1
3335	" "	8	NWSE	1839-09-20		A1
3336	" "	8	NWSW	1839-09-20		A1
3337	" "	8	SENW	1839-09-20		A1
3338	" "	8	W½NW	1839-09-20		A1
3333	" "	17	W½NW	1858-06-01	Walker	A1
3332	" "	17	NENW	1860-10-01	Walker	A1
3150	VINES, Andrew B	34	NE	1882-06-30		A1
3152	VINES, Andrew J	15	E½NW	1884-12-05		A4
3153	" "	15	NESW	1884-12-05		A4
3159	VINES, Benton F	14	NWSW	1889-10-07		A1
3160	" "	14	W½NW	1889-10-07		A1
3161	" "	15	SENE	1889-10-07		A1
3175	VINES, Eli	9	N½SE	1884-12-05		A4
3176	" "	9	S½NE	1884-12-05		A4
3177	VINES, Elisha B	26	E½NW	1884-03-20		A1
3178	" "	26	NESW	1884-03-20		A1
3179	" "	26	NWNE	1884-03-20		A1
3186	VINES, Francis M	15	W½NE	1891-06-30		A4
3210	VINES, Hosa	22	NWNW	1858-06-01		A1
3216	VINES, Jackson	13	NENE	1839-09-20		A1
3228	VINES, James	15	W½SE	1858-06-01		A1
3229	" "	26	N½SE	1884-11-13		A1
3230	" "	26	S½NE	1884-11-13		A1
3263	VINES, John	15	NENE	1850-04-01		A1
3258	" "	10	NENW	1858-06-01		A1
3259	" "	10	NESE	1858-06-01		A1
3260	" "	10	SWSE	1858-06-01		A1

ID	Individual in Patent	Sec.	Sec. Part	Date Issued	Other Counties	For More Info . . .
3261	VINES, John (Cont'd)	11	NW	1858-06-01		A1
3262	" "	11	NWSW	1858-06-01		A1
3264	" "	24	E½SW	1889-11-21		A4
3265	" "	24	SENW	1889-11-21		A4
3266	" "	24	SWSE	1889-11-21		A4
3234	VINES, John C	18	E½NW	1897-05-12	Walker	A4
3235	" "	18	NWNW	1897-05-12	Walker	A4
3236	" "	7	E	1897-05-12	Walker	A4 V3209
3274	VINES, Joseph	36	NENE	1860-04-02		A1
3272	" "	24	E½NE	1860-10-01		A1
3273	" "	24	NWNE	1860-10-01		A1
3268	VINES, Joseph L	18	NWSW	1891-06-30	Walker	A4
3280	VINES, Lot V	22	NESW	1884-03-20		A4
3281	" "	22	SWNE	1884-03-20		A4
3282	" "	22	W½SE	1884-03-20		A4
3287	VINES, Mary	15	NWSW	1859-12-10		A1
3288	" "	15	SWNW	1859-12-10		A1
3356	VINES, William	14	E½NE	1860-12-01		A1
3357	" "	14	N½SE	1860-12-01		A1
3358	" "	14	SENW	1860-12-01		A1
3359	" "	14	SWNE	1860-12-01		A1
3360	" "	3	E½SW	1860-12-01		A1
3363	" "	9	W½SW	1886-02-10		A1
3361	" "	3	SENW	1889-02-20		A1
3362	" "	3	SWSW	1889-02-20		A1
3148	WALDROP, Alvah P	18	E½SW	1895-12-14	Walker	A4
3149	" "	18	SWNW	1895-12-14	Walker	A4
3164	WALDROP, Calvin	13	NWSW	1839-09-20		A1
3168	" "	25	NENE	1839-09-20		A1
3169	" "	25	SWNE	1850-04-01		A1
3162	" "	13	N½SE	1858-06-01		A1
3163	" "	13	NESW	1858-06-01		A1
3165	" "	13	SWNE	1858-06-01		A1
3166	" "	24	W½NW	1860-10-01		A1
3167	" "	24	W½SW	1860-10-01		A1
3184	WALDROP, Fielding	24	SESE	1858-06-01		A1
3185	" "	25	NWSE	1858-06-01		A1
3299	WALDROP, Nancy	13	SESW	1834-10-21		A1
3317	WALDROP, Preston	26	NENE	1860-10-01		A1
3300	WALDRUP, Nancy	13	SENE	1834-10-01		A1
3303	WILLIAMS, Nathaniel	12	W½NE	1823-06-02		A1
3302	" "	10	E½SW	1839-09-20		A1
3305	" "	5	SWNW	1858-06-01		A1 F
3306	" "	6	S½NE	1858-06-01	Walker	A1 F
3304	" "	5	E½NW	1860-12-01		A1
3339	WILLIAMS, Thomas	1	SWSE	1837-03-30		A1
3340	" "	12	NENW	1837-03-30		A1
3231	WYATT, James	21	W½SW	1824-04-14		A1

Patent Map

T17-S R6-W
Huntsville Meridian

Map Group 19

Township Statistics

Parcels Mapped	:	220
Number of Patents	:	151
Number of Individuals	:	118
Patentees Identified	:	113
Number of Surnames	:	61
Multi-Patentee Parcels	:	20
Oldest Patent Date	:	6/2/1823
Most Recent Patent	:	1/23/1913
Block/Lot Parcels	:	2
Parcels Re - Issued	:	1
Parcels that Overlap	:	1
Cities and Towns	:	0
Cemeteries	:	4

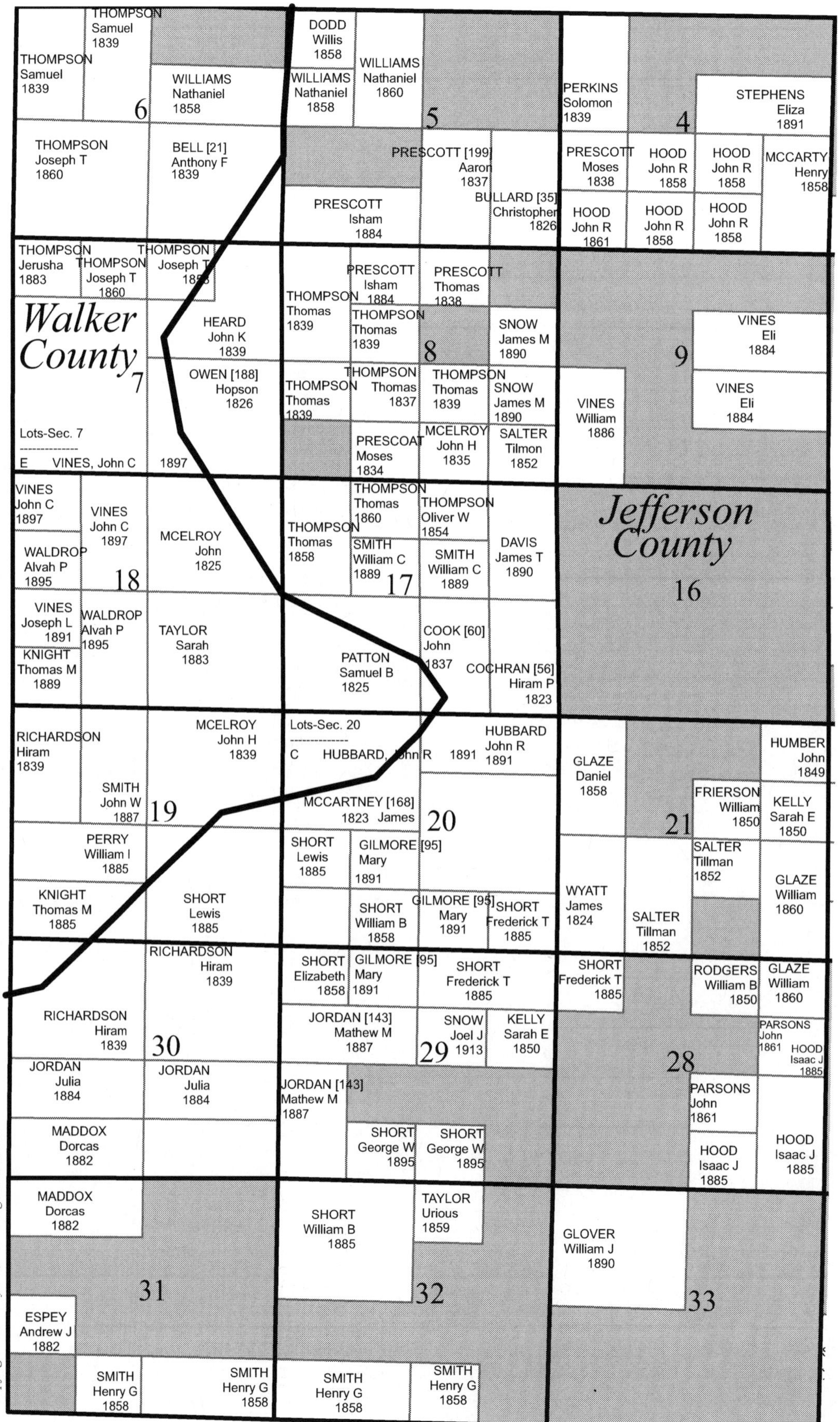

Helpful Hints

1. This Map's INDEX can be found on the preceding pages.
2. Refer to Map "C" to see where this Township lies within Jefferson County, Alabama.
3. Numbers within square brackets [ ] denote a multi-patentee land parcel (multi-owner). Refer to Appendix "C" for a full list of members in this group.
4. Areas that look to be crowded with Patentees usually indicate multiple sales of the same parcel (Re-issues) or Overlapping parcels. See this Township's Index for an explanation of these and other circumstances that might explain "odd" groupings of Patentees on this map.

Legend

Patent Boundary

Section Boundary

No Patents Found (or Outside County)

1., 2., 3., ... Lot Numbers (when beside a name)

[ ] Group Number (see Appendix "C")

Scale: Section = 1 mile X 1 mile (generally, with some exceptions)

Road Map

T17-S R6-W
Huntsville Meridian

Map Group 19

Cities & Towns

None

Cemeteries

Atwood Cemetery
Dug Hill Cemetery
Prescott Cemetery
Weaver Cemetery

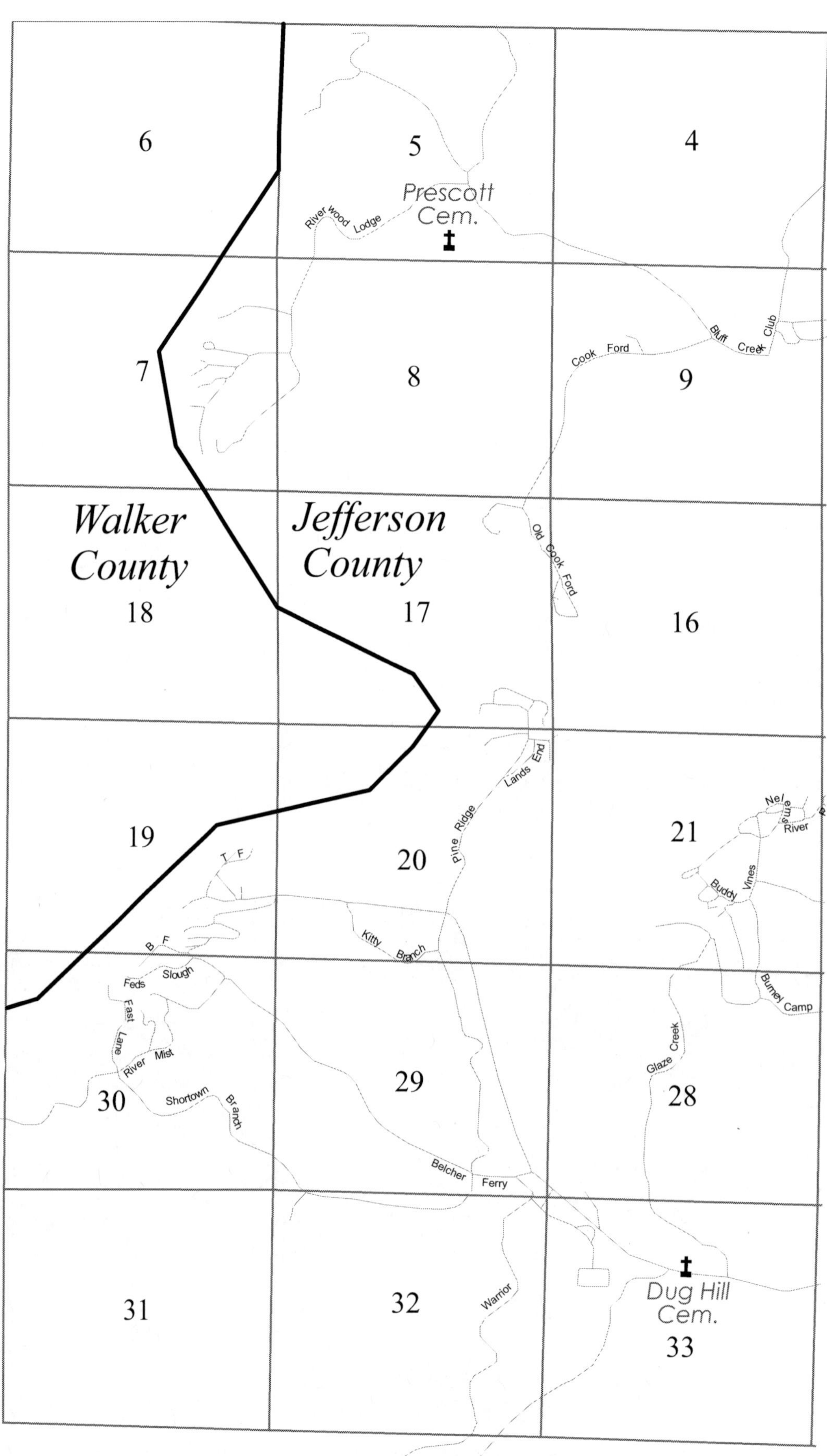

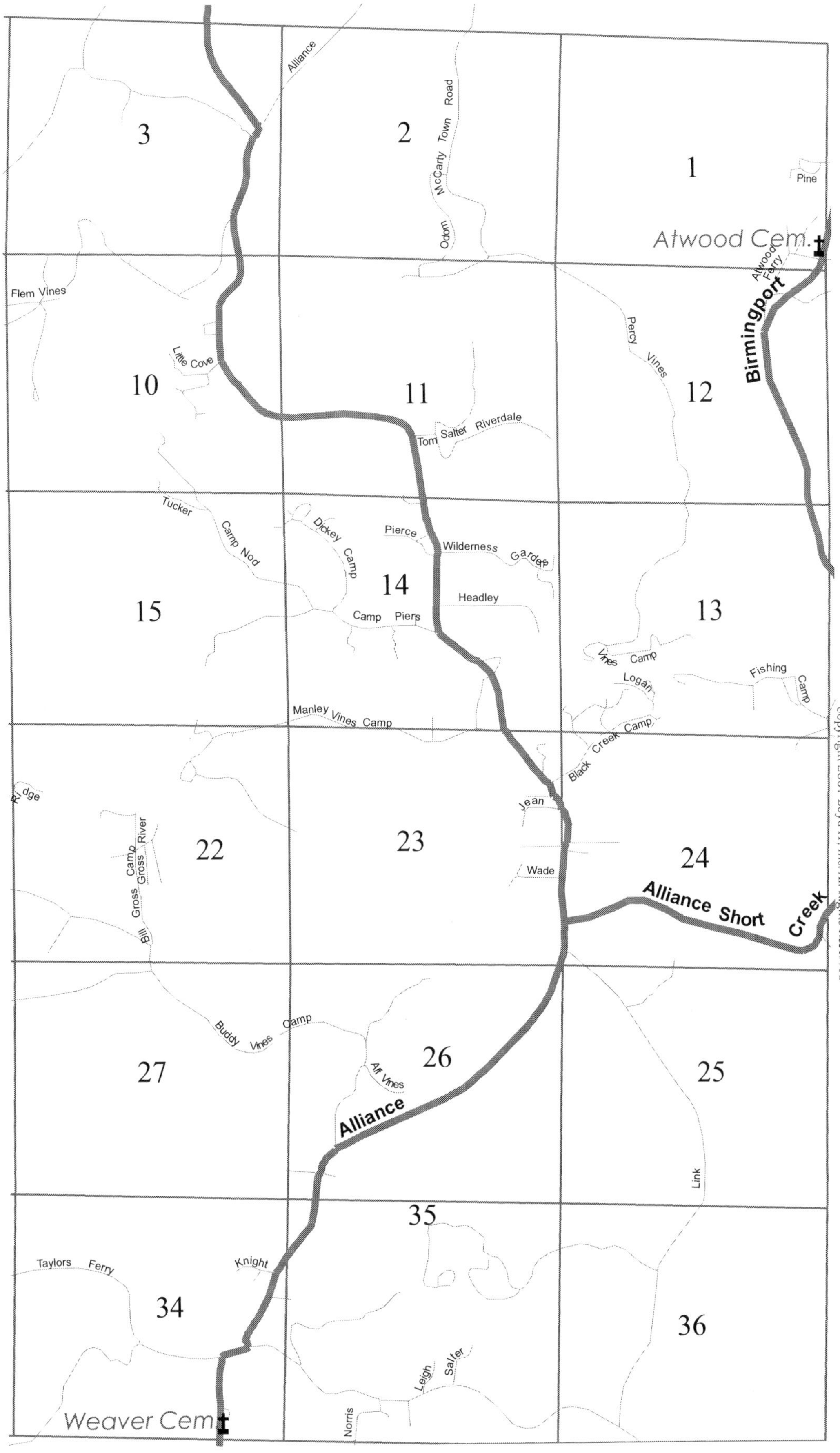

3
Alliance
2
McCarty Town Road
Odom
1
Pine
Atwood Cem.
Atwood Ferry
Flem Vines
Birmingport
Percy Vines
Little Cove
10
11
12
Tom Salter Riverdale
Tucker
Camp Nod
Dickey Camp
Pierce
Wilderness Garden
14
Headley
15
Camp Piers
13
Vines Camp
Logan
Fishing Camp
Manley Vines Camp
Black Creek Camp
Ridge
Jean
Bill Gross Camp
Gross River
22
23
24
Wade
Alliance Short Creek
Buddy Vines Camp
27
Alf Vines
26
25
Alliance
Link
35
Taylors Ferry
Knight
34
36
Leigh
Salter
Norris
Weaver Cem.

Helpful Hints

1. This road map has a number of uses, but primarily it is to help you: a) find the present location of land owned by your ancestors (at least the general area), b) find cemeteries and city-centers, and c) estimate the route/roads used by Census-takers & tax-assessors.
2. If you plan to travel to Jefferson County to locate cemeteries or land parcels, please pick up a modern travel map for the area before you do. Mapping old land parcels on modern maps is not as exact a science as you might think. Just the slightest variations in public land survey coordinates, estimates of parcel boundaries, or road-map deviations can greatly alter a map's representation of how a road either does or doesn't cross a particular parcel of land.

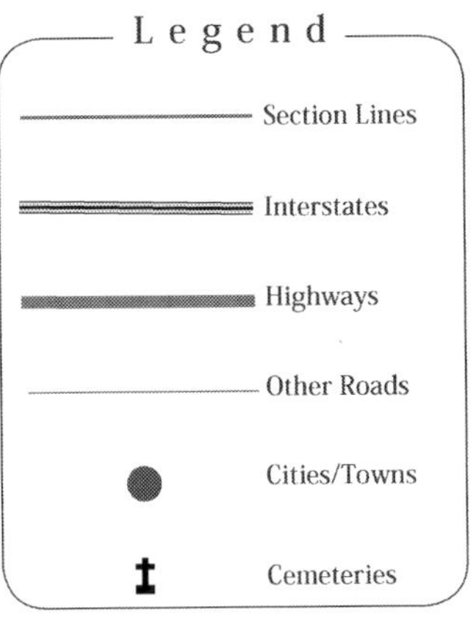

Scale: Section = 1 mile X 1 mile
(generally, with some exceptions)

Historical Map

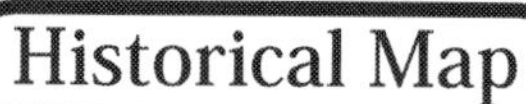

T17-S R6-W
Huntsville Meridian

Map Group 19

Cities & Towns

None

Cemeteries

Atwood Cemetery
Dug Hill Cemetery
Prescott Cemetery
Weaver Cemetery

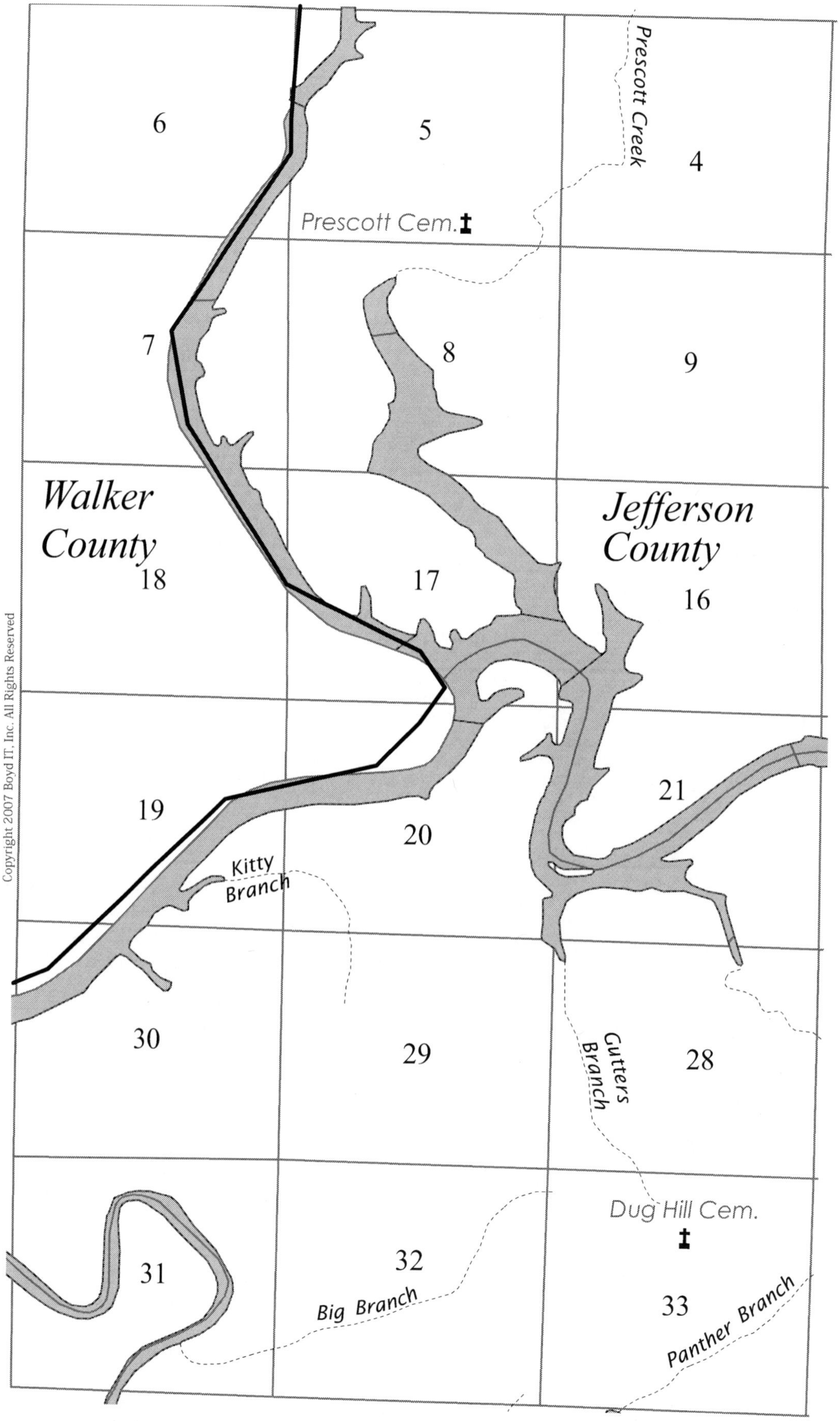

6
5
4
Prescott Creek
Prescott Cem.
7
8
9
Walker County
Jefferson County
18
17
16
19
20
21
Kitty Branch
30
29
28
Gutters Branch
31
32
33
Dug Hill Cem.
Big Branch
Panther Branch

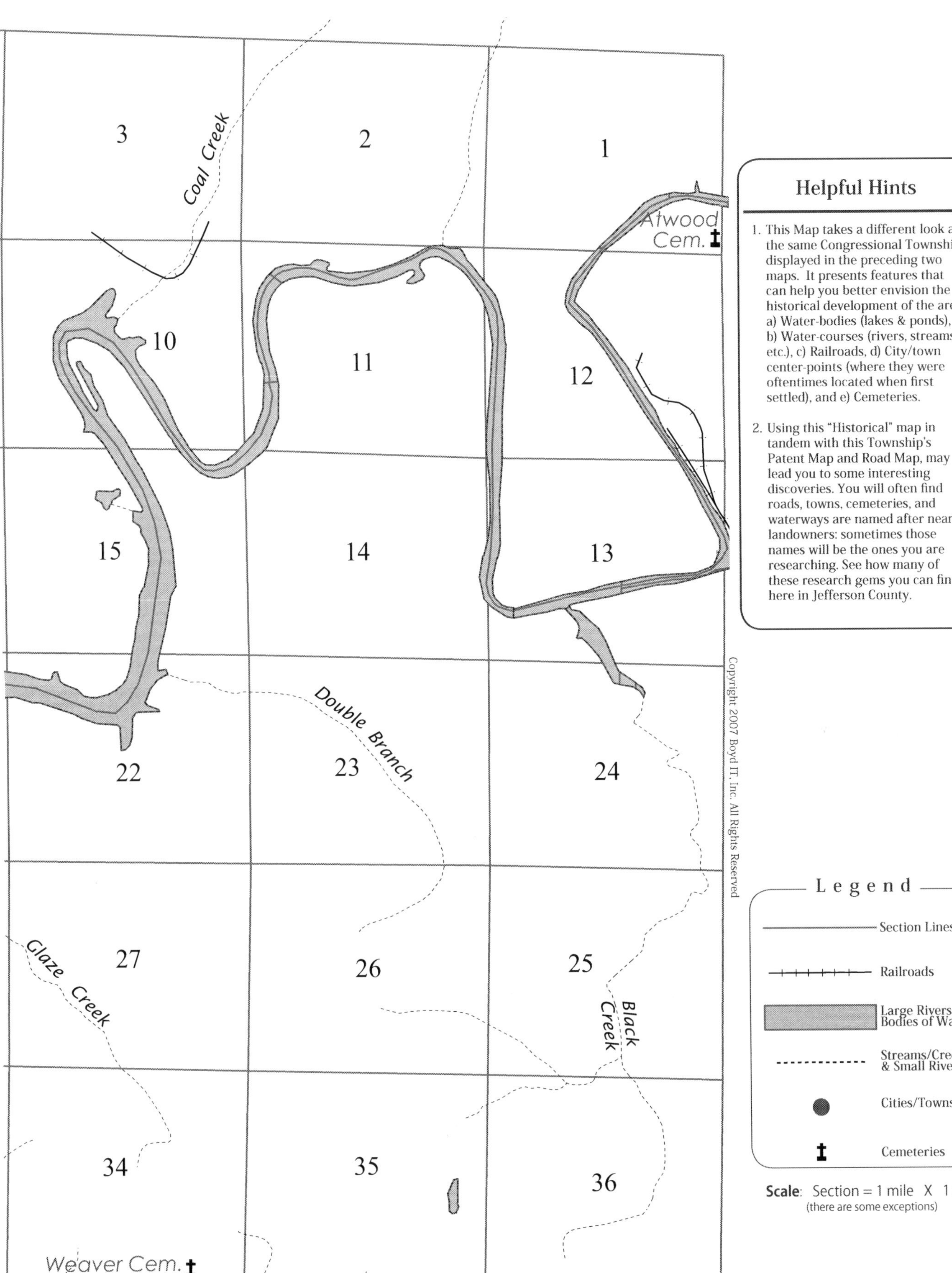
3
2
1
Coal Creek
Atwood Cem.
10
11
12
15
14
13
22
23
24
Double Branch
27
26
25
Glaze Creek
Black Creek
34
35
36
Weaver Cem.
Copyright 2007 Boyd IT, Inc. All Rights Reserved
Helpful Hints
1. This Map takes a different look at the same Congressional Township displayed in the preceding two maps. It presents features that can help you better envision the historical development of the area: a) Water-bodies (lakes & ponds), b) Water-courses (rivers, streams, etc.), c) Railroads, d) City/town center-points (where they were oftentimes located when first settled), and e) Cemeteries.
2. Using this "Historical" map in tandem with this Township's Patent Map and Road Map, may lead you to some interesting discoveries. You will often find roads, towns, cemeteries, and waterways are named after nearby landowners: sometimes those names will be the ones you are researching. See how many of these research gems you can find here in Jefferson County.
Legend
Section Lines
Railroads
Large Rivers & Bodies of Water
Streams/Creeks & Small Rivers
Cities/Towns
Cemeteries
Scale: Section = 1 mile X 1 mile
(there are some exceptions)

Map Group 20: Index to Land Patents

Township 17-South Range 5-West (Huntsville)

After you locate an individual in this Index, take note of the Section and Section Part then proceed to the Land Patent map on the pages immediately following. You should have no difficulty locating the corresponding parcel of land.

The "For More Info" Column will lead you to more information about the underlying Patents. See the *Legend* at right, and the "How to Use this Book" chapter, for more information.

LEGEND

"For More Info . . . " column

A = Authority (Legislative Act, See Appendix "A")
B = Block or Lot (location in Section unknown)
C = Cancelled Patent
F = Fractional Section
G = Group (Multi-Patentee Patent, see Appendix "C")
V = Overlaps another Parcel
R = Re-Issued (Parcel patented more than once)

(A & G items require you to look in the Appendixes referred to above. All other Letter-designations followed by a number require you to locate line-items in this index that possess the ID number found after the letter).

ID	Individual in Patent	Sec.	Sec. Part	Date Issued	Other Counties	For More Info . . .
3432	ADAMS, Jesse	18	SENE	1839-09-20		A1
3444	ARNETT, John W	17	NWSE	1892-01-11		A1
3445	" "	17	W½NE	1892-01-11		A1
3449	ATWOOD, Joseph H	6	SENW	1858-06-01		A1
3446	BLACKWELL, John W	19	E½SW	1891-06-18		A1
3447	" "	19	W½SE	1891-06-18		A1
3412	CARMICHAEL, James A	34	SE	1888-02-04		A4
3487	CARMICHAEL, Stephen A	34	SW	1886-04-10		A4
3488	CHAPMAN, Susanah C	24	SW	1884-03-20		A4
3505	CHAPMAN, William D	10	SW	1884-11-13		A1
3456	COLE, Larkin	8	SENW	1839-09-20		A1
3489	COOLEY, Susaner E	10	N½NE	1885-06-20		A4 G61
3490	" "	10	N½NW	1885-06-20		A4 G61
3392	COOPER, George	2	N½NE	1878-04-09		A4
3393	" "	2	NENW	1878-04-09		A4
3394	" "	2	SENE	1878-04-09		A4
3480	CUNNINGHAM, Robert J	4	S½SE	1884-03-20		A1
3408	EATON, Humphrey P	1	N½SW	1858-06-01		A1
3409	" "	1	SWNW	1858-06-01		A1
3410	" "	2	N½SE	1858-06-01		A1
3426	EATON, James S	12	NWNW	1878-06-13		A4
3481	EATON, Roland B	28	E½SE	1889-11-21		A4
3482	" "	28	NESW	1889-11-21		A4
3483	" "	28	NWSE	1889-11-21		A4
3435	GILLEN, John	7	E½NW	1827-09-10		A1
3389	GLASGOW, Emeline T	14	SE	1884-03-20		A4
3427	GLASGOW, James S	24	NW	1884-11-13		A1
3491	GOODWIN, Thomas	5	S½SE	1860-07-02		A1
3492	" "	5	SESW	1860-07-02		A1
3493	" "	8	N½NW	1860-07-02		A1
3413	GOOLSBY, James A	30	E½NE	1890-03-19		A4
3414	" "	30	E½SE	1890-03-19		A4
3382	HANBY, David	6	NWSE	1850-04-01		A1 G118
3383	HANLY, David	6	SWSE	1850-04-01		A1 G122
3401	HARDEN, Hampton G	19	SWNE	1892-04-29		A4
3486	HARVEY, Scott	34	NW	1884-11-13		A1
3386	HICKS, Edward	12	NESW	1878-04-09		A4
3387	" "	12	S½NW	1878-04-09		A4
3388	" "	12	SWNE	1878-04-09		A4
3418	HICKS, James	1	S½SW	1860-12-01		A1
3419	" "	1	SWSE	1860-12-01		A1
3420	" "	2	SESE	1860-12-01		A1
3423	HICKS, James M	12	E½NE	1888-02-04		A4
3424	" "	12	E½SE	1888-02-04		A4
3433	HIGGINS, Jesse C	22	W½NW	1891-06-08		A4
3434	" "	22	W½SW	1891-06-08		A4

ID	Individual in Patent	Sec.	Sec. Part	Date Issued	Other Counties	For More Info . . .
3506	HIGGINS, William	14	E½NW	1889-11-21		A4
3507	" "	14	W½NE	1889-11-21		A4
3367	HIX, Adaree	14	S½SW	1858-06-01		A1
3368	" "	23	NENW	1858-06-01		A1
3508	HIX, William	12	NWNE	1858-06-01		A1
3369	HOGAN, Amanda C	36	E½SE	1889-08-16		A4
3473	HUEY, Melmouth T	32	SW	1891-06-29		A4
3395	KEMP, George W	12	S½SW	1885-05-25		A4
3396	" "	12	W½SE	1885-05-25		A4
3436	KEMP, John M	30	NENW	1884-11-13		A1
3437	" "	30	NWSW	1884-11-13		A1
3438	" "	30	W½NW	1884-11-13		A1
3382	LEDYARD, William J	6	NWSE	1850-04-01		A1 G118
3383	" "	6	SWSE	1850-04-01		A1 G122
3485	LEE, Samuel	8	NE	1837-03-20		A1 G158
3484	" "	8	NESE	1839-09-20		A1
3474	MCCARTY, Michael	4	NWSW	1837-03-30		A1
3475	" "	4	SWNW	1837-03-30		A1
3378	MCFERRIN, Cynthia C	8	NESW	1896-09-04		A4 G171
3379	" "	8	NWSE	1896-09-04		A4 G171
3380	" "	8	S½SE	1896-09-04		A4 G171
3457	MCMILLAN, Lemuel G	19	E½NE	1824-05-10		A1
3402	MILLER, Henry A	10	SE	1884-11-13		A1
3509	MILLER, William O	24	SE	1883-10-01		A4
3415	MUDD, James A	4	SENW	1850-04-01		A1
3425	NICHOLS, James P	4	N½NW	1890-03-19		A4
3469	NICHOLS, Mathew M	5	E½NE	1891-10-07		A1
3470	" "	5	N½SE	1891-10-07		A1
3495	NICHOLS, Thomas J	6	NE	1889-10-07		A1
3416	NORRIS, James D	36	NE	1886-04-10		A4
3517	NORRIS, William W	26	E½NW	1884-03-20		A4
3518	" "	26	W½NE	1884-03-20		A4
3485	OBAR, George R	8	NE	1837-03-20		A1 G158
3494	PALMER, Thomas H	28	NE	1884-03-20		A1
3461	PARKER, Louisa H	5	NWNW	1902-03-07		A4 G193
3461	PARKER, Monroe D	5	NWNW	1902-03-07		A4 G193
3496	PARSONS, Thomas J	7	E½SE	1897-09-22		A4
3497	" "	7	NWSE	1897-09-22		A4
3498	" "	7	SWNE	1897-09-22		A4
3439	PENN, John	20	E½SW	1884-11-13		A1
3440	" "	20	SENW	1884-11-13		A1
3462	PENWELL, Louisa J	28	NW	1886-03-10		A1
3403	PHILLIPS, Henry J	30	W½NE	1876-04-01		A4
3404	" "	30	W½SE	1876-04-01		A4
3476	POOL, Noah A	26	W½NW	1883-04-10		A4
3431	RAGIN, Jeremiah	7	SWSE	1852-01-01		A1
3500	SALTER, Tilman	36	NESW	1860-04-02		A1
3501	" "	36	NWSE	1860-04-02		A1
3502	" "	36	S½NW	1860-04-02		A1
3390	SHOEMAKER, Flem B	31	W½NE	1891-10-07		A1
3391	" "	31	W½SE	1891-10-07		A1
3407	SHOEMAKER, Hiram W	17	NW	1891-06-18		A1
3417	SHOEMAKER, James H	32	SE	1889-10-07		A1
3463	SHOEMAKER, Martin R	20	SE	1884-11-13		A1
3464	" "	5	E½NW	1890-04-15		A1
3465	" "	5	W½NE	1890-04-15		A1
3478	SHOEMAKER, Rhody F	31	E½NW	1891-10-07		A1
3479	" "	31	E½SW	1891-10-07		A1
3503	SHOEMAKER, Washington	26	NWSW	1858-06-01		A1 V3374
3504	" "	27	SESE	1858-06-01		A1
3370	SNEAD, Ambrose H	5	NESW	1894-12-07		A4
3371	" "	5	SWNW	1894-12-07		A4
3372	" "	5	W½SW	1894-12-07		A4
3374	STEPHENS, Benjamin R	26	N½SW	1884-11-13		A1 V3503
3375	" "	26	NWSE	1884-11-13		A1
3376	" "	26	SESW	1884-11-13		A1
3385	STEPHENS, Edmund W	26	S½SE	1884-03-20		A4
3406	TATE, Henry	6	E½SW	1837-03-20		A1 G218
3405	" "	7	NENE	1839-09-20		A1
3406	TATE, Jacob	6	E½SW	1837-03-20		A1 G218
3411	" "	7	NWNE	1839-09-20		A1
3382	TUTHILL, George A	6	NWSE	1850-04-01		A1 G118
3383	" "	6	SWSE	1850-04-01		A1 G122

ID	Individual in Patent	Sec.	Sec. Part	Date Issued	Other Counties	For More Info . . .
3454	TYLER, Joshua A	36	S½SW	1886-04-10		A4
3455	" "	36	SWSE	1886-04-10		A4
3421	VANCE, James J	18	S½NW	1889-11-21		A4
3422	" "	18	SWNE	1889-11-21		A4
3510	VANCE, William	32	NE	1889-11-21		A4
3384	VIENS, Dawson	17	SWSE	1834-10-16		A1
3428	VIENS, James	17	W½SW	1837-03-20		A1
3441	VIENS, John	19	NESE	1835-10-01		A1
3377	VINES, Benjamin	22	SE	1884-03-20		A4
3397	VINES, George W	3	SWNW	1860-07-02		A1
3398	" "	4	N½SE	1860-07-02		A1
3399	" "	4	NESW	1860-07-02		A1
3400	" "	4	SENE	1860-07-02		A1
3429	VINES, James	18	SESE	1839-09-20		A1
3430	" "	19	N½NW	1859-12-10		A1
3442	VINES, John	19	SESE	1839-09-20		A1
3443	" "	9	N½SW	1858-06-01		A1
3489	VINES, John D	10	N½NE	1885-06-20		A4 G61
3490	" "	10	N½NW	1885-06-20		A4 G61
3448	VINES, Johnson	22	NE	1882-07-25		A4
3450	VINES, Joseph	18	NWSW	1839-09-20		A1
3451	" "	18	SWSE	1839-09-20		A1
3452	" "	19	NWNE	1839-09-20		A1
3453	" "	19	S½NW	1858-06-01		A1
3458	VINES, Levi	30	E½SW	1891-04-08		A4
3459	" "	30	SENW	1891-04-08		A4
3460	" "	30	SWSW	1891-04-08		A4
3466	VINES, Mary A	8	NWSW	1890-07-03		A4 G226
3467	" "	8	S½SW	1890-07-03		A4 G226
3468	" "	8	SWNW	1890-07-03		A4 G226
3471	VINES, Mcdaniel	20	W½NW	1883-08-13		A4
3472	" "	20	W½SW	1883-08-13		A4
3477	VINES, Noah J	18	S½SW	1884-03-20		A4
3511	VINES, William	18	NENW	1850-04-01		A1
3512	" "	18	NWNE	1852-01-01		A1
3515	" "	4	SWSW	1853-08-01		A1
3513	" "	18	NWNW	1858-06-01		A1
3514	" "	4	SESW	1858-06-01		A1
3516	" "	7	E½SW	1858-06-01		A1
3466	VINES, William M	8	NWSW	1890-07-03		A4 G226
3467	" "	8	S½SW	1890-07-03		A4 G226
3468	" "	8	SWNW	1890-07-03		A4 G226
3373	WALDROP, Andrew J	20	NENW	1839-09-20		A1
3499	WILLIAMS, Thomas	7	SENE	1850-09-02		A1
3378	WINES, Cynthia C	8	NESW	1896-09-04		A4 G171
3379	" "	8	NWSE	1896-09-04		A4 G171
3380	" "	8	S½SE	1896-09-04		A4 G171
3381	WOBARR, Daniel	4	NWNE	1839-09-20		A1

Patent Map

T17-S R5-W
Huntsville Meridian

Map Group 20

Township Statistics

Parcels Mapped	:	152
Number of Patents	:	99
Number of Individuals	:	94
Patentees Identified	:	89
Number of Surnames	:	57
Multi-Patentee Parcels	:	13
Oldest Patent Date	:	5/10/1824
Most Recent Patent	:	3/7/1902
Block/Lot Parcels	:	0
Parcels Re - Issued	:	0
Parcels that Overlap	:	2
Cities and Towns	:	0
Cemeteries	:	2

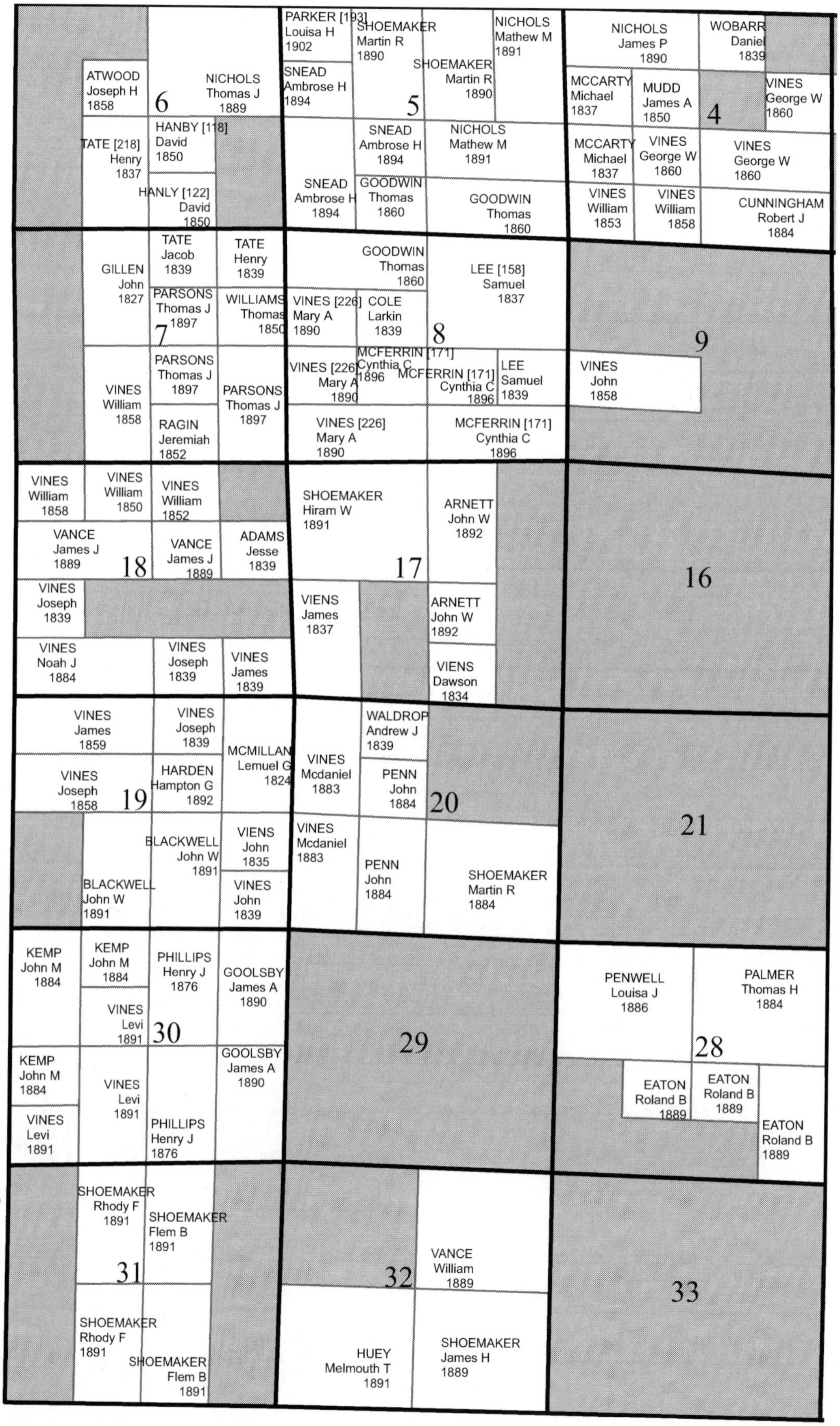

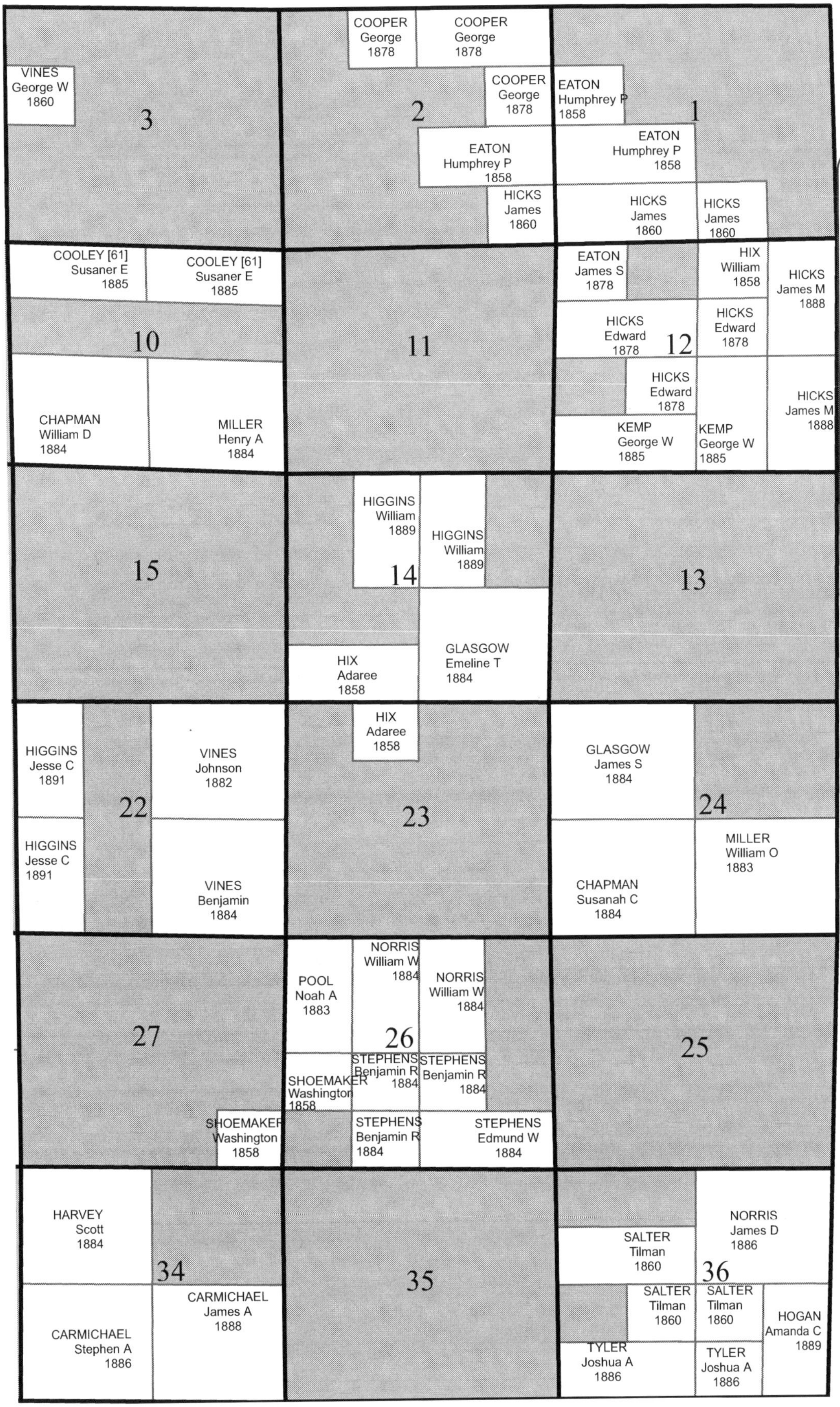

VINES George W 1860

3

COOPER George 1878

COOPER George 1878

COOPER George 1878

2

EATON Humphrey P 1858

HICKS James 1860

EATON Humphrey P 1858

1

EATON Humphrey P 1858

HICKS James 1860

HICKS James 1860

COOLEY [61] Susaner E 1885

COOLEY [61] Susaner E 1885

10

CHAPMAN William D 1884

MILLER Henry A 1884

11

EATON James S 1878

HIX William 1858

HICKS James M 1888

HICKS Edward 1878

12

HICKS Edward 1878

HICKS Edward 1878

HICKS James M 1888

KEMP George W 1885

KEMP George W 1885

15

HIGGINS William 1889

HIGGINS William 1889

14

HIX Adaree 1858

GLASGOW Emeline T 1884

13

HIGGINS Jesse C 1891

22

HIGGINS Jesse C 1891

VINES Johnson 1882

VINES Benjamin 1884

HIX Adaree 1858

23

GLASGOW James S 1884

24

CHAPMAN Susanah C 1884

MILLER William O 1883

27

SHOEMAKER Washington 1858

POOL Noah A 1883

NORRIS William W 1884

NORRIS William W 1884

26

SHOEMAKER Washington 1858

STEPHENS Benjamin R 1884

STEPHENS Benjamin R 1884

STEPHENS Benjamin R 1884

STEPHENS Edmund W 1884

25

HARVEY Scott 1884

34

CARMICHAEL Stephen A 1886

CARMICHAEL James A 1888

35

SALTER Tilman 1860

NORRIS James D 1886

36

SALTER Tilman 1860

SALTER Tilman 1860

HOGAN Amanda C 1889

TYLER Joshua A 1886

TYLER Joshua A 1886

Helpful Hints

1. This Map's INDEX can be found on the preceding pages.
2. Refer to Map "C" to see where this Township lies within Jefferson County, Alabama.
3. Numbers within square brackets [ ] denote a multi-patentee land parcel (multi-owner). Refer to Appendix "C" for a full list of members in this group.
4. Areas that look to be crowded with Patentees usually indicate multiple sales of the same parcel (Re-issues) or Overlapping parcels. See this Township's Index for an explanation of these and other circumstances that might explain "odd" groupings of Patentees on this map.

Legend

Patent Boundary

Section Boundary

No Patents Found (or Outside County)

1., 2., 3., ... Lot Numbers (when beside a name)

[ ] Group Number (see Appendix "C")

Scale: Section = 1 mile X 1 mile (generally, with some exceptions)

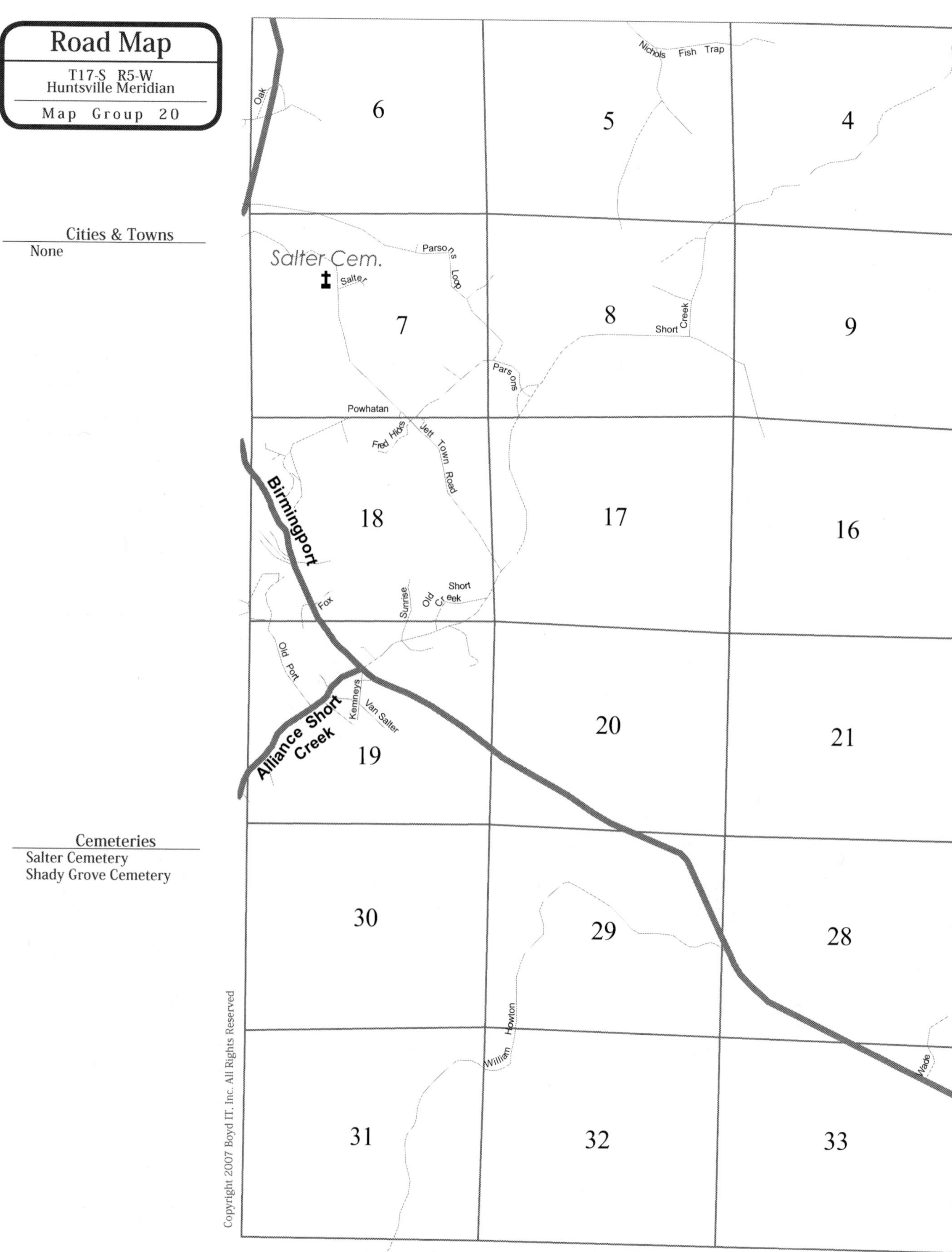
Road Map
T17-S R5-W
Huntsville Meridian
Map Group 20
Cities & Towns
None
Cemeteries
Salter Cemetery
Shady Grove Cemetery
6
5
4
7
8
9
18
17
16
19
20
21
30
29
28
31
32
33
Oak
Nichols Fish Trap
Salter Cem.
Salter
Parsons Loop
Short Creek
Parsons
Powhatan
Fred Hicks
Jett Town Road
Birmingport
Fox
Sunrise
Old Cr
Short eek
Old Port
Keimeys
Van Salter
Alliance Short Creek
Howton
William
Wade
Copyright 2007 Boyd IT, Inc. All Rights Reserved

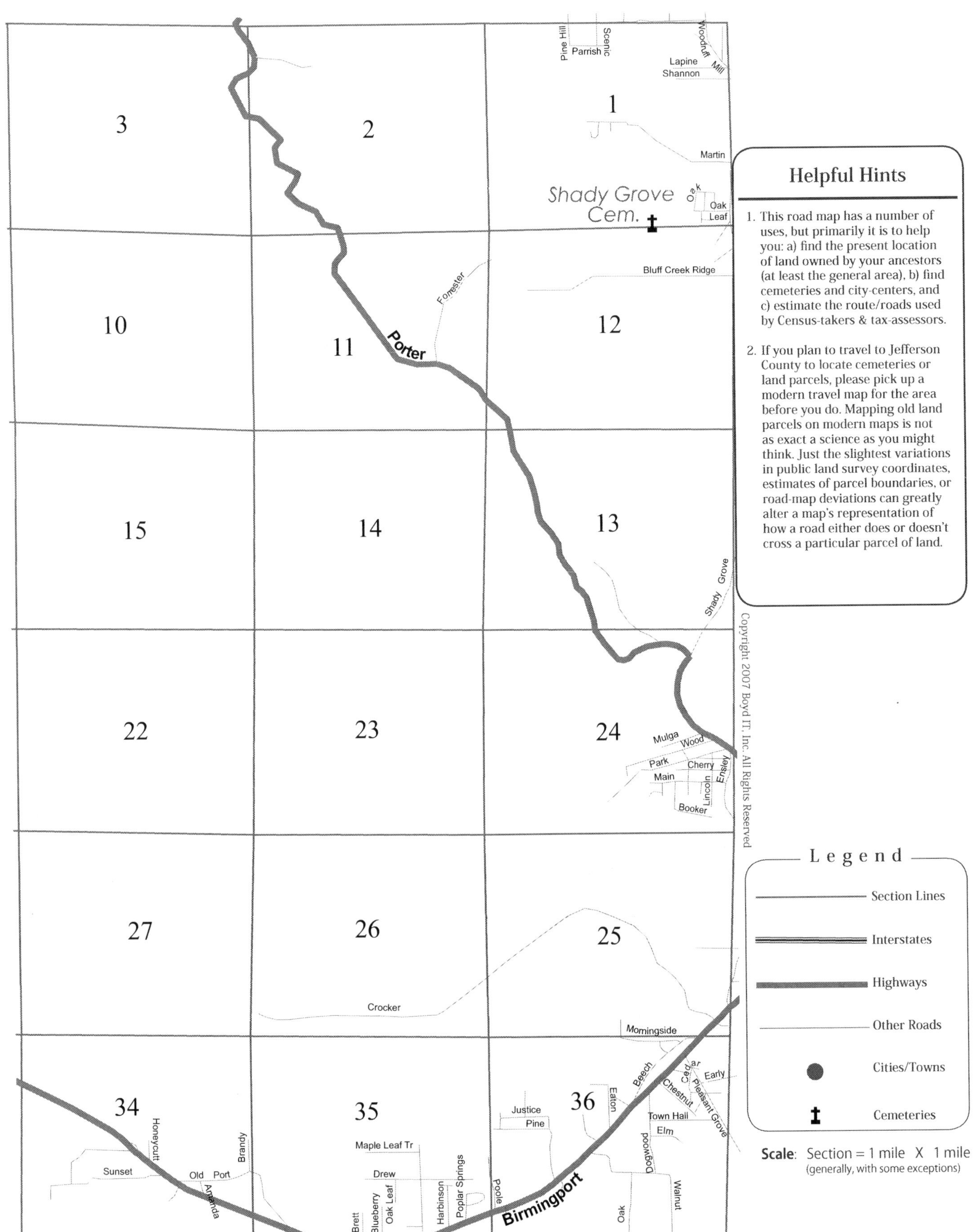
3
2
1
10
11
12
15
14
13
22
23
24
27
26
25
34
35
36
Pine Hill
Scenic
Parrish
Woodruff
Lapine
Mill
Shannon
Martin
Shady Grove Cem.
Oak
Oak
Leaf
Bluff Creek Ridge
Forester
Porter
Shady Grove
Mulga
Wood
Park
Cherry
Main
Ensley
Lincoln
Booker
Crocker
Morningside
Beech
Cedar
Early
Chestnut
Pleasant Grove
Eaton
Town Hall
Elm
Justice
Pine
Dogwood
Walnut
Oak
Birmingport
Poole
Harbinson
Poplar Springs
Maple Leaf Tr
Drew
Brett
Blueberry
Oak Leaf
Honeycutt
Brandy
Sunset
Old Port
Amanda
Helpful Hints
1. This road map has a number of uses, but primarily it is to help you: a) find the present location of land owned by your ancestors (at least the general area), b) find cemeteries and city-centers, and c) estimate the route/roads used by Census-takers & tax-assessors.
2. If you plan to travel to Jefferson County to locate cemeteries or land parcels, please pick up a modern travel map for the area before you do. Mapping old land parcels on modern maps is not as exact a science as you might think. Just the slightest variations in public land survey coordinates, estimates of parcel boundaries, or road-map deviations can greatly alter a map's representation of how a road either does or doesn't cross a particular parcel of land.
Copyright 2007 Boyd IT, Inc. All Rights Reserved
Legend
Section Lines
Interstates
Highways
Other Roads
Cities/Towns
Cemeteries
Scale: Section = 1 mile X 1 mile
(generally, with some exceptions)

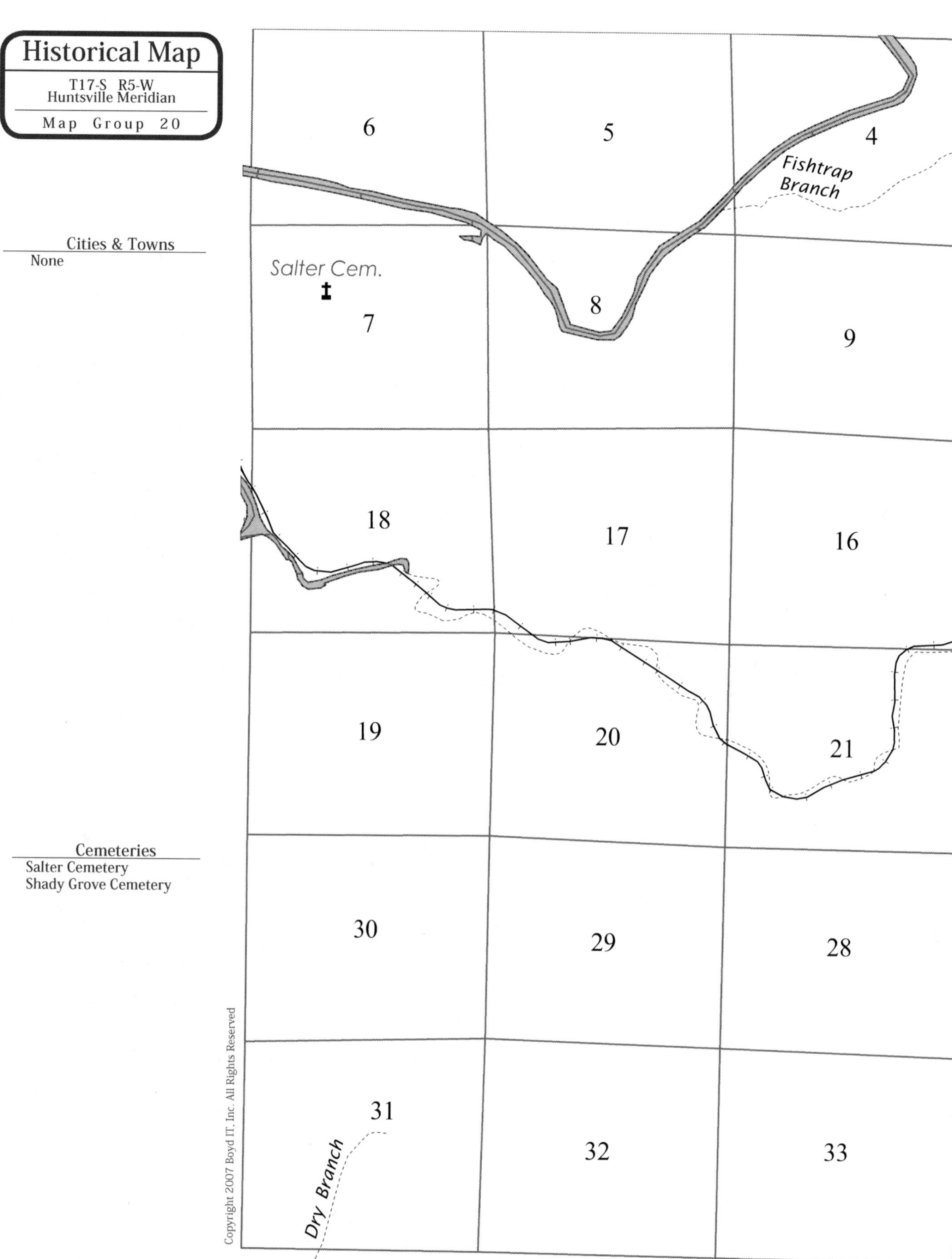
Historical Map
T17-S R5-W
Huntsville Meridian
Map Group 20
Cities & Towns
None
Cemeteries
Salter Cemetery
Shady Grove Cemetery
6
5
4
Fishtrap Branch
Salter Cem.
7
8
9
18
17
16
19
20
21
30
29
28
31
32
33
Dry Branch
Copyright 2007 Boyd IT, Inc. All Rights Reserved

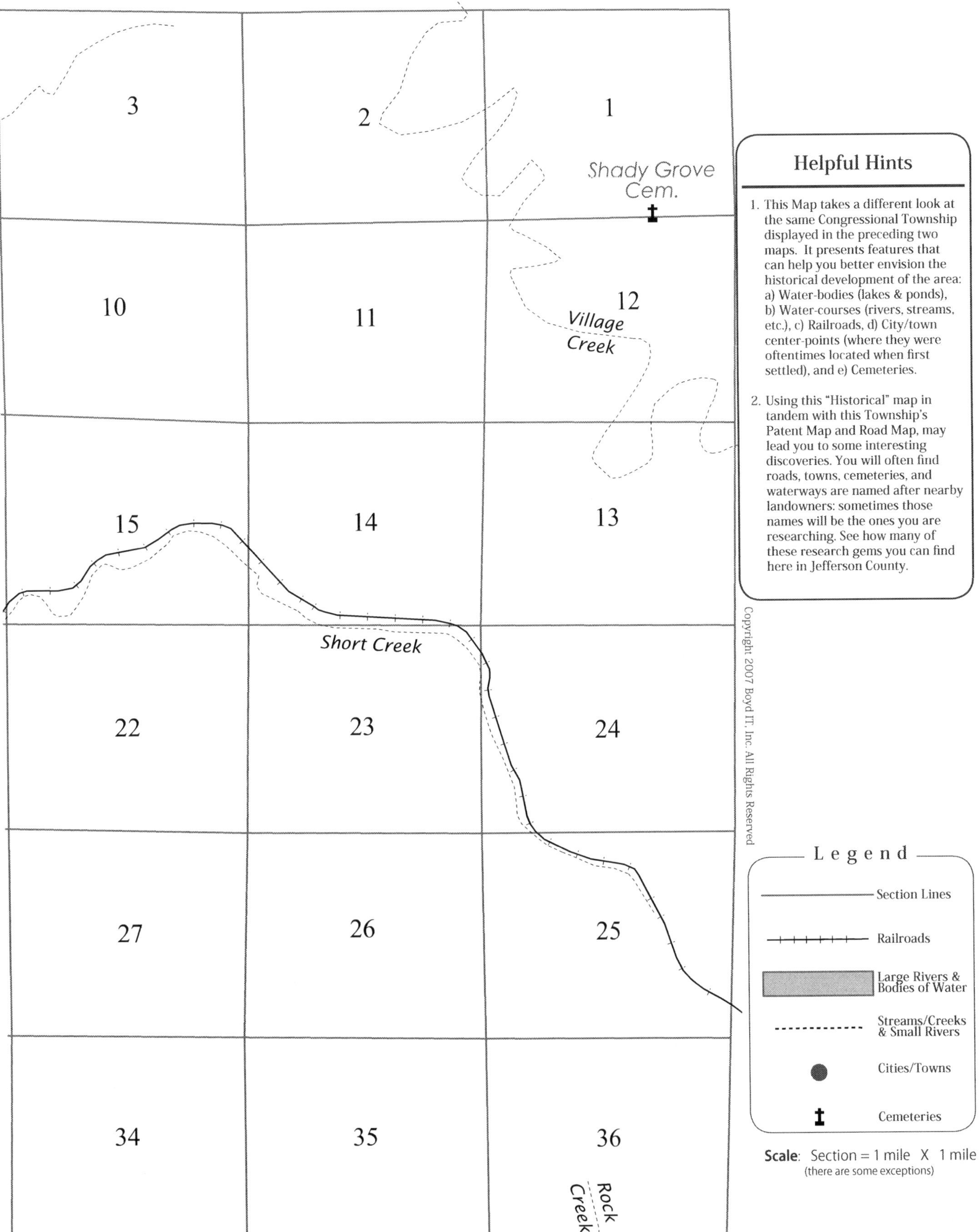

Helpful Hints

1. This Map takes a different look at the same Congressional Township displayed in the preceding two maps. It presents features that can help you better envision the historical development of the area: a) Water-bodies (lakes & ponds), b) Water-courses (rivers, streams, etc.), c) Railroads, d) City/town center-points (where they were oftentimes located when first settled), and e) Cemeteries.
2. Using this "Historical" map in tandem with this Township's Patent Map and Road Map, may lead you to some interesting discoveries. You will often find roads, towns, cemeteries, and waterways are named after nearby landowners: sometimes those names will be the ones you are researching. See how many of these research gems you can find here in Jefferson County.

Legend

- Section Lines
- Railroads
- Large Rivers & Bodies of Water
- Streams/Creeks & Small Rivers
- Cities/Towns
- Cemeteries

Scale: Section = 1 mile X 1 mile
(there are some exceptions)

Map Group 21: Index to Land Patents

Township 17-South Range 4-West (Huntsville)

After you locate an individual in this Index, take note of the Section and Section Part then proceed to the Land Patent map on the pages immediately following. You should have no difficulty locating the corresponding parcel of land.

The "For More Info" Column will lead you to more information about the underlying Patents. See the *Legend* at right, and the "How to Use this Book" chapter, for more information.

LEGEND

"For More Info . . . " column

A = Authority (Legislative Act, See Appendix "A")
B = Block or Lot (location in Section unknown)
C = Cancelled Patent
F = Fractional Section
G = Group (Multi-Patentee Patent, see Appendix "C")
V = Overlaps another Parcel
R = Re-Issued (Parcel patented more than once)

(A & G items require you to look in the Appendixes referred to above. All other Letter-designations followed by a number require you to locate line-items in this index that possess the ID number found after the letter).

ID	Individual in Patent	Sec.	Sec. Part	Date Issued	Other Counties	For More Info . . .
3658	ALRED, Moses	34	W½NW	1837-03-20		A1
3707	ANTHONY, Whitfield	20	NWSE	1878-06-13		A4
3708	" "	20	SENW	1878-06-13		A4
3718	ARNETT, William J	2	SE	1876-04-01		A4
3608	BAGLEY, Joab	27	SESE	1849-09-01		A1
3609	" "	34	NENE	1850-09-02		A1
3577	BATSON, George W	10	NE	1858-06-01		A1
3578	" "	3	SWSE	1858-06-01		A1
3714	BATSON, William	10	NW	1858-06-01		A1
3715	" "	9	NENE	1858-06-01		A1
3703	BIVENS, Valentine	12	SENE	1849-09-01		A1
3704	" "	12	SWNE	1853-08-01		A1
3639	BRADSHAW, John W	22	SESW	1858-06-01		A1
3640	" "	27	NENW	1858-06-01		A1
3594	BROWN, James	36	SENE	1858-06-01		A1
3595	" "	36	SESW	1858-06-01		A1
3651	BROWN, Lucinda	26	SESW	1880-02-20		A4
3652	" "	26	SWSE	1880-02-20		A4
3730	BUCKALEW, Zebedee	8	NENW	1881-10-19		A1
3731	" "	8	NWNE	1881-10-19		A1
3732	" "	8	W½NW	1881-10-19		A1
3681	BUCKELEW, Richard C	8	SWSE	1883-09-15		A4
3539	CARMICHAEL, Benjamin F	28	NESE	1884-03-20		A1
3540	" "	28	SENE	1884-03-20		A1
3549	CARMICHAEL, Daniel L	25	E½NW	1830-11-01		A1
3596	CARMICHAEL, James	30	SW	1878-04-09		A4
3597	CARMICHAEL, James F	17	E½NW	1858-06-01		A1
3598	" "	17	NWSE	1858-06-01		A1
3599	" "	17	W½NE	1858-06-01		A1
3712	CARMICHEAL, William B	20	N½NW	1884-11-13		A1
3713	" "	20	SWNW	1884-11-13		A1
3600	CARMICLE, James F	27	SWSE	1858-06-01		A1
3601	" "	35	W½NW	1858-06-01		A1
3616	CHRISTIAN, John	18	SENW	1839-09-20		A1
3617	" "	18	W½SE	1839-09-20		A1
3657	CLICK, Mathew M	3	SWNE	1850-04-01		A1
3646	COLLIER, Joshua	18	N½NW	1896-08-15		A4
3647	" "	18	SWNW	1896-08-15		A4
3610	CONNER, John A	12	NENE	1880-02-20		A4
3611	" "	12	NESE	1880-02-20		A4
3719	CONNER, William M	8	E½NE	1858-06-01		A1
3720	" "	8	NESE	1858-06-01		A1
3721	" "	8	SESE	1858-06-01		A1
3722	" "	9	N½NW	1858-06-01		A1
3723	" "	9	SWSW	1858-06-01		A1
3536	CRUM, Benjamin	23	E½SE	1831-01-04		A1

ID	Individual in Patent	Sec.	Sec. Part	Date Issued	Other Counties	For More Info . . .
3537	CRUM, Benjamin (Cont'd)	23	NWSE	1834-10-14		A1
3538	" "	24	NWSW	1834-10-16		A1
3550	CRUM, David	23	W½NE	1834-10-14		A1
3548	CRUMLY, Charles W	14	E½SE	1883-07-03		A4
3575	CRUMLY, Flora A	26	W½SW	1858-06-01		A1
3604	DACUS, Jarrel D	33	E½NE	1823-07-09		A1
3570	DEATON, Elizabeth W	6	E½NW	1861-01-01		A1
3571	" "	6	SWNE	1861-01-01		A1
3572	" "	6	SWNW	1861-01-01		A1
3573	" "	6	W½SE	1861-01-01		A1
3669	DOWNEY, Peyton D	35	E½NE	1858-06-01		A1
3670	" "	36	NWSW	1858-06-01		A1
3671	" "	36	SWNW	1858-06-01		A1
3672	" "	8	NWSE	1883-07-03		A4
3673	" "	8	SWNE	1883-07-03		A4
3694	DOWNEY, Samuel W	27	S½SW	1859-04-01		A1
3527	EARLY, Allen	36	E½SE	1837-03-20		A1
3591	ECHOLS, Isaac N	14	E½NE	1858-06-01		A1
3592	" "	14	SWNE	1858-06-01		A1
3593	" "	14	W½SE	1858-06-01		A1
3618	EUBANK, John	24	SWSE	1839-09-20		A1
3682	EUBANK, Robert	36	NENW	1839-09-20		A1
3579	EZEKIEL, George W	6	SESE	1884-12-05		A1
3643	EZEKIEL, Joseph	8	N½SW	1881-09-01		A1
3644	" "	8	SENW	1881-09-01		A1
3659	FIELDS, Moses	33	SWSW	1837-04-01		A1
3660	" "	34	SWSW	1839-09-20		A1
3552	FRANKLIN, Doctor B	12	N½NW	1883-07-03		A4
3553	" "	12	NWNE	1883-07-03		A4
3554	" "	12	SWNW	1883-07-03		A4
3716	FRANKLIN, William H	2	E½NE	1883-09-15		A4
3691	FRETWELL, Samuel	20	W½NE	1858-06-01		A1
3692	" "	21	NWNW	1858-06-01		A1
3622	GILLILAND, John	10	N½SW	1858-06-01		A1
3567	GLASGOW, Elizabeth	2	SENW	1876-04-01		A4
3568	" "	2	SWNE	1876-04-01		A4
3569	" "	2	W½NW	1876-04-01		A4
3619	GLASGOW, John F	2	NENW	1876-02-01		A4
3620	" "	2	NWNE	1876-02-01		A4
3695	GLASGOW, Sarah E	20	E½SW	1882-07-25		A4
3696	" "	20	SWSE	1882-07-25		A4
3711	GODFREY, Wiley	27	NWNE	1858-06-01		A1
3709	GODFREY, Wiley B	28	NWSE	1889-12-28		A1
3710	" "	28	SWNE	1889-12-28		A1
3675	GOLDSBY, Reuben	28	SWNW	1849-09-01		A1
3623	GOOLSBY, John H	20	SESE	1884-11-13		A1
3655	GOOLSBY, Mary	28	W½SW	1882-06-30		A1
3676	GOOLSBY, Reuben	21	SESW	1839-09-20		A1
3677	" "	28	E½SW	1839-09-20		A1
3699	GOOLSBY, Susan	32	E½NE	1891-06-30		A4
3532	GOSSET, Bayless	23	SENW	1858-06-01		A1
3533	" "	23	SW	1858-06-01		A1
3534	" "	23	SWNW	1858-06-01		A1
3535	" "	26	NWNW	1860-04-02		A1
3557	GOSSETT, Eber S	14	S½SW	1883-07-03		A4
3656	GOSSETT, Mary R	26	SWNW	1889-03-02		A1
3678	GOULSBY, Reuben	28	E½NW	1858-06-01		A1
3679	" "	28	NWNW	1858-06-01		A1
3680	" "	29	E½NE	1858-06-01		A1
3729	GOULSBY, Zachariah S	20	W½SW	1858-06-01		A1
3674	HARDIN, Pleasant	30	NE	1891-11-03		A4
3686	HARDIN, Robert W	30	NW	1889-08-16		A4
3546	HAWKINS, Calvin	24	W½NW	1881-10-19		A1
3727	HAWKINS, Williamson	25	NWNW	1858-06-01		A1
3581	HEATON, Henry O	4	NE	1858-06-01		A1
3605	HEMBREE, Jeptha T	4	S½SE	1878-04-09		A4
3541	HENDERSON, Benjamin	4	N½SE	1885-03-16		A1
3542	HICKS, Berryman	6	W½SW	1889-08-10		A4
3631	HICKS, John	6	E½SW	1860-07-02		A1
3632	" "	7	E½NW	1860-07-02		A1
3531	HIGGINS, Andrew J	7	SE	1860-12-01		A1
3633	HILL, John	4	SWNW	1858-06-01		A1
3634	" "	4	W½SW	1858-06-01		A1

ID	Individual in Patent	Sec.	Sec. Part	Date Issued	Other Counties	For More Info . . .
3635	HILL, John (Cont'd)	5	E½NE	1858-06-01		A1
3636	" "	5	NESE	1858-06-01		A1
3558	HOGAN, Eli	27	NWSE	1858-06-01		A1
3559	" "	27	SWNE	1858-06-01		A1
3648	HOGAN, Laraet	32	SW	1876-02-01		A4
3661	HOGAN, Nancy C	32	NW	1876-02-01		A4
3653	ISRAEL, Mary A	20	NESE	1885-03-30		A4
3654	" "	20	SENE	1885-03-30		A4
3613	JOHNSON, John C	10	SWSW	1858-06-01		A1
3614	" "	15	NWNW	1858-06-01		A1
3615	" "	9	SESE	1858-06-01		A1
3641	JOHNSON, John W	4	E½SW	1876-02-01		A4
3724	JOHNSON, William S	4	E½NW	1883-09-15		A4
3725	" "	4	NWNW	1883-09-15		A4
3555	JONES, Dorathy	26	NWSE	1881-04-11		A4 G141
3555	JONES, Mannon G	26	NWSE	1881-04-11		A4 G141
3701	KENNEDY, Thomas L	26	NESW	1891-09-01		A4
3702	" "	26	SENW	1891-09-01		A4
3563	LOVETT, Elijah B	22	NWSE	1850-04-01		A1
3561	" "	22	E½NE	1858-06-01		A1
3562	" "	22	NESE	1858-06-01		A1
3564	" "	22	SWSE	1858-06-01		A1
3565	" "	23	NWNW	1858-06-01		A1
3566	" "	27	NENE	1858-06-01		A1
3520	MARTIN, Alexander K	25	E½SW	1858-06-01		A1
3521	" "	36	NENE	1858-06-01		A1
3522	" "	36	NESW	1858-06-01		A1
3523	" "	36	NWNE	1858-06-01		A1
3524	" "	36	NWNW	1858-06-01		A1
3525	" "	36	SENW	1858-06-01		A1
3526	" "	36	SWNE	1858-06-01		A1
3606	MILLER, Jesse C	22	W½NE	1883-07-03		A4
3607	MILLER, Jesse T	24	NENW	1881-04-11		A4
3637	MILLER, John	24	SENW	1875-10-01		A4
3638	" "	24	SWNE	1875-10-01		A4
3642	MILLER, Jonathan W	24	E½SE	1875-11-20		A4
3576	MORROW, George	23	NENW	1839-09-20		A1
3528	ROGERS, Allen	34	NWSW	1839-09-20		A1
3612	ROGERS, John B	34	E½NW	1837-03-20		A1
3584	RUSSELL, Hiram	33	SESE	1854-07-15		A1
3582	" "	27	NESE	1858-06-01		A1
3583	" "	33	NESE	1858-06-01		A1
3585	" "	34	E½SW	1858-06-01		A1
3683	RUSSELL, Robert	34	SE	1858-06-01		A1
3684	" "	34	SENE	1858-06-01		A1
3650	SAMPLES, Lilla E	18	E½SE	1889-10-07		A1 G208
3650	SAMPLES, Olin W	18	E½SE	1889-10-07		A1 G208
3705	SELF, Vinson G	9	NWSW	1858-06-01		A1
3706	" "	9	SWNW	1858-06-01		A1
3645	SHARP, Joseph R	22	NESW	1883-10-01		A4
3547	SHOEMAKER, Charles T	12	SESE	1884-12-05		A4
3574	SHOEMAKER, Fleming	21	NWNE	1839-09-20		A1
3586	SHOEMAKER, Hiram	28	S½SE	1858-06-01		A1
3587	" "	33	NENW	1858-06-01		A1
3588	" "	33	NWNE	1858-06-01		A1
3589	" "	33	SWNE	1858-06-01		A1
3590	SHOEMAKER, Hiram W	28	N½NE	1884-03-20		A1
3603	SHOEMAKER, James W	27	W½NW	1858-06-01		A1
3664	SHOEMAKER, Oliver	12	SESW	1858-06-01		A1
3665	" "	12	W½SE	1858-06-01		A1
3666	" "	12	W½SW	1858-06-01		A1
3667	" "	13	NENW	1858-06-01		A1
3668	" "	13	W½NW	1858-06-01		A1
3662	SHOEMAKER, Oliver L	14	N½SW	1883-07-03		A4
3663	" "	14	S½NW	1883-07-03		A4
3688	SHOEMAKER, Russum	13	SESE	1858-06-01		A1
3689	" "	13	W½SE	1858-06-01		A1
3690	" "	24	N½NE	1858-06-01		A1
3687	" "	12	NESW	1876-04-01		A4
3543	SMITH, Bryant	6	E½NE	1891-11-03		A4
3544	" "	6	NESE	1891-11-03		A4
3545	" "	6	NWNE	1891-11-03		A4
3717	SMITH, William H	11	SESE	1858-06-01		A1

ID	Individual in Patent	Sec.	Sec. Part	Date Issued	Other Counties	For More Info . . .
3728	SNOW, Willis J	22	SESE	1850-09-02		A1
3697	STAGG, Sarah E	18	NE	1885-03-16		A4
3726	STATHAM, William	36	W½SE	1837-03-20		A1
3698	STATON, Sarah	35	NWNE	1858-06-01		A1
3685	THOMAS, Robert	2	N½SW	1876-04-01		A4
3693	THOMAS, Samuel J	2	S½SW	1883-07-03		A4
3529	VARNON, Alonzo W	14	N½NW	1883-07-03		A4
3530	" "	14	NWNE	1883-07-03		A4
3551	VIENS, Dawson	17	E½SW	1837-03-20		A1
3519	WHEELER, Albert J	10	SESW	1885-03-16		A1
3621	WHEELER, John F	10	W½SE	1876-02-01		A4
3700	WHEELER, Thomas D	10	E½SE	1883-07-03		A4
3556	WILKES, Dukelin	36	SWSW	1891-06-08		A4
3626	WILKS, John H	26	NENE	1852-01-01		A1
3624	" "	23	E½NE	1858-06-01		A1
3625	" "	23	SWSE	1858-06-01		A1
3627	" "	26	NESE	1858-06-01		A1
3628	" "	26	SENE	1858-06-01		A1
3629	" "	26	SESE	1858-06-01		A1
3630	" "	26	W½NE	1858-06-01		A1
3560	WILSON, Elias	20	NENE	1839-09-20		A1
3580	WOODRUFF, George W	34	W½NE	1858-06-01		A1
3602	YOUNG, James M	22	W½SW	1889-10-07		A1
3649	YOUNG, Lawson	22	NW	1875-11-20		A4 C

Patent Map

T17-S R4-W
Huntsville Meridian

Map Group 21

Township Statistics

Parcels Mapped	:	214
Number of Patents	:	142
Number of Individuals	:	120
Patentees Identified	:	118
Number of Surnames	:	74
Multi-Patentee Parcels	:	2
Oldest Patent Date	:	7/9/1823
Most Recent Patent	:	8/15/1896
Block/Lot Parcels	:	0
Parcels Re - Issued	:	0
Parcels that Overlap	:	0
Cities and Towns	:	2
Cemeteries	:	6

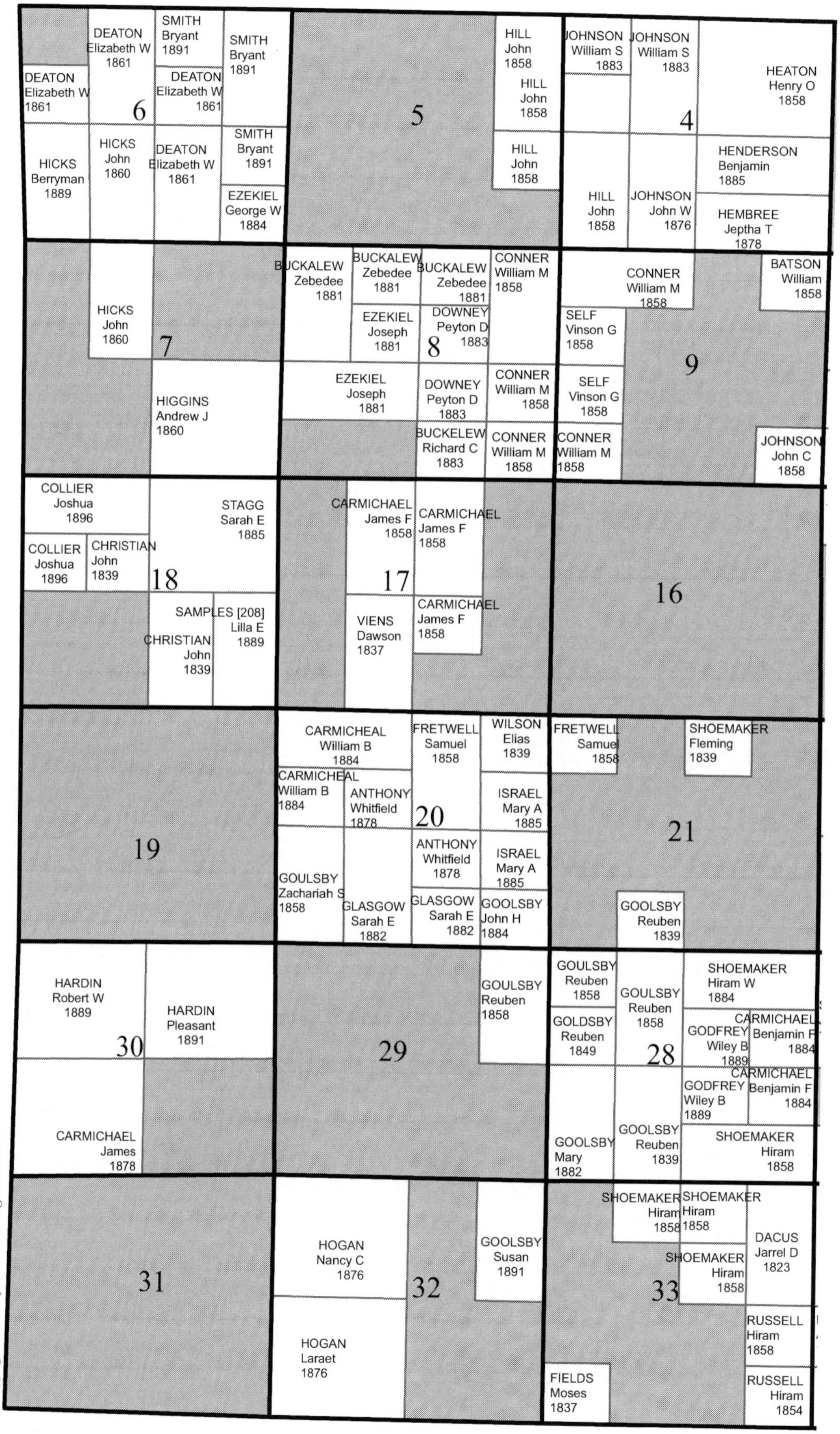

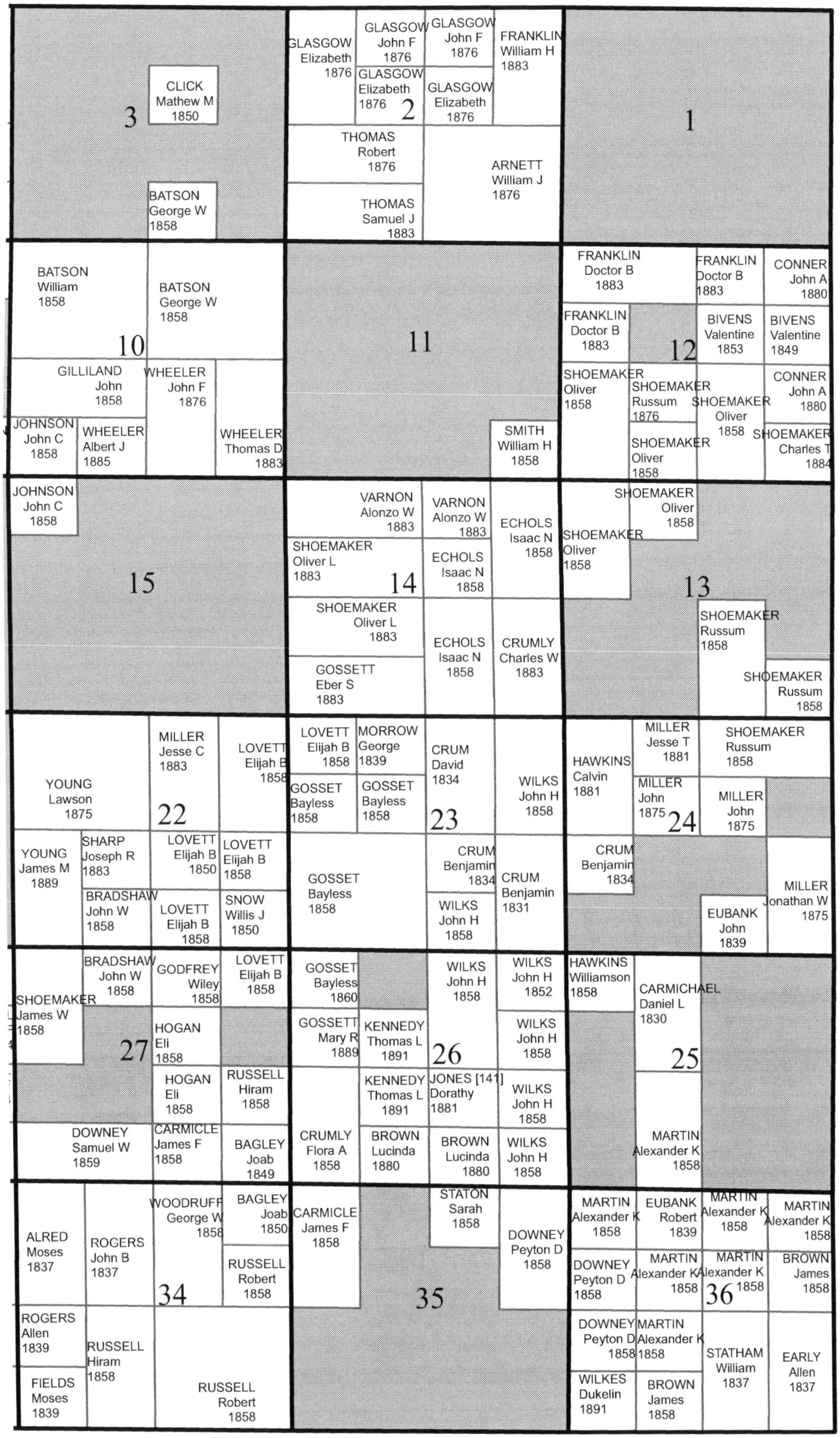

3
CLICK Mathew M 1850
BATSON George W 1858

2
GLASGOW Elizabeth 1876
GLASGOW John F 1876
GLASGOW John F 1876
FRANKLIN William H 1883
GLASGOW Elizabeth 1876
GLASGOW Elizabeth 1876
THOMAS Robert 1876
ARNETT William J 1876
THOMAS Samuel J 1883

1

10
BATSON William 1858
BATSON George W 1858
GILLILAND John 1858
WHEELER John F 1876
JOHNSON John C 1858
WHEELER Albert J 1885
WHEELER Thomas D 1883

11
SMITH William H 1858

12
FRANKLIN Doctor B 1883
FRANKLIN Doctor B 1883
CONNER John A 1880
FRANKLIN Doctor B 1883
BIVENS Valentine 1853
BIVENS Valentine 1849
SHOEMAKER Oliver 1858
SHOEMAKER Russum 1876
SHOEMAKER Oliver 1858
CONNER John A 1880
SHOEMAKER Oliver 1858
SHOEMAKER Charles T 1884

15
JOHNSON John C 1858

14
VARNON Alonzo W 1883
VARNON Alonzo W 1883
ECHOLS Isaac N 1858
SHOEMAKER Oliver L 1883
ECHOLS Isaac N 1858
SHOEMAKER Oliver L 1883
ECHOLS Isaac N 1858
CRUMLY Charles W 1883
GOSSETT Eber S 1883

13
SHOEMAKER Oliver 1858
SHOEMAKER Oliver 1858
SHOEMAKER Russum 1858
SHOEMAKER Russum 1858

22
YOUNG Lawson 1875
MILLER Jesse C 1883
LOVETT Elijah B 1858
YOUNG James M 1889
SHARP Joseph R 1883
LOVETT Elijah B 1850
LOVETT Elijah B 1858
BRADSHAW John W 1858
LOVETT Elijah B 1858
SNOW Willis J 1850

23
LOVETT Elijah B 1858
MORROW George 1839
CRUM David 1834
WILKS John H 1858
GOSSETT Bayless 1858
GOSSETT Bayless 1858
GOSSETT Bayless 1858
CRUM Benjamin 1834
CRUM Benjamin 1831
WILKS John H 1858

24
HAWKINS Calvin 1881
MILLER Jesse T 1881
SHOEMAKER Russum 1858
MILLER John 1875
MILLER John 1875
CRUM Benjamin 1834
MILLER Jonathan W 1875
EUBANK John 1839

27
BRADSHAW John W 1858
GODFREY Wiley 1858
LOVETT Elijah B 1858
SHOEMAKER James W 1858
HOGAN Eli 1858
HOGAN Eli 1858
RUSSELL Hiram 1858
DOWNEY Samuel W 1859
CARMICLE James F 1858
BAGLEY Joab 1849

26
GOSSETT Bayless 1860
WILKS John H 1858
WILKS John H 1852
GOSSETT Mary R 1889
KENNEDY Thomas L 1891
WILKS John H 1858
KENNEDY Thomas L 1891
JONES [141] Dorathy 1881
WILKS John H 1858
CRUMLY Flora A 1858
BROWN Lucinda 1880
BROWN Lucinda 1880
WILKS John H 1858

25
HAWKINS Williamson 1858
CARMICHAEL Daniel L 1830
MARTIN Alexander K 1858

34
ALRED Moses 1837
ROGERS John B 1837
WOODRUFF George W 1858
BAGLEY Joab 1850
RUSSELL Robert 1858
ROGERS Allen 1839
RUSSELL Hiram 1858
FIELDS Moses 1839
RUSSELL Robert 1858

35
CARMICLE James F 1858
STATON Sarah 1858
DOWNEY Peyton D 1858

36
MARTIN Alexander K 1858
EUBANK Robert 1839
MARTIN Alexander K 1858
MARTIN Alexander K 1858
DOWNEY Peyton D 1858
MARTIN Alexander K 1858
MARTIN Alexander K 1858
BROWN James 1858
DOWNEY Peyton D 1858
MARTIN Alexander K 1858
STATHAM William 1837
EARLY Allen 1837
WILKES Dukelin 1891
BROWN James 1858

Helpful Hints

1. This Map's INDEX can be found on the preceding pages.
2. Refer to Map "C" to see where this Township lies within Jefferson County, Alabama.
3. Numbers within square brackets [ ] denote a multi-patentee land parcel (multi-owner). Refer to Appendix "C" for a full list of members in this group.
4. Areas that look to be crowded with Patentees usually indicate multiple sales of the same parcel (Re-issues) or Overlapping parcels. See this Township's Index for an explanation of these and other circumstances that might explain "odd" groupings of Patentees on this map.

Legend

Patent Boundary
Section Boundary
No Patents Found (or Outside County)
1., 2., 3., ... Lot Numbers (when beside a name)
[ ] Group Number (see Appendix "C")

Scale: Section = 1 mile X 1 mile (generally, with some exceptions)

Road Map

T17-S R4-W
Huntsville Meridian

Map Group 21

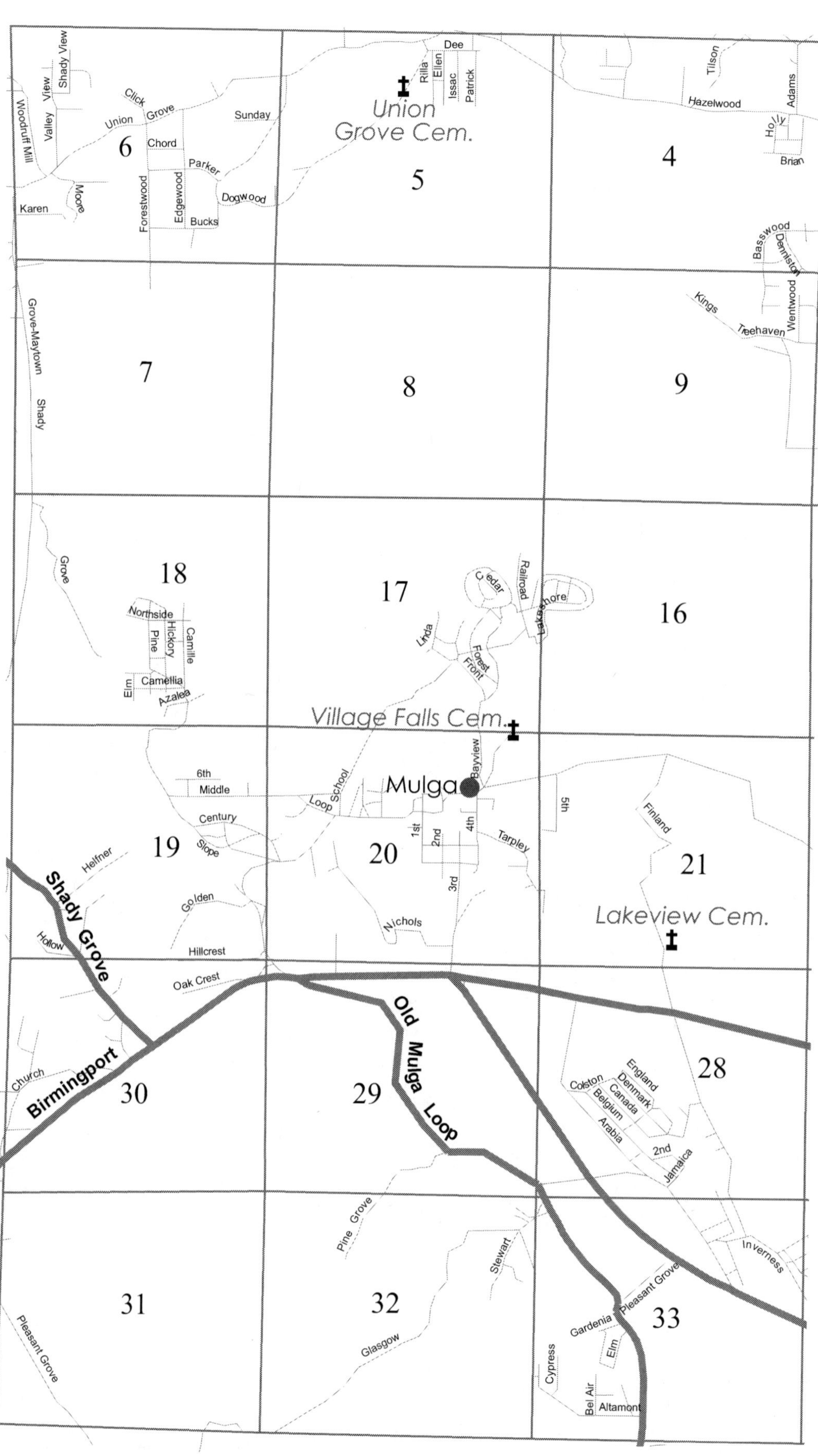

Cities & Towns

Docena
Mulga

Cemeteries

Crumley Chapel Cemetery
George Washington Memorial Gardens Cemetery
Lakeview Cemetery
Midway Cemetery
Union Grove Cemetery
Village Falls Cemetery

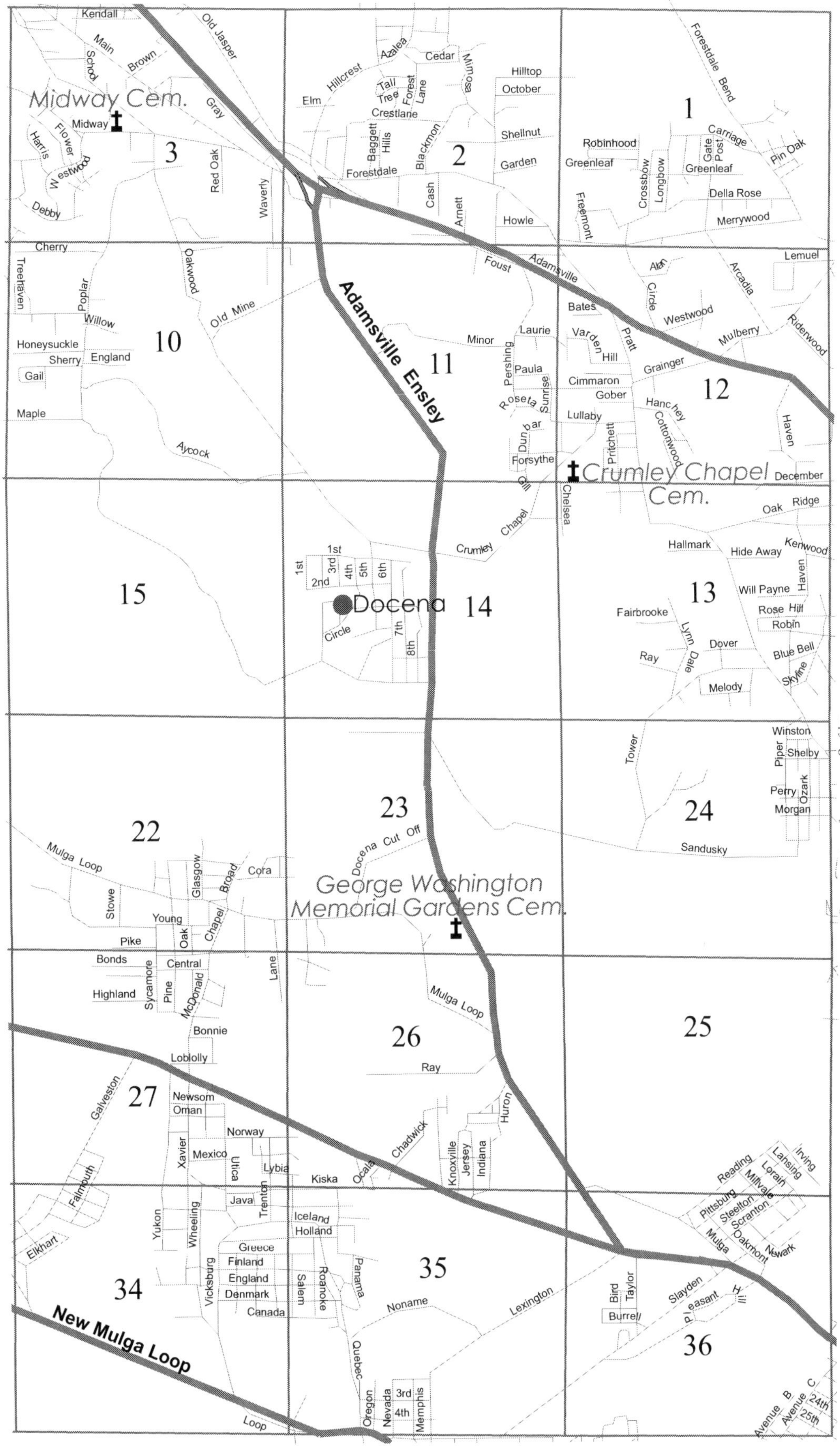

Helpful Hints

1. This road map has a number of uses, but primarily it is to help you: a) find the present location of land owned by your ancestors (at least the general area), b) find cemeteries and city-centers, and c) estimate the route/roads used by Census-takers & tax-assessors.

2. If you plan to travel to Jefferson County to locate cemeteries or land parcels, please pick up a modern travel map for the area before you do. Mapping old land parcels on modern maps is not as exact a science as you might think. Just the slightest variations in public land survey coordinates, estimates of parcel boundaries, or road-map deviations can greatly alter a map's representation of how a road either does or doesn't cross a particular parcel of land.

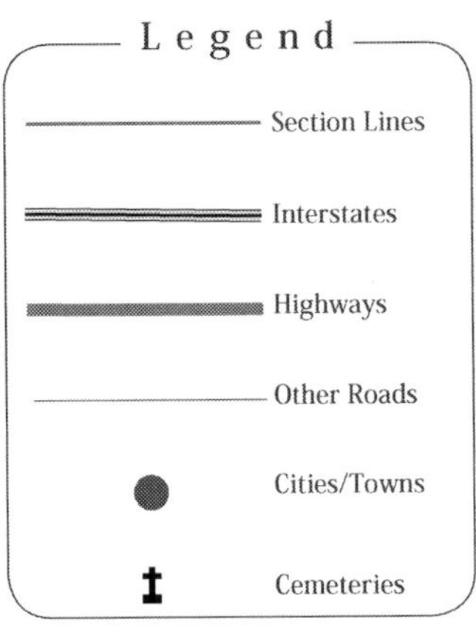

Scale: Section = 1 mile X 1 mile (generally, with some exceptions)

Historical Map

T17-S R4-W
Huntsville Meridian

Map Group 21

Cities & Towns

Docena
Mulga

Cemeteries

Crumley Chapel Cemetery
George Washington Memorial Gardens Cemetery
Lakeview Cemetery
Midway Cemetery
Union Grove Cemetery
Village Falls Cemetery

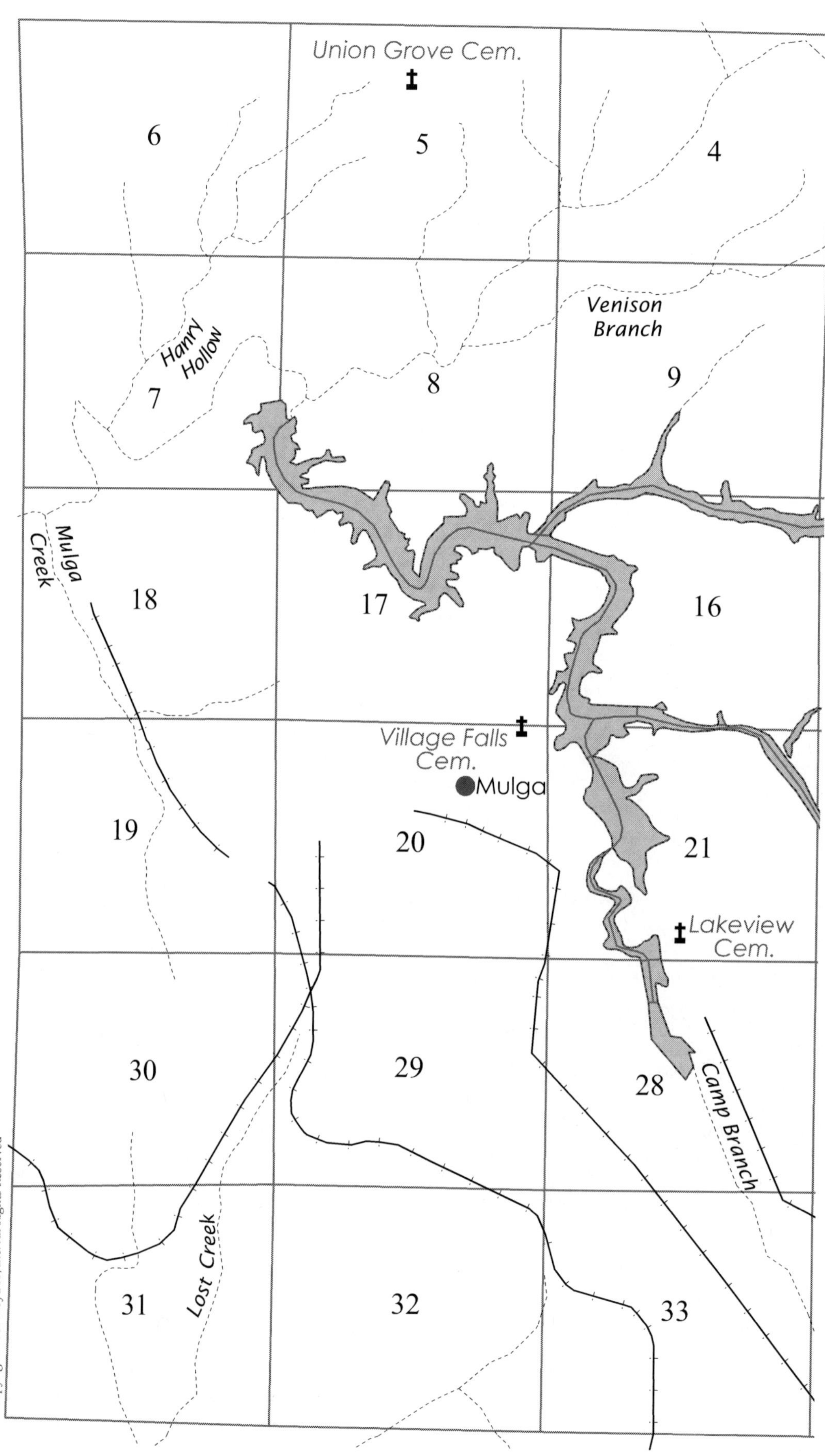

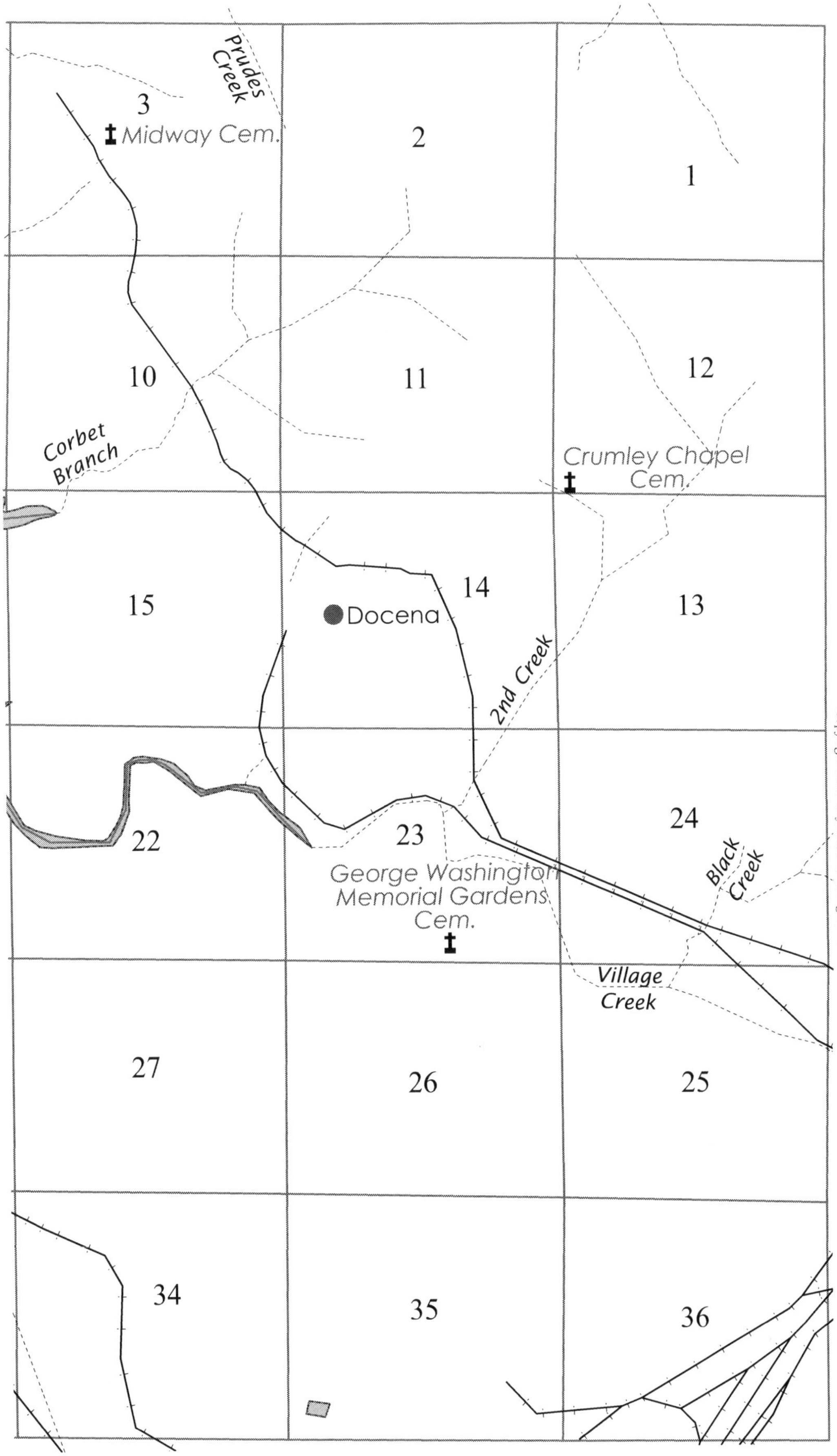

Prudes Creek
3
Midway Cem.
2
1
10
11
12
Corbet Branch
Crumley Chapel Cem.
15
Docena
14
13
2nd Creek
22
23
24
George Washington Memorial Gardens Cem.
Black Creek
Village Creek
27
26
25
34
35
36

Helpful Hints

1. This Map takes a different look at the same Congressional Township displayed in the preceding two maps. It presents features that can help you better envision the historical development of the area: a) Water-bodies (lakes & ponds), b) Water-courses (rivers, streams, etc.), c) Railroads, d) City/town center-points (where they were oftentimes located when first settled), and e) Cemeteries.

2. Using this "Historical" map in tandem with this Township's Patent Map and Road Map, may lead you to some interesting discoveries. You will often find roads, towns, cemeteries, and waterways are named after nearby landowners: sometimes those names will be the ones you are researching. See how many of these research gems you can find here in Jefferson County.

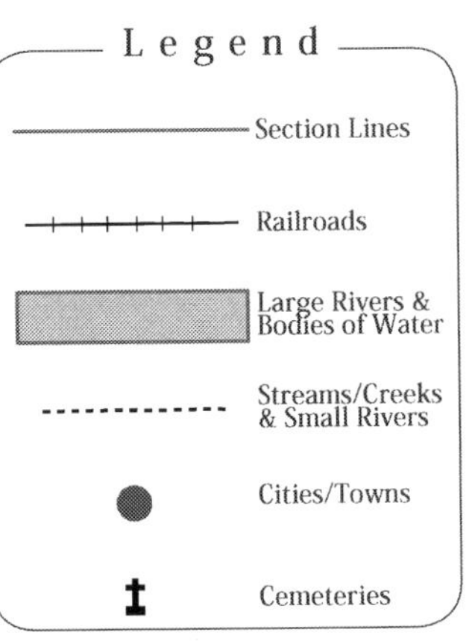

Scale: Section = 1 mile X 1 mile
(there are some exceptions)

Map Group 22: Index to Land Patents

Township 17-South Range 3-West (Huntsville)

After you locate an individual in this Index, take note of the Section and Section Part then proceed to the Land Patent map on the pages immediately following. You should have no difficulty locating the corresponding parcel of land.

The "For More Info" Column will lead you to more information about the underlying Patents. See the *Legend* at right, and the "How to Use this Book" chapter, for more information.

LEGEND

"For More Info . . . " column

A = Authority (Legislative Act, See Appendix "A")
B = Block or Lot (location in Section unknown)
C = Cancelled Patent
F = Fractional Section
G = Group (Multi-Patentee Patent, see Appendix "C")
V = Overlaps another Parcel
R = Re-Issued (Parcel patented more than once)

(A & G items require you to look in the Appendixes referred to above. All other Letter-designations followed by a number require you to locate line-items in this index that possess the ID number found after the letter).

ID	Individual in Patent	Sec.	Sec. Part	Date Issued	Other Counties	For More Info . . .
3904	ABERCROMBIE, Nicholas	2	W½SW	1878-04-09		A4
3781	ADAMS, Elias	29	E½NE	1824-05-19		A1
3938	ADKINS, Thomas M	26	SWSE	1837-04-01		A1
3739	ANDREWS, Allen	20	SENE	1884-03-10		A4
3764	AYRES, Daniel	14	W½SE	1833-06-02		A1 G6
3811	AYRES, Jacob	1	E½NW	1826-06-01		A1
3846	BAGLEY, Joab	26	SESW	1853-08-01		A1
3845	" "	26	N½SW	1854-07-15		A1
3812	BAKER, Jacob H	32	S½SE	1854-07-15		A1
3743	BARRY, Armstead	29	E½SE	1823-06-02		A1 G16
3891	BEAM, Michael	31	E½SW	1824-05-18		A1
3802	BIBB, Irena	11	N½NE	1837-03-20		A1
3737	BILLINGSLEA, Alfred	2	E½NW	1885-03-16		A1
3908	BROTHERS, Paul	2	E½SE	1878-04-09		A4
3907	" "	2	E½NE	1892-03-01		A1
3765	BROWN, David	27	W½NE	1823-06-02		A1 G28
3805	BROWN, Isaac M	4	N½SE	1882-06-10		A1
3806	" "	4	SWSE	1885-06-20		A4
3822	BROWN, James	31	NENW	1858-06-01		A1
3823	" "	31	NWNW	1858-06-01		A1
3824	" "	31	SWNW	1858-06-01		A1
3733	BUCKELEW, Abner J	6	SESW	1881-04-11		A4
3734	" "	6	SWSE	1881-04-11		A4
3788	BURFORD, George	12	NWSW	1889-11-21		A4
3847	BURFORD, John	13	E½SE	1831-01-04		A1
3850	BUTLER, John G	10	NENW	1839-09-20		A1
3852	" "	3	SWSW	1839-09-20		A1 C R3896
3851	" "	3	SESW	1912-11-11		A1
3877	CAPERS, Joseph	20	NENE	1881-04-11		A1
3789	CARMICHAEL, George J	29	SWNW	1837-03-30		A1
3790	CLIFT, George W	1	N½SE	1858-06-01		A1
3791	" "	1	SESW	1858-06-01		A1
3792	" "	12	NENW	1858-06-01		A1
3793	" "	12	SWNW	1858-06-01		A1
3900	COBB, Nancy L	6	E½SE	1883-07-03		A4
3981	CONWAY, Wilson W	6	SENW	1876-04-01		A4
3982	" "	6	SWNE	1876-04-01		A4
3816	COUNTS, Jacob W	14	NWNW	1883-09-15		A4
3825	CRAUSWELL, James E	18	W½NE	1881-04-11		A1
3950	CUMMING, William	19	W½NW	1837-03-20		A1 G68
3764	DACUS, Jarrel	14	W½SE	1833-06-02		A1 G6
3801	DEMENT, Ira	12	NWNE	1889-10-07		A1
3834	DOLLAR, James P	4	N½SW	1860-10-01		A1
3859	DUPUY, John M	24	E½SW	1837-04-01		A1
3860	" "	24	W½SE	1837-04-01		A1
3861	" "	25	E½NW	1837-04-01		A1

ID	Individual in Patent	Sec.	Sec. Part	Date Issued	Other Counties	For More Info . . .
3862	DUPUY, John M (Cont'd)	25	W½NE	1837-04-01		A1
3906	DYER, Otis	1	W½NE	1826-06-10		A1
3923	EARL, Samuel S	26	E½NW	1837-11-07		A1
3924	EARLE, Samuel S	33	NENW	1839-09-20		A1
3926	" "	34	SWNW	1839-09-20		A1
3925	" "	34	NWNW	1849-08-01		A1
3944	EARLEY, Thomas P	17	SWNW	1858-06-01		A1
3951	EARLEY, William	31	W½SW	1824-10-20		A1 R3952
3952	" "	31	W½SW	1914-12-14		A1 R3951
3948	EASTIS, Wiley	4	NWNW	1834-10-14		A1
3757	ECHOLS, Charles L	18	N½SE	1881-04-11		A1
3758	" "	18	SESW	1881-04-11		A1
3759	" "	18	SWSE	1881-04-11		A1
3826	ECHOLS, James F	18	W½NW	1891-10-07		A1
3848	ECHOLS, John	18	SWSW	1858-06-01		A1
3849	" "	19	NWNE	1858-06-01		A1
3870	ECHOLS, John W	20	NWNW	1875-11-20		A4
3871	" "	20	S½NW	1880-12-30		A4
3872	" "	20	SWNE	1880-12-30		A4
3899	ECHOLS, Nancy	18	NWSW	1881-06-01		A1
3969	ECHOLS, William P	8	S½NE	1881-09-01		A1 V3986, 3984
3983	ECHOLS, Winston C	8	NESE	1881-12-10		A1
3984	" "	8	SENE	1881-12-10		A1 V3969
3985	ECHOLS, Winston W	8	SENW	1881-09-01		A4
3986	" "	8	SWNE	1881-09-01		A4 V3969
3949	EUBANK, William C	18	SESE	1858-06-01		A1
3937	FARRIS, Thomas J	24	NWSW	1834-10-14		A1
3799	FERGUSON, Henry	33	E½NE	1824-05-18		A1
3854	FERGUSON, John H	27	E½SW	1824-05-04		A1
3800	FLANAGAN, Hiram M	3	NWNW	1834-11-04		A1
3873	FRANKLIN, John W	10	N½SE	1886-02-10		A1
3786	FREEMAN, Frances A	6	NESW	1885-11-13		A1
3934	FRIEL, Thomas	12	SENW	1883-07-03		A4
3853	GARY, John	12	E½SW	1824-05-10		A1
3954	GILL, William	12	NWNW	1839-09-20		A1
3742	GOING, Amos	20	N½SW	1881-04-11		A1
3935	GOODWIN, Thomas	30	E½SE	1823-06-02		A1
3766	GUTHREY, David	4	S½SW	1858-06-01		A1
3959	HAMNER, William	25	E½SE	1823-06-02		A1 G116
3957	" "	25	E½SW	1823-06-02		A1
3960	" "	25	W½SE	1823-06-02		A1 G116
3958	" "	25	W½SW	1823-06-02		A1
3798	HANCOCK, Hardy H	6	SWSW	1858-06-01		A1
3827	HANEY, James	12	W½SE	1823-07-09		A1
3961	HANNA, William	25	E½NE	1824-04-12		A1
3855	HARRIS, John	4	NWNE	1858-06-01		A1
3856	" "	4	SWNW	1858-06-01		A1
3787	HAWKINS, Frank	30	NENW	1881-06-01		A1
3817	HAWKINS, James A	14	NWSW	1858-06-01		A1
3818	" "	14	SWNW	1858-06-01		A1
3819	" "	15	E½SE	1858-06-01		A1
3878	HAWKINS, Josiah	30	N½NE	1881-04-11		A4
3901	HAWKINS, Nathaniel	22	W½NW	1854-07-15		A1
3946	HAWKINS, Washington A	21	E½NE	1854-07-15		A1
3962	HAWKINS, William	28	E½SW	1823-06-02		A1
3963	" "	28	W½SE	1823-06-02		A1
3964	" "	28	W½SW	1823-06-02		A1
3965	" "	33	W½NW	1823-06-02		A1
3979	HAWKINS, Williamson	29	SWNE	1837-03-30		A1
3980	" "	33	NWNE	1839-09-20		A1
3971	" "	20	NENW	1844-07-10		A1
3972	" "	20	NWNE	1853-08-01		A1
3976	" "	21	S½SW	1854-07-15		A1
3977	" "	21	SWSE	1854-07-15		A1
3970	" "	20	E½SE	1858-06-01		A1
3973	" "	20	NWSE	1858-06-01		A1
3974	" "	21	N½SW	1858-06-01		A1
3975	" "	21	NWSE	1858-06-01		A1
3978	" "	29	NWNE	1858-06-01		A1
3857	HAYS, John	10	NE	1885-05-04		A1
3863	HILL, John M	6	NWSE	1889-12-28		A1
3909	HILL, Reuben R	6	NWNW	1881-09-01		A1
3910	" "	6	NWSW	1881-09-01		A1

ID	Individual in Patent	Sec.	Sec. Part	Date Issued	Other Counties	For More Info . . .
3911	HILL, Reuben R (Cont'd)	6	SWNW	1881-09-01		A1
3912	HILL, Reuben T	18	E½NE	1881-06-01		A1
3828	HOLMES, James	23	E½NW	1824-05-18		A1
3889	HOLMES, Mary	14	NENW	1883-04-10		A4
3936	HORN, Thomas	17	E½SW	1824-04-12		A1
3763	HOUK, Coonrod	5	NWNE	1835-10-01		A1
3767	HOUK, David	4	E½NE	1826-06-10		A1
3768	" "	4	NENW	1839-09-20		A1
3955	HUDSON, William H	22	E½NE	1823-06-02		A1
3752	HUGHES, Caleb	12	E½NE	1824-04-30		A1
3956	HUTSON, William H	23	W½NW	1823-06-02		A1
3874	ISAACS, John W	6	NENE	1858-06-01		A1
3858	JOHNSTON, John	5	E½NE	1824-04-30		A1
3841	JONES, Jesse	22	E½SE	1823-06-02		A1
3843	" "	26	W½NW	1823-06-02		A1
3842	" "	22	SW	1824-05-10		A1
3794	KELLY, Gersham	34	W½NE	1834-10-01		A1
3795	KELLY, Gershom P	10	SW	1858-06-01		A1
3796	" "	15	N½NW	1858-06-01		A1
3797	" "	9	E½SE	1858-06-01		A1
3893	KELLY, Moses	10	SENW	1858-06-01		A1
3894	" "	10	W½NW	1858-06-01		A1
3895	" "	3	NESW	1858-06-01		A1
3896	" "	3	SWSW	1858-06-01		A1 R3852
3897	" "	4	SESE	1858-06-01		A1
3898	" "	9	E½NE	1858-06-01		A1
3740	KILLOUGH, Allen	27	W½NW	1823-06-02		A1 G145
3771	KILLOUGH, David	27	E½NW	1823-06-02		A1 G146
3769	" "	28	E½SE	1823-06-02		A1
3770	" "	34	E½NW	1826-05-15		A1
3803	KILLOUGH, Isaac	23	SW	1823-06-02		A1
3804	" "	27	W½SW	1824-05-10		A1
3885	KILLOUGH, Margaret	34	E½SE	1823-06-02		A1
3886	" "	34	W½SE	1823-06-02		A1
3887	KILLOUGH, Margarett	34	E½NE	1824-04-14		A1
3748	KYLE, Baker	22	NENW	1883-10-01		A4
3813	LAND, Jacob	17	E½NE	1858-06-01		A1
3814	" "	17	E½SE	1858-06-01		A1
3815	" "	8	S½SE	1858-06-01		A1
3875	LANE, John W	13	E½SW	1823-06-02		A1 G150
3876	" "	13	W½SW	1823-06-02		A1 G150
3764	LOCKHART, Benjamin	14	W½SE	1833-06-02		A1 G6
3888	LOCKHART, Martin	20	S½SW	1881-04-11		A1
3864	MARTIN, John	34	E½SW	1823-06-02		A1
3865	" "	34	W½SW	1823-06-02		A1
3945	MASON, Viney	10	S½SE	1889-03-01		A4
3916	MASTERS, Robert	5	NESE	1839-09-20		A1
3917	MAVERICK, Samuel	24	W½NW	1823-06-02		A1
3918	" "	31	E½NE	1823-06-02		A1
3919	" "	31	W½NE	1823-06-02		A1
3920	" "	32	E½NE	1823-06-02		A1
3921	" "	32	E½NW	1823-06-02		A1
3922	" "	32	W½NW	1823-06-02		A1
3966	MCCARTEY, William	8	SWNW	1854-07-15		A1
3959	MCCARTNEY, James	25	E½SE	1823-06-02		A1 G116
3960	" "	25	W½SE	1823-06-02		A1 G116
3771	" "	27	E½NW	1823-06-02		A1 G146
3740	" "	27	W½NW	1823-06-02		A1 G145
3881	MCCOO, Leonard	20	SWSE	1891-12-01		A4 R3882
3882	MCCOW, Leonard	20	SWSE	1894-03-10		A4 C R3881
3830	MCCOY, James	1	E½NE	1826-06-01		A1
3883	MCDANIEL, Mack	6	NENW	1885-08-05		A1
3884	" "	6	NWNE	1885-08-05		A1
3953	MCDUFF, William F	32	NWSW	1844-07-10		A1
3879	MCGUIRE, Josiah	14	E½SE	1823-06-02		A1
3880	MCMILLION, Lemuel G	33	NWSW	1854-07-15		A1
3782	MCWILLIAMS, Elizabeth	31	NWSE	1839-09-20		A1
3783	" "	31	SENW	1839-09-20		A1
3831	MCWILLIAMS, James	33	E½SE	1824-04-30		A1
3839	MCWILLIAMS, James W	31	SWSE	1853-08-01		A1
3840	" "	32	NESE	1853-08-01		A1
3835	" "	29	NWNW	1860-04-02		A1
3836	" "	30	S½NE	1860-04-02		A1

ID	Individual in Patent	Sec.	Sec. Part	Date Issued	Other Counties	For More Info . . .
3837	MCWILLIAMS, James W (Cont'd)	30	SENW	1860-04-02		A1
3838	" "	30	SW	1860-04-02		A1
3774	MILES, Dorothy	4	E½SW	1824-04-14		A1 C
3941	MITCHELL, Thomas	14	E½NE	1823-06-02		A1
3939	" "	12	SWNE	1839-09-20		A1
3940	" "	12	SWSW	1839-09-20		A1
3820	MUDD, James A	26	NWSE	1854-07-15		A1
3821	" "	26	SWSW	1854-07-15		A1
3744	MURPHY, Armstead	28	E½NW	1823-06-02		A1
3745	" "	28	W½NW	1823-06-02		A1
3967	NABOURS, William	28	E½NE	1823-06-02		A1
3968	" "	28	W½NE	1823-06-02		A1
3832	NATIONS, James	12	E½SE	1823-06-02		A1
3765	" "	27	W½NE	1823-06-02		A1 G28
3833	" "	27	E½NE	1824-04-26		A1
3902	NATIONS, Nathaniel	13	E½NE	1823-06-02		A1
3903	" "	13	W½NE	1823-06-02		A1
3760	OGWIN, Charles W	8	NESW	1876-04-01		A4
3761	" "	8	NWSE	1876-04-01		A4
3866	OGWIN, John	8	W½SW	1875-10-01		A4
3754	OWEN, Caleb	24	E½NW	1823-06-02		A1
3755	" "	24	W½NE	1823-07-09		A1
3753	" "	24	E½NE	1824-05-04		A1
3875	OWEN, David	13	E½SW	1823-06-02		A1 G150
3876	" "	13	W½SW	1823-06-02		A1 G150
3773	" "	14	W½NE	1824-04-12		A1
3772	" "	13	W½SE	1824-04-14		A1
3931	OWEN, Stephen M	13	E½NW	1823-06-02		A1
3932	" "	23	SE	1823-06-02		A1
3942	OWEN, Thomas	26	E½SE	1824-04-12		A1 R3943
3943	" "	26	E½SE	1920-01-29		A1 R3942
3775	PARSONS, Edmund	32	NWSE	1837-04-01		A1
3776	" "	32	SWSW	1837-04-01		A1
3784	POTTER, Elizabeth	23	E½NE	1823-06-02		A1 G198
3929	POTTER, Sarah	13	W½NW	1824-05-27		A1
3785	POWELL, Elza	18	E½NW	1881-04-11		A1
3915	POWELL, Robert J	6	SENE	1889-10-07		A1
3947	POWELL, Wilborn G	8	NENW	1889-10-07		A1
3844	REGAN, Jesse	18	NESW	1881-04-11		A1
3738	ROEBUCK, Alfred H	33	SWNE	1839-09-20		A1
3735	RUSSELL, Absalom	29	W½SE	1823-06-02		A1
3736	" "	30	W½SE	1823-06-02		A1
3927	SENTELL, Samuel	22	W½SE	1823-06-02		A1
3741	SIMMONS, Amanda	2	W½NE	1878-04-09		A4
3784	SIMS, Edward	23	E½NE	1823-06-02		A1 G198
3777	" "	23	W½NE	1823-06-02		A1
3743	" "	29	E½SE	1823-06-02		A1 G16
3778	" "	29	E½SW	1823-06-02		A1
3779	" "	29	W½SW	1823-06-02		A1
3780	" "	32	W½NE	1823-06-02		A1
3746	SMITH, Augustus	4	SENW	1884-12-05		A1
3747	" "	4	SWNE	1884-12-05		A1
3950	SMITH, Eldred	19	W½NW	1837-03-20		A1 G68
3905	SPENCER, Octavius	31	E½SE	1853-08-01		A1
3750	STAGGS, Benjamin	14	SENW	1839-09-20		A1
3751	" "	14	SWSW	1839-09-20		A1
3829	STAGGS, James M	1	SWSW	1839-09-20		A1
3988	STAGGS, Zachariah	1	NESW	1839-09-20		A1
3989	" "	22	W½NE	1839-09-20		A1
3867	STOVALL, John	27	E½SE	1838-08-28		A1
3913	TANKERSLY, Richard	33	SWSW	1854-07-15		A1
3749	TANNEHILL, Benjamin H	32	E½SW	1824-05-20		A1
3756	TARRANT, Carter	33	W½SE	1824-10-20		A1 G216
3756	TARRANT, Henry M	33	W½SE	1824-10-20		A1 G216
3928	THOMPSON, Sarah A	30	W½NW	1875-11-20		A4
3868	VANZANDT, John	24	SWSW	1839-09-20		A1
3869	" "	25	W½NW	1839-09-20		A1
3807	VARNON, Isaac	5	SWSW	1858-06-01		A1
3808	" "	7	NENE	1858-06-01		A1
3809	" "	7	S½NE	1858-06-01		A1
3810	" "	8	NWNW	1858-06-01		A1
3987	WADE, Woodson	22	SENW	1883-08-13		A1
3762	WATTS, Clinton	7	NWNW	1839-09-20		A1

ID	Individual in Patent	Sec.	Sec. Part	Date Issued	Other Counties	For More Info . . .
3890	WHITTINGTON, Melvin P	19	E½NW	1831-06-01		A1
3930	WILLIAMS, Sharp	2	E½SW	1878-04-09		A4
3933	WILLIAMS, Tharp	2	W½SE	1891-10-07		A1
3892	WILSON, Miles V	8	SESW	1883-07-03		A4
3914	WOODRUFF, Richard	11	S½NE	1837-03-20		A1

Patent Map

T17-S R3-W
Huntsville Meridian

Map Group 22

Township Statistics

Parcels Mapped	:	257
Number of Patents	:	218
Number of Individuals	:	161
Patentees Identified	:	158
Number of Surnames	:	116
Multi-Patentee Parcels	:	12
Oldest Patent Date	:	6/2/1823
Most Recent Patent	:	1/29/1920
Block/Lot Parcels	:	0
Parcels Re - Issued	:	4
Parcels that Overlap	:	3
Cities and Towns	:	1
Cemeteries	:	5

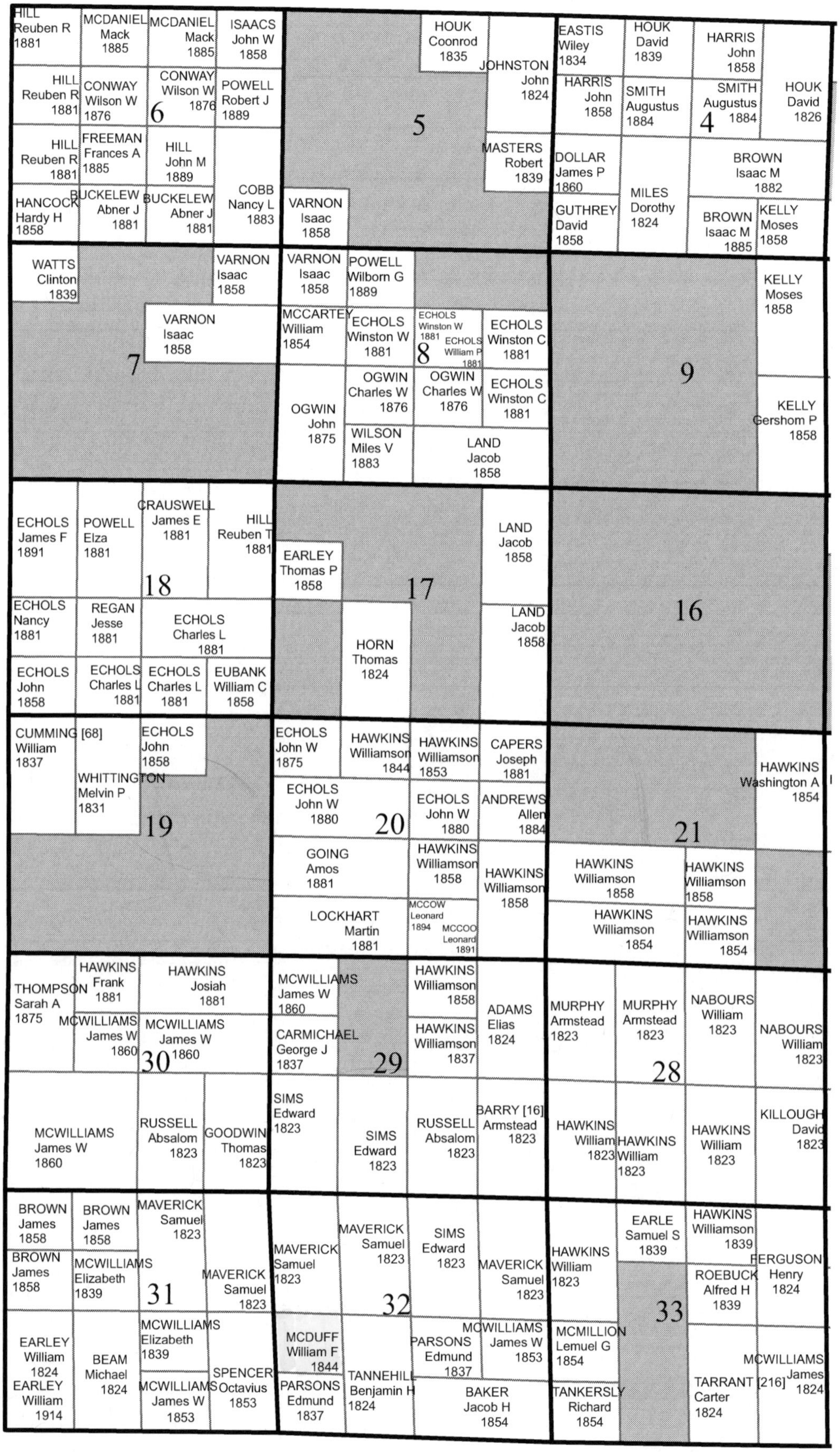

Helpful Hints

1. This Map's INDEX can be found on the preceding pages.
2. Refer to Map "C" to see where this Township lies within Jefferson County, Alabama.
3. Numbers within square brackets [ ] denote a multi-patentee land parcel (multi-owner). Refer to Appendix "C" for a full list of members in this group.
4. Areas that look to be crowded with Patentees usually indicate multiple sales of the same parcel (Re-issues) or Overlapping parcels. See this Township's Index for an explanation of these and other circumstances that might explain "odd" groupings of Patentees on this map.

Legend

- Patent Boundary
- Section Boundary
- No Patents Found (or Outside County)
- 1., 2., 3., ... Lot Numbers (when beside a name)
- [ ] Group Number (see Appendix "C")

Scale: Section = 1 mile X 1 mile (generally, with some exceptions)

Road Map

T17-S R3-W
Huntsville Meridian

Map Group 22

Cities & Towns

Birmingham

Cemeteries

Emanuel Cemetery
Fraternal Cemetery
Knesses Israel Cemetery
Oak Hill Cemetery
Roberts Cemetery

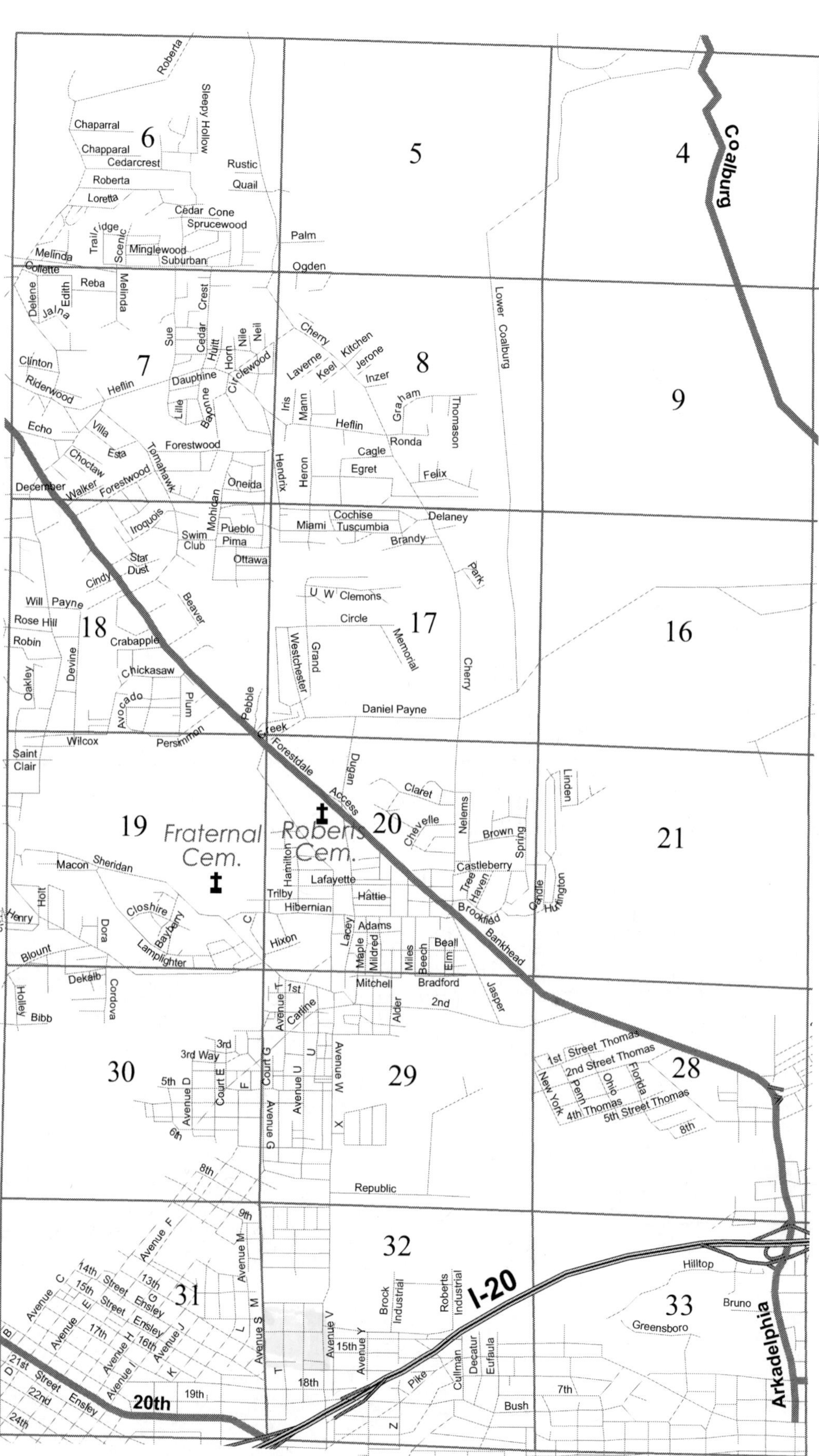

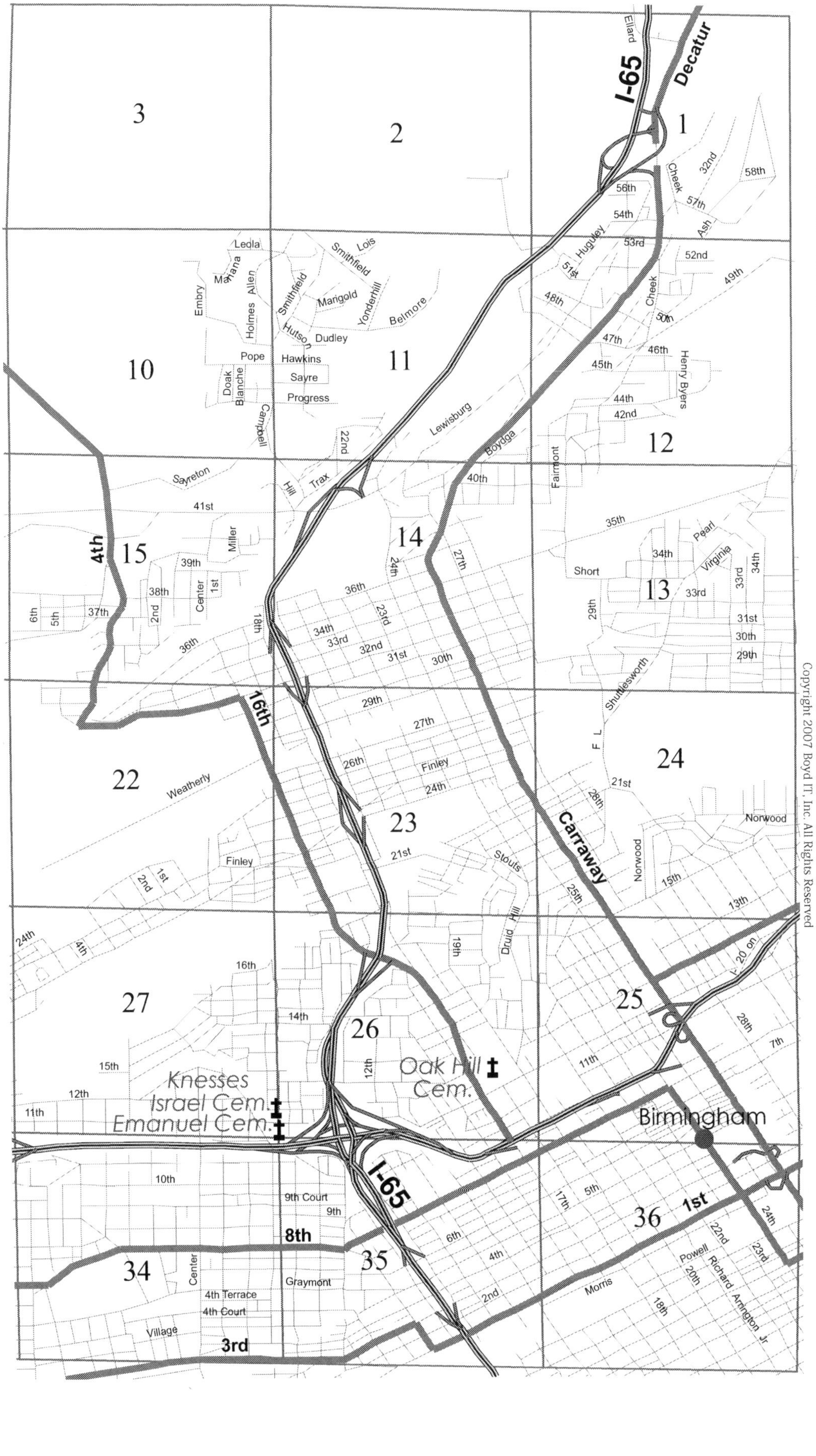

Helpful Hints

1. This road map has a number of uses, but primarily it is to help you: a) find the present location of land owned by your ancestors (at least the general area), b) find cemeteries and city-centers, and c) estimate the route/roads used by Census-takers & tax-assessors.

2. If you plan to travel to Jefferson County to locate cemeteries or land parcels, please pick up a modern travel map for the area before you do. Mapping old land parcels on modern maps is not as exact a science as you might think. Just the slightest variations in public land survey coordinates, estimates of parcel boundaries, or road-map deviations can greatly alter a map's representation of how a road either does or doesn't cross a particular parcel of land.

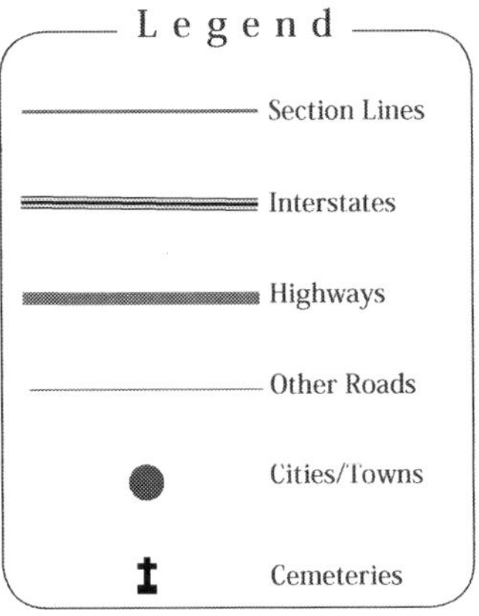

Scale: Section = 1 mile X 1 mile
(generally, with some exceptions)

Historical Map

T17-S R3-W
Huntsville Meridian

Map Group 22

Cities & Towns
Birmingham

Cemeteries
Emanuel Cemetery
Fraternal Cemetery
Knesses Israel Cemetery
Oak Hill Cemetery
Roberts Cemetery

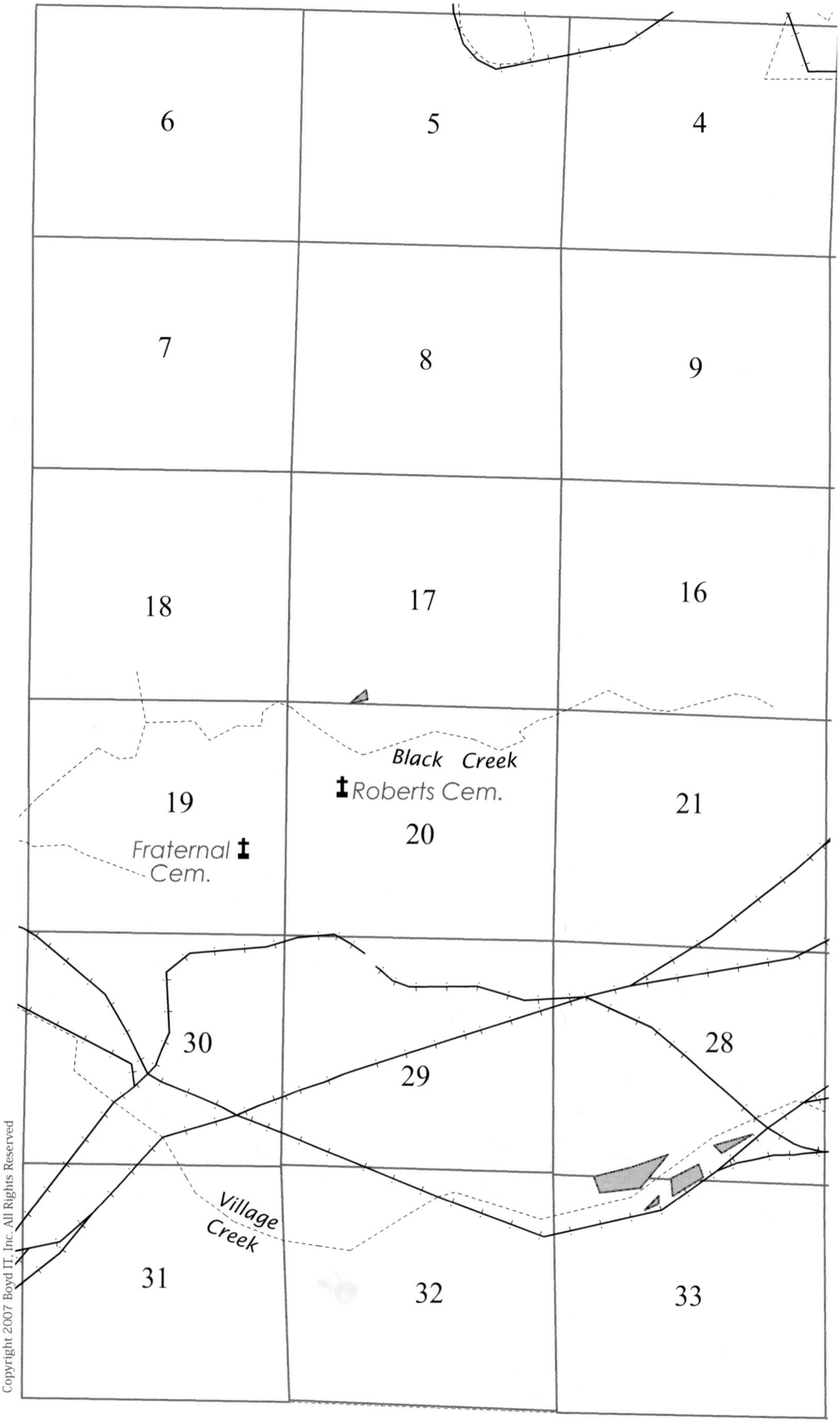

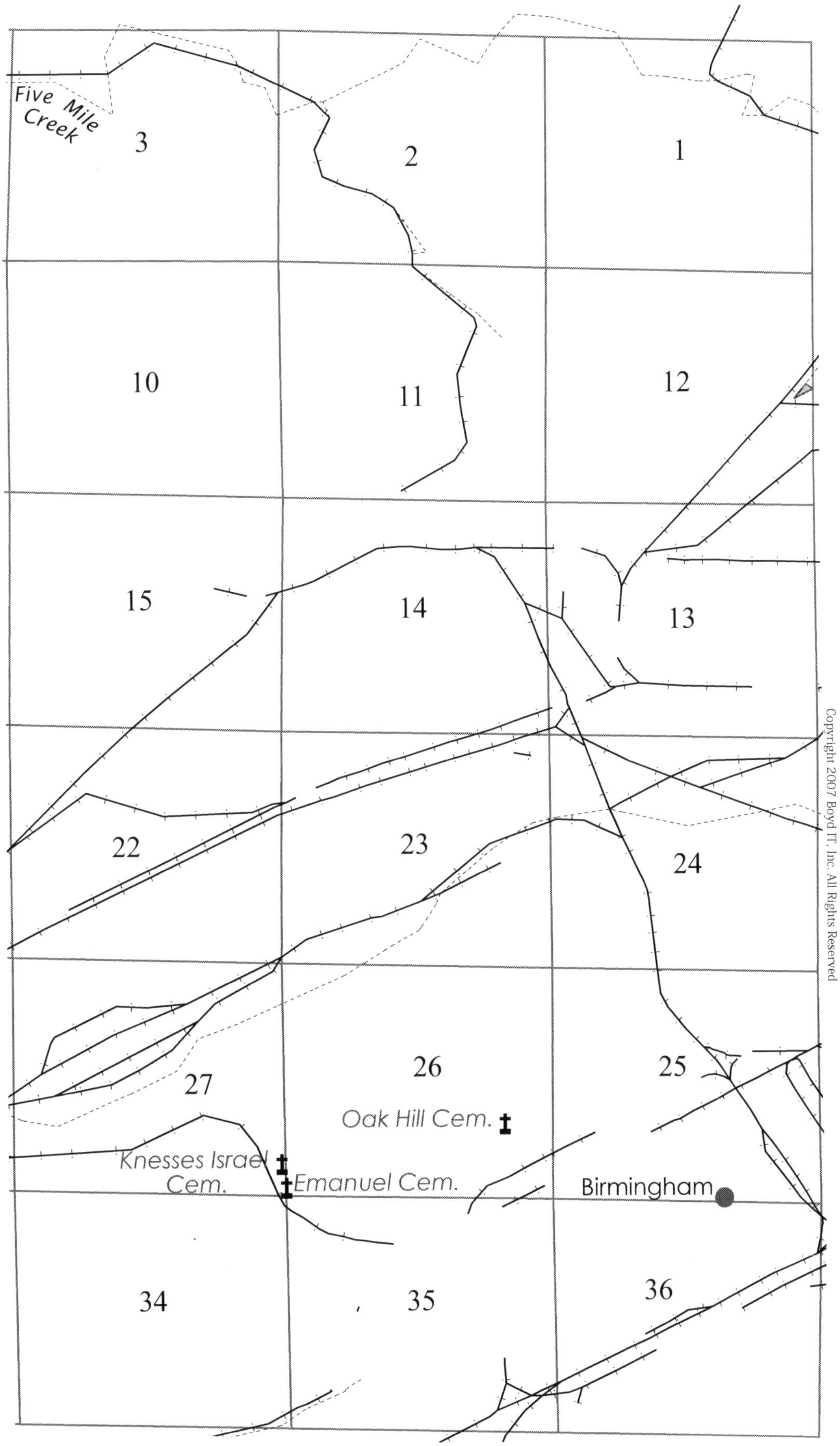

Five Mile Creek
3
2
1
10
11
12
15
14
13
22
23
24
27
26
25
Oak Hill Cem.
Knesses Israel Cem.
Emanuel Cem.
Birmingham
34
35
36

Helpful Hints

1. This Map takes a different look at the same Congressional Township displayed in the preceding two maps. It presents features that can help you better envision the historical development of the area: a) Water-bodies (lakes & ponds), b) Water-courses (rivers, streams, etc.), c) Railroads, d) City/town center-points (where they were oftentimes located when first settled), and e) Cemeteries.

2. Using this "Historical" map in tandem with this Township's Patent Map and Road Map, may lead you to some interesting discoveries. You will often find roads, towns, cemeteries, and waterways are named after nearby landowners: sometimes those names will be the ones you are researching. See how many of these research gems you can find here in Jefferson County.

Legend

Section Lines
Railroads
Large Rivers & Bodies of Water
Streams/Creeks & Small Rivers
Cities/Towns
Cemeteries

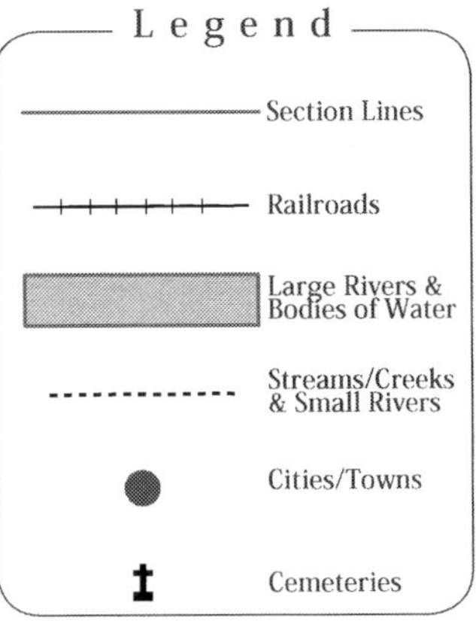

Scale: Section = 1 mile X 1 mile
(there are some exceptions)

Map Group 23: Index to Land Patents

Township 17-South Range 2-West (Huntsville)

After you locate an individual in this Index, take note of the Section and Section Part then proceed to the Land Patent map on the pages immediately following. You should have no difficulty locating the corresponding parcel of land.

The "For More Info" Column will lead you to more information about the underlying Patents. See the *Legend* at right, and the "How to Use this Book" chapter, for more information.

LEGEND

"For More Info . . . " column

A = Authority (Legislative Act, See Appendix "A")
B = Block or Lot (location in Section unknown)
C = Cancelled Patent
F = Fractional Section
G = Group (Multi-Patentee Patent, see Appendix "C")
V = Overlaps another Parcel
R = Re-Issued (Parcel patented more than once)

(A & G items require you to look in the Appendixes referred to above. All other Letter-designations followed by a number require you to locate line-items in this index that possess the ID number found after the letter).

ID	Individual in Patent	Sec.	Sec. Part	Date Issued	Other Counties	For More Info . . .
4088	ARMSTRONG, James C	8	SWSE	1889-10-07		A1
4198	ARMSTRONG, Robert	22	SWNE	1858-06-01		A1
4199	" "	23	S½SW	1858-06-01		A1
4029	AYERS, Cyrus	36	E½NE	1883-07-03		A4
4172	AYRES, Moses	5	W½SE	1823-05-01		A1
4173	" "	8	W½NW	1823-05-01		A1
4117	AYRS, John	8	E½NW	1826-06-01		A1
4115	BAGLEY, Joab	24	NENW	1852-01-01		A1
4116	" "	31	SWSE	1854-07-15		A1
4113	BAGWELL, Jason	36	E½SE	1890-07-03		A4 G8
4113	BAGWELL, Jeremiah	36	E½SE	1890-07-03		A4 G8
4113	BAGWELL, Mary	36	E½SE	1890-07-03		A4 G8
4235	BAGWELL, Wiley	23	NWSW	1834-11-04		A1
4236	" "	23	SENW	1834-11-04		A1
4113	BAGWELL, Wilson	36	E½SE	1890-07-03		A4 G8
4274	BAKER, William R	25	NWNW	1848-04-15		A1
4272	" "	24	W½SE	1849-08-01		A1
4271	" "	24	SESW	1853-08-01		A1
4270	" "	24	NESE	1858-06-01		A1
4273	" "	25	NENW	1858-06-01		A1
4275	" "	25	SWNW	1858-06-01		A1
4276	" "	26	SWNE	1858-06-01		A1
4007	BARRY, Armstead	20	E½NE	1823-05-01		A1 G14
4008	" "	20	W½NE	1823-05-01		A1 G15
4217	BARTON, Thomas	15	E½NE	1823-05-01		A1 G17
4214	" "	15	W½NE	1823-05-01		A1
4215	" "	15	W½NW	1823-05-01		A1
4213	" "	15	NWSW	1844-07-10		A1
4212	" "	10	W½NE	1858-06-01		A1
4216	" "	3	W½SE	1858-06-01		A1
4058	BAYLES, George L	9	E½SE	1823-06-02		A1
4060	" "	9	W½SE	1824-05-04		A1
4059	" "	9	NE	1858-06-01		A1
4002	BEARDEN, Ansel	33	SWSE	1858-06-01		A1
4003	" "	33	SWSW	1858-06-01		A1
4009	BEARDIN, Arthur	33	NESW	1858-06-01		A1
4010	" "	33	NWSE	1858-06-01		A1
4011	" "	34	SWSW	1858-06-01		A1
4241	BIBB, William C	32	NENE	1867-11-20		A1 G22 V3992
4242	" "	32	SE	1867-11-20		A1 G22
4243	" "	32	SESW	1867-11-20		A1 G22
4043	BOYLES, Elbert H	13	E½NE	1837-03-20		A1
4087	BRANTLEY, James	15	SWSW	1834-10-21		A1
4077	BRITT, Hiram H	28	SESE	1876-03-15		A1
4082	BROWN, Isaiah C	14	SW	1890-03-08		A1 R4218
4084	BROWN, Jackson	34	W½SE	1824-04-28		A1

ID	Individual in Patent	Sec.	Sec. Part	Date Issued	Other Counties	For More Info . . .
4120	BROWN, John	11	E½NW	1823-05-01		A1
4121	" "	11	W½NE	1823-05-01		A1
4123	" "	2	E½SE	1823-05-01		A1
4124	" "	2	W½SE	1823-05-01		A1
4122	" "	11	W½NW	1824-04-12		A1
4119	" "	11	E½NE	1824-04-26		A1
4237	BROWN, William	21	E½SW	1823-05-01		A1
4238	" "	34	NWSW	1839-09-20		A1
4018	BROWNLEE, Benjamin	36	W½SW	1887-04-20		A4
4017	" "	36	E½SW	1893-04-03		A4
4203	BROWNLEE, Samuel	24	SESE	1890-03-19		A4
4241	BUFFINGTON, William C	32	NENE	1867-11-20		A1 G22 V3992
4242	" "	32	SE	1867-11-20		A1 G22
4243	" "	32	SESW	1867-11-20		A1 G22
4189	BURWELL, Orrin S	35	SWNE	1850-09-02		A1
4188	" "	2	NENW	1852-01-01		A1
4239	BUTTLER, William	33	NE	1858-06-01		A1
4240	" "	34	NWNW	1858-06-01		A1
4026	BYARS, Catharine	3	NENE	1860-04-02		A1
4178	CANTERBERRY, Nelson	5	E½NW	1823-05-01		A1 G43
4177	" "	5	E½SW	1823-05-01		A1
4125	CEMP, John	3	W½NE	1824-10-20		A1
4016	CLARK, Bartholomew	17	E½NE	1827-04-10		A1
4019	CLEMENTS, Benjamin	1	W½NW	1823-05-01		A1 G49
4020	" "	2	E½NE	1823-05-01		A1 G49
4073	CLEMENTS, Hardy	1	E½NW	1823-05-01		A1 G51
4074	" "	1	W½SW	1823-05-01		A1 G51
4007	" "	20	E½NE	1823-05-01		A1 G14
4075	" "	29	W½SW	1823-05-01		A1 G50
4190	COBB, Peter M	33	E½SE	1824-05-10		A1
4090	COKER, James	31	E½NE	1824-04-28		A1
4089	" "	24	NENE	1835-10-01		A1
4244	COKER, William	13	W½NE	1837-03-20		A1 R3990
4155	CONDEN, Josiah	24	W½SW	1824-05-21		A1
4157	COWDEN, Josiah	26	E½NE	1824-04-14		A1
4156	" "	23	E½SE	1824-04-22		A1
4076	CROCKER, Harriet	26	NWSW	1889-08-02		A4
4245	CUMMINGS, William	34	NESW	1850-04-01		A1
4248	CUMMINS, William	34	NENE	1854-07-15		A1
4246	" "	26	SWSW	1858-06-01		A1
4247	" "	27	SWSE	1858-06-01		A1
4249	" "	34	SENE	1858-06-01		A1
4250	" "	35	NWNW	1858-06-01		A1
4169	DANIEL, Mary	14	S½SE	1838-08-28		A1
4075	DANIEL, William	29	W½SW	1823-05-01		A1 G50
4241	DONELSON, Presley W	32	NENE	1867-11-20		A1 G22 V3992
4242	" "	32	SE	1867-11-20		A1 G22
4243	" "	32	SESW	1867-11-20		A1 G22
4127	DUPUY, John M	30	W½NW	1837-04-01		A1
4128	" "	30	W½SW	1837-04-01		A1
4139	DUPUY, John W	19	E½NW	1839-09-20		A1 G78
4140	" "	19	W½NE	1839-09-20		A1 G78
4030	EASTIS, Daniel	23	SENE	1852-01-01		A1
4290	EASTIS, Willis	34	SWNE	1853-11-15		A1
4288	" "	34	E½SE	1858-06-01		A1
4289	" "	34	SESW	1858-06-01		A1
4251	EDWARDS, William	36	W½NE	1883-07-03		A4
4091	ELLARD, James	4	NWSE	1883-07-03		A4
4143	ELLARD, Jonathan	10	W½SE	1824-04-22		A1
4144	" "	11	E½SW	1824-04-22		A1
4145	" "	15	E½NW	1824-04-22		A1
4170	ELLARD, Merit	24	SENE	1854-07-15		A1
4286	ELLARD, William W	17	SWNE	1853-08-01		A1
4285	" "	17	NWNE	1858-06-01		A1
4167	FERGUSON, Martin	14	N½SE	1837-03-20		A1
4072	FRANKLIN, Green B	26	NWNE	1852-01-01		A1
3990	FRENCH, Aaron	13	W½NE	1829-04-01		A1 R4244
4150	GARRITT, Joseph	10	SWNW	1839-09-20		A1
4241	GILMER, George N	32	NENE	1867-11-20		A1 G22 V3992
4242	" "	32	SE	1867-11-20		A1 G22
4243	" "	32	SESW	1867-11-20		A1 G22
4252	GORE, William	9	E½NW	1858-06-01		A1
4154	GRAHAM, Joshua	6	W½SE	1823-06-02		A1

ID	Individual in Patent	Sec.	Sec. Part	Date Issued	Other Counties	For More Info . . .
4062	GREEN, George L	18	E½SW	1839-09-20		A1 G105
4063	" "	18	SESE	1839-09-20		A1 G105
4064	" "	18	W½SE	1839-09-20		A1 G105
4061	" "	9	SESW	1839-09-20		A1
4065	" "	8	E½SW	1840-11-10		A1 G105
4108	GREEN, Jane Y	4	S½SW	1858-06-01		A1
4109	" "	4	SWSE	1858-06-01		A1
4110	" "	5	SESE	1858-06-01		A1
4111	" "	8	E½NE	1858-06-01		A1
4112	" "	9	W½NW	1858-06-01		A1
4066	GREENE, George L	17	W½SW	1841-01-09		A1
4092	HALE, James	20	E½SW	1824-04-05		A1 G108
4093	" "	29	W½NW	1824-04-05		A1 G107
4093	HALE, Samuel	29	W½NW	1824-04-05		A1 G107
4139	HALE, Samuel W	19	E½NW	1839-09-20		A1 G78
4140	" "	19	W½NE	1839-09-20		A1 G78
4208	" "	20	W½NW	1839-09-20		A1
4094	HALL, James	19	W½SE	1823-05-01		A1 G109
4095	" "	30	E½NE	1823-05-01		A1 G109
4204	HALL, Samuel	19	E½SE	1823-05-01		A1 G111
4094	" "	19	W½SE	1823-05-01		A1 G109
4205	" "	20	W½SW	1823-05-01		A1 G111
4095	" "	30	E½NE	1823-05-01		A1 G109
4206	" "	30	W½NE	1823-05-01		A1 G111
4209	HALL, Samuel W	19	W½NW	1824-05-24		A1
4014	HAMILTON, Audley	1	W½NE	1823-05-01		A1 G115
4015	" "	2	W½NE	1823-05-01		A1 G115
4012	" "	2	E½SW	1824-04-12		A1 R4013
4013	" "	2	E½SW	1920-06-29		A1 R4012
4073	HAMILTON, Audly	1	E½NW	1823-05-01		A1 G51
4019	" "	1	W½NW	1823-05-01		A1 G49
4074	" "	1	W½SW	1823-05-01		A1 G51
4020	" "	2	E½NE	1823-05-01		A1 G49
4264	HAMNER, William	31	E½NW	1823-05-01		A1 G116
4265	" "	31	W½NE	1823-05-01		A1 G117
4263	" "	31	W½NW	1823-05-01		A1
4083	HARRISON, Isham	15	E½SE	1830-11-01		A1
4031	HENLY, Darby	20	E½SE	1823-05-01		A1
4152	HICKMAN, Joseph	31	E½SW	1823-05-01		A1 G131
4151	" "	31	W½SW	1823-05-01		A1
4269	HICKMAN, William P	31	NWSE	1837-11-07		A1
4159	HODGES, Leroy H	26	E½SW	1858-06-01		A1
4160	" "	26	W½SE	1858-06-01		A1
4218	HORNE, Thomas	14	SW	1823-07-09		A1 R4082
4070	KELLY, Gershom	29	W½NE	1824-05-24		A1
4174	KELLY, Moses	30	E½SW	1823-05-01		A1 G144
3994	KILLOUGH, Abner	32	SENW	1858-06-01		A1
3995	" "	32	SWNE	1858-06-01		A1
3996	" "	33	NWNW	1858-06-01		A1
3991	" "	29	S½SE	1861-08-01		A1
3992	" "	32	N½NE	1861-08-01		A1 V4241
3993	" "	32	NENW	1861-08-01		A1
4191	KING, Peyton	29	E½SW	1824-04-14		A1
4004	LATHAM, Anthony	22	NWNE	1839-09-20		A1
4005	" "	23	NWSE	1854-07-15		A1
4006	LATHEM, Anthony	23	SWSE	1858-06-01		A1
4153	LINN, Joseph	30	E½NW	1826-06-10		A1
4048	LLOYD, Emery	28	W½NW	1823-05-01		A1
4171	LOVELESS, Milton	8	SESE	1858-06-01		A1
4196	LOVELESS, Richard	8	NWSW	1837-03-30		A1 R4069
4062	" "	18	E½SW	1839-09-20		A1 G105
4063	" "	18	SESE	1839-09-20		A1 G105
4064	" "	18	W½SE	1839-09-20		A1 G105
4065	" "	8	E½SW	1840-11-10		A1 G105
4194	" "	17	SENW	1854-07-15		A1
4193	" "	17	NENW	1858-06-01		A1
4195	" "	8	N½SE	1858-06-01		A1
4197	" "	9	N½SW	1858-06-01		A1
4041	MANSON, Edward D	36	W½SE	1892-04-20		A4
4039	MARSHALL, Edmund	2	NWNW	1880-02-20		A4
4129	MARTIN, John	31	E½SE	1824-05-25		A1
4210	MARTIN, Solomon	29	E½NE	1824-04-26		A1
4096	MASSEY, James	32	NWNW	1837-11-07		A1

ID	Individual in Patent	Sec.	Sec. Part	Date Issued	Other Counties	For More Info . . .
4079	MCADAMS, Isaac	10	W½SW	1824-04-12		A1
4080	MCADORY, Isaac	36	E½NW	1883-07-03		A4
4081	" "	36	W½NW	1884-12-05		A4
4152	MCADORY, James	31	E½SW	1823-05-01		A1 G131
4008	MCCARTNEY, James	20	W½NE	1823-05-01		A1 G15
4264	" "	31	E½NW	1823-05-01		A1 G116
4178	" "	5	E½NW	1823-05-01		A1 G43
4114	MCCLAIN, Jesse	20	SENW	1837-04-01		A1
4097	MCCOY, James	6	E½SW	1823-06-02		A1
4292	MCMATH, Winder H	32	SWNW	1858-06-01		A1
4291	" "	32	NESW	1861-08-01		A1
4293	" "	32	W½SW	1861-08-01		A1
4021	MILLER, Benjamin	17	SE	1823-05-01		A1
4046	MILNER, Elisha C	12	S½SE	1882-10-30		A1
4221	MITCHEL, Thomas	7	W½NW	1824-04-12		A1
4219	" "	17	W½NW	1839-09-20		A1
4220	" "	18	E½NE	1839-09-20		A1
4224	MITCHELL, Thomas	7	E½NW	1823-05-01		A1
4225	" "	7	W½SW	1823-05-01		A1
4222	" "	18	W½NW	1826-06-10		A1
4223	" "	6	W½SW	1826-12-20		A1
4226	" "	8	W½NE	1839-09-20		A1
4049	MONTGOMERY, Ervin N	24	NESW	1853-08-01		A1
4054	MONTGOMERY, Francis	27	E½SE	1824-05-20		A1
4053	" "	24	SWNW	1835-10-01		A1
4052	" "	24	SENW	1858-06-01		A1
4136	MONTGOMERY, John S	26	NENW	1858-06-01		A1
4137	" "	26	W½NW	1858-06-01		A1
4165	MONTGOMERY, Martha	10	SENW	1854-07-15		A1
4164	" "	10	N½NW	1858-06-01		A1
4166	" "	3	S½SW	1858-06-01		A1
4201	MONTGOMERY, Robert	34	E½NW	1826-05-15		A1
4200	MONTGOMERY, Robert B	34	NWNE	1848-07-01		A1
4233	MONTGOMERY, Washington	14	W½NW	1824-05-27		A1
4234	" "	26	SENW	1834-10-14		A1
4241	MOSES, Alfred H	32	NENE	1867-11-20		A1 G22 V3992
4242	" "	32	SE	1867-11-20		A1 G22
4243	" "	32	SESW	1867-11-20		A1 G22
4071	MURRAY, Gibson W	29	E½NW	1825-09-10		A1
4098	MURRAY, James	21	W½NE	1823-05-01		A1
4101	" "	22	E½SE	1823-05-01		A1 G178
4102	" "	23	W½NW	1823-05-01		A1 G178
4100	" "	22	W½SE	1824-05-04		A1
4099	" "	22	E½NE	1824-05-10		A1
4103	MURRY, James	21	W½SE	1824-05-18		A1
4268	NABORS, William	5	NESE	1854-07-15		A1
4266	NABORS, William M	4	N½SW	1858-06-01		A1
4267	" "	4	NW	1858-06-01		A1
4130	NORTON, John	29	NWSE	1839-09-20		A1
4265	ORR, Jonathan	31	W½NE	1823-05-01		A1 G117
4078	OWEN, Hopson	6	W½NW	1826-12-20		A1
4211	OWEN, Stephen M	7	E½SE	1823-05-01		A1 G189
4227	OWEN, Thomas	5	W½SW	1823-05-01		A1
4228	" "	7	E½NE	1823-05-01		A1
4211	" "	7	E½SE	1823-05-01		A1 G189
4229	" "	7	W½NE	1823-05-01		A1
4230	" "	7	W½SE	1823-05-01		A1
4231	OWENS, Thomas	7	E½SW	1823-05-01		A1
4126	PARKER, John D	26	E½SE	1885-06-20		A4
4032	PEARSON, David	28	E½NE	1858-06-01		A1 V4187, 4183
4033	" "	28	SW	1858-06-01		A1
4034	" "	28	W½SE	1858-06-01		A1
4035	PIERSON, David	22	E½NW	1839-09-20		A1
4036	" "	28	E½NW	1853-08-01		A1
4037	" "	29	NESE	1853-08-01		A1
4038	PRATT, David	4	N½NE	1883-07-03		A4
3998	REAVIS, Allen	19	E½SW	1824-05-24		A1
4134	REED, John	30	E½SE	1823-05-01		A1
4135	" "	30	W½SE	1823-05-01		A1
4202	REED, Robert	20	W½SE	1823-05-01		A1
4279	REED, William	21	W½SW	1823-05-01		A1
4175	REESE, Nancy	21	E½NW	1823-05-01		A1
4176	" "	21	W½NW	1823-05-01		A1

ID	Individual in Patent	Sec.	Sec. Part	Date Issued	Other Counties	For More Info . . .
4056	ROEBUCK, George J	1	SENE	1858-06-01		A1
4057	" "	2	SENW	1858-06-01		A1
4277	SADDLER, William R	13	E½SE	1823-05-01		A1
4278	" "	24	W½NE	1823-05-01		A1
4050	SHOEMAKER, Evander	18	NESE	1839-09-20		A1
4168	SHUTTLESWORTH, Martin	34	SWNW	1834-10-14		A1
4014	SIMS, Edward	1	W½NE	1823-05-01		A1 G115
4217	" "	15	E½NE	1823-05-01		A1 G17
4204	" "	19	E½SE	1823-05-01		A1 G111
4015	" "	2	W½NE	1823-05-01		A1 G115
4205	" "	20	W½SW	1823-05-01		A1 G111
4101	" "	22	E½SE	1823-05-01		A1 G178
4102	" "	23	W½NW	1823-05-01		A1 G178
4174	" "	30	E½SW	1823-05-01		A1 G144
4206	" "	30	W½NE	1823-05-01		A1 G111
4042	" "	6	E½SE	1823-05-01		A1
4241	SMITH, Frank J	32	NENE	1867-11-20		A1 G22 V3992
4242	" "	32	SE	1867-11-20		A1 G22
4243	" "	32	SESW	1867-11-20		A1 G22
4158	SNELL, Larkin M	6	E½NW	1891-06-19		A4
4044	SNOW, Eli	6	E½NE	1823-05-01		A1
4045	" "	6	W½NE	1824-05-04		A1
4092	SPEER, Charles	20	E½SW	1824-04-05		A1 G108
4027	" "	19	E½NE	1824-04-14		A1
4051	STAGGS, Ezekiel	5	E½NE	1823-06-02		A1
4067	STARNES, George	9	SWSW	1839-09-20		A1
4068	STARNES, George W	20	NENW	1839-09-20		A1
4069	" "	8	NWSW	1839-09-20		A1 R4196
4024	TARRANT, Benjamin	5	W½NE	1823-05-01		A1
4025	" "	5	W½NW	1823-05-01		A1
4118	TARRANT, John B	12	N½SE	1880-02-20		A4
4280	THURSTON, William S	3	NESW	1858-06-01		A1
4281	" "	3	NWSW	1858-06-01		A1
4282	" "	3	SWNW	1858-06-01		A1
4283	" "	4	E½SE	1858-06-01		A1
4284	" "	4	S½NE	1858-06-01		A1
4028	TRUSS, Columbus	14	SENE	1889-12-28		A1
3997	TURNER, Alexander	10	SENE	1839-09-20		A1
4161	TURNER, Lewis	23	NESW	1858-06-01		A1
4162	TURNER, Lucy	14	SENW	1858-06-01		A1
4163	" "	14	SWNE	1858-06-01		A1
4207	TURNER, Samuel	22	SESW	1849-05-01		A1
4138	VANZANDT, John	18	W½SW	1839-09-20		A1
4001	WALDROP, Andrew J	2	SWSW	1854-07-15		A1
3999	" "	12	S½NE	1858-06-01		A1
4000	" "	12	S½NW	1858-06-01		A1
4131	WALDROP, John P	22	NESW	1858-06-01		A1
4132	" "	27	NENW	1858-06-01		A1
4133	" "	27	NWNE	1858-06-01		A1
4232	WIDEMAN, Thomas	24	NWNW	1884-03-20		A1
4104	WILSON, James	1	E½SW	1858-06-01		A1
4105	" "	1	W½SE	1858-06-01		A1
4106	" "	12	N½NW	1858-06-01		A1
4107	" "	2	NWSW	1858-06-01		A1
4040	WOOD, Edmund	21	NESE	1839-09-20		A1
4055	WOOD, Frank	2	SWNW	1883-10-01		A4
4085	WOOD, James B	13	NWNW	1858-06-01		A1
4086	" "	14	NENE	1858-06-01		A1
4141	WOOD, John	10	E½SE	1823-05-01		A1
4142	" "	11	W½SW	1823-05-01		A1
4179	WOOD, Obadiah W	22	W½SW	1854-07-15		A1
4180	" "	27	NWSW	1860-04-02		A1
4181	" "	27	SENW	1860-04-02		A1
4182	" "	28	NESE	1860-04-02		A1
4183	" "	28	SENE	1860-04-02		A1 V4032
4184	WOOD, Obediah W	21	SESE	1853-08-01		A1
4185	" "	27	NWNW	1853-08-01		A1
4186	" "	27	SWNW	1853-08-01		A1
4187	" "	28	NENE	1853-08-01		A1 V4032
4192	WOOD, Richard H	1	NENE	1854-07-15		A1
4287	WOOD, William	12	N½NE	1880-02-20		A4
4255	WOOD, William H	11	NWSE	1849-09-01		A1
4253	" "	10	NENE	1853-08-01		A1

ID	Individual in Patent	Sec.	Sec. Part	Date Issued	Other Counties	For More Info . . .
4256	WOOD, William H (Cont'd)	11	SESE	1853-08-01		A1
4258	" "	12	E½SW	1858-06-01		A1
4260	" "	12	SWSW	1858-06-01		A1
4261	" "	3	NESE	1858-06-01		A1
4254	" "	11	NESE	1860-04-02		A1
4257	" "	11	SWSE	1860-04-02		A1
4259	" "	12	NWSW	1860-04-02		A1
4262	" "	3	SESE	1860-04-02		A1
4022	WORTHINGTON, Benjamin P	18	E½NW	1858-06-01		A1
4023	" "	18	W½NE	1858-06-01		A1
4146	YORK, Jonathan	15	E½SW	1824-04-28		A1
4147	" "	22	W½NW	1824-05-04		A1
4047	YORKE, Emanuel	10	E½SW	1823-05-01		A1
4148	YORKE, Jonathan	15	W½SE	1823-05-01		A1
4149	" "	21	E½NE	1823-05-01		A1

Patent Map

T17-S R2-W
Huntsville Meridian

Map Group 23

Township Statistics

Parcels Mapped	:	304
Number of Patents	:	252
Number of Individuals	:	173
Patentees Identified	:	170
Number of Surnames	:	118
Multi-Patentee Parcels	:	35
Oldest Patent Date	:	5/1/1823
Most Recent Patent	:	6/29/1920
Block/Lot Parcels	:	0
Parcels Re - Issued	:	4
Parcels that Overlap	:	5
Cities and Towns	:	0
Cemeteries	:	9

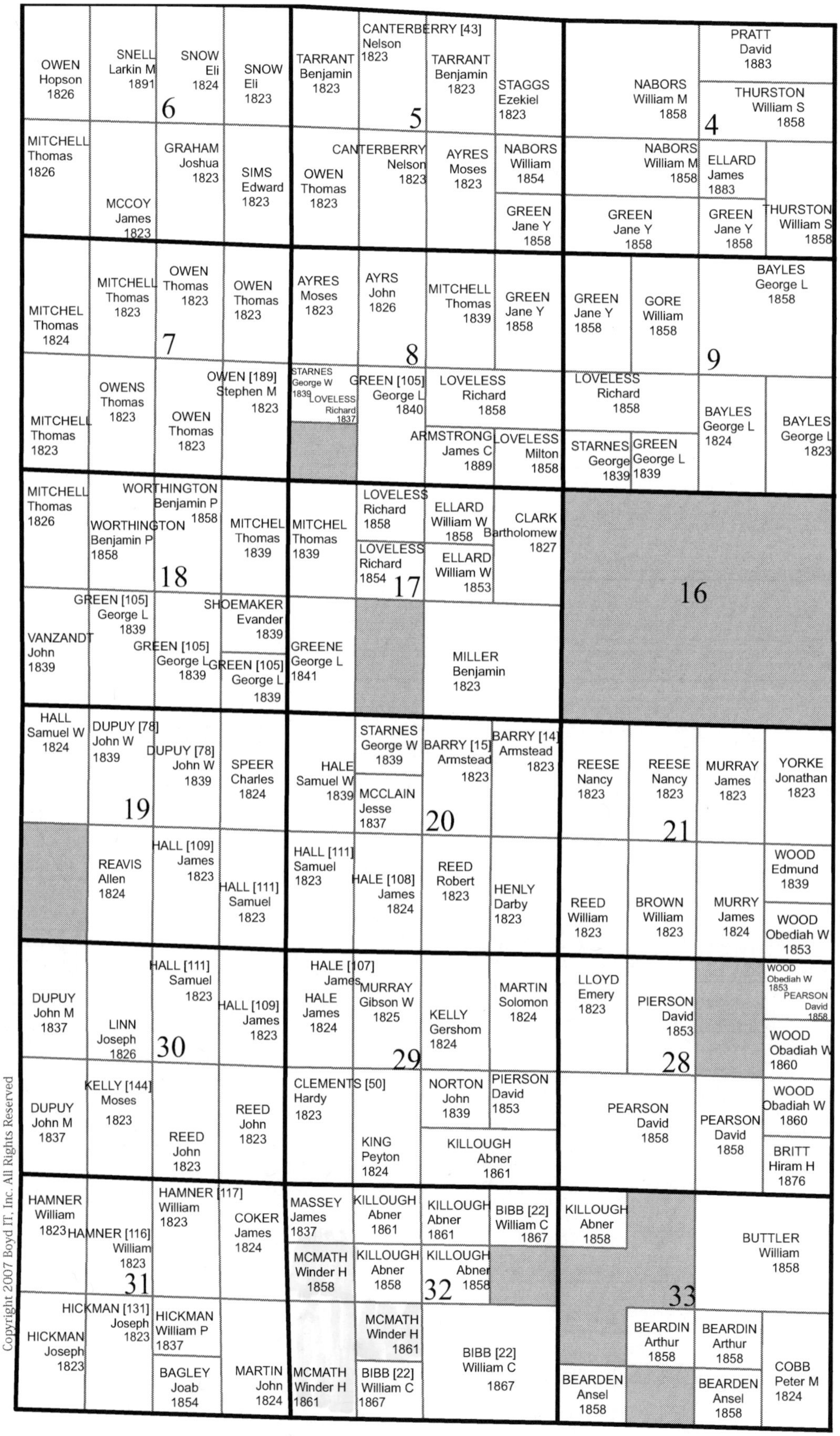

6
OWEN Hopson 1826
SNELL Larkin M 1891
SNOW Eli 1824
SNOW Eli 1823
MITCHELL Thomas 1826
MCCOY James 1823
GRAHAM Joshua 1823
SIMS Edward 1823

5
TARRANT Benjamin 1823
CANTERBERRY [43] Nelson 1823
TARRANT Benjamin 1823
STAGGS Ezekiel 1823
CANTERBERRY Nelson 1823
OWEN Thomas 1823
AYRES Moses 1823
NABORS William 1854
GREEN Jane Y 1858

4
PRATT David 1883
NABORS William M 1858
THURSTON William S 1858
NABORS William M 1858
ELLARD James 1883
GREEN Jane Y 1858
GREEN Jane Y 1858
THURSTON William S 1858

7
MITCHEL Thomas 1824
MITCHELL Thomas 1823
OWEN Thomas 1823
OWEN Thomas 1823
MITCHELL Thomas 1823
OWENS Thomas 1823
OWEN Thomas 1823
OWEN [189] Stephen M 1823

8
AYRES Moses 1823
AYRS John 1826
MITCHELL Thomas 1839
GREEN Jane Y 1858
STARNES George W 1839
LOVELESS Richard 1837
GREEN [105] George L 1840
LOVELESS Richard 1858
ARMSTRONG James C 1889
LOVELESS Milton 1858

9
GREEN Jane Y 1858
GORE William 1858
BAYLES George L 1858
LOVELESS Richard 1858
BAYLES George L 1824
BAYLES George L 1823
STARNES George 1839
GREEN George L 1839

18
MITCHELL Thomas 1826
WORTHINGTON Benjamin P 1858
WORTHINGTON Benjamin P 1858
MITCHEL Thomas 1839
GREEN [105] George L 1839
SHOEMAKER Evander 1839
VANZANDT John 1839
GREEN [105] George L 1839
GREEN [105] George L 1839

17
MITCHEL Thomas 1839
LOVELESS Richard 1858
ELLARD William W 1858
CLARK Bartholomew 1827
LOVELESS Richard 1854
ELLARD William W 1853
GREENE George L 1841
MILLER Benjamin 1823

16

19
HALL Samuel W 1824
DUPUY [78] John W 1839
DUPUY [78] John W 1839
SPEER Charles 1824
REAVIS Allen 1824
HALL [109] James 1823
HALL [111] Samuel 1823

20
HALE Samuel W 1839
STARNES George W 1839
BARRY [15] Armstead 1823
BARRY [14] Armstead 1823
MCCLAIN Jesse 1837
HALL [111] Samuel 1823
HALE [108] James 1824
REED Robert 1823
HENLY Darby 1823

21
REESE Nancy 1823
REESE Nancy 1823
MURRAY James 1823
YORKE Jonathan 1823
REED William 1823
BROWN William 1823
MURRY James 1824
WOOD Edmund 1839
WOOD Obediah W 1853

30
DUPUY John M 1837
LINN Joseph 1826
HALL [111] Samuel 1823
HALL [109] James 1823
DUPUY John M 1837
KELLY [144] Moses 1823
REED John 1823
REED John 1823

29
HALE [107] James
HALE James 1824
MURRAY Gibson W 1825
KELLY Gershom 1824
MARTIN Solomon 1824
CLEMENTS [50] Hardy 1823
NORTON John 1839
PIERSON David 1853
KING Peyton 1824
KILLOUGH Abner 1861

28
LLOYD Emery 1823
PIERSON David 1853
WOOD Obediah W 1853
PEARSON David 1858
WOOD Obadiah W 1860
PEARSON David 1858
PEARSON David 1858
WOOD Obadiah W 1860
BRITT Hiram H 1876

31
HAMNER William 1823
HAMNER [116] William 1823
HAMNER [117] William 1823
COKER James 1824
HICKMAN [131] Joseph 1823
HICKMAN Joseph 1823
HICKMAN William P 1837
BAGLEY Joab 1854
MARTIN John 1824

32
MASSEY James 1837
KILLOUGH Abner 1861
KILLOUGH Abner 1861
BIBB [22] William C 1867
MCMATH Winder H 1858
KILLOUGH Abner 1858
KILLOUGH Abner 1858
MCMATH Winder H 1861
BIBB [22] William C 1867
MCMATH Winder H 1861
BIBB [22] William C 1867

33
KILLOUGH Abner 1858
BUTTLER William 1858
BEARDIN Arthur 1858
BEARDIN Arthur 1858
COBB Peter M 1824
BEARDEN Ansel 1858
BEARDEN Ansel 1858

3
THURSTON William S 1858
THURSTON William S 1858
THURSTON William S 1858
CEMP John 1824
BYARS Catharine 1860
WOOD William H 1858
MONTGOMERY Martha 1858
BARTON Thomas 1858
WOOD William H 1860

2
MARSHALL Edmund 1880
BURWELL Orrin S 1852
HAMILTON [115] Audley 1823
WOOD Frank 1883
ROEBUCK George J 1858
CLEMENTS [49] Benjamin 1823
WILSON James 1858
HAMILTON Audley 1824
WALDROP Andrew J 1854
HAMILTON Audley 1920
BROWN John 1823
BROWN John 1823

1
CLEMENTS [49] Benjamin 1823
HAMILTON [115] Audley 1823
WOOD Richard H 1854
ROEBUCK George J 1858
CLEMENTS [51] Hardy 1823
CLEMENTS [51] Hardy 1823
WILSON James 1858
WILSON James 1858

10
MONTGOMERY Martha 1858
BARTON Thomas 1858
WOOD William H 1853
GARRITT Joseph 1839
MONTGOMERY Martha 1854
TURNER Alexander 1839
MCADAMS Isaac 1824
ELLARD Jonathan 1824
WOOD John 1823
YORKE Emanuel 1823

11
BROWN John 1824
BROWN John 1823
BROWN John 1823
BROWN John 1824
ELLARD Jonathan 1824
WOOD John 1823
WOOD William H 1849
WOOD William H 1860
WOOD William H 1860
WOOD William H 1853

12
WILSON James 1858
WOOD William 1880
WALDROP Andrew J 1858
WALDROP Andrew J 1858
WOOD William H 1860
WOOD William H 1858
TARRANT John B 1880
WOOD William H 1858
MILNER Elisha C 1882

15
BARTON [17] Thomas 1823
BARTON Thomas 1823
ELLARD Jonathan 1824
BARTON Thomas 1823
BARTON Thomas 1844
HARRISON Isham 1830
YORK Jonathan 1824
YORKE Jonathan 1823
BRANTLEY James 1834

14
MONTGOMERY Washington 1824
WOOD James B 1858
TURNER Lucy 1858
TURNER Lucy 1858
TRUSS Columbus 1889
HORNE Thomas 1823
FERGUSON Martin 1837
BROWN Isaiah C 1890
DANIEL Mary 1838

13
WOOD James B 1858
COKER William 1837
BOYLES Elbert H 1837
FRENCH Aaron 1829
SADDLER William R 1823

22
YORK Jonathan 1824
PIERSON David 1839
LATHAM Anthony 1839
MURRAY James 1824
ARMSTRONG Robert 1858
WALDROP John P 1858
MURRAY James 1824
MURRAY [178] James 1823
WOOD Obadiah W 1854
TURNER Samuel 1849

23
MURRAY [178] James 1823
BAGWELL Wiley 1834
EASTIS Daniel 1852
BAGWELL Wiley 1834
TURNER Lewis 1858
LATHAM Anthony 1854
COWDEN Josiah 1824
ARMSTRONG Robert 1858
LATHEM Anthony 1858

24
WIDEMAN Thomas 1884
BAGLEY Joab 1852
SADDLER William R 1823
COKER James 1835
MONTGOMERY Francis 1835
MONTGOMERY Francis 1858
ELLARD Merit 1854
MONTGOMERY Ervin N 1853
BAKER William R 1858
CONDEN Josiah 1824
BAKER William R 1853
BAKER William R 1849
BROWNLEE Samuel 1890

27
WOOD Obediah W 1853
WALDROP John P 1858
WALDROP John P 1858
WOOD Obediah W 1853
WOOD Obadiah W 1860
WOOD Obadiah W 1860
MONTGOMERY Francis 1824
CUMMINS William 1858

26
MONTGOMERY John S 1858
MONTGOMERY John S 1858
FRANKLIN Green B 1852
COWDEN Josiah 1824
MONTGOMERY Washington 1834
BAKER William R 1858
CROCKER Harriet 1889
HODGES Leroy H 1858
HODGES Leroy H 1858
PARKER John D 1885
CUMMINS William 1858

25
BAKER William R 1848
BAKER William R 1858
BAKER William R 1858

34
MONTGOMERY Robert 1826
MONTGOMERY Robert B 1848
CUMMINS William 1854
BUTTLER William 1858
SHUTTLESWORTH Martin 1834
EASTIS Willis 1853
CUMMINS William 1858
BROWN William 1839
CUMMINGS William 1850
BROWN Jackson 1824
EASTIS Willis 1858
BEARDIN Arthur 1858
EASTIS Willis 1858

35
CUMMINS William 1858
BURWELL Orrin S 1850

36
MCADORY Isaac 1884
AYERS Cyrus 1883
EDWARDS William 1883
MCADORY Isaac 1883
BAGWELL [8] Jason 1890
BROWNLEE Benjamin 1887
BROWNLEE Benjamin 1893
MANSON Edward D 1892

Helpful Hints

1. This Map's INDEX can be found on the preceding pages.
2. Refer to Map "C" to see where this Township lies within Jefferson County, Alabama.
3. Numbers within square brackets [ ] denote a multi-patentee land parcel (multi-owner). Refer to Appendix "C" for a full list of members in this group.
4. Areas that look to be crowded with Patentees usually indicate multiple sales of the same parcel (Re-issues) or Overlapping parcels. See this Township's Index for an explanation of these and other circumstances that might explain "odd" groupings of Patentees on this map.

Legend

Patent Boundary
Section Boundary
No Patents Found (or Outside County)
1., 2., 3., ... Lot Numbers (when beside a name)
[ ] Group Number (see Appendix "C")

Scale: Section = 1 mile X 1 mile (generally, with some exceptions)

Road Map

T17-S R2-W
Huntsville Meridian

Map Group 23

Cities & Towns

None

Cemeteries

- Bass Cemetery
- Bush Cemetery
- East Lake Cemetery
- Forest Hill Cemetery
- Greenwood Cemetery
- Higgins Cemetery
- Inglenook Cemetery
- McElwain Cemetery
- Mount Zion Cemetery

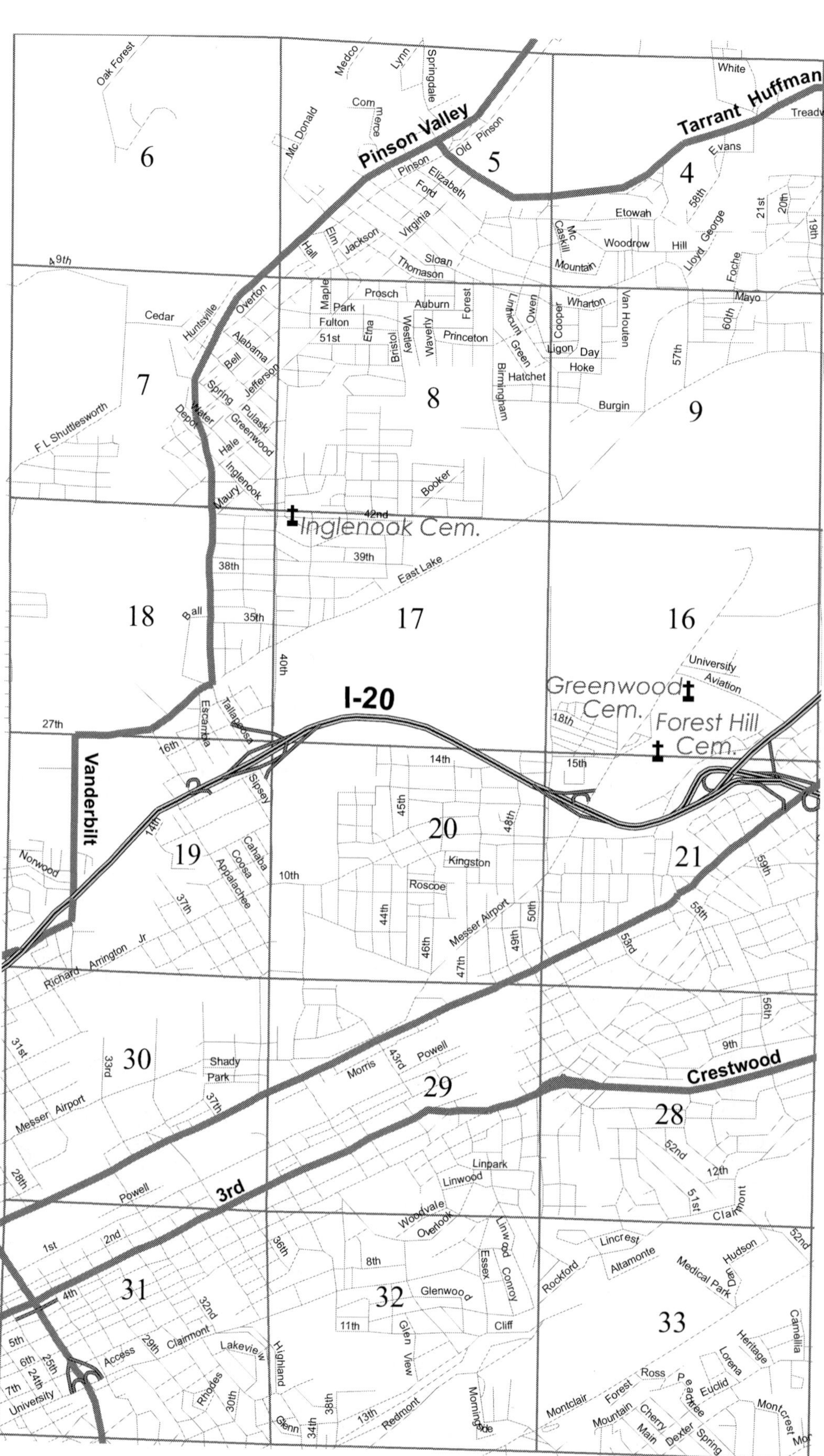

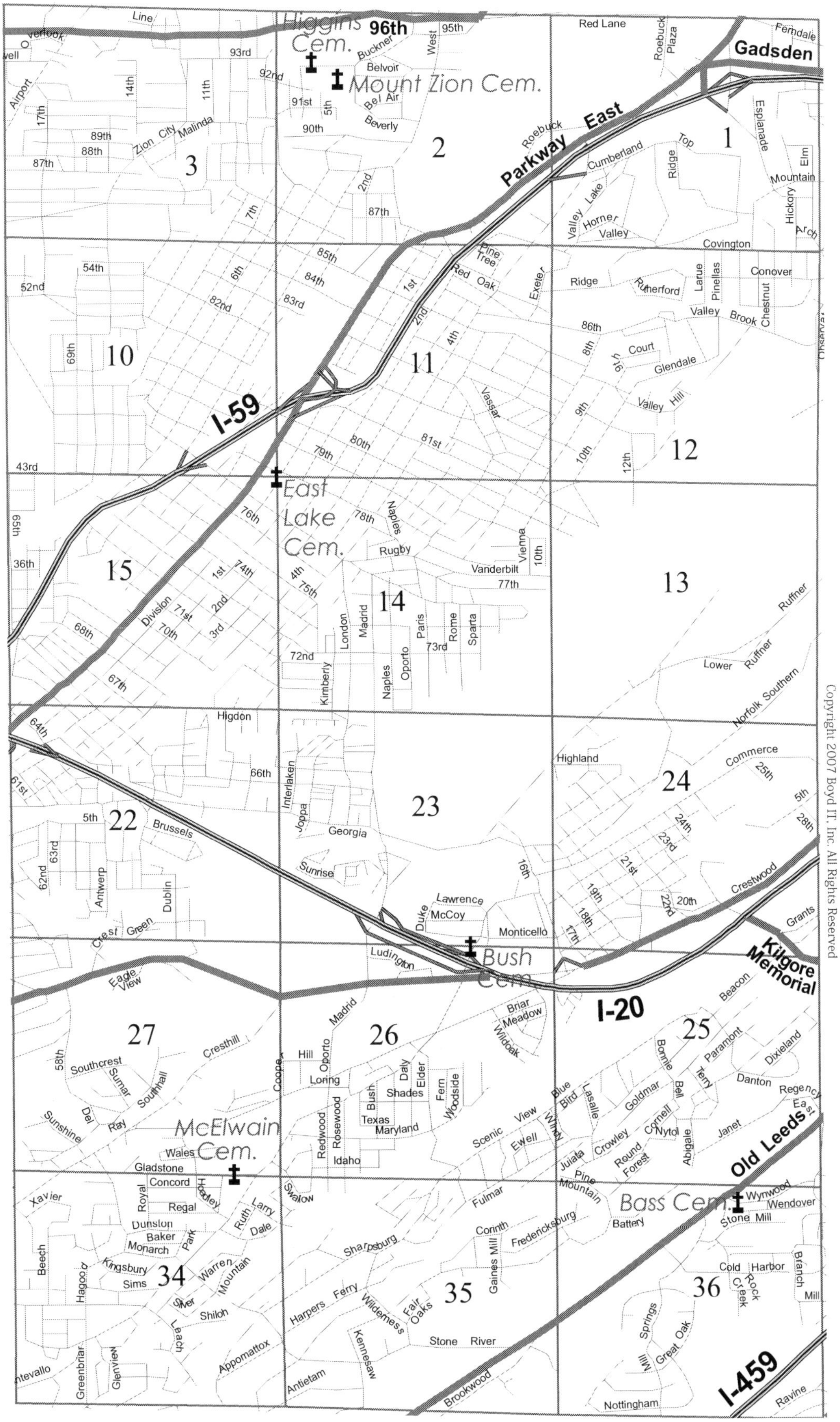

Helpful Hints

1. This road map has a number of uses, but primarily it is to help you: a) find the present location of land owned by your ancestors (at least the general area), b) find cemeteries and city-centers, and c) estimate the route/roads used by Census-takers & tax-assessors.

2. If you plan to travel to Jefferson County to locate cemeteries or land parcels, please pick up a modern travel map for the area before you do. Mapping old land parcels on modern maps is not as exact a science as you might think. Just the slightest variations in public land survey coordinates, estimates of parcel boundaries, or road-map deviations can greatly alter a map's representation of how a road either does or doesn't cross a particular parcel of land.

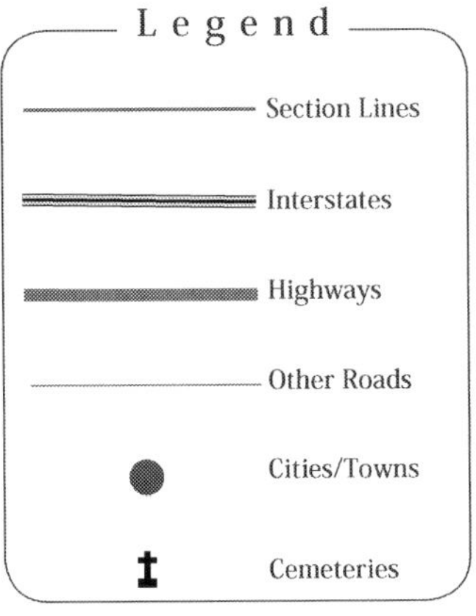

Scale: Section = 1 mile X 1 mile
(generally, with some exceptions)

Historical Map

T17-S R2-W
Huntsville Meridian

Map Group 23

Cities & Towns
None

Cemeteries
Bass Cemetery
Bush Cemetery
East Lake Cemetery
Forest Hill Cemetery
Greenwood Cemetery
Higgins Cemetery
Inglenook Cemetery
McElwain Cemetery
Mount Zion Cemetery

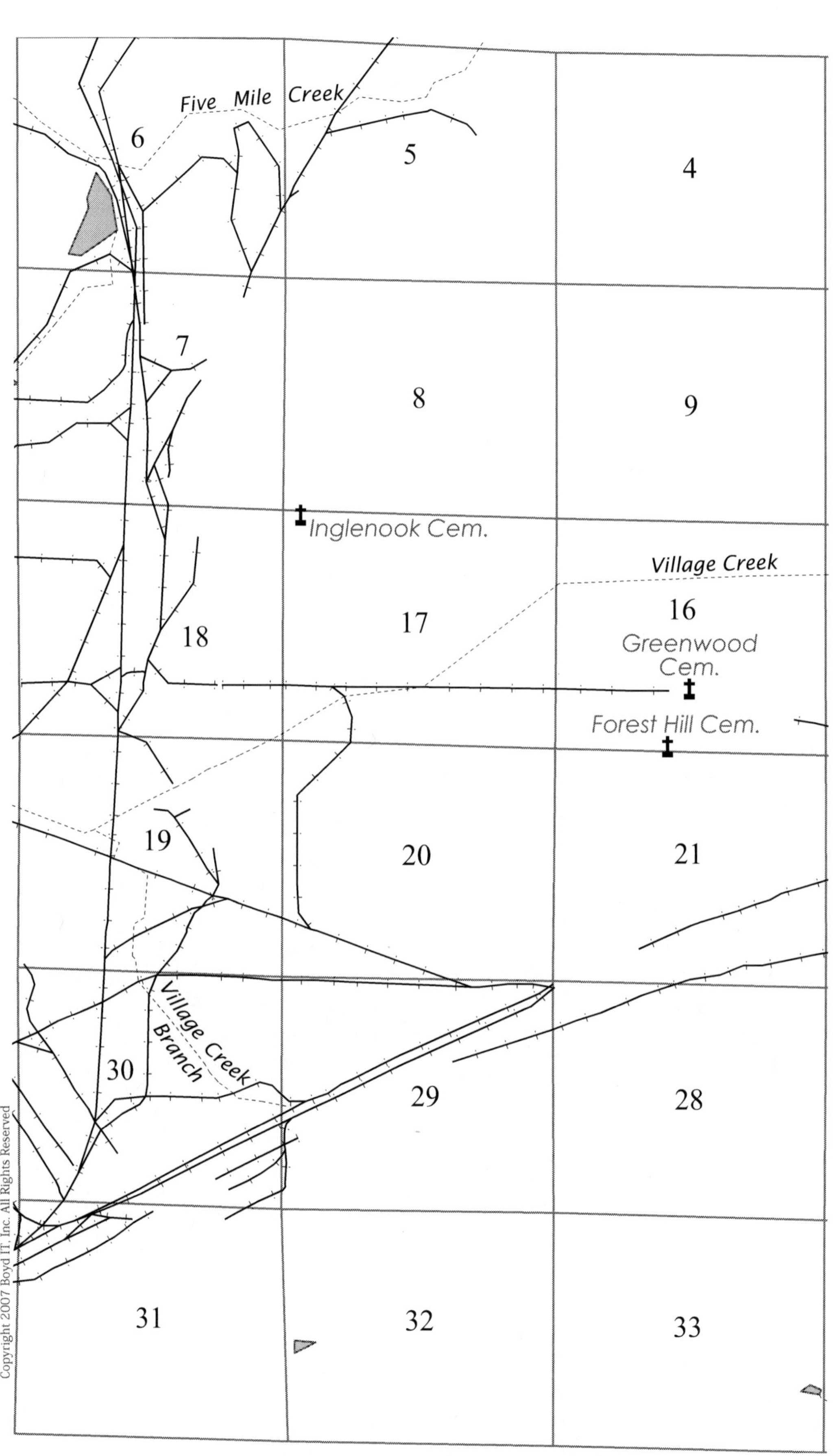

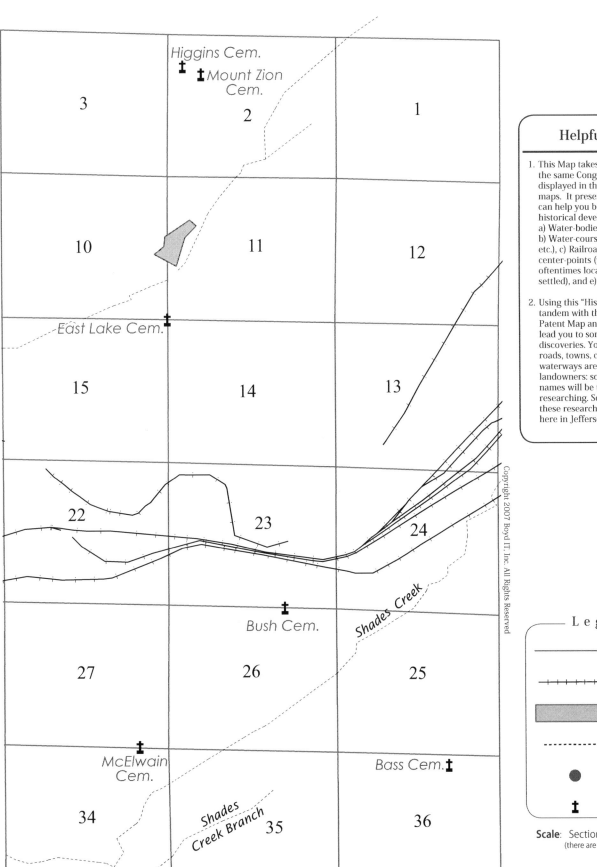

Higgins Cem.
Mount Zion Cem.

3 2 1

10 11 12

East Lake Cem.

15 14 13

22 23 24

Shades Creek

Bush Cem.

27 26 25

McElwain Cem.

Bass Cem.

34 35 36

Shades Creek Branch

Helpful Hints

1. This Map takes a different look at the same Congressional Township displayed in the preceding two maps. It presents features that can help you better envision the historical development of the area: a) Water-bodies (lakes & ponds), b) Water-courses (rivers, streams, etc.), c) Railroads, d) City/town center-points (where they were oftentimes located when first settled), and e) Cemeteries.

2. Using this "Historical" map in tandem with this Township's Patent Map and Road Map, may lead you to some interesting discoveries. You will often find roads, towns, cemeteries, and waterways are named after nearby landowners: sometimes those names will be the ones you are researching. See how many of these research gems you can find here in Jefferson County.

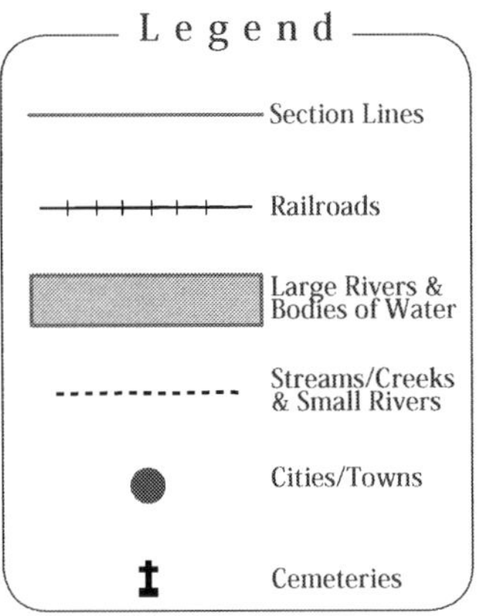

Scale: Section = 1 mile X 1 mile
(there are some exceptions)

Map Group 24: Index to Land Patents

Township 17-South Range 1-West (Huntsville)

After you locate an individual in this Index, take note of the Section and Section Part then proceed to the Land Patent map on the pages immediately following. You should have no difficulty locating the corresponding parcel of land.

The "For More Info" Column will lead you to more information about the underlying Patents. See the *Legend* at right, and the "How to Use this Book" chapter, for more information.

LEGEND

"For More Info . . . " column

A = Authority (Legislative Act, See Appendix "A")
B = Block or Lot (location in Section unknown)
C = Cancelled Patent
F = Fractional Section
G = Group (Multi-Patentee Patent, see Appendix "C")
V = Overlaps another Parcel
R = Re-Issued (Parcel patented more than once)

(A & G items require you to look in the Appendixes referred to above. All other Letter-designations followed by a number require you to locate line-items in this index that possess the ID number found after the letter).

ID	Individual in Patent	Sec.	Sec. Part	Date Issued	Other Counties	For More Info . . .
4438	ALLEN, Matthew	1	SENE	1858-06-01		A1
4482	APPLEBERRY, Thomas	20	W½NE	1884-12-05		A4
4301	AYERS, Alonzo	30	W½SW	1890-01-08		A4
4303	BASS, Andrew	5	SWSW	1839-09-20		A1
4313	BASS, Burrel	7	SESE	1834-10-14		A1
4312	" "	7	NWNE	1858-06-01		A1
4314	" "	7	SWNE	1858-06-01		A1
4315	" "	8	E½SW	1858-06-01		A1
4316	" "	8	W½SE	1858-06-01		A1
4317	" "	8	W½SW	1858-06-01		A1
4319	BASS, Burrell	21	SWNE	1839-09-20		A1
4320	BASS, Calvin	11	SWNE	1848-07-01		A1
4383	BASS, Jane	5	NWSW	1858-06-01		A1
4384	" "	6	SENE	1858-06-01		A1
4385	" "	8	E½NW	1858-06-01		A1
4424	BASS, Lewis G	2	E½NW	1858-06-01		A1
4425	" "	2	E½SW	1858-06-01		A1
4426	" "	2	NWNE	1858-06-01		A1
4427	" "	2	W½SW	1858-06-01		A1
4464	BASS, Pinckney T	12	NWSW	1860-04-02		A1 R4459
4465	" "	12	SENW	1860-04-02		A1
4466	" "	12	W½NW	1860-04-02		A1 R4460
4505	BASS, William J	10	W½NW	1858-06-01		A1
4506	" "	9	S½NE	1858-06-01		A1
4333	BAYLES, Elbert H	7	NESE	1837-11-07		A1
4308	BEARDEN, Arthur	32	SWNE	1834-10-14		A1
4304	BECKHAM, Andrew J	26	E½SE	1883-05-21		A4
4471	BELL, Robert	2	NWSE	1848-07-01		A1
4492	BRADFORD, Thomas J	12	W½NE	1882-09-15		A1
4321	BROWN, Calvin	18	SESE	1891-06-19		A4
4340	BYERS, Francis	4	NE	1858-06-01		A1
4419	BYERS, Joseph	4	NENW	1849-08-01		A1
4420	BYRAM, Joseph	36	SENW	1852-01-01		A1
4497	CAMERON, William	36	E½SE	1823-05-01		A1
4498	" "	36	SWNE	1839-09-20		A1
4394	CAMPBELL, John	36	E½SW	1824-04-14		A1
4374	CANTRELL, James R	20	NWSW	1889-11-21		A4
4375	" "	20	S½SW	1889-11-21		A4
4376	" "	20	SWNW	1889-11-21		A4
4468	CARZELIUS, Richard	10	NENE	1893-08-14		A4
4416	CHAPMAN, John W	26	N½NW	1883-05-21		A4
4417	" "	26	NWNE	1883-05-21		A4
4477	COWDEN, Robert S	18	NWSE	1854-07-15		A1
4512	CRAWFORD, William T	2	SWNE	1894-10-22		A4
4481	CROCKER, Stewart	6	SWSW	1858-06-01		A1
4341	DEPOISTER, George C	22	E½NW	1885-03-16		A1

ID	Individual in Patent	Sec.	Sec. Part	Date Issued	Other Counties	For More Info . . .
4342	DEPOISTER, George C (Cont'd)	22	N½SW	1891-11-23		A4
4395	DEVERNEY, John	26	E½NE	1883-05-21		A4
4354	DOTSON, Ira G	14	E½SE	1891-10-07		A1
4355	" "	14	SENE	1891-10-07		A1
4356	" "	14	SWSE	1891-10-07		A1
4396	EARLE, John	30	NWNW	1892-10-18		A4 G80
4450	EDMUNDSON, Parthena	6	W½NE	1823-05-01		A1
4357	ELLARD, Isaac	4	SE	1889-12-28		A1
4499	ELLARD, William	21	SESW	1858-06-01		A1
4363	ELLERD, Jackson	30	E½SE	1885-05-25		A4
4331	ELLINGTON, Drury	10	NESW	1839-09-20		A1
4332	" "	10	SWSW	1839-09-20		A1
4493	FAGASON, Thomas P	5	NESW	1849-05-01		A1
4494	FAGERSON, Thomas P	18	SESW	1852-01-01		A1
4472	FATIO, Robert	34	N½NW	1883-05-21		A4
4473	" "	34	NWNE	1883-05-21		A4
4474	FOSTER, Robert R	10	NENW	1858-06-01		A1
4475	" "	10	NWNE	1858-06-01		A1
4476	" "	15	NENW	1858-06-01		A1
4478	FOSTER, Robert W	10	SWNE	1839-09-20		A1
4479	" "	15	SENW	1841-01-09		A1
4325	FOUST, David C	6	SESW	1876-04-01		A4
4326	" "	6	SWSE	1876-04-01		A4
4322	FRANKLIN, Cary A	10	NWSW	1894-10-22		A4
4318	FURGASON, Burrel L	6	NENE	1884-12-05		A4
4381	GILBERT, James W	10	SENW	1903-06-12		A4
4294	GLASS, Abner	32	E½SW	1889-08-16		A4
4335	GLASS, Elisha	32	NWSW	1883-07-03		A4
4336	" "	32	SWNW	1883-07-03		A4
4366	GLASS, James	28	S½SW	1884-11-20		A1
4429	GLASS, Mahala	28	E½SE	1884-11-20		A1
4430	GLASS, Manson	34	S½NW	1880-02-20		A4
4461	GODWIN, Pinckney	3	SENE	1858-06-01		A1
4295	GOODWIN, Abraham	3	NENE	1838-08-28		A1
4348	GOODWIN, Henry	4	NWNW	1839-03-15		A1
4349	" "	5	SWNE	1844-07-10		A1 R4435
4397	GOODWIN, John	3	SESE	1838-08-28		A1
4434	GOODWIN, Marion F	5	E½NW	1858-06-01		A1
4435	" "	5	SWNE	1858-06-01		A1 R4349
4462	GOODWIN, Pinckney	2	SWNW	1858-06-01		A1
4463	" "	3	NWNE	1858-06-01		A1
4484	GOODWIN, Thomas	4	SWNW	1837-04-01		A1
4488	" "	5	SESE	1837-04-01		A1
4483	" "	4	SENW	1858-06-01		A1
4485	" "	4	W½SW	1858-06-01		A1
4486	" "	5	NESE	1858-06-01		A1
4487	" "	5	NWNE	1858-06-01		A1
4495	GOODWIN, Wesley	6	E½NW	1858-06-01		A1
4496	" "	6	NESW	1858-06-01		A1
4368	GORE, James M	18	E½NE	1858-06-01		A1
4489	GORE, Thomas	18	NWNW	1858-06-01		A1
4490	" "	19	E½NW	1858-06-01		A1
4491	" "	19	W½NW	1858-06-01		A1
4500	GORE, William	18	NESE	1880-02-20		A4
4347	GRACE, Harrison	30	SWNE	1887-04-20		A4
4396	GRACE, Leana	30	NWNW	1892-10-18		A4 G80
4469	GRAY, Richard	26	N½SW	1883-05-21		A4
4470	" "	26	NWSE	1883-05-21		A4
4351	GREEN, Hilton	18	SENE	1883-05-25		A4 C
4352	" "	18	SWNW	1883-05-25		A4 C R4379
4353	" "	18	SWSE	1883-05-25		A4 C R4409
4350	GREENBERG, Henry	2	E½NE	1891-12-01		A1
4431	GRIFFIN, Marcus L	30	NENW	1890-01-08		A4
4399	HAACK, John	34	N½SE	1883-05-25		A4
4400	" "	34	SWSE	1883-05-25		A4
4391	HAGOOD, Joe	30	SENE	1884-03-20		A4
4390	" "	30	N½NE	1889-11-21		A4
4501	HALE, William H	20	S½SE	1889-11-21		A4
4310	HALL, Berry	30	W½SE	1883-07-03		A4
4421	HARDING, Judson M	22	E½SE	1885-08-05		A1
4422	" "	22	SESW	1885-08-05		A1
4423	" "	22	SWSE	1885-08-05		A1
4467	HARRIS, Reuben T	32	N½NW	1880-02-20		A4

ID	Individual in Patent	Sec.	Sec. Part	Date Issued	Other Counties	For More Info . . .
4369	HARVEY, James M	24	S½SW	1883-08-10		A4
4299	HENRY, Allen	30	SENW	1891-06-19		A4
4311	HENRY, Bunk	34	S½SW	1881-12-30		A1
4367	HERREN, James	35	E½SE	1823-05-01		A1 G129
4358	HERRING, Isaac	18	SWNE	1854-07-15		A1
4359	" "	7	NESW	1858-06-01		A1
4360	" "	7	SENW	1858-06-01		A1
4428	HERRING, Lewis W	25	E½SE	1858-06-01		A1
4365	HUNEYCUTT, James E	2	NWNW	1884-12-05		A4
4367	LANE, John W	35	E½SE	1823-05-01		A1 G129
4418	" "	36	W½SW	1823-05-01		A1 G148
4402	LATHEM, John	32	NWSE	1858-06-01		A1
4509	LINDSEY, William	2	E½SE	1858-06-01		A1
4510	" "	2	SWSE	1858-06-01		A1
4447	MARTIN, Nichodemus	6	NWSW	1908-11-05		A4
4344	MASKE, George L	32	SENE	1888-02-29		A1
4345	MASKE, George W	32	N½NE	1888-02-29		A1
4418	MASON, Job	36	W½SW	1823-05-01		A1 G148
4513	MCADAMS, William W	7	SESW	1838-08-28		A1
4323	MCCOMBE, David A	15	NESE	1839-09-20		A1
4324	" "	22	SENE	1839-09-20		A1
4328	MCCOMBS, David	15	NWNE	1834-10-21		A1
4327	" "	10	SESE	1835-10-01		A1
4370	MCCOMBS, James M	14	SESW	1882-10-30		A1
4371	" "	14	SWNW	1882-10-30		A1
4372	" "	14	W½SW	1882-10-30		A1
4413	MCCOMBS, John T	14	E½NW	1882-10-30		A1
4414	" "	14	W½NE	1882-10-30		A1
4433	MCCOMBS, Marcus L	22	SWNE	1884-12-05		A4
4432	" "	22	N½NE	1889-03-01		A4
4508	MCCOMBS, William L	22	SWSW	1913-08-14		A1
4364	MCDANAL, Jake	34	SESE	1881-12-30		A1
4403	MCDANAL, John R	35	NWSE	1858-06-01		A1
4404	" "	35	S½NE	1858-06-01		A1
4405	" "	35	SENW	1858-06-01		A1
4502	MCDANAL, William H	35	E½SW	1858-06-01		A1
4503	" "	35	NWSW	1858-06-01		A1
4504	" "	35	SWSE	1858-06-01		A1
4300	MCDONALD, Allen	36	W½NW	1858-06-01		A1
4444	NAVE, Moses	20	NWNW	1891-06-08		A4
4436	PARKER, Martin	24	NESE	1881-12-30		A1
4437	" "	24	SENE	1881-12-30		A1
4361	PERRY, Isaac	8	E½NE	1876-04-01		A4
4362	" "	8	E½SE	1885-08-05		A4
4480	PIERCE, Salmon	6	NWNW	1884-01-15		A1
4388	POE, Jesse R	24	N½NE	1881-12-30		A1
4393	POOL, John C	36	NENW	1884-03-20		A4
4443	POOL, Mitchell	36	W½SE	1824-05-20		A1
4442	" "	36	NWNE	1852-01-01		A1
4441	" "	12	NENW	1853-08-01		A1
4373	POOLE, James	22	NWSE	1841-01-09		A1
4296	RATLIFF, Abraham	22	W½NW	1891-05-29		A4
4392	REAM, John A	24	S½SE	1883-05-21		A4
4343	ROEBUCK, George J	6	SWNW	1858-06-01		A1
4386	ROSS, Jesse H	14	NESW	1883-07-03		A4
4387	" "	14	NWSE	1883-07-03		A4
4455	ROWAN, Peyton	11	E½SE	1858-06-01		A1
4456	" "	11	NESW	1858-06-01		A1
4457	" "	11	NWSE	1858-06-01		A1 V4346
4458	" "	11	SENE	1858-06-01		A1
4459	" "	12	NWSW	1858-06-01		A1 R4464
4460	" "	12	W½NW	1858-06-01		A1 R4466
4452	RYAN, Peter C	29	E½NW	1858-06-01		A1
4453	" "	29	NWNE	1858-06-01		A1
4454	" "	29	SWNW	1858-06-01		A1
4511	SADDLER, William R	18	W½SW	1823-05-01		A1
4406	SANSON, John	12	E½SE	1860-04-02		A1
4407	" "	13	NENE	1860-04-02		A1
4451	SHAGER, Peder P	34	N½SW	1883-05-21		A4
4329	SHIPMAN, David	26	S½NW	1883-05-21		A4
4330	" "	26	SWNE	1883-05-21		A4
4334	SIMS, Elijah	4	E½SW	1882-11-20		A4
4380	STOVALL, James	7	W½SW	1826-12-01		A1

ID	Individual in Patent	Sec.	Sec. Part	Date Issued	Other Counties	For More Info . . .
4377	STOVALL, James (Cont'd)	18	E½NW	1837-11-07		A1
4379	" "	18	SWNW	1837-11-07		A1 R4352
4378	" "	18	NWNE	1839-09-20		A1
4411	STOVALL, John	7	E½NE	1823-05-01		A1
4410	" "	6	E½SE	1824-05-10		A1
4412	" "	7	W½SE	1824-05-24		A1
4408	" "	18	NESW	1837-11-07		A1
4409	" "	18	SWSE	1839-09-20		A1 R4353
4302	TAYLOR, Alphus L	8	W½NE	1883-10-01		A4
4346	TAYLOR, George W	11	W½SE	1858-06-01		A1 V4457
4389	THOMPSON, Joe D	30	E½SW	1883-07-03		A4
4445	THOMPSON, Ned	20	E½NE	1890-03-19		A4
4446	" "	20	N½SE	1890-03-19		A4
4448	VON MINDIN, NICOLAUS	34	E½NE	1883-05-21		A4
4449	" "	34	SWNE	1883-05-21		A4
4306	WALD, Anthony	24	NWSE	1883-05-21		A4
4307	" "	24	SWNE	1883-05-21		A4
4297	WALDROP, Albert N	12	E½SW	1882-09-09		A1
4298	" "	12	W½SE	1882-09-09		A1
4338	WARE, Floyd	20	E½NW	1892-12-15		A4
4339	" "	20	NESW	1892-12-15		A4
4337	WATSON, Ezekiel	12	E½NE	1884-03-20		A1
4415	WATSON, John T	24	NW	1882-10-30		A1
4514	WEEMS, William	5	E½NE	1839-09-20		A1
4515	" "	5	NWSE	1839-09-20		A1
4507	WEEMS, William J	28	W½SE	1875-11-20		A4
4398	WILLIAMS, John H	24	N½SW	1883-05-21		A4
4439	WILLIAMS, Micaiah	26	S½SW	1883-05-21		A4
4440	" "	26	SWSE	1883-05-21		A4
4305	WILSON, Andrew	8	W½NW	1824-05-04		A1
4401	WOODALL, John J	5	SESW	1837-03-20		A1
4309	WORTHINGTON, Benjamin	6	NWSE	1852-01-01		A1
4382	WYATT, James	36	E½NE	1824-04-26		A1

Patent Map

T17-S R1-W
Huntsville Meridian

Map Group 24

Township Statistics

Parcels Mapped	:	222
Number of Patents	:	163
Number of Individuals	:	138
Patentees Identified	:	136
Number of Surnames	:	99
Multi-Patentee Parcels	:	3
Oldest Patent Date	:	5/1/1823
Most Recent Patent	:	8/14/1913
Block/Lot Parcels	:	0
Parcels Re - Issued	:	5
Parcels that Overlap	:	2
Cities and Towns	:	1
Cemeteries	:	4

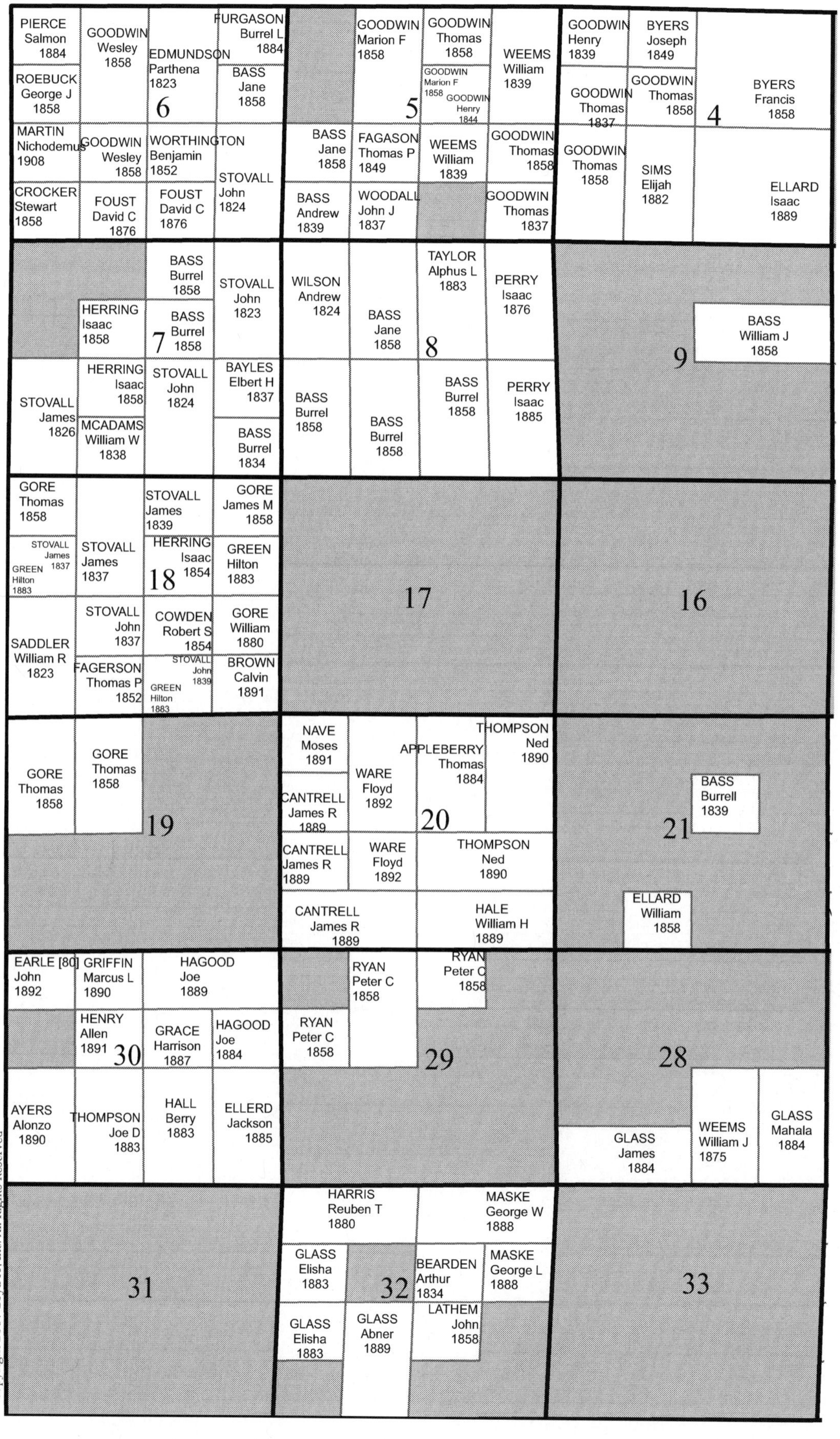

6
PIERCE Salmon 1884
GOODWIN Wesley 1858
EDMUNDSON Parthenia 1823
FURGASON Burrel L 1884
BASS Jane 1858
ROEBUCK George J 1858
MARTIN Nichodemus 1908
GOODWIN Wesley 1858
WORTHINGTON Benjamin 1852
STOVALL John 1824
CROCKER Stewart 1858
FOUST David C 1876
FOUST David C 1876

5
GOODWIN Marion F 1858
GOODWIN Thomas 1858
GOODWIN Marion F 1858
GOODWIN Henry 1844
WEEMS William 1839
BASS Jane 1858
FAGASON Thomas P 1849
WEEMS William 1839
GOODWIN Thomas 1858
BASS Andrew 1839
WOODALL John J 1837
GOODWIN Thomas 1837

4
GOODWIN Henry 1839
BYERS Joseph 1849
GOODWIN Thomas 1837
GOODWIN Thomas 1858
BYERS Francis 1858
GOODWIN Thomas 1858
SIMS Elijah 1882
ELLARD Isaac 1889

7
BASS Burrel 1858
STOVALL John 1823
HERRING Isaac 1858
BASS Burrel 1858
HERRING Isaac 1858
STOVALL John 1824
BAYLES Elbert H 1837
STOVALL James 1826
MCADAMS William W 1838
BASS Burrel 1834

8
WILSON Andrew 1824
TAYLOR Alphus L 1883
PERRY Isaac 1876
BASS Jane 1858
BASS Burrel 1858
BASS Burrel 1858
BASS Burrel 1858
PERRY Isaac 1885

9
BASS William J 1858

18
GORE Thomas 1858
STOVALL James 1839
GORE James M 1858
STOVALL James 1837
GREEN Hilton 1883
STOVALL James 1837
HERRING Isaac 1854
GREEN Hilton 1883
STOVALL John 1837
COWDEN Robert S 1854
GORE William 1880
SADDLER William R 1823
FAGERSON Thomas P 1852
STOVALL John 1839
GREEN Hilton 1883
BROWN Calvin 1891

17

16

19
GORE Thomas 1858
GORE Thomas 1858

20
NAVE Moses 1891
WARE Floyd 1892
APPLEBERRY Thomas 1884
THOMPSON Ned 1890
CANTRELL James R 1889
CANTRELL James R 1889
WARE Floyd 1892
THOMPSON Ned 1890
CANTRELL James R 1889
HALE William H 1889

21
BASS Burrell 1839
ELLARD William 1858

30
EARLE [80] John 1892
GRIFFIN Marcus L 1890
HAGOOD Joe 1889
HENRY Allen 1891
GRACE Harrison 1887
HAGOOD Joe 1884
AYERS Alonzo 1890
THOMPSON Joe D 1883
HALL Berry 1883
ELLERD Jackson 1885

29
RYAN Peter C 1858
RYAN Peter C 1858
RYAN Peter C 1858

28
GLASS James 1884
WEEMS William J 1875
GLASS Mahala 1884

31

32
HARRIS Reuben T 1880
MASKE George W 1888
GLASS Elisha 1883
BEARDEN Arthur 1834
MASKE George L 1888
GLASS Elisha 1883
GLASS Abner 1889
LATHEM John 1858

33

GOODWIN Pinckney 1858
GOODWIN Abraham 1838
HUNEYCUTT James E 1884
BASS Lewis G 1858
BASS Lewis G 1858
GREENBERG Henry 1891
GOODWIN Pinckney 1858
GOODWIN Pinckney 1858
CRAWFORD William T 1894
ALLEN Matthew 1858
3
2
1
BASS Lewis G 1858
BASS Lewis G 1858
BELL Robert 1848
LINDSEY William 1858
LINDSEY William 1858
GOODWIN John 1838

BASS William J 1858
FOSTER Robert R 1858
FOSTER Robert R 1858
CARZELIUS Richard 1893
BASS Pinckney T 1860
POOL Mitchell 1853
BRADFORD Thomas J 1882
WATSON Ezekiel 1884
GILBERT James W 1903
FOSTER Robert W 1839
10
11
BASS Calvin 1848
ROWAN Peyton 1858
ROWAN Peyton 1858
BASS Pinckney T 1860
BASS Pinckney T 1860
12
FRANKLIN Cary A 1894
ELLINGTON Drury 1839
ROWAN Peyton 1858
ROWAN Peyton 1858
ROWAN Peyton 1858
ROWAN Peyton 1858
WALDROP Albert N 1882
WALDROP Albert N 1882
TAYLOR George W 1858
ELLINGTON Drury 1839
MCCOMBS David 1835
SANSON John 1860

FOSTER Robert R 1858
MCCOMBS David 1834
MCCOMBS John T 1882
MCCOMBS John T 1882
SANSON John 1860
FOSTER Robert W 1841
MCCOMBS James M 1882
DOTSON Ira G 1891
15
14
13
MCCOMBE David A 1839
MCCOMBS James M 1882
ROSS Jesse H 1883
ROSS Jesse H 1883
DOTSON Ira G 1891
MCCOMBS James M 1882
DOTSON Ira G 1891

DEPOISTER George C 1885
MCCOMBS Marcus L 1889
WATSON John T 1882
POE Jesse R 1881
RATLIFF Abraham 1891
MCCOMBS Marcus L 1884
MCCOMBE David A 1839
22
23
24
WALD Anthony 1883
PARKER Martin 1881
DEPOISTER George C 1891
POOLE James 1841
WILLIAMS John H 1883
WALD Anthony 1883
PARKER Martin 1881
MCCOMBS William L 1913
HARDING Judson M 1885
HARDING Judson M 1885
HARDING Judson M 1885
HARVEY James M 1883
REAM John A 1883

CHAPMAN John W 1883
CHAPMAN John W 1883
DEVERNEY John 1883
SHIPMAN David 1883
SHIPMAN David 1883
27
26
25
GRAY Richard 1883
GRAY Richard 1883
BECKHAM Andrew J 1883
HERRING Lewis W 1858
WILLIAMS Micaiah 1883
WILLIAMS Micaiah 1883

FATIO Robert 1883
FATIO Robert 1883
MINDIN Nicolaus Von 1883
POOL John C 1884
POOL Mitchell 1852
WYATT James 1824
MCDONALD Allen 1858
GLASS Manson 1880
MINDIN Nicolaus Von 1883
MCDANAL John R 1858
MCDANAL John R 1858
BYRAM Joseph 1852
CAMERON William 1839
34
35
36
SHAGER Peder P 1883
HAACK John 1883
MCDANAL William H 1858
MCDANAL John R 1858
CAMPBELL John 1824
LANE [148] John W 1823
POOL Mitchell 1824
MCDANAL William H 1858
HERREN [129] James 1823
HENRY Bunk 1881
HAACK John 1883
MCDANAL Jake 1881
MCDANAL William H 1858
CAMERON William 1823

Helpful Hints

1. This Map's INDEX can be found on the preceding pages.
2. Refer to Map "C" to see where this Township lies within Jefferson County, Alabama.
3. Numbers within square brackets [ ] denote a multi-patentee land parcel (multi-owner). Refer to Appendix "C" for a full list of members in this group.
4. Areas that look to be crowded with Patentees usually indicate multiple sales of the same parcel (Re-issues) or Overlapping parcels. See this Township's Index for an explanation of these and other circumstances that might explain "odd" groupings of Patentees on this map.

Legend

Patent Boundary
Section Boundary
No Patents Found (or Outside County)
1., 2., 3., ... Lot Numbers (when beside a name)
[ ] Group Number (see Appendix "C")

Scale: Section = 1 mile X 1 mile (generally, with some exceptions)

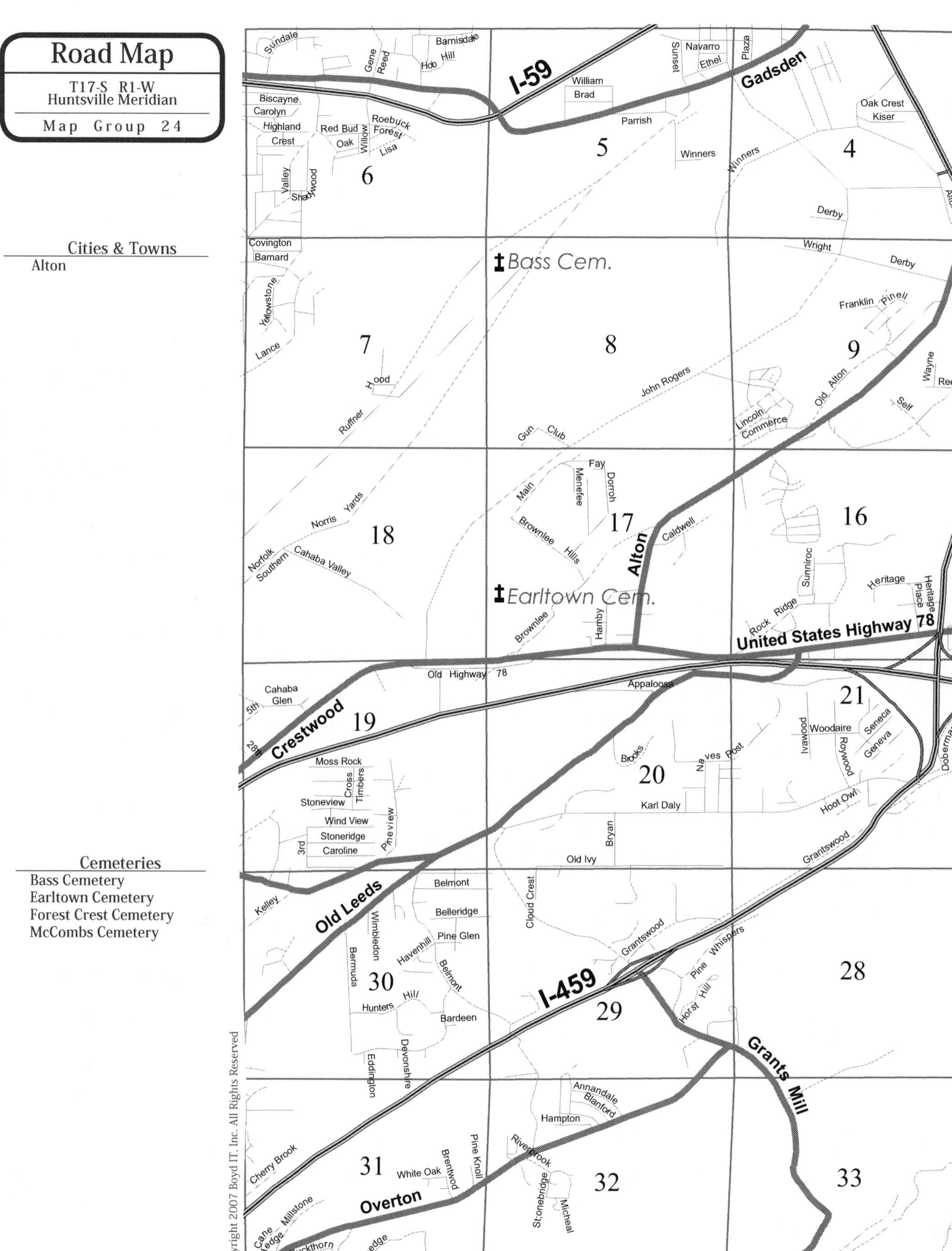
Road Map
T17-S R1-W
Huntsville Meridian
Map Group 24
Cities & Towns
Alton
Cemeteries
Bass Cemetery
Earltown Cemetery
Forest Crest Cemetery
McCombs Cemetery
I-59
Gadsden
United States Highway 78
Old Highway 78
Crestwood
Old Leeds
I-459
Grants Mill
Overton
Alton
Bass Cem.
Earltown Cem.
4
5
6
7
8
9
16
17
18
19
20
21
28
29
30
31
32
33
Sundale
Barnisdale
Hill
Hob
Gene
Reed
Biscayne
Carolyn
Highland
Crest
Red Bud
Oak
Willow
Roebuck
Forest
Lisa
Valley
Shadywood
William
Brad
Parrish
Sunset
Navarro
Ethel
Plaza
Winners
Oak Crest
Kiser
Clayton
Pine
Derby
Wright
Covington
Barnard
Yellowstone
Lance
Hood
Ruffner
Gun
Club
John Rogers
Franklin
Pinell
Old Alton
Wayne
Reese
Self
Lincoln
Commerce
Norris
Yards
Norfolk
Southern
Cahaba Valley
Main
Menefee
Fay
Dorroh
Brownlee
Hills
Caldwell
Hamby
Sunniroc
Rock
Ridge
Heritage
Heritage
Place
Cahaba
Glen
5th
28th
Appaloosa
Moss Rock
Cross
Timbers
Stoneview
Wind View
Stoneridge
Caroline
Pineview
3rd
Brooks
Post
Karl Daly
Bryan
Old Ivy
Ivawood
Woodaire
Roywood
Seneca
Geneva
Doberman
Hoot Owl
Grantswood
Kelley
Belmont
Belleridge
Pine Glen
Wimbledon
Bermuda
Havenhill
Belmont
Hunters
Hill
Bardeen
Cloud Crest
Grantswood
Pine
Whispers
Horst
Hill
Edington
Devonshire
Annandale
Blanford
Hampton
Riverbrook
Stonebridge
Micheal
Pine Knoll
Brentwood
White Oak
Cherry Brook
Cane
Hedge
Millstone
Buckthorn
Hillsedge
Nameless

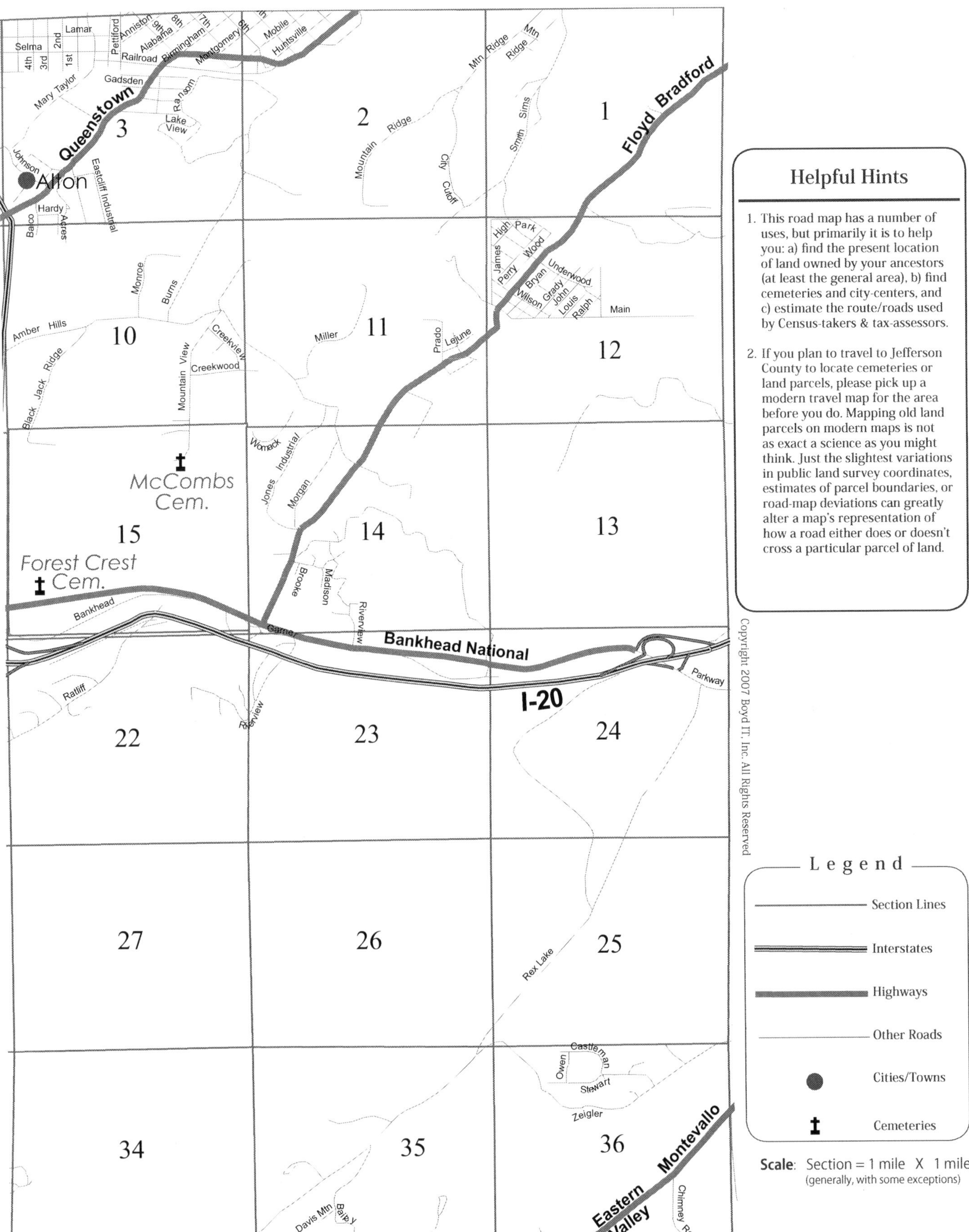

Helpful Hints

1. This road map has a number of uses, but primarily it is to help you: a) find the present location of land owned by your ancestors (at least the general area), b) find cemeteries and city-centers, and c) estimate the route/roads used by Census-takers & tax-assessors.

2. If you plan to travel to Jefferson County to locate cemeteries or land parcels, please pick up a modern travel map for the area before you do. Mapping old land parcels on modern maps is not as exact a science as you might think. Just the slightest variations in public land survey coordinates, estimates of parcel boundaries, or road-map deviations can greatly alter a map's representation of how a road either does or doesn't cross a particular parcel of land.

Legend

- Section Lines
- Interstates
- Highways
- Other Roads
- Cities/Towns
- Cemeteries

Scale: Section = 1 mile X 1 mile
(generally, with some exceptions)

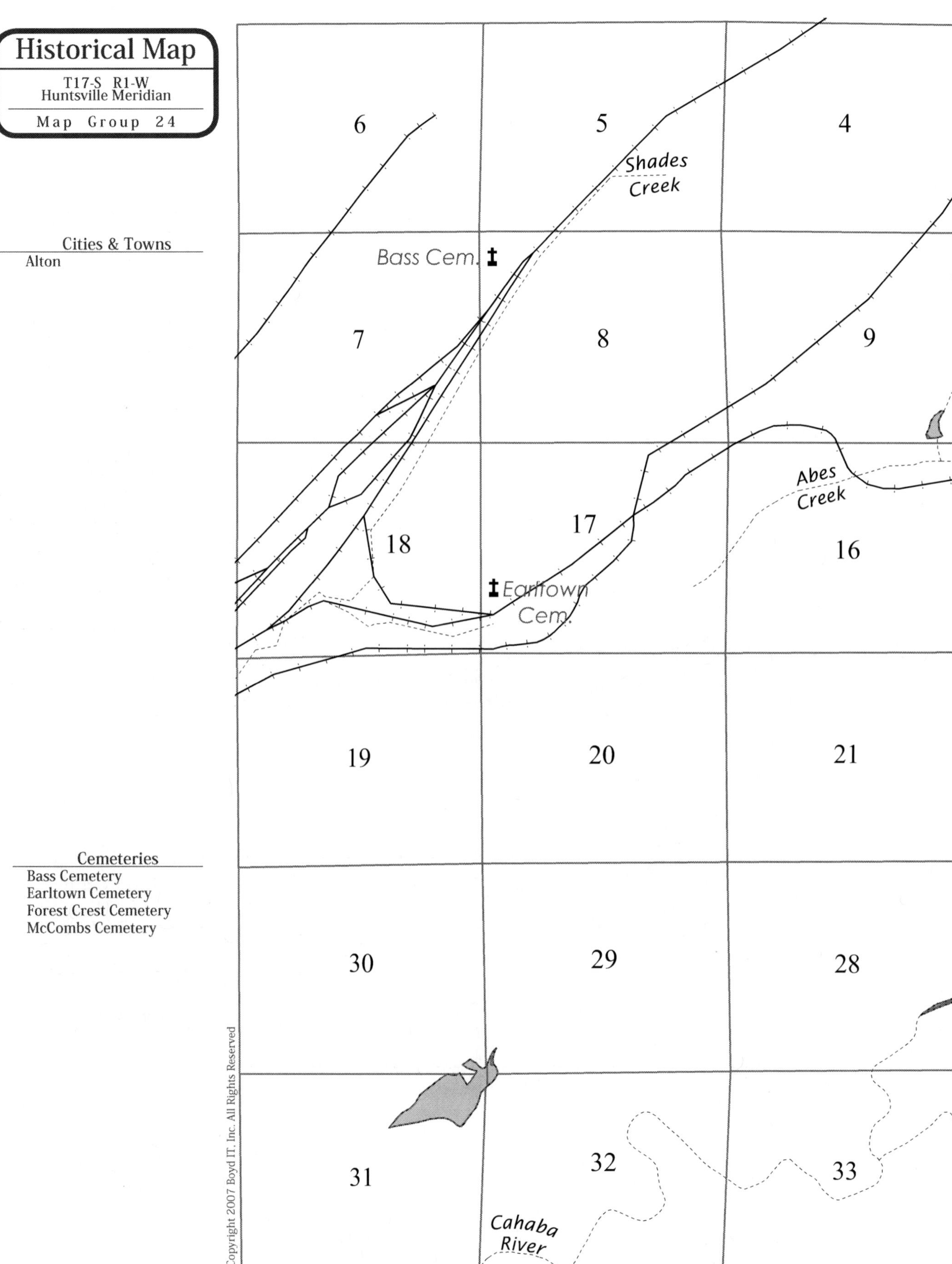
Historical Map
T17-S R1-W
Huntsville Meridian
Map Group 24
Cities & Towns
Alton
Cemeteries
Bass Cemetery
Earltown Cemetery
Forest Crest Cemetery
McCombs Cemetery
6
5
4
Shades Creek
Bass Cem.
7
8
9
18
17
16
Abes Creek
Earltown Cem.
19
20
21
30
29
28
31
32
33
Cahaba River
Copyright 2007 Boyd IT, Inc. All Rights Reserved

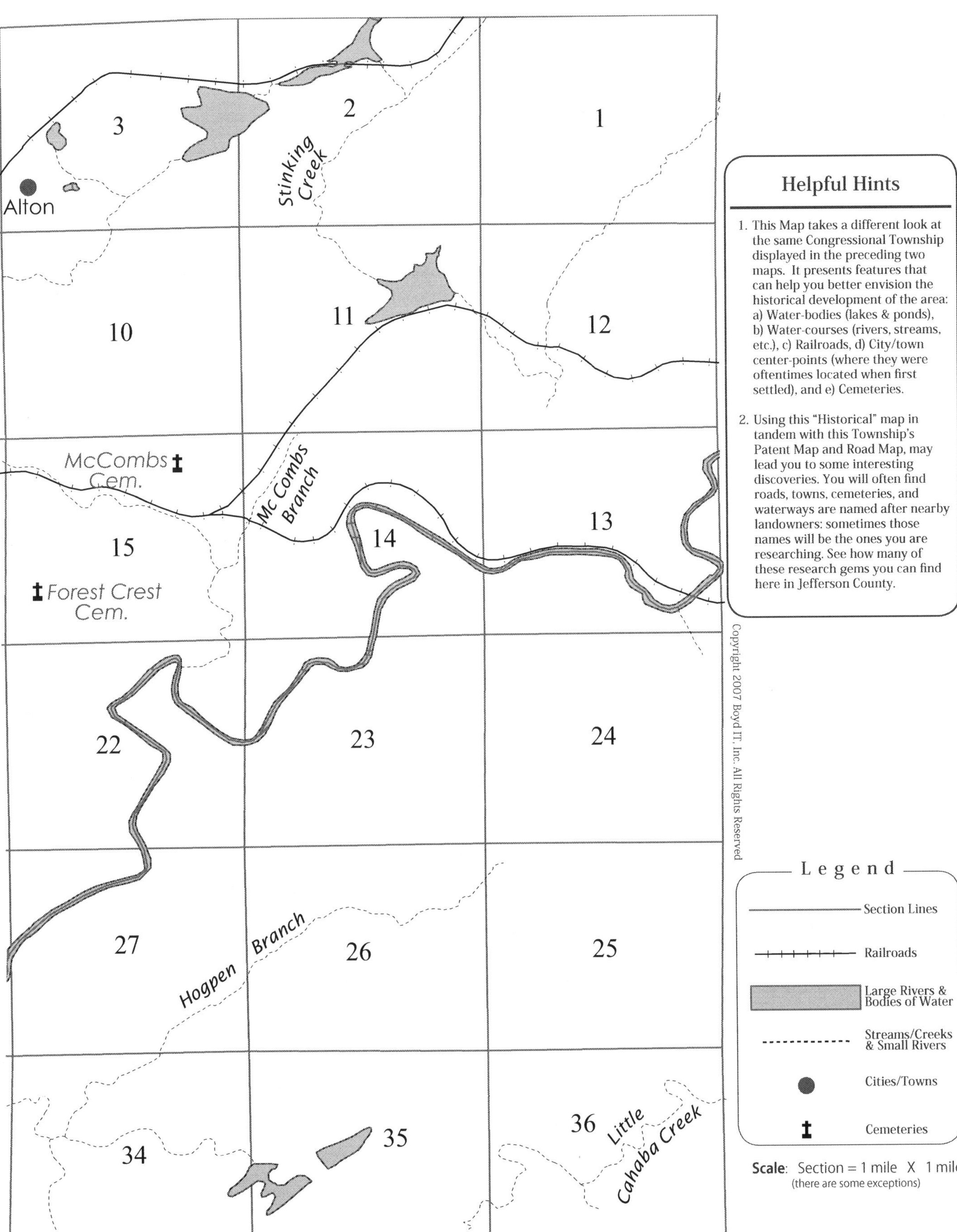
3
2
1
Alton
Stinking Creek
10
11
12
McCombs Cem.
Mc Combs Branch
15
14
13
Forest Crest Cem.
22
23
24
27
Hogpen Branch
26
25
34
35
36
Little Cahaba Creek
Helpful Hints
1. This Map takes a different look at the same Congressional Township displayed in the preceding two maps. It presents features that can help you better envision the historical development of the area: a) Water-bodies (lakes & ponds), b) Water-courses (rivers, streams, etc.), c) Railroads, d) City/town center-points (where they were oftentimes located when first settled), and e) Cemeteries.
2. Using this "Historical" map in tandem with this Township's Patent Map and Road Map, may lead you to some interesting discoveries. You will often find roads, towns, cemeteries, and waterways are named after nearby landowners: sometimes those names will be the ones you are researching. See how many of these research gems you can find here in Jefferson County.
Copyright 2007 Boyd IT, Inc. All Rights Reserved
Legend
Section Lines
Railroads
Large Rivers & Bodies of Water
Streams/Creeks & Small Rivers
Cities/Towns
Cemeteries
Scale: Section = 1 mile X 1 mile
(there are some exceptions)

Map Group 25: Index to Land Patents

Township 17-South Range 1-East (Huntsville)

After you locate an individual in this Index, take note of the Section and Section Part then proceed to the Land Patent map on the pages immediately following. You should have no difficulty locating the corresponding parcel of land.

The "For More Info" Column will lead you to more information about the underlying Patents. See the *Legend* at right, and the "How to Use this Book" chapter, for more information.

LEGEND

"For More Info . . . " column

- **A** = Authority (Legislative Act, See Appendix "A")
- **B** = Block or Lot (location in Section unknown)
- **C** = Cancelled Patent
- **F** = Fractional Section
- **G** = Group (Multi-Patentee Patent, see Appendix "C")
- **V** = Overlaps another Parcel
- **R** = Re-Issued (Parcel patented more than once)

(A & G items require you to look in the Appendixes referred to above. All other Letter-designations followed by a number require you to locate line-items in this index that possess the ID number found after the letter).

ID	Individual in Patent	Sec.	Sec. Part	Date Issued	Other Counties	For More Info . . .
4606	ALLEN, Matthew	6	SWNW	1858-06-01		A1
4535	ARMSTRONG, Elbert	15	SESE	1860-07-02	St. Clair	A1
4536	" "	22	E½NE	1860-07-02		A1
4537	" "	22	NWNE	1860-07-02		A1
4544	ARMSTRONG, Greenberry	22	E½NW	1858-06-01		A1
4545	" "	22	NESW	1858-06-01		A1
4520	BEERS, Anthony	8	E½NW	1881-07-20		A4
4521	" "	8	W½NE	1881-07-20		A4
4569	BLACK, John	18	NWSE	1883-10-01		A4
4570	" "	18	SENW	1883-10-01		A4
4571	" "	18	SWNE	1883-10-01		A4
4630	CAMERON, William	31	W½NW	1823-03-01		A1
4628	" "	31	E½NW	1823-05-01		A1
4631	" "	31	W½SW	1823-05-01		A1
4629	" "	31	W½NE	1824-04-26		A1
4611	CAST, Permelia A	6	NE	1882-09-15		A1
4539	CASTE, Forney	6	S½SW	1884-05-15		A1
4540	" "	6	W½SE	1884-05-15		A1
4607	CASTE, Nancy A	6	NWSW	1889-05-10		A1
4541	CHAMLESS, George	18	SESE	1892-01-18		A4
4534	COPELAND, Douglas	20	W½SW	1823-06-02		A1
4642	CRUMP, Zachariah	31	NESW	1852-01-01		A1
4522	DOROUGH, Benjamin F	18	W½SW	1881-12-30		A1
4608	DOROUGH, Nathaniel	32	N½NE	1880-02-20	Shelby	A4
4632	DOROUGH, William F	28	NENW	1885-03-30	Shelby	A4
4633	" "	28	NWNE	1885-03-30	Shelby	A4
4640	EPPERSON, William T	22	NWSE	1881-07-20		A4
4641	" "	22	SWNE	1881-07-20		A4
4525	FALKNER, Carrol	7	SWSW	1841-01-09		A1
4598	FRANKLIN, Mahala	6	N½NW	1882-12-20		A1
4599	" "	6	NESW	1882-12-20		A1
4600	" "	6	SENW	1882-12-20		A1
4625	FULLER, Trion	22	W½NW	1824-04-12		A1
4626	FULLER, Tryon	21	E½NE	1823-05-01		A1 G91
4627	" "	21	W½NE	1823-05-01		A1 G91
4560	GIVENS, James A	15	E½SW	1823-05-01	St. Clair	A1 V4575, 4619
4561	" "	15	W½NW	1823-05-01	St. Clair	A1
4559	" "	15	E½NW	1823-07-09	St. Clair	A1
4554	GREEN, Hilton	18	SENE	1883-06-26		A4
4555	" "	18	SWNW	1883-06-26		A4
4556	" "	18	SWSE	1883-06-26		A4
4562	HAGWOOD, James A	6	E½SE	1888-02-04		A4
4564	HAMILTON, James	20	E½SE	1823-05-01		A1
4565	" "	20	W½SE	1823-05-01		A1
4572	HARAN, John M	22	E½SE	1885-05-04		A1
4573	" "	22	SWSE	1885-05-04		A1

ID	Individual in Patent	Sec.	Sec. Part	Date Issued	Other Counties	For More Info . . .
4542	HARDING, George	32	SESE	1860-07-02	Shelby	A1
4543	" "	32	W½SE	1860-07-02	Shelby	A1
4528	HERRING, Crawford	8	SESE	1894-10-22		A4
4596	HERRING, Lewis W	30	NWSW	1858-06-01		A1
4597	" "	30	SWNW	1858-06-01		A1
4602	HERRING, Mary	18	E½SW	1883-07-03		A4
4639	HERRING, William P	32	N½NW	1858-06-01	Shelby	A1
4518	HUCHINGSON, Amos S	21	NESW	1834-10-21		A1
4619	HURST, Spencer	15	NESW	1858-06-01	St. Clair	A1 V4560
4622	JOHNSON, Taylor	8	W½SW	1883-05-21		A4
4634	JOHNSON, William H	8	NESW	1883-05-21		A4
4635	" "	8	NWSE	1883-05-21		A4
4617	JONES, Seborn W	29	SENW	1840-11-10		A1
4557	LATHAM, Isaac	8	NENE	1883-10-20		A1
4523	LOCKHART, Benjamin	20	E½SW	1823-05-01		A1
4567	MASON, Job	30	E½SE	1823-05-01		A1
4568	" "	30	W½SE	1823-05-01		A1
4516	MASSENGILL, A A	18	N½NE	1883-05-21		A4 G162
4516	MASSENGILL, Henry A	18	N½NE	1883-05-21		A4 G162
4516	MASSENGILL, Thaddeus J	18	N½NE	1883-05-21		A4 G162
4566	MCCARTNEY, James	20	E½NE	1823-05-01		A1 G165
4533	MCGUIRE, Davidson	21	NWSE	1839-09-20		A1
4616	MCGUIRE, Sarah J	20	N½NW	1858-06-01		A1
4517	MCLAUGHLIN, Alexander	21	E½NW	1823-05-01		A1
4529	MCLAUGHLIN, Daniel	30	E½SW	1823-06-02		A1
4546	MCLAUGHLIN, Hezekiah B	8	NESE	1880-02-20		A4
4547	" "	8	SENE	1880-02-20		A4
4558	MCLAUGHLIN, Isaac	19	SESE	1850-04-01		A1
4563	MCLAUGHLIN, James F	15	E½NE	1858-06-01	St. Clair	A1
4566	MCLAUGHLIN, John	20	E½NE	1823-05-01		A1 G165
4574	" "	21	W½NW	1823-05-01		A1
4601	MCLAUGHLIN, Marion F	22	S½SW	1891-06-30		A4
4636	MCLAUGHLIN, William H	17	SESE	1848-04-15		A1
4637	" "	17	SESW	1858-06-01		A1
4638	" "	17	SWSE	1858-06-01		A1
4519	MOOR, Ann H	17	N½SE	1861-08-01		A1
4548	MOOR, Hezekiah B	15	NESE	1858-06-01	St. Clair	A1
4549	" "	15	NWSE	1858-06-01	St. Clair	A1
4550	" "	15	SWNE	1858-06-01	St. Clair	A1
4551	" "	21	NESE	1858-06-01		A1
4552	" "	21	SESE	1858-06-01		A1
4553	" "	22	NWSW	1858-06-01		A1
4531	NEAL, David	29	W½NW	1823-05-01		A1
4532	" "	29	W½SW	1823-05-01		A1
4538	NELSION, Elias	8	W½NW	1883-05-25		A4
4612	OBAR, Robert	18	NESE	1852-01-01		A1
4603	OBARR, Mathis	17	NENW	1858-06-01		A1
4604	" "	8	SESW	1858-06-01		A1
4605	" "	8	SWSE	1858-06-01		A1
4575	OLIVER, John	15	SESW	1858-06-01	St. Clair	A1 V4560
4576	" "	15	SWSE	1858-06-01	St. Clair	A1
4577	" "	17	E½NE	1861-08-01		A1
4578	PATTON, John	30	SENW	1839-09-20		A1
4586	RAY, Joseph	21	W½SW	1823-05-01		A1
4623	ROWAN, Thomas	20	SWNW	1858-06-01		A1
4579	SANSON, John	18	N½NW	1860-04-02		A1
4580	" "	7	E½SW	1860-04-02		A1
4581	" "	7	NWSW	1860-04-02		A1
4620	SCOTT, Stafford	30	NENW	1880-02-20		A4
4621	" "	30	NWNW	1884-12-05		A4
4526	SEAL, Chapman	29	NENE	1852-01-01		A1
4530	SEAL, Daniel	29	SWNE	1850-04-01		A1
4618	SHOOK, Solomon	20	SENW	1839-09-20		A1
4626	SIMS, Edward	21	E½NE	1823-05-01		A1 G91
4627	" "	21	W½NE	1823-05-01		A1 G91
4587	SMITH, Lester C	28	E½NE	1885-05-04	Shelby	A1
4588	" "	28	S½SW	1885-05-04	Shelby	A1
4589	" "	28	SE	1885-05-04	Shelby	A1
4590	" "	28	SWNE	1885-05-04	Shelby	A1
4591	" "	32	N½SW	1885-05-04	Shelby	A1
4592	" "	32	NESE	1885-05-04	Shelby	A1
4593	" "	32	S½NE	1885-05-04	Shelby	A1
4594	" "	32	S½NW	1885-05-04	Shelby	A1

ID	Individual in Patent	Sec.	Sec. Part	Date Issued	Other Counties	For More Info . . .
4595	SMITH, Lester C (Cont'd)	32	SWSW	1885-05-04	Shelby	A1
4585	SPARKS, Joseph K	20	W½NE	1823-05-01		A1
4527	THOMPSON, Clayton	29	NESW	1837-04-01		A1
4582	WALLACE, John	30	E½NE	1823-05-01		A1
4583	" "	30	W½NE	1824-05-20		A1
4609	WATSON, Obadiah	28	N½SW	1885-05-25	Shelby	A4
4610	" "	28	S½NW	1885-05-25	Shelby	A4
4524	WHITE, Bradley	31	NENE	1852-01-01		A1
4584	WORTHINGTON, John	30	SWSW	1850-04-01		A1
4613	WORTHINGTON, Robert	21	SESW	1858-06-01		A1
4614	" "	28	NWNW	1858-06-01	Shelby	A1
4615	" "	29	NWNE	1858-06-01		A1
4624	WORTHY, Thomas	15	NWNE	1835-10-01	St. Clair	A1

Patent Map

T17-S R1-E
Huntsville Meridian

Map Group 25

Township Statistics

Parcels Mapped	:	127
Number of Patents	:	90
Number of Individuals	:	77
Patentees Identified	:	74
Number of Surnames	:	55
Multi-Patentee Parcels	:	4
Oldest Patent Date	:	3/1/1823
Most Recent Patent	:	10/22/1894
Block/Lot Parcels	:	0
Parcels Re - Issued	:	0
Parcels that Overlap	:	3
Cities and Towns	:	2
Cemeteries	:	1

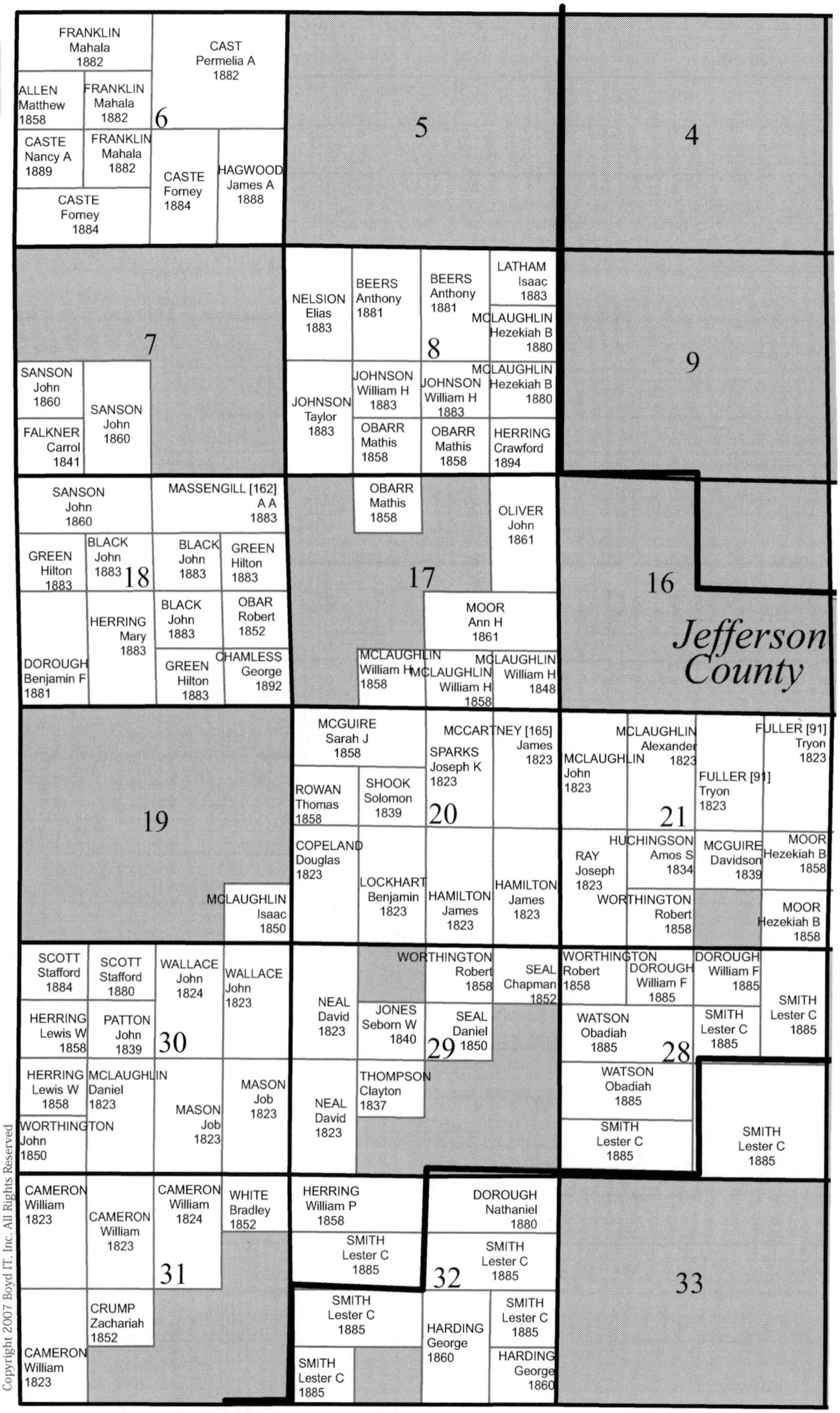

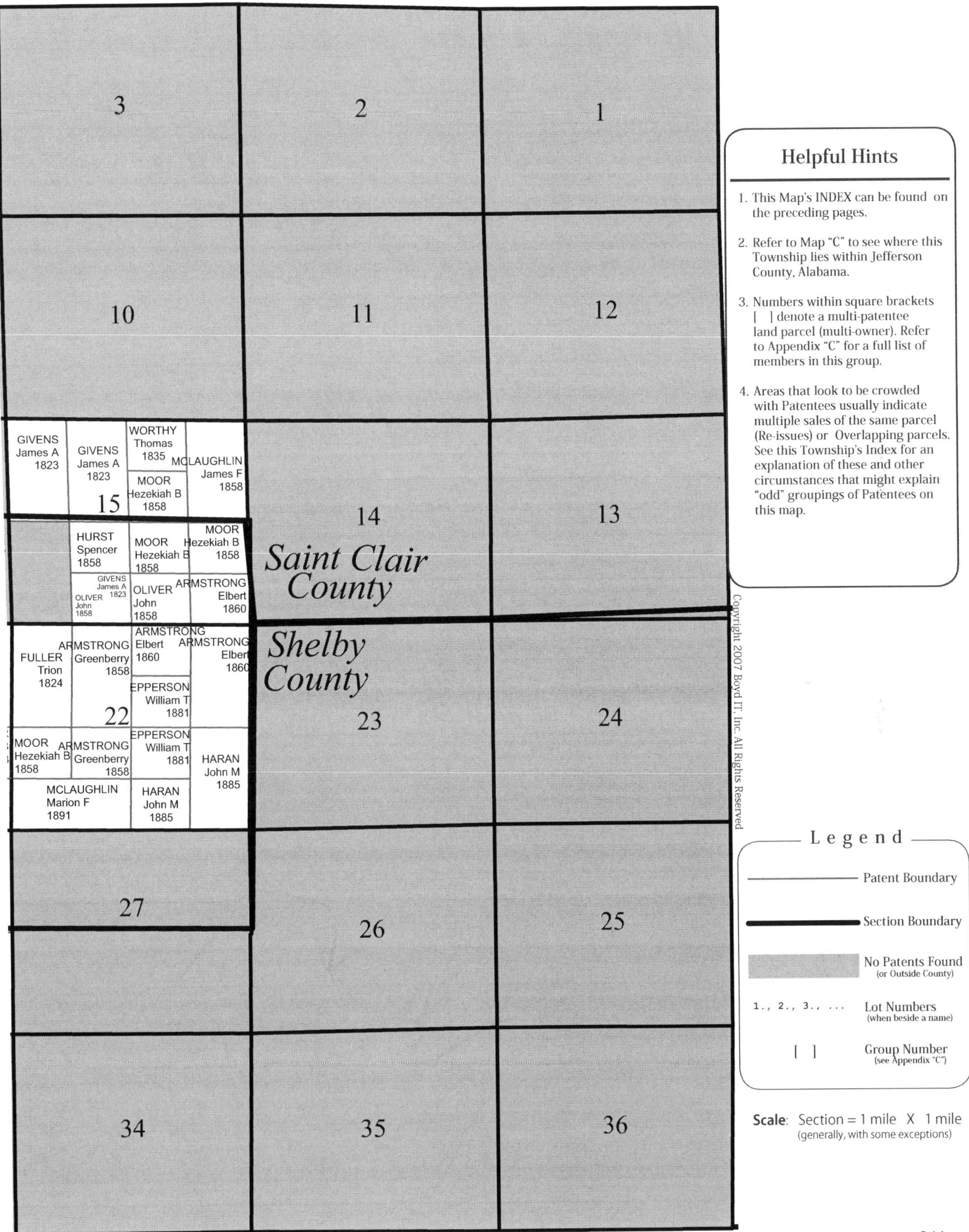

Helpful Hints

1. This Map's INDEX can be found on the preceding pages.
2. Refer to Map "C" to see where this Township lies within Jefferson County, Alabama.
3. Numbers within square brackets [ ] denote a multi-patentee land parcel (multi-owner). Refer to Appendix "C" for a full list of members in this group.
4. Areas that look to be crowded with Patentees usually indicate multiple sales of the same parcel (Re-issues) or Overlapping parcels. See this Township's Index for an explanation of these and other circumstances that might explain "odd" groupings of Patentees on this map.

Legend

- Patent Boundary
- Section Boundary
- No Patents Found (or Outside County)
- 1., 2., 3., ... Lot Numbers (when beside a name)
- [ ] Group Number (see Appendix "C")

Scale: Section = 1 mile X 1 mile (generally, with some exceptions)

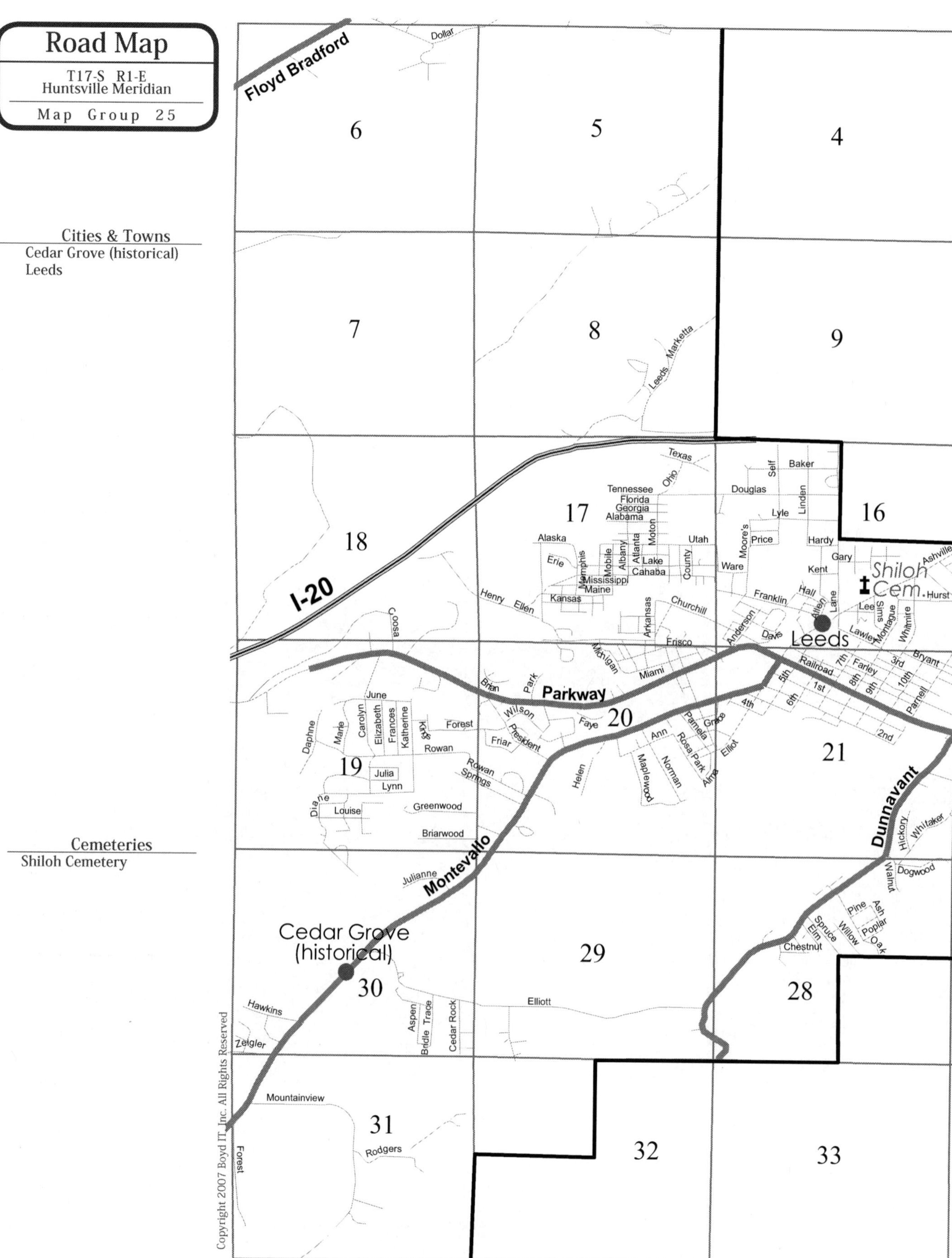
Road Map
T17-S R1-E
Huntsville Meridian
Map Group 25
Cities & Towns
Cedar Grove (historical)
Leeds
Cemeteries
Shiloh Cemetery
Floyd Bradford
Dollar
6
5
4
7
8
9
Leeds Marketta
18
17
16
I-20
Texas
Ohio
Tennessee
Florida
Georgia
Alabama
Alaska
Erie
Memphis
Mobile
Albany
Atlanta
Moton
Lake
Cahaba
Mississippi
Maine
Kansas
Utah
County
Henry Ellen
Arkansas
Churchill
Frisco
Self
Baker
Douglas
Linden
Lyle
Moore's
Price
Hardy
Gary
Kent
Ware
Franklin
Hall
Allen
Lane
Anderson
Davis
Leeds
Shiloh Cem.
Ashville
Hurst
Lee
Sims
Montague
Whitmire
Lawley
Bryant
Coosa
Michigan
Miami
Parkway
Brian
Park
Wilson
President
Faye
20
Railroad
7th
8th
9th
10th
3rd
Farley
1st
5th
6th
4th
Parnell
2nd
21
June
Daphne
Marie
Carolyn
Elizabeth
Frances
Katherine
Forest
Friar
Rowan
Rowan Springs
19
Julia
Lynn
Diane
Louise
Greenwood
Briarwood
Ann
Grace
Pamela
Rosa Park
Elliot
Helen
Maplewood
Norman
Alma
Dunnavant
Hickory
Whitaker
Walnut
Dogwood
Montevallo
Julianne
Cedar Grove (historical)
29
30
Pine
Ash
Spruce
Elm
Willow
Poplar
Oak
Chestnut
28
Elliott
Hawkins
Aspen
Bridle Trace
Cedar Rock
Zeigler
Mountainview
31
Rodgers
Forest
32
33

3 2 1

10 11 12

15 14 13

Clayton
Minor
Maitland
Owens
Millie
Swafford
Sunset
Spruiell
Moss
Veasey
Lewis
Dorrough
Poole
Tree
Azalea
Thornton
Pear
Beech
Shale
Borden
Oakridge
Leaf
East Grove
Goldenrod
Berry
Ivy
Holly
Vine

Saint Clair County

Shelby County

Jefferson County

22 23 24

27 26 25

34 35 36

Helpful Hints

1. This road map has a number of uses, but primarily it is to help you: a) find the present location of land owned by your ancestors (at least the general area), b) find cemeteries and city-centers, and c) estimate the route/roads used by Census-takers & tax-assessors.

2. If you plan to travel to Jefferson County to locate cemeteries or land parcels, please pick up a modern travel map for the area before you do. Mapping old land parcels on modern maps is not as exact a science as you might think. Just the slightest variations in public land survey coordinates, estimates of parcel boundaries, or road-map deviations can greatly alter a map's representation of how a road either does or doesn't cross a particular parcel of land.

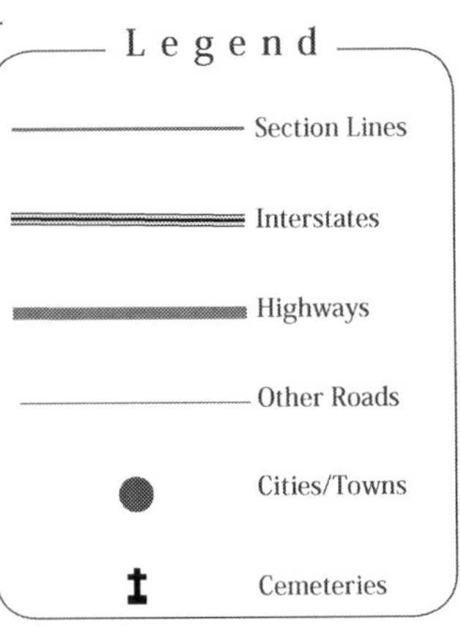

Scale: Section = 1 mile X 1 mile
(generally, with some exceptions)

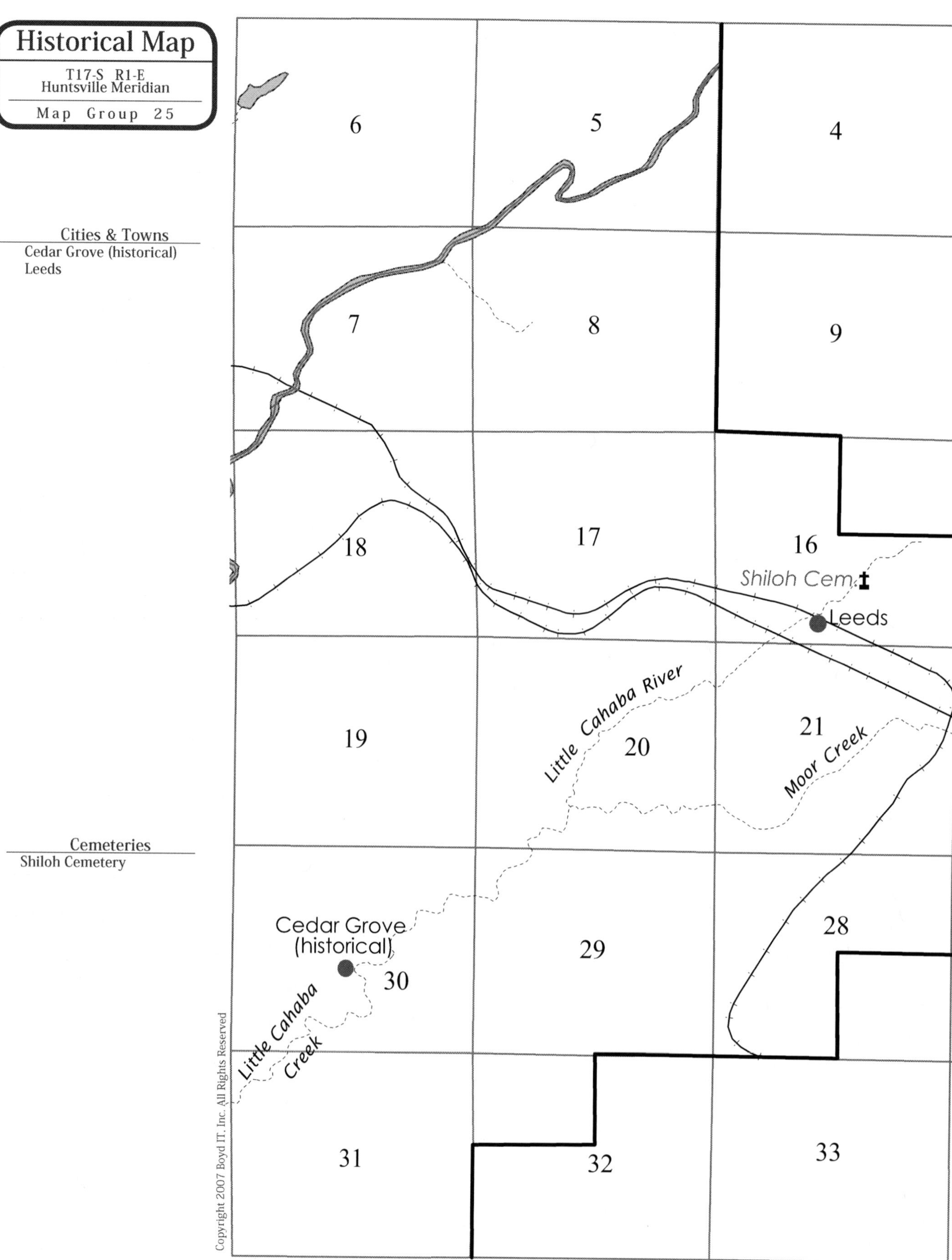
Historical Map
T17-S R1-E
Huntsville Meridian
Map Group 25
Cities & Towns
Cedar Grove (historical)
Leeds
Cemeteries
Shiloh Cemetery
6
5
4
7
8
9
18
17
16
Shiloh Cem.
Leeds
19
20
21
Little Cahaba River
Moor Creek
Cedar Grove (historical)
29
28
30
Little Cahaba Creek
31
32
33

Helpful Hints

1. This Map takes a different look at the same Congressional Township displayed in the preceding two maps. It presents features that can help you better envision the historical development of the area: a) Water-bodies (lakes & ponds), b) Water-courses (rivers, streams, etc.), c) Railroads, d) City/town center-points (where they were oftentimes located when first settled), and e) Cemeteries.
2. Using this "Historical" map in tandem with this Township's Patent Map and Road Map, may lead you to some interesting discoveries. You will often find roads, towns, cemeteries, and waterways are named after nearby landowners: sometimes those names will be the ones you are researching. See how many of these research gems you can find here in Jefferson County.

Legend

Scale: Section = 1 mile X 1 mile
(there are some exceptions)

Map Group 26: Index to Land Patents

Township 18-South Range 8-West (Huntsville)

After you locate an individual in this Index, take note of the Section and Section Part then proceed to the Land Patent map on the pages immediately following. You should have no difficulty locating the corresponding parcel of land.

The "For More Info" Column will lead you to more information about the underlying Patents. See the *Legend* at right, and the "How to Use this Book" chapter, for more information.

LEGEND

"For More Info . . . " column

A = Authority (Legislative Act, See Appendix "A")
B = Block or Lot (location in Section unknown)
C = Cancelled Patent
F = Fractional Section
G = Group (Multi-Patentee Patent, see Appendix "C")
V = Overlaps another Parcel
R = Re-Issued (Parcel patented more than once)

(A & G items require you to look in the Appendixes referred to above. All other Letter-designations followed by a number require you to locate line-items in this index that possess the ID number found after the letter).

ID	Individual in Patent	Sec.	Sec. Part	Date Issued	Other Counties	For More Info . . .
4653	ERNEST, Melvina A	14	N½NE	1888-11-08	Tuscaloosa	A1
4643	GILBERT, Andrew	13	NESE	1890-01-08	Tuscaloosa	A4
4644	" "	13	SENE	1890-01-08	Tuscaloosa	A4
4651	GILBERT, John T	12	A	1858-06-01	Tuscaloosa	A1 F
4654	GILLIAN, William F	13	NW	1891-12-01	Tuscaloosa	A1 F
4655	" "	13	NWNE	1891-12-01	Tuscaloosa	A1 F
4648	PATTON, James H	13	SESE	1850-09-02	Tuscaloosa	A1
4649	" "	24	E½NE	1858-06-01		A1
4650	" "	24	SESE	1860-12-01		A1
4645	PHILLIPS, James E	14	E½NW	1860-07-02	Tuscaloosa	A1
4646	" "	14	NWSW	1860-07-02	Tuscaloosa	A1
4647	" "	14	SWNW	1860-07-02	Tuscaloosa	A1
4652	REID, Levi	24	SWSE	1858-06-01		A1
4656	REID, William T	12	SE	1861-01-01	Tuscaloosa	A1 F
4657	" "	12	SW	1861-01-01	Tuscaloosa	A1 F
4658	" "	13	NENE	1861-07-01	Tuscaloosa	A1

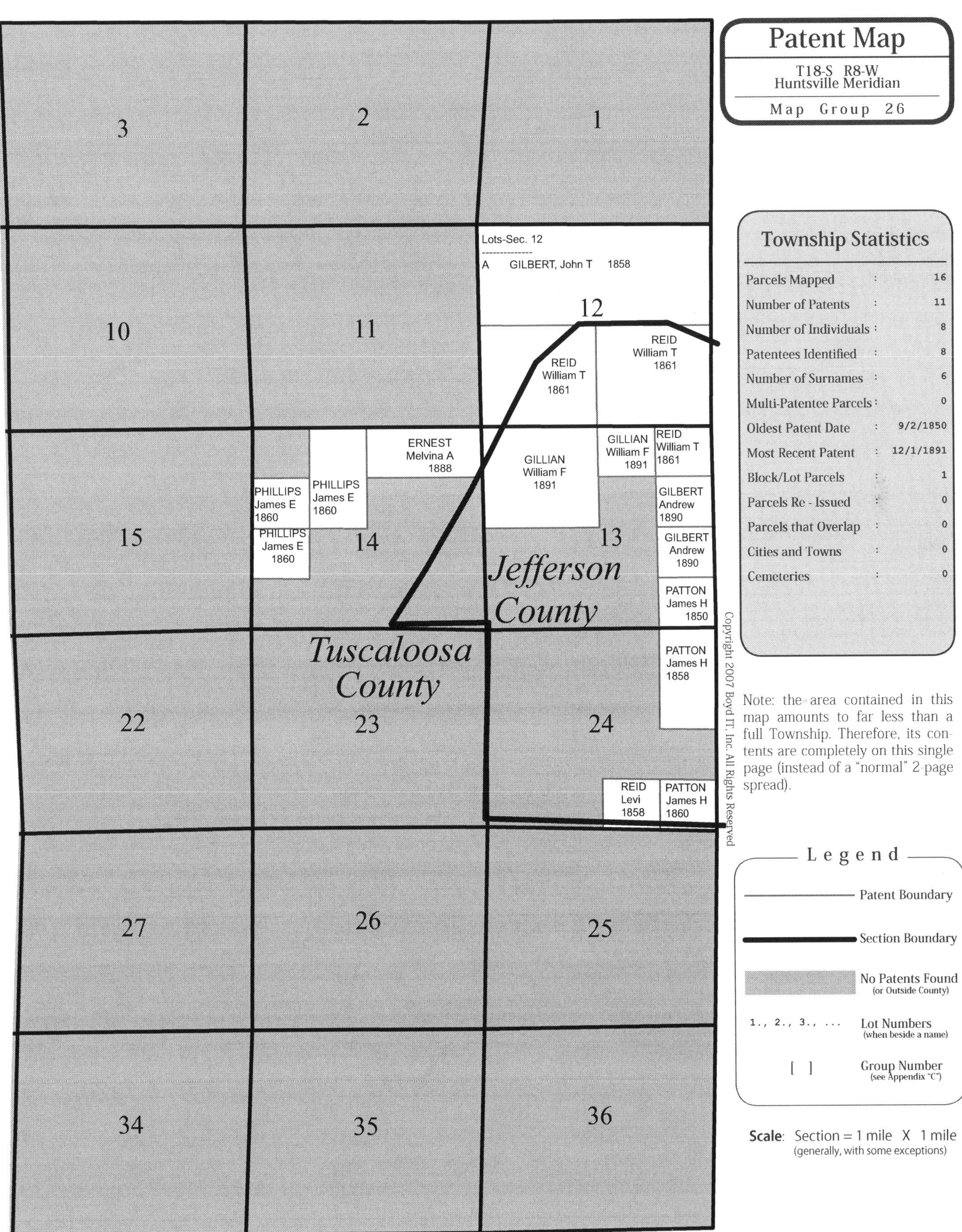
Patent Map
T18-S R8-W
Huntsville Meridian
Map Group 26
3
2
1
10
11
Lots-Sec. 12
A GILBERT, John T 1858
12
REID William T 1861
REID William T 1861
15
ERNEST Melvina A 1888
PHILLIPS James E 1860
PHILLIPS James E 1860
PHILLIPS James E 1860
14
GILLIAN William F 1891
GILLIAN William F 1891
REID William T 1861
GILBERT Andrew 1890
GILBERT Andrew 1890
13
PATTON James H 1850
Jefferson County
Tuscaloosa County
22
23
24
PATTON James H 1858
REID Levi 1858
PATTON James H 1860
27
26
25
34
35
36
Copyright 2007 Boyd IT, Inc. All Rights Reserved
Township Statistics
Parcels Mapped : 16
Number of Patents : 11
Number of Individuals : 8
Patentees Identified : 8
Number of Surnames : 6
Multi-Patentee Parcels : 0
Oldest Patent Date : 9/2/1850
Most Recent Patent : 12/1/1891
Block/Lot Parcels : 1
Parcels Re - Issued : 0
Parcels that Overlap : 0
Cities and Towns : 0
Cemeteries : 0
Note: the area contained in this map amounts to far less than a full Township. Therefore, its contents are completely on this single page (instead of a "normal" 2-page spread).
Legend
Patent Boundary
Section Boundary
No Patents Found (or Outside County)
1., 2., 3., ... Lot Numbers (when beside a name)
[ ] Group Number (see Appendix "C")
Scale: Section = 1 mile X 1 mile (generally, with some exceptions)

Road Map

T18-S R8-W
Huntsville Meridian

Map Group 26

Note: the area contained in this map amounts to far less than a full Township. Therefore, its contents are completely on this single page (instead of a "normal" 2-page spread).

Cities & Towns
None

Cemeteries
None

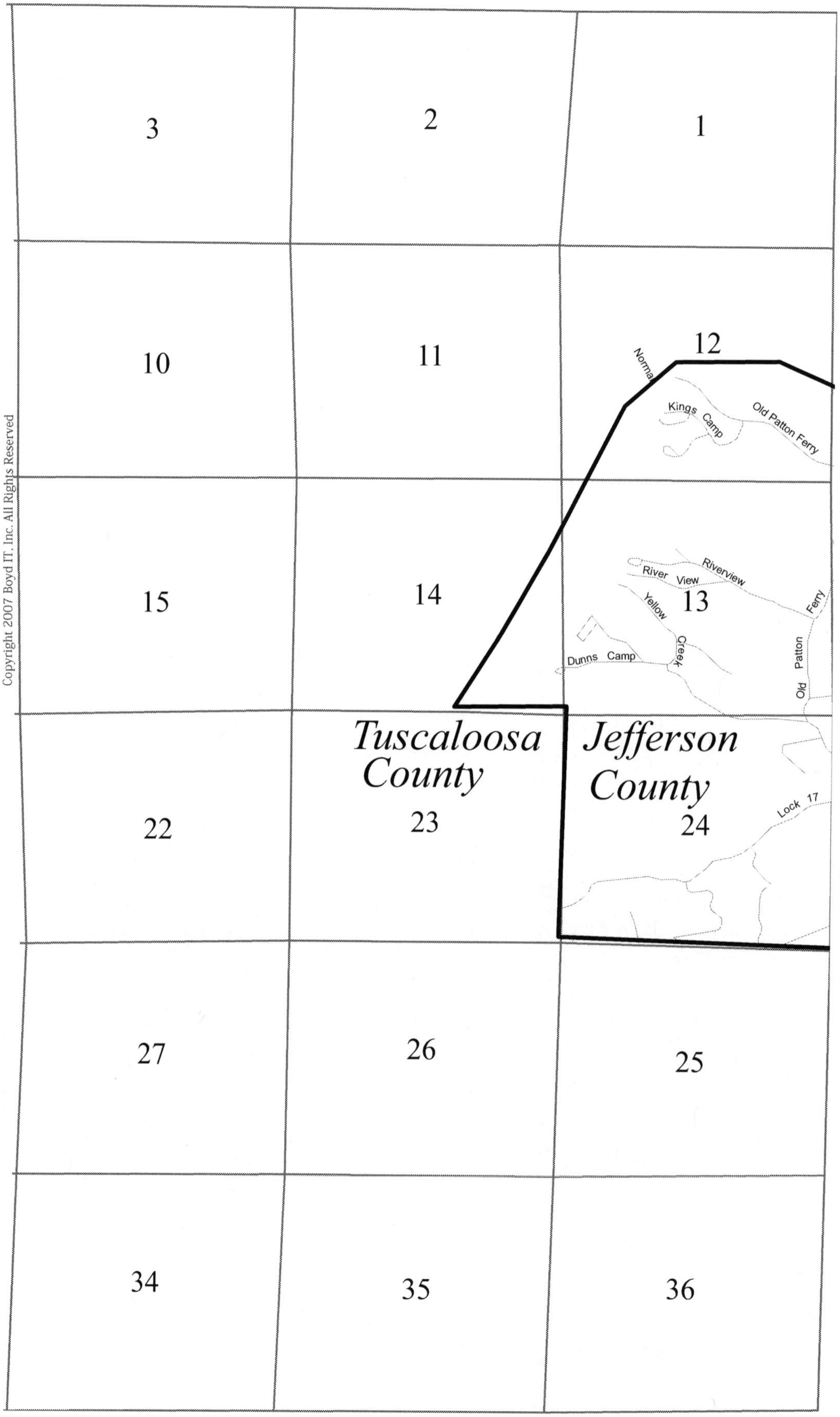

Legend
- Section Lines
- Interstates
- Highways
- Other Roads
- Cities/Towns
- Cemeteries

Scale: Section = 1 mile X 1 mile
(generally, with some exceptions)

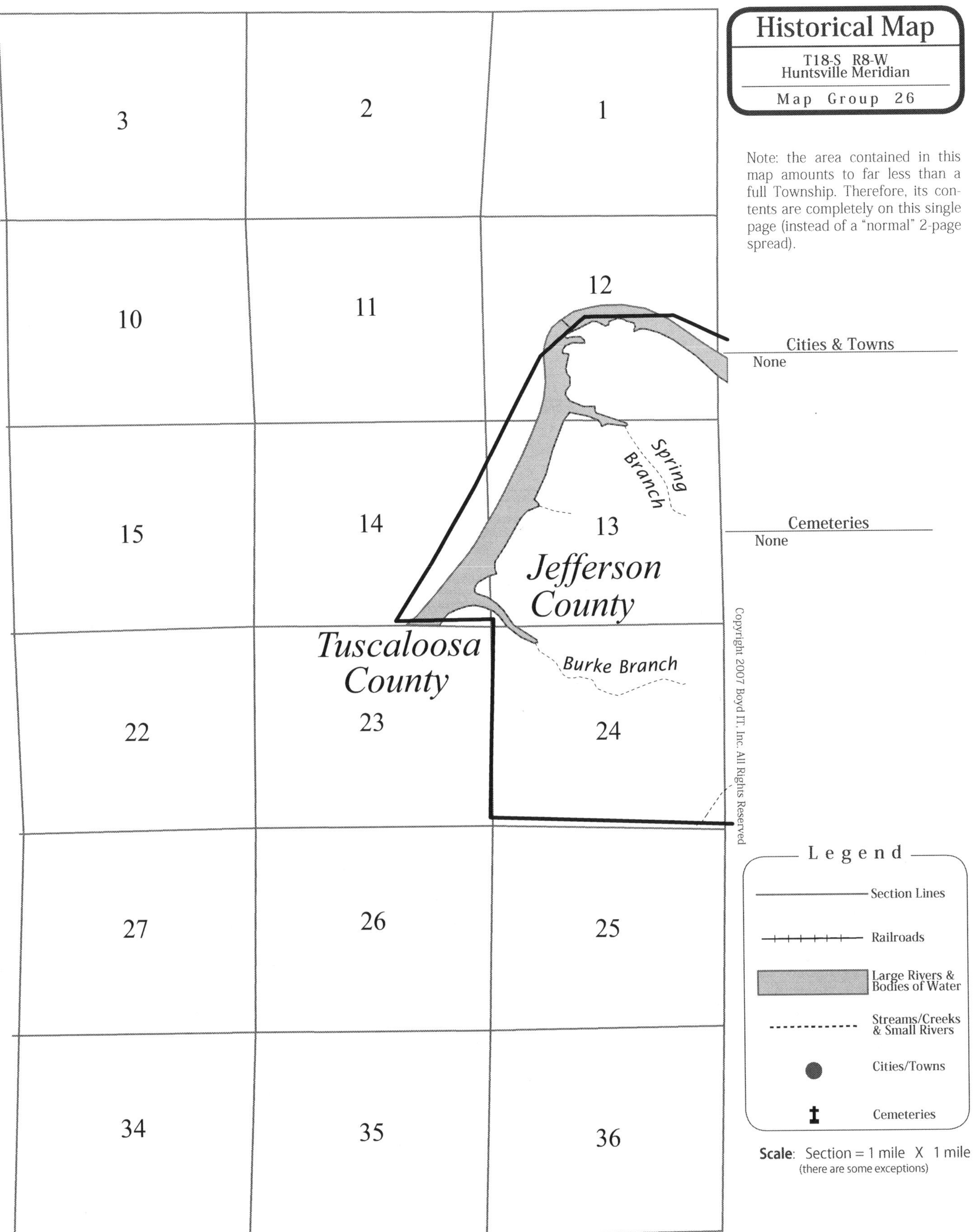

Note: the area contained in this map amounts to far less than a full Township. Therefore, its contents are completely on this single page (instead of a "normal" 2-page spread).

Scale: Section = 1 mile X 1 mile
(there are some exceptions)

Map Group 27: Index to Land Patents

Township 18-South Range 7-West (Huntsville)

After you locate an individual in this Index, take note of the Section and Section Part then proceed to the Land Patent map on the pages immediately following. You should have no difficulty locating the corresponding parcel of land.

The "For More Info" Column will lead you to more information about the underlying Patents. See the *Legend* at right, and the "How to Use this Book" chapter, for more information.

LEGEND

"For More Info . . . " column

A = Authority (Legislative Act, See Appendix "A")
B = Block or Lot (location in Section unknown)
C = Cancelled Patent
F = Fractional Section
G = Group (Multi-Patentee Patent, see Appendix "C")
V = Overlaps another Parcel
R = Re-Issued (Parcel patented more than once)

(A & G items require you to look in the Appendixes referred to above. All other Letter-designations followed by a number require you to locate line-items in this index that possess the ID number found after the letter).

ID	Individual in Patent	Sec.	Sec. Part	Date Issued	Other Counties	For More Info . . .
4675	ABSTEN, David A	29	SWNW	1859-04-01		A1
4676	ABSTON, David A	30	SENE	1858-06-01	Tuscaloosa	A1
4760	ALABAMA, State Of	21	SW	1909-01-25		A2
4761	" "	21	W½SE	1909-01-25		A2
4737	BOYD, Mary A	28	NWNE	1850-04-01		A1
4690	BURCHFIELD, Isaac J	33	S½SW	1904-07-15		A4
4691	" "	33	SWSE	1904-07-15		A4
4763	BURCHFIELD, Thomas	35	NESW	1834-10-16		A1
4764	" "	35	NWSE	1839-09-20		A1
4668	BURTON, Caroline E	13	E½NW	1893-04-29		A4 G37
4669	" "	13	W½NE	1893-04-29		A4 G37
4674	BURTON, Columbus	18	SW	1897-11-05		A4
4683	BURTON, Edmund B	35	NWNW	1834-11-04		A1
4695	BURTON, James B	20	S½SE	1899-02-25		A4
4696	" "	28	NWNW	1899-02-25		A4
4697	" "	29	NENE	1899-02-25		A4
4714	BURTON, John M	20	E½SW	1858-06-01		A1
4715	" "	29	NENW	1858-06-01		A1
4716	" "	29	NWNE	1858-06-01		A1
4753	CAIN, Robert	12	NESE	1852-01-01		A1
4713	DAVIS, John L	5	SWSW	1839-09-20	Tuscaloosa	A1
4703	DUNN, James M	4	N½NW	1904-07-27	Tuscaloosa	A4
4704	" "	4	NWNE	1904-07-27	Tuscaloosa	A4
4705	DUNN, James T	4	SWNE	1860-10-01	Tuscaloosa	A1
4734	DUNN, Marion J	5	SESW	1883-07-03	Tuscaloosa	A4
4735	" "	8	C	1883-07-03	Tuscaloosa	A4 F
4736	" "	8	NWNW	1883-07-03	Tuscaloosa	A4 R4733
4754	DUNN, Samuel	4	N½SE	1892-11-15	Tuscaloosa	A1
4767	DUNN, William A	19	NESE	1915-11-19		A4
4768	" "	19	SENE	1915-11-19		A4
4769	" "	20	W½SW	1915-11-19		A4
4782	FOX, William R	28	SESE	1861-07-01		A1
4679	FRANKLIN, David M	11	SWSE	1884-03-20		A4
4680	" "	14	E½NW	1884-03-20		A4
4681	" "	14	NWNE	1884-03-20		A4
4730	FRANKLIN, Lewis	2	S½NW	1858-06-01		A1
4773	FRANKLIN, William M	26	E½SW	1890-07-03		A4
4774	" "	26	S½SE	1890-07-03		A4
4776	FRANKLIN, William O	21	NESE	1890-07-03		A4
4777	" "	21	S½NE	1890-07-03		A4
4778	" "	21	SENW	1890-07-03		A4
4770	FREELAND, William	1	SESE	1859-04-01		A1
4724	FRIERSON, Joseph H	10	NWNW	1850-04-01		A1 F
4725	" "	9	NENE	1850-04-01		A1 F
4660	GANUS, Alvah F	20	E½NE	1919-06-25		A4
4661	" "	20	NESE	1919-06-25		A4

ID	Individual in Patent	Sec.	Sec. Part	Date Issued	Other Counties	For More Info . . .
4662	GANUS, Alvah F (Cont'd)	21	SWNW	1919-06-25		A4
4663	GILBERT, Andrew	18	W½NW	1890-01-08		A4
4666	GILBERT, Bookter	26	SWSW	1834-10-16		A1
4667	" "	35	SENW	1834-10-16		A1
4692	GILBERT, Jackson M	27	E½NE	1885-03-30		A4
4718	GILBERT, John T	35	SESW	1839-09-20		A1
4719	" "	7	D	1858-06-01	Tuscaloosa	A1 F
4775	GILBERT, William N	7	NENW	1891-11-23	Tuscaloosa	A4
4779	GILBERT, William Q	22	W½SE	1885-03-30		A4
4780	" "	27	NENW	1885-03-30		A4
4781	" "	27	NWNE	1885-03-30		A4
4672	GWIN, Chesley B	21	N½NE	1884-12-05		A4
4673	" "	21	N½NW	1884-12-05		A4
4772	HARDYMAN, William	12	S½SE	1884-03-20		A4
4665	HARRIS, Benjamin	36	SWNW	1884-03-20		A4
4749	HARRIS, Nancy	33	E½NE	1861-07-01		A1
4765	HARRIS, Thomas C	1	W½NW	1891-06-29		A4
4771	HARRIS, William H	36	SE	1913-10-22		A4 C
4712	HEARD, John K	10		1839-09-20		A1 F
4738	HENDON, Matilda C	30	SESE	1861-07-01	Tuscaloosa	A1
4698	HOSMER, James H N	33	NW	1914-01-17		A4
4709	HOWTON, John B	8	S½SW	1891-06-29	Tuscaloosa	A1 F
4710	" "	8	SE	1891-06-29	Tuscaloosa	A1 F
4668	HOWTON, Joseph A	13	E½NW	1893-04-29		A4 G37
4669	" "	13	W½NE	1893-04-29		A4 G37
4731	HOWTON, Lewis	15	N½SE	1884-12-05		A4
4732	" "	15	S½NE	1884-12-05		A4
4762	HOWTON, Thomas B	23	NW	1882-06-30		A1
4671	HUMBER, Charles	2	NWNW	1839-09-20		A1 G135
4670	HUMBER, Charles C	1	NWSW	1839-09-20		A1
4711	HUMBER, John	1	SENW	1839-09-20		A1
4717	HUMBER, John P	3	NW	1858-06-01	Tuscaloosa	A1 F
4726	HUMBER, Joseph	11	NENE	1884-03-20		A4
4727	" "	2	E½SE	1884-03-20		A4
4728	" "	2	SENE	1884-03-20		A4
4685	JACKSON, Henry	1	NESW	1884-12-05		A4
4686	" "	1	SWNE	1884-12-05		A4
4687	" "	1	W½SE	1884-12-05		A4
4684	JOHNSTON, Eveline	3	NE	1890-08-29	Tuscaloosa	A4
4755	JONES, Samuel H	4	SENE	1852-01-01	Tuscaloosa	A1
4659	JORDAN, Abner W	1	SESW	1858-06-01		A1
4739	JORDAN, Mortimer	3		1839-03-15	Tuscaloosa	A1 F
4740	" "	4	S½SE	1839-03-15	Tuscaloosa	A1
4741	" "	4	SW	1839-03-15	Tuscaloosa	A1 F R4742
4743	" "	5	SE	1839-03-15	Tuscaloosa	A1 F
4744	" "	8		1839-03-15	Tuscaloosa	A1 F
4745	" "	9		1839-03-15		A1 F
4742	" "	4	SW	1839-09-20	Tuscaloosa	A1 R4741
4746	" "	9	SW	1839-09-20		A1 F
4747	" "	9	W½NW	1840-11-10		A1
4706	LAFOY, Jessie M	33	E½SE	1892-04-20		A4
4707	" "	33	NESW	1892-04-20		A4
4708	" "	33	NWSE	1892-04-20		A4
4748	PARSONS, Nancy A	15	NW	1891-11-23		A4
4751	PATTEN, Reuben B	19	SESE	1890-07-03		A4
4752	" "	30	NENE	1890-07-03	Tuscaloosa	A4
4664	PATTON, Andrew	27	NWNW	1839-09-20		A1 G194
4699	PATTON, James H	17	N½	1849-05-01	Tuscaloosa	A1 F
4702	" "	7	S½	1850-09-02	Tuscaloosa	A1 F
4700	" "	30	NWSW	1858-06-01	Tuscaloosa	A1
4701	" "	30	W½NW	1858-06-01	Tuscaloosa	A1
4664	REID, Levi	27	NWNW	1839-09-20		A1 G194
4689	RICHARDSON, Hiram	17		1837-11-07	Tuscaloosa	A1 F
4729	RIED, Levi	28	NENW	1852-01-01		A1
4733	ROBINS, Lorenzo D	8	NWNW	1858-06-01	Tuscaloosa	A1 R4736
4677	STAGGS, David F	10	E½NW	1899-08-16		A4
4678	" "	10	W½NE	1899-08-16		A4
4693	TACKET, Jacob	28	SWSE	1861-07-01		A1
4694	" "	33	NWNE	1861-07-01		A1
4688	THOMPSON, Henry	21	SESE	1852-01-01		A1
4756	THOMPSON, Samuel	2	E½SW	1839-09-20		A1
4757	" "	2	W½SE	1839-09-20		A1
4758	" "	3	SW	1839-09-20	Tuscaloosa	A1 C F

ID	Individual in Patent	Sec.	Sec. Part	Date Issued	Other Counties	For More Info . . .
4759	THOMPSON, Samuel (Cont'd)	3	W½SE	1917-07-26	Tuscaloosa	A1
4766	THOMPSON, Thomas S	1	NENW	1839-09-20		A1
4671	WARE, Nimrod W	2	NWNW	1839-09-20		A1 G135
4750	WILKEY, Perry A	24	SE	1884-03-20		A4
4671	WILLIAMS, Benjamin	2	NWNW	1839-09-20		A1 G135
4784	WINCHESTER, Wiloby	5	N½NW	1858-06-01	Tuscaloosa	A1
4783	" "	4	S½NW	1861-01-01	Tuscaloosa	A1
4785	" "	5	SENE	1861-01-01	Tuscaloosa	A1
4720	WOODDIEL, John	28	SENW	1839-09-20		A1
4682	WRIGHT, David	22	SWSW	1859-12-10		A1
4721	WRIGHT, John	36	NESW	1860-10-01		A1
4722	" "	36	SENW	1860-10-01		A1
4723	" "	36	W½NE	1860-10-01		A1

Patent Map

T18-S R7-W
Huntsville Meridian

Map Group 27

Township Statistics

Parcels Mapped	:	127
Number of Patents	:	90
Number of Individuals	:	76
Patentees Identified	:	72
Number of Surnames	:	44
Multi-Patentee Parcels	:	4
Oldest Patent Date	:	10/16/1834
Most Recent Patent	:	6/25/1919
Block/Lot Parcels	:	2
Parcels Re - Issued	:	2
Parcels that Overlap	:	0
Cities and Towns	:	0
Cemeteries	:	1

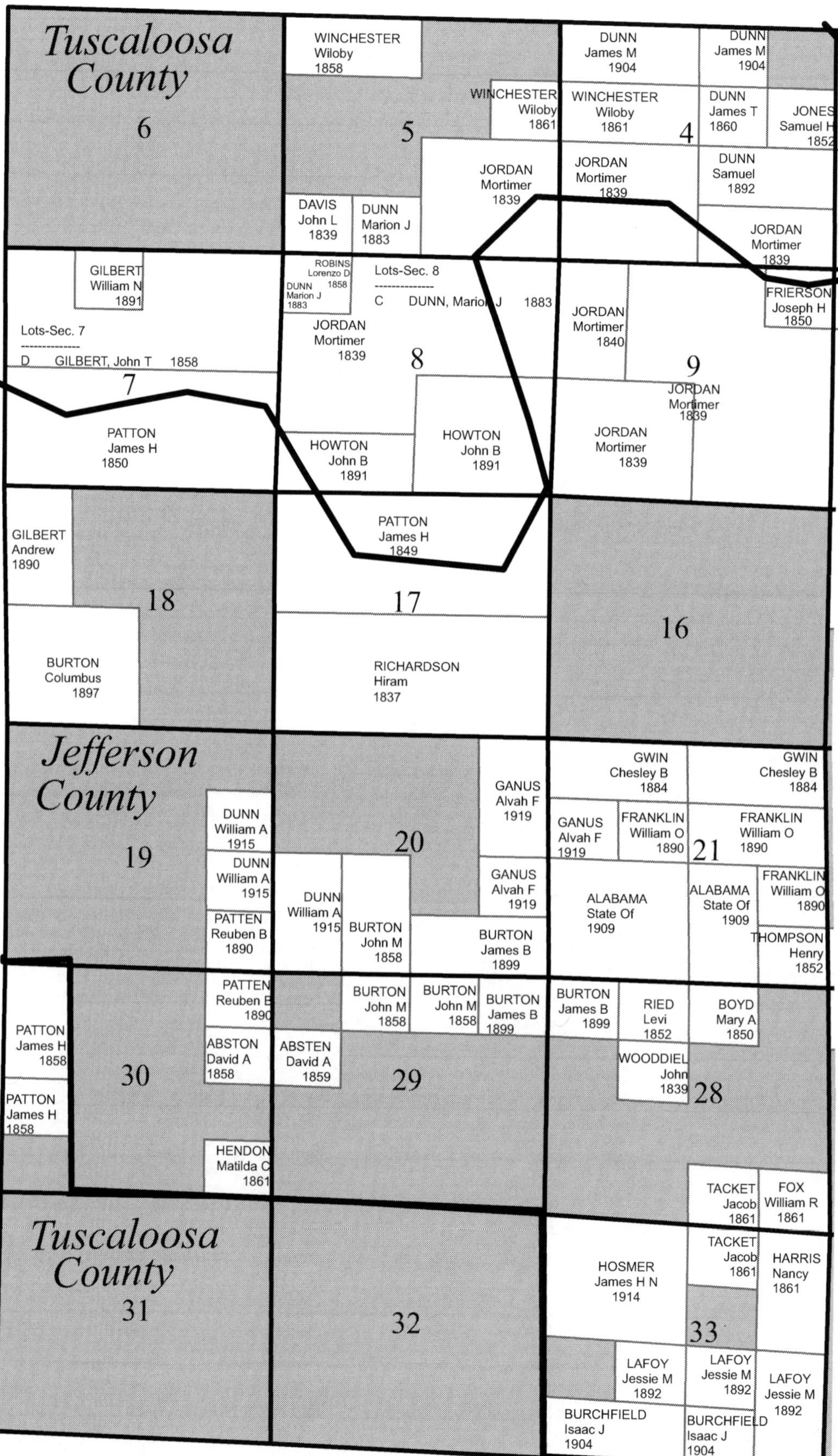

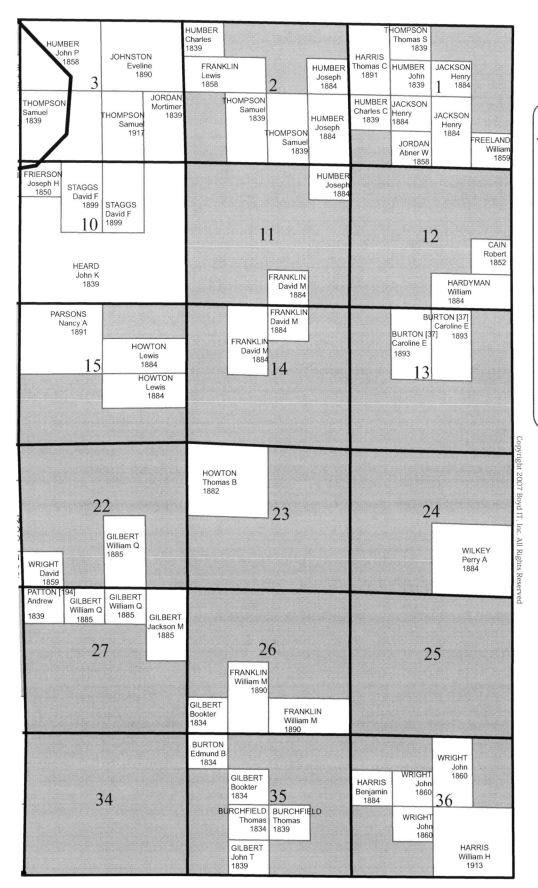

3
HUMBER John P 1858
JOHNSTON Eveline 1890
THOMPSON Samuel 1839
THOMPSON Samuel 1917
JORDAN Mortimer 1839

2
HUMBER Charles 1839
FRANKLIN Lewis 1858
HUMBER Joseph 1884
THOMPSON Samuel 1839
THOMPSON Samuel 1839
HUMBER Joseph 1884

1
THOMPSON Thomas S 1839
HARRIS Thomas C 1891
HUMBER John 1839
JACKSON Henry 1884
HUMBER Charles C 1839
JACKSON Henry 1884
JACKSON Henry 1884
JORDAN Abner W 1858
FREELAND William 1859

10
FRIERSON Joseph H 1850
STAGGS David F 1899
STAGGS David F 1899
HEARD John K 1839

11
HUMBER Joseph 1884
FRANKLIN David M 1884

12
CAIN Robert 1852
HARDYMAN William 1884

15
PARSONS Nancy A 1891
HOWTON Lewis 1884
HOWTON Lewis 1884

14
FRANKLIN David M 1884
FRANKLIN David M 1884

13
BURTON [37] Caroline E 1893
BURTON [37] Caroline E 1893

22
GILBERT William Q 1885
WRIGHT David 1859

23
HOWTON Thomas B 1882

24
WILKEY Perry A 1884

27
PATTON [194] Andrew 1839
GILBERT William Q 1885
GILBERT William Q 1885
GILBERT Jackson M 1885

26
FRANKLIN William M 1890
GILBERT Bookter 1834
FRANKLIN William M 1890

25

34

35
BURTON Edmund B 1834
GILBERT Bookter 1834
BURCHFIELD Thomas 1834
BURCHFIELD Thomas 1839
GILBERT John T 1839

36
WRIGHT John 1860
HARRIS Benjamin 1884
WRIGHT John 1860
WRIGHT John 1860
HARRIS William H 1913

Helpful Hints

1. This Map's INDEX can be found on the preceding pages.
2. Refer to Map "C" to see where this Township lies within Jefferson County, Alabama.
3. Numbers within square brackets [ ] denote a multi-patentee land parcel (multi-owner). Refer to Appendix "C" for a full list of members in this group.
4. Areas that look to be crowded with Patentees usually indicate multiple sales of the same parcel (Re-issues) or Overlapping parcels. See this Township's Index for an explanation of these and other circumstances that might explain "odd" groupings of Patentees on this map.

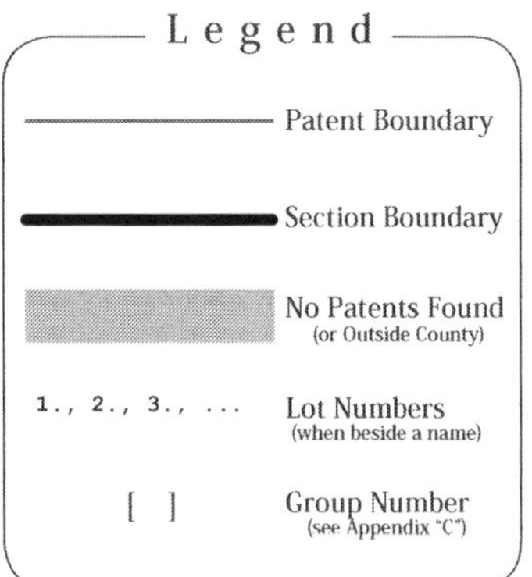

Scale: Section = 1 mile X 1 mile (generally, with some exceptions)

Road Map

T18-S R7-W
Huntsville Meridian

Map Group 27

Cities & Towns
None

Cemeteries
Providence Cemetery

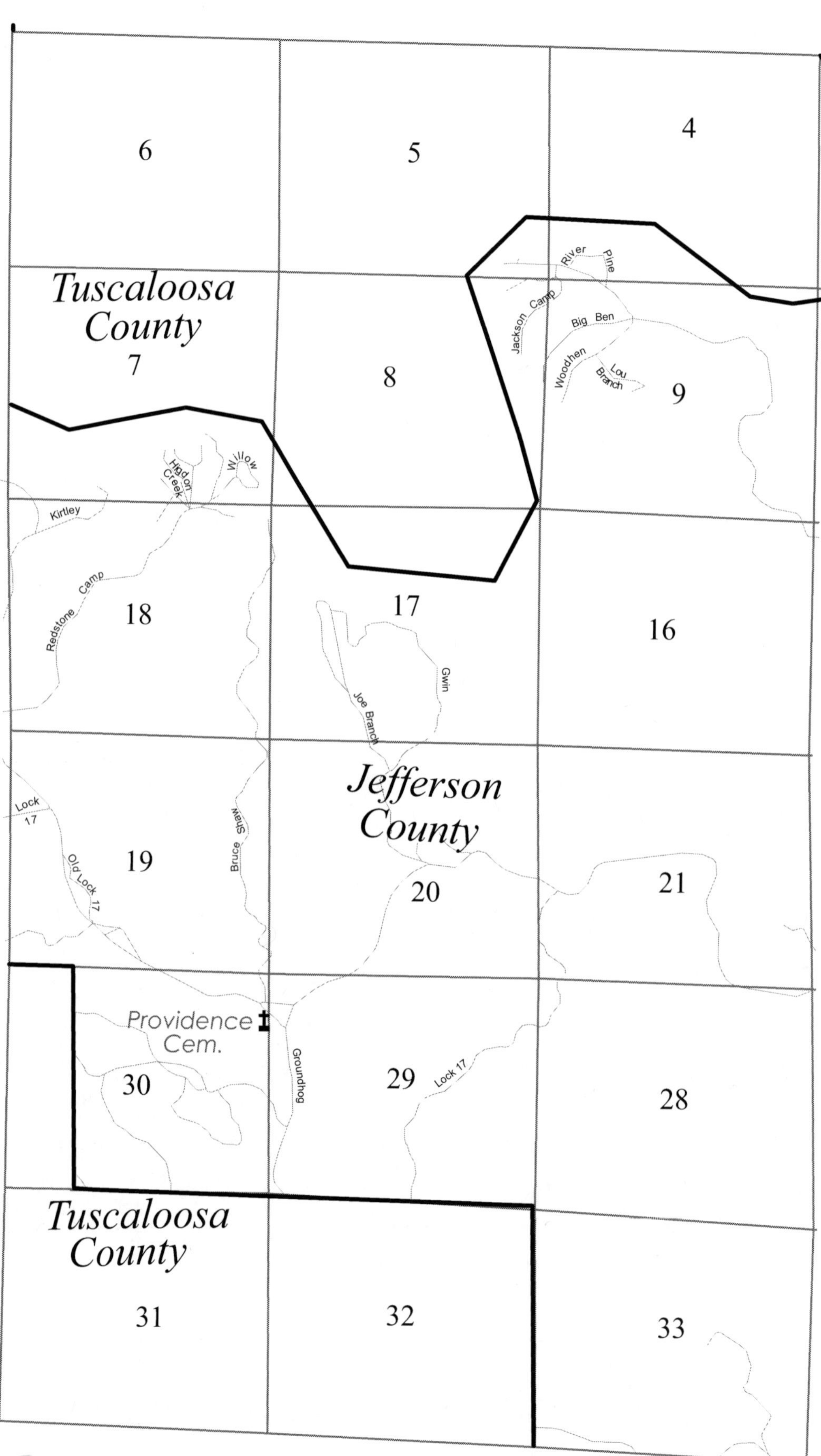

Jay Payne
Bells
Camp
Julian
Greenwood
Johnson Camp
Henderson Camp
Cedar Valley
3
2
1
Perry Loop
Camp Oliver
Little Shoals
Smith Camp
Gosset Camp
Stonehedge
Clear Valley
10
11
12
Greer
15
14
13
Nancy Ann Bend
22
23
24
Paul Allman
Lock 17
27
26
25
34
Betty Hill
35
36

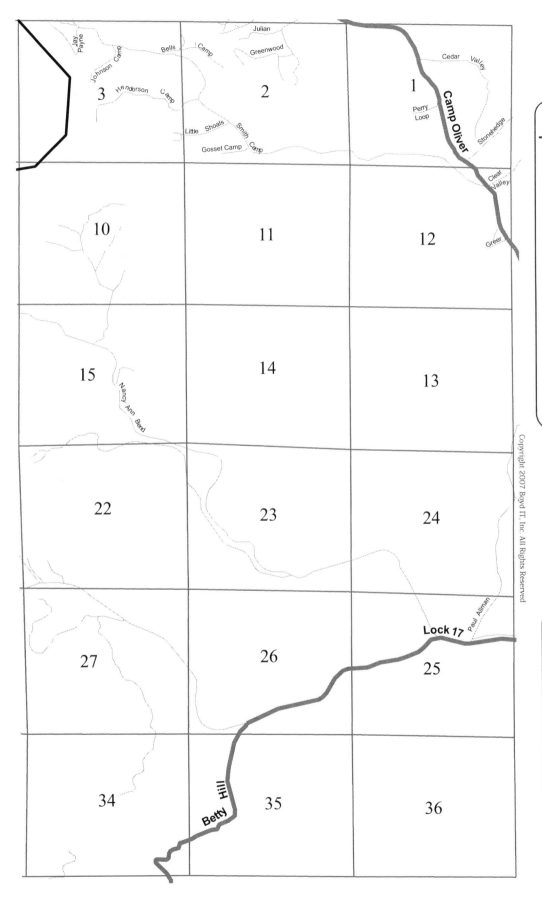

Helpful Hints

1. This road map has a number of uses, but primarily it is to help you: a) find the present location of land owned by your ancestors (at least the general area), b) find cemeteries and city-centers, and c) estimate the route/roads used by Census-takers & tax-assessors.
2. If you plan to travel to Jefferson County to locate cemeteries or land parcels, please pick up a modern travel map for the area before you do. Mapping old land parcels on modern maps is not as exact a science as you might think. Just the slightest variations in public land survey coordinates, estimates of parcel boundaries, or road-map deviations can greatly alter a map's representation of how a road either does or doesn't cross a particular parcel of land.

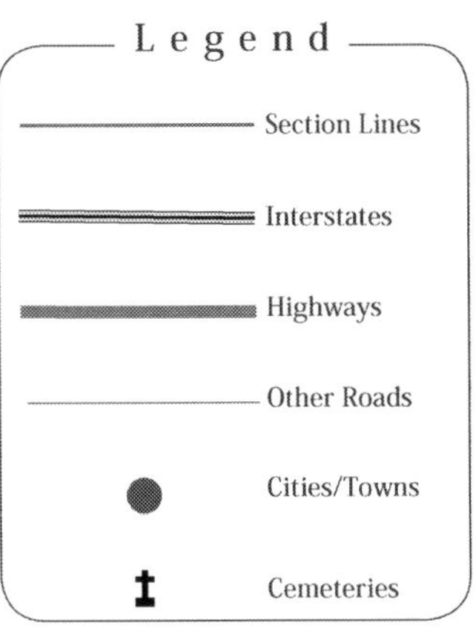

Scale: Section = 1 mile X 1 mile
(generally, with some exceptions)

Cities & Towns
None

Cemeteries
Providence Cemetery

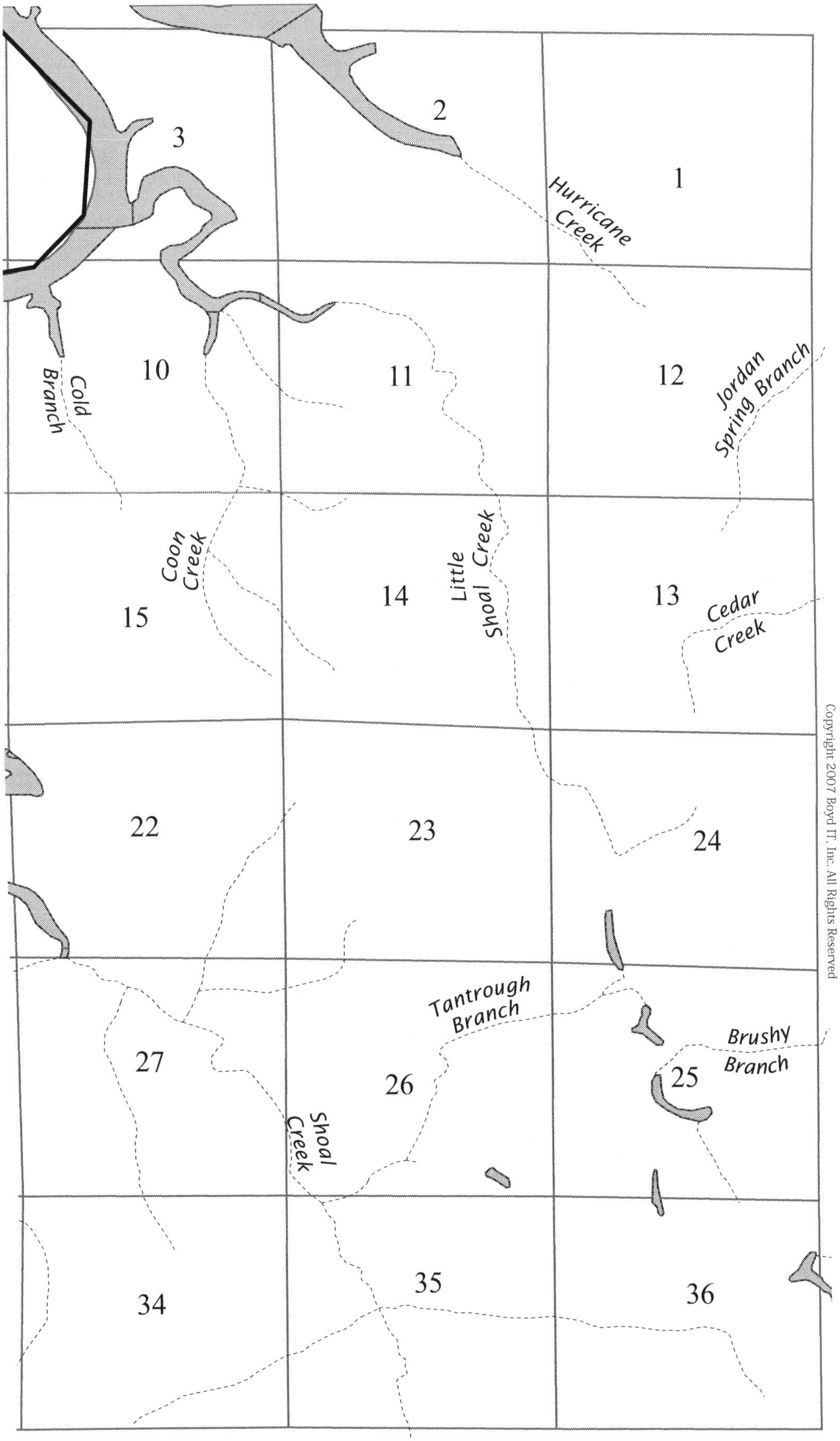

3
2
1
Hurricane Creek
10
11
12
Cold Branch
Jordan Spring Branch
Coon Creek
Little Shoal Creek
15
14
13
Cedar Creek
22
23
24
Tantrough Branch
Brushy Branch
27
26
25
Shoal Creek
34
35
36

Helpful Hints

1. This Map takes a different look at the same Congressional Township displayed in the preceding two maps. It presents features that can help you better envision the historical development of the area: a) Water-bodies (lakes & ponds), b) Water-courses (rivers, streams, etc.), c) Railroads, d) City/town center-points (where they were oftentimes located when first settled), and e) Cemeteries.
2. Using this "Historical" map in tandem with this Township's Patent Map and Road Map, may lead you to some interesting discoveries. You will often find roads, towns, cemeteries, and waterways are named after nearby landowners: sometimes those names will be the ones you are researching. See how many of these research gems you can find here in Jefferson County.

Legend
Section Lines
Railroads
Large Rivers & Bodies of Water
Streams/Creeks & Small Rivers
Cities/Towns
Cemeteries

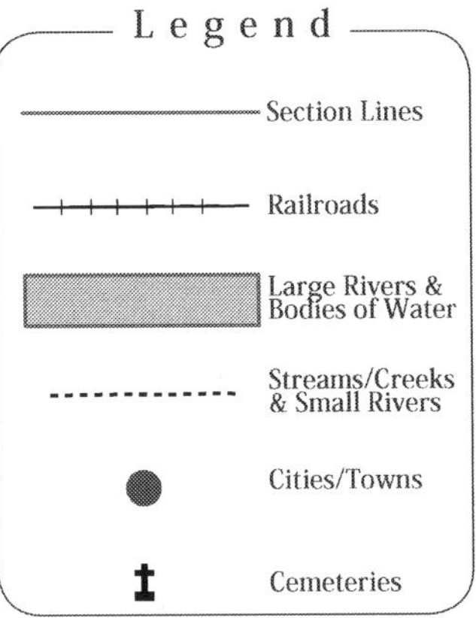

Scale: Section = 1 mile X 1 mile
(there are some exceptions)

Map Group 28: Index to Land Patents

Township 18-South Range 6-West (Huntsville)

After you locate an individual in this Index, take note of the Section and Section Part then proceed to the Land Patent map on the pages immediately following. You should have no difficulty locating the corresponding parcel of land.

The "For More Info" Column will lead you to more information about the underlying Patents. See the *Legend* at right, and the "How to Use this Book" chapter, for more information.

LEGEND

"For More Info . . . " column

- **A** = Authority (Legislative Act, See Appendix "A")
- **B** = Block or Lot (location in Section unknown)
- **C** = Cancelled Patent
- **F** = Fractional Section
- **G** = Group (Multi-Patentee Patent, see Appendix "C")
- **V** = Overlaps another Parcel
- **R** = Re-Issued (Parcel patented more than once)

(A & G items require you to look in the Appendixes referred to above. All other Letter-designations followed by a number require you to locate line-items in this index that possess the ID number found after the letter).

ID	Individual in Patent	Sec.	Sec. Part	Date Issued	Other Counties	For More Info . . .
4806	ALLMAN, Coleman F	18	S½NW	1884-12-05		A4
4807	" "	18	W½SW	1884-12-05		A4
4877	BATSON, John H	34	NENE	1885-12-10		A4
5000	BATSON, William H	20	E½SW	1888-02-04		A4
5001	" "	20	SENW	1888-02-04		A4
5002	" "	20	SWSE	1888-02-04		A4
4803	BELL, Amon	35	SESE	1839-09-20		A1
4852	BROWN, James	25	E½NW	1823-06-02		A1
4851	" "	24	E½SW	1824-05-20		A1
4889	BROWN, Joseph	24	E½NW	1823-07-09		A1 G31
4890	" "	24	W½SE	1823-07-09		A1 G31
4888	" "	24	E½NE	1824-10-20		A1
4894	BROWN, Joseph M	24	NESE	1839-09-20		A1
4889	BROWN, Thomas	24	E½NW	1823-07-09		A1 G31
4890	" "	24	W½SE	1823-07-09		A1 G31
4832	BURCHFIELD, Gilbert B	31	NWNW	1839-09-20		A1
4853	BURCHFIELD, James	26	NWSW	1839-09-20		A1
4925	BURCHFIELD, Nathaniel	33	SWSE	1839-09-20		A1
4854	CAIN, James	18	NWNW	1850-09-02		A1 G41
4829	CARGILE, George	22	SENE	1858-06-01		A1
4830	" "	22	SWNE	1858-06-01		A1
4831	" "	22	W½SE	1858-06-01		A1
4826	" "	22	NENE	1861-07-01		A1
4827	" "	22	NESE	1861-07-01		A1
4828	" "	22	NESW	1861-07-01		A1
4881	CARRINGTON, John R	12	SESE	1858-06-01		A1
4891	CARRINGTON, Joseph	12	NWSE	1858-06-01		A1
4892	" "	12	S½NE	1858-06-01		A1
4872	CHILDRESS, John C	10	NENE	1839-09-20		A1
4994	COKER, William B	34	NWNW	1835-10-01		A1
4819	CROOKS, Francis M	36	N½SE	1885-07-27		A1
4820	" "	36	NESW	1885-07-27		A1
4821	" "	36	SWSE	1885-07-27		A1
4998	CROOKS, William	34	SESW	1839-09-20		A1
4923	FIELDS, Moses	25	NENE	1849-08-01		A1
4999	FORBIS, William G	8	SESW	1834-10-21		A1
4905	FORRESTER, Lewis	26	E½SW	1860-10-01		A1
4906	" "	26	N½NE	1860-10-01		A1
4907	" "	26	NWSE	1860-10-01		A1
4908	" "	26	SWSW	1860-10-01		A1
4794	FRANKLIN, Alfred J	21	SWSW	1839-09-20		A1
4816	FRANKLIN, Eleana G	17	NWSE	1849-08-01		A1
4815	" "	17	NESW	1858-06-01		A1
4817	" "	17	SESW	1858-06-01		A1
4818	FRANKLIN, Ephraim P	20	NWSW	1840-11-10		A1
4834	FRANKLIN, Greenberry	28	SWSW	1839-09-20		A1

ID	Individual in Patent	Sec.	Sec. Part	Date Issued	Other Counties	For More Info . . .
4833	FRANKLIN, Greenberry F	29	NE	1837-03-20		A1 G86
4873	FRANKLIN, John	30	SWSE	1852-01-01		A1
4909	FRANKLIN, Lewis	28	W½NW	1839-09-20		A1
4833	FRANKLIN, Owen	29	NE	1837-03-20		A1 G86
4934	" "	29	NWSE	1837-03-30		A1
4935	" "	29	SENW	1839-09-20		A1
4933	FRANKLIN, Owen A	13	NESE	1860-07-02		A1
4979	FRANKLIN, Thomas	28	NWSW	1834-11-04		A1 C R4980
4980	" "	28	NWSW	1923-04-28		A1 R4979
4985	FRANKLIN, Thomas G	33	W½NE	1834-10-01		A1
4984	" "	28	SWSE	1839-09-20		A1
4981	" "	21	SESW	1883-08-13		A1
4983	" "	28	E½NW	1883-08-13		A1
4982	" "	22	W½SW	1889-11-21		A4
4989	FRANKLIN, Thomas J	27	NWNW	1852-01-01		A1
4990	" "	28	SWNE	1854-07-15		A1
4991	" "	4	E½SE	1861-07-01		A1
4992	" "	4	SWSE	1861-07-01		A1
4845	FRAZIER, Isaiah D	14	NESW	1861-07-01		A1
4846	" "	14	NWSE	1861-07-01		A1
4835	FREELAND, Hampton	17	NW	1837-03-20		A1 G87
4893	FREELAND, Joseph	8	SWSW	1839-09-20		A1
4887	FREELAND, Joseph B	6	NWSE	1848-07-01		A1
4924	FREELAND, Nancy S	7	SWNW	1858-06-01		A1
4950	FREELAND, Samuel	8	SWSE	1839-09-20		A1
4995	GILLMORE, William C	21	S½NE	1859-12-10		A1
4811	GILMORE, Edmond M	5	NESW	1858-06-01		A1
4812	" "	8	NWNE	1858-06-01		A1
4951	GILMORE, Samuel	5	SE	1837-03-20		A1 G97
5006	GLAZE, William M	2	SW	1890-10-11		A4
4798	GOLDEN, Allen	4	NWSW	1839-09-20		A1
4796	" "	10	NWSW	1858-06-01		A1
4799	" "	4	SWSW	1858-06-01		A1 R4800
4801	" "	9	NESE	1858-06-01		A1
4800	" "	4	SWSW	1860-10-01		A1 R4799
4795	" "	10	NESW	1861-07-01		A1
4797	" "	10	S½NW	1861-07-01		A1
4855	GOLDING, James E	9	E½NW	1858-06-01		A1
4858	GOODWIN, James M	36	NENW	1861-07-01		A1
4896	GOODWIN, Joshua	36	SWSW	1853-08-01		A1
4897	GOODWIN, Joshua R	25	SWNE	1852-01-01		A1
4898	" "	26	SWSE	1858-06-01		A1
4899	" "	35	NENW	1858-06-01		A1
4900	" "	35	NWNE	1858-06-01		A1
4921	GOODWIN, Martin	36	NWNW	1860-10-01		A1
4930	GOODWIN, Oliver P	36	NWSW	1860-10-01		A1
4931	" "	36	SWNW	1860-10-01		A1
4874	GWIN, John	14	E½NE	1885-03-16		A4
4875	" "	14	NESE	1885-03-16		A4
4876	" "	14	NWNE	1885-03-16		A4 R4978
4922	HAMMOND, Mary	32	SW	1885-07-27		A1
4835	HARDIMAN, Lewis	17	NW	1837-03-20		A1 G87
5004	HARDYMAN, William	7	W½SW	1884-03-20		A4
4859	HIGGINS, James M	34	SESE	1853-08-01		A1
5007	HIGGINS, William T	35	N½SW	1858-06-01		A1
5008	" "	35	SENW	1858-06-01		A1
5009	" "	35	SWNE	1858-06-01		A1
4986	HORNE, Thomas	29	E½SW	1824-05-27		A1
4808	HOWTON, Curtis	28	E½SW	1833-08-12		A1
4809	" "	33	NENW	1839-09-20		A1
4810	" "	33	W½NW	1858-06-01		A1
4883	HOWTON, John W	20	E½SE	1882-10-30		A1
4884	" "	20	S½NE	1882-10-30		A1
4886	HOWTON, Jonathan	33	SESW	1850-09-02		A1
4914	HOWTON, Lewis	33	SENW	1839-09-20		A1
4910	" "	29	SWSE	1858-06-01		A1
4911	" "	32	NENW	1858-06-01		A1
4912	" "	32	NWSE	1858-06-01		A1
4913	" "	32	W½NE	1858-06-01		A1
4916	HOWTON, Lucy E	32	E½NE	1884-03-20		A4
4917	" "	32	NESE	1884-03-20		A4
4943	HOWTON, Robert	32	S½SE	1884-03-20		A4
4996	HOWTON, William C	32	NWNW	1891-11-23		A4

ID	Individual in Patent	Sec.	Sec. Part	Date Issued	Other Counties	For More Info . . .
4997	HOWTON, William C (Cont'd)	32	S½NW	1891-11-23		A4
4863	HUEY, Jesse G	22	SESW	1858-06-01		A1
4864	" "	27	NENW	1858-06-01		A1
4865	" "	28	E½NE	1858-06-01		A1
4866	" "	28	NWNE	1858-06-01		A1
4867	" "	28	NWSE	1858-06-01		A1
4952	HUEY, Samuel	23	SE	1840-04-10		A1 G134 R4956
4956	HUEY, Samuel T	23	SE	1837-03-20		A1 G133 R4952
4955	" "	24	W½SW	1861-07-01		A1
4956	HUEY, Thomas	23	SE	1837-03-20		A1 G133 R4952
4987	" "	14	SWSE	1839-09-20		A1
4988	" "	24	SWNE	1839-09-20		A1
4952	" "	23	SE	1840-04-10		A1 G134 R4956
5010	HUMBER, Willis B	4	NENE	1860-12-01		A1
5011	" "	4	NW	1860-12-01		A1
5012	" "	4	W½NE	1860-12-01		A1
4836	HUTCHINS, Henry C	30	NESW	1890-01-08		A4
4837	" "	30	NWSE	1890-01-08		A4
4838	" "	30	SWNE	1890-01-08		A4
4961	JOHNSON, Starling T	10	S½SE	1858-06-01		A1 C R4964
4962	" "	10	S½SW	1858-06-01		A1 C R4965
4856	LAIRD, James K	22	SESE	1882-06-30		A1
4804	LEE, Amos	23	E½NE	1823-06-02		A1
4805	MCWILLIAMS, Andrew L	24	SESE	1899-12-07		A1
4857	MEIGS, James L	26	NWNW	1882-06-30		A1
4967	MILLER, Stephen	23	SESW	1839-09-20		A1
4968	" "	26	E½NW	1839-09-20		A1
4969	" "	26	SWNW	1839-09-20		A1
4970	" "	27	E½NE	1839-09-20		A1
4971	" "	27	E½SE	1839-09-20		A1
4901	PALMORE, Levi	34	E½NW	1860-10-01		A1
4902	" "	34	NESW	1860-10-01		A1
4903	" "	34	SWNW	1860-10-01		A1
4904	" "	34	W½NE	1860-10-01		A1
4870	PARSONS, John B	34	SENE	1860-10-01		A1
4871	" "	34	W½SE	1860-10-01		A1
4915	PARSONS, Littleton	25	NWSW	1839-09-20		A1
4932	PARSONS, Oliver P	36	NENE	1860-12-01		A1
4953	PARSONS, Samuel	34	NESE	1858-06-01		A1
4954	" "	35	SWSW	1858-06-01		A1
4948	PARSONS, Samuel F	30	E½SE	1883-07-03		A4
4972	PARSONS, Theophilus	25	NESW	1837-03-30		A1
4976	" "	26	SENE	1839-09-20		A1
4973	" "	25	NWSE	1852-01-01		A1
4974	" "	25	SWSW	1858-06-01		A1
4975	" "	26	E½SE	1858-06-01		A1
4993	PARSONS, Wiley F	36	S½NE	1905-11-08		A4
4822	PAYNE, Francis M	10	N½NW	1889-12-28		A1
4847	REEVES, Jackson R	12	NW	1891-06-29		A4
4977	REEVES, Thomas D	14	E½NW	1883-08-13		A4
4978	" "	14	NWNE	1883-08-13		A4 R4876
4802	RILEY, Allen W	34	SWSW	1885-03-30		A4 G201
4802	RILEY, Amanda M	34	SWSW	1885-03-30		A4 G201
4860	RILEY, James	14	SESW	1885-03-16		A4
4861	" "	14	SWNW	1885-03-16		A4
4862	" "	14	W½SW	1885-03-16		A4
4843	ROBERTS, Isaac	17	SESE	1848-07-01		A1
4844	" "	20	N½NE	1861-01-01		A1
4919	ROBERTS, Marshall B	6	SESW	1890-07-03		A4
4920	" "	6	W½SW	1890-07-03		A4
4918	" "	6	NESW	1891-06-30		A4
4963	ROBERTS, Starling T	10	N½SE	1858-06-01		A1
4964	" "	10	S½SE	1905-11-27		A1 R4961
4965	" "	10	S½SW	1905-11-27		A1 R4962
4966	ROBERTS, Startling F	17	SWSE	1849-05-01		A1
4813	SMITH, Edmund C	10	SENE	1849-08-01		A1
4814	" "	3	N½SE	1859-12-10		A1
4839	SMITH, Henry G	6	N½NE	1858-06-01		A1
4850	SMITH, Jacob	3	SWSW	1859-04-01		A1
4848	" "	3	S½NW	1859-12-10		A1
4849	" "	3	SWNE	1859-12-10		A1
4927	SMITH, Oliver M	3	NESW	1839-09-20		A1
4926	" "	11	SESW	1849-05-01		A1

ID	Individual in Patent	Sec.	Sec. Part	Date Issued	Other Counties	For More Info . . .
4928	SMITH, Oliver M (Cont'd)	8	E½NW	1860-10-01		A1
4929	" "	8	NESW	1860-10-01		A1
4951	SMITH, William L	5	SE	1837-03-20		A1 G97
5005	" "	8	NENE	1839-09-20		A1
4868	SNOW, Joel	25	NWNE	1839-09-20		A1
4869	" "	26	SWNE	1839-09-20		A1
4878	SNOW, John H	17	NWNE	1839-09-20		A1
4936	SPEARS, Penelton E	18	E½SW	1860-10-01		A1
4937	" "	18	W½SE	1860-10-01		A1
4842	STRINGFELLOW, Hiram A	28	E½SE	1890-01-08		A4
4825	TAYLOR, Frederick	2	SWSE	1858-06-01		A1
4823	" "	2	E½SE	1861-01-01		A1
4824	" "	2	NWSE	1861-01-01		A1
4792	VAN HAUSE, ALFRED E	7	NENW	1850-04-01		A1 R4793
4793	VAN HOOSE, ALFRED E	7	NENW	1850-04-01		A1 R4792
4854	VANHOUSE, Jesse	18	NWNW	1850-09-02		A1 G41
4840	VINES, Hezekiah	12	N½NE	1883-08-13		A4
4841	" "	12	NESE	1883-08-13		A4
4882	VINES, John T	2	NW	1884-03-20		A1
4786	WALDROP, Albert G	11	NWSW	1835-10-01		A1
4787	" "	11	SWSE	1839-09-20		A1
4791	" "	23	NENW	1858-06-01		A1
4788	" "	11	SWSW	1859-04-01		A1
4789	" "	12	SWSE	1859-04-01		A1
4790	" "	14	NWNW	1859-04-01		A1
4879	WALDROP, John P	11	SWNE	1852-01-01		A1
4895	WALDROP, Joseph	10	W½NE	1823-06-02		A1
4942	WALDROP, Richard	13	NE	1837-03-20		A1 G227
4938	WALDROP, Richard S	13	NENW	1858-06-01		A1
4939	" "	13	W½SE	1858-06-01		A1
4940	" "	14	SESE	1858-06-01		A1
4941	" "	24	NWNE	1858-06-01		A1
4945	WALDROP, Robert	11	W½NW	1823-06-02		A1
4946	" "	19	E½SE	1823-06-02		A1
4942	" "	13	NE	1837-03-20		A1 G227
4944	" "	11	SENW	1839-09-20		A1
4947	" "	23	NWNE	1840-11-10		A1
4957	WILKEY, Samuel	29	NWNW	1839-09-20		A1
4958	" "	30	NENW	1852-01-01		A1
4959	" "	30	NWNE	1883-07-03		A4
4960	" "	30	NWNW	1883-07-03		A4
4949	WILKEY, Samuel F	30	S½NW	1890-07-03		A4
4885	WOOD, John	24	W½NW	1823-06-02		A1
4880	WOODSON, John P	33	NWSE	1839-09-20		A1
5003	WRIGHT, William H	22	NW	1885-05-20		A4

Patent Map

T18-S R6-W
Huntsville Meridian

Map Group 28

Township Statistics

Parcels Mapped	:	227
Number of Patents	:	166
Number of Individuals	:	121
Patentees Identified	:	119
Number of Surnames	:	59
Multi-Patentee Parcels	:	10
Oldest Patent Date	:	6/2/1823
Most Recent Patent	:	4/28/1923
Block/Lot Parcels	:	0
Parcels Re - Issued	:	7
Parcels that Overlap	:	0
Cities and Towns	:	0
Cemeteries	:	1

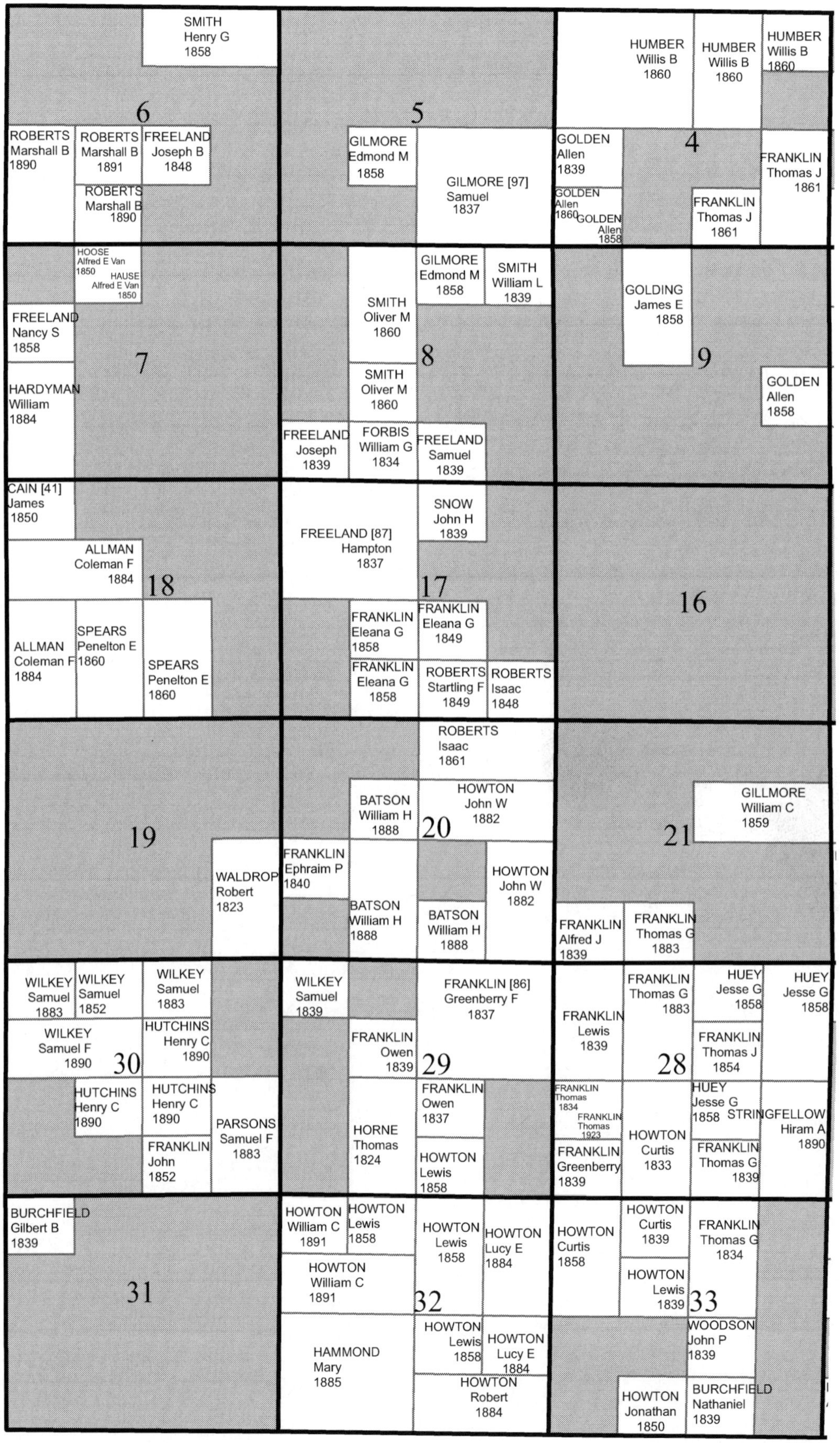

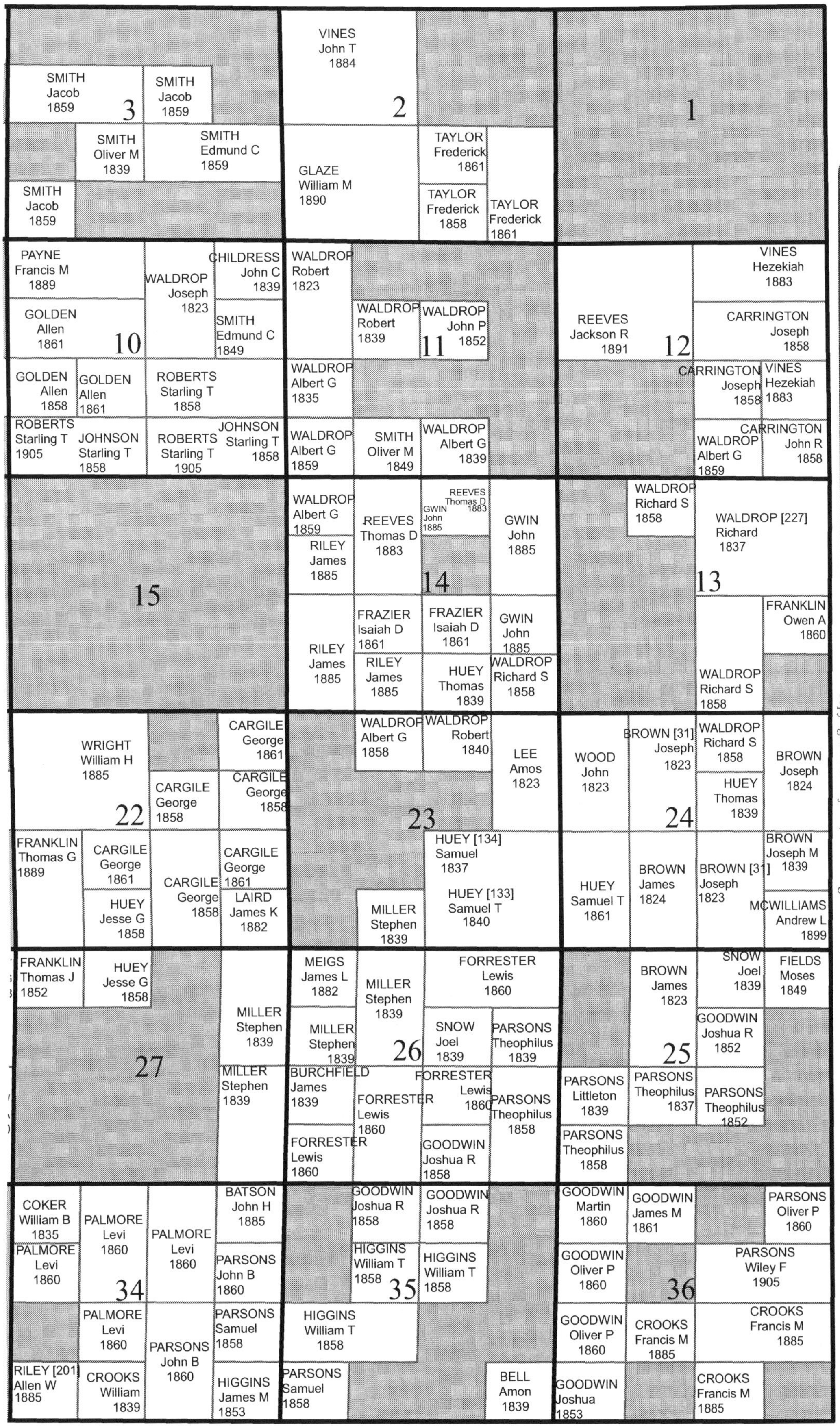

3
SMITH Jacob 1859
SMITH Jacob 1859
SMITH Oliver M 1839
SMITH Edmund C 1859
SMITH Jacob 1859

2
VINES John T 1884
GLAZE William M 1890
TAYLOR Frederick 1861
TAYLOR Frederick 1858
TAYLOR Frederick 1861

1

10
PAYNE Francis M 1889
WALDROP Joseph 1823
CHILDRESS John C 1839
GOLDEN Allen 1861
SMITH Edmund C 1849
GOLDEN Allen 1858
GOLDEN Allen 1861
ROBERTS Starling T 1858
ROBERTS Starling T 1905
JOHNSON Starling T 1858
ROBERTS Starling T 1905
JOHNSON Starling T 1858

11
WALDROP Robert 1823
WALDROP Robert 1839
WALDROP John P 1852
WALDROP Albert G 1835
WALDROP Albert G 1859
SMITH Oliver M 1849
WALDROP Albert G 1839

12
VINES Hezekiah 1883
REEVES Jackson R 1891
CARRINGTON Joseph 1858
CARRINGTON Joseph 1858
VINES Hezekiah 1883
WALDROP Albert G 1859
CARRINGTON John R 1858

15

14
WALDROP Albert G 1859
REEVES Thomas D 1883
REEVES Thomas D 1883
GWIN John 1885
GWIN John 1885
RILEY James 1885
FRAZIER Isaiah D 1861
FRAZIER Isaiah D 1861
GWIN John 1885
RILEY James 1885
RILEY James 1885
HUEY Thomas 1839
WALDROP Richard S 1858

13
WALDROP Richard S 1858
WALDROP [227] Richard 1837
FRANKLIN Owen A 1860
WALDROP Richard S 1858

22
WRIGHT William H 1885
CARGILE George 1861
CARGILE George 1858
CARGILE George 1858
FRANKLIN Thomas G 1889
CARGILE George 1861
CARGILE George 1858
CARGILE George 1861
HUEY Jesse G 1858
LAIRD James K 1882

23
WALDROP Albert G 1858
WALDROP Robert 1840
LEE Amos 1823
HUEY [134] Samuel 1837
HUEY [133] Samuel T 1840
MILLER Stephen 1839

24
WOOD John 1823
BROWN [31] Joseph 1823
WALDROP Richard S 1858
BROWN Joseph 1824
HUEY Thomas 1839
HUEY Samuel T 1861
BROWN James 1824
BROWN [31] Joseph 1823
BROWN Joseph M 1839
MCWILLIAMS Andrew L 1899

27
FRANKLIN Thomas J 1852
HUEY Jesse G 1858
MILLER Stephen 1839
MILLER Stephen 1839

26
MEIGS James L 1882
MILLER Stephen 1839
FORRESTER Lewis 1860
MILLER Stephen 1839
SNOW Joel 1839
PARSONS Theophilus 1839
BURCHFIELD James 1839
FORRESTER Lewis 1860
FORRESTER Lewis 1860
PARSONS Theophilus 1858
FORRESTER Lewis 1860
GOODWIN Joshua R 1858

25
BROWN James 1823
SNOW Joel 1839
FIELDS Moses 1849
GOODWIN Joshua R 1852
PARSONS Littleton 1839
PARSONS Theophilus 1837
PARSONS Theophilus 1852
PARSONS Theophilus 1858

34
COKER William B 1835
PALMORE Levi 1860
PALMORE Levi 1860
BATSON John H 1885
PALMORE Levi 1860
PARSONS John B 1860
PALMORE Levi 1860
PARSONS Samuel 1858
PARSONS John B 1860
RILEY [201] Allen W 1885
CROOKS William 1839
HIGGINS James M 1853

35
GOODWIN Joshua R 1858
GOODWIN Joshua R 1858
HIGGINS William T 1858
HIGGINS William T 1858
HIGGINS William T 1858
PARSONS Samuel 1858
BELL Amon 1839

36
GOODWIN Martin 1860
GOODWIN James M 1861
PARSONS Oliver P 1860
GOODWIN Oliver P 1860
PARSONS Wiley F 1905
GOODWIN Oliver P 1860
CROOKS Francis M 1885
CROOKS Francis M 1885
GOODWIN Joshua 1853
CROOKS Francis M 1885

Helpful Hints

1. This Map's INDEX can be found on the preceding pages.
2. Refer to Map "C" to see where this Township lies within Jefferson County, Alabama.
3. Numbers within square brackets [ ] denote a multi-patentee land parcel (multi-owner). Refer to Appendix "C" for a full list of members in this group.
4. Areas that look to be crowded with Patentees usually indicate multiple sales of the same parcel (Re-issues) or Overlapping parcels. See this Township's Index for an explanation of these and other circumstances that might explain "odd" groupings of Patentees on this map.

Legend

Patent Boundary
Section Boundary
No Patents Found (or Outside County)
1., 2., 3., ... Lot Numbers (when beside a name)
[ ] Group Number (see Appendix "C")

Scale: Section = 1 mile X 1 mile (generally, with some exceptions)

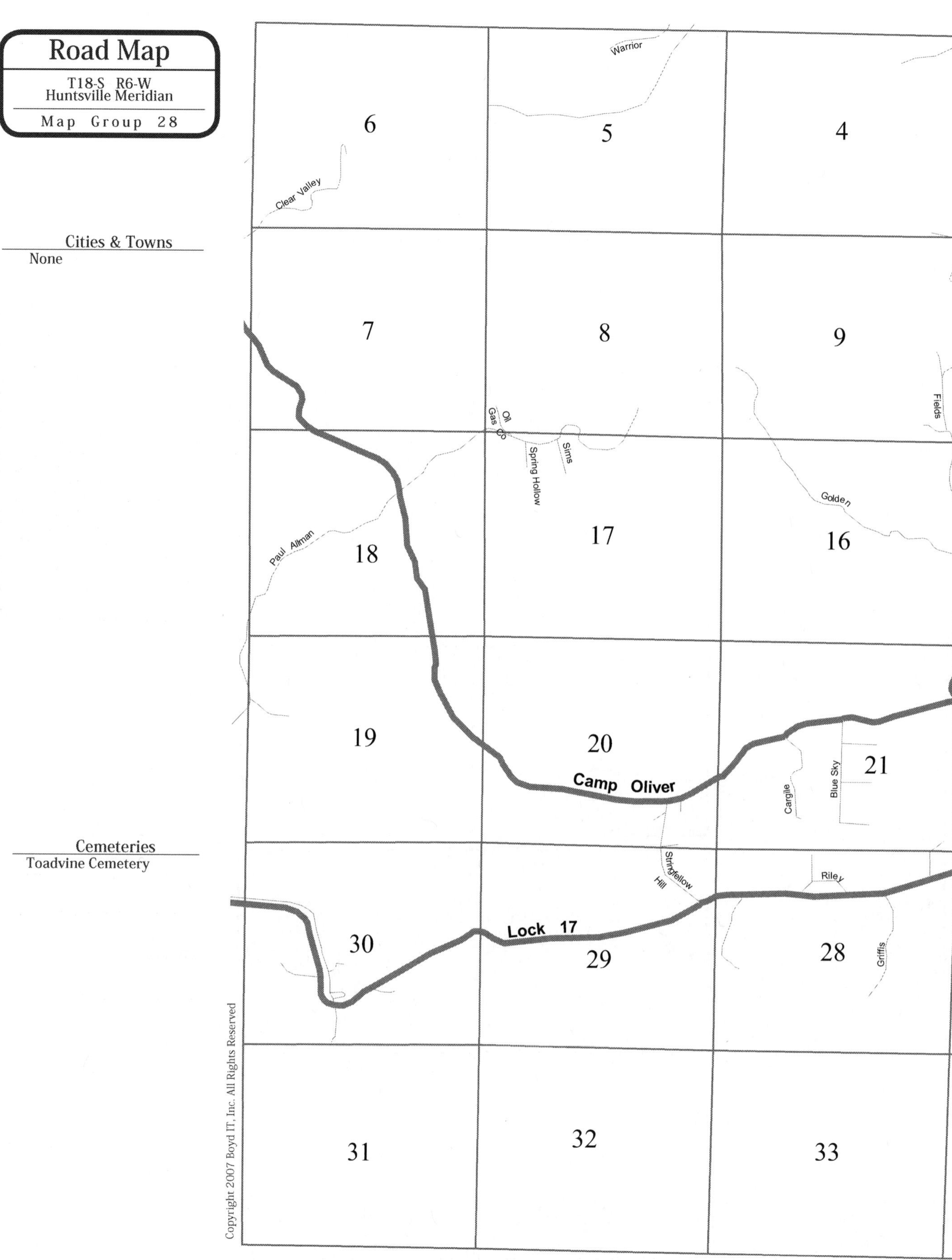
Road Map
T18-S R6-W
Huntsville Meridian
Map Group 28
Cities & Towns
None
Cemeteries
Toadvine Cemetery
6
5
4
Warrior
Clear Valley
7
8
9
Oil Gas Co
Sims
Spring Hollow
Fields
Golden
Paul Allman
18
17
16
19
20
21
Camp Oliver
Cargile
Blue Sky
Stringfellow Hill
Riley
Lock 17
30
29
28
Griffis
31
32
33

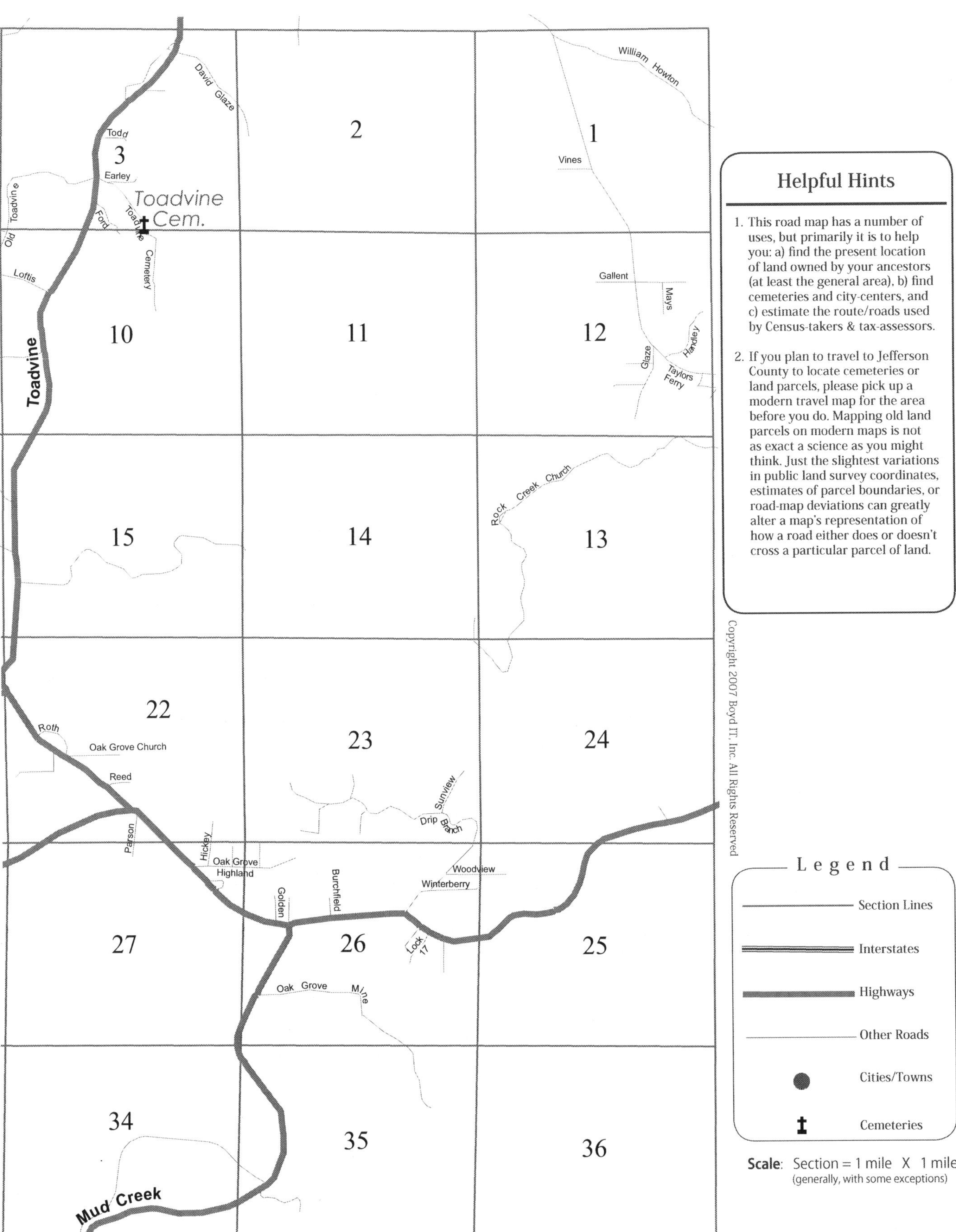
David Glaze
William Howton
Todd
Earley
Old Toadvine
Ford
Toadvine
Toadvine Cem.
Cemetery
Loftis
Vines
Gallent
Mays
Handley
Glaze
Taylors Ferry
Toadvine
Rock Creek Church
Roth
Oak Grove Church
Reed
Parson
Hickey
Oak Grove Highland
Golden
Burchfield
Sunview
Drip Branch
Woodview
Winterberry
Lock 17
Oak Grove Mine
Mud Creek
1
2
3
10
11
12
13
14
15
22
23
24
25
26
27
34
35
36
Helpful Hints
1. This road map has a number of uses, but primarily it is to help you: a) find the present location of land owned by your ancestors (at least the general area), b) find cemeteries and city-centers, and c) estimate the route/roads used by Census-takers & tax-assessors.
2. If you plan to travel to Jefferson County to locate cemeteries or land parcels, please pick up a modern travel map for the area before you do. Mapping old land parcels on modern maps is not as exact a science as you might think. Just the slightest variations in public land survey coordinates, estimates of parcel boundaries, or road-map deviations can greatly alter a map's representation of how a road either does or doesn't cross a particular parcel of land.
Copyright 2007 Boyd IT, Inc. All Rights Reserved
Legend
Section Lines
Interstates
Highways
Other Roads
Cities/Towns
Cemeteries
Scale: Section = 1 mile X 1 mile
(generally, with some exceptions)

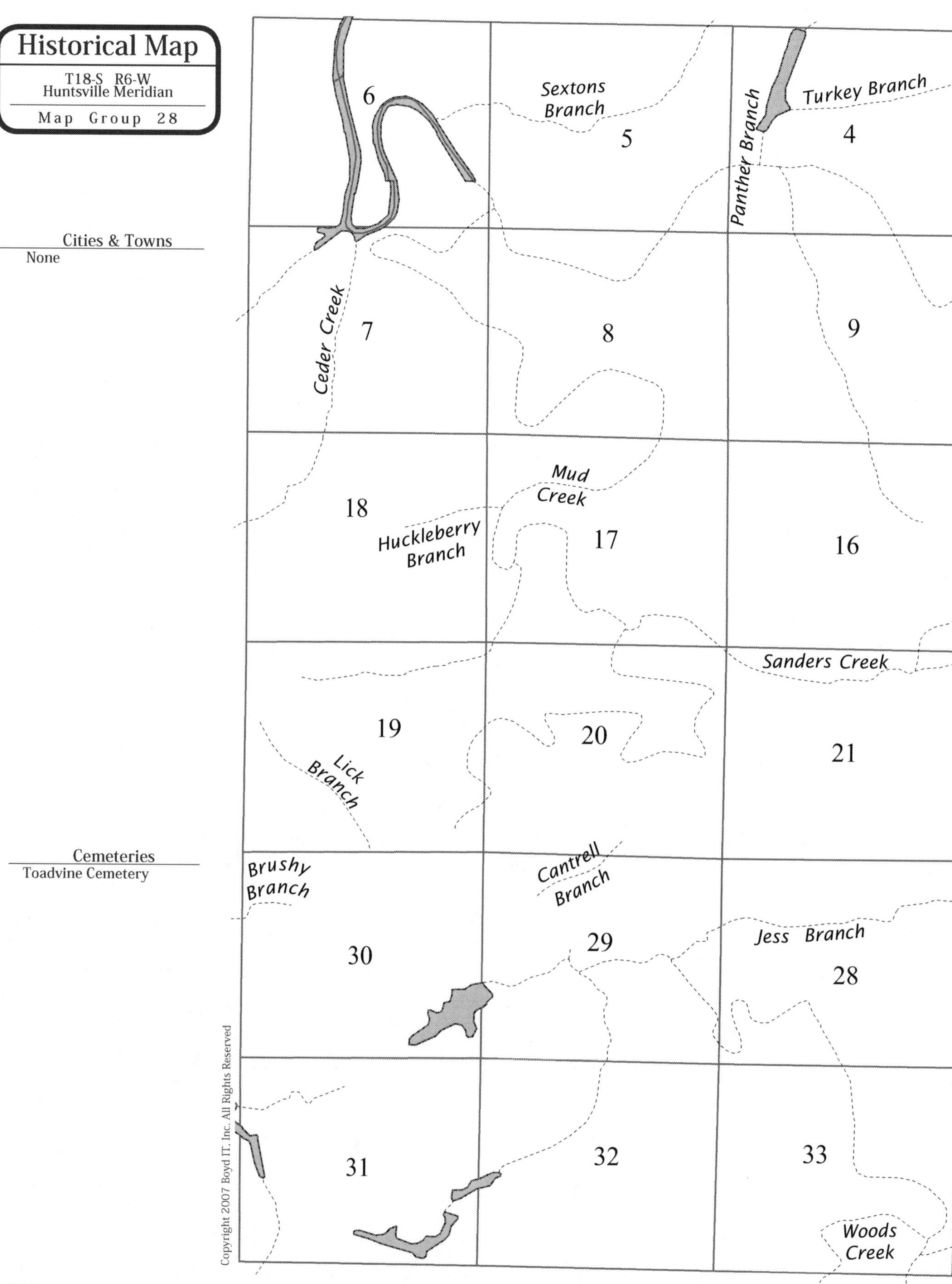
Historical Map
T18-S R6-W
Huntsville Meridian
Map Group 28
Cities & Towns
None
Cemeteries
Toadvine Cemetery
6
Sextons Branch
5
Panther Branch
Turkey Branch
4
Ceder Creek
7
8
9
Mud Creek
18
Huckleberry Branch
17
16
Sanders Creek
19
Lick Branch
20
21
Brushy Branch
Cantrell Branch
Jess Branch
30
29
28
31
32
33
Woods Creek
Copyright 2007 Boyd IT, Inc. All Rights Reserved

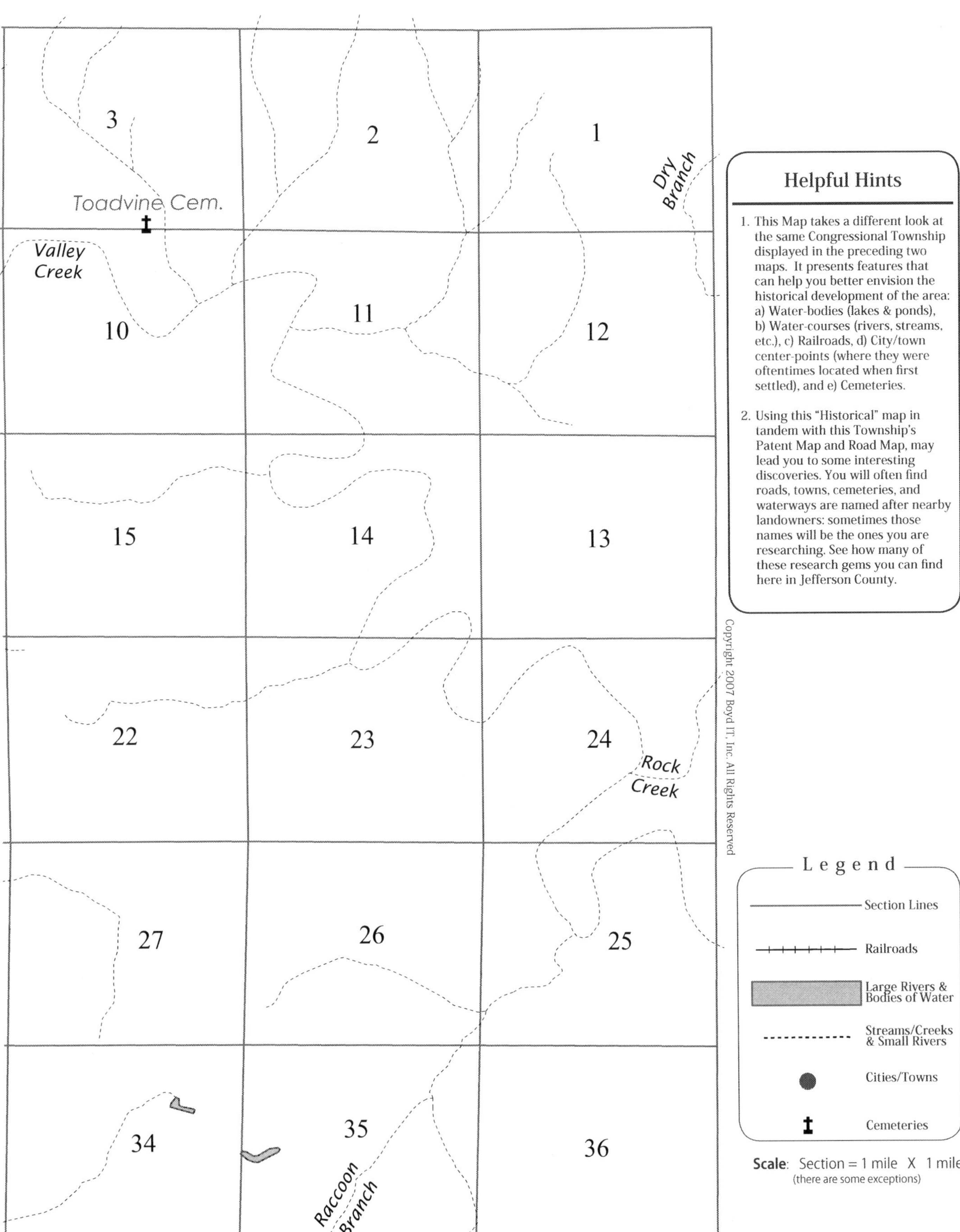

Helpful Hints

1. This Map takes a different look at the same Congressional Township displayed in the preceding two maps. It presents features that can help you better envision the historical development of the area: a) Water-bodies (lakes & ponds), b) Water-courses (rivers, streams, etc.), c) Railroads, d) City/town center-points (where they were oftentimes located when first settled), and e) Cemeteries.
2. Using this "Historical" map in tandem with this Township's Patent Map and Road Map, may lead you to some interesting discoveries. You will often find roads, towns, cemeteries, and waterways are named after nearby landowners: sometimes those names will be the ones you are researching. See how many of these research gems you can find here in Jefferson County.

Map Group 29: Index to Land Patents

Township 18-South Range 5-West (Huntsville)

After you locate an individual in this Index, take note of the Section and Section Part then proceed to the Land Patent map on the pages immediately following. You should have no difficulty locating the corresponding parcel of land.

The "For More Info" Column will lead you to more information about the underlying Patents. See the *Legend* at right, and the "How to Use this Book" chapter, for more information.

LEGEND

"For More Info . . . " column

A = Authority (Legislative Act, See Appendix "A")
B = Block or Lot (location in Section unknown)
C = Cancelled Patent
F = Fractional Section
G = Group (Multi-Patentee Patent, see Appendix "C")
V = Overlaps another Parcel
R = Re-Issued (Parcel patented more than once)

(A & G items require you to look in the Appendixes referred to above. All other Letter-designations followed by a number require you to locate line-items in this index that possess the ID number found after the letter).

ID	Individual in Patent	Sec.	Sec. Part	Date Issued	Other Counties	For More Info . . .
5180	ALABAMA, State Of	8	SESW	1910-06-06		A5
5051	BATSON, George W	10	E½SE	1884-03-20		A4
5052	" "	10	NWSE	1884-03-20		A4
5053	" "	10	SWNE	1884-03-20		A4
5182	BATSON, Thomas J	12	S½NE	1890-07-03		A4
5183	" "	12	SWSE	1890-07-03		A4
5058	BROWN, Isaac	13	SWNE	1849-05-01		A1
5054	" "	12	NESW	1850-04-01		A1
5057	" "	13	NWSW	1850-04-01		A1
5059	" "	20	SWNW	1852-01-01		A1
5062	" "	24	SWNW	1854-07-15		A1
5055	" "	12	NWSE	1858-06-01		A1
5056	" "	12	SESW	1858-06-01		A1
5060	" "	24	NENW	1858-06-01		A1
5061	" "	24	NWNE	1858-06-01		A1
5074	BROWN, James	19	W½NE	1838-08-28		A1
5101	BROWN, John	19	E½NE	1838-08-28		A1
5137	BROWN, Joseph M	18	SWSE	1839-09-20		A1
5097	CALDWELL, Joab	34	S½SW	1883-10-01		A4
5096	" "	34	NWSW	1884-12-05		A4
5098	" "	34	SWNW	1884-12-05		A4
5104	CLARK, John	23	SE	1858-06-01		A1
5105	" "	25	W½NW	1858-06-01		A1
5181	CLARK, Thomas H	12	E½SE	1831-06-01		A1
5108	DABBS, John G	22	SW	1885-03-16		A1
5190	DABBS, William B	26	N½NW	1901-12-30		A4 R5194
5191	" "	26	NWNE	1901-12-30		A4 R5195
5192	" "	26	SENW	1901-12-30		A4 R5196
5075	DEASE, James	14	NWNE	1850-04-01		A1
5076	DEES, James	11	W½SE	1858-06-01		A1
5077	" "	14	SWNW	1858-06-01		A1 R5174
5165	DEES, Richard	17	NESE	1858-06-01		A1
5166	" "	17	W½SE	1858-06-01		A1
5167	" "	20	NWNW	1858-06-01		A1
5168	" "	20	W½SW	1858-06-01		A1
5194	DOBBS, William H	26	N½NW	1890-03-19		A4 C R5190
5195	" "	26	NWNE	1890-03-19		A4 C R5191
5196	" "	26	SENW	1890-03-19		A4 C R5192
5063	FIELDS, Isaac	17	W½NW	1839-09-20		A1
5064	" "	4	SWNW	1840-11-10		A1
5207	FIELDS, William T	13	NW	1858-06-01		A1
5208	" "	30	N½NE	1883-10-01		A4
5163	FRANKLIN, Owen A	18	NWSW	1860-07-02		A1
5164	" "	18	SWNW	1860-07-02		A1
5021	HALL, Arthur	26	N½SW	1884-03-20		A1
5022	" "	26	SWNW	1884-03-20		A1

ID	Individual in Patent	Sec.	Sec. Part	Date Issued	Other Counties	For More Info . . .
5023	HALL, Arthur (Cont'd)	26	SWSE	1884-03-20		A1 R5043
5124	HAMAKER, John	32	W½SE	1839-09-20		A1
5125	" "	33	SWSW	1839-09-20		A1
5115	" "	2	W½SW	1850-09-02		A1
5116	" "	23	NENE	1850-09-02		A1
5113	" "	10	SWSE	1853-08-01		A1
5117	" "	23	NWNE	1853-08-01		A1
5123	" "	32	SWNE	1853-08-01		A1
5126	" "	7	NENE	1853-08-01		A1
5111	" "	10	E½SW	1858-06-01		A1
5114	" "	10	SWSW	1858-06-01		A1
5118	" "	23	SENW	1858-06-01		A1
5119	" "	23	SWNE	1858-06-01		A1
5127	" "	7	SENE	1858-06-01		A1
5128	" "	8	NWNW	1858-06-01		A1
5112	" "	10	SENW	1860-04-02		A1
5120	" "	23	W½SW	1860-04-02		A1
5121	" "	32	SENE	1860-04-02		A1
5122	" "	32	SESE	1860-04-02		A1
5197	HAMAKER, William	9	E½SW	1858-06-01		A1
5198	" "	9	NWSW	1858-06-01		A1
5199	" "	9	SENE	1858-06-01		A1
5200	" "	9	W½NE	1858-06-01		A1
5201	" "	9	W½SE	1858-06-01		A1
5209	HOGAN, William T	2	NENW	1891-06-29		A4
5210	" "	2	W½NW	1891-06-29		A4
5027	HOUGHTON, Carroll P	17	SESE	1910-04-18		A1
5044	HOWTON, David W	30	S½NE	1858-06-01		A1
5149	JORDAN, Mortimer	24	E½SW	1854-07-15		A1
5151	" "	24	S½SE	1854-07-15		A1
5150	" "	24	NESE	1858-06-01		A1
5169	JORDAN, Richmond	17	E½NE	1858-06-01		A1
5170	" "	17	NENW	1858-06-01		A1
5171	" "	17	NWNE	1858-06-01		A1
5172	" "	8	SE	1858-06-01		A1
5080	JOURDEN, James	15	NENE	1852-01-01		A1
5029	JUSTICE, Charles	13	NESE	1850-09-02		A1
5032	" "	13	SWSW	1850-09-02		A1
5034	" "	14	NESE	1852-01-01		A1
5028	" "	13	E½SW	1858-06-01		A1
5030	" "	13	NWNE	1858-06-01		A1
5031	" "	13	SENE	1858-06-01		A1
5033	" "	13	W½SE	1858-06-01		A1
5035	" "	14	SENE	1858-06-01		A1
5036	" "	8	NESW	1884-03-10		A4
5037	" "	8	W½SW	1884-03-10		A4
5038	JUSTICE, Charles M	21	NWSE	1858-06-01		A1
5039	" "	21	SWNE	1858-06-01		A1
5040	" "	21	SWSE	1858-06-01		A1
5041	" "	28	NWNE	1858-06-01		A1
5099	JUSTICE, John A	12	W½NW	1884-03-20		A1
5100	" "	12	W½SW	1884-03-20		A1
5135	JUSTICE, Joseph E	12	E½NW	1889-12-28		A1
5136	" "	12	N½NE	1889-12-28		A1
5186	JUSTICE, William A	8	E½NW	1882-09-09		A1
5187	" "	8	SWNW	1882-09-09		A1
5017	LEE, Amos	7	E½SW	1826-05-15		A1
5065	MAYFIELD, Israel	20	SE	1858-06-01		A1
5066	" "	20	SENE	1858-06-01		A1
5067	" "	29	NENE	1858-06-01		A1
5068	" "	29	W½NE	1858-06-01		A1
5018	MCCLAIN, Andrew	4	SW	1858-06-01		A1
5019	" "	4	SWSE	1858-06-01		A1
5020	" "	5	NESE	1858-06-01		A1
5147	MCCLAIN, Marcus D	8	E½NE	1890-01-08		A4
5148	" "	8	NWNE	1890-01-08		A4
5188	MCCLAIN, William A	4	E½NW	1892-01-30		A4
5189	" "	4	SWNE	1892-01-30		A4
5090	MCCLERKIN, Jane	19	NWNW	1859-04-01		A1
5087	MCCLINTON, James R	18	NESE	1882-09-09		A1
5088	" "	18	SENE	1882-09-09		A1
5138	MCMICKEN, Joseph T	6	E½NW	1884-11-13		A1
5139	" "	6	W½NE	1884-11-13		A1

ID	Individual in Patent	Sec.	Sec. Part	Date Issued	Other Counties	For More Info . . .
5145	MEEKS, Littleberry	22	N½NW	1860-12-01		A1
5154	MEEKS, Noah S	2	SE	1890-01-08		A4
5025	NABERS, Benjamin G	25	SW	1839-09-20		A1
5024	" "	25	SE	1858-06-01		A1
5081	NAIL, James	34	E½NW	1858-06-01		A1
5082	" "	34	N½NE	1858-06-01		A1
5083	" "	34	SENE	1858-06-01		A1
5084	" "	35	NESW	1858-06-01		A1
5085	" "	35	NWNW	1858-06-01		A1
5086	" "	35	S½NW	1858-06-01		A1
5152	NAIL, Nicholas L	32	N½NE	1883-08-13		A4
5153	" "	32	NESE	1883-08-13		A4
5026	PARSONS, Bennett	36	SE	1885-03-16		A4
5046	PARSONS, Elias M	30	N½SE	1891-06-29		A4
5047	" "	30	N½SW	1891-06-29		A4
5049	PARSONS, Ervin	32	E½SW	1858-06-01		A1
5072	PARSONS, Jackson A	20	E½NW	1884-03-20		A1
5073	" "	20	E½SW	1884-03-20		A1
5132	PARSONS, John	31	SENW	1853-08-01		A1
5130	" "	31	NWNW	1853-11-15		A1
5129	" "	31	NENW	1858-06-01		A1
5131	" "	31	NWSW	1858-06-01		A1 V5193
5146	PARSONS, Littleton	30	NW	1837-03-20		A1
5161	PARSONS, Oliver P	30	SWSW	1858-06-01		A1
5193	PARSONS, William B	31	W½SW	1858-06-01		A1 V5131
5106	PRICE, John D	13	SESE	1858-06-01		A1
5107	" "	24	NENE	1858-06-01		A1
5092	RAGAN, Jeremiah	9	NENW	1858-06-01		A1
5093	" "	9	NWNW	1858-06-01		A1
5094	" "	9	SENW	1858-06-01		A1
5095	" "	9	SWNW	1858-06-01		A1
5091	" "	9	NENE	1899-12-07		A1
5184	REIVES, Thomas	18	SENW	1852-01-01		A1
5016	RILEY, Allen W	6	SESE	1860-12-01		A1
5102	RILEY, John C	6	E½NE	1882-07-25		A4
5103	" "	6	NESE	1882-07-25		A4
5089	SALTER, James	2	E½SW	1884-03-20		A4
5013	SANDERS, Absolom	10	NWNW	1850-04-01		A1
5014	" "	9	SWSW	1850-09-02		A1
5050	SCOTT, George	34	SE	1885-05-25		A4
5143	SHOEMAKER, Lindsey A	27	W½NW	1858-06-01		A1
5144	" "	28	SESE	1858-06-01		A1
5202	SHOEMAKER, William	21	N½NE	1858-06-01		A1
5203	SPAULDING, William	4	E½SE	1892-01-25		A1
5204	" "	4	NWSE	1892-01-25		A1
5205	" "	4	SENE	1892-01-25		A1
5155	SPENCER, Octavius	14	W½SE	1853-08-01		A1
5156	" "	22	N½NE	1858-06-01		A1
5157	" "	25	E½NW	1858-06-01		A1
5158	" "	25	NE	1858-06-01		A1
5159	SPENCER, Octavus	14	SW	1839-09-20		A1
5160	" "	15	E½SE	1839-09-20		A1
5206	STAGGS, William	14	SESE	1850-04-01		A1
5042	THOMPSON, David	26	S½SW	1885-03-16		A1
5043	" "	26	SWSE	1885-03-16		A1 R5023
5048	THOMPSON, Ephraim	26	E½SE	1888-10-25		A4
5078	THOMPSON, James H	24	NWSE	1885-07-27		A1
5079	" "	24	S½NE	1885-07-27		A1
5141	THOMPSON, Lina	22	S½NE	1884-03-20		A1
5142	" "	22	S½NW	1884-03-20		A1
5211	THOMPSON, William W	2	NE	1889-08-16		A4
5133	TUCKER, Johnson J	29	SWNW	1839-09-20		A1
5134	TUCKER, Johnston J	29	NWSW	1839-09-20		A1 R5215
5140	VINES, Josephus	6	SWNW	1858-06-01		A1
5173	VINES, Rufus F	14	E½NW	1884-03-20		A4
5174	" "	14	SWNW	1884-03-20		A4 R5077
5015	WALDROP, Albert D	28	SWSW	1850-09-02		A1
5109	WALDROP, John H	20	NENE	1839-09-20		A1
5110	" "	28	SWNW	1839-09-20		A1
5162	WALDROP, Oliver Z	32	NW	1883-10-01		A4
5175	WALDROP, Samuel A	28	NESW	1884-03-20		A4
5176	" "	28	NWSE	1884-03-20		A4
5177	" "	28	SENW	1884-03-20		A4

ID	Individual in Patent	Sec.	Sec. Part	Date Issued	Other Counties	For More Info . . .
5178	WALDROP, Samuel A (Cont'd)	28	SWNE	1884-03-20		A4
5212	WALDROP, Zachariah	28	NESE	1840-11-10		A1
5214	" "	28	SENE	1840-11-10		A1
5213	" "	28	NWSW	1858-06-01		A1
5215	" "	29	NWSW	1858-06-01		A1 R5134
5216	" "	29	SENE	1858-06-01		A1
5217	" "	29	SWSE	1858-06-01		A1
5045	WATSON, David	35	W½SE	1824-05-04		A1
5069	WOOD, Jack	26	NENE	1888-02-04		A4
5071	" "	26	SWNE	1888-02-04		A4
5070	" "	26	SENE	1889-03-01		A4
5179	WOODS, Simeon D	22	SE	1885-03-16		A1
5185	YOUNG, Thomas	29	E½SE	1915-08-31		A1

Patent Map

T18-S R5-W
Huntsville Meridian

Map Group 29

Township Statistics

Parcels Mapped	:	205
Number of Patents	:	136
Number of Individuals	:	86
Patentees Identified	:	86
Number of Surnames	:	48
Multi-Patentee Parcels	:	0
Oldest Patent Date	:	5/4/1824
Most Recent Patent	:	8/31/1915
Block/Lot Parcels	:	0
Parcels Re - Issued	:	6
Parcels that Overlap	:	2
Cities and Towns	:	0
Cemeteries	:	2

MCMICKEN Joseph T 1884
MCMICKEN Joseph T 1884
VINES Josephus 1858
6
RILEY John C 1882
RILEY John C 1882
RILEY Allen W 1860
5
MCCLAIN Andrew 1858
MCCLAIN William A 1892
FIELDS Isaac 1840
4
MCCLAIN William A 1892
SPAULDING William 1892
MCCLAIN Andrew 1858
SPAULDING William 1892
SPAULDING William 1892
MCCLAIN Andrew 1858

HAMAKER John 1853
HAMAKER John 1858
7
LEE Amos 1826
HAMAKER John 1858
JUSTICE William A 1882
JUSTICE William A 1882
MCCLAIN Marcus D 1890
MCCLAIN Marcus D 1890
8
JUSTICE Charles 1884
JUSTICE Charles 1884
ALABAMA State Of 1910
JORDAN Richmond 1858
RAGAN Jeremiah 1858
RAGAN Jeremiah 1858
RAGAN Jeremiah 1858
RAGAN Jeremiah 1858
HAMAKER William 1858
RAGAN Jeremiah 1899
HAMAKER William 1858
9
HAMAKER William 1858
HAMAKER William 1858
SANDERS Absolom 1850
HAMAKER William 1858

FRANKLIN Owen A 1860
REIVES Thomas 1852
18
MCCLINTON James R 1882
FRANKLIN Owen A 1860
MCCLINTON James R 1882
BROWN Joseph M 1839
FIELDS Isaac 1839
JORDAN Richmond 1858
JORDAN Richmond 1858
JORDAN Richmond 1858
17
DEES Richard 1858
DEES Richard 1858
HOUGHTON Carroll P 1910
16

MCCLERKIN Jane 1859
BROWN James 1838
BROWN John 1838
19
DEES Richard 1858
PARSONS Jackson A 1884
BROWN Isaac 1852
20
WALDROP John H 1839
MAYFIELD Israel 1858
DEES Richard 1858
PARSONS Jackson A 1884
MAYFIELD Israel 1858
SHOEMAKER William 1858
JUSTICE Charles M 1858
21
JUSTICE Charles M 1858
JUSTICE Charles M 1858

PARSONS Littleton 1837
FIELDS William T 1883
HOWTON David W 1858
30
PARSONS Elias M 1891
PARSONS Elias M 1891
PARSONS Oliver P 1858
TUCKER Johnson J 1839
WALDROP Zachariah 1858
TUCKER Johnston J 1839
29
MAYFIELD Israel 1858
MAYFIELD Israel 1858
WALDROP Zachariah 1858
YOUNG Thomas 1915
WALDROP Zachariah 1858
JUSTICE Charles M 1858
WALDROP John H 1839
WALDROP Samuel A 1884
28
WALDROP Samuel A 1884
WALDROP Zachariah 1840
WALDROP Zachariah 1858
WALDROP Samuel A 1884
WALDROP Samuel A 1884
WALDROP Zachariah 1840
WALDROP Albert D 1850
SHOEMAKER Lindsey A 1858

PARSONS John 1853
PARSONS John 1858
PARSONS John 1853
31
PARSONS William B 1858
PARSONS John 1858
WALDROP Oliver Z 1883
NAIL Nicholas L 1883
HAMAKER John 1853
HAMAKER John 1860
32
PARSONS Ervin 1858
HAMAKER John 1839
NAIL Nicholas L 1883
HAMAKER John 1860
33
HAMAKER John 1839

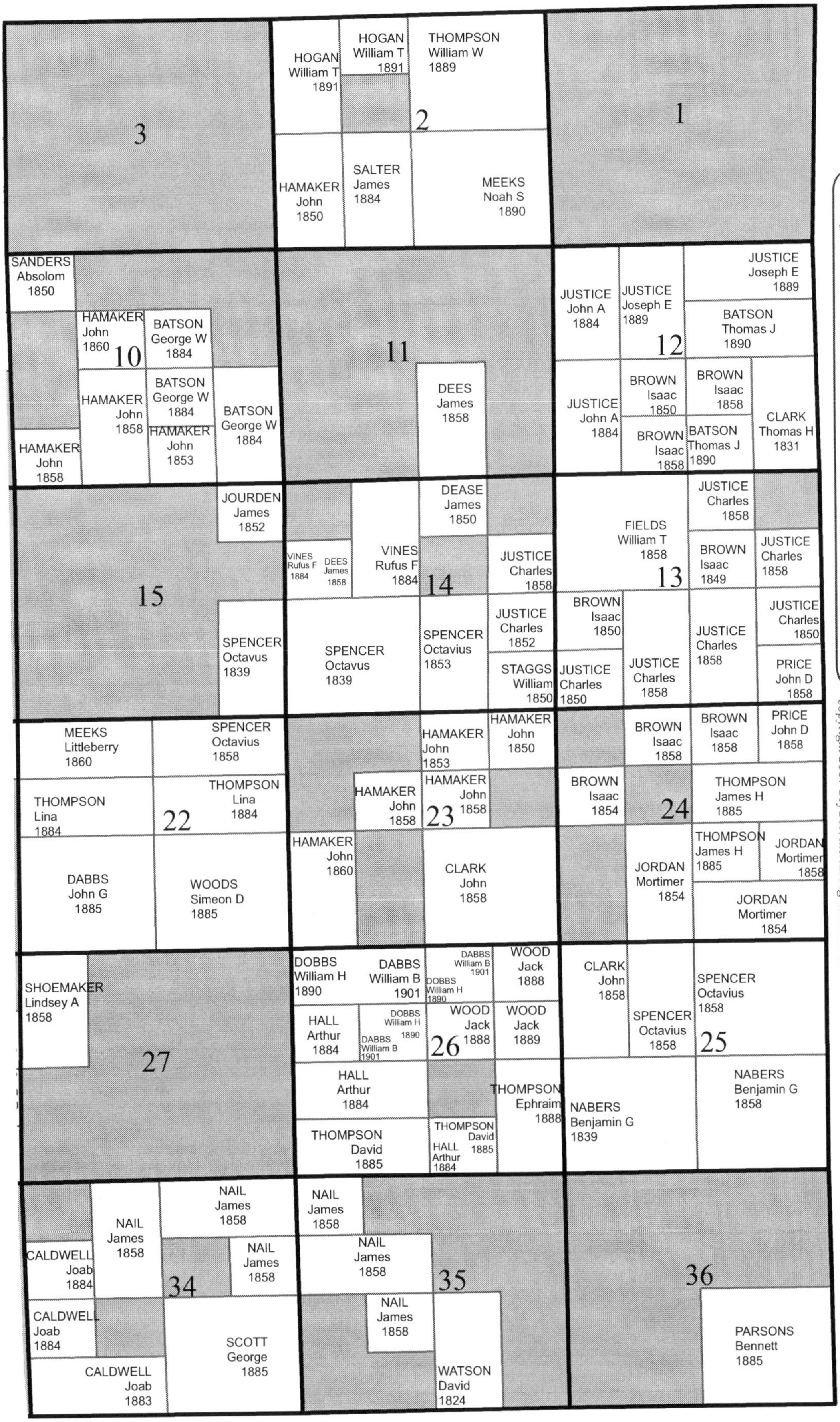

3

2
HOGAN William T 1891
HOGAN William T 1891
THOMPSON William W 1889
HAMAKER John 1850
SALTER James 1884
MEEKS Noah S 1890

1

10
SANDERS Absolom 1850
HAMAKER John 1860
BATSON George W 1884
HAMAKER John 1858
BATSON George W 1884
BATSON George W 1884
HAMAKER John 1853
HAMAKER John 1858

11
DEES James 1858

12
JUSTICE John A 1884
JUSTICE Joseph E 1889
JUSTICE Joseph E 1889
BATSON Thomas J 1890
JUSTICE John A 1884
BROWN Isaac 1850
BROWN Isaac 1858
BROWN Isaac 1858
BATSON Thomas J 1890
CLARK Thomas H 1831

15
JOURDEN James 1852
SPENCER Octavus 1839

14
DEASE James 1850
VINES Rufus F 1884
DEES James 1858
VINES Rufus F 1884
JUSTICE Charles 1858
SPENCER Octavus 1839
SPENCER Octavius 1853
JUSTICE Charles 1852
STAGGS William 1850

13
FIELDS William T 1858
JUSTICE Charles 1858
BROWN Isaac 1849
JUSTICE Charles 1858
BROWN Isaac 1850
JUSTICE Charles 1850
JUSTICE Charles 1858
JUSTICE Charles 1850
JUSTICE Charles 1858
PRICE John D 1858

22
MEEKS Littleberry 1860
SPENCER Octavius 1858
THOMPSON Lina 1884
THOMPSON Lina 1884
DABBS John G 1885
WOODS Simeon D 1885

23
HAMAKER John 1853
HAMAKER John 1850
HAMAKER John 1858
HAMAKER John 1858
HAMAKER John 1860
CLARK John 1858

24
BROWN Isaac 1858
BROWN Isaac 1858
PRICE John D 1858
BROWN Isaac 1854
THOMPSON James H 1885
THOMPSON James H 1885
JORDAN Mortimer 1858
JORDAN Mortimer 1854
JORDAN Mortimer 1854

27
SHOEMAKER Lindsey A 1858

26
DOBBS William H 1890
DABBS William B 1901
DABBS William B 1901
DOBBS William H 1890
WOOD Jack 1888
HALL Arthur 1884
DOBBS William H 1890
DABBS William B 1901
WOOD Jack 1888
WOOD Jack 1889
HALL Arthur 1884
THOMPSON Ephraim 1888
THOMPSON David 1885
THOMPSON David 1885
HALL Arthur 1884

25
CLARK John 1858
SPENCER Octavius 1858
SPENCER Octavius 1858
NABERS Benjamin G 1839
NABERS Benjamin G 1858

34
NAIL James 1858
NAIL James 1858
CALDWELL Joab 1884
NAIL James 1858
CALDWELL Joab 1884
SCOTT George 1885
CALDWELL Joab 1883

35
NAIL James 1858
NAIL James 1858
NAIL James 1858
WATSON David 1824

36
PARSONS Bennett 1885

Helpful Hints

1. This Map's INDEX can be found on the preceding pages.
2. Refer to Map "C" to see where this Township lies within Jefferson County, Alabama.
3. Numbers within square brackets [ ] denote a multi-patentee land parcel (multi-owner). Refer to Appendix "C" for a full list of members in this group.
4. Areas that look to be crowded with Patentees usually indicate multiple sales of the same parcel (Re-issues) or Overlapping parcels. See this Township's Index for an explanation of these and other circumstances that might explain "odd" groupings of Patentees on this map.

Legend

Patent Boundary
Section Boundary
No Patents Found (or Outside County)
1., 2., 3., ... Lot Numbers (when beside a name)
[ ] Group Number (see Appendix "C")

Scale: Section = 1 mile X 1 mile (generally, with some exceptions)

Road Map

T18-S R5-W
Huntsville Meridian

Map Group 29

Cities & Towns
None

Cemeteries
Valley Creek Cemetery
Virginia Mines Cemetery

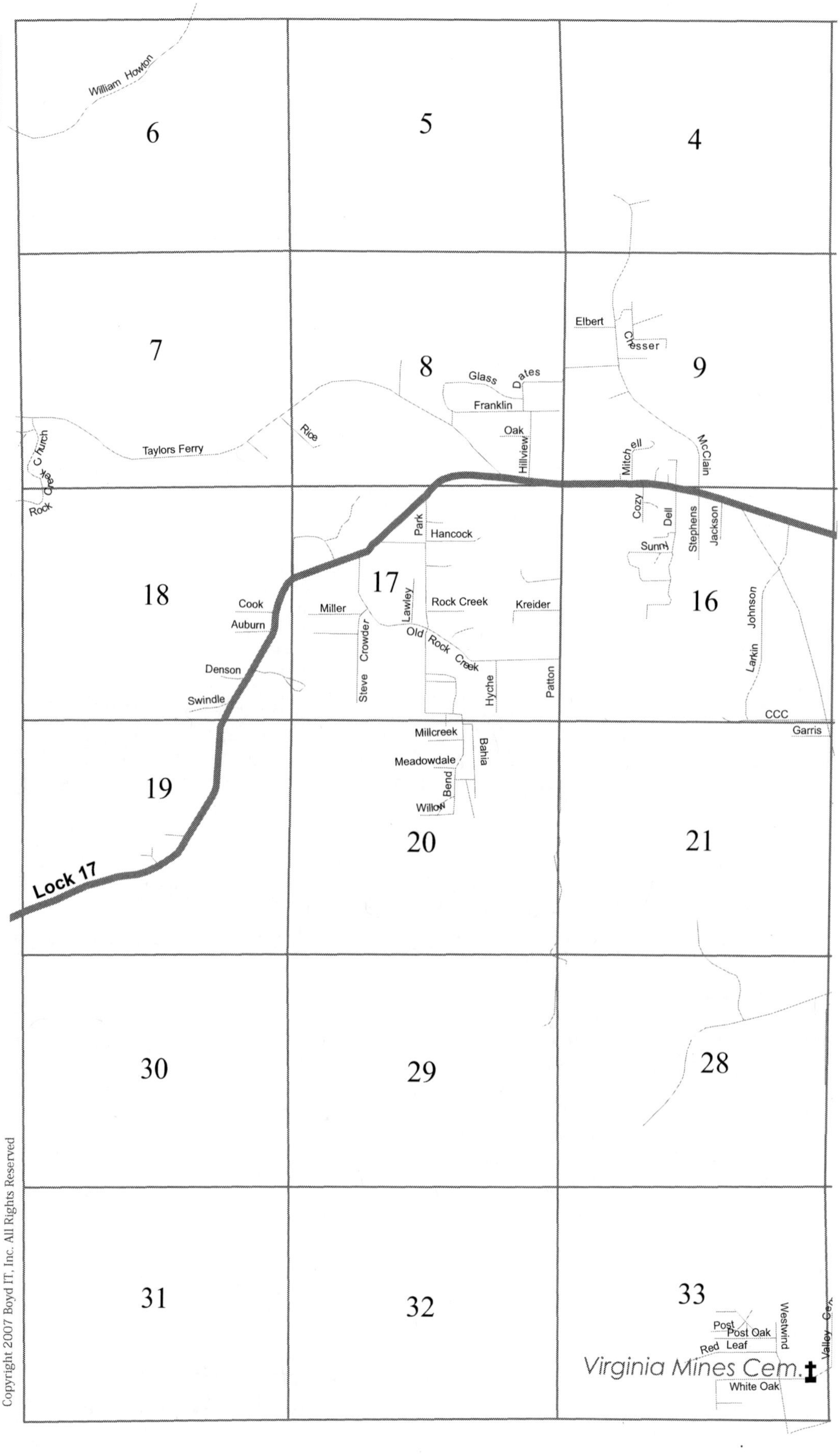

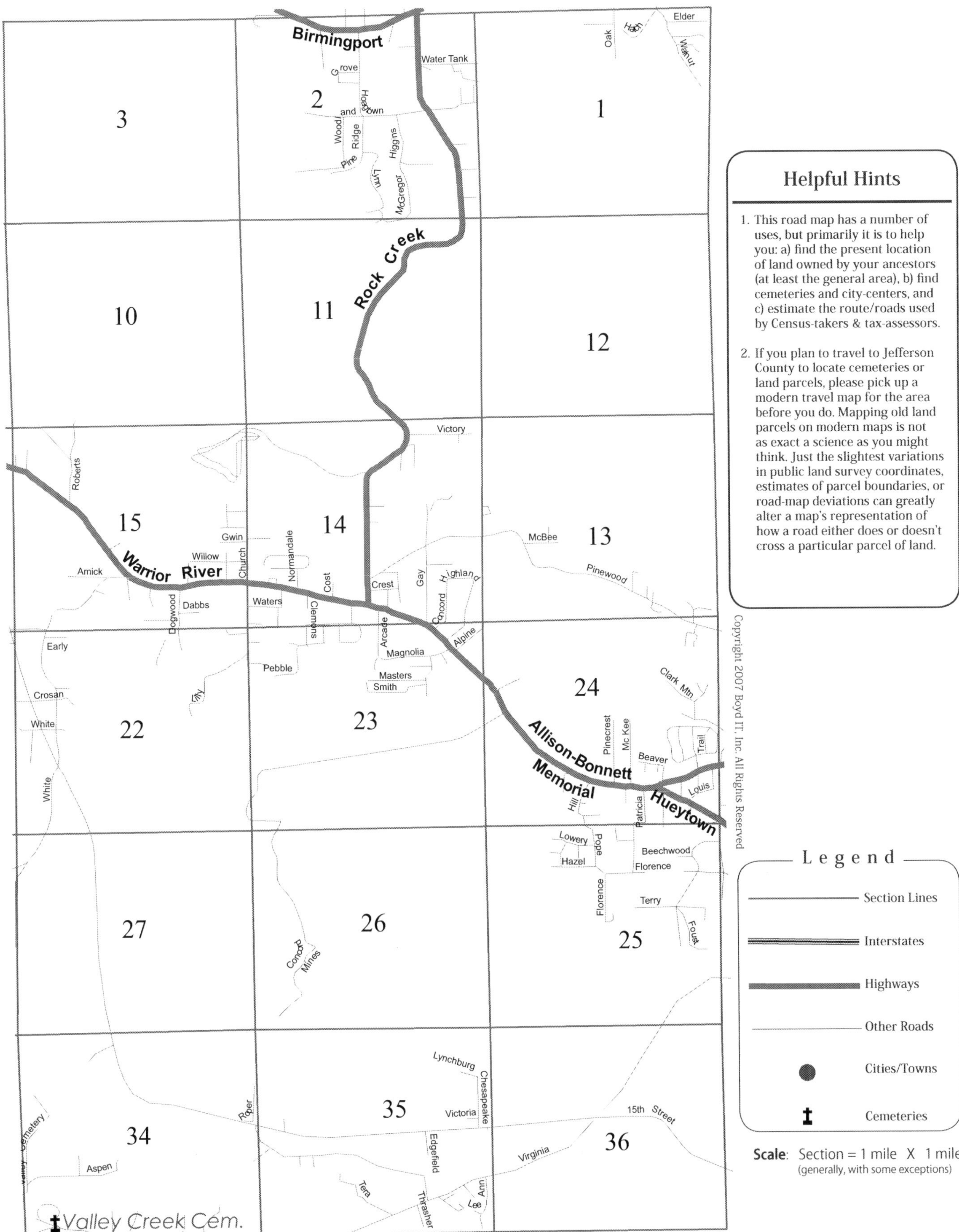

Helpful Hints

1. This road map has a number of uses, but primarily it is to help you: a) find the present location of land owned by your ancestors (at least the general area), b) find cemeteries and city-centers, and c) estimate the route/roads used by Census-takers & tax-assessors.

2. If you plan to travel to Jefferson County to locate cemeteries or land parcels, please pick up a modern travel map for the area before you do. Mapping old land parcels on modern maps is not as exact a science as you might think. Just the slightest variations in public land survey coordinates, estimates of parcel boundaries, or road-map deviations can greatly alter a map's representation of how a road either does or doesn't cross a particular parcel of land.

Scale: Section = 1 mile X 1 mile
(generally, with some exceptions)

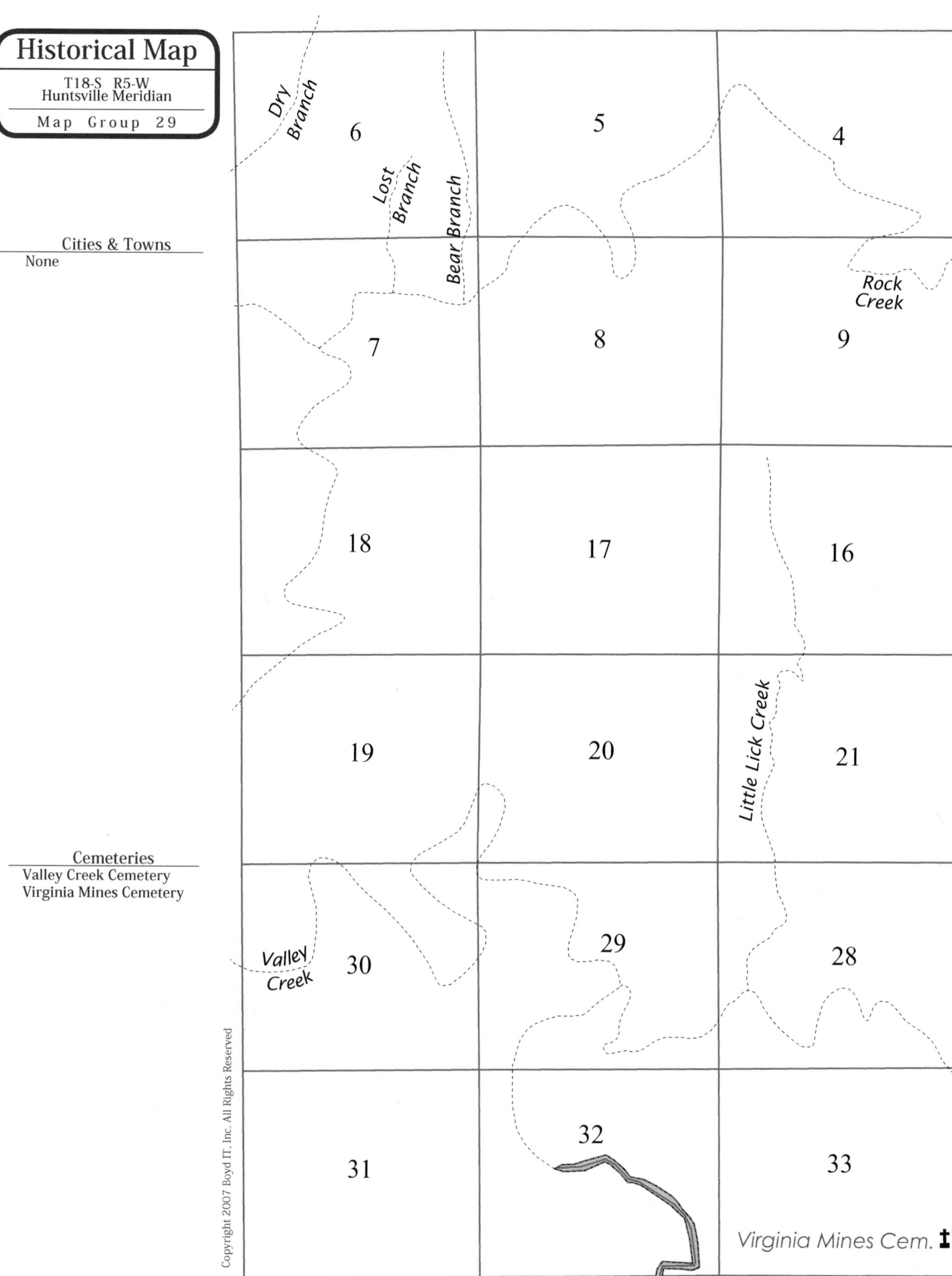
Historical Map
T18-S R5-W
Huntsville Meridian
Map Group 29
Cities & Towns
None
Cemeteries
Valley Creek Cemetery
Virginia Mines Cemetery
Dry Branch
Lost Branch
Bear Branch
Rock Creek
Little Lick Creek
Valley Creek
Virginia Mines Cem.
6
5
4
7
8
9
18
17
16
19
20
21
30
29
28
31
32
33
Copyright 2007 Boyd IT, Inc. All Rights Reserved

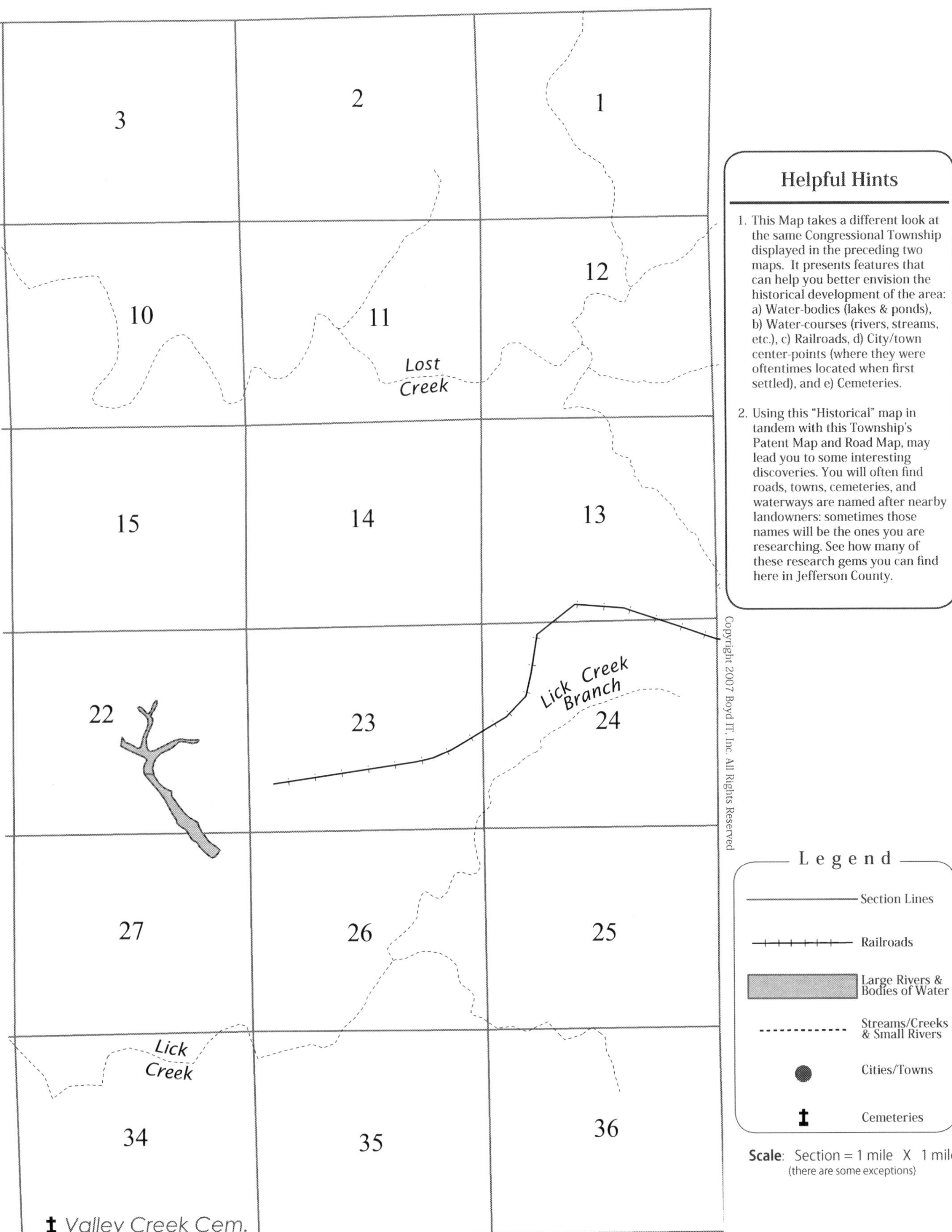

Helpful Hints

1. This Map takes a different look at the same Congressional Township displayed in the preceding two maps. It presents features that can help you better envision the historical development of the area: a) Water-bodies (lakes & ponds), b) Water-courses (rivers, streams, etc.), c) Railroads, d) City/town center-points (where they were oftentimes located when first settled), and e) Cemeteries.

2. Using this "Historical" map in tandem with this Township's Patent Map and Road Map, may lead you to some interesting discoveries. You will often find roads, towns, cemeteries, and waterways are named after nearby landowners: sometimes those names will be the ones you are researching. See how many of these research gems you can find here in Jefferson County.

Legend

- Section Lines
- Railroads
- Large Rivers & Bodies of Water
- Streams/Creeks & Small Rivers
- Cities/Towns
- Cemeteries

Scale: Section = 1 mile X 1 mile
(there are some exceptions)

Map Group 30: Index to Land Patents

Township 18-South Range 4-West (Huntsville)

After you locate an individual in this Index, take note of the Section and Section Part then proceed to the Land Patent map on the pages immediately following. You should have no difficulty locating the corresponding parcel of land.

The "For More Info" Column will lead you to more information about the underlying Patents. See the *Legend* at right, and the "How to Use this Book" chapter, for more information.

LEGEND

"For More Info . . . " column

A = Authority (Legislative Act, See Appendix "A")
B = Block or Lot (location in Section unknown)
C = Cancelled Patent
F = Fractional Section
G = Group (Multi-Patentee Patent, see Appendix "C")
V = Overlaps another Parcel
R = Re-Issued (Parcel patented more than once)

(A & G items require you to look in the Appendixes referred to above. All other Letter-designations followed by a number require you to locate line-items in this index that possess the ID number found after the letter).

ID	Individual in Patent	Sec.	Sec. Part	Date Issued	Other Counties	For More Info . . .
5372	ALLEN, Thomas M	8	S½NE	1884-12-05		A4
5245	ANTHONY, George L	18	S½NE	1891-06-08		A4 G5
5245	ANTHONY, Sarah A	18	S½NE	1891-06-08		A4 G5
5316	ATWOOD, Joseph H	27	SENE	1839-09-20		A1
5311	AYRES, Joseph	26	SE	1837-03-20		A1
5309	" "	22	SESE	1854-07-15		A1
5310	" "	23	SWSW	1854-07-15		A1
5308	" "	22	NESE	1858-06-01		A1
5278	BAGLEY, Joab	2	SWSE	1858-06-01		A1
5263	BALL, James	22	W½SW	1839-09-20		A1
5409	BANKS, Willis	20	E½SE	1825-09-01		A1
5408	BARKSDALE, William W	36	N½SE	1873-08-01		A1
5285	BASS, John	25	SW	1913-07-31		A1
5234	BROWN, David	8	SWSW	1839-09-20		A1
5233	" "	2	SESW	1840-11-10		A1
5254	BROWN, Isaac	9	NWSW	1854-07-15		A1
5252	" "	8	E½SW	1858-06-01		A1
5253	" "	8	NWSW	1858-06-01		A1
5255	" "	9	SWNW	1858-06-01		A1
5256	" "	9	SWSW	1858-06-01		A1
5314	BROWN, Joseph	27	E½SW	1839-09-20		A1
5315	" "	27	SWSW	1839-09-20		A1
5363	BROWN, Robert W	2	E½NW	1858-06-01		A1
5364	" "	2	NENE	1858-06-01		A1
5365	" "	2	NWNW	1858-06-01		A1
5386	BROWN, William	10	W½SE	1837-03-20		A1
5387	" "	15	SW	1915-08-11		A1 G34
5379	BROWN, William A	18	N½SE	1893-06-13		A1
5380	" "	18	N½SW	1893-06-13		A1
5381	BROWN, William B	10	SW	1858-06-01		A1
5382	" "	9	E½SE	1858-06-01		A1
5383	" "	9	SESW	1858-06-01		A1
5384	" "	9	SWSE	1858-06-01		A1
5226	BURGIN, Andrew W	4	E½SE	1882-06-30		A1
5273	BURGIN, James T	12	N½SE	1885-03-16		A1
5395	BURGIN, William M	12	E½SW	1858-06-01		A1
5257	CALDWELL, Isaac	4	W½NE	1884-12-05		A4
5258	" "	4	W½SE	1884-12-05		A4
5396	CAPPS, William M	6	SW	1883-07-03		A4
5321	CHAPMAN, Lewis	8	SE	1891-06-30		A4
5247	CLEMENTS, Hardy	31	NE	1912-11-11		A1
5329	CLICK, Matthew M	13	SESW	1839-09-20		A1
5287	CROOKS, John	17	E½SE	1858-06-01		A1
5288	" "	17	SESW	1858-06-01		A1
5289	" "	17	SWSE	1858-06-01		A1
5290	" "	17	W½NE	1858-06-01		A1 R5320

ID	Individual in Patent	Sec.	Sec. Part	Date Issued	Other Counties	For More Info . . .
5291	CROOKS, John (Cont'd)	20	NENE	1858-06-01		A1
5292	" "	20	NENW	1858-06-01		A1
5277	DABBS, Jesse T	18	NW	1891-11-23		A4
5294	DAVIS, John	21	SW	1912-02-15		A1 G71
5378	DICKENSON, Wiley	35	N½NE	1837-03-20		A1
5267	DICKINSON, James	25	W½NE	1837-03-20		A1
5266	" "	25	SWNW	1838-08-28		A1
5264	" "	25	NESE	1839-09-20		A1
5265	" "	25	NWNW	1839-09-20		A1
5351	DOWNEY, Peter	36	E½NE	1858-06-01		A1
5352	" "	36	NWNE	1858-06-01		A1
5349	DRAKE, Ozias	2	NWSE	1839-09-20		A1
5390	DRAKE, William G	12	W½SW	1839-09-20		A1
5280	DRAPER, John B	36	SWNE	1854-07-15		A1
5223	DUPUY, Alfred H	35	SWNW	1853-08-01		A1
5389	EARLY, William	8	N½NE	1884-12-05		A4
5222	ENGLISH, Alexander	11	SE	1915-08-09		A1
5388	EUBANK, William C	1	NESE	1849-05-01		A1
5243	EUBANKS, George	34	NESW	1834-10-14		A1
5244	" "	34	NWSE	1834-10-14		A1
5340	FIELDS, Moses	12	NW	1915-08-09		A1
5294	GILLEN, John	21	SW	1912-02-15		A1 G71
5312	GLENN, Joseph B	6	E½NW	1883-07-03		A4
5313	" "	6	W½NE	1883-07-03		A4
5353	GLENN, Rebecca	6	E½NE	1883-07-03		A4 G99
5354	" "	6	N½SE	1883-07-03		A4 G99
5353	GLENN, Sarah	6	E½NE	1883-07-03		A4 G99
5354	" "	6	N½SE	1883-07-03		A4 G99
5248	GOYNE, Harrison W	33	E½SE	1836-02-15		A1
5295	GOYNE, John	23	SE	1833-06-08		A1
5296	" "	23	SESW	1839-09-20		A1
5297	HAGER, John	36	SESW	1885-10-30		A1
5298	" "	36	SWSE	1885-10-30		A1
5268	HALL, James	11	NW	1915-08-09		A1 G110
5299	HAMAKER, John	34	SWSE	1853-08-01		A1
5300	HARDIN, John	21	NE	1917-11-14		A1 G124
5259	HARRISON, Isham	32	E½SE	1825-08-05		A1
5260	" "	32	W½SE	1825-08-05		A1
5235	HAWKINS, David	22	NENE	1858-06-01		A1
5236	" "	23	NW	1858-06-01		A1
5237	" "	23	NWSW	1858-06-01		A1
5366	HAWKINS, Samuel	13	NESW	1850-09-02		A1
5367	" "	13	NW	1858-06-01		A1
5231	HENLY, Darby	35	E½SW	1825-08-05		A1
5232	" "	35	W½SW	1825-08-05		A1
5230	" "	27	W½SE	1832-01-02		A1
5286	HODGES, John C	14	NWNE	1849-08-01		A1
5318	HODGES, Joseph	14	NW	1832-01-02		A1
5317	" "	14	N½SW	1837-03-20		A1
5370	HODGES, Stephen	22	W½NE	1839-09-20		A1
5369	" "	18	SWSE	1853-08-01		A1
5368	" "	18	SESW	1858-06-01		A1
5373	HOLCOMB, Thomas M	35	S½NE	1837-03-20		A1
5357	HUGHES, Robert	36	NENW	1854-07-15		A1
5358	" "	36	NESW	1858-06-01		A1
5359	" "	36	SENW	1858-06-01		A1
5397	IRION, William M	36	SESE	1890-04-15		A1
5319	JENNINGS, Leander	17	SENW	1858-06-01		A1
5320	" "	17	W½NE	1858-06-01		A1 R5290
5327	JOHNSON, Mastin	1	SENW	1839-09-20		A1
5328	" "	1	SWNE	1839-09-20		A1
5330	JORDAN, Mortimer	19	E½NW	1839-09-20		A1
5331	" "	19	E½SW	1839-09-20		A1
5332	" "	19	NE	1839-09-20		A1
5334	" "	19	W½SE	1839-09-20		A1
5335	" "	20	E½SW	1839-09-20		A1
5336	" "	20	SENW	1852-01-01		A1
5333	" "	19	SWNW	1853-08-01		A1
5338	" "	6	NENW	1853-08-01		A1 C
5337	" "	30	SESW	1858-06-01		A1
5339	JORDAN, Mortimere	20	W½SW	1834-10-01		A1
5279	JUSTICE, John A	18	SESE	1892-06-25		A1
5269	KELLY, James	27	W½NE	1839-09-20		A1

ID	Individual in Patent	Sec.	Sec. Part	Date Issued	Other Counties	For More Info . . .
5375	LACEY, Thomas S	12	SENE	1889-12-28		A1
5227	LEE, Archelaus	15	S½NE	1837-03-20		A1
5400	LEWIS, William R	1	SESE	1852-01-01		A1
5401	" "	12	NENE	1852-01-01		A1
5281	LOVE, John B	2	W½NE	1884-12-05		A4
5224	LOVELESS, Andrew M	36	SWSW	1882-10-30		A1
5376	LOVELESS, Vinson	35	SESE	1858-06-01		A1
5377	" "	36	NWSW	1858-06-01		A1
5225	MARTIN, Andrew	1	NWSE	1839-09-20		A1
5301	MARTIN, John	12	SESE	1852-01-01		A1
5302	" "	13	NENE	1852-01-01		A1
5242	MCDONALD, Franklin R	2	NWSW	1883-07-03		A4
5261	MCDONALD, Jacob	4	N½SW	1889-11-21		A4
5262	" "	4	S½SW	1889-11-21		A4
5218	MCGEHEE, Abner	20	W½SE	1825-08-05		A1
5220	" "	30	E½NE	1825-09-01		A1
5219	" "	29	NE	1833-06-08		A1
5398	MCMILLAN, William	15	N½NE	1837-03-20		A1
5228	NABERS, Benjamin	28	W½SE	1839-09-20		A1
5229	NABORS, Benjamin	19	W½SW	1839-09-20		A1
5270	NELSON, James	2	SENE	1839-09-20		A1
5360	OWEN, Robert	23	S½NE	1850-04-01		A1
5374	OWEN, Thomas	10	E½SE	1915-08-09		A3 G191
5399	PATTERSON, William	12	W½NE	1823-07-09		A1
5394	PAULLING, William K	19	E½SE	1826-06-10		A1
5246	PEIRCE, George	24	SW	1832-01-02		A1
5293	PRICE, John D	18	SWSW	1858-06-01		A1
5325	REGIN, Martha	8	NW	1884-12-05		A4
5371	RICHARDS, Thomas H	18	N½NE	1888-05-25		A4
5276	RILEY, Jefferson	33	W½SE	1834-10-01		A1
5322	ROBERTSON, Manoah	2	SWNW	1858-06-01		A1
5323	" "	3	NESE	1858-06-01		A1
5324	" "	3	SENE	1858-06-01		A1
5355	ROBERTSON, Reuben	2	NESW	1858-06-01		A1
5356	" "	2	SWSW	1858-06-01		A1
5403	ROBERTSON, William	14	S½SW	1837-03-20		A1
5402	" "	14	E½NE	1839-09-20		A1
5404	" "	20	SENE	1839-09-20		A1
5405	" "	21	W½NW	1839-09-20		A1
5406	" "	22	SENE	1839-09-20		A1
5221	RUSSELL, Absalom	1	SW	1915-08-12		A1 G205
5249	RUSSELL, Hiram	3	NENW	1854-07-15		A1 R5361
5250	" "	3	W½NW	1858-06-01		A1
5251	" "	4	E½NE	1858-06-01		A1
5350	RUSSELL, Perry G	35	NESE	1837-03-30		A1
5361	RUSSELL, Robert	3	NENW	1858-06-01		A1 R5249
5362	" "	3	W½NE	1858-06-01		A1
5272	RUTLEDGE, James	22	NWSE	1839-09-20		A1
5238	SANDERS, David	28	NESW	1834-10-14		A1
5239	" "	28	SWSW	1834-10-14		A1
5241	SANDERS, Elijah H	28	NWSW	1837-03-20		A1 G209
5241	SANDERS, Owen	28	NWSW	1837-03-20		A1 G209
5387	SANDERS, Philip	15	SW	1915-08-11		A1 G34
5385	SANDERS, William B	28	SESW	1837-03-30		A1
5268	SHARP, Edward G	11	NW	1915-08-09		A1 G110
5306	SMITH, John	33	E½NW	1834-10-01		A1
5305	" "	28	E½SE	1839-09-20		A1
5307	" "	34	SESW	1839-09-20		A1
5303	" "	27	NENE	1853-08-01		A1
5304	" "	27	SWNW	1858-06-01		A1
5282	SMITH, John B	22	SESW	1854-07-15		A1
5283	" "	22	SWSE	1854-07-15		A1
5284	" "	35	NWNW	1858-06-01		A1
5407	SNOW, William	22	NESW	1839-09-20		A1
5300	" "	21	NE	1917-11-14		A1 G124
5391	SNOW, William H	10	E½NE	1858-06-01		A1
5392	" "	10	NW	1858-06-01		A1
5393	" "	10	W½NE	1858-06-01		A1
5271	SPENCER, James O	4	S½NW	1883-08-13		A4
5326	SPENCER, Mary M	4	N½NW	1885-08-05		A1
5342	SPENCER, Octavius	28	NW	1838-08-28		A1
5341	" "	1	SWSE	1853-08-01		A1
5343	" "	31	SWSW	1854-07-15		A1

ID	Individual in Patent	Sec.	Sec. Part	Date Issued	Other Counties	For More Info . . .
5344	SPENCER, Octavus	28	E½NE	1839-09-20		A1
5345	" "	30	NW	1839-09-20		A1
5346	" "	30	W½NE	1839-09-20		A1
5347	" "	30	W½SE	1839-09-20		A1
5348	" "	31	E½SE	1839-09-20		A1
5240	STEWART, Elias	34	NW	1832-01-02		A1
5374	TARRANT, George	10	E½SE	1915-08-09		A3 G191
5274	TARRANT, James	27	NWNW	1839-09-20		A1
5275	" "	27	NWSW	1839-09-20		A1
5221	THOMAS, Benjamin	1	SW	1915-08-12		A1 G205
5294	WORTHINGTON, Benjamin	21	SW	1912-02-15		A1 G71

Patent Map

T18-S R4-W
Huntsville Meridian

Map Group 30

Township Statistics

Parcels Mapped	:	192
Number of Patents	:	166
Number of Individuals	:	117
Patentees Identified	:	109
Number of Surnames	:	81
Multi-Patentee Parcels	:	10
Oldest Patent Date	:	7/9/1823
Most Recent Patent	:	11/14/1917
Block/Lot Parcels	:	0
Parcels Re - Issued	:	2
Parcels that Overlap	:	0
Cities and Towns	:	3
Cemeteries	:	8

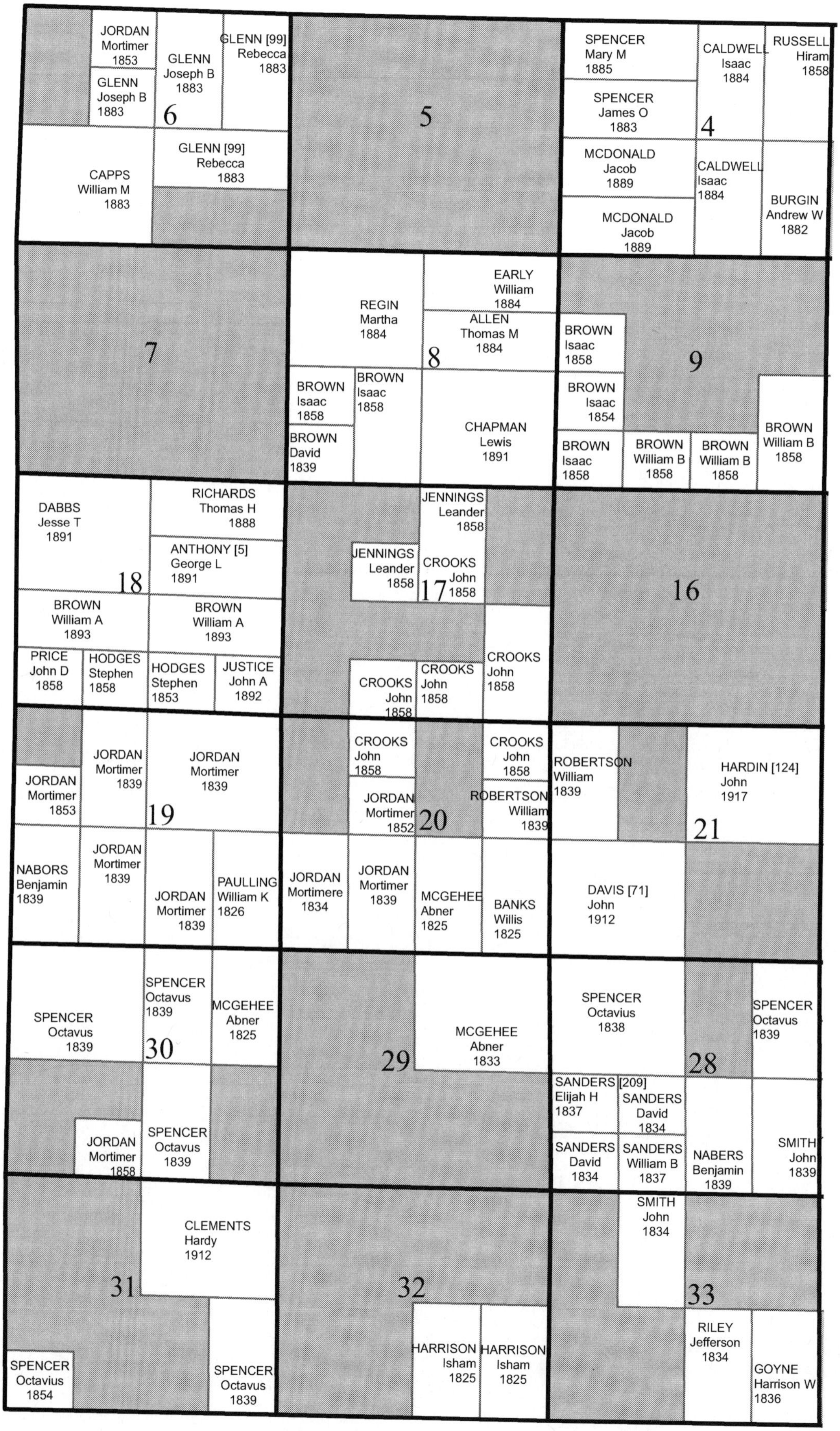

RUSSELL Hiram 1858
RUSSELL Robert 1858
RUSSELL Hiram 1854
RUSSELL Robert 1858
ROBERTSON Manoah 1858
3
ROBERTSON Manoah 1858

BROWN Robert W 1858
BROWN Robert W 1858
LOVE John B 1884
BROWN Robert W 1858
NELSON James 1839
ROBERTSON Manoah 1858
2
MCDONALD Franklin R 1883
ROBERTSON Reuben 1858
DRAKE Ozias 1839
ROBERTSON Reuben 1858
BROWN David 1840
BAGLEY Joab 1858

JOHNSON Mastin 1839
JOHNSON Mastin 1839
1
RUSSELL [205] Absalom 1915
MARTIN Andrew 1839
EUBANK William C 1849
SPENCER Octavius 1853
LEWIS William R 1852

SNOW William H 1858
SNOW William H 1858
SNOW William H 1858
10
BROWN William B 1858
BROWN William 1837
OWEN [191] Thomas 1915

HALL [110] James 1915
11
ENGLISH Alexander 1915

FIELDS Moses 1915
PATTERSON William 1823
LEWIS William R 1852
LACEY Thomas S 1889
12
DRAKE William G 1839
BURGIN William M 1858
BURGIN James T 1885
MARTIN John 1852

MCMILLAN William 1837
LEE Archelaus 1837
15
BROWN [34] William 1915

HODGES Joseph 1832
HODGES John C 1849
ROBERTSON William 1839
14
HODGES Joseph 1837
ROBERTSON William 1837

HAWKINS Samuel 1858
MARTIN John 1852
13
HAWKINS Samuel 1850
CLICK Matthew M 1839

HODGES Stephen 1839
HAWKINS David 1858
ROBERTSON William 1839
22
SNOW William 1839
RUTLEDGE James 1839
AYRES Joseph 1858
BALL James 1839
SMITH John B 1854
SMITH John B 1854
AYRES Joseph 1854

HAWKINS David 1858
OWEN Robert 1850
23
HAWKINS David 1858
AYRES Joseph 1854
GOYNE John 1839
GOYNE John 1833

24
PEIRCE George 1832

TARRANT James 1839
KELLY James 1839
SMITH John 1853
SMITH John 1858
ATWOOD Joseph H 1839
27
TARRANT James 1839
BROWN Joseph 1839
HENLY Darby 1832
BROWN Joseph 1839

26
AYRES Joseph 1837

DICKINSON James 1839
DICKINSON James 1837
DICKINSON James 1838
25
DICKINSON James 1839
BASS John 1913

STEWART Elias 1832
34
EUBANKS George 1834
EUBANKS George 1834
SMITH John 1839
HAMAKER John 1853

SMITH John B 1858
DICKENSON Wiley 1837
DUPUY Alfred H 1853
HOLCOMB Thomas M 1837
35
HENLY Darby 1825
HENLY Darby 1825
RUSSELL Perry G 1837
LOVELESS Vinson 1858

HUGHES Robert 1854
DOWNEY Peter 1858
DOWNEY Peter 1858
HUGHES Robert 1858
DRAPER John B 1854
36
LOVELESS Vinson 1858
HUGHES Robert 1858
BARKSDALE William W 1873
LOVELESS Andrew M 1882
HAGER John 1885
HAGER John 1885
IRION William M 1890

Helpful Hints

1. This Map's INDEX can be found on the preceding pages.
2. Refer to Map "C" to see where this Township lies within Jefferson County, Alabama.
3. Numbers within square brackets [ ] denote a multi-patentee land parcel (multi-owner). Refer to Appendix "C" for a full list of members in this group.
4. Areas that look to be crowded with Patentees usually indicate multiple sales of the same parcel (Re-issues) or Overlapping parcels. See this Township's Index for an explanation of these and other circumstances that might explain "odd" groupings of Patentees on this map.

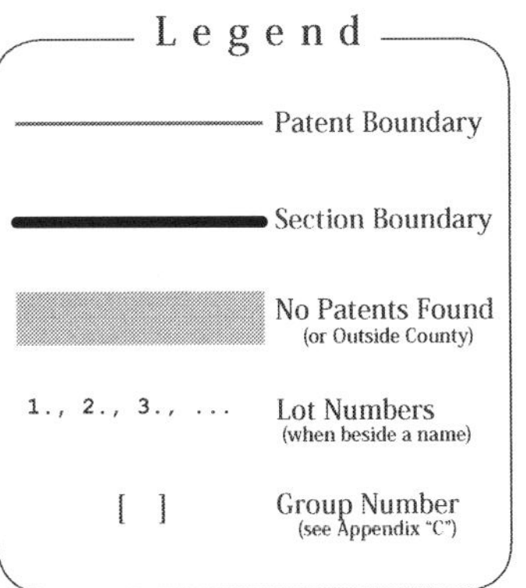

Scale: Section = 1 mile X 1 mile
(generally, with some exceptions)

Road Map

T18-S R4-W
Huntsville Meridian

Map Group 30

Cities & Towns

Dolomite
Fairfield
Pleasant Grove

Cemeteries

Brighton Cemetery
Highland Memorial Gardens
Joley Cemetery
Martin Luther King Junior Memorial Cemetery
Mason Cemetery
Oakdale Cemetery
Union Cemetery
Valhalla Cemetery

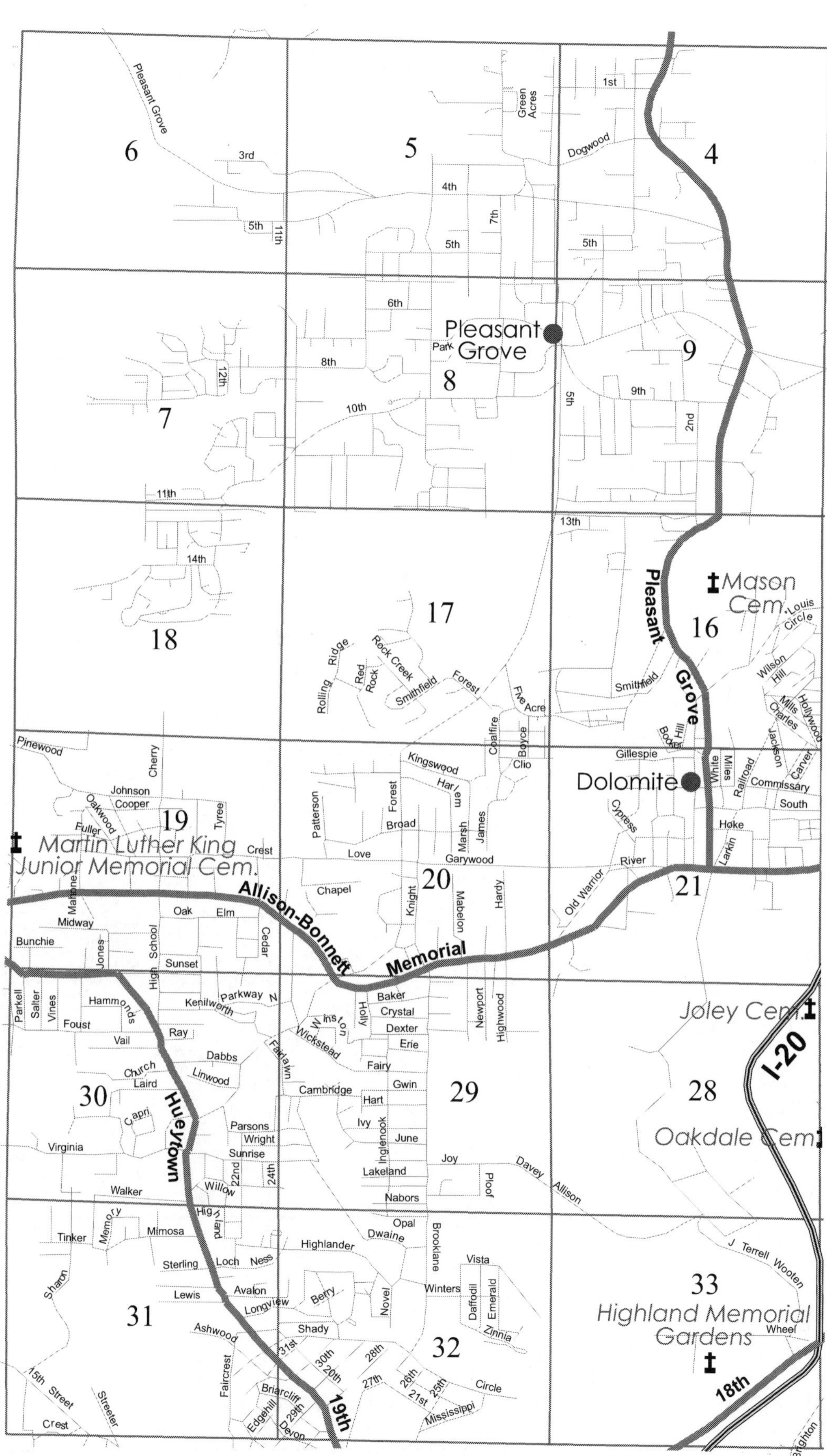

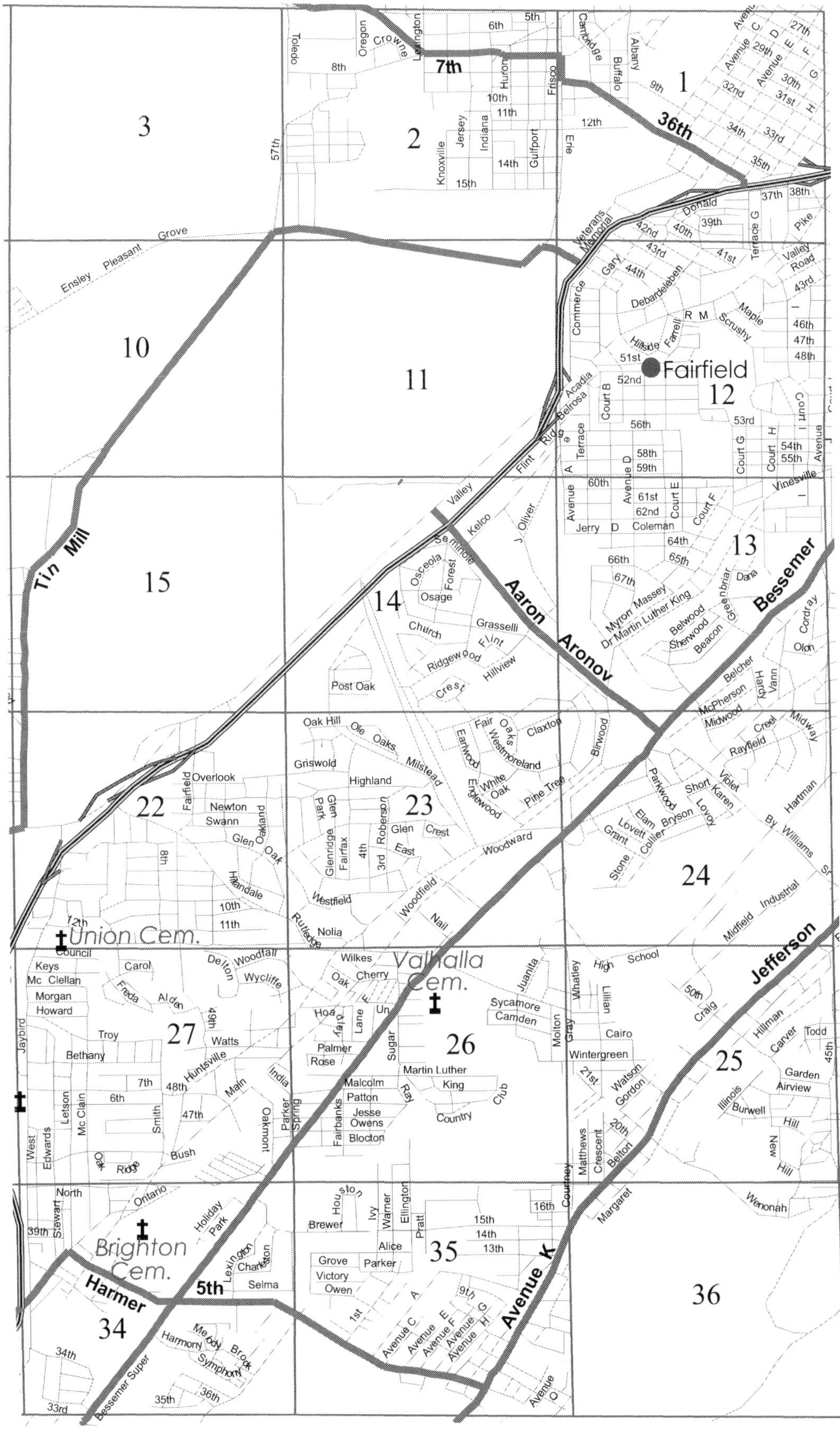

Helpful Hints

1. This road map has a number of uses, but primarily it is to help you: a) find the present location of land owned by your ancestors (at least the general area), b) find cemeteries and city-centers, and c) estimate the route/roads used by Census-takers & tax-assessors.

2. If you plan to travel to Jefferson County to locate cemeteries or land parcels, please pick up a modern travel map for the area before you do. Mapping old land parcels on modern maps is not as exact a science as you might think. Just the slightest variations in public land survey coordinates, estimates of parcel boundaries, or road-map deviations can greatly alter a map's representation of how a road either does or doesn't cross a particular parcel of land.

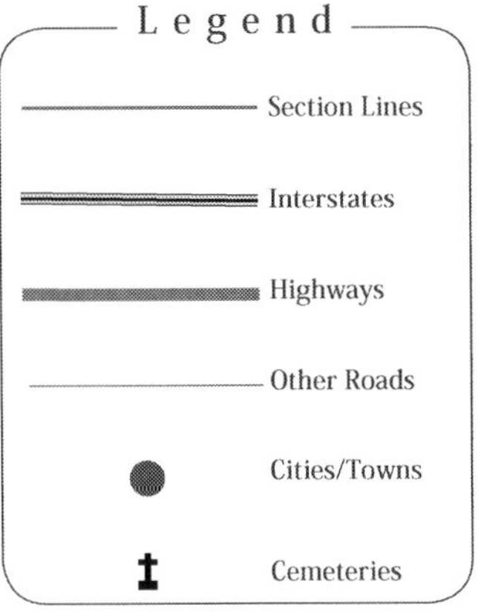

Scale: Section = 1 mile X 1 mile
(generally, with some exceptions)

Historical Map

T18-S R4-W
Huntsville Meridian

Map Group 30

Cities & Towns

- Dolomite
- Fairfield
- Pleasant Grove

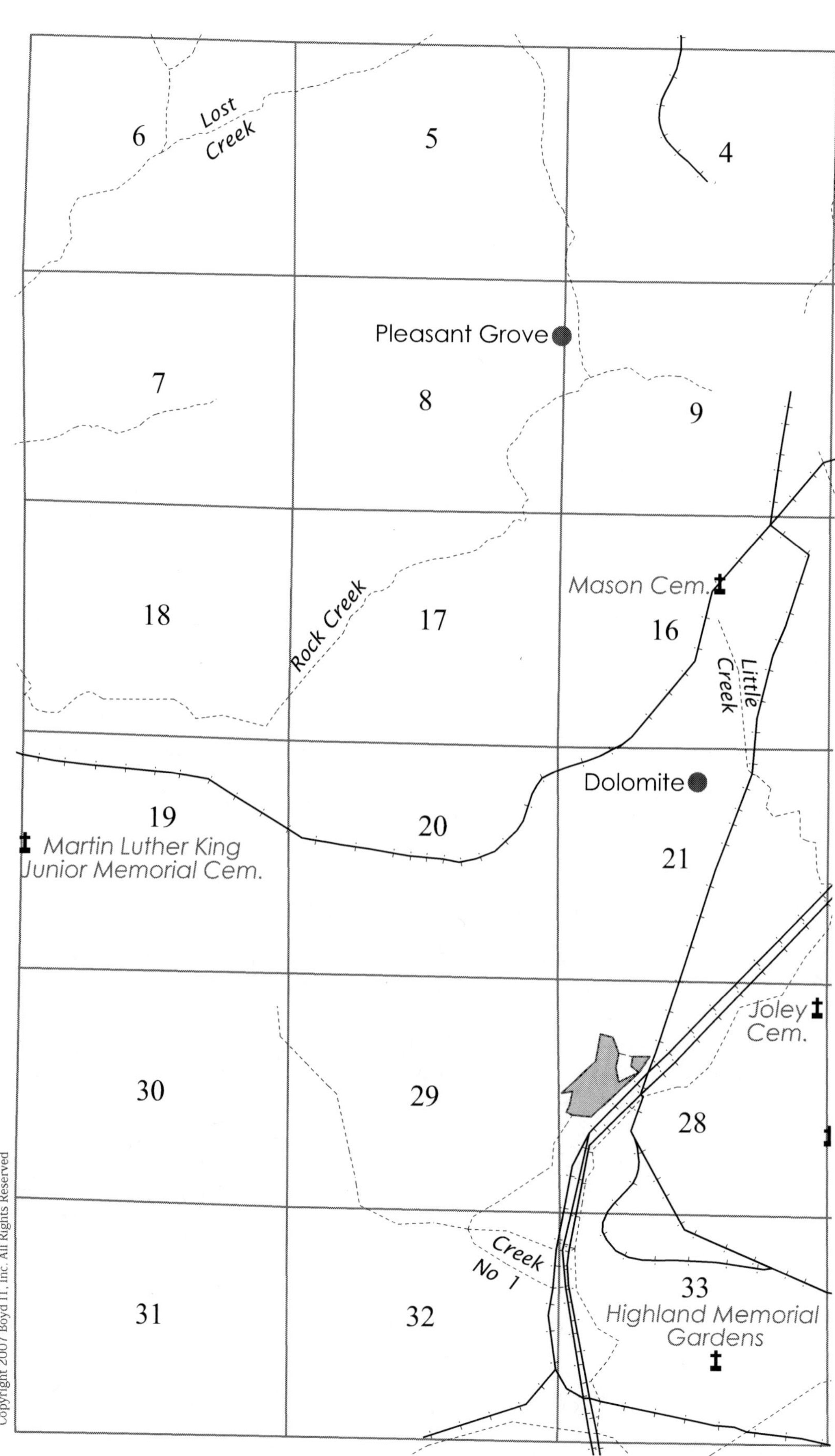

Cemeteries

- Brighton Cemetery
- Highland Memorial Gardens
- Joley Cemetery
- Martin Luther King Junior Memorial Cemetery
- Mason Cemetery
- Oakdale Cemetery
- Union Cemetery
- Valhalla Cemetery

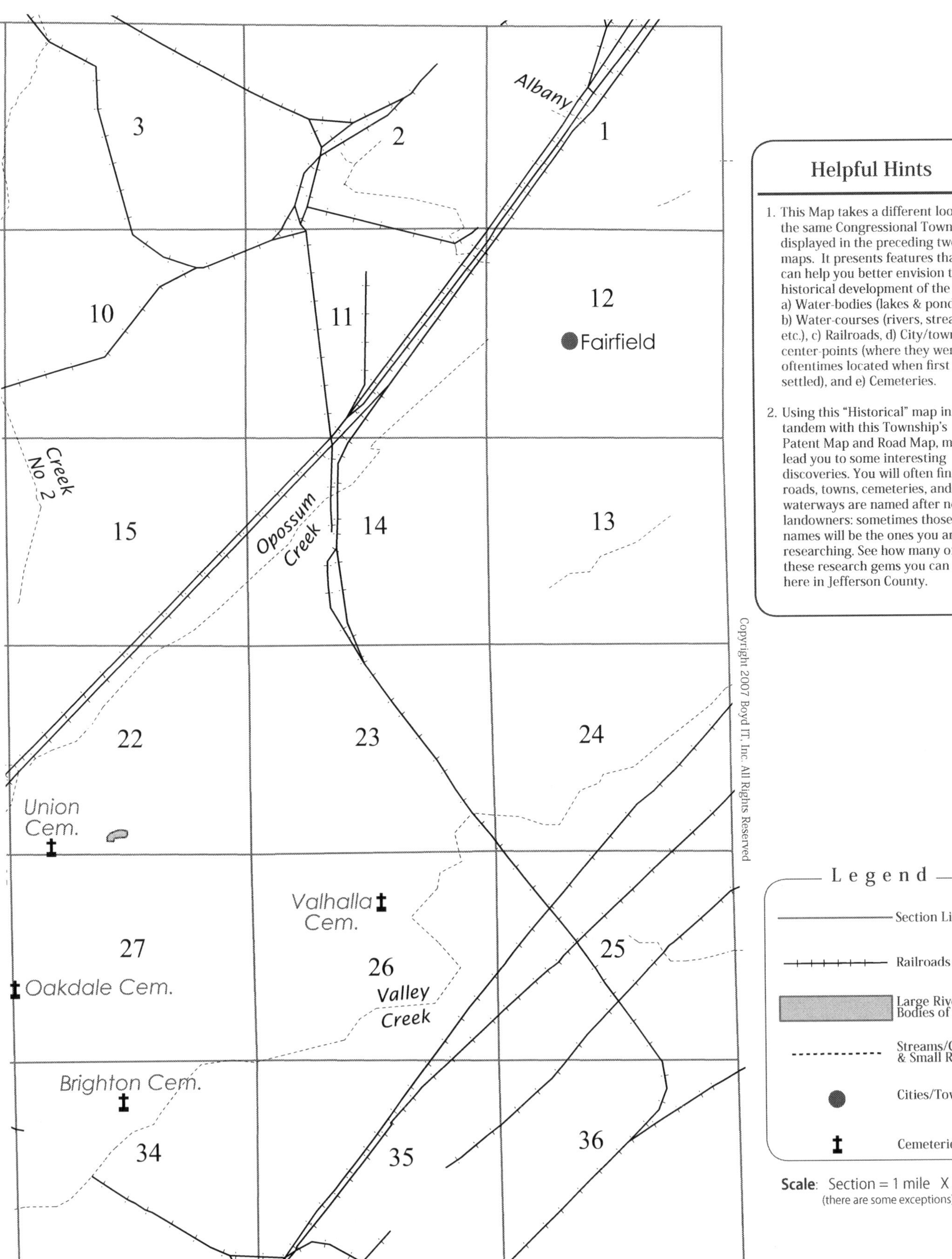

Helpful Hints

1. This Map takes a different look at the same Congressional Township displayed in the preceding two maps. It presents features that can help you better envision the historical development of the area: a) Water-bodies (lakes & ponds), b) Water-courses (rivers, streams, etc.), c) Railroads, d) City/town center-points (where they were oftentimes located when first settled), and e) Cemeteries.

2. Using this "Historical" map in tandem with this Township's Patent Map and Road Map, may lead you to some interesting discoveries. You will often find roads, towns, cemeteries, and waterways are named after nearby landowners: sometimes those names will be the ones you are researching. See how many of these research gems you can find here in Jefferson County.

Legend

- Section Lines
- Railroads
- Large Rivers & Bodies of Water
- Streams/Creeks & Small Rivers
- Cities/Towns
- Cemeteries

Scale: Section = 1 mile X 1 mile
(there are some exceptions)

Map Group 31: Index to Land Patents

Township 18-South Range 3-West (Huntsville)

After you locate an individual in this Index, take note of the Section and Section Part then proceed to the Land Patent map on the pages immediately following. You should have no difficulty locating the corresponding parcel of land.

The "For More Info" Column will lead you to more information about the underlying Patents. See the *Legend* at right, and the "How to Use this Book" chapter, for more information.

LEGEND

"For More Info . . . " column

A = Authority (Legislative Act, See Appendix "A")
B = Block or Lot (location in Section unknown)
C = Cancelled Patent
F = Fractional Section
G = Group (Multi-Patentee Patent, see Appendix "C")
V = Overlaps another Parcel
R = Re-Issued (Parcel patented more than once)

(A & G items require you to look in the Appendixes referred to above. All other Letter-designations followed by a number require you to locate line-items in this index that possess the ID number found after the letter).

ID	Individual in Patent	Sec.	Sec. Part	Date Issued	Other Counties	For More Info . . .
5410	ADAMS, Ace	28	NENE	1834-10-16		A1 G3
5586	ADKINS, Reuben G	35	NESW	1858-06-01		A1
5587	" "	35	NWSE	1858-06-01		A1
5588	" "	35	SWNE	1858-06-01		A1
5632	ADKINS, Thomas M	25	SESW	1858-06-01		A1 C R5633
5634	" "	35	NENE	1858-06-01		A1 C R5635
5636	" "	36	NWNW	1858-06-01		A1 C R5637
5631	" "	25	NESE	1859-04-01		A1
5633	" "	25	SESW	1859-04-01		A1 R5632
5635	" "	35	NENE	1859-04-01		A1 R5634
5637	" "	36	NWNW	1859-04-01		A1 R5636
5489	BAKER, Jacob H	24	E½SE	1858-06-01		A1
5490	" "	24	SWSE	1858-06-01		A1
5519	BASS, John	30	E½SW	1823-06-02		A1 G18
5549	BEAM, Michael	6	W½NW	1824-05-18		A1
5548	BENNETT, Micajah	31	SESE	1858-06-01		A1
5452	BETTER, Edward L	28	SESE	1885-03-16		A1
5652	BIBB, William C	12	N½SE	1867-11-20		A1 G22
5653	" "	12	NE	1867-11-20		A1 G22
5654	" "	12	SENW	1867-11-20		A1 G22
5655	" "	12	SW	1867-11-20		A1 G22
5659	BRADFORD, William D	34	E½NW	1824-05-24		A1
5431	BROWN, Bennett S	26	NESW	1894-05-04		A1
5480	BROWN, Isaac	4	W½SW	1823-07-09		A1
5493	BROWN, James	8	E½SW	1823-06-02		A1
5494	" "	8	W½NE	1823-06-02		A1
5495	" "	8	W½NW	1823-06-02		A1
5496	" "	8	W½SW	1823-06-02		A1
5538	BRUCE, Linza B	32	SENE	1889-12-28		A1
5652	BUFFINGTON, William C	12	N½SE	1867-11-20		A1 G22
5653	" "	12	NE	1867-11-20		A1 G22
5654	" "	12	SENW	1867-11-20		A1 G22
5655	" "	12	SW	1867-11-20		A1 G22
5460	BURFORD, Frank	26	SENE	1883-10-01		A4
5461	" "	26	SWNE	1884-12-05		A4
5638	BURFORD, Washington	10	W½SE	1839-09-20		A1
5639	" "	15	NENE	1839-09-20		A1
5640	" "	15	SENW	1839-09-20		A1
5641	BURFORD, Washington C	21	NESE	1858-06-01		A1
5642	" "	21	SENE	1858-06-01		A1
5643	" "	22	S½NW	1858-06-01		A1
5520	BURKS, John	20	W½SW	1825-09-01		A1
5513	BUTLER, Jesse	19	E½NW	1823-06-02		A1 G38
5479	BYARS, Henry K	12	SESE	1858-06-01		A1
5497	BYARS, James C	15	NENW	1853-08-01		A1
5410	BYARS, John	28	NENE	1834-10-16		A1 G3

ID	Individual in Patent	Sec.	Sec. Part	Date Issued	Other Counties	For More Info . . .
5556	BYARS, Nathan	14	E½SE	1839-09-20		A1 G39
5552	" "	23	NENE	1839-09-20		A1
5550	" "	13	SW	1858-06-01		A1
5551	" "	14	SWSE	1858-06-01		A1
5553	" "	23	SENE	1858-06-01		A1
5554	" "	24	NENE	1858-06-01		A1
5555	" "	24	NWNW	1858-06-01		A1
5621	BYARS, Stripling	22	W½SE	1826-05-15		A1
5651	BYARS, William	27	SWSW	1839-09-20		A1
5657	CARITHERS, William	36	NESE	1839-09-20		A1 G44
5658	CARTER, William	32	SWSW	1839-09-20		A1
5468	CLEMENTS, Hardy	19	E½SW	1823-06-02		A1 G54
5469	" "	19	W½NW	1823-06-02		A1 G54
5470	" "	20	E½NW	1823-06-02		A1 G53
5471	" "	20	W½NW	1823-06-02		A1 G53
5512	CLEMENTS, Jesse B	10	W½NW	1823-06-02		A1 G55
5410	COLLY, William	28	NENE	1834-10-16		A1 G3
5432	COOPER, Cader	22	E½SW	1823-07-09		A1
5434	" "	22	W½SW	1824-10-20		A1 R5435
5433	" "	22	SWNE	1839-09-20		A1
5435	" "	22	W½SW	1915-08-11		A1 R5434
5578	CULP, Peter H	25	SENW	1858-06-01		A1
5514	CUNNINGHAM, Jesse	33	NE	1860-04-02		A1
5515	" "	34	W½NW	1860-04-02		A1
5436	DIFFEY, Charles C	23	SESE	1839-09-20		A1
5557	DISON, Nathan J	34	NESW	1885-12-10		A4
5558	" "	34	NWSE	1885-12-10		A4
5652	DONELSON, Presley W	12	N½SE	1867-11-20		A1 G22
5653	" "	12	NE	1867-11-20		A1 G22
5654	" "	12	SENW	1867-11-20		A1 G22
5655	" "	12	SW	1867-11-20		A1 G22
5576	DOWNEY, Peter	25	SESE	1858-06-01		A1
5577	" "	30	W½SW	1858-06-01		A1
5523	DUPEY, John M	12	NWNW	1853-11-15		A1
5525	DUPUY, John M	1	W½SW	1823-06-02		A1
5524	" "	1	E½SW	1839-09-20		A1
5526	" "	11	E½SW	1839-09-20		A1
5527	" "	11	W½SW	1839-09-20		A1
5668	DUPUY, William L	1	SWSE	1839-09-20		A1
5598	EARLE, Samuel S	22	NESE	1854-07-15		A1
5597	" "	22	NENE	1858-06-01		A1
5599	" "	22	SESE	1858-06-01		A1
5600	" "	23	N½SW	1858-06-01		A1
5601	" "	23	NENW	1858-06-01		A1
5602	" "	23	NWNE	1858-06-01		A1
5603	" "	23	S½NW	1858-06-01		A1
5542	EARNEST, Margaret L	26	SWSW	1891-06-19		A4
5656	EUBANK, William C	6	NWSW	1853-08-01		A1
5472	FANCHER, Henry F	34	SESW	1883-04-10		A4
5473	" "	34	SWSE	1883-04-10		A4
5474	" "	34	W½SW	1883-04-10		A4
5544	FORREST, Mary A	5	NWSW	1853-08-01		A1
5475	GILL, Henry H	27	NWSW	1858-06-01		A1
5534	GILL, Joseph K	27	SESW	1858-06-01		A1
5535	" "	27	SWSE	1858-06-01		A1
5662	GILL, William	23	NESE	1858-06-01		A1
5663	" "	26	SESW	1858-06-01		A1
5664	" "	26	SWSE	1858-06-01		A1
5665	" "	35	NENW	1858-06-01		A1
5652	GILMER, George N	12	N½SE	1867-11-20		A1 G22
5653	" "	12	NE	1867-11-20		A1 G22
5654	" "	12	SENW	1867-11-20		A1 G22
5655	" "	12	SW	1867-11-20		A1 G22
5532	GILMORE, John W	24	S½NW	1883-07-03		A4
5455	GLENN, Elias	33	NWSE	1852-01-01		A1
5482	GLENN, Isaac	34	S½NE	1858-06-01		A1
5516	GLENN, Jesse J	26	N½SE	1858-06-01		A1
5451	GOODE, Edward	10	W½SW	1824-05-04		A1
5556	GOYNE, John R	14	E½SE	1839-09-20		A1 G39
5529	" "	27	NENW	1839-09-20		A1
5415	GRACE, Baylis E	15	NWNW	1839-09-20		A1
5426	" "	28	E½NW	1839-09-20		A1
5427	" "	28	W½SW	1839-09-20		A1

ID	Individual in Patent	Sec.	Sec. Part	Date Issued	Other Counties	For More Info . . .
5428	GRACE, Baylis E (Cont'd)	29	NESE	1839-09-20		A1
5424	" "	24	SWNE	1849-08-01		A1
5425	" "	24	SWSW	1849-08-01		A1
5417	" "	15	NWSW	1853-08-01		A1
5422	" "	24	NESW	1854-07-15		A1
5416	" "	15	NWSE	1858-06-01		A1
5418	" "	15	SWNW	1858-06-01		A1
5419	" "	15	SWSW	1858-06-01		A1
5420	" "	21	N½NE	1858-06-01		A1
5421	" "	22	N½NW	1858-06-01		A1
5423	" "	24	NWSW	1858-06-01		A1
5591	GREEN, Robert N	12	SWNW	1854-07-15		A1
5593	" "	14	NWSE	1854-07-15		A1
5594	" "	14	SENW	1854-07-15		A1
5589	" "	11	E½SE	1858-06-01		A1
5590	" "	11	SWSE	1858-06-01		A1
5592	" "	14	NE	1858-06-01		A1
5581	GRIFFIN, Phillip T	23	SESW	1858-06-01		A1
5582	" "	23	SWNE	1858-06-01		A1
5583	" "	23	W½SE	1858-06-01		A1
5584	" "	26	NENW	1858-06-01		A1
5498	HALL, James	15	E½SW	1826-05-15		A1
5410	HALL, Samuel W	28	NENE	1834-10-16		A1 G3
5615	HALL, Stephen	10	E½NW	1823-06-02		A1 G113 V5533
5616	" "	10	W½NE	1823-06-02		A1 G113
5512	" "	10	W½NW	1823-06-02		A1 G55
5613	" "	11	E½NW	1823-06-02		A1
5614	" "	11	NE	1823-06-02		A1
5617	" "	2	E½SE	1823-06-02		A1 G112
5618	" "	2	W½SE	1823-06-02		A1 G112
5448	HANBY, Dewitt M	32	E½SW	1889-12-28		A1
5440	HAWKINS, David	10	NESW	1839-09-20		A1
5441	" "	11	NWSE	1839-09-20		A1
5442	" "	15	W½NE	1839-09-20		A1
5562	HAWKINS, Nathaniel	28	SWNW	1853-11-15		A1
5564	" "	5	NWNE	1854-07-15		A1
5565	" "	5	SENW	1854-07-15		A1
5559	" "	21	E½SW	1858-06-01		A1
5560	" "	21	W½SE	1858-06-01		A1
5561	" "	28	E½SW	1858-06-01		A1
5563	" "	28	W½SE	1858-06-01		A1
5443	HEIFNER, David	15	SENE	1839-09-20		A1
5437	HENLEY, Darby	19	E½NE	1823-06-02		A1
5438	" "	19	W½NE	1823-06-02		A1
5439	" "	19	W½SE	1823-06-02		A1 G127
5519	HODGE, John	30	E½SW	1823-06-02		A1 G18
5536	IGOW, Joseph L	36	SESE	1858-06-01		A1
5462	JACOBS, George	36	E½NW	1892-01-20		A4
5463	" "	36	N½NE	1892-01-20		A4
5476	JACOBS, Henry	36	SESW	1891-11-23		A4
5477	" "	36	SWNW	1891-11-23		A4
5478	" "	36	W½SW	1891-11-23		A4
5488	JOHNSON, Ivy	32	W½SE	1885-03-16		A4
5410	JONES, Charles P	28	NENE	1834-10-16		A1 G3
5617	KELLY, Moses	2	E½SE	1823-06-02		A1 G112
5618	" "	2	W½SE	1823-06-02		A1 G112
5585	KEMP, Rebecca	5	SWNE	1854-07-15		A1
5483	KILLAUGH, Isaac	4	E½SW	1824-05-24		A1
5484	KILLOUGH, Isaac	10	E½NE	1823-06-02		A1
5485	" "	11	W½NW	1823-06-02		A1
5449	LACEY, Drury S	27	SWNW	1858-06-01		A1
5537	LACEY, Joshua	7	E½SE	1823-06-02		A1
5669	LACY, William	7	SWNE	1839-09-20		A1
5487	LANDRUM, Isham	5	W½NW	1824-05-25		A1
5595	LANE, Sampson	7	E½SW	1823-06-02		A1 G154
5596	" "	7	W½SE	1823-06-02		A1 G154
5486	LE FEVRE, ISAAC	34	NESE	1888-07-24		A1
5670	LEWIS, William R	6	SWSW	1852-01-01		A1
5660	LINTHICUM, William G	21	SESE	1839-09-20		A1
5661	" "	28	W½NE	1839-09-20		A1
5499	LITTLE, James	36	S½NE	1894-12-07		A4
5410	MARTIN, John	28	NENE	1834-10-16		A1 G3
5528	" "	7	SWSW	1837-04-01		A1

ID	Individual in Patent	Sec.	Sec. Part	Date Issued	Other Counties	For More Info . . .
5539	MARTIN, Louis D	7	NWNE	1852-01-01		A1
5504	MASSEY, James	13	NENW	1850-04-01		A1
5491	MASSEY, James A	24	NWSE	1889-11-21		A4
5492	" "	24	SESW	1889-11-21		A4
5531	MASSEY, John T	12	SWSE	1858-06-01		A1
5622	MASSEY, Thomas A	13	SWNW	1849-08-01		A1
5626	MASSEY, Thomas D	36	NESW	1891-05-29		A4
5627	" "	36	W½SE	1891-05-29		A4
5615	MCCARTNEY, James	10	E½NW	1823-06-02		A1 G113 V5533
5616	" "	10	W½NE	1823-06-02		A1 G113
5439	" "	19	W½SE	1823-06-02		A1 G127
5517	MCCLINTOCK, John A	34	SESE	1858-06-01		A1
5518	" "	35	SWSW	1858-06-01		A1
5511	MCWILLIAMS, James W	6	NWNE	1853-08-01		A1
5510	" "	5	NENW	1854-07-15		A1
5410	MITCHELL, Roland	28	NENE	1834-10-16		A1 G3
5652	MOSES, Alfred H	12	N½SE	1867-11-20		A1 G22
5653	" "	12	NE	1867-11-20		A1 G22
5654	" "	12	SENW	1867-11-20		A1 G22
5655	" "	12	SW	1867-11-20		A1 G22
5543	MUNKUS, Marion F	26	SESE	1896-01-14		A4
5429	NABERS, Benjamin G	30	N½SE	1858-06-01		A1
5430	" "	30	SENE	1858-06-01		A1
5456	NABERS, Francis D	20	NENE	1853-08-01		A1
5457	" "	20	NESW	1853-08-01		A1
5458	" "	20	SWNE	1853-08-01		A1
5481	NABERS, Isaac G	30	NENE	1852-01-01		A1
5545	NABORS, Matilda	20	SE	1858-06-01		A1
5546	" "	20	SENE	1858-06-01		A1
5547	" "	20	SESW	1858-06-01		A1
5459	NABOURS, Francis	8	E½NE	1825-12-01		A1
5500	NORMENT, James M	29	E½SW	1858-06-01		A1
5501	" "	29	W½SE	1858-06-01		A1
5502	" "	32	E½NW	1858-06-01		A1
5503	" "	32	W½NE	1858-06-01		A1
5413	ONEAL, Albert P	34	N½NE	1885-03-16		A4
5619	OWEN, Stephen M	1	W½NE	1823-06-02		A1
5580	PARTAIN, Philemon	12	NENW	1850-04-01		A1
5579	" "	1	N½SE	1858-06-01		A1
5657	PEELER, Montraville	36	NESE	1839-09-20		A1 G44
5470	PIERCE, George	20	E½NW	1823-06-02		A1 G53
5471	" "	20	W½NW	1823-06-02		A1 G53
5521	PITTS, John C	28	NESE	1858-06-01		A1
5522	" "	28	SENE	1858-06-01		A1
5530	RANDOLPH, John	32	E½SE	1885-03-30		A4
5607	ROCKETT, Sarah W	26	NWSW	1854-07-15		A1
5608	" "	26	SWNW	1854-07-15		A1
5609	" "	27	NESE	1854-07-15		A1
5610	" "	23	SWSW	1860-04-02		A1 G203
5611	" "	26	NWNW	1860-04-02		A1 G203
5612	" "	27	E½NE	1860-04-02		A1 G203
5410	ROCKETT, Thomas W	28	NENE	1834-10-16		A1 G3
5610	" "	23	SWSW	1860-04-02		A1 G203
5611	" "	26	NWNW	1860-04-02		A1 G203
5612	" "	27	E½NE	1860-04-02		A1 G203
5414	ROEBUCK, Alfred H	33	E½SW	1858-06-01		A1
5464	ROEBUCK, George	33	NESE	1852-01-01		A1
5411	SANDIFORD, Adelia	5	E½SE	1823-06-02		A1
5412	" "	5	W½SE	1823-06-02		A1
5541	SANDIFORD, Lowry	8	E½NW	1823-06-02		A1
5540	" "	5	E½SW	1824-05-04		A1
5629	SCOTT, Thomas J	27	SENW	1853-11-15		A1
5628	" "	27	NESW	1858-06-01		A1
5630	" "	27	W½NE	1858-06-01		A1
5672	SHACKLEFORD, Zadok D	5	SWSW	1839-09-20		A1
5513	SHARP, Edward G	19	E½NW	1823-06-02		A1 G38
5450	" "	19	W½SW	1823-06-02		A1
5468	SIMS, Edward	19	E½SW	1823-06-02		A1 G54
5469	" "	19	W½NW	1823-06-02		A1 G54
5454	" "	7	E½NE	1823-06-02		A1
5595	" "	7	E½SW	1823-06-02		A1 G154
5596	" "	7	W½SE	1823-06-02		A1 G154
5453	" "	19	E½SE	1823-07-09		A1

ID	Individual in Patent	Sec.	Sec. Part	Date Issued	Other Counties	For More Info . . .
5652	SMITH, Frank J	12	N½SE	1867-11-20		A1 G22
5653	" "	12	NE	1867-11-20		A1 G22
5654	" "	12	SENW	1867-11-20		A1 G22
5655	" "	12	SW	1867-11-20		A1 G22
5574	SPENCER, Octavius	7	N½NW	1852-01-01		A1
5575	" "	7	SENW	1852-01-01		A1
5571	" "	6	E½NE	1853-08-01		A1
5572	" "	6	E½NW	1853-08-01		A1
5573	" "	6	SWNE	1853-08-01		A1
5567	" "	21	SWSW	1854-07-15		A1
5568	" "	28	NWNW	1854-07-15		A1
5566	" "	21	NW	1858-06-01		A1
5569	" "	29	W½NW	1858-06-01		A1
5570	" "	29	W½SW	1858-06-01		A1
5623	SPENCER, Thomas B	6	E½SE	1858-06-01		A1
5624	" "	6	SESW	1858-06-01		A1
5625	" "	6	SWSE	1858-06-01		A1
5410	STEALE, Jonathan	28	NENE	1834-10-16		A1 G3
5410	TERRIL, James T	28	NENE	1834-10-16		A1 G3
5505	TURNER, James	30	S½SE	1858-06-01		A1
5506	" "	31	E½NE	1858-06-01		A1
5507	" "	31	NESE	1858-06-01		A1
5508	" "	32	NWSW	1858-06-01		A1
5509	" "	32	W½NW	1858-06-01		A1
5604	TURNER, Samuel	29	SENE	1858-06-01		A1
5605	" "	29	SESE	1858-06-01		A1
5606	" "	32	NENE	1858-06-01		A1
5644	WALKER, William A	14	N½NW	1854-07-15		A1
5646	" "	14	S½SW	1854-07-15		A1
5645	" "	14	N½SW	1858-06-01		A1
5647	" "	14	SWNW	1858-06-01		A1
5648	" "	15	E½SE	1858-06-01		A1
5649	" "	15	SWSE	1858-06-01		A1
5650	" "	22	NWNE	1858-06-01		A1
5465	WARE, George	30	E½NW	1823-06-02		A1
5466	" "	30	W½NE	1823-06-02		A1
5467	" "	30	W½NW	1823-06-02		A1
5671	WEEMS, William	5	E½NE	1824-04-30		A1
5620	WHARTON, Stephen	20	NWNE	1839-03-15		A1
5444	WILLIAMS, David	31	E½SW	1858-06-01		A1
5445	" "	31	SENW	1858-06-01		A1
5446	" "	31	SWNE	1858-06-01		A1
5447	" "	31	W½SE	1858-06-01		A1
5666	WILLIAMS, William J	24	NENW	1883-07-03		A4
5667	" "	24	NWNE	1883-07-03		A4
5533	WILLINGHAM, John	10	SENW	1850-09-02		A1 V5615

Patent Map

T18-S R3-W
Huntsville Meridian

Map Group 31

Township Statistics

Parcels Mapped	:	263
Number of Patents	:	189
Number of Individuals	:	136
Patentees Identified	:	124
Number of Surnames	:	102
Multi-Patentee Parcels	:	24
Oldest Patent Date	:	6/2/1823
Most Recent Patent	:	8/11/1915
Block/Lot Parcels	:	0
Parcels Re - Issued	:	4
Parcels that Overlap	:	2
Cities and Towns	:	0
Cemeteries	:	4

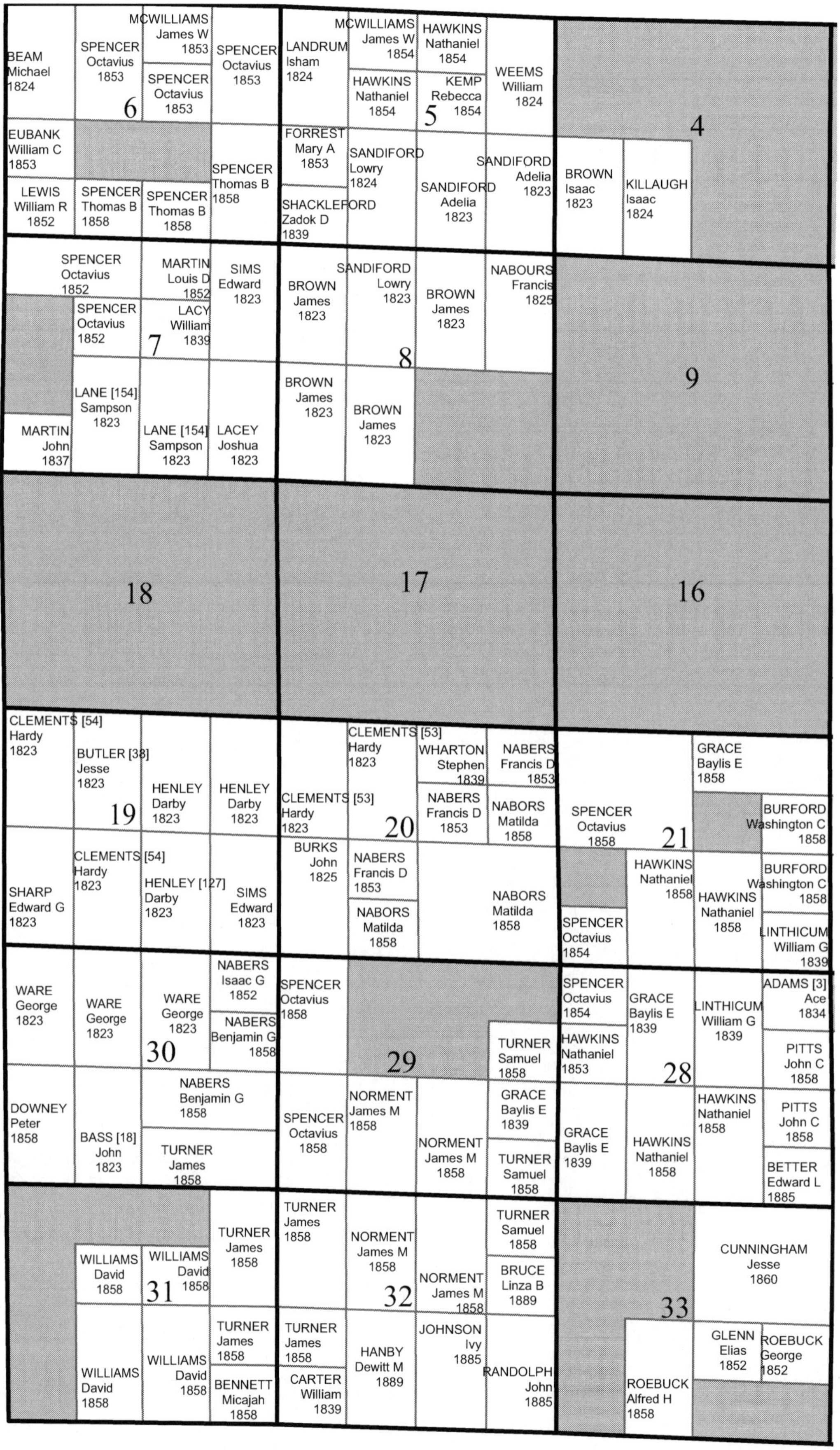

6
BEAM Michael 1824
SPENCER Octavius 1853
MCWILLIAMS James W 1853
SPENCER Octavius 1853
SPENCER Octavius 1853
EUBANK William C 1853
SPENCER Thomas B 1858
LEWIS William R 1852
SPENCER Thomas B 1858
SPENCER Thomas B 1858

5
LANDRUM Isham 1824
MCWILLIAMS James W 1854
HAWKINS Nathaniel 1854
HAWKINS Nathaniel 1854
KEMP Rebecca 1854
WEEMS William 1824
FORREST Mary A 1853
SANDIFORD Lowry 1824
SANDIFORD Adelia 1823
SANDIFORD Adelia 1823
SHACKLEFORD Zadok D 1839

4
BROWN Isaac 1823
KILLAUGH Isaac 1824

7
SPENCER Octavius 1852
MARTIN Louis D 1852
SIMS Edward 1823
SPENCER Octavius 1852
LACY William 1839
LANE [154] Sampson 1823
MARTIN John 1837
LANE [154] Sampson 1823
LACEY Joshua 1823

8
BROWN James 1823
SANDIFORD Lowry 1823
BROWN James 1823
NABOURS Francis 1825
BROWN James 1823
BROWN James 1823

9

18

17

16

19
CLEMENTS [54] Hardy 1823
BUTLER [38] Jesse 1823
HENLEY Darby 1823
HENLEY Darby 1823
SHARP Edward G 1823
CLEMENTS [54] Hardy 1823
HENLEY [127] Darby 1823
SIMS Edward 1823

20
CLEMENTS [53] Hardy 1823
WHARTON Stephen 1839
NABERS Francis D 1853
CLEMENTS [53] Hardy 1823
NABERS Francis D 1853
NABORS Matilda 1858
BURKS John 1825
NABERS Francis D 1853
NABORS Matilda 1858
NABORS Matilda 1858

21
GRACE Baylis E 1858
SPENCER Octavius 1858
BURFORD Washington C 1858
HAWKINS Nathaniel 1858
BURFORD Washington C 1858
HAWKINS Nathaniel 1858
SPENCER Octavius 1854
LINTHICUM William G 1839

30
WARE George 1823
WARE George 1823
WARE George 1823
NABERS Isaac G 1852
NABERS Benjamin G 1858
DOWNEY Peter 1858
NABERS Benjamin G 1858
BASS [18] John 1823
TURNER James 1858

29
SPENCER Octavius 1858
TURNER Samuel 1858
NORMENT James M 1858
GRACE Baylis E 1839
SPENCER Octavius 1858
NORMENT James M 1858
TURNER Samuel 1858

28
SPENCER Octavius 1854
GRACE Baylis E 1839
LINTHICUM William G 1839
ADAMS [3] Ace 1834
HAWKINS Nathaniel 1853
PITTS John C 1858
HAWKINS Nathaniel 1858
PITTS John C 1858
GRACE Baylis E 1839
HAWKINS Nathaniel 1858
BETTER Edward L 1885

31
TURNER James 1858
WILLIAMS David 1858
WILLIAMS David 1858
TURNER James 1858
WILLIAMS David 1858
WILLIAMS David 1858
BENNETT Micajah 1858

32
TURNER James 1858
NORMENT James M 1858
TURNER Samuel 1858
BRUCE Linza B 1889
NORMENT James M 1858
TURNER James 1858
JOHNSON Ivy 1885
HANBY Dewitt M 1889
CARTER William 1839
RANDOLPH John 1885

33
CUNNINGHAM Jesse 1860
GLENN Elias 1852
ROEBUCK George 1852
ROEBUCK Alfred H 1858

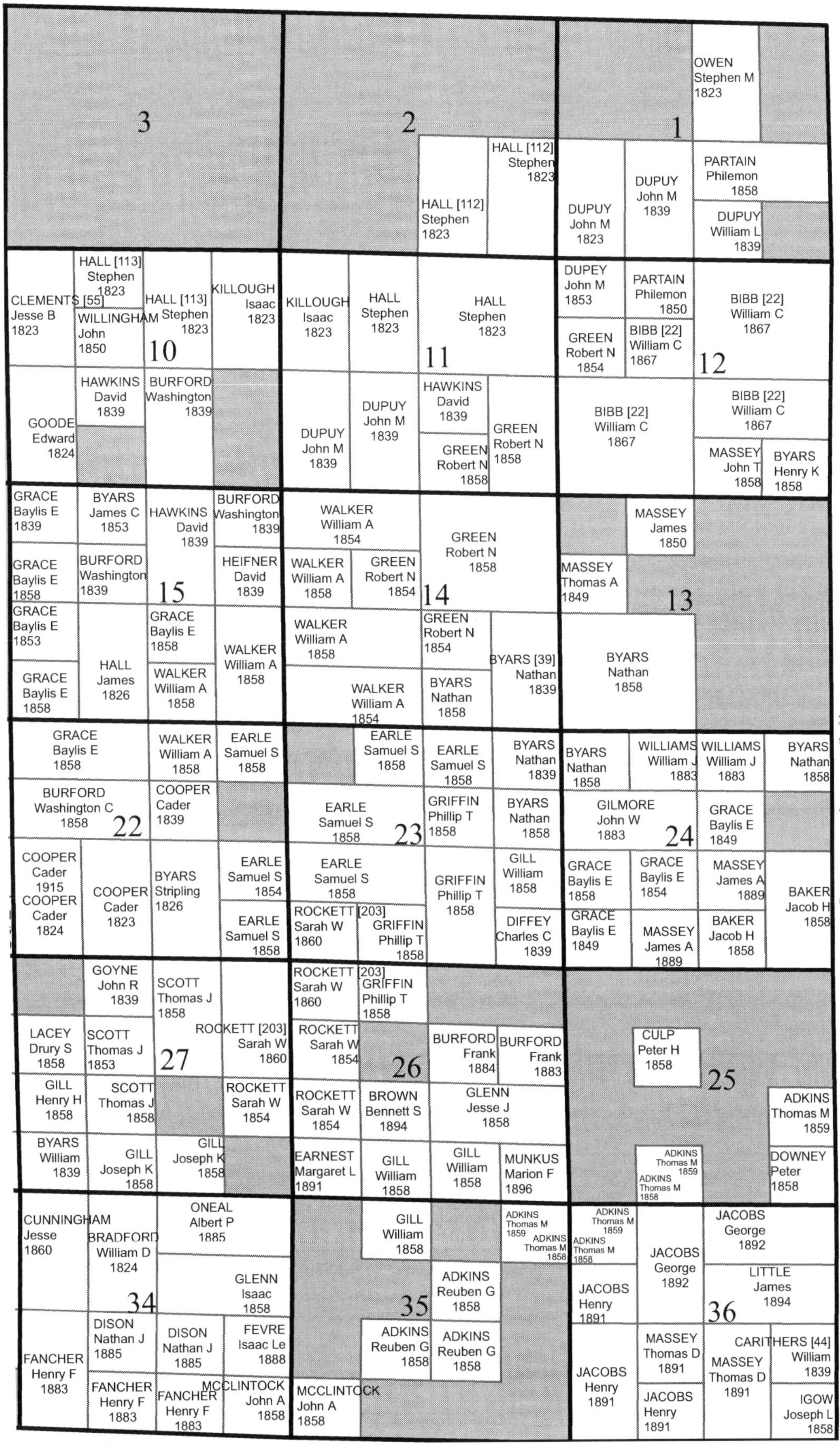

3
2
1
OWEN Stephen M 1823
HALL [112] Stephen 1823
HALL [112] Stephen 1823
DUPUY John M 1823
DUPUY John M 1839
PARTAIN Philemon 1858
DUPUY William L 1839
HALL [113] Stephen 1823
CLEMENTS [55] Jesse B 1823
WILLINGHAM John 1850
HALL [113] Stephen 1823
KILLOUGH Isaac 1823
10
KILLOUGH Isaac 1823
HALL Stephen 1823
HALL Stephen 1823
11
DUPEY John M 1853
PARTAIN Philemon 1850
GREEN Robert N 1854
BIBB [22] William C 1867
BIBB [22] William C 1867
12
GOODE Edward 1824
HAWKINS David 1839
BURFORD Washington 1839
DUPUY John M 1839
DUPUY John M 1839
HAWKINS David 1839
GREEN Robert N 1858
GREEN Robert N 1858
BIBB [22] William C 1867
BIBB [22] William C 1867
MASSEY John T 1858
BYARS Henry K 1858
GRACE Baylis E 1839
BYARS James C 1853
HAWKINS David 1839
BURFORD Washington 1839
WALKER William A 1854
GREEN Robert N 1858
MASSEY James 1850
GRACE Baylis E 1858
BURFORD Washington 1839
15
HEIFNER David 1839
WALKER William A 1858
GREEN Robert N 1854
14
MASSEY Thomas A 1849
13
GRACE Baylis E 1853
GRACE Baylis E 1858
WALKER William A 1858
WALKER William A 1858
GREEN Robert N 1854
BYARS [39] Nathan 1839
BYARS Nathan 1858
GRACE Baylis E 1858
HALL James 1826
WALKER William A 1858
WALKER William A 1854
BYARS Nathan 1858
GRACE Baylis E 1858
WALKER William A 1858
EARLE Samuel S 1858
EARLE Samuel S 1858
EARLE Samuel S 1858
BYARS Nathan 1839
BYARS Nathan 1858
WILLIAMS William J 1883
WILLIAMS William J 1883
BYARS Nathan 1858
BURFORD Washington C 1858
22
COOPER Cader 1839
EARLE Samuel S 1858
23
GRIFFIN Phillip T 1858
BYARS Nathan 1858
GILMORE John W 1883
24
GRACE Baylis E 1849
COOPER Cader 1915
COOPER Cader 1824
COOPER Cader 1823
BYARS Stripling 1826
EARLE Samuel S 1854
EARLE Samuel S 1858
EARLE Samuel S 1858
ROCKETT [203] Sarah W 1860
GRIFFIN Phillip T 1858
GRIFFIN Phillip T 1858
GILL William 1858
DIFFEY Charles C 1839
GRACE Baylis E 1858
GRACE Baylis E 1854
GRACE Baylis E 1849
MASSEY James A 1889
MASSEY James A 1889
BAKER Jacob H 1858
BAKER Jacob H 1858
GOYNE John R 1839
SCOTT Thomas J 1858
ROCKETT [203] Sarah W 1860
GRIFFIN Phillip T 1858
LACEY Drury S 1858
SCOTT Thomas J 1853
27
ROCKETT [203] Sarah W 1860
ROCKETT Sarah W 1854
26
BURFORD Frank 1884
BURFORD Frank 1883
CULP Peter H 1858
25
GILL Henry H 1858
SCOTT Thomas J 1858
ROCKETT Sarah W 1854
ROCKETT Sarah W 1854
BROWN Bennett S 1894
GLENN Jesse J 1858
ADKINS Thomas M 1859
BYARS William 1839
GILL Joseph K 1858
GILL Joseph K 1858
EARNEST Margaret L 1891
GILL William 1858
GILL William 1858
MUNKUS Marion F 1896
ADKINS Thomas M 1859
ADKINS Thomas M 1858
DOWNEY Peter 1858
CUNNINGHAM Jesse 1860
BRADFORD William D 1824
ONEAL Albert P 1885
GILL William 1858
ADKINS Thomas M 1859
ADKINS Thomas M 1858
ADKINS Thomas M 1859
ADKINS Thomas M 1858
JACOBS George 1892
JACOBS George 1892
GLENN Isaac 1858
34
ADKINS Reuben G 1858
35
JACOBS Henry 1891
LITTLE James 1894
36
DISON Nathan J 1885
DISON Nathan J 1885
FEVRE Isaac Le 1888
ADKINS Reuben G 1858
ADKINS Reuben G 1858
MASSEY Thomas D 1891
CARITHERS [44] William 1839
MASSEY Thomas D 1891
FANCHER Henry F 1883
FANCHER Henry F 1883
FANCHER Henry F 1883
MCCLINTOCK John A 1858
MCCLINTOCK John A 1858
JACOBS Henry 1891
JACOBS Henry 1891
IGOW Joseph L 1858

Helpful Hints

1. This Map's INDEX can be found on the preceding pages.
2. Refer to Map "C" to see where this Township lies within Jefferson County, Alabama.
3. Numbers within square brackets [ ] denote a multi-patentee land parcel (multi-owner). Refer to Appendix "C" for a full list of members in this group.
4. Areas that look to be crowded with Patentees usually indicate multiple sales of the same parcel (Re-issues) or Overlapping parcels. See this Township's Index for an explanation of these and other circumstances that might explain "odd" groupings of Patentees on this map.

Legend

- Patent Boundary
- Section Boundary
- No Patents Found (or Outside County)
- 1., 2., 3., ... Lot Numbers (when beside a name)
- [ ] Group Number (see Appendix "C")

Scale: Section = 1 mile X 1 mile (generally, with some exceptions)

Road Map

T18-S R3-W
Huntsville Meridian

Map Group 31

Cities & Towns

None

Cemeteries

Elmwood Cemetery
Grace Hill Cemetery
Oakland Cemetery
Shadowlawn Memorial Park

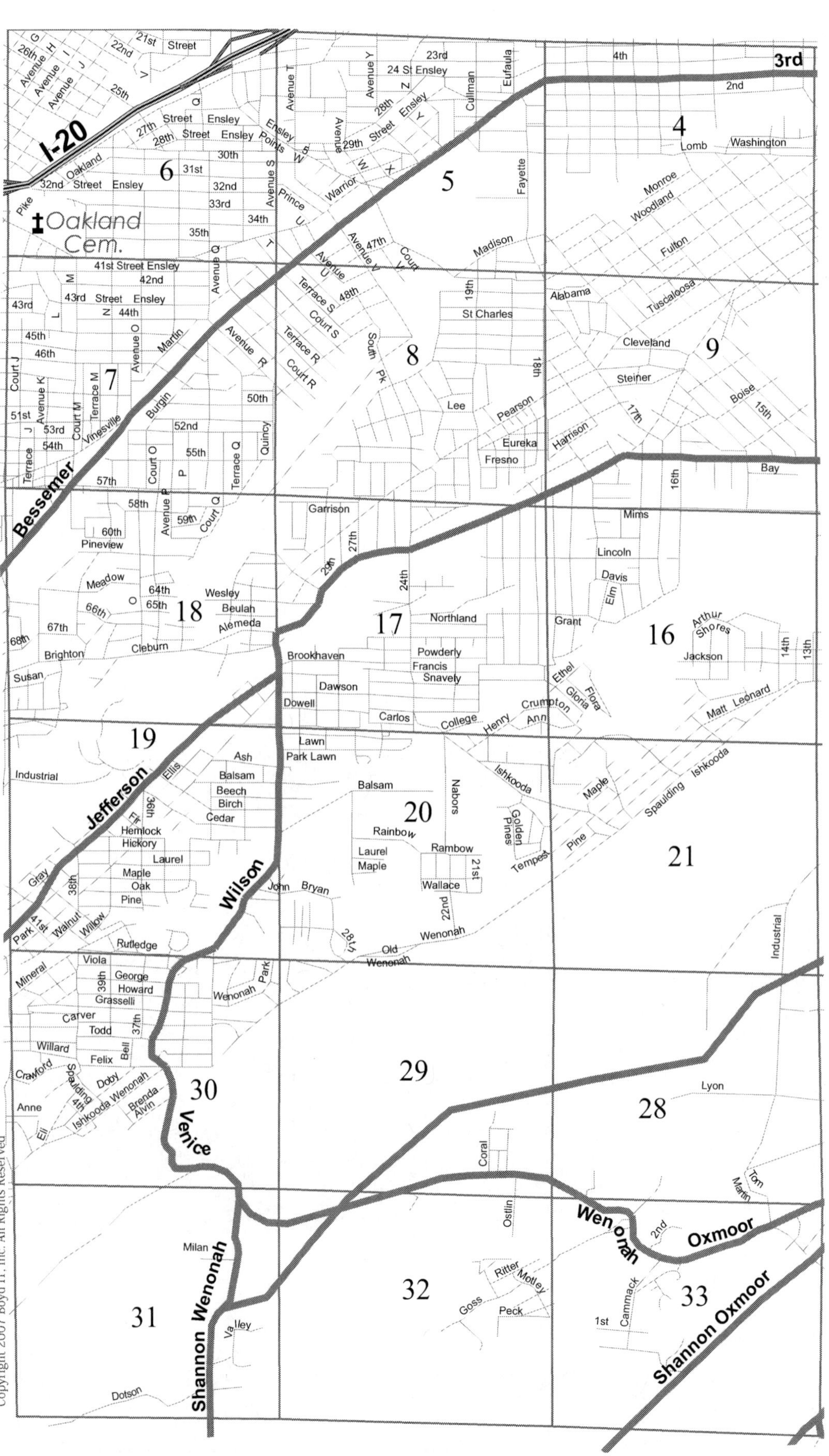

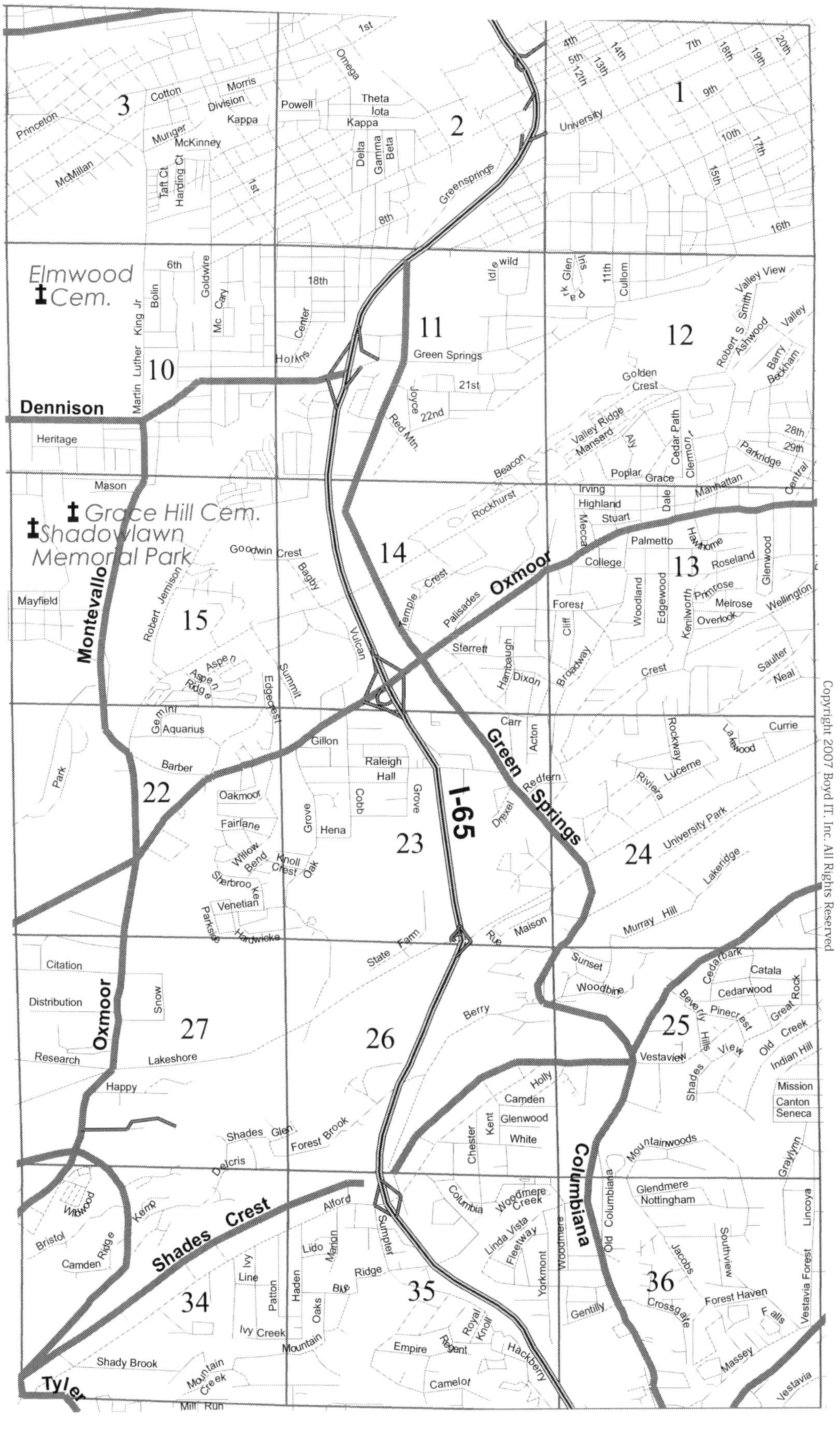

Helpful Hints

1. This road map has a number of uses, but primarily it is to help you: a) find the present location of land owned by your ancestors (at least the general area), b) find cemeteries and city-centers, and c) estimate the route/roads used by Census-takers & tax-assessors.

2. If you plan to travel to Jefferson County to locate cemeteries or land parcels, please pick up a modern travel map for the area before you do. Mapping old land parcels on modern maps is not as exact a science as you might think. Just the slightest variations in public land survey coordinates, estimates of parcel boundaries, or road-map deviations can greatly alter a map's representation of how a road either does or doesn't cross a particular parcel of land.

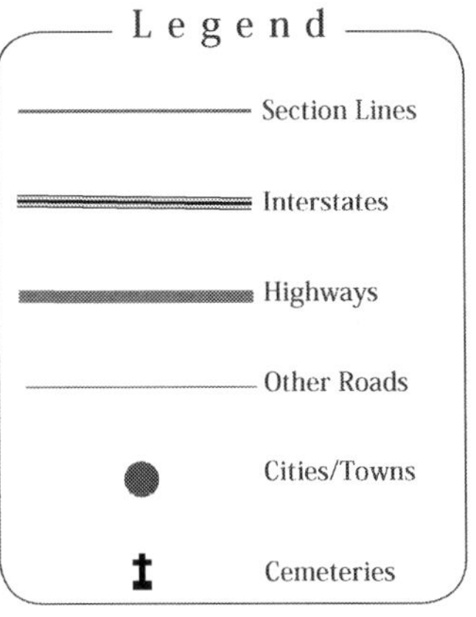

Scale: Section = 1 mile X 1 mile (generally, with some exceptions)

Historical Map

T18-S R3-W
Huntsville Meridian

Map Group 31

Cities & Towns
None

Cemeteries
Elmwood Cemetery
Grace Hill Cemetery
Oakland Cemetery
Shadowlawn Memorial Park

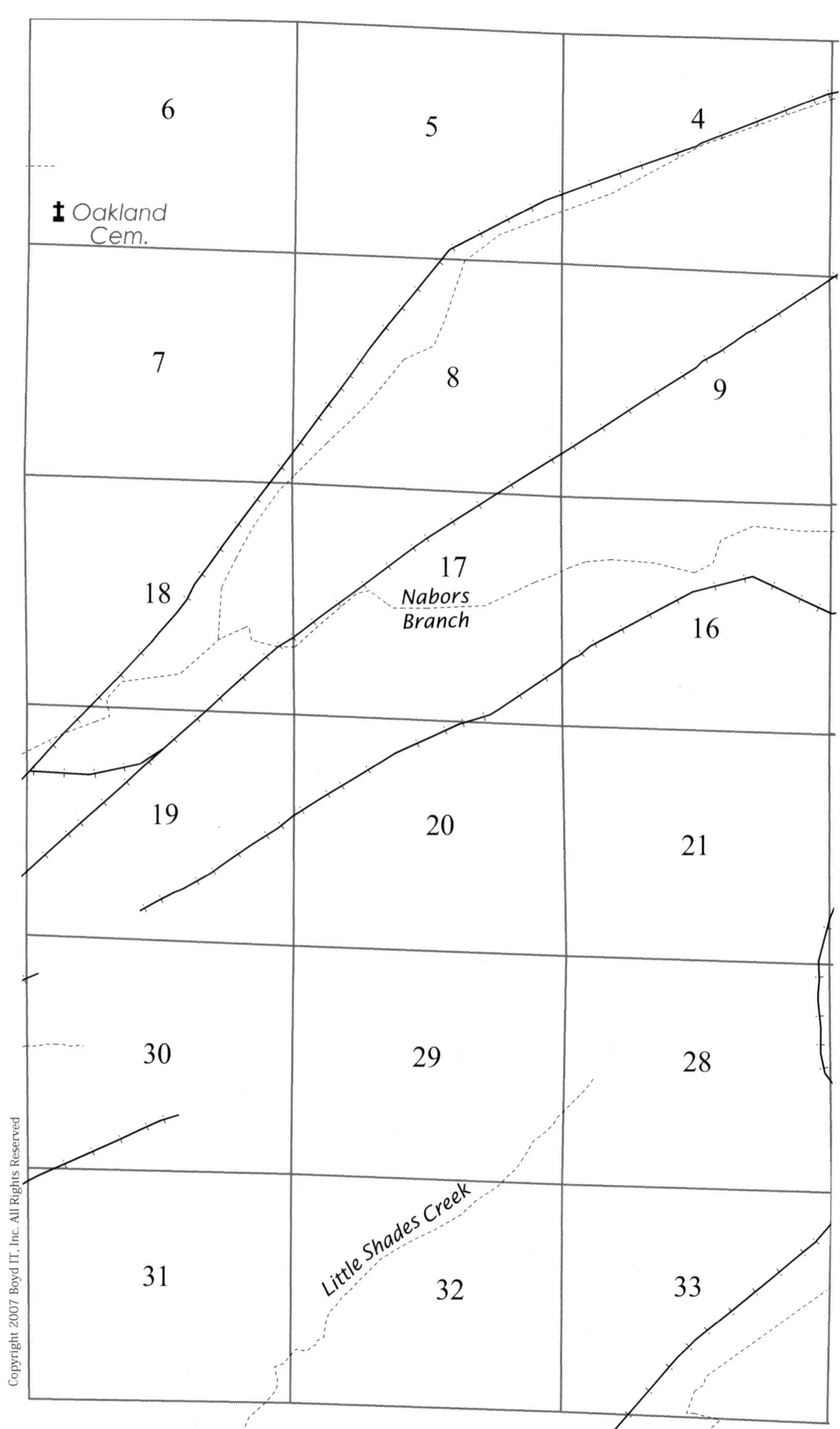

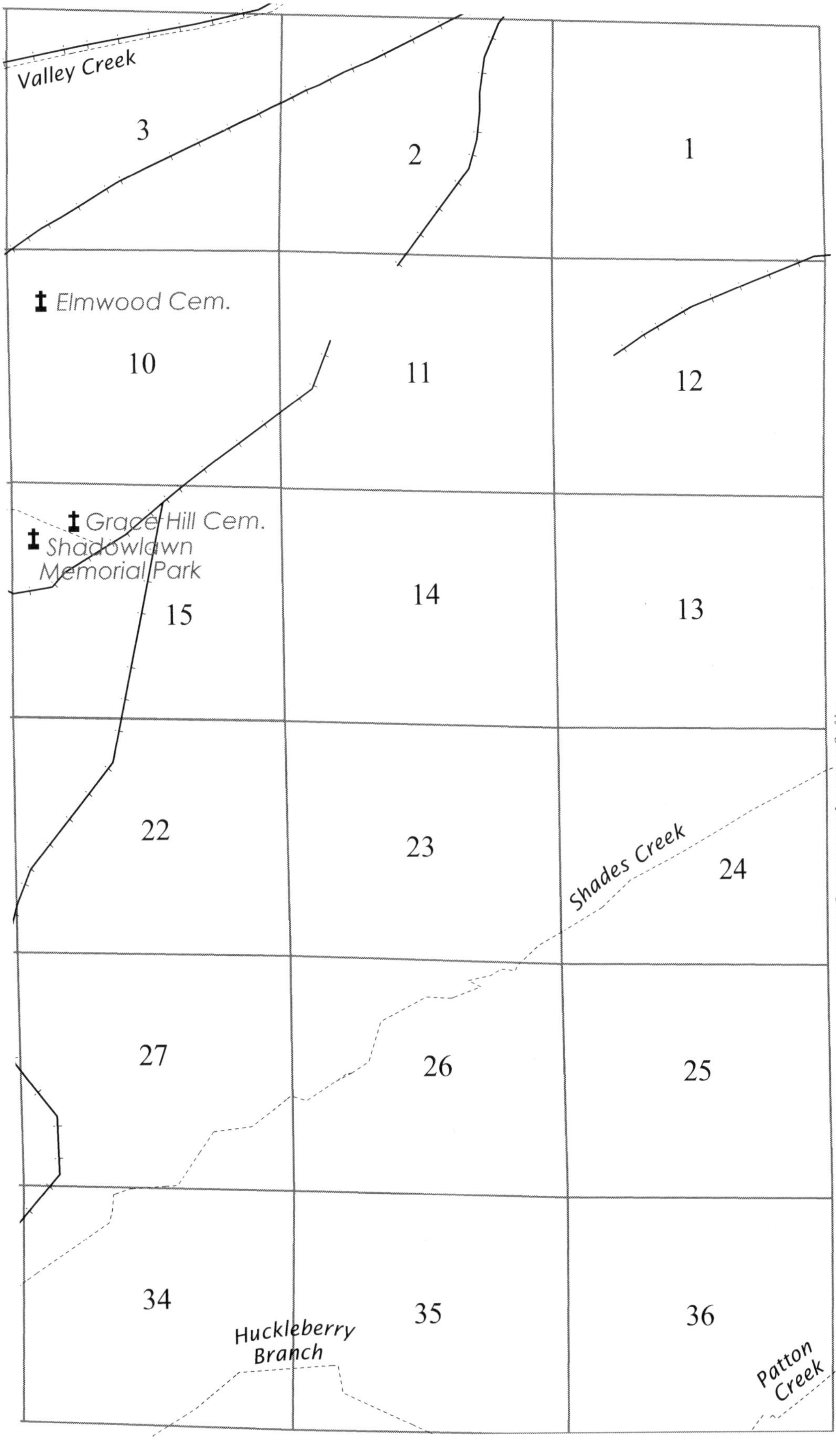

Valley Creek

3 2 1

Elmwood Cem.

10 11 12

Grace Hill Cem.

Shadowlawn Memorial Park

15 14 13

22 23 24

Shades Creek

27 26 25

34 35 36

Huckleberry Branch

Patton Creek

Helpful Hints

1. This Map takes a different look at the same Congressional Township displayed in the preceding two maps. It presents features that can help you better envision the historical development of the area: a) Water-bodies (lakes & ponds), b) Water-courses (rivers, streams, etc.), c) Railroads, d) City/town center-points (where they were oftentimes located when first settled), and e) Cemeteries.

2. Using this "Historical" map in tandem with this Township's Patent Map and Road Map, may lead you to some interesting discoveries. You will often find roads, towns, cemeteries, and waterways are named after nearby landowners: sometimes those names will be the ones you are researching. See how many of these research gems you can find here in Jefferson County.

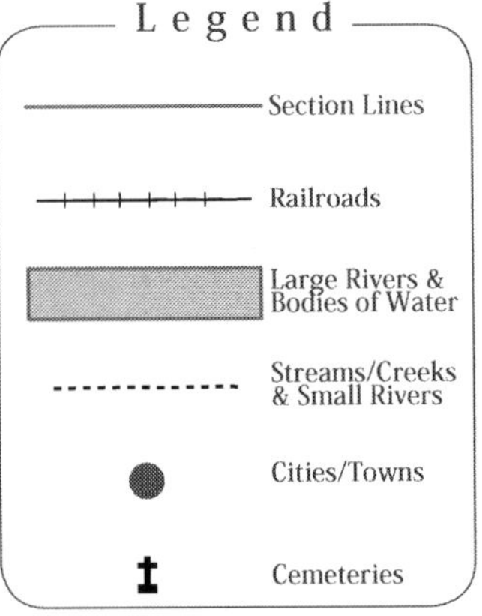

Scale: Section = 1 mile X 1 mile
(there are some exceptions)

Map Group 32: Index to Land Patents

Township 18-South Range 2-West (Huntsville)

After you locate an individual in this Index, take note of the Section and Section Part then proceed to the Land Patent map on the pages immediately following. You should have no difficulty locating the corresponding parcel of land.

The "For More Info" Column will lead you to more information about the underlying Patents. See the *Legend* at right, and the "How to Use this Book" chapter, for more information.

LEGEND

"For More Info . . . " column

A = Authority (Legislative Act, See Appendix "A")
B = Block or Lot (location in Section unknown)
C = Cancelled Patent
F = Fractional Section
G = Group (Multi-Patentee Patent, see Appendix "C")
V = Overlaps another Parcel
R = Re-Issued (Parcel patented more than once)

(A & G items require you to look in the Appendixes referred to above. All other Letter-designations followed by a number require you to locate line-items in this index that possess the ID number found after the letter).

ID	Individual in Patent	Sec.	Sec. Part	Date Issued	Other Counties	For More Info . . .
5721	ACTON, Emberson	35	SESE	1853-11-15	Shelby	A1
5780	ACTON, John V	34	SESW	1858-06-01		A1
5858	ACTON, William	34	NWSW	1852-01-01		A1
5859	" "	34	SENW	1852-01-01		A1
5861	" "	35	NENW	1852-01-01	Shelby	A1
5862	" "	35	NESW	1858-06-01	Shelby	A1
5864	" "	35	SENW	1858-06-01	Shelby	A1
5857	" "	34	NENE	1860-03-01		A1
5863	" "	35	NWSW	1860-03-01	Shelby	A1
5855	" "	27	S½SW	1860-07-02		A1
5856	" "	27	SESE	1860-07-02		A1
5860	" "	34	SWNE	1860-07-02		A1
5874	ACTON, Zephaniah W	33	NESE	1858-06-01		A1
5875	" "	34	NESW	1858-06-01		A1
5876	" "	34	SWNW	1858-06-01		A1
5848	ADKINS, Thomas M	30	NWSW	1859-04-01		A1
5849	" "	30	SWNW	1859-04-01		A1
5674	ARMSTRONG, Abraham	13	NWNW	1839-03-15		A1
5675	ARMSTRONG, Absalom	11	SENE	1837-04-01		A1
5782	ARMSTRONG, Joseph	12	E½SE	1885-05-04		A1
5783	" "	12	SWSE	1885-05-04		A1
5795	ARMSTRONG, Lanzalot	26	NESE	1860-12-01		A1
5796	" "	26	SENE	1860-12-01		A1
5870	ARMSTRONG, William T	10	SE	1891-05-29		A4
5765	BAGLEY, Joab	6	NWNE	1854-07-15		A1
5815	BAGLEY, Nancy	2	N½NW	1883-07-03		A4
5814	" "	2	N½NE	1895-06-03		A4
5673	BAGWELL, Aaron	28	E½NE	1891-04-08		A1 R5843
5766	BAGWELL, John	12	NWNE	1839-09-20		A1
5797	BAGWELL, Larkin	12	E½SW	1889-03-01		A4
5798	" "	12	W½SW	1889-03-14		A1
5751	BAKER, Jacob H	19	SWNW	1858-06-01		A1
5752	" "	19	W½SW	1858-06-01		A1
5686	BEARDEN, Ansel	4	NENW	1858-06-01		A1
5688	BEARDEN, Arter	20	N½NW	1883-08-13		A4
5687	" "	20	N½NE	1884-12-05		A4
5811	BRAGG, More	25	E½SW	1858-06-01	Shelby	A1
5812	" "	25	NWSE	1858-06-01	Shelby	A1
5813	" "	25	SWNE	1858-06-01	Shelby	A1
5842	BRAZIER, Samuel T	26	S½SE	1889-10-07		A1
5712	BROWN, Elijah	6	NENW	1854-07-15		A1
5713	" "	6	NESW	1858-06-01		A1
5714	" "	6	SENW	1858-06-01		A1
5767	BROWN, John	4	NENE	1839-09-20		A1
5800	BULLOCK, Lenard H	26	NWSE	1889-08-02		A4
5801	" "	26	SWNE	1889-08-02		A4

ID	Individual in Patent	Sec.	Sec. Part	Date Issued	Other Counties	For More Info . . .
5738	BYARS, Henry K	18	S½NW	1889-08-16		A4
5739	" "	18	SWNE	1889-08-16		A4
5768	BYARS, John	17	E½NE	1837-03-20		A1
5784	BYERS, Joseph	5	SESE	1858-06-01		A1
5785	" "	5	SWSW	1858-06-01		A1
5786	" "	8	NENE	1858-06-01		A1
5677	CALDWELL, Alexander	34	NENW	1839-09-20		A1
5678	" "	34	NWNE	1839-09-20		A1
5845	CALLAWAY, Stewart B	30	E½NE	1893-06-13		A1
5846	" "	30	E½SE	1893-06-13		A1
5836	CAMAK, Samuel	26	NESW	1884-11-13		A1
5837	" "	26	S½SW	1884-11-13		A1
5838	" "	26	SENW	1884-11-13		A1
5701	CUMMINS, Daniel H	3	NESW	1858-06-01		A1
5702	" "	4	NESE	1858-06-01		A1
5703	" "	4	SENE	1858-06-01		A1
5792	DIMMICK, Joseph O	24	NWNW	1883-05-25		A4
5793	" "	24	NWSE	1883-05-25		A4
5794	" "	24	SWNE	1883-05-25		A4
5708	DODD, David	1	SESE	1858-06-01		A1 V5769
5735	DODD, Henry B	14	NENW	1882-06-30		A1
5736	" "	14	NWNE	1882-06-30		A1
5737	" "	14	SWNE	1891-06-08		A4
5740	DUKE, Henry M	14	E½SE	1882-10-20		A4
5741	" "	14	NESW	1889-03-01		A4
5742	" "	14	NWSE	1889-03-01		A4
5865	DUKE, William H	34	SE	1882-10-30		A1
5753	EASTIS, James A	14	W½NW	1883-10-20		A1
5787	EDWARDS, Joseph	10	NWNW	1894-06-20		A4
5769	FLOWERS, John C	1	E½SE	1858-06-01		A1 V5708
5770	" "	1	NESW	1858-06-01		A1
5771	" "	1	NWSE	1858-06-01		A1
5772	" "	1	SWNE	1858-06-01		A1
5773	" "	1	W½SW	1858-06-01		A1
5719	GLASS, Elisha	11	SE	1837-03-20		A1 G98
5717	" "	15	NWSE	1858-06-01		A1
5718	" "	15	SWNE	1858-06-01		A1
5719	GLASS, Mary	11	SE	1837-03-20		A1 G98
5679	GLENN, Alexander M	12	W½NW	1883-10-01		A4
5824	GOODE, Robert	8	E½SE	1860-07-02		A1
5825	" "	8	SENE	1860-07-02		A1
5826	" "	9	NESW	1860-07-02		A1
5827	" "	9	S½NW	1860-07-02		A1
5828	" "	9	W½SW	1860-07-02		A1
5754	GOODWIN, James E	20	S½SE	1893-05-26		A4
5728	HANNA, Gaberrilla A	12	NWSE	1884-12-05		A4 G123
5729	" "	12	SWNE	1884-12-05		A4 G123
5680	HARRIS, Allen	22	SWNW	1858-06-01		A1
5700	HODGES, Daniel F	4	SESE	1858-06-01		A1
5745	HOWARD, Isaac	25	SWNW	1839-09-20	Shelby	A1
5839	HOWARD, Samuel	24	S½SW	1891-06-29		A4
5840	" "	24	SWSE	1891-06-29		A4
5791	IGOW, Joseph L	31	NWSW	1858-06-01		A1
5709	JEFFERSON, Dicy	24	NENW	1881-12-10		A1 G138
5710	" "	24	NWNE	1881-12-10		A1 G138
5709	JEFFERSON, Green	24	NENW	1881-12-10		A1 G138
5710	" "	24	NWNE	1881-12-10		A1 G138
5731	JOHNSON, Hannah	4	SWNE	1883-07-03		A4
5716	JONES, Elijah S	18	SWSW	1854-07-15		A1
5715	" "	18	NWSW	1858-06-01		A1
5808	JONES, Mary E	32	SENW	1891-06-08		A4
5819	JONES, Perry L	32	N½NW	1899-11-04		A4
5746	JORDAN, Isaac	24	E½NE	1881-12-10		A1
5820	KING, Peyton	5	E½SW	1824-04-22		A1
5711	LEE, Edward	32	SWSW	1837-04-01		A1
5816	LEE, Perry H	32	E½SW	1858-06-01		A1
5817	" "	32	NWSW	1858-06-01		A1
5818	" "	32	SWNW	1858-06-01		A1
5841	LOWERY, Samuel R	20	S½SW	1894-12-07		A4
5730	MARKE, George W	20	S½NE	1884-03-20		A1
5829	MASSEY, Robert J	30	E½NW	1892-01-18		A4
5830	" "	30	W½NE	1892-01-18		A4
5683	MCADOREY, Anna	10	NE	1891-01-15		A4

ID	Individual in Patent	Sec.	Sec. Part	Date Issued	Other Counties	For More Info . . .
5844	MCADORY, Stephen	10	S½SW	1891-09-01		A4
5774	MCCABE, John J	18	SESE	1891-06-18		A1
5696	MCKEEVER, Carrie A	20	NWSW	1900-08-09		A4
5697	" "	20	SWNW	1900-08-09		A4
5873	MCMATH, Winder H	6	NENE	1861-08-01		A1
5725	MERKEL, Frank L	24	NWSW	1891-12-01		A1
5778	MILNER, John T	6	S½NE	1873-12-10		A1
5872	MILNER, Willis J	6	N½SE	1870-09-20		A1
5699	MOORE, Cupit	2	S½NE	1885-03-30		A4
5689	MORRIS, Augustus G	18	NESW	1891-06-29		A4
5690	" "	18	NWSE	1891-06-29		A4
5681	NATIONS, Anderson L	28	E½SW	1892-06-21		A1
5682	" "	28	S½SE	1892-06-21		A1
5777	NATIONS, John	3	S½NW	1837-03-20		A1
5850	NATIONS, Thomas	3	N½NW	1837-03-20		A1
5781	NELSON, Joseph A	5	NWNE	1858-06-01		A1
5691	OATES, Augustus	30	NESW	1889-10-07		A1
5692	" "	30	NWSE	1889-10-07		A1
5693	" "	30	S½SW	1889-10-07		A1
5835	OTTS, Samuel B	6	S½SE	1890-12-18		A1
5732	OWENS, Harvey	20	N½SE	1893-12-02		A4
5733	OWENS, Henderson	20	NESW	1894-05-11		A4
5734	" "	20	SENW	1894-05-11		A4
5684	PALMER, Annie L	10	N½SW	1889-10-07		A1 G192
5685	" "	10	S½NW	1889-10-07		A1 G192
5684	PALMER, Cora C	10	N½SW	1889-10-07		A1 G192
5685	" "	10	S½NW	1889-10-07		A1 G192
5684	PALMER, Mamie A	10	N½SW	1889-10-07		A1 G192
5685	" "	10	S½NW	1889-10-07		A1 G192
5755	PARKER, James E	4	NWNE	1883-07-03		A4
5823	PATTON, Rafe	30	NWNW	1895-10-22		A4
5720	PHELAN, Ellis	6	S½SW	1870-09-20		A1
5832	PIERCE, Salmon	14	SENW	1883-10-20		A1
5833	" "	14	SWSE	1883-10-20		A1
5834	" "	34	SENE	1884-12-05		A1
5757	PLEDGER, James R	34	SWSW	1835-10-01		A1
5799	PLEDGER, Lemuel	33	SESE	1834-10-14		A1
5698	POOL, Celia A	14	W½SW	1884-03-20		A1
5728	POOLE, Gaberrilla A	12	NWSE	1884-12-05		A4 G123
5729	" "	12	SWNE	1884-12-05		A4 G123
5807	POOLE, Lucinda M	12	E½NE	1883-10-01		A4
5867	PULLEN, William	7	E½NE	1824-04-26		A1
5868	" "	8	W½NW	1824-04-26		A1
5869	RILEY, William	8	NWNE	1885-03-30		A4
5851	ROTH, Wendel	18	N½NW	1885-09-10		A4
5760	ROWAN, James	8	E½NW	1823-06-02		A1
5847	RUTHERFORD, Thomas J	4	SW	1858-06-01		A1
5758	SCOTT, James R	4	W½SE	1889-03-16		A4
5788	SHACKELFORD, Joseph H	7	E½SW	1860-04-02		A1
5789	" "	7	S½NW	1860-04-02		A1
5790	" "	7	SWSW	1860-04-02		A1
5821	SOUTH, Philip	5	W½SE	1824-04-22		A1
5694	TANNEHILL, Benjamin H	4	W½NW	1826-05-15		A1
5759	TILERSON, James R	18	E½NE	1895-01-31		A4
5779	TIMMONS, John	6	NWSW	1858-06-01		A1
5695	VEAZEY, Brown J	28	W½NW	1890-07-03		A4
5761	WALKER, James S	33	E½NE	1823-05-01		A1
5704	WATKINS, Daniel	7	NWSW	1839-09-20		A1
5705	" "	8	NESW	1858-06-01		A1
5706	" "	8	SWNE	1858-06-01		A1
5707	" "	8	W½SE	1860-07-02		A1
5722	WATKINS, Enoch A	8	S½SW	1883-07-03		A4
5822	WATKINS, Pleasant H	8	NWSW	1880-02-20		A4
5843	WATKINS, Stephen H	28	E½NE	1888-02-29		A1 R5673
5852	WELDON, William A	26	N½NW	1885-03-16		A4
5853	" "	26	NWSW	1885-03-16		A4
5854	" "	26	SWNW	1885-03-16		A4
5743	WHITE, Henry	30	SWSE	1890-08-16		A1
5762	WHITEHEAD, James	23	NWSE	1835-10-01		A1
5676	WIDEMAN, Absalom	23	SWSE	1858-06-01		A1
5726	WIDEMAN, Franklin	17	NWSW	1858-06-01		A1
5727	" "	17	SWNW	1858-06-01		A1
5744	WIDEMAN, Henry	14	SESW	1837-04-01		A1

ID	Individual in Patent	Sec.	Sec. Part	Date Issued	Other Counties	For More Info . . .
5750	WIDEMAN, Jackson	22	W½NE	1883-09-15		A4
5749	" "	22	E½NE	1884-12-05		A4
5747	WIDEMAN, Jackson H	22	N½NW	1858-06-01		A1
5748	" "	22	SENW	1858-06-01		A1
5871	WILEY, William	17	W½NE	1837-03-20		A1
5763	WILLIAMS, James	18	NWNE	1891-06-29		A4
5809	WILLIS, Mary	24	E½SE	1858-06-01		A1
5810	" "	25	E½NE	1858-06-01	Shelby	A1
5831	WINSTEAD, Robert S	4	SENW	1889-08-02		A4
5802	WIRE, Lorenzo D	29	E½SW	1858-06-01		A1
5803	" "	29	NWSW	1858-06-01		A1
5804	" "	29	S½NW	1858-06-01		A1
5805	" "	29	SWNE	1858-06-01		A1
5806	" "	29	W½SE	1858-06-01		A1
5723	WISE, Ephraim A	22	E½SE	1883-09-15		A4
5724	" "	22	W½SE	1884-12-05		A4
5756	WOOTEN, James F	14	E½NE	1882-10-30		A1
5775	WOOTTEN, John J	12	E½NW	1886-04-10		A4
5764	WRIGHT, Jesse	26	N½NE	1884-12-05		A4
5776	WRIGHT, John L	24	S½NW	1881-12-10		A1
5866	WRIGHT, William J	24	NESW	1881-12-10		A1

Patent Map

T18-S R2-W
Huntsville Meridian

Map Group 32

Township Statistics

Parcels Mapped	:	204
Number of Patents	:	147
Number of Individuals	:	128
Patentees Identified	:	124
Number of Surnames	:	90
Multi-Patentee Parcels	:	7
Oldest Patent Date	:	5/1/1823
Most Recent Patent	:	8/9/1900
Block/Lot Parcels	:	0
Parcels Re - Issued	:	1
Parcels that Overlap	:	2
Cities and Towns	:	0
Cemeteries	:	3

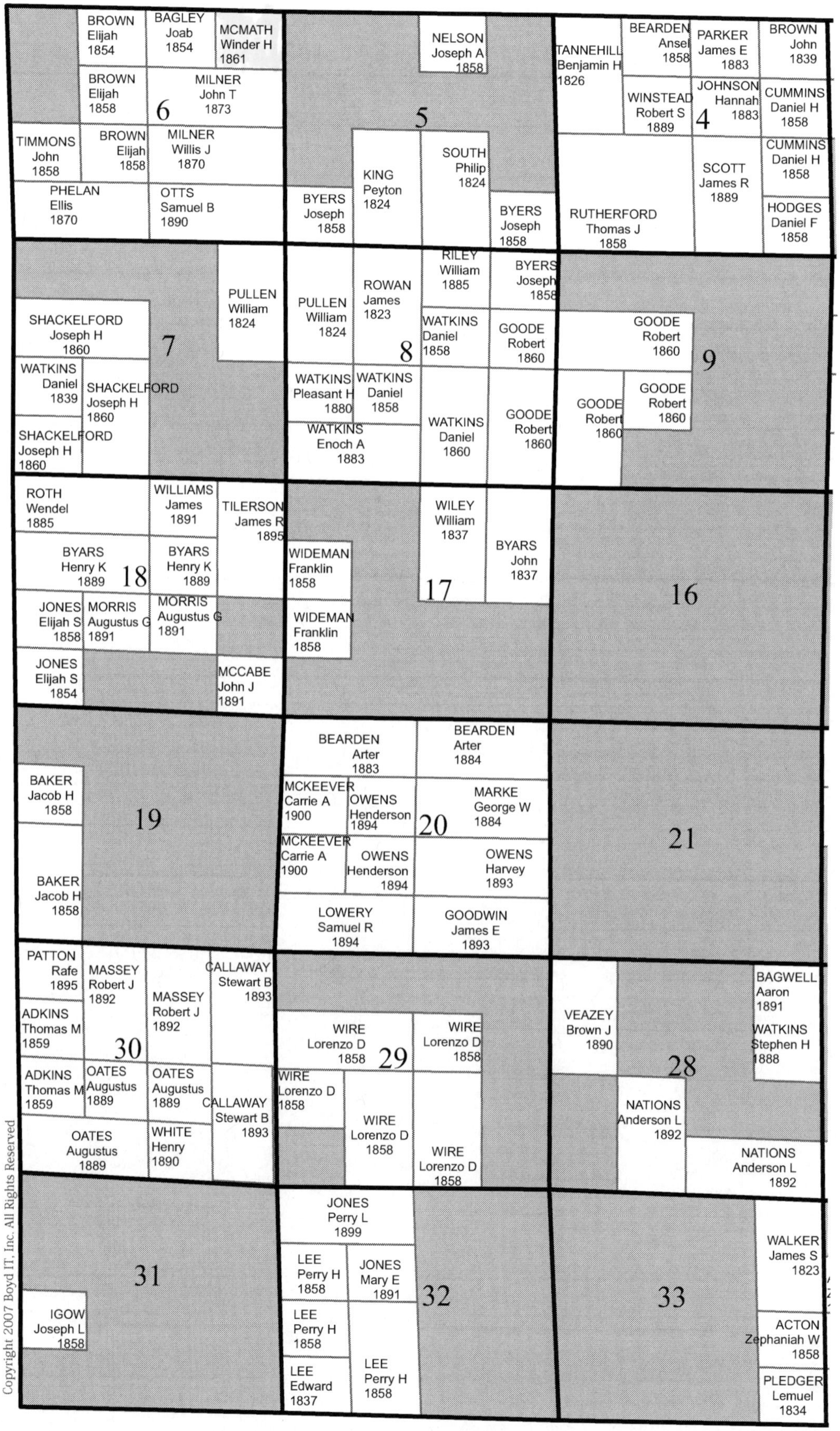

6
BROWN Elijah 1854
BAGLEY Joab 1854
MCMATH Winder H 1861
BROWN Elijah 1858
MILNER John T 1873
TIMMONS John 1858
BROWN Elijah 1858
MILNER Willis J 1870
PHELAN Ellis 1870
OTTS Samuel B 1890

5
NELSON Joseph A 1858
KING Peyton 1824
SOUTH Philip 1824
BYERS Joseph 1858
BYERS Joseph 1858

4
TANNEHILL Benjamin H 1826
BEARDEN Ansel 1858
PARKER James E 1883
BROWN John 1839
WINSTEAD Robert S 1889
JOHNSON Hannah 1883
CUMMINS Daniel H 1858
CUMMINS Daniel H 1858
SCOTT James R 1889
RUTHERFORD Thomas J 1858
HODGES Daniel F 1858

7
PULLEN William 1824
SHACKELFORD Joseph H 1860
WATKINS Daniel 1839
SHACKELFORD Joseph H 1860
SHACKELFORD Joseph H 1860

8
PULLEN William 1824
ROWAN James 1823
RILEY William 1885
BYERS Joseph 1858
WATKINS Daniel 1858
GOODE Robert 1860
WATKINS Pleasant H 1880
WATKINS Daniel 1858
WATKINS Enoch A 1883
WATKINS Daniel 1860
GOODE Robert 1860

9
GOODE Robert 1860
GOODE Robert 1860
GOODE Robert 1860

18
ROTH Wendel 1885
WILLIAMS James 1891
TILERSON James R 1895
BYARS Henry K 1889
BYARS Henry K 1889
JONES Elijah S 1858
MORRIS Augustus G 1891
MORRIS Augustus G 1891
JONES Elijah S 1854
MCCABE John J 1891

17
WIDEMAN Franklin 1858
WILEY William 1837
BYARS John 1837
WIDEMAN Franklin 1858

16

19
BAKER Jacob H 1858
BAKER Jacob H 1858

20
BEARDEN Arter 1883
BEARDEN Arter 1884
MCKEEVER Carrie A 1900
OWENS Henderson 1894
MARKE George W 1884
MCKEEVER Carrie A 1900
OWENS Henderson 1894
OWENS Harvey 1893
LOWERY Samuel R 1894
GOODWIN James E 1893

21

30
PATTON Rafe 1895
MASSEY Robert J 1892
MASSEY Robert J 1892
CALLAWAY Stewart B 1893
ADKINS Thomas M 1859
ADKINS Thomas M 1859
OATES Augustus 1889
OATES Augustus 1889
CALLAWAY Stewart B 1893
OATES Augustus 1889
WHITE Henry 1890

29
WIRE Lorenzo D 1858
WIRE Lorenzo D 1858
WIRE Lorenzo D 1858
WIRE Lorenzo D 1858
WIRE Lorenzo D 1858

28
VEAZEY Brown J 1890
BAGWELL Aaron 1891
WATKINS Stephen H 1888
NATIONS Anderson L 1892
NATIONS Anderson L 1892

31
IGOW Joseph L 1858

32
JONES Perry L 1899
LEE Perry H 1858
JONES Mary E 1891
LEE Perry H 1858
LEE Edward 1837
LEE Perry H 1858

33
WALKER James S 1823
ACTON Zephaniah W 1858
PLEDGER Lemuel 1834

Helpful Hints

1. This Map's INDEX can be found on the preceding pages.
2. Refer to Map "C" to see where this Township lies within Jefferson County, Alabama.
3. Numbers within square brackets [ ] denote a multi-patentee land parcel (multi-owner). Refer to Appendix "C" for a full list of members in this group.
4. Areas that look to be crowded with Patentees usually indicate multiple sales of the same parcel (Re-issues) or Overlapping parcels. See this Township's Index for an explanation of these and other circumstances that might explain "odd" groupings of Patentees on this map.

Legend

- Patent Boundary
- Section Boundary
- No Patents Found (or Outside County)
- 1., 2., 3., ... Lot Numbers (when beside a name)
- [ ] Group Number (see Appendix "C")

Scale: Section = 1 mile X 1 mile (generally, with some exceptions)

Road Map

T18-S R2-W
Huntsville Meridian

Map Group 32

Cities & Towns

None

Cemeteries

Cahaba Heights Cemetery
Union Hill Cemetery
Wise Cemetery

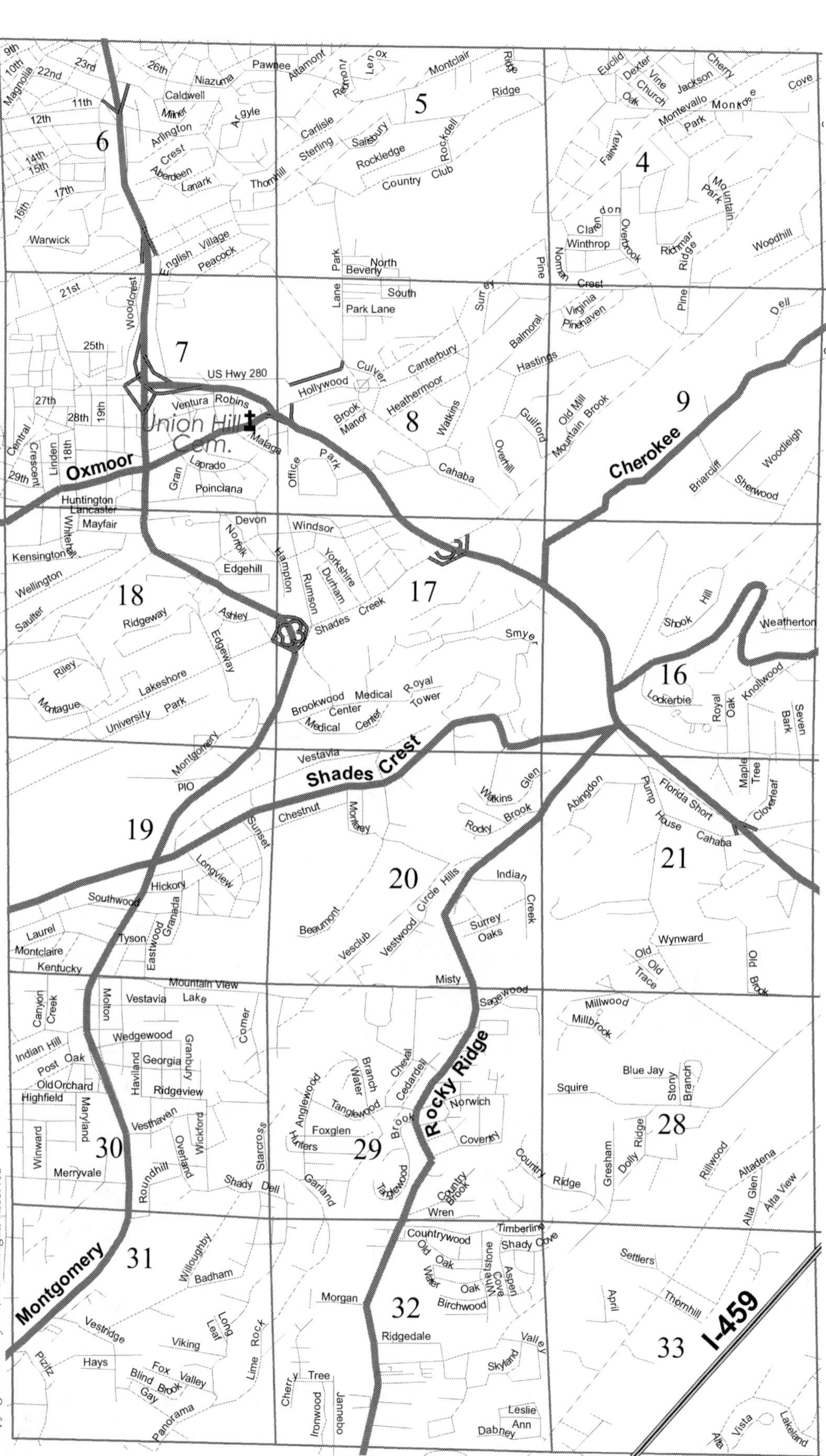

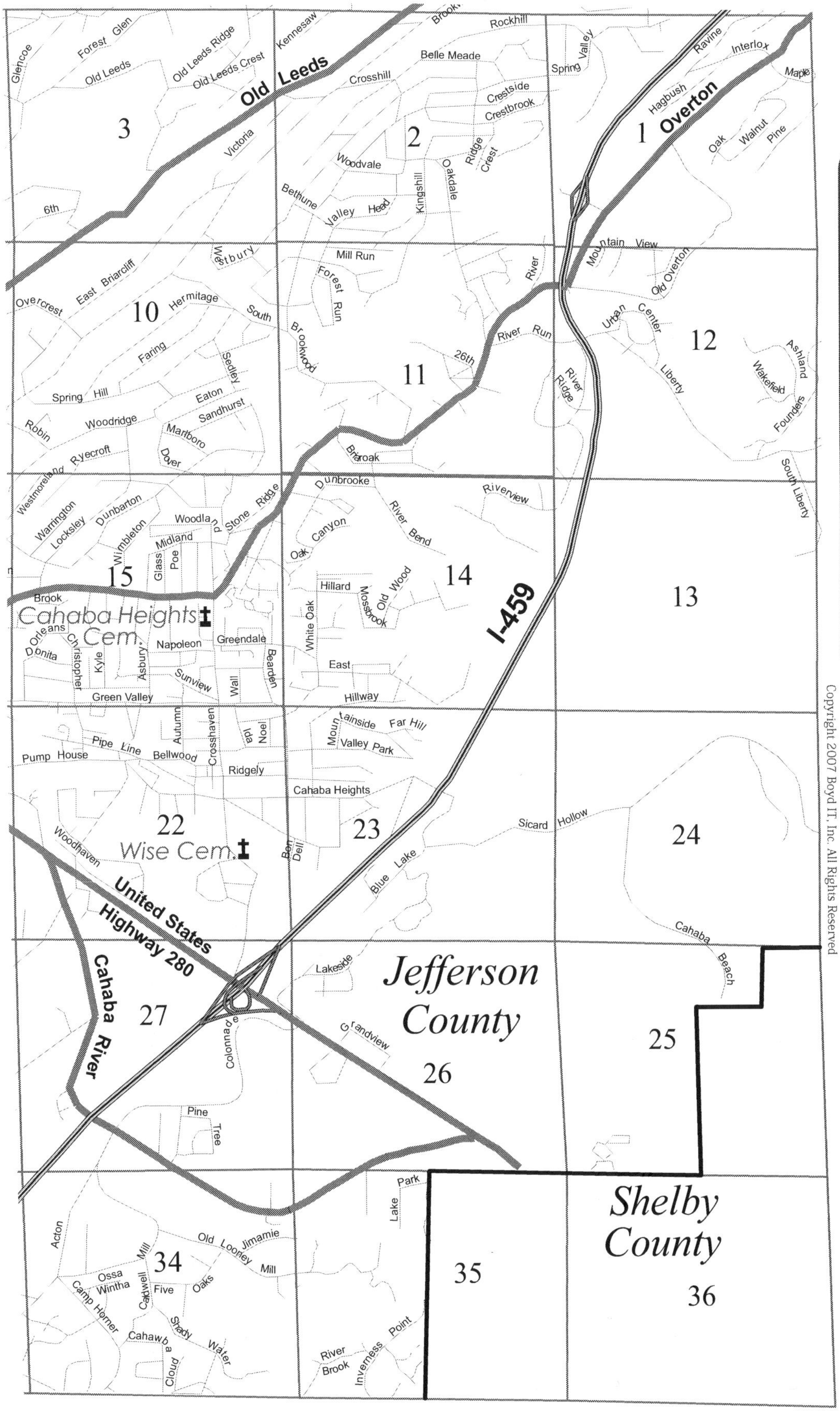

Glencoe
Forest Glen
Old Leeds
Old Leeds Ridge
Old Leeds Crest
Kennesaw
Old Leeds
Victoria
3
6th
Brook
Rockhill
Belle Meade
Crosshill
Crestside
Crestbrook
2
Woodvale
Ridge Crest
Oakdale
Kingshill
Bethune
Valley Head
Spring Valley
Ravine
Interlox
Maple
Hagbush
1 Overton
Oak
Walnut
Pine
Westbury
East Briarcliff
Overcrest
10
Hermitage
South
Faring
Sedley
Spring Hill
Eaton
Sandhurst
Woodridge
Robin
Marlboro
Ryecroft
Dover
Westmoreland
Mill Run
Forest Run
Brookwood
River
26th
River Run
11
Briaroak
Mountain View
Old Overton
Urban Center
12
Ashland
Wakefield
Liberty
River Ridge
Founders
South Liberty
Warrington
Locksley
Dunbarton
Wimbleton
Woodland
Stone Ridge
Midland
Glass
Poe
15
Brook
Cahaba Heights Cem.
Orleans
Donita
Christopher
Kyle
Asbury
Napoleon
Greendale
Sunview
Wall
Bearden
Green Valley
Dunbrooke
Oak Canyon
River Bend
Riverview
Hillard
Mossbrook
Old Wood
14
White Oak
East
Hillway
I-459
13
Pump House
Pipe Line
Bellwood
Autumn
Crosshaven
Ida
Noel
Ridgely
Mountainside
Far Hill
Valley Park
Cahaba Heights
22
Woodhaven
Wise Cem.
Ben Dell
23
Sicard Hollow
24
Blue Lake
United States Highway 280
Cahaba River
27
Colonnade
Lakeside
Jefferson County
Grandview
26
Cahaba Beach
25
Pine Tree
Park
Lake
Shelby County
Acton
Old Looney Mill
Jimamie
34
Ossa Wintha
Camp Horner
Caldwell
Five Oaks
Mill
Shady Water
Cahawba Cloud
35
36
River Brook
Inverness Point

Helpful Hints

1. This road map has a number of uses, but primarily it is to help you: a) find the present location of land owned by your ancestors (at least the general area), b) find cemeteries and city-centers, and c) estimate the route/roads used by Census-takers & tax-assessors.

2. If you plan to travel to Jefferson County to locate cemeteries or land parcels, please pick up a modern travel map for the area before you do. Mapping old land parcels on modern maps is not as exact a science as you might think. Just the slightest variations in public land survey coordinates, estimates of parcel boundaries, or road-map deviations can greatly alter a map's representation of how a road either does or doesn't cross a particular parcel of land.

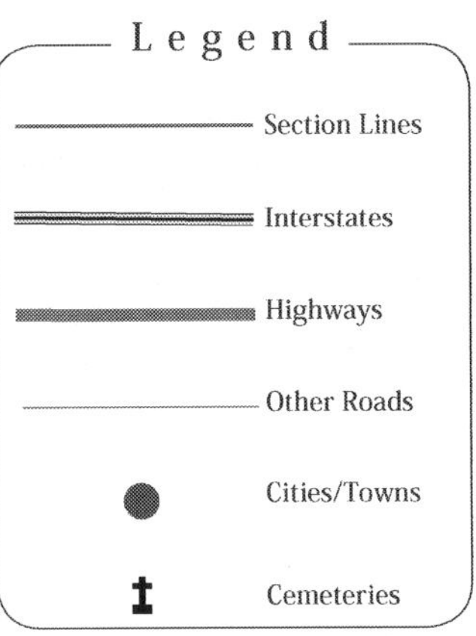

Scale: Section = 1 mile X 1 mile
(generally, with some exceptions)

Historical Map

T18-S R2-W
Huntsville Meridian

Map Group 32

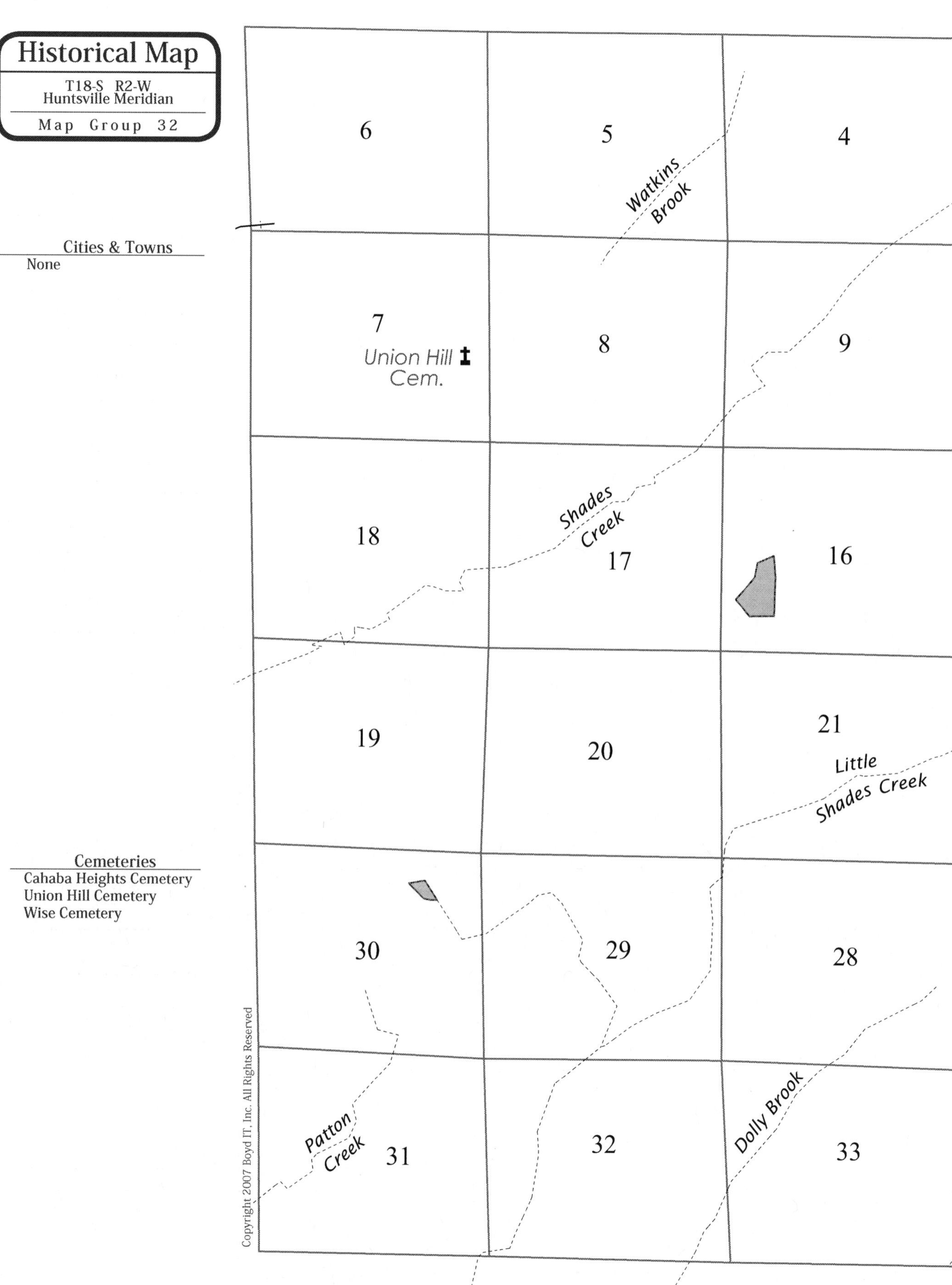

Cities & Towns

None

Cemeteries

Cahaba Heights Cemetery
Union Hill Cemetery
Wise Cemetery

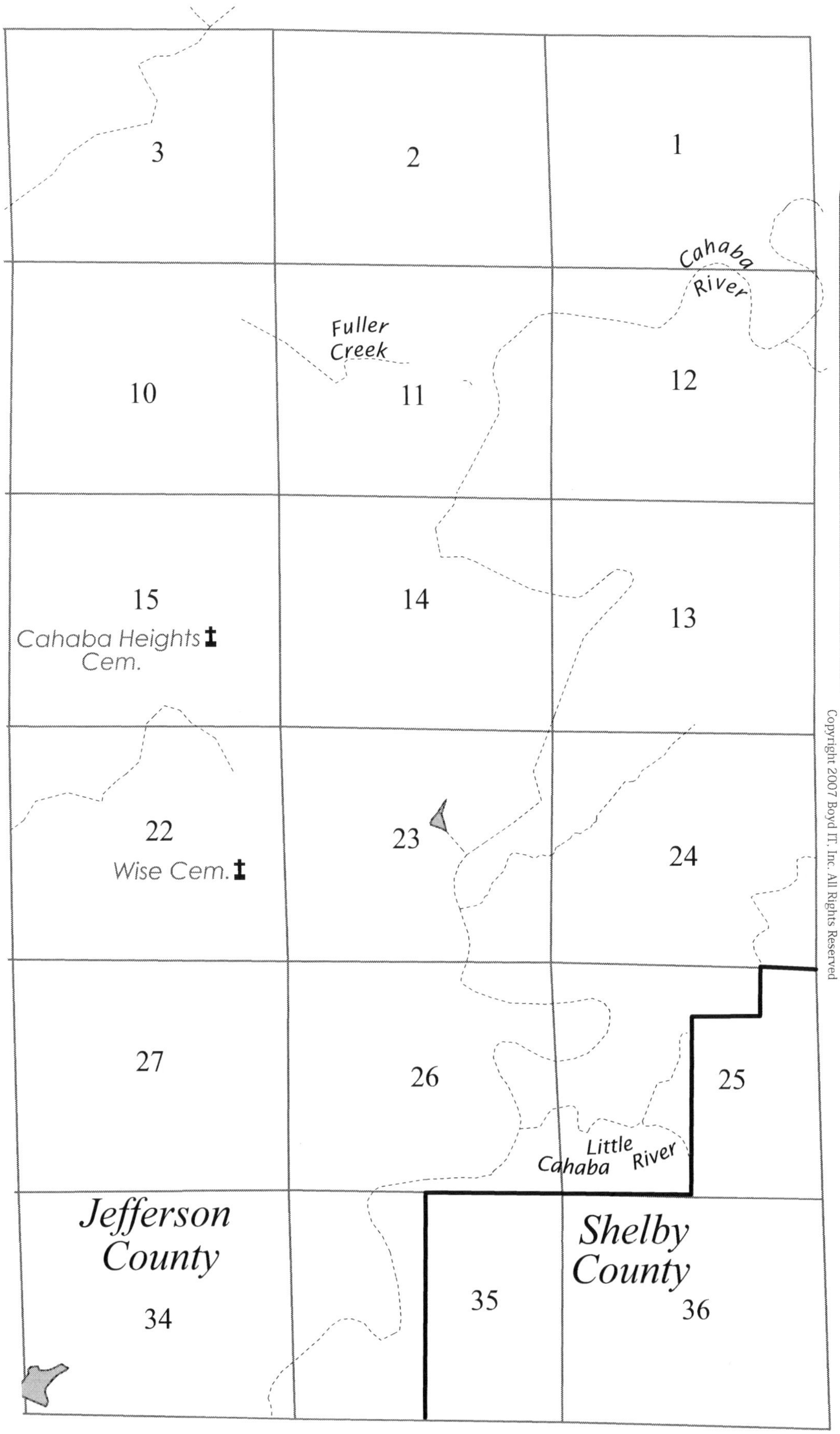

3
2
1
Cahaba River
Fuller Creek
10
11
12
15
14
13
Cahaba Heights Cem.
22
23
24
Wise Cem.
27
26
25
Little Cahaba River
Jefferson County
34
35
Shelby County
36

Helpful Hints

1. This Map takes a different look at the same Congressional Township displayed in the preceding two maps. It presents features that can help you better envision the historical development of the area: a) Water-bodies (lakes & ponds), b) Water-courses (rivers, streams, etc.), c) Railroads, d) City/town center-points (where they were oftentimes located when first settled), and e) Cemeteries.

2. Using this "Historical" map in tandem with this Township's Patent Map and Road Map, may lead you to some interesting discoveries. You will often find roads, towns, cemeteries, and waterways are named after nearby landowners: sometimes those names will be the ones you are researching. See how many of these research gems you can find here in Jefferson County.

Legend
Section Lines
Railroads
Large Rivers & Bodies of Water
Streams/Creeks & Small Rivers
Cities/Towns
Cemeteries

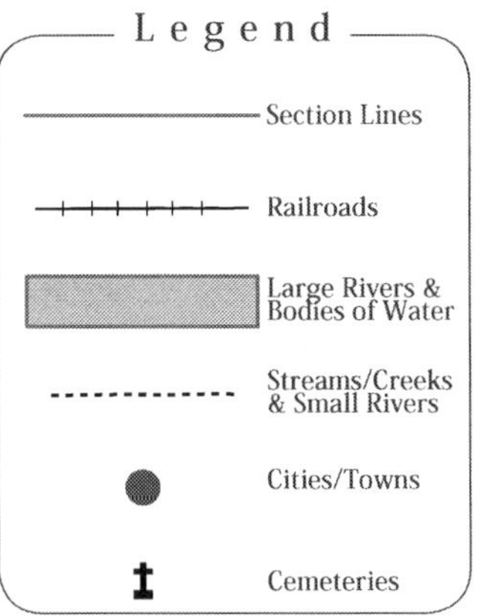

Scale: Section = 1 mile X 1 mile
(there are some exceptions)

Map Group 33: Index to Land Patents

Township 18-South Range 1-West (Huntsville)

After you locate an individual in this Index, take note of the Section and Section Part then proceed to the Land Patent map on the pages immediately following. You should have no difficulty locating the corresponding parcel of land.

The "For More Info" Column will lead you to more information about the underlying Patents. See the *Legend* at right, and the "How to Use this Book" chapter, for more information.

LEGEND

"For More Info . . . " column

A = Authority (Legislative Act, See Appendix "A")
B = Block or Lot (location in Section unknown)
C = Cancelled Patent
F = Fractional Section
G = Group (Multi-Patentee Patent, see Appendix "C")
V = Overlaps another Parcel
R = Re-Issued (Parcel patented more than once)

(A & G items require you to look in the Appendixes referred to above. All other Letter-designations followed by a number require you to locate line-items in this index that possess the ID number found after the letter).

ID	Individual in Patent	Sec.	Sec. Part	Date Issued	Other Counties	For More Info . . .
5898	BAGLEY, Francis	18	NESW	1882-09-09		A1
5899	" "	18	NWSE	1882-09-09		A1
5949	BAGLEY, Joseph	18	NESE	1881-12-10		A1
5950	" "	18	SENE	1881-12-10		A1
5904	BLITON, George W	4	N½SW	1883-05-21		A4
5905	" "	4	NWSE	1883-05-21		A4
5913	BRASHER, Isham H	4	N½NW	1884-03-10		A4 R5944
5972	BRASHER, Seaborn	6	N½SW	1882-10-30		A1
5921	BROWN, James F	6	NENW	1889-12-28		A1
5977	BRYANT, William	4	N½NE	1883-05-21		A4
5978	" "	4	SENE	1883-05-21		A4
5900	BYERS, Francis	6	NENE	1849-08-01		A1
5952	CALDWELL, Lazarus F	12	SE	1897-08-05	Shelby	A4
5917	CAMERON, James	1	E½NW	1824-05-10		A1
5979	CAMERON, William	1	W½NE	1823-05-01		A1
5953	CLINE, Lee W	12	NESW	1917-02-01	Shelby	A4
5954	" "	12	S½SW	1917-02-01	Shelby	A4
5966	COWDEN, Robert S	6	SWSW	1849-08-01		A1
5973	COX, Stephen	2	NESE	1858-06-01		A1
5980	CROSS, William	17	SW	1831-07-01	Shelby	A1 G63
5879	DESHAZO, Alfred L	18	S½SE	1885-03-16		A4
5901	DORMAN, George A	8	W½NW	1883-05-21		A4 R5880
5991	EASTIS, William M	14	S½SW	1900-08-09	Shelby	A4
5992	" "	14	W½SE	1900-08-09	Shelby	A4
5965	ELLICOTT, Peter F	4	E½SE	1883-05-21		A4
5894	ELLINGTON, Drewry A	15	SE	1858-06-01	Shelby	A1
5906	FRANKLIN, Greenberry	11	NENW	1854-07-15		A1
5914	FRIES, Jacob	2	E½SW	1823-05-01		A1 G89
5936	GILBERT, John	1	E½NE	1824-04-05		A1
5938	" "	11	E½NE	1824-04-05		A1
5940	" "	2	W½SW	1824-04-05		A1
5937	" "	10	E½SE	1824-04-12		A1
5939	" "	14	W½NW	1824-05-18	Shelby	A1
5981	GILBERT, William	10	W½SE	1823-05-01		A1
5983	" "	15	E½SW	1823-05-01	Shelby	A1 G92
5984	" "	15	W½NE	1823-05-01	Shelby	A1 G92
5985	" "	15	W½SW	1823-05-01	Shelby	A1 G92
5982	" "	15	E½NW	1824-04-12	Shelby	A1
5980	" "	17	SW	1831-07-01	Shelby	A1 G63
5886	GLASS, Calvin	6	S½NW	1884-12-05		A4
5907	GLASS, Henry R	18	W½NE	1894-11-21		A4
5941	GLASS, John	1	SESW	1858-06-01		A1
5942	" "	1	SWSE	1858-06-01		A1
5974	GLASS, Susan	6	NWNW	1884-03-20		A1
5955	GOAS, Lewis	8	E½NE	1883-05-21		A4
5959	GOLDEN, Martin	18	NWSW	1881-12-10		A1

ID	Individual in Patent	Sec.	Sec. Part	Date Issued	Other Counties	For More Info . . .
5960	GOLDEN, Martin (Cont'd)	18	SWNW	1881-12-10		A1
5881	HAMAKER, Anderson N	18	S½SW	1892-05-26		A4
5883	HARIS, Benjamin F	9	E½SE	1860-04-02		A1
5935	HARRIS, Joel	10	SESW	1834-11-04		A1
5922	HERREN, James	1	W½NW	1823-05-01		A1
5924	HERRING, James	2	E½NE	1823-05-01		A1 G130
5923	" "	2	W½SE	1824-04-05		A1
5943	HERRING, John	2	SENW	1834-10-14		A1
5887	HOPPER, Charles H	18	NENE	1883-05-21		A4
5888	" "	18	NWNW	1883-05-21		A4
5929	HOWARD, Jesse	19	NENE	1834-11-04	Shelby	A1
5925	HOWEN, James	2	W½NE	1824-04-05		A1
5958	INZER, Marcus L	3	SESE	1858-06-01		A1
5897	JACKSON, Emeline	18	E½NW	1881-12-30		A1
5895	JOHNSTON, Elizabeth	11	E½SW	1823-05-01		A1
5896	" "	11	W½SW	1823-05-01		A1
5944	LIGHTHALL, John	4	N½NW	1883-05-21		A4 C R5913
5946	" "	4	SWNE	1883-05-21		A4 C R5947
5945	" "	4	S½NW	1883-06-07		A4
5947	" "	4	SWNE	1883-06-07		A4 R5946
5882	LOONEY, Apsolum	1	SWSW	1848-07-01		A1
5902	LOWERY, George	1	N½SE	1858-06-01		A1
5903	LOWRY, George	15	W½NW	1828-07-30	Shelby	A1
5931	MASON, Job	10	W½SW	1823-06-02		A1
5932	" "	17	E½SE	1823-06-02	Shelby	A1
5948	MCDANAL, John	11	NWSE	1839-09-20		A1
5969	MCDANAL, Samuel	8	E½SE	1884-03-10		A4
5970	" "	8	NESW	1884-03-10		A4
5971	" "	8	NWSE	1884-03-10		A4
5986	MCDANAL, William H	2	NENW	1858-06-01		A1
5927	MCDANIEL, Jeremiah	10	SENW	1835-10-01		A1
5993	MCDANIEL, William	2	SESE	1850-04-01		A1
5928	MCDOWEL, Jeremiah	10	NESW	1834-10-16		A1
5962	MORGAN, Mattie	12	SENE	1907-04-01	Shelby	A4 G175
5962	MORGAN, William L	12	SENE	1907-04-01	Shelby	A4 G175
5963	NUNLEY, Moses	15	E½NE	1823-05-01	Shelby	A1
5926	OWEN, James W	2	NWNW	1885-06-20		A4
5956	OWEN, Luther C	14	NENE	1880-02-20	Shelby	A4
5957	" "	14	S½NE	1891-06-10	Shelby	A4
5911	OWENS, Irwin	8	SESW	1881-12-30		A1
5912	" "	8	SWSE	1881-12-30		A1
5987	PARKER, William H	14	E½SE	1904-07-02	Shelby	A1
5892	RAIMER, Douglas	4	S½SW	1883-05-21		A4
5893	" "	4	SWSE	1883-05-21		A4
5877	RINEHART, Abraham	19	N½SE	1858-06-01	Shelby	A1
5878	" "	19	S½NE	1858-06-01	Shelby	A1
5967	SHEPHERD, Robert S	12	NWNW	1835-10-01	Shelby	A1
5983	SIMS, Edward	15	E½SW	1823-05-01	Shelby	A1 G92
5984	" "	15	W½NE	1823-05-01	Shelby	A1 G92
5985	" "	15	W½SW	1823-05-01	Shelby	A1 G92
5924	" "	2	E½NE	1823-05-01		A1 G130
5914	" "	2	E½SW	1823-05-01		A1 G89
5930	SPARKS, Jesse	11	W½NW	1823-06-02		A1
5951	SPARKS, Joseph K	10	NE	1823-05-01		A1
5990	SPERRY, William L	8	W½SW	1883-05-21		A4
5915	STALNAKER, James B	12	N½NE	1920-08-10	Shelby	A4
5916	" "	12	SWNE	1920-08-10	Shelby	A4
5933	STANDIFER, Joel D	6	N½SE	1884-03-20		A1
5934	" "	6	S½NE	1884-03-20		A1
5988	STANDIFER, William J	6	S½SE	1884-11-13		A1
5989	" "	6	SESW	1884-11-13		A1
5964	VOSE, Orin B	8	E½NW	1883-05-21		A4
5880	WETHERS, Allen M	8	W½NW	1883-05-21		A4 R5901
5975	WHITBY, Thomas	10	W½NW	1882-10-30		A1
5884	WHITE, Bradley	2	SWNW	1854-07-15		A1
5885	" "	3	NESE	1854-07-15		A1
5890	WHITE, Daniel P	11	SENW	1835-10-01		A1
5889	" "	11	S½SE	1858-06-01		A1
5891	" "	14	NWNE	1858-06-01	Shelby	A1
5908	WHITE, Henry S	14	N½SW	1858-06-01	Shelby	A1
5909	" "	14	NENW	1858-06-01	Shelby	A1
5910	" "	14	SENW	1858-06-01	Shelby	A1
5918	WHITE, James D	12	NENW	1890-03-19	Shelby	A4

ID	Individual in Patent	Sec.	Sec. Part	Date Issued	Other Counties	For More Info . . .
5919	WHITE, James D (Cont'd)	12	NWSW	1890-03-19	Shelby	A4
5920	" "	12	S½NW	1890-03-19	Shelby	A4
5995	WHITE, William	11	SWNE	1834-10-14		A1
5994	" "	11	NWNE	1834-11-04		A1
5996	WHITEFIELD, William	17	SWSE	1835-10-01	Shelby	A1
5961	WILLIS, Mary	19	SW	1858-06-01	Shelby	A1
5968	WORTHINGTON, Robert	1	NWSW	1850-04-01		A1
5976	WORTHY, Thomas	1	NESW	1839-09-20		A1

Patent Map

T18-S R1-W
Huntsville Meridian

Map Group 33

Township Statistics

Parcels Mapped	:	120
Number of Patents	:	97
Number of Individuals	:	82
Patentees Identified	:	82
Number of Surnames	:	63
Multi-Patentee Parcels	:	7
Oldest Patent Date	:	5/1/1823
Most Recent Patent	:	8/10/1920
Block/Lot Parcels	:	0
Parcels Re - Issued	:	3
Parcels that Overlap	:	0
Cities and Towns	:	0
Cemeteries	:	1

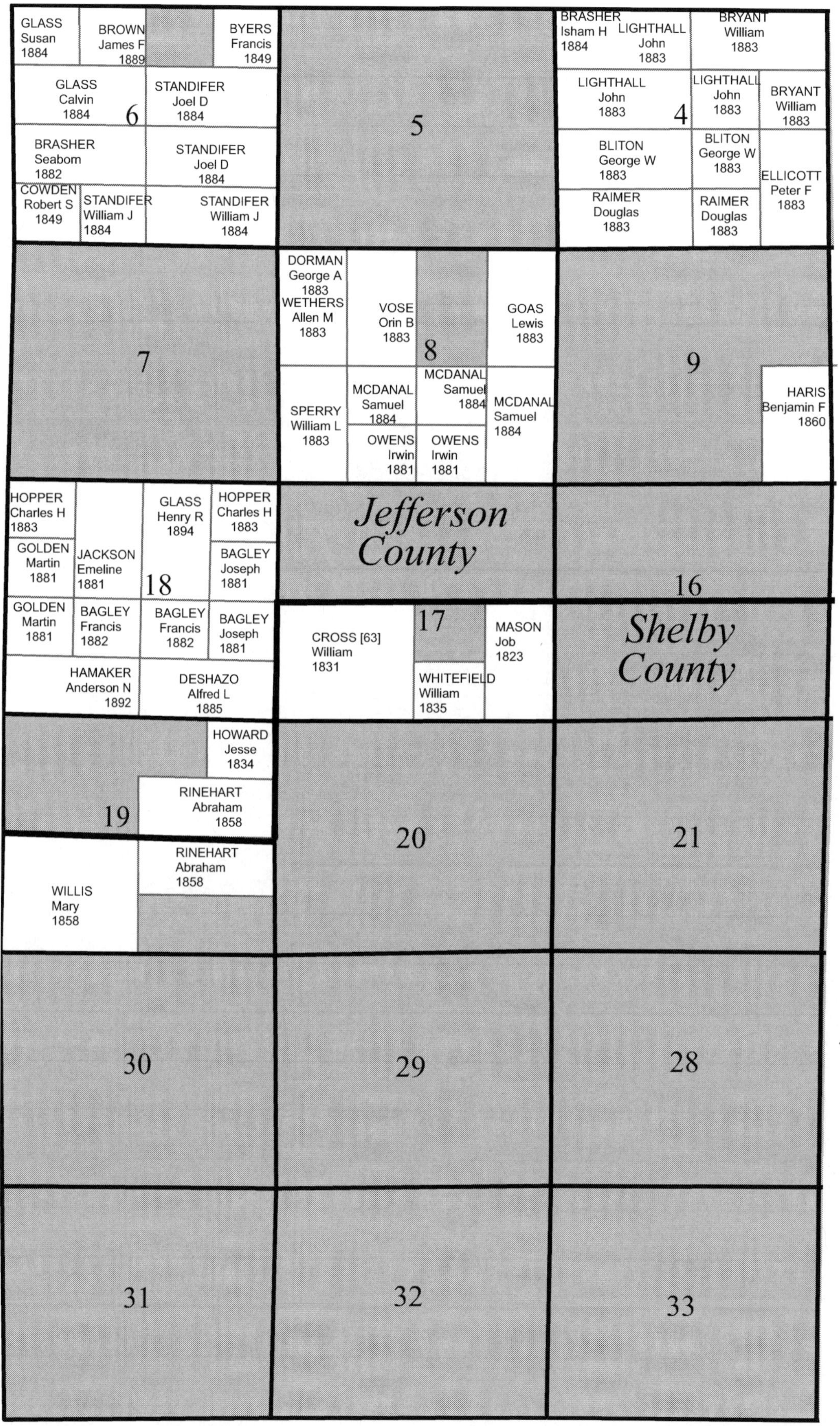

6
GLASS Susan 1884
BROWN James F 1889
BYERS Francis 1849
GLASS Calvin 1884
STANDIFER Joel D 1884
BRASHER Seaborn 1882
STANDIFER Joel D 1884
COWDEN Robert S 1849
STANDIFER William J 1884
STANDIFER William J 1884

5

4
BRASHER Isham H 1884
LIGHTHALL John 1883
BRYANT William 1883
LIGHTHALL John 1883
LIGHTHALL John 1883
BRYANT William 1883
BLITON George W 1883
BLITON George W 1883
ELLICOTT Peter F 1883
RAIMER Douglas 1883
RAIMER Douglas 1883

7

8
DORMAN George A 1883
WETHERS Allen M 1883
VOSE Orin B 1883
GOAS Lewis 1883
MCDANAL Samuel 1884
MCDANAL Samuel 1884
MCDANAL Samuel 1884
SPERRY William L 1883
OWENS Irwin 1881
OWENS Irwin 1881

9
HARIS Benjamin F 1860

18
HOPPER Charles H 1883
GLASS Henry R 1894
HOPPER Charles H 1883
GOLDEN Martin 1881
JACKSON Emeline 1881
BAGLEY Joseph 1881
GOLDEN Martin 1881
BAGLEY Francis 1882
BAGLEY Francis 1882
BAGLEY Joseph 1881
HAMAKER Anderson N 1892
DESHAZO Alfred L 1885

Jefferson County

17
CROSS [63] William 1831
MASON Job 1823
WHITEFIELD William 1835

16

Shelby County

19
HOWARD Jesse 1834
RINEHART Abraham 1858
RINEHART Abraham 1858
WILLIS Mary 1858

20

21

30

29

28

31

32

33

Helpful Hints

1. This Map's INDEX can be found on the preceding pages.
2. Refer to Map "C" to see where this Township lies within Jefferson County, Alabama.
3. Numbers within square brackets [ ] denote a multi-patentee land parcel (multi-owner). Refer to Appendix "C" for a full list of members in this group.
4. Areas that look to be crowded with Patentees usually indicate multiple sales of the same parcel (Re-issues) or Overlapping parcels. See this Township's Index for an explanation of these and other circumstances that might explain "odd" groupings of Patentees on this map.

Legend

- Patent Boundary
- Section Boundary
- No Patents Found (or Outside County)
- 1., 2., 3., ... Lot Numbers (when beside a name)
- [ ] Group Number (see Appendix "C")

Scale: Section = 1 mile X 1 mile (generally, with some exceptions)

Road Map

T18-S R1-W
Huntsville Meridian

Map Group 33

Cities & Towns
None

Cemeteries
Mount Hebron Cemetery

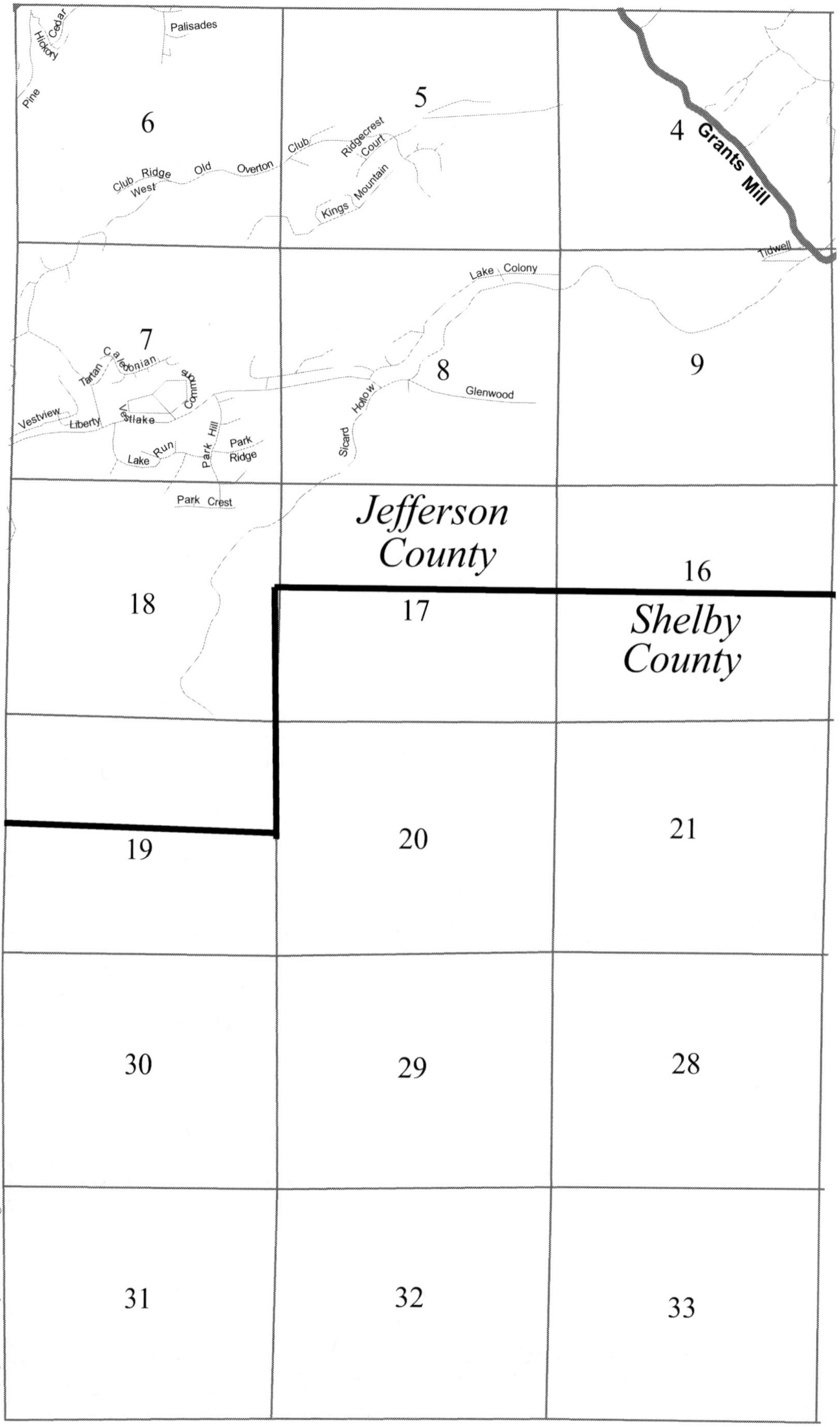

Hickory
Cedar
Palisades
Pine
6
5
4
Grants Mill
Club Ridge West
Old Overton
Club
Ridgecrest Court
Kings Mountain
Tidwell
Lake Colony
7
8
9
Caledonian
Tartan
Commons
Vestview
Liberty
Westlake
Park Hill
Park Ridge
Lake Run
Sicard Hollow
Glenwood
Park Crest
Jefferson County
18
17
16
Shelby County
19
20
21
30
29
28
31
32
33

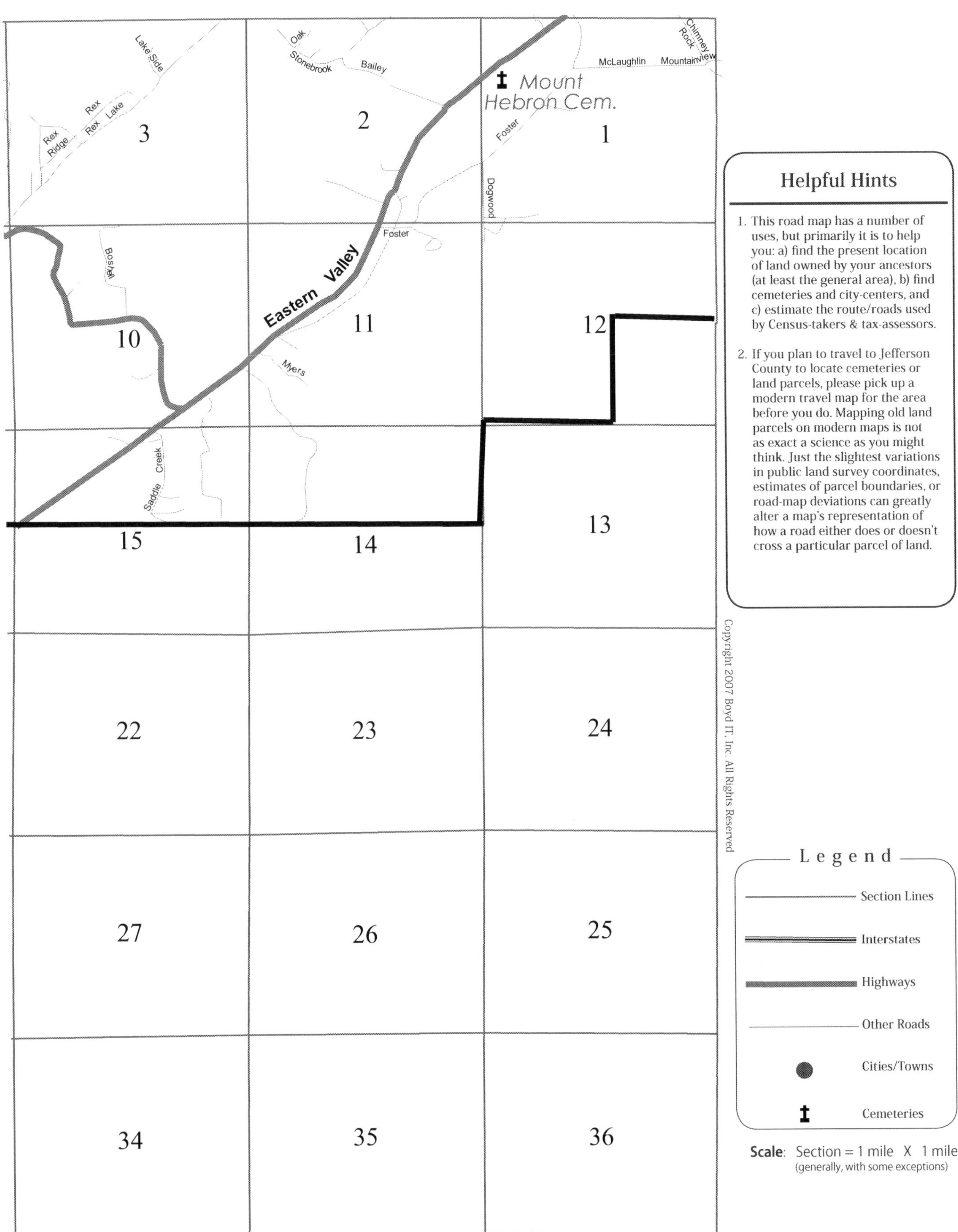

Lake Side
Rex
Rex Lake
Rex
Rex Ridge
3
Oak
Stonebrook
Bailey
2
Chimney Rock
McLaughlin
Mountainview
Mount Hebron Cem.
Foster
1
Dogwood
Boshell
Foster
Eastern Valley
10
11
12
Myers
Saddle Creek
15
14
13
22
23
24
27
26
25
34
35
36
Helpful Hints
1. This road map has a number of uses, but primarily it is to help you: a) find the present location of land owned by your ancestors (at least the general area), b) find cemeteries and city-centers, and c) estimate the route/roads used by Census-takers & tax-assessors.
2. If you plan to travel to Jefferson County to locate cemeteries or land parcels, please pick up a modern travel map for the area before you do. Mapping old land parcels on modern maps is not as exact a science as you might think. Just the slightest variations in public land survey coordinates, estimates of parcel boundaries, or road-map deviations can greatly alter a map's representation of how a road either does or doesn't cross a particular parcel of land.
Copyright 2007 Boyd IT, Inc. All Rights Reserved
Legend
Section Lines
Interstates
Highways
Other Roads
Cities/Towns
Cemeteries
Scale: Section = 1 mile X 1 mile
(generally, with some exceptions)

Historical Map

T18-S R1-W
Huntsville Meridian

Map Group 33

Cities & Towns

None

Cemeteries

Mount Hebron Cemetery

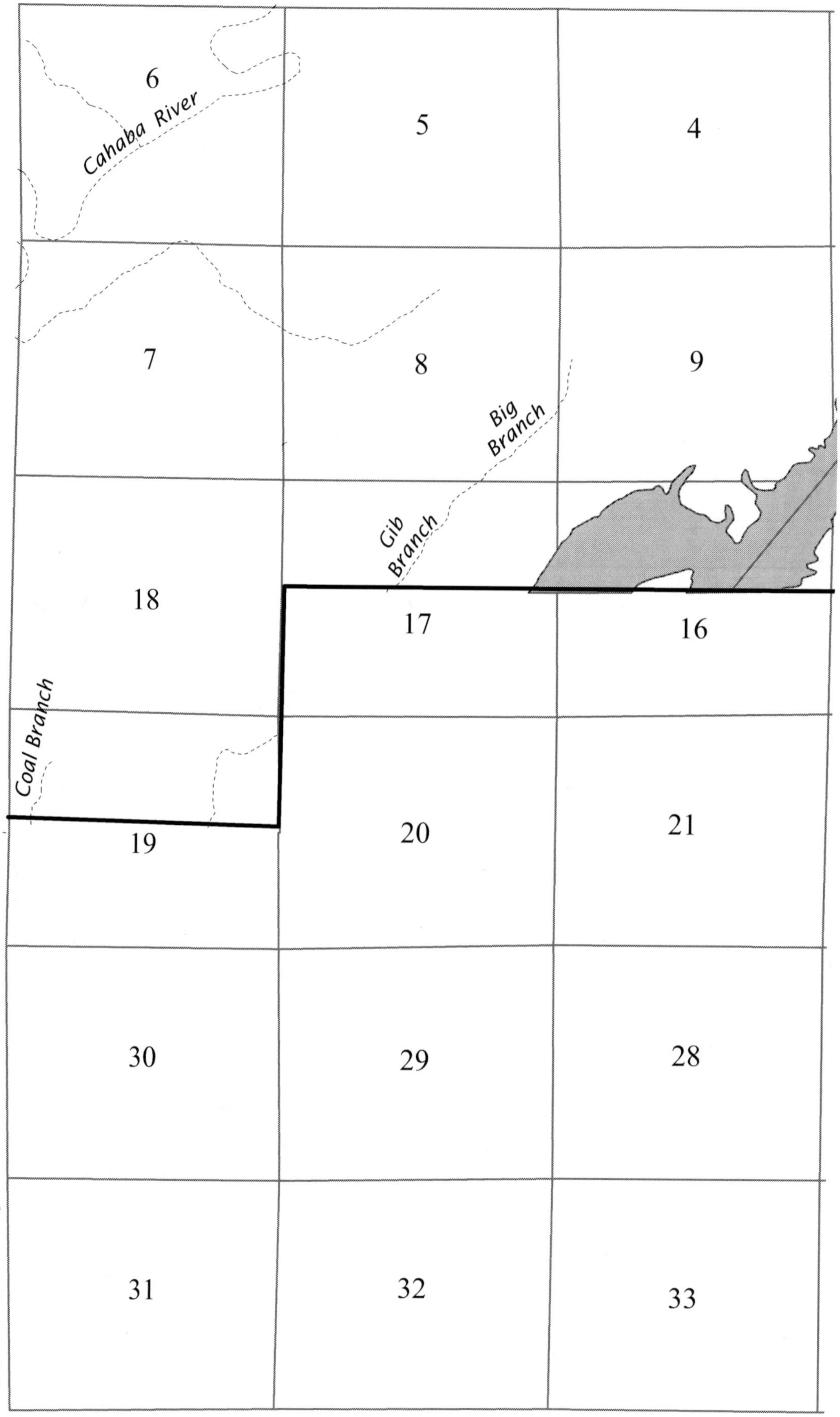

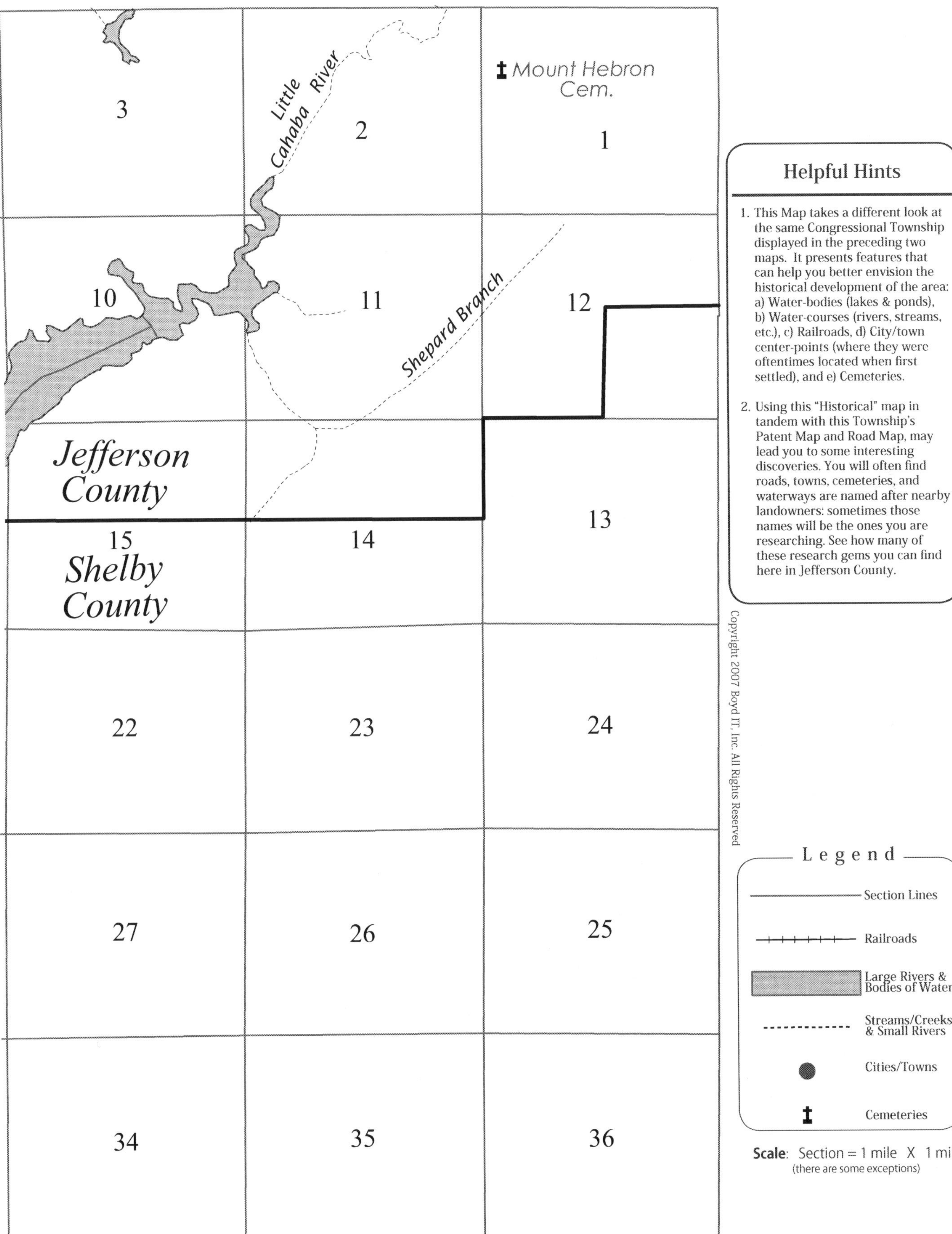

Helpful Hints

1. This Map takes a different look at the same Congressional Township displayed in the preceding two maps. It presents features that can help you better envision the historical development of the area: a) Water-bodies (lakes & ponds), b) Water-courses (rivers, streams, etc.), c) Railroads, d) City/town center-points (where they were oftentimes located when first settled), and e) Cemeteries.

2. Using this "Historical" map in tandem with this Township's Patent Map and Road Map, may lead you to some interesting discoveries. You will often find roads, towns, cemeteries, and waterways are named after nearby landowners: sometimes those names will be the ones you are researching. See how many of these research gems you can find here in Jefferson County.

Map Group 34: Index to Land Patents

Township 18-South Range 1-East (Huntsville)

After you locate an individual in this Index, take note of the Section and Section Part then proceed to the Land Patent map on the pages immediately following. You should have no difficulty locating the corresponding parcel of land.

The "For More Info" Column will lead you to more information about the underlying Patents. See the *Legend* at right, and the "How to Use this Book" chapter, for more information.

LEGEND

"For More Info . . . " column

A = Authority (Legislative Act, See Appendix "A")
B = Block or Lot (location in Section unknown)
C = Cancelled Patent
F = Fractional Section
G = Group (Multi-Patentee Patent, see Appendix "C")
V = Overlaps another Parcel
R = Re-Issued (Parcel patented more than once)

(A & G items require you to look in the Appendixes referred to above. All other Letter-designations followed by a number require you to locate line-items in this index that possess the ID number found after the letter).

ID	Individual in Patent	Sec.	Sec. Part	Date Issued	Other Counties	For More Info . . .
5999	FOWLER, Ewens T	6	SESW	1912-06-20	Shelby	A1
6000	" "	6	W½SW	1912-06-20	Shelby	A1
5997	LOWERY, David	6	E½SE	1858-06-01	Shelby	A1
5998	" "	6	SWSE	1858-06-01	Shelby	A1
6005	MCLAUGHLIN, William C	6	NENW	1858-06-01	Shelby	A1
6006	" "	6	W½NW	1858-06-01	Shelby	A1
6001	MORGAN, Job	6	NE	1894-06-09	Shelby	A4 V6004
6002	MORGAN, Lewis	6	NESW	1905-04-18	Shelby	A4
6003	" "	6	NWSE	1905-04-18	Shelby	A4
6004	SHERMAN, Napoleon D	6	NWNE	1891-06-29	Shelby	A1 V6001

MCLAUGHLIN William C 1858
MCLAUGHLIN William C 1858
SHERMAN Napoleon D 1891
MORGAN Job 1894
Jefferson County
6
Shelby County
5
FOWLER Ewens T 1912
MORGAN Lewis 1905
MORGAN Lewis 1905
LOWERY David 1858
FOWLER Ewens T 1912
LOWERY David 1858
7
8
18
17
19
20
30
29
31
32

Patent Map

T18-S R1-E
Huntsville Meridian

Map Group 34

Township Statistics

Parcels Mapped	:	10
Number of Patents	:	6
Number of Individuals	:	6
Patentees Identified	:	6
Number of Surnames	:	5
Multi-Patentee Parcels	:	0
Oldest Patent Date	:	6/1/1858
Most Recent Patent	:	6/20/1912
Block/Lot Parcels	:	0
Parcels Re - Issued	:	0
Parcels that Overlap	:	2
Cities and Towns	:	0
Cemeteries	:	0

Note: the area contained in this map amounts to far less than a full Township. Therefore, its contents are completely on this single page (instead of a "normal" 2-page spread).

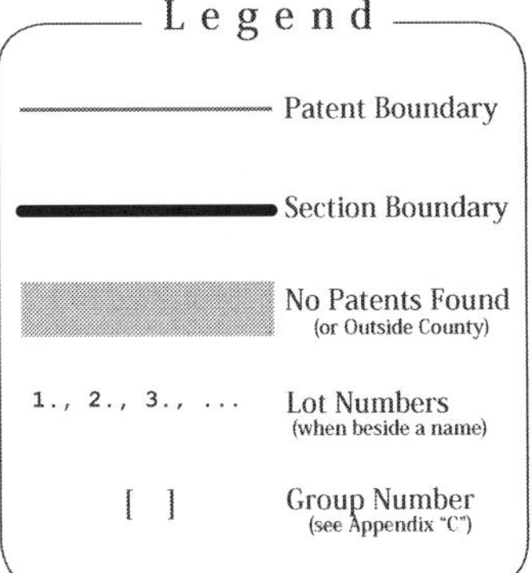

Scale: Section = 1 mile X 1 mile
(generally, with some exceptions)

Road Map

T18-S R1-E
Huntsville Meridian

Map Group 34

Note: the area contained in this map amounts to far less than a full Township. Therefore, its contents are completely on this single page (instead of a "normal" 2-page spread).

Cities & Towns

None

Cemeteries

None

Legend

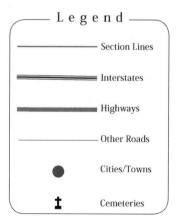

- Section Lines
- Interstates
- Highways
- Other Roads
- Cities/Towns
- Cemeteries

Scale: Section = 1 mile X 1 mile
(generally, with some exceptions)

Historical Map

T18-S R1-E
Huntsville Meridian

Map Group 34

Note: the area contained in this map amounts to far less than a full Township. Therefore, its contents are completely on this single page (instead of a "normal" 2-page spread).

Cities & Towns

None

Cemeteries

None

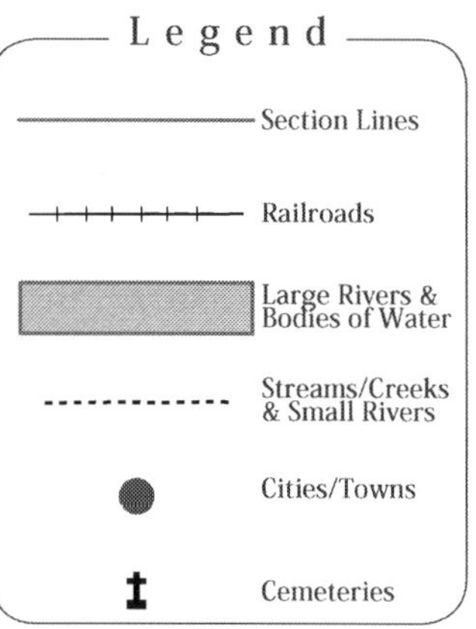

Scale: Section = 1 mile X 1 mile
(there are some exceptions)

Map Group 35: Index to Land Patents

Township 19-South Range 7-West (Huntsville)

After you locate an individual in this Index, take note of the Section and Section Part then proceed to the Land Patent map on the pages immediately following. You should have no difficulty locating the corresponding parcel of land.

The "For More Info" Column will lead you to more information about the underlying Patents. See the *Legend* at right, and the "How to Use this Book" chapter, for more information.

LEGEND

"For More Info . . . " column

A = Authority (Legislative Act, See Appendix "A")
B = Block or Lot (location in Section unknown)
C = Cancelled Patent
F = Fractional Section
G = Group (Multi-Patentee Patent, see Appendix "C")
V = Overlaps another Parcel
R = Re-Issued (Parcel patented more than once)

(A & G items require you to look in the Appendixes referred to above. All other Letter-designations followed by a number require you to locate line-items in this index that possess the ID number found after the letter).

ID	Individual in Patent	Sec.	Sec. Part	Date Issued	Other Counties	For More Info . . .
6013	AARON, Margaret	12	N½NW	1885-03-30		A4
6014	" "	12	NWSW	1885-03-30		A4
6015	" "	12	SWNW	1885-03-30		A4
6007	ALMON, George R	11	SWSE	1859-12-10		A1
6008	BURCHFIELD, John A	3	NWSE	1858-06-01	Tuscaloosa	A1
6009	" "	3	SESW	1858-06-01	Tuscaloosa	A1
6010	" "	3	SWSE	1858-06-01	Tuscaloosa	A1
6023	BURCHFIELD, William	2	NESE	1839-09-20		A1
6024	" "	2	SWNE	1839-09-20		A1
6025	FRANKLIN, William	2	SENW	1839-09-20		A1
6011	GWIN, Littleton C	2	NENW	1839-09-20		A1
6012	" "	2	NWNE	1839-09-20		A1
6016	PARSONS, Mary	2	SWNW	1858-06-01		A1
6019	STONE, Rauley	12	N½SE	1861-01-01		A1
6020	" "	12	NESW	1861-01-01		A1
6021	" "	12	S½NE	1861-01-01		A1
6022	" "	12	SENW	1861-01-01		A1
6017	WILLARD, Osbray	12	SESW	1883-10-20		A1
6018	" "	12	SWSE	1883-10-20		A1
6026	WOOD, William J	2	NWSE	1891-06-30		A4
6027	" "	2	S½SE	1891-06-30		A4
6028	" "	2	SESW	1891-06-30		A4

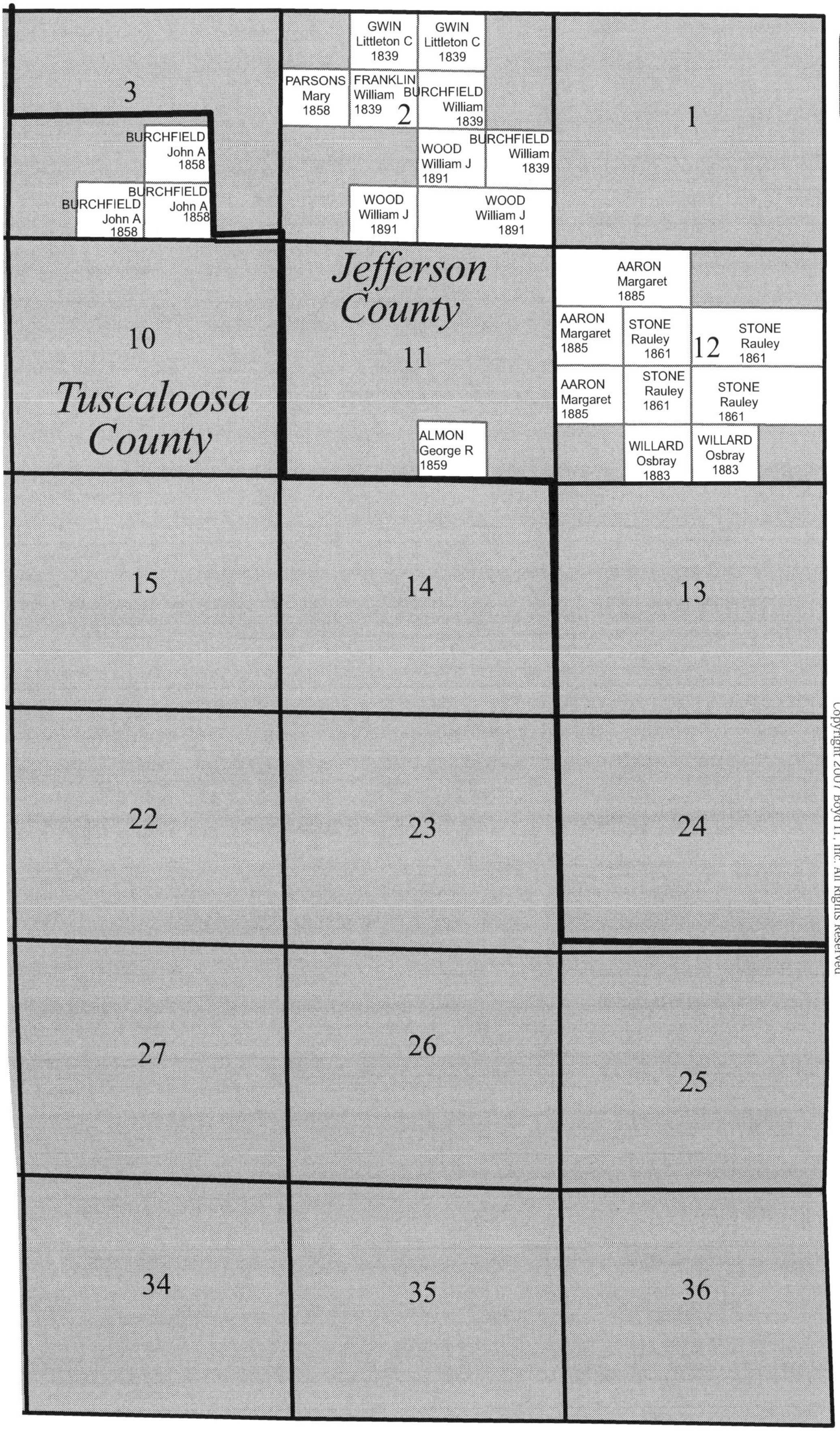

3

BURCHFIELD John A 1858

BURCHFIELD John A 1858

BURCHFIELD John A 1858

GWIN Littleton C 1839

GWIN Littleton C 1839

PARSONS Mary 1858

FRANKLIN William 1839

BURCHFIELD William 1839

2

WOOD William J 1891

BURCHFIELD William 1839

WOOD William J 1891

WOOD William J 1891

1

10

Tuscaloosa County

Jefferson County

11

ALMON George R 1859

AARON Margaret 1885

AARON Margaret 1885

STONE Rauley 1861

12

STONE Rauley 1861

AARON Margaret 1885

STONE Rauley 1861

STONE Rauley 1861

WILLARD Osbray 1883

WILLARD Osbray 1883

15

14

13

22

23

24

27

26

25

34

35

36

Patent Map

T19-S R7-W
Huntsville Meridian

Map Group 35

Township Statistics

Parcels Mapped	:	22
Number of Patents	:	12
Number of Individuals	:	10
Patentees Identified	:	10
Number of Surnames	:	9
Multi-Patentee Parcels	:	0
Oldest Patent Date	:	9/20/1839
Most Recent Patent	:	6/30/1891
Block/Lot Parcels	:	0
Parcels Re - Issued	:	0
Parcels that Overlap	:	0
Cities and Towns	:	0
Cemeteries	:	0

Note: the area contained in this map amounts to far less than a full Township. Therefore, its contents are completely on this single page (instead of a "normal" 2-page spread).

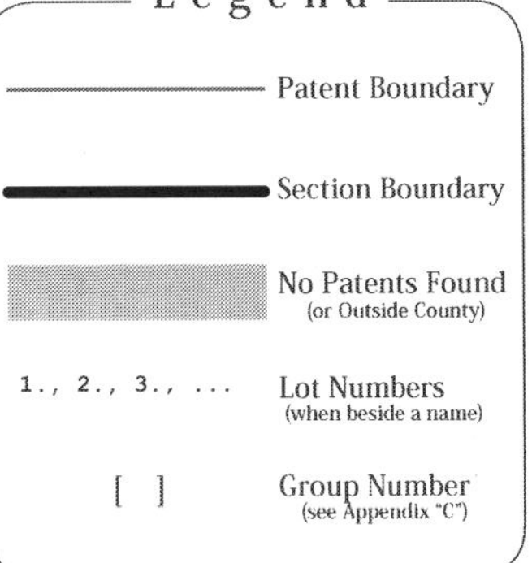

Scale: Section = 1 mile X 1 mile
(generally, with some exceptions)

Road Map

T19-S R7-W
Huntsville Meridian

Map Group 35

Note: the area contained in this map amounts to far less than a full Township. Therefore, its contents are completely on this single page (instead of a "normal" 2-page spread).

Cities & Towns
None

Cemeteries
None

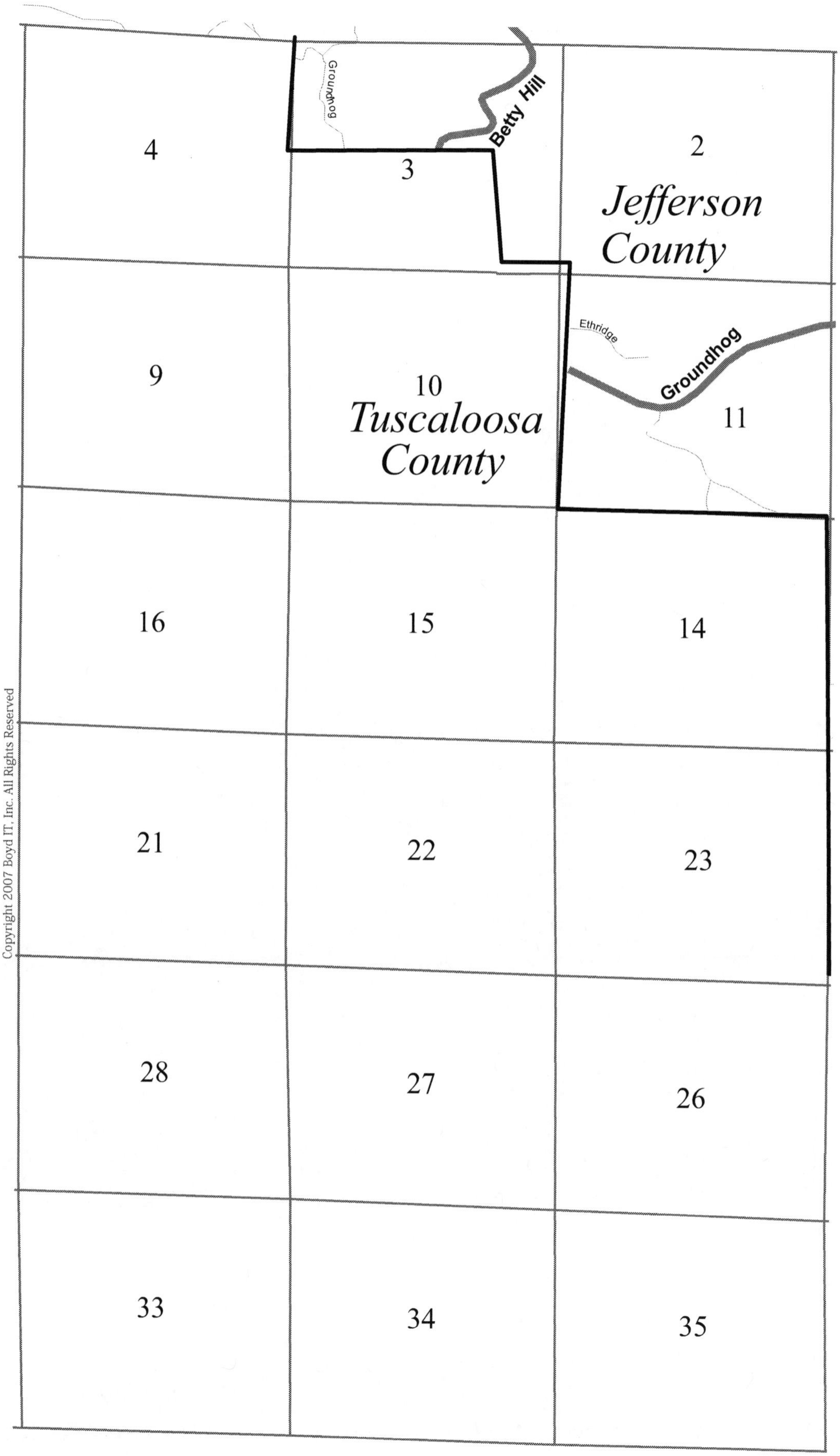

Legend

- Section Lines
- Interstates
- Highways
- Other Roads
- Cities/Towns
- Cemeteries

Scale: Section = 1 mile X 1 mile
(generally, with some exceptions)

Groundhog
Betty Hill
Jefferson County
Tuscaloosa County
Ethridge
Groundhog

4 3 2
9 10 11
16 15 14
21 22 23
28 27 26
33 34 35

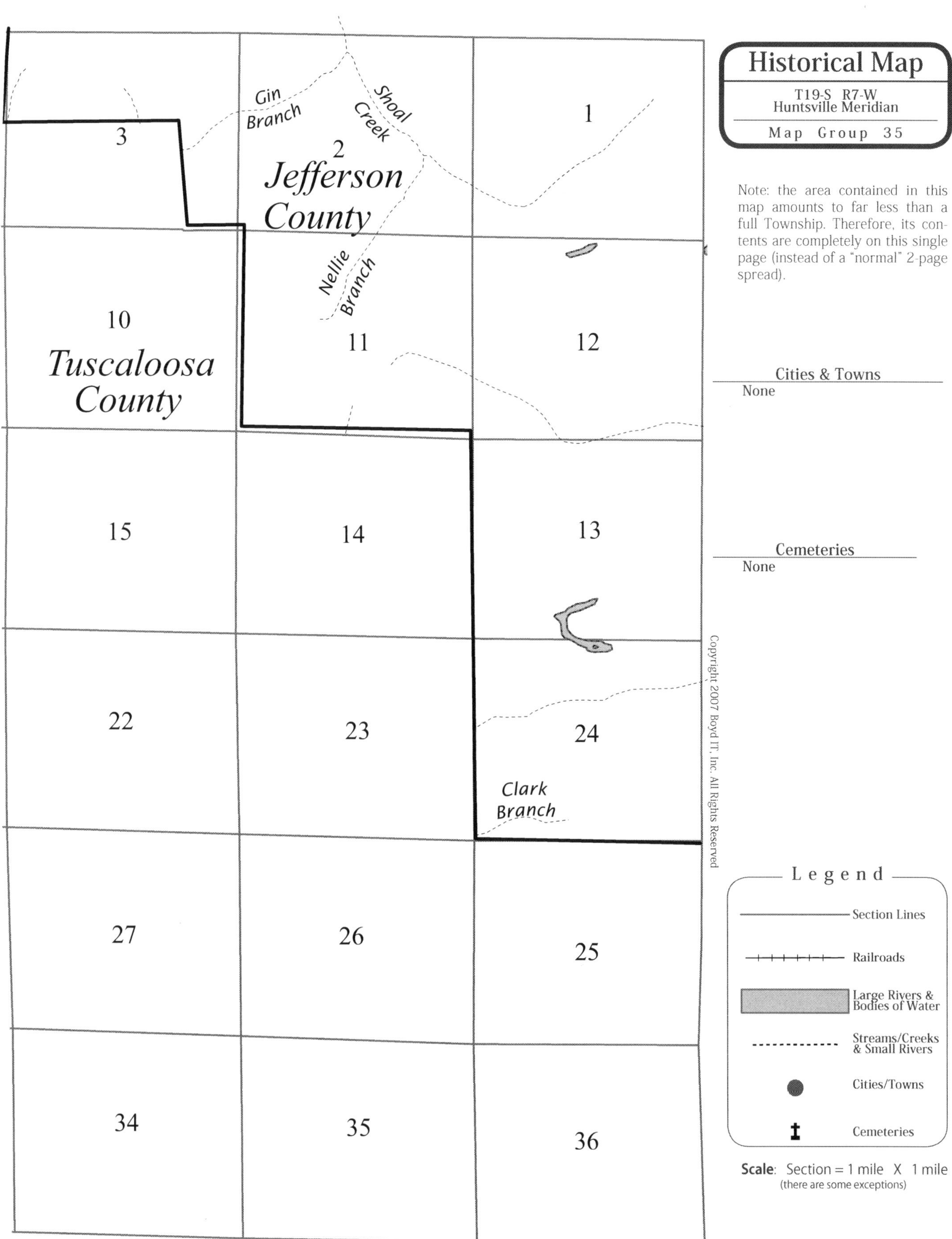

Note: the area contained in this map amounts to far less than a full Township. Therefore, its contents are completely on this single page (instead of a "normal" 2-page spread).

Cities & Towns

None

Cemeteries

None

Scale: Section = 1 mile X 1 mile
(there are some exceptions)

Map Group 36: Index to Land Patents

Township 19-South Range 6-West (Huntsville)

After you locate an individual in this Index, take note of the Section and Section Part then proceed to the Land Patent map on the pages immediately following. You should have no difficulty locating the corresponding parcel of land.

The "For More Info" Column will lead you to more information about the underlying Patents. See the *Legend* at right, and the "How to Use this Book" chapter, for more information.

LEGEND

"For More Info . . . " column

A = Authority (Legislative Act, See Appendix "A")
B = Block or Lot (location in Section unknown)
C = Cancelled Patent
F = Fractional Section
G = Group (Multi-Patentee Patent, see Appendix "C")
V = Overlaps another Parcel
R = Re-Issued (Parcel patented more than once)

(A & G items require you to look in the Appendixes referred to above. All other Letter-designations followed by a number require you to locate line-items in this index that possess the ID number found after the letter).

ID	Individual in Patent	Sec.	Sec. Part	Date Issued	Other Counties	For More Info . . .
6054	BARNETT, Erastus S	30	E½SW	1848-07-01	Tuscaloosa	A1 G13
6150	BROWN, Thomas	17	E½NW	1823-06-02		A1 G33
6151	" "	17	W½NW	1823-06-02		A1 G33
6163	BRYANT, William F	24	NE	1885-06-12		A4
6071	BURCHFIELD, James M	4	NW	1884-03-10		A4
6044	CARGILE, David R	22	NW	1890-01-08		A4
6119	CARGILE, Lewis	8	E½SE	1837-03-20		A1
6155	CARGILE, Tolaver R	14	NESW	1884-12-05		A4
6156	" "	14	S½NW	1884-12-05		A4
6157	" "	14	SWNE	1884-12-05		A4
6152	CLARKE, Thomas H	3	W½SW	1824-04-12		A1 R6153
6153	" "	3	W½SW	1915-08-11		A1 R6152
6088	COWEN, John G	10	SENW	1860-04-02		A1
6084	COWLEY, Jerrem	30	E½NW	1839-09-20	Tuscaloosa	A1
6085	" "	30	W½NE	1858-06-01	Tuscaloosa	A1
6086	" "	30	W½NW	1858-06-01	Tuscaloosa	A1
6054	COWLEY, Jerrom	30	E½SW	1848-07-01	Tuscaloosa	A1 G13
6087	COX, John	36	SWNE	1839-09-20		A1
6127	CROOKS, Nancy	20	NE	1858-06-01		A1
6128	" "	20	SENW	1858-06-01		A1
6045	DAVIS, Edward	10	E½SW	1824-05-20		A1
6046	" "	15	E½NW	1824-05-20		A1
6136	DAVIS, Ralph C	22	W½NE	1835-10-01		A1
6166	DAWSON, William H	36	SESE	1880-02-20		A4
6165	FORBIS, William G	8	W½NE	1827-07-02		A1
6066	GARNER, James	28	SWSW	1844-07-10		A1
6089	GOODWIN, John	23	SENE	1839-09-20		A1
6090	GOODWIN, John M	2	NENE	1858-06-01		A1
6092	" "	2	SENE	1858-06-01		A1
6091	" "	2	NESE	1860-10-01		A1
6093	" "	2	W½NE	1860-10-01		A1
6118	GOODWIN, Leander F	36	SWSE	1883-07-03		A4
6123	GOODWIN, Mark	10	E½SE	1837-03-20		A1
6124	" "	14	N½NW	1839-09-20		A1
6129	GOODWIN, Oliver P	1	NWNW	1891-10-07		A1
6189	GOODWIN, Wyche	11	SWSE	1839-09-20		A1
6037	GREEN, Caleb S	14	NWSW	1858-06-01		A1
6036	GREER, Caleb	11	NWSE	1854-07-15		A1
6032	HAMMONDS, Andrew J	10	NENW	1858-06-01		A1
6055	HAMMONDS, Francis M	14	SESW	1858-06-01		A1
6062	HAMMONDS, Isham	10	S½NE	1860-10-01		A1 V6070
6132	HAMMONDS, Peter	15	SWNW	1839-09-20		A1
6048	HARDYMAN, Edwin T	36	NESE	1891-06-30		A4
6049	" "	36	SENE	1891-06-30		A4
6033	HENDERSON, Azor	6	W½SW	1825-06-20		A1 R6074
6058	HERRING, George W	26	E½SW	1885-03-16		A4

ID	Individual in Patent	Sec.	Sec. Part	Date Issued	Other Counties	For More Info . . .
6059	HERRING, George W (Cont'd)	26	W½SE	1885-03-16		A4
6063	HORTON, James C	4	E½SE	1889-03-01		A4
6064	" "	4	NESW	1889-03-01		A4
6065	" "	4	NWSE	1889-03-01		A4
6159	HORTON, William C	17	NESW	1852-01-01		A1
6031	HOWTON, Alfred J	6	NWSE	1860-12-01		A1
6041	HOWTON, David A	18	E½SW	1884-03-20		A4
6042	" "	18	S½SE	1884-03-20		A4
6072	HOWTON, James M	6	SESW	1891-06-30		A4
6073	" "	6	SWSE	1891-06-30		A4
6074	" "	6	W½SW	1891-06-30		A4 R6033
6104	HOWTON, Jonathan	4	SWNE	1852-01-01		A1
6103	" "	4	NWNE	1858-06-01		A1
6102	" "	4	NENE	1861-07-01		A1
6108	HOWTON, Joseph M	6	NESW	1883-10-01		A4
6109	" "	6	NWNW	1883-10-01		A4
6110	" "	6	S½NW	1883-10-01		A4
6161	HOWTON, William C	17	SWNE	1850-09-02		A1
6160	" "	17	SESW	1858-06-01		A1
6162	" "	17	SWSE	1858-06-01		A1
6113	HYCH, Josiah	28	NWSW	1858-06-01		A1
6111	JOHNSON, Joseph M	4	S½SW	1885-07-27		A1
6112	" "	4	SWSE	1885-07-27		A1
6137	JOHNSON, Randolph	10	W½SE	1837-03-20		A1
6143	JOHNSTON, Robert	17	NWSE	1858-06-01		A1
6130	JONES, Perry A	26	E½NE	1892-01-18		A4
6131	" "	26	E½SE	1892-01-18		A4
6167	JONES, William H	26	E½NW	1891-06-19		A4
6168	" "	26	NWSW	1891-06-19		A4
6169	" "	26	SWNW	1891-06-19		A4
6029	LAWSON, Albert A	36	N½SW	1889-06-05		A4
6030	" "	36	S½SW	1889-06-05		A4
6050	LOVETT, Elijah B	5	SESW	1839-09-20		A1
6051	" "	8	NENW	1839-09-20		A1
6120	MARTIN, Lorenzo D	2	NWSW	1860-10-01		A1
6121	" "	2	W½NW	1860-10-01		A1
6053	MCFERRIN, Elizabeth	28	NENW	1860-10-01		A1
6154	MITCHELL, Thomas	5	E½SE	1823-06-02		A1
6115	NELSON, Lawner B	29	NESW	1860-10-01		A1
6116	" "	29	SENW	1860-10-01		A1
6117	" "	29	SWNE	1860-10-01		A1
6034	PARSONS, Barnet	14	SWSW	1839-09-20		A1
6035	" "	23	NWNE	1839-09-20		A1
6038	PARSONS, Celia	8	NESW	1852-01-01		A1
6039	" "	8	SWNW	1858-06-01		A1
6052	PARSONS, Elijah	7	SWSW	1850-04-01		A1
6061	PARSONS, Isaiah	4	NWSW	1839-09-20		A1
6077	PARSONS, James	34	SWSE	1852-01-01		A1
6075	" "	34	E½SE	1858-06-01		A1
6076	" "	34	NWSE	1858-06-01		A1
6078	" "	35	SW	1858-06-01		A1
6096	PARSONS, John T	8	NENE	1839-09-20		A1
6097	" "	8	SENW	1839-09-20		A1
6106	PARSONS, Joseph C	26	NWNW	1839-09-20		A1
6105	" "	26	NWNE	1840-11-10		A1
6107	PARSONS, Joseph K	27	NENE	1858-06-01		A1
6114	PARSONS, Josiah	5	SWSE	1839-09-20		A1
6122	PARSONS, Malissa J	14	SE	1889-08-02		A4
6126	PARSONS, Miles	26	SWSW	1839-09-20		A1
6125	PARSONS, Miles J	27	SWSW	1849-05-01		A1
6133	PARSONS, Pinkney R	34	NESW	1884-12-05		A4
6134	" "	34	SENW	1884-12-05		A4
6135	" "	34	W½NE	1884-12-05		A4
6145	PARSONS, Samuel	22	SESE	1840-11-10		A1
6146	" "	23	SESE	1840-11-10		A1
6148	" "	24	NWSW	1849-08-01		A1
6147	" "	24	NESW	1858-06-01		A1
6149	" "	24	S½NW	1858-06-01		A1
6172	PARSONS, William	35	NWNW	1850-04-01		A1
6170	" "	27	SESE	1860-04-02		A1
6171	" "	34	E½NE	1860-04-02		A1
6173	" "	35	SWNW	1860-04-02		A1
6158	PARSONS, William A	23	W½SW	1858-06-01		A1

ID	Individual in Patent	Sec.	Sec. Part	Date Issued	Other Counties	For More Info . . .
6079	RANEY, James	11	SESE	1853-08-01		A1
6081	" "	12	SWSW	1854-07-15		A1
6080	" "	12	NWSW	1883-08-13		A4
6067	RANEY, James H	2	S½SW	1884-12-05		A4
6068	" "	2	W½SE	1884-12-05		A4
6082	RICHARDSON, James	30	SWSW	1858-06-01	Tuscaloosa	A1
6083	" "	30	W½SE	1858-06-01	Tuscaloosa	A1
6141	ROBERTSON, Reuben	8	W½SE	1837-03-20		A1
6140	" "	6	NESE	1839-09-20		A1
6174	ROBERTSON, William	15	SWNE	1839-09-20		A1
6175	" "	15	SWSE	1839-09-20		A1
6142	ROBISON, Reuben	5	SWSW	1839-09-20		A1
6060	RODGERS, George W	10	SWSW	1885-08-05		A1
6164	RODGERS, William F	3	SESE	1850-09-02		A1
6047	ROGERS, Edward	9	NESE	1852-01-01		A1
6095	ROGERS, John	15	NWSE	1858-06-01		A1
6098	ROGERS, John W	22	NESE	1853-08-01		A1
6056	ROSS, Francis	15	NESE	1839-09-20		A1
6057	" "	22	NWSE	1839-09-20		A1
6144	ROSS, Robert M	15	SESW	1839-09-20		A1
6178	STAGGS, William	32	SWSE	1854-07-15	Tuscaloosa	A1
6176	" "	32	NWSE	1860-10-01	Tuscaloosa	A1
6177	" "	32	SESW	1860-10-01	Tuscaloosa	A1
6138	STONE, Rauley	18	NENW	1839-09-20		A1
6139	" "	7	SESE	1839-09-20		A1
6099	STRINGFELLOW, John W	20	E½SW	1890-01-08		A4
6100	" "	20	N½SE	1890-01-08		A4
6179	TRAVIS, William	21	NWNW	1839-09-20		A1
6040	TURNER, Daniel K	32	W½SW	1915-08-28	Tuscaloosa	A4 R6043
6043	TURNER, David K	32	W½SW	1889-11-21	Tuscaloosa	A4 C R6040
6069	WOOD, James H	10	NWSW	1837-03-30		A1
6070	" "	10	SWNE	1837-03-30		A1 V6062
6150	WOOD, John	17	E½NW	1823-06-02		A1 G33
6151	" "	17	W½NW	1823-06-02		A1 G33
6101	" "	3	E½SW	1823-07-09		A1
6187	WOOD, William	9	E½NE	1834-10-21		A1
6186	" "	8	SESW	1837-04-01		A1
6183	" "	3	SENW	1839-09-20		A1
6185	" "	3	W½SE	1839-09-20		A1
6181	" "	18	SENE	1850-04-01		A1
6182	" "	18	SWNE	1852-01-01		A1
6188	" "	9	W½NE	1852-01-01		A1
6180	" "	10	NWNW	1853-08-01		A1
6184	" "	3	SWNE	1858-06-01		A1
6094	WOODSON, John P	18	NENE	1839-09-20		A1

Patent Map

T19-S R6-W
Huntsville Meridian

Map Group 36

Township Statistics

Parcels Mapped :	161
Number of Patents :	126
Number of Individuals :	92
Patentees Identified :	91
Number of Surnames :	48
Multi-Patentee Parcels :	3
Oldest Patent Date :	6/2/1823
Most Recent Patent :	8/28/1915
Block/Lot Parcels :	0
Parcels Re - Issued :	3
Parcels that Overlap :	2
Cities and Towns :	0
Cemeteries :	0

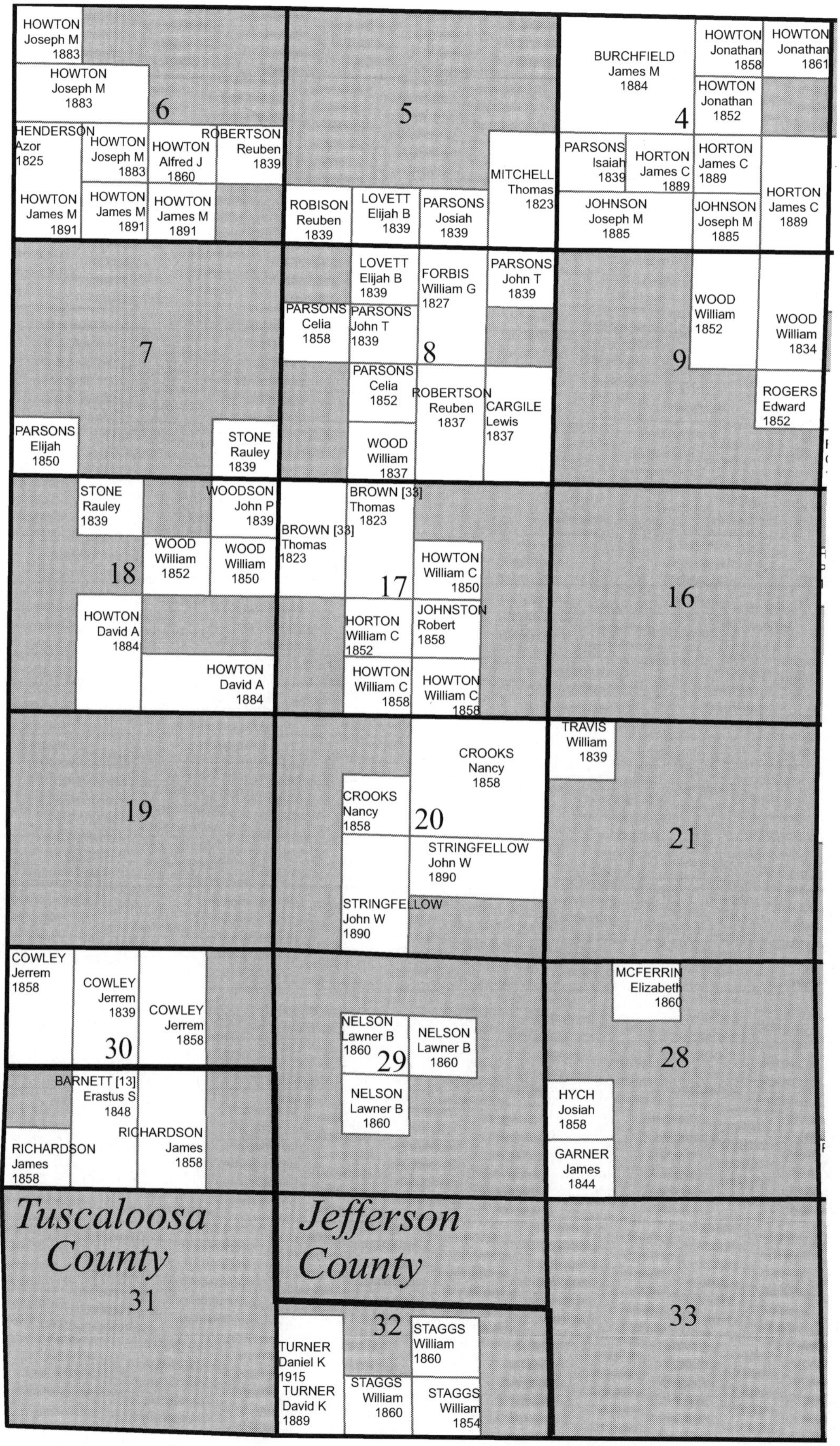

6
HOWTON Joseph M 1883
HOWTON Joseph M 1883
HENDERSON Azor 1825
HOWTON Joseph M 1883
HOWTON Alfred J 1860
ROBERTSON Reuben 1839
HOWTON James M 1891
HOWTON James M 1891
HOWTON James M 1891

5
ROBISON Reuben 1839
LOVETT Elijah B 1839
PARSONS Josiah 1839
MITCHELL Thomas 1823

4
BURCHFIELD James M 1884
HOWTON Jonathan 1858
HOWTON Jonathan 1861
HOWTON Jonathan 1852
PARSONS Isaiah 1839
HORTON James C 1889
HORTON James C 1889
JOHNSON Joseph M 1885
JOHNSON Joseph M 1885
HORTON James C 1889

7
PARSONS Elijah 1850
STONE Rauley 1839

8
LOVETT Elijah B 1839
FORBIS William G 1827
PARSONS John T 1839
PARSONS Celia 1858
PARSONS John T 1839
PARSONS Celia 1852
ROBERTSON Reuben 1837
CARGILE Lewis 1837
WOOD William 1837

9
WOOD William 1852
WOOD William 1834
ROGERS Edward 1852

18
STONE Rauley 1839
WOODSON John P 1839
WOOD William 1852
WOOD William 1850
HOWTON David A 1884
HOWTON David A 1884

17
BROWN [33] Thomas 1823
BROWN [33] Thomas 1823
HOWTON William C 1850
JOHNSTON Robert 1858
HORTON William C 1852
HOWTON William C 1858
HOWTON William C 1858

16

19

20
CROOKS Nancy 1858
CROOKS Nancy 1858
STRINGFELLOW John W 1890
STRINGFELLOW John W 1890

21
TRAVIS William 1839

30
COWLEY Jerrem 1858
COWLEY Jerrem 1839
COWLEY Jerrem 1858
BARNETT [13] Erastus S 1848
RICHARDSON James 1858
RICHARDSON James 1858

29
NELSON Lawner B 1860
NELSON Lawner B 1860
NELSON Lawner B 1860

28
MCFERRIN Elizabeth 1860
HYCH Josiah 1858
GARNER James 1844

Tuscaloosa County

31

Jefferson County

32
STAGGS William 1860
TURNER Daniel K 1915
TURNER David K 1889
STAGGS William 1860
STAGGS William 1854

33

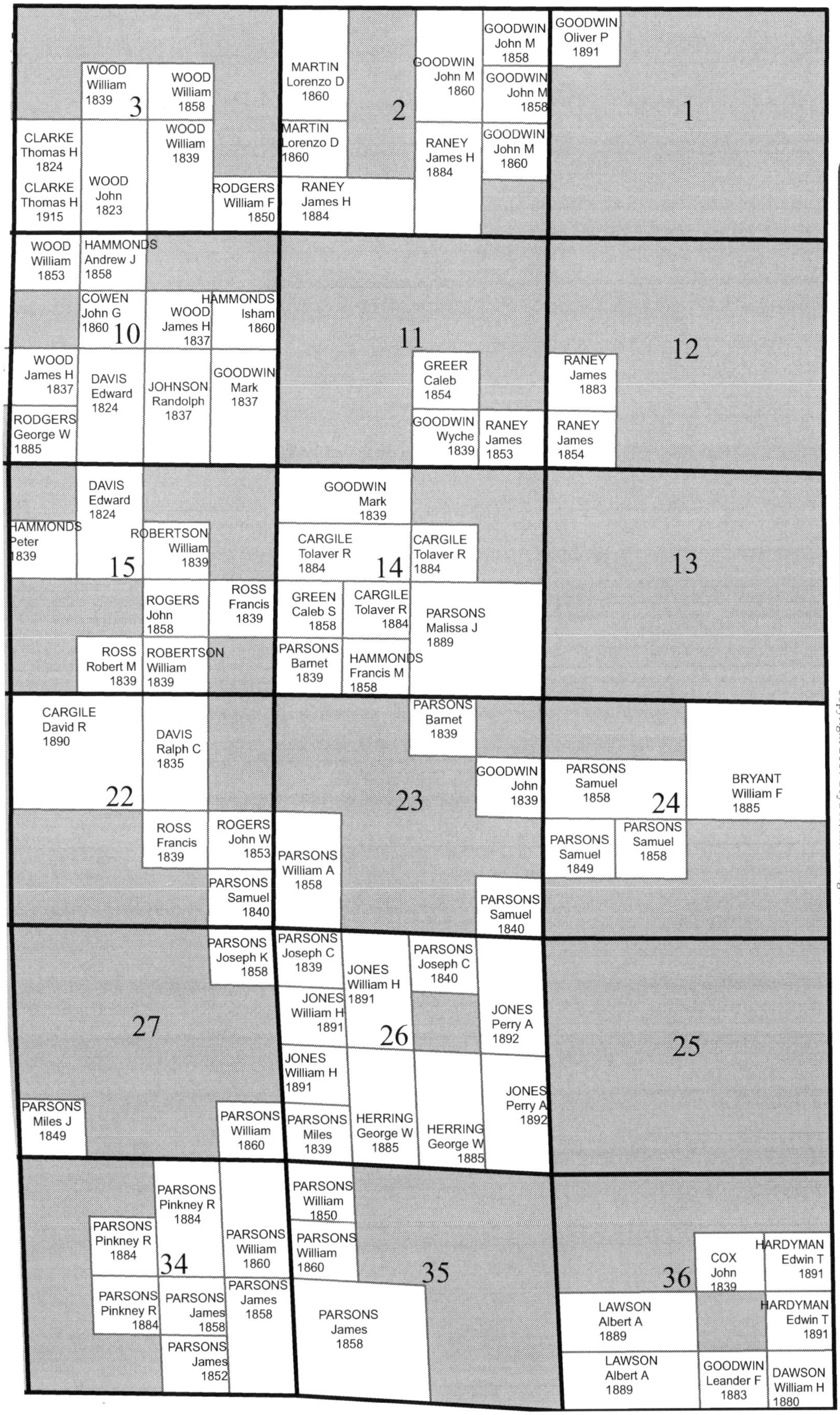

Helpful Hints

1. This Map's INDEX can be found on the preceding pages.
2. Refer to Map "C" to see where this Township lies within Jefferson County, Alabama.
3. Numbers within square brackets [ ] denote a multi-patentee land parcel (multi-owner). Refer to Appendix "C" for a full list of members in this group.
4. Areas that look to be crowded with Patentees usually indicate multiple sales of the same parcel (Re-issues) or Overlapping parcels. See this Township's Index for an explanation of these and other circumstances that might explain "odd" groupings of Patentees on this map.

Legend

- Patent Boundary
- Section Boundary
- No Patents Found (or Outside County)
- 1., 2., 3., ... Lot Numbers (when beside a name)
- [ ] Group Number (see Appendix "C")

Scale: Section = 1 mile X 1 mile (generally, with some exceptions)

Road Map

T19-S R6-W
Huntsville Meridian

Map Group 36

Cities & Towns
None

Cemeteries
None

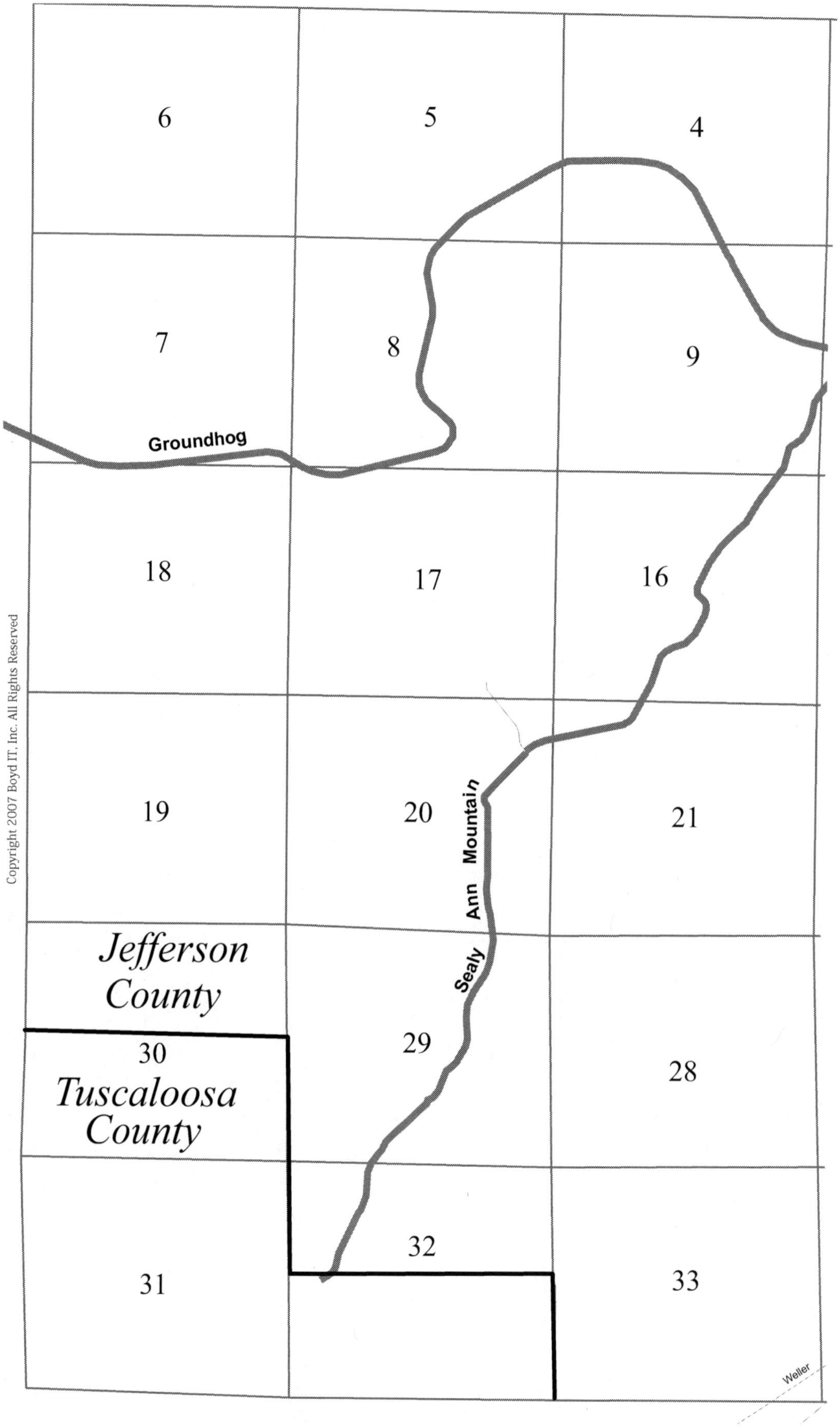

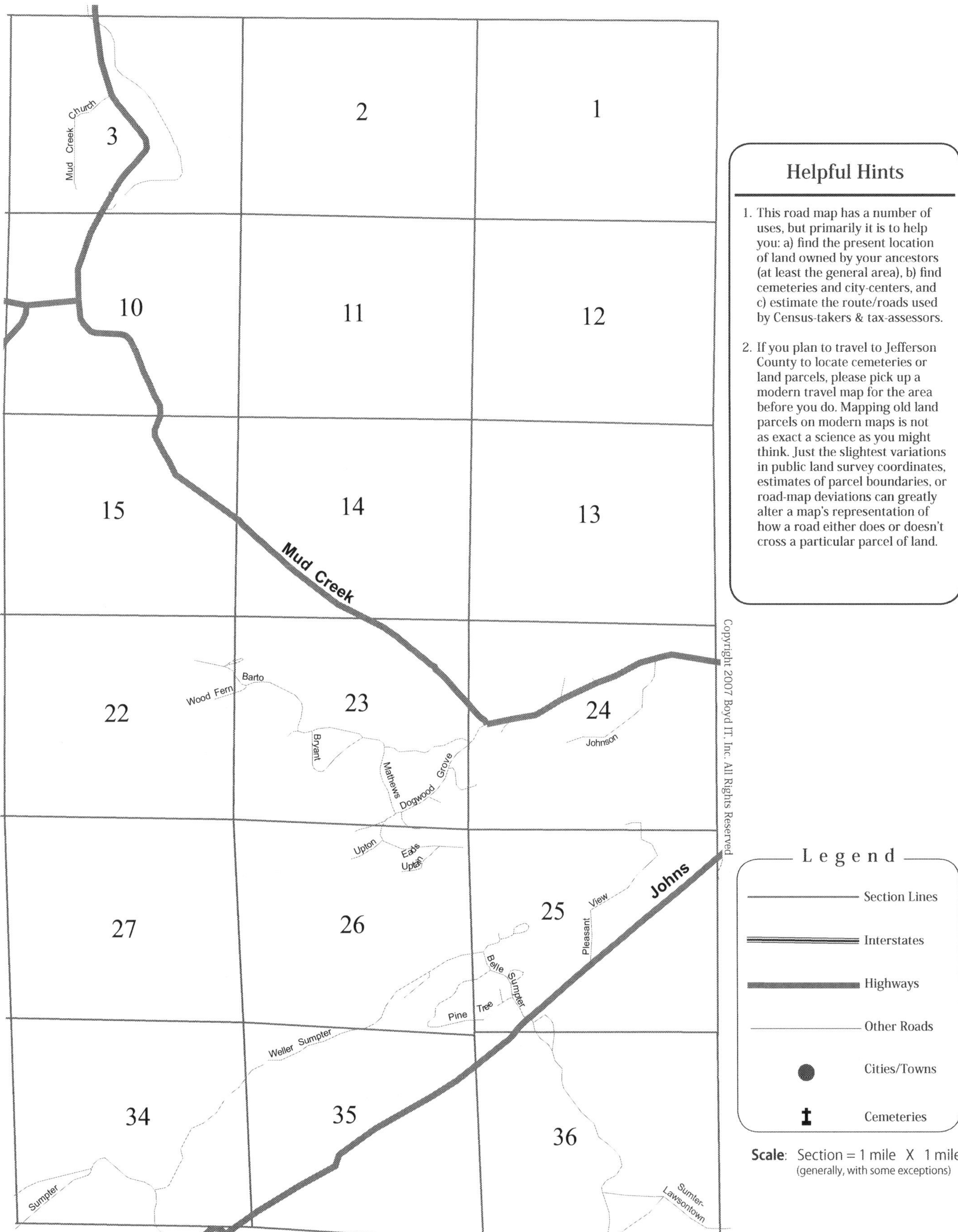
3
2
1
Mud Creek
Church
10
11
12
15
14
13
Mud Creek
22
23
24
Barto
Wood Fern
Bryant
Mathews
Dogwood
Grove
Johnson
27
26
25
Upton
Eads
Upton
Johns
View
Pleasant
Belle
Sumpter
Pine
Tree
34
35
36
Weller Sumpter
Sumpter
Sumter-Lawsontown
Helpful Hints
1. This road map has a number of uses, but primarily it is to help you: a) find the present location of land owned by your ancestors (at least the general area), b) find cemeteries and city-centers, and c) estimate the route/roads used by Census-takers & tax-assessors.
2. If you plan to travel to Jefferson County to locate cemeteries or land parcels, please pick up a modern travel map for the area before you do. Mapping old land parcels on modern maps is not as exact a science as you might think. Just the slightest variations in public land survey coordinates, estimates of parcel boundaries, or road-map deviations can greatly alter a map's representation of how a road either does or doesn't cross a particular parcel of land.
Copyright 2007 Boyd IT, Inc. All Rights Reserved
Legend
Section Lines
Interstates
Highways
Other Roads
Cities/Towns
Cemeteries
Scale: Section = 1 mile X 1 mile
(generally, with some exceptions)

Historical Map

T19-S R6-W
Huntsville Meridian

Map Group 36

Cities & Towns
None

Cemeteries
None

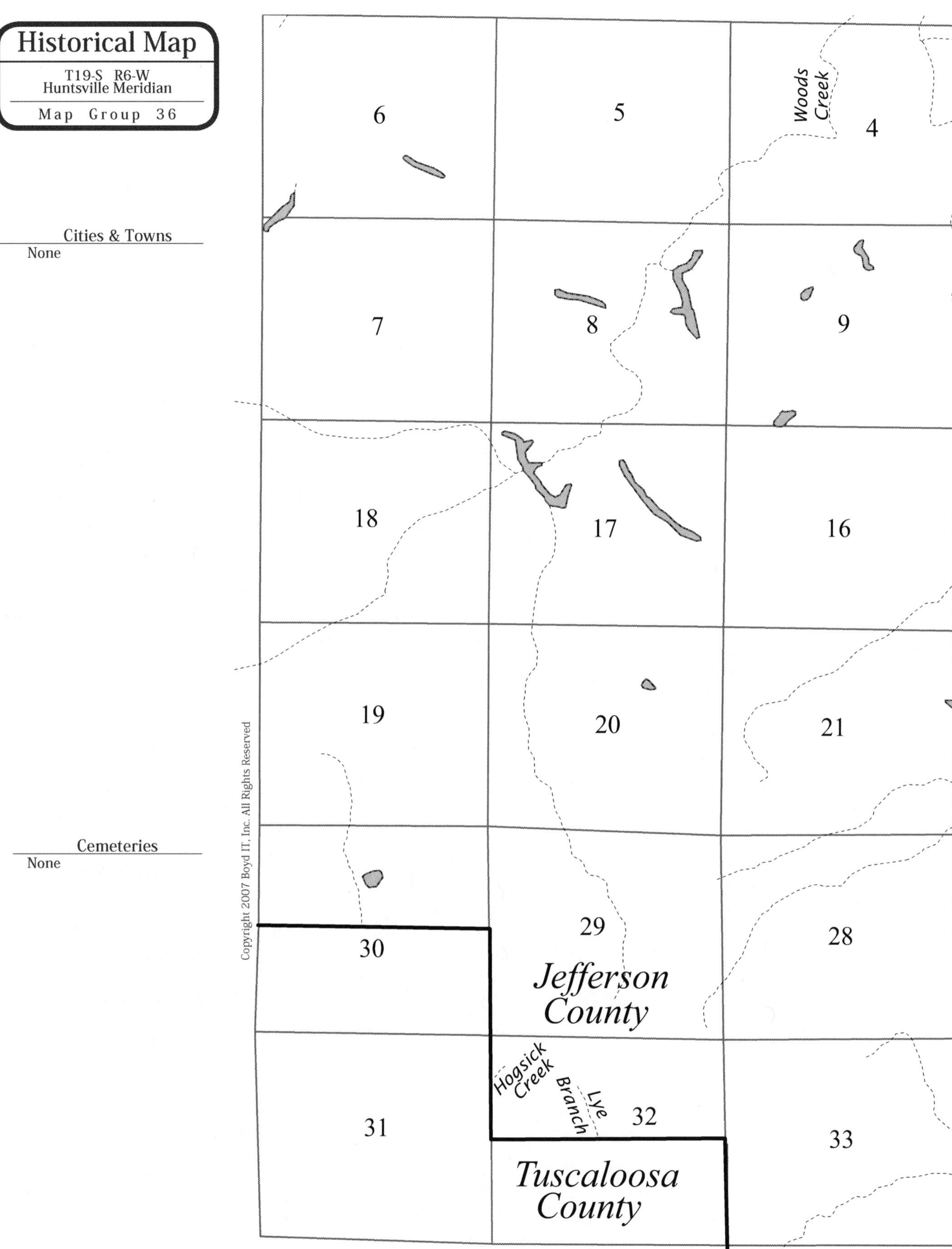

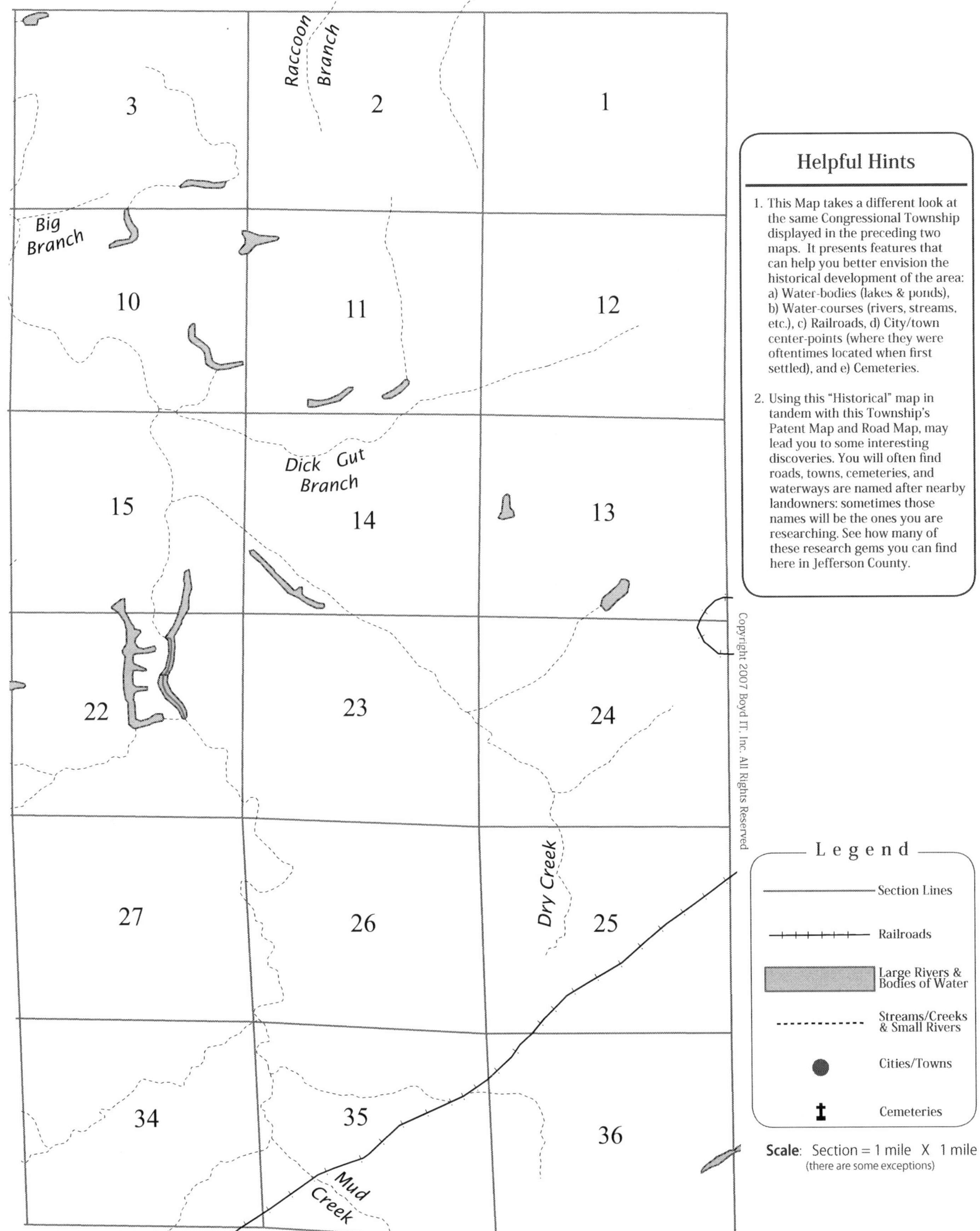

3
2
1
Raccoon Branch
Big Branch
10
11
12
Dick Gut Branch
15
14
13
22
23
24
Dry Creek
27
26
25
34
35
36
Mud Creek
Helpful Hints
1. This Map takes a different look at the same Congressional Township displayed in the preceding two maps. It presents features that can help you better envision the historical development of the area: a) Water-bodies (lakes & ponds), b) Water-courses (rivers, streams, etc.), c) Railroads, d) City/town center-points (where they were oftentimes located when first settled), and e) Cemeteries.
2. Using this "Historical" map in tandem with this Township's Patent Map and Road Map, may lead you to some interesting discoveries. You will often find roads, towns, cemeteries, and waterways are named after nearby landowners: sometimes those names will be the ones you are researching. See how many of these research gems you can find here in Jefferson County.
Copyright 2007 Boyd IT, Inc. All Rights Reserved
Legend
Section Lines
Railroads
Large Rivers & Bodies of Water
Streams/Creeks & Small Rivers
Cities/Towns
Cemeteries
Scale: Section = 1 mile X 1 mile
(there are some exceptions)

Map Group 37: Index to Land Patents

Township 19-South Range 5-West (Huntsville)

After you locate an individual in this Index, take note of the Section and Section Part then proceed to the Land Patent map on the pages immediately following. You should have no difficulty locating the corresponding parcel of land.

The "For More Info" Column will lead you to more information about the underlying Patents. See the *Legend* at right, and the "How to Use this Book" chapter, for more information.

LEGEND

"For More Info . . . " column

A = Authority (Legislative Act, See Appendix "A")
B = Block or Lot (location in Section unknown)
C = Cancelled Patent
F = Fractional Section
G = Group (Multi-Patentee Patent, see Appendix "C")
V = Overlaps another Parcel
R = Re-Issued (Parcel patented more than once)

(A & G items require you to look in the Appendixes referred to above. All other Letter-designations followed by a number require you to locate line-items in this index that possess the ID number found after the letter).

ID	Individual in Patent	Sec.	Sec. Part	Date Issued	Other Counties	For More Info . . .
6393	BIRD, William M	28	W½SW	1884-03-20		A4
6228	BRIDGES, George M	2	S½SE	1884-12-05		A4
6227	" "	2	N½SE	1885-06-20		A4
6372	BRIDGES, Thomas W	2	NW	1891-11-23		A4
6200	CALDWELL, Carroll H	4	SENW	1885-03-30		A4
6201	" "	4	SWNE	1885-03-30		A4
6242	CALDWELL, Hugh	4	NWNE	1885-03-16		A1
6290	CHAPEL, John	35	E½NE	1912-02-15		A1 G47 V6241
6365	COMPANY, Sims Scott And	25	W½NE	1825-09-01		A1
6366	" "	25	W½NW	1825-09-01		A1
6217	CONDRAY, Elijah	13	SWSE	1837-03-30		A1
6207	CONDRY, Cristenia	20	SENW	1839-09-20		A1
6226	COX, George A	34	NW	1891-06-08		A4
6236	COX, Hiram	21	SENE	1850-04-01		A1
6237	" "	21	SWNE	1858-06-01		A1
6238	" "	22	N½SW	1858-06-01		A1
6240	" "	22	SENW	1858-06-01		A1
6239	" "	22	NWSE	1882-07-25		A4
6291	COX, John	29	NWSW	1839-09-20		A1
6312	COX, Jordan P	20	E½SW	1891-06-29		A4
6313	" "	20	S½SE	1891-06-29		A4
6340	CRANE, Odam	31	SESE	1852-01-01		A1
6344	" "	32	SWSW	1852-01-01		A1
6343	" "	32	SWSE	1854-07-15		A1
6339	" "	31	NESE	1858-06-01		A1
6341	" "	32	E½SW	1858-06-01		A1
6342	" "	32	NWSW	1858-06-01		A1
6346	CROOKS, Rebecca S	28	SENE	1891-06-29		A1 G62
6348	CUMMINS, Ridley T	30	E½NE	1885-11-13		A1
6259	DENTON, James	24	E½SW	1839-09-20		A1 G74
6190	DICKEY, Aaron B	14	NWSW	1885-07-27		A1 R6208
6191	" "	14	SWNW	1885-07-27		A1
6397	DILLARD, William R	30	W½NE	1885-11-13		A1
6376	DUFF, Walter	35	E½SE	1915-08-09		A1 G75
6282	EARLEY, Jesse	14	NE	1885-03-16		A4
6347	HALL, Renny B	19	NWNW	1848-07-01		A1
6386	HALL, William J	8	SESE	1858-06-01		A1
6387	" "	9	W½SW	1858-06-01		A1
6260	HAMAKER, James	4	SWNW	1839-09-20		A1
6292	HAMAKER, John	10	SESE	1839-09-20		A1
6293	" "	10	SWSE	1839-09-20		A1
6294	" "	15	NWSE	1839-09-20		A1
6295	" "	15	SWNE	1839-09-20		A1
6296	" "	4	NWSW	1858-06-01		A1
6385	HAMAKER, William	4	SESW	1852-01-01		A1
6384	" "	10	N½SE	1883-07-03		A4

ID	Individual in Patent	Sec.	Sec. Part	Date Issued	Other Counties	For More Info . . .
6330	HARRIS, Mark M	11	W½SW	1823-05-01		A1 G125
6280	HOPKINS, James W	10	S½NE	1891-11-23		A4
6368	HOPKINS, Thomas	10	NENW	1883-10-01		A4
6369	" "	10	NWNE	1883-10-01		A4
6324	HOUSTON, Loyd	12	SWSW	1892-06-10		A4
6192	HOWELL, Alexander H	15	SWSE	1839-09-20		A1
6211	JOHNSTON, Duncan	5	W½NE	1823-05-01		A1
6353	JONES, Robert	12	NWNW	1890-04-15		A1
6350	JONES, Robert A	30	SESW	1876-04-01		A4
6351	" "	30	SWSE	1876-04-01		A4
6349	" "	30	NESW	1884-12-05		A4
6352	" "	30	SWSW	1884-12-05		A4
6334	JORDAN, Mortimer	12	W½NE	1853-08-01		A1
6335	JORDON, Mortimer	1	S½SE	1858-06-01		A1
6336	" "	12	E½NW	1858-06-01		A1
6358	LANE, Sampson	13	W½NW	1915-08-12		A1 G155
6262	LEDLOW, James	18	N½SW	1858-06-01		A1
6263	" "	18	SENW	1858-06-01		A1
6196	LETSON, Andrew J	18	E½SE	1883-10-20		A1
6220	MARTIN, Francis M	4	S½SE	1883-07-03		A4
6205	MCADORY, Charles	14	NWNW	1884-03-20		A4
6259	MCADORY, James	24	E½SW	1839-09-20		A1 G74
6278	" "	24	NWNE	1852-01-01		A1
6279	" "	24	W½SE	1852-01-01		A1
6267	" "	10	NWNW	1854-07-15		A1
6268	" "	13	E½SE	1854-07-15		A1
6269	" "	13	NENW	1854-07-15		A1
6271	" "	13	NWSE	1854-07-15		A1
6272	" "	13	NWSW	1854-07-15		A1
6274	" "	13	SESW	1854-07-15		A1
6275	" "	14	NESE	1854-07-15		A1
6276	" "	23	NESE	1854-07-15		A1
6277	" "	23	SENE	1854-07-15		A1
6270	" "	13	NESW	1858-06-01		A1
6273	" "	13	SENW	1858-06-01		A1
6290	MCASHAN, John	35	E½NE	1912-02-15		A1 G47 V6241
6376	" "	35	E½SE	1915-08-09		A1 G75
6298	MCCLINTON, John	14	SESE	1835-10-01		A1
6297	" "	13	SWSW	1839-09-20		A1
6202	MCDANIEL, Catherine	20	NESE	1885-03-16		A4
6203	" "	20	SENE	1885-03-16		A4
6206	MOORE, Charles P	32	NENW	1852-01-01		A1
6256	MOORE, James B	35	W½NE	1839-09-20		A1
6289	MOORE, John B	36	SW	1832-01-02		A1
6286	" "	15	NWSW	1852-01-01		A1
6287	" "	22	NWNW	1852-01-01		A1
6288	" "	22	SWNW	1852-01-01		A1
6396	MOORE, William	25	SESW	1834-10-01		A1
6395	" "	25	NESW	1837-04-01		A1
6394	" "	25	E½NW	1839-09-20		A1
6379	MOORE, William B	23	SESE	1854-07-15		A1
6377	" "	21	NENE	1858-06-01		A1
6378	" "	22	NENW	1858-06-01		A1
6380	" "	23	SWSE	1858-06-01		A1
6381	" "	26	NWNE	1858-06-01		A1
6406	MOORE, Willis W	23	NENE	1860-04-02		A1
6407	" "	23	W½NE	1860-04-02		A1
6360	MOSES, Samuel F	15	NESW	1858-06-01		A1
6361	" "	15	W½NW	1858-06-01		A1
6362	" "	22	NWNE	1858-06-01		A1
6261	NAIL, James L	28	N½NE	1876-04-01		A4
6346	NAIL, Rebecca S	28	SENE	1891-06-29		A1 G62
6235	OWEN, Harrison	22	S½NE	1889-08-16		A4
6198	PARSONS, Benjamin	15	SENE	1839-09-20		A1
6197	" "	15	NESE	1853-08-01		A1
6218	PARSONS, Ervin	5	NW	1858-06-01		A1
6219	" "	5	NWSW	1858-06-01		A1
6222	PARSONS, Garrett	26	NWSE	1839-09-20		A1
6223	" "	26	SW	1858-06-01		A1
6224	" "	26	SWSE	1858-06-01		A1
6225	" "	27	E½SE	1858-06-01		A1
6231	PARSONS, George	8	SWNE	1849-09-01		A1
6229	" "	8	NWNE	1858-06-01		A1

ID	Individual in Patent	Sec.	Sec. Part	Date Issued	Other Counties	For More Info . . .
6230	PARSONS, George (Cont'd)	8	SENW	1858-06-01		A1
6232	PARSONS, Green	8	NESW	1876-04-01		A4
6244	PARSONS, Isaac B	18	SESW	1883-07-03		A4
6245	" "	18	SWSE	1883-07-03		A4
6243	" "	18	NWSE	1891-06-30		A4
6246	" "	18	SWSW	1891-06-30		A4
6257	PARSONS, James B	30	N½NW	1876-04-01		A4
6258	" "	30	S½NW	1885-03-30		A4
6264	PARSONS, James M	8	SESW	1885-03-30		A4
6265	" "	8	SWSE	1885-03-30		A4
6266	" "	8	W½SW	1885-03-30		A4
6303	PARSONS, John	26	SENE	1837-03-30		A1
6299	" "	17	NENE	1839-09-20		A1
6300	" "	17	NESW	1839-09-20		A1 R6325
6302	" "	17	SENE	1839-09-20		A1
6301	" "	17	NWNE	1858-06-01		A1
6311	PARSONS, John W	2	S½SW	1891-06-29		A4
6314	PARSONS, Joseph	15	NENE	1839-09-20		A1
6320	PARSONS, Josiah L	17	NESE	1853-08-01		A1
6321	" "	17	SWNE	1858-06-01		A1
6322	PARSONS, Leander F	8	E½NE	1885-06-20		A4
6323	" "	8	N½SE	1885-06-20		A4
6328	PARSONS, Lucinda	20	NWNW	1852-01-01		A1
6325	" "	17	NESW	1858-06-01		A1 R6300
6326	" "	17	NWSE	1858-06-01		A1
6327	" "	17	SWSW	1858-06-01		A1
6354	PARSONS, Robert	18	NENE	1852-01-01		A1
6355	" "	18	SENE	1858-06-01		A1
6356	" "	18	W½NE	1858-06-01		A1
6357	" "	34	E½	1858-06-01		A1
6367	PARSONS, Stephen	15	E½NW	1839-09-20		A1
6383	PARSONS, William B	6	NWNW	1849-05-01		A1
6382	" "	6	NENW	1858-06-01		A1
6409	PARSONS, Zachariah T	10	SW	1884-12-05		A4
6212	PATTERSON, Edward	20	NENW	1858-06-01		A1
6213	" "	20	NWNE	1858-06-01		A1
6214	" "	27	W½NW	1858-06-01		A1
6283	PERSONS, Job	15	NWNE	1839-09-20		A1
6304	PERSONS, John	17	SESW	1839-09-20		A1
6305	" "	17	SWSE	1839-09-20		A1
6241	PETERSON, Hopson	35	SENE	1839-09-20		A1 V6290
6221	PRINCE, Francis M	26	N½NW	1889-10-07		A1
6204	PRUDE, Celia	24	SWNE	1839-09-20		A1
6388	RANEY, William J	29	E½SW	1858-06-01		A1
6389	" "	29	SENW	1858-06-01		A1
6390	" "	29	SWNE	1858-06-01		A1
6391	" "	29	SWSW	1858-06-01		A1
6392	" "	30	E½SE	1858-06-01		A1
6399	SADDLER, William R	24	E½SE	1823-05-01		A1
6398	" "	24	E½NE	1823-06-02		A1
6193	SADLER, Allions T	25	NENE	1844-07-10		A1
6199	SADLER, Caroline M	25	SENE	1849-05-01		A1
6400	SADLER, William R	12	E½NE	1824-10-20		A1 R6401
6401	" "	12	E½NE	1915-08-12		A1 R6400
6290	SCOTT, David	35	E½NE	1912-02-15		A1 G47 V6241
6233	SELLERS, Gurley	28	SESW	1884-03-10		A4
6234	" "	28	SWSE	1884-03-10		A4
6309	SELLERS, John	28	SENW	1876-04-01		A4
6310	" "	28	SWNE	1876-04-01		A4
6308	" "	28	N½NW	1885-09-10		A4
6332	SELLERS, Mary	28	NESW	1884-03-10		A4
6333	" "	28	NWSE	1884-03-10		A4 R6370
6331	" "	28	E½SE	1884-12-05		A4
6248	SHARP, Jacob	20	NWSW	1849-08-01		A1
6247	" "	19	NESE	1853-08-01		A1
6249	" "	20	SWNE	1858-06-01		A1
6250	" "	20	SWNW	1858-06-01		A1
6251	" "	20	SWSW	1858-06-01		A1
6252	" "	32	N½NE	1858-06-01		A1
6254	" "	32	SENW	1858-06-01		A1
6255	" "	32	W½NW	1858-06-01		A1
6253	" "	32	SENE	1875-06-01		A4
6345	SHAW, Pleasant	15	S½SW	1839-09-20		A1

ID	Individual in Patent	Sec.	Sec. Part	Date Issued	Other Counties	For More Info . . .
6330	SIMS, Edward	11	W½SW	1823-05-01		A1 G125
6284	SNOW, Joel G	26	S½NW	1858-06-01		A1
6285	" "	26	SWNE	1858-06-01		A1
6337	SPENCER, Octavius	1	E½NE	1854-07-15		A1
6338	" "	1	SWNE	1854-07-15		A1
6408	STAGGS, Willoughby	19	SESE	1844-07-10		A1
6402	TANNAHILL, William	36	NE	1832-01-02		A1
6404	TATUM, William	5	W½SE	1839-09-20		A1
6403	" "	31	SWSE	1852-01-01		A1
6195	TAYLOR, Anderson	22	S½SW	1883-08-13		A4
6194	" "	22	S½SE	1885-03-30		A4
6358	THOMAS, Benjamin	13	W½NW	1915-08-12		A1 G155
6208	THOMAS, Cubid	14	NWSW	1883-08-13		A4 R6190
6209	THOMAS, Cupid	14	SESW	1889-11-21		A4
6210	" "	14	W½SE	1889-11-21		A4
6330	THOMAS, John	11	W½SW	1823-05-01		A1 G125
6306	THOMAS, John R	35	SWSE	1859-04-01		A1
6307	" "	35	SWSW	1859-04-01		A1
6405	THOMAS, William	35	NWSE	1839-09-20		A1
6371	THOMPSON, Thomas	32	E½SE	1883-08-13		A4
6215	THORNE, Elias	14	NESW	1885-06-20		A4
6216	" "	14	SENW	1885-06-20		A4
6359	THORNE, Sampson	22	NESE	1884-03-10		A4
6281	TOWERS, Jasper	34	SW	1899-12-21		A1
6364	WALDROP, Samuel R	5	NENE	1837-04-01		A1
6363	" "	4	NENW	1839-09-20		A1
6318	WARE, Joshua S	12	NWSW	1884-03-20		A4
6319	" "	12	SWNW	1884-03-20		A4
6317	" "	12	E½SW	1889-11-21		A4
6329	WASHINGTON, Luxie	14	NENW	1889-11-21		A4
6375	WILLARD, Thomas	19	SWNE	1850-09-02		A1
6373	" "	19	NENE	1854-07-15		A1
6374	" "	19	SENE	1858-06-01		A1
6370	WILSON, Thomas J	28	NWSE	1894-06-15		A4 R6333
6315	WOOD, Joseph	32	NWSE	1875-06-01		A4
6316	" "	32	SWNE	1875-06-01		A4

Patent Map

T19-S R5-W
Huntsville Meridian

Map Group 37

Township Statistics

Parcels Mapped	:	220
Number of Patents	:	173
Number of Individuals	:	113
Patentees Identified	:	107
Number of Surnames	:	68
Multi-Patentee Parcels	:	6
Oldest Patent Date	:	5/1/1823
Most Recent Patent	:	8/12/1915
Block/Lot Parcels	:	0
Parcels Re - Issued	:	4
Parcels that Overlap	:	2
Cities and Towns	:	3
Cemeteries	:	3

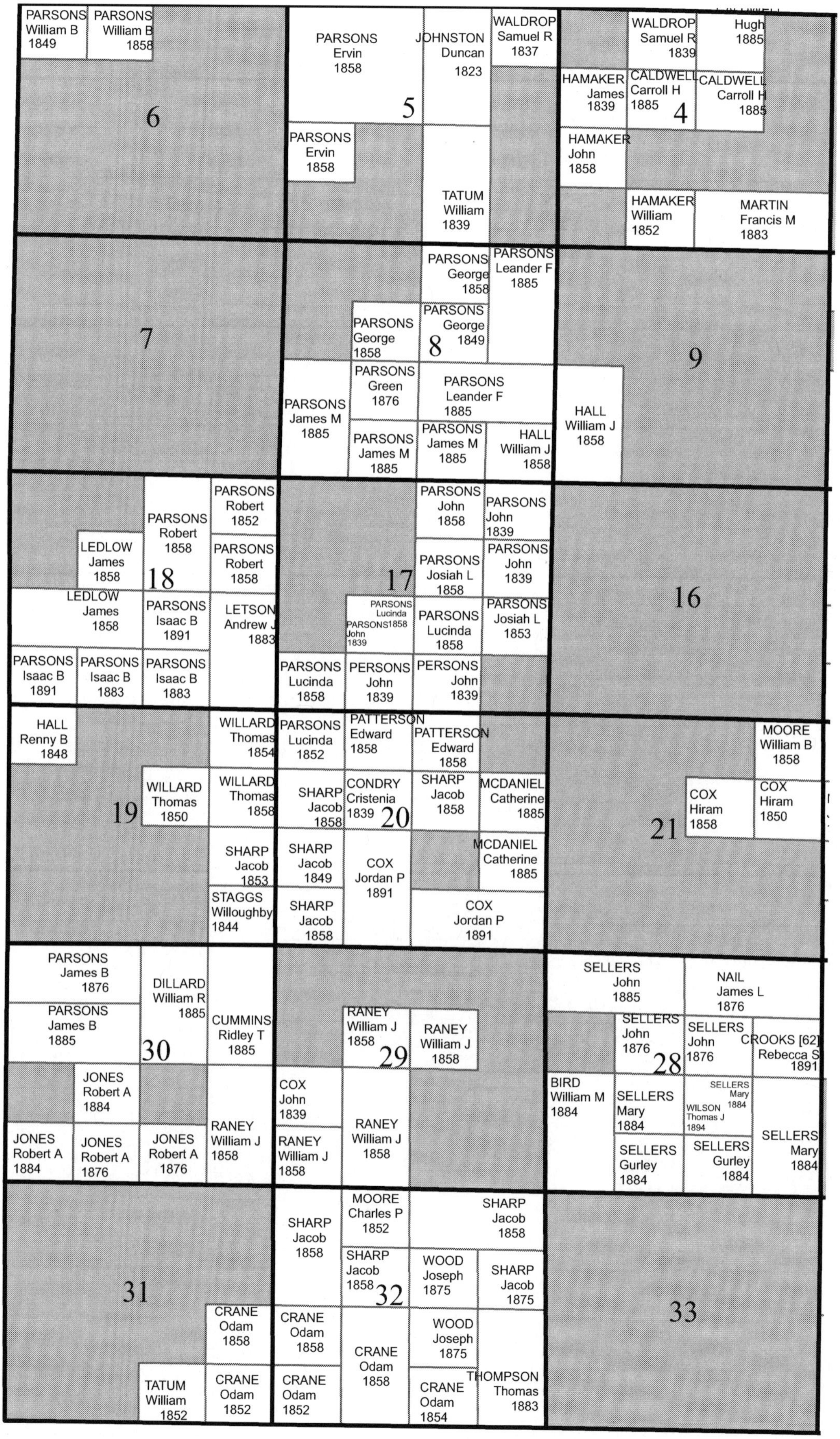

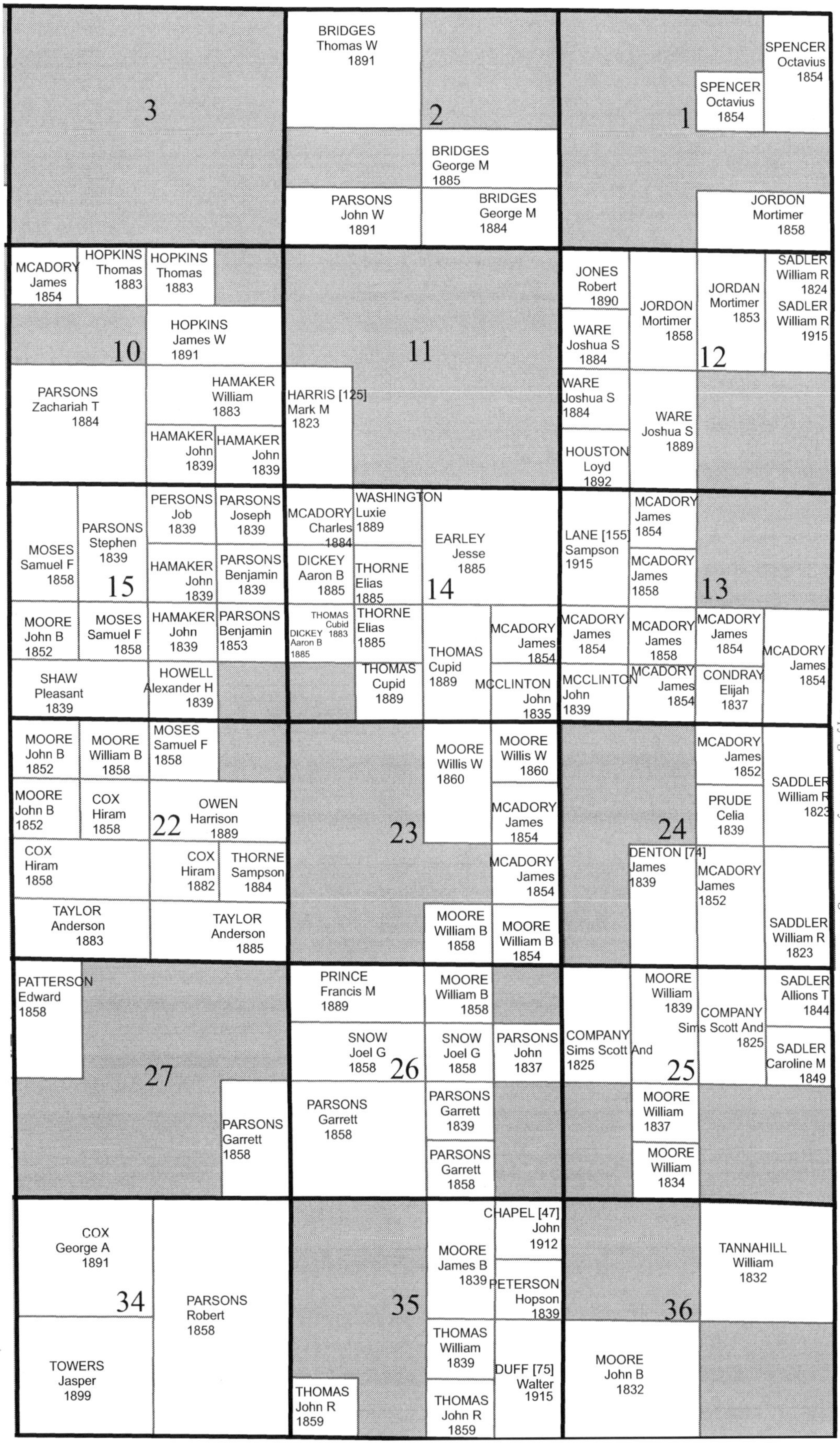

3
BRIDGES Thomas W 1891
2
BRIDGES George M 1885
PARSONS John W 1891
BRIDGES George M 1884
SPENCER Octavius 1854
SPENCER Octavius 1854
1
JORDON Mortimer 1858

MCADORY James 1854
HOPKINS Thomas 1883
HOPKINS Thomas 1883
HOPKINS James W 1891
10
PARSONS Zachariah T 1884
HAMAKER William 1883
HAMAKER John 1839
HAMAKER John 1839
11
HARRIS [125] Mark M 1823
JONES Robert 1890
WARE Joshua S 1884
WARE Joshua S 1884
HOUSTON Loyd 1892
JORDON Mortimer 1858
WARE Joshua S 1889
JORDAN Mortimer 1853
SADLER William R 1824
SADLER William R 1915
12

MOSES Samuel F 1858
PARSONS Stephen 1839
15
PERSONS Job 1839
PARSONS Joseph 1839
HAMAKER John 1839
PARSONS Benjamin 1839
MOORE John B 1852
MOSES Samuel F 1858
HAMAKER John 1839
PARSONS Benjamin 1853
SHAW Pleasant 1839
HOWELL Alexander H 1839
MCADORY Charles 1884
WASHINGTON Luxie 1889
DICKEY Aaron B 1885
THORNE Elias 1885
EARLEY Jesse 1885
14
THOMAS Cubid 1883
DICKEY Aaron B 1885
THORNE Elias 1885
THOMAS Cupid 1889
THOMAS Cupid 1889
MCADORY James 1854
MCCLINTON John 1835
LANE [155] Sampson 1915
MCADORY James 1854
MCADORY James 1858
13
MCADORY James 1854
MCADORY James 1858
MCADORY James 1854
MCADORY James 1854
MCCLINTON John 1839
MCADORY James 1854
CONDRAY Elijah 1837

MOORE John B 1852
MOORE William B 1858
MOSES Samuel F 1858
MOORE John B 1852
COX Hiram 1858
OWEN Harrison 1889
22
COX Hiram 1858
COX Hiram 1882
THORNE Sampson 1884
TAYLOR Anderson 1883
TAYLOR Anderson 1885
23
MOORE Willis W 1860
MOORE Willis W 1860
MCADORY James 1854
MCADORY James 1854
MOORE William B 1858
MOORE William B 1854
24
MCADORY James 1852
PRUDE Celia 1839
SADDLER William R 1823
DENTON [74] James 1839
MCADORY James 1852
SADDLER William R 1823

PATTERSON Edward 1858
27
PARSONS Garrett 1858
PRINCE Francis M 1889
MOORE William B 1858
SNOW Joel G 1858
26
SNOW Joel G 1858
PARSONS John 1837
PARSONS Garrett 1858
PARSONS Garrett 1839
PARSONS Garrett 1858
COMPANY Sims Scott And 1825
MOORE William 1839
COMPANY Sims Scott And 1825
SADLER Allions T 1844
SADLER Caroline M 1849
25
MOORE William 1837
MOORE William 1834

COX George A 1891
34
PARSONS Robert 1858
TOWERS Jasper 1899
35
MOORE James B 1839
CHAPEL [47] John 1912
PETERSON Hopson 1839
THOMAS William 1839
DUFF [75] Walter 1915
THOMAS John R 1859
THOMAS John R 1859
36
TANNAHILL William 1832
MOORE John B 1832

Helpful Hints

1. This Map's INDEX can be found on the preceding pages.
2. Refer to Map "C" to see where this Township lies within Jefferson County, Alabama.
3. Numbers within square brackets [ ] denote a multi-patentee land parcel (multi-owner). Refer to Appendix "C" for a full list of members in this group.
4. Areas that look to be crowded with Patentees usually indicate multiple sales of the same parcel (Re-issues) or Overlapping parcels. See this Township's Index for an explanation of these and other circumstances that might explain "odd" groupings of Patentees on this map.

Legend

Patent Boundary
Section Boundary
No Patents Found (or Outside County)
1., 2., 3., ... Lot Numbers (when beside a name)
[ ] Group Number (see Appendix "C")

Scale: Section = 1 mile X 1 mile (generally, with some exceptions)

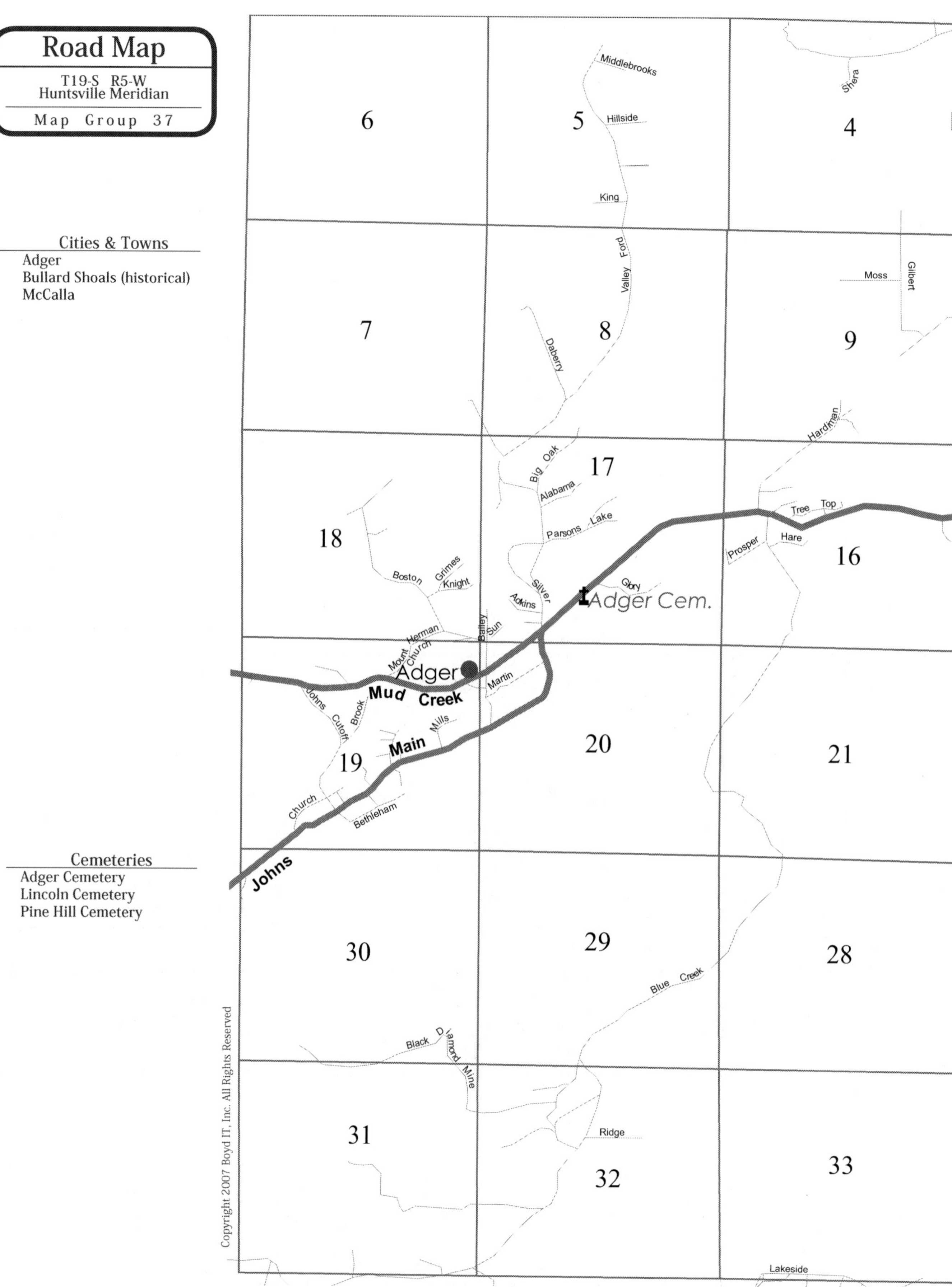
Road Map
T19-S R5-W
Huntsville Meridian
Map Group 37
Cities & Towns
Adger
Bullard Shoals (historical)
McCalla
Cemeteries
Adger Cemetery
Lincoln Cemetery
Pine Hill Cemetery
6
5
4
7
8
9
18
17
16
19
20
21
30
29
28
31
32
33
Middlebrooks
Hillside
King
Shera
Valley Ford
Moss
Gilbert
Daberry
Hardiman
Big Oak
Alabama
Parsons Lake
Tree Top
Hare
Prosper
Boston
Grimes
Knight
Silver
Adkins
Glory
Adger Cem.
Bailey
Sun
Herman
Mount Church
Adger
Martin
Mud Creek
Johns Cutoff
Brook
Mills
Main
Church
Bethlehem
Johns
Blue Creek
Black Diamond Mine
Ridge
Lakeside

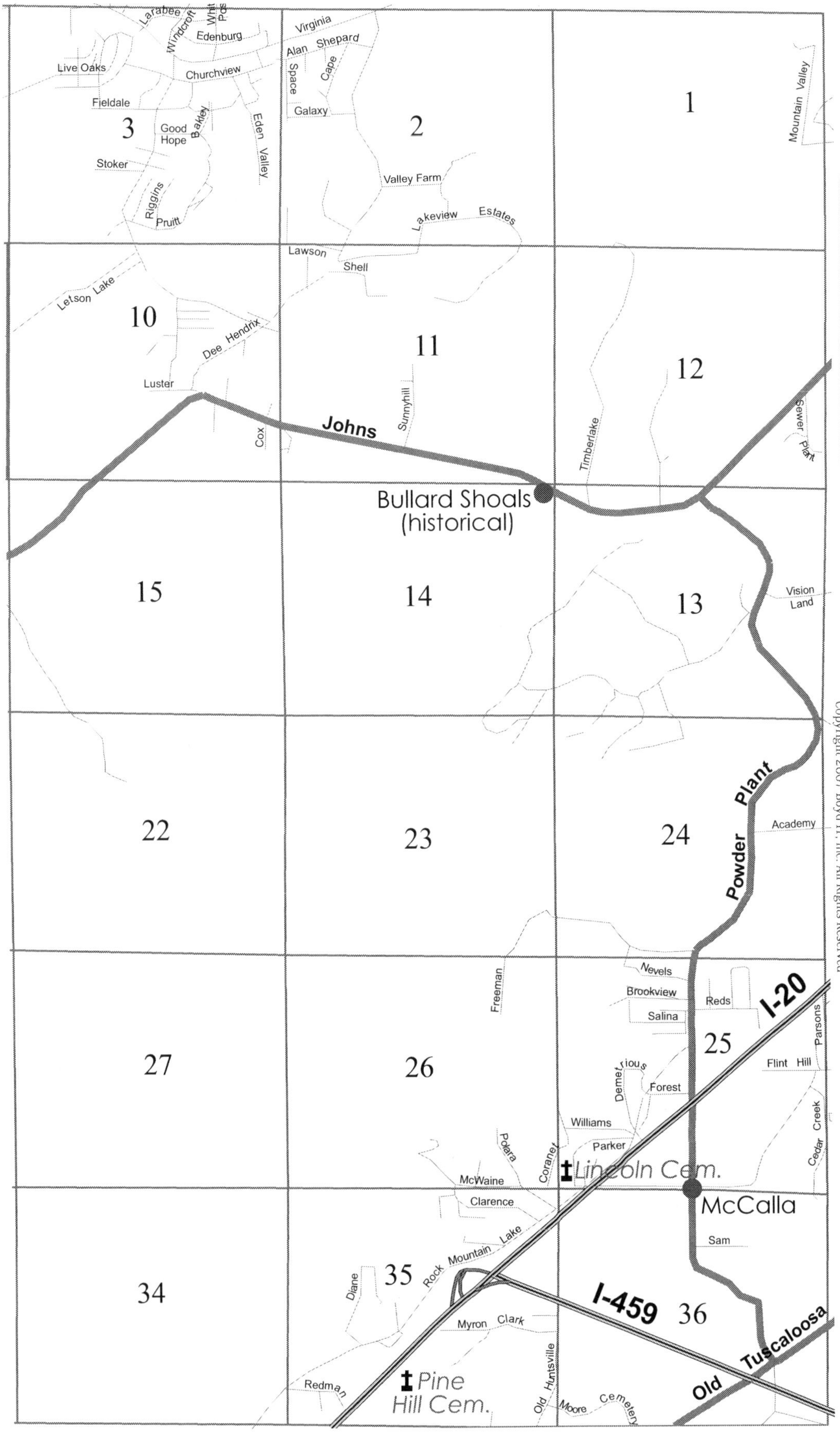

Larabee
Windcroft
Whit Pos
Edenburg
Virginia
Alan Shepard
Live Oaks
Churchview
Space
Cape
Fieldale
Galaxy
Mountain Valley
1
3
Good Hope
Bakley
Eden Valley
2
Stoker
Valley Farm
Riggins
Pruitt
Lakeview Estates
Lawson
Shell
Letson Lake
10
Dee Hendrix
11
12
Luster
Sunnyhill
Timberlake
Sewer Plant
Cox
Johns
Bullard Shoals (historical)
15
14
13
Vision Land
22
23
24
Powder Plant
Academy
Nevels
Freeman
Brookview
Reds
I-20
Salina
Parsons
25
27
26
Demetrious
Flint Hill
Forest
Cedar Creek
Williams
Parker
Polara
Coranet
Lincoln Cem.
McWaine
McCalla
Clarence
Sam
Lake
Rock Mountain
34
Diane
35
I-459
36
Myron
Clark
Old Tuscaloosa
Redman
Pine Hill Cem.
Old Huntsville
Moore
Cemetery

Helpful Hints

1. This road map has a number of uses, but primarily it is to help you: a) find the present location of land owned by your ancestors (at least the general area), b) find cemeteries and city-centers, and c) estimate the route/roads used by Census-takers & tax-assessors.

2. If you plan to travel to Jefferson County to locate cemeteries or land parcels, please pick up a modern travel map for the area before you do. Mapping old land parcels on modern maps is not as exact a science as you might think. Just the slightest variations in public land survey coordinates, estimates of parcel boundaries, or road-map deviations can greatly alter a map's representation of how a road either does or doesn't cross a particular parcel of land.

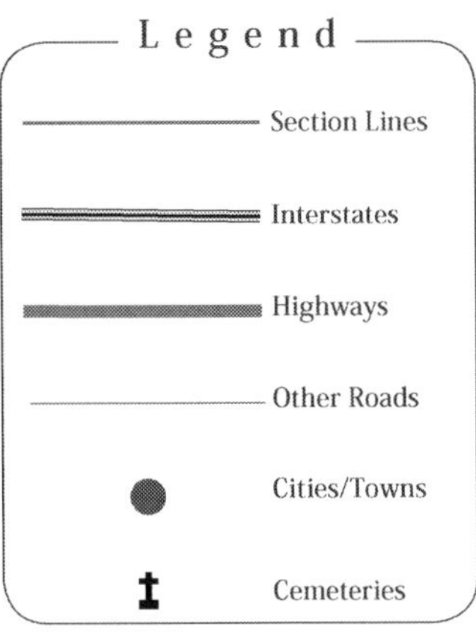

Scale: Section = 1 mile X 1 mile
(generally, with some exceptions)

Historical Map

T19-S R5-W
Huntsville Meridian

Map Group 37

Cities & Towns

Adger
Bullard Shoals (historical)
McCalla

Cemeteries

Adger Cemetery
Lincoln Cemetery
Pine Hill Cemetery

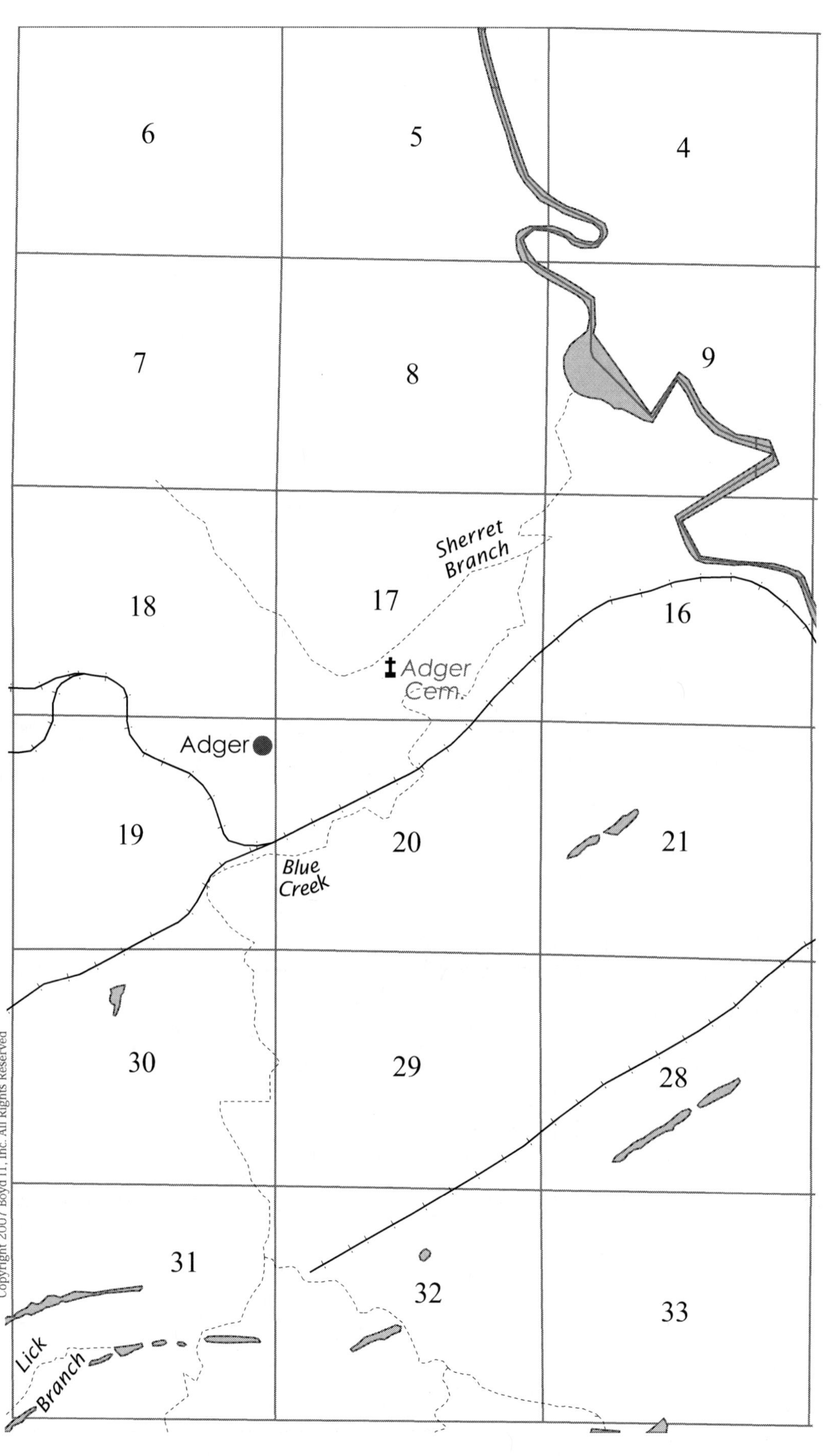

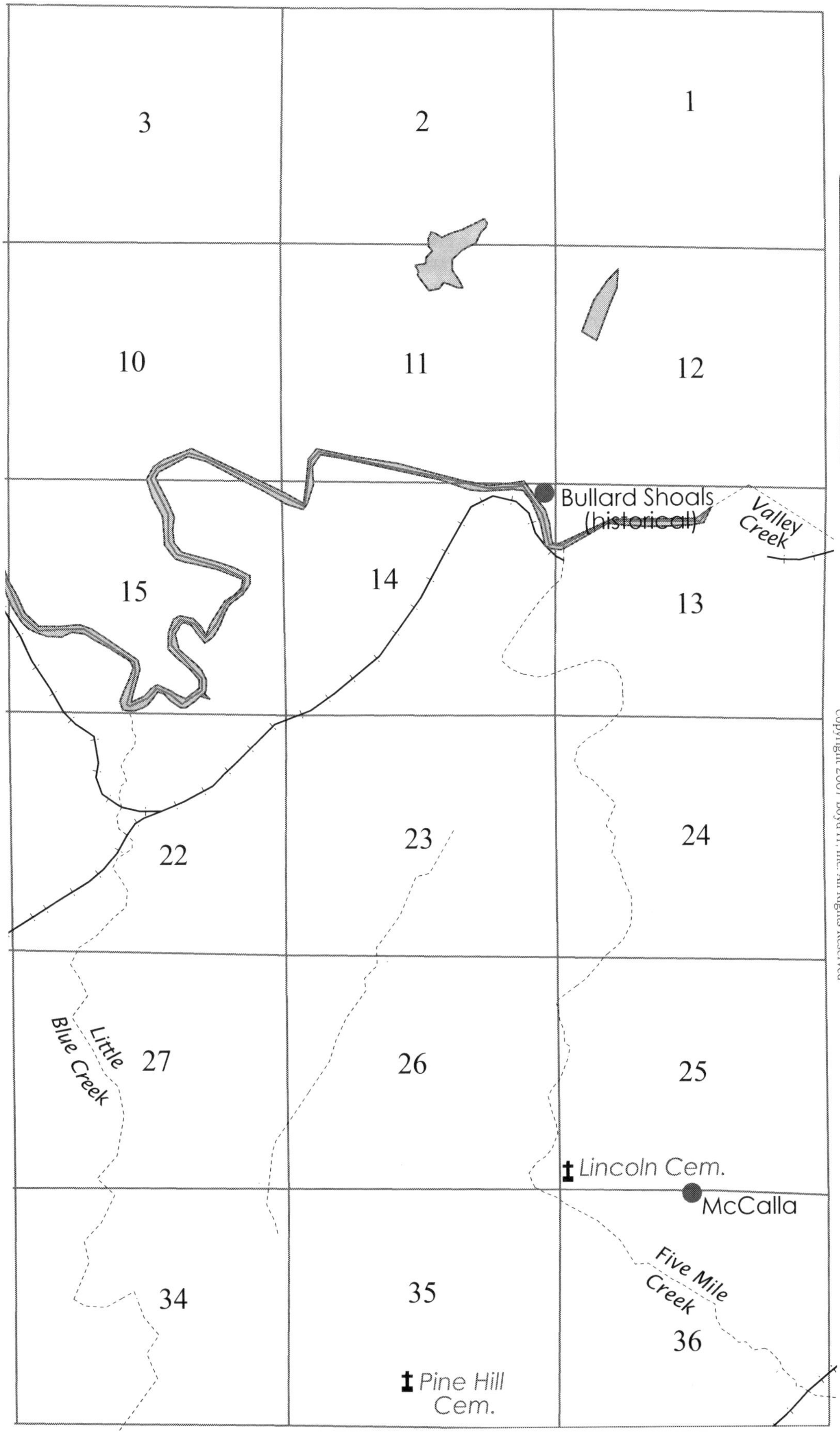

3
2
1
10
11
12
Bullard Shoals (historical)
Valley Creek
15
14
13
22
23
24
Little Blue Creek
27
26
25
Lincoln Cem.
McCalla
Five Mile Creek
34
35
36
Pine Hill Cem.

Helpful Hints

1. This Map takes a different look at the same Congressional Township displayed in the preceding two maps. It presents features that can help you better envision the historical development of the area: a) Water-bodies (lakes & ponds), b) Water-courses (rivers, streams, etc.), c) Railroads, d) City/town center-points (where they were oftentimes located when first settled), and e) Cemeteries.

2. Using this "Historical" map in tandem with this Township's Patent Map and Road Map, may lead you to some interesting discoveries. You will often find roads, towns, cemeteries, and waterways are named after nearby landowners: sometimes those names will be the ones you are researching. See how many of these research gems you can find here in Jefferson County.

Legend
Section Lines
Railroads
Large Rivers & Bodies of Water
Streams/Creeks & Small Rivers
Cities/Towns
Cemeteries

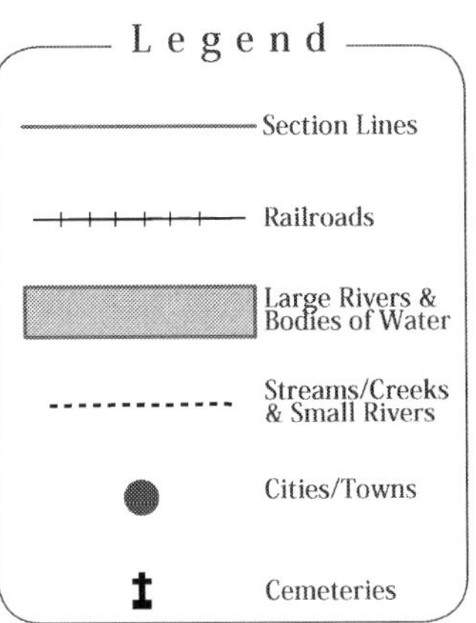

Scale: Section = 1 mile X 1 mile
(there are some exceptions)

Map Group 38: Index to Land Patents

Township 19-South Range 4-West (Huntsville)

After you locate an individual in this Index, take note of the Section and Section Part then proceed to the Land Patent map on the pages immediately following. You should have no difficulty locating the corresponding parcel of land.

The "For More Info" Column will lead you to more information about the underlying Patents. See the *Legend* at right, and the "How to Use this Book" chapter, for more information.

LEGEND

"For More Info . . . " column

A = Authority (Legislative Act, See Appendix "A")
B = Block or Lot (location in Section unknown)
C = Cancelled Patent
F = Fractional Section
G = Group (Multi-Patentee Patent, see Appendix "C")
V = Overlaps another Parcel
R = Re-Issued (Parcel patented more than once)

(A & G items require you to look in the Appendixes referred to above. All other Letter-designations followed by a number require you to locate line-items in this index that possess the ID number found after the letter).

ID	Individual in Patent	Sec.	Sec. Part	Date Issued	Other Counties	For More Info . . .
6500	ABANATHY, James M	24	E½NW	1858-06-01		A1
6501	" "	24	NWNE	1858-06-01		A1
6686	ABARNATHY, Wilson	23	NENE	1858-06-01		A1
6687	" "	23	W½SE	1858-06-01		A1
6688	" "	23	W½SW	1858-06-01		A1
6689	" "	24	NWNW	1858-06-01		A1
6584	ABERNATHY, Richard	12	SWNW	1837-03-30		A1
6583	" "	12	SENW	1839-09-20		A1
6604	ABERNATHY, Samuel V	24	W½SW	1828-02-20		A1
6603	" "	23	E½SE	1839-09-20		A1
6605	ABERNATHY, Starling	14	SWNE	1839-09-20		A1
6606	" "	23	SWNW	1839-09-20		A1
6662	ABERNATHY, William	23	SWNE	1834-11-04		A1
6690	ABERNATHY, Wilson	35	NWNW	1839-09-20		A1
6422	ACKER, Amos	8	W½NW	1834-10-01		A1
6531	ADAMS, John	7	E½SE	1834-10-01		A1
6530	" "	18	NWNE	1839-09-20		A1
6532	" "	31	NW	1912-01-29		A1 G4 V6674
6490	ALEXANDER, Isaac	24	SENE	1839-09-20		A1
6615	ALLINDER, Thomas	35	SENW	1839-09-20		A1
6616	" "	35	SWNE	1839-09-20		A1
6610	" "	23	SENE	1858-06-01		A1
6611	" "	24	NESE	1858-06-01		A1
6612	" "	24	SWNW	1858-06-01		A1
6613	" "	24	SWSE	1858-06-01		A1
6614	" "	26	E½NE	1858-06-01		A1
6617	ARCHER, Thomas	2	NWNE	1839-09-20		A1
6560	ARMSTRONG, Margret	22	NENW	1886-02-10		A1
6663	AYRES, William	4	W½SE	1914-11-27		A1 G7
6492	BAKER, Jacob H	18	NWSE	1853-08-01		A1
6665	BAKER, William	20	SWSE	1839-09-20		A1
6502	BARBOUR, James M	24	SWNE	1889-10-07		A1
6491	BARGER, Isaac	15	NENW	1837-04-01		A1
6477	BELL, George W	12	SESE	1892-01-18		A4
6478	" "	12	SESW	1892-01-18		A4
6479	" "	12	W½SE	1892-01-18		A4
6536	BELL, John	34	SWSW	1837-03-20		A1
6535	" "	23	NWNW	1839-09-20		A1
6533	" "	11	SWSE	1858-06-01		A1
6534	" "	14	NENW	1858-06-01		A1
6663	BURGIN, Thomas	4	W½SE	1914-11-27		A1 G7
6410	CALDWELL, Absalom	6	SE	1833-06-08		A1
6619	CARROL, Thomas	7	W½SE	1834-10-01		A1
6557	COKER, Loving	31	W½SW	1824-05-10		A1
6411	COLDWELL, Absalom	34	W½SE	1837-03-30		A1
6412	COLWELL, Absalom	6	W½SW	1825-08-05		A1

ID	Individual in Patent	Sec.	Sec. Part	Date Issued	Other Counties	For More Info . . .
6414	COLWELL, Alexander	35	SWNW	1839-09-20		A1
6495	CONDRY, James	34	E½NW	1824-05-21		A1
6472	COWARD, George	1	SESW	1853-08-01		A1
6473	COX, George	21	SWNE	1839-09-20		A1
6668	CULBERTSON, William D T	27	SE	1912-01-29		A1 G67
6666	" "	10	E½NW	1915-04-13		A1 G66
6667	" "	34	NE	1921-09-02		A1 G65
6480	DAILEY, Henry	13	SWSE	1859-04-01		A1
6524	DENTON, James W	20	SENW	1839-09-20		A1
6671	DENTON, William I	20	W½NE	1824-05-18		A1
6496	DICKINSON, James	20	E½SE	1837-03-20		A1
6532	DUFF, James	31	NW	1912-01-29		A1 G4 V6674
6415	DUPEY, Alfred M	11	NESW	1854-07-15		A1
6416	" "	11	SWNE	1854-07-15		A1
6539	DUPEY, John M	12	NENE	1854-07-15		A1
6553	EDWARDS, Lamech	21	E½NW	1837-03-20		A1
6554	" "	9	E½NW	1837-03-20		A1
6669	GABLE, William F	36	E½SE	1884-12-05		A4
6667	GALLAWAY, Robert	34	NE	1921-09-02		A1 G65
6593	GALLOWAY, Robert	23	E½NW	1824-05-24		A1
6594	" "	23	E½SW	1824-05-24		A1
6481	GOODWIN, Henry M	26	E½SE	1885-03-30		A4
6551	GOODWIN, Joseph	36	E½NW	1858-06-01		A1
6552	" "	36	NWNE	1858-06-01		A1
6437	GUNNELL, Benjamin	2	NW	1837-03-20		A1
6482	HALCOMBE, Hosea	22	E½SW	1824-05-18		A1
6666	HALL, James	10	E½NW	1915-04-13		A1 G66
6580	HALL, Raney B	1	N½NE	1854-07-15		A1
6581	" "	1	NWSE	1854-07-15		A1
6582	" "	1	SWNE	1854-07-15		A1
6663	HENDLEY, Darby	4	W½SE	1914-11-27		A1 G7
6595	HIGGINBOTHOM, Robert	12	W½SW	1827-03-20		A1
6447	HILL, Bird	22	W½NW	1876-09-30		A1
6608	HOLCOMB, Tartom P	15	SESE	1837-04-01		A1
6463	HOLCOMBE, Darius I	22	W½SE	1837-03-20		A1
6485	HOLCOMBE, Hosea	26	W½NW	1832-01-10		A1
6486	" "	27	W½NE	1837-03-20		A1
6484	" "	26	NWNE	1838-08-28		A1
6483	" "	14	SWSW	1839-03-15		A1
6461	HOUSTON, Daniel W	28	SESW	1884-12-05		A4
6462	" "	28	SWSE	1884-12-05		A4
6596	HUMBER, Robert	27	NENW	1852-01-01		A1
6670	HUNT, William	27	E½NE	1837-03-20		A1
6460	IVY, Charles A	24	NENE	1889-10-07		A1
6431	JONES, Belson	12	NESE	1858-06-01		A1
6432	JONES, Benjamin F	1	NWSW	1860-07-02		A1
6433	" "	1	S½NW	1860-07-02		A1
6434	" "	2	E½SE	1860-07-02		A1
6435	" "	2	S½NE	1860-07-02		A1
6436	" "	2	SWSE	1860-07-02		A1
6592	JONES, Robert B	8	E½SW	1913-05-21		A1 G142
6602	JONES, Samuel N	32	SESE	1889-03-01		A4
6568	JORDON, Mortimer	6	NESW	1858-06-01		A1
6569	" "	6	SENW	1858-06-01		A1
6570	" "	6	W½NW	1858-06-01		A1
6499	KELLY, James	8	E½NE	1832-01-02		A1
6465	KEVELING, Dominick	6	W½NE	1889-10-07		A1
6672	LACEY, William	10	E½SW	1825-09-01		A1
6541	LANDIFER, John S	11	NESE	1853-08-01		A1
6547	LANE, John W	5	W½NE	1824-10-20		A1 G149
6546	" "	5	W½SE	1825-08-05		A1 G151
6467	LAWLEY, Elisha	31	W½SE	1823-06-02		A1
6673	LAWLEY, William	31	NESE	1837-03-30		A1
6674	" "	31	SWNW	1837-03-30		A1 V6532
6532	LOLLY, John	31	NW	1912-01-29		A1 G4 V6674
6425	LOVELESS, Andrew M	2	NENE	1882-10-30		A1
6517	MCADORY, James	7	W½SW	1834-10-01		A1
6505	" "	18	E½NW	1839-09-20		A1
6507	" "	18	SWNE	1852-01-01		A1
6510	" "	19	E½SW	1852-01-01		A1
6515	" "	19	W½SE	1852-01-01		A1
6503	" "	17	SESW	1853-08-01		A1
6513	" "	19	SENW	1853-08-01		A1

ID	Individual in Patent	Sec.	Sec. Part	Date Issued	Other Counties	For More Info . . .
6514	MCADORY, James (Cont'd)	19	W½NE	1853-08-01		A1
6516	" "	20	NWSW	1853-08-01		A1
6509	" "	18	W½SW	1854-07-15		A1
6511	" "	19	NENW	1854-07-15		A1
6512	" "	19	NESE	1854-07-15		A1
6504	" "	17	SWSW	1858-06-01		A1
6506	" "	18	E½SE	1858-06-01		A1
6508	" "	18	SWSE	1858-06-01		A1
6656	MCADORY, Thomas	31	SESW	1839-09-20		A1
6648	" "	21	NWNE	1849-08-01		A1
6641	" "	15	SENW	1853-08-01		A1
6645	" "	2	NWSE	1853-08-01		A1
6633	" "	10	NWSE	1854-07-15		A1
6634	" "	10	SWSE	1854-07-15		A1
6635	" "	14	NWSW	1854-07-15		A1
6636	" "	14	SWNW	1854-07-15		A1
6637	" "	15	NESE	1854-07-15		A1
6638	" "	15	NESW	1854-07-15		A1
6639	" "	15	NWSW	1854-07-15		A1
6642	" "	15	SWSE	1854-07-15		A1
6646	" "	21	NENE	1854-07-15		A1
6650	" "	21	SESW	1854-07-15		A1
6652	" "	22	NENE	1854-07-15		A1
6653	" "	22	NWNE	1854-07-15		A1
6654	" "	28	NENW	1854-07-15		A1
6655	" "	28	SWNW	1854-07-15		A1
6640	" "	15	SENE	1858-06-01		A1
6643	" "	15	SWSW	1858-06-01		A1
6644	" "	15	W½NE	1858-06-01		A1
6647	" "	21	NESE	1858-06-01		A1
6649	" "	21	SENE	1858-06-01		A1
6651	" "	21	W½SE	1858-06-01		A1
6684	MCADORY, William R	20	NENW	1853-08-01		A1
6676	MCCRAW, William	33	SESE	1839-09-20		A1 C R6677
6677	" "	33	SESE	1889-07-09		A1 R6676
6427	MCFALL, Arthur	25	NESE	1839-09-20		A1
6540	MCFALL, John	26	W½SW	1837-03-20		A1
6548	MCFALLS, John W	36	NWSW	1839-09-20		A1
6549	" "	36	SWSW	1839-09-20		A1
6426	MCLAUGHLIN, Andrew	9	W½NW	1834-10-01		A1
6428	MCLUER, Arthur	11	SESW	1854-07-15		A1
6429	" "	14	NWNW	1854-07-15		A1
6601	MCLUER, Samuel L	1	SENE	1839-09-20		A1
6494	MOORE, James B	33	SWSE	1858-06-01		A1
6664	MOORE, William B	30	SWNW	1849-08-01		A1
6475	MORROW, George	3	SE	1837-03-20		A1 G176
6474	MORROW, George M	26	SWSE	1889-08-13		A4
6550	MORROW, John W	26	E½NW	1834-10-16		A1
6564	MORROW, Matthew	26	E½SW	1837-03-20		A1
6565	" "	26	NWSE	1839-09-20		A1
6566	" "	26	SWNE	1839-09-20		A1
6438	NABERS, Benjamin	34	E½SW	1838-08-28		A1
6439	" "	34	NWSW	1839-09-20		A1
6487	NABERS, Howard	21	NESW	1839-09-20		A1
6600	NABERS, Samuel C	3	W½NW	1839-09-20		A1
6440	NABORS, Benjamin	3	E½NW	1839-09-20		A1
6471	NABOURS, Francis D	5	E½NW	1834-10-01		A1 G179
6547	NABOURS, William	5	W½NE	1824-10-20		A1 G149
6679	" "	4	W½SW	1825-09-01		A1
6678	" "	4	E½NW	1834-10-01		A1
6609	NORWOOD, Thomas A	14	SESE	1858-06-01		A1
6469	OWEN, Fleming	32	E½SW	1882-10-30		A1
6470	" "	32	W½SE	1882-10-30		A1
6493	OWEN, Jacob	28	W½NE	1883-07-03		A4
6598	OWEN, Rose W	28	W½SW	1882-10-30		A1
6620	OWEN, Thomas H	20	E½SW	1853-11-15		A1
6621	" "	20	NWSE	1853-11-15		A1
6623	" "	29	NENW	1853-11-15		A1
6626	" "	29	W½NW	1853-11-15		A1
6627	" "	30	SESE	1853-11-15		A1
6628	" "	32	NENW	1853-11-15		A1
6624	" "	29	SE	1854-07-15		A1
6625	" "	29	SENE	1854-07-15		A1

ID	Individual in Patent	Sec.	Sec. Part	Date Issued	Other Counties	For More Info . . .
6629	OWEN, Thomas H (Cont'd)	32	SENW	1854-07-15		A1
6631	" "	33	NWNW	1854-07-15		A1
6630	" "	33	E½NW	1858-06-01		A1
6622	" "	28	NWNW	1882-10-30		A1
6675	OWEN, William M	32	W½NE	1898-07-25		A1
6567	OWENS, Minus	14	NESE	1890-01-08		A4
6518	PATTERSON, James	35	W½SE	1823-07-09		A1
6680	PATTERSON, William	29	E½SW	1834-10-21		A1
6683	" "	29	W½NE	1837-03-20		A1
6681	" "	29	NENE	1837-03-30		A1
6682	" "	29	SENW	1837-03-30		A1
6519	PETERSON, James	35	N½NE	1858-06-01		A1
6520	" "	36	W½NW	1858-06-01		A1
6576	PETERSON, Peter	35	E½SE	1824-05-25		A1
6449	PHILIPS, Caroline M	30	E½NW	1852-01-01		A1
6450	" "	30	NENE	1852-01-01		A1
6452	" "	30	NWNW	1852-01-01		A1
6455	" "	30	W½NE	1852-01-01		A1
6448	" "	20	SWSW	1853-08-01		A1
6456	" "	31	NESW	1853-08-01		A1
6451	" "	30	NESE	1854-07-15		A1
6453	" "	30	SENE	1854-07-15		A1
6454	" "	30	SWSE	1854-07-15		A1
6457	" "	31	SWNE	1854-07-15		A1
6458	" "	31	SESE	1858-06-01		A1 G196
6459	" "	32	W½SW	1858-06-01		A1 G196
6458	PHILIPS, Reuben	31	SESE	1858-06-01		A1 G196
6459	" "	32	W½SW	1858-06-01		A1 G196
6521	PIERCE, James	12	NWNE	1834-10-21		A1
6668	PITTS, William	27	SE	1912-01-29		A1 G67
6561	POTTER, Mark L	28	NENE	1882-10-30		A1
6562	" "	28	NWSE	1882-10-30		A1
6618	PRIDE, Thomas B	22	E½SE	1837-03-20		A1
6558	REDER, Margaret	25	NWSE	1858-06-01		A1
6559	" "	25	SWNE	1858-06-01		A1
6468	RILEY, Elizabeth	8	W½NE	1834-10-01		A1
6522	ROCKETT, James	24	SESW	1834-10-14		A1
6587	ROCKETT, Richard	10	W½NW	1825-09-01		A1
6590	" "	14	E½SW	1831-06-01		A1
6585	" "	1	SWSE	1837-03-30		A1
6586	" "	10	NENE	1837-03-30		A1
6588	" "	12	NENW	1837-03-30		A1
6589	" "	12	NWNW	1853-08-01		A1
6591	" "	3	SWSW	1889-07-09		A1
6488	ROY, Isaac A	36	SESW	1858-06-01		A1
6489	" "	36	W½SE	1890-01-08		A4
6525	ROY, Jasper W	24	SESE	1900-10-12		A1
6413	RUSSELL, Absalom	4	W½NE	1915-04-13		A1 G205
6423	SADDLER, Anderson M	22	W½SW	1858-06-01		A1
6424	" "	27	NWNW	1858-06-01		A1
6421	SADLER, Allions T	30	NWSE	1839-09-20		A1
6657	SADLER, Thomas	18	W½NW	1915-04-13		A1 G207
6657	SADLER, William R	18	W½NW	1915-04-13		A1 G207
6685	" "	7	E½SW	1924-04-11		A1
6475	SANDERS, Philip	3	SE	1837-03-20		A1 G176
6578	" "	3	W½NE	1837-03-30		A1
6577	" "	3	E½NE	1915-06-25		A1
6579	SHAW, Pleasant	34	SWNW	1858-06-01		A1
6632	SHAW, Thomas L	28	E½SE	1884-03-20		A4
6658	SIMPSON, Thompson R	10	W½NE	1837-03-20		A1
6592	SIMS, Edward	8	E½SW	1913-05-21		A1 G142
6464	SMITH, David	20	W½NW	1853-08-01		A1
6543	SMITH, John	1	NESW	1854-07-15		A1
6537	SPARKES, John H	27	SWNW	1858-06-01		A1
6538	" "	28	SENE	1858-06-01		A1
6523	SPARKS, James	27	E½SW	1837-03-20		A1
6418	SPENCER, Alfred S	11	NWNW	1854-07-15		A1
6419	" "	2	SESW	1854-07-15		A1
6420	" "	3	NWSW	1854-07-15		A1
6417	" "	10	E½SE	1858-06-01		A1
6542	SPENCER, John S	1	SWSW	1854-07-15		A1
6572	SPENCER, Octavius	5	W½NW	1837-03-20		A1
6573	" "	6	E½NE	1837-03-20		A1

ID	Individual in Patent	Sec.	Sec. Part	Date Issued	Other Counties	For More Info . . .
6574	SPENCER, Octavius (Cont'd)	6	NENW	1854-07-15		A1
6575	SPENCER, Octavus	6	SESW	1839-09-20		A1
6599	TARRANT, Samuel A	17	W½NE	1853-08-01		A1
6607	TARRANT, Stephen	32	E½NE	1883-07-03		A4
6555	TAYLOR, Lewis	28	NESW	1883-07-03		A4
6556	" "	28	SENW	1883-07-03		A4
6441	THOMAS, Benjamin	4	E½NE	1825-08-05		A1
6546	" "	5	W½SE	1825-08-05		A1 G151
6446	" "	8	W½SW	1825-08-05		A1
6443	" "	8	NWSE	1834-10-01		A1
6444	" "	8	SESE	1834-10-01		A1
6442	" "	8	NESE	1837-03-20		A1
6445	" "	8	SWSE	1837-03-20		A1
6413	" "	4	W½NE	1915-04-13		A1 G205
6544	THOMAS, John	1	E½SE	1823-05-01		A1
6545	" "	14	E½NE	1823-05-01		A1
6571	THOMPSON, Nancy	22	SENE	1885-03-16		A4
6597	TILLMAN, Robert J	2	NESW	1889-10-07		A1
6668	TORRENT, Roland	27	SE	1912-01-29		A1 G67
6659	TOURY, Walter	34	NWNW	1839-09-20		A1
6660	TOWERY, Walter	27	W½SW	1837-03-20		A1
6661	TRUSS, Warren	4	E½SW	1915-04-13		A1 G222
6476	VEITCH, George	12	S½NE	1885-08-05		A1
6466	WALKER, Elias G	32	NESE	1858-06-01		A1
6527	WARE, Jeptha M	11	SENE	1854-07-15		A1
6528	" "	11	SESE	1854-07-15		A1
6526	" "	11	NWSE	1858-06-01		A1
6529	" "	12	NESW	1858-06-01		A1
6563	WARREN, Mary E	36	E½NE	1885-03-16		A1
6430	WHITE, Asbury	24	NESW	1894-10-22		A4
6498	WOOD, James H	5	E½SE	1834-10-01		A1
6497	" "	4	E½SE	1837-03-30		A1
6471	WOOD, William	5	E½NW	1834-10-01		A1 G179
6661	WORTHINGTON, Benjamin	4	E½SW	1915-04-13		A1 G222

Patent Map

T19-S R4-W
Huntsville Meridian

Map Group 38

Township Statistics

Parcels Mapped	:	281
Number of Patents	:	245
Number of Individuals	:	154
Patentees Identified	:	147
Number of Surnames	:	108
Multi-Patentee Parcels	:	15
Oldest Patent Date	:	5/1/1823
Most Recent Patent	:	4/11/1924
Block/Lot Parcels	:	0
Parcels Re - Issued	:	1
Parcels that Overlap	:	2
Cities and Towns	:	1
Cemeteries	:	4

6
JORDON Mortimer 1858
SPENCER Octavius 1854
JORDON Mortimer 1858
KEVELING Dominick 1889
SPENCER Octavius 1837
COLWELL Absalom 1825
JORDON Mortimer 1858
SPENCER Octavius 1839
CALDWELL Absalom 1833

5
NABOURS [179] Francis D 1834
SPENCER Octavius 1837
LANE [149] John W 1824
LANE [151] John W 1825
WOOD James H 1834

4
NABOURS William 1834
RUSSELL [205] Absalom 1915
THOMAS Benjamin 1825
TRUSS [222] Warren 1915
NABOURS William 1825
AYRES [7] William 1914
WOOD James H 1837

7
MCADORY James 1834
SADLER William R 1924
CARROL Thomas 1834
ADAMS John 1834

8
ACKER Amos 1834
RILEY Elizabeth 1834
KELLY James 1832
THOMAS Benjamin 1825
JONES [142] Robert B 1913
THOMAS Benjamin 1834
THOMAS Benjamin 1837
THOMAS Benjamin 1837
THOMAS Benjamin 1834

9
EDWARDS Lamech 1837
MCLAUGHLIN Andrew 1834

18
SADLER [207] Thomas 1915
MCADORY James 1839
ADAMS John 1839
MCADORY James 1852
MCADORY James 1854
BAKER Jacob H 1853
MCADORY James 1858
MCADORY James 1858

17
TARRANT Samuel A 1853
MCADORY James 1858
MCADORY James 1853

16

19
MCADORY James 1854
MCADORY James 1853
MCADORY James 1853
MCADORY James 1852
MCADORY James 1852
MCADORY James 1854

20
SMITH David 1853
MCADORY William R 1853
DENTON William I 1824
DENTON James W 1839
MCADORY James 1853
OWEN Thomas H 1853
OWEN Thomas H 1853
DICKINSON James 1837
PHILIPS Caroline M 1853
BAKER William 1839

21
EDWARDS Lamech 1837
MCADORY Thomas 1849
MCADORY Thomas 1854
HILL Bird 1876
COX George 1839
MCADORY Thomas 1858
NABERS Howard 1839
MCADORY Thomas 1858
MCADORY Thomas 1858
MCADORY Thomas 1854

30
PHILIPS Caroline M 1852
PHILIPS Caroline M 1852
PHILIPS Caroline M 1852
PHILIPS Caroline M 1852
MOORE William B 1849
PHILIPS Caroline M 1854
SADLER Allions T 1839
PHILIPS Caroline M 1854
PHILIPS Caroline M 1854
OWEN Thomas H 1853

29
OWEN Thomas H 1853
OWEN Thomas H 1853
PATTERSON William 1837
PATTERSON William 1837
PATTERSON William 1837
OWEN Thomas H 1854
OWEN Thomas H 1854
PATTERSON William 1834

28
OWEN Thomas H 1882
MCADORY Thomas 1854
OWEN Jacob 1883
POTTER Mark L 1882
MCADORY Thomas 1854
TAYLOR Lewis 1883
SPARKES John H 1858
TAYLOR Lewis 1883
POTTER Mark L 1882
SHAW Thomas L 1884
OWEN Rose W 1882
HOUSTON Daniel W 1884
HOUSTON Daniel W 1884

31
ADAMS [4] John 1912
LAWLEY William 1837
PHILIPS Caroline M 1854
COKER Loving 1824
PHILIPS Caroline M 1853
LAWLEY Elisha 1823
LAWLEY William 1837
MCADORY Thomas 1839
PHILIPS [196] Caroline M 1858

32
OWEN Thomas H 1853
OWEN William M 1898
TARRANT Stephen 1883
OWEN Thomas H 1854
PHILIPS [196] Caroline M 1858
OWEN Fleming 1882
OWEN Fleming 1882
WALKER Elias G 1858
JONES Samuel N 1889

33
OWEN Thomas H 1854
OWEN Thomas H 1858
MOORE James B 1858
MCCRAW William 1889
MCCRAW William 1839
BELL John 1837

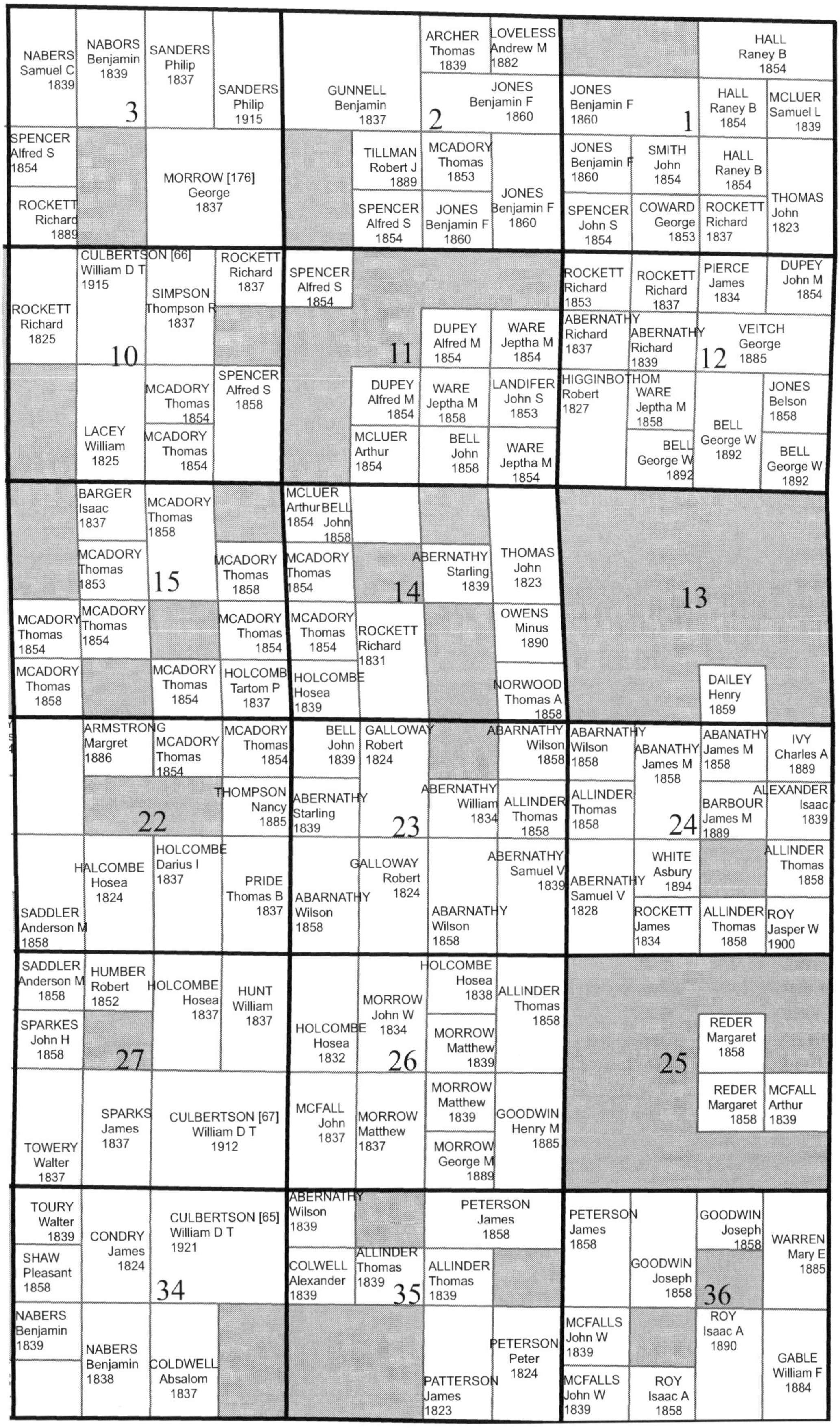

3
NABERS Samuel C 1839
NABORS Benjamin 1839
SANDERS Philip 1837
SANDERS Philip 1915
SPENCER Alfred S 1854
ROCKETT Richard 1889
MORROW [176] George 1837

2
GUNNELL Benjamin 1837
ARCHER Thomas 1839
LOVELESS Andrew M 1882
JONES Benjamin F 1860
TILLMAN Robert J 1889
MCADORY Thomas 1853
JONES Benjamin F 1860
SPENCER Alfred S 1854
JONES Benjamin F 1860

1
HALL Raney B 1854
JONES Benjamin F 1860
HALL Raney B 1854
MCLUER Samuel L 1839
JONES Benjamin F 1860
SMITH John 1854
HALL Raney B 1854
THOMAS John 1823
SPENCER John S 1854
COWARD George 1853
ROCKETT Richard 1837

10
CULBERTSON [66] William D T 1915
ROCKETT Richard 1837
ROCKETT Richard 1825
SIMPSON Thompson R 1837
MCADORY Thomas 1854
SPENCER Alfred S 1858
LACEY William 1825
MCADORY Thomas 1854

11
SPENCER Alfred S 1854
DUPEY Alfred M 1854
WARE Jeptha M 1854
DUPEY Alfred M 1854
WARE Jeptha M 1858
LANDIFER John S 1853
MCLUER Arthur 1854
BELL John 1858
WARE Jeptha M 1854

12
ROCKETT Richard 1853
ROCKETT Richard 1837
PIERCE James 1834
DUPEY John M 1854
ABERNATHY Richard 1837
ABERNATHY Richard 1839
VEITCH George 1885
HIGGINBOTHOM Robert 1827
WARE Jeptha M 1858
JONES Belson 1858
BELL George W 1892
BELL George W 1892
BELL George W 1892

15
BARGER Isaac 1837
MCADORY Thomas 1858
MCADORY Thomas 1853
MCADORY Thomas 1858
MCADORY Thomas 1854
MCADORY Thomas 1854
MCADORY Thomas 1854
MCADORY Thomas 1858
MCADORY Thomas 1854
HOLCOMB Tartom P 1837

14
MCLUER Arthur 1854
BELL John 1858
MCADORY Thomas 1854
ABERNATHY Starling 1839
THOMAS John 1823
MCADORY Thomas 1854
ROCKETT Richard 1831
OWENS Minus 1890
HOLCOMBE Hosea 1839
NORWOOD Thomas A 1858

13
DAILEY Henry 1859

22
ARMSTRONG Margret 1886
MCADORY Thomas 1854
MCADORY Thomas 1854
THOMPSON Nancy 1885
HALCOMBE Hosea 1824
HOLCOMBE Darius I 1837
PRIDE Thomas B 1837
SADDLER Anderson M 1858

23
BELL John 1839
GALLOWAY Robert 1824
ABARNATHY Wilson 1858
ABERNATHY Starling 1839
ABERNATHY William 1834
ALLINDER Thomas 1858
GALLOWAY Robert 1824
ABERNATHY Samuel V 1839
ABARNATHY Wilson 1858
ABARNATHY Wilson 1858

24
ABARNATHY Wilson 1858
ABANATHY James M 1858
ABANATHY James M 1858
IVY Charles A 1889
ALLINDER Thomas 1858
ALEXANDER Isaac 1839
BARBOUR James M 1889
WHITE Asbury 1894
ALLINDER Thomas 1858
ABERNATHY Samuel V 1828
ROCKETT James 1834
ALLINDER Thomas 1858
ROY Jasper W 1900

27
SADDLER Anderson M 1858
HUMBER Robert 1852
HOLCOMBE Hosea 1837
HUNT William 1837
SPARKES John H 1858
SPARKS James 1837
CULBERTSON [67] William D T 1912
TOWERY Walter 1837

26
HOLCOMBE Hosea 1838
MORROW John W 1834
ALLINDER Thomas 1858
HOLCOMBE Hosea 1832
MORROW Matthew 1839
MCFALL John 1837
MORROW Matthew 1839
MORROW Matthew 1837
GOODWIN Henry M 1885
MORROW George M 1889

25
REDER Margaret 1858
REDER Margaret 1858
MCFALL Arthur 1839

34
TOURY Walter 1839
CULBERTSON [65] William D T 1921
CONDRY James 1824
SHAW Pleasant 1858
NABERS Benjamin 1839
NABERS Benjamin 1838
COLDWELL Absalom 1837

35
ABERNATHY Wilson 1839
PETERSON James 1858
COLWELL Alexander 1839
ALLINDER Thomas 1839
ALLINDER Thomas 1839
PETERSON Peter 1824
PATTERSON James 1823

36
PETERSON James 1858
GOODWIN Joseph 1858
WARREN Mary E 1885
GOODWIN Joseph 1858
MCFALLS John W 1839
ROY Isaac A 1890
GABLE William F 1884
MCFALLS John W 1839
ROY Isaac A 1858

Helpful Hints

1. This Map's INDEX can be found on the preceding pages.
2. Refer to Map "C" to see where this Township lies within Jefferson County, Alabama.
3. Numbers within square brackets [ ] denote a multi-patentee land parcel (multi-owner). Refer to Appendix "C" for a full list of members in this group.
4. Areas that look to be crowded with Patentees usually indicate multiple sales of the same parcel (Re-issues) or Overlapping parcels. See this Township's Index for an explanation of these and other circumstances that might explain "odd" groupings of Patentees on this map.

Legend

Patent Boundary
Section Boundary
No Patents Found (or Outside County)
1., 2., 3., ... Lot Numbers (when beside a name)
[ ] Group Number (see Appendix "C")

Scale: Section = 1 mile X 1 mile (generally, with some exceptions)

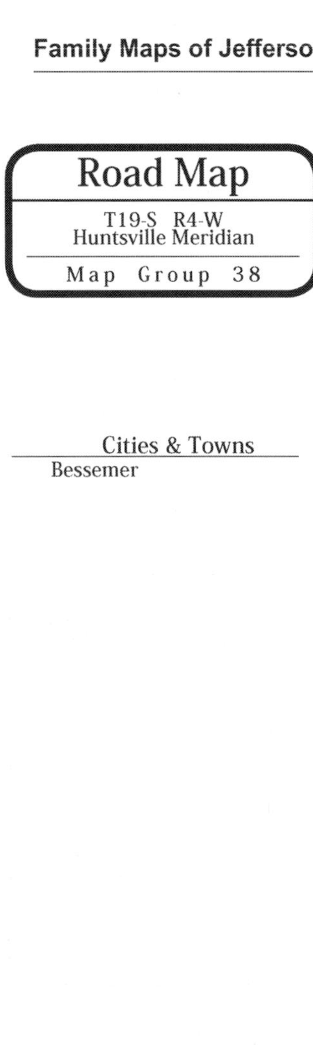

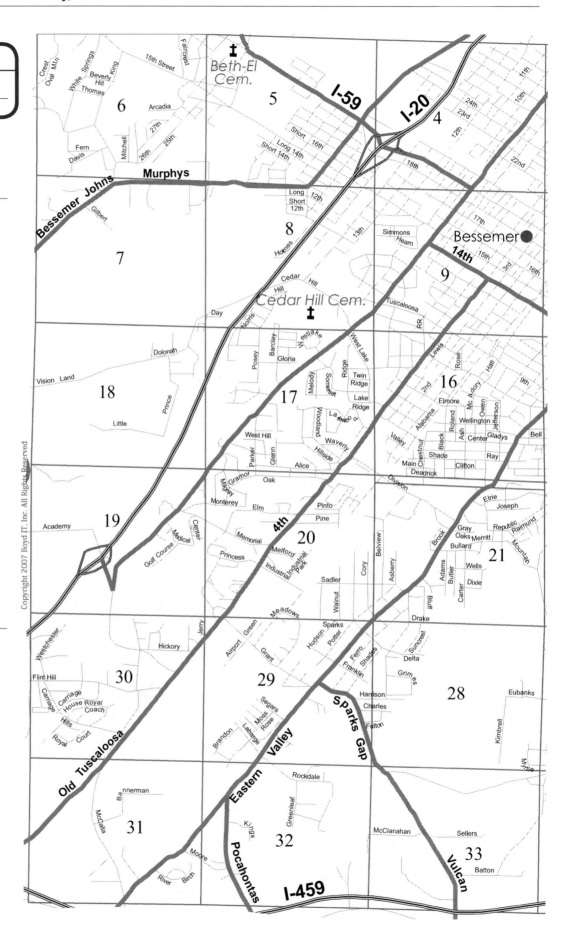

Road Map

T19-S R4-W
Huntsville Meridian

Map Group 38

Cities & Towns

Bessemer

Cemeteries

Beth-El Cemetery
Cedar Hill Cemetery
Sadlers Cemetery
Union Cemetery

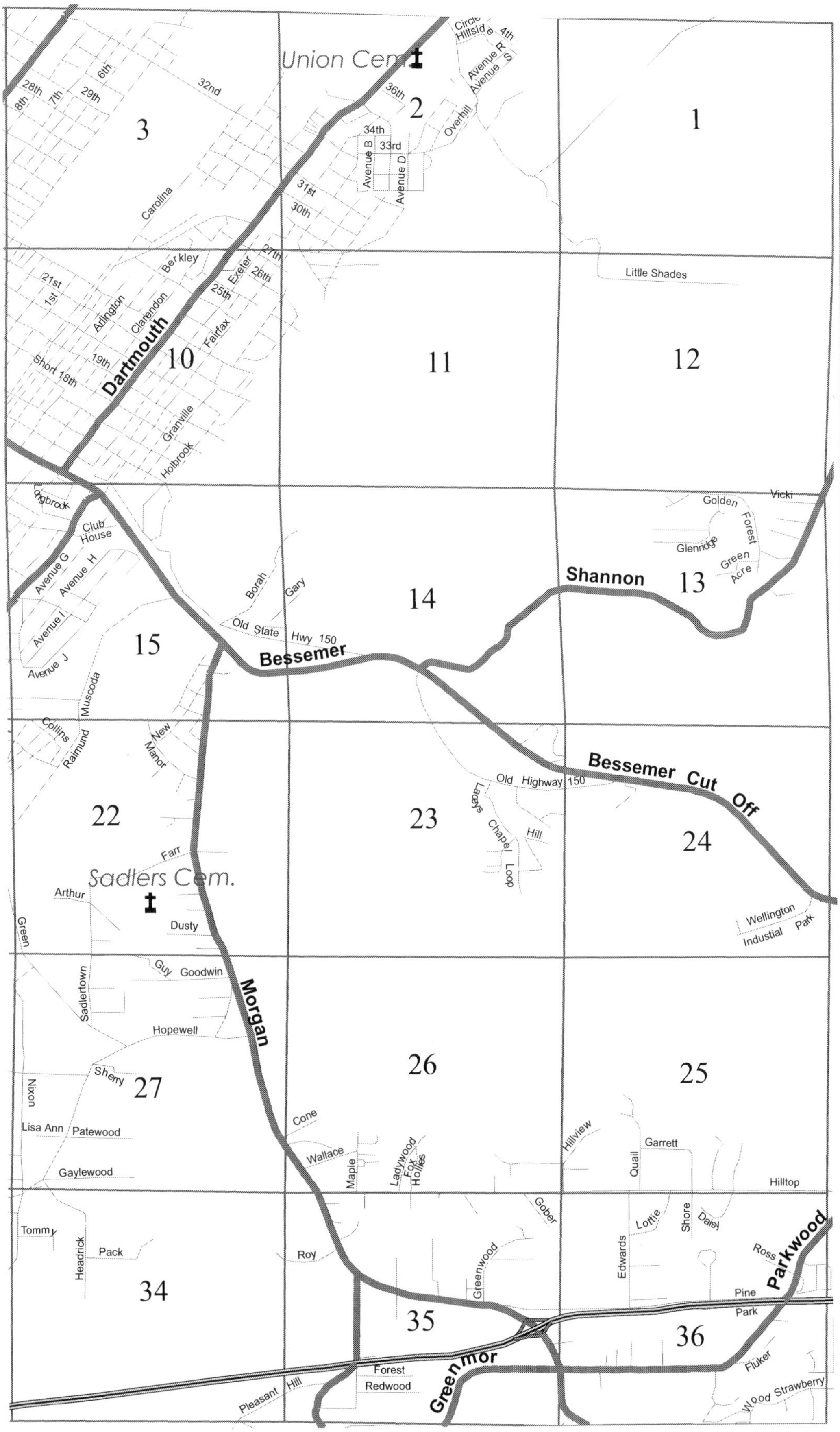

Helpful Hints

1. This road map has a number of uses, but primarily it is to help you: a) find the present location of land owned by your ancestors (at least the general area), b) find cemeteries and city-centers, and c) estimate the route/roads used by Census-takers & tax-assessors.

2. If you plan to travel to Jefferson County to locate cemeteries or land parcels, please pick up a modern travel map for the area before you do. Mapping old land parcels on modern maps is not as exact a science as you might think. Just the slightest variations in public land survey coordinates, estimates of parcel boundaries, or road-map deviations can greatly alter a map's representation of how a road either does or doesn't cross a particular parcel of land.

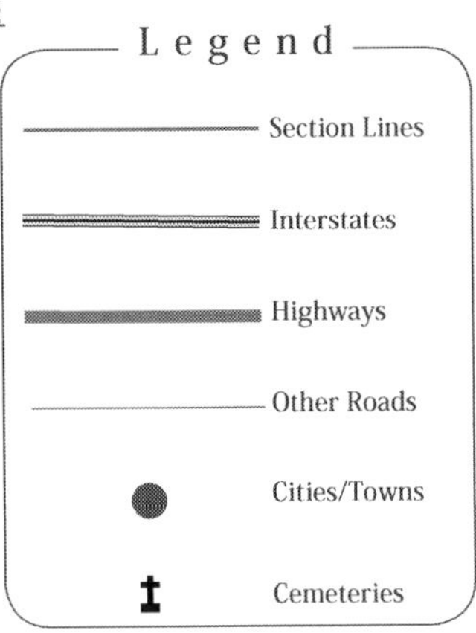

Scale: Section = 1 mile X 1 mile
(generally, with some exceptions)

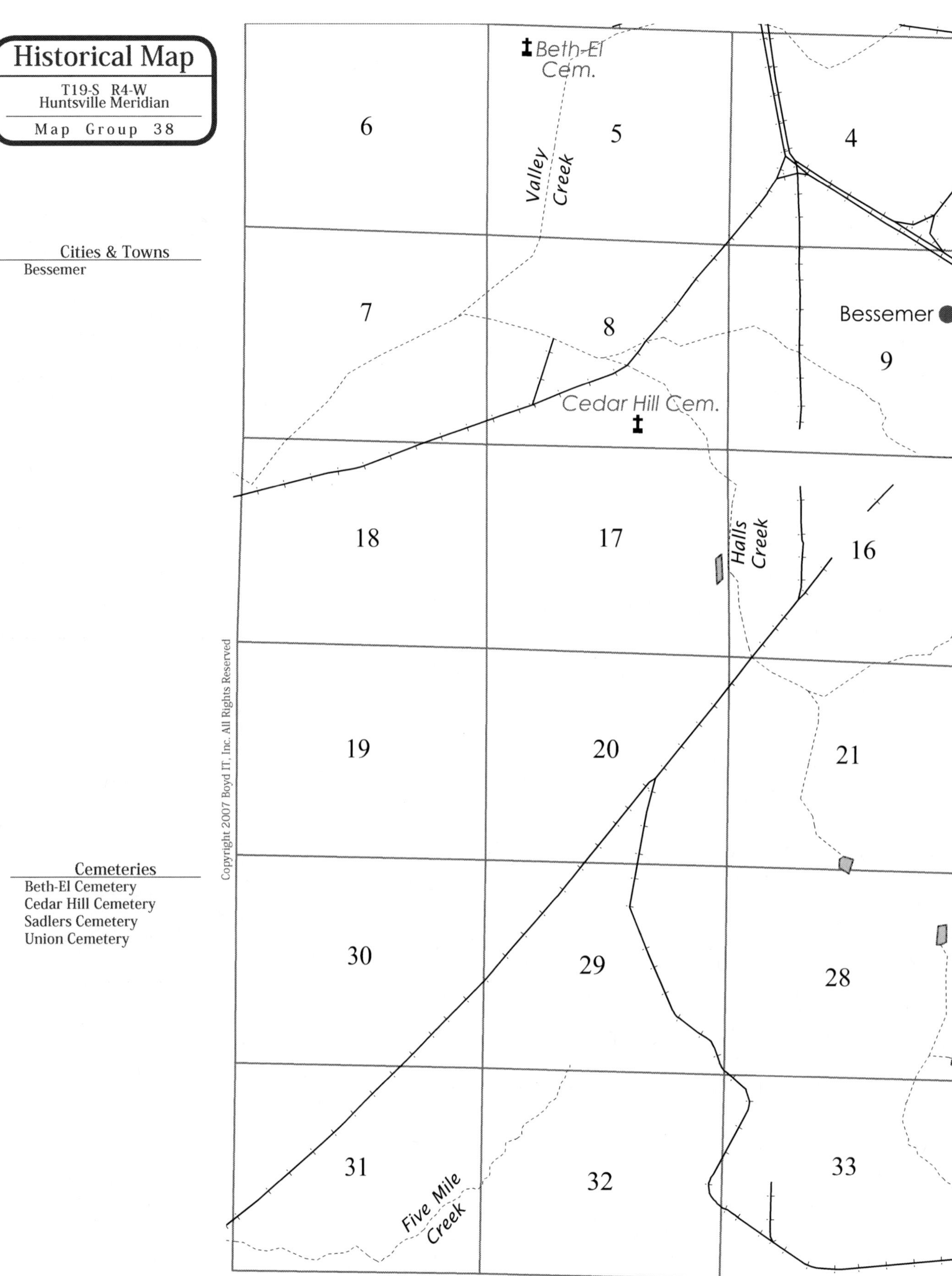
Historical Map
T19-S R4-W
Huntsville Meridian
Map Group 38
Cities & Towns
Bessemer
Cemeteries
Beth-El Cemetery
Cedar Hill Cemetery
Sadlers Cemetery
Union Cemetery
Beth-El Cem.
Valley Creek
Cedar Hill Cem.
Bessemer
Halls Creek
Five Mile Creek
6
5
4
7
8
9
18
17
16
19
20
21
30
29
28
31
32
33

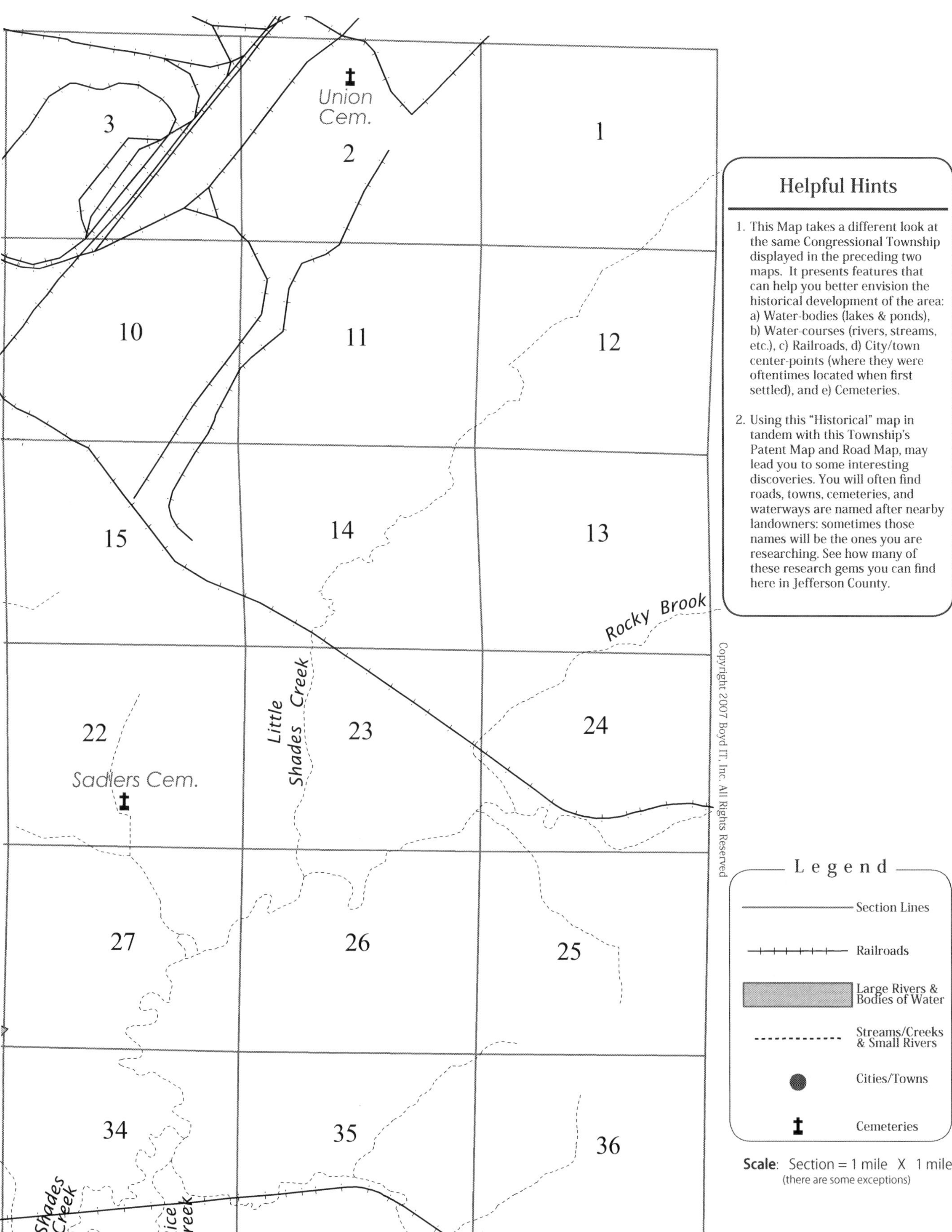

Helpful Hints

1. This Map takes a different look at the same Congressional Township displayed in the preceding two maps. It presents features that can help you better envision the historical development of the area: a) Water-bodies (lakes & ponds), b) Water-courses (rivers, streams, etc.), c) Railroads, d) City/town center-points (where they were oftentimes located when first settled), and e) Cemeteries.

2. Using this "Historical" map in tandem with this Township's Patent Map and Road Map, may lead you to some interesting discoveries. You will often find roads, towns, cemeteries, and waterways are named after nearby landowners: sometimes those names will be the ones you are researching. See how many of these research gems you can find here in Jefferson County.

Legend

- Section Lines
- Railroads
- Large Rivers & Bodies of Water
- Streams/Creeks & Small Rivers
- Cities/Towns
- Cemeteries

Scale: Section = 1 mile X 1 mile
(there are some exceptions)

Map Group 39: Index to Land Patents

Township 19-South Range 3-West (Huntsville)

After you locate an individual in this Index, take note of the Section and Section Part then proceed to the Land Patent map on the pages immediately following. You should have no difficulty locating the corresponding parcel of land.

The "For More Info" Column will lead you to more information about the underlying Patents. See the *Legend* at right, and the "How to Use this Book" chapter, for more information.

LEGEND

"For More Info . . . " column

A = Authority (Legislative Act, See Appendix "A")
B = Block or Lot (location in Section unknown)
C = Cancelled Patent
F = Fractional Section
G = Group (Multi-Patentee Patent, see Appendix "C")
V = Overlaps another Parcel
R = Re-Issued (Parcel patented more than once)

(A & G items require you to look in the Appendixes referred to above. All other Letter-designations followed by a number require you to locate line-items in this index that possess the ID number found after the letter).

ID	Individual in Patent	Sec.	Sec. Part	Date Issued	Other Counties	For More Info . . .
6744	ABERNATHY, David	30	SW	1837-03-20		A1 G1
6742	" "	30	NWSE	1839-03-15		A1
6743	" "	30	SENW	1839-09-20		A1
6744	ABERNATHY, James	30	SW	1837-03-20		A1 G1
6882	ALLEY, Thomas K	13	N½SW	1858-06-01		A1
6739	ARMSTRONG, Daniel R	6	SESW	1888-02-04		A4
6740	" "	6	SWSE	1888-02-04		A4
6839	ARMSTRONG, Lancelot	10	NWNE	1858-06-01		A1
6840	" "	2	SWSW	1858-06-01		A1
6841	" "	3	S½SE	1858-06-01		A1
6842	" "	3	SESW	1858-06-01		A1
6847	AVERY, Mary	29	N½NE	1859-04-01		A1
6848	" "	29	NENW	1859-04-01		A1
6885	AVERY, Tobias	18	N½SE	1885-12-10		A4
6886	" "	18	S½NE	1885-12-10		A4
6887	AVERY, Tony	20	N½NW	1891-06-29		A4
6797	BAILEY, James	24	NESW	1837-11-07	Shelby	A1
6793	" "	1	NWSW	1850-09-02		A1
6791	" "	1	NESW	1858-06-01		A1
6792	" "	1	NWSE	1858-06-01		A1
6794	" "	1	S½NW	1858-06-01		A1
6795	" "	1	SWSW	1858-06-01		A1
6796	" "	2	SESE	1858-06-01		A1
6802	BAILEY, James F	24	NENE	1882-10-30	Shelby	A1
6827	BAILEY, John S	11	NWNE	1858-06-01		A1
6828	" "	11	SENE	1858-06-01		A1
6829	" "	11	SWNE	1858-06-01		A1
6873	BAILEY, Samuel W	24	N½NW	1882-10-30	Shelby	A1
6876	BAILEY, Susan J	2	NESE	1894-06-15		A4
6877	" "	2	SENE	1894-06-15		A4
6878	BAILEY, Thomas	24	NWSW	1853-08-01	Shelby	A1 R6767
6749	BALLARD, Delilia	8	N½SE	1837-03-20		A1
6774	BARKSDALE, George T	14	S½NE	1892-10-08		A4
6890	BIBB, William C	28		1867-11-20		A1 G22 C R6891
6891	" "	28		1915-08-13		A1 G22 R6890
6730	BRASWELL, Bolivar S	8	E½NW	1895-01-31		A4
6731	" "	8	NESW	1895-01-31		A4
6732	" "	8	NWNW	1895-01-31		A4
6738	BRASWELL, Crawford	30	NENE	1893-07-19		A4
6798	BRASWELL, James	18	S½SE	1897-11-22		A4
6799	" "	18	S½SW	1897-11-22		A4
6844	BRASWELL, Lushus J	4	SWSW	1890-04-15		A1
6745	BROCK, David	29	SWNW	1858-06-01		A1
6746	" "	30	SENE	1858-06-01		A1
6855	BROCK, Pinckney L	32	NESW	1858-06-01		A1
6856	" "	32	SESE	1858-06-01		A1

ID	Individual in Patent	Sec.	Sec. Part	Date Issued	Other Counties	For More Info . . .
6857	BROCK, Pinckney L (Cont'd)	32	W½SE	1858-06-01		A1
6729	BROOKS, Berry	4	SENW	1891-11-23		A4
6736	BUCKLEY, Charles W	34	S½NW	1882-10-30		A1
6890	BUFFINGTON, William C	28		1867-11-20		A1 G22 C R6891
6891	" "	28		1915-08-13		A1 G22 R6890
6750	BURNS, Dorcus D	7	E½	1860-07-02		A1
6692	BYRAM, Alden M	31	NE	1858-06-01		A1
6693	" "	32	SWNW	1858-06-01		A1
6751	BYRAM, Ebenezer	1	S½SE	1858-06-01		A1
6752	" "	1	SESW	1858-06-01		A1
6694	CALDWELL, Alexander	19	NESE	1859-04-01		A1
6695	" "	20	W½SW	1859-04-01		A1
6710	CALDWELL, Amanda	24	NESE	1882-12-20	Shelby	A1 G42 R6709
6709	" "	24	NESE	1887-07-01	Shelby	A1 R6710
6720	CALDWELL, Augustus	19	SESW	1860-07-02		A1
6721	" "	19	W½SE	1860-07-02		A1
6722	" "	30	NENW	1860-07-02		A1
6710	CALDWELL, Benjamin V	24	NESE	1882-12-20	Shelby	A1 G42 R6709
6893	CARTER, William	9	SW	1837-03-20		A1 G45
6892	" "	6	NENE	1839-09-20		A1
6816	COLLEY, John	2	NESW	1890-04-15		A1
6817	" "	2	NWSE	1890-04-15		A1
6818	" "	2	W½NE	1890-04-15		A1
6843	COLLINS, Lewis	14	N½SW	1890-07-03		A4 V6715, 6896
6775	COWARD, George W	29	NWSE	1858-06-01		A1
6776	" "	29	SWNE	1858-06-01		A1
6780	COWARD, Harvey	20	E½SW	1882-11-20		A4
6782	CRAIGER, Henry	12	N½NW	1896-07-09		A4
6768	CROTWELL, George	30	NWNW	1858-06-01		A1
6890	DONELSON, Presley W	28		1867-11-20		A1 G22 C R6891
6891	" "	28		1915-08-13		A1 G22 R6890
6714	DORMAN, Andrew J	32	NWNW	1888-08-29		A1
6823	DUPEY, John M	6	SWSW	1854-07-15		A1
6824	" "	7	NWNW	1854-07-15		A1
6698	DUPUY, Alfred	4	N½NW	1839-09-20		A1
6871	EARLE, Samuel S	14	NENW	1889-10-22		A1
6872	EARLE, Samuel T	4	W½NE	1826-05-15		A1 G81
6872	FARRAR, Thomas W	4	W½NE	1826-05-15		A1 G81
6786	FISHER, Henry R	20	S½NW	1892-02-08		A4
6787	" "	20	W½NE	1892-02-08		A4
6812	FORD, Jane	27	SESE	1853-08-01		A1
6853	GALLAGHER, Neil	34	NWNW	1885-03-16		A1
6715	GILL, Andrew J	14	NESW	1884-12-05		A4 V6843
6716	" "	14	NWSE	1884-12-05		A4
6781	GILL, Henry B	2	E½NW	1890-03-19		A4 G93
6835	GILL, Joseph M	5	NESE	1839-09-20		A1
6836	" "	5	SESE	1839-09-20		A1
6837	" "	9	NWNE	1839-09-20		A1
6838	GILL, Joseph R	12	S½NW	1890-03-19		A4
6781	GILL, Margaret A	2	E½NW	1890-03-19		A4 G93
6896	GILL, William	14	NWSW	1890-03-19		A4 V6843
6897	" "	14	SENW	1890-03-19		A4
6898	" "	14	W½NW	1890-03-19		A4
6901	GILL, William K	17	NWNE	1848-07-01		A1
6890	GILMER, George N	28		1867-11-20		A1 G22 C R6891
6891	" "	28		1915-08-13		A1 G22 R6890
6757	GLENN, Elias	14	SWSE	1853-08-01		A1
6760	" "	23	SWNE	1853-08-01		A1
6758	" "	23	NESW	1858-06-01		A1
6759	" "	23	SENW	1858-06-01		A1
6761	" "	3	NWSW	1858-06-01		A1
6762	" "	3	W½NW	1858-06-01		A1
6763	" "	4	NESE	1858-06-01		A1
6764	" "	4	SENE	1858-06-01		A1
6831	GLENN, Joseph B	22	E½SE	1858-06-01		A1
6754	GOODE, Edward	22	S½NW	1837-03-20		A1
6833	GOODE, Joseph H	20	SENE	1837-11-07		A1
6834	" "	21	NWNW	1837-11-07		A1
6864	GOODE, Robert	20	NENE	1834-10-14		A1
6881	GOODE, Thomas	15	SWSW	1839-09-20		A1
6900	GOODE, William	5	SWSE	1854-07-15		A1
6899	" "	5	S½SW	1858-06-01		A1
6832	GOODWIN, Joseph	29	SENW	1853-08-01		A1

ID	Individual in Patent	Sec.	Sec. Part	Date Issued	Other Counties	For More Info . . .
6846	GOODWIN, Mark	30	NWNE	1837-03-30		A1
6845	" "	19	SESE	1839-09-20		A1
6788	GREEN, Hugh	32	NENW	1853-08-01		A1
6789	" "	8	W½NE	1858-06-01		A1
6699	GRIFFIN, Alfred	20	NESE	1852-01-01		A1
6700	" "	20	SESE	1858-06-01		A1
6701	" "	20	W½SE	1858-06-01		A1
6702	" "	21	SWNW	1858-06-01		A1
6858	HALL, Renney B	6	SWNW	1858-06-01		A1
6811	HARD, James W	30	SWNW	1903-10-01		A4
6874	HARMAN, Scintha	29	SWSE	1858-06-01		A1
6803	HARMON, James	29	SESW	1852-01-01		A1
6866	HENRY, Samuel	6	SWNE	1839-09-20		A1
6893	HOOPER, Toliver	9	SW	1837-03-20		A1 G45
6888	HUBBARD, Wiley N	34	NENW	1884-12-05		A4
6889	" "	34	NWNE	1884-12-05		A4
6894	HUBBARD, William D	34	SENE	1884-12-05		A4
6725	JONES, Belson	7	NWSW	1858-06-01		A1
6726	" "	7	SWNW	1858-06-01		A1
6783	JONES, Henry	11	NESW	1858-06-01		A1
6784	" "	11	NWSE	1858-06-01		A1
6785	" "	11	SENW	1858-06-01		A1
6820	JONES, John	34	NENE	1848-04-15		A1
6821	" "	34	NWSE	1848-04-15		A1
6822	" "	34	SWNE	1849-05-01		A1
6851	KELLY, Moses	10	NENE	1839-09-20		A1
6852	" "	11	NENE	1839-09-20		A1
6741	LANEY, Daniel S	8	S½SE	1837-03-20		A1
6691	LEATHERWOOD, Agilla	6	SENW	1854-07-15		A1
6895	LINTHICUM, William G	4	NENE	1839-09-20		A1
6825	MATHENY, John M	8	NWSW	1889-10-07		A1
6826	" "	8	SWNW	1889-10-07		A1
6753	MAXWELL, Edmond C	18	W½NW	1858-06-01		A1
6756	MCCLELEN, Elias B	33	SWSW	1858-06-01		A1
6813	MCCLINTOCK, John A	2	NWNW	1858-06-01		A1
6814	" "	3	NENE	1858-06-01		A1
6719	MCFALL, Arthur	19	SWSW	1839-09-20		A1
6815	MCLINTOCK, John A	10	SW	1892-06-10		A4
6869	MCLINTOCK, Samuel R	3	SWSW	1860-04-02		A1
6870	" "	4	SESE	1860-04-02		A1
6867	MCLUER, Samuel L	6	NWSW	1839-09-20		A1
6804	MILSTEAD, James M	34	E½SW	1884-12-05		A4
6805	" "	34	S½SE	1884-12-05		A4
6717	MONFEE, Andrew	10	S½NE	1892-06-10		A4
6718	" "	10	S½SE	1892-06-10		A4 R6737
6708	MORROW, Alphonso R	10	W½NW	1885-09-10		A1
6903	MORROW, William S	10	E½NW	1885-08-05		A1
6890	MOSES, Alfred H	28		1867-11-20		A1 G22 C R6891
6891	" "	28		1915-08-13		A1 G22 R6890
6765	NABORS, Elihu	1	NENW	1858-06-01		A1
6766	" "	1	NWNE	1858-06-01		A1
6819	NELMS, John G	22	N½NW	1837-03-20		A1
6849	PATTON, Mathew	14	E½SE	1889-08-02		A4
6850	PATTON, Matthew	12	E½SW	1858-06-01		A1
6859	PATTON, Robert B	11	E½SE	1858-06-01		A1
6860	" "	11	SWSE	1858-06-01		A1
6861	" "	12	W½SW	1858-06-01		A1
6862	" "	13	NWNW	1858-06-01		A1
6863	" "	14	N½NE	1858-06-01		A1
6868	PATTON, Samuel	12	SE	1883-07-03		A4
6880	PATTON, Thomas G	12	S½NE	1883-07-03		A4
6879	" "	12	N½NE	1885-03-30		A4
6875	PEARSON, Shadrach H	8	S½SW	1892-08-27		A4
6779	PHILLIPS, Harriett	18	N½SW	1890-01-08		A4 G197
6779	PHILLIPS, Sidney	18	N½SW	1890-01-08		A4 G197
6790	RAY, Isaac A	23	NENW	1850-09-02		A1
6854	RAY, Perry H	32	NWSW	1899-08-14		A4
6769	READING, George	24	SWSW	1837-03-30	Shelby	A1
6806	REDDING, James	24	SENE	1834-10-01	Shelby	A1
6703	ROEBUCK, Alfred H	4	NWSW	1858-06-01		A1
6704	" "	5	E½NE	1858-06-01		A1
6705	" "	8	SENE	1858-06-01		A1
6770	ROEBUCK, George	4	SWNW	1854-07-15		A1

ID	Individual in Patent	Sec.	Sec. Part	Date Issued	Other Counties	For More Info . . .
6771	ROEBUCK, George (Cont'd)	5	NWSE	1854-07-15		A1
6807	ROSS, James	6	NWNW	1891-06-30		A4
6808	ROSS, James T	17	E½NE	1858-06-01		A1
6809	" "	17	SWNE	1858-06-01		A1
6810	" "	6	NWSE	1888-02-04		A4
6755	SANDIFORD, Edward L	8	NENE	1839-09-20		A1
6706	SELLARS, Allison	2	NWSW	1883-10-01		A4
6707	" "	2	SWNW	1883-10-01		A4
6890	SMITH, Frank J	28		1867-11-20		A1 G22 C R6891
6891	" "	28		1915-08-13		A1 G22 R6890
6772	SMITH, George	24	S½NW	1884-12-05	Shelby	A4
6773	" "	24	W½NE	1884-12-05	Shelby	A4
6904	SMITH, William	4	SESW	1858-06-01		A1
6905	" "	4	SWSE	1858-06-01		A1
6906	" "	9	E½NW	1858-06-01		A1
6907	" "	9	NWSE	1858-06-01		A1
6908	" "	9	SWNE	1858-06-01		A1
6727	STACKS, Benjamin J	24	SESW	1882-10-30	Shelby	A1
6728	" "	24	SWSE	1882-10-30	Shelby	A1
6865	TARRANT, Samuel A	6	NESW	1854-07-15		A1 G217
6724	VANHOOSE, Azor	29	NESW	1839-09-20		A1
6735	VENS, Charles	30	SWSE	1913-06-07		A4
6872	WALTON, Jacob	4	W½NE	1826-05-15		A1 G81
6734	WARREN, Bures A	22	S½SW	1883-10-01		A4
6733	" "	22	N½SW	1885-03-30		A4
6830	WELCH, John W	2	NENE	1894-05-15		A4
6902	WEST, William L	22	NWSE	1911-10-19		A4 R6712
6800	WIDEMAN, James C	2	SESW	1885-03-16		A1
6801	" "	2	SWSE	1885-03-16		A1
6883	WIDEMAN, Thomas	6	E½SE	1889-10-07		A1 F
6884	" "	6	SENE	1889-10-07		A1 F
6767	WILDER, Garret	24	NWSW	1839-03-15	Shelby	A1 C R6878
6696	WILLIAMS, Alexander E	4	NESW	1891-06-29		A1
6697	" "	4	NWSE	1891-06-29		A1
6747	WILLIAMS, David	6	NENW	1858-06-01		A1
6748	" "	6	NWNE	1858-06-01		A1
6777	WILLIAMS, Hanibal	18	E½NW	1899-04-17		A4
6778	" "	18	N½NE	1899-04-17		A4
6737	WILLIS, Charles W	10	S½SE	1911-10-12		A4 R6718
6711	WINFIELD, Americus A	22	NWNE	1885-03-30		A4
6712	" "	22	NWSE	1885-03-30		A4 R6902
6713	" "	22	S½NE	1885-03-30		A4
6723	WOLF, Augustus	30	E½SE	1884-12-05		A4
6865	WRITE, Thomas J	6	NESW	1854-07-15		A1 G217

Patent Map

T19-S R3-W
Huntsville Meridian

Map Group 39

Township Statistics

Parcels Mapped	:	218
Number of Patents	:	151
Number of Individuals	:	138
Patentees Identified	:	128
Number of Surnames	:	89
Multi-Patentee Parcels	:	9
Oldest Patent Date	:	5/15/1826
Most Recent Patent	:	8/13/1915
Block/Lot Parcels	:	0
Parcels Re - Issued	:	5
Parcels that Overlap	:	3
Cities and Towns	:	1
Cemeteries	:	1

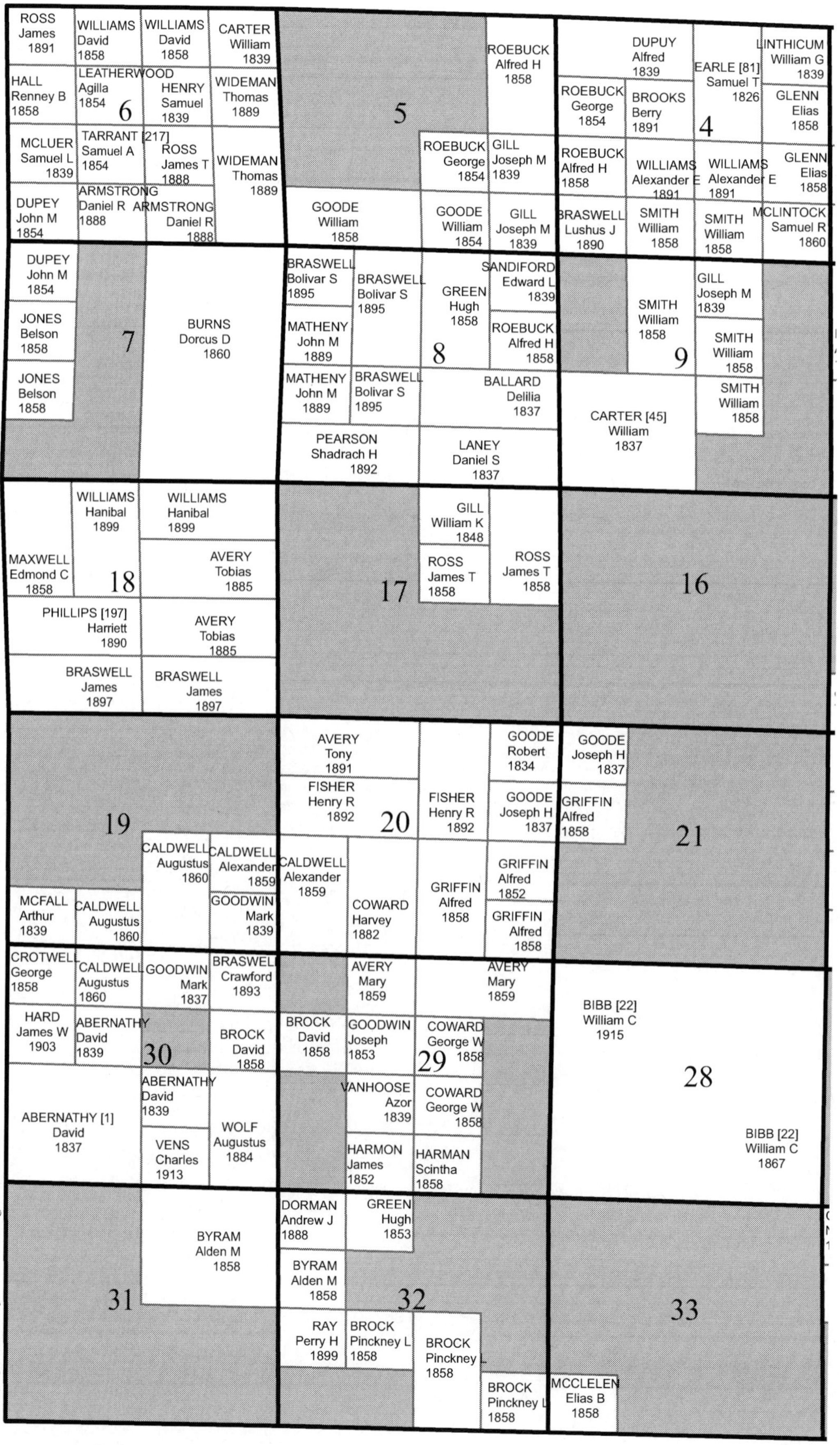

6
ROSS James 1891
WILLIAMS David 1858
WILLIAMS David 1858
CARTER William 1839
HALL Renney B 1858
LEATHERWOOD Agilla 1854
HENRY Samuel 1839
WIDEMAN Thomas 1889
MCLUER Samuel L 1839
TARRANT [217] Samuel A 1854
ROSS James T 1888
WIDEMAN Thomas 1889
ARMSTRONG Daniel R 1888
ARMSTRONG Daniel R 1888
DUPEY John M 1854

5
ROEBUCK Alfred H 1858
ROEBUCK George 1854
GILL Joseph M 1839
GOODE William 1858
GOODE William 1854
GILL Joseph M 1839

4
DUPUY Alfred 1839
LINTHICUM William G 1839
EARLE [81] Samuel T 1826
ROEBUCK George 1854
BROOKS Berry 1891
GLENN Elias 1858
ROEBUCK Alfred H 1858
WILLIAMS Alexander E 1891
WILLIAMS Alexander E 1891
GLENN Elias 1858
BRASWELL Lushus J 1890
SMITH William 1858
SMITH William 1858
MCLINTOCK Samuel R 1860

7
DUPEY John M 1854
JONES Belson 1858
JONES Belson 1858
BURNS Dorcus D 1860

8
BRASWELL Bolivar S 1895
BRASWELL Bolivar S 1895
GREEN Hugh 1858
SANDIFORD Edward L 1839
MATHENY John M 1889
ROEBUCK Alfred H 1858
MATHENY John M 1889
BRASWELL Bolivar S 1895
BALLARD Delilia 1837
PEARSON Shadrach H 1892
LANEY Daniel S 1837

9
SMITH William 1858
GILL Joseph M 1839
SMITH William 1858
SMITH William 1858
CARTER [45] William 1837

18
WILLIAMS Hanibal 1899
WILLIAMS Hanibal 1899
MAXWELL Edmond C 1858
AVERY Tobias 1885
PHILLIPS [197] Harriett 1890
AVERY Tobias 1885
BRASWELL James 1897
BRASWELL James 1897

17
GILL William K 1848
ROSS James T 1858
ROSS James T 1858

16

19
MCFALL Arthur 1839
CALDWELL Augustus 1860
CALDWELL Augustus 1860
CALDWELL Alexander 1859
GOODWIN Mark 1839

20
AVERY Tony 1891
FISHER Henry R 1892
FISHER Henry R 1892
GOODE Robert 1834
GOODE Joseph H 1837
CALDWELL Alexander 1859
COWARD Harvey 1882
GRIFFIN Alfred 1858
GRIFFIN Alfred 1852
GRIFFIN Alfred 1858

21
GOODE Joseph H 1837
GRIFFIN Alfred 1858

30
CROTWELL George 1858
CALDWELL Augustus 1860
GOODWIN Mark 1837
BRASWELL Crawford 1893
HARD James W 1903
ABERNATHY David 1839
BROCK David 1858
ABERNATHY David 1839
ABERNATHY [1] David 1837
WOLF Augustus 1884
VENS Charles 1913

29
AVERY Mary 1859
AVERY Mary 1859
BROCK David 1858
GOODWIN Joseph 1853
COWARD George W 1858
VANHOOSE Azor 1839
COWARD George W 1858
HARMON James 1852
HARMAN Scintha 1858

28
BIBB [22] William C 1915
BIBB [22] William C 1867

31
BYRAM Alden M 1858

32
DORMAN Andrew J 1888
GREEN Hugh 1853
BYRAM Alden M 1858
RAY Perry H 1899
BROCK Pinckney L 1858
BROCK Pinckney L 1858
BROCK Pinckney L 1858

33
MCCLELEN Elias B 1858

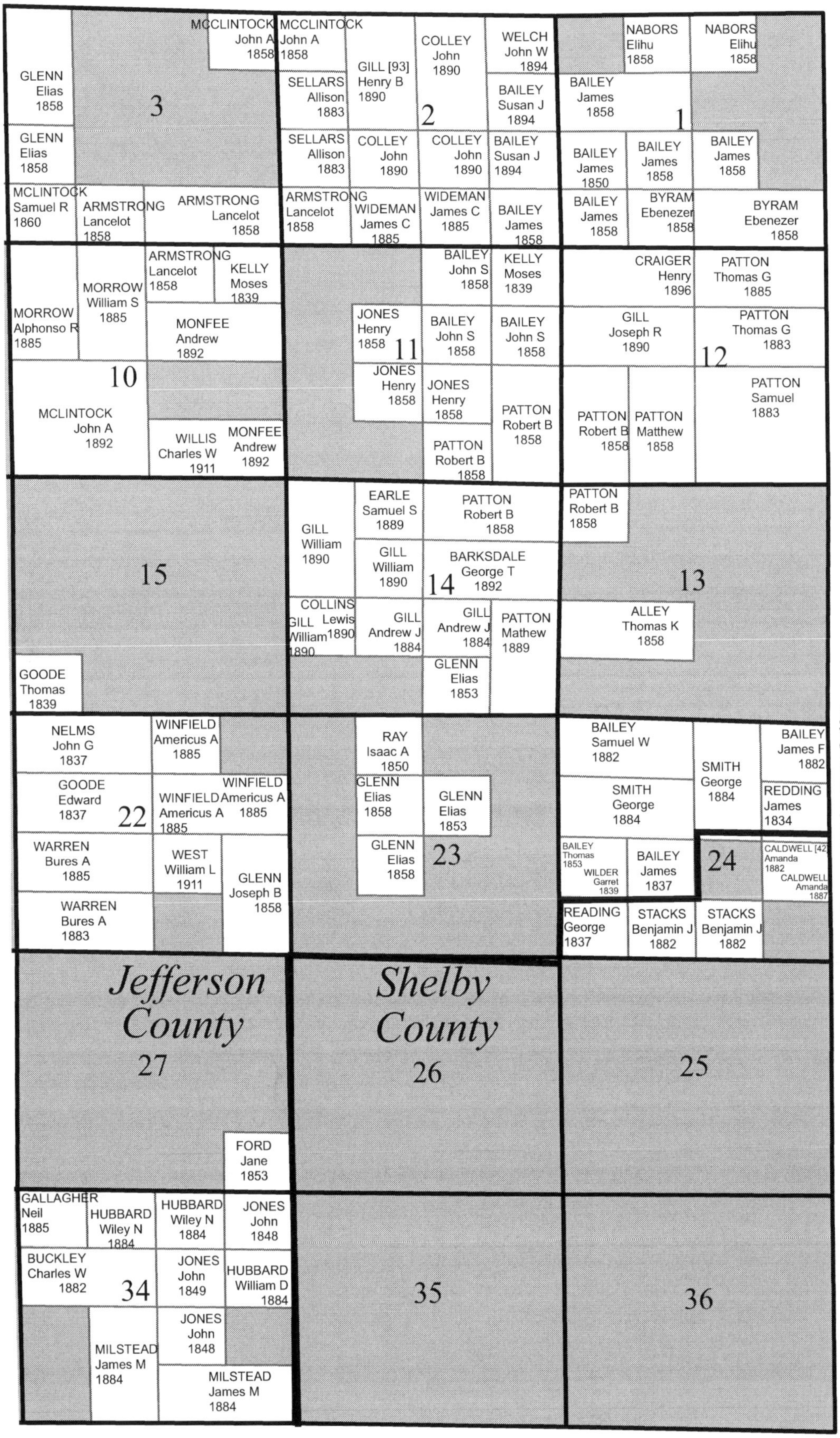

Helpful Hints

1. This Map's INDEX can be found on the preceding pages.
2. Refer to Map "C" to see where this Township lies within Jefferson County, Alabama.
3. Numbers within square brackets [ ] denote a multi-patentee land parcel (multi-owner). Refer to Appendix "C" for a full list of members in this group.
4. Areas that look to be crowded with Patentees usually indicate multiple sales of the same parcel (Re-issues) or Overlapping parcels. See this Township's Index for an explanation of these and other circumstances that might explain "odd" groupings of Patentees on this map.

Legend

- Patent Boundary
- Section Boundary
- No Patents Found (or Outside County)
- 1., 2., 3., ... Lot Numbers (when beside a name)
- [ ] Group Number (see Appendix "C")

Scale: Section = 1 mile X 1 mile (generally, with some exceptions)

Road Map

T19-S R3-W
Huntsville Meridian

Map Group 39

Cities & Towns
Shannon

Cemeteries
Jefferson Garden of Memories

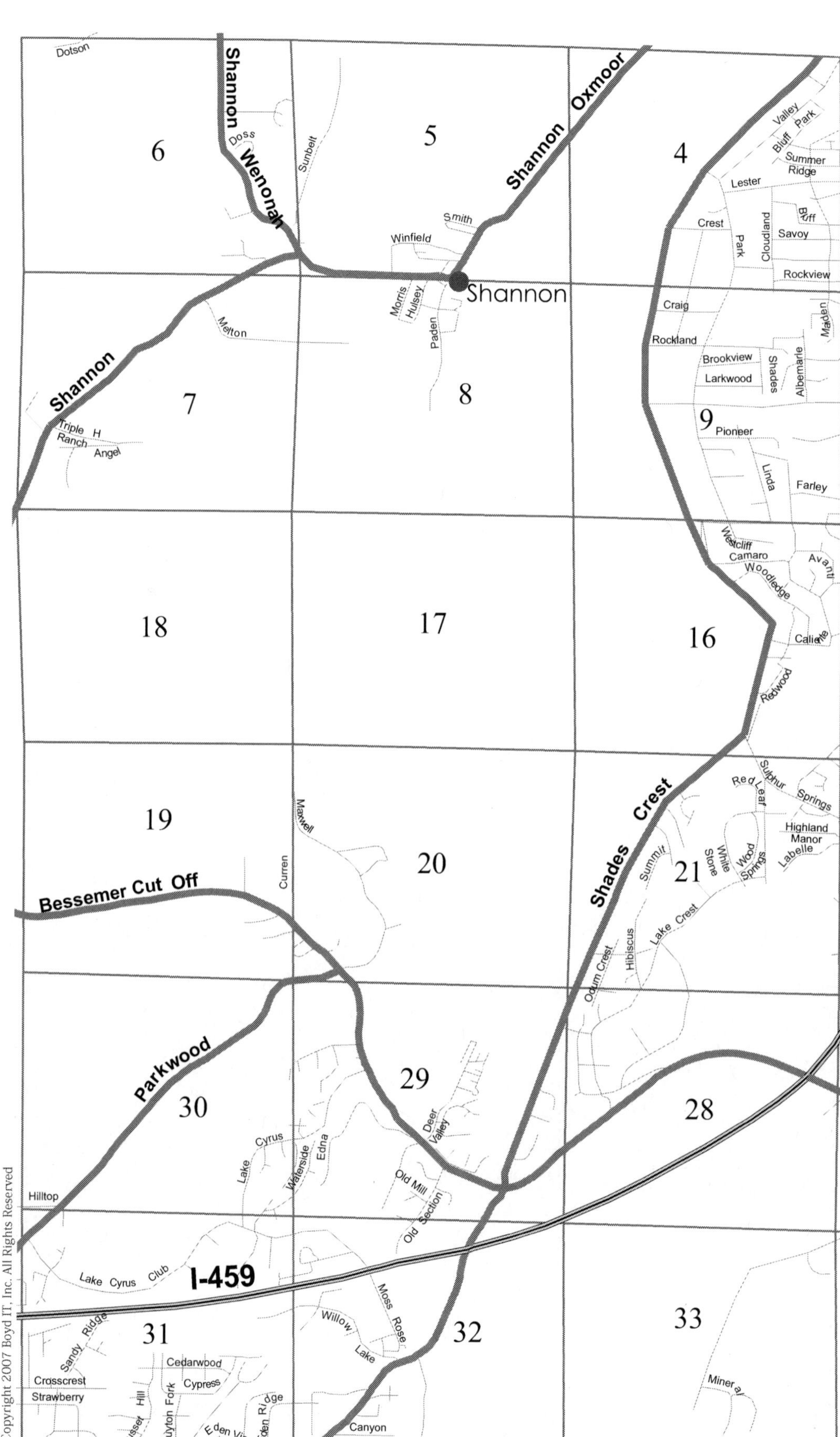

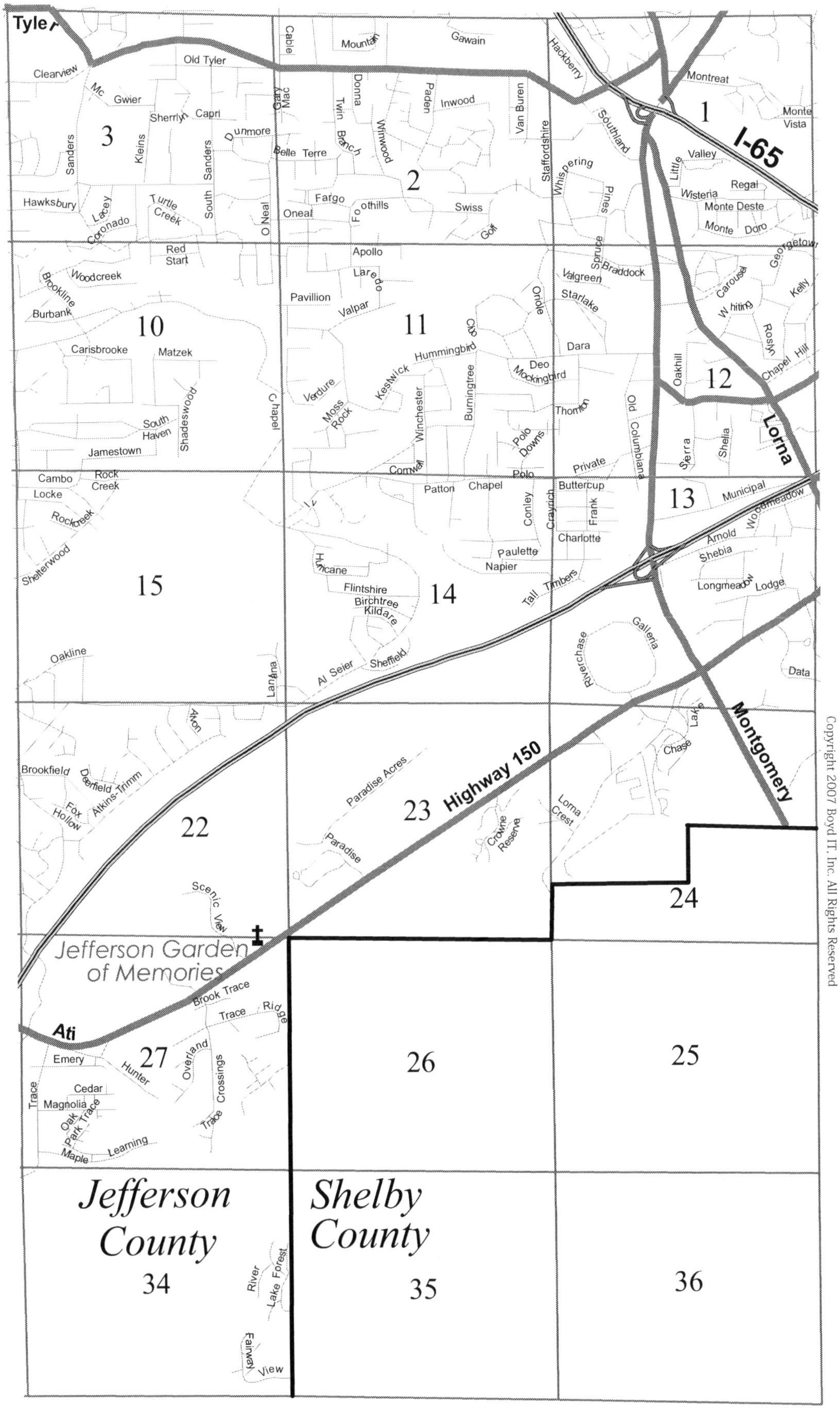

1 2 3 10 11 12 13 14 15 22 23 24 25 26 27 34 35 36

I-65

Highway 150

Lorna

Montgomery

Jefferson Garden of Memories

Jefferson County

Shelby County

Tyler
Old Tyler
Clearview
Mc Gwier
Sherry
Capri
Dunmore
Sanders
Kleins
South Sanders
Hawksbury
Lacey
Coronado
Turtle Creek
O Neal
Cable
Mountain
Gawain
Cary
Donna
Twin Branch
Paden
Inwood
Winwood
Van Buren
Belle Terre
Fargo
Oneal
Foothills
Swiss
Golf
Staffordshire
Whispering
Hackberry
Southland
Pines
Montreat
Monte Vista
Valley
Little
Wisteria
Regal
Monte Deste
Monte Doro
Red Start
Woodcreek
Brookline
Burbank
Carisbrooke
Matzek
South Haven
Shadeswood
Jamestown
C Chapel
Apollo
Laredo
Pavillion
Valpar
Hummingbird
Keswick
Verdure
Moss Rock
Winchester
Burningtree
Oriole
Valgreen
Braddock
Spruce
Starlake
Dara
Deo
Mockingbird
Thornton
Polo Downs
Old Columbiana
Oakhill
Georgetown
Carousel
Whiting
Kelly
Roslyn
Chapel Hill
Serra
Shelia
Private
Cambo
Rock Creek
Locke
Rockcreek
Shelterwood
Cornwall
Patton
Chapel
Polo
Buttercup
Conley
Crayrich
Frank
Charlotte
Municipal
Woodmeadow
Arnold
Shebia
Longmeadow
Lodge
Hurricane
Paulette
Napier
Flintshire
Birchtree
Kildare
Tall Timbers
Oakline
Lanana
Al Seier
Sheffield
Riverchase
Galleria
Data
Avon
Brookfield
Deerfield
Atkins-Trimm
Fox Hollow
Paradise Acres
Paradise
Crowne Reserve
Lorna Crest
Lake
Chase
Scenic View
Brook Trace
Trace
Ridge
Ati
Emery
Hunter
Overland
Crossings
Trace
Cedar
Magnolia
Oak Park Trace
Maple
Learning
River
Lake Forest
Fairway
View

Helpful Hints

1. This road map has a number of uses, but primarily it is to help you: a) find the present location of land owned by your ancestors (at least the general area), b) find cemeteries and city-centers, and c) estimate the route/roads used by Census-takers & tax-assessors.

2. If you plan to travel to Jefferson County to locate cemeteries or land parcels, please pick up a modern travel map for the area before you do. Mapping old land parcels on modern maps is not as exact a science as you might think. Just the slightest variations in public land survey coordinates, estimates of parcel boundaries, or road-map deviations can greatly alter a map's representation of how a road either does or doesn't cross a particular parcel of land.

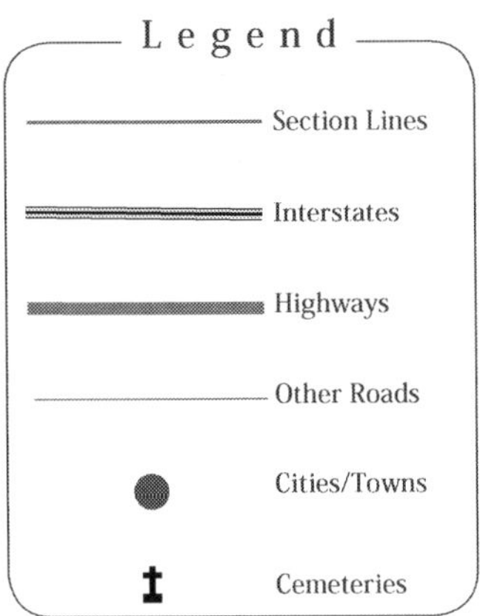

Scale: Section = 1 mile X 1 mile
(generally, with some exceptions)

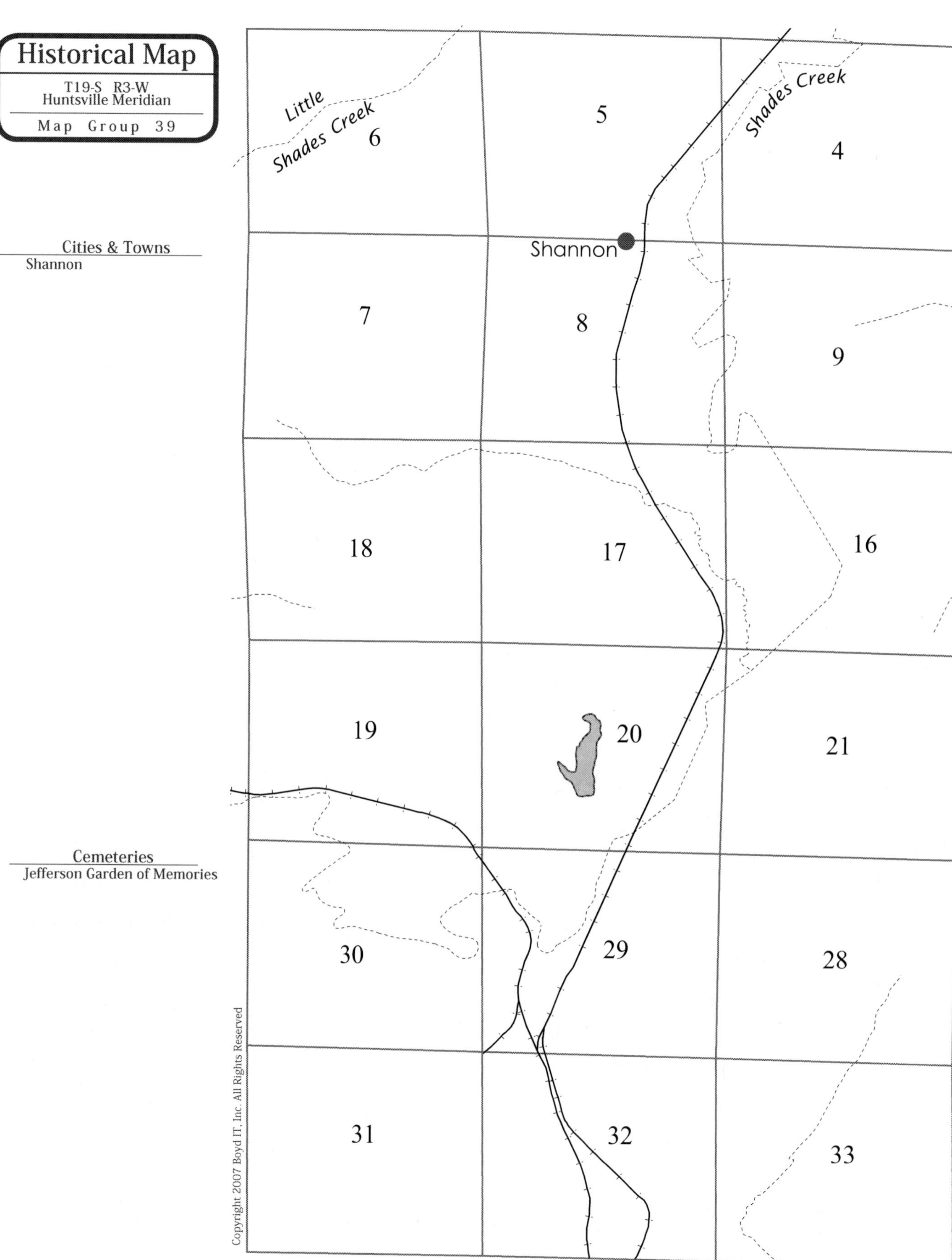
Historical Map
T19-S R3-W
Huntsville Meridian
Map Group 39
Cities & Towns
Shannon
Cemeteries
Jefferson Garden of Memories
Little Shades Creek
Shades Creek
Shannon
6
5
4
7
8
9
18
17
16
19
20
21
30
29
28
31
32
33
Copyright 2007 Boyd IT, Inc. All Rights Reserved

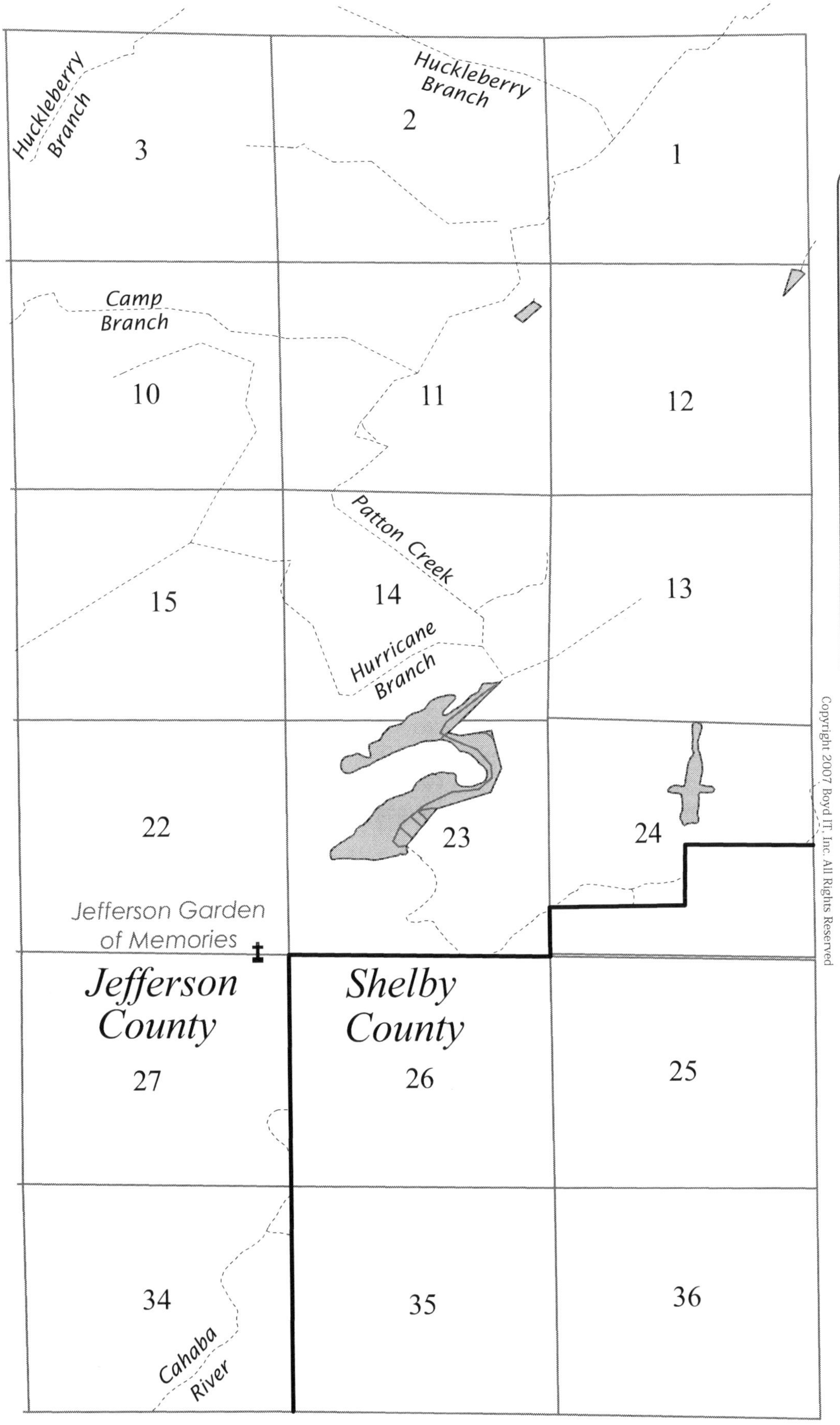

Huckleberry Branch
Huckleberry Branch
3
2
1
Camp Branch
10
11
12
Patton Creek
15
14
13
Hurricane Branch
22
23
24
Jefferson Garden of Memories
Jefferson County
Shelby County
27
26
25
34
35
36
Cahaba River

Helpful Hints

1. This Map takes a different look at the same Congressional Township displayed in the preceding two maps. It presents features that can help you better envision the historical development of the area: a) Water-bodies (lakes & ponds), b) Water-courses (rivers, streams, etc.), c) Railroads, d) City/town center-points (where they were oftentimes located when first settled), and e) Cemeteries.

2. Using this "Historical" map in tandem with this Township's Patent Map and Road Map, may lead you to some interesting discoveries. You will often find roads, towns, cemeteries, and waterways are named after nearby landowners: sometimes those names will be the ones you are researching. See how many of these research gems you can find here in Jefferson County.

Legend
Section Lines
Railroads
Large Rivers & Bodies of Water
Streams/Creeks & Small Rivers
Cities/Towns
Cemeteries

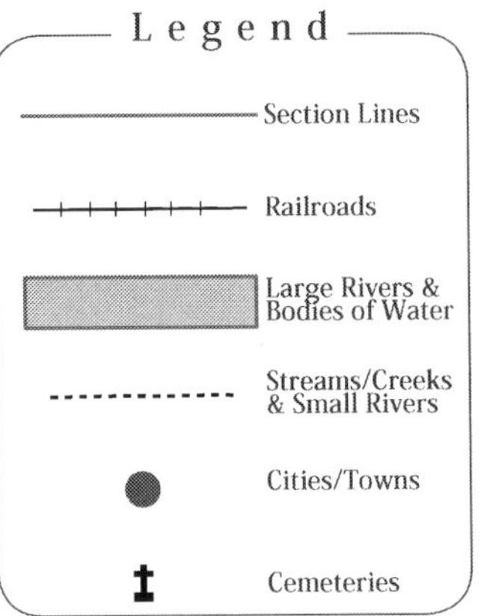

Scale: Section = 1 mile X 1 mile
(there are some exceptions)

Map Group 40: Index to Land Patents

Township 19-South Range 2-West (Huntsville)

After you locate an individual in this Index, take note of the Section and Section Part then proceed to the Land Patent map on the pages immediately following. You should have no difficulty locating the corresponding parcel of land.

The "For More Info" Column will lead you to more information about the underlying Patents. See the *Legend* at right, and the "How to Use this Book" chapter, for more information.

LEGEND

"For More Info . . . " column

A = Authority (Legislative Act, See Appendix "A")
B = Block or Lot (location in Section unknown)
C = Cancelled Patent
F = Fractional Section
G = Group (Multi-Patentee Patent, see Appendix "C")
V = Overlaps another Parcel
R = Re-Issued (Parcel patented more than once)

(A & G items require you to look in the Appendixes referred to above. All other Letter-designations followed by a number require you to locate line-items in this index that possess the ID number found after the letter).

ID	Individual in Patent	Sec.	Sec. Part	Date Issued	Other Counties	For More Info . . .
6909	ACTON, Aaron C	18	E½SE	1883-07-03		A4
6918	ACTON, John	8	E½SW	1824-04-30		A1
6920	" "	8	SWSE	1837-04-01		A1
6919	" "	8	SESE	1890-07-03		A4
6926	ACTON, Mariah E	18	NWSE	1883-07-03		A4 G2
6927	" "	18	SWNE	1883-07-03		A4 G2
6928	ACTON, Needham	8	E½NW	1885-03-16		A4
6934	ACTON, Samuel	5	SENE	1853-11-15		A1
6935	" "	5	SWNE	1858-06-01		A1
6936	" "	6	NESE	1858-06-01		A1
6937	" "	6	SENE	1858-06-01		A1
6938	" "	8	NWSW	1858-06-01		A1
6939	" "	8	SWNW	1858-06-01		A1
6954	ACTON, Thomas M	18	N½NE	1883-07-03		A4
6926	ACTON, William M	18	NWSE	1883-07-03		A4 G2
6927	" "	18	SWNE	1883-07-03		A4 G2
6923	BAILEY, John S	18	N½NW	1882-10-30		A1
6940	BAILEY, Samuel M	19	E½NW	1858-06-01	Shelby	A1
6941	" "	19	NWNW	1858-06-01	Shelby	A1
6942	" "	19	W½NE	1858-06-01	Shelby	A1
6947	BAILEY, Stephen H	6	NWSW	1890-07-03		A4
6948	" "	6	S½NW	1890-07-03		A4 V6915
6949	" "	6	SWNE	1890-07-03		A4
6953	BAILEY, Thomas	6	NENE	1858-06-01		A1
6951	" "	18	SESW	1883-10-01		A4
6952	" "	18	SWSE	1883-10-01		A4
6955	BELL, William	5	SWSW	1839-09-20		A1
6956	" "	8	NWNW	1839-09-20		A1
6912	BYRAM, Ebenezer	6	SWSW	1858-06-01		A1
6957	BYRAM, William H	6	E½SW	1887-04-20		A4
6958	" "	6	W½SE	1887-04-20		A4
6910	CALDWELL, Alexander	4	E½SW	1830-11-01	Shelby	A1
6922	CALDWELL, John	4	W½SE	1883-10-01	Shelby	A4
6921	" "	4	E½SE	1885-03-16	Shelby	A4
6933	DAVENPORT, Robert P	4	W½SW	1833-08-12	Shelby	A1
6943	DAVENPORT, Samuel W	18	SENE	1834-10-14		A1
6945	" "	8	E½NE	1837-03-20		A1
6944	" "	7	NENE	1839-03-15		A1
6911	DAVIS, Bennett	9	SWNW	1852-01-01	Shelby	A1
6959	JONES, William Y	4	S½NW	1882-10-30	Shelby	A1
6932	KILLOUGH, Richmond	9	NWNW	1834-10-01	Shelby	A1
6913	LEE, Edward	5	NW	1837-03-20		A1 G157
6916	LEE, James F	18	N½SW	1884-12-05		A4
6931	LEE, Needham	8	W½NE	1837-03-20		A1
6930	" "	8	NESE	1837-04-01		A1
6929	" "	6	SESE	1839-03-15		A1

ID	Individual in Patent	Sec.	Sec. Part	Date Issued	Other Counties	For More Info . . .
6946	LEE, Sarah	19	SENE	1860-04-02	Shelby	A1
6914	PILLARS, Granville	6	N½NW	1893-05-26		A4 V6915
6924	PLEDGER, Lemuel	4	E½NE	1824-05-25	Shelby	A1
6925	" "	4	W½NE	1825-09-01	Shelby	A1
6917	REDDING, James	19	SWNW	1834-10-14	Shelby	A1
6913	ROY, Margaret	5	NW	1837-03-20		A1 G157
6915	SPRADLEY, James B	6	NW	1890-04-15		A1 V6948, 6914
6950	WHARTON, Stephen	8	NWSE	1834-10-14		A1

Patent Map

T19-S R2-W
Huntsville Meridian

Map Group 40

Township Statistics

Parcels Mapped	:	51
Number of Patents	:	40
Number of Individuals	:	31
Patentees Identified	:	29
Number of Surnames	:	16
Multi-Patentee Parcels	:	3
Oldest Patent Date	:	4/30/1824
Most Recent Patent	:	5/26/1893
Block/Lot Parcels	:	0
Parcels Re - Issued	:	0
Parcels that Overlap	:	3
Cities and Towns	:	0
Cemeteries	:	0

Note: the area contained in this map amounts to far less than a full Township. Therefore, its contents are completely on this single page (instead of a "normal" 2-page spread).

Legend

Patent Boundary

Section Boundary

No Patents Found (or Outside County)

1., 2., 3., ... Lot Numbers (when beside a name)

[ ] Group Number (see Appendix "C")

Scale: Section = 1 mile X 1 mile (generally, with some exceptions)

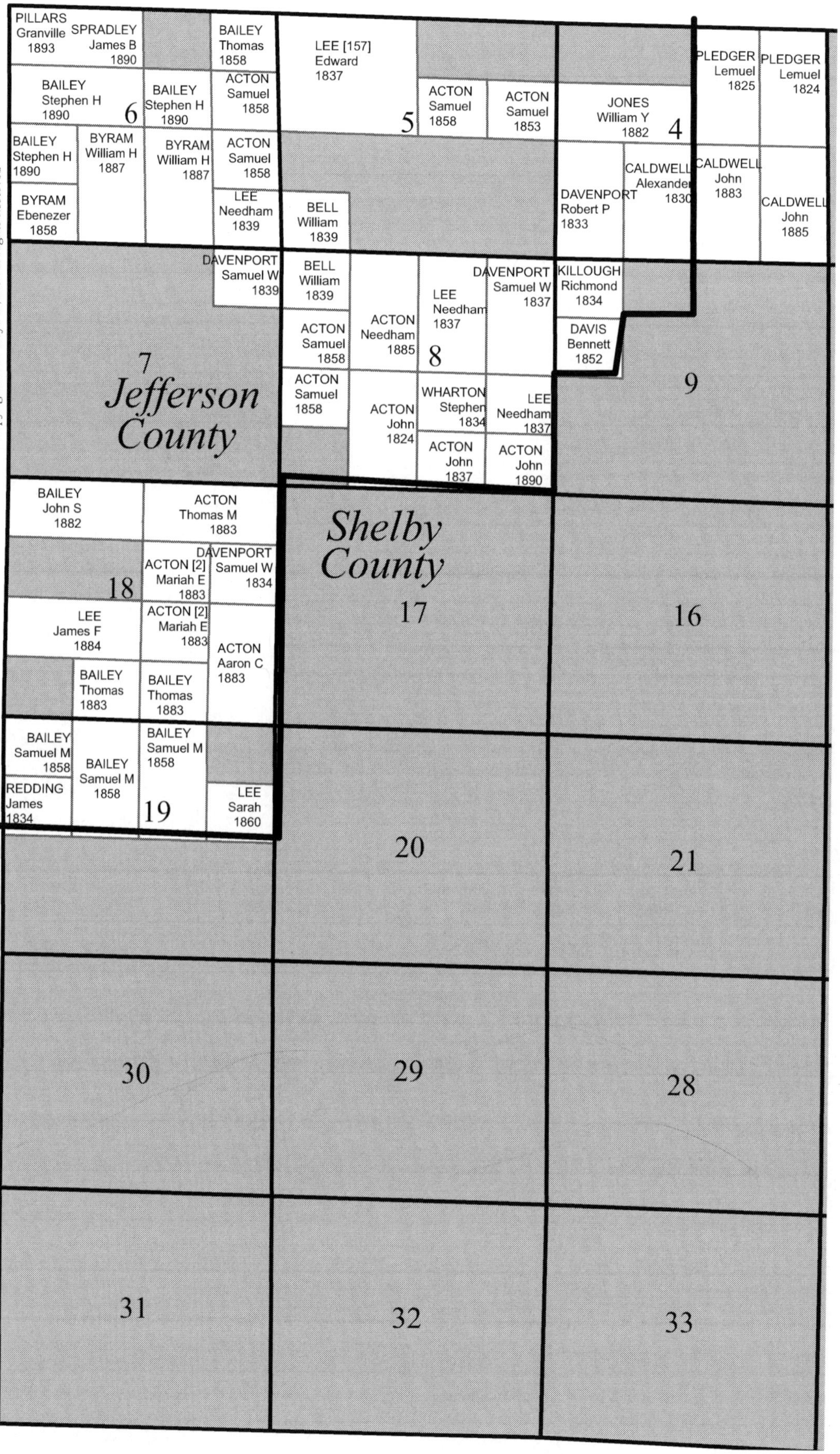

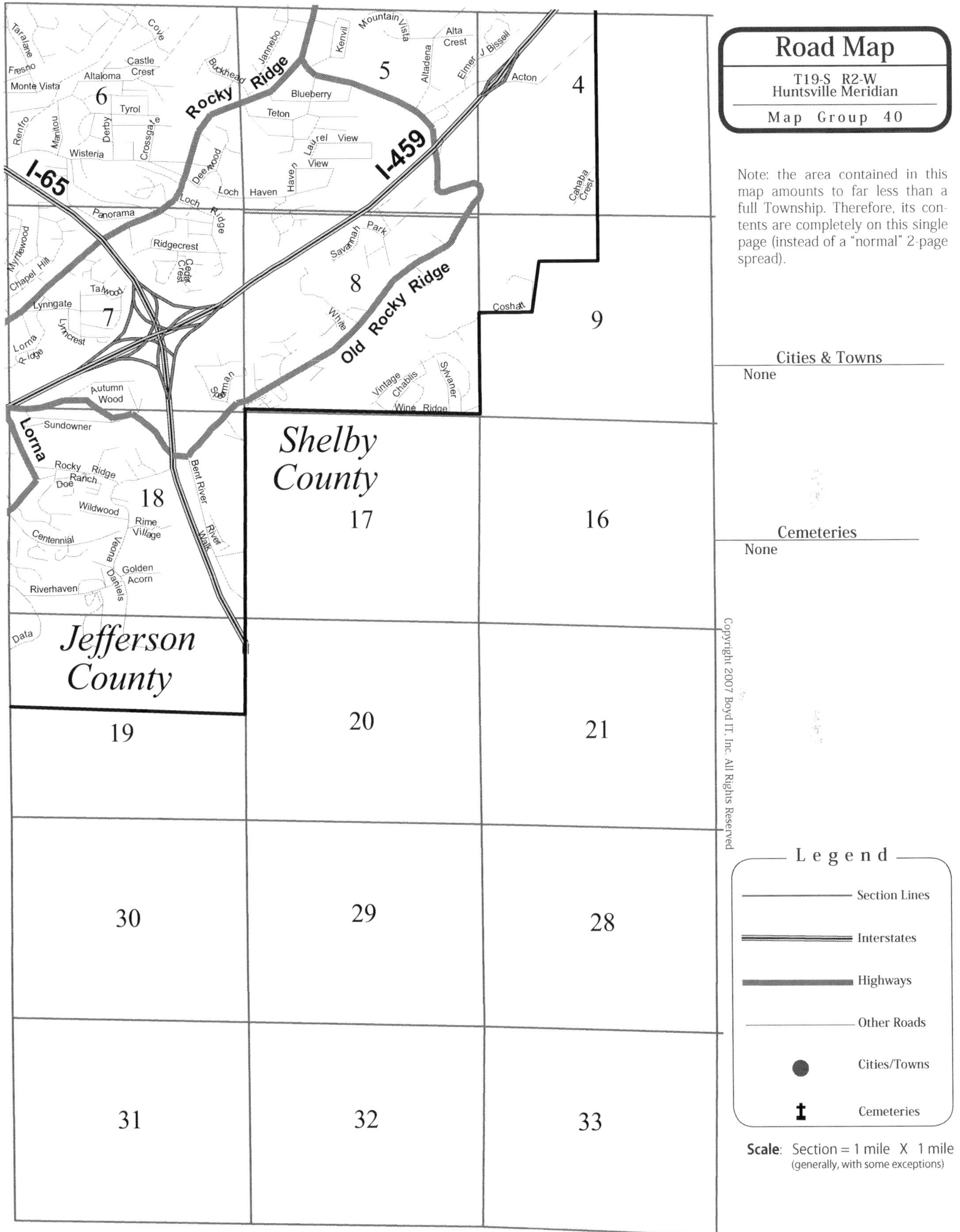
Road Map
T19-S R2-W
Huntsville Meridian
Map Group 40
Note: the area contained in this map amounts to far less than a full Township. Therefore, its contents are completely on this single page (instead of a "normal" 2-page spread).
Cities & Towns
None
Cemeteries
None
Legend
Section Lines
Interstates
Highways
Other Roads
Cities/Towns
Cemeteries
Scale: Section = 1 mile X 1 mile
(generally, with some exceptions)
Copyright 2007 Boyd IT, Inc. All Rights Reserved
Shelby County
Jefferson County
I-65
I-459
Rocky Ridge
Old Rocky Ridge
Lorna
6
5
4
7
8
9
18
17
16
19
20
21
30
29
28
31
32
33
Taralane
Cove
Fresno
Monte Vista
Altaloma
Castle Crest
Tyrol
Renfro
Manitou
Derby
Crossgate
Wisteria
Buckhead
Jannebo
Kenvil
Mountain Vista
Altadena
Alta Crest
Elmer
J Bissell
Acton
Blueberry
Teton
Laurel View
View
Haven
Haven
Deerwood
Loch
Loch Ridge
Canaba Crest
Panorama
Ridgecrest
Cedar Crest
Savannah Park
Myrtlewood
Chapel Hill
Tarwood
Lynngate
Lynncrest
Lorna Ridge
White
Coshatt
Spearman
Vintage
Chablis
Sylvaner
Wine Ridge
Autumn Wood
Sundowner
Rocky Ridge Ranch
Doe
Wildwood
Rime Village
Bent River
River Walk
Centennial
Veona
Daniels
Golden Acorn
Riverhaven
Data

Historical Map

T19-S R2-W
Huntsville Meridian

Map Group 40

Note: the area contained in this map amounts to far less than a full Township. Therefore, its contents are completely on this single page (instead of a "normal" 2-page spread).

Cities & Towns

None

Cemeteries

None

Legend

- Section Lines
- Railroads
- Large Rivers & Bodies of Water
- Streams/Creeks & Small Rivers
- Cities/Towns
- Cemeteries

Scale: Section = 1 mile X 1 mile
(there are some exceptions)

Map Group 41: Index to Land Patents

Township 20-South Range 6-West (Huntsville)

After you locate an individual in this Index, take note of the Section and Section Part then proceed to the Land Patent map on the pages immediately following. You should have no difficulty locating the corresponding parcel of land.

The "For More Info" Column will lead you to more information about the underlying Patents. See the *Legend* at right, and the "How to Use this Book" chapter, for more information.

LEGEND

"For More Info . . . " column

A = Authority (Legislative Act, See Appendix "A")
B = Block or Lot (location in Section unknown)
C = Cancelled Patent
F = Fractional Section
G = Group (Multi-Patentee Patent, see Appendix "C")
V = Overlaps another Parcel
R = Re-Issued (Parcel patented more than once)

(A & G items require you to look in the Appendixes referred to above. All other Letter-designations followed by a number require you to locate line-items in this index that possess the ID number found after the letter).

ID	Individual in Patent	Sec.	Sec. Part	Date Issued	Other Counties	For More Info . . .
6993	ARMSTRONG, William C	12	E½NE	1889-11-21		A4
6994	" "	12	NENW	1889-11-21		A4
6995	" "	12	NWNE	1889-11-21		A4
6960	BURNS, Alonzo W	2	E½NE	1891-06-29		A1
6961	CURRY, David B	10	SWNW	1858-06-01		A1
6996	CURRY, William	10	W½SW	1853-08-01		A1
6976	GOODWIN, Mark	4	W½SW	1860-07-02		A1
6984	HARKEY, Rufus	12	E½SE	1884-12-05		A4
6975	HERRING, Lee L	10	E½NE	1885-03-16		A1
6997	HERRING, William	11	S½SE	1858-06-01		A1
6998	" "	13	NWNW	1858-06-01		A1
6971	KIMBREL, James W	4	E½NW	1891-06-19		A4
6972	" "	4	W½NE	1891-06-19		A4
6967	MCMATH, James H	1	NESE	1858-06-01		A1
6968	" "	1	SENE	1858-06-01		A1
6977	MOSES, Moses B	12	SENW	1873-12-10		A1
6978	" "	12	SWNE	1873-12-10		A1
6988	MOSES, Sarah D	12	N½SW	1873-12-10		A1
6969	PARSONS, James	3	NWNE	1858-06-01		A1
6991	PARSONS, Wesley	2	NWNW	1884-12-05		A4
6992	" "	2	SWSW	1884-12-05		A4
6989	PARSONS, Wesley A	2	NWSW	1883-07-03		A4
6990	" "	2	SWNW	1883-07-03		A4
6970	RAY, James	10	SESE	1849-08-01		A1
6973	REAVES, Jesse T	10	E½NW	1885-06-12		A4
6974	" "	10	W½NE	1885-06-12		A4
6985	REAVES, Sarah A	2	NESE	1891-06-18		A1
6986	" "	2	S½SE	1891-06-18		A1
6987	" "	2	SESW	1891-06-18		A1
6979	SALMONS, Nelson	13	NENE	1858-06-01		A1
6962	SELLERS, Gurley	10	NESE	1858-06-01		A1
6963	" "	10	SESW	1858-06-01		A1
6964	" "	10	SWSE	1858-06-01		A1
6965	" "	11	SESW	1858-06-01		A1
6966	" "	11	W½SW	1858-06-01		A1
6983	SHARP, Robert M	10	NESW	1858-06-01		A1
6980	WILLARD, Olins S	2	E½NW	1885-11-13		A1
6981	" "	2	NESW	1885-11-13		A1
6982	" "	2	SWNE	1885-11-13		A1

Patent Map

T20-S R6-W
Huntsville Meridian

Map Group 41

Township Statistics

Parcels Mapped	:	39
Number of Patents	:	23
Number of Individuals	:	22
Patentees Identified	:	22
Number of Surnames	:	16
Multi-Patentee Parcels	:	0
Oldest Patent Date	:	8/1/1849
Most Recent Patent	:	6/29/1891
Block/Lot Parcels	:	0
Parcels Re - Issued	:	0
Parcels that Overlap	:	0
Cities and Towns	:	0
Cemeteries	:	0

Note: the area contained in this map amounts to far less than a full Township. Therefore, its contents are completely on this single page (instead of a "normal" 2-page spread).

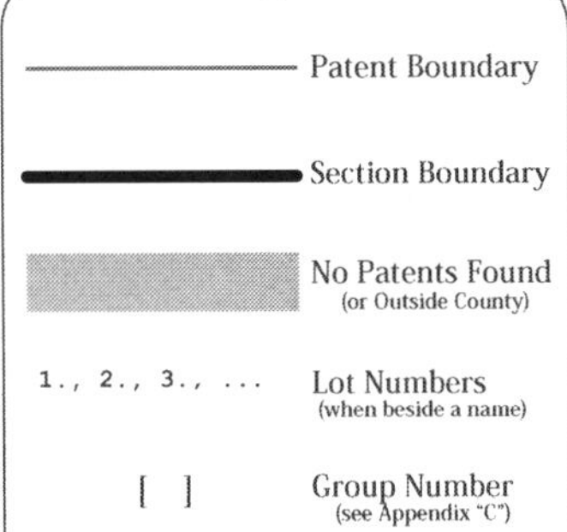

Scale: Section = 1 mile X 1 mile
(generally, with some exceptions)

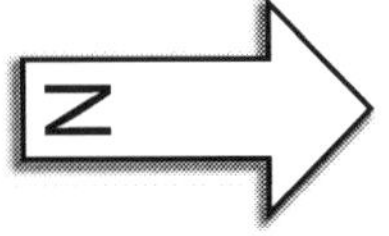

Road Map

T20-S R6-W
Huntsville Meridian

Map Group 41

Note: the area contained in this map amounts to far less than a full Township. Therefore, its contents are completely on this single page (instead of a "normal" 2-page spread).

Cities & Towns

None

Cemeteries

None

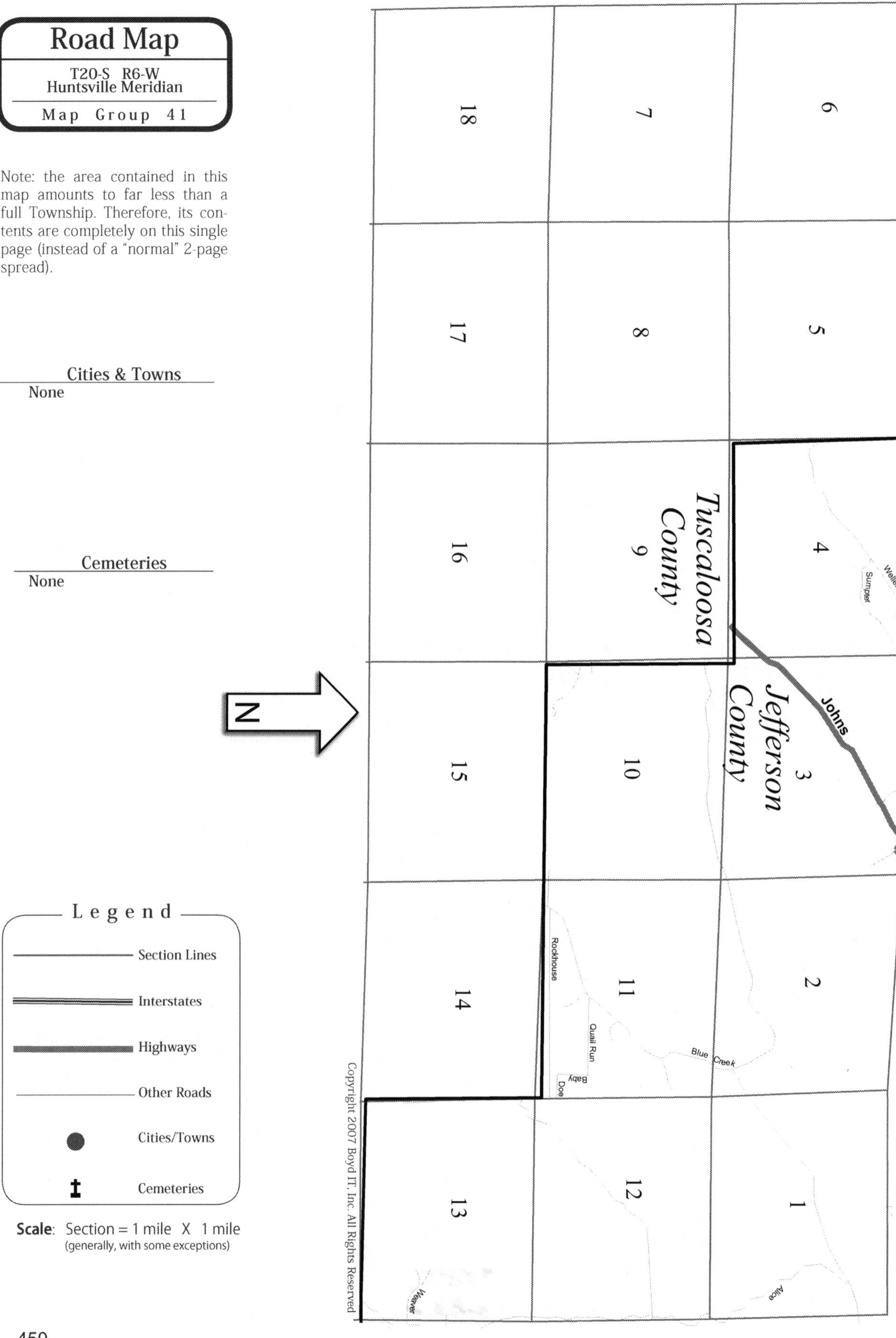

Scale: Section = 1 mile X 1 mile
(generally, with some exceptions)

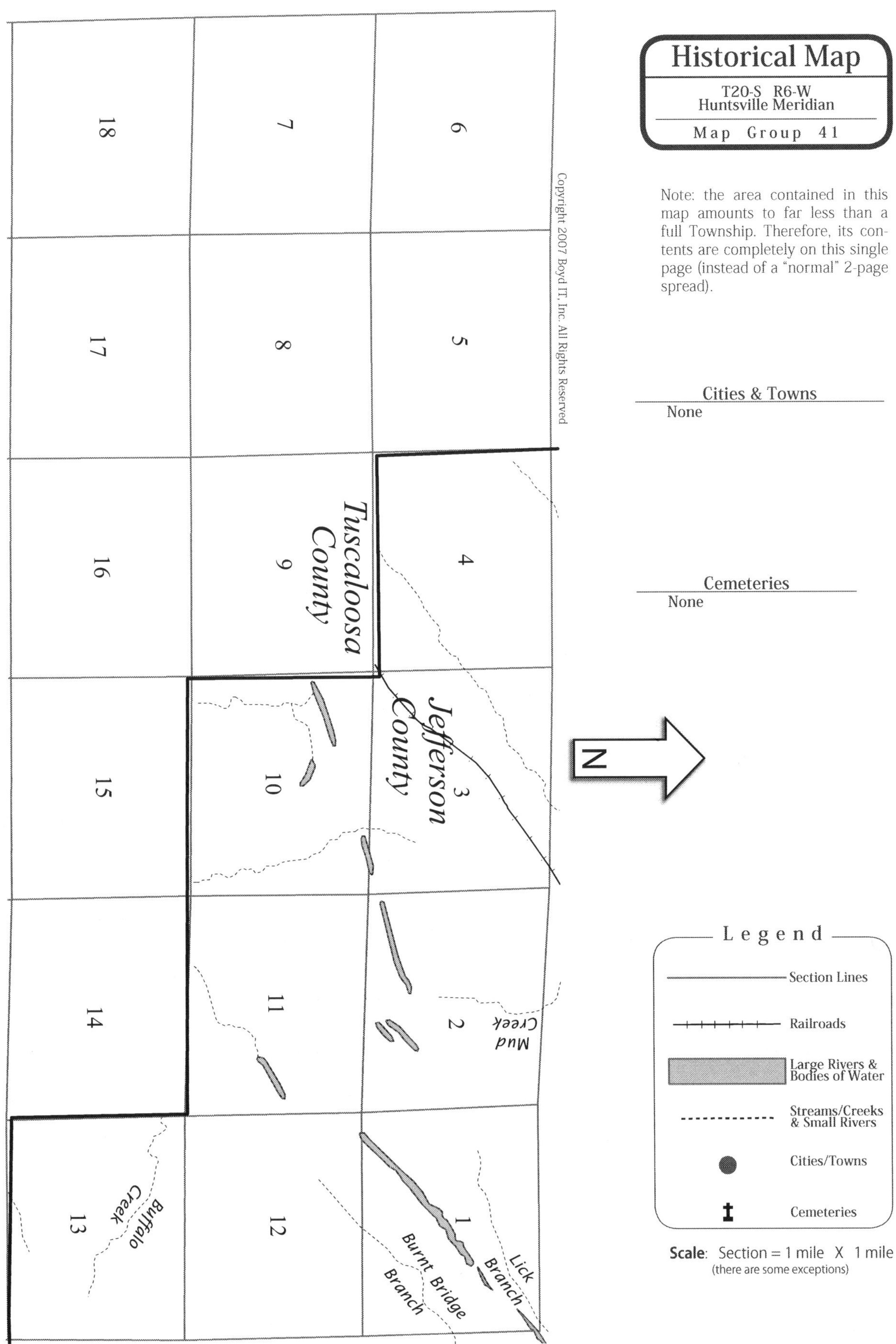
18
7
6
17
8
5
16
9
4
15
10
3
14
11
2
13
12
1
Tuscaloosa County
Jefferson County
Mud Creek
Buffalo Creek
Burnt Bridge Branch
Lick Branch
N
Copyright 2007 Boyd IT, Inc. All Rights Reserved
Historical Map
T20-S R6-W
Huntsville Meridian
Map Group 41
Note: the area contained in this map amounts to far less than a full Township. Therefore, its contents are completely on this single page (instead of a "normal" 2-page spread).
Cities & Towns
None
Cemeteries
None
Legend
Section Lines
Railroads
Large Rivers & Bodies of Water
Streams/Creeks & Small Rivers
Cities/Towns
Cemeteries
Scale: Section = 1 mile X 1 mile
(there are some exceptions)

Map Group 42: Index to Land Patents

Township 20-South Range 5-West (Huntsville)

After you locate an individual in this Index, take note of the Section and Section Part then proceed to the Land Patent map on the pages immediately following. You should have no difficulty locating the corresponding parcel of land.

The "For More Info" Column will lead you to more information about the underlying Patents. See the *Legend* at right, and the "How to Use this Book" chapter, for more information.

LEGEND

"For More Info . . . " column

A = Authority (Legislative Act, See Appendix "A")
B = Block or Lot (location in Section unknown)
C = Cancelled Patent
F = Fractional Section
G = Group (Multi-Patentee Patent, see Appendix "C")
V = Overlaps another Parcel
R = Re-Issued (Parcel patented more than once)

(A & G items require you to look in the Appendixes referred to above. All other Letter-designations followed by a number require you to locate line-items in this index that possess the ID number found after the letter).

ID	Individual in Patent	Sec.	Sec. Part	Date Issued	Other Counties	For More Info . . .
7100	ABERNATHY, James W	36	NW	1891-06-29		A4
7104	ARMSTRONG, John	7	NWNE	1859-12-10		A1
7151	ARMSTRONG, Nancy M	6	SESW	1885-07-27		A1
7152	" "	6	SWSE	1885-07-27		A1
7173	ARMSTRONG, Robert	22	SESW	1837-03-30		A1
7170	" "	14	NWSW	1839-09-20		A1
7171	" "	15	E½NE	1839-09-20		A1
7172	" "	15	SWNE	1839-09-20		A1
7178	ARMSTRONG, Samuel	18	W½SE	1837-03-20		A1
7183	ARMSTRONG, Sarah	6	W½SW	1885-03-30		A4
7207	BAKER, William	27	NWSW	1858-06-01		A1
7208	" "	27	SENW	1858-06-01		A1
7209	" "	28	SESE	1858-06-01	Tuscaloosa	A1
7053	BLACK, Ephraim W	35	E½SE	1837-03-30		A1
7054	" "	36	NWSW	1837-03-30		A1
7130	BRACKNER, Joseph	4	NWNW	1904-07-15		A4
7040	BUCK, David	33	W½NE	1823-05-01	Tuscaloosa	A1
7219	CARROLL, Zedekiah	20	SENW	1834-10-14	Tuscaloosa	A1
7117	CHILTON, John M	28	NENW	1889-10-07	Tuscaloosa	A1 C
7118	" "	28	NWNE	1889-10-07	Tuscaloosa	A1 C
7041	COOLEY, David L	17	N½NE	1858-06-01		A1
7042	" "	9	NESW	1858-06-01		A1
7043	" "	9	S½NW	1858-06-01		A1
7127	COWLEY, John W	22	NESE	1890-04-15		A1
7159	CRANE, Odam	5	NENW	1858-06-01		A1
7160	" "	5	SENW	1858-06-01		A1
7012	CURRY, Alexander	2	NWNW	1852-01-01		A1
7180	CURRY, Samuel	8	SESE	1837-03-30		A1
7029	DAVIS, Daniel	10	NWSE	1837-03-20		A1
7032	" "	15	W½SW	1837-03-20		A1
7031	" "	15	NWNW	1839-09-20		A1
7034	" "	22	NWNE	1839-09-20		A1
7028	" "	10	NENE	1861-08-01		A1
7030	" "	10	SWNE	1861-08-01		A1
7033	" "	2	SWSW	1861-08-01		A1
7035	" "	9	E½SE	1861-08-01		A1
7036	" "	9	NWSE	1861-08-01		A1
7047	DAVIS, Edward	22	SWNE	1839-09-20		A1
7013	DICKEY, Alexander H	9	SESW	1839-09-20		A1
7015	DICKEY, Alexander K	17	SENE	1839-09-20		A1
7128	DICKEY, John W	34	NWSW	1904-08-23		A1
7218	DICKEY, Wiseman	9	SWSW	1837-04-01		A1
7186	EASTIN, Thomas	24	NESW	1839-09-20		A1
7188	" "	24	NWSE	1839-09-20		A1
7184	" "	13	SWSW	1858-06-01		A1
7185	" "	23	E½NE	1858-06-01		A1

ID	Individual in Patent	Sec.	Sec. Part	Date Issued	Other Counties	For More Info . . .
7187	EASTIN, Thomas (Cont'd)	24	NW	1858-06-01		A1
7189	" "	24	NWSW	1858-06-01		A1
7138	ELLIS, Lewis L	17	W½SE	1839-09-20		A1
7135	" "	17	SENW	1858-06-01		A1
7136	" "	17	SESW	1858-06-01		A1
7137	" "	17	SWNE	1858-06-01		A1
7139	" "	20	NENW	1858-06-01	Tuscaloosa	A1
7206	ELLIS, William B	10	NWNW	1881-04-11		A1
7112	FINLEY, John	24	S½SW	1889-08-16		A4 R7057
7145	FINLEY, Marion A	24	W½NE	1889-08-13		A4
7019	FLEMING, Andrew J	8	S½NW	1885-03-16		A4
7048	GEESLIN, Edy	20	W½NE	1837-03-20	Tuscaloosa	A1
7027	GENTRY, Columbus W	36	N½NE	1904-07-02		A4
7022	GRAY, Bartley T	8	SWSE	1891-06-08		A4
7129	GREEN, Joselin B	33	NENW	1839-09-20	Tuscaloosa	A1
7026	HAGELGANS, Christ	26	SENW	1891-06-18		A1
7087	HAWKINS, James B	26	E½SE	1889-10-07		A1
7216	HICKS, Willis	10	SWNW	1839-09-20		A1
7217	" "	11	NWSW	1839-09-20		A1
7037	HOFFMAN, Daniel	9	NWSW	1834-10-21		A1
7046	HOLCOMB, Earley	4	NENE	1908-11-12		A4
7140	HOLCOMBE, Louis H	4	N½SE	1904-02-12		A1
7044	HOWARD, Dorsey	24	NESE	1858-06-01		A1
7045	" "	24	SESE	1858-06-01		A1
7014	HOWEL, Alexander H	10	SENE	1835-10-01		A1
7038	HUFFMAN, Daniel	22	SWSE	1858-06-01		A1
7039	HUFFMAN, Daniel J	27	NENW	1853-08-01		A1
7051	HUNT, Elijah M	27	SWSW	1849-05-01		A1
6999	KENNEDY, Absalom M	18	E½NE	1883-10-20		A1
7000	" "	18	E½SW	1883-10-20		A1
7001	" "	18	SWNE	1883-10-20		A1
7002	" "	18	SWSW	1883-10-20		A1
7007	" "	8	E½NE	1883-10-20		A1
7008	" "	8	E½SW	1883-10-20		A1
7009	" "	8	NWSE	1883-10-20		A1
7010	" "	8	SWNE	1883-10-20		A1
7011	" "	8	SWSW	1883-10-20		A1
7003	" "	22	SESE	1884-12-05		A1
7004	" "	26	NENW	1884-12-05		A1
7005	" "	34	NENW	1884-12-05		A1
7006	" "	34	SWNW	1884-12-05		A1
7017	KILLOUGH, Allen	1	E½NW	1824-04-30		A1
7190	KIMBREL, Thomas	27	SWNW	1850-09-02		A1
7052	KNOX, Elisha	20	E½NE	1837-03-20	Tuscaloosa	A1 G147
7066	LAWLESS, Hiram	18	E½SE	1837-03-20		A1
7095	LAWSON, James	6	NENW	1860-07-02		A1
7096	" "	6	NWNE	1860-07-02		A1
7091	LAWSON, James H	6	NWNW	1885-07-27		A1
7092	" "	6	SENW	1885-07-27		A1
7093	" "	6	SWNE	1885-07-27		A1
7023	LOCKHART, Benjamin	1	W½NW	1824-01-19		A1
7116	LOVELESS, John	12	W½NE	1827-07-02		A1
7161	LOVELESS, Ozias G	5	NESW	1858-06-01		A1
7163	" "	5	NWSE	1858-06-01		A1
7164	" "	5	SWNE	1858-06-01		A1
7162	" "	5	NWNE	1859-04-01		A1
7018	LOWE, Amos	8	NESE	1890-01-08		A4
7021	MAHAN, Anthony	34	NENE	1848-07-01		A1
7052	MALLORY, Thomas	20	E½NE	1837-03-20	Tuscaloosa	A1 G147
7083	MCBRIDE, James A	18	E½NW	1894-09-25		A4
7084	" "	18	NWNE	1894-09-25		A4
7085	" "	18	SWNW	1894-09-25		A4
7097	MCGILL, James	10	NENW	1881-09-01		A4
7098	" "	10	NWNE	1881-09-01		A4
7061	MCKENNEY, Harris	10	SWSE	1834-10-01		A1
7020	MCKINNEY, Anslem	10	E½SW	1824-05-21		A1
7062	MCKINNEY, Harris	28	NENE	1837-04-01	Tuscaloosa	A1
7024	MCLEOD, Charles	14	SWNE	1854-07-15		A1
7094	MCMATH, James H	6	SWNW	1858-06-01		A1
7110	MCMATH, John D	14	SWSW	1850-09-02		A1
7200	MITCHELL, Thomas	33	NENE	1837-04-01	Tuscaloosa	A1
7088	MOORE, James B	1	SWNE	1839-09-20		A1
7089	" "	2	E½SE	1839-09-20		A1

ID	Individual in Patent	Sec.	Sec. Part	Date Issued	Other Counties	For More Info . . .
7090	MOORE, James B (Cont'd)	2	NENE	1839-09-20		A1
7108	MOORE, John B	2	SESW	1839-09-20		A1
7105	" "	1	NWNE	1844-07-10		A1
7106	" "	1	SWSW	1852-01-01		A1
7107	" "	2	NESW	1854-07-15		A1
7119	MOSES, John	22	NESW	1838-08-28		A1
7120	" "	22	NWSE	1839-09-20		A1
7121	" "	27	NWNW	1839-09-20		A1
7149	MOSES, Meradith	17	E½SE	1833-08-12		A1
7204	NICHOLAS, William A	36	S½SE	1890-01-08		A4
7205	" "	36	SESW	1890-01-08		A4
7060	NORWOOD, Hannah	4	S½SE	1878-04-09		A4
7181	NORWOOD, Samuel F	4	S½NE	1891-09-15		A4
7057	OGLESBERRY, George	24	S½SW	1858-06-01		A1 R7112
7179	OGLESBERRY, Samuel B	34	NESW	1858-06-01		A1
7210	OLDHAM, William E	12	NESE	1890-04-15		A1
7211	" "	12	S½SE	1890-04-15		A1
7049	PHILLIPS, Elbert	26	W½SW	1904-07-02		A4
7056	PIERSON, George H	34	SE	1891-12-01		A1
7141	PRUDE, Margaret	11	NESW	1852-01-01		A1
7142	" "	11	SWSW	1852-01-01		A1
7143	PRUDE, Margarett	11	SESW	1839-09-20		A1
7144	" "	14	NWNE	1839-09-20		A1
7109	RODGERS, John C	26	NE	1891-09-01		A4
7212	RUPE, William	15	E½NW	1915-08-09		A1
7101	RUSSELL, Jeremiah	11	NW	1918-07-18		A1 G206
7102	RUSSELL, Jesse C	28	NESE	1853-11-15	Tuscaloosa	A1
7103	" "	28	SENE	1853-11-15	Tuscaloosa	A1
7067	SADDLER, Isaac W	11	NENE	1853-11-15		A1
7070	" "	12	NESW	1853-11-15		A1
7077	" "	2	SENE	1853-11-15		A1
7068	" "	11	SWNE	1854-07-15		A1
7069	" "	12	NENE	1854-07-15		A1
7071	" "	12	NWSE	1854-07-15		A1
7072	" "	12	SENE	1854-07-15		A1
7073	" "	12	SESW	1854-07-15		A1
7074	" "	13	NESE	1854-07-15		A1
7075	" "	13	NWNW	1854-07-15		A1
7076	" "	13	SENE	1854-07-15		A1
7078	" "	24	SENE	1854-07-15		A1
7080	SADLER, Isaac W	11	SENE	1839-09-20		A1
7079	" "	1	NWSW	1852-01-01		A1
7081	" "	13	SESE	1858-06-01		A1
7082	" "	24	NENE	1858-06-01		A1
7153	SALMONS, Nelson	18	NWNW	1858-06-01		A1
7154	" "	7	SWSW	1858-06-01		A1
7174	SELLARS, Robert J	6	NESE	1885-03-16		A4
7175	" "	6	SENE	1885-03-16		A4
7099	SELLENGER, James	20	W½NW	1826-06-01	Tuscaloosa	A1
7025	SELLERS, Charley A	34	NWNW	1904-09-28		A4
7148	SELLERS, Mary P	6	NENE	1889-10-07		A1
7176	SELLERS, Robert J	6	NESW	1883-07-03		A4
7177	" "	6	NWSE	1883-07-03		A4
7213	SELLERS, William	8	N½NW	1883-07-03		A4
7214	" "	8	NWNE	1889-11-21		A4
7123	SHEPHERD, John	9	SWSE	1834-11-04		A1
7113	SHEPHERD, John H	34	NWNE	1890-04-15		A1
7114	" "	34	S½NE	1890-04-15		A1
7115	" "	34	SENW	1890-04-15		A1
7131	SQUIRE, Joseph	10	SENW	1881-06-01		A1
7132	" "	2	NWSW	1881-09-01		A1
7133	" "	2	SWNW	1881-09-01		A1
7150	STROUP, Moses	27	SESW	1858-06-01		A1
7146	TANNEHILL, Marion	17	NESW	1854-07-15		A1
7147	" "	17	SWSW	1854-07-15		A1
7157	TANNEHILL, Ninian	27	SWNE	1852-01-01		A1
7155	" "	26	SWNW	1858-06-01		A1
7156	" "	27	SENE	1858-06-01		A1
7158	" "	33	W½SE	1858-06-01	Tuscaloosa	A1
7101	" "	11	NW	1918-07-18		A1 G206
7055	THOMAS, Etheldred W	1	E½NE	1827-04-10		A1
7122	THOMAS, John R	3	N½NE	1859-04-01		A1
7202	THOMAS, Tristram S	15	NWNE	1834-10-01		A1

ID	Individual in Patent	Sec.	Sec. Part	Date Issued	Other Counties	For More Info . . .
7203	THOMAS, Tristram S (Cont'd)	15	SWNW	1834-10-01		A1
7215	THOMAS, William	10	E½SE	1837-03-20		A1
7016	THOMPSON, Alice C	4	SW	1892-01-18		A4
7167	THOMPSON, Richard E	4	NENW	1891-06-30		A4
7168	" "	4	NWNE	1891-06-30		A4
7169	" "	4	S½NW	1891-06-30		A4
7086	TURNER, James A	18	NWSW	1901-12-04		A4
7063	TYLOR, Henry N	36	N½SE	1860-04-02		A1
7064	" "	36	NESW	1860-04-02		A1
7065	" "	36	S½NE	1860-04-02		A1
7126	VANDIFORD, John	26	NWNW	1905-03-30		A4
7134	VINES, Josephus	2	SENW	1914-01-30		A1
7166	VINES, Ransom M	2	NENW	1895-04-09		A1
7111	VINING, John D	6	SESE	1905-03-27		A1
7165	VINING, Peter L	8	NWSW	1905-03-27		A1
7050	WEED, Elihu	35	SWSE	1858-06-01		A1
7124	WEED, John T	26	E½SW	1891-06-18		A1
7125	" "	26	W½SE	1891-06-18		A1
7182	WEED, Samuel	36	SWSW	1890-01-08		A4
7201	WILLIAMS, Thomas	1	E½SW	1826-12-01		A1
7197	WILLIAMS, Thomas L	23	NWNW	1853-08-01		A1
7194	" "	14	E½SW	1853-11-15		A1
7196	" "	23	NENW	1853-11-15		A1
7195	" "	14	W½SE	1854-07-15		A1
7191	" "	10	W½SW	1858-06-01		A1
7192	" "	14	E½NE	1858-06-01		A1
7193	" "	14	E½SE	1858-06-01		A1
7198	" "	23	SWNW	1858-06-01		A1
7199	" "	23	W½NE	1858-06-01		A1
7058	WRIGHT, George W	27	NESW	1858-06-01		A1
7059	" "	27	NWSE	1858-06-01		A1

Patent Map

T20-S R5-W
Huntsville Meridian

Map Group 42

Township Statistics

Parcels Mapped	:	221
Number of Patents	:	166
Number of Individuals	:	118
Patentees Identified	:	117
Number of Surnames	:	82
Multi-Patentee Parcels	:	2
Oldest Patent Date	:	5/1/1823
Most Recent Patent	:	7/18/1918
Block/Lot Parcels	:	0
Parcels Re - Issued	:	1
Parcels that Overlap	:	0
Cities and Towns	:	0
Cemeteries	:	0

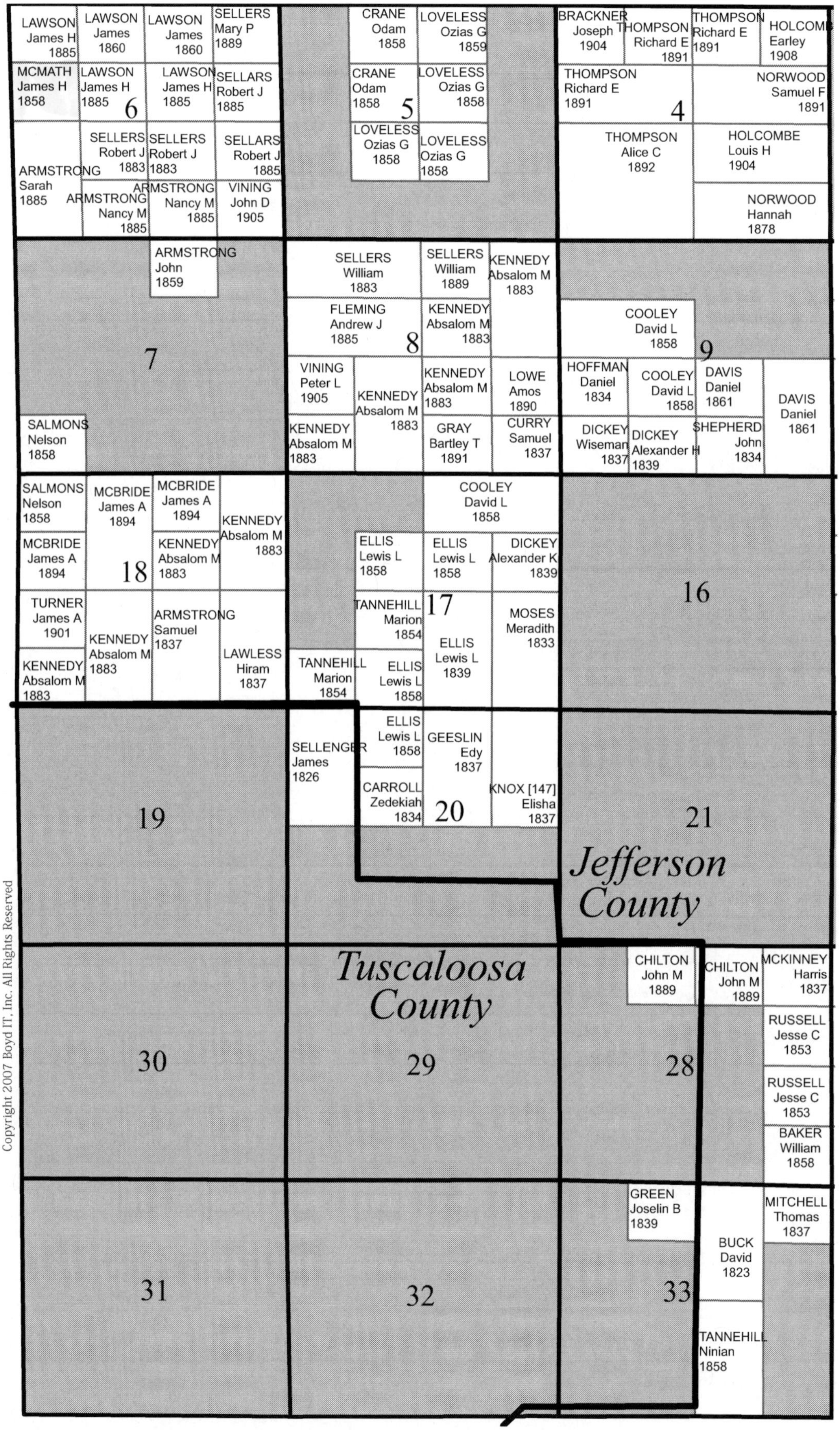

3

THOMAS John R 1859

2

CURRY Alexander 1852

VINES Ransom M 1895

SQUIRE Joseph 1881

VINES Josephus 1914

SQUIRE Joseph 1881

MOORE John B 1854

DAVIS Daniel 1861

MOORE John B 1839

MOORE James B 1839

SADDLER Isaac W 1853

MOORE James B 1839

1

LOCKHART Benjamin 1824

KILLOUGH Allen 1824

MOORE John B 1844

THOMAS Etheldred W 1827

MOORE James B 1839

SADLER Isaac W 1852

WILLIAMS Thomas 1826

MOORE John B 1852

10

ELLIS William B 1881

MCGILL James 1881

MCGILL James 1881

DAVIS Daniel 1861

HICKS Willis 1839

SQUIRE Joseph 1881

DAVIS Daniel 1861

HOWEL Alexander H 1835

WILLIAMS Thomas L 1858

MCKINNEY Anslem 1824

DAVIS Daniel 1837

MCKENNEY Harris 1834

THOMAS William 1837

11

RUSSELL [206] Jeremiah 1918

SADDLER Isaac W 1853

SADDLER Isaac W 1854

SADLER Isaac W 1839

HICKS Willis 1839

PRUDE Margaret 1852

PRUDE Margaret 1852

PRUDE Margarett 1839

12

LOVELESS John 1827

SADDLER Isaac W 1854

SADDLER Isaac W 1854

SADDLER Isaac W 1853

SADDLER Isaac W 1854

OLDHAM William E 1890

SADDLER Isaac W 1854

OLDHAM William E 1890

15

DAVIS Daniel 1839

RUPE William 1915

THOMAS Tristram S 1834

ARMSTRONG Robert 1839

THOMAS Tristram S 1834

ARMSTRONG Robert 1839

DAVIS Daniel 1837

14

PRUDE Margarett 1839

MCLEOD Charles 1854

WILLIAMS Thomas L 1858

ARMSTRONG Robert 1839

WILLIAMS Thomas L 1853

WILLIAMS Thomas L 1854

WILLIAMS Thomas L 1858

MCMATH John D 1850

13

SADDLER Isaac W 1854

SADDLER Isaac W 1854

SADDLER Isaac W 1854

EASTIN Thomas 1858

SADLER Isaac W 1858

22

DAVIS Daniel 1839

DAVIS Edward 1839

MOSES John 1838

MOSES John 1839

COWLEY John W 1890

ARMSTRONG Robert 1837

HUFFMAN Daniel 1858

KENNEDY Absalom M 1884

23

WILLIAMS Thomas L 1853

WILLIAMS Thomas L 1853

WILLIAMS Thomas L 1858

WILLIAMS Thomas L 1858

EASTIN Thomas 1858

24

EASTIN Thomas 1858

FINLEY Marion A 1889

SADLER Isaac W 1858

SADDLER Isaac W 1854

EASTIN Thomas 1858

EASTIN Thomas 1839

EASTIN Thomas 1839

HOWARD Dorsey 1858

FINLEY John 1889

OGLESBERRY George 1858

HOWARD Dorsey 1858

27

MOSES John 1839

HUFFMAN Daniel J 1853

KIMBREL Thomas 1850

BAKER William 1858

TANNEHILL Ninian 1852

TANNEHILL Ninian 1858

BAKER William 1858

WRIGHT George W 1858

WRIGHT George W 1858

HUNT Elijah M 1849

STROUP Moses 1858

26

VANDIFORD John 1905

KENNEDY Absalom M 1884

RODGERS John C 1891

TANNEHILL Ninian 1858

HAGELGANS Christ 1891

PHILLIPS Elbert 1904

WEED John T 1891

WEED John T 1891

HAWKINS James B 1889

25

34

SELLERS Charley A 1904

KENNEDY Absalom M 1884

SHEPHERD John H 1890

MAHAN Anthony 1848

KENNEDY Absalom M 1884

SHEPHERD John H 1890

SHEPHERD John H 1890

DICKEY John W 1904

OGLESBERRY Samuel B 1858

PIERSON George H 1891

35

BLACK Ephraim W 1837

WEED Elihu 1858

36

GENTRY Columbus W 1904

ABERNATHY James W 1891

TYLOR Henry N 1860

BLACK Ephraim W 1837

TYLOR Henry N 1860

TYLOR Henry N 1860

WEED Samuel 1890

NICHOLAS William A 1890

NICHOLAS William A 1890

Helpful Hints

1. This Map's INDEX can be found on the preceding pages.
2. Refer to Map "C" to see where this Township lies within Jefferson County, Alabama.
3. Numbers within square brackets [ ] denote a multi-patentee land parcel (multi-owner). Refer to Appendix "C" for a full list of members in this group.
4. Areas that look to be crowded with Patentees usually indicate multiple sales of the same parcel (Re-issues) or Overlapping parcels. See this Township's Index for an explanation of these and other circumstances that might explain "odd" groupings of Patentees on this map.

Legend

Patent Boundary

Section Boundary

No Patents Found (or Outside County)

1., 2., 3., ... Lot Numbers (when beside a name)

[ ] Group Number (see Appendix "C")

Scale: Section = 1 mile X 1 mile (generally, with some exceptions)

Road Map

T20-S R5-W
Huntsville Meridian

Map Group 42

Cities & Towns

None

Cemeteries

None

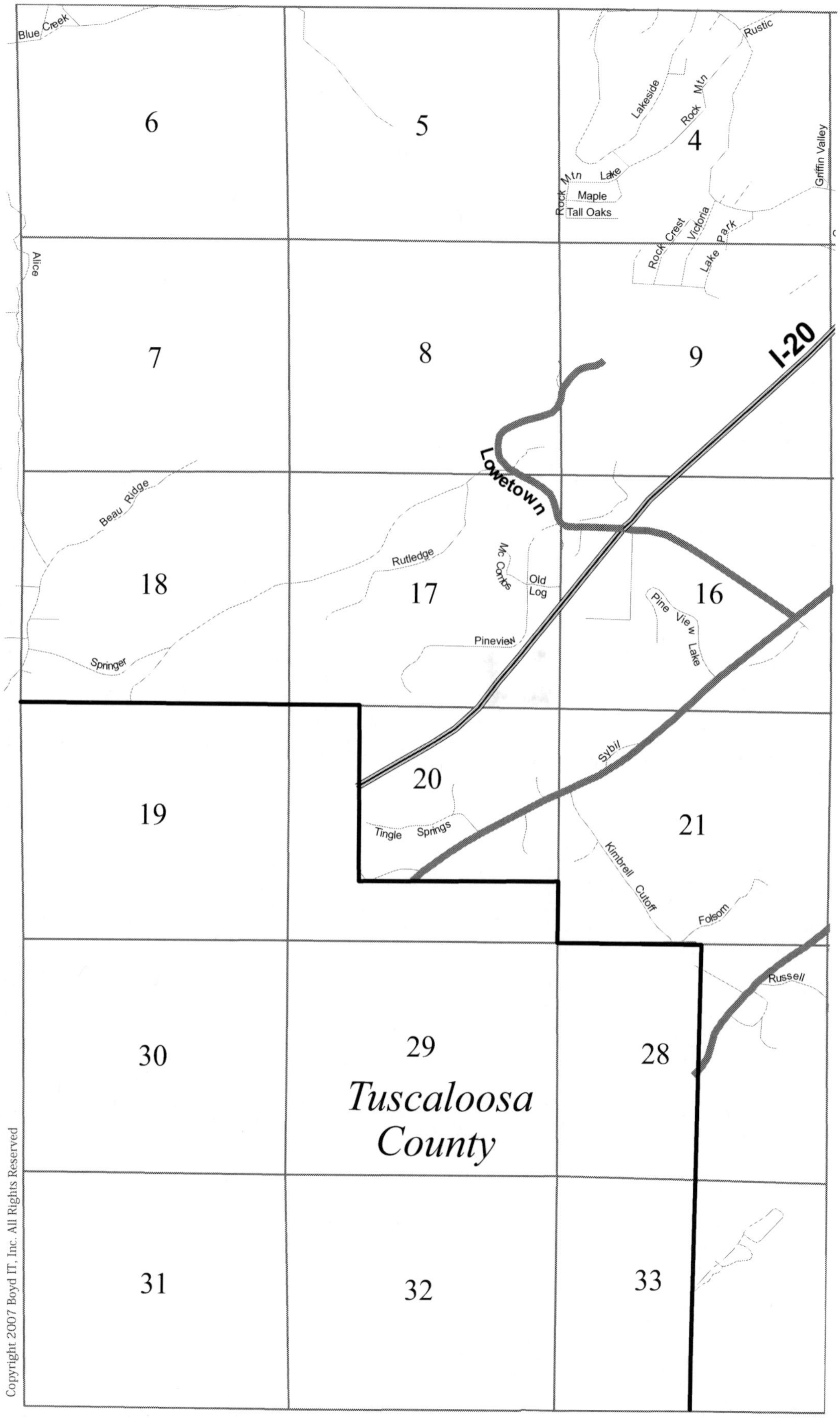

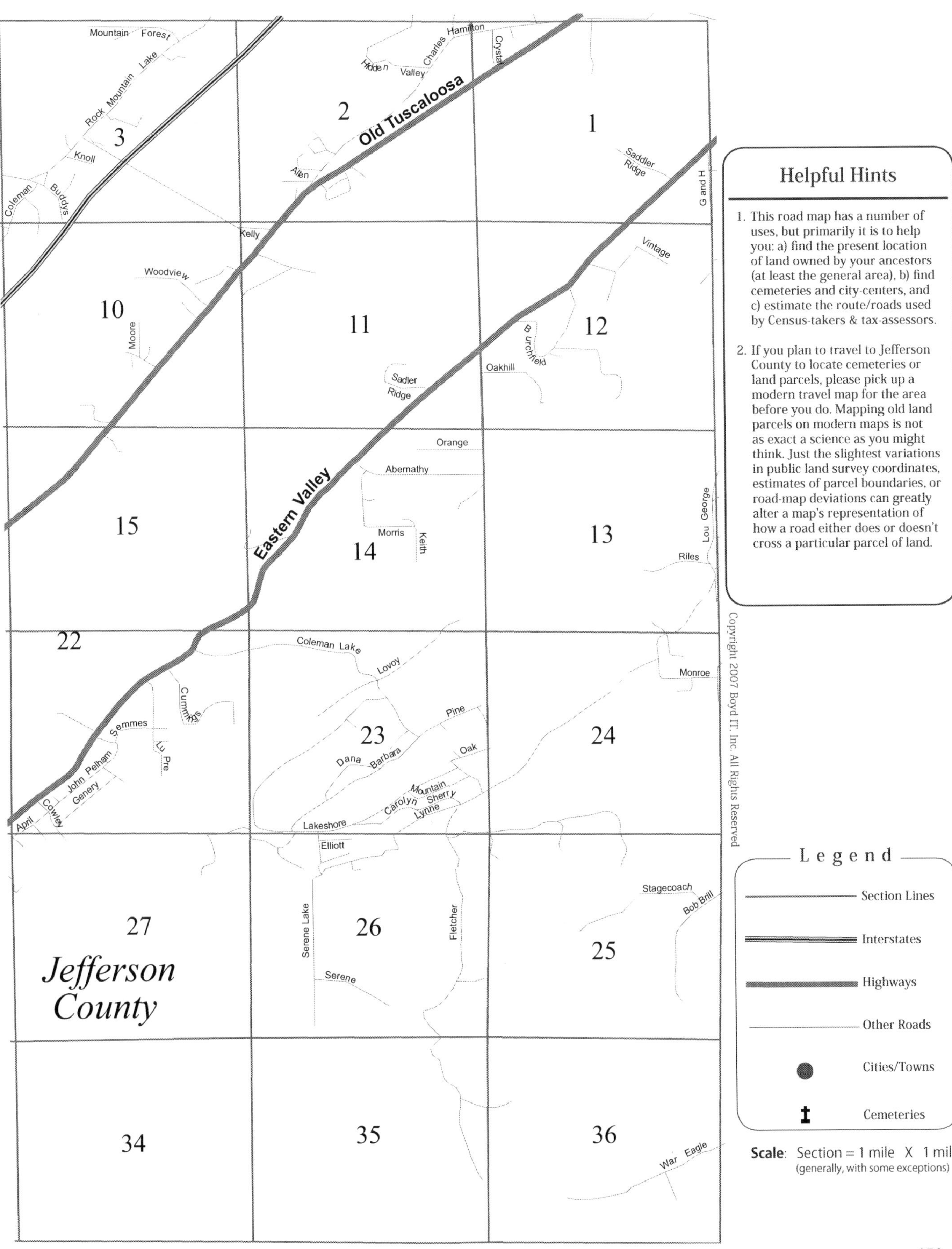

Helpful Hints

1. This road map has a number of uses, but primarily it is to help you: a) find the present location of land owned by your ancestors (at least the general area), b) find cemeteries and city-centers, and c) estimate the route/roads used by Census-takers & tax-assessors.

2. If you plan to travel to Jefferson County to locate cemeteries or land parcels, please pick up a modern travel map for the area before you do. Mapping old land parcels on modern maps is not as exact a science as you might think. Just the slightest variations in public land survey coordinates, estimates of parcel boundaries, or road-map deviations can greatly alter a map's representation of how a road either does or doesn't cross a particular parcel of land.

Legend

- Section Lines
- Interstates
- Highways
- Other Roads
- Cities/Towns
- Cemeteries

Scale: Section = 1 mile X 1 mile (generally, with some exceptions)

Historical Map

T20-S R5-W
Huntsville Meridian

Map Group 42

Cities & Towns
None

Cemeteries
None

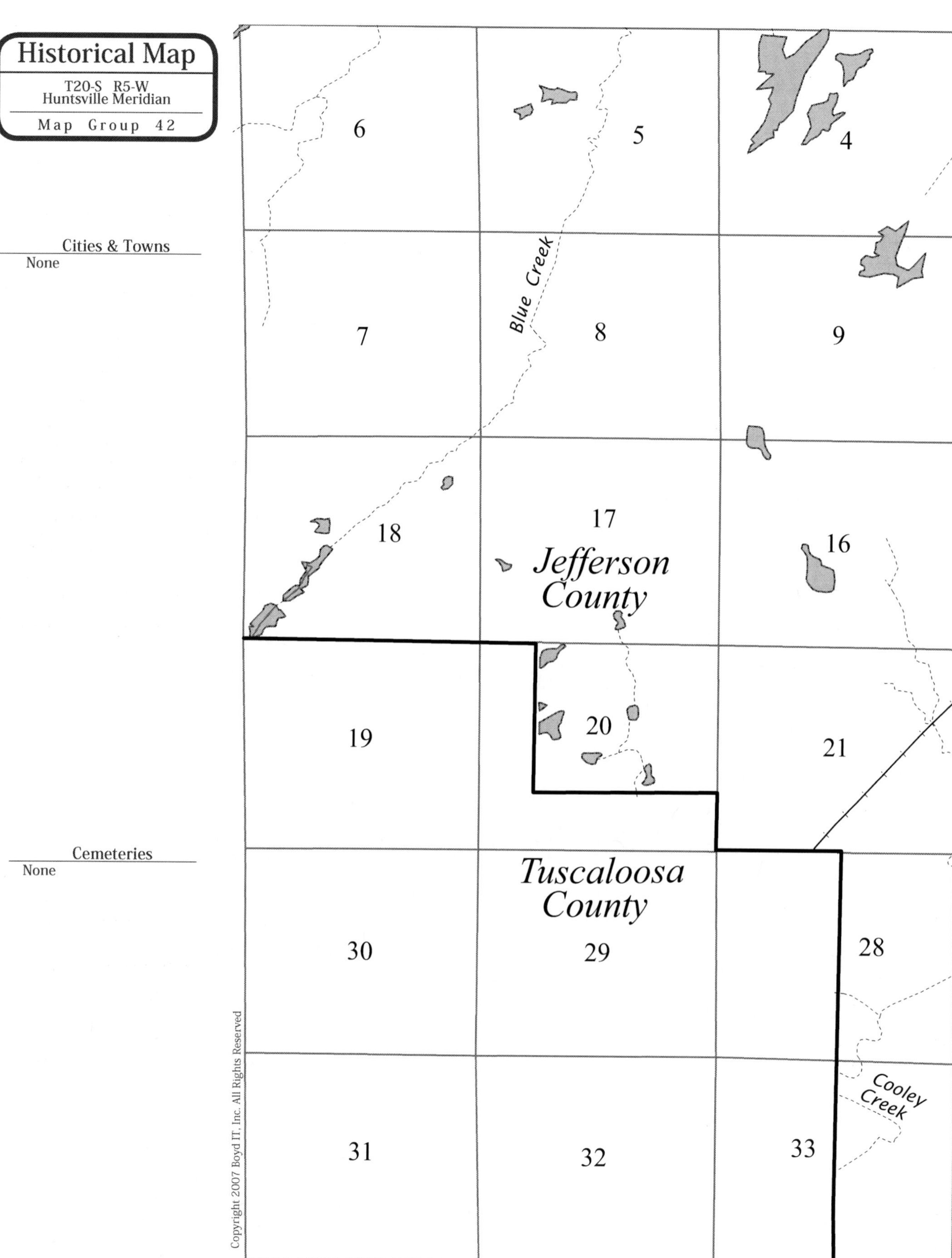

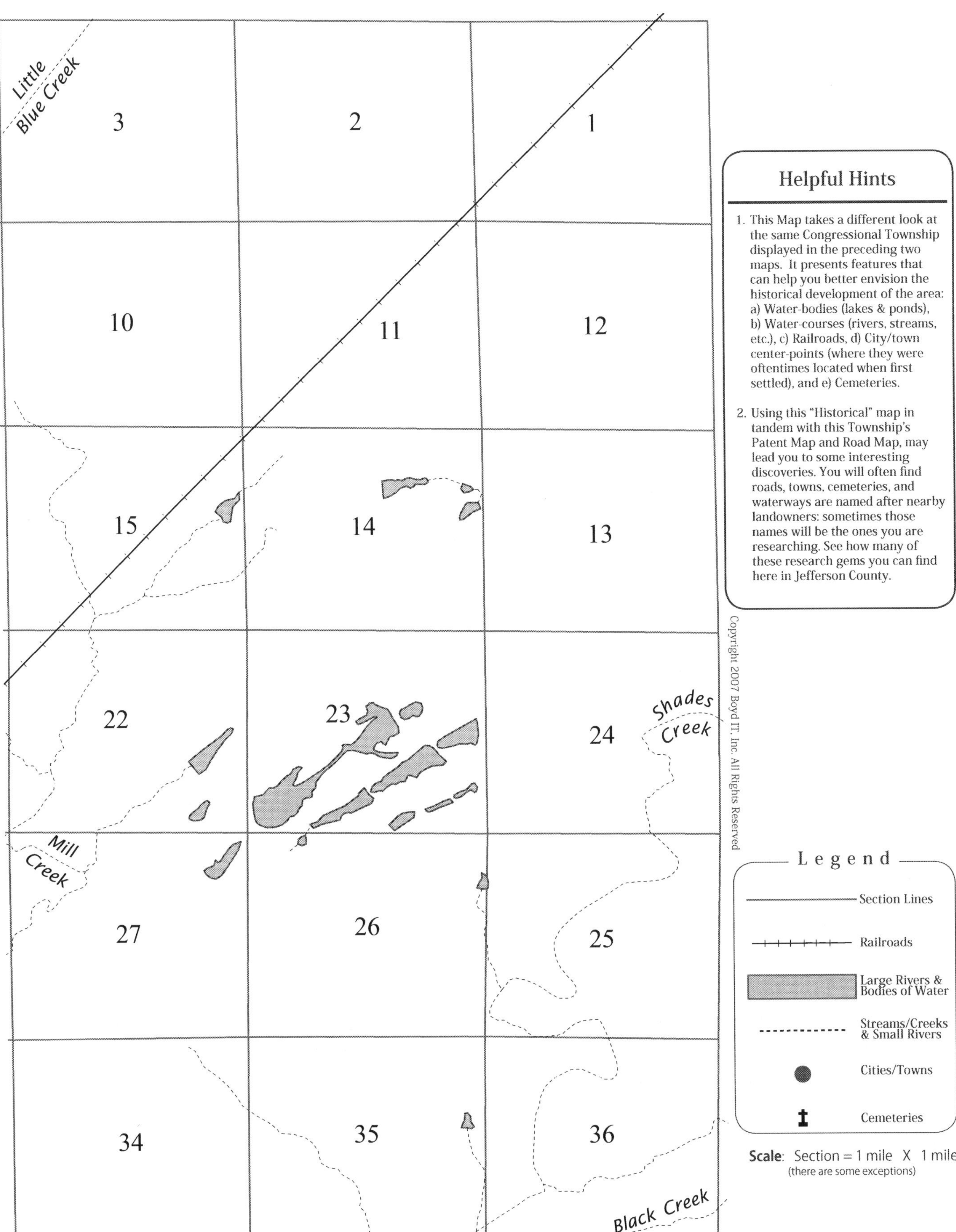
Little Blue Creek
3
2
1
10
11
12
15
14
13
22
23
24
Shades Creek
Mill Creek
27
26
25
34
35
36
Black Creek
Helpful Hints
1. This Map takes a different look at the same Congressional Township displayed in the preceding two maps. It presents features that can help you better envision the historical development of the area: a) Water-bodies (lakes & ponds), b) Water-courses (rivers, streams, etc.), c) Railroads, d) City/town center-points (where they were oftentimes located when first settled), and e) Cemeteries.
2. Using this "Historical" map in tandem with this Township's Patent Map and Road Map, may lead you to some interesting discoveries. You will often find roads, towns, cemeteries, and waterways are named after nearby landowners: sometimes those names will be the ones you are researching. See how many of these research gems you can find here in Jefferson County.
Copyright 2007 Boyd IT, Inc. All Rights Reserved
Legend
Section Lines
Railroads
Large Rivers & Bodies of Water
Streams/Creeks & Small Rivers
Cities/Towns
Cemeteries
Scale: Section = 1 mile X 1 mile
(there are some exceptions)

Map Group 43: Index to Land Patents

Township 20-South Range 4-West (Huntsville)

After you locate an individual in this Index, take note of the Section and Section Part then proceed to the Land Patent map on the pages immediately following. You should have no difficulty locating the corresponding parcel of land.

The "For More Info" Column will lead you to more information about the underlying Patents. See the *Legend* at right, and the "How to Use this Book" chapter, for more information.

LEGEND

"For More Info . . . " column

- **A** = Authority (Legislative Act, See Appendix "A")
- **B** = Block or Lot (location in Section unknown)
- **C** = Cancelled Patent
- **F** = Fractional Section
- **G** = Group (Multi-Patentee Patent, see Appendix "C")
- **V** = Overlaps another Parcel
- **R** = Re-Issued (Parcel patented more than once)

(A & G items require you to look in the Appendixes referred to above. All other Letter-designations followed by a number require you to locate line-items in this index that possess the ID number found after the letter).

ID	Individual in Patent	Sec.	Sec. Part	Date Issued	Other Counties	For More Info . . .
7409	ABERNATHY, William W	7	SESW	1858-06-01		A1
7408	" "	18	SENE	1888-05-25		A4
7256	ARMSTRONG, Dennis	5	SESE	1858-06-01		A1
7257	" "	9	NWNW	1858-06-01		A1
7279	ARMSTRONG, Henry	1	E½NW	1858-06-01		A1
7281	ARMSTRONG, Holcomb C	28	NWSW	1919-10-07	Shelby	A4
7283	ARMSTRONG, Hugh	2	NESE	1854-07-15		A1
7269	ARNOLD, Ezekiel	30	SWSE	1858-06-01		A1
7270	" "	31	NW	1858-06-01		A1
7271	" "	31	NWNE	1858-06-01		A1
7265	BASS, Elijah	3	E½SW	1918-07-18		A1
7264	" "	3	E½NW	1921-09-02		A1
7323	BELL, John	3	W½NW	1839-09-20		A1
7366	BLANKINGSHIP, Richard L	22	N½SW	1894-07-12		A4
7345	BLANKINSHIP, John W	14	W½SW	1899-04-28	Shelby	A4
7391	BROWNLEE, William	19	NWSW	1839-09-20		A1
7255	BURNS, Demsy B	30	W½NW	1885-03-30		A4
7315	BUTLER, Jasper L	6	S½NE	1878-04-09		A4
7284	CALDWELL, Hughey	10	E½SW	1858-06-01		A1
7285	" "	10	W½NW	1858-06-01		A1
7333	CHILTON, John M	28	NENW	1893-12-22	Shelby	A1
7334	" "	28	NWNE	1893-12-22	Shelby	A1
7282	COLWELL, Huey	15	NWNW	1853-08-01		A1
7298	COOLEY, James E	10	E½NW	1891-06-19		A4
7353	COOLEY, Martha E	12	NENE	1890-01-08	Shelby	A4
7223	CROSS, Andrew B	30	NWSE	1921-11-22		A1
7393	DANIEL, William	5	NESE	1834-10-14		A1
7392	" "	4	W½SE	1837-04-01		A1
7261	DAVIDSON, Edwin	32	N½SW	1858-06-01	Shelby	A1
7262	" "	32	SENW	1858-06-01	Shelby	A1
7394	DEMOTT, William	2	SESE	1904-12-20		A4
7395	" "	2	SWSW	1916-04-19		A4
7352	DICKEY, Martha	9	NENW	1839-09-20		A1
7245	DRAPER, Daniel D	4	NWNW	1839-09-20		A1
7246	" "	5	E½NE	1839-09-20		A1
7244	" "	4	NENW	1858-06-01		A1
7377	DRAPER, Solomon	4	NWSW	1839-09-20		A1
7378	" "	5	NWSE	1839-09-20		A1
7324	DRENNON, John	8	N½SW	1891-06-30		A4
7325	FARRINGTON, John	4	SWNW	1834-10-14		A1
7412	FARRINGTON, Willis	8	NENE	1854-07-15		A1
7230	FERRINGTON, Barney	32	SWNE	1849-08-01	Shelby	A1
7413	FERRINGTON, Willis	10	NWSW	1839-09-20		A1
7299	FIELDS, James G	31	SESW	1858-06-01		A1
7300	" "	31	SWSE	1858-06-01		A1
7241	FULTON, Charley E	20	NENE	1903-05-19		A4

ID	Individual in Patent	Sec.	Sec. Part	Date Issued	Other Counties	For More Info . . .
7231	GANONS, Benjamin F	6	E½SE	1884-12-05		A4
7258	GEORGE, Dennis	18	SWNE	1858-06-01		A1
7259	" "	19	SENW	1892-11-23		A1
7274	GEORGE, George K	17	S½NW	1858-06-01		A1
7329	GEORGE, John K	17	NESW	1854-07-15		A1
7350	GEORGE, Lewis	18	SENW	1834-10-01		A1
7349	" "	17	SWNE	1839-09-20		A1
7351	" "	19	NENW	1850-04-01		A1
7383	GEORGE, Thomas W	20	NWNE	1858-06-01		A1
7396	GEORGE, William	20	N½NW	1885-03-30		A4
7416	GEORGE, Zachariah L	29	NESW	1858-06-01		A1
7417	" "	29	NWSE	1858-06-01		A1
7418	" "	29	SWNE	1858-06-01		A1
7414	" "	18	N½NW	1885-03-30		A4
7415	" "	18	SWNW	1890-07-03		A4
7397	GINERY, William	12	NESE	1890-03-19	Shelby	A4
7398	" "	12	SENE	1890-03-19	Shelby	A4
7227	GREEN, Barbara E	12	SESE	1890-03-19	Shelby	A4 G103
7228	GREEN, Barbra E	12	SESW	1885-12-10	Shelby	A4 G104
7229	" "	12	SWSE	1885-12-10	Shelby	A4 G104
7316	GREEN, Jesse Q	6	SESW	1889-03-26		A1
7370	GREENE, Samuel E	20	S½NE	1893-05-05		A4
7371	" "	20	W½SE	1893-05-05		A4
7400	HALL, William J	30	E½NW	1891-01-15		A4 G114
7263	HARKNESS, Eli L	30	W½NE	1885-03-30		A4
7302	HARMON, James L	32	S½SW	1893-05-05	Shelby	A4
7303	" "	32	SWSE	1893-05-05	Shelby	A4
7317	HARMON, Joel	3	NWSE	1839-09-20		A1
7326	HARMON, John	32	E½SE	1888-02-04	Shelby	A4
7327	" "	32	SENE	1888-02-04	Shelby	A4
7387	HARMON, William A	32	NENW	1893-05-05	Shelby	A4
7388	" "	32	NWNE	1893-05-05	Shelby	A4
7389	" "	32	W½NW	1893-05-05	Shelby	A4
7407	HILL, William T	28	SWNE	1914-11-16	Shelby	A4
7242	HINTON, Coleman	17	NENW	1858-06-01		A1
7243	" "	8	S½SW	1858-06-01		A1
7359	HOLLINGSWORTH, Needham W	12	NWSE	1885-06-12	Shelby	A4
7360	" "	12	S½NW	1885-06-12	Shelby	A4
7361	" "	12	SWNE	1885-06-12	Shelby	A4
7379	HORNE, Thomas	2	E½SW	1824-05-27		A1
7221	HORTON, Amos J	12	N½SW	1885-08-05	Shelby	A4 G132
7222	" "	12	SWSW	1885-08-05	Shelby	A4 G132
7328	HORTON, John	18	E½SE	1858-06-01		A1
7221	HORTON, Joseph A	12	N½SW	1885-08-05	Shelby	A4 G132
7222	" "	12	SWSW	1885-08-05	Shelby	A4 G132
7236	JOHNSON, Beulah	20	SESW	1895-02-23		A4 G139
7405	JUDD, William S	14	NE	1890-03-19	Shelby	A4
7266	LAWLEY, Elijah	9	NWSW	1839-09-20		A1
7267	" "	9	SENW	1839-09-20		A1
7278	LAWLEY, Harrison	9	SWNW	1839-09-20		A1
7401	LAWLEY, William	9	E½SW	1839-09-20		A1
7402	" "	9	W½SE	1839-09-20		A1
7226	LEATHERWOOD, Aquilla	1	NESE	1860-04-02		A1
7363	LEATHERWOOD, Paul C	22	SWSW	1858-06-01		A1
7364	" "	27	W½NW	1858-06-01	Shelby	A1
7365	" "	28	E½NE	1858-06-01	Shelby	A1
7319	LEMMONS, John A	20	W½SW	1891-11-23		A4
7330	LOVELESS, John	5	SESW	1837-03-30		A1
7332	" "	8	NWNW	1837-04-01		A1
7331	" "	5	W½SW	1839-09-20		A1
7403	LOVELESS, William	8	E½NW	1891-02-16		A4
7404	" "	8	NWNE	1891-06-08		A4
7307	MASSEY, James P	8	NWSE	1858-06-01		A1
7308	" "	8	S½NE	1858-06-01		A1
7286	MCADORY, Isaac W	6	NESW	1882-10-30		A1
7380	MCADORY, Thomas	6	NWSW	1839-09-20		A1
7346	MCCLENDON, Jones	20	E½SE	1888-02-04		A4
7236	MCDANIEL, Beulah	20	SESW	1895-02-23		A4 G139
7236	MCDANIEL, Stokely A	20	SESW	1895-02-23		A4 G139
7276	MCKINNEY, Green	8	SWNW	1890-07-03		A4
7301	MCMATH, James H	32	NWSE	1848-04-15	Shelby	A1
7357	MCMEANS, Mary S	30	E½NE	1884-12-05		A4
7237	MCPHAUL, Calvin	2	SWSE	1875-10-01		A4

ID	Individual in Patent	Sec.	Sec. Part	Date Issued	Other Counties	For More Info . . .
7306	MERRITT, James	4	SENW	1834-11-04		A1
7385	MILES, Tilman L	3	SWSW	1839-09-20		A1
7386	" "	4	NESW	1839-09-20		A1
7295	MOORE, James B	4	NENE	1858-06-01		A1
7296	" "	4	W½NE	1858-06-01		A1
7297	" "	9	E½NE	1858-06-01		A1
7320	MOORE, John B	3	NWSW	1839-09-20		A1
7321	" "	4	E½SE	1839-09-20		A1
7322	" "	4	SWSW	1840-11-10		A1
7347	MOORE, Joseph T	2	NWSW	1858-06-01		A1
7348	" "	3	NESE	1858-06-01		A1
7318	NICHOLAS, Joel	28	SWSW	1858-06-01	Shelby	A1
7338	NICHOLAS, John	30	SESE	1858-06-01		A1
7354	NICHOLAS, Mary	28	NWNW	1858-06-01	Shelby	A1
7355	" "	29	NENE	1858-06-01		A1
7356	" "	29	SENE	1858-06-01		A1
7339	NICHOLS, John	29	NWSW	1858-06-01		A1
7340	" "	30	NESE	1858-06-01		A1
7312	PETERSON, James	2	NWNE	1834-10-16		A1
7310	" "	2	E½NE	1839-09-20		A1
7311	" "	2	E½NW	1839-09-20		A1
7313	" "	2	NWSE	1839-09-20		A1
7314	" "	2	SWNE	1839-09-20		A1
7309	" "	1	NWNW	1858-06-01		A1
7238	PHILIPS, Caroline M	6	NENE	1854-07-15		A1
7239	" "	5	NWNW	1858-06-01		A1 G196
7239	PHILIPS, Reuben	5	NWNW	1858-06-01		A1 G196
7369	PIERCE, Riley	9	E½SE	1826-06-10		A1
7227	PITTS, Barbara E	12	SESE	1890-03-19	Shelby	A4 G103
7228	PITTS, Barbra E	12	SESW	1885-12-10	Shelby	A4 G104
7229	" "	12	SWSE	1885-12-10	Shelby	A4 G104
7335	PITTS, John M	28	E½SW	1858-06-01	Shelby	A1
7336	" "	28	NWSE	1858-06-01	Shelby	A1
7358	RAGSDALE, Milton C	6	W½SE	1884-12-05		A4
7381	RODGERS, Thomas	20	SWNW	1897-07-27		A4
7220	ROUNSLEY, Alfred	22	NE	1890-03-08		A1
7272	ROUNSLEY, Francis J	22	E½SE	1890-03-08		A1
7273	" "	22	NWSE	1890-03-08		A1
7253	RUSSELL, David	4	SENE	1839-09-20		A1
7254	" "	4	SESW	1839-09-20		A1
7260	SADBERRY, Doctor A	14	NW	1890-08-29	Shelby	A4
7288	SADDLER, Isaac W	6	NWNE	1853-11-15		A1
7287	" "	19	SWNW	1854-07-15		A1
7289	" "	6	SWSW	1854-07-15		A1
7290	" "	7	NWNW	1854-07-15		A1
7268	SADLER, Elisha	18	NESW	1891-12-01		A1
7277	SADLER, Harriet	18	NWNE	1884-03-20		A4
7291	SADLER, Isaac W	19	NESW	1858-06-01		A1
7292	" "	19	NWNW	1858-06-01		A1
7384	SIMPSON, Thompson R	9	W½NE	1837-04-01		A1
7224	SMITHSON, Anson	10	SWSW	1839-09-20		A1
7225	" "	9	SWSW	1839-09-20		A1
7232	SMITHSON, Benjamin W	17	E½NE	1858-06-01		A1
7233	" "	17	NESE	1858-06-01		A1
7234	" "	17	NWNE	1858-06-01		A1
7235	" "	8	SWSE	1858-06-01		A1
7293	SMITHSON, James A	10	SE	1892-01-18		A4 C R7294
7294	" "	10	SE	1915-04-13		A4 R7293
7337	SMITHSON, John N	10	NE	1891-06-18		A1
7382	SPARKS, Thomas	1	NWSW	1839-09-20		A1
7249	STEEDMAN, Daniel W	27	SESE	1858-06-01	Shelby	A1
7250	" "	27	W½SE	1858-06-01	Shelby	A1
7247	" "	27	NESE	1860-04-02	Shelby	A1
7248	" "	27	SENE	1860-04-02	Shelby	A1
7399	STURDIVANT, William H	14	E½SW	1899-08-16	Shelby	A4
7362	TANNAHILL, Ninian	8	E½SE	1831-01-04		A1
7341	THOMPSON, John	1	SWSE	1858-06-01		A1
7342	" "	12	NENW	1890-01-08	Shelby	A4
7343	" "	12	NWNE	1890-01-08	Shelby	A4
7344	" "	12	NWNW	1894-10-22	Shelby	A4
7406	THORINGTON, William S	28	S½NW	1889-10-07	Shelby	A1
7240	TURNER, Charles	18	S½SW	1889-10-07		A1
7251	TYLER, Daniel Z	22	SESW	1893-05-26		A4

ID	Individual in Patent	Sec.	Sec. Part	Date Issued	Other Counties	For More Info . . .
7252	TYLER, Daniel Z (Cont'd)	22	SWSE	1893-05-26		A4
7280	TYLER, Henry N	30	SW	1894-10-22		A4
7304	TYLER, James M	20	NESW	1885-05-20		A4
7305	" "	20	SENW	1885-05-20		A4
7367	TYLER, Richard L	28	E½SE	1895-10-09	Shelby	A4
7368	" "	28	SWSE	1895-10-09	Shelby	A4
7374	TYLER, Samuel S	21	W½SE	1858-06-01		A1
7372	" "	21	E½SW	1861-08-01		A1
7373	" "	21	SWSW	1861-08-01		A1
7390	TYLER, William A	22	NW	1894-12-07		A4
7400	WALDROP, Margaret A	30	E½NW	1891-01-15		A4 G114
7375	WEED, Samuel	18	W½SE	1858-06-01		A1
7376	" "	19	NE	1858-06-01		A1
7410	WILSON, William	17	NWNW	1859-12-10		A1
7411	" "	18	NENE	1859-12-10		A1
7275	WYATT, George	14	SE	1889-12-28	Shelby	A1

Patent Map

T20-S R4-W
Huntsville Meridian

Map Group 43

Township Statistics

Parcels Mapped	:	199
Number of Patents	:	159
Number of Individuals	:	126
Patentees Identified	:	120
Number of Surnames	:	82
Multi-Patentee Parcels	:	8
Oldest Patent Date	:	5/27/1824
Most Recent Patent	:	11/22/1921
Block/Lot Parcels	:	0
Parcels Re - Issued	:	1
Parcels that Overlap	:	0
Cities and Towns	:	0
Cemeteries	:	4

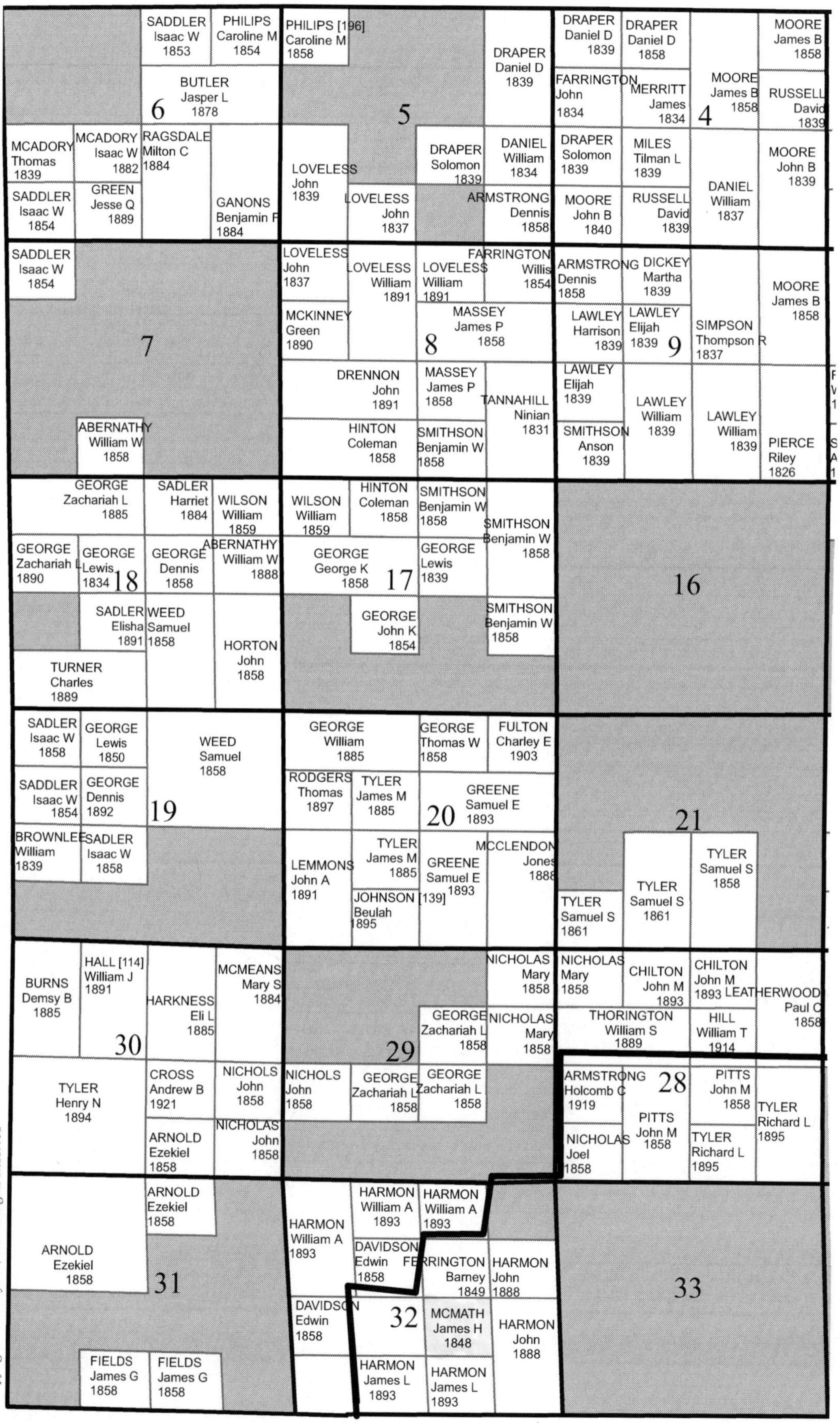

SADDLER Isaac W 1853
PHILIPS Caroline M 1854
BUTLER Jasper L 1878
6
MCADORY Thomas 1839
MCADORY Isaac W 1882
RAGSDALE Milton C 1884
SADDLER Isaac W 1854
GREEN Jesse Q 1889
GANONS Benjamin F 1884
PHILIPS [196] Caroline M 1858
5
DRAPER Daniel D 1839
LOVELESS John 1839
LOVELESS John 1837
DRAPER Solomon 1839
DANIEL William 1834
ARMSTRONG Dennis 1858
DRAPER Daniel D 1839
DRAPER Daniel D 1858
FARRINGTON John 1834
MERRITT James 1834
MOORE James B 1858
4
MOORE James B 1858
RUSSELL David 1839
DRAPER Solomon 1839
MILES Tilman L 1839
MOORE John B 1839
MOORE John B 1840
RUSSELL David 1839
DANIEL William 1837
SADDLER Isaac W 1854
7
ABERNATHY William W 1858
LOVELESS John 1837
LOVELESS William 1891
LOVELESS William 1891
FARRINGTON Willis 1854
MCKINNEY Green 1890
MASSEY James P 1858
8
DRENNON John 1891
MASSEY James P 1858
TANNAHILL Ninian 1831
HINTON Coleman 1858
SMITHSON Benjamin W 1858
ARMSTRONG Dennis 1858
DICKEY Martha 1839
MOORE James B 1858
LAWLEY Harrison 1839
LAWLEY Elijah 1839
9
SIMPSON Thompson R 1837
LAWLEY Elijah 1839
LAWLEY William 1839
LAWLEY William 1839
SMITHSON Anson 1839
PIERCE Riley 1826
GEORGE Zachariah L 1885
SADLER Harriet 1884
WILSON William 1859
GEORGE Zachariah L 1890
GEORGE Lewis 1834
18
GEORGE Dennis 1858
ABERNATHY William W 1888
SADLER Elisha 1891
WEED Samuel 1858
HORTON John 1858
TURNER Charles 1889
WILSON William 1859
HINTON Coleman 1858
SMITHSON Benjamin W 1858
SMITHSON Benjamin W 1858
GEORGE George K 1858
17
GEORGE Lewis 1839
GEORGE John K 1854
SMITHSON Benjamin W 1858
16
SADLER Isaac W 1858
GEORGE Lewis 1850
WEED Samuel 1858
SADDLER Isaac W 1854
GEORGE Dennis 1892
19
BROWNLEE William 1839
SADLER Isaac W 1858
GEORGE William 1885
GEORGE Thomas W 1858
FULTON Charley E 1903
RODGERS Thomas 1897
TYLER James M 1885
GREENE Samuel E 1893
20
LEMMONS John A 1891
TYLER James M 1885
GREENE Samuel E 1893
MCCLENDON Jones 1888
JOHNSON [139] Beulah 1895
21
TYLER Samuel S 1861
TYLER Samuel S 1861
TYLER Samuel S 1858
BURNS Demsy B 1885
HALL [114] William J 1891
HARKNESS Eli L 1885
MCMEANS Mary S 1884
30
TYLER Henry N 1894
CROSS Andrew B 1921
NICHOLS John 1858
ARNOLD Ezekiel 1858
NICHOLAS John 1858
NICHOLAS Mary 1858
GEORGE Zachariah L 1858
NICHOLAS Mary 1858
29
NICHOLS John 1858
GEORGE Zachariah L 1858
GEORGE Zachariah L 1858
NICHOLAS Mary 1858
CHILTON John M 1893
CHILTON John M 1893
LEATHERWOOD Paul C 1858
THORINGTON William S 1889
HILL William T 1914
ARMSTRONG Holcomb C 1919
28
PITTS John M 1858
PITTS John M 1858
TYLER Richard L 1895
NICHOLAS Joel 1858
TYLER Richard L 1895
ARNOLD Ezekiel 1858
ARNOLD Ezekiel 1858
31
FIELDS James G 1858
FIELDS James G 1858
HARMON William A 1893
HARMON William A 1893
HARMON William A 1893
DAVIDSON Edwin 1858
FERRINGTON Barney 1849
HARMON John 1888
DAVIDSON Edwin 1858
32
MCMATH James H 1848
HARMON John 1888
HARMON James L 1893
HARMON James L 1893
33

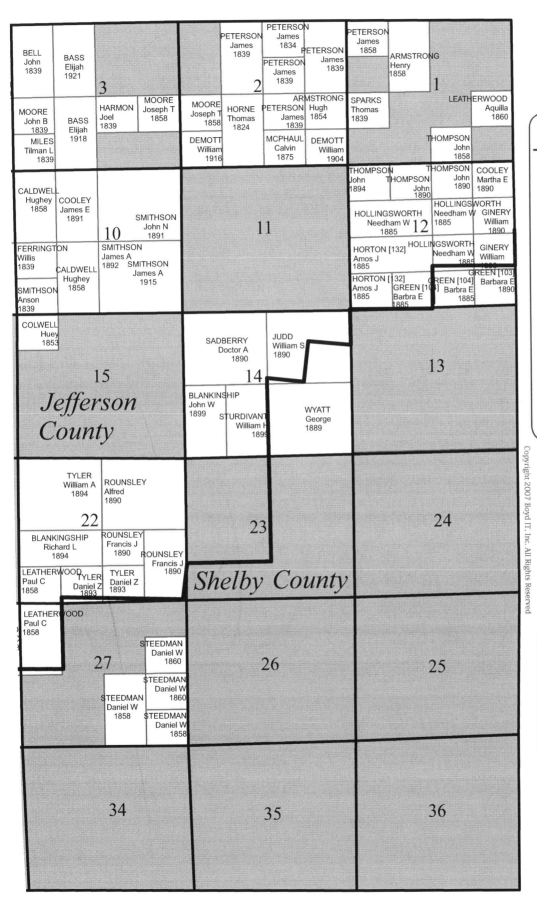

Helpful Hints

1. This Map's INDEX can be found on the preceding pages.
2. Refer to Map "C" to see where this Township lies within Jefferson County, Alabama.
3. Numbers within square brackets [ ] denote a multi-patentee land parcel (multi-owner). Refer to Appendix "C" for a full list of members in this group.
4. Areas that look to be crowded with Patentees usually indicate multiple sales of the same parcel (Re-issues) or Overlapping parcels. See this Township's Index for an explanation of these and other circumstances that might explain "odd" groupings of Patentees on this map.

Legend

- Patent Boundary
- Section Boundary
- No Patents Found (or Outside County)
- 1., 2., 3., ... Lot Numbers (when beside a name)
- [ ] Group Number (see Appendix "C")

Scale: Section = 1 mile X 1 mile (generally, with some exceptions)

Road Map

T20-S R4-W
Huntsville Meridian

Map Group 43

Cities & Towns
None

Cemeteries
Fairington Cemetery
George Cemetery
Massey Cemetery
Smithson Cemetery

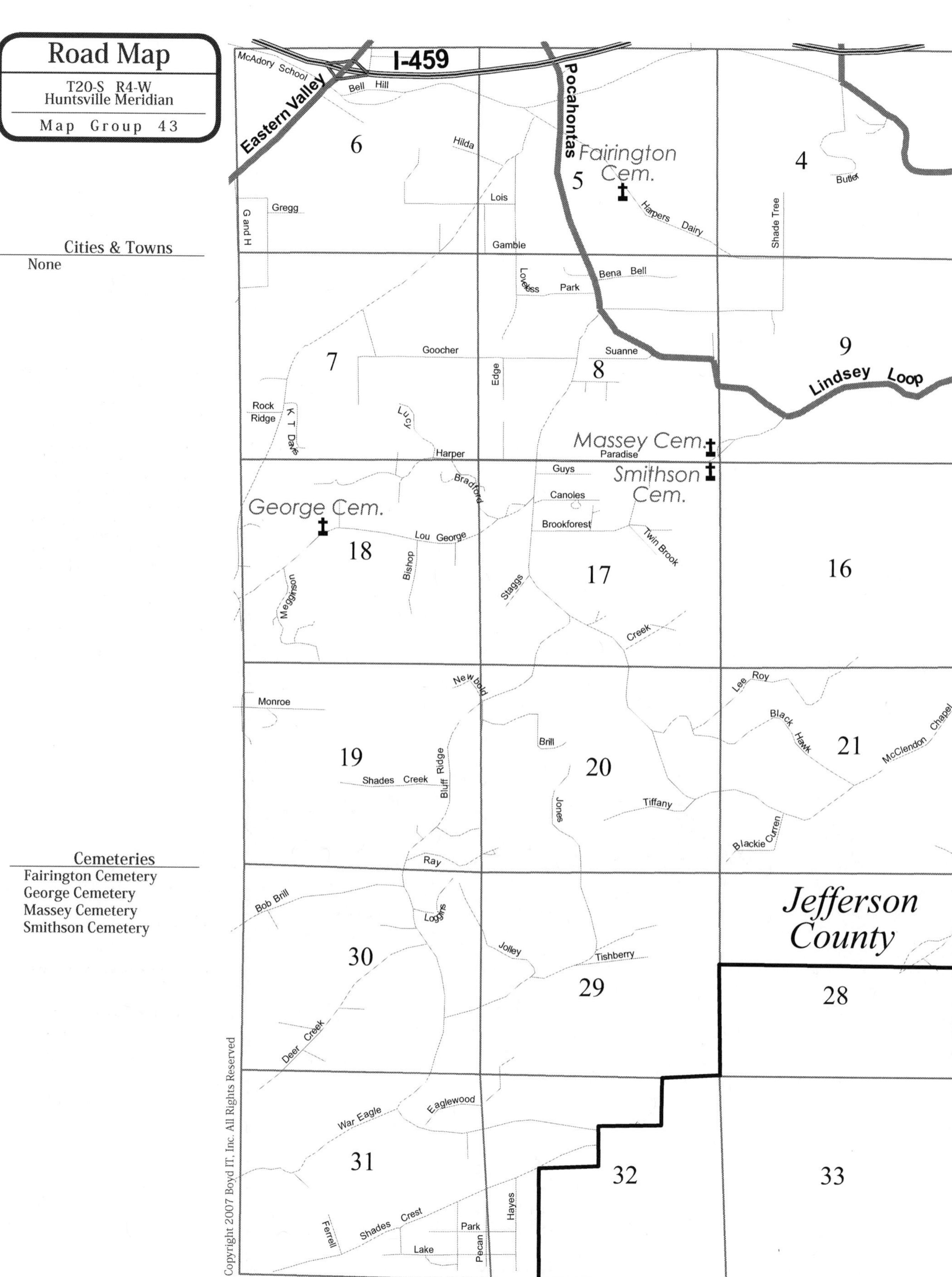

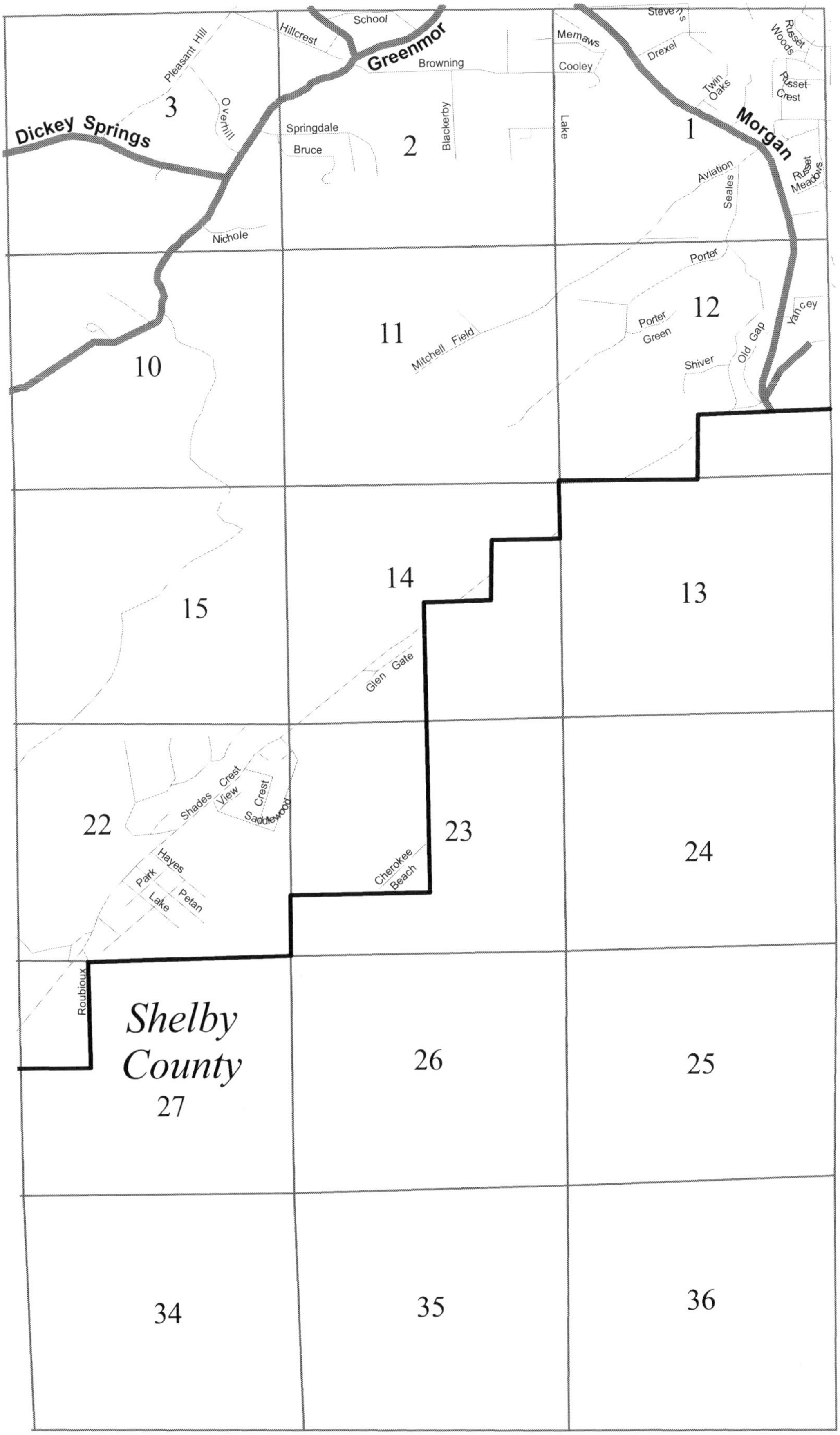

Helpful Hints

1. This road map has a number of uses, but primarily it is to help you: a) find the present location of land owned by your ancestors (at least the general area), b) find cemeteries and city-centers, and c) estimate the route/roads used by Census-takers & tax-assessors.

2. If you plan to travel to Jefferson County to locate cemeteries or land parcels, please pick up a modern travel map for the area before you do. Mapping old land parcels on modern maps is not as exact a science as you might think. Just the slightest variations in public land survey coordinates, estimates of parcel boundaries, or road-map deviations can greatly alter a map's representation of how a road either does or doesn't cross a particular parcel of land.

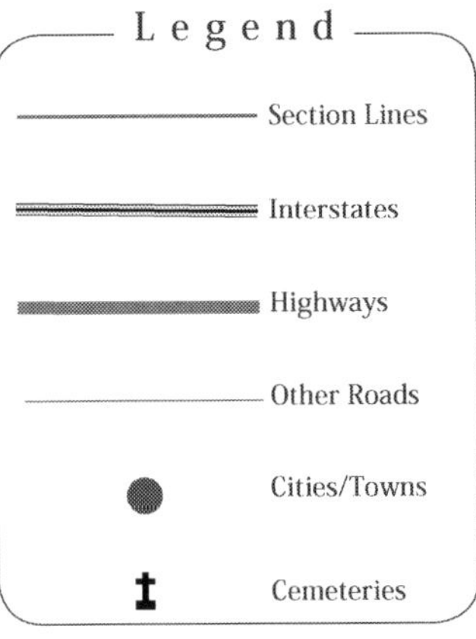

Scale: Section = 1 mile X 1 mile
(generally, with some exceptions)

Historical Map

T20-S R4-W
Huntsville Meridian

Map Group 43

Cities & Towns

None

Cemeteries

Fairington Cemetery
George Cemetery
Massey Cemetery
Smithson Cemetery

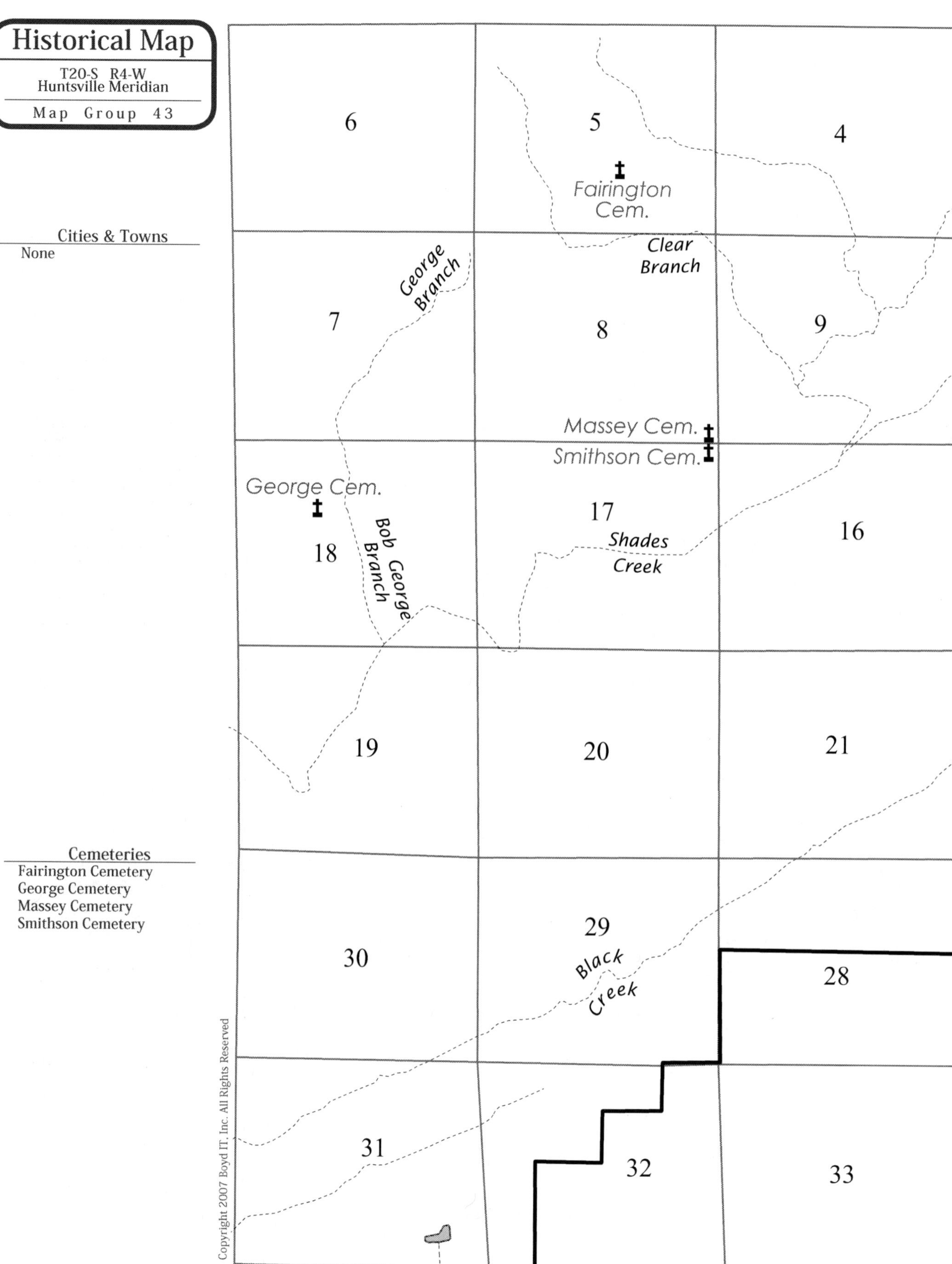

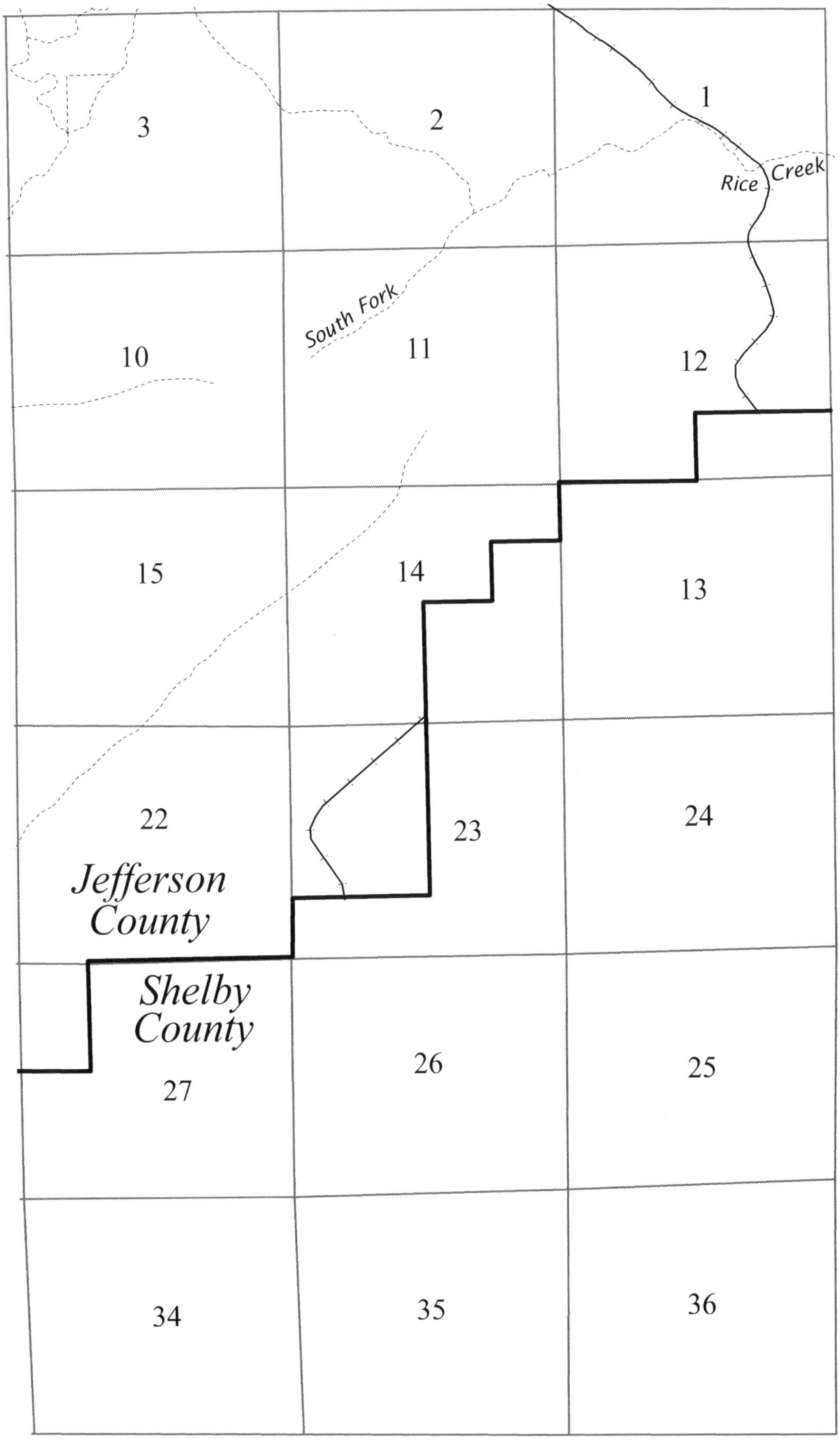

3 2 1

Rice Creek

South Fork

10 11 12

15 14 13

22 23 24

Jefferson County

Shelby County

27 26 25

34 35 36

Helpful Hints

1. This Map takes a different look at the same Congressional Township displayed in the preceding two maps. It presents features that can help you better envision the historical development of the area: a) Water-bodies (lakes & ponds), b) Water-courses (rivers, streams, etc.), c) Railroads, d) City/town center-points (where they were oftentimes located when first settled), and e) Cemeteries.

2. Using this "Historical" map in tandem with this Township's Patent Map and Road Map, may lead you to some interesting discoveries. You will often find roads, towns, cemeteries, and waterways are named after nearby landowners: sometimes those names will be the ones you are researching. See how many of these research gems you can find here in Jefferson County.

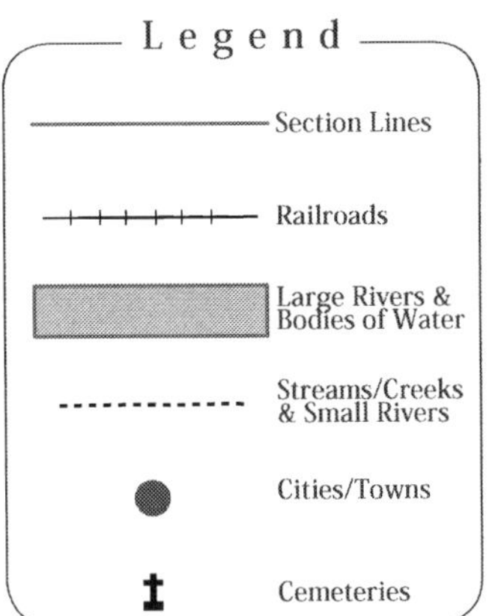

Scale: Section = 1 mile X 1 mile
(there are some exceptions)

Map Group 44: Index to Land Patents

Township 20-South Range 3-West (Huntsville)

After you locate an individual in this Index, take note of the Section and Section Part then proceed to the Land Patent map on the pages immediately following. You should have no difficulty locating the corresponding parcel of land.

The "For More Info" Column will lead you to more information about the underlying Patents. See the *Legend* at right, and the "How to Use this Book" chapter, for more information.

LEGEND

"For More Info . . . " column

A = Authority (Legislative Act, See Appendix "A")
B = Block or Lot (location in Section unknown)
C = Cancelled Patent
F = Fractional Section
G = Group (Multi-Patentee Patent, see Appendix "C")
V = Overlaps another Parcel
R = Re-Issued (Parcel patented more than once)

(A & G items require you to look in the Appendixes referred to above. All other Letter-designations followed by a number require you to locate line-items in this index that possess the ID number found after the letter).

ID	Individual in Patent	Sec.	Sec. Part	Date Issued	Other Counties	For More Info . . .
7426	ALLEN, Thomas	7	NWNW	1858-06-01	Shelby	A1
7423	BARBEAU, Laura A	6	N½NE	1885-03-30	Shelby	A4 G12
7424	BISHOP, Malachi	6	N½SW	1858-06-01	Shelby	A1
7425	" "	6	SWNW	1858-06-01	Shelby	A1
7423	FEENKER, Laura A	6	N½NE	1885-03-30	Shelby	A4 G12
7419	GRANT, Alexander	6	NENW	1884-03-10	Shelby	A4
7422	GRANT, John G	6	NWNW	1884-03-10	Shelby	A4
7427	GREEN, Thomas J	6	SESW	1892-01-20	Shelby	A4
7431	HOUSTON, William	6	E½SE	1883-10-01	Shelby	A4
7432	" "	6	W½SE	1889-11-21	Shelby	A4
7429	MARTIN, William B	7	E½NE	1858-06-01	Shelby	A1
7430	" "	7	N½SE	1858-06-01	Shelby	A1
7420	NABORS, James B	6	S½NE	1902-11-21	Shelby	A4
7428	PORTER, Thursday A	6	SWSW	1885-08-05	Shelby	A4
7421	STANDLAND, James H	6	SENW	1858-06-01	Shelby	A1

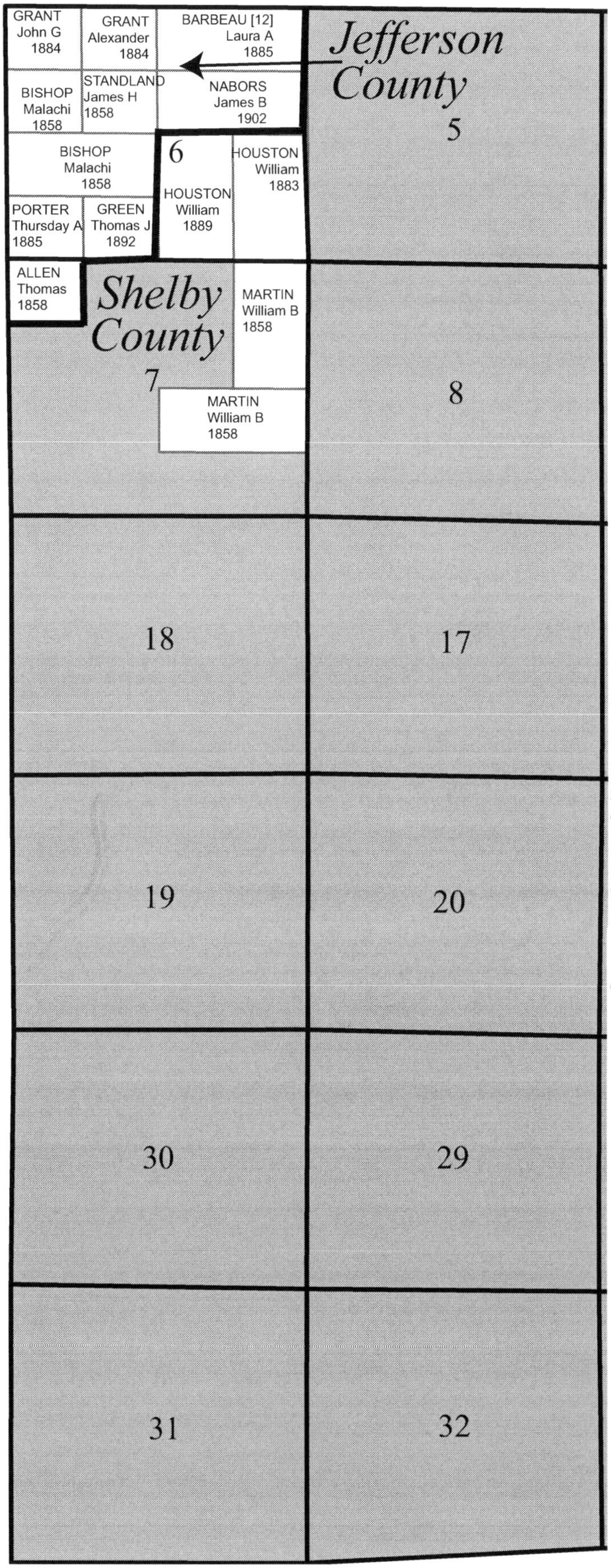

GRANT John G 1884
GRANT Alexander 1884
BARBEAU [12] Laura A 1885
BISHOP Malachi 1858
STANDLAND James H 1858
NABORS James B 1902
BISHOP Malachi 1858
6
HOUSTON William 1883
HOUSTON William 1889
PORTER Thursday A 1885
GREEN Thomas J 1892
ALLEN Thomas 1858
Shelby County
MARTIN William B 1858
7
MARTIN William B 1858
Jefferson County
5
8
18
17
19
20
30
29
31
32

Patent Map

T20-S R3-W
Huntsville Meridian

Map Group 44

Township Statistics

Parcels Mapped	:	14
Number of Patents	:	13
Number of Individuals	:	12
Patentees Identified	:	11
Number of Surnames	:	11
Multi-Patentee Parcels	:	1
Oldest Patent Date	:	6/1/1858
Most Recent Patent	:	11/21/1902
Block/Lot Parcels	:	0
Parcels Re - Issued	:	0
Parcels that Overlap	:	0
Cities and Towns	:	0
Cemeteries	:	0

Note: the area contained in this map amounts to far less than a full Township. Therefore, its contents are completely on this single page (instead of a "normal" 2-page spread).

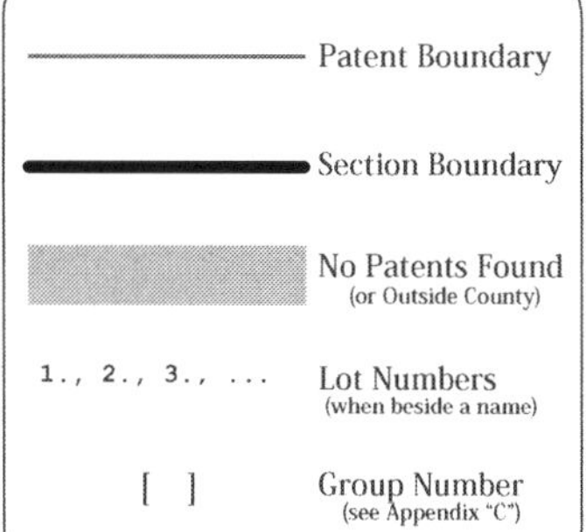

Scale: Section = 1 mile X 1 mile
(generally, with some exceptions)

Road Map

T20-S R3-W
Huntsville Meridian

Map Group 44

Note: the area contained in this map amounts to far less than a full Township. Therefore, its contents are completely on this single page (instead of a "normal" 2-page spread).

Cities & Towns
None

Cemeteries
None

Legend

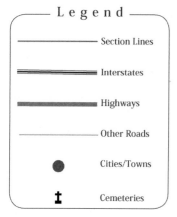

- Section Lines
- Interstates
- Highways
- Other Roads
- Cities/Towns
- Cemeteries

Scale: Section = 1 mile X 1 mile
(generally, with some exceptions)

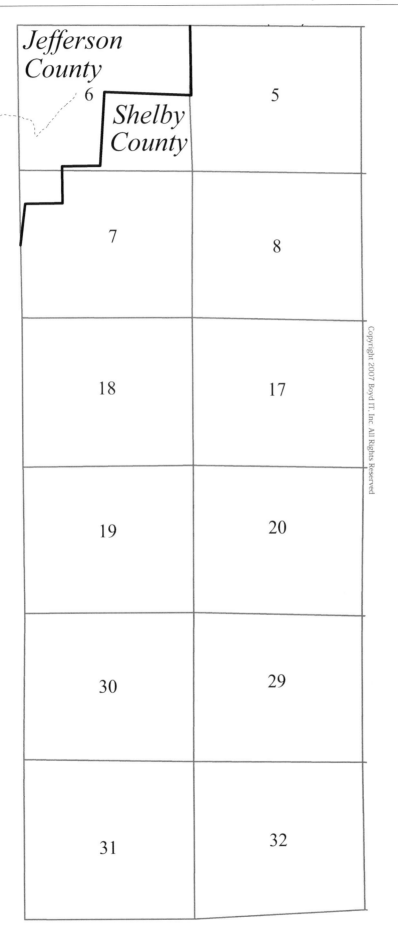

Jefferson County

Shelby County

6

5

7

8

18

17

19

20

30

29

31

32

Historical Map

T20-S R3-W
Huntsville Meridian

Map Group 44

Note: the area contained in this map amounts to far less than a full Township. Therefore, its contents are completely on this single page (instead of a "normal" 2-page spread).

Cities & Towns

None

Cemeteries

None

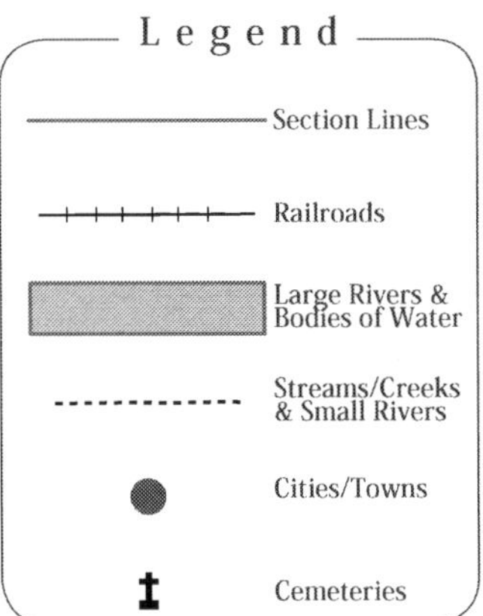

Scale: Section = 1 mile X 1 mile
(there are some exceptions)

Appendices

Appendix A - Acts of Congress Authorizing the Patents Contained in this Book

The following Acts of Congress are referred to throughout the Indexes in this book. The text of the Federal Statutes referred to below can usually be found on the web. For more information on such laws, check out the publishers's web-site at *www.arphax.com,* go to the "Research" page, and click on the "Land-Law" link.

Ref. No.	Date and Act of Congress	Number of Parcels of Land
1	April 24, 1820: Sale-Cash Entry (3 Stat. 566)	5478
2	January 1, 1999: No Authority Available ()	2
3	March 3, 1873: Sale-Coal Land (17 Stat. 607)	1
4	May 20, 1862: Homestead EntryOriginal (12 Stat. 392)	1950
5	September 4, 1841: Grant-Certain Land to State (5 Stat. 453)	1

Appendix B - Section Parts (Aliquot Parts)

The following represent the various abbreviations we have found thus far in describing the parts of a Public Land Section. Some of these are very obscure and rarely used, but we wanted to list them for just that reason. A full section is 1 square mile or 640 acres.

Section Part	Description	Acres
<none>	Full Acre (if no Section Part is listed, presumed a full Section)	640
<1-??>	A number represents a Lot Number and can be of various sizes	?
E½	East Half-Section	320
E½E½	East Half of East Half-Section	160
E½E½SE	East Half of East Half of Southeast Quarter-Section	40
E½N½	East Half of North Half-Section	160
E½NE	East Half of Northeast Quarter-Section	80
E½NENE	East Half of Northeast Quarter of Northeast Quarter-Section	20
E½NENW	East Half of Northeast Quarter of Northwest Quarter-Section	20
E½NESE	East Half of Northeast Quarter of Southeast Quarter-Section	20
E½NESW	East Half of Northeast Quarter of Southwest Quarter-Section	20
E½NW	East Half of Northwest Quarter-Section	80
E½NWNE	East Half of Northwest Quarter of Northeast Quarter-Section	20
E½NWNW	East Half of Northwest Quarter of Northwest Quarter-Section	20
E½NWSE	East Half of Northwest Quarter of Southeast Quarter-Section	20
E½NWSW	East Half of Northwest Quarter of Southwest Quarter-Section	20
E½S½	East Half of South Half-Section	160
E½SE	East Half of Southeast Quarter-Section	80
E½SENE	East Half of Southeast Quarter of Northeast Quarter-Section	20
E½SENW	East Half of Southeast Quarter of Northwest Quarter-Section	20
E½SESE	East Half of Southeast Quarter of Southeast Quarter-Section	20
E½SESW	East Half of Southeast Quarter of Southwest Quarter-Section	20
E½SW	East Half of Southwest Quarter-Section	80
E½SWNE	East Half of Southwest Quarter of Northeast Quarter-Section	20
E½SWNW	East Half of Southwest Quarter of Northwest Quarter-Section	20
E½SWSE	East Half of Southwest Quarter of Southeast Quarter-Section	20
E½SWSW	East Half of Southwest Quarter of Southwest Quarter-Section	20
E½W½	East Half of West Half-Section	160
N½	North Half-Section	320
N½E½NE	North Half of East Half of Northeast Quarter-Section	40
N½E½NW	North Half of East Half of Northwest Quarter-Section	40
N½E½SE	North Half of East Half of Southeast Quarter-Section	40
N½E½SW	North Half of East Half of Southwest Quarter-Section	40
N½N½	North Half of North Half-Section	160
N½NE	North Half of Northeast Quarter-Section	80
N½NENE	North Half of Northeast Quarter of Northeast Quarter-Section	20
N½NENW	North Half of Northeast Quarter of Northwest Quarter-Section	20
N½NESE	North Half of Northeast Quarter of Southeast Quarter-Section	20
N½NESW	North Half of Northeast Quarter of Southwest Quarter-Section	20
N½NW	North Half of Northwest Quarter-Section	80
N½NWNE	North Half of Northwest Quarter of Northeast Quarter-Section	20
N½NWNW	North Half of Northwest Quarter of Northwest Quarter-Section	20
N½NWSE	North Half of Northwest Quarter of Southeast Quarter-Section	20
N½NWSW	North Half of Northwest Quarter of Southwest Quarter-Section	20
N½S½	North Half of South Half-Section	160
N½SE	North Half of Southeast Quarter-Section	80
N½SENE	North Half of Southeast Quarter of Northeast Quarter-Section	20
N½SENW	North Half of Southeast Quarter of Northwest Quarter-Section	20
N½SESE	North Half of Southeast Quarter of Southeast Quarter-Section	20

Section Part	Description	Acres
N½SESW	North Half of Southeast Quarter of Southwest Quarter-Section	20
N½SESW	North Half of Southeast Quarter of Southwest Quarter-Section	20
N½SW	North Half of Southwest Quarter-Section	80
N½SWNE	North Half of Southwest Quarter of Northeast Quarter-Section	20
N½SWNW	North Half of Southwest Quarter of Northwest Quarter-Section	20
N½SWSE	North Half of Southwest Quarter of Southeast Quarter-Section	20
N½SWSE	North Half of Southwest Quarter of Southeast Quarter-Section	20
N½SWSW	North Half of Southwest Quarter of Southwest Quarter-Section	20
N½W½NW	North Half of West Half of Northwest Quarter-Section	40
N½W½SE	North Half of West Half of Southeast Quarter-Section	40
N½W½SW	North Half of West Half of Southwest Quarter-Section	40
NE	Northeast Quarter-Section	160
NEN½	Northeast Quarter of North Half-Section	80
NENE	Northeast Quarter of Northeast Quarter-Section	40
NENENE	Northeast Quarter of Northeast Quarter of Northeast Quarter	10
NENENW	Northeast Quarter of Northeast Quarter of Northwest Quarter	10
NENESE	Northeast Quarter of Northeast Quarter of Southeast Quarter	10
NENESW	Northeast Quarter of Northeast Quarter of Southwest Quarter	10
NENW	Northeast Quarter of Northwest Quarter-Section	40
NENWNE	Northeast Quarter of Northwest Quarter of Northeast Quarter	10
NENWNW	Northeast Quarter of Northwest Quarter of Northwest Quarter	10
NENWSE	Northeast Quarter of Northwest Quarter of Southeast Quarter	10
NENWSW	Northeast Quarter of Northwest Quarter of Southwest Quarter	10
NESE	Northeast Quarter of Southeast Quarter-Section	40
NESENE	Northeast Quarter of Southeast Quarter of Northeast Quarter	10
NESENW	Northeast Quarter of Southeast Quarter of Northwest Quarter	10
NESESE	Northeast Quarter of Southeast Quarter of Southeast Quarter	10
NESESW	Northeast Quarter of Southeast Quarter of Southwest Quarter	10
NESW	Northeast Quarter of Southwest Quarter-Section	40
NESWNE	Northeast Quarter of Southwest Quarter of Northeast Quarter	10
NESWNW	Northeast Quarter of Southwest Quarter of Northwest Quarter	10
NESWSE	Northeast Quarter of Southwest Quarter of Southeast Quarter	10
NESWSW	Northeast Quarter of Southwest Quarter of Southwest Quarter	10
NW	Northwest Quarter-Section	160
NWE½	Northwest Quarter of Eastern Half-Section	80
NWN½	Northwest Quarter of North Half-Section	80
NWNE	Northwest Quarter of Northeast Quarter-Section	40
NWNENE	Northwest Quarter of Northeast Quarter of Northeast Quarter	10
NWNENW	Northwest Quarter of Northeast Quarter of Northwest Quarter	10
NWNESE	Northwest Quarter of Northeast Quarter of Southeast Quarter	10
NWNESW	Northwest Quarter of Northeast Quarter of Southwest Quarter	10
NWNW	Northwest Quarter of Northwest Quarter-Section	40
NWNWNE	Northwest Quarter of Northwest Quarter of Northeast Quarter	10
NWNWNW	Northwest Quarter of Northwest Quarter of Northwest Quarter	10
NWNWSE	Northwest Quarter of Northwest Quarter of Southeast Quarter	10
NWNWSW	Northwest Quarter of Northwest Quarter of Southwest Quarter	10
NWSE	Northwest Quarter of Southeast Quarter-Section	40
NWSENE	Northwest Quarter of Southeast Quarter of Northeast Quarter	10
NWSENW	Northwest Quarter of Southeast Quarter of Northwest Quarter	10
NWSESE	Northwest Quarter of Southeast Quarter of Southeast Quarter	10
NWSESW	Northwest Quarter of Southeast Quarter of Southwest Quarter	10
NWSW	Northwest Quarter of Southwest Quarter-Section	40
NWSWNE	Northwest Quarter of Southwest Quarter of Northeast Quarter	10
NWSWNW	Northwest Quarter of Southwest Quarter of Northwest Quarter	10
NWSWSE	Northwest Quarter of Southwest Quarter of Southeast Quarter	10
NWSWSW	Northwest Quarter of Southwest Quarter of Southwest Quarter	10
S½	South Half-Section	320
S½E½NE	South Half of East Half of Northeast Quarter-Section	40
S½E½NW	South Half of East Half of Northwest Quarter-Section	40
S½E½SE	South Half of East Half of Southeast Quarter-Section	40

Section Part	Description	Acres
S½E½SW	South Half of East Half of Southwest Quarter-Section	40
S½N½	South Half of North Half-Section	160
S½NE	South Half of Northeast Quarter-Section	80
S½NENE	South Half of Northeast Quarter of Northeast Quarter-Section	20
S½NENW	South Half of Northeast Quarter of Northwest Quarter-Section	20
S½NESE	South Half of Northeast Quarter of Southeast Quarter-Section	20
S½NESW	South Half of Northeast Quarter of Southwest Quarter-Section	20
S½NW	South Half of Northwest Quarter-Section	80
S½NWNE	South Half of Northwest Quarter of Northeast Quarter-Section	20
S½NWNW	South Half of Northwest Quarter of Northwest Quarter-Section	20
S½NWSE	South Half of Northwest Quarter of Southeast Quarter-Section	20
S½NWSW	South Half of Northwest Quarter of Southwest Quarter-Section	20
S½S½	South Half of South Half-Section	160
S½SE	South Half of Southeast Quarter-Section	80
S½SENE	South Half of Southeast Quarter of Northeast Quarter-Section	20
S½SENW	South Half of Southeast Quarter of Northwest Quarter-Section	20
S½SESE	South Half of Southeast Quarter of Southeast Quarter-Section	20
S½SESW	South Half of Southeast Quarter of Southwest Quarter-Section	20
S½SESW	South Half of Southeast Quarter of Southwest Quarter-Section	20
S½SW	South Half of Southwest Quarter-Section	80
S½SWNE	South Half of Southwest Quarter of Northeast Quarter-Section	20
S½SWNW	South Half of Southwest Quarter of Northwest Quarter-Section	20
S½SWSE	South Half of Southwest Quarter of Southeast Quarter-Section	20
S½SWSE	South Half of Southwest Quarter of Southeast Quarter-Section	20
S½SWSW	South Half of Southwest Quarter of Southwest Quarter-Section	20
S½W½NE	South Half of West Half of Northeast Quarter-Section	40
S½W½NW	South Half of West Half of Northwest Quarter-Section	40
S½W½SE	South Half of West Half of Southeast Quarter-Section	40
S½W½SW	South Half of West Half of Southwest Quarter-Section	40
SE	Southeast Quarter Section	160
SEN½	Southeast Quarter of North Half-Section	80
SENE	Southeast Quarter of Northeast Quarter-Section	40
SENENE	Southeast Quarter of Northeast Quarter of Northeast Quarter	10
SENENW	Southeast Quarter of Northeast Quarter of Northwest Quarter	10
SENESE	Southeast Quarter of Northeast Quarter of Southeast Quarter	10
SENESW	Southeast Quarter of Northeast Quarter of Southwest Quarter	10
SENW	Southeast Quarter of Northwest Quarter-Section	40
SENWNE	Southeast Quarter of Northwest Quarter of Northeast Quarter	10
SENWNW	Southeast Quarter of Northwest Quarter of Northwest Quarter	10
SENWSE	Souteast Quarter of Northwest Quarter of Southeast Quarter	10
SENWSW	Southeast Quarter of Northwest Quarter of Southwest Quarter	10
SESE	Southeast Quarter of Southeast Quarter-Section	40
SESENE	SoutheastQuarter of Southeast Quarter of Northeast Quarter	10
SESENW	Southeast Quarter of Southeast Quarter of Northwest Quarter	10
SESESE	Southeast Quarter of Southeast Quarter of Southeast Quarter	10
SESESW	Southeast Quarter of Southeast Quarter of Southwest Quarter	10
SESW	Southeast Quarter of Southwest Quarter-Section	40
SESWNE	Southeast Quarter of Southwest Quarter of Northeast Quarter	10
SESWNW	Southeast Quarter of Southwest Quarter of Northwest Quarter	10
SESWSE	Southeast Quarter of Southwest Quarter of Southeast Quarter	10
SESWSW	Southeast Quarter of Southwest Quarter of Southwest Quarter	10
SW	Southwest Quarter-Section	160
SWNE	Southwest Quarter of Northeast Quarter-Section	40
SWNENE	Southwest Quarter of Northeast Quarter of Northeast Quarter	10
SWNENW	Southwest Quarter of Northeast Quarter of Northwest Quarter	10
SWNESE	Southwest Quarter of Northeast Quarter of Southeast Quarter	10
SWNESW	Southwest Quarter of Northeast Quarter of Southwest Quarter	10
SWNW	Southwest Quarter of Northwest Quarter-Section	40
SWNWNE	Southwest Quarter of Northwest Quarter of Northeast Quarter	10
SWNWNW	Southwest Quarter of Northwest Quarter of Northwest Quarter	10

Section Part	Description	Acres
SWNWSE	Southwest Quarter of Northwest Quarter of Southeast Quarter	10
SWNWSW	Southwest Quarter of Northwest Quarter of Southwest Quarter	10
SWSE	Southwest Quarter of Southeast Quarter-Section	40
SWSENE	Southwest Quarter of Southeast Quarter of Northeast Quarter	10
SWSENW	Southwest Quarter of Southeast Quarter of Northwest Quarter	10
SWSESE	Southwest Quarter of Southeast Quarter of Southeast Quarter	10
SWSESW	Southwest Quarter of Southeast Quarter of Southwest Quarter	10
SWSW	Southwest Quarter of Southwest Quarter-Section	40
SWSWNE	Southwest Quarter of Southwest Quarter of Northeast Quarter	10
SWSWNW	Southwest Quarter of Southwest Quarter of Northwest Quarter	10
SWSWSE	Southwest Quarter of Southwest Quarter of Southeast Quarter	10
SWSWSW	Southwest Quarter of Southwest Quarter of Southwest Quarter	10
W½	West Half-Section	320
W½E½	West Half of East Half-Section	160
W½N½	West Half of North Half-Section (same as NW)	160
W½NE	West Half of Northeast Quarter	80
W½NENE	West Half of Northeast Quarter of Northeast Quarter-Section	20
W½NENW	West Half of Northeast Quarter of Northwest Quarter-Section	20
W½NESE	West Half of Northeast Quarter of Southeast Quarter-Section	20
W½NESW	West Half of Northeast Quarter of Southwest Quarter-Section	20
W½NW	West Half of Northwest Quarter-Section	80
W½NWNE	West Half of Northwest Quarter of Northeast Quarter-Section	20
W½NWNW	West Half of Northwest Quarter of Northwest Quarter-Section	20
W½NWSE	West Half of Northwest Quarter of Southeast Quarter-Section	20
W½NWSW	West Half of Northwest Quarter of Southwest Quarter-Section	20
W½S½	West Half of South Half-Section	160
W½SE	West Half of Southeast Quarter-Section	80
W½SENE	West Half of Southeast Quarter of Northeast Quarter-Section	20
W½SENW	West Half of Southeast Quarter of Northwest Quarter-Section	20
W½SESE	West Half of Southeast Quarter of Southeast Quarter-Section	20
W½SESW	West Half of Southeast Quarter of Southwest Quarter-Section	20
W½SW	West Half of Southwest Quarter-Section	80
W½SWNE	West Half of Southwest Quarter of Northeast Quarter-Section	20
W½SWNW	West Half of Southwest Quarter of Northwest Quarter-Section	20
W½SWSE	West Half of Southwest Quarter of Southeast Quarter-Section	20
W½SWSW	West Half of Southwest Quarter of Southwest Quarter-Section	20
W½W½	West Half of West Half-Section	160

Appendix C - Multi-Patentee Groups

The following index presents groups of people who jointly received patents in Jefferson County, Alabama. The Group Numbers are used in the Patent Maps and their Indexes so that you may then turn to this Appendix in order to identify all the members of the each buying group.

Group Number 1
ABERNATHY, David; ABERNATHY, James

Group Number 2
ACTON, Mariah E; ACTON, William M

Group Number 3
ADAMS, Ace; BYARS, John; COLLY, William; HALL, Samuel W; JONES, Charles P; MARTIN, John; MITCHELL, Roland; ROCKETT, Thomas W; STEALE, Jonathan; TERRIL, James T

Group Number 4
ADAMS, John; DUFF, James; LOLLY, John

Group Number 5
ANTHONY, George L; ANTHONY, Sarah A

Group Number 6
AYRES, Daniel; DACUS, Jarrel; LOCKHART, Benjamin

Group Number 7
AYRES, William; BURGIN, Thomas; HENDLEY, Darby

Group Number 8
BAGWELL, Jason; BAGWELL, Jeremiah; BAGWELL, Mary; BAGWELL, Wilson

Group Number 9
BAILEY, Fannie; BAILEY, Livingston

Group Number 10
BAIRD, Robert; GEE, William J

Group Number 11
BANKSTON, Sarah A C; THOMAS, David W; THOMAS, Sarah A C

Group Number 12
BARBEAU, Laura A; FEENKER, Laura A

Group Number 13
BARNETT, Erastus S; COWLEY, Jerrom

Group Number 14
BARRY, Armstead; CLEMENTS, Hardy

Group Number 15
BARRY, Armstead; MCCARTNEY, James

Group Number 16
BARRY, Armstead; SIMS, Edward

Group Number 17
BARTON, Thomas; SIMS, Edward

Group Number 18
BASS, John; HODGE, John

Group Number 19
BEARD, Alexander; LANE, John W

Group Number 20
BELCHER, J A; CORNELIUS, William P

Group Number 21
BELL, Anthony F; HEARD, John K

Group Number 22
BIBB, William C; BUFFINGTON, William C; DONELSON, Presley W; GILMER, George N; MOSES, Alfred H; SMITH, Frank J

Group Number 23
BIVINS, Robert; HARDIN, John

Group Number 24
BLACK, Fannie F; BLACK, Jacob

Group Number 25
BOYD, Archibald C; BOYD, Martha J

Group Number 26
BRADFORD, Thomas C; TALLEY, Nicholas

Group Number 27
BRADFORD, William; TRUSS, Warren

Group Number 28
BROWN, David; NATIONS, James

Group Number 29
BROWN, Elijah; MARKS, Nicholas M

Group Number 30
BROWN, George; MARKS, Nicholas M

Group Number 31
BROWN, Joseph; BROWN, Thomas

Group Number 32
BROWN, Lida; WILLIAMS, Lida

Group Number 33
BROWN, Thomas; WOOD, John

Group Number 34
BROWN, William; SANDERS, Philip

Group Number 35
BULLARD, Christopher; PRESCOTT, Aaron

Group Number 36
BURNS, Polly A; BURNS, Thomas W

Group Number 37
BURTON, Caroline E; HOWTON, Joseph A

Group Number 38
BUTLER, Jesse; SHARP, Edward G

Group Number 39
BYARS, Nathan; GOYNE, John R

Group Number 40
BYRD, Dona; BYRD, Hilliard D

Group Number 41
CAIN, James; VANHOUSE, Jesse

Group Number 42
CALDWELL, Amanda; CALDWELL, Benjamin V

Group Number 43
CANTERBERRY, Nelson; MCCARTNEY, James

Group Number 44
CARITHERS, William; PEELER, Montraville

Group Number 45
CARTER, William; HOOPER, Toliver

Group Number 46
CAWOOD, Moses; WALKER, James S

Group Number 47
CHAPEL, John; MCASHAN, John; SCOTT, David

Group Number 48
CLARK, Samuel; TOWNBY, John

Group Number 49
CLEMENTS, Benjamin; HAMILTON, Audly

Group Number 50
CLEMENTS, Hardy; DANIEL, William

Group Number 51
CLEMENTS, Hardy; HAMILTON, Audly

Group Number 52
CLEMENTS, Hardy; NEAL, Zacheriah

Group Number 53
CLEMENTS, Hardy; PIERCE, George

Group Number 54
CLEMENTS, Hardy; SIMS, Edward

Group Number 55
CLEMENTS, Jesse B; HALL, Stephen

Group Number 56
COCHRAN, Hiram P; MCELROY, John

Group Number 57
COCHRAN, Hiram P; WOOD, John

Group Number 58
COOK, Calliedonia A; COOK, James R

Group Number 59
COOK, Charles M; COOK, Skiddie V

Group Number 60
COOK, John; MCELROY, John H

Group Number 61
COOLEY, Susaner E; VINES, John D

Group Number 62
CROOKS, Rebecca S; NAIL, Rebecca S

Group Number 63
CROSS, William; GILBERT, William

Group Number 64
CRUMP, John; SCOTT, David

Group Number 65
CULBERTSON, William D T; GALLAWAY, Robert

Group Number 66
CULBERTSON, William D T; HALL, James

Group Number 67
CULBERTSON, William D T; PITTS, William; TORRENT, Roland

Group Number 68
CUMMING, William; SMITH, Eldred

Group Number 69
CUNNINGHAM, James; REED, Robert

Group Number 70
CUNNINGHAM, James; SIMS, Edward

Group Number 71
DAVIS, John; GILLEN, John; WORTHINGTON, Benjamin

Group Number 72
DAVIS, Ruth; GLAZE, William

Group Number 73
DELANY, Baker; MCCARTNEY, James

Group Number 74
DENTON, James; MCADORY, James

Group Number 75
DUFF, Walter; MCASHAN, John

Group Number 76
DULANY, Baker; LANE, John W

Group Number 77
DULANY, Baker; SCOTT, David

Group Number 78
DUPUY, John W; HALE, Samuel W

Group Number 79
DYER, Otis; MITCHELL, Thomas

Group Number 80
EARLE, John; GRACE, Leana

Group Number 81
EARLE, Samuel T; FARRAR, Thomas W; WALTON, Jacob

Group Number 82
EASTIS, Balas E; EASTIS, Mary L

Group Number 83
ERWIN, John; SCOTT, David

Group Number 84
FARR, David; GILLEN, John

Group Number 85
FIELDS, Nancy M; FIELDS, William C

Group Number 86
FRANKLIN, Greenberry F; FRANKLIN, Owen

Group Number 87
FREELAND, Hampton; HARDIMAN, Lewis

Group Number 88
FRIEDMAN, Bernard; LOVEMAN, Emanuel

Group Number 89
FRIES, Jacob; SIMS, Edward

Group Number 90
FULLER, Trion; PERKINS, William

Group Number 91
FULLER, Tryon; SIMS, Edward

Group Number 92
GILBERT, William; SIMS, Edward

Group Number 93
GILL, Henry B; GILL, Margaret A

Group Number 94
GILL, Joseph; GILL, Louisa

Group Number 95
GILMORE, Mary; GILMORE, William C

Group Number 96
GILMORE, Nancy; GILMORE, Samuel W

Group Number 97
GILMORE, Samuel; SMITH, William L

Group Number 98
GLASS, Elisha; GLASS, Mary

Group Number 99
GLENN, Rebecca; GLENN, Sarah

Group Number 100
GOODWIN, Theopholus; JONES, Reuben

Group Number 101
GORMAN, William; SCOTT, David

Group Number 102
GRAHAM, John; GRAHAM, Permelia A

Group Number 103
GREEN, Barbara E; PITTS, Barbara E

Group Number 104
GREEN, Barbra E; PITTS, Barbra E

Group Number 105
GREEN, George L; LOVELESS, Richard

Group Number 106
GREENE, Augustus C; GREENE, Sarah

Group Number 107
HALE, James; HALE, Samuel

Group Number 108
HALE, James; SPEER, Charles

Group Number 109
HALL, James; HALL, Samuel

Group Number 110
HALL, James; SHARP, Edward G

Group Number 111
HALL, Samuel; SIMS, Edward

Group Number 112
HALL, Stephen; KELLY, Moses

Group Number 113
HALL, Stephen; MCCARTNEY, James

Group Number 114
HALL, William J; WALDROP, Margaret A

Group Number 115
HAMILTON, Audley; SIMS, Edward

Group Number 116
HAMNER, William; MCCARTNEY, James

Group Number 117
HAMNER, William; ORR, Jonathan

Group Number 118
HANBY, David; LEDYARD, William J; TUTHILL, George A

Group Number 119
HANBY, Gabriel; MCGEHEE, William

Group Number 120
HANBY, John; TATUM, Jesse

Group Number 121
HANCOCK, Josiah; HARRISON, Joseph D

Group Number 122
HANLY, David; LEDYARD, William J; TUTHILL, George A

Group Number 123
HANNA, Gaberrilla A; POOLE, Gaberrilla A

Group Number 124
HARDIN, John; SNOW, William

Group Number 125
HARRIS, Mark M; SIMS, Edward; THOMAS, John

Group Number 126
HARRISON, Joseph D; MICHAEL, Barney

Group Number 127
HENLEY, Darby; MCCARTNEY, James

Group Number 128
HENRY, John; MCGEHEE, William

Group Number 129
HERREN, James; LANE, John W

Group Number 130
HERRING, James; SIMS, Edward

Group Number 131
HICKMAN, Joseph; MCADORY, James

Group Number 132
HORTON, Amos J; HORTON, Joseph A

Group Number 133
HUEY, Samuel T; HUEY, Thomas

Group Number 134
HUEY, Samuel; HUEY, Thomas

Group Number 135
HUMBER, Charles; WARE, Nimrod W; WILLIAMS, Benjamin

Group Number 136
INGLE, Peter; SCOTT, David

Group Number 137
ISAACS, Allen M; ISAACS, John W

Group Number 138
JEFFERSON, Dicy; JEFFERSON, Green

Group Number 139
JOHNSON, Beulah; MCDANIEL, Beulah; MCDANIEL, Stokely A

Group Number 140
JOHNSON, William R; JOHNSON, Zama P

Group Number 141
JONES, Dorathy; JONES, Mannon G

Group Number 142
JONES, Robert B; SIMS, Edward

Group Number 143
JORDAN, Mathew M; JORDAN, Nancy

Group Number 144
KELLY, Moses; SIMS, Edward

Group Number 145
KILLOUGH, Allen; MCCARTNEY, James

Group Number 146
KILLOUGH, David; MCCARTNEY, James

Group Number 147
KNOX, Elisha; MALLORY, Thomas

Group Number 148
LANE, John W; MASON, Job

Group Number 149
LANE, John W; NABOURS, William

Group Number 150
LANE, John W; OWEN, David

Group Number 151
LANE, John W; THOMAS, Benjamin

Group Number 152
LANE, John W; TRUSS, Warren

Group Number 153
LANE, John W; WALKER, James S

Group Number 154
LANE, Sampson; SIMS, Edward

Group Number 155
LANE, Sampson; THOMAS, Benjamin

Group Number 156
LANIER, Lucy J; LANIER, William B

Group Number 157
LEE, Edward; ROY, Margaret

Group Number 158
LEE, Samuel; OBAR, George R

Group Number 159
LOCKHART, Benjamin; SCOTT, David

Group Number 160
MADDOX, Elizabeth; MADDOX, John

Group Number 161
MADISON, Benjamin; MATTHEWS, Charles L

Group Number 162
MASSENGILL, A A; MASSENGILL, Henry A; MASSENGILL, Thaddeus J

Group Number 163
MASSEY, Jonathan; MCCARTNEY, James

Group Number 164
MCANALLY, Elizabeth; MCANALLY, William

Group Number 165
MCCARTNEY, James; MCLAUGHLIN, John

Group Number 166
MCCARTNEY, James; NASH, George

Group Number 167
MCCARTNEY, James; NEAL, Zacheriah

Group Number 168
MCCARTNEY, James; SIMS, Edward

Group Number 169
MCCARTNEY, James; WALKER, James S

Group Number 170
MCCARTY, Benajah; MCCARTY, James

Group Number 171
MCFERRIN, Cynthia C; WINES, Cynthia C

Group Number 172
MCGEHEE, William; TRUSS, Warren

Group Number 173
MELTON, Laura J; MELTON, Thomas J

Group Number 174
MILLER, Fannie; MILLER, Jasper

Group Number 175
MORGAN, Mattie; MORGAN, William L

Group Number 176
MORROW, George; SANDERS, Philip

Group Number 177
MULVEHILL, Mary; MULVEHILL, Peter E

Group Number 178
MURRAY, James; SIMS, Edward

Group Number 179
NABOURS, Francis D; WOOD, William

Group Number 180
NASH, George; SCOTT, David

Group Number 181
NASH, George; SIMS, Edward

Group Number 182
NASH, George; SIMS, Francis

Group Number 183
NEIGHBOURS, William; SCOTT, David

Group Number 184
ODOM, Emma L; ODOM, James P

Group Number 185
ORR, Jonathan; PERKINS, William

Group Number 186
ORR, Jonathan; ROBERTSON, Anderson

Group Number 187
ORR, Jonathan; WILSON, William

Group Number 188
OWEN, Hopson; THOMPSON, Thomas

Group Number 189
OWEN, Stephen M; OWEN, Thomas

Group Number 190
OWEN, Stephen; SCOTT, David

Group Number 191
OWEN, Thomas; TARRANT, George

Group Number 192
PALMER, Annie L; PALMER, Cora C; PALMER, Mamie A

Group Number 193
PARKER, Louisa H; PARKER, Monroe D

Group Number 194
PATTON, Andrew; REID, Levi

Group Number 195
PEARSON, John B; PEARSON, Lucresy

Group Number 196
PHILIPS, Caroline M; PHILIPS, Reuben

Group Number 197
PHILLIPS, Harriett; PHILLIPS, Sidney

Group Number 198
POTTER, Elizabeth; SIMS, Edward

Group Number 199
PRESCOTT, Aaron; PRESCOTT, Thomas

Group Number 200
REED, Robert; TURNER, William S

Group Number 201
RILEY, Allen W; RILEY, Amanda M

Group Number 202
ROBERTSON, William H; STEEL, Jonathan

Group Number 203
ROCKETT, Sarah W; ROCKETT, Thomas W

Group Number 204
ROEBUCK, Mattie; WILSON, Mattie; WILSON, Toney

Group Number 205
RUSSELL, Absalom; THOMAS, Benjamin

Group Number 206
RUSSELL, Jeremiah; TANNEHILL, Ninian

Group Number 207
SADLER, Thomas; SADLER, William R

Group Number 208
SAMPLES, Lilla E; SAMPLES, Olin W

Group Number 209
SANDERS, Elijah H; SANDERS, Owen

Group Number 210
SCOTT, David; STAGGS, Ezekiel

Group Number 211
SCOTT, David; TRUSS, Warren

Group Number 212
SCOTT, David; WILSON, William

Group Number 213
SELF, Elijah; SELF, Nathaniel

Group Number 214
SIMS, Edward; WOOD, Joshua

Group Number 215
SMITH, John; TAYLOR, Nehemiah

Group Number 216
TARRANT, Carter; TARRANT, Henry M

Group Number 217
TARRANT, Samuel A; WRITE, Thomas J

Group Number 218
TATE, Henry; TATE, Jacob

Group Number 219
TAYLOR, James; TAYLOR, Penina

Group Number 220
THOMAS, Kate; THOMAS, William H

Group Number 221
TRUSS, Arthur; TRUSS, John; TRUSS, Thomas K

Group Number 222
TRUSS, Warren; WORTHINGTON, Benjamin

Group Number 223
TURNER, Benjamin; TURNER, Elijah; TURNER, Sarah

Group Number 224
TURNER, Rachel; TURNER, Richard

Group Number 225
VANN, James W; VANN, Mary A

Group Number 226
VINES, Mary A; VINES, William M

Group Number 227
WALDROP, Richard; WALDROP, Robert

Group Number 228
WALDROP, Terril F; WALDROP, Thomas L

Group Number 229
WALTERS, Elizabeth A; WALTERS, Robert B

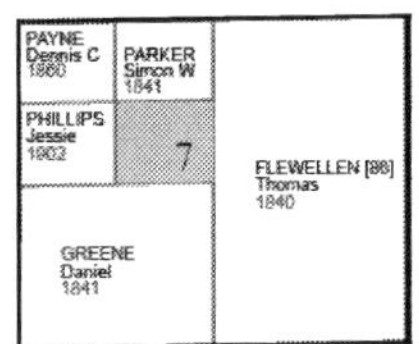

Extra! Extra! (about our Indexes)

We purposefully do not have an all-name index in the back of this volume so that our readers do not miss one of the best uses of this book: finding misspelled names among more specialized indexes.

Without repeating the text of our "How-to" chapter, we have nonetheless tried to assist our more anxious researchers by delivering a short-cut to the two county-wide Surname Indexes, the second of which will lead you to all-name indexes for each Congressional Township mapped in this volume :

For your convenience, the "How To Use this Book" Chart on page 2 is repeated on the reverse of this page.

We should be releasing new titles every week for the foreseeable future. We urge you to write, fax, call, or email us any time for a current list of titles. Of course, our web-page will always have the most current information about current and upcoming books.

Arphax Publishing Co.
2210 Research Park Blvd.
Norman, Oklahoma 73069
(800) 681-5298 toll-free
(405) 366-6181 local
(405) 366-8184 fax
info@arphax.com

www.arphax.com

How to Use This Book - A Graphical Summary

Part I

"The Big Picture"

Map A ▸ *Counties in the State*
Map B ▸ *Surrounding Counties*
Map C ▸ *Congressional Townships (Map Groups) in the County*
Map D ▸ *Cities & Towns in the County*
Map E ▸ *Cemeteries in the County*
Surnames in the County ▸ *Number of Land-Parcels for Each Surname*
Surname/Township Index ▸ Directs you to Township Map Groups in Part II

The Surname/Township Index can direct you to any number of **Township Map Groups**

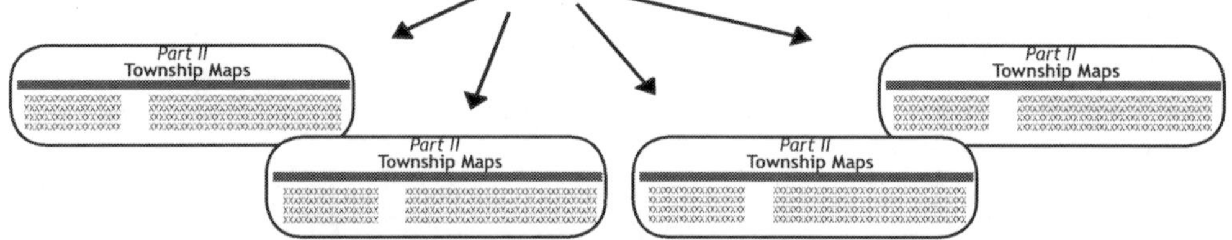

Part II

Township Map Groups

(1 for each Township in the County)

Each Township Map Group contains all four of of the following tools . . .

Land Patent Index ▸ *Every-name Index of Patents Mapped in this Township*
Land Patent Map ▸ *Map of Patents as listed in above Index*
Road Map ▸ *Map of Roads, City-centers, and Cemeteries in the Township*
Historical Map ▸ *Map of Railroads, Lakes, Rivers, Creeks, City-Centers, and Cemeteries*

Appendices

Appendix A ▸ *Congressional Authority enabling Patents within our Maps*
Appendix B ▸ *Section-Parts / Aliquot Parts (a comprehensive list)*
Appendix C ▸ *Multi-patentee Groups (Individuals within Buying Groups)*

Made in the USA
Columbia, SC
22 April 2021

36575616R00274